International Directory of
COMPANY
HISTORIES

International Directory of

COMPANY HISTORIES

VOLUME 18

Editor

Jay P. Pederson

ST. JAMES PRESS

AN IMPRINT OF GALE

DETROIT • NEW YORK • TORONTO • LONDON

STAFF

Jay P. Pederson, *Editor*

Miranda H. Ferrara, *Project Manager*
Kristin Hart, Tina Grant, *Contributing Editors*
Peter M. Gareffa, *Managing Editor, St. James Press*

The paper used in this publication meets the minimum
requirements of American National Standard for Information Sciences—
Permanence Paper for Printed Library Materials, ANSI Z39.48-1984.

This book is printed on recycled paper that meets Environmental Protection Agency Standards.

Library of Congress Catalog Number: 89-190943

British Library Cataloguing in Publication Data

International directory of company histories. Vol. 18
I. Jay P. Pederson
338.7409

ISBN 1-55862-352-3

Printed in the United States of America
Published simultaneously in the United Kingdom

St. James Press is an imprint of Gale

Cover photograph: Aerial view of the Hong Kong business district
(courtesy Hong Kong Trade Development Council)

10 9 8 7 6 5 4 3 2 1

CONTENTS _____

Company Histories

PREFACE

The St. James Press series *The International Directory of Company Histories (IDCH)* is intended for reference use by students, business people, librarians, historians, economists, investors, job candidates, and others who seek to learn more about the historical development of the world's most important companies. To date, *IDCH* has covered over 2,900 companies in eighteen volumes.

Inclusion Criteria

Most companies chosen for inclusion in *IDCH* have achieved a minimum of US$100 million in annual sales and are leading influences in their industries or geographical locations. Companies may be publicly held, private, or non-profit. State-owned companies that are important in their industries and that may operate much like public or private companies also are included. Wholly owned subsidiaries and divisions are profiled if they meet the requirements for inclusion. Entries on companies that have had major changes since they were last profiled may be selected for updating.

The *IDCH* series highlights 10% private and non-profit companies, and features updated entries on approximately 25 companies per volume.

Entry Format

Each entry begins with the company's legal name, the address of its headquarters, its telephone and fax numbers, and its web site. A statement of public, private, state, or parent ownership follows. A company with a legal name in both English and the language of its headquarters country is listed by the English name, with the native-language name in parentheses.

The company's founding or earliest incorporation date, the number of employees, and the most recent sales figures available follow. Sales figures are given in local currencies with equivalents in U.S. dollars. For some private companies, sales figures are estimates. The entry lists the exchanges on which a company's stock is traded, as well as the company's principal Standard Industrial Classification codes.

Entries also contain a *Company Perspectives* box which provides a short summary of the company's mission, goals, and ideals, a list of *Principal Subsidiaries*, *Principal Divisions*, *Principal Operating Units*, and articles for *Further Reading*.

American spelling is used throughout *IDCH*, and the word "billion" is used in its U.S. sense of one thousand million.

Sources

Entries have been compiled from publicly accessible sources both in print and on the Internet such as general and academic periodicals, books, annual reports, and material supplied by the companies themselves.

Cumulative Indexes

IDCH contains two indexes: the **Index to Companies**, which provides an alphabetical index to companies discussed in the text as well as companies profiled, and the **Index to Industries**, which allows researchers to locate companies by their principal industry. Both indexes are cumulative and specific instructions for using them are found immediately preceding each index.

Suggestions Welcome

Comments and suggestions from users of *IDCH* on any aspect of the product as well as suggestions for companies to be included or updated are cordially invited. Please write:

The Editor
International Directory of Company Histories
St. James Press
835 Penobscot Building
Detroit, Michigan 48226-4094

ABBREVIATIONS FOR FORMS OF COMPANY INCORPORATION

A.B.	Aktiebolaget (Sweden)
A.G.	Aktiengesellschaft (Germany, Switzerland)
A.S.	Atieselskab (Denmark)
A.S.	Aksjeselskap (Denmark, Norway)
A.Ş.	Anomin Şirket (Turkey)
B.V.	Besloten Vennootschap met beperkte, Aansprakelijkheid (The Netherlands)
Co.	Company (United Kingdom, United States)
Corp.	Corporation (United States)
G.I.E.	Groupement d'Intérêt Economique (France)
GmbH	Gesellschaft mit beschränkter Haftung (Germany)
H.B.	Handelsbolaget (Sweden)
Inc.	Incorporated (United States)
KGaA	Kommanditgesellschaft auf Aktien (Germany)
K.K.	Kabushiki Kaisha (Japan)
LLC	Limited Liability Company (Middle East)
Ltd.	Limited (Canada, Japan, United Kingdom, United States)
N.V.	Naamloze Vennootschap (The Netherlands)
OY	Osakeyhtiöt (Finland)
PLC	Public Limited Company (United Kingdom)
PTY.	Proprietary (Australia, Hong Kong, South Africa)
S.A.	Société Anonyme (Belgium, France, Switzerland)
SpA	Società per Azioni (Italy)

ABBREVIATIONS FOR CURRENCY

DA	Algerian dinar		M$	Malaysian ringgit
A$	Australian dollar		Dfl	Netherlands florin
Sch	Austrian schilling		NZ$	New Zealand dollar
BFr	Belgian franc		N	Nigerian naira
Cr	Brazilian cruzado		NKr	Norwegian krone
C$	Canadian dollar		RO	Omani rial
RMB	Chinese renminbi		P	Philippine peso
DKr	Danish krone		Esc	Portuguese escudo
E£	Egyptian pound		SRls	Saudi Arabian riyal
Fmk	Finnish markka		S$	Singapore dollar
FFr	French franc		R	South African rand
DM	German mark		W	South Korean won
HK$	Hong Kong dollar		Pta	Spanish peseta
Rs	Indian rupee		SKr	Swedish krona
Rp	Indonesian rupiah		SFr	Swiss franc
IR£	Irish pound		NT$	Taiwanese dollar
L	Italian lira		B	Thai baht
¥	Japanese yen		£	United Kingdom pound
W	Korean won		$	United States dollar
KD	Kuwaiti dinar		B	Venezuelan bolivar
LuxFr	Luxembourgian franc		K	Zambian kwacha

International Directory of

COMPANY

HISTORIES

ABC Rail Products Corporation

200 South Michigan Avenue, Suite 1300
Chicago, Illinois 60604
U.S.A.
(312) 322-0360
Fax: (312) 322-0377

Public Company
Incorporated: 1987 as ABC Rail Corporation
Employees: 1,449
Sales: $240.6 million (1996)
Stock Exchanges: NASDAQ
SICs: 3312 Blast Furnaces & Steel Mills; 3531
  Construction Machinery; 3743 Railroad Equipment

A leader in the engineering, manufacturing, and marketing of original and replacement products for the freight railroad, public transit, and intercity high-speed passenger rail industries, ABC Rail Products Corporation manufactures specialty trackwork, such as switches, turnouts, and rail crossings, metal brake shoes, and wheels for locomotives and rail cars. During the mid-1990s, ABC Rail operated ten manufacturing facilities in the United States and ranked as the largest manufacturer of specialty trackwork in North America, the second-largest manufacturer of freight railcar and locomotive wheels in North America, and the only manufacturer of metal brake shoes in the United States. Through a series of strategic alliances and joint ventures, the company ascended to market leadership during the 1990s, experiencing promising growth domestically and abroad.

Although ABC Rail originated in 1902 with the American Brake Shoe and Foundry Company, the modern version of the company began business during what industry pundits hailed as the decade of the railroad industry's resurgence. After decades of losing ground to the trucking industry and exhibiting signs of stagnation and decay, the U.S. railroad industry began to show signs of life during the 1980s, beginning in 1980 when deregulation sparked growth in the rail transportation business. In the wake of deregulation, rail carriers throughout the country began

recording consistent growth as they trimmed their payrolls and invested in new technologies that enabled them to operate with fewer employees. Employment in the industry shrank from 458,000 in 1980 to 190,000 by 1994, yet the industry's aggregate revenue ton-miles rose from 919 million to 1.2 billion during the same span, resulting in a 200 percent increase in productivity for carriers nationwide. Invigorated by the benefits realized from the adoption of new technologies, the railroad industry at last began to take market share away from the trucking industry in 1995 for the first time since 1920. Integral to this rejuvenation of the railroad industry were the companies who designed and manufactured the equipment that bolstered railroad companies' profitability. One such company was ABC Rail, a late comer to the trend sweeping through the industry during the 1980s, but a company that reigned as a market leader during the mid-1990s.

Formation of ABC Rail in 1987

ABC Rail entered into the business world in 1987 when the company was formed to acquire the assets of the Rail Products Group operating within Abex Corporation, which was one of the units composing the conglomerate IC Industries. Through a leveraged buyout completed in July 1987, the rail products assets belonging to Abex were organized into an independent company christened ABC Rail Corporation. Organized to serve the railroad industry during its decade of resurgence, ABC Rail entered into business on its own at the right time, but for several years the company floundered, as it struggled with financial problems exacerbated by a 1989 leveraged recapitalization and a $20 million equity distribution.

Entering the 1990s, the company continued to struggle, unable to establish a solid foundation from which to grow in the new decade. Financially weak, ABC was further crippled by declining prices in 1990 and 1991 for the trackwork it produced and by anemic market conditions. By 1991, after four years of attempting to carve a lasting niche for itself, ABC appeared to be headed nowhere, at least in light of the optimistic expectations that marked its creation. Better times were ahead, however, beginning in 1991 when the company received the financial backing of Kohlberg & Co., an investment firm that funnelled $5 million of equity into the company. The infusion of capital represented a turning point in the company's history, marking the true beginning of its rise as a market leader. Shortly after Kohlberg & Co. entered the scene, ABC Rail's management endeavored to eradicate the ills that had afflicted the company since its inception in 1987. The company instituted a program aimed at slashing marketing and administrative expenses, restructuring the company's trackwork operations, and adjusting its product mix to favor more expensive, higher profit-margin equipment. The changes worked. From the company's fiscal 1992 forward, consistent growth became a common occurrence, lifting ABC Rail's stature within the industry and refueling management's focus on serving the blossoming railroad industry.

ABC Rail and Cogifer in the 1990s

ABC Rail's growth from 1992 forward was largely achieved through a series of affiliations and joint ventures that significantly expanded its operations and extended its geographic presence to foreign shores. By entering into joint ventures and alliances, ABC Rail pursued a less risky path toward expansion, yet realized substantial gains in its technology base and marketing and distribution capabilities. One of the first and longest-lasting of these pivotal collaborative agreements was struck in February 1992, when ABC Rail and France-based Cogifer, S.A. formed a business relationship that promised to introduce ABC Rail to a lucrative segment of the rail industry. Historically, specialty trackwork manufacturers like ABC Rail directed the bulk of their marketing and production energies toward freight carriers rather than dividing their efforts equally between freight and rail transit system operators. As a result, equipment sold to rail transit system operators generally was freight specialty trackwork modified for rail transit system operators. By the early 1990s, however, the demand for European-style high speed and light rail technology was growing; recognizing this trend, ABC Rail's management began looking for an experienced partner. Cogifer, a European specialty trackwork producer, represented a perfect match for ABC Rail. The company was the leading supplier of European-style high-speed and light rail specialty trackwork to customers across the globe and specifically a supplier of trackwork for the high-speed *Train à Grande Vitesse* (TGV) trains in France and other parts of Europe. As rail transit customers in North America were increasingly seeking equipment to provide smooth, quiet service on high-speed and light rail systems, ABC Rail was intent on capturing a share of the burgeoning market.

The relationship with Cogifer was manifested by the formation of two 50-50 joint venture companies in February 1992 and December 1993, both of which were called ABC Rail-Cogifer Technologies. Through these partnership agreements, and a joint marketing agreement that named Cogifer as ABC Rail's exclusive worldwide representative for the sale of its products, ABC Rail gained access to Cogifer's design concepts and expertise in high-speed and light rail technology. With this technology, ABC Rail hoped to penetrate the intercity, "Amtrak-type" rail passenger market and the growing market for high-speed freight railroad switches.

Strengthened by its affiliation with Cogifer, ABC Rail next took steps to facilitate the development of further business alliances. In December 1993, during the same month it formed its second joint venture company with Cogifer, ABC Rail completed its initial public offering of stock, thereby gaining the financial resources to aggressively pursue growth. Shortly thereafter, the company began fleshing out its operations. In February 1994, ABC Rail acquired two specialty trackwork manufacturing facilities, giving it a total of ten plants scattered across the country. The first of the two new plants was Santa Fe Railway's manufacturing, warehousing, and distribution operations, located in Newton, Kansas. For the second facility, ABC teamed up with Cogifer to form a new manufacturing joint venture to acquire a 110,000-square-foot plant in Cincinnati, Ohio. Originally owned exclusively by Cogifer, the facility had the capability to manufacture a broad line of trackwork products. Next, the company entered into a five-year strategic alliance with Burlington Northern in July 1994 to provide the railroad company with an uninterrupted supply of track materials. Buoyed by this added business, ABC Rail recorded the first appreciable gain in annual sales since the 1990s had begun. In 1991, the company generated $150 million in sales and proceeded to post stagnant results for the next two years, collecting $143 million in 1992 and $148 million in 1993. In 1994, however, sales rose encouragingly, reaching $187 million while the company's net income swelled to more than $5 million after consecutive losses in 1991 and 1992.

Mid-1990s Expansion

Demonstrating an unprecedented vitality in the mid-1990s, ABC Rail at last was able to tackle projects that promised to add to its revenue volume and profit levels in meaningful amounts. In May 1995, the company acquired five wheel assembly plants from General Electric Railcar Wheel and Parts Services Corporation, gaining facilities in Lewistown, Pennsylvania, Calera, Alabama, Chicago Heights, Illinois, Corsicana, Texas, Riverside, California, and Kansas City, Kansas. Construction of a wheel machining plant was begun during the company's 1995 fiscal year and by the following year the plant was ready to operate. As construction of this plant was underway, the company entered into another joint venture, teaming up with Standard Car Truck in September 1995 to form a company named Anchor Brake Shoe. The joint venture company, which was formed to execute the composition brake shoe business of both ABC and Standard Car Truck, represented one of only two brake shoe suppliers in the United States.

By the end of 1995, sales had risen strongly to $243 million, and the company occupied enviable positions in several key markets. ABC Rail ranked as the largest manufacturer of specialty trackwork in North America, its dominance strengthened by the departure of the second-largest manufacturer in 1992. Specialty trackwork, which accounted for roughly half of the company's business during the mid-1990s, consisted of replacement track for freight railroads and track switches or turnouts, which direct trains from one track to another, as well as crossings, which allow one set of railroad tracks to cross through another. ABC Rail also ranked as the second-largest manufacturer of freight railcar and locomotive wheels in North America, producing 28-, 33-, 36-, and 38-inch diameter wheels for freight railcars and 40-inch diameter wheels for diesel locomotives. The production of railcar and locomotive wheels represented ABC Rail's second-largest product category, accounting for approximately 45 percent of the company's business during the mid-1990s. The balance of ABC Rail's business was derived from the manufacture of composition and metal brake shoes, which exert friction directly on the railroad wheel to generate braking power. Operating as the only manufacturer of metal brake shoes in the United States, ABC Rail derived roughly five percent of its business from the manufacture of brake shoes.

Firmly established as one of the strongest companies in its various markets during the mid-1990s, ABC Rail moved resolutely forward in 1996, continuing to seek the benefits of pursuing growth through joint ventures and strategic alliances. In May 1996, the company deepened its involvement in one of the world's largest markets by establishing additional business in China. Previously, ABC Rail had completed several projects in China, providing in one instance technical expertise for the manufacture of composition brake shoes. ABC Rail had also sold railroad wheels produced at the company's Calera, Alabama, foundry to China and supplied trackwork manganese castings, forming what promised to be a lucrative business relationship with China. As the late-1990s neared, China was expected to invest more than $30 billion in upgrading and expanding its massive rail system, creating a wealth of business for companies like ABC Rail. In May 1996, ABC Rail took strides toward capturing a share of the rail business in China when the company entered into a joint venture with China's Ministry of Railroads to manufacture 160,000 railroad wheels at a plant west of Beijing in Datong, Shanxi Province. With a 40 percent interest in the joint venture company (which operated as Datong ABC Castings Company Ltd.), ABC Rail was expected to expand its wheel manufacturing business with China into neighboring Asian countries.

On the domestic front, ABC Rail completed a pivotal acquisition in June 1996 when it purchased Deco Industries, Inc., a manufacturer of electric, pneumatic, and hydraulic retarder equipment, radar, and other components at its production facility in Milwaukee, Wisconsin. In addition to the Milwaukee facility, ABC Rail also obtained control of Norristown, Pennsylvania-based Deco Automation, which designed computerized railroad yard systems and produced the hardware, software, and electrical-mechanical interface equipment for yard control systems. As a result of the Deco acquisition, ABC Rail could add another feather to its cap, becoming the largest operator in the rail classification yard market.

Plans for the Future

Later in the year, ABC Rail broadened its business scope further by reaching an agreement in principle to acquire American Systems Technologies, Inc. Based in Verona, Wisconsin, American Systems Technologies ranked as the leading private company in the railway signal system installation and maintenance field, giving ABC Rail yet another facet to its rapidly expanding business. As the company prepared for the late 1990s and the completion of its first decade of business, plans for future growth called for the formation of additional strategic alliances and joint ventures. Although there was much to be achieved in the United States, ABC Rail was also formulating its future plans around expanding its foreign business, particularly in South America where the deregulation and privatization of railroad industries offered strong growth opportunities. Encouraged by these opportunities, ABC Rail's management scanned the horizons of the late 1990s, intent on shoring up the company's leading market positions both domestically and abroad.

Principal Subsidiaries

Datong ABC Castings Company LTD. (China; 40%); Deco Industries, Inc.; Deco Automation; ABC Rail-Cogifer Technologies (50%).

Further Reading

"ABC Rail Announces Agreement in Principle to Acquire American Systems Technologies, Inc.," *PR Newswire,* October 16, 1996, p. 1.
"ABC Rail Products Acquires DECO," *Railway Age,* June 1996, p. 27.
"ABC Rail Products Corp.," *Railway Age,* February 1994, p. 22.
"ABC Rail Products Corp.," *Railway Age,* May 1995, p. 22.
"ABC Rail Products," *Railway Age,* October 1995, p. 8.
"ABC Rail Products," *Railway Age,* May 1996, p. 24.
"ABC Rail Products," *Railway Age,* August 1996, p. 23.
"Burlington Northern," *Railway Age,* July 1994, p. 6.
"Standard Car Truck and ABC Rail Products," *Railway Age,* September 1995, p. 30.
"Strategic Plant Upgrades Expected to Result in Lower Q1 Sales and Substantial Earnings Decline for ABC Rail," *PR Newswire,* October 22, 1996, p. 1.
Vazzano, Sheri, "Investigators Probing On-Job Death of Duluth, Minnesota Crane Operator," *Knight-Ridder/Tribune Business News,* February 24, 1994, p. 2.

—Jeffrey L. Covell

Alex Lee Inc.

120 Fourth Street, S.W.
Hickory, North Carolina 28602
U.S.A.
(704) 323-4424
Fax: (704) 323-4435

Private Company
Incorporated: 1992
Employees: 5,400
Sales: $1.27 billion (1995)
SICs: 5141 Groceries, General Line; 5411 Retail
    Supermarkets & Convenience Food Stores

Alex Lee Inc. is a holding company formed in 1992 to serve as the parent company for three food and food distribution firms in North Carolina. Of the three, the oldest, largest, and original firm is Merchants Distributors Inc. (MDI), the 23rd-largest retail food wholesaler in the United States in 1995 and the 76th-largest general line grocery firm. The second, Institution Food House (IFH), also a wholesale food distributor, was rated the 18th-largest U.S. food "broadliner" (distributors with the widest range of goods) in 1991 and the 125th-largest general line grocery firm in 1995. Alex Lee's third operating unit, Lowes Food Stores, was the 84th-largest supermarket and convenience store firm in the United States in 1995. Alex Lee Inc. as a whole ranked 26th among all general line grocery firms in the United States in 1995.

MDI has historically sold food and nonfood grocery items to independent supermarkets in North and South Carolina. In 1993 its 833 retail customers in North Carolina, South Carolina, Virginia, Tennessee, and Georgia made MDI the largest source of sales for Alex Lee. IFH, which accounted for about one-tenth of Alex Lee's total sales in 1995, began originally as a purveyor of volume food products to public school systems. By the early 1990s, it had two primary sources of revenue: so-called street sales to independent restaurants, school systems, and health care institutions (representing 68 percent of total volume); and sales to chain or national accounts, primarily restaurants (representing 32 percent of total volume). Overall, full-menu restaurants accounted for 47 percent of IFH's total sales in 1991, followed by chains (20 percent), bakeries and delis (7 percent), schools (7 percent), health care institutions (6 percent), catering and cafeteria accounts (4 percent), upscale restaurants (3 percent), and other accounts (6 percent). In 1996 Alex Lee's smallest unit, Lowes Food Stores, operated about fifty-five supermarkets and convenience stores in North Carolina and Virginia.

Merchants Distributors Inc., 1931–59

In 1931, a 27-year-old Lebanese immigrant named Moses George opened a wholesale produce and food distribution business in Shelby, North Carolina, with the goal of becoming a low-cost/low-price middleman between local food processors and the buying public. Although the Depression was quickly becoming more severe than anyone could have predicted, George's enterprise, Merchants Distributors Inc. (MDI), survived on the public's continuing need for basic food goods. George's only concession to circumstance was the relocation of his business a hundred miles north to Hickory, North Carolina, where he reopened MDI from a cramped 2,500-square-foot storefront on the town's Main Avenue.

Throughout the 1920s and 1930s the U.S. food store industry underwent a radical sea change. The traditional mom-and-pop grocery store, in which a limited selection of goods was sold from tables and barrels, was giving way to large "self-service" grocery store chains like A&P, Kroger, and Piggly-Wiggly. As grocers began introducing such innovations as merchandise displayed on customer-accessible shelves, price tagging, shopping baskets, and on-the-premises butcher shops, ice cream parlors, and bakeries, the supermarket concept took hold. From the beginning, however, smaller independent merchants saw the threat posed by the chains and began organizing to create the economies of scale that would enable them to compete. In 1926, the Independent Grocers Alliance (IGA) was formed in the Midwest to enable non-chain stores to pool their resources and buy groceries in volume from food distributors; in the East the Wakefern Cooperative (which later became Pathmark Stores) was founded after World War II to strengthen its members' buying power against the grocery chains of New York and New Jersey.

It was within the battle for survival between the new chain foodstores and the independents that George found his niche. Throughout the 1930s and early 1940s he positioned MDI to become a leading distributor of food and groceries for the independent supermarkets of North and South Carolina. By the time of his premature death in 1947 he had hired six of the seven men who would lead MDI's explosive growth in the coming years. With George's three children—Alex, Lee, and Josephine—now at the company's helm, MDI continued to expand its territory in the 1950s, shipping flour, corn, meal, salt and pepper, sugar, grits, snuff, shoelaces, milk, potatoes, and a broad range of other food and grocery lines from its Main Avenue facility to customers throughout the Carolinas.

Expansion, 1960–65

By 1960, MDI's 130-plus employees were shipping 11,000 items to more than 400 independent supermarkets in a 100-to-150-mile radius around Hickory, an area encompassing Asheville and Greensboro to the west and east, and the Virginia line and Greenville, South Carolina, to the north and south. With the business quadrupling in a few years, reaching the $16-million level in 1960, MDI (with Alex George now as president) had become one of the largest wholesale food distribution operations in the southeast. A larger facility was clearly needed to house the growing business, and in the late 1950s MDI announced plans for a new million-dollar, four-acre warehouse and office building on Twelfth Street in Hickory.

The new plant, unveiled in March 1960, was state of the art. Eight rail cars and 20 trucks could be unloaded simultaneously at the facility's expansive dock area, 237 boxcars full of food could be stored in the warehouse at one time, and the contents of the entire warehouse could be stocked, sold off to customers, and restocked seventeen times a year. One hundred loading carts wound slowly through the warehouse on a chain-pulled system that enabled workers to fill customers' orders with minimal strain; specialized cold storage rooms were maintained for specific perishables like bananas and tomatoes so they could be ripened just before shipment to customers; and an early IBM punch card computer system automated the entire order placement, order fulfillment, product packing, and billing process.

The local Hickory paper celebrated the warehouse's opening with an entire issue, and a "Grand Opening and Food and Specialty Show" was organized to announce MDI's expansion, with more than one hundred food manufacturers, packers, and canners turning out to celebrate the company's growing clout in the regional distribution business. By the mid-1960s, MDI had grown into a full-line grocery wholesaler with a continually growing share of the southeastern food distribution business. Asked in 1960 to account for MDI's success, Alex George enthused to the *Hickory Daily Record* that "our ability to get good men is the secret to the growth of MDI. Take a look at these men. Look how long they have worked with us. Their contribution cannot be overlooked or overestimated."

Institution Food House and
Lowes Food Stores, 1966–91

By mid-decade Alex and Lee George had decided to expand MDI's market from its traditional independent grocery store customer to the institutional food market. The first customers of the resulting operation, MDI Foodservice, were public school systems, but at the 1965 National-American Wholesale Grocers' Association convention in Chicago the George brothers met Norman James, another Hickory food distributor whose James Wholesale Company also sold food to area schools. After exploratory discussions the three agreed to merge MDI Foodservice and James Wholesale as Institution Food House (IFH). By the end of the year, IFH had rented an unused MDI warehouse in downtown Hickory and consolidated the James Wholesale and MDI Foodservice merchandise there.

On January 2, 1966, IFH was officially born with Lee George as president and Norman James as vice-president. Beginning with only fourteen employees IFH took all early orders by hand, building its small customer base into close to $1 million in revenue by the end of its first year. By the summer of 1966 IFH had held the first of its many annual food shows to generate publicity and drum up new customers. Within five years IFH sales had edged beyond $5 million, and it began to expand, acquiring fifteen acres for a new warehouse outside Hickory. The 50,000-square-foot facility opened in 1973 and provided IFH with room for three thousand different items and 15,000 square feet of freezer and cooler space. Like MDI's 1960 warehouse unveiling, the new IFH facility represented the latest in food storage and distribution technology. Products could be easily stored and relocated via a numbered rack system; state-of-the-art materials-handling equipment enhanced storage and order-filling efficiency; a computerized billing and inventory system streamlined paperwork; and all product could be loaded and unloaded inside without exposing personnel or product to the elements.

When Norman James died in the early 1970s, the George brothers bought out his interest in IFH and began to operate it as a subsidiary of MDI. They next merged IFH with the Frosty Acres Brands group (now known as F.A.B. Inc.) of Norcross, Georgia, retaining its labels and advertising to maintain brand loyalty. In 1982, *Institutional Distribution* magazine ranked IFH, whose sales had now climbed to $55 million, the 48th-largest institutional food distributor in the nation. Its sales area stretched 100 miles around Hickory, its sales force had grown to 30, and its product offerings had increased to 3,500, now including everything from fresh meat and smallwares to chemicals. In 1982 IFH purchased Brothers Foods of Dillon, South Carolina, a $5-million food distributor that expanded IFH's sales region into the South Carolina market.

That same year, CEO Alex George named Dennis Hatchell president of MDI and began laying plans for MDI's second major merger: the purchase of Lowes Food Stores. Lowes traced its origins back to 1921, when Lucius S. Lowe founded the North Wilkesboro Hardware Store to sell general merchandise such as snuff, ladies' shoes, and horse collars to Hickory, North Carolina, residents. When Lucius's son Jim returned from military service in 1946, he joined with his sister's husband, Carl Buchan, to run the business, and Lowe's expanded into groceries, dry goods, notions, and other products. In May of 1954 Jim Lowe decided to open a food store proper, appropriately named Lowes Food Store, but seven months later he sold out to the store's manager, J. C. Faw. While Carl Buchan focused on developing Lowes Hardware into the Lowe's Companies, Inc. home improvement super chain that by 1995 would number 350 stores, Faw focused on the expansion of his part of Lucius Lowe's legacy. He opened the second Lowes Food Store in 1960 and in succeeding years progressively expanded the chain before selling it at last to MDI in 1984. Once only a food distributor, MDI now competed head to head with such southeastern grocery store giants as Food Lion and Winn-Dixie. Within five years of the purchase Alex George had initiated a major expansion program for Lowes, shifting Dennis Hatchell from the presidency of MDI to the lead position at Lowes and relocating Lowes' headquarters from North Wilkesboro to a new facility in Winston-Salem, North Carolina.

In the mid-1980s, the U.S. food distribution industry remained, as *Forbes* magazine described it, "a plodding business with micromargins." Fierce competition was squeezing industry profits, slow growth in food prices was forcing distributors to cut costs and lay off employees, and consolidation seemed to offer the only route to growth for industry firms. Since 1979, the number of U.S. wholesale food operators had dropped by two-thirds to 325, and experts were predicting that the industry would shrink even more, to 100 firms, by 1990. Drastic efficiency measures were needed for industry firms to stay afloat, and a growing number followed MDI's pioneering lead by increasingly relying on enterprise-wide automation and inventory control systems to maintain profitability.

In 1986 MDI's sister firm, IFH, was forced to cope with the aftermath of its decision four years earlier to purchase Brothers Foods. Although the purchase had enabled its volume in the Dillon area to grow to $9 million by 1986 (out of total IFH sales of $96 million), in July of that year a fire destroyed the office, cooler, and some of the dry space area, presenting IFH's new executive vice president, Robert S. Donaldson, with an opportunity to earn his stripes. Disaster was averted when emergency deliveries of produce and dry groceries from IFH's Hickory facilities enabled IFH-Dillon to fill all its orders without interruption. Working out of trailers installed on the burned-out Dillon plant, IFH's sales reps transmitted customer orders to Hickory, which then flew customers' invoices back to Dillon. Low-temperature produce and grocery trailers were parked at the Dillon site to store customers' goods. IFH held on to its Dillon customers.

Within 18 months of Donaldson's arrival, Alex George had named him president of IFH, making him, at age thirty-three, perhaps the youngest president of a major U.S. food service distributor. Rather than rebuild IFH's Dillon facility on the original Brothers Foods site, George and Donaldson chose to build a new 90,000-square-foot facility in Florence, South Carolina, a few miles south of Dillon. The new site opened in January 1988 and, because of its proximity to Interstate 95, IFH now had ready access to the Myrtle Beach, South Carolina, market as well as direct access to potential customers in Georgia and Florida. Five months after the Dillon fire IFH again expanded by acquiring food service distributor Thomas & Howard of Charlotte, North Carolina. Although IFH had planned to use the Thomas & Howard facility to pursue business with chain store customers, it lost a major chain store account and, unable to replace it, was forced to close the Charlotte facility in January of 1988, transferring its remaining accounts to IFH's facilities in Hickory and Dillon.

Donaldson set about transforming IFH's corporate image, which had been marred by poor truck departure times and low product in-stock rates. He retained a public relations firm to create a new company logo and developed a new mission statement that unambiguously declared IFH's goal to become "a strong regional food service distributor through innovation, development of resources, and by being known for superior customer service and integrity." Donaldson also announced specific goals, known as "IFH Business Values," to improve the company's focus on customers and organizational excellence and to instill a commitment to innovation and integrity. He also initiated a customer-feedback program to enhance IFH's responsiveness to customers' needs. By 1991, IFH was selling almost 7,500 different products—dry goods, frozen meat, bakery items, seafood, fruits and vegetables, beverages, and more—to its 3,500 customers, who now included supermarket delis, bakeries, independent full-menu restaurants, and chain restaurants and food stores such as Kentucky Fried Chicken and Piggly-Wiggly, in addition to its original school and health care customers.

In an aggressive move to expand its territory IFH purchased 80 percent of the restaurants in the 150-unit Western Steer Family Restaurant chain of Claremont, North Carolina, in early 1991. In one fell swoop, a sales territory that had once comprised only North and South Carolina now spanned eleven states, stretching as far north as Maryland, as far south as Miami, Florida, and as far west as Knoxville, Tennessee, and Cincinnati, Ohio. Aided by Donaldson's commitment to utilizing the latest in electronic data interchange and inventory and transaction software, between 1986 and 1991 IFH's sales had ballooned 90 percent to almost $182 million.

Alex Lee Inc., 1992–96

In August 1992 the MDI-IFH-Lowes triumvirate was placed under the umbrella of a new holding company structure named Alex Lee Inc., after the first names of Moses George's two sons. The founder's grandson, Boyd Lee George—who had previously held the position of chairman and president of MDI—was named chairman and president of the new entity while staying on as MDI's chairman. In announcing the move, Boyd George described the new corporate structure as "strictly a structural-type" move to streamline the financial structure of the three sister companies and promised that it would have no effect on the three firms' day-to-day operations.

In the early 1990s the U.S. food industry as a whole continued to be buffeted by consolidation, withering competition, and razor-thin profit margins. The once unquestioned dominance of the supermarket was being dramatically eroded by warehouse food clubs, mass merchants, and deep discount drugstores. In 1992, for example, Albertson's, the fifth-largest U.S. grocery chain, announced it was dropping its traditional food supplier (Super Food Services) in favor of its own distribution network, and in 1993 food wholesalers like MDI lost a major source of income when many food manufacturers began eliminating traditional special-price promotion programs. Food distributors could now no longer profit from the purchase of stockpiles of specially priced goods that could later be resold to supermarkets at higher prices. Moreover, the nation's chain supermarkets—many of which now operated their own distribution networks—

were winning the war for market share from the independents on which MDI had traditionally staked its growth.

Alex Lee won a major coup in November 1993, however, when IGA, the third-largest supermarket chain in sales in North America, announced that MDI had been selected as one of two food wholesalers to service its distribution system. And in October 1995, Alex Lee announced that it would build a brand new $60-million-dollar grocery distribution facility (to be completed in late 1997) in Hickory, a few miles north of the site it had occupied since 1960. Local authorities fell over themselves devising the right mix of incentives to land the new facility, and the final decision was made only when an earlier site became the subject of heated annexation disputes, and representatives of Caldwell County and the communities of Hickory and Granite Falls finally offered $5.5 million in economic incentives to win Alex Lee's commitment. In August 1996, Alex Lee floated a $60 million investors' issue to pay for the expansion.

In November, Boyd George named Dennis Hatchell the new president and chief operating officer of Alex Lee and tapped Margaret Urquhart, an experienced supermarket and drug store industry executive, to replace Hatchell as president of Lowes Food Stores. Only the second woman to run a grocery store chain of fifty or more stores, Urquhart launched a major program to broaden Lowes' share of a market dominated by industry giants. In 1996, she opened two Lowes "FreshSmart" stores, which featured expanded offerings of produce, seafood and meats, prepared and organic foods, and such nonfood services as flower sales and photo processing. She also returned Lowes to the television advertising market after a five-year absence. Under the new company slogan "Quality, Service, the Right Price," she increased Lowes' responsiveness to customer preferences with a toll-free feedback phone line, improved aisle signage, and implemented a "Quick Checkout" policy to speed customers on their way. Buoyed by Urquhart's hands-on campaign to steal the thunder of the big southeastern U.S. foodstore

chains, in 1996 Lowes announced plans to build new stores in new markets.

Principal Subsidiaries

Merchants Distributors Inc. (MDI); Institution Food House (including Western Steer); Lowes Food Stores.

Further Reading

Ballard, Tanya, "Lowes Foods Sets Up Shop in Reidsville," *Rockingham News & Record,* October 4, 1996, p. 1R.

Bent, Jennifer, "Company President 'Walks the Talk,'" *Wautauga Democrat,* September 9, 1996.

Coleman, Zach, "Lowes President Stars in Television Ads," *Winston-Salem Journal,* October 7, 1996.

Dolan, Kerry A., "Food Distributors," *Forbes,* January 1, 1996, p. 13.

"Dream of Long Ago Materializes into Huge Food Distribution Center Here," *Hickory Daily Record,* March 31, 1960, pp. 7, 10.

Eckmann, Katy, "Lowe's First Lady," *AdWeek,* October 7, 1996.

Gomlak, Norman, "Food Distribution Center Set for Caldwell, Reports Say," *Charlotte Observer,* October 3, 1995, p. 1C.

Gutner, Toddi, "Food Distributors," *Forbes,* January 4, 1993, p. 152.

——, "Food Distributors," *Forbes,* January 3, 1994, p. 148.

"Institution Food House: Great Distributor Organization," *Institutional Distribution: The Magazine of Foodservice Distribution,* August 1992.

King, Ralph, Jr., "Food Distributors," *Forbes,* January 12, 1987, p. 130.

Ledbetter, Amy, "Lowes Foods Store Cuts 4,000 Prices," *Statesville Record and Landmark,* June 26, 1996, p. 1.

"MDI Prepares for Big Event," *Hickory Daily Record,* March 29, 1960, p. 1.

"New Lowes FreshSmart Marks Beginning of Grandfather Center Development," *Mountain Times,* September 12, 1996.

"Two Food Retailers Hit Market," *American Banker-Bond Buyer,* August 5, 1996.

—Paul S. Bodine

Allwaste, Inc.

5151 San Felipe
Houston, Texas 77056
U.S.A.
(713) 623-8777
Fax: (713) 625-7085
Web site: http://www.allwaste.com

Public Company
Incorporated: 1978 as Allwaste of Texas, Inc.
Employees: 4,057
Sales: $382.2 million (1996)
Stock Exchanges: New York
SICs: 4212 Local Trucking without Storage; 4953 Refuse
Systems; 7699 Repair Shops & Related Services, Not
Elsewhere Classified

Allwaste, Inc. provides industrial and commercial customers with a range of environmental and industrial services in North America and Austria. These included, in the mid-1990s, on-site industrial cleaning and waste management; waste transportation and processing; wastewater pretreatment, site remediation; container cleaning, maintenance and repairs; and emergency spill response services. Allwaste has grown chiefly through acquisition, having purchased about 90 businesses in its first decade as a public company.

Private Company, 1977–86

Allwaste was founded in 1977 by Raymond L. "Bubba" Nelson, Jr. After earning a degree in industrial management from McNeese State University, he had gone to work driving a garbage truck for the family business, Nelson Industrial Services of Sulphur, Louisiana. This enterprise had expanded to 16 trucks by 1971, when it was sold to Browning-Ferris Industries Inc. (BFI) for $2 million in stock. As part of the agreement, Nelson stayed on to run the company, but he later moved to Houston to help Browning-Ferris acquire similar family-owned garbage operations.

While in Houston, Nelson saw an opportunity in industrial waste removal and started Allwaste in 1977 with a single air mover, a powerful industrial vacuum cleaner, mounted on a truck chassis, that he operated himself. Purchased for $85,000 with his BFI stock as collateral, this device was used to remove waste from petrochemical-refinery smokestacks and tanks and steel-mill blast furnaces. "Before, they used buckets and shovels, but air moving cut the time needed to do the job by 80 percent," Nelson later told a reporter. Nelson soon added electrical utilities to his roster of clients.

Allwaste had a fleet of 14 air movers serving Texas petrochemical plants before the collapse of oil prices in the early 1980s almost swamped the fledgling firm under a torrent of debt. By firing one-quarter of his employees, calling on customers himself, and cutting other expenses, Nelson kept the company afloat until the local economy recovered. Interviewed by *Forbes* in 1990, he recalled, "The experience taught me that big is not necessarily beautiful in this business. Now we try to have all our locations three or four trucks underequipped. If one location has an onslaught of business, he can call his buddy next door."

Headlong Growth, 1986–88

By 1986 Allwaste was operating from five locations in three states. Nelson took the company public in December 1986 in a stock offering that raised about $7 million for Allwaste. Revenues grew from $9.2 million in fiscal 1985 (the year ended August 31, 1985) to $13.1 million in fiscal 1986, while net income increased from $143,000 to $581,000.

During the next two years Allwaste acquired about 25 small, family-run waste companies, keeping the owners on as managers, a strategy he later described as "not any different than what Browning-Ferris Industries and Waste Management did in the Seventies." It entered the trailer-tank cleaning field in October 1987 by acquiring Independent Tank Cleaning Services, Inc. of Atlanta. Also in that year the firm entered the growing asbestos abatement business. Allwaste had become the nation's leader in the vacuuming of industrial waste by the end of 1988. It was providing services from 20 facilities located in the southern and western United States and Canada, primarily for the refining, petrochemical, utility, steel, pulp and paper mining and manufacturing industries.

Allwaste's revenues soared from $27.1 million in fiscal 1987 to a startling $86 million in fiscal 1988, when net income reached $6.5 million. The company netted another $10.9 million from a February 1988 secondary public stock offering and ended the fiscal year with a 45 percent average annual return on invested capital over the last three years and a 77 percent average return on equity for the preceding five years. It was ranked second that year by *Forbes* among the 200 best small companies in the United States. Its stock, trading at about 30 times earnings, had risen fivefold since the company had gone public less than three years earlier.

Expansion by Acquisition, 1989–90

Allwaste acquired 14 companies in 1989 and earned $13.5 million during the fiscal year on revenues of $131.5 million. It became the largest glass recycler in North America by acquiring Cleveland-based The Bassichis Co. in April 1989 and began providing dewatering and sludge-processing services by acquiring a Paducah, Kentucky, company. To fund its acquisitions, the company raised $30 million in a public offering of convertible bonds. In December of that year its common stock split two for one.

By March 1990 Allwaste had acquired 37 companies since its initial public offering, mostly for stock rather than cash. Air-moving services and asbestos removal each was accounting for about one third of the company's sales. The rest came chiefly from cleaning truck tanks, recycling glass, and manufacturing the Guzzler, a superstrong vacuum machine in great demand. Early that year the company entered the railway-car cleaning business by purchasing Richmond Tank Car Co. of Angleton, Texas. For fiscal 1990 Allwaste reported record net income of $15.4 million on record revenues of $152.7 million. In September 1990 the company sold its Guzzler Manufacturing Inc. unit to a British firm for about $48 million.

Company president Clayton K. Trier, a former accountant, was largely credited by *Forbes* for Allwaste's outstanding record of growth by acquisition. The company's methods were challenged, however, in *Barron's* by a professor of accounting who concluded the company was "paying at least as much attention to collecting other waste-collection companies as to actually collecting or cleaning up waste" and "indulging in hazardous accounting practices that tend to inflate corporate profits." Ac-

cording to the author, Abraham J. Briloff, under legitimate but misleading accounting rules Allwaste had recorded only a tiny fraction of its costs for acquisitions in fiscal 1989 on its balance sheet. Trier resigned shortly after this article was published and was succeeded by Nelson, who was also chairman.

Trimming the Sails, 1991–93

During 1991 Allwaste acquired seven more companies, but it was a poor-performing year for the nation's economy, and in the fiscal year the company earned only $3.2 million on $166.6 million in revenues. One reason was the growing awareness by industries that asbestos removal might be more hazardous than simply leaving the material in place. In December 1990 Allwaste announced it planned to drop the asbestos-removal division, reporting a loss of about $2.4 million in discontinued operations and a one-time charge of nearly twice that amount. In May 1991, Allwaste sold its asbestos plants in Charlotte and Tampa for $2.9 million and in August sold its remaining asbestos abatement operations to IAM/Environmental for $4.4 million. Allwaste's revenues increased to $234 million and its net income to $11.5 million in fiscal 1992, during which it acquired eight companies.

Allwaste added the cleaning of 350-gallon stainless-steel intermediate-bulk containers to its services by acquiring a Cleveland company in June 1990. It also began leasing these containers, but in December 1992 sold, for $8.1 million, its 3,000 IBC containers to a unit of Hoover Group Inc. and immediately signed a marketing pact by which Hoover, a manufacturer of the containers, would lease and sell them, while Allwaste would become the recommended container cleaner for Hoover clients.

Allwaste earned net income of $10.2 million in fiscal 1993 on revenues of $243.6 million. Nelson attributed the company's decentralized chain of command as a primary reason for its success despite a recession for petroleum refineries and other smokestack industries served by environmental cleanup companies. There were only three layers of management between Nelson and the 63 local managers of the nationwide industrial operation comprising Allwaste's environmental services division, which was accounting for 70 percent of the company's revenues.

Further Restructuring, 1994–96

During fiscal 1994 Allwaste earned $13.1 million in net income on revenues of $286.9 million. The 1994 revenue figure was restated to reflect the September 1995 sale of glass operations, which had brought in about $63 million the previous year. Allwaste sold this business, Strategic Materials, Inc. to Equus II Inc. for about $57.1 million, so that, in the company's words, "our focus could be targeted on America's huge, heavy-industrial customer bases." Allwaste continued to own warrants in Equus's stock.

Using the funds from its glass-recycling sale, Allwaste bought 13 companies in fiscal 1995, including a California company cleaning and repairing heat exchangers, a Canadian pumping service, and a company performing in-plant services for Amoco refineries. It also installed a new management team, including Robert Chiste, who succeeded Nelson as president and chief executive officer. Chiste announced that the firm would be moving into the high-tech and health-care industries.

Allwaste lost $1.1 million in fiscal 1995 on record revenues of $344.2 million. The disappointing result rested, in great part, on pretax charges totaling $11.9 million that related to a wastewater treatment plant, investments in the former asbestos abatement business, the firm's Mexican operations, and operating plants and equipment. In fiscal 1996 the company had net income of $10.4 million, including an extraordinary gain of $3.8 million from the sale of glass-recycling operations, on revenue of $382.2 million. Allwaste's long-term debt was $137.8 million in February 1996.

The first of several small Allwaste start-up firms, Allies Staffing, was formed in September 1995 to provide contract labor during peak demand periods, both for the parent company and third-party firms. This was supplemented the following month by SafeSeal, specializing in online leak-sealing services for refineries and petrochemical plants. AllQuest Energy Services, performing lighting retrofits and improving the efficiency of heating, ventilation, and air conditioning, was started in January 1996. AllQuest Water Resources, upgraded and operating wastewater treatment facilities, was organized the following month. AllQuest Technologies was formed in April 1996 for chemical cleaning and AllQuest Pipeline Services in May to upgrade natural-gas-pipeline compressor systems. Allwaste announced that month that these companies were being placed under a subsidiary known as AllQuest Enterprises.

In August 1996 Allwaste announced that its board had adopted a poison-pill plan intended to make hostile takeover bids for the company prohibitively expensive. According to its provisions shareholders would receive 10-year rights allowing them to buy Allwaste shares at a discount if a person or group acquired 15 percent or more of the company's stock or began a tender or exchange offer to acquire 20 percent or more of the company's stock. Allwaste said the plan had not been adopted in response to any specific effort to acquire the company.

Allwaste's Operations in the Mid-1990s

On-site industrial and waste management accounted for 55 percent of Allwaste's revenues in fiscal 1995; container services for 14 percent; transportation, roll off, and tank rental for 12 percent, and excavation and site remediation for 11 percent. Industrial cleaning and waste management services were being performed from 98 locations in North America and under long-term contracts at customer facilities at 11 locations. These included air-moving and liquid vacuuming; hydroblasting and gritblasting; dredging, dewatering, and sludge processing; sludge pumping; chemical cleaning; and jet rodding. The customers were primarily in the petrochemical and refining, electric power, pulp and paper, and automotive industries.

Container services were being conducted from 31 locations in the United States. They included the cleaning of over-the-highway tank-trailers, intermodal containers, and railcar tanks, and the cleaning, repair, and maintenance of intermediate bulk containers. Wastewater pretreatment services also were being provided. Allwaste also was providing transportation of wastes from customer sites to designated landfills, recycling and recla-

mation facilities, and treatment, storage, and disposal facilities. It owned containers used to collect and transport materials and operated liquid-tank transports equipped with vacuum pumps. It operated four facilities accepting nonhazardous commercial and industrial waste products, primarily from third parties, and provided excavation and site remediation, including site preparation, construction, and maintenance of industrial settlement ponds and lagoons.

Principal Subsidiaries

Ace/Allwaste Environmental Services of Indiana, Inc.; Allies Staffing, Inc.; All Safety and Supply, Inc.; Allwaste Access Services, Inc.; Allwaste Asbestos Abatement, Inc.; Allwaste Asbestos Abatement Holdings, Inc.; Allwaste Asbestos Abatement of New England, Inc.; Allwaste Environmental Services, Inc.; Allwaste Environmental Services/Central Florida, Inc.; Allwaste Environmental Services/Chesapeake, Inc.; Allwaste Environmental Services/North Atlantic, Inc.; Allwaste Environmental Services/North Central, Inc. (Illinois); Allwaste Environmental Services/North Central, Inc. (Iowa); Allwaste Environmental Services/South Central, Inc.; Allwaste Environmental Services/West Coast, Inc.; Allwaste Environmental Services of Atlanta, Inc.; Allwaste Environmental Services of Denver, Inc.; Allwaste Environmental Services of Louisiana, Inc.; Allwaste Environmental Services of Missouri, Inc.; Allwaste Environmental Services of Ohio, Inc.; Allwaste Environmental Services of Oklahoma, Inc.; Allwaste Environmental Services of Sarnia, Ltd. (Canada); Allwaste Environmental Services of Texas, Inc.; Allwaste Explosive Services, Inc.; Allwaste Intermountain Plant Services, Inc.; Allwaste/ NAL, Inc.; Allwaste of Canada, Ltd. (Canada); Allwaste of Hawaii, Ltd.; Allwaste Oilfield Services, Inc.; Allwaste Railcar Cleaning, Inc.; Allwaste Recovery Systems, Inc.; Allwaste Services of Birmingham, Inc.; Allwaste Services of Charlotte, Inc.; Allwaste Services of El Paso, Inc.; Allwaste Services of Memphis, Inc.; Allwaste Services of Mobile, Inc.; Allwaste Services of Savannah, Inc.; Allwaste Services of Virginia, Inc.; Allwaste Servicios Industriales de Control Ecologico S.A. de C.V. (Mexico); Allwaste Tank Cleaning, Inc.; Allwaste Tank Services S.A. de C.V. (Mexico); Allwaste Transportation and Remediation, Inc.; Allwaste/Whiting, Inc.; ALRC, Inc.; ALW Enterprises, Inc.; APLC, Inc.; BEC/Allwaste, Inc.; Brown Williams Construction, Inc.; Bryson Environmental Services, Inc.; Calipo de Mexico, S.A. de C.V. (Mexico); Calipo, Ltd.; Calipo Reclamation, Ltd. (Canada); Calipo Reingungsges m.b.H. (Austria); Canadian Cargo Clean, Ltd. (Canada); Clean America, Inc.; CPC Heat Exchanger Services, Inc.; Enviro-Jet Services, Inc. (Canada); Honey-Bee Sanitation, Inc. (Canada); Hydrowash Recycling Systems, Inc.; Industrial Construction Services Co., Inc.; Industrial Pond Services, Inc.; J. D. Meagher/Allwaste, Inc.; James & Luther Services, Inc.; Jesco Industrial Services, Inc.; Madsen-Barr-Allwaste, Inc.; Oil Recycling, Inc.; Oneida Asbestos Abatement, Inc.; Oneida Asbestos Removal, Inc.; Roussel Rental Equipment, Inc.; Southern Scaffold, Inc.; Thompson Environmental Management, Inc.; Western Hydro Vac, Inc.

Further Reading

"Allwaste: Turning Garbage into Gold," *Business Week,* September 7, 1987, p. 100.

Antosh, Nelson, "Allwaste Creates 6 Companies," *Houston Chronicle,* September 28, 1996, pp. C1, C8.

——, "Allwaste Looking to Expand to Make Up for Sold Division," *Houston Chronicle,* September 4, 1995, p. C4.

"Brave Analyst," *Forbes,* December 26, 1988, p. 155.

Briloff, Abraham J., "Muddying the Waters," *Barron's,* October 8, 1990, pp. 14–15, 56.

Payne, Chris, "Allwaste Shifts Strategy as Waste Boom Wanes," *Houston Business Journal,* August 30, 1993, p. 1.

Petty, John Ira, "Allwaste Reassigns Key Players," *Houston Post,* December 21, 1993, p. C3.

——, "Forbes Names Allwaste Inc. Second among Small Firms," *Houston Post,* October 30, 1989, p. C1.

——, "Tank Car Firm Sells Last Unit to Allwaste," *Houston Post,* December 15, 1989, p. C1.

Sabota, Danni, "Allwaste Agrees to Sell Container Fleet in Marketing Deal with Atlanta Firm," *Houston Business Journal,* December 28, 1992, p. 11.

——, "Local Company Bottles Up Profits in Glass Recycling Business," *Houston Business Journal,* May 2, 1992, p. 17.

Simon, Ruth, "An Air Moving Experience," *Forbes,* March 5, 1990, pp. 112, 114, 116–117.

Vogel, Todd, "Bubba Nelson Fights for the Dirty Jobs," *Business Week,* May 22, 1989, p. 96.

—Robert Halasz

Alpine Lace Brands, Inc.

111 Dunnell Road
Maplewood, New Jersey 07040
U.S.A.
(201) 378-8600
Fax: (201) 378-8887
Web site: http://www.alpinelace.com

Public Company
Incorporated: 1986
Employees: 127
Sales: $145.0 million (1995)
Stock Exchanges: NASDAQ
SICs: 2022 Cheese, Natural, Processed & Imitation; 2099
   Food Preparations, Not Elsewhere Classified

Alpine Lace Brands, Inc., is a leading manufacturer of re-duced-fat and fat-free deli cheeses and meats. The company's operations are two-fold: First, it markets, distributes, packages, converts, and manufactures branded cheeses and specialty food products. Its PreMonde Alpine Lace line, for example, includes such items as Ched-R-Lo, Colbi-Lo, Monti-Jack-Lo, Muenster, and Sharp R.F. Cheddar cheese products. Secondly, the com-pany engages in cheese and dairy products trading. Its subsid-iary MCT Dairies, Inc., trades cheese and dairy products do-mestically and internationally. Usually the principal in transactions, MCT Dairies buys and sells bulk domestic and imported cheeses, whey powders, dairy flavorings, and but-termilk to manufacturers, processors, distributors, and cheese and dairy traders. The subsidiary also exports cheese and dairy products through U.S. government-assisted programs. Marolf Dakota Farms Cheese, Inc., another subsidiary, slices and pack-ages Alpine Lace cheese products.

Humble Beginnings, 1983

Although the items listed on the labels of low-fat cheeses and dairy products were often very appealing to the health conscious, the taste and textures of early "healthy cheeses" were not always palatable to consumers. Yet, food brokers Carl and Marion Wolf successfully positioned Alpine Lace Brands as a leader in low-fat, fat-free, and low-sodium cheese and dairy products. In less than 20 years since its founding, the company established international distribution of its product line and immediate customer recognition of the Alpine Lace brand name, making it one of the top-selling brands of light cheese and dairy products. "The biggest challenge," explained founder Carl Wolf in *Dairy Foods,* "is to have consumers try low-fat cheese and dairy products."

In 1983, Carl and Marion Wolf obtained the marketing rights for Alpine Lace brand reduced-cholesterol and reduced-salt cheese for their company First World Cheeses. The hus-band-and-wife team developed a reduced-fat cheddar cheese and then a low-fat Swiss cheese, which they started selling to a limited number of stores. At first, they marketed their products exclusively to supermarket deli sections where competition from national brands was not as formidable. First World Cheeses became a public company three years later in 1986 and sold merchandise nationally since 1987.

In 1989 First World Cheeses purchased Marolf Dakota Farms, Inc. As a wholly owned subsidiary headquartered in Sturgis, North Dakota, Marolf Dakota Farms served as a skim milk and cheese producer for the company, eventually becom-ing the packaging and converting facility for bulk cheese for Alpine Lace. Another subsidiary, Mountain Farms, Inc., con-verted cheese products for the company as well.

Competing with National Brands During the 1990s

During the 1990s, First World Cheeses' products began to compete effectively with national brands. In 1991, the company changed its name from First World Cheeses to Alpine Lace Brands, Inc. Still headquartered in Maplewood, New Jersey, Alpine Lace Brands marketed its products as having substantial nutritional benefits—fat free, reduced fat, or reduced sodium— as compared to other cheeses. Alpine Lace's products were distributed both to supermarket delis and dairy cases, as well as to club stores and food service accounts. They also were fea-tured as ingredients in food products.

Company Perspectives:

Alpine Lace Brands, Inc., develops and markets an expanding line of Fat Free, Reduced Fat and/or Reduced Sodium cheese and delicatessen meat products sold under the Alpine Lace brand name. Alpine Lace products are available in virtually 100 percent of supermarkets and delicatessens nationwide, and provide nutritionally superior benefits over regular cheeses and delicatessen meats while addressing consumer demands regarding taste, quality, and freshness. The company's Marolf Dakota Farms Cheese, Inc., subsidiary slices and packages Alpine Lace cheese for dairy case and club store sales, while its MCT Dairies, Inc., subsidiary engages in the cheese and dairy commodity trading business.

Though Alpine Lace brand products were priced somewhat higher than conventional cheese items—about 16 cents per slice of American-flavor cheese compared to 14 cents for a slice of Kraft American singles—they still sold well. Net sales for 1991 totaled $113.7 million, and pre-tax earnings were $1.4 million that year. Stockholders' equity was recorded at $6.6 million.

By 1992, Alpine Lace products were sold in 45 percent of supermarkets, including major chains such as A&P, Vons, Ralphs, and Great Food. The company controlled 20 percent of the market and was the second-largest light cheese brand.

That year the company introduced Alpine Lace Free N' Lean Fat Free cheese spreads, featuring cream cheese, cream cheese with chives, cream cheese with garlic and herbs, cheddar, and cheddar with jalapeno. The line of products contained only thirty calories and less than 0.5 grams of fat per one ounce serving. In addition, Free N' Lean products could be microwaved, baked, or reheated. Other manufacturers' low-fat cream cheeses could not.

Alpine Lace Brands launched the new line with a major merchandising campaign in New York. In addition to a press conference and sampling of the Free N' Lean products, the company offered free bagels and cream cheese to New York commuters at train stations and at the Staten Island Ferry's terminal. In all, the company treated commuters to more than 50,000 bagels.

The Free N' Lean line was made with fat replacement technology acquired in May 1990 from Dr. Aly Gamay. The technology allowed the removal of cream from and the addition of flavorings and texture to the cheese product. Gamay told *Supermarket News:* "The whole system basically involves cultured vegetable gum and a special series of flavorings that are particularly adaptable [to cheese made of skim milk]. If you take the fat out of milk and cheese, it becomes bitter. What we've been able to do is add back or mimic the feel and also the sweetness of the fat." Other products under development at this time included fat-free grated Parmesan cheese, butter, sour cream, toppings, and whipped cream.

Net sales for 1992 totaled $117.8 million, and pre-tax earnings were $0.2 million. Selling, general, and administration expenses added up to $32.7 million. In 1993, net sales were higher—$129.8 million—but pre-tax earnings resulted in a loss of $5.2 million. As a result, Alpine Lace Brands sold its holdings in its Mountain Farms, Inc., subsidiary. Mountain Farms's operating losses prompted Alpine Lace Brands to sell all its common stock, which represented 65 percent of the subsidiary's outstanding shares. J.R. Simplot, a dairy products company, purchased Mountain Farms on February 14, 1994. At that time, Alpine Lace contracted Mountain Farms to convert no less than 3 million pounds of cheese annually in a three-year supply agreement, which was terminated in 1994 owing to Mountain Farms's continued operational troubles and subsequent restructuring.

Alpine Lace likewise initiated a restructuring plan for Marolf Dakota Farms Cheese, Inc., in 1994 to increase efficiency and productivity at that subsidiary. Alpine Lace Brands ended skim-milk cheese production at the Marolf Dakota Farms facility, as well as discontinued the Marolf Dakota Farms Cheese brand line. The subsidiary became solely a cheese packaging operation. With these changes, the net sales for Alpine Lace Brands grew to $132.4 million in 1994. In all, sales increased $2.5 million or 2 percent from 1993. Gross profit grew from 20 percent in 1993 to 24.8 percent in 1994. Operating expenses dropped $5.2 million, and administration expenses decreased more than 27.9 percent. Pre-tax earnings—before special charges—recovered to $1.1 million.

In 1995, Marolf Dakota Farms Cheese, Inc., purchased a high-speed slicing production line to improve quality and increase productivity. Also that year, Alpine Lace Brands was granted a patent for the chemical process used in manufacturing low-fat and fat-free cheeses. Upon receipt of the patent, the company brought suit against its major competitors—namely, Kraft, Borden, Beatrice Cheese, and Schreiber Foods—for patent infringement. Alpine Lace Brands requested relief and damages owing to these manufacturers producing products using the recently patented process. A federal court, however, found in favor of Kraft. Alpine Lace planned to appeal the decision to the U.S. Court of Appeals for the Federal Circuit in Washington, D.C.

New Products and International Expansion

Alpine Lace Brands introduced a variety of new or improved products in 1995. The company, said Wolf at the time, "made important strides in the dairy case through new item distribution and product innovation." Branching from cheese and dairy products, the company launched a fat-free, reduced-sodium turkey breast under the Alpine Lace brand name. This product, manufactured without nitrates, claimed to be 63 percent lower in sodium and only 22 calories per ounce. Kim Alexis, a supermodel and spokesperson for the company, was featured in television commercials for the new fat-free turkey. In addition, the company announced a reduced-fat feta cheese under the Alpine Lace brand name. With 33 percent less fat, the feta cheese sold in prepackaged seven- to nine-ounce chunks. At its introduction, Alpine Lace Brands was the only national distributor of a reduced-fat feta cheese. In addition, the company offered a fancy-shredded, ziplock-packaged fat-free Parmesan cheese for the first time in 1995. Alpine Lace Brands also developed enhanced fat-free shredded mozzarella and cheddar cheeses with improved melting and taste. New, bolder packaging was instituted to note the enhancements on products.

Alpine Lace Brands also established an industrial and food service business in 1995 and expanded its channels of distribution, including co-branding, licensing, and industrial and international sales. The company achieved Kosher—certification for its fat-free bulk cheeses used as industrial ingredients. It planned to increase further its Kosher line of deli products and formed an industrial/co-branding division, headed by Marion Wolf, to assist with these efforts. Another area under the new division's control involved negotiations with restaurant chains for their use of Alpine Lace brand cheeses in appetizers, entrees, or desserts. In November 1995, Alpine Lace also marketed a line of low-fat food—such as cheese loaves, cheese sauces, and salsa—with exercise celebrity Richard Simmons. These stable, nonrefrigerated items were co-branded products with Simmons and sold under his Slimmons name.

In addition to new and improved product lines, Alpine Lace Brands expanded its sales territory in 1995. The company further developed its presence in Canada and Puerto Rico and added an international division charged with evaluating international markets and the distribution channels for these markets. The company named vice-president and general manager of the Branded Division George Wenger as head of the new division.

The product line growth and international expansion of 1995 resulted in net sales of $145 million that year—an increase of 9.6 percent from the preceding year. Pre-tax earnings in 1995 totaled $4.4 million. And stockholders' equity grew from a deficiency of $0.5 million in 1994 to a surplus of $5.1 million. As Wolf reported to the company's shareholders in the 1995 annual report: "Fiscal 1995 was an extremely successful year for Alpine Lace. The company reported substantial growth in its profits and solid gains in its revenues. We controlled overhead expenses, expanded our product lines and distribution channels, incorporated new divisions within the company, and refined our Fat Free and Reduced Fat cheesemaking technologies. The year's achievements enhanced our position as the leading marketer of nutritionally superior deli cheeses and meats, and poised us for further growth in 1996."

Indeed, in 1996 expansion continued. Internationally, MCT Dairies moved in the same direction as Alpine Lace Brands in the preceding year with the appointment of Kevin Colson as director of international sales and marketing. Colson brought experience and familiarity in international sales to the company, especially in the Mexican and South American markets. The cultivation of the company's product line advanced as well. By 1996 Alpine Lace Brands offered more than 200 sizes and types of cheeses to consumers. In March of that year, the company further developed low-fat cheeses with improved melting points. "Rather than an onslaught of new products, we're improving the quality of our existing products," Carl Wolf told *Dairy Foods* in February 1996. Nevertheless, Alpine Lace

Brands still introduced a new low-fat turkey, then launched a 97 percent fat-free ham in 1996.

The company controlled 50 percent of the low-fat cheese market in 1996 and expected a 17 percent sales growth. In February of that year, Alpine Lace Brand products were available in 99 percent of all U.S. supermarkets. Despite this enviable position, the company remained chagrined with consumer distrust regarding the taste of light cheese products. Thus, Alpine Lace Brands expected to increase its merchandising efforts in 1996 through new field merchandisers and electronic signs, among other promotions, to win over doubting consumers. The company, for instance, contracted Texan chef Pam Mycoskie to write a cookbook featuring recipes using Alpine Lace products and explored ways to incorporate the Internet into its marketing strategy. Nonetheless, as Carl Wolf noted, "With one of the most recognizable and reputable names in the cheese industry and [with] consumer lifestyle and consumption patterns turning toward healthier living, we have great hopes for the future."

Principal Subsidiaries

Marolf Dakota Farms Cheese, Inc.; MCT Dairies, Inc.

Further Reading

"Alpine Lace Brands in Licensing Agreement with Richard Simmons," *Business Wire,* October 24, 1995, p. 10241241.
"Alpine Lace Brands, Inc., Announces Its Co-Branding Project with Snack Appeal, Inc.," *Business Wire,* June 18, 1996, p. 6181308.
"Alpine Lace Brands to Seek Acquisitions, Joint Ventures," *Business Wire,* July 23, 1996, p. 7231469.
"Alpine Lace Products to Be Served on Amtrak Trains," *Business Wire,* December 23, 1996, p. 12231067.
"Alpine Lace, Simplot Dairy in Deal," *Supermarket News,* March 28, 1994, p. 46.
Anderson, Peggy, "Alpine Lace Grows a Healthy Business: Company Jockeys for Bigger Slice of Deli Market," *Dairy Foods,* February 1996, p. 19.
"Clear Container Delivers 'Deli Fresh' Appearance," *Prepared Foods,* August 1994, p. 177.
"Consumer Reports Rates Alpine Lace American Slices Best," *Business Wire,* April 24, 1996, p. 4241328.
"Fat-Free Turkey Joins Alpine Line," *Supermarket News,* July 15, 1995, p. 30.
Goldstein, Seth, "Goodtimes Sweats Its Way to the Top: Richard Simmons Helps Vendor to Move Product," *Billboard,* July 22, 1995, p. 6.
"No-Fat Foods: Less Than Meets the Eye," *Consumer Reports,* May 1993, p. 282.
"Shops Contact Alpine Lace," *ADWEEK* (Eastern edition), November 18, 1996, p. 6.
Sparks, Debra, "Alpine Lace: Bigger Cheese," *Financial World,* September 26, 1995, p. 18+.
Turcsik, Richard, "Alpine Lace Offers Fat-Free Spreads," *Supermarket News,* May 4, 1992, p. 146.

—Charity Anne Dorgan

Altera Corporation

2610 Orchard Parkway
San Jose, California 95134
U.S.A.
(408) 894-7000
Fax: (408) 828-0463
Web site: http://www.altera.com

Public Company
Incorporated: 1984
Employees: 923
Sales: $401.6 million (1995)
Stock Exchanges: NASDAQ
SICs: 3674 Semiconductors & Related Devices

Founded in 1983, Altera Corporation is a leading maker of high-density programmable logic devices (PLDs), based on metal-oxide semiconductor technology (CMOS). These logic chips are circuits used in a variety of devices to produce electrical signals. The specific technology associated with programmable logic chips requires less power than other chips, and is more efficient than custom logic chips, reducing development time and time-to-market. Altera's products are used by makers of communications, computer, and industrial equipment. In addition to PLDs, Altera also creates software to help customers program standard integrated circuits.

Rodney Smith—a British applications engineer and then Fairchild Semiconductor manager—founded Altera in 1983 with $500,000 in seed money. Joining Smith as founding members were three others with considerable semiconductor industry experience: Robert Hartmann of Signetics Corp., James Sansbury of Hewlett-Packard Co., and Paul Newhagen of Fairchild Semiconductor Corp. The name "Altera" was introduced in 1984, standing for the word "alterable." That year, the company introduced its first generation of chips.

Altera's sales strategy, from the beginning, has been to offer a range of standard programmable parts for the IBM PC AT with inexpensive development tools, allowing customers to self-design and program custom logic circuits that meet their specific needs. This strategy was formulated to meet the industry need created by the delay associated with custom chips, due to the high percentage of silicon designs that require revision toward the end of the design cycle. With erasable, reprogrammable chips, revision can proceed immediately and repeatedly until all design bugs have been eliminated. A relationship with Intel Corp. began in August 1984, when the companies agreed to swap certain designs. In 1985, Intel began to market a group of Altera's logic microchips.

1988: Altera Goes Public

In 1988, Altera went public, and calendar sales for the year reached $38 million. The company also purchased a minority interest in Cypress Semiconductor's wafer fabrication facility (fab), and introduced a new generation of chips. The company launched the industry's first erasable programmable logic device (EPLD), which provided a complete interface to the PS/2's Micro Channel Bus. This new device allowed vendors to save time and board space. New EPLD programming software—usable on IBM PC AT and compatible computers—accompanied the device. Later that year, Altera came forth with another innovation, MAX (multiple-array matrix), a new architecture for ultra-violet-erasable programmable logic devices that doubled the timing and quadrupled the density of previous AND/OR EPLD arrays. The new devices presented up to 5,000 gates, system speeds of up to 40 MHz, and over 200,000 unique programmable elements. Because the structure of the new PLDs differed so much from previous PLD devices, which used the AND/OR architecture, Altera offered a tool-kit addition to quicken the learning curve for designers. The package, which was workable on IBM Personal Computer ATs and compatibles, contained a graphics-design editor, a design-processing engine, a timing simulator, and programming software modules, all controlled by a supervisor task-control module.

Altera's key competitor, Xilinx, introduced similar technology in 1988. No longer was Altera alone in its market niche of programmable logic. Altera's relationship with Xilinx would be a heated rivalry over the coming years.

17

The Semiconductor Industry During the 1980s

The U.S. semiconductor market at this time was dominated by five large companies: Advanced Micro Devices, Inc., Intel Corp., Motorola, Inc., National Semiconductor Corp., and Texas Instruments, Inc. However, companies such as Altera and Xilinx were seen as formidable ''upstarts.'' Altera consistently ranked among the top five public semiconductor companies in the categories of net profits and gross margins (with margins reaching an impressive 60 percent). The company had been able to carve a niche due to specialization, focusing on top-notch design of PLDs and spending its research and design budget on new product development. In 1989, sales rose 55 percent to $59 million, with $11 million net.

Looking primarily to Japan, Altera stepped up its overseas sales techniques in 1989. Lacking a Japanese office or distributor, the company hired two distributors with unique entrepreneurial approaches to aggressively promote Altera's product line to the Japanese market. The majority of Japanese sales were handled by JMC, a 9-year-old company led by Haruki Kamiyama. Kamiyama, the youngest member of a Japanese trade delegation that visited the U.S. around this time, was an entrepreneur committed to selling U.S. technology in Japan. Altera's other Japanese distributor, Paltek, focused primarily on market development, largely through the efforts of one representative—a Japanese-speaking American whose previous career stints included teaching English, working as a circus clown, and acting in Japanese soap operas. Trained in physics, this representative was able to use language skills and technical know-how to design products and customer services, and to effectively communicate with Japanese markets. Because almost all semiconductor business in Japan goes through distributors (as opposed to the United States, where 75 percent of business is done directly with customers), these two distributors were key to Altera's 1989 growth in Japanese business. By 1990, 15 percent of the company's business was due to sales in Japan.

Sales in 1990 were $78.3 million, a 33 percent increase, with net income of $13.4 million. In June of that year, Altera made its first cash investment in a fab. The company invested $7.4

million in Cypress Semiconductor's Round Rock, Texas facility, receiving in exchange guaranteed IC production capability, a portion of the fab's CMOS capacity, access to next-generation products whenever they come on-line, and the right to purchase up to 20 percent of the fab over time. Cypress received the rights to Altera's next generation of MAX products (Altera was already producing Cypress's line of programmable logic devices, SRAMs, and other products). Altera President Rodney Smith told *Computer Design* that the production purchasing option with Cypress would save Altera approximately $30 million in construction costs over sharing production with another vendor. Although Altera had never before entered into this type of relationship with a fab, the company already had exchange and foundry agreements with Intel, Texas Instruments, and Sharp. These arrangements enabled the company to continue producing state-of-the-art chips with no production facilities.

Altera's partners also benefit from these relationships. For example, Texas Instruments used Altera's erasable programmable logic chip to design a compact, high-resolution video camera that was flexible enough to be used under different lighting systems, and for uses ranging from closed-circuit security to industrial inspection and monitoring systems. The chip proved a low-cost, high-yield option.

In 1991, another new chip generation was introduced. The Max 7000 family of ultraviolet-erasable programmable logic devices provided between 4,000 and 40,000 gates, increasing up to five times the capacity of previous high-density programmable chips. Sales surpassed the $100 million mark, reaching $106.9 million with net income of $17.8 million.

Challenges During the 1990s

The year 1992 included the development of another new chip generation, as well as a series of challenges for Altera. The slowdown of Japanese business caused by overseas economic conditions, as well as competitive pricing by rival companies, led Altera to drop its chip prices. A drop in sales brought the company down to $101.5 million with net income of only $11.5 million. The crisis was short-lived, however; sales in Japan increased by 87 percent in 1993. At this time, Altera's Japanese sales accounted for about 20 percent of business, with NEC serving as the company's largest customer, and Matsushita, Sony, Mitsubishi Electric, and Toshiba among the company's biggest clients. Altera's Japanese-bound chips primarily serviced two types of products: telecommunications equipment, including digital telephone exchanges and cellular telephone base stations; and professional audio visual equipment such as portable camcorders.

Also in 1992, a class action lawsuit was filed against Altera and some current and former officers and directors. The suit alleged violations of federal security laws, and was settled out of court in July 1994.

Overall 1993 revenues surged to $140.3 million, with an 84 percent increase in net income to $21.2 million. That year, the company also invented a system to protect delicate leads from ruin during burn-in and test processes, as well as after customer purchase. The device also reduced time-to-market by facilitating programming and prototyping. The company also developed two compatible sockets, one for use on PC boards and the other for programming EPLDs in carriers.

As new products aged, manufacturing costs went down and Altera was able to drop prices on its products over time. In 1993, such a discount was passed on to Altera's customers, with 30 percent price cuts on the volume-driven FLEX 8000 family of PLDs. At the end of 1993, Altera and Xilinx each introduced Pentium-compatible products, seeking to migrate programmable array logic (PAL) markets toward programmable logic device solutions. Altera's product targeted the high-density macrocell portion of the PLD business, while Xilinx's was aimed at the low-density segment. Altera also released the MAX 7000E family of complex PLDs, which featured architectural improvements of circuit performance of complex PLDs, as well as enhanced routability and usability features. At this time, Altera was the number three volume manufacturer of programmable CMOS logic devices, with a 15 percent market share. Ahead of Altera was Advanced Micro Devices, and in the number one position was competitor Xilinx, Inc., with a 24 percent share.

For Altera, 1994 was a year characterized by new product innovations and an ongoing effort to beat the competition with presence in new market segments. Seeking to gain a lead, Altera increased its market share to 20 percent in 1994 with the purchase of Intel's PLD business, for about $50 million in cash and stock. In addition, the Intel acquisition delivered new customers and 15 new products to Altera. Further, Altera established itself as a programmable logic vendor supporting Microsoft's Windows NT operating system by releasing MAX PLUS II version 4.0, representing a shift to the fully 32-bit software environment. MAX PLUS II incorporates VHDL very-high-speed integrated circuit hardware description language synthesis. This VHDL standard was promoted when 11 companies joined to form Analog VHDL International (AVI), an industry group that helped develop the IEEE 1076.1 standard (the analog extension of VHDL).

Altera Battles Xilinx

Altera also made a first step into the reconfigurable hardware products market in 1994. The company introduced a high-capacity programmable logic add-in board for PCs—the Reconfigurable Interconnect Peripheral Processor (RIPP 10). This ISA bus board supports up to 100,000 gates of reconfigurable logic, allowing up to eight Altera FLEX 8188 devices. The company also put forth the industry's highest density single-die device, the 16,000-gate EPF51500 PLD, which was immediately followed by Xilinx's introduction of a 25,000-gate device. In April, the company introduced the largest capacity PLD on the market and the first off-the-shelf PLD/MCM—the 50,000-gate PLD multichip module PEF8050M, targeted at the ASIC prototyping market, as well as imaging applications and reconfigurable hardware products (RHPs).

Altera and Xilinx continued to race each other for introduction of industry-leading products. In June 1994, both companies came forth with products moving their devices to unprecedented 5 nanosecond pin-to-pin delay time range. Xilinx targeted new markets with faster speed devices, while Altera's EPM7032 was aimed at applications requiring logic integration

in systems with next-generation microprocessors. In July, Altera made its first overtures to the military market, offering four PLDs as military standard compliant. Although defense spending was decreasing, a new emphasis on upgrading existing programs made design engineers receptive to off-the-shelf solutions to integrate system features into smaller board space, while keeping design costs low. As add-in card designers began to look toward PCI-compliant PLDs, Xilinx and Altera both claimed to introduce the industry's first programmable logic devices that were fully compliant with the Peripheral Component Interconnect (PCI) specification.

In August 1994, competitor Advanced Micro Devices filed a suit against Altera. AMD charged Altera with violating six of AMD's programmable logic device technology patents. Altera followed with a countersuit, stating that AMD infringed upon at least two perhaps as many as six of Altera's PLD patents. The case would be decided against AMD in 1996. Another suit had been initiated against Altera by Xilinx in June 1993, also regarding patent infringement. In the winter of 1994, Judge Aguilar indicated plans to appoint a special master with the technical background necessary to sort out the companies' claims regarding master-slave configurations and interconnect patents. Altera filed a separate suit against Xilinx and the case continued to boomerang with multiple countersuits probing the company patents over the next couple of years. In 1994, Xilinx continued to lead the CMOS PLD market with a 29 percent share, while Altera retained 18 percent, followed by AMD with 16 percent.

Another innovation in the MAX family, the MAX 9000 architecture, was introduced in October 1994. The 9000 family more than doubled the density of currently available EPLDs, reaching system speeds of up to 80Mhz, and increasing cell utilization. Sales in 1994 neared $200,000, with almost 50 percent of revenues derived from foreign sales. Data communications and telecom customers comprised about 44 percent of sales. The $58 million increase in sales over 1993 represented the largest one-year increase in Altera's history. International semiconductor shipments reached $100 billion, along with sales of CMOS PLDs (the newly preferred method for implementing logic design).

In 1995, Altera came out with its MAX 9000 family of erasable PLDs. After a 30 percent drop in the price of the MAX 7000 family of erasable PLDs, the company's sales burst to more than twice the previous year's, reaching an incredible $401.6 million with $86.9 million in net income. By this time, Altera had 881 employees, as compared to 370 just five years earlier. Also in 1995, Altera and Xilinx announced that their chips could service the lucrative $3 billion DSP semiconductor market, competing with dedicated and general-purpose DSP chips. Altera introduced Flexible Logic Element matrix (FLEX) 10000, another programmable logic architecture which sent the market over the 100,000 gate barrier. The device was created with what Altera called a "sea of programmable bits" architecture, using the embedded/standard logic block combination.

The company put a new face on an old model in 1995, augmenting the three-year-old MAX 7000 line with the MAX 7000S family. This new line of CPLDs was based on a new 0.5 micron, triple-layer metal process developed with Altera's foundry partners. The MAX 7000, since its introduction in 1992 when it generated $5 million in sales, had grown to an $80 million sales product by 1994, making it Altera's most successful CPLD line. Also in 1995, while industry reports bemoaned longer lead times in the field programmable gate array (FPGA) market, Altera announced that it had reduced lead times for two devices—the 12,000-gate EPF81188A and 16,000-gate EPF81500A—from 20 weeks to 10 weeks.

Altera and Xilinx once again were neck-and-neck in their announcements of industry landmark products, with Xilinx's introduction of the industry's fastest FPGA and Altera's announcement of the highest gate count FPGA shipped in volume.

Partnerships in the Mid-1990s

Joining six intellectual property providers, Altera launched the Altera Megafunctions Partners Program (AMPP) in August 1995. Megafunctions are hardware description language (HDL)-based designs of system-level functions that may be compiled in MAX-PLUS II software and targeted to Altera's device architectures. This new alliance was charged with the development of synthesizable function blocks for Altera's PLDs. The five other partners in AMPP—Eureka Technology, CAST Inc., RAVIcad, Silicon Engineering, and Advacel— were provided with access to Altera's 21,000 design seats.

In another partnership development, Altera entered into a U.S. joint venture wafer fabrication site, to be located in Camas, Washington, with foundry partner Taiwan Semiconductor Manufacturing Corp. (TSMC). The agreement caused TSMC to displace Sharp as Altera's biggest wafer supplier. Later, the companies were joined by Analog Devices and Integrated Silicon Solutions, Inc., forming a joint venture company named WaferTech.

The industry's largest capacity chip was introduced by Altera in 1996. The 10K100 has 10 million transistors. Also that year, the company unveiled MegaCore and OpenCore, software programs which allowed engineers to evaluate MegaCore functions prior to licensing them. A major industry slowdown in computers led to downsizing, and Altera was no exception. An oversupply of inventory and reduction of chip demand led to revenue decline during the year's first quarter, and the company cut its workforce by 11 percent in June, eliminating about 100 positions. At the same time, the company authorized the repurchase of up to two million company shares.

Forging a new union, Altera joined Synopsis in a five-year agreement to jointly develop and market designer tools to support complex programmable logic devices (CPLDs). The partnership targeted two market segments: second wave designers changing to HDL-based designs for CPLDs and FPGAs, and gate array designers migrating to programmable logic for designs with gate densities of 100,000 or less.

The end of 1996 gave signs of a semiconductor industry downturn, similar to those of the 1980s and early 1990s. Several semiconductor manufacturers, including Altera, closed for the Christmas holidays, asking employees to take vacation days, borrow vacation days from the next year, and/or take time off without pay.

Predictions for Future Growth

In 1983, Altera brought a new idea to the market, introducing the reprogrammable logic device. In the 1990s, that innovation is a billion-dollar industry, bustling with competition. Altera's niche is, and always has been, its emphasis on new-product development, through an investment in research and development over production. A market research firm, Dataquest, estimated in 1994 that the overall semiconductor market would grow at a compound annual growth rate of 15 percent a year through 1998. And, according to *Money,* analysts believed in 1996 that CPLD sales would grow 25 percent over the next five years. By 1996, the CPLD market had reached $1.6 billion, and Altera was well-protected from competition, due to the complexity of its chips—fueled by its long-time emphasis on research and development over production—as well as its close customer relationships. It seems likely that if the industry downturn reverses itself and the market grows more lucrative and technologically advanced Altera will be at the forefront.

Further Reading

"Altera to Cut Employment 11%," *Wall Street Journal,* June 26, 1996, p. B6.

"Altera 2Q Sales up 26%, Net 24%," *Electronic News,* July 22, 1996, p. 16.

Case, John, "Intimate Relations," *Inc.,* August, 1990, pp. 64–72.

Cohen, Sarah, "Washington Fab Venture Lures 2 More," *Electronic News,* July 1, 1996, p. 6.

DeTar, Jim, "Altera, Partners Launch PLD Program," *Electronic News,* August 14, 1995, p. 49.

Keating, Peter, "Coming off the Ropes, These Techs Pack Punch," *Money,* December 1996, pp. 76–78.

Lineback, J. Robert, "Altera's Speedy Way to Tailor Add-Ons to IBM's PS/2," *Electronics,* February 18, 1988, pp. 99–102.

Mayer, John H., "Altera Buys into Cypress Fab Capability," *Computer Design,* June 18, 1990, p. 34.

Rice, Valerie, "Where They Are Now: 1987's Superstars Revisited," *Electronic Business,* September 4, 1989, pp. 35–38.

——, "Breaking into Japan: Small U.S. companies Find Success in a Demanding Market," *Electronic Business,* November 27, 1989, pp. 60–62.

"Trial Prospects Grow for Xilinx, Altera," *Electronic News,* December 12, 1994, p. 65.

Wiegner, Kathleen K., "Roll-Your-Own Chips," *Forbes,* October 1, 1990, pp. 242–244.

"Xilinx, Altera Tout Faster, Larger Programmable Devices," *Electronic News,* October 16, 1995, pp. 52–53.

—Heidi Feldman

American Business Information, Inc.

5711 South 86th Circle
P.O. Box 27347
Omaha, Nebraska 68127
U.S.A.
(402) 593-4500
Fax: 402-331-1505
Web site: http://www.abii.com

Public Company
Incorporated: 1972
Employees: 870 (1995)
Sales: $86.77 million (1995)
Stock Exchanges: NASDAQ
SICs: 7379 Computer Related Services; 7375 Information
    Retrieval Services; 2741 Miscellaneous Publishing

American Business Information, Inc. (ABI) is a leading U.S. provider of marketing-related business information for small businesses and consumers and in 1995 was the eighth-largest firm in the large and fragmented computer-related services industry. In addition to database developers like American Business Information, the computer-related services industry includes data vendors, directory publishers, list brokers, marketing consultants, and ad agencies. In the mid-1990s, more than 450,000 customers—two-thirds of them repeat buyers—used American Business Information's varied data products to generate sales leads, reduce selling costs, improve marketing efficiency, and verify business credit information. With one of the largest and most accurate proprietary business information libraries in the world, American Business Information's databases are divided into 7,500 industry categories and provide the data for all its directories, list brokerage and market research services, and phone and on-line information services. The preponderance of American Business Information's sales come from its CD-ROM, computer diskette, prospect list, and mailing label products, and in the mid-1990s its bestselling CD-ROM titles included *The Ultimate Phone Book, American Manufac-*

turers Directory, 88 Million Households Phone Book, and *16 Million Businesses Phone Book.*

Mobile Homes, Phone Books, and the Great Untapped Market: 1972–80

After earning an MBA at the University of Nebraska, Lincoln, in 1971 American Business Information's Indian-born founder Vinod Gupta joined the Commodore Corporation, an Omaha-based mobile home manufacturer, as a marketing research analyst. When Commodore asked him to compile a list of mobile home dealers in its region, Gupta ordered AT&T's entire 4,800-volume catalog of national Yellow Pages phone books only to be told that Commodore would consider buying his list only if he did the work on his own time. Working with a colleague out of his garage, Gupta completed the list and offered to sell it to Commodore for $9,000 *or* give it to them outright in exchange for the right to market it to their competitors. Commodore chose the latter route, and armed with a $100 bank loan for postage, Gupta sent a sample list to the nation's mobile home makers to gauge their interest. Within a month, Gupta was deluged with checks totaling $13,000 and orders for another $9,000.

While holding down his Commodore job, Gupta hired two part-time employees and officially launched American Business Information, Inc., in 1972. By the end of its first year American Business Information had generated $22,000 in profit, and when Commodore's business began to slump in 1973, Gupta was freed to pursue his growing business full time. Following his success with his mobile home industry data, Gupta began compiling lists for the U.S. motorcycle, bicycle, boat, car, tractor, and CB radio industries and methodically inputting the nation's Yellow Pages into his master database. Because American Business Information was promising to give small businesses the same access as larger firms to data that would help them determine the size of potential markets, select optimal distribution channels, generate sales leads, allocate marketing resources in their territories, and prioritize and qualify customers, each of American Business Information's new lists was greeted with a flurry of orders. Gupta's visits to industry trade shows to "work

---

Company Perspectives:

The sources we use provide us with the most dependable and accurate information we can find, and we're able to identify virtually every business in the United States and Canada. But even though these are the best sources available, that's not good enough for us. It's our philosophy to contact every single company in our database to verify our information. As a matter of fact, we won't enter ANY information into our database until it's been personally verified.

It all adds up to more than 14 million telephone calls a year, just to verify and update our information. Sure, it's expensive, but it's the only way to make absolutely certain that we have correct information.

Aside from ensuring accuracy, however, telephone verification gives us a golden opportunity to gather more information. We are able to obtain such valuable information as the names of key executives, number of employees, suite number, and the exact line of business a company is in . . . important information that helps our customers stay one step ahead of their competition.

The result? The finest database of 11 million businesses in existence.

In terms of completeness, accuracy, and depth, no other source can compare to our database of virtually every U.S. and Canadian business. Our commitment to quality at every level of the compilation effort guarantees you the very best business marketing information available.

---

the exhibits'' only cemented his conviction that American small business's hunger for basic, comprehensive business-to-business data had barely been tapped.

Gupta soon discovered that there was more than one way to usefully package marketing data. Prior to the 1970s, sales and marketing costs for smaller U.S. businesses had traditionally been comparatively low, and only the largest American firms could afford to use expensive computerized data processing methods in their marketing programs. By the 1980s, however, marketing costs had skyrocketed, and computers were becoming cheap enough to help even smaller firms gather data on potential customers and target them with precision and efficiency. Gupta had followed the changing topography of business marketing closely and began to expand the available formats for his data, from simple alphabetic prospect lists that gave the name, address, and Yellow Pages heading of each company in an industry, to customized mailing labels, three-by-five index cards for telemarketer's cold-call notes, and, by 1977, magnetic tapes and diskettes for sorting and generating lists, labels, and cards.

Minding the Data Store: 1981–90

While American Business Information's staff painstakingly keyed in the entire industry-by-industry contents of the nation's phone directories, in 1981 Gupta began diversifying and specializing American Business Information's growing horde of

data. Experience had taught him that the average American Business Information customer ordered only a few thousand names and that rather than offer customers a list for their entire industry his data could be repackaged in more focused and effective ways. In 1981 American Business Information therefore published its first state directory—for businesses in Nebraska—and two years later offered a directory of national businesses categorized by the four-digit Standard Industrial Classification codes published by the U.S. government. By 1984, American Business Information had moved squarely into the emerging electronic information services industry with the introduction of On-Line Business Link, a master database of American Business Information business information available to callers around the clock for a competitive fee.

Although Gupta had been sifting, repackaging, and enhancing the phone companies' business data for more than a decade, in 1984 the phone industry finally sued him for copyright infringement. Southwestern Bell Media charged that American Business Information's practice of basing its databases on the information and subject headings found in the Yellow Pages amounted to an illegal arrogation of the phone company's proprietary information. After three years of legal investigation and motion filing, American Business Information and Southwestern Bell reached a settlement that allowed Gupta to continue using phone directory information, temporarily averting a major legal setback.

By the mid-1980s, the nation's roughly five thousand individual Yellow Pages had finally been digested by American Business Information's computers, and Gupta continued to expand on his phone directory data by leasing the data of other commercial list compilers and owners. In 1985 he also began to retain advertising agencies and list brokers to help market American Business Information's products. American Business Information published 14 updated state business directories in 1987 and increased the number to 36 in 1989. To gain the largest possible piece of the small business marketing information market, Gupta kept his prices low, charging four to sixteen cents a name depending on the number of names, the sophistication of content, and the data format the customer selected.

In 1988 Gupta launched a comprehensive $4.7 million, three-year ''data enhancement'' program to systematically add value to his basic business lists. The rate of change among U.S. businesses seemed only to increase, and American Business Information's primary data sources—phone books and association membership lists—were no longer reliable by themselves to support the guarantee of accuracy and timeliness that American Business Information needed to win return customers. American Business Information compilation staff began to annually contact every business in its database with more than one hundred employees as well as each business that had registered a change or deletion of its Yellow Pages listing from the previous year (roughly 40 percent of American Business Information's database). They also verified the accuracy of American Business Information's existing information and added additional data such as business size, number of employees, and primary business activity. American Business Information's database soon included not only name and address but the product brands sold by each business, the size of the original

Yellow Page ad, and the year the ad first appeared in the phone directory.

By 1988 American Business Information was also including the size of each business and the name of its owners or managers. Although the data enhancement portion of the program was complete by 1991, American Business Information's verification procedure became an ongoing process involving 14 million phone calls a year and the careful sifting of annual reports, government publications, business magazines, newsletters, and newspapers. As useful as American Business Information's affordable lists were proving for small business owners, larger companies (annual orders of $10,000 or more) still preferred information in directory-style books. Eager to win the business of these firms from the traditional marketing data companies, in 1988 Gupta released American Business Information's first *American Manufacturers Directory,* a hardbound reference tool that classified 125,000 U.S. manufacturing enterprises (with more than 25 employees) by name, city, and SIC code.

By 1989, American Business Information had expanded into the kind of customized, sophisticated market research services previously offered only by its larger competitors. Smaller firms desperate for data to determine sales goals, devise marketing plans, locate business sites, assign sales territories, budget marketing costs, or generate leads could now order American Business Information's "market opportunity reports," which characterized the size of a given market for a product and analyzed the customer's rate of penetration in a geographic area or industry group. American Business Information's "sales potential reports" analyzed a customer's sales history to determine its marketing success rates and return on investment and identified industries or geographic areas that offered the best promise for improved sales. The data could also be customized into statistical reports or color-coded maps, and American Business Information began offering to study a customer's in-house database to determine what information was missing or out of date. Finally, American Business Information's marketing services were now including a "namescan" feature that helped customers determine whether a proposed business name had been used or was eligible for legal protection as a new company name.

"They Shoot You": 1990–93

American Business Information's right to market products based on commercial phone directories was challenged again in 1990, when another BellSouth subsidiary sued American Business Information for copyright violation. BellSouth now demanded that American Business Information not only cease publishing its Yellow Pages-based information products but requested that the courts force it to destroy its databases and cough up cash damages for its alleged infringement. The suit struck at the heart of Gupta's data-gathering methods and, sensitive to its ramifications, American Business Information countersued, claiming that BellSouth's desire to view its phone directories as copyrighted material amounted to "monopolizing activity." In December 1991, American Business Information and BellSouth reached a partial settlement in which BellSouth agreed to withdraw its demand for damages and the destruction of American Business Information's databases in exchange for

American Business Information's abandonment of its antitrust counterclaim.

Gupta's pursuit of the elusive large, national business customer drove him to establish a direct sales staff in 1990, which by the end of 1991 had grown to 12 reps in eight branch offices around the country. To expand American Business Information's client base and strengthen its sales through third-party resellers, Gupta also purchased list broker CompilersPlus, Inc. in January 1990 and in 1991 acquired the assets of marketing data provider Trinet, Inc. and directory publisher Contacts Influential, Inc. The Trinet acquisition broadened Gupta's reach into the large-company data market, and Contacts Influential expanded American Business Information's burgeoning stable of customers; both strengthened American Business Information's ability to reach new customers through direct sales. In 1990 Gupta opened an American Business Information office in Toronto and began to include information on Canadian businesses in his master databases. Before the year was out, he also unveiled a "Business Info-Line" that allowed customers to dial an 800 number (for credit card billing) or 900 number (for phone statement billing) to get specific answers to business questions. For $3 for the first minute and $1.50 for each succeeding one callers could get the kind of directory assistance information Ma Bell could only dream of supplying—the number of Honda dealers in Dallas, for example, or specific business information on an "XYZ Corporation" located somewhere on the West Coast.

In 1990 Gupta began a two-year, $3.2 million expansion of American Business Information's facilities and data processing capabilities. To ensure the security of its data, American Business Information now operated redundant computer systems at its data centers in Omaha and nearby Carter Lake, Iowa, and by the end of 1991 American Business Information's data processing staff had grown to 62, including 26 systems analysts and programmers charged with maintaining and improving American Business Information's ability to sort, manage, and expand the databases from which each product line and service was culled. The data compilation, data enhancement and verification, and order fulfillment arms of American Business Information's operation utilized 1,500 proprietary software programs, and American Business Information's data entry employees could access the company's database at a rate of 1.2 million records per month.

By the early 1990s the CD-ROM had emerged as the method of choice for libraries and information-intensive businesses that needed to store and quickly access large amounts of business and research data. Keenly aware of the medium's potential, American Business Information introduced a "Business Lists-on-Disc" CD-ROM version of its business data in 1991, giving customers yet another format in which to search, sort, and access market-critical company information. By the end of the year, American Business Information's traditional data formats—prospect lists, mailing labels, index cards, and computer diskettes and tapes—were accounting for only 71 percent of total sales, while its newer products—hardbound state and business directories, CD-ROMs, list brokerage and market research services, and On-Line Business Link—were generating a full 29 percent. American Business Information also introduced *The Directory of Blue Chip Companies,* which contained data on 120,000 major businesses with one hundred or more employees; published its first *Directory of Public Companies,* which provided names, addresses, product lines, and sales figures for 9,000 publicly traded U.S. companies; and offered 49 new U.S. state business directories. By the end of 1991, American Business Information was employing 422 workers; mailing more than 15 million catalogs, letters, and other marketing pieces to 1.2 million prospective customers; and closing its second decade of unbroken profitability.

In early 1995 Gupta took American Business Information public, instantly transforming American Business Information's business strategy from measured, gradual growth to all-out, relentless expansion. Because as a public corporation, "if you miss a quarter, they shoot you," Gupta now had to demonstrate constant forward momentum to his shareholders in each quarterly report. As a result, while American Business Information's net sales had expanded between $3.5 and $10 million a year from 1987 to 1991, during 1993–95 alone they grew at an annual $14 to $17 million clip. In 1992, Gupta formed a joint venture with credit-reporting agency TRW that allowed American Business Information to incorporate credit information in its databases, and in 1993 it acquired Seminars International to form a new division, American Business Communications (ABC), that moved American Business Information into educational services (ABC was later sold to Baker University of Kansas for $3 million).

Vindication, Partnerships, and the Internet: 1994–97

In 1994, Gupta won his long legal struggle to justify American Business Information's use of Yellow Pages business data when the Supreme Court refused to hear BellSouth's copyright violation lawsuit, finally establishing that phone companies could not claim a copyright on the information contained in their directories. To further position American Business Information as a cutting-edge information supplier, Gupta released two new products that moved American Business Information squarely into the exploding computer software market. Priced at $19 each, *11 Million Businesses Phone Book* and *70 Million Households Phone Book* gave businesses and consumers alike ready access to the bulk of American Business Information's database via their CD-ROM drives.

With nearly 500,000 customers and revenues closing in on $100 million, American Business Information unleashed a stream of new industry-specific CD-ROM products in 1995–96, including *517,000 Physicians and Surgeons,* which gave medical industry marketers access to such key data as the medical speciality, patient volume, and education of virtually every physician in the United States, and *1.1 Million Professionals,* which offered purveyors of luxury goods a single-source database for some of the most highly paid professionals in the United States. With its first ten CD-ROM titles—sold through retailers like Best Buy and Egghead Software—American Business Information had become a leader in the CD-ROM directory product market, with six of the top ten CD-ROM directory titles in 1995 and 48 percent of all CD-ROM directory sales.

In 1995 Gupta announced alliances with Bloomberg Financial Markets, Microsoft, and America Online to exploit the growing popularity of the Internet and World Wide Web as distribution channels for American Business Information's products. The Bloomberg deal gave stockbrokers and other financial industry professionals access to American Business Information's business database via Bloomberg's online data network, and the agreements with Microsoft and America Online offered the general online user access to the same information through two of the largest U.S. consumer online services. By 1996, American Business Information and Disclosure, Inc., a provider of financial business information, had unveiled the "Big Business Database" on Disclosure's Internet site, a massive research catalog of 100,000 U.S. companies. Moreover, in July 1995 American Business Information launched its own Web home page that exposed potential customers to American Business Information's products through such free information services as "Lookup USA," a search engine for finding individuals or businesses anywhere in the United States. "What our people have done here, very quickly," Gupta explained, "is come up with an Internet product that will generate revenue for the company. . . . It's what I call the hook—the free service. . . . The initial strategy is to drive a lot of traffic to use our Web site. . . . The fact that our information can be used in your daily lives is going to help us." Lookup USA, which mirrored the information available in American Business Information's new InfoAccess 800-number service, was expected to draw a million users in 1996 alone and, perhaps more importantly, attract advertisers and thus new revenue to American Business Information's site.

In 1996, American Business Information released its "ultimate" CD-ROM product, *The 130 Million Listings Ultimate Phone Book,* which combined its *88 Million Households, 16 Million American Yellow Page Businesses,* 800 number, and nine-digit zip code products into one single-source reference tool. Gupta also expanded American Business Information's network of retail sellers by adding Staples and Office Depot to its network of outlets, hired a new vice president for its fields sales operation, and joined in the growing consolidation of the marketing information industry with four strategic acquisitions: Marketing Data Systems, Inc., a supplier of data warehousing, research and analysis services for target marketing uses; Digital Directory Assistance, the publisher of PhoneDisc, a competing CD-ROM directory product; County Data Corporation, the leading U.S. compiler of databases on new business formations; and DBA Holdings, Inc., the parent company of Database America Companies, Inc., a New Jersey-based supplier of data processing and analytical services for marketing applications. The number of daily average "hits" on American Business Information's web site was meanwhile exceeding expectations, and Gupta unveiled for-fee business profiles and credit reports to American Business Information's home page, which were to culminate, he predicted, in the company's first online sale of its data list and sales leads products.

To Gupta's delight, customer testimonials to the usefulness of American Business Information's products in finding lost family members and apprehending criminals began trickling into American Business Information's offices, providing him with invaluable material for his public relations campaigns. Moreover, American Business Information's new line of subscription products, which extended the life of its CD-ROM titles by including an annual subscription to monthly updates and data additions, were now accounting for 30 percent of American Business Information's total revenue. ''The potential market is $4 billion,'' Gupta enthused, ''if a company does $100 million, there's a lot of potential for growth.''

Principal Subsidiaries

B. J. Hunter; American Business Information Marketing; CD-ROM Technologies; Contacts Influential, Inc.; County Data Corporation.

Further Reading

Cox, Kathleen, ''The Grateful Graduate,'' *Span*, September 1994, pp. 29–31.

Graves, Jacqueline M., ''Building a Fortune on Free Data,'' *Fortune*, February 6, 1995.

Norris, Melinda, ''can Business Information Puts Phone Listings on Internet,'' *Omaha World-Herald*, March 31, 1996.

Von Daehne, Niklas, ''Data Wizard,'' *Success*, September 1995, p. 16.

—Paul S. Bodine

American Homestar Corporation

2450 South Shore Boulevard
Suite 300
League City, Texas 77573
U.S.A.
(713) 334-9700
Fax: (713) 334-9737

Public Company
Incorporated: 1971 as Mobile America Housing
   Corporation
Employees: 1,317
Sales: $208.7 million (1996)
Stock Exchanges: New York
SICs: 2451 Mobile Homes; 5271 Mobile Home Dealers;
   6719 Holding Companies, Not Elsewhere Classified

With its corporate headquarters located near Houston, Texas, American Homestar Corporation has become one of the leading producers of site-assembled manufactured housing in the United States. Committed to the goal of fulfilling the American dream of home ownership for working-class families, American Homestar designs, constructs, and markets pre-constructed homes through a growing network of over 300 retail outlets covering half of the 48 contiguous United States. Since its inception in 1971, the company has prevailed in a competitive market. Aggressive in its efforts to expand, it now dominates the industry in its core market areas: Louisiana, New Mexico, Arkansas, Oklahoma, and its home state of Texas.

Improved Quality and Changing Demographics Aid the Industry During the 1980s and 90s

Manufactured homes are complete single-family housing units fabricated in sections, or "floors." Constructed in a factory and then trailered to a site of their owner's choosing, they offer amenities comparable to those of site-built homes. While manufactured homes were once the focus of ridicule within the housing construction industry, they have successfully shed their association with the tacky, disordered trailer parks of the 1960s and

1970s. In fact, the quality and design of manufactured (as opposed to mobile) homes has improved to such an extent that the more upscale models have become almost indistinguishable from homes being constructed in newer, moderate-cost, single-family subdivisions in many parts of the country. According to the Manufactured Housing Institute, by 1996 there were 7.3 million manufactured homes in use in the United States, providing housing for over seven percent of the nation's population.

In recent years, manufactured homes have made up the fastest-growing segment of home sales in the United States, accounting for 33 percent of all single-family home sales in 1996. This figure, up from 25 percent in 1991, reflects the growing need for affordable housing for first-time homebuyers earning less than $50,000 per year. For this growing segment of the U.S. population, manufactured housing is an attractive alternative to condominium ownership or home or apartment rental. With the average cost of a new home approaching $125,000 by 1996, the $43,460 price-tag on a mid-range American Homestar manufactured home is attractive, even when factoring in the cost of land.

Manufactured housing provides growing families with a stable neighborhood and the pride of home ownership. And, as U.S. home-buyer demographics continue to shift away from young families and towards single adults, married adults with no children, and growing numbers of affluent retirees, manufactured homes fit the requirements of these new homeowners as well. Such homes serve as comfortable, yet low cost, vacation housing as well as efficient, low-maintenance residences for elderly individuals. Resort areas in the southern and western states have also witnessed an increase in the development of entire manufactured-home subdivisions. By producing both single- and the larger, multi-section manufactured homes, which range in price between $21,300 and $99,400 (excluding land costs), American Homestar is able to satisfy all segments of the growing U.S. housing market.

Answering the Need for Affordable Housing Since 1971

Responding to the changing requirements of U.S. home-buyers, American Homestar was founded in 1971 as Mobile

America Housing Corporation. Company founder and Texas native Finis Teeter, who had been selling manufactured housing since hiring on at Mobile Home Industries in 1969, decided to focus his area of operations in the southwest region. Establishing a 137,000-square-foot manufacturing facility in Fort Worth, Teeter began marketing middle-priced homes within the five-state area that has remained the company's core market. Teeter responded to the obviously unsatisfied need for affordable housing by setting up a retail network throughout the Southwest. The year 1971 would prove to be a banner one for both Teeter and the manufactured housing industry as a whole as unit sales peaked throughout the nation.

The company reincorporated as American Homestar Corporation in 1983. While the next few years would be rocky indeed—the industry as a whole saw shipments of manufactured homes drop nationwide from 295,079 in 1983 to only 179,713 in 1991—Teeter and his company kept their footing until economic conditions across the nation began to stabilize.

But it was not only a national recessionary economy that affected the company. During the late 1980s, Texas experienced a dramatic decline in its own economic fortunes as the state's oil industry went through the "bust" cycle after its earlier boom years. Within American Homestar's core market area the number of manufactured home-makers shrank from 54 in 1984 to 6 by the early 1990s. However, the state has since begun a financial comeback; along with other southern states—which have traditionally served as the manufactured homes industry's strongest sales territory—Texas has returned to its former glory, once again providing American Homestar with a lucrative market for its product.

Develops Manufacturing and Sales Networks in the 1990s

By 1994, despite the setbacks caused by the local Texas economy, American Homestar ran three manufacturing plants located throughout the Dallas/Fort Worth area. Under the umbrella of National Housing Systems, Inc., the company retailed its homes in Arkansas, Colorado, Kansas, Louisiana, Missouri, New Mexico, Oklahoma, and Texas via 34 company-owned retail centers. These company-owned centers were supplemented by 103 independent retailers in the same core market area.

Due to the high cost of materials and storage, as well as the cyclical nature of the construction industry, factory-built homes are usually not manufactured until an order has been received, either from an independent retailer or one of American Homestar's own sales centers. The average rate of production in the company is 23 floors per day; the decline in orders experienced by the slump in housing demand over the winter months is balanced by a corresponding increase in production during warmer weather. Sixty percent of total sales are generated by company-owned retailers, with the remainder written by its network of independents. New company-manufactured homes—medium to upper-priced houses that vary in features and design—comprise over 60 percent of the homes sold by American Homestar, which also resells used homes and homes from other manufacturers. Long-term company goals have continued to focus on increasing this percentage to 80 percent through enlargement of American Homestar's own manufacturing facilities.

Vertical Integration Achieved

The implementation of a management strategy known as "Vertical Integration"—the ability to design, manufacture, market, deliver, and finance its product—has been the key to the success of several competitors in the manufactured home industry, notably the Knoxville, Tennessee-based Clayton Homes. Teeter also recognized the benefits of this means of developing structural efficiency early on, and has guided American Homestar in the direction of vertical integration. In light of Teeter's success in this area, analysts have praised American Homestar as possessing one of the best-managed corporate organizations in the manufactured housing industry.

The company obtained a controlling interest in the newly formed Roadmaster Transport Company in 1992 as its first step towards vertical integration. Because of the specialized trucking needs of the manufactured home industry, Roadmaster was organized as a means of providing transit from factory to homesite. Deriving only a small percentage of its revenue from American Homestar—26 percent in 1996—Roadmaster generates most of its income by servicing other home manufacturers within its transit area. Under efficient management, it has become one of the largest transporters of manufactured homes in the southwest region.

1992: Merger with Oak Creek Homes

The year 1992 would be significant, not only for the company's diversification into the transport business, but also for its timely merger with another home manufacturer. Recognizing the increased potential for profits with an increase in production and retail size, CEO Teeter formed a joint venture with Oak Creek Homes, a major supplier of homes to American Homestar retailers. Under the joint name of American Homestar, Oak Creek CEO and primary shareholder Laurence A. Dawson Jr. worked with Teeter to open two new manufacturing plants to capture the still-increasing demand for manufactured homes. The Lancaster manufacturing facility was opened in December 1992 to produce lower-priced homes; upper-medium and higher-priced homes would be constructed at the 94,000-square-foot Burleson plant beginning in May 1993. Oak Creek Homes was acquired by American Homestar in August 1993. Under the acquisition, all corporate operations were combined; Dawson would be named co-CEO and director alongside chairman and CEO Teeter.

Providing its customers with adequate long-term financing for home purchases would also contribute to American Homestar's goal of vertical integration. Through its 50 percent ownership of 21st Century Mortgage, which was formed in early 1996, the company reaped the profits of $47 million in home mortgages by the end of the mortgage company's first fiscal year. Approximately half of the homes purchased through American Homestar retailers would eventually be financed by 21st Century. And through its ownership of Western Insurance Agency and Lifestar Reinsurance Ltd., the company was able to both service its customers' property/casualty and credit life insurance needs and profit from yet another financial transaction on the way to owning a home.

1994: Company Goes Public

Company management's efforts towards vertical integration paid off: while sales in 1992 had only contributed $27 million to revenues of $28.7 million, by 1994 they had reached $109 million, an increase of over 400 percent. Such rapid growth enabled American Homestar to consider an expansion of its sales territory through the acquisition of smaller manufactured homes producers. However, expansion into these new markets would necessitate an influx of capital. Accordingly, in July 1994 the company went public, offering 2 million shares on the New York over-the-counter market. While Teeter and Dawson would retain 45 percent of the company stock, the sale of the remaining 1.1 million shares would generate sufficient revenues to continue the implementation of their planned acquisition of other firms.

Formulating reorganization strategies were only a means to an end. American Homestar approached the year 2000 with several strategic goals, which included opening between eight to ten new retail centers through 1999, expanding its current network of independent retailers and strengthening retailer loyalties to its product, and further expanding its manufacturing capacity. The company also focused on maximizing the profit opportunities inherent in its vertical structure through earning manufacturing, retailing, and financial service profits on every home sold. The company's continued policy of aggressive acquisitions would ensure ever-increasing market opportunities for both its mortgage and insurance sectors.

By the mid-1990s American Homestar was reporting annual average growth rates of between 15 and 18 percent, with 1995 revenues of $187 million and sales in its core market area cresting between 35 and 45 percent. Sales of new homes for 1995 were reported at 3,127 units, evenly distributed between single-and multi-floored home models. Branching out into its first retail sales location in the state of Louisiana, the company worked towards its goal of establishing 40 new retail centers by 1997. And the September 1995 investment of $2.5 million in 21st Century Life, a venture with partners Vanderbilt Mortgage & Finance and Clayton Homes, would reap $22,000 in net income by the following year.

Aggressive Expansion Reaps Rewards

In 1996 American Homestar more than doubled the size of its manufacturing capacity through the acquisition of three firms: Guerdon Homes, Inc., which sells and produces manufactured homes within a 13-state region; Henderson, North Carolina's Heartland Homes, Inc.; and the 15-member Manu-Fac, Inc., retailer network, also located in North Carolina. This expansion made the company a major industry presence in 24 states through the addition of 215 new independent retailers and five additional manufacturing locations to its operations. Guerdon and Heartland, both manufacturers of upscale double-section homes, were predicted to especially enhance the company's overall sales figures. The trend within the manufactured home industry has been towards such larger, multi-section homes, which accounted for almost half of the industry's 1996 sales. These more upscale homes—sometimes boasting three bedrooms, luxury amenities, or innovative architectural elements—have become an increasingly attractive alternative to buyers considering more expensive site-built homes. With American Homestar's traditional mid-price homes serving both ends of the country's new homebuyer demographic profile (first-time homebuyers and retirees), the addition of multi-section homes was seen to be an effective way to expand company market share.

Reflecting an industry-wide trend towards consolidation, the acquisitions of Guerdon and Heartland made American Homestar an industry leader, not only in its core southwest and south central regions, but in the Pacific Northwest, Rocky Mountain area, and the southeastern United States as well. By the second quarter of fiscal 1997, with the multi-stage acquisition of Guerdon Homes completed, the company had diversified its geographical base to the point where it could boast 48 company-owned retail centers and 300 independent dealerships servicing customers in 24 states, with eight manufacturing plants at their disposal. Through this dramatic increase in its sales base, coupled with a 100 percent increase in its manufacturing capabilities, American Homestar seemed poised on the brink of rapid financial growth.

Looking Towards the Future

In both 1996 and 1997, American Homestar announced a 5-for-4 split of its stock, increasing its common shares outstanding and generating new funds for the continued implementation of its plan for aggressive expansion. Praising the company's stock—one of the lowest-valued stocks in the industry—as one of the best picks of 1997, industry analysts expected the company's earnings to rise at an annual rate of 20 percent into the next century. Company goals for fiscal 1997, which included the addition of ten new retail facilities, reflected such an optimistic outlook. By the first quarter of fiscal 1997, three new retail outlets had already been established; by the second quarter American Homestar had reported record gains as revenues rose 76 percent from 1996 levels to $89.3 million.

According to the industry's Manufactured Housing Institute, the 370,000 manufactured homes shipped in 1996—a 9 percent increase over the previous year and a 37 percent increase over the previous decade—generated $14 billion in sales for the industry. American Homestar's piece of this growing pie was $208 million, generated through the manufacture and sale of 3,593 new homes. While housing analysts have noted that fluctuations in the interest rate, as well as excess inventories caused by slow orders, might affect the manufactured home industry as it began its process of maturation, the nation's improving economic conditions and the product's value within the overall housing market would seem to ensure that American Homestar's long-range forecast is a bright one.

Principal Subsidiaries

Associated Retailers Group, Inc.; 21st Century Mortgage; Roadmaster Transport Company; Western Insurance Agency; Lifestar Reinsurance, Ltd. Nationwide Housing Systems.

Further Reading

Byrne, Harlan S., "Once a Joke, Manufactured Housing Has Gained Respect," *DowVision* (online), January 6, 1997.

Trager, Cara S., "Mobile Houses Provide Path to Affordability," *Newsday*, November 22, 1996.

—Pamela L. Shelton

Ameritech Corporation

30 South Wacker Drive
Chicago, Illinois 60606
U.S.A.
(312) 750-5000
Fax: (312) 207-1601
Web site: http://www.ameritech.com

Public Company
Incorporated: 1983 as American Information
    Technologies Corporation
Employees: 65,345
Sales: $13.4 billion
Stock Exchanges: New York Boston Chicago Pacific
    Philadelphia London Tokyo Amsterdam Basel Geneva
    Zürich
SICs: 4812 Radiotelephone Communications

Ameritech Corporation is one of the largest telecommunications companies in the United States. Ameritech's Bell Group, which provides exchange telecommunications and local and long-distance exchange access service for business and residential customers in the Midwest, is made up of Illinois Bell, Indiana Bell, Michigan Bell, Ohio Bell, and Wisconsin Bell; Ameritech Services and Ameritech Information Systems comprise the remaining operational sectors. As a whole, the corporation is structured into separate business units, which include consumer phone services, long-distance phone services, small-business services, advertising, and cellular services. Ameritech subsidiaries, offering communications-related products and services throughout the world, include Ameritech Mobile Communications, Inc., Ameritech Publishing Inc., Ameritech Development, and Ameritech International.

1982 Breakup of Ma Bell Creates Baby Bells

In 1982 the U.S. Department of Justice (DOJ) ended a 13-year antitrust suit against the world's largest corporation, American Telephone and Telegraph Company (AT&T). AT&T was required, under the landmark court-ordered consent decree, to divest itself of 22 local telephone operating companies. The key issue of the divestiture was to demonopolize the telecommunications industry and ensure equal access to the local exchange facilities by all long-distance carriers.

AT&T retained its Western Electric Manufacturing subsidiary, Bell Laboratories research facilities, as well as its long-distance operations, while the 22 local companies were divided into seven regional holding companies (RHCs). The Midwest regional Bell operating companies (BOCs), including Illinois Bell, Indiana Bell, Michigan Bell, Ohio Bell, and Wisconsin Bell, were assigned to the RHC American Information Technologies Corporation, called Ameritech for short. In 1991 the company formally changed its name to Ameritech.

According to the final judgment, all RHCs were initially limited to providing only basic phone service, which was strictly regulated. Any new telecommunications ventures had to be presented to the Federal Communications Commission (FCC); if approved, these unregulated businesses would be required to be operated through separate subsidiaries.

Ameritech, along with its six sibling RHCs, shared $147 billion in assets. The RHCs were, however, also ordered to share with AT&T any company debt, as well as the costs of antitrust suits initiated prior to January 1, 1984, the official date of divestiture.

William L. Weiss, named president and CEO of Illinois Bell in 1981, anticipated the solo operation of the Midwest RHC and diversified Ameritech operations into unregulated businesses as allowed by the court. In 1983 Ameritech incorporated several subsidiaries, including Ameritech Services, Inc., a support company owned equally by all the Midwest BOCs and designed to provide marketing, technical, and regulatory planning as well as new product development, purchasing, and national management services. The same year brought the formation of the Ameritech Development Corp., designed to target, research, and develop business-growth areas for all of Ameritech's "Baby Bells." Ameritech also moved into publishing telephone directories via Ameritech Publishing, Inc.

In October 1983 Ameritech Mobile Communications, Inc., a provider of wire-free cellular telephones, became the first in North America to offer cellular phone service. Within six months Ameritech's cellular phone test markets were a model for many competitors. Under previous mobile telephone systems, operating areas working from a single antenna could use only 12 channels; busy lines were the norm. In contrast, under Ameritech's cellular system regions were divided into small areas called "cells"; because each cell had its own antenna, Ameritech's Chicago-based system could accommodate up to 50,000 calls per hour. Company researchers forecasted that the total cellular service market could reach $3 billion by 1990, with equipment sales reaching $600 million. It came as no surprise that companies such as Motorola, General Electric, and Panasonic were soon jockeying for the chance to set up cellular systems.

By mid-1984 Ameritech led the RHCs in first-quarter earnings, and by November *Barron's* listed the corporation as recording the highest return on equity of all the RHCs. Weiss was credited for all the positive numbers; he kept operating expenses low by trimming his work force by 20 percent prior to divestiture. Ameritech concentrated on the telephone business, investing nearly $2 billion in new technology.

Ameritech did, nonetheless, run into some stumbling blocks on the road to independence. Modernization of Centrex, the company's central exchange switching system that linked local and long-distance carriers, was a must. However, deregulation allowed the increasing number of competitive carriers to buy their own switchboards, thereby sidestepping Centrex. In addition, the FCC had ordered Ameritech to charge access fees to users of its Centrex system, adding an additional disincentive to its use by other phone service providers. In response, Weiss launched a program to convert the corporation's central offices to electronic digital switching, which provided better technology and reduced maintenance costs.

Joins Move to Office Automation in Mid-1980s

In the meantime Ameritech's unregulated subsidiaries, less constrained by FCC and state restrictions, surged ahead. Ameritech Mobile expanded its cellular systems, moving into the retail sector. Following a 1985 agreement with Tandy Corporation, Tandy's Radio Shack stores marketed Ameritech cellular phones.

In 1985 Ameritech ventured into office automation systems with Real Com, an IBM Satellite Business Systems subsidiary. With Aetna Telecommunications Laboratories, Ameritech worked on simultaneous transmission of voice, video, and data via fiber-optic cables. In 1985 Ameritech Development purchased a minority interest in Davox Corporation, a producer of integrated voice and data communication systems. Despite growth potential, Weiss did not see Ameritech putting more than one-fifth of its resources into these newer ventures.

Ameritech Publishing, also on the upswing, acquired Cleveland-based Purchasing Directories, Inc., in 1985 and began publishing telephone directories in Ohio, Illinois, Indiana, and Michigan. Ameritech also acted as a consultant to AT&T in its efforts to publish a directory in Thailand.

Barely through the second year of operations, the RHCs were still legally bound to seek permission from the U.S. District Court before starting up businesses, and these new businesses had to fall within FCC decisions dubbed Computer I and II. These restrictions confined RHC operations to two areas: basic, or regulated, services comprised of local telephone hook-up and related maintenance; and enhanced, or non-regulated, services, which included the development and manufacture of telephone equipment.

In August 1985 an Ameritech attorney faced the FCC, asking the board to waive such restrictions. Computer III, announced in January 1986, ruled that RHCs could now provide enhanced communications and computer-generated data and storage through existing corporations. Accountability requirements included such safeguards as comparably efficient interconnection, open network architecture, and stringent cost-accounting methods, thereby assuring competing telecommunications companies fair access to local exchange facilities currently controlled by the RHCs. The equal access was necessary for non-Bell companies to offer comprehensive information packages.

Ameritech, following competitor Bell Atlantic's lead, began diversifying to the extent it was able. In January 1986 the corporation bought Applied Data Research Inc., a database management software producer for IBM mainframe computers. The corporation also purchased Speech Plus, Inc., a developer of speech-synthesis technology.

Ameritech Publishing extended its holdings with the May 1986 acquisition of Old Heritage Advertising & Publishing. Within two years the subsidiary expanded its coverage to 90 telephone directories in 15 states.

In 1986 the FCC loosened its reins still further, authorizing Ameritech to enter international telecommunications as well as foreign manufacturing and nontelecommunications businesses. Ameritech's movement was limited, however. It was required to establish a subsidiary to manufacture telecommunications products, provided that the subsidiary had no financial interest in the U.S. telecommunications industry, and such products could not be sold in the United States, Canada, or the U.S. Virgin Islands. In addition, Ameritech could not buy, sell, or patent technology manufactured by, or enter joint research projects with its foreign subsidiary, and it had to make available any software or technology from its foreign manufacturer to any U.S. companies that requested such information.

Satisfied with the ruling, Ameritech moved ahead in joint ventures with foreign concerns; through Applied Data Research Ameritech reached 40 nations. And in August 1986 Ameritech Publishing bought a portion of AT&T's international telephone directory businesses. Ameritech Development, always investigating opportunities, began consulting in Japan on several projects.

On the home front the company gradually expanded as well, with Ameritech Development joining David Systems of California in ongoing research and development into local network setups. Ameritech Mobile commissioned Motorola to develop a multi-feature cellular telephone, and by late 1986 was providing cellular service in Chicago-area commuter trains.

In September 1986 Ameritech Services and Siemens Communications Systems, Inc. sealed a three-year contract, the first of its kind to be made with other than the RHCs' usual suppliers. Under the agreement, Siemens agreed to supply to all Ameritech Baby Bells a mobile switching unit featuring business applications of the integrated services digital network (ISDN) for Ameritech's central offices.

Ameritech ended its third year as a strong competitor in the telecommunications industry. Conditions supporting the company's position varied. A new price flexibility because of state deregulation allowed Illinois Bell to project service fees based on cost without consulting regulator approval, thus speeding up local service. Ameritech's moderate moves into publishing and foreign manufacturing ventures kept the company on solid financial footing. CEO Weiss also decided to buy back some of Ameritech's stock, a wise decision according to industry analysts.

By 1987 Ameritech was putting its energies into fiber-optic and digital technologies, spending nearly 10 percent more than it had the previous year. The corporation planned to have nearly 150,000 miles of fiber-optic cable installed by year-end 1987, to serve one-fourth of its customers on digital switching lines. Through its newly established Ameritech Business Network, the company stepped up marketing of digital products designed to provide integrated information systems.

In August 1987, anticipating another change in regulatory status, Ameritech paid $5 million for the option to gain a 15 percent equity in a Canadian-based electronic messaging company. The purchase was Ameritech's effort to enter information database markets. Long-distance carrier MCI opposed the venture, charging that it violated the MFJ. Successfully securing DOJ approval, however, Ameritech, together with Bell Canada Enterprises and Telenet Communications, announced iNet, the first computer-based information management service to be offered in the United States. The service was available through data terminals, personal computers, and word processors equipped with a telephone line and modem.

In September 1987 Ameritech's Wisconsin Bell proposed two experimental ventures into pay-per-view cable television with Warner Cable Communications of Milwaukee. Using existing networks, Wisconsin Bell also planned to monitor gas, electric, and water meters in homes and offices. By October Ameritech Publishing was producing telephone directories in both western Pennsylvania and New York state. In December 1987 the corporation set up a Midwestern regional committee to review the company's regulated and unregulated subsidiaries and focus its changing areas of involvement.

Deregulation Sparks Corporate Restructuring

On the corporate level, Ameritech also initiated large-scale reorganization. In March 1988 the fully owned subsidiary Ameritech Applied Technologies, Inc. was formed with the goal of integrating and updating RHC computers to one standardized system. Despite its continued diversification, the corporation streamlined operations into ventures closely connected, both geographically and technologically, to its bread-and-butter business, the Bell telephone systems. While this restructuring was a reaction to the gradual loosening of government-enforced regulations, it was also a response to the fact that Ameritech lost more of its 1987 revenue to bypass technology than any other RHC. With the iNet system as a base, the company began modernizing all its exchange networks, developing electronic digital switching and fiber-optic transmission systems. Over 300,000 miles of fiber-optic cable were planned for use in serving customer lines and speeding up long-distance carriers' local access capabilities. Through its FiberHub system, for example, Ameritech routed long-distance calls from AT&T, Sprint, or MCI to their respective customer destinations via an electronic expressway interchange.

In step with these changes, Ameritech unloaded its 17 percent interest in the Canadian cellular service Cantel for $85 million, due to its distance from the company's Midwestern base. Ameritech Mobile, on the upswing, increased cellular service by 68 percent and covered 17 percent more territory. In September 1988 Ameritech Mobile Communications acquired the paging assets of both Multicom, Inc. and A Beeper Company, from sibling Bells. Through these acquisitions, Ameritech strengthened its Midwestern holdings.

Ameritech Development kept pace, buying the Midwest operations of Telephone Announcement Systems, Inc. in September 1988. Through the purchase the company also acquired Telephone Announcement's audiotex network, a voice-response system that gives information to callers via touch-tone telephones. Ameritech planned to extend the service throughout its operating area. With the October acquisition of Tigon Corporation, a Dallas voice-mail company, the company gained 200 corporate clients, a two-year jump on voice messaging technology, and a leadership position in the message servicing industry, which it planned to extend to its Midwest customers.

In the largest single transaction of 1988, Ameritech sold its software subsidiary, Applied Data Research, for $170 million, incurring an after-tax loss of $8.1 million. Two other major changes by year end included the formation of Ameritech Enterprise Holdings, a holding company for both Ameritech Audiotex Services, Inc. and Tigon Corporation. By this time Tigon had reached Japan and the United Kingdom with its voice-mail services. In January 1989 Ameritech Information Systems was formed to install business systems as well as to provide marketing and product and technical design support to large business customers in the Ameritech region.

Now facing its sixth year, Ameritech continued asking the FCC to remove all restrictions on information services. The previous year's gain had been the lift on information transmission—yet Ameritech, bound to transmit information generated by another company, was still unable to transmit its own information. Regardless of the 1987 pay-per-view cable trial in Wisconsin, the linkage of cable to existing networks was still forbidden. In a minor concession Ameritech was granted a waiver allowing the company to offer directory-assisted customer-name-and-address (CNA) service, provided that CNA revenues subsidized local telephone rates. However, as reported in the October 1989 issue of *Communications News*, Ameritech vice-chairman Ormand Wade said the court-imposed limitations not only inhibited competition, they weakened U.S. potential in the international telecommunications market.

Meanwhile, Ameritech continued research and development in information transmission, testing an electronic digital-loop carrier system designed to allow transmission of large amounts of data. Fiber-optic rings linked customer locations to central offices or long-distance carriers. Ameritech targeted a long-term investment of more than $200 million into Signaling System 7 (SS7), a database intended to support a new software-based intelligence system. In early 1990, with manufacturer Northern Telecom, Ameritech Information Systems worked directly with end users to test telephone audio deficiencies. Their tests resulted in new design standards to improve the transmission quality of telephones. Advancing in fiber optics, Ameritech also initiated the nation's first passive optic network.

One of the biggest breakthroughs in consumer-oriented technology was the introduction of Caller ID. First offered in Illinois in early 1992, the service enabled consumers to identify the caller prior to answering their telephone.

Pursues New Retail Markets in the 1990s

Heading into the 1990s Ameritech continued to aggressively pursue retail markets, an area that analysts expect to maintain steady growth through the year 2000. Ameritech Mobile offered cellular service through appliance centers and retail locations in Chicago, Detroit, Milwaukee, Columbus, and Cincinnati. The subsidiary also increased its Michigan-area paging operations, acquiring T-Com Inc. from Rochester Telephone Company. In February 1989 Ameritech's Tigon subsidiary negotiated a multimillion-dollar deal to supply Texas Instruments with voice-mail capability reaching 140 national and international locations. And in 1991 Ameritech acquired CyberTel, a St. Louis-based provider of paging and cellular services that would extend its range outside of the five-state Ameritech home area.

Ameritech also increased marketing in several new areas. With Sprint and Telesphere, Ameritech's audiotex services agreed to process "900" calls; with Teleline of Los Angeles, it entered negotiations to resell the VoiceQuest system. Ameritech Publishing announced a talking telephone directories service in the Midwest Bell regions, to be accessed through a number listed in Ameritech Pages Plus directories. By 1989 Ameritech was publishing directories in 30 states as well as English-language directories in Japan. The 1995 purchase of National Guardian Corp. (renamed SecurityLink) provided Ameritech entry into the $16 billion U.S. market for security monitoring services. The same year the company also joined forces with several entertainment providers to launch Americast, a cable television venture that offered residents in 33 states an alternative to standard cable fare, augmented with such two-

way services as home shopping, banking, travel planning services, and electronic games.

In addition, the corporation continued bidding with other RHCs in an effort to gain new national and international business. In December 1989 Illinois Bell took part in the first installation of ISDN service, linking the Andersen Consulting offices of Chicago and Tokyo. The following year, with Bell Atlantic and two New Zealand companies, it bought Telecom New Zealand from that country's government with the intent to offer a portion of their shares to the public. Another 1990 purchase was Wer Leifert Was? (Who Supplies What?), a publisher of industrial directories in Germany and Austria. Two years later Ameritech formed a partnership with France Télécom and Telekomunikacja S.A. of Poland to operate Centertel, a Polish-based cellular phone system.

As the U.S. entered a period of recession in the early 1990s, it became increasingly evident that costs of providing service would need to be cut in order to remain competitive. A five-year data center consolidation was proposed to reduce costs resulting from duplication of work; its intent was to install company-wide information systems, trimming the number of working data centers from 21 to 4. Meanwhile, as cutbacks occurred, Ameritech faced labor disputes. In August 1989 Ameritech union workers walked out, displeased with current wage-increase structures and health benefits. After several weeks Ameritech and the union reached agreements on the issues. Still working to strengthen its financial position, the corporation eliminated its subsidiary boards in November 1989. Going into the 1990s, Ameritech's greatest challenge remained centralizing its operations. As Ameritech Applied Technologies CEO Glen Arnold stated in *Computerworld*: "We've got to do for Ameritech what Ameritech can do for other customers."

The year 1993 would prove pivotal for Ameritech as it confronted the task of centralization head on by restructuring around eleven customer-centered business units rather than by state. A new corporate logo was unveiled at that year's shareholder meeting as a symbol of the corporation's transformation from a technology-driven organization to one committed to satisfying the needs of its growing customer base. In March of that year, it filed its "Customers First" plan with the FCC. In it, Ameritech offered to open its five Great Lakes-area Baby Bell networks to competition in exchange for the freedom to compete in the long-distance market. After a three-year wait, President Bill Clinton would authorize such action by signing the Telecommunications Act of 1996. The Act allowed not only local and long-distance service, but also cable television markets open to full competition between rival carriers.

1996 and the Addition of Long-Distance Service

Ameritech was quick to capitalize on the 1996 Act, signing a five-year contract with WorldCom Inc., the fourth largest long-distance carrier in the United States, to provide them with long-distance capacity. By February it had begun offering long-distance service to its 1.9 million cellular subscribers. Meanwhile, regional long-distance supplier MFS Communications Co. was accepted by Ameritech as a competitor in the company's home region, satisfying a necessary condition that local competition be present before the company could expand its consumer offerings to include long-distance services. MFS expected to be equipped to begin local phone service by early 1997. Telecommunications giants AT&T and MCI expressed dissatisfaction with their own stalled approval as competitors for local telephone service, a result of Ameritech's efforts to develop recognition in the long-distance market before other carriers gained momentum in the local sphere. As Illinois Commerce Commission chairman Dan Miller declared in *Business Week,* "Something like 90 percent of people still think AT&T is their local phone company. That's why this issue of timing is so important." By May AT&T was able to signal a nationwide price war when it announced its September entry into the lucrative local phone service market in Ameritech's five-state area, focusing its strategy on key service areas like Chicago and offering aggressive pricing strategies that included three months of unlimited local-toll calling.

Meanwhile, 1994 saw the retirement of Weiss and the appointment of Richard Notebaert as chief executive officer of the corporation. In addition to Ameritech's entry into domestic long-distance service, Notebaert would plot a course that led the company increasingly towards international telecommunications. The previous year had heralded a partnership that resulted in NetCom GSM and cellular service in Norway; by December of that year Ameritech also gained a stake in Hungary's state-run Matav, the first privatized telephone company to be organized within a former communist bloc country. Notebaert continued this trend: negotiations with China Communications System Company, Inc. (Chinacom) yielded a 1995 agreement to construct both fiber-optic and cellular telephone networks throughout mainland China, and the following year saw a partnership between Ameritech and Belgacom that marked Ameritech's accomplishment of extending its customer base to every continent. By 1994, matching this extensive customer base with improvements in technology, Ameritech's U.S. cellular customers were able to use their cellular phones both domestically and within Europe.

Recognizing the crucial role that communications was expected to play in the coming century, Ameritech re-envisioned its role: from a provider of local wired telephone service throughout the five-state Great Lakes region of the Midwest, it accepted the breakup of a lucrative monopoly in exchange for the chance to flex its technological and corporate muscle by both expanding into global markets and broadening its local services. From wired phones, cellular phones and pagers, security systems, and intercorporate communications networks to more recent ventures into the $26 million cable television market, Ameritech continued to maintain an expanding role in the ever-enlarging communications market, fueled by a vision of the future that resulted in continued financial success.

Principal Subsidiaries

Ameritech Bell Group; Ameritech Services, Inc.; Ameritech Information Systems, Inc.; Illinois Bell; Indiana Bell; Michigan Bell; Ohio Bell; Wisconsin Bell; Ameritech Mobile Communications, Inc.; Ameritech Publishing Inc.; Ameritech Credit Corp.; Tigon Corporation; Ameritech Audiotex Services, Inc.; Ameritech Development Corp.; Ameritech International; SecurityLink; Ameritech New Media, Inc.

Further Reading

Kuttner, Bob, "Ma Bell's Broken Home," *The New Republic,* March 17, 1982.
Leopold, George, "Will the FCC Free 'The Bell Operating Company Seven?,' " *Electronics,* January 20, 1986.
Mikolas, Mark, "Still Yearning to Be Free at Divestiture + 3 1/2," *Telephone Engineer and Management,* September 15, 1987.
Militzer, Kenneth, and Martin Wolf, "Deregulation in Telecommunications," *Business Economics,* July 1985.
Pauly, David, et. al., "Ma Bell's Big Breakup," *Newsweek,* January 18, 1982.
Therrien, Lois, "Ameritech's Audacious Gamble," *Business Week,* November 1, 1993.
Samuels, Gary, "Timing Is All," *Forbes,* November 6, 1995.

—Frances E. Norton
—updated by Pamela L. Shelton

Au Bon Pain Co., Inc.

19 Fid Kennedy Ave.
Boston, Massachusetts 02210
U.S.A.
(617) 423-2100
Fax: (617) 423-7879
Web site: http://www.boston.com:80/aubonpain

Public Company
Incorporated: 1981
Employees: 1,587
Sales: $226.5 million (1995)
Stock Exchanges: NASDAQ
SICs: 5812 Eating Places; 5461 Retail Bakeries; 6794
  Patent Owners and Lessors

A relatively small player in the overall retail food service industry, Au Bon Pain Co., Inc. is a leader of the bakery café category. The company's upscale urban cafés operate under two banners: Au Bon Pain (literally ''where the good bread's at''), with over 280 units in the United States, Chile, Thailand, the Philippines, and Indonesia; and Saint Louis Bread Company, a 59-store chain acquired in 1993. French-baked goods like croissants, baguettes, and pastries form the core of the chain's menu, which has expanded over the course of its 20-year history to include sandwiches, salads, soups, gourmet coffees, and other beverages. Although Au Bon Pain has since the mid-1980s registered an impressive record of sales growth that continued into the early 1990s, its internal operations have been spotty. Revenues increased at an average annual rate of over 35 percent from the time of the chain's initial public stock offering in 1991 to 1995, but a steady string of profit increases ended in the latter year with a $1.6 million shortfall. Co-chairmen Louis I. Kane and Ronald M. Shaich forecast ''improved operating results in 1996'' following a comprehensive reorganization encompassing everything from the managers to the menu.

Late 1970s Origins

The company was founded in 1976 by Pavallier, a French manufacturer of baking equipment. Established as a showcase for the foreign company's ovens in Boston's historic Faneuil Hall Marketplace, the Au Bon Pain shop was staffed with French bakers who painstakingly produced authentic baked goods like flaky croissants, mouth-watering pastries, and crusty loaves of bread.

In 1978, the concept caught the attention of Louis I. Kane, a venture capitalist who was involved with a Columbo Frozen Yogurt franchise also located in the mall. That year, his family-owned Kane Financial Corp. paid $1.5 million for Au Bon Pain and set out to turn the original concept upside-down, selling baked goods instead of ovens. The 40-something Harvard graduate likely realized that U.S. demand for French breads and pastries was on the rise. Wholesale revenues in this category rose 40 percent from 1977 to 1982. By 1984, sales of loaves and croissants attained $1.7 billion in U.S. sales.

Kane soon found, however, that the bakery business—and especially the elaborate specialty bread craft—was not well-suited to retail food service. It was very labor intensive, for instance, requiring an entire night of dough preparation and attentive baking, yielding a product with a shelf life of only 24 hours. By 1980, Kane had added two new shops in choice locations, had developed a thriving wholesale trade, and was generating over $1 million in sales, but was still unable to cover his overhead.

That's when Ronald M. Shaich (pronounced ''shake''), a 20-something fellow Harvard MBA graduate and native Bostonian, entered the picture. Shaich, who had set up and operated a non-profit convenience store as an undergraduate, was managing a Cookie Jar franchise in Boston in 1981. In an effort to boost morning sales, he asked Kane for permission to sell Au Bon Pain's breads in his cookie shop. After four months of observing Shaich's operational know-how, Kane invited his young colleague to help overhaul Au Bon Pain, which by this time was nearing bankruptcy.

Reorganization, Concept Development in 1980s

Kane assumed the title of chief executive officer with responsibility for site selection and financing. As president, Shaich was in charge of internal operations. With additional help from Shaich's father, Joseph P., the new partners reorga-

---

Company Perspectives:

Au Bon Pain believes in the careful selection of talented and entrepreneurial individuals. It is our firm belief that people are our most valuable resource.

Au Bon Pain Co., Inc.'s success relies on team members who can make a major contribution to our company's growth. In return, we are committed to providing an environment in which everyone can develop to their fullest potential.

Au Bon Pain supports a strong commitment to quality. This is the cornerstone of our Corporate Philosophy. The quality of our products and service will be second to none in the world. But, equally important, we want our commitment to quality to go beyond our products and encompass all of our business activities.

Au Bon Pain maintains a pledge to open communication. We strive to achieve open and meaningful dialogue between all team members. Our pledge is demonstrated throughout the company by our "open door policy." Every employee is encouraged to meet with any level of management to resolve issues and plan career paths within the company.

Au Bon Pain believes that the company and its participants must all succeed together.

---

nized their tiny chain as Au Bon Pain, Inc. and developed a multifaceted plan to invigorate the stalling firm. In an effort to focus squarely on the core retail business, the partners discontinued the wholesale division.

Perhaps most importantly, Shaich sought to simplify the tedious and costly bread-making process. Assembling a team of Au Bon Pain's French bakers, along with researchers from the Massachusetts Institute of Technology and the American Institute of Baking, the company developed a method of forming and freezing the bread dough for later baking. This process promoted uniformity from shop to shop, allowed for more precise stock control, and eliminated the need to have a professional baker on staff at each unit. Furthermore, by removing some equipment, it freed floor space previously devoted to production for seating, displays, and counters. Specially designed ovens later brought virtually full automation to what had been a labor-intensive craft. In 1983, Au Bon Pain centralized dough production at a Boston facility.

These technological breakthroughs nearly halved overhead, bringing not only profitability but also freeing capital for growth. Au Bon Pain resumed its wholesale business under the St. Patisse brand. By 1985 the company's more than 30 cafés in the northeast U.S. were generating an estimated $15 million in annual revenues.

Kane and Shaich were very particular when it came to site selection, placing Au Bon Pain's cafés, carts, and kiosks in high-traffic, upscale, urban office buildings and shopping centers like Boston's Copley Place, New York's Empire State Building, and Cleveland's Tower City Center. Airports, with their high concentration of hurried business travelers, com-

prised another ideal location. Au Bon Pain "clustered" its metropolitan outlets, hoping that "saturation marketing" would promote brand identification as well as operating efficiencies. In 1989, nearly 40 percent of its 76 units were located in the Boston area.

Cafés featured black and white ceramic tile, brass fixtures, and soothing classical music. Marble counters evoked images of handmade pastry. The 1,000 to 3,500-square-foot cafés' dining rooms averaged 60 seats. In order to boost lunch time sales, the company added gourmet coffees and sandwiches like brie and ham on a croissant or tarragon chicken on a baguette. The corporate slogan, "Good food, served quickly," reflected Au Bon Pain's use of fresh, quality ingredients and its commitment to serve customers in under three minutes. By mid-decade, sandwiches and beverages were generating more revenues than the core baked goods.

With the key elements of their French bakery café concept in place by mid-decade, Kane and especially Shaich turned their attention to a nagging dilemma: personnel. Shaich had in fact made a clean sweep of the employee roster in 1981, sacking "everyone who didn't care about the business." This move was predicated on his conviction that "friendliness and personalized service" were two of the keys to repeat business within Au Bon Pain's target market of white collar professionals. Nevertheless, the ensuing years had been plagued by high employee turnover, especially at the store manager level, and low morale, which in turn undermined training efforts and eroded motivation. Shaich found himself promoting unqualified employees to fill frequent vacancies at the fast-growing chain, then micro-managing these novices. A regional shortage of competent labor only exacerbated the predicament. These internal problems were manifested in poor customer service, causing an untenable, yet deeply intractable situation.

With the help of Harvard Business School professor and business consultant Len Schlesinger, Shaich and Kane undertook a comprehensive analysis and transformation of Au Bon Pain's compensation plan, testing several formulas throughout the early 1980s and finally settling on a program in 1986. (An in-depth article by *Inc.* magazine's Bruce G. Posner detailed the process in July 1987.) They combated turnover among hourly employees with increased training, premium wages (for the foodservice industry), and seniority bonuses. In order to give each manager a vested interest in his shop's bottom-line performance, they adapted a concept that had been used successfully by restaurant chains like Golden Corral steakhouse and Chick-fil-A Inc. In addition to a base salary, managers received a minority stake in their café, usually 20 to 30 percent. Along with this increased income potential came increased responsibility for everything from inventory to staffing to advertising. Following a successful test of this "manager/partner" plan in 1986, Au Bon Pain took the concept chainwide in 1987. The 1988 institution of a "mystery shopper" evaluation program helped keep front-line employees on their best behavior.

In a 1988 follow-up interview with Bruce Posner of *Inc.*, Shaich pronounced the new compensation plan a success, noting that same store revenues had increased by an average of 24 percent from 1986 to 1987. The trend continued throughout the remainder of the decade, with chainwide sales jumping from

$30 million in 1986 to $70 million in 1990 on a doubling of locations from 40 to 80. Moreover, Shaich, Kane, and the other members of the executive team were freed to ponder larger corporate issues, including the company's 1991 initial public stock offering.

Acquisitions Fuel Continued Growth in 1990s

Au Bon Pain common made its debut June 6, 1991, with 1.875 million new shares at $9 per share, rising to over $13 by that fall. The proceeds were used to fund a series of acquisitions that contributed to a near tripling of the size of the chain in the early 1990s. Au Bon Pain had made two relatively small acquisitions in the late 1980s, including the two-unit Cafe Creations of Philadelphia in 1987 and the Washington, D.C.-based Potomac Foods' four-store Le Cafe chain.

But these purchases paled in comparison to the 1992 acquisition of Warburtons Bakery Cafe, Inc., a $16 million (sales) chain of over 100 units in Chicago, Pittsburgh and Boston. In 1993, Au Bon Pain paid $24 million for Missouri's Saint Louis Bread Co., a 20-unit chain of bakery cafes in and around the Midwestern hub for which it was named. Although both Au Bon Pain and Saint Louis Bread used the same basic menu and concept, the new affiliate differed slightly from its parent in both its site selection and its target customer base. Saint Louis Bread concentrated its cafes in suburban areas and cultivated a more family-oriented clientele. By maintaining that strategic focus, Au Bon Pain hoped to penetrate two previously under-exploited markets: the suburbs and the Midwest. It cemented this commitment with the 1994 acquisition of ABP Midwest Inc., a 19-unit franchisee based in Madison, Wisconsin. This purchase boosted the parent company's presence in northern Illinois, Minnesota, and Wisconsin.

While investing large sums in unit growth via acquisition, Au Bon Pain was also plowing capital into operations during the early 1990s. In 1992, the company completed its installation of a customized, chainwide computer network. The database management system processed and tracked sales, inventory, payroll, food costs, and average order amounts, among other factors, thereby enabling individual store managers as well as top corporate executives to monitor day-to-day operations. The construction of a new frozen dough plant in Missouri was completed in 1996, but implementation of the facility was delayed until that fall. A catering department launched in 1991 grew from less than $1 million in revenues during its startup year to over $5.5 million by the end of 1993. Au Bon Pain also went international during this period with franchising of the French bakery cafe concept in Chile late in 1992 and the addition of franchisees in Thailand, the Philippines, and Indonesia by the end of 1995.

Although they raised costs in the short term, the massive cash outlays represented by Au Bon Pain's acquisitions, computerization, bread plant, and international foray were logical investments in the company's efficiency and competitiveness. And indeed, Au Bon Pain performed well during this period, despite what Shaich called "an extraordinarily difficult environment for the retail food industry." Revenues increased from $67.9 million in 1991 to $182.9 million in 1994, and net income multiplied from $2.6 million to $7.8 million during the same

period. However, this apparently healthy bottom line belied several underlying difficulties.

Au Bon Pain executives and industry analysts found a number of problem areas both within and beyond management control. Following the "clustering" strategy that had worked so well for Au Bon Pain, the parent company expanded its Saint Louis Bread chain from 20 units in 1993 to 59 by the end of 1995. But instead of promoting brand awareness, this ambitious plan backfired, resulting in cannibalization without the hoped-for efficiencies. At the same time, comparable store sales began to stagnate, while food costs (especially for basics like flour, coffee, butter and lettuce) and personnel expenses rose. Throw in increasing competition from the likes of Seattle-based Starbucks coffeehouses, and you had a recipe for disaster. Having been named "Gold Chain 1994" by *Nation's Restaurant News*, Au Bon Pain suffered a $1.6 million loss in 1995.

Reorganization Begins in 1995

Au Bon Pain attacked its problems from several angles, implementing a reorganization program in 1995. The company hired several new top executives, added new products to the menu, reined in unit growth, remodeled existing stores, and emphasized international franchising. The management shuffle actually started in 1994, when Ronald Shaich became the sole chief executive officer. (Sixty-three-year-old Louis Kane retained the title of co-chairman.) That same year, the company hired former Burger King vice president Samuel Yong as president of Au Bon Pain International, as well as new leaders of wholesale and operations. Au Bon Pain created new divisional presidencies for both Au Bon Pain and Saint Louis Bread mid-decade, installing Robert C. Taft in the former and Richard Postle in the latter. With 21 years' experience in food service, Taft had previously served as president and CEO of the Papa Gino's chain of pizzerias, while Postle had held top positions with Wendy's and Checkers.

Au Bon Pain also scaled back its 1996 growth plans from a proposed 50 to 60 units to 18 to 20 (8 Au Bon Pains, 10 to 12 Saint Louis Breads), and closed nine less than satisfactory units by the end of 1995. In reducing its emphasis on unit growth at Au Bon Pain, the parent company shifted its focus to remodeling existing stores in a warmer scheme featuring primary colors. Menu updates included bagels, new hot sandwiches, and soups in a fresh-baked "bread bowl." In 1995, Au Bon Pain agreed to make Peet's Coffee, headquartered in Berkeley, California, its exclusive brew. Other operational improvements cited in that year's annual report included "newly automated production, labor and food cost management tools; a more effective centralized training program; an ongoing 'customer intercept' system which tracks customer satisfaction; and a re-engineered partner manager compensation plan." Building on its presence in South America and Southeast Asia, Au Bon Pain hoped to expand its global reach via franchising to the United Kingdom, Eastern Europe, and the Middle East.

Notwithstanding their 1995 earnings setback and subsequent retrenchment, Co-chairmen Louis I. Kane and Ronald M. Shaich predicted that Au Bon Pain's bakery cafe chains would more than triple to a combined total of 1,000 units by the year 2005.

Principal Subsidiaries

Au Bon Pain Foundation, Inc.; Pain Francais, Inc. (75%); Saint Louis Bread Company, Inc.; ABP Midwest Manufacturing Co., Inc.

Further Reading

Allen, Robin Lee, "Au Bon Pain Pins Hopes on New President, Image," *Nation's Restaurant News*, December 2, 1996, pp. 3–4.

"Au Bon Pain Acquires Saint Louis Bread Co.," *Nation's Restaurant News*, November 22, 1993, pp. 1–2.

"Au Bon Pain Cools Unit Growth As It Works on Performance," *Nation's Restaurant News*, January 1, 1996, p. 12.

"Au Bon Pain Inks Deal To Buy Warburton Bakeries," *Nation's Restaurant News*, May 11, 1992, p. 3.

Baum, David, "Au Bon Pain Gains Quick Access to Sales Data," *InfoWorld*, August 10, 1992, p. 46.

"A Chain of Shopkeepers," *Bakery Production and Marketing*, January 24, 1990, p. 92.

Glass, John, "Stock in Au Bon Pain Shows Short Appeal," *Boston Business Journal*, September 2, 1991, p. 7.

Keegan, Peter O., "Louis I. Kane & Ronald M. Shaich: Au Bon Pain's Own Dynamic Duo," *Nation's Restaurant News*, September 19, 1994, p. 172.

Kolb, Patricia Moore, "Au Bon Pain's Gamble Pans Out; As Chains Add Bakeries, This One Is Already There," *Restaurant Business*, August 10, 1986, pp. 209–211.

McLaughlin, John, "Au Bon Pain Is on a Health Kick," *Restaurant Business*, October 10, 1992, p. 36.

Papernik, Richard L., "Au Bon Pain Mulls Remedies, Pares Back Expansion Plans," *Nation's Restaurant News*, August 28, 1995, pp. 3–4.

Posner, Bruce G., "May the Force Be with You," *Inc.*, July 1987, pp. 70–75.

——, "Rising Dough at Au Bon Pain," *Inc.*, May 1988, p. 14.

Sanson, Michael, "Have Your Cake and Eat Healthy Too," *Restaurant Hospitality*, July 1992, p. 75.

"Taft Appointed President of Au Bon Pain Division," *Nation's Restaurant News*, November 11, 1996, p. 2.

—April Dougal Gasbarre

Bacardi Limited

65 Pitts Bay Road, P.O. Box #HM720
Pembroke HM08
Bermuda
(441) 295-4345
Fax: (441) 292-0562
Web site: http://www.bacardi.com

Private Company
Incorporated: 1919 as Compania Ron Bacardi, S.A.
Employees: 2,500
Sales: $800 million (est. 1996)
SICs: 2085 Distilled and Blended Liquors; 5182 Wines
     and Distilled Beverages

Just say "Bacardi" and several images immediately spring to mind: Daiquiris and Rum & Cokes, tropical breezes, palm trees, and even fruit bats. Family-owned and operated since 1862, Bacardi Limited turned rum consumption from "Yo, ho, ho and a bottle of rum" to a sophisticated spirit sipped straight or on the rocks. Shipping upwards of 25 million cases of rum blends annually to 180 countries worldwide, Bacardi eyed greater market domination with the introduction of Bacardi Breezers, Bacardi Limón, and other new products in the mid-1990s. The first to produce a smooth, light-colored rum in the mid-1800s, Don Facundo Bacardi turned his blending process, called the "marriage of rums," into a reported billion-dollar empire.

From Rum Sales to Manufacturing, 1830 to 1875

Bacardi, the giant liquor conglomerate, began with the emigration of Facundo Bacardi y Maso from Spain in 1830. Born in Sitges, Catalonia, Bacardi arrived in the Caribbean port city of Santiago de Cuba, then a Spanish colony populated by many fellow Catalans. There the 14-year-old Bacardi began importing and selling wine. While working for an Englishman named John Nunes, who owned a local distillery, Facundo started tinkering with ways to upgrade the quality of *aguardiente* (fire water). Also known as rumbullion (then shortened to "rum"), Facundo

hoped to "civilize" the dark liquor from its early incarnations as a coarse, harsh liquid swilled by buccaneers. As rum production had changed little in the last 200 or so years, Facundo decided it was time to elevate the spirit into something smoother and more refined.

In 1843 Facundo married a young woman named Amalia, the daughter of a French Bonapartist fighter, and soon began a family. Around this time his rum experiments had paid off and he offered samples of his newfangled light rum to relatives and friends. Facundo's secret formula enabled him to ferment, distill, and blend from molasses a rum one could drink straight, almost like wine, without mixers or additives. Since molasses was a byproduct of processing sugarcane, Cuba's largest export, there were ample quantities around the island. On February 4, 1862, Facundo, his brother Jose, and a French wine merchant joined forces to buy Nunes' tin-roofed distillery for $3,500, which had the necessities (a still of cast-iron, fermenting tanks, and aging barrels) for creating and selling a Bacardi brand of rum. Buying the old distillery lock, stock, and barrel, Facundo also received an added bonus in the deal—a colony of fruit bats—who later came to represent the Bacardi name.

The Bacardi enterprise was a family affair, and Facundo's three sons—Emilio, Facundo (Jr.), and Jose—joined the company when they came of age and learned their father's secret formula for making what was fast becoming the Caribbean's finest rum. Emilio, the oldest, worked in the office; Facundo Jr. worked in the distillery; and Jose, the youngest, eventually worked in selling and promoting his father's products. Facundo Jr., in honor of his father and to celebrate the new family business, planted a coconut palm tree just outside the distillery. As the Bacardi boys learned their father's trade, another young man named Enrique Schueg y Chassin, who had been born the same year Don Facundo purchased the Santiago distillery, was maturing and would soon join both the business and the family. In the ensuing years, as the business thrived, young Facundo's coconut palm did, too, and became an enduring symbol of the Bacardi family and its spirits operation.

Just before Don Facundo and his partners bought the Nunes distillery, an Australian named T. S. Mort perfected the first machine-chilled cold storage unit. Three years after Bacardi was established, Thaddeus Lowe debuted the world's first ice machine. Though these two inventions seemed completely unrelated to Don Facundo's premium rum, they later helped Bacardi conquer the social drinking marketplace by making ice and cold mixers commonplace. Yet such thoughts were far from Don Facundo and his family's minds, for they had no idea how widespread the appeal of their smooth, fine rum would one day become. Instead, they greeted Bacardi's increasing popularity in Santiago and the neighboring villages as a pleasant surprise.

As was proper in the day, customers brought their own jugs and bottles to the distillery, which Bacardi family members promptly filled and returned. With business booming, Don Facundo decided the current method of distribution wasn't good enough and set out to find an alternative. Meanwhile, back in Spain, Queen Isabella, who ascended the throne in 1843 at the age of 13, was deposed. For Bacardi and his family, as with most Catalans living on the Spanish-controlled colony, the insurrection mirrored their own growing unrest. As civil war raged in Spain in 1872, Emilio, who had become a Cuban freedom fighter, was caught and exiled to an island off the coast of Morocco. During his absence, in 1875, hostilities grew and a rebellion swept through Cuba, though the family business was untouched. Four years after his capture, Emilio returned to Cuba and learned Bacardi rum had earned a gold medal at the Philadelphia Exposition of 1876.

A Changing Landscape, 1877 to 1931

As the 1880s dawned, Don Facundo retired and turned Bacardi over to Emilio, Facundo Jr., Jose, and Enrique, who was now his son-in-law. The company's distribution problems had been solved with a suggestion from Dona Amalia, to provide Bacardi products with a distinctive, easily recognized label. As many of Santiago's residents couldn't read, Dona Amalia recommended using a symbol to represent Bacardi. The Bacardi logo was then born, sporting a most unlikely mascot, the fruit bat.

Before the turn of the century, as Bacardi flourished, Cuba was again engaged in battle to gain its independence from Spain. Emilio, fighting for his country, was banished a second time and Enrique went with him into exile. The United States joined the fray after a mysterious explosion on the U.S. battleship *Maine* sparked the Spanish-American War in 1898. After defeating the Spanish fleet at Manila, the U.S. and Spain signed the Treaty of Paris, which ceded Cuba, Guam, the Philippines, and Puerto Rico to the U.S. for $20 million. In 1901 Cuba became an independent republic, and Emilio returned home to the Bacardi family and business.

Emilio was elected mayor of Santiago while Bacardi continued buying sugarcane fields and expanding its operations through several bottling facilities. In 1906 Emilio was elected to the Cuban Senate and the next year Jose, the youngest Bacardi son who had represented the company's interests in Havana, died. Though the family mourned his loss, the business continued to prosper and in 1910 Emilio returned to his father's homeland to begin Bacardi's first international venture: a new bottling facility in Barcelona, Spain. By the end of the next decade on May 2, 1919, Compania Ron Bacardi, S.A. was incorporated with Emilio as president, and Facundo Jr. and Enrique as vice presidents.

As Bacardi set out to conquer the world—especially the United States—with its premium rum, a roadblock called Prohibition stood in its way. Though temperance had been gaining ground for the last several years, the Prohibition amendment was officially ratified less than four months earlier on January 16, 1919. If the Bacardis could not sell their spirits to the U.S., nothing stopped Americans from coming to Cuba for liquor. Havana soon became known as "the unofficial U.S. saloon" and Bacardi rum was one of its biggest attractions. Bacardi's international sales were also strong in a world whose population topped 1.8 billion by 1922. This same year, both the family and the business suffered the loss of patriarch Emilio, followed two years later by Facundo Jr. Enrique, though not a family member by blood, took the reins of the burgeoning company and served as its president.

The dawn of the 1930s brought further international expansion for Bacardi as its bottling operation in Spain was a huge success. Realizing Bacardi rum could be distilled and sold from any facility with the appropriate equipment, Enrique began to open what soon became a network of distribution points. First came the establishment of a new subsidiary in Mexico in 1931, which was nearly bankrupt through a severe recession. Enrique's son-in-law, Jose Bosch, intervened and kept the operation afloat until the economy improved and the small company turned profitable.

After Prohibition, 1933–59

When Prohibition was repealed in December 1933 Bacardi was ready to fill the gap. Enrique promptly sent his son-in-law Jose to New York City to pave the way for Bacardi's distribution in the United States. Back in Cuba the political climate was once again boiling as Fulgencio Batista y Zaldivar, the country's army chief of staff, became Cuba's de facto ruler after a military coup. Unfettered by its tropical roots, Bacardi entered the U.S. marketplace in a bang—selling over 80,000 cases in 1934. To save the company the United States' expensive import duty tax (nearly $1 per bottle), Jose Bosch decided to open another Bacardi facility in Old San Juan, Puerto Rico. Under American control since the Treaty of Paris in 1901, Puerto Rico was considered U.S. soil and its exports duty free. Under the name Bacardi Corporation, the new company soon moved to larger accommodations across the bay in Catano.

The 1940s brought several milestones for Bacardi, both in expansion and brand recognition. Much of the company's U.S. business had begun through word-of-mouth praise from visitors to the Caribbean, especially those flying Pan American Airways, which used Bacardi in some of its ads, "Fly Pan Am to Cuba and you can be bathing in Bacardi in hours." To capitalize on Bacardi's growing reputation and enhance its brand at the same time, Enrique and Jose initiated advertising on Bacardi's excellent qualities as a mixer. Two of the more popular variations were the Daiquiri, named after a Cuban village where an American mining engineer mixed Bacardi, crushed ice, and lime juice in 1896; and the Cuba Libre or Rum & Coke, created by an American army lieutenant in honor of Cuba's new independence. The latter concoction gained widespread attention when the Andrews Sisters made "Rum & Coca-Cola" a hit in 1944.

The same year "Rum & Coca-Cola" sailed up the charts, Bacardi Imports was established in New York City to coordinate the increasing demand for Bacardi, and both Cuba and the United States joined the Allied war effort. By the end of the decade, dark clouds loomed on the horizon for Bacardi. In 1947, with the reintroduction of whiskey in the United States, rum sales plummeted 47 percent in a one-year period. Next came the death of Enrique Schueg in 1950, at which time Jose Bosch assumed the role of CEO. In 1953 when drinkers had become concerned over the caloric content of liquor, Bosch introduced a new advertising tact comparing the calories of a Daiquiri with those in a glass of milk. This successful spin was soon followed by ad campaigns directed to blacks and Hispanics, and in 1956 the company broke barriers by using a woman in its ads, who advised homemakers to serve a Daiquiri with the evening meal.

It was around this time (there were two dissenting versions) that the first Pina Colada was mixed in Puerto Rico, using Bacardi rum, varied fruit juices, and coconut milk. As the 1950s came to an end, Cuba was once again seized by revolution—this time to unseat Batista, who had returned to power in 1952. Regarded by many as a puppet of the United States, whose continued interference in Cuban affairs spawned guerrilla uprisings, Batista ruled until 1959 when rebels led by Fidel Castro and his brother Che Guevara overthrew his dictatorship.

The New Bacardi, 1960–89

Bosch, no fan of Batista, was shocked when the new Castro government seized Bacardi's assets, valued at $76 million, in 1960. Luckily for Bacardi, it not only had its Mexican, Puerto Rican, New York, and recently established Brazilian operations to fall back on, but its registered trademark (which Castro tried to seize, to no avail). Bacardi's shareholders, all descendants of Don Facundo, reconstituted the company in 1960 as Bacardi & Company Limited, headquartered in Nassau, the Bahamas. Another company, Bacardi International Limited, was also formed and headquartered in Bermuda. In 1962 the company sold 10 percent of its shares in an IPO (initial public offering).

Trying to stave off competitors with Bacardi's reputation as a mixer, the company launched a new advertising campaign once again expounding its rum's versatility. "Enjoyable always and all ways" was supposed to be taken literally, to use Bacardi's light-colored rum as a substitute for anything, even

vodka in heavyweight drinks like highballs. The formula worked and Bacardi's sales grew by 10 percent annually throughout the 1960s, when the company finally broke into the top ten of distilled spirits brands. In 1964 Bacardi sold over one million cases of rum; this figure doubled by 1968.

By the end of 1970, 2.6 million cases of Bacardi were sold. Aiming to further dominate the U.S. spirits market, Bacardi aggressively campaigned its rum as the mixer of choice, featured in joint promotions with Coca-Cola, Canada Dry Ginger Ale, Dr. Pepper, 7Up, Pepsi, Perrier, and Schweppes' tonic water. In a well-played game of one-upmanship, Bacardi won the battle against Smirnoff vodka as the nation's biggest-selling distilled spirit. In 1976 after a dispute with the Bacardi family, Jose Bosch resigned as president of the company. The following year Bosch and a group of his supporters sold their company stock (amounting to 12 percent or so) to an outsider, Hiram Walker. Unfortunately, this break with family tradition was the first in a series of squabbles that rocked the Bacardi empire over the next decade-and-a-half.

Bacardi's rums sold just shy of 8 million cases in 1978 and by 1980 reigned as the number-one liquor brand in the United States. During this period, consumers were once again weight-conscious and accordingly, Bacardi relaunched its status as a low calorie diet drink mixer. By 1985 Bacardi was selling over 18 million cases a year, with old rival Smirnoff selling less than 14 million. In 1986, three years after Bacardi Capital was created to manage and invest company funds, a group of inexperienced brokers lost $50 million speculating in the bond market. Regrouping, Bacardi chairman Alfred O'Hara and president Manuel Luis Del Valle (nonfamily members brought in to run the company in the 1970s) commenced a controversial stock buyback, which divided the company and inspired a storm of controversy. Many of the 500 family shareholders cried foul, several Bacardi family members were ousted, and O'Hara and Del Valle—despite the ruckus—succeeded. Spending more than $241 million, they bought back or converted shares from Bacardi's IPO in 1962 as well as those sold to Hiram Walker in 1977.

The Bacardi of the Future, 1990 and Beyond

When the 1990s began Bacardi was once again a private company. Having weathered the Bacardi Capital scandal and increasing family discord, the company was faced by falling market share and sales. In an effort to jazz up its image Bacardi Frozen Tropical Fruit Mixers and Bacardi Breezers were introduced to wide acclaim. Two years later came Rum & Coke in a can, and a majority interest in Martini & Rossi for $1.4 billion. Bacardi hoped the diversification would help its European operations; as a result of the purchase, Bacardi became the fifth largest wine-and-spirits company in the world. Before the Martini & Rossi acquisition, Bacardi was bringing in close to $500 million annually, yet was nowhere near complacent. Its next new product launch, Bacardi Limón, was aimed at younger drinkers of flavored liquors like Absolut's Citron and Stoli's Limonaya. Introduced in 1995 with an $11 million advertising campaign, Bacardi Limón took off and was considered one of the hottest high-proof new brands of the year.

By the mid-1990s Bacardi had bottling facilities located in Australia, Austria, France, Germany, New Zealand, Switzerland, the United Kingdom, and the United States, while its spirits were still manufactured in the Bahamas, Mexico, Puerto Rico, and Spain—with Brazil, Canada, Martinique, Panama, and Trinidad added to the list. The company's brands, of which Bacardi Breezers and Bacardi Limón were the latest newcomers, had grown to accommodate virtually all tastes. First and foremost was Bacardi's four premium rum blends: Bacardi Light, the original, comparative to gin and vodka as a mixer; Bacardi Dark (full-bodied, its amber color achieved by blackening the inside of wooden aging barrels) and Bacardi Black (charcoal-filtered just once before elongated aging; later renamed Bacardi Select), which competed with whiskey and bourbon; Bacardi Añejo, a golden rum blend named for the Castillian word meaning "aged" that appealed to upscale brown spirits-drinkers; and Bacardi Reserve, a twice-filtered blend for brandy and cognac drinkers.

By 1996 all of Bacardi's products were given a more hip look with updated labels and bottle caps as Bacardi Spice (to compete with Seagram's Captain Morgan) made its way to the market with several more prototypes in the works. As the company headed into the 21st century it was once again a family-run empire, with Don Facundo's heirs calling the shots. Manuel Jorge Cutillas and brother Eduardo occupied the top posts, while the company created alliances with partners in Hong Kong, Japan, Malaysia, the Philippines, Russia, Taiwan, and Thailand to introduce its products. Another global project was the debut of Club Bacardi, the company's web site. Well-positioned for the future, the name Bacardi conjured up far more than a refined, dry rum; Bacardi was not just a premium spirit but an institution here to stay.

Principal Subsidiaries

Bacardi & Co. (Bahamas); Bacardi Corp. (Puerto Rico); Bacardi-Martini, U.S.A. Inc.; Bacardi International (Bermuda); Bacardi y Compania (Mexico).

Further Reading

"Bacardi Has Long-Term Plans for Spice Market," *Grocer,* August 12, 1995, p. 25.

"A Bat, with a Coat of Arms," *Financial World,* November 22, 1994, p. 80.

Behar, Richard, "Hangover," *Forbes,* July 14, 1986, p. 33.

Holleran, Joan, "Bacardi Breakthrough," *Beverage Industry,* July 1996, p. 32.

Hornik, Richard, "Rum Deal in an Old Family Farm; the Bacardis Tussle Over Taking Their Liquor Company Private," *Time,* May 25, 1987, p. 56.

Khermouch, Gerry, "Bacardi's Proof Positive," *Brandweek,* March 11, 1996, p. 30.

Simley, John, "Bacardi," *Encyclopedia of Consumer Brands,* edited by Janice Jorgensen, Detroit, St. James Press, 1993, pp. 24–26.

Whitefield, Mimi, "A Renovated Bacardi Plans New Generation of Snappy Niche Beverages," *Knight-Ridder/Tribune Business News,* March 26, 1995.

—Taryn Benbow-Pfalzgraf

Ⅲ Baldwin

Baldwin Piano & Organ Company

422 Wards Corner Road
Loveland, Ohio 45140-8390
U.S.A.
(513) 576-4500
Fax: (513) 576-4546
Web site: email:bpao.com

Public Company
Founded: 1862
Employees: 1,500
Sales: $122.6 million (1995)
Stock Exchanges: NASDAQ
SICs: 3931 Musical Instruments; 3674 Semiconductors &
    Related Devices; 6141 Personal Credit Institutions

At first glance Baldwin Piano & Organ Company would appear to be a rather staid, traditional manufacturer of musical instruments, but a closer examination of its more than 125 years in business reveals a fascinating history of breathtaking highs and devastating lows. In its early years, the company combined innovative marketing and financing techniques with high-quality instruments to capture a leading share of the piano market. A 1970s-era diversification into financial services transformed the company into a $9 billion conglomerate known as Baldwin-United Corp. But bad management in the 1980s led to one of the largest bankruptcies in American history. Baldwin Piano & Organ (BP&O) emerged from the fiasco focused on its core business, keyboard instruments, only to find intense foreign competition and a shrinking customer base. Nevertheless, Baldwin has managed to eke out admirable returns; sales rose from $110.1 million in 1992 to $122.6 million in 1995, and net income slid from a high of $5.9 million in 1992 to just $345,000 in 1994, rebounding to just under $4 million in 1995. A new CEO, 48-year-old Karen L. Hendricks, hoped to lead a return to consistent growth in profitability.

Prelude: 19th-Century Origins

The company is named for founder Dwight Hamilton Baldwin, who was born in Pennsylvania in 1821. Hoping to be-

come an itinerant minister, this pious Presbyterian took courses at Ohio's Oberlin College. When advisors judged him too frail for this demanding vocation, Baldwin left Oberlin to become a traveling music teacher. With his wife, Emerine Summers, Baldwin finally settled in Cincinnati and took a teaching post with the city's public school system in the 1850s.

Having saved a $2,000 nest egg over the course of his seven-year career in music education, Baldwin invested the money in a retail piano shop in 1862. The showroom carried Chickering, Steinway, Decker Brothers, and Vose pianos as well as Estey Reed organs. A limited number of instruments manufactured by The Ohio Valley Piano Co. were sold under the D.H. Baldwin & Co. name.

A company history published in the June 1987 edition of *Music Trades Magazine* noted Baldwin's particular knack for hiring quality employees. In 1865 he engaged Civil War veteran Lucien Wulsin as a bookkeeper. Wulsin accepted a partnership in the company in 1873, and with Baldwin established sales outlets in Louisville and Indianapolis as well as other smaller cities in the tri-state area.

It was not until after they lost their Steinway franchise in 1887 that the colleagues decided to begin designing and building their own keyboard instruments. They started out manufacturing organs in Chicago, incorporating the Hamilton Organ Company in 1889, and establishing the Baldwin Piano Company in Cincinnati the following year. The partners shipped their first self-made piano in 1891, and two years later formed the Ellington Piano Company. This separate subsidiary and trademark built mid-range models without compromising the high-quality image cultivated by the Baldwin brand.

When D. H. Baldwin and his wife died within a few weeks of each other in 1899, his 80 percent stake in the various companies passed to the Presbyterian Church. Wulsin and three other minority shareholders purchased the businesses and merged them to form The Baldwin Corp.

Crescendo: Keys to Growth in the Early Twentieth Century

Up until this time, Baldwin had focused its sales efforts on building a chain of company-owned retail outlets. But soon

Company Perspectives:

As a leader in the U.S. keyboard market, Baldwin Piano & Organ Company manufactures and markets a full range of quality keyboard instrument featuring the Baldwin, Wurlitzer, and Chickering trademarks. From artist-accepted concert grand pianos to innovative digital keyboards, renowned Baldwin instruments are found in homes, churches, academic institutions, and concert halls across the nation.

Baldwin expands on its core business by providing in-house installment financing of musical products. With an emphasis on superior service, Keyboard Acceptance Corporation continues to grow. It is unique, due in part, to the fact that Baldwin is the only U.S. musical products manufacturer to offer consumer financing of its instruments.

Through its Special Products Division, Baldwin offers electronic and electromechanical design and manufacturing services for Original Equipment Manufacturers. With quality services and on-time delivery, Baldwin is expanding its business in this growth industry.

Baldwin headquarters are located in Loveland, Ohio, a suburb of Cincinnati. Its products are manufactured at five facilities in North America by 1,500 dedicated employees.

after the turn of the century, Wulsin adopted a growth strategy that had been unsuccessfully pioneered by the Singer Sewing Machine Company and also used by a competitor in the piano market, W.W. Kimball Co. of Chicago. This "consignment/installment plan," which Baldwin had started testing as early as 1875, called for independent retailers to carry instruments on consignment, only paying shipping costs until the keyboards were sold. This aspect of the program allowed retailers to carry large, expensive, and impressive inventories without much risk or cost. Furthermore, Baldwin assumed additional risk by financing individual customers' purchases. Dealers kept down payments and interest as their portion of the profit, while the manufacturer managed the loans and reaped the principal.

But it was not just savvy marketing that drove Baldwin's rise to the top of the piano industry. Beginning with the Paris Exposition of the Arts and Manufacturers in 1900, the well-built instruments earned top honors at World's Fairs in St. Louis (1904), London (1914), Brussels (1958), Seattle (1964), and New York (1964–65). Baldwin pianos soon captured the attention of well-known artists around the world, beginning with turn-of-the-century stars like Marcella Sernbrich and Vladimir de Pachmann and including Leonard Bernstein, Liberace, Aaron Copland, André Previn, Dave Brubeck, Lawrence Welk, Zubin Mehta, Carly Simon, and Bruce Hornsby, among many others. Baldwin took pains to emphasize that these were not compensated endorsements, but "a professional judgment and commitment" to the instrument.

Lucien Wulsin held the reins at Baldwin until his death in 1912, when he was succeeded by George Armstrong. The "scholarly" Armstrong led Baldwin for about 14 years, guiding a period when player pianos fueled rapid growth. By 1926, Baldwin's annual sales approached $10 million, half of that figure generated by player pianos. Lucien Wulsin took Bal-

dwin's helm that year, the second of three successive generations of Lucien Wulsins to lead the company through most of the twentieth century.

However, the "roaring twenties" ended even earlier for Baldwin and its keyboard industry competitors than they did for the rest of the country. The 1927 introduction of the radio decimated player piano sales, sending many keyboard manufacturers into bankruptcy. The Great Depression followed fast on the heels of this industry-specific downturn, sealing the fate of many of those piano companies that had not already succumbed. Baldwin's endurance and eventual resurgence was credited to Armstrong, who in the early 1920s had set aside significant funds for "unforeseen contingencies." By the end of the 1930s, Baldwin led the U.S. piano industry in dollar volume, with an estimated $4 million in sales and net income of $159,000.

Armstrong's "rainy day" fund not only kept the company afloat, but also enabled Lucien Wulsin to direct trailblazing sound reproduction studies in cooperation with the University of Cincinnati's Physics Department. These experiments stopped in 1941, when Baldwin's facilities were enlisted to help the war effort by manufacturing wooden aircraft wings. While the company was able to apply veneering skills honed during this period to piano manufacturing in the postwar era, war work was not the windfall it was to some other industries; in fact, Baldwin's sales only amounted to about $7 million at the war's end.

Postwar consumer demand, as well as a new line of electronic organs for residential and church use, drove sales to over $33 million by 1954. Seeking lower labor costs, more relaxed building codes, and less limited room to grow, Baldwin began to move its manufacturing operations from Cincinnati later that decade. Plants in Arkansas, Mississippi, and later Mexico had replaced the original factory by 1968.

By that time, the second Lucien Wulsin had been superseded as CEO by his son (also Lucien), who led Baldwin from 1964 until 1980, overseeing the most infamous period in the venerable company's history.

Allegro: Diversification into Financial Services Begins in Late 1960s

Given Baldwin's decades of experience financing pianos, the company's late 1960s diversification into other financial services seemed quite logical. Lucien Wulsin got the ball rolling with the 1968 acquisition of Denver's Central Bank & Trust Co. He was joined in this quest by Morley P. Thompson, appointed president of the company in 1970. Having graduated from the Harvard Business School in 1950, Thompson had started out as a door-to-door piano salesman. His skill at shuffling money among subsidiaries to limit corporate taxes and generate acquisition funds won him a reputation as a financial "wizard."

Thompson would not be satisfied with a mere sideline in finance; he wanted to fashion a major conglomerate out of the nation's largest keyboard company. Under his guidance, Baldwin acquired literally dozens of financial services firms in the 1970s and early 1980s. At its peak, the company controlled over 200 insurance companies, savings and loan institutions, and investment firms. Some of its larger deals included a 1977 merger with Cincinnati investment company United Corp. to form Baldwin-United Corp. and the October 1981 acquisition of Sperry & Hutchinson, best known for its "S&H Green Stamps." Baldwin's most popular financial product was the single-premium deferred annuity (SPDA), a life insurance policy that amassed interest tax-free until withdrawals began. From 1980 to 1983, Baldwin sold 165,000 of these policies, or over $4 billion worth, at interest rates of at least 7.5 percent and up to 14.5 percent. By 1982, keyboard instruments constituted a mere three percent of Baldwin-United's $3.6 billion revenues.

Decrescendo: Baldwin-United Files for Bankruptcy in Early 1980s

Although Thompson employed a complex array of transactions to maximize income and minimize costs, several factors fouled up his plans. Fundamentally, the company was paying higher interest rates than it was earning on its own investments. Thompson's fiscal juggling allowed the company to generate tax credits on the losses, but with little profit against which to count those credits, Thompson began to register some tax credits as profits in 1979.

In the absence of net income at his own companies, Thompson set out on a quest to acquire companies with positive cash flow. In March 1982, Baldwin acquired Mortgage Guaranty Insurance Corp. (MGIC), a Wisconsin-based residential mortgage insurer that ranked at the top of its field. Baldwin-United took out nearly $600 million in short-term loans from eight banks to help pay the $1.2 billion price tag. When MGIC's profits slid more than 20 percent, Thompson started siphoning liquid assets from insurance subsidiaries' reserve funds to service the debt, a move that drew the attention of insurance regulators in three states.

Thompson may have been known as a financial magician, but no sleight-of-hand could help him come up with the $440 million short-term debt payment that finally came due March 1983. The full extent of Baldwin's troubles began to come to light that May, the same month that Thompson took a "leave of absence." (By the end of the year, he would be acting as treasurer for American Laundry Machinery, a Cincinnati-based manufacturer of laundry and dry cleaning equipment.) Robert S. "Dick" Harrison, executive vice-president and chief financial officer, replaced Thompson on an interim basis. That July, insurance commissioners from Arkansas and Indiana seized control of Baldwin-United's six insurance companies, effectively freezing the vast majority of the company's assets. In June 1983 the board of directors called in Victor Palmieri, an expert at bankruptcy reorganization, to guide the proceedings. Palmieri did not pull any punches, telling *Time* magazine that "Things at Baldwin were more confused than anyone could have imagined."

Baldwin-United's $9 billion in liabilities exceeded the *combined* debt loads of the four largest bankruptcies to precede it, including Wickes, Itel, Braniff Airlines, and Penn Central. The market value of Lucien Wulsin's stake in Baldwin-United shrunk from $19.8 million in November 1982 to $1 million by late 1983. Laura Saunders of *Forbes* called it "a classic corporate disaster," and *Fortune's* Steven Flax agreed, saying it was an "amazing, appalling story." It took until August 1985 for Baldwin-United to file a reorganization plan. In the meantime,

Baldwin Piano & Organ was among the $1.4 billion in assets sold off to settle claims against the parent company.

Reprise: Management Buyout Brings Return to Roots in Mid-1980s

In June 1984, R. S. Harrison, who notwithstanding his brief stint as interim CEO of Baldwin-United had been CEO of Baldwin Piano & Organ since 1974, joined with BP&O President Harold Smith to execute a leveraged buyout of the subsidiary from its troubled parent. All but $4 million of the $65 million buyout was financed with help from Security Pacific Business Credit and General Electric Credit Corp. Despite this relatively small cash contribution, Harrison retained about 25 percent of the privately-held company, and Smith kept a 23 percent stake. *Barron's* Lauren R. Rublin characterized the move as a "rescue," but being extricated from the Baldwin-United mess did not by any means guarantee smooth sailing for BP&O. Although it continued to lead the keyboard industry, it faced a number of problems endemic to that market.

Forbes' s Laura Saunders cited demographics as a key factor of the piano industry's problems, noting that "From 1965 to 1975, the birth rate per 1,000 women dropped from 96 to 66. Since most pianos are bought for elementary school children, the effect of that should have been obvious." Other issues, like high interest rates and rising raw materials costs, accelerated the contraction of the overall keyboard market. U.S. acoustic piano sales peaked in 1978 at 282,000 new units, according to the American Music Conference, a Chicago-based trade group. That number declined by 30 percent, to less than 200,000 by 1983, and was down to 151,300 by 1985. Traditional manual multiple keyboard organs were sinking even faster: unit sales peaked in 1974 at 234,000, and were down to 50,000 by 1986.

Competition on several fronts further complicated these fundamental difficulties. Saunders noted the "diminished cultural cachet of playing the piano," and it was undeniable that other, largely more passive forms of entertainment like radio, television, computers, video games, and VCRs had whittled away at leisure time previously devoted to piano playing. Domestic piano companies also faced competition from low-cost foreign manufacturers, who by 1986 controlled 43 percent of the acoustic piano market. Leaders of this foreign assault included Yamaha, Kawai, and Samick. In the midst of these challenges, Baldwin Piano & Organ's sales slid from $116 million in 1981 to $90 million by 1985.

Harrison and Smith formulated several strategies for survival in these difficult circumstances. In October 1986, they sold 19.4 percent of the company, about 1.2 million shares, to generate about $9 million in debt reduction funds. At the same time, they initiated cost-reduction efforts, moving the corporate headquarters to Loveland, Ohio, for example. In order to utilize excess production capacity, BP&O reapplied its electronic, woodworking, and technological know-how to related businesses. By the mid-1980s, the company was creating printed circuit boards and electro-mechanical assemblies for heat pumps, vending machines, and clocks. By October 1987, they had reduced debt by more than $40 million.

Baldwin used several strategies to combat foreign competition. In 1988, the company increased its share of the U.S.

keyboard market via the acquisition of the Wurlitzer Co., which was itself near bankruptcy. While the merger with third-ranking Wurlitzer was not without pitfalls, it did help to increase Baldwin's leading share of U.S. keyboard sales from 19 percent in 1986 to more than 26 percent by 1991. Baldwin also moved some manufacturing to countries like South Korea, where rock-bottom labor costs reigned. It even started making pianos under contract with Yamaha in 1986. The company also enjoyed a measure of good luck: keyboard sales rebounded slightly in 1986 and 1987 after bottoming-out in the early 1980s.

BP&O's sales rebounded in the late 1980s, rising from less than $100 million mid-decade to a high of $135 million in 1988. Net income more than doubled during the period, to over $7.1 million in 1987.

Progression: New Leadership for the 1990s and Beyond

For the most part, Baldwin carried on the strategies formulated in the late 1980s through the early 1990s. Manufacturing, selling, and financing of acoustic pianos continued to constitute the vast majority of sales and net income, while electronic and digital pianos, organs, clocks, and circuit boards were considered small but vital operations. But as corporate revenues dipped to $103.2 million in 1991 and net income slid to $4.4 million, it became clear that BP&O would have to adopt an ongoing strategy of market analysis in order to ensure steady growth and profitability.

In 1994, the company hired 48-year-old Karen L. Hendricks to succeed R. S. Harrison as CEO and president. With more than twenty years' experience in consumer goods, Hendricks brought a renewed focus on marketing to Baldwin. In 1995, the company consolidated sales of its three primary brands—Baldwin, Chickering, and Wurlitzer—targeting each trademark at a particular price point. This strategy not only clarified brand strategies, but also yielded manufacturing, distribution, and back office efficiencies. Management also hoped to more fully develop the company's OEM electronics division. Although BP&O's annual sales and earnings had not fully recovered from

their late 1980s gusto by the end of 1995, CEO Hendricks expressed her confidence that the company was "Poised For Progress" in 1996 and beyond.

Principal Subsidiaries

Keyboard Acceptance Corp.; Wurlitzer Co.; Baldwin Piano Company (Canada) Ltd.; Fabricantes Tecnicos, S.A. (Mexico); Korean American Musical Instrument Corp. (South Korea).

Further Reading

Bolton, Douglas, "Baldwin Upbeat on Wurlitzer Deal," *Cincinnati Business Courier* February 15, 1988, pp. 1–2.

Flax, Steven, "Baldwin-United Back from the Dead," *Fortune*, September 16, 1985, pp. 46–50.

Hillstrom, Kevin, *Encyclopedia of American Industry*, vol. 1, Detroit: Gale Research, 1994, pp. 1310–1314.

Klose, Roland, "Baldwin Bounces Back from Creditors' Catcalls As Analysts Applaud Return Performance," *Memphis Business Journal*, November 14–18, 1988, pp. 1, 32–33.

"Low Flier; Grim Days at Baldwin-United," *Fortune*, May 30, 1983, p. 12.

Marcial, Gene G., "These Ivories Could Be Golden," *Business Week*, April 15, 1991, p. 88.

Meeks, Fleming, "Hard Choices," *Forbes*, October 31, 1988, pp. 126–127.

"Mournful Music; Baldwin Goes Bankrupt," *Time*, October 10, 1983, p. 53.

Paton, Huntley, "Wall Street Tunes in to Baldwin Stock," *Cincinnati Business Courier*, June 27, 1988, pp. 1–2.

Rublin, Lauren R. "Ragtime to Riches: Baldwin Is Back and Picking Up the Pieces," *Barron's*, January 12, 1987, pp. 13, 18, 20, 22.

"Sad Note: The Sale of Baldwin Piano," *Fortune*, January 9, 1984, p. 12.

Saunders, Laura, "Mood Indigo," *Forbes*, August 29, 1983, pp. 50–51.

Thompson, Morley P., *D.H. Baldwin; The Multibank Music Company*, New York: Newcomen Society, 1974.

"Vanishing Magic; Baldwin-United Will Sell MGIC," *Fortune*, October 17, 1983, p. 10.

Wulsin, Lucien, *Dwight Hamilton Baldwin (1821–1899) and the Baldwin Piano*, New York: Newcomen Society, 1953.

—April Dougal Gasbarre

BASF Aktiengesellschaft

Carl-Bosch-Strasse 38
67056 Ludwigshafen
Germany
(49) 621-60-99 9 38
Fax: (49) 621-60-92 6 93
Web site: http://www.basf.com

Public Company
Incorporated: 1952 as Badische Anilin- und Soda-Fabrik
 A.G.
Employees: 106,565
Sales: DM46.23 billion (US$32 billion) (1995)
Stock Exchanges: Munich Frankfurt Bonn Hamburg
 Zurich Basel Geneva Paris Vienna Brussels Antwerp
 London Amsterdam
SICs: 2812 Alkalies & Chlorine; 2819 Industrial
 Inorganic Chemicals, Not Elsewhere Classified; 2821
 Plastics Materials, Nonvulanizable Elastomers &
 Synthetic Resins; 2834 Pharmaceutical Preparations;
 2851 Paints, Varnishes, Lacquers, Enamels & Allied
 Products; 2865 Cyclic Organic Crudes &
 Intermediates, Organic Dyes & Pigments; 2879
 Pesticides & Agricultural Chemicals, Not Elsewhere
 Classified; 6719 Offices of Holding Companies, Not
 Elsewhere Classified

Since its founding in 1865 Badische Anilin- und Soda-Fabrik AG (now known as BASF Aktiengesellschaft) has been a major influence in the world chemical industry. As one of the three largest German chemical companies, BASF exerted an influence from 1924 to 1947 that extended far beyond dyes and nylons. When joined with Bayer and Hoechst to form the world's largest chemical cartel, one of the most powerful cartels in history, BASF was instrumental in helping to secretly re-arm Germany.

For its role during these years the chemical cartel, known as the I.G. Farben, was broken up by the Allies, and BASF again existed as an independent company. Despite the fact that almost half of its plant in Ludwigshafen, Germany, was reduced to rubble during World War II, BASF was able to reestablish its presence in the chemical industry. It is now the world's second-largest chemical company (after Hoechst). In addition to its flagship production facilities in Ludwigshafen (the world's largest chemical site), BASF operates major facilities in Antwerp, Belgium; Nanjing, China; Tarragona, Spain; and Geismar, Louisiana. BASF holds a significant share of the international market in chemicals, natural gas, plastics, pharmaceuticals, crop protection agents, and its original product, dyes.

Early History in the Late 19th Century

BASF was founded in 1861 by Frederick Engelhorn, a jeweler, along the banks of the Rhine River at Mannheim. Using the discoveries of the English scientist William Perkins, BASF became one of the first companies to manufacture dyes from coal tar. Its specialty was the bright bluish purple known as indigo. The attraction of BASF's process lay in the fact that it took coal tar, a messy byproduct of gas distillation, and transformed it into something that replaced a more expensive and unreliable organic substance.

BASF's synthetic dyes were less expensive, brighter, and easier to use than organic dyes. Profits from these dyes were used to finance BASF's diversification into inorganic chemicals later in the century as well as new production facilities across the river in Ludwigshafen.

By the early 20th century journalists were calling BASF "The World's Greatest Chemical Works." In 1910 the company employed over 8,000 people and by 1926 this number had grown to 42,000. Its production facilities in Ludwigshafen alone covered 2,787 acres. American journalists were impressed by BASF's charity and reported that, "The company has given a great deal of attention to welfare work; especially to housing, hygiene and the care of the sick."

BASF's sanatoriums and dispensaries, along with its main production facilities, were financed in part by business arrangements that would be illegal today in either Germany or the United States. Beginning around 1900 leaders of the German

---

Company Perspectives:

The BASF Group is one of the world's leading chemical companies, achieving sales of $32 billion in 1995. BASF offers a full range of chemical and chemical-related products. We have built major strengths in science and the process of innovation, and we are using these strengths to assure our future success. Ingrained in our culture is applying the process of innovation—or change—to all aspects of the business.

---

chemical industry began to dream of what was, in effect, the merger of most German chemical companies. Should this cartel be formed, said Carl Duisberg, the man who eventually set up the I.G. Farben, "... the now existing domination of the German chemical industry, especially the dye industry, over the rest of the world would then, in my opinion, be assured."

Cartels Formed in Early 20th Century

By 1904 two major cartels had been formed. The first of these cartels included Bayer and BASF; the second cartel was anchored by Hoechst. Not only did these firms avoid competition and fix prices, but they also set up a quota system and even shared their profits. For instance, a marketing agreement was reached for the sale of indigo, which was one of the most profitable dyes.

Both cartels played an important role during World War I. Not only was dye necessary for garments, but the basic chemical formulas for dyes could be altered slightly to make mustard gas and munitions. Companies such as BASF provided gas and explosives for German troops and, previous to the United States' entry into the war, they initiated economic activities that stunted the growth of the chemical companies important to the U.S. war effort. For instance, BASF had sold aniline at below market prices to U.S. firms in order to discourage aniline production by U.S. companies. As part of the dye cartel it had also engaged in a practice called "full-line forcing." If a dealer wanted to purchase item A for example, available only from BASF, the dealer was forced to purchase the whole product line, effectively eliminating U.S. producers.

After the war the German government recognized the importance of the chemical industry, especially the dye industry. Not only did the chemical industry bring in needed foreign currency, but it was critical to defense. Since the build-up of the chemical industry was so important to Germany, the cartels were granted government loans as well as a ten-year tax deferment. The cartels also received a special allotment of coal, which was very scarce at the time.

I.G. Farben Formed in 1925

In 1925 the top executives in the chemical industry decided that the duplication of product lines and the maintenance of separate sales forces was wasteful. As a result, hundreds of German chemical companies (including Bayer and Hoechst)

formally merged with BASF. This new corporation, headquartered at Ludwigshafen, was renamed the Interessengemeinschaft Farbenindustrie, or I.G. Farben. BASF ceased to exist as a legal entity; it operated for the next 26 years as "Betriebsgemeinschaft Oberrhein," or the upper Rhine operating unit of I.G. Farben.

The I.G. Farben set quotas and pooled profits. But this large trust was more than an economic entity—it was a political one. I.G. Farben's executives feared that leftists might triumph in Germany's unstable political climate and that I.G. Farben itself would be nationalized. This led to the I.G. Farben's support for Adolph Hitler. As early as 1931 its directors made secret contributions to the Nazi Party.

Notorious World War II Years

The I.G. Farben profited handsomely from its support of Hitler and his foreign policy, and it grew tremendously during World War II. By 1942 the cartel was making a yearly profit that was 800 million marks more than its entire combined capitalization in 1925, the year of its founding. Not only was the I.G. Farben given possession of chemical companies in foreign lands (the I.G. Farben had control of Czechoslovakian dye works a week after the Nazi invasion), but the captured lands also provided its factories in Germany with slave labor. In order to take advantage of slave labor, I.G. Farben plants were built next to Maidanek and Auschwitz.

At its peak, the I.G. Farben had controlling interest in 379 German firms and 400 foreign companies. It has been noted that one of the historic restraints on Germany was its lack of colonies to supply necessary products, such as rubber. During this time the I.G. Farben, synthesizing many of the country's chemical needs with a native product, provided Germany with the self-sufficiency it lacked during World War I.

Near the end of the war the BASF production facilities at Ludwigshafen were bombed extensively. While factories built during the war were often camouflaged, the old BASF factories were more visible to American bombers, which often flew over Ludwigshafen on the way back from other bombing raids and dropped any leftover bombs on the ammonia and nitrogen works. During the war BASF factories sustained the heaviest damage in the I.G. Farben with 45 percent of BASF buildings destroyed.

Postwar Rebuilding of BASF

With the surrender of Germany, I.G. Farben's problems had only just begun. Immediately after the war many members of the Vorstand, or board of directors of the I.G. Farben, were arrested and indicted for war crimes. There was a large amount of written evidence incriminating the Vorstand, most of it written by the directors themselves. I.G. Farben executives were in the habit of keeping copious records, not only of meetings and phone calls, but also of their private thoughts on the I.G. Farben's dealings with the government. Despite the quantity of written evidence and testimony from concentration camp survivors, the Vorstand was dealt with leniently by the judges at Nuremberg. Journalists covering the 1947 proceedings attributed the light sentences, none of which was longer than four years, to the fact that all the sentences in the trials were becoming less severe towards the end, and to the judges' unwillingness to lower the standards for active participation in war crimes to include businessmen.

The Potsdam Agreement referred to the necessity of dismantling the I.G. Farben in the interests of "peace and democracy." But from the very beginning the Allies disagreed over the fate of the I.G. Farben. The British and French favored a breakup of the company into large separate companies, while many U.S. officials advocated that the company be divided into smaller and therefore less influential firms. Negotiations over the cartel's fate lasted for several years. The French and British plan eventually prevailed.

After operating under Allied supervision from 1947 to 1952, the I.G. Farben was divided in 1952 into three large firms—Bayer, Hoechst, and BASF—and nine smaller firms. After this reorganization BASF was once again a small corporation located on its original Ludwigshafen site. Its share of the 30,000 I.G. Farben patents had been taken away; some of its trade secrets had been sold for as little as $1.00. It was isolated from its previous suppliers in Eastern Europe and, in fact, most of its basic supplies, such as coal, were insufficient. The 55 percent of its buildings that had not been destroyed were filled with outdated equipment. Leading BASF from its refounding until 1965 was board chairman Carl Wurster, who started at the company as a chemist.

West Germany, lacking money to import chemicals from abroad, was in dire need for chemicals produced at home. By 1957, BASF's sales of nitrogen and ammonia products were approaching their wartime levels. BASF initially lagged behind both Bayer and Hoechst in profits, in part because its product line included such items as fertilizers, plastics, and synthetics which were easily challenged on the market by competitors. Between 1957 and 1962 sales grew 59 percent, less than either Bayer or Hoechst. As prices for plastics and fertilizers stabilized in 1963, however, sales for the company increased 19 percent in one year.

BASF's growth during the postwar period was impressive. In the 10 years after the dissolution of the I.G. Farben, the company increased its capital from DM81 million to DM200 million. Employing only 800 workers in the late 1940s, it employed 45,000 by 1963. Although BASF had lost all of its patents in 1952, within 10 years it had recovered a large number of them.

Impressive Growth in the 1960s and 1970s

BASF began its second decade of independence from the I.G. Farben with a switch to oil as a base for most of its old, coal-based formulas. With the purchase of Rheinisch Olefinwerke, BASF added petroleum to the long list of raw materials it was able to provide for itself. The company soon became the world's largest producer of plastic, and provided an astonishing 10 percent of the international requirement for synthetic fibers.

Despite these gains, BASF was still faced with problems. It was the possessor of the old I.G. Farben soda and nitrogen works, but these products were often in oversupply. BASF competed with other European producers who were not burdened with this product and who were situated in more petro-

leum-rich countries. Nevertheless, the company reached DM1 billion in sales during 1965. Bernard Timm, the newly appointed board chairman with a background as a physicist, attributed the company's performance in 1965 to a judicious mix of plastics, farm chemicals, raw materials for coatings, dyes, and raw materials for fibers.

In 1969, another significant year for the company, BASF purchased Wintershall, which had half of the German potash market and produced a quarter of the country's natural gas. This acquisition was the largest in German history, and with it BASF jumped over Bayer to become the nation's second largest chemical company. A large new plastics plant at Antwerp made PVC, polyethylene, and caprolatum (a nylon intermediary) at an accelerated rate.

Following the impressive growth of BASF during the 1960s, the 1970s started slowly. After much encouragement by the state of South Carolina to build a $200 million dye and plastics plant in an impoverished area near Hilton Head, the company's plans were thwarted by an unlikely coalition of outside agitators, local residents, and Southern gentry who feared damage to the beautiful Carolina coastline. In 1971 large investments in fibers and plastics were lost due to overcapacity. Synthetic fibers, whose prices were low in relation to the petroleum used in their manufacture, continued to plague BASF throughout the decade.

Despite the problems with fibers, however, the company continued to grow. The growth plan favored by Timm, who served as board chairman until 1974, and Matthias Seefelder, chairman from 1974 to 1983 and a chemist by trade, featured vertical integration, expansion abroad, and emphasis on consumer products. Of the three successors to the I.G. Farben, BASF was the one left with the least attractive product line. In order to remedy this situation, BASF marketed its line of magnetic cassette tapes (a product it claims to have invented) and then ventured into videotapes. As for vertical integration, the company had ample access to raw materials and chose to modify existing raw materials rather than diversify into unfamiliar fields.

U.S. Expansion in the 1980s

Since there was little room to grow in Germany, the expansion into foreign markets was a cornerstone of BASF's strategy for growth. And the 1980s were a decade of significant growth for BASF in the United States. In order to avoid U.S. tariffs BASF formed numerous partnerships with American companies and acquired others. Wyandotte Chemicals Corporation of Wyandotte, Michigan, had been a major acquisition in 1969. The 1980s began with the purchase of Fritzsche Dodge and Olcott, Inc., the third largest U.S. producer of flavors and fragrances, not to mention Cook Industrial Coatings and Allegheny Ludlums. This last acquisition put BASF among the top 15 pigment manufacturers in the U.S. The 1985 purchase of American Enka doubled BASF's fiber capacity. Although BASF's 1980s foreign ventures were by no means limited to the United States, its emphasis on U.S. expansion was understandable. At the time, the United States consumed one-third of the world's chemical production. The company's holdings in the United States also cushioned BASF against fluctuations in the value of the deutschemark and the dollar.

In 1986 the increasing importance of its U.S. operations was highlighted when BASF consolidated all North American operations under a new subsidiary called BASF Corporation. Within the entire BASF Group, the new company ranked second in size only to the flagship BASF A.G., and generated 20 percent of overall group sales. Nearly all—90 percent—of the BASF Corporation's sales were generated from products it produced in North America.

The very year of its consolidation, BASF Corporation was in the news when the Oil, Chemical and Atomic Worker's union decided to strike at a plant located in Geismar, Louisiana. Union allegations of unsafe working conditions prompted the U.S. Congress to investigate conditions at the plant. The union announced a campaign of negative publicity directed against the company. The strike surprised the management at BASF which, with the exception of World War II, generally treated workers well. Asked about the labor difficulties, a highly ranked BASF executive said, ''We haven't had a strike since 1924, except a work stoppage in 1947 to protest our president being tried for war crimes.'' The strike—which evolved into a lockout—dragged on and on until it was finally settled with a union victory in 1989.

Transformation of BASF in the 1990s

After Hans Albers had served as board chairman from 1983 to 1990, he was succeeded by Jürgen Strube. The year 1990 was a fitting one for a change in leadership; it was the 125th anniversary of the company founding, and represented the beginning of one of the most remarkable periods in BASF history, a period of furious activity—restructurings, acquisitions, divestments, joint ventures, and immense capital expenditures, all on a scale unprecedented in BASF history.

Strube took over BASF after it had posted one of its strongest years ever in 1989, with sales of DM46.16 billion and net income after taxes of DM20.2 billion. Sales would then fall for each of the next four years, while net income fell for the next three. The levels of 1989 would not be surpassed until 1995. The reasons for BASF's struggles were many: a cyclical downturn in the chemical industry in the early 1990s, to which the company was still highly vulnerable; a serious recession in Germany, brought on in part by the cost of German reunification; health care reform efforts in Europe, which led to the increasing use of generic drugs to contain costs, with BASF's proprietary drug sales suffering as a result; and the Common Agricultural Policy reform effort, which reduced the amount of farmed land and the amount of chemicals used in farming it, thus hurting the sale of BASF agricultural products. The German reunification also affected BASF in a more direct way when it took over—for nothing—Synthesewerk Schwarzheide, one of the largest chemical businesses in the former East Germany. BASF converted it into BASF Schwarzheide GmbH, but then had to spend DM1.4 billion to modernize and expand its facilities.

Strube quickly responded to the crisis by initiating a serious cost-cutting program and by identifying businesses BASF should divest. Cost-cutting efforts included the closure of a number of plants and a gradual workforce reduction that saw BASF's employee numbers fall from a high of 136,990 in 1989 to 106,266 in 1994, a reduction of more than 22 percent.

Divested operations were identified as those where BASF was not competitive. These included the Auguste Victoria coal mine, which BASF had used to supply itself with coal since 1907, sold in 1990 to Ruhrkohle A.G.; the flavors and fragrances business of Fritzsche Dodge and Olcott, which was no longer viewed as a good fit; and the advanced materials division, which was not profitable enough to retain.

Strube also wanted to make BASF less susceptible to the cyclical downturns of the chemical industry by bolstering the company's noncyclical businesses. The company's consumer products area was beefed up with the 1991 acquisition of AGFA-Gevaert's magnetic tape operations, which were reorganized with BASF's existing magnetic tape business to form BASF Magnetics GmbH, producer of tapes, videocassettes, and diskettes. A more important and daring venture began in 1990 when Wintershall, BASF's oil and gas subsidiary, entered into an agreement with Gazprom—the world's largest natural gas producer, based in Russia—to build and operate pipelines for distributing Gazprom natural gas to the German market, directly challenging Ruhrgas, Germany's near-monopoly natural gas supplier. After committing itself to invest more than DM4.5 billion over the next decade in what was described as the largest project in company history, BASF could boast of already attaining 10 percent market share in its first year of operation (1995), and aimed to reach 15 percent by 2000.

The natural gas venture was perceived by BASF as a very-long-term investment, as were the company's large expenditures in China. Although other countries were also targeted by BASF for significant investment in the 1990s—including Japan, Russia, India, Malaysia, and Korea—it was China which saw astounding expenditure levels. BASF's first plant in China opened in 1992 in Nanjing, a production facility for unsaturated polyester resins. By 1995 the company had committed DM600 million to various Chinese ventures, including plants for making pigments, textile dyes, polystyrene, and vitamins, all through various joint ventures. In 1996 another joint venture was formed, this one to build a US$4-billion petrochemical facility, also in Nanjing, in what was the single biggest investment in China yet by a chemical company.

Meanwhile, acquisitions bolstered BASF's plastics operations. In 1992 the polystyrene-resins operation of Mobil was acquired for US$300 million. Then, two years later, BASF paid US$90 million for Imperial Chemical's polypropylene operations in Europe. Also in 1994, a new steam cracker located in Antwerp became operational after an outlay of DM1.5 billion, the largest single capital expenditure in BASF history. Further moves in plastics came in 1996 when two joint ventures were formed, one with Hoechst in polypropylene and one with Shell in polyethylene. Because of German antitrust laws, these had to be set up as separate businesses, with the joint venture partners being able to have only limited control over their operations.

Early in 1994 BASF reached the important decision to retain its struggling pharmaceuticals business as a core business and to pour money into its growth. The next three years saw a flurry of activity in this area. In 1994 a new biotechnology and genetic engineering research center was opened by BASF Bioresearch Corporation in Worcester, Massachusetts, to develop drugs for fighting cancer and immune system diseases. BASF gained a foothold in generic drugs that same year by acquiring the German generic drug maker Sagitta Arzneimittel, and by entering into a 50-50 joint venture with IVAX to market generic drugs. The following year BASF's pharmaceutical sector received a huge boost with the acquisition of Boots Pharmaceuticals, based in England, for US$1.3 billion. Boots was merged into BASF's existing drug operations, forming the new Knoll Pharmaceuticals.

Following the Boots acquisition, BASF created a new Health and Nutrition sector to highlight the importance of both pharmaceuticals and agricultural products to the company's future. Included in this sector were pharmaceuticals, fine chemicals (notably vitamins), crop protection agents (herbicides, fungicides, etc.), and fertilizers. In 1996, crop protection was beefed up when BASF paid US$780 million for the North American corn herbicides business of Sandoz, which was ordered divested as part of the merger of Sandoz and Ciba to form Novartis. Another joint venture was also initiated that year in an agreement with Lynx Therapeutics, based in California, to form BASF-Lynx Bioscience A.G., for research in biotechnology and genetic engineering for the development of new pesticides and drugs. BASF planned to invest more than DM100 million (US$66 million) in this venture, in which it held a 51 percent stake. Also in 1996, the FDA approved the antiobesity drug sibutramine—developed by Boots—from which the company expected annual worldwide sales of DM800 million (US$525 million).

As part of the restructuring that created the Health and Nutrition sector, BASF in 1995 also created an Information Systems sector. This was short-lived, as magnetic tape products were identified as a noncore business and sold early in 1997 to KOHAP of Korea. Another noncore business was potash and in 1996 BASF's holding in Kali und Salz was sold to Potash Corp. of Saskatchewan. Also in 1996, BASF purchased Zeneca's textile dye operations for US$208 million, making BASF third worldwide in textile dyes, trailing only DyStar (the merger of Bayer and Hoechst textile dye businesses) and Ciba's spun-off specialty chemical division.

By 1997, BASF was operating five main sectors: Plastics and Fibers, Colorants and Finishing Products, Health and Nutrition, Chemicals, and Oil and Gas. The company had plans to spend more than DM20 billion (US$13 billion) on acquisitions in the coming years, concentrating on businesses that will counter the cyclical chemical area—notably its Health and Nutrition sector—and on strengthening itself outside Europe. Another long-term goal was to set up early in the 21st century a more streamlined structure in Europe (where the conglomerate had more than 100 separate companies), one similar to that of the integrated BASF Corporation in the United States. There was certainly little doubt that BASF's visionary and aggressive approach would continue to make it one of the most important chemical companies in the world.

Principal Subsidiaries

BASF Lacke & Farben AG; BASF Magnetics GmbH; BASF Schwarzheide GmbH; Comparex Informationssysteme GmbH; Elastogran GmbH; Knoll AG; Rheinische Olefinwerke GmbH (50%); Wintershall AG; BASF Argentina S.A.; BASF Australia Ltd.; BASF Antwerpen N.V. (Belgium); BASF S.A. (Brazil); BASF Química Colombiana S.A. (Colombia); BASF France S.A.

(France); BASF Peintures & Encres S.A. (France); BASF India Ltd.; BASF Italia S.p.A. (Italy); BASF Vernici e Inchiostri S.p.A. (Italy); BASF Japan Ltd.; Mitsubishi Chemical BASF Company Ltd. (Japan; 50%); Hyosung-BASF Co., Ltd. (Korea; 50%); BASF (Malaysia) Sdn. Bhd.; BASF de México, S.A. de C.V. (Mexico); BASF plc (U.K.); BASF Corporation (U.S.A.).

Principal Divisions

Operating Divisions: Fertilizers; Potash and Salt; Crop Protection; Pharmaceuticals; Foam Plastics and Reactive Resins; Polyurethanes; Polyolefins and PVC; Engineering Plastics; Oil and Gas; Raw Materials Purchasing; Industrial Chemicals; Intermediates; Fine Chemicals; Basic Chemicals; Dispersions; Colorants and Process Chemicals; Specialty Chemicals; Textile and Leather Dyes and Chemicals; Coatings; Fiber Products. Regional Divisions: Central Europe; East Asia; Japan; South-East Asia, Australia; South America; Eastern Europe, Africa, West Asia; Northern Europe; Southern Europe; North America Chemicals; North America Coatings; North America Polymers; North America Consumer Products and Life Science/Central America.

Further Reading

Alperowicz, Natasha, Lyn Tattum, and Emma Chynoweth, ''Managing the Business Cycle at BASF: Gas Deal Provides Hope for Improving Results,'' *Chemical Week*, December 16, 1992, pp. 22–26.

Alperowicz, Natasha, Michael Roberts, and Debbie Jackson, ''Domestic Pressures Turn the Screw on German Chemical Firms,'' *Chemical Week*, March 31, 1993, pp. 34–35.

Baker, John, ''BASF Invests in Chinese Future,'' *ECN-European Chemical News*, October 7, 1996, p. 25.

''BASF: Change, Focus, Speed,'' supplement to *ECN-European Chemical News*, November 1995.

''BASF Claims Top Spot Among Investors in Korea,'' *Chemical Marketing Reporter*, September 23, 1996, p. 5.

BASF Milestones in Its History, Ludwigshafen, Germany: BASF Aktiengesellschaft, 1995.

''BASF Targets Acquisitions That Cut Cycles: The Company Also Wants to Structure European Business Like That of US,'' *Chemical Market Reporter*, November 18, 1996, pp. 7, 41.

Chandler Jr., Alfred D., ''The Enduring Logic of Industrial Success,'' *Harvard Business Review*, March/April 1990, p. 130.

Gibson, Paul, ''How the Germans Dominate the World Chemical Industry,'' *Forbes*, October 13, 1980, p. 155.

Hayes, Peter, *Industry and Ideology: I.G. Farben in the Nazi Era*, London: Cambridge University Press, 1987.

Layman, Patricia L., ''For BASF, Big Is Still Better,'' *Chemical and Engineering News*, September 16, 1996, pp. 13–15, 18.

Milmo, Sean, ''BASF, Lynx Form Biotech Collaboration,'' *Chemical Marketing Reporter*, October 28, 1996, p. 7.

''The Money Pit: Investing in Eastern Europe,'' *Economist*, June 22, 1991, pp. 74–75.

Reier, Sharon, ''Hundred Years War: How BASF Allied Itself with the Russians to Battle Germany's Gas Monopoly,'' *Financial World*, September 14, 1993, pp. 28–30.

Richman, Louis S., ''Hans Albers: BASF,'' *Fortune*, August 3, 1987, p. 50.

Schroter, Harm G., ''The German Question, the Unification of Europe, and the European Market Strategies of Germany's Chemical and Electrical Industries, 1990–1992,'' *Business History Review*, Autumn 1993, p. 369.

—updated by David E. Salamie

Bassett Furniture Industries, Inc.

P.O. Box 626
Bassett, Virginia 24055
U.S.A.
(703) 629-6000
Fax: (703) 629-6400

Public company
Incorporated: 1902 as Bassett Furniture Co.
Employees: 6,800
Sales: $490.8 million (1995)
Stock Exchanges: NASDAQ
SICs: 2511 Wood Household Furniture; 2515 Mattresses & Bedsprings; 2512 Upholstered Wood Household Furniture

Bassett furniture is sold through major retailers, with 14 percent of the company's revenue coming from J.C. Penney stores in 1995. Bassett Furniture Industries, Inc. also operates more than two dozen Bassett Direct Plus Galleries, furniture superstores that carry only the Bassett lines. In addition to Bassett, the company manufactures furniture under the Impact, Weiman, and Mount Airy brand names.

In 1995, Bassett Furniture Industries had earnings of $22.9 million on sales of $490.8 million, The company had manufacturing operations in 15 states.

Nineteenth-Century Origins

As the 19th century came to a close, the Bassett family of Henry County, Virginia, owned two sawmills that had been built to provide track ties and bridge timbers to the Norfolk & Western railroad. However, ever since the railroad from Roanoke to Winston-Salem was completed in 1892, the Bassetts had been looking for new buyers for the abundant hardwood in the area. Much of the marketing was done by John D. Bassett, who negotiated the family's first non-railroad contract with the Turner-White Coffin Co. in Winston-Salem. From there, he went to High Point, Carolina, where he was able to obtain two minor contracts with small furniture companies. That success led him to Jamestown, New York, and Grand Rapids, Michigan, two of the major furniture-producing areas of the day.

For the next half dozen years, J. D. Bassett continued to develop relationships with Northern furniture makers. Then in 1902, Bassett, 36, called a family meeting that was attended by two brothers, Samuel and Charles C. Bassett, and a brother-in-law, Reed L. Stone. At the meeting, J. D. Bassett proposed that the family go into the business of making furniture. As he recalled years later, "Here I was, shipping raw lumber from Henry County to Jamestown, New York, and to Grand Rapids, Michigan, where factories converted that lumber into finished furniture to be shipped everywhere, including the South. It seemed to me that furniture certainly could be made in Henry County at a tremendous advantage."

At the time, the Southern economy was still recovering from the Civil War, and the Bassetts knew almost nothing about making furniture. But Bassett figured the savings in freight alone would give them an advantage over Northern manufacturers. "I was convinced that the time for such a venture in Henry County was ripe because the South was then recovering rapidly," Bassett recalled. "Among the necessary commodities, furniture was in growing demand. I believed that this demand would continue for many years to come."

The four family members raised $27,500—somewhat less than J. D. Bassett figured they needed—and formed the Bassett Furniture Co. They decided to start with basic bedroom furniture because it seemed less complicated to make and none of them really knew anything about the business, except J. D. Bassett, who had absorbed what he could on the road. Up to that point, J. D. Bassett had also been a teacher, a tobacco farmer, and a drummer for a wholesale grocery business. He also owned his own grocery, the Bassett Mercantile Co., that doubled as the local post office, which later resulted in the small, western Virginia community becoming known as Bassett.

The Bassett Furniture Co. was set up in a wooden shed, later to be sheathed in metal. J. D. Bassett, president of the fledgling company, paid a traveling designer from Grand Rapids $100 to develop working prints, and hired about 50 of his rural Virginia

52

neighbors, who were paid 5-cents an hour, to work in the factory, which was soon turning out beds, dressers, washstands, and chifforobes made of oak. He also signed contracts to sell the furniture through stores in Virginia, West Virginia, and North Carolina. Company records show that beds originally wholesaled for $1.50 each.

In its first year, the Bassett Furniture Co. earned $15,000 on sales of $76,000. The next year, 1903, the company earned $25,000 on sales of a little more than $100,000. By the end of the third year, the family members had recouped their entire investment and the company was debt free. Even in 1907, with the nation in the grip of a financial panic, the Bassett Furniture Co. reported net income of $606. That same year, the company made its first outside acquisition, buying the American Furniture Co. of Martinsville, Virginia, for 10,000 shares of Bassett stock. J. D. Bassett also established his own bank, the Bank of Bassett Inc., capitalized at $13,000, which later became the First National Bank of Bassett.

By 1911, the economy had recovered and the Bassett Furniture Co. added sales representatives in several major Northern cities, including New York, Detroit, and Chicago. The company also paid its first dividends to shareholders, declaring a 5 percent dividend in February and an additional 5 percent in July.

Six years later, on Dec. 31, 1917, disaster struck when fire destroyed the Bassett Furniture Co. factory. But the company soon resumed operations in a modern brick building with motor-driven woodworking equipment, abandoning the belt-driven line-shaft system that had been a hallmark of the industrial revolution. In 1920, the board of directors voted to increase capital stock to $1 million; the Bassett Furniture Co. had become a million-dollar business in 18 years. J. D. Bassett was then earning $5,000 a year as president.

Bassett Versus Bassett, the 1920s

In 1921, J. D. Bassett took the unusual step of forming a second furniture business, the J.D. Bassett Manufacturing Co., apparently to test the abilities of his oldest son, William M. Bassett. J. D. Bassett was president of both companies, but his son was named vice president of the J.D. Bassett Manufacturing Co. and was largely responsible for day-to-day operations. The J.D. Bassett Manufacturing Co. developed its own sales staff

and retail distribution network but, confusingly, both companies used the same trade name, "Bassett."

In 1923, William Bassett succeeded his father as president of J.D. Bassett Manufacturing Co., while J. D. Bassett's second son, John Douglas Bassett (later known as J. D. Bassett, Jr.) became vice president. By then, the Bassett furniture businesses had become totally self-sufficient. In 1920, J.D. Bassett and his partners in the Bassett Furniture Co. had purchased the Valley Veneer Co. to produce veneers exclusively for Bassett furniture. In 1923, J. D. Bassett formed the Bassett Mirror Co., which set up operations in a 15,000-square-foot building next to the Bassett Furniture Co.

Fire struck again in 1925, this time destroying a large part of the J.D. Bassett Manufacturing Co. When the business was rebuilt, it added a facility to manufacture dining room furniture—marking the first time the Bassett name would venture outside bedroom furnishing.

Two years later, in 1927, William Bassett, apparently unhappy with his prospects in the growing Bassett family of businesses, left his job as head of the J.D. Bassett Manufacturing Co. John Douglas Bassett succeeded him as president. William Bassett then bought the Craig Furniture Co. in nearby Martinsville, which he renamed the W.M. Bassett Furniture Co.

Other family members had also left the fold to form their own furniture companies, including J.D. Bassett's son-in-law, Thomas Bahnson Stanley, a future governor of Virginia, who started the Stanley Furniture Co. in 1924 on land adjacent to the Bassett plants. That same year, J. Clyde Hooker, the son-in-law of J.D. Bassett's brother, Charles, formed the Hooker-Bassett Furniture Co. in Martinsville, which later became the Hooker Furniture Corp.

J.D. Bassett also backed another son-in-law, Taylor Vaughan, and his brother, B. C. Vaughan, when they formed their respective furniture businesses, the Vaughan Furniture Co. and the Vaughan-Bassett Co. Cabell Philpott, the son of a Bassett Furniture Co, board member, also worked for Bassett before leaving to form the United Furniture Co. in Lexington, North Carolina.

In *Foresight, Founders and Fortitude: The Growth of Industry in Martinsville and Henry County, Virginia,* Dorothy Cleal and Hiram H. Herbert noted, "At first J. D.'s attitude about competition appears paradoxical. With a strong wedge in the southern furniture field, why did he risk weakening his position by inviting competition, even in his own family?" They go on to suggest that Bassett was more consumed by a "personal struggle" to establish the South as the dominant furniture-making region in the United States. "If this is so," the authors concluded, "then it must be deduced that J. D. Bassett, Sr., had phenomenal foresight. By the time he died in 1965 at the age of 98 he was able to see dramatic changes taking place in America's preference for furniture produced in the South as opposed to furniture produced in the North, the cradle of the American furniture industry."

Bassett Furniture Industries Forms in 1930

Two years after William Bassett bought his own furniture business, and John Douglas Bassett rose to the presidency of the J.D. Bassett Manufacturing Co., J. D. Bassett called another family meeting. With the Depression beginning, he suggested the three Bassett furniture businesses could be more efficiently run as a single enterprise. Readily agreeing with that assessment, in 1930, the Bassetts and their investors formed Bassett Furniture Industries, Inc., a holding company for all three furniture manufacturers.

The accounting firm of Ernst & Ernst conducted an inventory of each business and placed a value of $1.875 million on the consolidated companies, which issued 187,500 shares of preferred stock. J. D. Bassett was named president of the new corporation. John Douglas Bassett, by then known as J. D., Jr., was vice president, and William Bassett, secretary-treasurer. Later that year, J.D. Bassett was elected chairman of the board and William Bassett succeeded to the presidency.

Despite the rigors of the Depression, the new corporation adopted an aggressive position in the industry. In 1931, Bassett Furniture Industries formed the Bassett Chair Co. Three years later, it acquired the Ramsey Furniture Co., later to be known as Bassett Superior Lines, in a public auction for $117,000. Bassett Furniture Industries, although forced to cut back on its workers' hours and wages, continued to operate throughout the Depression, at one point bringing in a railroad carload of Virginia hams for its employees.

In 1938, Bassett Furniture Industries introduced its massive and elaborate Waterfall design. Two years later, with the nation in the midst of an economic boom following the outbreak of war in Europe, the company raised more than $2 million in an offering of common stock. The proceeds were used to retire the preferred stock in the Bassett Furniture Co., the J.D. Bassett Manufacturing Co., and the William M. Bassett Furniture Co., making them wholly owned subsidiaries of the holding company. Later that year, the three furniture companies, along with the Bassett Chair Co. and Bassett Superior Lines, were merged into a single enterprise.

The following year, when the United States entered World War II, Bassett Furniture Industries realized that furniture was not going to be a high priority item in a time of government rationing. As they did when the market for railroad ties dried up in 1892, the Bassetts had to find another market. Although the company was unsuccessful in its efforts to obtain government contracts, J. D. Bassett, Jr. negotiated a sizable contract with the Yellow Cab and Coach Co. in Detroit to manufacture wooden truck bodies.

When the war ended in 1945, the nation experienced another economic boom—and rising expectations. Cleal and Herbert explained: "Throughout the nation there had been countless war-time marriages, and now the couples wanted homes of their own. . . With the new homes came demands for furniture to fill them." Bassett Furniture Industries invested $6 million to modernize its plants, all internally financed. The Bassett Chair Co. also began manufacturing coffee tables and other occasional pieces to fit the changing American lifestyle, culminating in 1957 with the formation of the Bassett Table Co. By 1960,

corporate-wide sales had reached $60 million, employment had risen to more than 3,000, and Bassett Furniture Industries had become the world's largest manufacturer of wood furniture.

Marketing, however, was beginning to pose headaches for the growing company. In 1959, there were still four separate marketing organizations for Bassett products—the Bassett Furniture Co., J.D. Bassett Manufacturing Co., William M. Bassett Furniture Co., and the Bassett Table Co. All three organizations handled sales for Bassett Superior Lines. As a result, a salesman for one Bassett line often found himself vying for retail space with another. Differences in design were usually minor, which left furniture dealers confused and often angry.

William Bassett, then chairman and chief executive of Bassett Furniture Industries, also worried that Bassett-branded furniture would find its way into cut-rate discount stores—a new force in American retailing—if the internal competition continued. Under his direction, top salesmen from the three companies were organized into a single sales force to represent the entire Bassett line in a three-state trial area. The test was so successful that the program was expanded nationwide within a year. William Bassett also died in 1960, after 30 years at the helm of Bassett Industries, and was succeeded as chairman and chief executive by his younger brother, J. D. Bassett, Jr.

In 1960, Bassett Furniture Industries also initiated its first nationwide marketing campaign, advertising in consumer magazines with a combined readership of 70 million to establish the Bassett image. By 1964, when Bassett Furniture Industries became the first furniture manufacturer to advertise in *Reader's Digest,* the marketing program was reaching more than 445 million readers. In addition to *Reader's Digest,* with its 22 million readers, Bassett advertised in *Ebony, Seventeen, Brides Magazine, Better Homes & Gardens, Sunset, Modern Bride, Good Housekeeping,* and *Bride & Home.* In 1963, Bassett Furniture Industries had also rounded out its product line by acquiring the Prestige Furniture Corp. in Newton, North Carolina, which made upholstered furniture. Afterwards, Bassett Industries could claim to make and sell furniture for every room of the house.

J. D. Bassett, Jr., then 65, died unexpectedly in 1966. He was succeeded as chairman and chief executive by John Edwin Bassett, Sr., a cousin and the son of Charles C. Bassett, one of the original founders of the Bassett Furniture Co. in 1902.

Expansion Through Acquisitions, 1960s–80s

In 1967, Bassett Furniture Industries opened its first retail outlet, a freestanding showroom on Interstate 85 between High Point and Thomasville, North Carolina. That same year, the company formed Bassett Furniture Industries of North Carolina, a wholly owned subsidiary, to manufacture juvenile furniture in Statesville, North Carolina. Two years later, Bassett Furniture Industries acquired the Art Furniture Manufacturing Co. in Macon, Georgia, and the Art Table Co. in Barnesville, Georgia. Those companies were reorganized as Bassett Furniture Industries of Georgia. The expansion continued in 1969 with the purchase of the Taylorcraft Furniture Co. in Taylorsville, North Carolina, which became a subsidiary of the Prestige

Furniture Corp. Bassett Furniture Industries' sales topped $139 million in 1969.

Bassett Furniture Industries continued to expand through acquisitions during the 1970s. In 1971, the company entered the mattress market by purchasing the E.B. Malone Bedding Co. That same year, it purchased the National Mount Airy Furniture Co., a manufacturer of upscale furniture in Mount Airy, North Carolina, followed by acquisition of the Weiman Co., a manufacturer of heirloom-quality furniture in Christianburg, Virginia, in 1979.

In 1984, Bassett Furniture Industries launched its Bassett Gallery program, a cooperative marketing program for retail dealers who were willing to set aside a portion of their floor space exclusively to settings of Bassett Furniture. The company also acquired Impact Furniture Inc., a manufacturer of low-end occasional and bedroom furniture in Hickory, North Carolina, followed by the purchase of Motion Chair Inc., a maker of recliners, in 1986.

The 1990s

In 1993, Bassett Furniture Industries built the first U.S. finishing plant for 100 percent polyester furniture in Catawba County, North Carolina. The furniture was marketed under the brand names Vision One by Bassett and Nova by Impact.

Two years later, Bassett Furniture Industries introduced its first ready-to-assemble line of furniture, a line of home-office furniture that was carried by the Staples chain of office superstores. Matt Johnson, then national sales manager for the division launching the home-office line, said the growth of home-based businesses convinced Bassett Furniture Industries that consumers would pay more for a better grade of furniture than traditional ready-to-assemble products. However, Johnson said the company had no plans to expand its ready-to-assemble line. In 1995, the company also launched its Bassett Direct Plus Dealership program of franchised furniture superstores that carry only the Bassett line.

Principal Subsidiaries

Burkeville Veneer Co.; Impact Furniture Co.; National Mount Airy Furniture Co.; Weiman Co.

Further Reading

Allegrezza, Ray, "Bassett Breaks into RTA," *HFN The Weekly Newspaper for the Home Furnishing Network,* June 26, 1995, p. 11.

Cleal, Dorothy & Hiram H. Herbert, *Foresight, Founders and Fortitude: The Growth of Industry in Martinsville and Henry County, Virginia,* Bassett, Virginia: Bassett Printing Corp., 1970.

—Dean Boyer

Benihana, Inc.

8665 NW 53rd Terrace
Miami, Florida 33166
U.S.A.
(305) 593-0770
Fax: (305) 592-6371

Public Company
Incorporated: 1964 as Benihana of Tokyo
Employees: 1,763
Sales: $81.6 million (fiscal year ending March 31, 1996)
Stock Exchanges: NASDAQ
SICs: 5810 Retail Eating & Drinking Places

Benihana, Inc. owns and licenses restaurants in the Benihana and Benihana Grill chain of Japanese dinnerhouses. The restaurants specialize in an exhibition-style of Japanese cooking called teppanyaki. Customers sit around a communal table at which a Benihana chef slices their seafood, steak, chicken, and vegetables with lightning speed, grills their meal right in front of them, and then tosses it accurately onto their plates. The restaurants are decorated with Samurai armor and valuable art, and Shoji rice paper screens partition the dining areas. For the fiscal year ending March 31, 1996, the company had sales of over $81 million, an all-time high. By December 1996, Benihana operated a total of 49 licensed and wholly owned restaurants in 20 states as well as in Bogota, Columbia, and Aruba, Netherlands Antilles.

Early History, from Tokyo to New York

The founder of Benihana, Inc. was a 25-year-old Olympic wrestler from Japan named Hiroaki Rocky Aoki. He got his start in the restaurant business by working after school in his family's coffee shop in downtown Tokyo. His mother named the family business Benihana after a red flower that survived the bombing of Tokyo during World War II. Rocky was a scrapper, defending himself in the streets and schoolyards against bigger boys. He got hooked on wrestling, became a national university champion, and earned a place on the 1960 Olympic team.

Although he didn't compete because he was over his weight limit, he did fall in love with New York when the plane stopped there on the way to the Games in Rome. That fall he left Japan for the United States.

In 1964, Aoki graduated from New York Community College's School of Hotel and Restaurant Management. During the summer he earned money driving the only ice cream truck in Harlem. The job was not easy, as he explained in an article in *Management Review.* "Every time I robbed, I get up earlier the next day and work later to make up. Every time I lose money, I get more challenge." With that philosophy, he managed to save $10,000 during the summer, which, along with a loan, was enough to start his first restaurant, Benihana of Tokyo.

Aoki's concept for his new restaurant, derived from specialty restaurants he knew of in Japan, was part entertainment and part food service. He wanted to offer Americans food they were familiar with, such as chicken, steak, and shrimp, prepared in a novel setting. He chose the teppanyaki table—a stainless steel grill surrounded by a wooden eating surface—where customers could watch a knife-wielding, joke-telling chef prepare and serve their food. His parents and brothers came from Japan to help him get started.

Unfortunately, New Yorkers equated Japanese food with raw fish and weren't comfortable sitting at a table with strangers. They ignored the midtown Manhattan eatery until the restaurant critic of the *New York Herald Tribune* gave it a glowing review. Suddenly, everyone in New York, including the Beatles and Muhammad Ali, wanted to sit around one of Benihana of Tokyo's four teppanyaki tables. Within six months after the review the restaurant had paid for itself, and Aoki quickly opened another restaurant in a larger, fancier building. The new location provided the same teppanyaki-style cooking but was decorated with valuable art, Samurai armor, heavy wooden ceiling beams brought from Japan by Aoki's father, and sliding Shoji screens to provide some privacy.

1965–80: Building a Company

The Benihana concept combined reasonable prices with good food, and, by preparing what was eaten right at the table, held waste to a minimum. Profits were good, and, in 1968, Aoki opened his first Benihana of Tokyo outside New York City—in downtown Chicago. That location made $700,000 in its first year and continued to be one of the company's top earning outlets.

Between 1969 and 1972, the company opened six more of its own restaurants and licensed franchisees to open another ten. In a joint venture with the Las Vegas Hilton, the company developed Benihana Village, a 38,000-square-foot complex of restaurants, bars, and other entertainment venues. In 1972, the company grossed $12 million and the Harvard Business School selected Benihana of Tokyo as a case study of an entrepreneurial success story.

With business going so well, Rocky Aoki could devote time to his other interests which included racing balloons and powerboats, collecting items ranging from vintage cars to slot machines and learning backgammon. "Rocky wanted to play," Joel Schwartz, the company's president, explained in a 1989 *Forbes* article. To help oversee the chain's operations and expansion, Aoki brought in a management company, Hardwicke Cos., as a partner in 1976. The relationship lasted only four years and, in 1980, Aoki ended the partnership, paying $3.7 million to break the contract. As Rod Willis of *Management Review* explained in a 1986 article, "He [Aoki] felt the company's management style clashed with his predominately Oriental workforce, and he wanted to maintain control over each restaurant's quality." The following year Aoki settled, without admitting any guilt, a Securities and Exchange Commission charge that he had improperly traded in Hardwicke stock while serving as vice-president of Hardwicke.

The 1980s: Ups and Downs

To help pay off the debt incurred in the split with Hardwicke, Aoki decided to take part of the company public. He accomplished this by having Benihana of Tokyo (BOT) form Benihana National Corporation (BNC) in 1982 and then taking the latter company public the following year. Investors paid the Miami-based BNC $11 for a unit consisting of two common shares and a warrant to buy another at $6. With the $5.5 million raised by selling half a million of these units, BNC bought 11 restaurants from Aoki in exchange for 60 percent of the BNC common stock and $2.5 million to pay BOT's debt. Later in the year, BNC bought another three restaurants from BOT for $7 million.

In spite of the new corporate structure, Benihana of Tokyo and Benihana National Corporation remained under the management of the same group of executives. As corporate president, Joel Schwartz continued to oversee the day to day operation of both companies. Aoki, who served as chairman of both entities, retained 51 percent of the common stock in BNC and kept about 30 restaurants in the privately held BOT. Aoki developed new concepts for the Benihana food chain but he also continued to play hard, becoming a championship-level backgammon player and setting a world record in off-shore powerboat racing. The Double Eagle V, a 400,000 cubic-foot gas balloon, displayed the Benihana logo as it became the first crewed balloon to successfully cross the Pacific Ocean, with Aoki as one of the crew members.

One of Aoki's new concepts was Benihana National Classics, a line of Chinese gourmet frozen foods, introduced in 1984 and sold in supermarkets. Chinese cuisine was chosen when the company found that Japanese food didn't freeze well. Within a year the Classics were the best-selling Oriental frozen foods in the United States, with sales in one quarter alone reaching more than $40 million and profits climbing to over $4 million. The company's stock took off, going as high as $21.50 in 1985. In December of that year, *Restaurant and Institution* magazine named Benihana of Tokyo the most popular family-style restaurant in America. At that time, Benihana of Tokyo and Benihana National together operated or franchised restaurants in 60 locations, from Seattle to New Jersey, serving a total of 25,000 customers a day.

Benihana National's frozen food success quickly attracted the attention of major food companies. When Campbell Soup and Stouffer's began offering their own lines of Oriental frozen foods, however, Benihana couldn't compete. The company lost $11 million on frozen foods between 1985 and 1987 and finally sold the business, for $4.5 million, to the small company that had been producing the dinners for them.

Frozen food, however, was not Aoki's only new idea. In 1985, Benihana National opened its first seafood restaurant, The Big Splash, just north of Miami. Aoki believed the sea would be the primary supplier of food in the future, and, borrowing an idea from a Malaysian fish market, came up with the concept of a seafood marketplace/restaurant. Customers could choose from hundreds of varieties of fresh seafood, decide how they wanted it cooked, and watch it being prepared. The idea was so popular initially that a second Big Splash was opened. The seafood restaurants soon experienced difficulty, however, registering losses of $2.7 million during 1987. The wide variety of options ran completely counter to the tight focus and minimal waste of the Benihana steakhouses. At the Miami location, the majority of customers were retirees who resented the high prices and preferred to eat fish they were familiar with. "All we sold was salmon and red snapper," Aoki told Eric Schmukler in a March 1989 *Forbes* article. The company closed its Big Splash outlets in March 1988. The 1988 fiscal year was a hard one for Benihana, as the company recorded a loss of nearly $7 million.

Despite the company's financial problems with Classics and Big Splash, the Benihana restaurants themselves were still popular. By the end of fiscal 1989, the publicly owned Benihana National Corp. reported profits of some $1.8 million on sales of $34 million at its 20 restaurants, with Aoki's privately-held Benihana of Tokyo taking in similar revenues.

1990–94: Making a Turnaround

Rocky Aoki kicked off the new decade by opening a gallery in one of the Miami Benihana restaurants to display a portion of what was becoming known in the art world as the Rocky Aoki Collection. Having spent more than a year consolidating his diverse collections, Aoki told *Antiques & Collecting*, ''I think it's a natural to have a gallery here. More than 90,000 people eat in this restaurant every year; why not provide them with something beautiful to look at, not to mention buy, if they so desire.'' In a 300-square-foot space that had been the restaurant's gift shop, diners could view etchings by Icarts, lamps by Tiffany and Handel, and bronzes by Remington.

The publicity about Aoki's collection helped generate business for the restaurant, and overall company revenues continued to grow. Profits, however, were less than a million dollars a year, and BNC stock fell below $1 a share. Angry at the situation, some shareholders sued. As Marilyn Alva reported in a 1992 *Restaurant Business* article, the shareholders claimed Aoki and his management team were in a conflict of interest by managing the two companies. The complainants further maintained that Benihana management had misappropriated the assets of Benihana National Corporation, passing them through Benihana of Tokyo for their personal benefit. The shareholders, however, were ultimately unsuccessful in trying to take control of the company away from Aoki.

Meanwhile, Benihana management took advantage of a health-conscious American public's growing interest in Japanese food and entertainment. With the tag line, ''We have been the restaurant of the '90s since the '60s,'' Aoki and Schwartz instituted a major advertising campaign stressing the fact that Benihana had always offered healthful food. Soon afterwards, in 1993, the Atlanta Benihana of Tokyo restaurant added an 18-seat sushi bar and 35-seat Karaoke dining room to draw more customers on weekday nights. Despite the higher labor and food costs associated with sushi, the company reported an increase in beverage sales, and a lot of sampling of the $.99 sushi pieces by people waiting to eat at the traditional teppanyaki tables.

Learning from its experience a decade earlier, in 1994 Benihana National Corp. decided to get into the frozen food business again. This time, however, by entering into a licensing agreement with Campbell Soup Co., the company hooked up with a major marketer rather than trying to compete with the big names. The new product was a line of frozen stir-fry kits featuring the Benihana trademark. The dinners served six people and sold for about $8.00. As Peter McMullin, an analyst with Southeast Research Partners, told *Florida Review.Net,* ''This time the strategy makes sense because it is linking with a high profile food company to help strengthen the distribution side and offsetting the razor-thin margins of retail by manufacturing with a low cost producer like Campbell.'' By the end of the fiscal year, revenues were over $70 million, with profits up 41 percent to $2.4 million.

1995 and Beyond: A New Company

At the beginning of 1995, Benihana National announced it would buy Aoki's 21 Benihana of Tokyo restaurants on the U.S. mainland, along with the U.S. rights to the Benihana trademark, for about $6.15 million. On May 16, a newly created subsidiary, Benihana Inc., acquired the BOT restaurants and, through a merger, simultaneously acquired Benihana National. BNC shareholders received one share in the new holding company for each of their shares of Benihana National. Aoki continued to serve as chairman of the new company and Schwartz as president.

Benihana Inc. now owned or licensed the 43 Benihana restaurants in the continental United States along with a franchise in Honolulu. It also had the rights to develop or license Benihana restaurants in Central and South America and the Caribbean Islands. Aoki kept private his Benihana of Tokyo restaurants in Hawaii, Britain, and Thailand.

During 1995, the new company took several steps to attract more customers. Benihana introduced weekend luncheon service and, following the success in Atlanta, opened sushi bars in seven locations. The company also instituted a national Karaoke contest for its patrons. In the fall, the company opened its first smaller format unit, called the Benihana Grill, in Sacramento. At 3,800 square feet, the Grill format was less than half the size of the traditional Benihana, and enabled the company to open units in smaller locations, particularly in urban areas. Schwartz had been refining this format since 1989 as an alternative to the company's more common free-standing, special use restaurant buildings. The Benihana Grill was designed to accommodate 10 to 12 teppanyaki tables, compared to the 18 tables in the typical Benihana. Analyst Peter McMullin remarked, ''Initial indications are encouraging even before the grand opening. With the lower capital costs of approximately $500,000 versus a stand-alone restaurant cost of $2 million, this could become an enormous growth vehicle for Benihana.''

The new hours and offerings helped increase guest counts in existing restaurants by 8.7 percent and same store sales by an average of 7.7 percent for fiscal 1996. This rise, plus the addition of the Benihana of Tokyo restaurants and the new Benihana Grill, resulted in annual revenues of over $81 million.

Benihana's growth came primarily from increased traffic in its existing restaurants, and the company continued to support that strategy. Early in 1996, in an effort to gain a larger share of the ethnic market, the company launched Spanish-language television advertisements in Miami and Los Angeles. In May, Benihana kicked off a two-year, $5 million ad campaign, focusing on the entertainment value of teppanyaki cooking. ''We want to bring the Benihana name to a different audience,'' company president Joel Schwartz told *Nation's Restaurant News* in a May 6, 1996 article. ''The ads show that Benihana is a place the entire family can come to and have a good time—a place they will see the chef perform and flip shrimp.'' Individual restaurants also developed innovative marketing techniques. A visit and meal at the Benihana in Bethesda, Maryland, for example, is one of the activities in the county's social studies curriculum for third graders learning about Japan.

The company did not depend entirely on its existing restaurants for growth. During 1996, it also signed leases for several more Benihana Grills and expanded its franchise operations, including restaurants in Bogota, Columbia, and Aruba, Netherlands Antilles. Benihana's track record of steady growth in same store sales, rising customer count, and profitability appeared to be continuing into the late 1990s as revenues for the first half of fiscal 1997 were up over eight percent from the year before.

Further Reading

Alva, Marilyn, ''Very Rocky Business: Aoki Besieged by Shareholder Suits,'' *Restaurant Business*, February 10, 1992.

''Benihana Buying Founder Aoki's Units,'' *Nation's Restaurant News*, January 16, 1995, p. 14.

''Benihana Profits Rise 67% for First Nine Months of Fiscal '95,'' *Nation's Restaurant News*, February 12, 1996, p. 12.

''Benihana Testing Stir-Fry Kits,'' *Supermarket News*, October 17, 1994, p. 28.

Card, Keith A., ''The Rocky Aoki Collection,'' *Antiques & Collecting*, November 1990, p. 36.

Hayes, Jack, ''Sushi Bar, Karaoke Boost Benihana's Midweek Traffic,'' *Nation's Restaurant News*, March 15, 1993, p. 50.

''More Ticker Tape: Benihana National Corp.,'' *Nation's Restaurant News*, May 29, 1995, p. 12.

''Operators Up Ante for Hispanic Markets,'' *Nation's Restaurant News*, January 29, 1996, p. 18.

Papiernik, Richard L., ''Benihana Reports Profits Up 17% in First Quarter,'' *Nation's Restaurant News*, August 26, 1996, p. 12.

Russo, Catherine, ''Benihana Recovers From Frozen Foods,'' *Florida Review.Net,* November 17, 1995, http://www.review.net/BFT/news/BFTlede.11.17.html.

Schmukler, Eric, ''Rocky's Road,'' *Forbes*, March 20, 1989, p. 80.

''Shareholders OK Reorganization Plan for Benihana Corp.,'' *Nation's Restaurant News*, May 15, 1995, p. 2.

''Social Studies Field Trips: Benihana of Tokyo, Montgomery County (Md.) Public Schools,'' http://www.mcps.k-12.md.us/FT/Benihana.html.

Willis, Rod, ''Rocky Aoki: Samurai Restaurateur,'' *Management Review*, May 1986, p. 17.

Zuber, Amy, ''Benihana's New Ad Campaign: A Slice of Theater,'' *Nation's Restaurant News*, May 6, 1996, p. 16.

—Ellen D. Wernick

Berkshire Hathaway Inc.

1440 Kiewit Plaza
Omaha, Nebraska 68131
U.S.A.
(402) 346-1400
Fax: (402) 346-3375

Public Company
Incorporated: 1889 as Berkshire Cotton Manufacturing
    Company
Employees: 35,000 (1996)
Assets: $35.5 billion (est. 1996)
Stock Exchanges: New York
SICs: 2711 Newspaper Publishing & Printing; 2731
    Book Publishing & Printing; 6331 Fire, Marine &
    Casualty Insurance; 6719 Holding Companies, Not
    Elsewhere Classified

Berkshire Hathaway Inc. and its subsidiaries are involved in several different businesses, the most significant of which is property, casualty, and auto insurance (GEICO) both directly and through reinsurance. Berkshire's other businesses include publishing (the *Buffalo News*, World Book, Childcraft; manufacturing (See's Candies, Campbell Hausfeld, Kirby, Fechheimer Brothers Company); retailing (Borsheim's, Helzberg's Diamond Shops, Nebraska Furniture Mart, R.C. Willey Home Furnishings, H.H. Brown Shoe Company, Dexter Shoe), and banking (Mutual Savings & Loan Association). Investing through its insurance subsidiaries, Berkshire often buys major shares of other publicly traded companies (American Express, Capital Cities/ABC, Coca-Cola, Gillette, Salomon Inc., Washington Post, and Wells Fargo); its chairman, Warren Buffett, is renowned for his expertise in selecting stocks with hidden appeal and staying power.

Humble Beginnings, 1889 Through the 1940s

Berkshire Hathaway Inc. began as a textile company, incorporated as Berkshire Cotton Manufacturing Company in Massachusetts in 1889. In 1929 several other New England textile manufac-

turers with much common ownership—Valley Falls Company, Coventry Company, Greylock Mills, and Fort Dummer Mills—merged into the company, which was then renamed Berkshire Fine Spinning Associates. This operation accounted for about 25 percent of the fine cotton textile production in the United States.

The glory years of the New England textile industry were numbered. The Great Depression of the 1930s contributed to its decline, as did competition from the South and overseas. Wages were lower in the South, and Southern workers had fewer alternatives than New Englanders for working in the textile mills. Further, market factors favored the coarser types of goods produced in the South, while wage differentials between the U.S. and foreign competition were often significant.

The New England textile business recovered somewhat during World War II, thanks to military demand for its products, and had a similar brief recovery during the Korean conflict. Still, the industry declined again after each of these upswings.

Diversification Is Good for the Soul, the 1950s and 1960s

In 1955 Berkshire Fine Spinning merged with Hathaway Manufacturing Company, a New Bedford, Massachusetts, textile maker dating back to 1888. The resulting company, Berkshire Hathaway Inc., had more than 10,000 employees and nearly six million square feet of plant space, but its financial performance was dismal. Berkshire Hathaway closed its extensive operations in Adams, Massachusetts, in 1958, and the same year sold its curtain plant in Warren, Rhode Island, to Pilgrim Curtain Company. The company recovered a bit the following year; a contract negotiated between Berkshire and its unionized employees in 1959 marked the first wage increase for New England textile workers since 1956.

By late 1959 and into 1960, the company was operating profitably and had a backlog of unfilled orders. Depressed conditions returned quickly, however, and in 1961 Berkshire cut its work week to four days at several plants and showed a loss for the year. In 1962 the company closed three plants in Rhode Island and showed even greater losses, due to depressed prices for its products. The financial hemorrhaging continued into the mid-1960s, despite cuts in Berkshire's workforce and

Company Perspectives:

Berkshire Hathaway Inc. is a holding company with an ever-increasing number of subsidiaries engaged in a myriad of business activities. Originally in textiles, Berkshire's reach has extended to insurance, retailing, manufacturing, publishing, and banking. Run by the dynamic Warren Buffett and his partner Charles Munger, Berkshire's name and reputation have become synonymous with its legendary investment portfolio, which has garnered excellent results far in excess of the S & P 500 and other indicators.

an extensive plant modernization. In 1965 came a major change in the company's management: a partnership led by investor Warren Buffett had purchased enough stock to control the company, and in a resulting dispute Seabury Stanton, a 50-year Berkshire employee, resigned as president. Kenneth V. Chace, a vice-president who had been with the company 18 years, replaced Stanton. After Buffett gained control of Berkshire, its operations were gradually moved from New Bedford to Omaha, Nebraska, where Buffett was based.

Berkshire Hathaway was profitable in 1965 and 1966, but profits fell sharply as it began its 1967 fiscal year. The company was actively shopping for acquisitions to help it diversify, and in 1967 it entered the insurance business, buying National Indemnity Company and National Fire & Marine Insurance Company for a total of $8.5 million. Acquisition of the two Omaha-based companies, which primarily handled automobile insurance, was expected to help Berkshire overcome the cyclical nature of the textile business. In 1968 the company made another significant acquisition, of Sun Newspapers, a group of Omaha-area weeklies. In 1969 it bought Illinois National Bank & Trust Company of Rockford. Buffett, who became Berkshire's chairman in 1969, tended to acquire companies whose management and products he liked, rather than buying companies with the intention of making major changes. Both Buffett's company and his reputation as an expert investor continued to grow for decades to come.

From Medium to Large, 1970–79

Berkshire Hathaway's expansion and diversification continued at a steady pace. During 1969 and 1970 it bought controlling interests in Blue Chip Stamps (which owned See's Candies, a chocolate maker and retailer) and Wesco Financial Corporation, a savings and loan operator. Berkshire's insurance operations grew with the formation of Cornhusker Casualty Company as part of the National Indemnity group in 1970 and Lakeland Fire and Casualty Company (now National Indemnity Company of Minnesota) also as part of that group, in 1971. Additionally, in 1971, Berkshire acquired Home & Automobile Insurance Company (now National Liability and Fire Insurance Company) and in 1972 formed Texas United Insurance Company, which it later merged into National Indemnity. Four years later, in 1976, the National Fire & Marine subsidiary acquired its only wholly owned subsidiary, Redwood Fire & Casualty Insurance Company and Berkshire began buying shares in GEICO (Government Employees Insurance Company).

In 1977 Berkshire continued to acquire related businesses, this time Cypress Insurance Company, and then the Kansas Fire & Casualty Company was formed. The same year, it made another move into the newspaper business by purchasing, through Blue Chip Stamps, the *Buffalo Evening News,* a six-day afternoon paper. The *News* competed against a morning paper with a Sunday edition, at a time when morning papers were outstripping evening papers in popularity. After the acquisition by Berkshire, the *News* increased competition by publishing a Sunday edition and within five years had bested its rival, the *Courier-Express,* which then went out of business.

Berkshire formed another insurance company, Continental Divide Insurance Company, in 1978. Through a merger with Diversified Retailing Company, Berkshire acquired two more insurers, Columbia Insurance Company and Southern Casualty Insurance Company, in 1978; Southern Casualty was later merged into National Indemnity. Even with Warren Buffett's growing reputation, not every company was eager to become part of Berkshire; CSE Corporation, the holding company for Civil Service Employees Insurance Company, turned down an informal takeover offer in 1979. Because Berkshire didn't execute hostile takeovers, the acquisition wasn't pursued.

From Large to XXL, the 1980s

In 1980 Berkshire spun off Illinois National Bank & Trust, a move required by the Bank Holding Company Act of 1969. A year later the company sold Sun Newspapers to Chicago publisher Bruce Sagan and began work on a rather unheard of practice. The next year, 1982, Berkshire instituted an unusual corporate philanthropy program that won praise from shareholders by allowing them to direct a portion of the company's charitable contributions. With this policy, Buffett said he hoped to foster an ''owner mentality'' among shareholders. Shareholders responded enthusiastically, with more than 95 percent of eligible shares participating in each year since the program's inception. The amount directed to charities of their choice was $2 a share in 1981 (the figure rose to $6 a share by 1989). Buffett's own favorite causes included population control and nuclear disarmament.

During the early 1980s the textile business continued to languish, and the insurance industry was hit by poor sales and price cutting. Berkshire's performance, however, was buoyed by the performance of its investment portfolio. Buying significant but noncontrolling blocks of stock in such companies as The Washington Post Company, Media General, and additional shares of GEICO Corporation, Berkshire's holdings grew in value by 21 percent in 1981—a year in which the Dow Jones Industrial Average declined by 9.2 percent—and earnings grew 23 percent per share.

In 1983 the 60 percent-owned Blue Chip Stamps merged with Berkshire Hathaway, the same year the company acquired 90 percent of the Nebraska Furniture Mart, a high-volume Omaha discount retailer and the largest U.S. home furnishings store founded by a Russian immigrant, Rose Blumkin. The Blumkin family retained management and the remaining ownership of the store, and Buffett had been known to promote it during annual shareholder meetings, often running buses to the store (a practice continued to this day). Also in 1983, another insurance company, National Indemnity Company of Florida, was formed and added to the National Indemnity group.

The mid-1980s proved a heady time for Berkshire with several monumental agreements and the sad denouement of its textiles business. Early in 1985 the company participated in Capital Cities Communications' acquisition of the American Broadcasting Company (ABC). Buffett agreed to put up $517.5 million in financing for the deal and came out with an 18 percent share of the merged company, Capital Cities/ABC. The investment community saw the move as unusual for Buffett, who tended to hunt for undervalued companies and stay away from high-priced deals. Buffett, however, said he saw the investment climate changing, with good prospects for companies like television networks which had intangible assets rather than heavy investments in plants and equipment.

Then came the end of Berkshire Hathaway's money-losing textiles operation, which the company had tried to sell. After finding no buyer, Berkshire liquidated the conglomerate's originating business due to increasing lower-cost foreign competition. Buffett lauded the efforts of Kenneth Chace—who remained a Berkshire director—and of Garry Morrison, who had succeeded him as president of textiles. Buffett had kind words for the unionized textile workers as well, who had made only reasonable demands in view of the company's financial position.

Later the same year Berkshire agreed to acquire Scott & Fetzer Company, a Cleveland, Ohio-based diversified manufacturing and marketing company, for about $320 million. Scott & Fetzer's products included *World Book* and *Childcraft* encyclopedias, and Kirby vacuum cleaners. At the same time Berkshire's insurance business underwent several changes. In a tight market for insurance, many commercial insurance buyers needed a financially stable company to underwrite large risks, so National Indemnity, Berkshire Hathaway's largest insurance company, advertised in an insurance trade publication its willingness to write property and casualty policies with a premium of $1 million or more. The advertisement produced an explosion in large-premium business for Berkshire; the company wrote $184.5 million in net premiums for large accounts from August 1985 through December 1986, compared with virtually no such business previously.

Also during 1985, Berkshire reached an agreement with Fireman's Fund Insurance Company which allowed it a 7 percent participation in Fireman's business. John J. Byrne, an executive of GEICO—an insurer partly owned by Berkshire and that shared a long history with Buffett—left to become chairman of Fireman's Fund earlier in the year, and had arranged the deal. Another insurance move during 1985 was the establishment of Wesco-Financial Insurance Company by Berkshire's Wesco Financial Corporation subsidiary.

In 1986 Berkshire finalized its Scott & Fetzer deal and went on to acquire 84 percent of Fechheimer Bros. Company, a uniform manufacturer and distributor based in Cincinnati, Ohio. The next year as the stock market continued the upward rise begun earlier in the decade, Buffett's policy of buying undervalued stocks and holding them for the long-term paid off well. In August 1987 the *Wall Street Journal* reported that in the five years since the market's surge began, Berkshire's stock portfolio had grown in value by 748 percent, far surpassing the Dow Jones average (which increased 233.6 percent) and Standard & Poor's (S&P) 500 stock index (which gained 215.4 percent).

When the stock market crashed in October and wiped out the year's gains, Berkshire's portfolio weathered the storm and was up 2.8 percent for the period—while the S&P 500 experienced a 2.5 percent decline. Just before the crash, Berkshire had bought $700 million-worth of preferred stock (convertible to a 12 percent common stake) in Salomon Inc., the Wall Street investment firm whose fortunes were closely tied to the market. Even after the crash, however, Buffett expressed his confidence in Salomon's management and the investment's inherent value. Another major event of 1988 was the listing of Berkshire's stock on the New York Stock Exchange (NYSE). Although the stock had previously traded in the over-the-counter market, the move was designed to reduce transaction costs for shareholders.

Berkshire Hathaway became the highest-priced stock on the exchange, at about $4,300 a share, up from $12 a share when Buffett first bought the company. The price hit a high for the decade of more than $8,000 a share but the ever-dynamic Buffett always encouraged buyers to be in the market for the long haul over frequent trading. And Buffett was not of the do-as-I-say-not-as-I-do school, for both he and Berkshire have proven themselves to be long-term shareholders in other companies, leading some to view Buffett as a protector against hostile takeovers. During 1989 the company bought significant shares of the Gillette Company, USAir Group, and Champion International Corporation, with each purchase widely interpreted as a defense against takeovers. Another major purchase was 6.3 percent or $1 billion-worth of the Coca-Cola Company (making Berkshire Coke's second-largest shareholder) and an 80 percent interest in Borsheim's, an Omaha jewelry store run by the Friedman family, relatives of the Nebraska Furniture Mart's Blumkins.

As Berkshire grew, so did Buffett's recognition and reputation as a no-nonsense businessman. To many, part of Buffett's charm was speaking his mind, even if his opinions weren't always fashionable. Buffett's frank assessment of situations brought him both fans and foes, like when he pulled the Wesco Financial-owned Mutual Savings & Loan Association of Pasadena, California, out of the U.S. League of Savings Institutions in 1989. Buffett's move was in response to the League's lobby for more leniency during the federal bailout of the S & L industry, which Buffett likened to a "mugging" of taxpayers. Another of Buffett's business stratagems, to the chagrin of many corporate honchos, was his belief that executive compensation be tied to a company's performance, not its size.

The Mega-Conglomerate with a Down-Home Feel, 1990s

In the early 1990s Berkshire continued its trend of buying complementary companies and large blocks of stock: the acquisition of H.H. Brown Shoe Company; 31.2 million shares of Guinness PLC; and 82 percent of Central States Indemnity in 1991; Lowell Shoe Company for H.H. Brown, and 14.1 percent of General Dynamics Corp. in 1992. In a related though somewhat surprising move in 1991, Buffett was appointed interim chairman of Salomon Inc. (in which the company still owned stock). After serving 10 months and effecting a turnaround, Buffett was happily back at the helm of Berkshire Hathaway full-time, although both Buffett and Munger joined the board of the ailing USAir in 1992.

The following year, H.H. Brown added Dexter Shoe to its holdings, Buffett sold 10 million shares of Capital Cities/ABC, and net earnings posted a spectacular surge from 1992's $407.3 million (down from 1991's $439.9 million) to $688.1 million. In 1994, Berkshire added major stock holdings of two companies to its portfolio (4.9 percent of Gannett Co., Inc. and 8.3 percent of PNC Bank Corp.) and Buffett admitted to two expensive gaffes: a $222.5 million faux pas from unloading 10 million Cap Cities shares for $64 each when prices topped $85, and taking a $268.5 million writedown for its questionable USAir stock (both Buffett and Munger stepped down from the airline's board after a year). Though Buffett was perhaps too optimistic with USAir and a bit pessimistic about Cap Cities, neither setback made more than a tiny ripple in Berkshire's bottom line.

During the mid-1990s Berkshire Hathaway imperceptibly changed course from a strategic long-term investment conglomerate to one still very much interested in investing but leaning more heavily towards acquiring and actually operating these investment opportunities. As early as 1993 in its annual solicitation for attractive acquisitions, Berkshire had raised the stakes by including the statement "We would be likely to make an acquisition in the $2–3 billion range." By 1995, after the company acquired Helzberg's Diamond Shops and R.C. Willey Home Furnishings through stock swaps, the stakes had risen further— up to the $3–5 billion range. Meanwhile, as Berkshire's "permanent four" (Capital Cities/ABC, Coca-Cola, GEICO, and Washington Post) lost a hint of their luster in 1995, the retailing segment more than offset this slip with Borsheim's, Kirby, Nebraska Furniture Mart, and Scott Fetzer (which posted exceptional numbers for the entire decade) exceeding expectations.

Late in 1995 Berkshire began the process of taking GEICO, the seventh largest auto insurer in the nation, private. Buffett's long history (45 years) with GEICO came full circle—after years of mentoring from Ben Graham and Lorimer Davidson, 43 years after selling his original 350 shares, and 15 years since Berkshire paid $45.7 million for a 33.3 percent stake of GEICO (which grew to 50 percent in the ensuing years)—the company spent $2.3 billion to make GEICO its own. With the GEICO deal completed in January 1996, Berkshire Hathaway's insurance segment mushroomed in both float and potential earnings, becoming more stalwart as the company's core segment. Number-wise, Berkshire finished 1995 with $29.9 billion in assets, a good-sized leap from the previous year's $21.3 billion, while Berkshire stock traded at $36,000 per share, over three-and-a-half times higher than 1992's mere $10,000 a share.

News in 1996 was the planned issuance of $100 million in new Class "B" stock (the company's original shares were now designated Class "A" stock), valued at one-thirtieth the price of its predecessor. The recapitalization was done in part, Buffett explained in the 1995 annual report, to discourage brokers from marketing unit trusts and seducing clients with the Berkshire name. Since most small investors found Berkshire's per share cost prohibitive, Buffett was attempting to make the company's stock available at a lower price without going through "expense-laden unit trusts" pretending to be Berkshire "clones." Yet what folks needed to remember, according to Buffett, was not *book* value, but *intrinsic* value. By measuring intrinsic value, an economic indicator rather than an accounting concept,

investors had a better handle on worth and whether or not something was a good long-term risk. In these terms, Buffett hoped to double Berkshire's per-share intrinsic value (of Class A stock) every five years, which was still a rather daunting task. Yet if anyone could do it, it was Warren Buffett, Charlie Munger, and Berkshire Hathaway.

As no one foretold the riches Berkshire had gained in just the last 10 years, few would hazard a guess of where the company would be by the year 2000. In this case, however, saying the sky was the limit would not be portentous. As for Chairman Buffett's future, when asked by a Harvard Business School student when he planned to retire, Buffett quipped "About five to ten years after I die." Such was the singular spirit and humor of the man—perhaps the world's most celebrated and successful businessman and investor—running Berkshire Hathaway.

Principal Subsidiaries

BHR; Berskhire Hathaway Credit Corporation; Berkshire Hathaway Life Insurance Co.; Blue Chip Stamps; Borsheim's; H.H. Brown Shoe Co.; Buffalo News; Campbell Haufeld; Carefree; Dexter Shoe Companies; Fechheimer Bros. Co.; France; Halex; Helzberg's Diamond Shops; K & W Products; Meriem; Mrs. B's Clearance and Factory Outlet Warehouse; Nebraska Furniture Mart; Northland; Powerwinch; Precision Steel Products; Quikut; ScottCare; Scott Fetzer Company; Scott Fetzer Financial Group; Scot Labs; Stahl; See's Candies; Wayne; Wesco Financial; Western Enterprises; Western Plastics; R.C. Willey Home Furnishings; and World Book; Columbia Insurance Co.; Continental Divide Insurance Co.; Cornhusker Casualty Co.; Cypress Insurance Co.; Kansas Fire & Casualty Co.; National Indemnity Co.; National Indemnity Co. of Florida; National Indemnity Co. of Minnesota; National Fire & Marine Insurance Co.; National Liability & Fire Insurance Co.; Redwood Fire & Casualty Co.; Wesco Financial Corp.

Further Reading

Collins, Linda, J., "Berkshire's Buffett Sees More Competition Ahead," *Business Insurance,* May 7, 1990, p. 67.

Grant, Linda, "The $4 Billion Regular Guy," *Los Angeles Times,* April 7, 1991, p. 36.

Hagstrom, Robert G., Jr., *The Warren Buffett Way: Investment Strategies of the World's Greatest Investor,* New York: John Wiley & Sons, 1994.

Kilpatrick, Andrew, *Warren Buffett: The Good Guy of Wall Street,* New York: Donald I. Fine, 1992.

Kilpatrick, Andy, *Of Permanent Value: The Story of Warren Buffett,* Birmingham, Alabama: Andy Kilpatrick Publishing Empire, 1994.

Laing, Jonathan R., "The Collector: Investor Who Piled Up $100 Million in the '60s Piles Up Firms Today," *The Wall Street Journal,* March 31, 1977.

Loomis, Carol J., "The Inside Story of Warren Buffett," *Fortune,* April 11, 1988.

Lowenstein, Roger, *Warren Buffett: The Making of an American Capitalist,* New York: Random House, 1995.

Sosnoff, Martin, "Larry the Tortoise, Warren the Hare," *Forbes,* January 27, 1997.

—Trudy Ring
—updated by Taryn Benbow-Pfalzgraf

BET Holdings, Inc.

1900 W Place NE
Washington, D.C. 20018-1211
U.S.A.
(202) 608-2000
Fax: (202) 608-2595
Web site: http://www.betnetworks.com

Public Company
Incorporated: 1979 as Black Entertainment Television
Employees: 452
Sales: $115.2 million (1995)
Stock Exchanges: New York
SICs: 4841 Cable & Other Pay Television Services; 6719
    Holding Companies, Not Elsewhere Classified

BET Holdings, Inc., with its centerpiece Black Entertainment Television cable television network, is well on its way to becoming the nation's preeminent media empire targeting the growing African American consumer market. Under the leadership of founder Robert L. Johnson, BET has expanded beyond its low-cost television format to include the BET on Jazz cable television channel, the pay-per-view Action movie channel, direct merchandising, and beauty products, as well as magazines, with the upscale general interest *Emerge* and the teen lifestyle *YSB* ("Young Sisters & Brothers"). BET has also entered original film production through United Image Entertainment, a joint venture with actor/director Tim Reid (of "WKRP in Cincinnati" fame) and boxing promoter Butch Lewis; BET Pictures, a joint venture with Blockbuster Entertainment; and BET Film Productions, a joint venture with LIVE Entertainment and the Encore Media unit of cable television giant Tele-Communications Inc. (TCI). In 1996, Johnson further expanded the BET brand name, in a partnership with Microsoft's MSN online service, to include World Wide Web content. More than 90 percent of BET's $115 million in 1995 revenues was generated through its core cable television network, which reached more than 47 million homes over more than 2,500 cable television systems in 1996, with revenues split approximately equally between advertising and subscriber fees. In the mid-1990s, CEO and Chairman Johnson owned 40.65 percent of the company; 20 percent of BET was owned by long-time backer TCI. BET has been a publicly traded company since 1991, when it became the first black-owned company to be traded on the New York Stock Exchange.

Founding a Media Empire in 1979

The cable television industry was still in its infancy when Robert L. Johnson first began to develop the idea of a television network devoted to the interests of the black community. Johnson's business experience, however, was largely limited to a childhood newspaper route. The ninth of ten children of a working class family (his father worked at a battery factory, his mother worked on an assembly line) in Freeport, Illinois, Johnson attended college at the University of Illinois. Johnson next attended Princeton University's Woodrow Wilson School of Public and International Affairs, where he earned a master's degree in public administration in 1972. From 1973 to 1976, Johnson served as press secretary to Walter E. Fauntroy, then congressional delegate for Washington, D.C. Johnson left that post to become vice-president of government relations for the National Cable Television Association (NCTA), a position he held until 1979.

Johnson's lobbying work for the NCTA gave him an insider's perspective on the nascent cable television industry, as well as contacts with major industry players. These contacts would serve Johnson well when he left the NCTA to begin a new venture: the building of Black Entertainment Television. The idea for a television network providing programming geared toward the country's black population, then an estimated $75 billion consumer market, came to Johnson one night while sharing a taxi. His fellow passenger showed him a proposal for forming a cable television channel with programming for the nation's senior citizen population. Johnson, then 33 years old, liked the idea, but reasoned that it could also be applied to the black community. His fellow passenger gave him permission to use the proposal. "So I took it, and wherever he had the word 'elderly,' I put the word 'black,' and it worked," Johnson told the *Chicago Tribune*.

Company Perspectives:

BET Holdings, Inc.'s mission is simply to become the pre-eminent media company serving black consumers, thereby creating substantial value for its shareholders.

Johnson secured a $15,000 loan from a Washington bank to launch his channel, which he dubbed Black Entertainment Television. Next, Johnson approached John Malone, head of TCI, which was then the third largest cable franchise in the country and beginning to compete for expansion into the urban market. Johnson believed, as he told the *Washington Post,* that "[o]perators out franchising would want to tell city officials that they could serve a black audience." In November 1979, TCI agreed to give Johnson $180,000 in return for a 20 percent stake in BET, as well as a $380,000 loan to finance the channel's start. Malone also gave Johnson a piece of business advice, as Johnson told the *Washington Post:* "Get your revenues up and keep your costs down." Johnson took Malone's advice to heart.

Johnson expected to achieve revenues by selling airtime to advertisers. These advertisers would be led to BET because it offered access to the black consumer markets. Analysis indicated that the black population watched more television than the white population and tended to be more fiercely brand loyal. And, Johnson told *Broadcasting,* "Blacks will watch black programming before they will watch white programming, everything else being equal." Indeed, Johnson would later tell *Forbes:* "The idea for BET was not conceived out of idealism, but as a business opportunity that had been ignored." By the time of the TCI investment, Anheuser Busch had signed on as BET's first major advertiser. That company was joined by Sears, Pepsi, Kellogg's, and Time, Inc. as BET neared its launch. Johnson also was able to secure channels for BET on a number of cable systems, including industry leaders American TV and Communications Corp., United Cable TV Corp., and Warner Cable, as well as on TCI. Expectations for the cable industry itself were high: with many rural and suburban areas already wired, cable was preparing to move into the more lucrative urban areas. BET was expected to profit from this shift, which would bring cable to the nation's largely urban black population.

But BET's birth, in January 1980, was inauspicious. The company's broadcasts were limited to two, and later three, hours on Friday nights in a spot given to BET on what would subsequently become the USA Network. Despite Johnson's pronouncement to the *Washington Post* that BET would be "a special channel that will showcase the full creative range of black entertainment," BET's early programming centered around a low-cost mix of gospel music and low-budget films from the previous decade. "Some of the product I have happens to be so-called 'blaxploitation,'" Johnson admitted at the time, "but this is a one-step-backward, two-steps-forward kind of thing." Johnson hoped to turn a profit within three years.

BET remained in its 11 p.m. to 2 a.m. weekly spot for more than two years. In 1982, however, TCI brought in a new investor, Taft Broadcasting Co. (later Great American Broadcasting Inc.), parent of Hanna Barbera Productions and other programming providers. Taft's investment of $360,000 for a 20 percent interest in BET enabled the network to move to its own satellite signal, and in August of that year the company expanded programming to six hours a day, seven days per week. The company added music videos (provided free by record companies) to its programming mix and began producing its own programs, including the popular "Bobby Jones Gospel Hour" and "Video Soul" hosted by Donnie Simmons.

By 1984, the network was reaching more than seven million homes on 365 cable systems. The company had yet to turn a profit, despite instituting a 3 cents per subscriber fee, which was not uncommon among cable networks. Profitability would come only when BET could reach 11 million subscribers. Yet, Johnson was experiencing difficulty finding cable providers to offer his network. One problem BET faced was the limited number of channels available on cable systems at the time. Cable operators servicing primarily white, suburban, and rural areas were less likely to add BET to their limited roster. A larger problem was the continued delay in wiring the country's cities, precisely where BET's core audience was located. In the mid-1980s, many cities—including the principal markets of New York, Chicago, Washington, D.C., and Los Angeles—still did not have cable services up and running. BET's limited programming hours also made it difficult for cable operators that did not have the technology to allow them to switch a channel between BET and another network. Hampered by a lack of funds (its partners contributed relatively small amounts of cash loans) BET was also criticized for its programming content, which had grown to include reruns of network programs, but had not yet fulfilled Johnson's promise of original, creative black programming.

Johnson soon began, however, to expand BET's offerings. BET launched its own news division in 1984, establishing a Washington news bureau and reaching an agreement with ABC to carry that network's national and international footage. Other programs included a weekly half-hour entertainment magazine, a weekly call-in talk show, and a one-hour show featuring celebrity and political guests. BET received a new boost in September 1984, when Time, Inc.'s HBO division provided BET with the use of one of its satellite transponders in return for 16 percent of the company (with TCI's and Taft's shares shrinking to match that and Johnson holding the remaining 52 percent). BET was then able to make the move to 24-hour programming. Videos, especially those featuring the black artists still largely ignored by MTV and other networks, figured prominently in BET's lineup. The network's daily broadcast was built around an eight-hour grouping of programs, of which six hours were music videos, repeated three times a day. Infomercials also became an important source of BET's revenues.

A Landmark IPO in the 1990s

By late 1985 BET was still reaching fewer than ten million subscribers. But, by then, cable was finally reaching the urban market and, by 1986, the company finally became profitable when its subscriber base topped 12 million. Profits in the year ending July 31, 1987 were reported to be $960,000. Two years later, BET's subscriber base grew to 22 million and its shows were showing up on the Nielsen ratings, which was important for generating advertising revenues. Johnson also convinced cable operators to increase their fees to 5 cents per subscriber. With revenues topping an estimated $23 million, BET moved from leased facilities into its own, newly built $10 million production studio.

Johnson's biggest move, however, came two years later. Taft, by then called Great American Broadcasting Inc., was struggling to pay down debt incurred in its own leveraged buyout and sought to sell off its BET shares to raise cash. Johnson complied by taking BET public, in the process becoming the first black-owned company ever to be listed on the New York Stock Exchange. The 4.25 million shares, which had initially been valued at $11 to $13 per share, began trading at $17 per share and closed at $23.5. Johnson retained 56 percent of the newly public company's voting rights, with 37 percent of its Class A shares. His original $15,000 was now worth more than $250 million.

By the time of its initial public offering (IPO), BET's revenues had grown to nearly $51 million, and its net profit soared to $9.3 million. BET had even more reason to cheer as the cable industry began moving to new technology, allowing cable operators to double the number of channels they offered. In addition, with the coming deregulation of the cable industry, BET became increasingly attractive to cable operators competing for the urban markets. Advertisers were also recognizing BET, now available to more than 30 million households, as a potent force for reaching the black consumer market, whose purchasing power had grown dramatically in the preceding decade.

Joint Ventures, New Markets, and the Future

With BET on "cruise control," as Johnson told the *Washington Post*, Johnson turned his attention to expanding BET, now reorganized as BET Holdings, into a media empire. He expanded into publishing, buying a controlling interest in the respected, general interest magazine *Emerge* and launching the youth-oriented magazine *YSB* under BET's newly formed Paige Publications subsidiary. BET also moved into film production, forming its first joint venture, United Image Entertainment, with actor/director Tim Reid of "WKRP in Cincinnati" fame. In 1993, with revenues topping $71 million, BET launched BET Direct, a direct marketing firm developed in conjunction with the Home Shopping Channel, and began featuring its own home shopping program on its BET network. Among the products featured was BET's own line of beauty products, Color Code.

Johnson's empire continued to grow with the acquisition of the Action pay-per-view station, which reached seven million homes by 1996. BET formed two more joint ventures to produce films: family-oriented movies through the BET Pictures partnership with Blockbuster Entertainment; and a third joint venture, BET Film Productions, with Encore and LIVE Entertainment. Another subsidiary, BET International, was formed to bring BET programming overseas, into markets including almost all of the Caribbean, as well as South Africa and the United Kingdom.

By 1995, BET's subscriber base had swelled to more than 43 million households, generating more than $115 million in revenues for a net profit of nearly $20 million. The network was given a big boost the following year when it grabbed the first post-trial O.J. Simpson interview—with three million viewers tuned in, BET had its largest audience ever. Debra Lee was named president and placed in charge of day-to-day operations while Johnson, as CEO and chairman, continued exploring new areas in which to take the company. BET on Jazz, a 24-hour cable network devoted to jazz music programming, debuted in early 1996.

In April 1996, BET repurchased all of Time-Warner's stock for $58 million. A third network was added to BET's stable with the launch of BET Movies/STARZ!3, in partnership with TCI's Liberty Media subsidiary's Encore division. BET's move into cyberspace, in a joint venture with Microsoft to provide content for Microsoft's MSN online service, as well as CD-ROM and interactive television content, was uploaded in early 1996. Johnson was also making plans to extend the BET brand name into the restaurant business, with the first of a proposed chain of black-oriented, Planet Hollywood-style restaurants. Although the company's core television network continued to produce 94 percent of its revenues and all of its profits, Robert Johnson's slow, but steady, hand seemed certain to craft his BET empire into a multimedia powerhouse.

Principal Divisions

Avalon Pictures (BET Action pay-per-view); BET Cable Network; BET Direct; BET Film Productions; BET on Jazz; BET Pictures; Paige Publications; United Image Entertainment.

Further Reading

"BET: Still Small, But Determined," *Broadcasting,* February 18, 1985, p. 67.

Guy, Pat, "Great Reception for BET," *USA Today,* October 31, 1991, Money Sec., p. 1B.

Litvan, Laura M., "A Broadcaster's Vision," *Nation's Business,* February 1995, p. 13.

Sanger, Elizabeth, "Betting on BET," *Newsday,* February 25, 1996, Money & Careers Sec., p. 1.

Shales, Tom, "Beyond 'Benson': Black-Oriented Channel from a Cable Pioneer," *Washington Post,* November 30, 1979, p. C1.

Sloan, Allan, "Wide Profits in 'Narrowcasting,' " *The Recorder,* October 7, 1991, p. 14.

Span, Paula, "Robert Johnson's Cable Vision," *Washington Post,* June 25, 1989, p. L34.

Waxler, Caroline, "Bob Johnson's Brainchild," *Forbes,* April 22, 1996, p. 98.

—M. L. Cohen

Blyth Industries, Inc.

100 Field Point Road
Greenwich, Connecticut 06830
U.S.A.
(203) 661-1926
Fax: (203) 661-1969
Web site: http://www.blythindustries.com

Public Company
Incorporated: 1977
Employees: 2,000
Sales: $331.34 million (1996)
Stock Exchanges: New York
SICs: 3999 Manufacturing Industries, Not Elsewhere
   Classified; 5199 Nondurable Goods, Not Elsewhere
   Classified; 5999 Miscellaneous Retail Stores, Not
   Elsewhere Classified

Blyth Industries, Inc. lights the way through the highly fragmented, and traditionally private, candle industry. With its Candle Corporation of America and other subsidiaries, Blyth designs, manufactures, and markets candles for nearly every market segment, as well as related items such as outdoor citronella products, potpourri and other fragrance products, candle accessories, and gift wrapping and gift bags. From a $3 million maker of religious and institutional candles, Blyth has grown into an industry powerhouse, with sales expected to near $500 million by 1997. Blyth's products are sold under a variety of brand names targeting the entire spectrum of candle sales, from food service/institutional and religious markets, to mass merchandise and retail candles, to high-end specialty markets. Candle and home fragrance sales are generally grouped under Blyth's Candle Corporation of America subsidiary and feature brand names such as Colonial Candle of Cape Cod, Mrs. Baker's Original Recipe, Carolina Designs Ltd., Ambria, L'Aroma, Old Harbor, Aromatics, and Eternalux. Another subsidiary, Tulsa, Oklahoma-based Jeanmarie Creations, Inc., acquired in 1995, designs and produces decorative gift bags and "convenience" gift wrap products such as gift sacks, poly-gift bags, bike bags, and metallized tissue sheets and shreds. A fast-growing subsidiary of Blyth is its direct-selling arm, PartyLite Gifts, Inc., which, like Mary Kay, Amway, Tupperware, and others, operates through independent representatives, who host PartyLite Shows to sell Colonial Candle of Cape Cod brand candles and such decorative candle accessories as candle holders, silk floral arrangements, and wall sconces.

Domestic sales account for approximately 90 percent of Blyth's revenues, with each brand segment represented by its own sales group. Blyth candles are sold through more than 20,000 department, gift, and specialty stores and more than 2,000 mass merchandisers. Major sellers of Blyth products include Wal-Mart, Mervyn's, Bloomingdale's, Nordstrom, Home Depot, J.C. Penney, and Target. In addition, the company supplies more than 1,000 food service and religious market distributors, including Kraft General Foods and Sysco Corporation. With its domestic business solidly in place, Blyth is seeing its fastest growth in the international market, with sales (including PartyLite Gift representatives) in more than 50 countries on six continents. Blyth has been particularly successful in bringing its consumer candles to Europe, a relatively untapped market. The company holds 25 percent equity positions in two United Kingdom companies, Colony Gift Corporation, Ltd. and Eclipse Candles, Ltd., with options to acquire full ownership positions.

Headquartered in Greenwich, Connecticut, Blyth's manufacturing operations are located in Chicago, North Carolina, Florida, and Massachusetts. Between 1995 and 1996, the company's employees grew from 1,400 to more than 2,000. Blyth's growth can be expected to continue: In 1996, the company reached agreement with Hallmark Cards, Inc. for a joint marketing and distribution partnership. Under the agreement, Blyth will purchase Hallmark's candlemaking production facilities, replacing Hallmark's Canterbury brand of candles with Blyth's Colonial and Mrs. Baker brands in the more than 5,000 Hallmark Gold Crown retail stores. Blyth is led by Chairman, President, and CEO Robert Goergen, who has also headed a venture capital firm, the Ropert Group, since 1978 and has been chairman of XTRA Corp., a trailer leasing company, since 1990.

Company Perspectives:

While we have grown from a small regional operation to a leader in all significant market segments, we have not lost sight of the principles that brought us to where we are today—a commitment to quality for every market segment, entrepreneurial enthusiasm, tenacious examination of every detail, fiscal responsibility, and patience. We continually challenge ourselves to maintain high levels of performance in our existing businesses, while exploring new avenues for potential expansion.

Marketing 101 in the 1960s and 1970s

As late as the 1970s, it was barely possible to speak of a candlemaking "industry." The candle market was highly fragmented among many small, privately held companies, each of which tended to be limited to producing for a specific market segment. Since the introduction of gas and then electric lighting, candle use had become increasingly marginalized, limited primarily to religious ceremonies or candlelight dinners. Despite an upsurge in candle use during the 1960s, driven by the hippie and "flower power" cultures, estimates suggested that the candle industry was worth barely more than $60 million per year. The majority of candle sales were in religious and food service/institutional products; the consumer market was largely untapped.

Enter Robert Goergen. When Goergen took over a small candle maker in 1977, he was just 37 years old and already had a varied career behind him. Goergen originally studied to become a nuclear physicist, but after taking a degree in physics from the University of Rochester, he decided he did not like that field. Instead, in 1960, Goergen enrolled in the Wharton School at the University of Pennsylvania, where he earned a master's degree in business, with honors, in only one year. While in school, Goergen had worked for Procter & Gamble, and upon receiving his degree, Procter & Gamble made him a supervisor over a 16-member crew in its manufacturing operations. But Goergen's career goals sought a more rapid rise than would have been available to him at Procter & Gamble. He entered the army, and then left military service after six months to join the McCann-Erickson advertising agency. Toward the middle of the 1960s, Goergen had risen to become a senior account executive, in charge of the Coca-Cola account.

Goergen had long set his ambitions, however, on the business side, and in 1966 he left McCann-Erickson for a position with the McKinsey & Co. consulting firm. With McKinsey, Goergen gained the experience in retail marketing strategy and in mergers and acquisitions of consumer goods industries that would prove crucial to his later success. Yet, after rising to principal partner in less than four years, Goergen made a new career move. As he told *Forbes,* "When I finished my reports for management I was out of the picture and had to start all over again. I got a good salary but I wasn't staying around long enough to reap the big rewards. That's when I decided to get into venture capital."

Goergen was hired by Donaldson, Lufkin & Jenrette in 1973 and named administrative manager of DLJ's Sprout venture

capital investment group. Goergen found early success when he convinced his partners to invest $500,000 in start-up Royce Electronics, formed to distribute Japanese-made citizens' band (CB) radios. As the CB craze built in the mid-1970s, Royce's revenues jumped to $40 million per year. In 1975, just before the CB market became overcrowded, and then bust, Royce was merged into Masco Corp., netting the Sprout partners $7.5 million on their two-year-old investment. Meanwhile, Goergen's success with DLJ led him to make personal, "hobby" investments in companies too small to capture DLJ's interest. One of these investments, made in 1976, was in Candle Corporation of America, a small, family-owned Brooklyn, New York company with about $3 million in sales, primarily to the religious candle market. But when that company started losing money, Goergen and three partners each put up $25,000 and bought the company. Goergen was made chairman.

Building a Better Candle in the 1980s

Goergen explained the leap from investment to management to the *Fairfield County Business Journal* this way: "I had to personally guarantee company loans, so that really focused my attention." Goergen's first step was to change the name of the company, to Blyth Industries, an existing unit of Candle Corporation of America, telling *Investor's Business Daily,* "We didn't want to say 'candle' or 'America' in the name, because we wanted to move toward a broader product line." Blyth's first move was to expand the company into consumer sales. To accomplish this, the company acquired four small candle makers between 1977 and 1981, adding $16 million in revenues and adding the gift market to Blyth's food service and religious market base. Each acquisition followed a similar pattern: The company would tighten the newly acquired company's manufacturing process, strengthen management, develop new distribution channels, and step up new product development. With the increased revenues, Blyth next turned to a new acquisition.

By 1982, these acquisitions had helped raise Blyth's sales to $26 million. But Goergen was also learning how to market candles, explaining to *Forbes,* "This is not a demand product— you have to push it." The company's marketing push was to create candles as an "affordable luxury" product. Toward this end, the company began expanding its product line as well as the nature of the consumer candle market itself.

Apart from candles made by the tiny artisan shops, candle manufacturers still produced almost exclusively white, unscented candles. As a consumer product, candles were most likely to be found on the dining room table. But Blyth set out to change the market. Between 1982 and 1985, the company focused on developing new products, introducing colors (to match the colors in a consumer's home) and then fragrances to its candles. The company also introduced its own line of outdoor citronella-scented candles, replacing the standard glass holder with pails and colorful ceramic pots.

By the mid-1980s, Blyth had achieved strong internal growth. But, to step up production, the company began to look outside the company to fuel its expansion. Goergen next directed Blyth's energies toward consolidating the candle industry, creating a critical mass of products and retailers. In 1986 Blyth made its first major acquisition, of Old Harbor Candles, then a subsidiary of Towle Manufacturing. The following year, Blyth acquired the Lenox Candle assets, including its Carolina brand, from Brown-Forman subsidiary Lenox Inc., strengthening Blyth's distribution to the retail and specialty store channels. The Lenox acquisition also placed Blyth in the lead among major candle manufacturers, ahead of Hallmark and Colonial Candle of Cape Cod. Both of the new subsidiaries kept their former management, operating as independent business units. In 1988, the company introduced a new subsidiary, Atmospherix Ltd., as it expanded its line of fragrance products.

Blyth's next major acquisition came in 1990, with the purchase of former rival Colonial Candle of Cape Cod from General Housewares Corp. Colonial brought Blyth deeper penetration into the department store channel. The purchase also included Colonial's direct-selling PartyLite Gifts unit. By then, Goergen had crafted the company's unique industry position as a single-source supplier of candles, fragrances, and accessories across the full range of industry distribution channels. Two years later, Blyth made its next acquisition, of Aromatic Industries, a subsidiary of The Mennen Company. Aromatic, which was based in California, was one of the country's leading producers of potpourri and other home fragrance products, which further complemented the Blyth line of products. By then Blyth's revenues had reached $87.3 million. Net income for the year was $3.9 million, continuing the company's unbroken record of profitability since Goergen assumed its leadership.

Burning Brighter in the 1990s

With the company's wide assortment of candle designs, colors, and fragrances, and with its variety of accessories ranging from candle holders to potpourri, Blyth helped move candles beyond the living and dining room into the bedroom, bathroom, and throughout the consumer's home. Aided by its insect-repelling citronella candles, Blyth was also able to extend sales from the typical candle buying seasons, Christmas and Easter, to more year-round revenues. The company also matched its segmented approach—from the high-end Colonial brand, to the mid-market Carolina brand, and the low-end Old Harbor brand—with a commitment to quality, describing the range of its products, in its first annual report, as "good, better, best." And the company profited as well from the disposable nature of its products. As Goergen told *Forbes:* "We are in the razor business, except our razor blades burn."

Having consolidated its position as the leader of the candle industry, Blyth entered the next phase of the company's development, stepping up the introduction of new products, expanding its distribution channels, and improving its customer service and production efficiency. The company's sales built quickly, to $116 million by January 1993 and to $157.5 million by January 1994, producing net incomes of nearly $6 million and more than $9 million, respectively. To fuel continued growth and to expand production capacity to meet the growing demand for its products, Blyth went public in 1994, raising more than $50 million. Goergen retained 42 percent of the company.

By then, the candle industry itself was growing by about 15 percent per year, aided by increases in the home decorating market. With cash raised from its public offering, Blyth added production capacity, building a new plant in Chicago, another in

North Carolina, and buying a third in Massachusetts. The company next turned its focus on its international sales, which accounted for only five percent of total sales in 1994. To Goergen, the European market was especially promising, since, as he told *Investor's Business Daily,* candles there were "still white and unscented." In 1995, Blyth purchased 25 percent equity investments in two British candle companies, Colony Gift Corporation, Ltd. and Eclipse Candles, Ltd., whose product lines complemented Blyth's domestic product base. On the domestic front, Blyth expanded its product lineup again, buying an 80 percent stake in Tulsa, Oklahoma-based Jeanmarie Creations, a maker of decorative wrapping paper, gift bags, and other accessories.

Through 1995, the company's revenues rose again, from $215 million for the year ending January 1995, to $331 million for the year ending January 1996. Net income also continued to grow, to $13.3 million and to $24 million. By then, the company had made a secondary offering, of 1.5 million shares in October 1995. One month later, Blyth announced a two-for-one stock split. Proceeds from the new offering were earmarked for new capital investments and to make some $150 million in intended new acquisitions over the next several years. Goergen's $25,000 investment was now worth more than $380 million.

In 1996, the company took two new steps to increase its share of the candle market. The first was its introduction of a new line of coordinated candles, potpourri, and home fragrances. Sold under the Ambria brand name, the new line was targeted especially at mass merchandisers such as Wal-Mart, extending the square footage given to Blyth products in such stores. The next step came with the announcement of the company's partnership agreement with Hallmark, with the first shipment of Blyth products to Hallmark stores begun in June 1996. The Hallmark partnership was not yet expected to add greatly to Blyth's revenues, predicted to reach $470 million for the year, for 1996. The full impact of the partnership, which offered the potential of adding Blyth products to more than 5,000 Hallmark Gold Crown stores, would not be known until the end of its 1997 fiscal year.

Principal Subsidiaries

Candle Corporation of America; Jeanmarie Creations, Inc. (80%); PartyLite Gifts, Inc.; Colony Gift Corporation, Ltd. (United Kingdom; 25%); Eclipse Candles, Ltd. (United Kingdom; 25%).

Further Reading

"Development Banking a la DLJ," *Forbes,* April 15, 1977, p. 56.

McElroy, Camille, "Blyth Industries Expands Across Market Lines," *Fairfield County Business Journal,* November 28, 1994, p. 8.

Galarza, Pablo, "Blyth Industries, Inc.," *Investor's Daily Business,* July 25, 1994, p. A6.

Gubernick, Lisa, "Razor Blades That Burn," *Forbes,* May 20, 1996, p. 278.

Maio, Patrick J., "Blyth Industries, Inc.," *Investor's Daily Business,* June 19, 1996, p. A4.

——, "Blyth Industries, Inc.," *Investor's Daily Business,* November 30, 1995, p. A6.

—M. L. Cohen

THE BOSTON BEER COMPANY

Boston Beer Company

75 Arlington Street
Boston, Massachusetts 02116
U.S.A.
(617) 482-1332
Fax: (617) 482-5527
Web site: http://www.samadams.com

Public Company
Incorporated: 1984
Employees: 196
Sales: $169.36 million (1995)
Stock Exchanges: New York
SICs: 2082 Malt Beverages

The leading specialty brewer in the United States, Boston Beer Company has made Samuel Adams known for being more than a signatory of the Declaration of Independence or a rebellious participant in the Boston Tea Party. Headquartered in Boston, Massachusetts, Boston Beer brews and markets Samuel Adams Boston Lager, an all-malt Pilsner-style beer based on a hundred-year-old formulation that continues to be the most popular ''craft'' beer on the market. In a competitive malt liquor market driven by increasingly discriminating upscale consumers, small ''microbreweries'' such as Boston Beer have become the dominant force. And Boston Beer's pivotal role in sparking the microbrewery boom of the 1990s has become the stuff of business legend; although its success has propelled it over the top—technically, the annual production of a microbrewery must remain under 15,000 barrels—the company remains the yardstick by which industry success is measured. Within the domestic specialty beer market, the company's sales are larger than the next five craft breweries combined.

Much of the success of Boston Beer has been its ability to foster and stay on top of a niche market for the second most popular beverage in the world (the first being tea). Unlike other microbrewers—skilled craftspeople who pride themselves on small-batch production and local distribution, often eschewing the ''business'' side of the business by leaving advertising to word of mouth—Boston Beer has been ambitious. A tiger in the industry, it went for the jugular, directly challenging high-priced imports like Heineken, St. Pauli Girl, and Beck's. Strategically avoiding head-to-head combat with domestic giants like Miller Brewery, Anheuser-Busch, and Budweiser, whose highly financed promotional ''lifestyle'' campaigns feature frogs, dogs, and buxom, bikini-clad beach babes, Boston Beer aimed for a share of the six percent import market. Instead of gearing its product toward twenty-something middle-class males, Samuel Adams is marketed toward connoisseurs, beer aficionados with an eye for quality and a taste for an exceptional product. Advertising the weaknesses of imported beers, that is, that foreign brews headed for the United States have fewer premium ingredients, a ''lighter'' taste, and are less fresh because of long shipping times (like other perishable foodstuffs, beer ''goes sour'' and loses its flavor and quality after as little as four months), the company has prided itself on the quality of ingredients and brewing skill it brings to its products. By directly tackling the premium imports, Boston Beer would create a new marketing niche, domestically brewed premium beer, and assume a leadership position within the growing specialty beer market.

Founded in 1984 on Life Savings and Hard Work

Boston Beer Company was founded by C. James Koch (pronounced *Cook*), a Cincinnati native who moved to Boston to study at Harvard's law and business schools. In the early 1980s, Koch (descended from five generations of brewmasters) noticed an increase in the sales of imported beers. In April 1984, with $100,000 of his own savings, $140,000 from supportive family and friends, and the sales savvy of Rhonda L. Kallman (his former secretary and, eventually, company marketing vice-president), 33-year-old Koch quit his well-paying job as management consultant to Boston Consulting Group. Armed with a recipe formulated by his great-great-grandfather, St. Louis-based brewer Louis Koch, he derived a beer that was more full bodied than typical U.S. brews. Koch's recipe adhered to rigorous German beer purity laws that demanded top-quality ingredients and long brewing and fermentation periods. After cooking up the first few batches on his kitchen stove, Koch contracted with 30-year-veteran Pittsburgh Brewing Co. to manufacture his brown-bottled, premium lager in their modern plant. Door-to-door marketing of the new beer began in downtown Boston in 1985, netting Koch a customer base of 25 restaurants and bars. Shipments of Samuel Adams Boston Lager were under way by April. Ironically, Koch was unable to find a distributor willing to carry his product, so was forced to buy a truck and do it himself.

Because of the brew's high retail cost—$20 per case, against Heineken's $17—these first sales were the hardest. Koch and Kallman used a personal approach, encouraging bartenders to sample their product and explaining why Samuel Adams was a higher quality brew from a better company. Their dogged persistence eventually won over the New England market. By 1987 the company was poised to enter the finicky Manhattan market where, Koch contended in the *Wall Street Journal,* "New Yorkers are well behind other cities in accepting quality American beers." He added, "But we've done so well elsewhere, we're ready to invest the time and money in educating New York." By 1988 Koch and Kallman had such a strong sales base that they were able to acquire $3 million from an investment banking firm for the purchase of an old brewery within Boston's Jamaica Plains section. Although efforts to establish a full-scale brewing operation there were quickly nixed because of the prohibitive costs associated with outfitting a brewery, the location would serve as a research and development facility, as well as a tourist attraction.

Boston Beer Goes National, 1990–92

Boston Beer soon saw its distribution networks grow to include Washington, D.C., and Chicago. In 1990, as part of its controlled, targeted expansion strategy, the company further expanded its market by reaching an agreement with Portland, Oregon-based Blitz-Weinhart Brewing to brew and distribute its product in the western United States. It also opened the Samuel Adams Brew House in Philadelphia, where the Samuel Adams flagship brand is still brewed. Distribution increased in 1992, when California's Pacific Wine Co. agreed to distribute Boston Beer products on the West Coast. With distribution now encompassing the 48 contiguous states, Koch watched 1992 sales increase 63 percent to $48.17 million, resulting in net income of $1.6 million.

Since upscale U.S. beer drinkers' tastes ran strongly to imports, marketing a new high-end brew required some creativity. As early as 1986 Koch earmarked a large portion of the company budget for marketing. He composed some quirky radio advertisements promoting the quality of his product. And he did some flag waving, touting Samuel Adams as a made-in-the-U.S.A. alternative to pricey foreign brews. But, more important, Koch recognized the value in focusing his efforts on a specific market segment, rather than the general beer-drinking public. In addition to catchy slogans like "Declare Your Independence from Foreign Beer," his ads were also an impassioned attempt to educate listeners about beer in general and about what made Samuel Adams unique, in particular.

Samuel Adams's rise to the top had stronger foundations than the flurry of interest generated by a clever ad campaign, however. Boston Beer made a quality product. The company uses only four age-old ingredients—hops, malt, yeast, and water—a time-honored four-vessel, all-malt process, and a secondary fermentation process called *krausening* to create a smoother brew. Use of relatively rare European-grown Hallertau Mittelfrueh, Spalt Spalt, Saaz, and Tettnang Tettnang hops provides a distinctive aroma and spicy edge. Boston Beer watched its flagship brand win numerous awards at Denver's annual Great American Beer Festival and more medals at the 1994 World Beer Championship than any other brew. Tellingly, Koch's 1993 advertising campaign, which claimed his product as the best beer in the United States "four years running," unleashed arguments and threats of litigation by rival microbrewers in an increasingly competitive beer industry. Similarly, ads claiming that Samuel Adams was the sole American beer imported into Germany ruffled feathers of more than one competitor who maintained a European market for their product. Ultimately, the hue and cry over Koch's jealous advertising strengthened the name recognition of his company's product as consumers went to the bar to find out what all the fuss was about.

Due to both clever ad strategies and quality products, Boston Beer watched its production increase from 294,000 barrels in 1992 to 714,000 by 1994. From 1992 to 1993 the company expanded its employee base from 87 to 110; the following year would see 170 people working to produce and promote Boston Beer products. These increases in production and staff were the result of increased sales; the company's sales staff, which numbered more than 90 people by the end of 1994, personally contacted customers whose collective beer tab earned the brewer a net income of more than $9 million. Well trained in brewing techniques—all company employees are required to spend a day brewing beer in Boston—company salespeople continually educate retailers about the quality of their products.

As sales and profits increased, so did the money the company allotted to advertising. Boston Beer sponsored bar beer nights that featured Samuel Adams t-shirt and cap giveaways, distributed coasters, table cards, restaurant umbrellas, and menu boards, and donated their product to charity events to increase public exposure. Samuel Adams was served at each of the social balls and dinners that accompanied President Clinton's ascension to the presidency in 1993. By 1995, along with other microbreweries like Mistik Beverages, Boston Beer began to consider the benefits of a television advertising campaign to tout its product; television testing was still under way through 1996.

Public Offering in 1995

Prompted by its forward momentum, Boston Beer made the decision to go public in 1995, offering 3.1 million shares that November. Of those, it held back 990,000 shares, directing these toward its loyal customers. These customers included not only the bar owners, shop owners, and wholesalers who distributed company products; every six-pack of Samuel Adams sold at retail came with a mail-in coupon for discounted shares in Boston Beer's growing operation. More than 130,000 customers were quick to invest in a piece of their favorite brew.

By the close of the year the company reported net income of $5.9 million on revenues of $151.3 million. Production was a record 961,000 barrels divided among an increasing array of products that included Samuel Adams Brand Ale, Boston Lager, Cream Stout, Honey Porter, and Triple Bock, as well as such tempting seasonal variations as Cranberry Iambic and Winter Lager. In addition, the company produced and marketed beers under the Boston Lightship brand. The Oregon Original brands, brewed by the company-owned Oregon Ale and Beer Company, had also been introduced to most major markets by 1995.

The Sincerest Form of Flattery

Not surprisingly, Boston Beer's success spawned a host of imitators. In fact, throughout the early 1990s approximately 55 new breweries were established each year. Of these, the company perceived a real threat in the similarly named Boston Beer Works. Although Boston Beer would sue the coattail brewery, it lost the suit in 1994.

In addition to encouraging other beer-brewing entrepreneurs, the major U.S. breweries did not respond to the advances made by Boston-based upstart Koch by lying down. Watching a segment of a relentlessly sluggish beer market mushroom almost overnight would tantalize any businessman. Beer giants Anheuser-Busch, Coors, and the Philip Morris-owned Miller Brewery used their leverage to try to restrict the supply of raw materials and national distribution network of the entire microbrewery industry, a $400 million market divided among almost 500 brewers by 1994. Their efforts would force many craft brewers to confine their distribution within regional markets, with a select few becoming the targets of takeovers as the giants maneuvered for a piece of the growing microbrew pie.

The "if you can't beat 'em, join 'em" strategy proved to be increasingly popular as well. Adopting an increasing array of small-scale guises, such as Miller's nonexistent Plank Road Brewery (Miller's original name in 1855), the major breweries attempted to cash in on the micro movement by introducing a battery of so-called "craft" beers into the high-end marketplace. Aesthetically appealing labels proclaiming brands like Red Dog, Killian, Blue Moon, Elk Mountain, Eisbock, Leinenkugel, Red Wolf House, and Augsburger could be seen filling retail beer shelves and popping up in point-of-sale tavern displays. Even importers responded to the competition by distributing "micros" of their own, such as Heineken's Tarwebok and Labatt's Moretti La Rossa.

The Future of the Beer Industry

Although Boston Beer's third quarter 1996 results once again showed record results, the 294,000 barrels sold were fewer than the company had expected for its product line, sending mini-shockwaves throughout the microbrewery industry. Other small-scale brewers, many of whom were fledgling

operations, wondered if the wave they had been riding had crested. While the overall beer market continued to stagnate because of the increasing influence of health-conscious consumers, however, the market for upscale craft beers remained on an ascent—albeit one not quite as steep—as these same consumers expressed a clear preference for quality malt liquor products when they did choose to indulge. On the strength of third quarter net sales of $46.1 million the company went ahead with the planned purchase of Cincinnati's historic Hudepohl-Schoenling Brewing Co., its Midwest contract brewery.

Throughout 1996 beer sales began to level off across the board, with both micros and large brewers alike posting more moderate increases in sales. Feeling an especially acute pinch due to lackluster Budweiser earnings, Anheuser-Busch fronted a group complaint to the Bureau of Alcohol, Tobacco and Firearms (BATF) leveled against Boston Beer, Pete's Brewing Co. (makers of Pete's Wicked Ale), and fellow top-gun brewer Miller. Accusing the two micros of false advertising in their reported claims to brew "in small batches" instead of through large-scale contracted breweries, Busch and associates also demanded that Miller's parentage of both Icehouse and Red Dog be legitimized on the label rather than cloaked by its fictitious alter-ego, the Plank Road Brewery.

In retaliation, in March 1996 Boston Beer petitioned the BATF to request "full disclosure" on all beer labels. This would end the widespread use of encoded freshness dates and require point of product origin to be clearly identified. Boston Beer has been among only a handful of brewers to print encoded freshness dates on their products so that they can be evaluated by consumers, a practice they initiated in 1989. The brewer also accepts product returns after expiration dates have been reached. Boston Beer's move to raise industry accountability to its own standards quickly got the nod from *Consumer Reports,* which praised both the company's packaging and product by voting Samuel Adams the best in the United States in its 1996 craft-brewed ale taste test.

Boston Beer also began efforts to bring its brew home to Boston, purchasing an abandoned brewery that it slated for renovation and planned for operation by January 1977. Meanwhile, the regional distribution of company-contracted brewing sites—which include Pittsburgh Brewing Co., upstate New York's F. X. Matt Brewing Co. and Genesee Brewing Co., Cincinnati's Hudepohl-Schoenling Brewing Co., and the Stroh-owned Blitz-Weinhart—continued to ensure the freshness of its products to its large customer base outside the greater Boston area.

Innovation Continues

In its position as microbrewery industry leader, Boston Beer has continued to encourage cultivation of the brewmeister's art. In 1995 it organized the first annual World Homebrew Championships, a summer gathering of 60 judges entrusted with the task of choosing the best among brews from around the world. Three category winners were announced in 1996 and their brews successfully marketed by the company under the names LongShot American Pale Ale, LongShot Hazelnut Brown Ale, and LongShot Black Lager. Boston Beer also entered into a working relationship with Seagram Beverage Company. Under the terms of the agreement, in exchange for ownership of both trademark and trade name and future royalties on sales, the company agreed to aid the liquor giant in the development and marketing, in 1997, of its new Devil Mountain craft beer line.

Commanding a sales force of 115 people by 1996, Boston Beer began to introduce its product line internationally; not only Germany, but also Ireland, Japan, and Hong Kong have welcomed Samuel Adams. In May of 1996 the company signed an agreement with England's Whitbread PLC to aid the United Kingdom's fourth largest brewery in the development of a craft brew catering to British tastes. The company also literally took to the skies, as Samuel Adams became American Airlines' in-flight beer on transcontinental flights beginning in mid-1996.

Industrywide Rankings Disguise Reality

Although pleased to have acquired an international profile, the company's efforts remained concentrated upon its domestic market. Its goals continued to be educating the consumer and developing a taste for a top-quality beer while maintaining profitability. Despite its ranking as one of the top ten brewers in the United States, Boston Brewery prides itself on being a small fish in an ocean containing a few large sharks; in the mid-1990s, the combined sales of the entire U.S. microbrewery industry accounted for less revenue than the total sales of Michelob Light in any one year. In a market dominated by a handful of giants, tenth-ranked Boston Brewery is, in the words of Koch, "like being the 12th largest car company." Anheuser-Busch's production had reached the millionth barrel by the first week of the year, the company CEO explained to Greg W. Prince in *Beverage World*. "When I tell people we're one five-hundredth of the beer business, . . . [they] are surprised at how small we really are."

Koch continued to indulge in the brewer's art, deriving new brews for the discerning palate. During 1995 he introduced three new products—Scotch Ale, Cherry Wheat, and Old Fezziwig Ale—increasing the company's product line to 14. Triple Bock, first introduced in 1994, is a dark, sherry-like barley beer that is aged in oak casks. An acquired taste, it is a sipping beer that boasts a 17 percent alcohol level.

Similarly, Boston Beer continued its commitment to satisfying a broader spectrum of discriminating consumers looking for a quality product. Its spicy Cherry Wheat Ale, introduced as a seasonal brew, became an annual product due to customer demand. The company's LongShot beers and Oregon Original brands continued to post record sales in a competitive market. Boston Beer was also encouraged by the fact that the market for specialty beers in the 1990s had expanded to include not only yuppie business people but twenty-something drinkers as well. These younger drinkers have gained their more sophisticated taste for malt liquors on the strength of the craft beer renaissance, a phenomenon directly attributable to Koch and Boston Beer.

Principal Subsidiaries

Oregon Ale and Beer Company.

Further Reading

Asimov, Eric, "Beer from Boston Brewery Makes Its Way to New York," *Wall Street Journal,* June 24, 1987.

Mamis, Robert A., "Market Maker," *Inc.,* December 1995.

McCune, Jenny C., "Finding Your Niche," *Small Business Reports,* January 1994.

Prince, Greg W., "Little Giants," *Beverage World,* December 1994.

—Pamela L. Shelton

Brightpoint, Inc.

6402 Corporate Drive
Indianapolis, Indiana 46278
U.S.A.
(317) 297-6100
Fax: (317) 297-6114
Web site: http://www.brightpoint.com

Public Company
Incorporated: 1989
Employees: 250
Sales: $280 million (1995)
Stock Exchanges: NASDAQ
SICs: 5065 Telephone Equipment, Wholesale

Brightpoint, Inc. is the second-largest independent U.S. distributor of cellular phone and cell phone accessories and in the mid-1990s was among the 50 fastest-growing companies in the United States. It acts as a middleman between the cellular carriers such as GTE, AT&T, and BellSouth—the companies that supply the actual transmission service for cell phone calls; the manufacturers of cell phone equipment and accessories, such as Nokia, Ericsson, and Motorola; and the cell-phone end-user or customer. In 1995, roughly 32 million subscribers used cell phone service in the United States, and Brightpoint's share of the total cellular equipment distribution market was 9.2 percent, second only to industry leader Cellstar Corporation of Texas.

Besides distributing nine lines of wireless phones, including car, portable, and handheld models (85 percent of its net sales in 1996) as well as 20 lines of wirelesss accessories such as batteries, chargers, and leather cases (15 percent), Brightpoint offers value-added services such as inventory management, same-day shipment, product training, cell phone programming, and custom packaging or "kitting." All told, its roughly seven to ten thousand customer accounts include agents, dealers, chain stores, resellers, exporters, direct marketers, expeditors, and by far the largest single category, cellular service providers. In 1996, Brightpoint distributed cell phones and accessories to customers in all 50 states, and through its international offices in Toronto; Manchester, England; Hong Kong; Sydney; and Johannesburg distributed equipment in 80 foreign countries.

The Birth of an Industry: 1984–89

The first test to determine the commercial feasibility of cellular communication technology was conducted in 1962, fifteen years after AT&T's Bell Laboratories introduced the idea of cellular transmission of radio communications signals. In 1970 the Federal Communications Commission (FCC) set aside radio frequencies for "land mobile communications," and by 1977 it had announced the construction of two cellular development systems in Baltimore/Washington and Chicago. As a U.S. cellular phone—or car phone, in its most common application—industry began to emerge in the 1980s, the FCC decided to authorize only two cell phone service carriers for each urban market, a decision that helped to keep the average monthly cost for cell phone service well above that of conventional phone lines for several years. Nevertheless, by 1985 roughly 300,000 U.S. cell phone subscribers were using cell phones throughout the United States.

In 1986, a young Indianapolis entrepreneur named Robert Laikin established a travel agency to cater to the corporate customers he had acquired through his first business enterprise, Tickets Up Front, a ticket agency for corporate clients. When a salesman for the communications firm Arnie Goldberg brought in an early model cell phone, Laikin became intrigued by the technology and agreed to buy one for his on-the-road business calls. He also invited Goldberg to call him if he ever wanted to go into business selling phones. Two weeks later Goldberg reappeared to take Laikin up on his offer and, using $20,000 from his ticket and travel agencies, Laikin and his partners bought a 50 percent share in the new business, Century Car Phones (later renamed Century Cellular Network, Inc.). By charging customers as much as $500 less per unit than his competitors, Goldberg began signing up new accounts in droves, and Century was soon expanding its monthly cell phone orders from one hundred to one thousand. By 1987 the number of cellular phone subscribers in the United States had grown to one million, and the average monthly cell phone subscription had dropped to a modest 50 dollars. Century rode the wave and by 1988 had become Indiana's leading cellular retailer. As the boom in cellular service grew, cell phone manufacturers struggled to keep up with demand, and retailers in small markets, like Century, found themselves wait-listed while the big urban markets were supplied. Dismayed by the practice, Laikin decided to establish his own low-cost cell phone supplier to buy Century's phones cheaply through bulk purchases from manufacturers. In partnership with Daniel Koerselman, a salesman for a car phone accessory firm, Laikin founded Wholesale Cellular USA in 1989. When the nation's cellular service carriers began reducing the commissions they paid local retailers like Century, however, Laikin began to view Wholesale rather than Century as his main chance for success in the cellular industry.

Wholesale Growth: 1989–93

Laikin's strategy for growing Wholesale Cellular read like a primer on successful business startups: The company's Midwest location capitalized on a trend afoot in the cell phone manufacturing industry, where firms were now beginning to look for new markets outside the major urban areas. Wholesale was strategically positioned to supply cell phones not only to Century but for agents in several Midwest states. Laikin also made sure to pay manufacturers promptly for all orders and was rewarded with first priority whenever manufacturers had to dole out cell phones during periods of short supply. Finally, Laikin kept Wholesale's costs to a minimum. With little real capital or collateral and a desk piled high with banks' loan rejections, Laikin was forced to operate with a low overhead and minimal inventory. To keep Wholesale's cash flow strong and steady, he made sure customers got their phones right away. Within a year of its birth, Wholesale had ceased to be merely a vehicle for Century's growth and was amassing sales of $12 million.

As the wireless industry expanded, the cellular service providers began reducing the number of operations they involved themselves in in order to concentrate on selling "minutes of use" rather than storing and, more often than not, essentially giving away expensive handsets to attract customers, who often discontinued service after only a few months. Hundreds of small third-party distributors like Wholesale began to occupy a larger segment of the middle market between the buying public and the cellular service carriers and phone manufacturers. Besides buying the cell phones from the manufacturers, these small, low-capital, usually privately owned distributors gradually began to

take on the "hardware" functions of the cellular service carriers. They maintained and managed their phone equipment inventory, programmed the cell phones for the individual markets they were destined to be used in, executed the delivery of the cell phone to customers, and sometimes activated the customers' cellular phone signal. As the price of cell phones dropped and the number of subscribers grew, competition among the industry's scattered distributors heated up, and low-cost firms like Wholesale could grab larger wedges of market share by buying phones in enormous volume, undercutting their competitors' prices. The wireless distribution industry began to consolidate rapidly, a trend that was only exacerbated when, in an economizing move, the cellular service carriers cut the number of suppliers they worked with. In an industry driven by rapid technological change, cutthroat competition, constantly falling prices, and hairline profit margins, only the distributors with the best management, the most financial resources, and the greatest flexibility stood any chance of surviving.

Wholesale Cellular was quickly establishing itself as that kind of company. By 1991, it had five hundred customers and sales of $32 million. By 1992, the number of cellular phone users in the United States had grown from zero only nine years before to ten million, and no fewer than 1,500 cellular systems were up and running across the country. With the adoption of wireless technology growing faster than virtually any previous technology—including color television, VCRs, and personal computers—at least one industry analyst anointed wireless technology "the product of the century." In 1992 Wholesale's sales leaped 50 percent to $48 million and then in 1993 another 60 percent to $77 million. As profits broke the $2 million mark, Laikin stepped down as president of Century in 1993 and in June entered the potentially gargantuan international wireless market by launching a Wholesale presence in Brazil.

"People Don't Like Wires": 1994–95

With net sales closing in on $169 million, Laikin took Wholesale public in April 1994 with an initial public offering (IPO) of common stock that raised $13.5 million. Like most IPOs, the decision to yield part ownership to public shareholders was driven by Laikin's desperate need for capital to keep his five-year-old juggernaut rolling. Laikin plowed part of the year's cash influx into the continuation of Wholesale's international expansion. The Chilean market was opened up in January, followed by Argentina in July, Columbia and Mexico in November, and Israel in December. In October Wholesale established an office and warehouse facility in Miami to serve its burgeoning Latin American customers. Moreover, Laikin was also pursuing a joint venture with the Indian information technology giant Pertech Computers Ltd. to distribute cellular equipment to the vast Indian middle class. In less than two years in the global marketplace, Wholesale's international business had grown to 10 percent of total sales.

Since Wholesale's inception, Laikin had been working double time to juggle the company's growing operations while visiting potential foreign markets and anticipating the latest developments in the wireless industry and cell phone technology. "I wanted to delegate," Laikin told the *Indianapolis Business Journal*, "I just had no time to delegate." On a friend's recommendation, he began exploring the possibility of bringing

J. Mark Howell, the chief accountant of the automobile auction firm Adesa Corporation, on board to manage Wholesale's finances. Howell initially resisted, but Laikin was persistent and in July 1994 Howell was named executive vice-president in charge of Wholesale's financial operations, administration, information services, and human resources.

By 1994, Wholesale's market-winning strategy had become clear. The cellular service providers who comprised the bulk of its customers paid Wholesale a flat dollar amount for each phone sold, and Wholesale negotiated directly for distribution rights with roughly 45 phone manufacturers—virtually all the major brands—to guarantee inventories of cell phone products, which were selected on the basis of quality, price, customer demand, product availability, and brand recognition. Wholesale's staff placed daily orders for equipment by phone or fax with the manufacturer, who then shipped them directly to Wholesale's warehouses in Indianapolis and Miami, where Wholesale's proprietary order fulfillment system shipped them in bulk to large buyers or singly to individual customers. By carefully avoiding dependence on any single supplier and by offering phones for every cellular transmission standard, Laikin could essentially eliminate the risk of being stuck with a product suddenly out of favor in the marketplace. Moreover, by resisting a contractual obligation to a single manufacturer (such as Cellstar's relationship with Motorola), Wholesale could market itself to manufacturers, service providers, and end users alike as a truly independent supplier.

Wholesale also assiduously expanded its order fulfillment services to encompass not only traditional product handling and warehousing but custom phone labeling, branding, and packaging; phone warranty and repair services; and overnight, "just-in-time" delivery. Laikin's quip that the cell phone industry's growth was being driven in part by the simple fact that "people don't like wires" was proven true when truly portable "walk-and-talk" cell phones began to become as common as the traditional car-mounted mobile phone. A whole new range of accessories became available for the new nonautomotive cell phone market, from antennas and carrying cases to batteries, rechargers, and "hands-free" kits, and all were integrated into Wholesale's distribution system. Because such accessories could normally be priced for a much greater profit margin than cell phones, Wholesale gained a welcome jolt of income, and by 1994 accessories were accounting for 12 percent of company sales.

In 1995 Wholesale also announced a five-year agreement with cellular service provider BellSouth Cellular Corporation and HSN Direct, the "infomercial" division of Home Shopping Network, Inc. to sell cellular phones and service. Under the plan, HSN Direct would initially produce 30-minute infomercials marketing BellSouth's "Mobile America" cellular service and products through an 800 number, with Wholesale fulfilling the orders.

In 1995 Wholesale also formed a joint venture, Wholesale Cellular Latina, with consumer electronics distributor German Garrido to distribute cell phones and accessories in Argentina, Bolivia, Chile, Ecuador, Paraguay, Peru, and Uruguay while expanding its warehousing facilities in Miami to absorb the additional traffic. As mid-year sales showed Wholesale on a course to break the $269 million mark for the year, Laikin

announced that a new $4 million headquarters, warehouse, and distribution complex would be constructed in Indianapolis, a few miles from its existing site.

Brightpoint, Inc.: 1995–97

As Wholesale's business continued to expand far beyond phone distribution, Laikin began to search for a new name to reflect the company's growing scope and potential. In September 1995, Wholesale Cellular USA was officially renamed Brightpoint, Inc. because, as Laikin's right-hand man, J. Mark Howell, explained, "we wanted a name that was not limiting in any way. We're just trying to get away from the perception of the company being a box-moving distributor." By August, Brightpoint had agreed to form a joint venture with India's Pertech Computers to begin distributing cell phones, pagers, and accessories in India in late 1995 and early 1996.

As Brightpoint expanded, it accumulated debt and a pressing need for additional growth capital. In October 1995, Laikin made a second stock offering to the public, this one for about $34 million, which resulted in increased equity of $59 million and the wherewithal to pay down its debt, fund the move to its new 90,000-square-foot office and distribution facility, and install a new management information system. In November it established a presence in mainland China and Hong Kong and expanded its Miami facility further. In December Brightpoint entered the Philippine, Malaysian, Singapore, and Taiwan markets for the first time. As the year drew to a close, Brightpoint announced the acquisition of the British firm Technology Resources International Ltd., which became part of a new operation, Brightpoint International Ltd. Headquartered in Manchester, England, it would conduct all Brightpoint's sales and marketing activities outside North and South America.

Meanwhile, the cellular phone industry was changing almost as rapidly as Brightpoint's efforts to keep up with it. New lightweight phone designs and the introduction of a new generation of digital cellular technology called PCS (personal cellular service) were beginning to fuel a booming phone replacement market as consumers began to substitute their older phones for the latest technology. New battery-less plug-in phones and long-life lithium ion batteries were giving Brightpoint new products to add to its line of accessories, and as cell phone service and equipment prices fell the consumer cell phone user was replacing the "power user" as the typical buyer, unleashing new demand for new phone styles, colors, features, and accessories. By the end of 1995, Brightpoint's sales had surpassed $260 million, and international customers in thirty-five countries were now accounting for 27 percent of its sales. Of Brightpoint's 6,000 customers, Nokia, BellSouth Cellular Corporation, Motorola, and AT&T Wireless Services were now accounting for 58 percent of its product purchases. On the strength of Brightpoint's 91 percent return on equity, *Forbes* magazine ranked it among the top three "Best Small Companies in America" in 1995.

The year 1996 was Brightpoint's best ever. Distributors were handling 30 percent of the cell phones and accessories being sold by the industry, with the remaining 70 percent shipped by the phone manufacturer to the service carrier or directly to retail stores like Radio Shack and Office Depot. Laikin wanted a piece of the retail pie too and announced in March that Brightpoint would be performing the repackaging and preprogramming of the "Cellular to Go" phone products marketed by U.S. Communications, Inc. in such mass retail outlets as Target, Kmart, and CompUSA. Brightpoint also announced that its own branded line of cell phone accessories named Brightlink would be sold in mass market retail outlets around the United States. Moreover, in 1996 Brightpoint agreed to provide the inventory management, order fulfillment, and packaging and telemarketing services for a new joint venture named Wireless LLC formed with paging service provider Metrocall Inc. and wireless developer America Unplugged of South Carolina. Finally, in late 1995 Brightpoint expanded its participation in the "Cellular to Go" venture by adding the Michigan chain Meijer, Inc. to its growing list of retail customers.

The year's biggest move, however, was the acquisition in early June of Allied Communications, Inc., the fourth-largest cell phone distributor in the United States and one of Brightpoint's sharpest competitors. In exchange for $42 million of Brightpoint stock, Allied added $150 million in sales to Brightpoint's kitty and vastly expanded its U.S. and Latin American presence. As Howell explained, the acquisition—which transformed Brightpoint from the third-largest to the second-largest U.S. cell phone distributor—gave the company more "purchasing power and financial stability, as well as more infrastructure." It also fit neatly with Brightpoint's new focus on retail sales, which Allied had specialized in. Now, Howell continued, "we can offer dealers one-stop shopping and speed of delivery." Of the hundreds of distributors that once crowded the wireless equipment distribution market, only five remained.

The feverish growth continued as the year wore on. Brightpoint secured a beachhead in the new PCS digital cellular technology standard by becoming the sole distributor of PCS phone equipment for BellSouth Mobility DCS in three southern states and won a contract with Omnipoint Communications Inc., the fifth-largest PCS operator in the United States, to provide phone packaging, inventory management, and order fulfillment services for Omnipoint's market of 40 million potential PCS customers. Finally, Brightpoint further consolidated its international strategy by acquiring distributor Hatadicorp Pty. Ltd. of Sydney, Australia, to form Brightpoint Australia Pty. Ltd. and increasing its ownership of Brightpoint International Ltd. to 100 percent.

Despite rapid growth, by 1997 the best days for Brightpoint and the cell phone industry at large seemed to lie ahead. The growth in U.S. cellular use was expected to continue at 20 percent annually, and the percentage of the U.S. population with cellular phones was expected to grow from 15 to at least 40 percent by 2002. Less than 1 percent of the potential international cellular market had been tapped by 1996, and the number of international subscribers was expected to top 180 million by the year 2000. By moving toward a fifty-fifty mix of international and domestic business, Brightpoint was poised to reap the benefits of this global growth, and analysts were predicting that its sales would break $1 billion by the end of the century.

Principal Subsidiaries

Brightpoint International Ltd.; Brightpoint Latin America.

Further Reading

"Agreement Signed to Buy Allied Communications Inc.," *Wall Street Journal*, January 24, 1996, p. A6.

Andrews, Greg, "Laikin Makes the Right Calls," *Indianapolis Business Journal*, February 19, 1996, p. 11A.

Cleary Gull Reiland & McDevitt, "Brightpoint, Inc.," stock report, Milwaukee: Cleary Gull Reiland & McDevitt Inc., November 18, 1996.

Cowen and Co., "Brightpoint, Inc.," stock report, Boston: Cowen and Co., November 16, 1995.

Dinnen, S. P., "Analysts Expect a Lot from Brightpoint," *Indianapolis Star/News*, October 28, 1996.

Galarza, Pablo, "Brightpoint: Cell Phone Peddler," *Financial World*, January 30, 1996, pp. 22–23.

Hancock Institutional Equity Services, "Great Lakes Review: Brightpoint, Inc.," stock report, San Francisco: Hancock Institutional Equity Services, January 4, 1996.

Heiken, Norman, "Dietrich, Laikin Bring Home Big Recognition," *Indianapolis Business Journal*, January 1, 1995, p. 10A.

Legg Mason Wood Walker, "Brightpoint, Inc.," stock report, Baltimore: Legg Mason Wood Walker, July 11, 1996.

Lynch, Jones and Ryan, Inc., "LJR Great Lakes Review: Brightpoint, Inc.," stock report, Cleveland: Lynch, Jones and Ryan, November 4, 1996.

McDonald and Company Securities, Inc., "Brightpoint, Inc.," stock reports, Cleveland: McDonald and Company Securities, Inc., July 2, 1996, and November 14, 1996.

NatCity Investments, Inc., "Brightpoint, Inc.," stock report, Indianapolis: NatCity Investments, Inc., March 29, 1996.

"Omnipoint Communications Inc. Selects Brightpoint, Inc. For PCS Equipment Distribution," *PR Newswire*, September 17, 1996.

Perrone, Ellen, "Cell Firm Makes Overseas Push," *Indianapolis Business Journal*, December 25, 1995, p. 8A.

Rauscher Pierce Refnes, Inc., "Brightpoint, Inc.," stock report, Dallas: Rauscher Pierce Refnes, Inc., March 7, 1996.

"Research Reports: Brightpoint, Inc.," *Barron's*, January 29, 1996, p. 53.

"Research Reports: Brightpoint, Inc.," *Barron's*, February 19, 1996, p. 50.

Sands Brothers and Co., Ltd., "Wireless Telecommunications Distribution and Value-Added Services Industry," stock report, New York: Sands Brothers and Co., Ltd., September 19, 1996.

Schneider, A. J., "Brightpoint Offering Fueled by Fast Growth," *Indianapolis Business Journal*, January 1, 1995, p. 13A.

——, "Wholesale Reaches 'Bright Point' in History," *Indianapolis Business Journal*, September 11, 1995, p. 4.

Silberg, Lurie, "A Wider Reach in Cellular," *HFN*, April 29, 1996, pp. 71, 75.

"Wireless: Brightpoint, Inc. Announces India Wireless Product Venture," *Cambridge Telecom Report*, 1995.

—Paul S. Bodine

British World Airlines Ltd.

Viscount House
Southend Airport
Essex
SS2 6YL
United Kingdom
44 (0) 1702 354435
Fax: 44 (0) 1702 331914
Web site: http://www.avnet.co.uk/ginsberg/air-bwa

Private Company
Incorporated: 1946 as Silver City Airways
Employees: 400
Sales: £45 million (1996)
SICs: 4516 Air Transportation, Scheduled; 4522 Air
Transportation, Nonscheduled

British World Airlines Ltd. has distinguished itself as an important regional airline. Its record of scheduled and charter service covering the far reaches of the British Isles, the British Empire, and beyond, in spite of the vagaries of its weather and the economy, has earned it a dedicated following of corporate and consumer clients. BWA joined an elite club of industry survivors upon its golden anniversary in 1996.

A Postwar Launch

Silver City Airways, headquartered in the airfield at Langley, was incorporated on November 25, 1946. Air Commander G. J. Powell served as managing director. The new airline took the nickname of the town of Broken Hill in New South Wales, Australia, where Zinc Corporation, one of the company's owners, operated mines. Although the link to Australia was to some extent the company's raison d'etre, the company's maiden voyage was a round trip to Johannesburg.

Having survived a tedious air war, British civilians were ready to fly again after WWII. However, nationalization curbed the role of independent carriers, until it became apparent that British Overseas Airways Corporation could not hope to restore routes to pre-war levels.

Silver City Airways bought three new four-engined Avro Lancastrians, the civil version of the Lancaster Mk.3 heavy bomber, which comprised the company's entire fleet at the time. After providing for a crew of four, Silver City fitted the plane with 13 passenger seats. Demobilization made crewmen familiar with the plane available. The Lancaster had carried a larger payload than any other aircraft in Europe; this and its high speed (over 250 mph) made it a likely choice. This aircraft remained in service with Silver City only until 1949. The company acquired three additional military transports in 1947. These were the Douglas Dakota III (known in the rest of the world as the civil DC-3 or military C-47); they were slated for shorter flights.

In 1947, the company relocated to Blackbushe as the growth of Heathrow Airport forced the airfield at their former home to be closed. In the same year, Silver City leased its first Bristol Freightmaster (originally known as the Type 170 or Wayfarer), which had been developed as a kind of giant bush plane for the RAF's Pacific operations. In its passenger configuration, it was called the Wayfarer and seated 32. Along with one of the Dakotas, it was dispatched by Silver City in a memorable mission to airlift Hindu refugees from Pakistan. After this successful trial, four were called into service. The airline participated in another significant operation when it supplied three of its Freightmasters to the Berlin Airlift.

Silver City performed the first cross channel car ferry operation with the Freightmaster. The 42-mile, 25-minute flight from Kent's Lympne Airport to Le Touquet in France took place on July 13, 1948. At the time, ferrying by sea was a tedious experience. The project generated a great amount of interest and in its first summer, the seasonal (and beginning the next year, scheduled) service ferried 180 vehicles; in 1949, over 2,500 (including a handful of motorcycles and bicycles) were carried.

The Mk 32, first delivered in spring 1953, increased Freighter's capacity to three cars and 23 passengers. Nearly 40,000 vehicles were ferried this year; the figure had grown to 70,000 by 1958. Nevertheless, other still larger cargo craft were examined, including the French Deux Ponts and the Blackburn Beverly.

New routes across the Channel were added, as well as service to Stranraer and Belfast in Ireland. One-way fares for all these flights were about £7 for vehicles and £2.50 for passengers. Silver City's grass field at Lympne could not sustain so many flights, and alternative operations were moved first to Southend in Essex and then, in 1953, to West Malling. The company built its own airport near Lydd, Kent, called "Ferryfield." Operational in July 1954, it was the first civil airport to be built after WWII. The company's headquarters remained at Southend, however.

In the late 1950s, Zinc Corporation sold the company to the British Aviation Services Group, a subsidiary of the P&O Shipping Group which traded under the name Britavia. The operations of Air Kruise, another acquisition, were taken over by Silver City in 1958. BASG had acquired the northern carriers Lancashire Aircraft Corporation, Manx Airlines, and Dragon Airways.

Amalgamation in the 1960s

In 1962 British United's holding company, Air Holdings, bought British Aviation Services, Silver City's parent, in a move to concentrate resources in the face of increased competition from surface ships. By the end of 1962, all Silver City planes were either repainted with British United colors or retired.

British United had been derived from several companies. In 1947, Freddie Laker had founded Air Charter and Aviation Traders at Croydon. They were the other antecedent of British World Airlines. In 1951 Air Charter bought Surrey Flying Services and Fairflight.

The Belgian national carrier SABENA had formed an agreement with Air Charter in 1957. Air Charter's cross channel freighter service was known as the Channel Air Bridge at the time. In 1959, the Airwork Group took over Air Charter, and on February 25 the Channel Air Bridge was reorganized as a company unto itself. In July 1960, the Airwork Group itself merged with Hunting Clan to form British United Airways.

The combination of British United Airways and Air Charter was known as British United Air Ferries (BUAF). The air ferries segment finally began to falter in 1964, losing some business to newly introduced hovercrafts. Interestingly, after a general strike in France and an outbreak of foot and mouth disease in Britain smote profits in 1968, the company set up a hovercraft ride over a grass field near its airfield at Lydd in order to attract nearby vacationers.

On October 1, 1967, BUAF became known as British Air Ferries (BAF). By this time, the company only controlled 5

percent of the car ferry market, compared to 27 percent five years earlier. It could no longer offer lower prices than sea carriers, although faster service seemed to ensure a niche. BAF's last car ferry occurred on New Year's Day, 1977. A similar downturn had reached the scheduled services in the early 1970s.

New Blood in the 1970s

T. D. "Mike" Keegan, who had founded Trans Meridian Air Cargo, bought a controlling interest in BAF in 1971. A former RAF Flight Sergeant, the energetic and strict Keegan was more visible than previous leadership.

The company's engineering unit, BAF Engineering, established in 1973, began to produce a series of unique products. Hawke Aircraft Parts produced a race car, ostensibly to promote BAF's lagging car ferry business, and produced a luxurious motor home known as the BAF Land Yacht. Only one example of each were made. These projects were in addition to the unit's role maintaining BAF's aircraft.

In late June 1977, Keegan sold Trans Meridian Air Cargo (but not BAF) to the Cunard Shipping Company for £3.4 million. Around the same time, BAF bought seven Heralds turboprops from the Royal Malaysian Air Force, one of the only sources for the reliable aircraft. The decade, which had begun with declines in ferry and passenger flights, ended with a whimper. At the beginning of 1979, British Island Airways took over several routes and aircraft from BAF, who laid off about 40 administrative employees.

Different Aircraft, Different Owners in the 1980s

In the early 1980s, BAF purchased most of the Vickers Viscounts owned by British Airways. As it did with the Herald, BAF lauded the turboprop's lower operating costs compared to the jets that most carriers used on international flights. At the same time, the company announced its intention to buy several of the new British Aerospace BAe 146 jet airliners for predicted service to southern Germany and France. As a result, the aircraft maker painted one of the test planes in BAF colors. However, the next BAe 146, a combination cargo/passenger variant, did not join the fleet for another eight years.

In 1983, Keegan sold BAF's commercial flying operations to the Jadepoint investment group for £2 million. Eventually all of BAF's flying operations were obtained by Jadepoint, as well as the Viscount travel marketers. Jadepoint soon acquired BAF Engineering as well, which was subsequently dubbed Jadepoint Aircraft Engineering for the next five years before resuming its prior identity.

In April 1983, the new owners established a one-plane operation, Jersey Air Ferries (JAF), in the Channel Islands. However, the JAF identity only lasted the summer. In 1983, Jadepoint bought five-year-old Guernsey Airlines from the bankrupt Inter City Airlines. The purchase gave BAF several new scheduled routes.

The company's experience in chartering to North Sea oil companies began shortly thereafter. It devoted two Viscount 800 turboprops, including one stand-by, for the four flights a day between Aberdeen and Sumburgh, which carried over 5,000 passengers a month. While BAF lauded the Viscount's low operating costs, customers enjoyed the plane's spaciousness.

In late 1983 Jadepoint entered the coach/air tour business with its "Skyrider" venture. Combination coach/air tours allowed British vacationers to holiday on the sunniest coasts of Europe on modest budgets. BWA had charted flights for inclusive tours—combination air/rail/coach packages—since the 1950s, when the packages were dubbed "Silver Arrow" services. However, their scope did not extend far beyond the Channel, only to Brussels or Paris.

In the mid-1980s, the company's aircraft leasing business produced £4 million a year in turnover. The company's first scheduled international service, from Gatwick to Rotterdam, began in 1985. However, administrative hindrances on the part of the Dutch caused the effort to be terminated two years later.

In 1987, a new base was established at Southampton to service Channel Islands routes. However, BAF began to show signs of a cash shortage, which resulted in the sale of Guernsey Airlines to Aurigny Aviation Holdings. It also announced the sale of some of its economical Viscount turboprops, and the discontinuation of the last of its own scheduled services (although it covered some routes for Virgin Atlantic).

These measures were not sufficient to stave off the company's going into Administration (British bankruptcy protection) in January 1988 due to the financial difficulties of its parent company, Jadepoint. The accounting firm Touche Ross managed the company during this period. However, the airline continued to produce a profit, as it always had, and picked up new contracts with Federal Express and Higgs Air Agency, the newspaper distributor.

A Shining Gold Anniversary, to 1996 and Beyond

Within a year Mostjet Ltd. was formed to purchase the assets of the company; Mostjet also acquired the assets of Baltic Airlines, also based at Southend. Ian Herman served as chief executive of this enterprise. However, BAF did not formally emerge from Administration until May 1989. It was the only British airline to ever accomplish the feat.

BAF planned to expand, and in 1991 it picked Neil Hansford as a new managing director. He had presided over the growth of TNT Express worldwide, a jet cargo service, for nine years. The company's CEO, Robert Sturman, joined in 1990.

A venture was proposed to operate a 747 freighter in cooperation with the American shippers Evergreen International. However, Evergreen had second thoughts about the project. The "Orient Express" project to link Hong Kong and several other southeast Asian cities also was aborted. To further Mostjet's difficulties, Federal Express canceled its contracts as it departed the European market in 1992.

Although its cargo business faced a very trying time, passenger service was up to an extent that the company briefly leased two Boeing 727s from Yugoslav Airlines before UN sanctions involving the combatants in the Balkans scuttled that deal. Two Adria Airways McDonnell Douglas MD-82s replaced them for the summers of 1992 and 1993.

Mostjet Ltd. was renamed British World Airlines Ltd. (BWA) on April 6, 1993. The new name replaced that of BAF as well, and the company executed a thorough redesign of its corporate image, including a sleek new leaping lion logo, and a new motto: "Chartering Excellence." BAF Engineering retained its name, however, for another couple of months before taking on the title "World Aviation Support" (WAS). Although WAS had expanded its expertise to cover maintenance duties for aircraft ranging from small piston-engined planes to large airliners, the company's specialty lay in servicing British Aerospace BAe 146 and One-Eleven types, both of which BWA also operated in its own flying operations.

BWA's marketing objectives continued to place a high priority on passenger flying, which was worth 70 percent of the company's business. Neil Hansford vacated his position as managing director at the end of 1993 in order to found the short-lived Euro Direct airline. Also in 1993, BWA opened the first scheduled route between Britain (Stansted) and Romania (Bucharest) by a British carrier in ten years. Although the service was popular, it was canceled after a year due to low margins. BWA won a £4 million a year contract ferrying British military personnel to and from bases in Germany in 1993.

BWA's performance for regular clients such as the Parcel Force and the Air Travel Group continued to earn it commendations and repeat business. It also supplied aircraft to larger carriers, such as Virgin, British Airways, and SABENA of Belgium, in times of peak demand. Profits in 1995 were £1 million on a turnover of £35 million.

In November 1995, its Shell Oil North Sea contract was renewed in the face of fierce competition as the airline committed to the purchase of new ATR 172 turboprops to replace its aging Viscounts, most of which continued to serve as freight carriers. The new turboprops consumed much less fuel per hour. The company has donated examples of its Viscount and Herald turboprops to aviation societies in England.

The thrust that pulled the company out of bankruptcy seems likely to propel it into the next half-century and beyond. Each decade seems to bring a new challenge to the company—new ownership, new aircraft types, and new markets—and BWA has repeatedly shown itself capable of rising to the occasion.

Principal Subsidiaries

World Aviation Support Ltd.

Further Reading

"A Short History of British World Airlines," http://www.avnet.co.uk/ginsberg/air-bwa/hist-bwa.htm.

Reed, Arthur, "New Horizons at 50," *Air Transport World,* March 1996, p. 93.

Wright, Alan J., *The British World Airlines Story,* Midland: England, 1996.

——, "British World's Golden Year," *Air International,* May 1996, pp. 268–274.

—Frederick C. Ingram

Brookstone®

Brookstone, Inc.

17 Riverside Street
Nashua, New Hampshire 03062
U.S.A.
(603) 880-9500
Fax: (603) 577-8005
Web site: http://www.streetlink.com/bkst

Public Company
Incorporated: 1973
Employees: 2,000
Sales: $196.3 million (1996)
Stock Exchanges: NASDAQ
SICs: 5399 Miscellaneous Merchandise Stores; 5961
    Catalog & Mail-Order Houses

Brookstone, Inc. is a retailer of diverse and interesting specialty products, many of which are exclusive to the company. It operates approximately 150 retail stores throughout the United States, while also selling its products through the rapidly expanding mail-order channel. Brookstone offers two different catalogs: an updated version of its original ''Hard-To-Find Tools'' collection, much of which is not available in the retail stores, as well as the ''Brookstone Collection'' catalog, which offers the merchandise found in its stores to customers out of range. Brookstone's catalogs generate 15 percent of the company's annual income; the remaining majority is derived from in-store sales.

The Early Years

In the early 1970s, a small advertisement appeared in the classified section of *Popular Mechanics* magazine, offering subscribers the chance to purchase a catalog containing hard-to-find tools. The catalog was targeted at woodworkers, do-it-yourself hobbyists, and collectors, and it contained high-quality items that were both functional and fun. The emergence of this catalog into the public domain marked Brookstone, Inc.'s foundation as a catalog marketer that would soon become known for its unique and useful items.

Circulation of Brookstone's catalog gradually increased throughout the next couple of years. During that time, customers near the company's New Hampshire-based headquarters began stopping in to the distribution center to acquire products on the spot, rather than waiting for shipment to their homes. It became quite clear that the demand for a retail store existed. Therefore, in 1973 Brookstone answered this demand by opening its first store in New Hampshire, near the company's mail-order distribution center.

Throughout the rest of the decade, Brookstone opened a few more retail stores in the New England area, but concentrated most of its efforts on catalog sales, which accounted for 80 percent of the company's yearly revenue. Of the few stores that were opened, most were managed by Brookstone employees who were more proficient in selling material out of the catalog than in working effectively on the sales floor. Furthermore, much of the merchandise found in Brookstone's catalogs did not lend itself well to the store environment, in that it did not effectively capture any more customers than those who already received the catalog and just happened to live nearby.

Retail Expansion into the 1980s and 1990s

Entering the 1980s, Brookstone decided that, for its stores to become more profitable, they would have to begin offering other types of merchandise not available in the catalog. Broadening from the hard-to-find tools designation, the company's stores began featuring all sorts of interesting and ingenious products, most of which were exclusive to Brookstone. New products appeared in the areas of leisure, games, massage, travel, and audio. As the widened range of product offerings gained popularity, Brookstone started opening more stores and the difference in sales figures between the catalog and the stores began to even out.

The company was still in a critical stage, however, in that it needed to boost revenues to cover its expansion expenses. In 1986, Brookstone was purchased by company insiders with the hope that taking on full financial responsibility would facilitate greater involvement in making the company more lucrative. Unfortunately, the company's stores still were not generating

---

Company Perspectives:

Brookstone is a nationwide specialty retailer recognized by its customers as a leader selling functional products, distinctive in quality and design. These products will make our customers' lives easier, better, more enjoyable, more comfortable or more fun. Brookstone stores focus on dramatic storewide themes, product demonstrations and compelling displays to encourage customer interaction with the product. Brookstone markets to upper-moderate and better income customers who appreciate quality, value and design that fulfill their personal and gift-giving needs.

---

enough profits to warrant the money being put into their expansion, and thus Brookstone had trouble dealing with the debt incurred from the leveraged buyout. Although overall sales figures were increasing each year, actual income plummeted and the company began losing substantial amounts of money. For example, in 1987 the company posted record sales of $93 million, while its actual income was −$9.7 million.

The negative earnings trend continued until 1990, when CEO Merwin Kaminstein began to renegotiate a deal with Brookstone's creditors that would help put the company back on a profitable path. He also researched the company's sales and started eliminating merchandise that was not selling well. The following year, Brookstone's stores underwent a major remodeling project, which focused on gaining more female customers and on cutting long-term costs. The stores' dark mahogany decors were replaced with a lighter veneer in an attempt to eliminate the "men's clubhouse" feeling within each location. Furthermore, adjustable shelving units were used in a manner that allowed for future change and flexibility, while also offering increased display space and a less crowded atmosphere for shoppers.

These efforts helped Brookstone survive the worst U.S. retail sales year in three decades, and for the first time in years the company achieved a positive income of $4.9 million from $104.6 million in 1991 sales. But Brookstone did not rest on that achievement, knowing that it still had to handle debt from the years of losses. In early 1992, the company drastically cut back its computer programming staff to save money, after deciding to upgrade the computer system used for retail sales. The system used at the time had been designed to handle the mail-order segment of the business, but was not equipped for the steadily increasing needs of the retail scene. The new system used existing software programs, which rendered Brookstone's programmers unnecessary.

Use of the new system helped the company save approximately $1 million annually and further separated the mail-order and retail businesses. The new computer system was an important addition for Brookstone, which needed a means of keeping up with a frenzied three-month period of booming sales surrounding each Christmas. Typically, the company was known to ride out a lull in sales for nine months out of each year and then achieve almost the entire year's earnings when bombarded with holiday shoppers.

The Mid-1990s and Beyond

In 1992, Brookstone began testing a new sales avenue when it opened five sales kiosks during the holiday season in shopping malls where Brookstone stores were already located. The kiosks were free-standing sales "booths" that featured a limited selection of Brookstone merchandise. Designed to capture shoppers as they walked by in the mall, these kiosks opened on November 1 and operated until the day after Christmas. After five were tested in Brookstone's stronger markets and were found to be successful additions, the company increased the number in operation each year thereafter.

By 1993, the company's sales had jumped to $143.7 million and management was enjoying the largest profits in history. That March, Brookstone entered the public arena again, selling shares of its stock for $10.50 each. After only four months, that figure had increased dramatically and shares were trading on NASDAQ as high as $12.63. Brookstone's recovery seemed to be sticking.

Ironically, the successful recovery that Brookstone achieved was due mainly to its retail segment, which originally had been the source of its problems. But by 1993, the company was operating approximately 100 stores across the United States, which were generating a huge 85 percent of the annual revenue. Its only remaining problem arose when it decided to circulate a new version of its catalog. In addition to the hard-to-find tools catalog, Brookstone started sending a catalog containing its retail items to areas of the country that were not served by a nearby store. Because of this addition, the company began to experience a need for access to retail merchandise for the catalog segment (and vice versa), but the two computer tracking and distribution systems were almost completely incompatible.

In 1994, Brookstone constructed a 200,000-square-foot distribution center in Mexico, Missouri, which was designed to handle all merchandise for both divisions of the company: retail stores and mail-orders. The company also switched all distribution to the United Parcel Service (UPS), which eliminated confusion that had arisen with the previous use of multiple carriers and methods. The across-the-board switch to UPS was also a benefit for mail-order customers, who began receiving orders faster and at no additional cost. Second-day air became standard delivery. Brookstone realized this was an important customer service tool, because most of its merchandise was classified as "non-essential" and was sold to people buying on impulse who wanted the product right away.

Another addition to Brookstone's customer service procedure came when it was announced that if an item was ever out of stock in a store location, the company would ship it directly to the customer from the distribution center at no cost. The reasoning behind such measures appeared in the 1994 annual report, when Brookstone's management stated: "We realize it is ultimately the customer who employs us. We are dedicated to ensuring complete customer satisfaction." Brookstone further strengthened their management team with the 1994 addition of Michael F. Anthony as president and chief operating officer, while Kaminstein remained as chairman and CEO.

Brookstone, Inc. entered the end of the century well positioned for continued future success. The company was operating approximately 150 stores in 32 different states and in Washington, D.C., as well as more than 100 sales kiosks each November and December. Catalog sales were solid as well, although accounting for only 15 percent of the company's total revenues. Having grown from a catalog advertised as ''for sale'' in small print in the back of another magazine, Brookstone had become a multimillion dollar enterprise made up of two separate businesses with a common theme: unique and interesting products that are both functional and fun for the customer. Operating on that basis, Brookstone seemed to be poised for unlimited future growth.

Principal Subsidiaries

Brookstone Company, Inc.; Brookstone Stores, Inc.; Brookstone Purchasing, Inc.; Brookstone Properties, Inc.; Brookstone By Mail, Inc.; Brookstone Holdings, Inc.

Further Reading

Bowman, Robert J., ''Putting the Pieces Together,'' *Distribution,* September 1994, p. 52.
''Companies To Watch: Brookstone,'' *Fortune,* August 23, 1993, p. 81.
Lindquist, Christopher, ''Changing the Game at Brookstone,'' *Computer World,* January 27, 1992, p. 77.
''New Fixtures Redefine Brookstone Image,'' *Chain Store Age Executive,* October 1981, p. 70.
''System Boosts In-Stock Positions at Brookstone,'' *Chain Store Age Executive,* November 1994, p. 42.

—Laura E. Whiteley

The Buckle, Inc.

2407 West 24th St.
Kearney, Nebraska 68847
U.S.A.
(308) 236-8491
Fax: (308) 236-4493
Web site: http://www.buckle.com

Public Company
Incorporated: 1948 as Mills Clothing, Inc.
Employees: 3,000
Sales: $206.4 million (1996)
Stock Exchanges: NASDAQ
SICs: 5611 Men's & Boys' Clothing Stores; 5621
   Women's Clothing Stores

Based in the north-central United States, The Buckle, Inc. is one of the leading retailers of medium-to-better-priced casual wear for men and women. Buckle outlets, which average approximately 4,600 square feet, are positioned within college towns and upscale shopping malls in metropolitan areas containing populations of between 20,000 to 250,000 individuals. The company's eye-catching blue, triangular logo is recognized throughout more than half the country, appearing on storefronts and on shopping bags containing a wide variety of brand-name denims, shirts, outerwear, shoes, accessories, and other sportswear. With its attention to personal customer attention—shoppers who enter Buckle stores are referred to as "guests" rather than customers—The Buckle has gained a strong base of customer loyalty in a highly competitive industry. Services such as free alterations, free gift-wrapping, and layaway options have enhanced its balanced product mix and have led to the repeat traffic that allowed it to prosper in a competitive industry.

The winning Buckle combination—popular brand-name merchandise coupled with a wide range of associated services—is designed to develop customer loyalty among its target market of fashion-conscious 12-to-24-year-olds. Key to the company's merchandising concept is denim, which has traditionally accounted for over one third of annual sales. The Buckle strives to provide its guests with a continually changing array of the most popular casual fashions, both in denim and related fabrics. Through its highly trained, personable sales staff, the company encourages multiple sales through the purchase of coordinating wardrobe components. While the merchandise mix remains relatively standardized from outlet to outlet, The Buckle allows individual stores to tailor inventories around local buying habits through its use of a company-wide computerized distribution system. This system also facilitates efforts by individual salespeople to search other branches for specific garments that are then speedily transferred where required. While slow-moving apparel items are occasionally marked down to make room for fresher stock, The Buckle does not hold storewide off-price sales at any time during the year.

Company Changes with the Times

The Buckle was founded in 1948 as Mills Clothing, Inc. Situated in downtown Kearney, Nebraska, this modest retail men's clothier went through several incarnations before assuming its present name and focus. In 1967 Mills Clothing opened a second store in Kearney under the name Brass Buckle, and the company's second Brass Buckle outlet was opened in Columbus, Nebraska, in 1976. Meanwhile, the original Mills Clothing Store would be renamed Brass Buckle in 1970, adopting the appropriate image as a jeans store offering a wide selection of denim apparel and coordinating shirts. All three outlets were furnished in a rustic motif, with built-in jeans bins and chrome display fixtures. In 1977, now focusing on the marketing of both men's and women's casual clothing, the Brass Buckle opened its first mall location, growing its outlets to 17 by the end of 1981. Company retail outlets would operate under the name The Buckle, Inc. after April 23, 1991.

The company's changing name reflected an adaptive, forward-thinking managerial perspective that allowed it the necessary flexibility to remain on the leading edge of changing fashion trends. To this end, while contracting for a limited number of private-label apparel products with which to stock its stores, The Buckle concentrated on developed relationships with vendors of such popular brands as Levi's, Girbaud, Lawman, Esprit, Guess?, and others that held name recognition with

Company Perspectives:

The Buckle team is focused on the delivery of our mission statement—"To create the most enjoyable shopping experience possible for our guests." We will remain open to constant changes in our business and continue to provide you with a unique specialty store.

the company's target market. In addition, it developed key relationships with both Pepe Clothing Co. and Lucky Brand Dungarees. The Buckle was one of Pepe's largest customers by 1991; in turn, it received quality, fashion-focused apparel at wholesale prices lower than those offered by the more well-known manufacturers.

As the Buckle's outlets spread throughout the inland United States, it developed a centralized, semi-automated distribution system within its corporate headquarters in Kearney. Using an efficient bar-coding system, incoming merchandise was received, sorted and packaged for transit, and reshipped to individual outlets, usually within one business day of receipt. Beginning in 1992, the company also began to warehouse a portion of its total inventory, thereby allowing individual stores to eliminate excessive inventories and replace individual items as needed. Such warehouse and distribution systems provided individual Buckle outlets with an ever-changing stock of products, and consumers with an uncluttered retail environment and a constantly changing array of new fashions. Every trip to The Buckle would reveal something new.

Motivated Teammates Make the Difference

At The Buckle, employees have always been highly valued assets, which may be one of the reasons why staff turnaround has been low. The company is organized around a tiered management system: ten district managers—who also serve as store managers—are supervised by three regional managers, who in turn are supervised by two vice-presidents of sales. Each outlet employs, in addition to the store manager, up to two assistant managers, between one and three full-time salespeople, and a staff of part-time salespeople as store volume and season demands. A seamstress also works on-site at most Buckle outlets as part of a team of dedicated personnel. None of the company's employees are represented by a union.

In addition to recruiting new managers from college campuses, The Buckle has traditionally held with the policy of promoting people from within company ranks: in 1967 Daniel J. Hirschfeld, who had been with the company since 1962, became company president and CEO; while Dennis Nelson, company president since 1991 (when Hirschfeld relinquished one of his two titles and its accordant responsibilities), first joined The Buckle in 1970 as a part-time sales staffer. Within its sales management team alone the company could boast almost 90 years of combined Buckle experience by 1996. The company has continued to rely upon the expertise of its employee team, not only in terms of day-to-day operations at individual outlets, but in overall buying decisions as well. Management was quick

to recognize an understanding of future fashion trends as crucial to the continued health of their business, and has consistently solicited the recommendations of store managers in such decisions due to their daily contact with customers.

Carefully Orchestrated Expansion Since the Early 1980s

The Buckle's strategy for expanding its retail market was to target high-traffic shopping malls near large universities and colleges or in economically vital cities with more than 20,000 residents. Particularly because of its reliance on college-aged consumers, business has traditionally been seasonal, with highest sales levels occurring during the periods November 15–December 30 and July 15–September 1. These two periods have combined to generate approximately 40 percent of the company's sales on an annual basis. The cost of opening a new Buckle location was estimated at $410,000 in 1996, $290,000 of which were construction costs and the remaining $120,000 relegated to starting inventory. Because of such high start-up costs, new store openings were scheduled to coincide with The Buckle's two busiest seasons. Most new stores became profitable within the first year of operation. Marketing to its new and existing customer base was done through both local radio and newspaper and via direct mail using a list generated through The Buckle Club, an in-store signup that boasts over 900,000 "members." Three mailing fliers were sent to customers throughout the course of each year, and a birthday club discount card was mailed during their birth month.

As expansion efforts increased, so did The Buckle's financial leverage. Shadowing a rise in sales from their 1988 level of just under $50 million to $57.4 million by the end of fiscal 1989, the company's net income would jump from $4.3 million to $4.8 million over the same period. And in 1989 The Buckle opened an additional six new outlets, while also beginning to alter its product mix with the inclusion of more higher-end clothing items. This change, coupled with a slight rise in retail prices, would cause the average annual sales per square foot in the company's retail outlets to increase from $221 to $238 over the course of the year.

The Buckle Gives Itself a Shiny New Image, 1990

In 1990 The Buckle got a new look, with redesigned store layouts, enhanced lighting arrays, and new fixtures that presented a more modern, forward-looking attitude. Beginning a five-year renovation schedule to update its older stores to appeal to savvy college-aged consumers, each of the company's newest outlets would boast this new look. A special buying opportunity with one of The Buckle's suppliers helped stock the company's newly designed retail spaces with fresh merchandise, while also contributing to net income by providing the opportunity for a higher-than-usual initial price markup.

Continuing its steady policy of expansion, the company opened new stores and beefed up the sales in existing stores. While newer Buckle locations tended toward higher-end malls that commanded higher costs of occupancy, this increased overhead was largely absorbed by corresponding increases in sales and prices. In tandem with its expansion, the company worked to streamline record-keeping and scheduling, refining its centralized system to increase efficiency among its many outlets and decrease managerial overhead. The decision to sell its internal Buckle credit card business to the Omaha-based First Credit Service Center in 1990 unburdened the company of the headaches associated with the delinquent portion of its accounts receivable balance, although the company would reintroduce a private label credit card in fiscal 1995. The Buckle invested in a new computer system during 1991 that further offset the increasing administrative and managerial functions required of such a large-scale operation. By year end 1990, the company was able to report a net income of $3.8 million on gross sales of $68.9 million.

Males in the 1990s Give Buckle a Boost

In 1987 The Buckle operated 45 stores in the north-central Midwest. Net sales for that year were posted at $38 million; only a year later, during which time the company continued refining its internal processes and opened 15 new outlets, that figure would increase to over $86.7 million, resulting in net income of $4.9 million.

Part of the reason for the company's successful expansion was the changing consumer market. Heading into the 1990s, young men, who had for years relied on blue jeans, T-shirts, and flannel shirts to get them through their college years, were becoming increasingly clued in to fashion. The color palette for menswear blossomed, expanding well beyond the traditional somber hues of navy, forest green and burgundy, and introducing even lavenders and pinks into men's closets. And styles—several layers of coordinating, oversized garments—also dictated an increased demand for menswear. The Buckle's trend of retailing the increasingly popular, and increasingly higher-end, denims and shirts would help boost its annual sales per square foot of retail space 5.9 percent during fiscal 1991 alone.

Company Goes Public in 1992

By the end of fiscal 1991 The Buckle had 5 million shares of stock outstanding, privately held. In early 1992 the company decided to undertake its first public offering, presenting an additional 1.7 million shares on the NASDAQ National Market System. With 89 stores then in operation, the company used the funds generated from the sale of stock to fund further expansion and continue the final three years of its existing store remodeling program.

The year 1992 welcomed the addition of 18 new Buckle outlets and an expanded market area that now included Tennessee, Ohio, Michigan, and Texas. The company also started its "Buckle Kids" line for younger customers, giving each store a more family-friendly orientation. By the end of fiscal 1992 the company was able to post net income of $7.9 million on sales of $112.9 million—a 30 percent jump over 1991 levels.

Through 1994 sales continued their steady climb despite some fluctuations in the Juniors market, moving from $129.6 million in 1993 to close at a year-end 1994 level of $145 million. Store openings also rose, with 27 new Buckle outlets opening for business in 1993 and an additional 16 during 1994. October 1994 witnessed the unveiling of the Buckle's "Primo Card," a frequent-shopper program that rewarded loyal customers with percentage-off savings. Unlike others in the retail fashion industry, The Buckle reported a strong Christmas in 1994, with sales up 7 percent over the five-week holiday shopping season.

By the close of fiscal 1995, with income of $9.8 million, the company's net sales had climbed to $172.3 million, an increase of almost 20 percent over the previous year. Advancements made during that year included the opening of 17 new outlets and The Buckle's inclusion as one of *Forbes* magazine's "World's Best Small Companies in America." The following year would only further the company's reputation as a leader in the field of casual apparel retailing. At the end of fiscal 1996 The Buckle posted $206.4 million in net sales, an increase of over 21 percent from the previous year.

Looking Forward

By 1996, in addition to opening 14 stores and incorporating the state of Wyoming within its growing market area, The Buckle had renovated the last of its existing stores. It now operated 181 stores in 22 states throughout the Midwest region, with plans for continued expansion toward both the East and West Coasts. Company management expected to continue its policy of targeting malls for expansion with higher traffic flows situated in increasingly larger urban areas than the company's historic markets had been. Management's success in choosing location speaks for itself: The Buckle, with its primary mission to act in the best interest of the consumer and a proven ability to adapt to a constantly changing retail climate, has closed only one store since 1982.

Further Reading

MacDonald, Laurie, "Buckled Up: Making It at the Mall," *Footwear News*, August 5, 1996.
"The World's Best Small Companies in America," *Forbes*, November 6, 1995.

—Pamela L. Shelton

Bugle Boy Industries, Inc.

2900 Madera Road
Simi Valley, California 93065
U.S.A.
(805) 582-1010
Fax: (805) 582-5236
Web site: http://www.bugleboy.com

Private Company
Incorporated: 1977 as Buckaroo International
Employees: 1,500
Sales: $481 million (1995)
SICs: 2321 Men's & Boys' Shirts; 2325 Men's & Boys'
Trousers & Slacks; 2331 Women's & Misses Blouses
& Shirts; 2369 Girls' & Children's Outerwear, Not
Elsewhere Classified

Bugle Boy Industries, Inc. is one of the United States' largest privately held apparel manufacturers. In the late 1980s, Bugle Boy became well known for its television advertising campaign featuring the catch phrase, "Excuse me, are those Bugle Boy jeans that you're wearing?" Specializing in moderately-priced casual clothing for young men and women, Bugle Boy markets its products through department stores and specialty retail chains. The company also operates its own factory outlet stores throughout the United States.

The Early Years

The beginnings of Bugle Boy International, Inc. can be traced to the mid-1970s, at which time Dr. William Mow was the head of Macrodata, a computer technology company that he had founded in 1969. Hoping to gain management support, Mow sold control of his company to a conglomerate based in Wisconsin. Unfortunately, he was taken advantage of, and his new owners filed suit against him in court for charges that were later settled in Mow's favor. At that time, however, he needed money to fund a defense for himself, and he decided to begin searching for a new business venture.

In 1976, a friend in the clothing business tipped Mow off that Asian clothing manufacturers and U.S. retailers were al-

ways in need of importers who could handle the transactions from both ends. Mow felt that he was well equipped to handle the position, because of his Chinese background and his ties to family in Taiwan. Therefore, he started an import company called Dragon International, which handled the admittance of apparel and other foreign merchandise into the United States.

A year later, Mow's desire to create things was unsatisfied by his importing business, and he was also uneasy with the instability and financial risk involved. He abandoned Dragon International and decided to join a friend in manufacturing clothing for a new company: Buckaroo International. The newly-formed company began marketing casual clothing for men under the Bugle Boy label.

The 1980s and the Birth of Bugle Boy Industries

Sales were slow for the first few years, partly because Buckaroo International's clothing line was too broad and somewhat overpriced. In early 1981, Mow's partner called it quits. Fortunately, Mow had kept in contact with many foreign suppliers from his time as an importer and, therefore, had an extensive international clothing industry network at his disposal. He also had the services of Vincent Nesi, who had joined Buckaroo International as a merchandiser when the company was formed. Nesi was well versed in sales and merchandising, whereas Mow's strengths lay in the manufacturing and financial aspects of the business.

In 1981, Mow changed Buckaroo's name to Bugle Boy Industries and asked Nesi to act as the company's president. The first thing the two men did was reevaluate the company's focus and address the problems that existed. Realizing that their casual men's clothing was overpriced for the consumer base it was targeting, they decided to focus instead on producing and marketing moderately-priced casual pants for men. This shift toward casual clothing, with a primary focus on men's slacks, helped increase sales dramatically, and soon annual sales had reached almost $10 million.

Beginning in 1983, Bugle Boy attempted to take advantage of growing trends in clothing for the younger generation when it introduced the wildly popular parachute pant to the public. As the name would suggest, the garment was a loose-fitting nylon

---

Company Perspectives:

Behind Bugle Boy's success is a simple philosophy: offer real value and quality to the consumer while maximizing retail profits. It is a philosophy that requires Bugle Boy to provide stylish and comfortable clothing at a moderate price. In a crowded marketplace, it also requires Bugle Boy to create an extremely savvy marketing strategy and to maintain bulletproof manufacturing and distribution operation systems.

---

pant that ballooned out in the top portion, thus creating the illusion of a parachute. Sales of this new item skyrocketed for a period of time, but ultimately the pants proved to be a passing fad. Nevertheless, Mow and Nesi were pleased. Bugle Boy had gained visibility during the parachute pant's run, and stores were more eager to stock its products thereafter.

The following year, sensing the potential gain of tapping into the market for younger buyers, the company unveiled a new division specializing in clothing for boys. This move was followed in 1985 by the introduction of the cargo pant, which was a khaki-like casual pant made of a washed-twill material and featuring oversized side pockets and buttons, snaps, or zippers. The cargo pant, much like the parachute pant, was greeted by tremendous positive reactions from retailers and consumers. It soon became a best-seller as well and solidified Bugle Boy's standing in the industry.

In 1986, Bugle Boy signed its first licensee agreement with another manufacturer, giving it rights to produce young men's and boys' shirts with the Bugle Boy label. A year later, realizing the potential profits to be gained by expanding its product offerings, Bugle Boy introduced its men's division, which included a full line of pants and shirts. These measures helped Bugle Boy's annual sales in 1987 increase to almost $190 million.

It was not until 1988, however, that Bugle Boy introduced what would come to be one of its most well-known and popular items. Jeans were added to Bugle Boy's product list at the same time that the company launched its first television advertising campaign. The ads featured a sexy female model who would stop her sports car to ask a man, "Excuse me, are those Bugle Boy jeans you're wearing?" The spots were an immediate hit with consumers. Also in 1988, Bugle Boy expanded its offerings to include a division of clothing for young women.

Because of Bugle Boy's subsequent sales increase, Mow relocated the company's corporate headquarters to Simi Valley, California, where he constructed a state-of-the-art automated distribution center. Three more foreign licensee agreements were signed, and Bugle Boy opened a retail store in Japan. The company seemed to possess unlimited potential for growth, and in 1990 it posted record sales of more than $500 million.

The 1990s and Beyond

In the early 1990s, Bugle Boy focused on providing the best possible service to its retailers and their customers. In 1991, the company provided Electronic Data Interchange (EDI) service to its retail clients, and the following year it made its Stock Replenishment Program (SRP) available as well. Both EDI and SRP worked to connect each retailer electronically to Bugle Boy's new distribution center, which facilitated faster and more efficient service and made it possible for stores to keep Bugle Boy's products in stock. In 1993, a continued increase in demand dictated that Bugle Boy expand even further its distribution space in Simi Valley.

The company then introduced a new series of commercials to accompany the roll-out of its latest product line, colored denim. Once again, the ads featured sexy female models and catchy phrases, such as, "We know what guys like." Interestingly, Bugle Boy chose to stick with the "sex sells" approach, even in the face of controversy that had been surrounding other companies in relation to their use of women and sex to sell product. Many of Bugle Boy's new advertisements hardly featured the product itself, but instead focused on the women and captions such as, "This is a commercial for Bugle Boy's new color denims. They wanted to show a bunch of male models, but we said showing nothing but beautiful women would work better." Despite the supposed controversy, once again the commercials and the new line were both a huge success.

In the next few years, after experiencing a slight decrease in sales since the high in 1990, Bugle Boy continued to expand both its product line and its capability to provide excellent service to its retailers. Its "Bugle Boy for Her" offerings had grown to include twill and denim bottoms, and cotton pique and yarn-dyed tops, jackets, and shorts. Furthermore, the company continued to license other manufacturers to produce products with the Bugle Boy tag. Van Mar, Inc. was licensed in early 1996 to create a line of Bugle Boy undergarments for women, which would be sold through the same retail channels as the rest of Bugle Boy's products. That same year, Bugle Boy expanded into footwear when it authorized Dynasty Footwear, Ltd. to produce a line of Bugle Boy shoes for men, women, and children.

Approaching the end of the century, Bugle Boy Industries, Inc. was well positioned for continued future growth. Primarily a marketer of men's and boys' casual clothing, Bugle Boy was beginning to enjoy strong recognition among female shoppers as well, as was indicated when the company received a high recognition rating from women in a 1996 jeans survey. Furthermore, late that year, the company expanded its scope once again when it licensed Tiger Accessories to manufacture and market Bugle Boy items for infants and toddlers. With a seemingly unlimited range of licensee options, and with many market areas still untouched, Bugle Boy Industries was poised for success.

Further Reading

Barrier, Michael, "From Riches to 'Rags'—And Riches," *Nation's Business,* January 1991, p. 34.
"Boy Gets Girls," *Advertising Age,* January 13, 1992, p. 6C.
Bugle Boy Corporate Website, http://www.bugleboy.com.
Magiera, Marcy, "Bugle Boy May Go In-House," *Advertising Age,* November 27, 1989, p. 112.

—Laura E. Whiteley

Buttrey Food & Drug Stores Co.

601 6th Street S.W.
Great Falls, Montana 59404
U.S.A.
(406) 761-3401
Fax: (406) 761-3001

Public Company
Incorporated: 1990 as Buttrey Holding Corp.
Employees: 2,652
Sales: $382.1 million (1995)
Stock Exchanges: NASDAQ
SICs: 5411 Grocery Stores; 5912 Drug Stores &
   Proprietary Stores; 6719 Holding Companies, Not
   Elsewhere Classified

The largest operator of food and drug stores in Montana, Buttrey Food & Drug Stores Co. is a seasoned retailer with a century of experience in its home state. During the mid-1990s, Buttrey operated 40 retail stores, 32 of which were combination food and drug stores that offered grocery, dairy, frozen food, meat and produce departments, over-the-counter drugs, health and beauty aids, and general merchandise. In addition to its stores in Montana, Buttrey also operated stores in Wyoming, North Dakota, and Idaho. Merchandise for the company's stores was delivered by a fleet of 28 tractors and 50 trailers, nearly all of which were refrigerated.

Early History

Established in 1896, Buttrey operated as an independent grocery store for 70 years until its acquisition by Melrose Park, Illinois-based Jewel Companies. Jewel's 1966 acquisition of Buttrey initiated a 25-year period during which Buttrey operated under a corporate umbrella. Buttrey's tenure as a subsidiary comprised two eras, the longest of which occurred under the Jewel umbrella. In 1984, the second era began when Salt Lake City-based American Stores Co. acquired the Buttrey chain. Historically, the Buttrey business had been a profitable one, but while under the stewardship of American Stores the

chain's financial health weakened as the communities it served suffered from their own financial difficulties. Positioned primarily in logging communities, Buttrey felt the downturn in the timber industry during the 1980s. By the late 1980s Buttrey regained profitability, but by that time American Stores was suffering from its own ills. American Stores' attempt to resolve its financial difficulties significantly altered Buttrey's future, marking a turning point in the supermarket chain's history.

American Stores' 1988 acquisition of Lucky Stores added a massive new supermarket chain in the company's Southern California region where it already operated a chain of Alpha Beta supermarkets. But the acquisition eventually lead to the sacrifice of American Stores' Buttrey division. The Lucky Stores acquisition saddled American Stores with nearly $3.4 billion dollars in debt. To ease the company's debt load, American Stores' management announced it would merge Lucky Stores and the Alpha Beta chain to realize the cost efficiencies of uniting its two Southern California retail chains. Buttrey, meanwhile, was operating in the wings, supported by its 44 stores and four home centers in Salt Lake City, Utah.

Buttrey was affected, however, when the U. S. Supreme Court entered the picture. In an April 30th, 1990, ruling the Supreme Court announced its decision to block the integration of American Stores' Lucky Stores and Alpha Beta operations. Unable to reduce its debt otherwise, American Stores looked toward divestiture as a means to trim its debt and immediately the Buttrey division emerged as the prime candidate.

Buttrey's 1990 Independence

In May 1990, American Stores announced, ''While Buttrey's sales and earnings have improved significantly, it is not yet performing at the levels desired by the company.'' This proclamation occurred concurrently with the announcement that the company was putting the Buttrey chain up for sale. At the time, the Buttrey chain comprised 44 stores operating in a 1,400-mile swath across five states. There were 26 stores in the company's home state of Montana, seven stores in eastern Washington, another seven stores in Wyoming, and two stores each in Idaho and North Dakota. These stores, which were generating roughly $475 million in sales at the time of the sale, were supported by two warehouses: one in Great Falls, a 285,000-square-foot facility that handled dry groceries, dairy, frozen food, meat, and deli items, and a second 235,000-square-foot facility located in Payson, Utah, that supplied general merchandise, drugs, health and beauty aids, and seasonal goods.

When the Buttrey chain was put on the block in May, industry observers listed two potential buyers: one of the chain's chief rivals, Albertson's, and an employee-led management group. By August, all conjecture about Buttrey's future owner was put to rest when an employee-led management group and a merchant banking firm acquired the chain for $184 million. Headed by Edward C. Agnew, who had been president and chief executive officer of Buttrey since August 1987, the management group acquired Buttrey through a leveraged buyout (LBO) with the financial assistance of Los Angeles-based merchant banker Freeman Spogli & Co., a heavy investor in the U.S. supermarket industry. By October 1990, with the deal completed, Buttrey reverted to private ownership. Commenting on the LBO of Buttrey, Agnew noted to a reporter from *Supermarket News,* "This purchase is the right thing for our customers, the communities we serve, and, especially, our employees. The new ownership structure allows us maximum flexibility to run our business in both the short and long term."

In the wake of the LBO that set it free to determine its own course, Buttrey searched for precisely what its future course would be. Initially, the company endeavored to increase its cash flow, and consequently re-evaluated all merchandise in its warehouse. By December 1990, Buttrey's management had decided to expand through acquisition and boost sales by remodeling many of the chain's stores. Noting as much, Agnew explained, "We made provisions in our capital structure to allow for prudent expansion as well as to complete our remodeling program." Specifically, the company's plans called for the remodeling of 14 stores during the ensuing three years and pursuit of acquisition opportunities that would strengthen its presence in markets where the chain already operated. Buttrey's expansion program, which in 1990 was slated to begin in two or three years, was expected to develop on two fronts. In larger, more populous markets the company intended to establish 45,000 square-foot stores, while 30,000 square-foot stores were selected for smaller communities.

The first store the company had opened since 1985 opened in Cut Bank, Montana, in January 1990 and served as the inspiration for the smaller store concept that was expected to extend Buttrey's presence into smaller markets. The extent of Buttrey's post-LBO plans were curbed by a variety of factors, however. The onset of a national recession and increased competition from mass merchandisers and club store operators conspired to hobble Buttrey's progress during the early 1990s. Although the company continued to remodel its chain of stores, sluggish sales and the debt incurred from the 1990 LBO precluded Buttrey from expanding either through internal means or through acquisition in any meaningful way during the early 1990s. To free itself from some of its financial pressures, the company sought the most expeditious path toward raising funds: converting to public ownership. In December 1991, Buttrey filed with the Securities and Exchange Commission for an initial public offering of 2.9 million shares at $17 per share.

The sale of stock was completed in February 1992 and exceeded expectations. Instead of entering the market at $17 per share, Buttrey's stock debuted at $21 per share, enabling the company to substantially reduce its outstanding debt. Following the conversion to public ownership, Buttrey continued with its ambitious remodeling program, announcing in early 1992 that it would renovate 11 stores in the immediate future at a cost of $735,000 per store. While the company continued to post lackluster sales in the midst of anemic economic conditions and mounting competition, two management changes were effected. In February 1993, Agnew, who had been serving as president and chief executive officer, succeeded Peter J. Sodini as chairman and retained his chief executive officer title. Agnew's promotion made room for Joseph H. Fernandez to move up Buttrey's managerial ladder to president and chief operating officer. Fernandez had began his career in the food industry in 1976 with Buttrey's former parent Jewel before being named executive vice president and chief operating officer of West Caldwell, New Jersey-based Kings Super Markets in 1991. By the end of 1993, Fernandez had assumed the chief executive position at Buttrey, putting in place the management team that would lead the company into the mid-1990s.

Mid-1990s Strategy

After several years of watching sales decline, Buttrey's management attempted to ameliorate the chain's lackluster performance in 1994. In July, the company agreed to sell all six of the stores in Washington to Seattle-based Associated Grocers for $19.2 million, stripping the company of 15 percent of its annual sales volume, or $64.3 million in sales. After shedding the six Washington stores, which the company said had been crimping profits, Buttrey recorded $382.1 million in sales for fiscal 1995, down from the $428.7 million collected in fiscal 1994, and down considerably from the $476 million the company generated when Freeman Spogli made its initial investment in 1990.

After nearly a half decade of allying itself financially with Buttrey, Freeman Spogli was ready to cut its ties to the supermarket chain in 1995. The merchant banker began looking for a buyer for the chain in early 1995 and in mid-April it appeared Buttrey and Freeman Spogli were going to go their separate ways. An acquisition proposal was received by Buttrey, but before industry analysts tired of speculating who the mystery purchaser was, the discussions with the potential buyer were terminated for undisclosed reasons. One month after discussions with Buttrey's unnamed suitor were abandoned, Buttrey sold its Payson, Utah, non-food warehouse, and in June announced it would expand through acquisitions to increase sales. According to Fernandez, increasing the company's sales volume was the number one priority in 1995.

Attempts to boost sales by adjusting prices, increasing the emphasis on selling perishable items, and redefining the company's general merchandising strategy had largely failed, so Buttrey re-dedicated itself to pursuing acquisition opportunities. During the ensuing year, Buttrey achieved only modest gains on the acquisition front, purchasing one store in Cheyenne, Wyoming, from Bismarck, North Dakota-based Dan's Supermarkets. In December 1995, however, encouraging news from Great Falls compensated for the lack of acquisitive activity. In

Great Falls, a Buttrey store featuring a new concept the company called ''Buttrey Big Fresh'' opened on November 15th and recorded immediate success. The concept featured expanded selections of produce, meat, seafood, delicatessen, bakery, and floral goods, and the chain's first food court. The ''Buttrey Big Fresh'' concept fueled hope that the company had at last found a recipe for higher sales.

Entering 1996, the success of the ''Buttrey Big Fresh'' and the ''Food Court at Buttrey'' concepts spurred confidence that the late 1990s would bring meaningful growth to the Montana chain. As the company mapped out its plans for the remainder of the decade, it announced its intentions to open a second in-store food court. Featuring Moose Brothers pizza, Chix fried and rotisserie chicken, Joey Pagoda's Oriental Express, Cinnamon Street gourmet cinnamon rolls, and a coffee bar, Buttrey's second food court was slated to open in March 1996.

After several anxious years of searching for a way to lift sales, the company's management was excited by the success of the ''Buttrey Big Fresh'' and ''Food Court at Buttrey'' concepts. Continued success with the second food court pointed toward the establishment of additional food courts during the late 1990s and, perhaps, solid growth in the future. Considering the company's dominant market position in Montana, any significant increase in the popularity of the Buttrey units would engender the boost in sales the company had long anticipated. Whether this would happen or not depended in large part on the marketing strength of its two new concepts, the long-term success of which remained to be determined in the late 1990s.

Principal Subsidiaries

Buttrey Food and Drug Company.

Further Reading

''Buttrey Cites Success with New Format,'' *Supermarket News,* December 4, 1995, p. 16.

''Buttrey Completes Depot Sale,'' *Supermarket News,* May 15, 1995, p. 62.

''Buttrey Names Agnew Chairman,'' *Supermarket News,* February 22, 1993, p. 6.

Farnsworth, Steve, ''Buttrey IPO to Pay Off Debt,'' *Supermarket News,* January 6, 1992, p. 6.

Harper, Roseanne, ''Buttrey to Open Second Food Court in March,'' *Supermarket News,* January 29, 1996, p. 24.

Tibbitts, Lisa A. ''Sale of Six Units Is Cited in Buttrey Revenue Drag,'' *Supermarket News,* September 4, 1995, p. 8.

Zweibach, Elliot, ''American Puts Buttrey Combo Chain on Block,'' *Supermarket News,* May 21, 1990, p. 6.

——, ''American Sells Off Buttrey to Management,'' *Supermarket News,* August 20, 1990, p. 1.

——, ''Buttrey Food LBO Has Been Completed,'' *Supermarket News,* November 5, 1990, p. 1.

——, ''Buttrey Receives Acquisition Proposal,'' *Supermarket News,* April 10, 1995, p. 1.

——, ''Buttrey's Post-LBO Strategy,'' *Supermarket News,* December 3, 1990, p. 1.

——, ''Buttrey to Seek Acquisitions this Year,'' *Supermarket News,* June 5, 1995, p. 11.

——, ''Buttrey to Sell Washington Stores,'' *Supermarket News,* July 4, 1994, p. 4.

—Jeffrey L. Covell

Canon Inc.

30-2, Shimomaruko 3-chome
Ohta-ku, Tokyo 146
Japan
(03) 3758-2111
Fax: (03) 5482-5133
Web site: http://www.canon.jp/head-e.html

Public Company
Incorporated: 1937 as Precision Optical Industry
    Company, Ltd.
Employees: 72,280
Sales: ¥2.17 trillion (US$21.03 billion) (1995)
Stock Exchanges: Tokyo Osaka Nagoya Kyoto Fukuoka
    Niigata Sapporo Luxembourg Frankfurt
SICs: 3571 Electronic Computers; 3577 Computer
    Peripheral Equipment, Not Elsewhere Classified; 3827
    Optical Instruments & Lenses; 3861 Photographic
    Equipment & Supplies

Although it scarcely predates World War II, Canon Inc. has already become one of the world's leading manufacturers of electronics, principally optical electronics. Year in and year out one of the top 10 companies receiving U.S. patents, Canon has a history of innovation that has brought it a leadership position in copiers, laser and bubble-jet printers, facsimile machines, cameras, and camcorders. In addition to a recent incursion into the production of personal computers, Canon also manufactures and markets binoculars, calculators, electronic typewriters and word processors, and medical, broadcasting, and semiconductor equipment.

Early History

The history of Canon dates back to 1933, when a young gynecologist named Takeshi Mitarai worked with some technician friends to develop cameras; to do so they founded Precision Optical Instruments Laboratory in Roppongi, Minato-ku, Japan. Their first major invention had applications that ranged far beyond the medical field. In 1934 Mitarai and his colleagues developed Japan's first 35-millimeter camera, closely patterned after the German Leica 35-millimeter camera, the industry standard. They named it the Kwanon, after a Buddhist figure representing mercy. In 1937 they incorporated their venture under the name Precision Optical Industry Company, Ltd.

In 1940 Precision Optical made a significant contribution to Japanese medical imaging technology when it developed the nation's first indirect x-ray camera, which played a major role in preventing spread of tuberculosis in Japan. When Japan went to war with the United States, the Japanese economy was entirely given over to supporting the military.

The company barely survived World War II. It was unable to manufacture its mainstay 35-millimeter cameras for the duration of the war, and only Mitarai's tireless efforts kept it afloat in the economic desolation that followed Japan's surrender in 1945. With raw materials rationed and capital scarce, Mitarai had to scramble just to keep his production lines going and the company's finances in order. He also drilled into his workers the importance of producing high-quality products, but his most important move may have been persuading the Allied occupation forces to stock Precision Optical cameras in their post exchanges and ships' stores. This arrangement laid the groundwork for Canon's later success as an exporter; U.S. servicemen bringing their cameras home with them gave the company its first foothold in the U.S. market. In 1947 Precision Optical changed its name to Canon Camera Company, Inc., using a transliteration of the original Kwanon.

Another international breakthrough for Canon occurred in the early 1950s, when news photographers covering the Korean War found that the best Japanese lenses were every bit as good as German lenses. The export market began to open up, and Canon prospered throughout the decade. The company created a U.S. subsidiary, based in New York, in 1955 and two years later it formed a European subsidiary, Canon Europa, headquartered in Geneva. In 1956 Canon added an 8-millimeter movie camera to its product lines, and in 1959 it became the first company in the world to manufacture an 8-millimeter camera with a built-in zoom lens.

Diversified into Business Machines in the 1960s

By the early 1960s Canon had become the dominant Japanese producer of middle-priced cameras, leaving the higher end of the market to Nikon. The company continued to grow, more than tripling in size between 1959 and 1963. In 1964 it ventured into business machines when it introduced the Canola 130 electronic calculator, the first in the world to use the now-standard ten-key keypad. In 1970 Canon and Texas Instruments produced the Pocketronic, the first all-electronic hand-held calculator. After entering the photocopier market in 1965 with the Canofax 1000, Canon became an innovator in the field when it introduced its first plain-paper copier in 1968. Until that time Xerox had dominated the copier market with its own process, known as xerography. Canon's diversification moves were significant enough to prompt a name change; ''Camera Company'' was dropped from the name in 1969 and the company became simply Canon Inc.

In spite of the company's engineering successes, however, Canon was plagued by weaknesses in marketing strategy in the late 1960s and early 1970s. Although it was a part of the spectacular overall penetration of the U.S. market by Japanese calculator makers, the company failed for the most part to distinguish itself from its competitors. It also frittered away its technical advances by failing to exploit their sales potential before rivals could catch up to them. This problem affected its copier lines as well as its calculators. In 1972 it developed the ''liquid dry'' copying system—so named because it uses plain paper and liquid developer but turns out dry copies—but doubted its own marketing strength and feared that competitors would infringe on its patents. Therefore, instead of selling the system itself, it licensed the technology to other manufacturers, effectively wasting its earnings potential. These mistakes hindered Canon's financial performance, and in 1975 it failed to pay a dividend for the first time since World War II.

New Product Development and Marketing Revitalized in the Mid-1970s

Into this leadership void stepped Ryuzaburo Kaku, the company's managing director. He won approval from Mitarai, who was still chairman and president, to change management and sales practices. Under Kaku, Canon began to streamline its operations and chain of command and market its products more aggressively. In 1976 the company introduced its revolutionary AE-1 35-millimeter camera, which used a microprocessor to focus automatically and set the length of exposure, with an advertising blitz led by television commercials featuring tennis star John Newcombe. ''It was a big gamble because 35-millimeter cameras had never before been advertised on TV,'' Mitarai said, but it paid off handsomely. According to *Fortune*, January 12, 1981, by 1981 the AE-1 had become so popular that one industry analyst called it ''the Chevrolet of the 35mm market.'' Kaku's emphasis on faster new product development led to laser beam printing technology in 1975 and a new retinal camera that made pupil-dilating drugs unnecessary in 1976. In 1977 Kaku was named president of the company, succeeding Mitarai, who remained chairman.

In 1982 Canon introduced the first personal copier, so called because all the essential reproduction components were contained in a cartridge that users could replace themselves. Again, it was accompanied by a massive ad campaign, this time starring actor Jack Klugman. In less than a decade, Canon's salesmanship had undergone a radical change from passive to highly aggressive. When Canon overtook Nikon as Japan's camera sales leader in the early 1980s, former Nikon chairman Kyojiro Iyanaga explained his rival's success by saying, ''We still make the best cameras. Canon just outmarketed us.''

Canon continued to introduce new products in the 1980s to compete effectively in mature markets. Much of its success, however, came in new markets, such as integrated office workstations and desktop publishing systems. Often that meant challenging large companies that were well entrenched in their markets. In 1982 it came out with an electronic typewriter, initiating a one-on-one competition with International Business Machines (IBM). Within a year, it captured 11 percent of that market, while IBM's share shrank from 26 to 17 percent. In 1983 it took on Xerox with a laser printer that offered similar quality at one-third the price. Canon also engaged Ricoh in a rivalry over facsimile machines in the early 1980s and laid the groundwork for a future duel with IBM in the computer business. It began a research push aimed at developing optical integrated circuits for personal computers of the future, and in 1984 Canon Sales started marketing the Apple Macintosh in Japan. Canon also joined with Apple to develop software for the Japanese market. Later in the decade, the company's optical chip efforts paid off when former Apple chief Steven Jobs chose Canon's chips for his new NeXT computer. In 1989 Canon acquired a 16.7 percent interest in NeXT Incorporated, along with the exclusive right to market the NeXT in Asia, for US$100 million.

In the camera area, Canon dropped to the number two position worldwide in 1985 when Minolta introduced the popular Maxxum, whose automated features included autofocus. By the end of the decade Canon was back on top after the 1987 launch of the EOS (electronic optical system) autofocus SLR followed in 1989 by the high-end EOS-1 autofocus SLR.

1990s and Beyond

Canon experienced rapid sales and profit growth from its low-water mark in 1975 through the end of the 1980s. Between 1975 and 1985, its annual sales grew sevenfold, to US$3.3 billion, and its profits showed a twentyfold increase, to US$136 million; by 1989, sales had reached US$8.18 billion and profits hit US$232 million. Following an exceptional year in 1990 which saw a 27.9 percent increase in sales (to US$12.73 billion) and a near doubling in profits (to US$452 million), succeeding years featured slower growth and reduced profits. Profit margins ranged from 1.1 to 1.9 percent from 1992 to 1994 after having ranged from 2.8 to 3.6 percent from 1988 to 1991.

The slowdown was partly attributable to the maturation of some of Canon's key product areas, notably copiers and cameras. The maturation in cameras—especially the SLR cameras Canon specialized in—affected Canon much less severely than other major camera makers (notably Minolta and Nikon), who relied on cameras for a much larger portion of overall sales than Canon did. In 1992, cameras comprised only 19 percent of overall Canon sales (compared to 44 and 43 percent for Minolta and Nikon, respectively), and by 1995 the percentage had dropped to 8.2 percent. Thus, the rapid growth in popularity of compact cameras, which began with Fuji's launch of the QuickSnap disposable camera in 1987 and was advanced by Konica's 1989 introduction of the Big Mini (the first super-compact camera), did not push Canon into the huge losses suffered by Minolta and Nikon in the early 1990s. Still, Canon quickly reacted to the new competition by developing its own compact camera, the Sure Shot, which grew into a full line of nearly a dozen models by the mid-1990s. In the meantime, however, Fuji had passed Canon as the world's top camera maker by 1992.

A larger factor in the 1990s slowdown was the recession in Japan and the appreciation of the yen, both of which affected all Japanese companies but hit the export-oriented electronic giants like Canon especially hard. In response, the company made a major commitment to advance its globalization, in particular by moving production out of Japan—whenever possible to where the products were sold. For example, Canon began to produce bubble-jet printers in Mexico in 1995, then started production of the same in Scotland the following year. The company also aggressively sought out new markets for its goods, setting a goal of increasing Asian-Pacific sales outside of Japan to 10 percent of overall sales, and marketing products to Russia for the first time in 1995 through the Finland-based Oy Canon AB subsidiary.

In the face of these years of slower growth, Canon continued its historic commitment to high expenditures on research and development (averaging about 5 percent of net sales) and risk-taking new product development. Back in 1977 a Canon engineer had accidently invented the bubble-jet printing technology, which Canon then somewhat belatedly marketed successfully in the early 1990s. The BJC-820 full-color bubble-jet printer was introduced in 1992, followed in 1994 by the innovative notebook computer with built-in color bubble-jet printer, a product developed in partnership with IBM. Canon's determination to become a major player in the personal computer field was seen as particularly risky, given the failure of NeXT (which exited the hardware business in 1993) and the highly competitive nature of the personal computer market. Of course, Canon's partnership strategy—which continued in 1994 with another venture with IBM to develop small computers based on IBM's PowerPC chip—was designed to alleviate some of the risk. Nonetheless, evidence existed that Canon was still willing to venture into territory few dared enter, notably its research into

the ferroelectric liquid crystal display (FLCD). Canon planned to invest more than ¥100 billion before seeing any return from its research into FLCD, an integral component to be used in flat, large-sized, high-definition computer and television screens—a projected replacement for the ubiquitous cathode ray tube.

Whether either FLCD or Canon's entry into the PC market would prove as successful as such previous innovations as plain-paper copying and bubble-jet printing was uncertain as Canon neared the 21st century. The company, however, had weathered the worst of the Japanese recession and maintained major shares of the copier, laser printer, bubble-jet printer, and SLR camera markets. This represented a tremendous achievement for less than 70 years in existence, with more Canon success seeming to be in store for the future.

Principal Subsidiaries

Canon Aptex Inc.; Canon Chemicals Inc.; Canon Components, Inc.; Canon Copyer Sales Co., Ltd.; Canon Electronics Inc.; Canon Precision Inc.; Canon Sales Co., Inc.; Canon Software Inc.; Copyer Co., Ltd.; Nagahama Canon Inc.; Nippon Typewriter Co., Ltd.; Oita Canon Inc.; Canon Australia Pty. Ltd.; Canon Finance Australia Pty. Ltd.; Canon Information Systems Research Australia Pty. Ltd.; CEE Canon East Europe Vertriebsgesellschaft m.b.H. (Austria); Canon Benelux N.V./ S.A. (Belgium); Canon do Brasil Indústria e Comércia Limitada (Brazil); Canon Canada, Inc.; Canon Dalian Business Machines, Inc. (China); Canon Zhuhai, Inc. (China); Oy Canon AB (Finland); Canon Bretagne S.A. (France); Canon France S.A.; Canon Photo Vidéo France S.A.; Canon Research Centre France S.A.; Canon Deutschland GmbH (Germany); Canon Euro-Photo Handelsgesellschaft m.b.H. (Germany); Canon Giessen GmbH (Germany); CPF Deutschland GmbH (Germany); Canon Electronic Business Machines (H.K.) Co., Ltd. (Hong Kong); Canon Hongkong Co., Ltd.; Canon Italia S.p.A. (Italy); Canon Marketing (Malaysia) Sdn. Bhd.; Canon Opto (Malaysia) Sdn. Bhd.; Canon Mexicana, S. de R.L. de C.V. (Mexico); Canon Benelux N.V. (Netherlands); Canon Europa N.V. (Netherlands); Canon Finance New Zealand Ltd.; Canon New Zealand Ltd.; Cannor A/S (Norway); Canon Panama, S.A.; Canon Marketing Services Pte. Ltd. (Singapore); Canon Singapore Pte. Ltd.; Canon España S.A. (Spain); Canon Svenska AB (Sweden); Canon S.A. (Switzerland); Canon (Schweiz) AG (Switzerland); Canon Inc., Taiwan; Canon Hi-Tech (Thailand) Ltd.; Canon Engineering (Thailand) Ltd.; Canon Manufacturing (UK) Ltd.; Canon Research Centre Europe Ltd. (U.K.); Canon (UK) Ltd.; Ambassador Office Equipment, Inc. (U.S.A.); Astro Office Products, Inc. (U.S.A.); Canon Business Machines, Inc. (U.S.A.); Canon Computer Systems, Inc. (U.S.A.); Canon Financial Services, Inc. (U.S.A.); Canon Information Systems, Inc. (U.S.A.); Canon Latin America, Inc. (U.S.A.); Canon Research Center America, Inc. (U.S.A.); Canon U.S.A., Inc.; Canon Virginia, Inc. (U.S.A.); Duplifax, Inc. (U.S.A.); FirePower Systems, Inc. (U.S.A.); MCS Business Machines, Inc. (U.S.A.).

Further Reading

Beauchamp, Marc, ''From Fuji to Everest,'' *Forbes*, May 2, 1988, p. 35.
The Canon Story 1996/97, Tokyo: Canon Inc., 1996.

Canon Today 1996, Lake Success: New York, Canon U.S.A., Inc., 1996.

Eisenstodt, Gale, " 'Crazy Is Praise for Us,' " *Forbes*, November 7, 1994, pp. 174–84.

Friedland, Jonathan, "Nothing Ventured . . .: Even Canon's Failed Products Serve a Purpose," *Far Eastern Economic Review*, February 24, 1994, pp. 76, 78.

——, "Out in Front," *Far Eastern Economic Review*, February 24, 1994, pp. 72–75.

Greenberg, Manning, "Canon Runs the Gamut from Video to Home Office," *HFD-The Weekly Home Furnishings Newspaper*, April 9, 1990, p. 150.

Johnstone, Bob, "If Anyone Can, Can Mitarai?," *Director*, July 1995, p. 17.

McCarthy, Joseph L., "Beyond the Box," *Chief Executive*, April 1995, pp. 32–35.

Murata, Taku, "Can Canon Become a PC Player?," *Tokyo Business Today*, January 1995, pp. 43–45.

—Douglas Sun
—updated by David E. Salamie

Cardinal Health, Inc.

655 Metro Place S., Ste. 925
Dublin, Ohio 43017
U.S.A.
(614) 761-8700
Fax: (614) 761-8919
Web site: http://www.healthtouch.com

Public Company
Incorporated: 1971
Employees: 4,800
Sales: $8.9 billion (1996)
Stock Exchanges: New York
SICs: 5122 Drugs—Wholesale; 5047 Medical
    Equipment—Wholesale; 6719 Holding Companies,
    Not Elsewhere Classified

Named for Ohio's crimson state bird, Cardinal Health, Inc. ranks among America's top three wholesale drug distributors, with 36 distribution facilities in 24 states. Under the direction of Robert Walter since 1971, the company has evolved from a rather inconsequential Ohio food distributor into a trend-setting member of the pharmaceutical industry. A steady stream of acquisitions—13 from 1979 to 1995—helped multiply Cardinal Health's sales from $429 million in 1986 to nearly $9 billion by 1995. By mid-decade, Cardinal came within about $1 billion in annual sales of breaking into the top spot, having an estimated 18 percent of the $57 billion wholesale market compared to the 19 percent stakes held by industry leaders McKesson Corp. and Bergen Brunswig Corp.

During the course of its growth spurt, Cardinal diversified from its core wholesale drug distribution business into specialty laboratory and pharmaceutical supplies, computer software, and retail drugstores. While it was not the country's largest drug distributor in terms of sales in the mid-1990s, Cardinal Health did rank highest in terms of market capitalization and profitability. A.G. Edwards investment analyst Donald Spindel asserted that "Cardinal has been the most innovative and the fastest growing. To me, they're really the top company in the industry."

1971 LBO Presages Transformation of Mid-Ohio Distributor

In 1971, just six months after his graduation from Harvard's MBA program, 26-year-old Robert Walter acquired Monarch Foods through a leveraged buyout. Walter hoped to build this small central Ohio grocery distribution company—which he renamed Cardinal Foods—into an industry leader through acquisitions, but soon discovered that he was too late: the market had already begun to consolidate. To make matters worse, Cardinal was compelled to withdraw ten tons of salmonella-infected, prepackaged roast beef mid-decade.

Since consolidation within the wholesale segment of the grocery business was out of the question, Walter attempted to shift his growth strategy, launching Mr. Moneysworth warehouse supermarkets. By the mid-1980s, Cardinal had three Mr. Moneysworth outlets and plans to open stores in Ohio, West Virginia, and Kentucky.

But Walter did not abandon the distribution industry. Rather, he turned to a business segment that was more profitable, more fragmented, and more ripe for consolidation: pharmaceuticals. The company made its first foray into pharmaceutical distribution in 1975, when it acquired Zanesville Distribution. Walter used the proceeds of a 1983 initial public offering to launch an acquisition spree that would gain steam over the next decade. During the 1980s, he targeted relatively small, privately-held distributors in adjacent states and regions for his friendly acquisitions. Reasoning that these local managers knew their markets and would work hard to maintain growth, Walter focused on successful companies with managers he characterized as "the kings in our company" in a 1993 interview with *Forbes* magazine's Reed Abelson. Walter operated Cardinal as a holding company, allowing affiliated companies to continue relatively autonomously. The new subsidiaries brought the parent company geographic growth and economies of scale. He told Abelson that "Knowing what I know now, I didn't know what I was doing. But it worked." Key acquisitions—focused in the eastern United States—included Ellicott Drug Co. (1984); James W. Daly, Inc. (1985); and John L. Thompson Sons & Co. (1986).

Company Perspectives:

With annual sales of almost $9 billion, Cardinal Health is one of the country's leading health care service providers. With its nationwide network of distribution facilities, the company is one of the largest wholesale distributors of pharmaceuticals and related health care products in the country. Cardinal Health has further extended its operational focus to include related businesses with several recent mergers. In fiscal 1996, the company acquired Pyxis Corporation, the largest manufacturer of unique, point-of-use systems which automate the distribution, management, and control of medications and supplies in hospitals and alternate care facilities; Medicine Shoppe International, Inc., the largest franchiser of independent retail pharmacies in the United States; and Allied Pharmacy Service, Inc., one of the largest providers of pharmacy management services to hospitals in the country.

Late 1980s Exit from Grocery Business

Walter gave up on the marginally profitable grocery business in 1988, when he sold the Cardinal Foods, Inc., Midland Grocery Co., and Mr. Moneysworth subsidiaries to Roundy's Inc., a cooperative wholesaler, for $27 million. Instead of declining, Cardinal's annual revenues actually increased by one-third that year, and its net income more than doubled.

In contrast with his entry into the grocery distribution business, Walter's foray into drug distribution proved well-timed, for retail drugstores and hospitals were increasing their purchases from distributors. Cardinal's acquisitions, while relatively small, were indicative of a budding trend toward consolidation in the distribution industry. Mergers and acquisitions shrunk the number of participants in this market by more than half, from 135 in 1984 to 80 in 1989 and less than 60 by 1995. By the end of the decade, Cardinal had accumulated a four percent stake in the $22 billion wholesale drug business. Sales mounted from $429 million in 1986 to $700 million in 1989, while net income grew from $6 million to $9 million during the same period.

Cardinal's profitable growth did not come exclusively from acquisitions. From 1986 to 1989, in fact, the company was able to increase productivity in nearly 80 percent of its operations. Computer automation was an important factor in this program. Cardinal employees developed IBM-compatible software to increase purchasing, inventorying, and distribution efficiency. A company executive told *Financial World*'s Jagannath Dubashi that the AccuNet system "can reduce the administrative costs of [a hospital's] pharmacy operations by as much as 80 percent." AccuNet not only helped Cardinal cut its own operating margins by 20 percent from 1988 to 1991, but also increased its level of customer service, offering its clients automated inventory management and up-to-date drug pricing information. Computer links with customers enabled Cardinal to fill and ship orders within 24 hours of receipt.

Ever-Larger Acquisitions Mark Early 1990s

Cardinal moved steadily up the ranks of the country's largest drug distributors and simultaneously increased its geographic reach in the early 1990s via significantly larger acquisitions. Purchase or perish was the theme in the market that by 1993 was dominated by seven major companies which monopolized 78 percent of the industry's estimated $40 billion sales. The addition of four new subsidiaries moved Cardinal from its bulkhead in the Northeast U.S. into the Mid-Atlantic and Southeastern states.

By the end of 1993 the company was ready to turn westward, but its rapid growth had caught the attention of well-established industry leaders McKesson Corp. and Bergen Brunswig Corp. When Walter made a move to acquire Alabama's Durr-Fillauer Medical, Bergen Brunswig quickly launched a bidding war with the upstart Ohio company. Under pressure from Bergen Brunswig, the price tag shot up from $250 million to $450 million in just four months. Although Walter lost the battle for Durr-Fillauer, he did not leave the contest empty-handed; Cardinal drew five of the target company's top managers to its ranks. Moreover, some industry observers criticized Bergen Brunswig for overpaying and praised Walter's self-control throughout the ego-charged competition.

Walter more than made up for this minor setback with several major acquisitions from 1994 to 1996. The merger of Cardinal and Whitmire Distribution in 1994 added over $2.25 billion in annual sales and made Cardinal America's third-largest drug distributor. With its strong distribution network in the western and central United States, Whitmire was a long-sought piece of Cardinal's nationwide puzzle. The parent company's geographic scope—32 distribution centers across the country—enabled it to compete for bigger business. In 1994, the company signed a $900 million contract to supply mass merchandiser Kmart's nearly 1,700 pharmacies. And in 1995, it earned the right to supply pharmaceutical goods to the 175-store Wakefern grocers' cooperative.

The acquisition of Medical Strategies in 1994 added Healthtouch computerized kiosks to Cardinal's repertoire. These electronic point-of-purchase machines offered pharmacy customers access to up-to-date data on illnesses and treatment options. The kiosks generated income via advertising and promoted featured products with coupons; Cardinal claimed that its more than 1,000 Healthtouch machines "increase incremental sales of the featured products by 20 percent on average."

Cardinal entered the retail drug industry late in 1995, when the parent company traded $348 million worth of its stock for full ownership of Medicine Shoppe International, a pharmacy franchiser with over 1,000 stores. Less than six months later, Cardinal announced its $870-million stock swap for Pyxis, the nation's leading manufacturer of automatic drug dispensing machines used in hospitals. Pyxis subsidiary Allied Pharmacy Management Inc. gave Cardinal entree into the health care information network business. PCI Services, Inc., a pharmaceutical packager, was acquired in July 1996 for $145 million in cash and $56 million of borrowed money. Reflecting on his company's recent activities, Walter noted that "Cardinal has been progressively expanding its business beyond the purely logistical side of drug distribution to providing a full range of value-added information, marketing and educational services to our customers.''

These acquisitions helped make Cardinal virtually impervious to the recession that gripped the country in the early years of the decade. For while customers like hospitals and drugstores—themselves under pressure from managed healthcare plans and other cost-conscious insurers—whittled away at drug distributors' gross profit margins, reducing them from over 17.5 percent in 1960 to 6.5 percent by 1992, Cardinal's increasing share of the market and high level of efficiency helped it maintain consistent growth in sales and profit.

Cardinal has also maintained healthy margins by focusing on the most profitable segments of its business. In the 1980s, for example, the company targeted independent drugstores who could not demand the volume discounts sought by larger chains. But as these retailers began to disappear from the pharmaceutical landscape, Cardinal sought out new profit centers: Pyxis' groundbreaking dispensers, Medicine Shoppe's retail pharmacies, and Healthtouch information systems, for example. Nevertheless, Cardinal was not completely impervious to the cost-cutting pressures that plagued the industry; its gross margins declined from 7 percent in 1992 to about 5.8 percent in 1996.

Fueled by its record-setting acquisitions, Cardinal's sales and net income multiplied rapidly in the early 1990s. Revenues doubled from $874 million in 1990 to almost $2 billion by 1993, then nearly quadrupled to $7.8 billion by 1995. Net income made similar advances, growing from $13 million in 1990 to $34 million in 1993 and $85 million in 1995. Employment more than tripled during this period and Cardinal's distribution centers nationwide increased from 6 to 32. In an early 1995 profile, *Financial World's* Jennifer Reingold characterized Cardinal as ''by far the healthiest'' of the drug distribution industry's five largest companies. Although it was not the sales leader, Cardinal topped the industry in profits and market capitalization. Cardinal Health stockholders—CEO Walter among the largest with about 8 percent of its stock—have been well-rewarded. According to *Forbes* magazine's 1996 analysis of U.S. companies' 10-year total return, Cardinal ranked 25th.

A Look to the Future

Although Cardinal appeared likely to continue its profitable growth pattern into the latter years of the decade, several uncertainties loomed. First, the company's bulk was likely to attract increased attention from antitrust regulators. Cardinal also faced the possibility that its success would make it a takeover target of one of the major pharmaceutical companies. A 48-year-old Robert Walter appeared to be paving the way for his retirement when he hired Abbott Labs' John Kane as president and chief operating officer in 1993. Walter's upcoming (although not necessarily imminent) retirement was another unknown; would the company survive in its highly competitive industry without the leader who guided it to the top ranks?

Principal Subsidiaries

Cardinal Distribution; Cardinal Specialty Companies; Allied Pharmacy Service, Inc.; Medicine Shoppe International, Inc.; Pyxis Corporation.

Further Reading

Abelson, Reed, ''It's My Money,'' *Forbes,* March 29, 1993, pp. 56–57.

Appleby, Chuck, ''Betting Against Health Care,'' *Hospitals & Health Networks,* June 20, 1996, pp. 34–37.

Autry, Ret, ''Cardinal Distribution,'' *Fortune,* June 3, 1991, pp. 104.

Byrne, Harlan S., ''Cardinal Distribution Co.: Acquisitions Carry Drug Wholesaler South and West,'' *Barron's,* November 11, 1991, pp. 47–48.

''Cardinal Health Plans to Buy Drugstore Franchiser,'' *New York Times,* August 29, 1995, p. C3.

''Cardinal to Buy Daly, Drug Wholesaler,'' *Supermarket News,* September 30, 1985, p. 14.

''Cardinal to Buy PCI in Stock Transaction Valued at $201 Million,'' *Wall Street Journal,* July 25, 1996, p. C20.

Dubashi, Jagannath, ''The Tie that Binds,'' *Financial World,* April 30, 1991, p. 66.

Freudenheim, Milt, ''Cardinal Health to Buy Pyxis in Stock Swap,'' *New York Times,* February 8, 1996, p. C1.

Jereski, Laura, ''Cardinal Health, Its Red-Hot Growth Slowing, Defends Its Flighty Price with Wider Margins,'' *Wall Street Journal,* January 16, 1996, p. C2.

Maturi, Richard, and Melynda Dovel Wilcox, ''Small Stocks with Big Ideas,'' *Changing Times,* March 1990, pp. 59–61.

Mehlman, William, ''Cardinal on Cutting Edge of Wholesale Drug Boom,'' *Insiders' Chronicle,* June 11, 1990, pp. 1–4.

Murray, Matt, ''Cardinal Health Takes Pulse of New Arenas for Growth,'' *Wall Street Journal,* February 28, 1996, p. B4.

Pearlman, Andrew, ''Cardinal Distribution: Popping Pills,'' *Financial World,* July 24, 1990, p. 18.

Reingold, Jennifer, ''Cardinal Rule,'' *Financial World,* January 31, 1995, pp. 36–38.

Reitman, Valerie, ''Cardinal Sets Whitmire Deal for $303 Million,'' *Wall Street Journal,* October 12, 1993, p. A2.

Rose, Frederick, ''Bergen Brunswig's Shares Jump 10 Percent on Rumors Cardinal Health May Bid,'' *Wall Street Journal,* February 27, 1995, p. B6.

Siwolop, Sana, ''Cardinal Doesn't Need Any Medicine,'' *Financial World,* September 19, 1989, p. 18.

Speer, Tibbett L. ''Just Say Grow,'' *Hospitals & Health Networks,* August 5, 1996, pp. 34–35.

Ukens, Carol, ''Wholesalers Push Inventory Consignment for Cost Efficiencies,'' *Drug Topics,* July 8, 1996, p. 108.

Vecchione, Anthony, ''Cardinal Health Signing Merger Deal with Pyxis,'' *Drug Topics,* February 19, 1996, p. 25.

Wright, J. Nils, ''Whitmire to Merge with Cardinal,'' *Business Journal Serving Greater Sacramento,* January 31, 1994, pp. 2–3.

Zimmerman, Susan, ''Roundy's to Buy Cardinal Food Unit,'' *Supermarket News,* March 28, 1988, p. 1.

—April Dougal Gasbarre

Catalina Marketing Corporation

<table>
<tr><td>

11300 Ninth Street North
St. Petersburg, Florida 33716-2329
U.S.A.
(813) 579-5000
Fax: (813) 570-8507
Web site: http://www.catalinamktg.com

Public Company
Incorporated: 1983
Employees: 577 (1996)
Sales: $134.2 million (1996)
Stock Exchanges: New York
SICs: 3577 Computer Peripheral Equipment, Not
   Elsewhere Classified

</td></tr>
</table>

Catalina Marketing Corporation, the parent company of the Catalina Marketing Network, was founded in 1983 by five marketing professionals on a trip to Catalina Island. With backgrounds in packaged-goods marketing, retailing, and scanner-based technology, the travelers lamented about the waste and misdirection of coupons; then they thought up an electronic alternative. From its inception in 1983 until 1987, Catalina Marketing consumed $12 million in venture capital and lost $7.7 million. In 1992, however, its store base grew to a comfortable size, and Catalina Marketing's stock became publicly traded at $20.00 per share. Since then, its shares have enjoyed a 148 percent return. Revenues grew from $51.7 million in 1992 to $134.2 million in 1996, and Catalina Marketing was named to *Forbes* magazine's list of the 200 best small companies in America during 1993, 1994, and 1995. "Being recognized by *Forbes* for three consecutive years," said George Off, president and chief executive officer of Catalina Marketing, in 1995, "is a true testimonial to our success in expanding the existing network with new products and channels of trade, and applying our basic technology to bring value to consumers, manufacturers, and retailers. It's evidence of the commitment of all our people to continued growth."

In 1993, the company moved its headquarters from Anaheim, California, to St. Petersburg, Florida. With 20 sales and support offices in the United States and others elsewhere in the world, the company employed 577 workers in the United States, the United Kingdom, France, and Mexico in 1996. Operating units as of 1996 included: Catalina Marketing Services, Catalina Marketing International, Health Resource Publishing, Catalina Electronic Clearing Services, and Catalina Online.

Catalina Marketing Services

Catalina Marketing Services began selling programs to supermarkets and mass merchandisers through the Catalina Marketing Network, the core of the company's services. The network was a proprietary electronic marketing system that utilized Universal Product Code (UPC) labeling and scanning to generate coupons or promotions for retail stores. Catalina's first coupons were considered responsive to consumer behavior and cost efficient because its system offered manufacturers and retailers accurate consumer targeting. The redemption rate of Catalina Marketing's coupons was reported as 9.4 percent compared with 2.5 percent for traditional coupons. Where traditional coupons—newspaper, direct mail, or freestanding inserts—were subject to waste, misredemption, and clutter, Catalina's coupons were more effective and more efficient. Richard S. Teitelbaum explained in *Fortune:* "Landfills of America overflow with Sunday newspaper ad inserts, and research shows that shoppers who actually cash in their Tender Vittles coupons are usually the same brand loyalists who would have bought the stuff anyway. Catalina Marketing lets food companies peek at a customer's shopping habits before they issue coupons—and thus pitch their discounts with surgical precision."

Catalina's network worked as follows: Retail chains contracted with Catalina Marketing for the installation of the Catalina Marketing Network in their stores, whether selected sites, nationally, or regionally. Catalina paid retailers distribution fees based on the coupons generated. Promotional instructions and performance data were sent or retrieved by two hub data processing facilities in the United States. Catalina printed promotions and was paid by manufacturers and retailers for each promotion that was distributed. In an interview with the *Supermarket News* in 1994, George Off, then Catalina's president and chief operating officer, revealed: "The success of our system is that it's simple. There's no hassle for the store."

99

Company Perspectives:

Catalina Marketing Corporation is the leading provider of in-store electronic marketing services. Through its proprietary network, Catalina Marketing provides consumer products manufacturers and retailers with cost-effective methods of delivering promotional incentives and advertising messages directly to consumers based on their purchasing behavior. The Catalina Marketing Network is also used as a mechanism to capture coupon scan data and electronically clear coupons for participating retailers.

Catalina Marketing Corporation offers consumer- and pharmaceutical-product manufacturers and retailers alternative ways to advertise and to issue promotional incentives to consumers based on their established purchasing behaviors. The company also assists these same manufacturers and retailers with long-term marketing strategies to build consumer loyalty, promote goods, or increase brand awareness and sales. In addition, the company captures coupon data and clears coupons electronically for retailers.

Ten years after Catalina Marketing's founding, the network remained the strength of company. Off told *Forbes*'s Matt Walsh in 1994, "Our base business is our best growth opportunity. If you look at what we sold [to manufacturers] last year, we operated at 16 percent of capacity. Good gosh! We'd have to hire trucks to take the money to the bank if we got that up to 30 percent capacity." Key programs of Catalina Marketing in 1996 included Checkout Coupon, Pay-for-Performance, and Checkout Direct.

Catalina Marketing's services started with Checkout Coupon, a program that provided custom coupons delivered to consumers at store cash registers using the store's bar code scanner and controller, Catalina software, databases, and thermal printers. Coupons were generated based on buying patterns of the individual consumer. If a consumer bought a given product, he or she might receive a coupon for the same product or a competitor's equivalent item. The system evaluated scanned data, matched the data to a given promotion, and directed a thermal printer to generate a coupon. Printing continued throughout checkout and was completed at the end of each shopper's transaction. Consumers received their coupons with their store receipts. The system only printed coupons or incentives relevant to the data collected from the scanned UPC code at point-of-sale.

Manufacturers appreciated the directness and potential of Catalina's coupons. One frozen food manufacturer, for example, issued Checkout Coupon incentives over a two-year period to convert consumers of the competition over to its brand and earned a 6.1 increase in market share. In 1992, Wally Meyer reported in a *Frozen Food Digest* article that Checkout Coupon "is a flexible program that can be custom-tailored to address . . . specific marketing goals and strategies. Checkout Coupon eliminates the wasted dollars associated with more traditional forms of couponing because every coupon is placed directly in the hands of the shoppers you want to reach. The Catalina Market-

ing Network is the only coupon verification system in the nation, offering a guaranteed pay for performance. With this system, consumers are rewarded only when they actually purchase the required product or products." In 1996 some of Catalina's clients in consumer-packaged goods included Borden, Campbell Soup, Coca-Cola, General Mills, Hershey, Kraft, Nabisco, Nestle, Pillsbury, Quaker Oats, Ralston Purina, and Tropicana.

Retailers were rewarded for using the network, too, so—from 1991 through 1996—Catalina's network expanded to more than three times as many stores. "The big advantage to us," revealed Kevin Davis, a vice-president of Ralphs Grocery, "is that we can tie in Ralphs' private-label items: If someone buys Oreos, we can give him or her a coupon for Ralphs' milk." In 1991 Catalina issued 780 million coupons through nearly 4,200 supermarkets; by 1996 the Catalina Marketing Network was installed in 10,400 supermarkets—including A&P/Farmer Jack, Kroger, Meijer, and Winn-Dixie—in the top 95 markets and touched 136 million shoppers each week.

Like Checkout Coupon, Catalina's Pay-for-Performance (PFP) program triggered rewards for consumers when they complied with advertised offers; for example, if a shopper bought three items, he or she might get a certificate for one free item for the next shopping excursion. Introduced in 1994, the Pay-for-Performance program became an independent program separate from Checkout Coupon in 1995, just one year after its introduction to the marketplace. From 1994 to 1995, Pay-for-Performance programs increased by 50 percent. Sales volumes for retailers grew anywhere from 20 to 80 percent owing to Catalina's Pay-for-Performance programs. According to Helene Monat, president of Catalina Marketing Services in 1995, "We've seen a boom in the demand for our PFP programs due to the industry's interest in more efficient promotions and incremental volume. Our programs have proven results and a low cost-per-unit moved. The establishment of category exclusivity for PFP programs separate from our Checkout Coupon program is significant because it allows more manufacturers to participate. They can run a PFP program even if Checkout Coupon has been booked for the cycle." Catalina's introduction of Integrated Price Labels in 1994 further supported Pay-for-Performance programs. Integrated Price Labels showed standard retail tag data, plus promotional messages advertising Pay-for-Performance program offered.

Another service, Checkout Direct, was a database marketing program that monitored purchase behaviors of households and delivered incentives, joining Catalina's network with retailers' check cashing or card-based shopper programs. Promotions were then issued based on observed buying patterns and supplemented Checkout Coupon programs with newspaper ads and on-shelf signs, among other promotions.

Catalina Marketing Services experienced growth in many areas since 1992, including store expansion and the development of new applications. In 1995, for example, Catalina Marketing Corporation announced that 87 Super Kmart centers were joining the network in the first quarter of 1996. This marked the network's entry into mass merchandising. "This is an important move for our company because Kmart's stature solidifies our role as a multi-channel delivery system including supermarkets, drug stores, and mass merchandisers,'' said Off.

Additionally, the Catalina Marketing Network proved itself flexible and able to be upgraded to support different or new applications. Catalina Marketing's more recent innovations included Checkout CallFree, free phone debit card certificates, in 1996; Checkout Prizes, an electronic instant-win sweepstakes based on consumer purchases; and SaveNOW!, instant discounts of particular products.

Checkout Prizes was awarded first in 1996 to Dillons supermarkets, a Kansas-based chain. Catalina Marketing initiated a sweepstakes to thank retailers for helping its network grow. Checkout Prizes is an instant sweepstakes game that electronically awards prizes to consumers when they check out. Lynn Lackey, a Dillons executive, said: ''As one of the newest retailers on the Catalina Marketing Network, we're especially enthusiastic about the savings opportunities network programs will provide our customers. Giving our shoppers a chance to win valuable prizes will create excitement in the store while introducing them to the benefits of the network.''

SaveNOW! also created interest among consumers for retailers. Retailers were paid for each discount delivered to shoppers. Catalina billed the appropriate manufacturers, then reimbursed the retailers for the discounts. Tested in May 1996 at Ralphs and Pathmark stores in Los Angeles and New York, SaveNOW! required that manufacturers indicate products to discount—and the levels of those discounts—by brand and/or size for two-week intervals. Catalina then incorporated discounts into ads, signs, and point-of-sale scanning systems. Discounts occurred automatically at scanning, with confirmation on each customer's register receipt. As Off explained: ''With more than ten years of experience in transaction-based promotions, Catalina Marketing has the in-place electronic network, established retail partners, and proven technology base to make paperless discounts a feasible, cost-efficient alternative to traditional marketing. We see SaveNOW! As an enhancement of our existing portfolio—where Checkout Coupon and our other offerings serve as long-term franchise building tools, this program can provide a timed, targeted, short-term life in a brand's sales.''

Catalina Marketing also launched a frequent shopper program in 1996, offering a flexible menu of turnkey electronic database marketing programs. The frequent shopper program was an initial attempt at loyalty marketing. Catalina offered data collection, store and warehousing analysis, consumer communication through a program designed to assist retailers in communicating with shoppers, thus promoting store loyalty and increasing profitability. The program bridged the Catalina Marketing Network and a store's card-based transactions or other frequent shopper programs. Basically, Catalina's frequent shopper system provided data collection of purchases and a method of communicating with a retailer's customers, then printing incentives based on a consumer's total spending and number of shopping trips. Said Brian Woolf, president of Retail Strategy Center Inc.: ''Retailers have recently begun to grasp the power of frequent shopper programs, but are often daunted by the expense and time it takes to set up a program. The Catalina Marketing frequent shopper service now provides a great turn-

key database marketing solution without the delays, and hardware and software expenses typically incurred when running an in-house frequent shopper program. Catalina Marketing is the company to bring this type of program to market because they have an established expertise and a proven track record of executing successful electronic marketing programs, and they have a solid, electronic network in place.''

Catalina Marketing International, 1992

Catalina Marketing International was founded in 1992 with the licensing of Checkout Coupon technology in the United Kingdom. Catalina Marketing International eventually became responsible for all overseas and Mexican operations of the Catalina network. The network reached 14 million shoppers outside of the United States each week in 1996 through 650 stores. Though basically the Checkout Coupon program available in North America, the international versions sported their own names; for example, Checkout Saver in ASDA chain stores in England; Ecobon in the Casino and Promodes chains in France; or Promo Cupon in Gigante and Aurrera chains in Mexico. Checkout Direct, Catalina's database monitoring program, also was introduced in the United Kingdom to track household purchases and deliver incentives accordingly. In 1996 Catalina Marketing International bought out the 46 percent minority interest in its U.K. operation. Off revealed at the time of the purchase: ''We've had great success in England. Our U.K. operation is positioned for excellent growth in sales and profits, making this the right time to increase our ownership position. We feel that our U.K. operation will continue to be a strong performer for the company, and look to it as a model for success as we move forward with our international expansion.''

Moving beyond Europe, Catalina Marketing launched a joint venture in Japan with Pacific Media K.K. in 1996 to introduce Checkout Coupon and electronic marketing programs through a new division called Catalina Marketing Japan. According to Off, ''Our electronic marketing programs have excellent potential in Japan, where research has shown that shoppers are searching for good values. This fact, along with the positive reception we've received from Japanese retailers and manufacturers, prompted our decision to move into this market. Japan has a total population of more than 120 million, and a $150 billion supermarket segment. Ninety-nine percent of stores in the country's large chains are equipped with point-of-sale scanners.''

Health Resource Publishing Company Debuts in 1995

Founded in 1995 as a test program in 40 stores in seven chains, Catalina's Health Resource Publishing Company delivered a prescription-based newsletter to pharmacy customers. Similar to Checkout Coupon premiums, these customized newsletters were based on consumers' individual drug purchases as indicated by the National Drug Code that corresponded to each prescription. The laser printer-generated $8\frac{1}{2} \times 14$-inch newsletter covered fifty product categories and included editorials, product ads, consumer information, and incentives for customers. One year after its establishment, the Catalina's newsletter system was installed by fourteen retailers for a total of 150 stores, with commitments from several others for future installations. Soon more than 230 pharmacies offered Health Resource. President of Health Resource Publishing Company Mike McClorey revealed: "Retailers are excited about the program because consumer response has been so positive, and that has enabled us to expand within existing chains and into new retailers. Personalized health care information is a big customer concern. Retailers trying to distinguish themselves are looking at value-added programs such as the *Health Resource* newsletter to offer this type of information to their shoppers." Health Resource Publishing Company is headquartered in St. Louis, Missouri.

Catalina Electronic Clearing Services

Another operating unit, Catalina Electronic Clearing Services, was founded in 1993 as the first automated coupon clearing system, serving more than 100 stores and nine supermarket chains in the United States. Essentially, Catalina Electronic Clearing Services improved past manual systems of processing coupons. Manual systems were inefficient—with each coupon being handled about 30 times—paper intensive, and subject to misredemption and chargeback problems. Catalina's system, however, captured data as coupons were scanned, tallying count and value information for manufacturers to issue redemption payment to retailers. In 1996 Catalina Electronic Clearing Services were reorganized, moving from a separate business unit to part of Catalina Marketing's core operations. According to Off, "We strongly believe that electronic coupon clearing will become the industry standard in the future, and by streamlining operations now, we are ensuring the long-term viability of our electronic clearing business. We are committed to maintaining our leadership position and growing this business."

Online Activities and the Future

With the advent of the Internet, Catalina Marketing Corporation instituted two vehicles for reaching its clients and consumers. The first, Supermarkets Online (http://www.supermarkets.com) is a cooperative Web site offering promotional and information services to consumers from retailers and manufacturers. Consumers see weekly specials, create shopping lists, or print coupons. (Coupons had security measures installed to ensure proper redemption: bar coding, chain-specific redemption, manufacturer expiration dates, sequential numbering, and personalization with a shopper's name.) Supermarkets Online was first available to consumers in California in 1996. By mid-June 1996 it was installed in 1,600 stores by eleven retailers—including Ralphs, Vons, Lucky, and Safeway—that participated in the lead-market launch. Catalina Marketing believed it to be the first third-party Internet project for retailers and manufacturers. David Rochon, Catalina Marketing Online vice-president, said: "Just as Catalina Marketing has spent the last twelve years building its in-store network, now the company is establishing an in-home network, which will give our clients and consumers better access to one another. We believe Catalina Marketing Online will provide retailers and manufacturers with a new way to offer added value, and will present consumers with shortcuts to make shopping easier, faster, and more enjoyable."

Catalina Marketing also launched a business-to-business web site (http://www.catalinamktg.com) offering news and issues relevant to the packaged goods industry and providing an interactive medium that profiled the Catalina Marketing Network's services. Really the company's home page, the Web site featured a bulletin board, hot issues, a shopping game, demonstrations of Catalina Marketing Network services, chats with industry experts, live discussions, and polls. "In developing our home page," noted Off, "we strived to provide a combination of topical information, effective business-to-business marketing tools, and entertainment. And I think we've accomplished this by providing user friendly access to company information as well as through engaging and interactive resource elements."

Principal Operating Units

Catalina Marketing Services; Catalina Marketing International (United Kingdom, Mexico, and Japan); Health Resource Publishing Company; Catalina Electronic Clearing Services; Catalina Online.

Further Reading

"Buy Theirs, Get Ours Free: Catalina Marketing," *The Economists*, September 5, 1992, p. 68.
"Catalina Adds 7 Chains to Network," *Supermarket News*, March 1, 1993, p. 16.
"Catalina Sets International Expansion," *Supermarket News*, February 12, 1996, p. 31.
De Santa, Richard, "Instore Marketing Continues to Surge," *Supermarket Business*, February 1996, p. 26.
Gelsi, Steve, "Catalina Adds Phone Cards to System," *Brandweek*, October 2, 1995, p. 6.
"IRI, Catalina Beginning Joint Venture," *Supermarket News*, December 7, 1992, p. 19.
Meyer, Wally, "Checkout Coupon Moves Product with a Multitude of Winning Strategies," *Frozen Food Digest*, July 1992, p. 16.
Millstein, Marc, "Catalina Foresees Steady Growth in Electronic Marketing," *Supermarket News*, May 2, 1994, p. 74.
Petersen, Laurie, "Click Here for Coupons," *Direct*, June 1, 1996, p. 45.
Sims, Calvin, "In Coupons, It's Catalina at the Checkout," *New York Times*, August 29, 1993, Sec. 3, p. 6.
Teitelbaum, Richard S., "Catalina Marketing," *Fortune*, May 18, 1992, p. 89.
Walsh, Matt, "Point-of-Sale Persuaders," *Forbes*, October 24, 1994, p. 232.
Zwiebach, Elliot, "Catalina to Launch Coupon Program," *Supermarket News*, August 31, 1992, p. 14.

—Charity Anne Dorgan

Central Parking Corporation

2401 21st Avenue South
Suite 200
Nashville, Tennessee 37212
U.S.A.
(615) 297-4255
Fax: (615) 297-6240

Public Company
Incorporated: 1968
Employees: 6,600
Sales: $143.32 million (1996)
Stock Exchanges: New York
SICs: 7521 Automobile Parking; 6719 Holding
    Companies, Not Elsewhere Classified

Central Parking Corporation is the leading parking services company in the United States, operating nearly 1,500 parking facilities with more than 600,000 parking spaces in 32 states, Washington, DC, and Puerto Rico, and in Europe, Mexico, and Asia. In addition to management and operation of parking facilities, the company offers various ancillary services, including consulting services for new construction projects, insurance for contracted facilities, and related privatized services such as parking meter enforcement and shuttle transportation. Led by founder Monroe Carell, Jr., Central Parking has brought professional management techniques to a highly fragmented, typically ''mom-and-pop'' industry, scoring high-profile parking contracts such as the new, 8,500-space Atlanta Braves stadium; the Prudential Center in Boston; Busch Stadium in St. Louis; Heathrow Airport in London; the 63-story MesseTurm complex in Frankfurt, Germany; and the 88-story City Centre complex in Kuala Lampur, Malaysia. Other clients include the Hyatt and Westin hotel chains, May Department Stores, and the Rouse Company. None of the company's contracts, however, accounts for more than five percent of Central Parking's revenues, and the company's contract retention rate is high, generally reaching 95 percent or more. The company operates parking facilities primarily under its Central Parking System subsidiary.

Central Parking owns, either independently or through joint venture partnerships, only about three percent of the parking facilities it operates. The largest share of facilities under Central Parking's watch are operated through management contracts. Central Parking's responsibilities under these contracts, which are generally short-term renewable contracts lasting one to three years, involve employee hiring and training, collections, accounting, marketing, and insurance. Wages, fees, taxes, and similar payments are paid by the owner of the facility, which also is responsible for maintenance and security. The facility owner pays the company a base monthly fee; Central Parking often receives a percentage of revenues above a certain amount. Since the early 1990s, however, the company has stepped up the number of facilities it operates under lease arrangements. Under a lease arrangement, the company rents the facility and is responsible for all aspects of the facility's operation. Rent is calculated as a flat annual rate or percentage of gross revenues, or a combination of the two. Leases generally are for ten years. Although they involve greater risk to the company, lease arrangements provide far higher profit margins than management contracts. In the mid-1990s, Central Parking has turned to increasing its rate of leased or owned facilities, converting its management contracts where possible.

Central Parking went public in October 1995 and recorded a three-for-two stock split in March 1996. The company posted revenues of $143 million for its 1996 fiscal year, generating a net income of $13.84 million. In December 1996, the company agreed to acquire New Jersey-based Square Industries, a public company with revenues of $65 million. After completion of the merger, that company's 117 facilities, located primarily in New York, New Jersey, and Pennsylvania, would add 61,000 parking spaces to the Central Parking empire.

The Professional Approach to Parking in the 1960s

Monroe Carell, Jr. held an electrical engineering degree from Vanderbilt University; his family also owned two parking lots in Nashville, Tennessee. In 1968, Carell gave up a career in engineering to manage the family's lots, incorporating the company as Central Parking Corporation. During the next decade, Carell expanded the company's operations, winning management contracts for a steadily growing number of parking facilities. The company was helped by the boom in new building construction that took place across the country during the 1970s and 1980s, as cities began urban renewal projects to revitalize their downtown areas. At the same time, more and more urban real estate was dedicated to parking garages and lots.

Central Parking stepped into the highly fragmented industry by offering a novel approach: promising, and delivering, professional service, with well-maintained facilities and well-trained staff. Under Central Parking management, a parking facility typically saw strong increases in revenues, winning the company a high customer retention rate. But Central Parking's employee recruitment, training, and compensation policies were essential components of the company's growth strategy. From the start, Central Parking sought out college-educated personnel who could be groomed as company managers. Central Parking developed its own intensive training procedures, formalized in 1986, and created a specific promotion path. The company also pursued a policy of performance-based compensation. "Since the beginning, we have paid people based on success," Carell told *Investor's Business Daily.* "Everyone has an individual contract." Managers were paid a base salary, but managers themselves held the key to their earnings potential, with performance-based bonuses capable of more than tripling their base salary. Managers were also encouraged by the company's policy of promoting from within the organization. New hires spent a year in the company's management trainee program, then were trained for an additional year as manager of a single facility. After that year, successful managers were promoted to area manager, in charge of several facilities, and from there to operations manager and to general manager.

Central Parking's growth continued into the 1980s; once the company established itself in one facility in a city, it typically grew to capture a major share of that city's private parking spaces, allowing the company to achieve greater economies of scale. Until the end of the decade, the company's growth was based largely on winning contracts for new parking construction. But the collapse of the new building market and a slump in the commercial real estate industry in the late 1980s led the company into new strategies for expansion.

"Take-Away" Growth in the 1990s

To continue its growth, Central Parking switched its emphasis to what Carell called a "take-away" strategy. By promising developers and other owners of parking facilities that the company could maximize parking revenues, Central Parking began increasing the number of facilities under its control by taking existing facility contracts from its competitors. At the same time, the company recognized the opportunity to shift its operating focus from management contracts to leasing arrangements,

thereby not only increasing the company's profits on a facility, but also providing a more stable and predictable income. With the commercial real estate slump sending occupancy rates plunging, developers were eager to relinquish the expense of operating parking facilities for their underused properties. Central Parking, in turn, was able to cut operating costs and gain economies of scale with its increased market share. The company also began marketing itself as a consultant for developers planning parking facilities.

By 1991, Central Parking operated in 630 locations and revenues had grown to $30.6 million. In that year, the company went international, winning a contract to provide consulting services to the Canary Wharf project in London. Later that year, the company expanded its London presence by winning the contract to manage Heathrow Airport's Terminal 4 parking facility, and it soon added the airport's Terminal 1 facility. By mid-decade, the company had built its United Kingdom base to nearly 90 facilities. The company also began a new type of service in the United Kingdom, that of providing privatized parking meter enforcement and ticketing services for three cities. This move, begun in 1994, positioned the company for further growth domestically, as increasing numbers of communities, eyeing the successful privatization of services such as the corrections system, began to consider privatizing meter enforcement and ticketing services as well. In 1991, the company entered a consulting agreement with Realty Parking Properties II L.P., in which the company agreed to provide information on potential parking facilities acquisitions. Central Parking received fees based on a property's acquisition cost and was required to lease and operate the acquired properties.

The following year, Central Parking added significantly to its facilities base when it acquired the management contract rights of Meyers Parking, a regional parking facilities operator with 104 facilities located primarily in New York and Boston. Meyers had been generating $34 million per year in revenues, but was losing money. Central Parking paid $8 million for the contract rights and brought the Meyers system back to profitability. But, by 1992, the company's move to emphasize leasing arrangements or outright ownership of its parking facilities was already providing the strongest fuel for growth: the company's parking revenues from leasing or ownership rose to form nearly $27 million of the company's $46 million in revenues, compared with $19 million from management contracts. By the end of 1993, the company leased or owned 356 of its total base of 948 facilities. Central Parking's revenues jumped to nearly $95.5 million for the year.

The company's next international move occurred in 1994, when it entered a joint venture partnership with Mexican developer Fondo Opcion to operate 16 parking facilities in Mexico. Back in the United States, Central Parking continued adding to its list of facilities. The company's agreement with Realty Parking Properties ended that year, and the company was freed from its obligation to offer that partnership first choice at purchasing properties that Central Parking located. In 1994, the company purchased four parking facilities. By the end of 1994, the company had added a net of 100 facilities, nearly 80 of which were added under leasing arrangements. With leasing and ownership producing three-quarters of the company's revenues, Central Parking's sales surpassed $112 million for the year and net earnings neared $9 million. With international sales nearing ten percent of revenues by 1994, the company stepped up its international growth, opening a business development office in Amsterdam, the Netherlands, in 1995 to expand the company's European presence.

After finishing its 1995 fiscal year with revenues topping $126 million, Central Parking went public in October 1995 to fund further expansion plans, which included not only stepping up its lease equity activities but also the acquisition of other parking services companies. The company's offering of 2.8 million shares, originally expected to trade at $15 per share, debuted instead at $18 per share and neared $21 per share by the end of the first day's trading. Shortly after the offering, the company paid $1.6 million for a Nashville garage and $10 million for property in Chicago, adding to the five facilities purchases made in the company's 1995 fiscal year.

In March 1996, the company added significantly to its European base with the announcement of a joint venture agreement with Wisser Service Holdings AG, a leading German supplier of business services, including building security and maintenance. The joint venture, operating as Central Parking System Deutschland, would bring Central Parking into Berlin, Dresden, and Frankfurt, and help raise the company's share of revenues from its international operations to 13.6 percent, despite the loss of a number of facilities in the United Kingdom. By the end of its 1996 fiscal year, Central Parking managed 1,359 facilities, including 37 owned by the company. Revenues increased to $143 million, providing net income of $13.8 million.

The start of Central Parking's 1997 fiscal year seemed to herald a new era of growth for the company. In November 1996, the company made a cash purchase of Civic Parking LLC, a St. Louis-based operator of four parking garages. One month later, Central Parking announced its agreement to acquire Square Industries, which, with 117 parking facilities and nearly $66 million in 1995 revenues, firmly positioned Central Parking as the leader in the U.S. parking services industry.

Principal Subsidiaries

Central Parking System, Inc.; Central Parking System of Mexico, S.A. De C.V. (50%); Central Parking System of the United Kingdom, Ltd.; Central Parking System Deutschland, GmbH (Germany; 50%); Central Parking System Realty, Inc.; Control Plus Parking System of UK, Ltd (United Kingdom); Larimer Square Parking Associates (50%); LoDo Parking Garage, LLC (50%); Servicios Corporativos Para Estacionamientos, S.A. De C.V. (Mexico; 50%).

Further Reading

Carey, Bill, "Central Parking Stock Takes Off," *Tennessean,* May 27, 1996, p. 1E.
——, "Central Parking Top of the Lot," *Tennessean,* December 10, 1996, p. 1E.
Maio, Patrick J., "Central Parking Corp.," *Investor's Daily Business,* September 24, 1996, p. A6.
——, "Profit Lots," *Investor's Daily Business,* January 16, 1996, p. A6.
Rudnitsky, Howard, "Take-Away Game," *Forbes,* July 29, 1996, p. 50.
Ward, Gethan, "Central Parking Buys Big Rival," *Nashville Banner,* December 10, 1996, p. D4.

—M. L. Cohen

CHEROKEE.

Cherokee Inc.

6835 Valjean Avenue
Van Nuys, California 91406
U.S.A.
(818) 908-9868
Fax: (818) 908-9191

Public Company
Incorporated: 1973
Employees: 15
Sales: $13.9 million
Stock Exchanges: NASDAQ
SICs: 6794 Patent Owners & Lessors

Cherokee Inc. is a licenser whose namesake brand appears on clothing, housewares, accessories, footwear, and other consumer goods in retail outlets around the world. During the first half of its 26-year history, the company evolved from a tiny shoe repair shop into a highly profitable, multimillion-dollar manufacturer of shoes and apparel. Heavy debt from a management-led leveraged buyout in the late 1980s led to multiple bankruptcy reorganizations. In the mid-1990s, the scaled-back company staked its future on the cultivation of the Cherokee label as a "megabrand" and the creation of a global licensing operation. In the process, Cherokee's sales have shrunk from a high of $236.9 million in 1991 to just under $14 million in 1995. After scoring annual profits of more than $10 million in the late 1980s, the firm failed to record a single year in the black from 1990 to 1995.

Corporate Foundations in 1970s

Cherokee was founded in 1971 by James Argyropoulos. With his family—including a twin brother—"Argy" had emigrated to Chicago from Greece in 1958 at the age of 14. Over the next four years, he learned the English language in high school and the shoemaking trade from his father. But Argy was not interested in becoming a cobbler when he graduated. At 18, he moved to Los Angeles to pursue a career as an electric guitarist for a rock 'n roll band. He chased that dream for about four years, until the financial demands of a new wife and baby drew him back into the footwear business.

Argyropoulos launched a shoe repair shop in 1968, and like his father before him was soon selling custom-made footwear to "hippies and flower children" from his Venice, California, garage. His comfortable leather and wood shoes, sandals, and clogs were embellished with hand-painted symbols. Especially popular was a geometric Indian motif. With orders growing, Argy founded the Cherokee Shoe Co. in 1971 and incorporated two years later.

Over the course of the 1970s, the twenty-something entrepreneur expanded his line to include sandals with an injection-molded sole known as the "Beep Bottom," as well as closed shoe lines. With orders from national department store chains like Macy's, Bloomingdales, and Dayton-Hudson, Argyropoulos was able to increase his production to 1.5 million pairs per year. Sales volume tripled from 1979 to nearly $34 million in 1980. It was around this time that the entrepreneur decided to pursue a major brand extension.

Union with Robert Margolis in 1983

Argyropoulos found a like-minded entrepreneur in skiing-buddy-turned-business-partner Robert Margolis. Margolis brought with him another partner, Jay Kester, and about a decade of experience in the bargain clothing segment. The three formed a joint venture, Cherokee Apparel Inc., in 1981. In acknowledgment of his new colleagues' expertise in the clothing industry, Argyropoulos put up 75 percent of the start-up funds, but only kept a 55 percent stake in the new affiliate.

Writing for *Forbes* magazine in 1986, journalist Ellen Paris described Argyropoulos and Margolis as "a natural fit," noting that "Margolis' contacts with the apparel buyers opened up shelf space for Cherokee shoes at important accounts like Burdine's in Florida. And Argyropoulos' shoe account contacts cleared rack space for Margolis' apparel lines in a chain like Nordstrom."

Company Perspectives:

As "dress down Friday" continues to sweep the nation, casual clothes are becoming more important. Now, corporate America is learning what CHEROKEE customers have known for years. When it comes to casual dressing—no one does it better than CHEROKEE!

Growth Follows 1983 Initial Public Offering

With a focus on women's and children's apparel, sales at the new affiliate soon outstripped shoe revenues, growing from $15.1 million in 1983 to $51.6 million in 1984. In 1983, Argyropoulos took Cherokee Shoe public and used $5.3 million of the $9 million proceeds to retire short-term debt and acquire the remaining 45 percent of Cherokee Apparel Corp. he did not own. The initial public offering was structured so that the principals would gain some cash without relinquishing control: the founder retained a one-third stake in his company, his twin brother Arthur Argyris (who had Anglicized his name) held another 10 percent, and Margolis (who became president of the reincarnated Cherokee Inc. in 1984) owned about 6 percent.

The partners used several strategies to bring their brand to national status in the early 1980s. National advertising via print and television helped support the company's business with nationwide department stores. Argyropoulos also hoped to expand a fledgling chain of Cherokee stores from its roots in California into a nationwide chain of 100 franchised outlets by the end of the decade.

By mid-decade it was apparent that brand licensing had become a very successful and prolific program. In exchange for a royalty of 7 percent—2 to 3 percent of which was earmarked for the corporate advertising budget—Cherokee sold other clothing manufacturers the right to use the trademark and Indian head logo on everything from menswear to accessories and children's clothing. By 1986, the company had over a dozen licensees, including international affiliates in New Zealand, Australia, and Canada.

In keeping with its thoroughly American name and image, all of Cherokee's clothing and footwear was made in the U.S.A. (The company did make a brief stab at importing, but soon found that Californian immigrant labor made up for its relative expense with quick turnarounds and reliable quality.) At the time of the merger, the company's sales ratio was about 60 percent shoes, 40 percent apparel. Within two years, that equation was turned on its head, with 65 percent of sales generated from women's clothing. Along with this corporate transformation came skyrocketing annual sales and a mounting stock price. Revenues tripled from $33.97 million in 1980 to $104 million in 1986, and net income multiplied tenfold, from $690,000 to $6.8 million during the same period. A tripling of Cherokee's stock price during this period left some analysts eagerly speculating that the apparel company was "another [Liz] Claiborne."

Forbes's Paris wrote admiringly of Argyropoulos' innate business sense, noting that while he was "only" a high school graduate, he was "what many eager business school applicants think they can somehow learn to be—a successful entrepreneur, creator of a dynamic business. We wish them luck. Entrepreneurs of this type are born, not made." Of course, Paris could not have predicted that those "eager business school" types would later cut the natural out of his own company.

Early in 1986, Argyropoulos announced ambitious financial performance goals for the remainder of the decade, among them 20 percent annual sales and earnings growth. That April brought a secondary equity offering totaling 2.5 million shares, 700,000 of which had been held by the principals. The cash-out reduced Argyropoulos' stake to 15 percent, while Argyris and Margolis held on to 1 percent each. Cherokee used part of the proceeds to purchase a controlling interest in clothing manufacturer Code Bleu from Bayly Corp. in December 1987 and outright control of shoemaker Pallmark International two months later.

Cherokee exceeded its founder's goals in fiscal 1987 (ending November 30), achieving year-over-year increases of 34 percent in sales and 53 percent in earnings. And while sales growth fell somewhat short of projections, at 16.6 percent on the 1988 fiscal year (which, since it ended May 31, overlapped the previous period), profits continued their upward climb at a 23 percent rate, to $12.8 million. It was the most prosperous 12 months in Cherokee's history, and would be its last profitable year for quite some time.

Leveraged Buyout in 1988

With the aid of investment firm Deutschman & Co.'s Green Acquisition Co., Cherokee president Robert Margolis led a corporate mutiny against Jimmy Argyropoulos in May 1988. The $150 million, $12.50 per share bid offered to exchange shares in the newly-formed Green Acquisition for Cherokee shares held by officers and directors Margolis, Jay Kester, and Cary Cooper, making them the principal officers of the privately-held Green in the process. The offer made no mention of Argyropoulos, even though he continued to own about 14.5 percent of the company.

When a special committee of Cherokee's board of directors rejected the bid in June, the executives—this time joined by Argyropoulos—brought a second, $13 per share, $156 million, offer to take the company private. By July, however, Argy had defected, asserting that the high debt the managers would have to assume in order to buy out their fellow shareholders would hamstring the company and require severe layoffs and other cutbacks. The special committee of the board agreed and rejected this second offer in August.

The third time proved a charm for Green Acquisition. In September, its $173.6 million bid for control was approved over the "nays" of Argyropoulos and a small cadre of loyal directors. Unwilling to admit defeat, the founder sought a "white knight" and solicited a court injunction to block the takeover, but both efforts were fruitless. Argy resigned from Cherokee that October, no doubt taking some solace in a $31 million settlement.

Margolis and company's leveraged buyout proceeded in two steps: in October 1988, the group paid about $84.7 million for a 50 percent stake. Green acquired the remaining equity for

$13.99 per share ($12 cash and an unsecured $1.99 per share bond) and merged the company in May 1989. This privatization process was financed almost entirely with debt, loading Cherokee with over $170 million in long-term liabilities. Interest on the loans was set at 15.75 percent.

Losses, Bankruptcy Reorganizations in Late 1980s, Early 1990s

Debt service proved a powerful impetus for growth in the post-LBO era. Cherokee adopted several new strategies and revised some old ones in its quest for increased cash flow. In an effort to raise sales volume, the clothing company began to lower its wholesale prices and concentrate more on mass merchandisers like Mervyn's and Wal-Mart, and less on its traditional department store customers. A long-resisted shift to overseas production helped cut production costs. Cherokee vastly increased its licensing programs as well, accumulating a total of 26 licensees authorized to make everything from belts to beach towels by 1989. Overseas licenses were a particular focus. By the end of the decade, the company had added affiliates in Mexico and Japan. Corky Newman, president of marketing and licensing, predicted that "The Cherokee label will be a dominant label in the Nineties and the Nineties is a decade of the megabrand," in a September 26, 1989 *WWD* article. The company also boosted its advertising budget from about $3 million in 1990 to $7 million in 1991.

While these efforts succeeded in increasing Cherokee's sales from $156.2 million in fiscal 1988 to over $236.9 million in fiscal 1991, the company lost over $2 million in the ensuing years, ending the latter year with a "negative tangible book value of $126.2 million." Despite an injection of cash from a public offering of 2.5 million shares at $6.50 each in early 1991, the company continued to struggle with its debt. In November 1992, Cherokee missed an interest payment on the $105 million liability that remained, and was forced to enter Chapter 11 bankruptcy negotiations with its creditors. The company emerged from the proceedings June 1, 1993, having reduced its annual fixed charges by $14 million.

Margolis resigned Cherokee's chairmanship and chief executive office that November, citing familial responsibilities and a desire to "pursue other entrepreneurial opportunities." Jay Kester, Margolis's long-time partner and Cherokee's president of worldwide marketing, followed suit later that month, giving virtually identical reasons for his departure. The board of directors selected Bryan Marsal, a management consultant, to act as interim CEO and hired Joseph M. Elles as president. Formerly general merchandising manager at Lee Apparel Co., Elles implemented several strategies in the hopes of getting Cherokee back on track.

A label overhaul abolished Cherokee's Indian-head logo, which Elles thought was inappropriate for the politically-correct 1990s. In an effort to streamline production, he eliminated 75 percent of the company's styles to focus primarily on jeans. He also instituted a market research program, increased the advertising budget, and raised inventory levels to better serve the department stores that he hoped to target. As he told *WWD's* Janet Ozzard in January 1994, Elles had high hopes for Cherokee, noting that "it would be a disappointment if we did not run

substantial double-digit [sales] growth" in the ensuing year. But these hopes evaporated along with Cherokee's revenues in the ensuing months. Results for the year ending May 31, 1993, showed a 19 percent decline in sales to $157.3 million and a near-doubling of its annual shortfall to $20.3 million. The disparity only grew worse in the following year, with revenues declining to $114.1 million and a $24.8 million loss. Elles resigned in November 1994 as the company once again sought bankruptcy protection.

His successor, Jim Novak, joined *WWD's* Kim-Van Dang in blaming high inventory costs for pushing the company into its second bankruptcy reorganization in as many years. Commenting for an April 1995 article, Novak said that "It was not a bad idea, but this company is not financially structured to handle [costly inventories]. The support was not here for him." Novak resurrected Cherokee's Indian-head logo and planned to reinstate many of the company's trouser and shirt lines, but early in 1995 former chairman and CEO Robert Margolis re-emerged with a radically different idea.

Licensing Sole Focus Beginning in 1995

By this time, Margolis had accumulated about one-fourth of Cherokee's devalued stock via an investment group. It only seemed natural for him to accept bondholders' requests that he reprise his role at the troubled company's helm. He started with a corporate "garage sale," pawning off everything from sewing machines to buttons and even the proverbial "garage," a 110,000-square-foot factory. Margolis used the $20 million proceeds to eliminate Cherokee's remaining debt. The elimination of all manufacturing operations shrunk the company's payroll from over 400 in 1993 to less than two dozen in 1995 and reduced its overhead to less than $2 million.

Margolis based his new strategy, which he dubbed "private label with a label," strictly on licensing the Cherokee brand and logo. But the company would not limit its client base to manufacturers, as it had in the past. Instead, it sought "strategic alliances" with retailers, to whom it would license the brand for whole categories of soft goods. This tactic followed the successful lead of such retailer-owned brands as J.C. Penney's Arizona and Wal-Mart's Kathy Lee. Cherokee's first major deal in this vein, a 1995 agreement with Dayton Hudson Corporation's Target chain, guaranteed it a minimum of $5.5 million in royalties for the fiscal year ended that May.

By 1997, Margolis could point to several signs that his innovative program was succeeding. The company had about 30 licensees, several of whom had confidently signed on since the latest corporate reincarnation. In January, the company announced net income of $2.8 million on sales of $3.7 million for the six-month period ending November 1996. The company optimistically instituted a quarterly dividend early that year, and forecast that it would have $8 million cash and be unencumbered by debt at year-end (May 1997).

Further Reading

Bloomfield, Judy, "Labels Stretching Out Via Licensing," *WWD*, June 7, 1989, pp. 20–21.
"Cherokee Files Initial Order," *Footwear News*, October 10, 1983, pp. 1–2.

"Cherokee Founder Left Out of $150 Million Buyout," *Daily News Record*, May 26, 1988, p. 2.

Cole, Benjamin Mark, "Cherokee Cedes Control in LBO; Drexel Underwriting Deal Gives Firm the Upper Hand," *Los Angeles Business Journal,* January 16, 1989, pp. 1–2.

Dang, Kim-Van, "New Frontiers for Cherokee," *WWD*, November 17, 1993, p. 16.

——, "Cherokee's New Chapter," *WWD*, April 12, 1995, p. 10.

——, "Cherokee's New Trail," *WWD*, July 5, 1995, p. 12.

Dodds, Lyn Strongin, "Home Is Where the Profits Are," *Financial World*, November 13, 1985, pp. 96–97.

Forman, Ellen, "Franchising: Racing on a Fast Track," *WWD*, March 6, 1986, pp. 7–8.

Jaffe, Thomas, "Smoke Signals?" *Forbes*, May 18, 1987, p. 267.

Lippincott, Liz, "Cherokee: Power Moves," *WWD*, July 28, 1993, p. 10.

MacIntosh, Jean, "Argyropoulos Opposes Cherokee Buyout Bid," *Footwear News*, July 25, 1988, pp. 1–2.

——, "Cherokee Emerges Stronger Than Ever," WWD, December 1, 1988, p. 13.

——, "Buyout Is a $31M Bonanza for Cherokee Founder," *WWD*, April 27, 1989, p. 8.

——, "Planning to Slice the Debt—A Bit," *WWD*, May 13, 1991, p. 7.

——, "Cherokee Loses $5.3M in Quarter, $9.8M in Year," *WWD*, September 3, 1992, p. 2.

"Margolis Rejoins Cherokee," *WWD*, May 8, 1995, pp. 2–3.

Marlow, Michael, "Cherokee: Back on the Public Path," *WWD*, May 13, 1991, pp. 6–7.

Newman, Morris, "Apparel Maker Cherokee Suffers Steep Stock Drop," *Los Angeles Business Journal*, September 26, 1994, pp. 5A–6A.

Ozzard, Janet, "Cherokee Blazes a New Trail," *WWD*, January 26, 1994, p. 16.

Rottman, Meg, "Cherokee's Initial Offer Comes in at $9 a Share," *Footwear News*, December 12, 1983, pp. 2–3.

——, "30.5% Of Cherokee Sales Are East of Mississippi," *Footwear News*, January 13, 1986, pp. 2–3.

——, "Argy Leaves All Cherokee Positions," *Footwear News*, October 24, 1988, pp. 1–2.

——, "Jim Argyropoulos: Looking Back, Thinking Ahead," *Footwear News Magazine*, February 1989, pp. S46–S49.

——, "Cherokee Group Feeling Strong After Year's Hurdles," *Footwear News*, February 6, 1989, pp. 4–6.

——, "Cherokee Rescinds Stock Offering Plans," *Footwear News*, October 8, 1990, pp. 4–5.

Rottman, Meg, and Jean MacIntosh, "Cherokee Stock Climbs After Takeover Attempt," *Footwear News*, May 30, 1988, pp. 2–3.

Ruben, Howard G. "Ex-Cherokee Executives Form Firm," *WWD*, March 8, 1989, p. 40.

Rutberg, Sidney, "Wall St. Analysts Beating Drums for Cherokee," *WWD*, February 13, 1986, p. 6.

—April Dougal Gasbarre

Ciber, Inc.

5251 DTC Parkway, Suite 1400
Englewood, Colorado 80111
U.S.A.
(303) 220-0100
Fax: (303) 220-7100
Web site: http://www.ciber.com

Public Company
Incorporated: 1974
Employees: 2,300
Sales: $156.8 million (1996)
Stock Exchanges: NASDAQ
SICs: 7371 Computer Programming Services

A leading, middle-tier information technology company, Ciber, Inc. provides computer consulting services that help corporate clients keep pace with the ever-changing capabilities of computer software. With more than 30 branch offices nationwide and a team of more than 2,100 consultants during the mid-1990s, Ciber was a company whose time had come during the 1990s, a decade that witnessed a meteoric rise in annual revenue volume from barely more than $10 million to the $156 million generated in 1996.

Origins in 1974

Ciber was founded in 1974 by three individuals, one of whom would remain with the company and guide its fortunes for its crucial first two decades. Of the three original founders of Ciber, Bobby G. Stevenson emerged as the key figure in Ciber's history, shaping a start-up computer consulting firm into a leading national force by the 1990s, when the computer consulting industry was generating more than $30 billion worth of business a year. A graduate of Texas Tech University, Stevenson spent the years between his formal education and the formation of Ciber working as a programmer analyst for International Business Machines Corporation (IBM) and LTV Steel in Houston. By the early 1970s, when Stevenson was in his early 30s, he and two other colleagues decided to make a go of it

on their own and organized Ciber, an acronym for "consultants in business, engineering, and research."

At the time, Stevenson and Ciber's other co-founders perceived a need in the corporate world for specialized, technical assistance in keeping pace with the technological advances in computer hardware and computer software. The trio saw an opportunity to provide contract computer consulting services to clients lacking either in the resources or the expertise to use the promising power of computers in their day-to-day operations. Through Ciber, the founders tapped into a market that would grow explosively in the decades ahead. Few realized at the time how important computers would become to the business world. As the use of computers increased and wave after wave of computer innovations swept away yesterday's technological vanguard, the need for sophisticated service firms like Ciber to implement the frequently indecipherable technology of tomorrow grew exponentially.

Although Ciber entered the business of computer consulting services at a relatively early time, the company's physical and financial growth did not mirror the growth of its industry. Ciber grew at a modest pace initially, then embraced a new business strategy during the mid-1980s that ignited prolific growth. Stevenson watched over Ciber during both of the company's two eras, heading the company during its contrastingly slower period of growth and leading the charge during its decided rise during the 1990s.

During Ciber's inaugural year of business, Stevenson served as the company's vice-president in charge of recruiting and managing the fledgling firm's technical staff, a post he would occupy until November 1977, when he was named Ciber's chief executive officer. From late 1977 into the 1990s, Stevenson was responsible for all of Ciber's operations. At first, Stevenson and the two other co-founders targeted their consulting services exclusively to the automotive industry, establishing Ciber's first office in the hotbed of automotive production in the United States, Detroit, Michigan. Ciber did not remain wedded to the automotive industry for long, however. A few short years after its formation, Ciber began tailoring its services to the oil and gas industry as well, a move that occurred at roughly the same time as the company's geographic expansion. Two years after the company opened its doors in Detroit, an office in Phoenix was opened. A year later, in 1977, an office was established in Houston. A Denver office was opened in 1979, followed by the opening of a Dallas office in 1980 and an Atlanta office in 1987. The following year, Ciber relocated its corporate headquarters to Englewood, Colorado. While executive officers circulated throughout Ciber's Englewood facility, the company embarked on the most prolific growth period in its history to that point.

Growth Strategy Developed in the 1980s

A year after the move to Englewood and 15 years after its founding, Ciber competed in the burgeoning industry of computer consulting services as a minor player. Total sales in 1989 amounted to a mere $13 million, small change when compared with the revenue volume generated by the country's leading computer consulting firms. By this point, however, Ciber executives were plotting an era of dramatic growth for their company. During the mid-1980s, Stevenson and other Ciber executives adopted a new growth strategy that focused on the development of a new range of services and the realization of both physical and financial growth through the acquisition of established computer consulting firms. Although the strategy embraced during the mid-1980s would take half a decade to manifest itself in any meaningful way, once the strategy for the future began to take shape in tangible form, Ciber began its resolute rise to the upper echelon of its industry.

By the end of 1989, when annual sales had slipped past the $10 million mark, the plans formulated midway through the decade moved from the drawing board to implementation. Ciber's expansion in 1990 included the opening of offices in Cleveland, Orlando, and Tampa, moves that were associated with the development of new clientele in the telecommunications industry. As Ciber focused its marketing efforts toward telecommunications providers during the early 1990s, securing contracts with industry giants such as AT&T, GTE, and U.S. West Communications, Inc., the company found itself occupying fertile ground in the computer consulting market. Not only were computers and their technology becoming increasingly sophisticated, progressing at a pace that demanded the help of experts such as Ciber's consultants, but the shifting dynamics of the corporate world also favored companies like Ciber.

The early years of the 1990s were marked by a national economic recession that forced many of the country's corporations to alter their business strategies. As business declined and profit margins shrank, downsizing became the mantra of business leaders from coast to coast. Payroll was trimmed, entire departments were cut from corporate budgets, and, as a consequence, many companies found themselves lacking the resources and skills to perform certain tasks in-house, creating a greater need for the specialized services offered by Ciber. To meet this demand, Ciber contracted out specialists to help the nation's largest corporations complete computer projects and cope with hardware and software problems as they arose. Ciber consultants wrote and maintained software that performed a host of chores, including inventory control, accounts payable, and customer support.

Although the conditions were ripe for rapid growth as the 1990s began, Ciber's stature at the start of the decade prohibited it to a certain degree from capturing a sizable share of the computer consulting market. The company was too small to realize the growth potential that surrounded it. Mac J. Slingerlend, who joined the company in 1989 as executive vice-president and chief financial officer before being named president and chief operating officer in 1996, reflected on Ciber's diminutive size years after the company had grown into a genuine national contender, noting, "We wanted to be a survivor. We were the smallest national player, and we needed to get larger quickly."

Explosive Growth in the 1990s

Getting larger quickly ranked as Ciber's chief objective during the first half of the 1990s, engendering a period of growth that lifted the company's revenue volume from the $13 million recorded when Slingerlend joined the company to more than $150 million by the time he was promoted to the twin posts of president and chief operating officer. Growth was achieved largely by purchasing established computer consulting firms, as Ciber embarked on an acquisition program that ranked it as the most active computer consulting acquirer in the nation during the first half of the 1990s. More than a dozen acquisitions were completed in six years' time, adding more than $70 million to the company's revenue base and greatly increasing the Colorado-based firm's national presence. Equally as important as the growth achieved through acquisition was the added expertise Ciber gained by swallowing up established computer consulting firms. During the 1990s, the push was on to grow larger quickly and to gain personnel that would enable Ciber to tackle more complex projects. Instead of just writing programs tailored to the specifications of its clients, Ciber executives were endeavoring to create a consulting firm that could identify problems and provide solutions, a transformation that would propel the company into the market for higher-margin services.

The majority of the acquisitions that helped Ciber expand its services and broaden its national presence were completed after the company's initial public offering of stock in March 1994. Once the company converted to public ownership (Stevenson retained control of more than 50 percent of the company's shares), acquisitions followed in steady succession. In June 1994, Ciber acquired all of the business operations of $16-million-in-sales C.P.U., Inc. for approximately $10 million. Based in Rochester, New York, C.P.U. operated as a computer consulting firm employing 190 consultants in six branch offices and served clients such as Northern Telecom and Xerox Corporation. The C.P.U. acquisition was Ciber's fifth of the decade and by far the largest. In the coming two years, as expansion picked up pace, annual sales more than doubled, and the company's net income, inflated by the move into more complex, higher-margin services, nearly quadrupled.

Following the C.P.U. acquisition, Ciber purchased Holmdel, New Jersey-based Interface Systems, Inc., a systems-consulting firm with 48 consultants and $5 million in annual revenue. Interface Systems was acquired in January 1995 and was followed by the May 1995 acquisition of Spencer & Spencer Systems, Inc., a 141-consultant, $13-million-in-sales computer programming provider with offices in St. Louis and Indianapolis. Next, in June 1995, Ciber reached across to the West Coast and acquired Concord, California-based Business Information Technology, Inc., a five-branch, 125-consultant computer consulting firm with $20 million in annual sales. A fourth acquisition was completed before the end of 1995 when Ciber purchased Broadway & Seymour, Inc., its Rochester, Minnesota office, and its 45 consultants. By the end of 1995, sales had increased from the $79.8 million generated in 1994 to more than $120 million, and company executives were set to launch Ciber's CIBR2000 division, a venture representative of the company's desire to provide more complex, higher-margin services.

Introduced in December 1995, CIBR2000 service was designed as a solution to a potentially devastating problem with wide-ranging ramifications. Many software programs written between the 1960s and 1990s used a two-digit date format to record calendar dates, thereby rendering a host of computer calculations inaccurate after 11:59:59 p.m., December 31, 1999. Without the ability to recognize "00" as the beginning of the new century, computer programs that performed calculations related to inventory control, invoices, interest payments, pension payments, contract expirations, license and lease renewals, and myriad other tasks would generate false reports, create computer "bugs," and perhaps cause systemwide shutdowns, all under the presumption that "00" signified the year 1900. Ciber's CIBR2000 division was created to solve the dilemma posed by the century date change and represented an area of substantial growth potential for the company during the latter half of the 1990s.

At the time CIBR2000 service was being introduced, Ciber employed roughly 1,800 consultants and operated 28 branch offices scattered throughout the country. More than half of the company's sales was derived from 20 clients, including industry stalwarts such as American Express Company, AT&T, Ford Motor Company, IBM, MCI Telecommunications, Mellon Bank, Monsanto Corp., U.S. West Communications, Inc., and Xerox Corporation.

On the acquisition front, 1996 proved to be a busy year, eclipsing the achievements of 1995. In March, the company acquired Columbus, Ohio-based OASYS, Inc., a provider of contract computer programming services that gave Ciber a new geographic location in Columbus supported by 20 information technology consultants. In May 1996, Ciber acquired Practical Business Solutions, Inc., an information technology company with offices in Boston and Providence, Rhode Island. Two months later, the company completed yet another acquisition, purchasing the Business Systems Development division of DataFocus, Inc., a computer consulting firm with offices in Fairfax, Virginia and Edison, New Jersey. Not stopping there, Ciber brought another company under its corporate umbrella in September, when it acquired Spectrum Technology Group, Inc., a management consulting firm based in Somerville, New Jersey that strengthened Ciber's management consulting and project management services.

Looking Ahead

Before the end of 1996, Ciber acquired an additional company, picking up Bellevue, Washington-based Technology Management Group, Inc. in November. By the end of the year, the company's acquisition spree had lifted the total number of its consultants to 2,100, a work force that operated out of more than 30 branch offices in more than 20 states. Looking ahead to the remainder of the decade, Ciber officials were targeting further acquisition candidates, intent on increasing the company's stature. Aside from the growth realized through future acquisitions, company executives were anticipating a substantial boost in business from CIBR2000 as the century drew to a close, particularly in 1998 and 1999. According to industry analysts, Ciber was headed toward annual sales growth in excess of 35 percent for the remainder of the 1990s, a prognostication that fueled confidence in Englewood, convincing Stevenson, Slingerlend, and other top executives that the years ahead would witness the continued ascendancy of Ciber.

Principal Subsidiaries

C.P.U., Inc.; Eurosystems International, Inc.; Business Information Technology, Inc.; Interface Systems, Inc.; Spencer & Spencer Systems, Inc.

Further Reading

"Ciber, Inc.," *The Wall Street Transcript*, May 13, 1996, p. 1.
Krause, Reinhardt, "Filling Clients' Need for High-Tech Skills," *Investor's Business Daily*, August 15, 1996, p. 20.

—Jeffrey L. Covell

CITIC Pacific Ltd.

Level 35, Two Pacific Place
88 Queensway
Hong Kong
(852) 2820 2111
Fax: (852) 2877 2771
Web site: http://www.citicpacific.com

Public Company
Incorporated: 1990
Employees: 5,000
Sales: HK$10.836 billion (1995)
Stock Exchanges: Hong Kong
SICs: 5012 Automobiles & Other Vehicles; 4899 Communications Services, Not Elsewhere Classified; 6552 Subdividers & Developers, Not Elsewhere Classified

In less than a decade, CITIC Pacific Ltd. has become the premier ''hong'' in Hong Kong, challenging the leadership of that territory's four largest trading houses. But CITIC Pacific is not the typical British-controlled conglomerate that has dominated Hong Kong's economy for the past century. Until 1996, CITIC Pacific was 43 percent controlled by private CITIC Hong Kong, which in turn is 100 percent controlled by the ruling cabinet of the People's Republic of China and its foreign investment company China International Trust and Investment Corporation (CITIC). From its formation as a largely passive investment vehicle—a so-called ''red-chip'' stock that gave investors financial and political ties to China's ruling party—CITIC Pacific has matured into a capitalist powerhouse with primary interests in infrastructure, real estate, trading and distribution, and Hong Kong's aviation industry. In its rise, CITIC Pacific has enjoyed a unique relationship with the mainland: its chairman, Larry Yung Chi-kin, is the son of China's vice-president and ''red capitalist'' Rong Yiren (Yung and Rong are different English transliterations of the same family name), himself a close ally of Deng Xiaoping, who died in early 1997. But CITIC Pacific is no puppet of the Chinese government; rather, Yung and CITIC Pacific have enjoyed from the com-

pany's inception an independence crucial to establishing CITIC Pacific as the soon-to-be former colony's top investment play. At the end of 1996, CITIC Pacific achieved still greater independence, when Yung and other management purchased an additional 15.5 percent of the company's shares from its Chinese parent, reducing CITIC Hong Kong's control to 26.5 percent. Yung took the majority of these shares, raising his own stake in the company to more than 18 percent.

Launched by Chinese Economic Reform in the 1980s

The China International Trust and Investment Corporation was established in 1979 as the first step in Deng Xiaoping's ''open door policy'' of economic reform. Deng chose Rong Yiren to form and lead CITIC, which would become China's primary domestic and foreign investment vehicle. Rong's own history was steeped in capitalism. Before the communist takeover in 1949, the Rongs had been one of Shanghai's wealthiest families, with control over much of that region's textile industry. Most of the Rong family left China when the communists took over, but Rong—who did not himself join the communist party— stayed in Shanghai and worked with the new government. Rong, and son Yung Chi-kin, were able to maintain much of their wealth through the 1950s. But the Cultural Revolution of the mid-1960s saw the family fall from grace. Rong was stripped of his property and son Yung was sent off to be ''re-educated,'' doing hard labor on collective farms in remote regions of the country.

The family's fortunes revived with Deng Xiaoping's rise to power. Rong and Yung were rehabilitated in 1972, and their personal property was restored to them. Yung went to Stanford to study business; in 1978, he moved to Hong Kong, where he ran a small company that manufactured electronic watch movements. While his father was launching CITIC, Yung was enjoying success as an entrepreneur: together with a group of Chinese and American friends, Yung invested in a small software company in California. That company merged with another software company, going public in 1984. Yung sold his shares in the company, netting US$50 million.

As talks between the British and Chinese governments finalized plans to return Hong Kong to Chinese control, CITIC launched its CITIC Hong Kong investment subsidiary. In 1987, Yung was placed in charge of the new company, with US$30 million in startup funds. From the outset, Yung insisted upon—and received—a large degree of independence, including the ability to make local investment decisions and the ability to hire his choice of management, giving Yung a unique position among other Chinese government-controlled companies. Under Yung, CITIC HK bought large shares of two primary Hong Kong businesses, Cathay Airlines and Hong Kong Telecommunications. Named CITIC HK's managing director, Yung was able to make these and other purchases at deeply discounted prices—with China's looming return to control, Hong Kong businesses were eager to establish ties with the government. And CITIC HK offered an attractive route to China's State Council, especially once Rong Yiren was named the country's vice president.

CITIC HK operated primarily as a passive investment vehicle. But China needed to go beyond regaining governmental control of Hong Kong, it needed to establish itself as a force in the powerful Hong Kong economy, and this meant taking a place in the territory's stock market. Yung took a backdoor to the market in 1990, when CITIC HK bought an inactive but listed holding company, Tylfull Co. Ltd. CITIC HK placed some of its assets, including shares of Cathay and Hong Kong Telecom, into the public company and renamed it as CITIC Pacific Ltd. The company quickly added to its holdings, building its share of Cathay Airlines—Hong Kong's premier international airline—to 12.5 percent; gaining 38.3 percent of Hong Kong Dragon Airlines, known as Dragonair, which was partly owned by Cathay and was the premier airline carrier along Hong Kong-China routes; and buying 20 percent of Macau Telephone. In addition to these investments, CITIC Pacific quickly established the second of its principal focus markets, buying up HK$647 million of Hong Kong real estate properties.

Top "Hong" in the 1990s

CITIC Pacific's ambitions went beyond simply building a portfolio of passive investments, however. In order to gain position in the Hong Kong economy, CITIC Pacific would need to establish itself as one of the territory's "hongs," or trading houses. The four principal hongs, Jardine Matheson, Hutchison Whampoa, Swire Pacific, and Wharf Holdings, were all conglomerates rooted in British control (although Hutchison and Wharf were by then run by Hong Kong entrepreneurs), with interests ranging widely beyond trading into the colony's infrastructure, manufacturing, and real estate. In order to achieve hong status, CITIC Pacific needed to diversify into more active holdings. The company took the first step toward that end in October 1991, when it took a 36 percent share in a consortium organized to make a HK$7 billion purchase of the private Hang Chong company. Hang Chong, itself a smaller version of a hong, had extensive real estate holdings in Hong Kong, as well as in Japan and the United States. But CITIC Pacific's real interest was in Hang Chong's primary subsidiary, Dah Chong Heng, with food and shipping interests, and a chain of 40 car dealerships that controlled 40 percent of the Hong Kong automobile market. CITIC Pacific's 36 percent interest in Hang Chong quadrupled the company's net assets.

Three months later, CITIC Pacific bought out the other members of the consortium (which included ultimate parent CITIC) and gained a more than 97 percent share of Hang Chong. Under terms of the deal, valued at HK$3 billion (US$385 million), CITIC Pacific also bought an additional 7.8 percent of Dragonair from CITIC, boosting CITIC Pacific's share of the airline to 46.1 percent, for HK$93 million (US$12 million). The company's sales, which had reached HK$118 million in 1991, skyrocketed to HK$7.8 billion in 1992. Net profits for the year were up 212 percent, to HK$1.2 billion.

The move was seen as a major step forward in China's economic stake in Hong Kong. It could also been seen as some assurance that the mainland would honor its commitment to the "one country, two systems" policy that was to govern the return of Hong Kong in 1997. With its large stake in Hong Kong's market, China would be less likely to dismantle the territory's economy. In turn, CITIC Pacific enhanced CITIC's credibility with the international financial community. Banks were reluctant to lend to the Chinese government; with CITIC Pacific, however, China had the opportunity to prove its integrity to investors. At the same time, investments in CITIC Pacific offered a more stable method of investing in the mainland. In January 1993, CITIC Pacific's position as the leading "red chip" (a term given to Hong Kong listed companies that were attractive investments because they were controlled by mainland parent companies, thereby giving investors entry into the mainland's political and economic arenas) enabled it to raise HK$7.2 billion. By then, however, CITIC Pacific had also turned "blue," after it was added to the territory's Hang Seng Index of blue chip stocks.

CITIC Pacific used that money to purchase a 12 percent share in Hong Kong Telecom from CITIC HK. Under terms of the deal, CITIC HK increased its ownership of CITIC Pacific to 46 percent; CITIC Pacific received a HK$3.3 billion loan from CITIC HK, as well as controlling shares in two mainland power plants and a 20 percent share in Hong Kong's Chemical Waste Treatment Centre. CITIC Pacific also made a separate purchase of a 51 percent share of the Shanghai Children's Food Factory. In another deal, the company entered a joint-venture with Swire for HK$2.85 billion real estate purchase in Hong Kong's Yau Yat Chuen area. In June 1993, CITIC Pacific also purchased a 20 percent stake in Chase Manhattan Bank's Manhattan Card Co. Hong Kong credit card business. Apart from further diversifying CITIC Pacific's assets, these deals helped boost the company's market capitalization to HK$24 billion, placing it in the top 20 of Hong Kong companies. The success of CITIC Pacific was also encouraging other China-backed companies to move into the Hong Kong market, a development that would soon come to haunt CITIC Pacific.

In the meantime, CITIC Pacific continued its aggressive expansion. With sales topping HK$10 billion for 1993, the company paid HK$3.06 billion (US$390 million) for a 50 percent share of a residential development on Hong Kong's Discovery Bay island. The company was also active on the infrastructure front, paying HK$104 million (US$13.3 million) for 25 percent of the Western Harbour Crossing, a tunnel project linking Hong Kong with the territory's Kowloon airport. The company also acquired 28.5 percent of another Hong Kong tunnel project, the Eastern Harbour Crossing, as well as gaining

50 percent of a mainland tunnel, in Shanghai. These moves were also seen as part of CITIC Pacific's attempt to counter criticism that the company was still not much more than a holding company for passive investments. The company slowed its acquisition growth to concentrate on taking a more active management role in the tunnel projects and its Hang Chong subsidiary. Revenues continued to grow, topping HK$12 billion in 1994. The diversity of CITIC Pacific's projects, which by then included a joint-venture with Japan's Isuzu to build cars and light trucks on the mainland, as well as a 20 percent stake in a joint venture to build an airport railway system, seemed to have finally elevated the company to true hong status.

Not all of CITIC Pacific's critics were convinced, however. Analysts faulted the company for having no clear investment strategy. And the company's trading subsidiary, Dah Chong Hong, in which CITIC Pacific had taken its most active management role, was suffering heavy losses. Nevertheless, the company continued to attract investors, in part because of its close ties with China's government; at the same time, however, the company—and Yung—were widely praised for refusing to exploit the political clout of its parent, relying instead on its own entrepreneurial skills to build the company. But competition from other mainland-backed companies was heating up, and as its position as the premier China investment vehicle came under attack, CITIC Pacific needed to step up its entrepreneurial activities. In 1995, the company began reducing its stake in its more passive holdings, such as Cathay Airlines and Hong Kong Telecom, raising a war chest of some HK$10 billion. The company's revenues, however, dropped to HK$10.83 billion for the year, dragged down by Dah Chong Hong's poor performance amid a weak retail market.

A Blue Chip for a Red Future

The following year saw CITIC Pacific's first real challenge from another mainland company. China National Aviation Corp. (CNAC), controlled by the mainland's civil aviation agency, which in turn had strong ties to the country's powerful military, announced its intention to establish a third Hong Kong airline. CNAC's ties with China's civil aviation agency would give it a decided advantage in winning important air routes to the mainland's major cities, possibly taking routes away from Dragonair. The move would directly threaten CITIC Pacific, which had been reducing its role in Cathay in favor of boosting its activities in Dragonair.

Meanwhile, the company continued to refocus its business, turning away from minority investments and investing its war chest instead into a new string of infrastructure deals, including a US$200 million purchase of 45 percent of Shanghai's Xu Pu Bridge. The company also added to its infrastructure portfolio with controlling interests in another two mainland power stations. In real estate, the company purchased, for HK$3.5 billion, the former British naval headquarters site in Central Hong Kong's Tamar Basin in order to build the company's 37-story headquarters, expected to be completed in 1998.

By May 1996, the situation with CNAC came to a head. In a sudden turnaround, CITIC Pacific agreed to sell a 17.6 percent stake in Dragonair to CNAC; at the same time, however, the company increased its share of Cathay, from 10 percent to 25 percent, for HK$6.3 billion. Analysts read several implications into the agreement. For one, it was believed that CITIC Pacific had been forced to sell the Dragonair holdings by its parent, CITIC, under direction of China's State Council—with the further implication that CITIC Pacific, despite its blue-chip status, continued to operate at the will of the Chinese government. For another, the agreement suggested a potential shift in the Chinese government's power base from the reform-oriented position of the ailing Deng Xiaoping (and Rong Yiren, who himself was 80 years old) to the more left-wing Old Guard, represented by CNAC and its parent, the Civil Aviation Administration of China.

The deal caught the Hong Kong investment community by surprise. Despite the fact that CITIC Pacific had relied on its own business skills, rather than Larry Yung's political ties, to build the company, a shift in the power base was nevertheless seen as harmful to CITIC Pacific's future. In response, the company stepped up its emphasis on its infrastructure portfolio, adding a purchase of 13 water treatment plants in mainland China for HK$1.26 billion in October 1996. But at the end of the year, Yung surprised the market again, when he led other members of CITIC Pacific management in buying up 15.5 percent—at a 28 percent discounted price—of the company from CITIC HK. Yung, who took most of the stock, increased his personal share of the company to 18.5 percent, making him the company's second largest shareholder. While some analysts suggested the deal was a way of rewarding Yung for acquiescing in the CNAC agreement, others pointed to the political situation on the mainland. Deng Xiaoping's death was announced in early 1997, suggesting that Yung's political allies were fading. Gaining tighter control of CITIC Pacific placed Yung in a stronger position to steer the company—especially after the imminent return of Hong Kong to Chinese control.

Further Reading

"CITIC Licks Wounds After Cathay Battle," *South China Morning Post*, May 5, 1996, p. 2.

Hewett, Gareth, "CITIC Pacific Undergoes Changes to Become Hong," *South China Morning Post*, January 27, 1996, p. 16.

Koo, Carolyn, "Heavier Seas for CITIC Pacific," *Institutional Investor*, International Edition, February 1996, p. 40.

Kraar, Louis, "The Man To Know in Hong Kong," *Fortune*, January 13, 1997, p. 102.

Leung, Alison, "Hong Kong's 'Red Chip' CITIC Seen Turning Blue," *Reuters World Service*, January 9, 1997.

Leung, James, "Firm Hand Steers China's Thriving Hong," *Asian Business*, April 1996, p. 26.

Poole, Teresa, "CITIC Pacific Storms Hong Kong," *The Independent*, January 18, 1993, p. 19.

Spain, Mark, "Chinese Challenge the Hongs," *The Independent*, October 1, 1991, p. 23.

Vines, Steve, "A Company Worth Being Seen With," *The Independent*, January 29, 1996, p. 17.

Whai, Quak Hiang, "CITIC Deal: A Larry Yung Special or a New Policy?" *Business Times*, January 6, 1997, p. 17.

—M. L. Cohen

Congoleum Corp.

3705 Quakerbridge Road
P.O. Box 3127
Mercerville, New Jersey 08619-0127
U.S.A.
(609) 584-3000
Fax: (609) 584-3555
Web site: http://www.congoleum.com

Public Company
Incorporated: 1911 as The United Roofing &
    Manufacturing Co.
Employees: 1,320
Sales: $263.1 million (1995)
Stock Exchanges: New York
SICs: 2821 Plastics Materials, Synthetic Resins &
    Nonvulcanizable Elastomers; 3081 Unsupported
    Plastics Film & Sheet

Congoleum Corp., a manufacturer of vinyl sheet and tile products is among the nation's largest manufacturers of resilient vinyl flooring products, for both commercial and residential markets. Its corporate history includes such industry highlights as the introduction of the first no-wax floor and the first chemically embossed vinyl-sheet floor. Throughout a complex corporate history the Congoleum name has remained a constant. In 1995 American Biltrite Inc. secured a majority of Congoleum's voting power, and its chairman and chief executive officer also became Congoleum's chairman, president, and chief executive officer. Therefore, although nominally independent and publicly traded, Congoleum became in effect a subsidiary of American Biltrite.

Congoleum and Nairn, 1886–1924

By 1910 a new type of smooth-surfaced floor covering known as printed felt base had come into existence as an economical alternative to floorcloth and linoleum. The United Roofing & Manufacturing Co. was formed in 1911 to manufac-

ture this waterproof floor covering, which was marketed under the registered name of Congoleum. Soon this entity became The Congoleum Co., a Pennsylvania corporation wholly controlled and operated by The Barrett Co. It was reincorporated in New York in 1919 as the Congoleum Co., Inc., with Barrett retaining a substantial interest until its holdings of preferred stock were reacquired by Congoleum in 1922. The company's plant, in 1920, was in Marcus Hook, Pennsylvania—a location the company still retained 75 years later. It had its general office in Philadelphia and display rooms and warehouses in New York City, Chicago, and San Francisco. Additional warehouses were located in Pittsburgh, Galveston, Minneapolis, and several other U.S. cities. Congoleum added to its line by acquiring Farr & Bailey Manufacturing Co., a Camden, New Jersey, linoleum maker, in 1920, and it purchased the Salem, New Jersey, plant of the Salem Manufacturing Co. in 1923 for additional felt-base production. It began making felt at a Maryland plant about the same time.

In 1924 Congoleum acquired Nairn Linoleum Co. and became Congoleum-Nairn, Inc. Michael Nairn was said to have been the founder in Scotland of the floorcloth industry. His son, Sir Michael Baker Nairn, was chairman of Michael Nairn & Co., Ltd. of Kirkaldy, Scotland, and in 1886 founded the Nairn Linoleum Co. Invented in 1860, linoleum constituted a more upscale product than printed felt base. Nairn's head office and linoleum plant were in Kearny, New Jersey.

Congoleum-Nairn, 1924–50

Congoleum-Nairn made Nairn's headquarters its own. A. W. Erickson of Congoleum became its chairman and Sir Michael Nairn its vice-chairman, but active management was headed by Alfred W. Hawkes, the president, who remained in this position until 1941. (He later became a U.S. senator from New Jersey.) Congoleum-Nairn had gross revenue of $10.4 million in 1925 and total income of $4.5 million, about half of which apparently came from patent royalties rather than from sales of its manufactured products. The years 1926 to 1930, during which the company suspended its annual dividend, were not as profitable, although it never lost money. It resumed its dividend in 1931 and sailed through the Great Depression with a comfortable profit each year.

By 1940 Congoleum-Nairn had become the leading producer of felt-base, smooth-surfaced floor coverings, which it sold under the tradenames Gold Seal Congoleum and Crescent Seal Congoleum. It was also producing a substantial quantity of linoleum under the tradenames Nairn, Nairn Sealex, and Nairn Treadlite. In addition it was producing linoleum paste, cement, self-polishing wax, and floor-laying and floor-maintenance accessories. It held minority interests in the Congoleum Co. of Canada, Ltd. and Michael Nairn of Greenwich, Ltd. (England). The Camden and Salem plants were discontinued in 1936 and 1939, respectively, with the former's production moved to Kearny and the latter's to Marcus Hook. Production at Salem revived in 1943, however, and continued until 1953.

Congoleum-Nairn introduced printed felt-base wall covering in 1944 and added a facility at its Kearny location in 1947 for the manufacture of asphalt tile. The creation of new households following World War II enabled sales to reach $60.4 million and net income $7.2 million in 1948, but the company could not maintain these record levels as new smooth-surfaced floor-covering products began to supplant linoleum and felt base. The 1948 sales figure was not topped until 1965.

Troubled Times and New Products, 1950–68

Forced by the competition to expand its line, Congoleum-Nairn in 1951 acquired Delaware Floor Products, Inc., a Wilmington manufacturer of vinyl plastic tile and rolls as well as felt-base floor coverings and also a manufacturer of sheet-vinyl coverings for sinks and counter tops. Congoleum also began producing rubber tile and desktop linoleum, plus cork and all-vinyl tile for the luxury market. In 1953 it acquired Sloane-Blabon Corp., another floor-covering maker, for $10.3 million, and in 1955 the equipment and inventories of the fibre-rug division of Patchogue-Plymouth Corp., creating a subsidiary called Loomweve Corp. to manufacture tufted carpeting, woven fibre rugs, and automotive flooring in Lawrence, Massachusetts.

The acquisitions were moving Congoleum-Nairn in the right direction, since by 1955 synthetic tiles were clearly supplanting linoleum in public favor. It shifted some of its linoleum production from sheets to squares in order to attract trade from do-it-yourselfers and brought out a linoleum tile with a special base and adhesive for use with concrete-slab construction. However, to meet intense competition from other tilemakers the company had to reduce its price for asphalt tiles by 13 percent and for vinyl plastic tiles by 10 percent in 1955, even though this sector of its business was barely profitable. In addition, Congoleum-Nairn was finding it more difficult to sell felt-base floor coverings because quality-conscious consumers increasingly found this enamel-top material inferior in wearability and other respects.

Shifting emphasis away from linoleum, Congoleum-Nairn moved its linoleum-making operations from the Kearny plant in 1957 to the former Sloane-Blabon factory in Trenton, New Jersey, retaining part of the Kearny facility to make asphalt and vinyl plastic tile. It installed at Marcus Hook what it called the largest rotogravure press in the world for a new plastic floor covering. Nevertheless, sales continued to skid—falling to a low of $41.1 million in 1960—and the company lost money in 1957, 1958, 1960, and 1961, the year it discontinued production in Wilmington. The annual dividend was suspended in 1958. At the 1960 annual meeting for shareholders an interior decorator who came armed with swatches called Congoleum-Nairn "moth-eaten," and a Brooklyn linoleum sales representative described the company's floor coverings as "dogs."

Congoleum-Nairn turned the corner in the early 1960s by reorganizing its distribution and merchandising operations and launching new products and new styles. Introduced in 1962, Cushionflor was a no-wax product—the first in its field—composed of a layer of chemically embossed vinyl foam bonded between a vinyl surface and a vinylized felt backing. It was advertised as having "the cushiony softness, warmth and quiet of carpeting" and proved the savior of the company. In December 1966 Congoleum-Nairn received two patents covering the chemically embossed vinyl-foam products it had been marketing and promptly instituted patent-infringement actions against four competitors, all of which were eventually settled on a basis favorable to the company. Profitable again since 1962, Congoleum-Nairn restored its annual dividend in 1965. It ended the year with $5.8 million in net income on record sales of $67 million. Sales reached $80.7 million in 1967.

Congoleum Industries, 1968–80

By 1968 Congoleum-Nairn had drawn a suitor in Milwaukee-based Bath Industries Inc., a holding company that acquired 42 percent of its stock. When Congoleum-Nairn's board of directors opposed a proposed merger Bath was able to push it through by removing nine of the directors and replacing them with its own nominees. Congoleum-Nairn became Congoleum Industries, a subsidiary of Bath Industries. Although the parent company included Bath Iron Works, one of the nation's oldest and most important shipyards, in 1969 two-thirds of its $189.8 million in revenues came from floor coverings and furniture and only about 28 percent from shipbuilding. Floor coverings and furniture accounted for 78 percent of the year's $7.6 million in profits and shipbuilding for only 18 percent. (The furniture sector included the former Mersman Bros. Corp., a Celina, Ohio, maker of occasional tables acquired by Congoleum-Nairn in 1963.)

At this time the bulk of Congoleum Industries' sales was coming from the repair and maintenance market rather than from new construction. It also was a major supplier of furniture for the mobile- and recreational-home market. Another lucrative income source, amounting to $1.7 million in 1969, came from royalties earned on its patents. In 1970 Congoleum Industries also added to its carpeting capacity by moving into a $10-million plant in Wilburton, Oklahoma, that had the industry's most technologically advanced printing and dyeing machines. That year sales of its floor and wall products reached $96.6 million, and its share of the growing market for cushioned vinyl-sheet flooring was estimated at 40 percent. It claimed over 400 different patterns and colors in flooring, ''more than anyone else in the business.'' In 1972 Congoleum Industries began a $20-million expansion of the Marcus Hook plant to provide new facilities for the manufacture of vinyl floor coverings.

Bath Industries acknowledged the preeminence of its Congoleum Industries unit by renaming itself Congoleum Corp. in 1975. Effective at the end of the year, Congoleum Industries was swallowed by the company and its operations divided into separate resilient-flooring, carpeting, and furniture divisions. Floor coverings remained the company's leading product sector in 1975, accounting for $169 million in revenues (42 percent of the total) and $25 million in net income (95 percent of the total). That year Congoleum Industries ceased producing vinyl asbestos tile. By this time tile was representing less than one percent of the parent firm's sales volume.

In 1976 Congoleum Corp. received $35 million in damages from Armstrong Cork Co., the industry leader in smooth-surfaced floor coverings, for violating the company's patents. This enabled Congoleum to pay down most of its long-term debt, which had swelled to a dangerous $75 million. The company had outstanding earnings in 1977 and 1978, sparked by its more-than-40-percent share of 1977's $1.7 billion in overall retail sales of resilient flooring. That year it collected $13.5 million in royalties on its flooring patents and was marketing resilient-flooring products through 65 independent wholesalers.

Aided by a backlog of naval shipyard contracts, Congoleum's sales soared to $558.6 million in 1978, and its net profits to $41.7 million. Resilient flooring remained its mainstay, however. That year the Home Furnishings Division, which consisted almost entirely of resilient flooring, accounted for $226 million in revenue and two-thirds of Congoleum's operating profits. Its operating margin of 21 percent was far higher than that of shipbuilding or Congoleum's other businesses.

Privately Held, 1980–95

In early 1980 Congoleum was acquired by Fibic Corp., a newly formed, privately held corporation organized by The First Boston Corp., with payment in cash of $38 for each share of common stock, or about $445 million in all. The new owners were First Boston, Inc., Century Capital Associates, various financial institutions loaning funds to the company, and members of Congoleum management. Headquarters were moved from Milwaukee to Portsmouth, New Hampshire.

First Boston sold its holdings in Congoleum in 1984 to the company's chief executives, Byron C. Radaker and Eddy G. Nicholson, in a leveraged buy out. Radaker and Nicholson, who said they owned or controlled 70 percent of Congoleum's stock,

sold the Bath Iron Works unit in 1986 to a New York investment concern in a leveraged buy out valued at estimates ranging from $500 million to $675 million. At the same time they sold the remaining three company businesses piecemeal for a total of $175 million. The flooring business, which retained the Congoleum Corp. name, was purchased by Hillside Industries Inc., a subsidiary of New York–based Hillside Capital Inc. Hillside paid $82 million for the business but had to add another $48 million later because Congoleum had difficulty paying down $55 million in acquisition debt.

Based in Mercerville, New Jersey—outside Trenton—Congoleum embarked on a capital-spending program in 1989. One benefit of this program was that the Marcus Hook plant, which in 1987 led all Delaware river valley polluters by pumping more than a million pounds of ozone-destroying compounds into the air, completely eliminated this noxious discharge by switching from hazardous solvents to water in its inks. In 1991 Congoleum announced it would spend between $45 million and $50 million to improve several of its vinyl-flooring plants, with the bulk of the funds used to install new equipment, such as improved ovens and an improved printing system. The company was unable to borrow from banks for these improvements but in 1991 secured a $57.5–million asset-based working-capital line from CIT Group Inc.

Congoleum had net sales of $158.3 million in fiscal 1990 (ended September 30, 1990), $152.4 million in fiscal 1991, and $164.2 million in fiscal 1992. It had net income of $3.1 million in 1990 but lost $4.2 million in 1991 and $1.6 million in 1992, chiefly because of heavy interest payments on its considerable debt. In February 1993 American Biltrite Inc. sold its Amtico Tile Division, a producer of resilient-floor tiles, to Congoleum, in return for a 40 percent stake, valued at $18.8 million, in the company. The acquisition was effected through a new company, Congoleum Holdings Inc., which combined Amtico's assets with Hillside Industries' stock into a reorganized Congoleum Corp. In the 10 months following the merger this company had net sales of $211.1 million and net income of $11.2 million. In 1994 Congoleum had net sales of $265.8 million and net income of $17.5 million.

Going Public Again in 1995

In February 1995 Congoleum completed a public offering of 4.65 million shares of Class A common stock at $13 a share, following which Congoleum Holdings was merged into Congoleum Corp. The proceeds of the sale ($56.2 million) and other company funds were used to acquire the 4.65 million shares of Class B common stock—with twice the voting power of Class A stock—held by Hillside Industries, also at $13 a share. Following these transactions American Biltrite held 82 percent of the Class B common stock and 57 percent of the combined voting power of the corporation. Hillside Capital held 18 percent of the Class B stock and 12 percent of the voting power. The biggest holders of the Class A common stock were Putnam Investments, Inc. and The Zweig Companies, with nine and seven percent, respectively. Roger S. Marcus, American Biltrite's chairman and chief executive officer, was president, chairman, and chief executive officer of Congoleum.

In 1996 Congoleum was manufacturing 40 vinyl tile and sheet products available in more than 1,000 combinations of designs and colors. These products were being used principally in the remodeling-and-replacement, commercial, manufactured-home and new-residential markets. A substantial amount of its vinyl tile was being sold through home centers and mass-market merchandisers. The majority of these tiles had an adhesive backing mainly for do-it-yourself customers, with the remainder sold "dry back" and generally installed by professionals in commercial and, to a lesser extent, residential settings. The sheet vinyl was almost exclusively for residential use. In addition, the company was producing through-chip inlaid products for the commercial market. Congoleum was selling these products through over 13,000 outlets by means of about 40 distributors providing about 100 distribution points in the United States and Canada. Retail prices ranged from below $3 to more than $45 per square yard.

Congoleum owned sheet-vinyl manufacturing plants in Marcus Hook and Trenton, a vinyl-tile plant in Trenton, and a felt plant (felt being still used in the backing of vinyl sheets) in Finksburg, Maryland. It was leasing its corporate and marketing offices in Mercerville. In 1995 Congoleum introduced Futura, which it called the flagship product of a new generation of residential flooring; Forum Wood Plank, a vinyl tile sold in plank form with a startlingly natural wood color and grain; and Ultraflor, a higher-priced, more-durable vinyl sheet for manufactured-housing builders.

Congoleum's net sales declined slightly to $263.1 million in 1995 in what the company attributed to a cyclical downturn in the homebuilding sector, accompanied by rising raw-material prices, and "a sluggish retail environment and higher interest rates." Net income fell to $9.4 million, with earnings negatively affected by a $1.5-million after-tax charge relating to a writeoff of accounts receivable from Color Tile, Inc. which filed for Chapter 11 bankruptcy protection in January 1996. Congoleum's long-term debt was $90 million in June 1996.

Principal Subsidiaries

Congoleum Intellectual Properties, Inc.; Congoleum International Incorporated (U.S. Virgin Islands).

Further Reading

"Bath Industries Sets Vote on Merger Plan with Congoleum-Nairn," *Wall Street Journal,* September 9, 1968.
"Congoleum," *Barron's,* January 23, 1995, p. 49.
"Congoleum-Nairn Holders Criticize Firm for Loss, Sales Drop," *Wall Street Journal,* June 2, 1960, p. 14.
"Congoleum: Still a Sitting Duck?" *Financial World,* February 1, 1979, pp. 20–21.
Ditlev-Simonsen, Cecilie, "Congoleum Gone, but Cash Remains," *Boston Globe,* August 23, 1986, p. 33.
Hals, Tom, "Congoleum Expands to Match the Rise in Manufactured Housing," *Philadelphia Business Journal,* p. 34.
Keresztes, Peter, "Results at Congoleum Show Plenty of Bounce," *Barron's,* February 6, 1978, pp. 33–34.
Laubsher, Harry W., "Bath Industries Inc.," *Wall Street Transcript,* August 31, 1970, p. 21605.
"Lease on Life," *Forbes,* May 1, 1976, pp. 44–45.
Millman, Gregory J., "Hock the Company? Why Not?" *CFO,* September 1991, pp. 72, 77.
Sherman, Joseph V., "Barely Scratching the Surface," *Barron's,* October 25, 1971, p. 11.
Solomon, Goody L., "Glossier Sheen," *Barron's,* February 25, 1963, p. 5.
Welling, Brenton, Jr., "Makers of Plastic Tiles, Linoleum Fight Fiercely Despite Building Boom," *Wall Street Journal,* March 11, 1955, pp. 1, 14.

—Robert Halasz

Credit Acceptance Corporation

25505 W. Twelve Mile Road
Suite 3000
Southfield, Michigan 48084-8339
U.S.A.
(810) 353-2700
Fax: (810) 353-9776

Public Company
Incorporated: 1972
Employees: 406
Sales: $85.08 million
Stock Exchanges: NASDAQ
SICs: 6141 Personal Credit Institutions; 6153 Short-Term
    Business Credit

Credit Acceptance Corporation is a pioneer provider of a range of credit financing services to automobile dealers selling used automobiles to consumers considered high credit risks. Such consumers typically lack access to traditional sources of credit and automobile financing. Services provided to dealers by Credit Acceptance include funding, receivables management, collection, sales training, and other products and services. In September 1996, Credit Acceptance held more than $920 million in installment contracts receivables, an increase of more than $300 million over the previous year. Credit Acceptance's network of participating dealers has been growing quickly as well, nearly doubling in 1996 to almost 5,000 dealers. Credit Acceptance works with dealers in 49 states as well as in the United Kingdom, which accounted for approximately 16 percent of participating dealers in 1995. During 1996, Credit Acceptance also received the necessary licenses to expand its operations into Canada. The company has seen strong growth since going public in 1992, increasing revenues from $18.7 million to $85.1 million in 1995. The company's profits have also been strong: net income for 1995 was more than $29.5 million. Credit Acceptance holds about two percent of the highly fragmented used automobile financing market, which has been estimated at more than $100 billion per year in the

mid-1990s. Credit Acceptance is led by chairman, CEO, and founder Donald A. Foss, who controls approximately 52 percent of the company's stock.

A Credit Pioneer in the 1970s

Don Foss, named to the *Forbes* list of the 400 wealthiest Michigan residents in 1996, graduated from Detroit High School in 1964. By 1967, Foss had opened his first used car lot. As was customary among used car dealers, Foss offered his customers financing on a 'buy-here, pay-here' basis. Despite the credit risk of many of his customers, Foss would often use personal funds in order to finance—and stimulate—automobile purchases. Foss quickly added more used car dealerships, each arranging its own financing with customers. In 1972, however, Foss decided to consolidate his financing services under one company, which he called Credit Acceptance Corporation. "The credit business was started over his compassion for people," a former Foss employee told the *Detroit News.* "He knew that if he could help enough people get what they wanted, he could get what he wanted."

For the next decade, Credit Acceptance existed primarily to provide financing for customers of Foss's dealerships. By 1986, however, Credit Acceptance began offering its services to used car dealers outside the company. The company also began attracting new car dealers eager to stimulate sales. Almost all of these dealerships were located in the Detroit area.

In 1988 Credit Acceptance began to expand the company's dealer base. Over the next four years the company doubled the number of dealers using Credit Acceptance services. This aggressive expansion was stimulated in two ways. The first was by instituting a sales and marketing division within Credit Acceptance that could attract new dealers while providing sales and training support to existing dealers. The second move was the incorporation of the company's Advance program as a supplement to the receivables management and collection services already offered by Credit Acceptance.

Under the Advance program, dealers were provided cash advances on car sales financed through Credit Acceptance. When the dealer sold a used vehicle, he received a cash down payment from the customer. A down payment typically represented 25 percent of the vehicle's purchase price. The dealer then assigned the purchase contract to Credit Acceptance, and Credit Acceptance paid the dealer a cash advance averaging 50 percent of the purchase value. The average loan was for $6,000. Credit Acceptance took over all of the collection risk from the dealer, overseeing collection on the account. Payments would go first toward paying the company's servicing fees and reimbursing the company's collection costs, which averaged 20 percent of the total contract amount, then toward recovering the cash advance. Once the cash advance was fully recovered, the dealer received the balance of the payments. In order to minimize risk to both the dealer and the company, Credit Acceptance purchased the vehicle financing contracts in blocks of 100. The dealer would receive the balance due once Credit Acceptance had been reimbursed for its cash advances, servicing fees, and collection costs on all of the 100 contracts in the block. The dealer's balance also included interest on the contract: interest rates were set by the dealer, and usually represented the maximum allowable rate for the dealer's state. Apart from the advance, dealers generally would see no cash on the purchase for the initial 19 to 21 months of the contracts. Contracts usually had a 36-month life.

The Advance program proved attractive to all of the parties involved in used vehicle purchases. The dealers saw a positive cash flow and were able to sell more vehicles, especially older model cars, as Credit Acceptance generally approved more than 90 percent of used vehicle financing contracts. Credit Acceptance also generated higher profits for dealers than other high-risk lenders. Customers also benefitted. The high approval rate put more customers with little credit or a damaged credit rating behind the wheel of a car. Paying off the finance contract also provided the customer with a means to establish or repair his or her credit rating.

Dealers flocked to the new Credit Acceptance plan. The number of used car dealers arranging financing through Credit Acceptance more than doubled in four years, and the number of new car dealers working with the company also grew. Business was boosted by improvements in U.S. automobile design and manufacturing, as better-built automobiles proved more durable and more attractive to consumers buying second-hand. The economic slowdown of the late 1980s and early 1990s also spurred sales of used automobiles over new automobiles. At the same time, staggering rises during the 1980s in the prices of new automobiles stimulated the used auto market. As families struggled with the effects of the recession, the Gulf War, and the wave of downsizing sweeping corporate America, the cost of new automobiles jumped from about 36 percent of a family's annual income in 1980 to 46 percent in 1990. Credit Acceptance's high acceptance rate of financing applications was another factor attracting dealers to the company.

Public in the 1990s

In the early 1990s, Credit Acceptance was the sole central lender in the high-risk financing market. Even after the company was joined by a growing list of competitors, the market remained highly fragmented, with enormous potential for growth. Credit Acceptance quickly expanded across the continental United States, gaining licenses in 46 states by 1992. The

company's dealer network grew rapidly, to 394 dealers in 1991, then nearly doubled in one year to 750 in 1992. The company's accounts receivable assets climbed from just $7 million in 1990 to more than $70 million in 1991. Revenues, the majority of which were generated by finance charges, passed $12 million for 1991. Net income on this revenue passed $5 million for the year. Credit Acceptance next prepared to expand even more aggressively in the high-risk lending market.

In order to fuel further growth, Foss took Credit Acceptance public in June 1992, selling 2.3 million shares and raising $27 million. The initial selling price was $12 per share. The company stepped up recruitment of new dealers and added new services to increase the company's attractiveness to both dealers and their customers. Among the new services Credit Acceptance offered were credit life and disability insurance and dual interest collateral protection programs offered through the company by third-party insurers. The company also set up a subsidiary offering vehicle service contracts through the dealers. Dealers were also offered floor plan financing and working capital loans. While vehicle financing remained the company's most important source of revenue, these new programs helped boost the company's dealer base to nearly 1,100 in 1993 and to more than 1,500 in 1994. The company's total assets from its financing contracts and other receivables climbed from $128 million in 1992 to $203 million in 1993. Revenues rose from $16 million to $25.7 million, while net income passed $12 million in 1993.

The company's stock split 2-for-1 by March 1993. By November of that year, Credit Acceptance's stock was selling for $40 per share. A second stock split, of 3-for-2, following in December 1993. The number of new-car dealers in Credit Acceptance's dealer base had risen to more than 50 percent, as new-car dealers expanded their used vehicle sales. "We take the risk out of financing for dealers," Foss told *Automotive News*, "We allow dealers to get into the business of financing older cars and later-model cars as well." By 1994, Credit Acceptance counted nearly 650 new-car dealers in its dealer base.

In 1994 the company also added a new program to increase its attractiveness to dealers. The program, called the Credit Acceptance Corp. Stock Option Plan for dealers, granted dealers the option to buy 1,000 shares of Credit Acceptance stock after they set up 100 automobile financing contracts with the company. Every additional 100 contracts gave the dealer an option to buy 100 more shares of company stock. Credit Acceptance registered 500,000 new shares for the program. As one analyst told *Crain's Detroit Business*, "I think it's a good way to build up a base of loyal customers and business friends. If the dealers exercise the option and hold the stock, they may say, 'Hey, I'm a stockholder in Credit Acceptance Corp.; maybe I'd better send them all the business I can.' "

Credit Acceptance next moved to enter the international market, setting up a subsidiary in the United Kingdom. Despite first-year losses, the company's U.K. subsidiary soon proved profitable, and the U.K. dealers quickly grew to represent a significant portion of the company's total dealer base, which more than doubled, from over 1,500 in 1994 to more than 3,300 in 1995. A key factor in the company's growth was its growing sales and marketing force. In 1990 the company had just two sales representatives. By 1995, the company had nearly 70 sales representatives and sales agents.

Credit Acceptance made a second public offering in September 1995, offering 5.5 million shares for a total price of nearly $135 million. By the end of that year, the company's receivables and other assets had climbed to $686 million, producing revenue of $85 million, and net income of nearly $30 million. By the company's third quarter the following year, its receivables approached $1 billion.

Despite Credit Acceptance's steady growth during the 1990s, the high-risk auto financing market remained largely untapped. Credit Acceptance, while still the largest in the high-risk market, was estimated to hold only about two percent of the market. In 1996 Credit Acceptance continued plans for international expansion when it secured the licenses to expand operations into Canada. By then, Foss, who still owned 12 Detroit-area dealerships, was worth more than $500 million on paper. And analysts agreed that Foss's and Credit Acceptance's background in used car sales gave it the edge in the booming high-risk financing market.

Principal Subsidiaries

Credit Acceptance Corporation Life Insurance Company; Buyers Vehicle Protection Plan, Inc.; Credit Acceptance Property and Casualty Agency, Inc.; Credit Acceptance Corporation UK, Ltd. (United Kingdom).

Further Reading

Jones, John A., "Credit Acceptance Gets Good Mileage on Used Car Sales," *Investor's Business Daily,* November 5, 1992, p. 32.

Maio, Patrick J., "Used Cars," *Investor's Business Daily,* March 22, 1995, p. A6.

Roush, Matt, "Stock Less Acceptable: Credit Acceptance Feeling Economic Worries," *Crain's Detroit Business,* January 22, 1996, p. 2.

——, "Stock Used to Woo Car Loans," *Crain's Detroit Business,* April 4, 1994, p. 3.

Smith, Joel J., "Detroit Used Car Dealer Makes Forbes' 400 List," *Detroit News,* October 1, 1996, p. B1.

Thomas, Charles M., "High-Risk Lenders Add Dealers, Aid Used Sales," *Automotive News,* June 27, 1994, p. 3.

—M. L. Cohen

Daewoo Group

541, Namdaemunno, 5-GA
Chung-gu Seoul
Republic of Korea
(02) 759-2114
Fax: (02) 753-9489
**Web site: http://www.daewoo.co.kr/daewoo/english/
daewoo.html**

Public Company
Incorporated: 1967
Employees: 196,000
Sales: US$57 billion (1995)
Stock Exchanges: Seoul
SICs: 1629 Heavy Construction, Not Elsewhere Classified;
3366 Copper Foundries; 3519 Internal Combustion Engines, Not Elsewhere Classified; 3531 Construction Machinery & Equipment; 3537 Industrial Trucks, Tractors, Trailers, & Stackers; 3542 Machine Tools, Metal Forming Types; 3545 Cutting Tools, Machine Tool Accessories, & Machinists Precision Measuring Devices; 3571 Electronic Computers; 3575 Computer Terminals; 3577 Computer Peripheral Equipment, Not Elsewhere Classified; 3585 Air Conditioning, Warm Air Heating Equipment, & Commercial & Industrial Refrigeration Equipment; 3625 Relays & Industrial Controls; 3631 Household Cooking Equipment; 3634 Electric Housewares & Fans; 3651 Household Audio & Video Equipment; 3661 Telephone & Telegraph Apparatus; 3674 Semiconductors & Related Devices; 3694 Electrical Equipment for Internal Combustion Engines; 3711 Motor Vehicles & Passenger Car Bodies; 3713 Truck & Bus Bodies; 3714 Motor Vehicle Parts & Accessories; 3731 Ship Building & Repairing; 3743 Railroad Equipment; 3873 Watches, Clocks, & Clockwork Operated Devices & Parts; 5045 Computers & Computer Peripheral Equipment & Software; 5065 Electronic Parts & Equipment; 5075 Warm Air Heating & Air Conditioning Equipment; 5082 Construction & Mining Machinery & Equipment, Except Petroleum, Wholesale; 5084 Industrial Machinery & Equipment

Daewoo Group was founded by Kim Woo Choong in March 1967. Daewoo means "Great Universe," and although the initial share capital of the company was a modest US$18,000, Kim and his colleagues held great hopes for their business. Today, Daewoo is South Korea's fourth-largest conglomerate, or *chaebol*, with principal operations in trading, motor vehicles, shipbuilding, heavy industry, aerospace, consumer electronics, telecommunications, and financial services.

Daewoo's success is inseparable from South Korea's rapid transformation from an agrarian country, racked by a long history of hostile invasions and lacking essential resources, to a land where the centrally planned "economic miracle" has become a fact of life. South Korea entered the 1960s with a crippling trade-deficit balance and a domestic market too poor to support indigenous industries. When Korea was divided by the Allies after World War II, the territory north of the 38th parallel inherited all of the country's natural resources. With a far stronger military force than its rivals in the South, North Korea waited less than two years after the withdrawal of U.S. peacekeeping troops to invade. Peace was eventually restored in 1953, but the fear of foreign invasion has remained with the South Koreans and, indeed, has acted as a powerful incentive in the search for economic prosperity.

The Daewoo Group is comprised of 25 subsidiary companies which are linked together in a complicated system of cross holdings. The major company in the group is Daewoo Corporation, which was licensed as a general trading company (GTC) by the Korean government in 1975. GTCs were set up to promote exports, and licenseholders were required to establish offices abroad. Daewoo has a network of over 100 branches worldwide, with some 3,500 different products traded in over 130 countries. In exchange for promoting Korean goods abroad, the Daewoo Corporation was able to finance its expansion through preferential loan agreements, reduced foreign exchange requirements, and improved government advice on exporting and marketing abroad.

The second-largest member of the group is Daewoo Heavy Industries, which was traditionally involved in construction equipment, industrial vehicles, and aerospace-industry products as well as the defense industry, but then added shipbuilding and heavy machinery in 1994 when Daewoo Shipbuilding and

Heavy Machinery was merged into it. Daewoo Heavy Industries and Daewoo Corporation are related through cross holdings of stock. Major contributions to the Daewoo Group are also made by Daewoo Motor, Daewoo Electronics, Daewoo Telecom, and Daewoo Securities, the largest brokerage firm in South Korea.

The Daewoo Group is a *chaebol*, a large conglomeration of companies with widespread interests reporting to a powerful head office, Daewoo Corporation. There are more than fifty *chaebols* in South Korea; the Big Four are the Hyundai Group, the LG Group (formerly Lucky-Goldstar), the Samsung Group, and Daewoo. In order to understand Daewoo's meteoric rise it is necessary to appreciate the place of the *chaebols* in the modern Korean economy. Successive governments used the *chaebols* as their main method of implementing economic strategies. Incentives were offered in the form of massive subsidies, apparently unlimited cheap credit, and protection against foreign competition. On the other hand, Daewoo was forced to take over ailing companies and to enter industry sectors that the company would have preferred to leave to more appropriate competitors.

Early History

Beginning in 1962 the South Korean government instigated a series of five-year plans and forced the *chaebols* to aim for a number of basic objectives. In common with their Far East competitors, Hong Kong and Taiwan, South Korea's government relied on a strategy that focused attention on the importance of exports as the method to decrease the country's balance-of-trade gap and to strengthen domestic production.

Daewoo began trading in 1967 at the start of the second five-year plan, and benefited from government-sponsored cheap loans on borrowing for exports. The company chose to concentrate on the labor-intensive clothing and textile industries, which would provide relatively high profit margins while utilizing South Korea's major asset, its large workforce. A factory was set up at Pusan and, in 1990, 3.6 million shirts were made there each month. Daewoo further contributed to the increases in South Korea's level of exports, which averaged 38.6 percent growth per annum during this period, by producing uncompli-

cated light manufacturing machines the construction of which, again, was labor intensive.

The third and fourth phases of Korea's economic recovery ran from 1973 to 1981. The country's most significant resource, labor, was then in high demand, and as wages increased, competitors from Malaysia and Thailand began to erode Korea's comparative advantage in labor-intensive production. The government responded by concentrating on mechanical and electrical engineering, shipbuilding, petrochemicals, and construction. This change in emphasis was designed to continue Korea's export-led expansion and to provide domestic industries with parts that previously had to be imported. A home-based defense industry was also a priority as plans were announced for the total withdrawal of the U.S. peacekeeping force.

Daewoo moved into construction, serving the new village program and, in a farsighted move, the rapidly growing African and Middle Eastern markets. During this period Daewoo achieved its GTC status and received significant investment help from the South Korean government. Subsidized loans and strict import controls aroused the anger of competing nations, but the *chaebols* were in need of protectionist policies if they were to survive this period of world recession, triggered by the oil crisis of 1973.

Government policy forced Daewoo into shipbuilding, an industry to which Hyundai and Samsung were more suited because of their greater expertise in heavy engineering. Kim's reluctance to take over the world's biggest dockyard, at Okpo, in 1980 is well documented, and his comment on the Korean government indicated a growing frustration as his entrepreneurial instinct was being stifled. "They tell you it's your duty and you have to do it even if there's no profit." Displaying characteristic vigor and enthusiasm, however, Kim soon saw Daewoo Shipbuilding and Heavy Machinery earn a reputation for competitively priced ships and oil rigs that were often delivered ahead of schedule.

Established Joint Ventures in 1980s to Expand Outside Korea

The 1980s were a decade of liberalization for South Korea's economy. Small private companies were encouraged, and Daewoo was made to divest two of the textile companies that had contributed to its success. Protectionist import controls were relaxed, and the government no longer practiced positive discrimination towards the shipbuilding industry. These moves were instigated to ensure an efficient allocation of resources in a free market and to force the *chaebols* to be more aggressive in their dealings abroad.

The great change in attitude shown by the Korean government to the *chaebols* is best illustrated by the fate of one of Daewoo's competitors, the Kukje Group, which went into liquidation in 1985. At that time the government saw the *chaebols* as barriers to economic efficiency and refused to supply Kukje with further credit. Small- and medium-sized companies were to be favored to ensure that the wealth in Korea's two industrial centers, Seoul and Pusan, eventually would be spread throughout the whole country. The only large industries to benefit from government support would be those that were internationally competitive and those that could further a more equitable distribution of income.

Daewoo responded to the challenge by establishing a number of joint ventures with U.S. and European companies. Kim's philosophy for the 1980s was that finished products would eventually lose their national identity as countries cooperated in design and manufacturing before exporting the goods to a further country. In 1986 Daewoo Heavy Industries launched a $40 million Eurobond issue in order to expand exports of machine tools, defense products, and aerospace interests. The president of Daewoo Heavy Industries, Kyung Hoon Lee, hoped that the money would enable his company to move away from simply licensing products from abroad and to enter a new phase of complimentary and long-term relationships with foreign companies.

The 50/50 joint venture with Sikorsky Aerospace illustrated the benefits of operating in partnership with a U.S. company. Daewoo started by building S-76 helicopters from parts imported from the United States and gradually began to produce these parts in Korea. As the South Korean government had always regarded the defense industry as being of utmost importance, Daewoo received generous subsidies to establish new factories. By the end of 1988, Daewoo had enough confidence in the skills it had learned in the Sikorsky project to announce that it was to begin work on civilian helicopters and airplanes, which would be considerably cheaper than those produced by their U.S. counterparts.

Daewoo used other methods to capture foreign markets. It had excellent experience in turning around faltering companies in Korea and was now, increasingly, applying this knowledge abroad. In 1986 Daewoo acquired a controlling interest in the U.S. ZyMOS Corporation as a means of gaining the technical knowledge necessary to expand its interests in semiconductor manufacturing and semiconductor design. Subsidiaries that actually produce goods abroad, rather than acting solely as sales agents, have also been established. Daewoo added a microwave-oven assembly plant in Lorraine, France, and set up a video-recorder company in Northern Ireland. Signaling that South Korea's economic recovery was reaching completion, Daewoo began considering investment in countries such as Bangladesh and Indonesia, where textiles can be produced as cheaply as Korea was able to do in the early 1960s. Other linkups included a deal with Caterpillar to export 100,000 forklifts by 1993, a marketing contract to sell IBM-compatible personal computers, and the production of parts for the European Airbus on behalf of British Aerospace.

The mid-1980s saw an increased emphasis on the motor vehicle industry. Although the government, fearful of arousing protectionist sympathies in its foreign markets, was reticent in announcing its ambitions publicly, it was clear that South Korea was aiming to become one of the world's major car exporters before the end of the decade. In 1986 the Japanese yen appreciated 25 percent against the dollar, making Daewoo's already cheap exports even more attractive. Daewoo established a 50/50 joint venture with General Motors, called Daewoo Motor, to produce an internationally competitive small car and components for a number of General Motors's existing vehicles. Daewoo was not deterred by the difficulties inherent in setting up the required high-technology production lines and relied on the experience gained in other parts of the group to construct sophisticated computer systems in a relatively short period of time.

The joint venture with General Motors was, initially, one of Daewoo's most profitable links with a foreign company. In 1987 247,000 Pontiac LeMans were built, and the car, based on a design by the German car giant Opel, was well received in the U.S. market. Demand for the LeMans and the slightly larger Oldsmobile Royale soon faltered, however, and there were rumors of friction between the management of the two companies. The venture was not as successful as Hyundai's foray into the international car market, and it appears that Daewoo underestimated the sophistication and technical standards required by the U.S. car buyer.

Late 1980s Crisis in Daewoo Shipbuilding

In 1989 heavy losses suffered by Daewoo Shipbuilding and Heavy Machinery made servicing the company's loans increasingly difficult. In an unprecedented demonstration against the traditional work ethic that had helped South Korea to economic prosperity, workers began an increasingly violent protest against years of long hours and low pay. The only solution available to Daewoo's management was to placate the workers with pay raises of more than 20 percent.

The reliance on shipbuilding as a way of cementing South Korea's export-led recovery looked even more dangerous as the rapidly appreciating South Korean won made exports more expensive. Demand for Daewoo's ships remained constant but the company was forced to sell ships at a loss as a way of guaranteeing a steady supply of orders. The situation was exacerbated by the bankruptcy of US Lines in 1986. A bad debt of $570 million marked the start of the crisis at the Okpo shipyard.

The Ministry of Trade and Industry, however, was no longer willing to bail out one of its most reliable *chaebols*, which was suffering as a direct result of the Daewoo Shipbuilding and Heavy Machinery acquisition forced on it by the government. Instead, the government promised a seven-year moratorium on Daewoo's debt to the Korean Development Bank and offered to provide a further W150 billion in exchange for a number of contributions from the company. Daewoo would have to refinance the shipyards by selling off four subsidiaries, including the profitable Korea Steel Company and Daewoo Investment and Finance, as well as selling Daewoo Shipbuilding and Heavy Machinery's headquarters in Seoul. Subsidiaries were forced to raise W85 billion on the Korean stock exchange, and Kim was ordered by the government to sell his W150 billion investment in Daewoo Securities, the country's largest stockbroker. The government also ordered workers to curb their demands for wage increases and asked to see proof of improved management before the deal to help Daewoo was agreed to.

Kim's response was typical of his personal style. He had already moved his office to the shipyard so that he could keep direct control of the worsening situation, and had begun to take tours around the premises by bicycle to ensure that he could implement changes and cut costs where necessary. By 1990 improvements at the shipyard were already visible, and by the mid-1990s Daewoo was one of the most efficient shipbuilders in the world and, with 10 percent of the world market, was also the world's leading shipbuilder.

1990s and Beyond

Daewoo entered the 1990s facing more problems than the downturn in the fortunes of its shipbuilding subsidiary. The company was highly leveraged, partly due to the ready availability of government loans, and was paying interest of W300 million a day—about US$500,000—on its debts. Daewoo had not marketed itself as well as competitors like Hyundai and, as a consequence, suffered from the lack of a strong brand image. Its heavy industries were now operating in stagnant markets and expenditure on research and development had to be increased if internationally competitive new products were to be successfully introduced. Continuing workers' demonstrations and changes in government policy further added to Daewoo's worries.

The company also had to deal with the unraveling of its relationship with General Motors. Sales of LeMans had fallen to 39,081 in 1990, a 39 percent drop from the peak of 1988. When GM and Daewoo could not agree on a plan to revive the venture, GM sold its half of Daewoo Motor to Daewoo in 1992 for US$170 million. As he had done in shipbuilding, Kim decided to take direct control of Daewoo Motor and quickly turned its fortunes around. He focused the company on improving the quality of its cars; added to the production lines were detailed checks at every step along the way and for a one-year period every Espero and Prince car made was taken on a grueling road test to identify problems. By 1993 Daewoo had regained the number two spot in the domestic car market, still trailing Hyundai but once again ahead of Kia, and by 1995 Daewoo Motor was making a slight profit.

As he was turning Daewoo Motor around, Kim embarked on a risky strategy of overseas expansion, aggressively seeking out opportunities for both marketing and manufacturing Daewoo products in the United States, Europe, and less-developed countries. He committed more than US$20 billion in numerous joint ventures and start-ups around the world.

More than half of this money—US$11 billion—was slated for Daewoo Motor ventures. In 1992 Daewoo entered into a joint venture with an automaker in Uzbekistan, which led to the opening in late 1995 of a US$800-million plant capable of producing 200,000 compact cars annually by 2000. US$250 million was spent to buy a state-owned carmaker in Romania, capable—after retooling—of making another 200,000 cars each year. In 1994 Daewoo Motor committed US$1 billion to a joint venture in India. The following year, the company outbid General Motors itself to buy 60 percent of Poland's state-owned FSO carmaker for US$1.1 billion. Manufacturing cars in these lesser-developed countries resulted in a lower-cost product that Kim hoped would succeed even in the brand-conscious West. Early indications were positive as Daewoo, in 1995, captured more than 1 percent of the British car market in the first month that it started selling Nexia and Espero sedans, exceeding its goal. After gaining this toehold in Europe, Kim then planned to enter the U.S. market in either 1997 or 1998. But by placing manufacturing in such countries as Poland and India, Daewoo would also be well-positioned to sell the cars in these same countries, which were experiencing much higher growth in demand for new cars than Western Europe or the United States. Overall, Kim set goals of quadrupling auto output to a total of 2 million vehicles by 2000, and of becoming one of the world's top ten automakers.

Automobiles, however, were not the only Daewoo product Kim aggressively moved overseas; consumer electronics became another key Daewoo transplant. But first, Daewoo Electronics revamped its product line. Quality problems had hampered sales of its higher-end electronics items, so Daewoo decided to focus on such lower-tech products as televisions, VCRs, and microwave ovens. Its aggressive yet systematic approach to overseas expansion then followed; by 1996 Daewoo Electronics had 20 production subsidiaries outside South Korea, with plans for 16 more. Non-Korean production stood at 19 percent but was slated to be increased to 60 percent by 2000. Daewoo strategically chose one country within each major target region for most of its production facilities. Southeast Asia was based in Vietnam (where Daewoo was the single largest foreign investor); the Americas, Mexico; Central and Eastern Europe, Poland; and Western Europe, France. Daewoo nearly made a huge step forward in late 1996 when a deal was announced whereby Daewoo Electronics would buy Thomson Multimedia, based in France. The acquisition would have made Daewoo the world's leading maker of televisions, but the deal was quickly scuttled after protests by French workers who were angered by the prospect of Thomson Multimedia falling into foreign hands.

The importance of Daewoo's moves in Europe, as well as the importance of Daewoo Motor, were shown in late 1995 when Kim moved to Vienna to concentrate solely on the Daewoo Group's overseas auto business. Placed at least temporarily in charge of the Daewoo Group was Kim's long-time ally, Yoon Young-Suk, who had headed up Daewoo Heavy Industries. Kim's move, however, fueled speculation that he was trying to distance himself from the ongoing corruption trials involving several heads of *chaebol*, as well as two former presidents of South Korea, Chun Doo Hwan and Roh Tae Woo. The *chaebol* leaders were accused of bribing Roh in an outgrowth of the overly cozy relationship between the Korean government and the *chaebol*. In late August 1996, eight of the *chaebol* leaders—including Kim—were found guilty of bribery; Kim was sentenced to two years in prison but immediately filed an appeal.

The late 1990s and early 21st century were slated to be a critical period for Daewoo. In addition to Kim's bribery conviction and possible jail sentence, Daewoo (and other *chaebol*) faced the possibility that the Korean government would intervene to reduce the power of the *chaebol*, which were beginning to be seen as impediments to the country's economic progress. Korean reunification, which was sure to profoundly affect the entire nation's future, seemed ever more likely and Daewoo had in 1995 become the first South Korean company allowed to enter into joint ventures in the north. These prospects, combined with the company's massive commitment to overseas expansion and a continuing heavy debt load, added up to a very uncertain future for the Daewoo Group.

Principal Subsidiaries

Daewoo Corporation; Daewoo Automotive Components, Ltd.; Daewoo Capital Management Co., Ltd.; Daewoo Development Co.; Daewoo Electric Motor Industries, Ltd.; Daewoo Electronics Co., Ltd.; Daewoo Engineering Company; Daewoo Heavy Industries, Ltd.; Daewoo Metal Co., Ltd.; Daewoo Motor Company, Ltd.; Daewoo Precision Industries, Ltd.; Daewoo Sang Sa; Daewoo Securities Co., Ltd.; Daewoo Telecom Co., Ltd.; Societe Algerienne d'Hotellerie, De Loisirs et d'Immobilier (Algeria); Daewoo Australia Pty. Limited; Universal Refining N.V. (Belgium); Daewoo do Brazil Imp. Exp. Ltd.; Daewoo Canada Ltd.; Daewoo Chile S.A.; Daewoo Motor Chile S.A.; Beijing Lufthansa Center Co., Ltd. (China); Qingdao Daewoo Stone Co., Ltd. (China); Daewoo (Latin America) Ltd. (Colombia); Daewoo France S.A.R.L.; Daewoo Handels GmbH (Germany); Daewoo Hong Kong Ltd.; Daewoo Italia S.R.L. (Italy); Daewoo Fukuoka Corp. (Japan); Myanmar Daewoo International Ltd.; Daewoo Corp. Amsterdam B.V. (Netherlands); Daewoo Nigeria Limited; Daewoo Singapore Pte. Ltd.; Nlle. Corp. Construction Corp. (Sudan); Union Daewoo Engineering & Construction Co., Ltd. (Thailand); Daewoo UK Ltd.; Daewoo America Development, Inc. (U.S.A.); Daewoo International America Corp. (U.S.A.).

Further Reading

Brull, Steven V., Catherine Keumhyun Lee, and Mia Trinephi, ''Daewoo's Tycoon of Television,'' *Business Week*, September 23, 1996, pp. 142H, 142J.

Cho Dong Sung, ''Government Entrepreneurs and Competition,'' in *Doing Business in Korea*, edited by Arthur Whitehill, Sydney: Croom Helm, 1987.

Clifford, Mark, ''The Daewoo Comrade: South Korean Firm Blazes Northern Trail,'' *Far Eastern Economic Review*, February 20, 1992, pp. 47–48.

——, ''Wheels Off the Wagon: South Korean-US Car Venture Unravels Amid Acrimony,'' *Far Eastern Economic Review*, January 23, 1992, pp. 44–45.

Glain, Steve, ''Strategic Move: Daewoo Group Shifts Its Focus to Markets in the Third World,'' *Wall Street Journal*, October 11, 1993, p. A1.

Hoon, Shim Jae, ''Going Global,'' *Far Eastern Economic Review*, November 2, 1995, pp. 46–50.

Kraar, Louis, ''Daewoo's Daring Drive into Europe, *Fortune*, May 13, 1996, p. 145.

——, ''Korea Goes for Quality,'' *Fortune*, April 18, 1994, p. 153.

Lee, Charles S., ''Improving a Miracle,'' *Far Eastern Economic Review*, June 20, 1996, pp. 48–49.

Lowry, Tom, *The South Korean Motor Industry: A Rerun of Japan?*, London, Economist Intelligence Unit, 1987.

McDermott, Michael, and Stephen Young, *South Korea's Industry: New Directions in World Markets*, London, Economist Intelligence Unit, 1989.

Mi-young, Ahn, ''Terrific Trio Lead Revival: Daewoo Has Pulled Itself Out of a Pit of Despair. Now Its Top Three Companies Are Flying High and Spearheading a Push Overseas,'' *Asian Business*, August 1994, pp. 12–13.

''Mr. Kim's Big Picture: Should Western Car Makers Be Frightened of Daewoo?,'' *Economist*, September 16, 1995, pp. 73–74.

''Mr. Kim's One-Man Empire,'' *Economist*, January 27, 1996, pp. 56–57.

Nakarmi, Laxmi, ''At Daewoo, a 'Revolution' at the Top,'' *Business Week*, February 18, 1991, pp. 68–69.

——, ''Exile of the Patriarch: Daewoo's Founder Is Off to Vienna—But Don't Count Him Out,'' *Business Week*, February 5, 1996, p. 58.

——, ''A Flying Leap toward the 21st Century?: Pressure from Competitors and Seoul May Transform the *Chaebol*,'' *Business Week*, March 20, 1995, pp. 78–80.

Schuman, Michael, ''Daewoo Strains Slim Finances to Invest Fast and Hard in Overseas Expansion,'' *Wall Street Journal*, May 29, 1996, p. B7A(W), p. A9A(E).

Sohn, Y. J., ''Another Asian Conquerer Ventures East,'' *Business Korea*, August 1996, pp. 34–35.

''A Tale of Two Kims: Daewoo,'' *Economist*, July 4, 1992, p. 61.

Thornton, Emily, ''Do or Die,'' *Far Eastern Economic Review*, June 13, 1996, pp. 54–58.

United Nations Industrial Development Organization, *The Republic of Korea*, London, United Nations, 1987.

—Andreas Loizou
—updated by David E. Salamie

DAISYTEK™

Daisytek International Corporation

500 N. Central Expwy.
Plano, Texas 75074-6763
U.S.A.
(972) 881-4700
Fax: (972) 881-7111
Web site: http://www.daisytek.com

Public Company
Incorporated: 1978
Employees: 348 full-time, 172 part-time
Sales: $464.17 million (fiscal year ending March 31, 1996)
Stock Exchanges: NASDAQ
SICs: 5045 Computers, Peripherals, and Software; 5112 Stationery and Office Supplies; 6719 Holding Companies, Not Elsewhere Classified

Daisytek International Corporation is the largest wholesale distributor of non-paper computer and office automation supplies and accessories in the United States. The company sells primarily nationally known, name-brand products manufactured by over 145 original equipment manufacturers. It distributes more than 6,000 products to approximately 20,000 customer locations from one superhub in Memphis, Tennessee, two regional centers in Canada, and one center in Mexico. Through a contractual arrangement with FedEx Corporation, approximately 85 percent of all shipments to U.S. customers are sent via FedEx. Daisytek's Memphis distribution center is located only a few miles from the main FedEx facility.

Daisytek was originally founded in 1978 in Texas primarily as a manufacturer of paper handling products for daisywheel printers. It also distributed non-paper computer and office automation supplies and accessories on a smaller scale. After four years the company was acquired by a young British entrepreneur, David A. Heap, who was primarily interested in the company's distribution operations. Heap came to Texas from the U.K., where he was chairman of ISA International plc, a

company he founded in the United Kingdom in 1970. ISA distributed computer supplies in Western Europe. Upon purchasing Daisytek in 1982, Heap became its chairman of the board, chief executive officer, and president.

Heap sought to reshape the company by focusing on the distribution of "consumable" supplies for computers. With the help of Mark C. Layton, a management consultant with Arthur Andersen & Co., Heap succeeded in divesting Daisytek of its manufacturing operations over the next few years. By 1988 the company had sold or discontinued all of its manufacturing operations to concentrate on its core business, distributing consumable computer supplies and related products. Layton was named vice-president of operations and became a member of the board of directors in 1988.

Company Focused on Distribution by 1990

Daisytek posted net sales of $112.9 million for the fiscal year ending March 31, 1990, the first full year that operations were devoted exclusively to distribution. Operating income was $2.2 million. Michael D. Scannell, one of Heap's associates from ISA and an employee of the company since 1984, was named president in 1990. Layton was promoted to executive vice-president, and Heap remained as chairman and CEO.

Once Daisytek was focused on distributing non-paper consumable computer and office supplies, it enjoyed steady growth in sales. The company's consistent growth was buttressed by the growing U.S. supplies industry, which was estimated to be growing at a compound annual rate of approximately 10 percent. Other outside factors contributing to a growing demand for office automation consumables included the increasing automation of the workplace, the rapid evolution and acceptance of laser and inkjet printing technologies, and later in the decade the increasing penetration of color printing technology into corporate and home office environments.

Daisytek distributed primarily nationally known, name-brand products manufactured by more than 100 original equipment manufacturers, including Hewlett-Packard, Canon, Digital Equipment Corporation, Epson, Lexmark (IBM), Xerox, Okidata, 3M, Panasonic, Kodak, and Sony. Among the non-paper consumable supplies distributed by the company were laser toner, copier toner, ink jet cartridges, printer ribbons, diskettes, computer tape cartridges and accessories, cleaning kits, and media storage files. By pursuing a strategy of "selling the razors rather than the blades," Daisytek was able to capitalize on the boom in office technology without exposing itself to the risks of rapidly changing technologies.

From fiscal year 1990 through fiscal year 1996, the company recorded a steady and substantial increase in net sales and gross profit. Sales for 1991 rose to $150.8 million, an increase of 33.6 percent. They increased by 21 percent in 1992 to $182.8 million, then surpassed the $200 million mark to reach $233.5 million in 1993. For 1994 they climbed to $276.7 million, an increase of 18.5 percent. Sales for 1995 jumped to $353.0 million and continued to exceed industry growth rates in 1996 when they reached $464.2 million.

Started Laying Foundation for Future Growth in 1991

Once the company had successfully focused itself on distribution and recorded profits in its first full year as a distributor, it began to implement a strategy that would lay the foundations for future growth. In 1991 it reincorporated in Delaware with an eye to eventually raising capital through a public stock offering. In November 1991 the company announced it was moving its national order center from Garland to Plano, Texas, another suburb of Dallas. By May 1992 plans were in place for an initial public offering (IPO) to gross $24.7 million.

In April 1991 the company initiated a $5 million technology strategy designed to create a paperless order fulfillment environment, by utilizing the powerful combination of computers and telephones, and at the same time implement an advanced management information system. It purchased state-of-the-art hardware in the form of an IBM AS/400, which it called EDDIE, and a RISC-based client server, which it called MOE. Soon the company's EDI network would be able to communicate electronically, automatically sending and receiving purchase orders, invoices, and acknowledgements in a paperless environment. In terms of management information, the EDI system provided Daisytek's management with information concerning sales, inventory levels, customer profiles, and other operations that helped the company operate as a low-cost, highly efficient wholesale distributor.

Established Memphis "Superhub" in 1992

Another part of the company's strategy was to consolidate its five U.S. regional distribution centers into a single "superhub" distribution center located in Memphis, Tennessee.

Established in 1992, this 176,000-square-foot facility contained automated conveyors, in-line scales for accuracy checking, computerized sorting equipment, powered material handling equipment, and scanning and bar-coding systems. Perhaps more importantly, it was located approximately four miles from the Federal Express hub facility. Through a contractual agreement, virtually all of Daisytek's U.S. package orders were shipped via Federal Express, with the exception of certain "heavyweight" packages or as otherwise requested by the customer. By establishing a close working relationship with Federal Express, Daisytek was able to offer its U.S. customers next-business-day delivery to most geographic areas and only charge them local ground delivery rates for the service.

In the meantime, the IPO announced in 1992 resurfaced in 1994, only to be put on hold again until more favorable market conditions prevailed. Some changes were made in upper management, as Mark Layton replaced Michael Scannell as president and also assumed the duties of chief operating officer (COO) and chief financial officer (CFO) in 1993. Scannell subsequently resigned from Daisytek in 1994 and returned to the United Kingdom to become president of ISA.

Daisytek Went Public in 1995

In January 1995 Daisytek completed its IPO, issuing 1.38 million shares of common stock and realizing net proceeds of $18.6 million, which was used to reduce outstanding debt. According to the prospectus distributed for the IPO, Daisytek was distributing over 4,800 products to approximately 20,000 customer locations, including value-added resellers, computer supplies dealers, office product dealers, computer and office product superstores, and other retailers. Based on industry sources, the company believed it was one of the two largest wholesale distributors of non-paper computer and office automation supplies and accessories in the United States.

At the time of the IPO the company was in the middle of a $2.2 million upgrade of its Memphis superhub. Completed by July 1995, the upgrade included several high technology enhancements to the facility, including an automated package routing system and a paperless order picking system. Among the benefits from the upgrade were increased package movement capacity, improved shipping accuracy, and an enhanced ability to perform value-added services for customers. Personnel productivity was expected to improve as a result of the upgrade, and shipping costs would be reduced.

Daisytek also invested in other technologies to improve service and marketing capabilities. At its sales center in Plano, inbound and outbound telemarketing was improved through the use of the latest in voice-response equipment, automated fax technology, and automated inventory management. The latest AT&T telecommunications technology, which provided automatic caller recognition and customer profiles, helped Daisytek sales representatives field more than 9,000 calls daily in 1995.

The telemarketing department, consisting of 100 to 150 full-time and part-time sales reps, was evenly split between inbound and outbound calls. Half of the sales reps focused on building strong customer relationships through outbound calls, while the other half fielded inbound traffic. In addition, the sales reps were divided into teams to handle critical business functions. One team, for example, was devoted to retail accounts such as large computer retailers and office product superstores. Their goal was to convince potential customers that Daisytek could more efficiently distribute a wide variety of small shipments to a larger number of store locations than product manufacturers could.

In addition to making extensive use of telemarketing, Daisytek marketed its services through a quarterly catalog known as the "Book of Deals." In 1995 it mailed approximately 35,000 catalog and contract price books to its active U.S. customers every quarter. In addition, it also distributed a Canadian Book of Deals and a Mexican Book of Deals. An electronic version, known as the Disk of Deals, was also utilized. An end-user catalog, published with a variety of cover options, could be purchased in bulk by resellers and printed with their name on it. The company also produced more than 100,000 direct marketing pieces each month in multiple languages. Its customer and prospect database numbered more than 150,000 companies.

With sales offices and distribution centers located in the United States, Canada, and Mexico, the company began to pursue an expansion strategy on a global level in 1995. It leased distribution space in Miami, Florida, to serve as an inventory gateway to the high-growth South American consumables market. In October 1996 Daisytek signed an agreement to acquire substantially all of the assets of Lasercharge Pty Ltd, a privately held company based in Sydney, Australia. Management hoped the acquisition would serve as a launching pad into the promising Australasia region and rapidly growing Pacific Rim market. Lasercharge was the largest wholesaler of computer and printer supplies in Australia, with annual revenues of approximately $20 million in U.S. dollars, and the two companies' vision and focus appeared to be nearly identical. At the time of the announcement, Mark Layton stated, "This move is another step in one of the company's strategic objectives of international expansion of its core business operations."

During 1996 Daisytek completed another $2.5 million upgrade of its material handling system at the Memphis superhub. In September, as it signed a four-year lease agreement, the company announced plans to expand the superhub from 176,000 square feet to 372,000 square feet. After seven years of above-average sales and earnings growth, Daisytek continued to pursue growth opportunities internationally. At the same time, it continued to keep tight rein on its costs to remain competitive in the U.S. market.

Further Reading

"Daisytek International Corporation Hopes to Raise $13 to $15 Million in Public Stock Offering," *Dallas (TX) Business Journal*, April 8, 1994.

"Daisytek International Corporation Moving National Order Center to Plano TX," *Jacksonville (FL) Business Journal*, November 15, 1991.

Goldstein, Alan, "Daisytek International Corp.," *Dallas Morning News*, May 12, 1995, p. 10D.

Hansen, Bruce, "Daisytek IPO Put on Hold," *Memphis Business Journal*, July 18, 1994, p. 1.

"Sydney, Australia-based Lasercharge serves as first step in Pacific Rim Expansion," *Business Wire*, October 15, 1996.

—David P. Bianco

Damark International, Inc.

7101 Winnetka Avenue North
Minneapolis, Minnesota 55428
U.S.A.
(612) 531-0066
Fax: (612) 531-0481
Web site: http://www.damark.com

Public Company
Incorporated: 1986
Employees: 1,336
Sales: $500 million (1995)
Stock Exchanges: NASDAQ
SICs: 5961 Catalog & Mail-order Houses

Damark International, Inc., a leading national direct marketer, was established in 1986 as a mail-order company selling closeout name-brand merchandise. "The Great Deal Company" rapidly added current items and promised "quality products, great prices, and hassle-free shopping." The single most important aspect of Damark's business is its customer benefits program. Preferred Buyers' Club members contributed 46 percent of sales in 1995 and are pivotal to the future of the company.

Roots in the Closeout Market

Damark was founded by Mark Cohn and David Russ in 1986. Russ—whom Cohn called "the quintessential American entrepreneur" in a 1994 *Twin Cities Business Monthly* article by Clark Froebe—had started his first business by the time he was 17 years old. Cohn, a native of Long Island, New York, arrived in Minnesota as part of a deal with his father. Cohn wanted to go to California but did not have the money for the move. He agreed to take a job with a Minneapolis subsidiary of his father's employer; if the position wasn't a fit, the move west would be financed. Cohn left the company but stayed in Minneapolis and worked for a VW Bug conversion kit company where Russ was the national sales manager.

When C.O.M.B. Company, a retail store and mail-order business that sold discount and closeout goods, recruited Russ, he

brought Cohn over to the company. The rapidly growing enterprise allowed Russ and Cohn a lot of freedom in decision making. But that changed when financier Irwin Jacobs bought 40 percent of the company in 1983. Theodore Deikel came on board and tightened up the operation. Cohn and Russ left C.O.M.B.

About a year later, Cohn joined Russ in another business venture. The two purchased some gold-plated German flatware for a fraction of its retail price and offered it to their former employer, C.O.M.B. The product took off, and Russ and Cohn earned North American distribution rights for the line. When the men tried to expand their wholesale business, they found that C.O.M.B. was the only company interested in the flatware; growth would have to come through adding new products.

Cohn and Russ found what they believed to be an ideal product for C.O.M.B., a Seiko computerized watch. It had retailed for $300; the men paid $50. C.O.M.B. rejected the watches, and Cohn and Russ had to sell the product themselves, with the help of some C.O.M.B. employees and an ad placed in the *Wall Street Journal.* Sales for the watch C.O.M.B. had rebuffed four different times soon reached $600,000. But the successful venture had some fallout in the form of an ultimatum from C.O.M.B.: Cohn and Russ had to decide between being suppliers or competitors. They decided and incorporated Damark International, Inc., a name derived by combining their first names.

In the early days of business, Cohn and Russ searched trade shows for closeout merchandise; later, manufacturers began approaching them with their products. Damark first sold through ads in national magazines and newspapers such as *Popular Mechanics, Popular Science,* and *USA Today.* A two-page new merchandise flier was shipped with each order. Damark employed eight people in 1986, and Cohn's garage and basement served as the company warehouse. But the number of products, names on the mailing list, and the length of their merchandise flier grew steadily.

The Catalog Business Begins, 1987

In 1987, the first Damark catalog was mailed out. Sales for that first full year of business were $5 million, but the company lost money due to expansion costs. In 1988, 12 million Damark catalogs were sent out and brought in the majority of business.

Still, over twenty percent of sales were made via newspaper and magazine advertisements. According to a 1989 *Catalog Business* article, Damark spent $1.5 million on ad space in 1988. The typical Damark customer, whether garnered from an ad or catalog response, was an educated, young, professional male, and computers and consumer electronics topped his purchase list. Damark products, which came from large volume purchases, closeouts, distributors overstock, and discontinued merchandise, were fully warranted. Slow moving products were marked down and re-advertised until they were sold. Revenues for 1988 grew to about five times that of the previous year.

Cohn explained to *Catalog Business* contributor Dee Henry that the key to the company's success was America's obsession with the new and improved. Products rapidly became obsolete as manufacturers added features, thus allowing Damark to offer brand-name consumer goods at greatly reduced prices. Cohn, already president and chief executive officer, assumed the position of chairman of the board at the end of 1989. Sales that year were $110 million.

Damark's rapid growth was aided by a general expansion of the mail-order business in the 1980s. In a 1990 *Star Tribune* article, Susan Feyder cited "toll-free phone numbers, 24-hour phone service, greater use of credit cards, and quicker shipping" as contributing factors for more Americans shopping from home. But according to Feyder, Damark grew at an even faster pace than the industry: the privately-held company had a compound annual growth rate of over 300 percent from 1986 to 1989. By 1990, Damark was sending one catalog each month to proprietary customers and another to prospects from rented lists. Brand-name electronics, household goods, hardware, and jewelry were offered at discounts of 60 to 70 percent off retail prices. And by then, catalog sales accounted for 90 percent of Damark's business.

The Drama of Rapid Growth in the Early 1990s

Early financing, engineered through a progression of small investors, proved troublesome for Damark. Froebe wrote in 1994: "Desperately seeking funds landed Cohn and Russ in a fix at one point, when a Wichita, Kansas-based vendor gained 51 percent of Damark in exchange for $1.5 million." The vendor intended to downsize and move the company to Kansas.

Russ and Cohn saved the company at the last minute with a $2.5 million line of credit from another private investor. In 1989, Damark bought out its last private investor by means of its first institutional financing.

Damark endeavored to become the nation's largest closeout catalog marketer by making a bid to buy C.O.M.B. in 1990. The purchase was complicated by an anti-trust law suit Damark filed in 1989 against C.O.M.B.'s owner, CVN Companies. Damark claimed the television shopping company had tried to prevent manufacturers and distributors from doing business with them. Ultimately, Fingerhut Companies, lead by former C.O.M.B. executive Theodore Deikel, purchased the mail order assets of C.O.M.B. from CVN's new owner, QVC Network Inc.

The year 1991 proved to be a mix of good and bad for Damark. The year began with the receipt of about $12 million in venture capital funds and the addition of new board members, who added strength to the company. And while many retailers staggered under an on-going economic recession, Damark profited from its "good value" image among increasingly cost-conscious buyers. But Damark made headlines early in the year when seven software makers filed a piracy suit against the company. Midway through the year David Russ left the company he helped found. Froebe reported that Russ's departure was partly due to a shift in Damark's product mix away from closeout to current items. The men also differed regarding the company's financial goals: Cohn emphasized earnings, and Russ advocated growth.

Late in 1991, Damark hired two professional business executives. Barry Marchessault, who had been with Disney's and Bloomingdales' catalog divisions, was named company president; Tasso Koken, formerly with Nobody Beats the Wiz, a large New York consumer electronics retailer, assumed the role of vice-president of merchandising. The year ended on a positive financial note: net sales reached $217.5 million, and net profits neared $1.0 million. The Damark mailing list had grown to 2.5 million names from less than 50,000 in 1987.

In February 1992, Damark announced plans to double the size of its year-old headquarters facility. In March, the company made its first public stock offering: 2.72 million shares of common stock starting at $12.50 per share. Purchases by institutional investors quickly drove the price up to $14.25. The initial public offering (IPO) brought Damark $23.7 million in new capital. But by mid-year, Damark stock had fallen to less than half the offering price. Computer price wars had driven down Damark's quarterly earnings estimates, as computer sales were one of the biggest contributors to the company's revenues. To make matters worse, stock prices of mail-order businesses were generally depressed by a pending Supreme Court action regarding the taxation of mail-order merchandise, and Cohn became a national media figure around the issue. Christopher Palmeri noted in *Forbes* magazine that "Mark Cohn suddenly seemed to pop up everywhere," with comments on the ruling which denied states the right to impose sales tax on out-of-state mail-order companies. Cohn's visibility became a sore spot for the company in light of the post-IPO downturn.

In October 1992, Cohn resumed the position of company president; the recently-hired Marchessault and Tasso stepped down. An overlap of responsibilities and differences in management style were cited as reasons for the change. Despite the shakeup, Lee Schafer reported in *Corporate Report Minnesota*: "A few days after the shakeup, Cohn struck a confident tone when announcing third quarter results." The company's earnings and sales estimates were up compared with the same period in 1991, and the future appeared to be bright. Two weeks later, however, Cohn backpedaled, issuing a brief statement saying the company was "not comfortable with fourth-quarter Street estimates." Cohn was uncharacteristically silent following the announcement, and Damark lost the support of the investment community. Damark stock fell to $3.75 per share. Net sales were $270.3 million, up 25.2 percent from 1991; net income was $1.64 million, up 55.5 percent from the previous year, but the company lost 44 cents per share. In spite of all the year's drama, Cohn retained the support of the board of directors.

From Products to Membership

Damark credited promotional marketing strategies such as free shipping and handling and free Federal Express delivery for boosting 1992 sales. Damark's membership program was also enhanced that year. The Preferred Buyers' Club (PBC) annual fee was increased to $50, and a 10 percent discount on purchases was added to the benefit package. The company club concept had originated in 1987. The first club membership fee was $25 per year and benefits included one catalog a month with exclusive product offers and price markdowns, a toll-free customer service line, and a 60-day lowest price guarantee.

In 1993, Damark bought C.O.M.B. from Fingerhut and gained assets of about $100 million and an active buyer list of 1.4 million—including 185,000 buyers' club customers. The typical C.O.M.B. customer was less affluent, more likely to be female, and made more household purchases than Damark's customers. Bolstered by a positive response from investors regarding the C.O.M.B. purchase, Damark planned a two-million-share stock offering; Damark stock was trading in the $20 range at the time of the November announcement. Revenues for 1993 were $364 million; earnings were $5.8 million—up 252 percent from the previous year. The $28.8 million netted on the stock offering was used to repay long-term debt related to the C.O.M.B. acquisition and to support business growth.

In 1993, Damark continued to work to gain increased customer satisfaction and loyalty in the profitable club segment of its market by adding third-party, non-competitive retail and service discounts to its benefit program. Due to the success of installment and deferred payment plans implemented late in 1992, a private-label credit card was issued in 1993. In 1994, PBC benefits were expanded and included discounts in eight categories: convenience, retail, entertainment, travel and hospitality, manufacturers, direct marketing, services, and health and fitness. About forty percent of telephone customers were being converted to club members. And the renewal rate among existing members had risen to 65 percent.

Damark reorganized operations in 1995, dividing into a membership group and a retail group. Merchandising, marketing, advertising, and planning functions were integrated in order to reduce shipping costs and turnaround times, and increase profitability in the catalog business. The restructuring facilitated increased support of the club aspect of the company and accelerated Damark's move toward becoming a membership-driven

business. Price increases amounting to 14 percent for postage rates and 55 percent for paper rates resulted in $4.6 million in additional costs in 1995. Even though net revenues for 1995 increased to $500 million, the company experienced its first net losses since going public: $1.9 million or 20 cents per share.

The growth of club membership and plans for expanded marketing boded well for the company's future. A record number of new Preferred Buyers' Clubs members—600,000 of them—were added in 1995; club members continued to be the most profitable, predictable, and loyal customers. Damark's use of sophisticated customer tracking techniques helped the company accumulate more than 8 million names on its proprietary customer list by the end of 1995. In 1996, Damark added two new clubs to its membership program. The Vacation Passport Club, the first Damark club solely based on non-merchandise services, offered benefits such as hotel discounts, airline frequent flyer miles, car rental discounts, and travel agency services. The Insiders Club upgraded the level of services already offered by the PBC. Damark club membership passed the one million mark in 1996. According to a 1996 article by Sally Apgar, Cohn planned to continue to introduce new clubs appealing to specific markets and to move gradually into sales over the Internet.

Further Reading

Apgar, Sally, "Club Damark," *Star Tribune* (Minneapolis), May 27, 1996, p. 1D.

——, "Damark to Reorganize Operations to Focus on Profitable Club Members," *Star Tribune* (Minneapolis), May 31, 1995, p. 1D.

——, "Discount Mail-Order Firm Damark International Going Public with Offering of 2.72 Million Shares," *Star Tribune* (Minneapolis), January 23, 1992, p. 1D.

——, "Institutional Investors Buy Big," *Star Tribune* (Minneapolis), March 26, 1992, p. 1D.

Beran, George, "Damark Stock Takes Nose Dive on Loss Report," *St. Paul Pioneer Press,* June 22, 1994.

Carideo, Tony, "Computer Sales Recover as Damark Adjusts to Meet the Competition," *Star Tribune* (Minneapolis), September 1, 1992, p. 2D.

——, "Mark Cohn's Confident that Damark Is Back on Track after a Tough 1992," *Star Tribune* (Minneapolis), September 1, 1992, p. 2D.

"Company News," *Star Tribune* (Minneapolis), January 8, 1991, p. 2D.

"Company News," *Star Tribune* (Minneapolis), April 11, 1991, p. 2D.

Collins, Thomas J., "Brooklyn Park Firm Sued for Alleged Piracy," *St. Paul Pioneer Press,* March 2, 1991, p. 10B.

"Corporate Capsule: Damark International Inc.," *Minneapolis/St. Paul CityBusiness,* July 16, 1993.

"Corporate Capsule: Damark International Inc.," *Minneapolis/St. Paul CityBusiness,* February 3, 1995.

"Damark Earnings Soar 252 Percent," *Star Tribune* (Minneapolis), January 27, 1994, p. 4D.

"Damark International Inc.," *Corporate Report Fact Book 1996,* p. 224.

"The Dean Report: Damark International, Inc.," W.A. Dean & Associates, 1996.

Feyder, Susan, "Damark Profits Come C.O.D.," *Star Tribune* (Minneapolis), January 15, 1990, p. 1D.

Froebe, Clark, "Reluctant Entrepreneur," *Twin Cities Business Monthly,* 1994, pp. 48–51.

Giombetti, Anthony F., "Mark Cohn, Founder of Damark International," *Twin Cities Business Opportunities,* November 1994, pp. 26–33.

Henry, Dee, "Damark Seizes Closeout Market," *Catalog Business,* March 1, 1989.

"Marketplace Pulse," *Star Tribune* (Minneapolis), April 5, 1989, p. 1D.

Marksjarvis, Gail, "Analyst Likes Damark for Its Customer Focus," *St. Paul Pioneer Press,* November 1, 1993.

——, "Best Buy and Fingerhut Outwit Tough Environment," *St. Paul Pioneer Press,* May 4, 1992.

——, "Damark 'Mistake' Ends in Exec Departure, *St. Paul Pioneer Press,* October 10, 1992, p. 12.

Merrill, Ann, "Damark Now Seeking to Manage Its Growth," *St. Paul Pioneer Press,* July 20, 1992.

——, "For Members Only: Damark Launches Best Buyers's Club," *Minneapolis/St. Paul CityBusiness,* June 12, 1992.

"Monday's People," *Star Tribune* (Minneapolis), December 11, 1989, p. 2D.

"Monday's People," *Star Tribune* (Minneapolis), March 18, 1991, p. 2D.

Nhan, Tawn, "Damark, Fingerhut Agree on Sale of COMB Assets," *St. Paul Pioneer Press,* June 22, 1993, p. 1E.

Palmeri, Christopher, "Media Star," *Forbes,* July 20, 1992, p. 328.

Peterson, Susan, E., "Damark No Longer in Market for QVC's C.O.M.B.," *Star Tribune* (Minneapolis), April 6, 1990, p. 1D.

——, "Fingerhut Buys C.O.M.B. Mail Order Business," *Star Tribune* (Minneapolis), May 9, 1990, p. 1D.

Schafer, Lee, "Damark, Cohn in Heaven," *Corporate Report Minnesota,* November 1993, p. 15.

——, "Mark Cohn's Odyssey," *Corporate Report Minnesota,* March 1993, pp. 34–37.

"Two Executives Join Damark International," *Star Tribune* (Minneapolis), December 10, 1991, p. 3D.

Waters, Jennifer, "Damark Plans to Double Size," *Minneapolis/St. Paul CityBusiness,* February 17, 1992.

—Kathleen Peippo

Dayton Hudson Corporation

777 Nicollet Mall
Minneapolis, Minnesota 55402
U.S.A.
(612) 370-6948
Fax: (612) 370-5521

Public Company
Incorporated: 1969
Employees: 213,000
Sales: $23.5 billion (1995)
Stock Exchanges: New York Pacific
SICs: 5311 Department Stores

Dayton Hudson Corporation operates the well-known Target discount stores, Mervyn's moderately priced retail stores, and the Dayton's, Hudson's, and Marshall Field department stores in the Midwest. From its impecunious beginnings in 1902 on a small plot of land in Minneapolis, the Dayton Hudson Corporation had grown by the late 1990s to become the fourth largest retailer in the United States, with stores in 38 states and annual sales of more than $23 billion. Its philanthropy has been and still is legendary. In 1989 Dayton Hudson received the America's Corporate Conscience Award for its magnanimity, and in the same year, U.S. President George Bush presented the chairman and chief executive officer, Kenneth A. Macke, with the National Medal of Arts Award in recognition of the corporation's generous financial support of the arts. Committed to minimizing packaging waste through wide-ranging recycling efforts, Dayton Hudson also has been recognized for its managerial efficiency. In 1984 the University of California's School of Business Administration named it ''best managed company in the U.S.A.''

Dayton Hudson bears the strong imprint of its founder, George Draper Dayton. Dayton's father, a physician in New York state, could not afford to send him to college, in part because the doctor freely gave his services to the poor. Hence Dayton set off on his own in 1873 at age 16 to work in a coal and lumberyard. A workaholic, he undermined his health and a

year later had to return to the family home to recuperate. Undeterred, he went on to become a banker. Less than ten years later, in 1883, he was rich enough to buy the Bank of Worthington in Minnesota. Meanwhile he had married and had become active in the Presbyterian Church.

Early Years

Dayton's connection with the Presbyterian Church proved to be instrumental to the rise of his Dayton Company. In 1893, the year of a recession that sent local real estate prices tumbling, the Westminster Presbyterian Church in Minneapolis burned down. The insurance did not cover the cost of a new building, and the only other source of income, a corner lot next to the demolished church, was unsalable because the real estate market was doing poorly. The congregation prevailed on the Dayton family, who were faithful members of the church, to purchase it so the building of a new church could proceed. Dayton bought it and eventually erected a six-story building on the lot. Casting about for tenants, he decided to buy the nearby Goodfellow Dry Goods store and set it up in the new building. In the spring of 1902 the store was known as the Goodfellow Dry Goods store; it was then named the Dayton Dry Goods store, then simply the Dayton Company, the forerunner of Dayton Hudson Corporation.

Eventually the store would expand to fill the six-story edifice. Dayton, with no previous experience in the retail trade, wielded tight control of the company until his death in 1938. His principles of thrift and sobriety and his connections as a banker enabled the company to grow. As long as he was at the helm, the store was run as a family enterprise. Every Christmas Eve he would hand out candy to each employee of the store. Obsessed with punctuality, he was known to lock the doors at the onset of a meeting, forcing latecomers to wait and apologize to him in person afterwards. The store was run on strict Presbyterian guidelines: no liquor was sold, the store was closed on Sunday, no business travel or advertising was permitted on the Sabbath, and the Dayton Company refused to advertise in a newspaper that sponsored liquor ads.

This approach did not stifle business; the Dayton Company became extremely successful. A multimillion-dollar business by the 1920s, the Dayton Company decided it was ready to expand, purchasing J.B. Hudson & Son, a Minneapolis-based jeweler, in 1929, just two months before the historic stock market crash.

The Dayton Company managed to weather the Great Depression, although its jewelry company operated in the red for its duration. Dayton's son David had died in 1923 at age 43, and George turned more and more of the company business over to another son, Nelson. George Draper Dayton died in 1938. He left only a modest personal fortune, having given away millions of dollars to charity. In 1918 the Dayton Foundation had been established with $1 million.

Nelson Dayton took over the presidency of the Dayton Company in 1938, when it was already a $14 million business, and saw it grow to a $50 million enterprise. World War II did not hamper business; rather, Dayton's turned the war into an asset. Consumer goods were so scarce that it was no longer necessary to persuade shoppers to buy what merchandise was available. Sales volume increased dramatically thanks to Dayton's managers, who obtained goods to keep the store full. Nelson Dayton was scrupulous about complying with the government's wartime control of business and when, for instance, the government carried out its drive for scrap metal, he ordered the store's electric sign dismantled and added to the scrap heap. Until Nelson Dayton's death in 1950, the company was run along the strict moral lines of his father, its founder. In January 1944 Dayton's became one of the first stores in the nation to offer to its workers a retirement policy, followed in 1950 by a comprehensive insurance policy.

Sheds Conservative Image in the 1950s

With Nelson Dayton's death in 1950, the Dayton Company embarked on a new era. Instead of one-man rule, the company was led by a team of five Dayton cousins, although one of them, Nelson's son Donald Dayton, assumed the title of president. The prohibition of liquor in the store's dining rooms was dropped, and soon the Dayton Company would be completely secularized, advertising and doing business on Sunday.

The new management of the Dayton Company undertook radical and costly innovations. In 1954 the J.L. Hudson Company, which would eventually merge with Dayton's, opened the world's largest shopping mall in suburban Detroit. It was a great success, and two years later the Dayton Company decided to build a mall on a 500-acre plot of land outside of Minneapolis. Horrified to learn that Minneapolis had only 113 good shopping days a year, the architect decided to build a mall under cover; Southgate, the first enclosed shopping mall in history, was the result.

The safe, conservative management style favored by George Draper Dayton and his son Nelson passed into history; a younger, more aggressive management pushed for radical expansion and innovation would follow in its wake. The company established the large discount chain Target in 1962, and in 1966 decided to enter the highly competitive market of retail bookselling, opening B. Dalton Bookstores.

In 1967 the company, by then known as Dayton Corporation, made its first public stock offering. That year, it acquired San Francisco's Shreve and Company, which merged with J.B. Hudson to form Dayton Jewelers. In 1968 it bought the Pickwick Book Shops in Los Angeles and merged them with B. Dalton. Also in 1968 the company acquired department stores in Oregon and Arizona. The following year brought the acquisition of J.E. Caldwell, a Philadelphia-based chain of jewelry stores, and Lechmere, a Boston retailer.

Acquires Detroit Department Store in 1969

The year 1969 also saw a major acquisition: the Detroit-based J.L. Hudson Company, a department store chain that had been in existence since 1881. The merger resulted in Dayton Hudson Corporation, the 14th-largest retailer in the United States. Dayton Hudson stock was listed on the New York Stock Exchange.

With the merger, the Dayton Foundation changed its name to the Dayton Hudson Foundation. Since 1946, five percent of the Dayton Company's taxable income was donated to the foundation, which continued to be the case after the merger. The foundation inspired the Minneapolis Chamber of Commerce in 1976 to establish the Minneapolis 5% Club, which eventually included 23 companies, each donating five percent of their respective taxable incomes to charities. By the close of 1996 the foundation had donated over $352 million to social and arts-based programs.

Dayton Hudson bought two more jewelers in 1970—C.D. Peacock, Inc., of Chicago, and J. Jessop and Sons of San Diego. Company revenues surpassed $1 billion in 1971.

Mervyn's, a line of moderate-price department stores, merged with Dayton Hudson in 1978. That year Dayton Hudson became the seventh-largest general merchandise retailer in the United States, its revenues topping $3 billion in 1979.

Dayton Hudson bought Ayr-Way, an Indianapolis-based chain of 50 discount stores, in 1980, and converted those units to Target stores. In 1982 the company sold Dayton Hudson Jewelers, and in 1986 it divested itself of B. Dalton.

The late 1980s found the company the focus of an unsolicited takeover bid by the Dart Group, which would involve lawsuits by both parties before a stock market crash in October 1987 ended the takeover attempt. A second attempt at takeover of the company would be made nine years later, when rival J.C. Penney Co. offered more than $6.5 billion for the retailer. The offer, which analysts considered an undervaluation of the company's worth, was rebuffed. Meanwhile, Dayton Hudson continued its acquisitions, purchasing the Marshall Field stores from BATUS Inc. in 1990 for about $1 billion. Venerable Marshall Field's was as much a landmark in the Chicago area as Dayton's was in Minneapolis and the Hudson stores were in Detroit; the acquisition would add 24 department stores to the Dayton Hudson group while also doubling its department store retail space.

Diversifies into New Retail Markets in 1990s

While Dayton, Hudson, and Marshall Field department stores offered the monied customer more costly and sophisticated merchandise, the popular Target and Mervyn's catered to the budget-conscious customer, offering apparel and recreational items on a self-service basis. With the approach of the twenty-first century, Target continued to be Dayton Hudson Corporation's biggest moneymaker, combining a successful business mix of clean, easy-to-navigate stores with quality, trend-responsive merchandise. The year 1990 saw the opening of the first of over 50 expanded Target Greatland stores; in 1995, following the lead of such rivals as Wal-Mart and Kmart, the company opened its first SuperTarget, which combined the chain's successful general merchandise mix with a grocery store. Along with expanding its traditional department stores along the East Coast, six new SuperTargets were planned for 1996 alone.

The proliferation of shopping malls and the recessionary economy of the early 1990s caused sharp changes in consumer spending patterns throughout the United States. By 1996 the country could boast 4.97 billion square feet of retail space—an average of 19 square feet per person nationwide—but retailers felt the pinch caused by such a large number of stores courting increasingly spending-shy consumers. This situation most negatively affected the mid-range and upper-range sales volumes generated by stores on the level of Mervyn's, Dayton's, Marshall Field's, and Hudson's. In response, Dayton Hudson developed new merchandising, customer service, and advertising strategies in an effort to stabilize these units' falling sales volumes. Mervyn's focused increase reliance upon national brands, coupling this with the growing use of print advertising and market expansion through the acquisition of six Jordan Marsh stores and five Lord & Taylor stores in south Florida. Dayton's, Hudson's, and Marshall Fields courted the upscale consumer through an increased mix of unique, quality merchandise, an increased emphasis on customer service, and an increased sales-floor staff, all of which heralded a return to the "old fashioned service" on which Dayton Hudson was founded. Meanwhile, the Department Store unit worked to reduce inventories and invest in remodeling and technologically enhancing some of its older stores.

In 1994 Target executive Robert J. Ulrich was named chairman and chief executive officer of Dayton Hudson. In that same year the company began a new strategy: developing a "boundless" corporate structure wherein resources and marketing and management expertise could be shared by each of the three divisions to create a more efficient organization.

Poised Towards Future with Efficient Organization

By 1997 the Dayton Hudson Corporation consisted of three major operating units: Target, with 735 discount stores in 38 states, represented the company's primary area of growth; the moderately priced Mervyn's chain operated 300 stores in 16 states, and the upscale Department Store Company operating 22 Hudson's, 19 Dayton's, and 26 Marshall Field's stores. Such broad-based expansion from the first six-story building in which Dayton was housed no doubt would have stunned the company's founder. Capital expansion, as well as more varied retailing, had taken their place alongside the old policies of thrift and sobriety.

Dayton Hudson's three units operate autonomously. Significant investment is made for the long term; in 1990 alone the company's capital spending program amounted to $1 billion. While there has been some speculation that the company was considering the sale of its Mervyn unit due to sluggish returns on investment, the Target stores are seen as a continuing source of growth and high profitability for the corporation.

Principal Operating Units

Department Store Division; Mervyn's; Target.

Further Reading

Dayton, George Draper, II, *Our Story: With Histories of the Dayton, McDonald and Winchell Families*, Wayzata, Minnesota, [n.p.], 1987.
Chandler, Susan, " 'Speed Is Life' at Dayton Hudson," *Business Week*, March 27, 1995, pp. 84–85.

—Sina Dubovoj
—updated by Pamela L. Shelton

DH Technology, Inc.

15070 Avenue of Science
San Diego, California 92128
U.S.A.
(619) 451-3485
Fax: (619) 451-3573
Web site: http://www.dhtech.com

Public Company
Incorporated: 1977 as DH Associates
Employees: 1,025
Sales: $98.9 million (1995)
Stock Exchanges: NASDAQ
SICs: 3577 Computer Peripheral Equipment, Not
   Elsewhere Classified; 3679 Electronic Components,
   Not Elsewhere Classified

DH Technology, Inc. is the United States' leading designer
and supplier of printheads and other printing components. The
company manufactures and distributes printers and related
mechanisms that are used in such applications as freight and bar
code labels, airline ticketing, bank and ATM transaction
printers, lottery ticket printers, and retail point-of-sale transac-
tion/receipt printers. DH Technology's domestic operations are
separated into four main divisions: DHPrint produces impact,
thermal, and laser printers and mechanisms; DHTech designs
and manufactures printheads and other printer components;
DHDesign is responsible for the creation of customer-specific
printing products; and DHServ handles all repair and maintenance activities. The company has experienced sales increases
throughout the past decade, and has been recognized as one of
the country's top 200 small companies numerous times by
Forbes magazine.

The Early Years

The beginnings of DH Technology can be traced to 1977,
when Donald Hebert and Helmut Falk decided to create a
company to design and produce new printing technology products. They formed DH Associates (named after each of their
first initials), and began to explore different ideas in commercial
printing technology. Their collaborative efforts resulted in the
advent of printheads utilizing dot matrix technology, a type of
impact printing that incorporates the arrangement of small ink
dots to form an image on the printed page.

DH Associates began producing impact printer components,
which were then supplied to other computer and printer manufacturers for use in their own products. A major boost during the
early years was the company's status as one of the main suppliers of printheads to the well-known Wang Laboratories, Inc. By
the early 1980s, the market for DH Associates' products had
expanded dramatically, due to the increasing success and rapid
growth of the information processing industry. DH attempted to
keep pace by expanding its assortment of product offerings to
include many different models of dot matrix printheads that met
the needs of producers of numerous types of impact printers.

In 1983, six years after its inception, the company was
restructured and named DH Technology, Inc. At that point,
Hebert took on a role as the vice-president of product development, while Falk focused most of his attention on the managerial aspects of the business and stepped up to become the
company's chairman. In May of the following year, DH Technology initiated a public offering of its stock as a means of
generating revenues to fund future expansion.

Expansion Efforts in the 1980s

Using the new base of operating income gained by the public
offering, in 1985 DH purchased Micro Peripherals, Inc. of Salt
Lake City, Utah, a designer and producer of dot matrix printers.
Prior to the acquisition, DH had functioned primarily as a
supplier of printer components to other manufacturers. The
addition of Micro Peripherals, however, entered DH into the
business of producing and selling the actual printer product
itself. This change was beneficial because it offered the company diversity and enabled it to avoid relying solely on one
product. Furthermore, DH now had a constant and reliable
outlet for its printhead products, as the company's two new

divisions began working together to manufacture Micro Peripherals' printers.

Meanwhile, Falk had been serving as DH's acting CEO while the company searched for a new addition to its management team. In late 1985, William H. Gibbs joined DH as its new president and CEO, bringing with him both a wealth of experience in the industry and a strategic plan to increase DH's growth potential. Prior to his arrival at DH, Gibbs had served as the president and COO at Computer and Communications Technology, and had spent the six years prior to that at Datapoint Corporation. Upon assuming the administrative helm at DH, Gibbs began working to strengthen the company's management and to increase its customer base.

Within a year, DH Technology had undergone some important changes. Most notably, the company attempted to lower its operating costs by consolidating its many operations locations to its headquarters base in San Diego, California, and also to Tijuana, Mexico. In the process, other facilities in California, Utah, and Puerto Rico were closed. Also, Micro Peripherals was renamed DHDesign, and was restructured so as to focus its resources on the development of customer-specific products. Essentially, the division's marketing philosophy shifted from a production-driven attempt to locate buyers for its product, to an alternative market-driven process of developing applications to meet the needs of existing customers. DH's original printhead design and manufacturing operations were renamed DHTech, and continued as another division of the steadily expanding parent company.

Sales of DH products increased as the company's customer base expanded to include everything from manufacturers of data and word processing printers, to point-of-sale receipt printers in the retail arena, bank teller machines, and lottery ticket printers. Not only had DH increased its product line to include a diverse array of printhead models and types, but it was also supplying components to numerous manufacturers throughout the United States, Europe, and South America. With this worldwide success, and a dramatically increased bottom line since Gibbs's arrival, in 1987 Falk celebrated the company's tenth anniversary by retiring from his post as chairman. Gibbs was left to fill that role in addition to his other duties as president and CEO.

Also in 1987, DH secured many key contracts to develop specialty printing products for applications such as airline ticketing and a new U.S. Postal Service mail forwarding system. At that point, DH was becoming one of the most prominent printing technology suppliers in the country, and a good deal of the other domestic printer manufacturers either utilized DH components or licensed technology from the company. Because of this, DH created a new division called DHServ, to handle the repair and maintenance of all types of printheads. Meanwhile, DH continued to market its products using a customer-specific technology development approach, with a new focus on gaining more international business.

In 1988, DH's revenues increased 78 percent from figures the year before, due mainly to an important acquisition made early in the year. In April 1988, DH purchased Eaton Printer Products of Riverton, Wyoming, formerly a division of Eaton Corporation, for approximately $6.4 million. This added thermal printers to DH's product line, which the company began supplying to gasoline stations and convenience stores to print receipts. Eaton was renamed DHPrint, and began full shipment of new products under that name by the end of the year.

Meanwhile, DHDesign had entered into a joint venture agreement with Samsung Electronics in Korea to develop new printers for personal computers. DHTech was producing hundreds of thousands of printheads for over 100 customers worldwide, and in turn this widespread distribution of DH products gave DHServ more business when it came time for repairs or maintenance. Earnings per share doubled, and in 1989 DH Technology was listed in both *Business Week*'s top 100 and in *Forbes*'s top 200 list of growth companies in the United States. Annual sales neared the $50 million mark, most of which were generated in the domestic market, but also from increasing business in Europe, South America, Asia, Canada, and Mexico.

Aggressively striving to maintain its position as a leader in the print technology market, DH then decided to move all of its manufacturing and assembly operations to its facilities in Tijuana, Mexico. This move helped the company save production costs and undercut its Japanese competitors by taking advantage of the Mexican maquiladora program, which allowed U.S. companies to use less expensive Mexican labor. In 1989 DH also set up a new division called DHEurope, with its goal being to gain new sales opportunities overseas as Europe began to loosen its import regulations. Domestic business also continued to increase, as DHPrint obtained several large printing contracts from large banks on the West Coast and other companies in the freight industry.

The 1990s and Beyond

As DH Technology entered the 1990s, the increasing popularity and prevalence of laser printing technology caused some people to worry that the demand for DH's products would start to decline. But the high cost of laser printing was in DH's favor, because it made dot matrix a more cost-effective and attractive option for most of the company's customers. According to the August 1990 edition of *Money* magazine, "Lots of people think dot matrix is dead because of laser printers, but they're wrong. Dot matrix is cheaper and more reliable, so it's used for printing lottery tickets, grocery store receipts and automated teller machine records." Most experts agreed that it would be years before laser printers began to penetrate into the area of low-end applications, of which DH held over 50 percent of the market.

Nevertheless, DH made moves to expand its scope to include laser printing products. In late 1990, the company purchased Identification Business, Inc. (IBI), a business based in St. Louis, Missouri, that dealt in bar code tags and label applications. With the acquisition, DH strengthened its presence in the bar code market, while also expanding its product line to include laser technology. IBI continued to function as a separate division of DH Technology.

Early the next year, DH completed another important acquisition with the purchase of Datac plc, a designer and manufacturer of computer peripherals that was based in the United Kingdom. Datac plc dealt mainly in specialty printer products and hand-held data collection devices. Not only did this addition strengthen DH's standing in Europe, the Datac acquisition also included Datacos pty, a branch that provided a direct sales and marketing network in Australia. These new avenues of international marketing and distribution provided a means of filling the role that had previously been served by the DHEurope division; therefore, in 1992 that division was dissolved.

After achieving a 500 percent increase in sales of bar code products since the company had acquired IBI, DH began to focus more attention on expanding that aspect of its business. In 1992, a portable printer and a hand-held data collection computer were introduced into the bar code application product line. Within two years of that, DH had completed the acquisition of two more bar code product manufacturers. Stadia Colorado Corporation was purchased in February 1994 for approximately $6.5 million, and in August of that same year DH also bought Cognitive Solutions, Inc. of Paso Robles, California, and all of its technology rights, for $10 million.

The company's expansion efforts helped it achieve 1995 sales of almost $100 million. Profits were used to purchase the privately-held Mos Magnetics of San Diego, California, which entered DH into the market for magnetic heads such as those used in credit card and airline ticket readers. As DH Technology reached its 20th anniversary, it was well poised for continued future growth in the industry. The company's operations were strategically positioned across the globe, with locations in the United States, Mexico, England, and Australia. Furthermore, with a hold on approximately 65 percent of the domestic printhead market, and with its skill in bar code, thermal, impact, and laser printing technology development, DH Technology possessed the diversity and experience to continue as a leader in its industry.

Principal Subsidiaries

DH Tecnologia de Mexico, S.A. de C.V. (Mexico); DH Technology plc (United Kingdom); DH Technology pty. (Australia); Identification Business, Inc.; Stadia Colorado Corporation; Cognitive Solutions, Inc.

Principal Divisions

DHDesign; DHPrint; DHTech; DHServ.

Further Reading

Autry, Ret, "Companies to Watch: DH Technology," *Fortune,* July 16, 1990, p. 75.

Smith, Marguerite T., "Answered Prayers: Why Little Stocks Are Moving Among the Giants Again," *Money,* August 1990, p. 53.

"Taking Stock: DH Technology, Inc.," *San Diego Business Journal,* August 21, 1989, p. 31.

"Taking Stock: DH Technology, Inc.," *San Diego Business Journal,* April 16, 1990, p. 31.

"Taking Stock: DH Technology, Inc.," *San Diego Business Journal,* April 8, 1991, p. 31.

"Taking Stock: DH Technology, Inc.," *San Diego Business Journal,* June 3, 1991, p. 30.

—Laura E. Whiteley

Dialogic Corporation

300 Littleton Road
Parsippany, New Jersey 07054
U.S.A.
(201) 334-8450
Fax: (201) 334-1257
Web Site: www.dialogic.com

Public Company
Incorporated: 1983
Employees: 650
Sales: $168.6 million (1995)
Stock Exchanges: NASDAQ
SICs: 3672 Printed Circuit Boards; 7372 Prepackaged
Software

Dialogic Corporation, which has been credited with creating the computer telephony industry, is a world leader in computer telephony (CT) components. More than one-third of all computer-assisted telephone transmissions—including voice, fax, data, voice recognition, text-to-speech synthesis, and call management—are answered by computer networks incorporating Dialogic products. The company's 250 products cover the entire range of computer telephony applications, and are approved for use in some 50 countries. Since pioneering CT in the early 1980s, Dialogic has shipped more than two million ports, that is, connections to telephone lines, as well as helping to establish the Signal Computing System Architecture (SCSA) software standard for CT applications.

Dialogic does not provide end-user systems, but rather building blocks for the CT industry. Sales are made through a customer base including value-added resellers (VARs), original equipment manufacturers (OEMs), telephone and wireless communications providers, and software applications developers. The company's more than 3,000 customers include small system integrators, major telecommunications companies, Post Telephone and Telegraph (PTT) companies, and computer companies, including Deutsche Telekom, Northern Telecom, Fujitsu, IBM, Motorola, NEC, and Hewlett Packard. The company's two main product lines are its two- and four-port voice processing hardware, used for unified messaging, voice mail, and interactive voice response applications, and its DIALOG/HD high-density 16- to 60-port voice and network interface hardware, used in high-volume telecommunications networks.

Dialogic is led by cofounder and chairman Nicholas Zwick and by president and CEO Howard G. Bubb. Sales of the company's products neared $170 million in 1995, spurred in part by several mergers and acquisitions, including Gammalink in 1994; Spectron Microsystems and the Computer Integrated Technology (CIT) group of Digital Equipment Corporation in 1995; and Dianatel in 1996. Dialogic, headquartered in Parsippany, New Jersey, has operations in 13 countries in North and South America, Europe, and Asia.

The Call of the Future in 1983

The company was founded 1983 by three engineers, Nicholas Zwick and James Shinn, both of whom had worked for Advanced Micro Devices, and Kenneth Burkhardt, formerly with Unisys. At the time, the telecommunications and computer industries operated separately. The telecommunications industry relied on closed private branch exchange (PBX) systems to control both private and public telephone networks. The computer industry was based primarily on equally closed mainframe systems. The rise of the personal computer and client/server markets in the 1980s, however, opened new opportunities.

Zwick, Shinn, and Burkhardt were among the first to recognize the inevitable merging of the telecommunications and computer industries, and Dialogic was founded to provide building block solutions for linking voice processing to computers. "They knew that the same trends that revolutionized computing would fuel the creation of a whole new industry," as Howard Bubb told *Investor's Business Daily*.

Rather than focus on providing end-user products, Dialogic created hardware and software components that would then be used by a variety of manufacturers and resellers to build end-user systems. The company also provided strong technical support services to its VAR, OEM, and systems integrator customers. In this way, Dialogic avoided direct competition with

---

Company Perspectives:

Dialogic was founded in 1983 on a simple vision: to bridge the once separate telecommunications and computer networks by building standards-based components for voice and fax processing.

---

telecommunications and computer industry providers—indeed, the company's founding charter contained a clause forbidding it from competing with its customers. In turn, the company's customers helped raise Dialogic's products to the industry standard. By the end of the decade, Dialogic's products controlled between 60 and 70 percent of the new market. Its products were supported by more software and hardware vendors than all of its competitors combined. Discussing Dialogic's success with *Teleconnect,* Zwick said: "First, we stuck to our product and market focus. Our long-term goal was to be a building block supplier. We simply would not abandon this goal for mere short-term opportunities."

CTI held the promise of revolutionizing business and consumer communications. The integration of telephone technology with computer technology offered a dazzling array of possibilities for sharing voice and data communications among networks, desktop computers, the Internet, and the telephone. CTI, among other potential applications, would allow international voice calls and full-duplex (two-way) conference calling without long-distance charges. Local-area networks (LANs) could be used to route voice-mail messages over the Internet in the same way as e-mail messages. Facsimile machines and voice-mail were two early innovations provided by CTI; in the future, CTI promised expanded voice synthesis applications, such as allowing fax messages to be converted to speech, or voice messages to be converted to fax messages. Early implementation of CTI allowed the creation of call centers: when a customer placed a call to a bank, credit card agent, telephone provider, or other system, the call would bring up the customer's account information on the operator's computer screen. Fulfilling the promise of CTI, however, required several important factors: advances in the basic technology, the "opening" of systems to allow third-party add-ons to basic components, and the establishing of hardware and software standards.

Fulfilling the Promise in the 1990s

During the 1980s, Dialogic's main customer relationships came through its Toolkit Developer's Program. A developer was responsible for designing an application generator for its hardware components. The application generator was software that gave third-party developers a head start on developing the end-user software and hardware systems based on Dialogic components, allowing developers to create applications more quickly and easily. These developers—called Solutions Developers by Dialogic—were usually distinguished by an expertise in a specific industry, such as banking, health care, cable television, or insurance. As Shinn told *Teleconnect,* "There doesn't seem to be an industry that can't come up with an innovative application using our tools." Dialogic would provide not only

technical support, but sales and marketing support as well. This system, however, remained relatively closed to developers other than those specifically chosen by Dialogic.

By the beginning of the 1990s, Dialogic faced new competition. The industry that the company had pioneered spawned a host of new companies developing competing technology. At the same time, Dialogic feared that its dominant position in the market might cause customers to turn to the competition. As Bubb told *Electronic News,* "People don't want to be held hostage to us." In response, Dialogic moved to open its architecture, announcing the company's Open Platform Environment (OPEN) in 1991. This move was mirrored in the computer market as well: IBM opened its personal computer architecture in the 1980s, creating a flood of machines based on IBM technology that came to dominate the personal computer market; in contrast, rival Apple maintained a closed architecture until the mid-1990s, dooming the company to dwindling market share. With OPEN, Dialogic hoped not only to build on its relationships with its developers, but also to encourage far-reaching applications for its products, solidifying the company's base in the coming—and inevitable—standards wars. "Solutions Developers see our Open Platform Environment as assuring them of choice and of second sourcing," Shinn told *Teleconnect.* "The open Platform Environment lets Solutions Developers differentiate their voice processing systems by adding bits and pieces of new technology arising as a result of the now-open architecture." By opening its architecture to competing companies, Dialogic also hoped to expand the market itself, increasing Dialogic's revenues despite the competition.

In further support of OPEN, Dialogic also established a new developer relationship, called Technology Developers. These developers were companies that made specialty products that Dialogic itself didn't produce, but which could be based on Dialogic components. Early Technology Developers included Gammalink, based in Sunnyvale, California, and Brooktrout Technology, based in Wellesley Hills, Massachusetts, both makers of facsimile boards, and several voice recognition product makers, such as Voice Control Systems of Dallas, Texas, and Berkeley Speech Technologies of Berkeley, California. Opening Dialogic's architecture was seen as a bold move. "It's like having a monkey on our back," Shinn told *Teleconnect,* "Either we keep up with what we've announced. Or we lose our dominant position and become a 'me-too' player."

The implementation of OPEN helped boost Dialogic's revenues from $50.8 million in 1991 to nearly $65.5 million in 1992. The company's income also proved strong, rising from $5.2 million in 1991 to $6.5 million the following year. By then, however, Dialogic found itself in a standards battle between Dialogic's pulse-code expansion bus (PEB) and the multivendor integration protocol (MVIP) touted by chief competitors Natural MicroSystems and Rhetorex. Both systems sought to create the protocol and physical connection standards for the communications backplane—a ribbon connector allowing voice processing boards to work with various computer bus systems. (A bus refers to the wiring system used to carry data to and from a computer processor, while also defining protocols for attaching peripheral components such as memory, hard drives, and others to the processor.) Setting up standards was seen as a necessity for the industry: applications developers were reluctant to invest in creating new telephony software programs without industry-wide standards, and without software to drive them, sales of hardware would remain limited. Despite some claims that MVIP offered a superior standard, Dialogic's large installed base gave the company an advantage.

Dialogic moved to build on that advantage in 1993, with the announcement of the formation of a new standards group, Signal Computing System Architecture (SCSA). Joining Dialogic to create the SCSA standard were some 70 other computer telephony companies, a group that would grow to more than 250 over the next two years. The SCSA group drafted its hardware standard by the end of 1993, and completed software specifications in September 1994. The SCSA standard provided seamless integration of telephony hardware components and software applications across a variety of vendors. Dialogic began shipping SCSA-based components in 1994, and the first end-user SCSA-based products began appearing in 1995.

The company's revenues continued to grow, reaching $95.6 million in 1993 and passing $127 million in 1994. Dialogic went public in 1994, selling 3.75 million shares. The IPO was made in part to complete the acquisition of Gammalink, which was announced in 1993. Dialogic's move to acquire Gammalink, which would continue to operate as a separate entity, was made in order to add Gammalink's facsimile board capacity to Dialogic's product line, allowing the company to step up the integration of voice-mail and fax capabilities.

At the start of 1995, Dialogic made two more strategic acquisitions. The first was of Digital Equipment Corp.'s CIT group and that company's computer integrated telephony server technologies. The acquisition, formed as Dialogic's CT division, brought out its first product, CT-Connect, in 1995. CT Connect allowed the integration of enterprise-wide personal computer networks to PBX systems using a Windows NT-based server. Dialogic's second acquisition in 1995 was of Spectron MicroSystems, the company that had developed the industry standard SPOX digital signal processing (DSP) operating system used by Motorola, Texas Instruments, Intel, and other industry heavyweights. The acquisition of DSP software was seen as a method for further coordinating standards development, while broadening the company's product range. At the same time, Dialogic joined with Digital Equipment Corp., Ericsson Business Networks, Hewlett-Packard, and Northern

Telecom to form the Enterprise Computer Telephony Forum (ECTF) to further the implementation of industry-wide CT standards.

Acquisitions, Alliances, and a Bright Future

Dialogic closed 1995 with revenues nearing $170 million and a net income of more than $16 million. The following year, the company entered strategic alliances with two more companies, Israel-based VocalTec, Inc., a pioneer in Internet telephone software, and Artisoft, Inc., based in Tucson, Arizona. In June 1996, the company also acquired Dianatel, based in San Jose, California, a maker of digital trunk interface products. Meanwhile, releases of SCSA-based products began to take off in 1996, and analysts began to predict a long-awaited boom in the CTI industry, with estimates that the industry would reach more than $5 billion in sales by 1998. With the computer telephony revolution gaining momentum, Dialogic, which controlled more than half of the non-proprietary segment of the industry, was braced for a sales explosion.

Principal Subsidiaries

GammaLink, Inc.; Spectron MicroSystems, Inc.; Dianatel, Inc.

Further Reading

Fioravante, Janice, "Dialogic Corp.," *Investor's Business Daily,* February 15, 1995, p. A5.

Leibowitz, Ed, "The Dialogic VAR Parade," *Teleconnect,* April 1993, p. 40.

——, "New American Cowboys," *Teleconnect,* December 1990, p. 40.

——, "No End-User Systems," *Teleconnect,* May 1991, p. S4.

Parets, Robin Taylor, "Dialogic Corp.," *Investor's Daily Business,* March 26, 1996, p. A6.

Phillips, Barry, "Computer & Phone—Making a Mixed Marriage Work," *Computer & Communications Magazine,* November 1, 1994, p. 72.

Rettig, Hillary, "Dialogic Rides Crest of Computer Telephony Wave," *Network Computing,* July 15, 1996, p. 70.

Rodriguez, Karen, "SCSA Gains Speed as Telephony Standard," *InfoWorld,* January 9, 1995, p. 47.

Zipper, Stuart, "PC Call Standards Processing Fight," *Electronic News,* April 13, 1992, p. 17.

—M. L. Cohen

Discount Auto Parts, Inc.

4900 Frontage Road South
Lakeland, Florida 33801
U.S.A.
(941) 687-9226
Fax: (941) 284-2063

Public Company
Incorporated: 1972
Employees: 3,150
Sales: $307.5 million (1996)
Stock Exchanges: New York
SICs: 5531 Automobile & Home Supply Stores

Discount Auto Parts, Inc. is one of the Southeast's leading specialty retailers of automotive replacement parts, maintenance items, and accessories for the do-it-yourself customer. At the end of fiscal 1996 (May 28, 1996) the company was operating 314 stores, of which 276 were in Florida, its home base. In the highly-fragmented, $65-billion-a-year automotive market Discount Auto Parts hoped to become for car owners what Home Depot had become for homeowners. Its prices generally were substantially below manufacturers' suggested retail prices and either at or below those of its competitors. In 1996 the company could boast 20 unbroken years of annual increases in sales and operating income.

Private Company, 1971–92

Discount Auto Parts was founded by Herman Fontaine, his son Denis, a lawyer and one-time judge, and other members of his family in 1971, when they opened an 800-square-foot store in Eloise, Florida. Growth was modest in the company's first years but more rapid after Denis Fontaine, described in one publication as "hard-charging and charismatic," succeeded his father as president and chief executive officer in 1978. Sales and income increased every year from 1977, and the company opened an average of 17 stores each year between fiscal years 1977 and 1982. In 1982 the company bought 16 franchised Aid Auto stores.

By 1989 there were 100 Discount Auto Parts stores in Florida. Net sales grew from $90.4 million in fiscal 1990 to $108.8 million in fiscal 1991 and $141.2 million in fiscal 1992. Net income grew from $7.5 million to $8.6 million and $12.2 million in these years, respectively. Discount Auto Parts went public in August 1992, raising $64 million from the sale of common stock, nearly half of which was used to pay down the company's long-term debt of $63.3 million—nearly twice its equity. The existing shareholders, for the most part members of the Fontaine family, were rewarded with $26 million. Denis Fontaine and his brother Peter continued to control the company, each holding 35 percent of the common stock.

Continued Growth, 1992–93

At the end of fiscal 1992 Discount Auto Parts was operating 139 stores throughout Florida. Each store carried a line of brand-name replacement parts for domestic and imported cars, vans, and light trucks, such as starters, alternators, brake pads, brake shoes, and water pumps, as well as maintenance items and accessories. By March 1993 Discount Auto Parts had become the nation's 14th-largest supplier in its field to the do-it-yourselfer and the largest in Florida, where it claimed 12 percent of the market. By this time the standard 5,200-square-foot stores were being phased out in favor of "mini-depots" averaging 7,600 square feet, or "depots" three times that size, the first of which opened in Miami in 1991. The entire chain was being supplied by a 150,000-square-foot distribution center in Lakeland, also the site of corporate headquarters. This center was doubled in size by the end of the year.

Discount Auto Parts' large warehouse enabled it to purchase in bulk at a substantial discount and pass on the savings to its customers. It also drew in customers by offering such services as free testing of electrical parts, free battery charging, free used motor-oil collection, and free use of specialty tools. Customer service was enhanced by the company's "team" concept of rigorous training for its employees, who were rewarded with a program of promotion from within and a generous benefits package that included profit sharing and, even for part-time workers, tuition reimbursement.

During fiscal 1993 Discount Auto Parts earned $13.6 million in net income on revenues of $176.8 million. From 1989 to 1983 the company had average annual revenue growth of 25.5 percent and average annual income growth of 20.8 percent. It ended the fiscal year with 175 stores and in that calendar year opened its first outlets outside of Florida, in Georgia. In its annual report the company said it had retained all of its district managers and its management team during the last year, 90 percent of its store managers, and 84 percent of its assistant store managers.

Discount Auto Parts in 1994

During fiscal 1994 Discount Auto Parts became the largest Florida-based retailer in state receipts, its net sales advancing to $207.6 million and its net income to $14.3 million. The number of its stores grew to 208, with 18 new ones added in the last quarter of the fiscal year alone. Seventy percent of the outlets now were mini-depots, intended to draw customers from a three-mile radius. The company opened its first store in Alabama and increased the number of its Georgia stores to 12. It also installed a $3-million custom-made point-of-sale computer system to continually track the inventory of parts sold and thereby allow company purchasers to make more accurate ordering decisions. The system automatically calculated the price of sales items and markdowns and also kept track of payroll and employees' hours.

The typical Discount Auto Parts customer was described at this time as an 18-to-30-year-old male with a household income in the range of $30,000 a year. Customers generally fell into one of three broad categories: basic customers, who changed their own oil and put in new car mats now and then; the chain's core clientele, who changed batteries, water pumps, and radiator hoses; and a third group, who were described as liking to get under the hood and tear the engine apart.

Team management remained a prime company concern. Each Tuesday and Friday corporate headquarters was left largely vacant as top managers fanned out throughout Florida to visit stores, sometimes without warning. "We go out and see what's working, what management decisions have gone awry," Peter Fontaine told a reporter for the *Tampa Bay Business Journal.* "Then we all meet back here and talk about it over coffee and doughnuts on Saturday morning." During the fiscal year the company spent about $2 million on internal and external training of employees. Denis Fontaine died of cancer in June 1994 and was succeeded as president and chief executive officer by Peter Fontaine.

One of the few negatives for Discount Auto Parts in fiscal 1994 was that its gain in same-store sales fell to four percent after two years of double-digit growth. However, new stores accounted for about $25 million of the $30.8 million in the company's sales increase. There was a decline of one percent in gross profit margins, which the company attributed chiefly to its policy of offering the lowest everyday price in a market and the lowest sale price on some high-volume items. On the other hand, Discount Auto Parts reduced its selling and administrative costs from 24.5 percent to 24.1 percent of the total, the third straight decline in expenses in this sector.

The 195 mini-depot stores were stocking 12,000 items and the 13 depots 14,500 items. Its own private-labels items, including oil, batteries, belts, hoses, and windshield-washer fluid under the Discount Auto and Power Pak names, accounted for 13 percent of sales. All the stores were being supplied from the Lakeland warehouse on a weekly basis, but not always directly, since about 10 percent of its products were going first to the depots, then to surrounding mini-depots.

Record Revenues and Income, 1995–96

Fiscal 1995 was another record-breaking year for Discount Auto Parts. Net sales rose to $253.7 million and net income to $20.6 million. The company opened its first store in South Carolina and expanded its total number of stores to 248. As the result of a second public offering of common stock in September 1995, the company sold nearly 3.5 million shares at $30 each. Net company proceeds from this sale were used primarily to pay outstanding debts.

During fiscal 1996 Discount Auto Parts had record revenue of $207.5 million and net income of $22.5 million. It ended this period with 66 new stores, bringing the total to 276 in Florida, 32 in Georgia, five in Alabama, and one in South Carolina. The depot stores—18 at the end of February 1996—averaged 13,182 square feet of space and 16,000 items, while the standard size had been totally phased out in favor of mini-depots averaging 5,110 square feet of selling space and holding 13,500 items. The company's long-term debt was $50.4 million at the end of the fiscal year. Peter Fontaine owned 63 percent of the company's stock in 1995.

On October 1, 1996, Discount Auto Parts and Q Lube, Inc., a subsidiary of Quaker State Corp., announced they had signed a letter of intent to jointly develop locations that would offer fast lube and automotive maintenance services as well as the retail sale of automotive parts. The fast lube/automotive maintenance centers would be located adjacent to either existing or newly developed Discount Auto Parts stores, with 10 to 20 to be opened by the end of 1997. A week later, Discount Auto Parts announced it would be title sponsor for one of Daytona International Speedway's premier events, the NASCAR Goody's Dash Series Discount Auto Parts 200 race, to be contested on February 14, 1997.

Discount Auto Parts in 1996

At the end of September 1996, the number of Discount Auto Parts stores had reached 336, and the company planned to open 85 to 90 in fiscal 1997, bringing the total to about 400. It was adhering to a strategy of owning the vast majority of its store locations and owned approximately 89 percent of its locations. The company-owned Lakeland distribution center, which was to be doubled in size by the end of fiscal 1998, also housed the company's headquarters and administrative offices. Almost all stores were within a six-hour drive of this center.

In order to establish and maintain customers for a lifetime, Discount Auto Parts was offering a variety of inducements, including computerized catalogs. Stores were being located on neighborhood sites easily accessible from a number of major roadways and arteries. They were open 364 days a year, typically from 8 A.M. to 9 P.M., with some higher-volume stores offering extended hours. Hard parts available included brake shoes, brake pads, belts, hoses, starters, alternators, batteries, shock absorbers, struts, carburetors, transmission parts, clutches, electronic components, and suspension, chassis, and engine parts; maintenance items such as oil, antifreeze, brake- and power-steering fluids, engine additives, paints, and waxes; and accessories such as floor mats, seat covers, and stereos and speakers. Even complete engines were being offered. Representative manufacturers included General Electric, TRW, AC Delco, Champion, Purulator, Prestone, Quaker State, Pennzoil, Valvoline, STP, and Turtle Wax.

Discount Auto Parts said it was following an everyday low-price strategy with prices generally at or below those of its competitors in the market area served by each store. Pricing in depot stores was generally even lower. Special promotional pricing was offered on selected products. The company said that it was achieving cost reductions by volume purchases, efficiencies in its distribution system, and higher productivity at the store level.

One of Discount Auto Parts' guiding principles was "First build the team, then the team will build the business." For new employees ("team members") there was an intensive week-long training and orientation program, to be followed over two years by "Parts Pro" certification and a "Tech 2000" program in order to qualify for promotion. Team members identified as potential store managers were eligible for the "DAP University" five-day training program at company headquarters. All store managers were required to participate in Dale Carnegie training courses. Virtually all full-time employees for more than a year were eligible to buy shares of the company's stock at a discount and make contributions to its profit-sharing plan.

Further Reading

Casey, Jerry, "Motorhead Heaven," *Florida Trend,* November 1993, p. 35.

"Discount Auto Cracks $200 Million with 208 Stores," *Automotive Marketing,* November 1994, p. 38.

"Discount Auto Leads Market in Sales, Income," *Automotive Marketing,* November 1993, p. 52.

Minkoff, Jerry, "Discount Auto Parts Maps Growth," *Discount Merchandiser,* February 1994, p. 30.

"Q Lube and Discount Auto Parts to Enter Joint Venture Agreement," *PR Newswire,* October 1, 1996, p. 1001.

Roach, Loretta, "Sunny Skies for Discount Auto Parts," *Discount Merchandiser,* April 1995, pp. 16, 19.

Smith, Katherine Snow, "Pedal to the Metal," *Tampa Bay Business Journal,* June 17, 1994, p. 1.

Turner, Alison, "Discount Auto Parts to Raise $58 Million with Initial Offer," *South Florida Business Journal,* August 10, 1992, p. 3.

Zipser, Andy, "Customer Driven," *Barron's,* March 8, 1993, pp. 38–39.

—Robert Halasz

Drypers Corporation

1415 West Loop North
Houston, Texas 77055
U.S.A.
(713) 682-6848
Fax: (713) 682-3104

Public Company
Incorporated: 1987 as Veragon Corporation
Employees: 600
Sales: $163.9 million (1995)
Stock Exchanges: NASDAQ
SICs: 2676 Sanitary Paper Products

Drypers Corporation is the third-largest manufacturer of disposable diapers and related products in the United States. The company's product line includes disposable diapers, disposable training pants, and pre-moistened wipes, most of which are marketed under the Drypers name. In the diaper market, Drypers is led by industry giants Procter & Gamble and Kimberly-Clark, to which it is a distant third place finisher holding less than a 10 percent share of the domestic market. But the company has successfully created a niche for itself by creating quality products that sell at significantly lower prices than those of its competition.

The Early Years

Drypers Corporation was formed in 1987 under the name Veragon Corporation, although the company's roots can actually be traced back three years earlier to when the company's founders launched another diaper business in Vancouver, Washington, called VMG Products. VMG was the brainchild of three college friends, David Pitassi, Walter Klemp, and Tim Wagner, all of whom shared an entrepreneurial spirit and dreamed of starting their own business. Following college, Pitassi took a job with Procter & Gamble, where he learned about the disposable-diaper business and the underdeveloped value-priced segment of the market. Both Klemp, a Coopers & Lybrand accountant, and Wagner, who held a job with a Port-

land adhesives company, joined Pitassi in a search for investors to back their own diaper-manufacturing project, which would focus on producing a quality product at a low price.

The three men soon set up a limited partnership with a group of investors who agreed to fund the company's start-up and then remain involved until they regained their initial investment. It was agreed that at that point, the investors would relinquish most of the company's earnings and its control to the founders. In mid-1985, VMG began shipping its diapers to West Coast supermarkets, selling them at prices significantly lower than those of the national brands such as Procter & Gamble (Pampers, Luvs) and Kimberly-Clark (Huggies).

VMG was instantly successful, and within months the fledgling company had reached its projected sales figures for five years down the road. Strangely enough, though, this success led to immediate problems for the three founders, who had no real financial stake in the company. To keep up with demand, they realized that it would be necessary to increase their production facilities and plow more money into expansion. Their partners, however, had agreed only to the initial investment, and refused to reinvest until after they had recaptured their original money. Heated debates ensued until late-1985, when the investors met and voted to oust the company's three founders. Wagner accepted a new job with VMG, but Pitassi and Klemp left with bitter feelings.

Post-VMG: A New Era in the Late 1980s

It was not long before Pitassi and Klemp had begun planning a new venture to take the place of VMG. They relocated to Houston, Texas, where there wasn't already another regional diaper brand with which to compete. The two men spent all of 1986 searching for investors, actually turning down some prospects because they sensed too many similarities to their first experience in Washington. Finally, by mid-1987 they had raised almost $2.5 million to fund the purchase of equipment and the initial production and distribution costs of their new enterprise, Veragon Corporation. One of their first moves was to hire Terry Tognietti as their chief operations officer, after wooing him away from Procter & Gamble where he had helped introduce the first "Luvs" brand boy/girl diaper product. Once Tognietti was in place, Veragon moved forward in its plan to produce and sell a high-quality product at a low price that consumers would appreciate. The company began shipping its new diapers under the name "Drypers" in the summer of 1988.

One of Veragon's most important assets was the relationships it formed with the Houston retailers that stocked its product. National-brand diapers were not typically a moneymaker for retailers, due to the fact that they were sold for little more than the wholesale price that the big companies charged for them. Retailers had no room to negotiate these terms, however, because consumers wanted diapers and thus the stores had to stock them, regardless of the fact that they weren't profitable items. Veragon decided to use the retailers' disenchantment with diaper products to its advantage. Because it was a local Houston company, it saved money on distribution costs, and the company also used local raw materials, which saved money on production as well. Therefore, Veragon was able to sell its product to retailers at a considerably lower price than Procter & Gamble and Kimberly-Clark, while still maintaining a retail price-point that was about one dollar cheaper than the national brands. Sales of Veragon's Drypers would be profitable for the stores, whose managers knew it. Soon almost everyone agreed to stock the Drypers product.

Another marketing strategy that proved successful for the young diaper company was its effort to mold advertisements and promotions to the needs of the individual stores that stocked the product. While Huggies, Luvs, and Pampers ran general advertisements on a national scale, Drypers focused on bringing customers into individual stores, which further strengthened its relationship with the retailers. These relationships proved themselves to be crucial when Veragon experienced its first attack by Procter & Gamble and Kimberly-Clark.

Drypers biggest selling point was its retail price—about one dollar less than that of its competitors. As the product gained popularity in the Houston area, though, the big companies issued $2-off coupons for their Pampers, Luvs, and Huggies in that region, attempting to destroy the Drypers price advantage. Pitassi came up with a genius counterattack strategy, however, which drew upon Veragon's strong relationships with its retailers. He convinced stores to apply any diaper maker's coupon to the purchase of Drypers, which turned the big companies' coupon attacks against themselves. Veragon ran local newspaper advertisements inviting customers to "Pamper, Hug, and Luv Us," and use their coupons to try out the new Drypers product. The marketing ploy worked like a charm, and Veragon was soon running at full production capacity to keep up with the heightened demand.

Veragon achieved first-year revenues of $101,000, which almost tripled the following year as 1990 revenues jumped to $285,000. In 1991, the company changed its name from Veragon Corp. to Drypers Corp. It was during that year that Drypers hit it big, as sales not only surpassed the $1 million mark, but actually topped off at $35 million. Drypers had spent the year exercising another brilliant marketing plan, which once again involved using Procter & Gamble's and Kimberly-Clark's own promotions to Drypers' advantage. Both big companies ran "educational" advertisements on a nationwide scale, which attempted to convince customers that certain characteristics of diapers were beneficial and necessary to have a dry and happy baby. For example, the big companies spent millions to explain the advantage of boy/girl-differentiated diapers. Drypers' advertisements simply acted as a follow-up; the big companies had already convinced the consumer to buy boy/girl diapers, and Drypers' ads focused on selling its own boy/girl products as opposed to those of the other companies.

Even though Drypers often opted to ride the coattails of its large competitors, the small company actually came up with some interesting innovations of its own as well. For example, Drypers attempted to appeal to working parents whose children went to day care facilities when it added a blank space on its packaging so parents could label and identify their diapers with their children's names. The company also introduced "perfume-free" products in the early 1990s, which were accompanied by an advertising campaign based on the idea that the perfumes used in most diaper products can be irritating to babies' sensitive skin.

Nationwide Expansion in the 1990s

If Drypers was a small annoyance to Procter & Gamble and Kimberly-Clark in their Texas markets during its first few years, it became an actual headache in 1992 when it expanded its distribution scope nationwide. 1992 saw Drypers acquire two other regional diaper makers, in an attempt to join forces and compete with the big companies, rather than compete against each other. Ironically, Drypers first acquisition was VMG, Pitassi and Klemp's first diaper company. With the purchase, Drypers gained access to the market in the Pacific Northwest. Then in late 1992, Drypers purchased an Ohio-based company called UltraCare Products, which possessed a distribution network throughout the Midwest.

By the end of the year, Drypers' sales had doubled to $77 million. The company possessed over 5 percent of the market for diapers in the United States, making it the country's third largest diaper manufacturer. Drypers had experienced a growth rate of over 49,000 percent since its inception in 1987, earning it the number one spot on *Inc.* magazine's 1993 list of fastest-growing private companies. 1993 sales broke the $150 million mark, nearly doubling in the space of one year. Meanwhile, private label and value-priced goods and merchandise were gaining popularity with consumers, shedding the "cheap" image that had often plagued generic brands in the past. Consumers were looking for quality products that they could afford, and were turning to discounted brands like Drypers more and more often.

In early 1994 Drypers went public, offering its stock at $14.50 per share. Industry analysts projected great things for the "little" diaper company, and its stock was quickly rounded up by people hoping to jump aboard early and earn huge returns in the future. Even Robert Sanborn, who had managed the leading U.S. stock fund for the three previous years, chose Drypers as one of the top five picks for the following year. Suddenly the name Drypers was becoming well-known around the country, and so the company decided to capitalize on the name recognition factor and combine all four of its regional diaper brands under the Drypers name. Around the country, Baby's Choice,

Cozies, Wee-Fits, and Drypers were rolled under one umbrella and tagged with the Drypers name.

Unfortunately, the nationwide change of all regional brands to the name Drypers acted against the company, rather than in its favor. Many customers weren't adequately informed of the switch, and thus didn't follow their brand as it became Drypers. But even more detrimental was the poor timing of the switch, which coincided with two other major changes. First, the company opted to make a switch from thick to thin diapers, which when combined with the name change made it confusing for consumers to relocate their previous brand once it became Drypers. Also, the price of raw materials suddenly skyrocketed during the middle of the confusion, which brought on a price increase. These factors all hurt Drypers, and in fiscal 1995 the company experienced its first annual sales decrease, from $173.6 million in 1994 to $163.9 million in 1995.

Furthermore, a new price war being waged between Procter & Gamble and Kimberly-Clark combined with Drypers heightened production costs to virtually destroy the company's retail price advantage. In fact, the big companies' promotional prices were often below the everyday prices for the Drypers brand. Without its low price advantage to appeal to its customers, Drypers quickly began to lose market share. The company suffered losses of $15.5 million in 1995, and after debuting at $14.50 per share the previous year its stock plummeted to lows of less than $4 per share. Rumors began to surface that Drypers would either seek bankruptcy protection or sell its holdings to another company.

Amazingly, however, the tide turned once again for the struggling company in late 1995. The price war between Procter & Gamble and Kimberly-Clark subsided, and the cost of raw materials decreased dramatically as well. Drypers made a last ditch effort to stay afloat. Internally, the company reorganized so as to decrease its operating costs. This included the consolidation of its production operations to its facilities in Ohio and Washington. It also secured a large line of credit to handle

expenses, and earned approximately $9 million when it initiated a preferred stock placement offering. Drypers once again set its retail prices lower than those of competitors, and used its new earnings and credit to reinstate its promotional and advertising campaigns and recapture its customer base.

By early 1996, Drypers had regained almost 7 percent of the market for diapers in the United States, its largest share ever. The company was planning the rollout of a new diaper containing baking soda to control odors, and was also working to increase its presence in the international market with continued expansion into Latin America. Drypers executives hoped that these measures would further aid the company in making a solid comeback. As the company entered the end of the decade, it had been seasoned by its string of ups and downs throughout its short history, and thus seemed well-equipped to handle the pressure of maintaining a profitable enterprise in the face of fierce competition.

Principal Subsidiaries

Drypers Limited; Drypers, S.A.; Hygienic Products International, Inc.; UltraCare Products, Inc.; UltraCare Products International, Inc.; VMG Holdings, Inc.; VRG Leasing Corp.; New Dry, S.A.; Seler, S.A.

Further Reading

Calkins, Laurel Brubaker, "Drypers Files Private Placement Offering with SEC," *Houston Business Journal,* December 14, 1992, p. 25.

Ellis, Junius, "The Top Fund Manager Since '91 Picks Five Stocks to Gain 66%," *Money,* December 1994, p. 191.

Neff, Jack, "Diaper Battle Puts EDLP on Injured List," *Advertising Age,* August 14, 1995, p. 3.

Posner, Bruce G., "Targeting the Giant," *Inc.,* October 1993, p. 92.

Stein, Tom, "Outselling the Giants: How Aggressive Upstarts Toppled the Competition," *Success,* May 1996, p. 38.

Sullivan, R. Lee, "Diaper Guerrillas," *Forbes,* July 1, 1996, p. 58.

—Laura E. Whiteley

Eaton Vance Corporation

24 Federal Street
Boston, Massachusetts 02110
U.S.A.
(617) 482-8260
Fax: (617)-482-5360

Public Company
Incorporated: 1981
Employees: 369
Sales: $1.6 billion (1995)
Stock Exchanges: NASDAQ
SICs: 6282 Investment Advice

The origins of Eaton Vance Corporation date to the activities of Charles F. Eaton Jr., founder of Eaton & Howard Inc., a Boston investment house. Born in Princeton, Maine, on February 3, 1898, Eaton graduated from Phillips Exeter Academy in 1919 and from Harvard University in 1923. From 1922 to 1924 he served as assistant secretary treasurer of First National Corporation in Boston. In 1924, he left First National to found Eaton & Howard, Inc., becoming president and director of the investment firm in 1931.

Under Vance's direction, the company created and managed several investment funds, including the Stock Fund, founded in 1931 to invest primarily in corporate common stocks. In 1932, the company formed two funds, the Balanced Fund that sought capital growth through a blend of holdings in bonds and preferred and common stock, and the Income Fund as a general investors trust. In 1962, Eaton & Howard established the Growth Fund, which invested principally in common stocks of aggressive growth companies. The company also created the Special Fund in 1967 as a diversified fund comprising securities that appeared to have potential for substantial capital appreciation. To expand its market niche, in 1975 the Special Fund acquired the Foundation Stock Fund, Inc. of St. Louis, Missouri.

On May 1, 1979, the company was acquired and incorporated by Vance Sanders & Company, thus becoming Eaton &

Howard, Vance Sanders Inc. Founder Eaton Vance remained as the new company's vice chairman. On February 20, 1981, the reconstituted company then formed Eaton Vance Corp. as a holding company, and incorporated in the state of Maryland to operate other businesses in real estate, oil and gas, precious metals, and investment counseling services.

Growth During the 1980s

By late 1983, the first year of the historic bull market, the firm's investment and mutual fund subsidiary had grown to manage 23 mutual funds and various individual and institutional accounts totalling $2.3 billion in assets. The company's success in the investment business rode the crest of the mutual fund boom. For the year ended August 1983, the total return for the mutual fund industry, including 538 stock and bond funds, averaged 56 percent. With the exception of the October 1987 stock market debacle, the bull market continued throughout the 1980s and into the 1990s.

The passage of the Tax Reform Act of 1984, however, posed substantial difficulties for the mutual fund industry's tax-managed funds by closing several tax loopholes. Although six leading industry managers abandoned their tax sheltering funds, converting them to conventional funds, Eaton Vance, the largest tax-managed fund with $499 million in assets, continued to seek tax protection for shareholders. Tax-managed funds operated by converting ordinary income from dividends into capital gains taxable at lower rates and only when shares were redeemed. As a result, they were taxed as corporations instead of as managed investments. Corporate taxes were then avoided through trading maneuvers and using the 85 percent dividend exclusion provision. Further, the funds kept all earnings, which allowed shareholders to avoid taxable dividends.

The 1984 tax law attacked these strategies in several ways. The law allowed the 85 percent dividend exclusion only when investors held stock for 46 days, instead of 16, and prohibited the exclusion if the fund borrowed money to purchase the stock. More prohibitive, the new tax law exacted an accumulated earnings tax on investment firms and disallowed trading losses as a deduction from the taxes. Although this provision served to kill many tax-managed funds, Eaton Vance decided to continue its Tax-Managed Trust.

In 1987, the company's group of funds outpaced many of its competitors despite the October 19th stock market plunge. In spite of record earnings, the company's stock tumbled from a high of 32 in March to just 13 in late October 1987. Nevertheless, like other fund distributors the company's success stemmed mostly from selling "spread" funds, earning brokers a 4 percent sales commission from Eaton itself rather than from the fund's shareholders. The company recovered commissions by charging Eaton shareholders a surrender fee when they redeemed shares. The deferred sales commission not only accounted for a substantial portion of Eaton's pretax income, but also protected its earnings by discouraging redemptions. By 1988, Eaton Vance had more than $6 billion under management.

Throughout the 1980s the rapid growth of the mutual fund industry was accompanied by expansion of municipal bond tax-exempt funds. In 1988, investors poured $4.2 billion into long-term national and single-state tax-exempt funds, while selling $21.5 billion of mutual funds, including $5.7 billion of fixed-income funds after the 1987 stock market plunge. The growing popularity of tax-exempt funds stemmed from nervous investors eschewing the stock market following the October 1987 stock market crash as well as others seeking tax relief or fearing rising state and federal income taxes. As a result of these trends, Eaton Vance's small Municipal Bond Fund L.P. grew about 20 percent in 1987 to $63 million.

Eaton Vance organized its Municipal Bond Fund as a limited partnership, a unique structure that provided fund holders added tax benefits. Whereas most funds established themselves as corporations and could only deduct losses against gains, Eaton Vance could pass these losses directly to fund holders, providing them a loss to offset any capital gain. This benefit allowed shareholders to claim lower taxes on capital gains. In addition, Eaton Vance's Municipal Bond Fund permitted investors to withdraw their principal investment without adverse tax consequences. In the late 1980s, the Municipal Bond Fund rivaled stock equity returns, posting a 33.89 percent one-year total return; a 79.7 percent return for three years; and 79.7 percent for five years. The fund invested mainly in long-term

revenue issues with an average maturity of 26 years. By 1988, Eaton Vance also had more than $6 billion under management.

In 1989, Eaton Vance's Prime Rate Reserves, the largest of new funds organized to purchase bank loans, suspended sales temporarily in order to invest a growing pool of assets. The fund's principal underwriter, Eaton Vance Distributors, announced that from almost $1.6 billion in assets, only $960 million had been invested. The closed-end fund engaged in several high-return, high-risk leveraged loans, requiring a minimum investment of $5,000. The inability to invest its assets stemmed primarily from the time needed to close on loan participation, which typically took several weeks.

In addition, like other prime rate funds that invested in bank loans, the company's Prime Rate Reserve failed to yield returns matching the prime lending rate. To close the gap, Eaton Vance innovated a method enabling the fund to boost its yield. In 1990, the company began leveraging the $2 billion fund by selling debt obligations at low interest rates and reinvesting the proceeds in higher yielding bank loans. The difference between the two rates increased the fund's yield. A large share of the fund's assets comprised highly leveraged transactions that earned 1.5 percent over the prime rate, or over 2.5 percent over the London interbank rate. In addition, Eaton Vance formed a $300 million credit-enhanced commercial paper program guaranteed by the fund's assets. Although mutual funds sometimes applied preferred stock and bank loans for leveraging returns, Prime Rate Reserves became the first to use commercial paper. The company's vice-president, Richard D'Addario, responsible for structuring the deal, believed the fund could obtain higher rates in the commercial paper market than in using bank lines. The use of commercial paper allowed the fund to borrow at cheaper rates, both enhancing the yield and allowing liquidity.

Good News, Bad News, the 1990s

By the late 1980s, Eaton Vance's core products included 34 low-risk, tax-free funds, making the company a giant in the industry. In 1990, the company began marketing its funds through banks, accounting in 1992 for about 15 percent of its $3 billion in total sales, or $450 million. By 1993 more than 60 banks were selling Eaton Vance funds. Because the company did no advertising, it relied on a cadre of 23 staff members to work with banks and provide extensive customer education. This initial success stemmed largely from Eaton Vance's fee structure. Rather than up-front load charges, customers could pay deferred sales charges, levied only when the funds were withdrawn.

In 1992, Eaton Vance affiliated with Lloyd George Management with the introduction of the Greater China Growth Fund. With offices in Hong Kong, London, and Bombay, Lloyd George Management enabled Eaton Vance to distribute mutual funds globally. Eaton Vance initially purchased a 6 percent stake in Lloyd George, which it later increased to 24 percent in 1995.

By 1993, Eaton Vance had doubled its assets under management in five years to $12 billion. Although impressive, this growth was slightly less than similar companies in the mutual fund industry. Nevertheless, earnings improved considerably from a low of 98 cents a share in 1989 to $2.49 a share in 1992, and operating income recorded a similar steep increase. Despite these gains, the company ran into difficulty with the Internal Revenue Service (IRS) over its fund sales and management fees. More than 90 percent of fund sales and 60 percent of management fees came from its primary product—B shares or mutual funds sold by brokers without a commission. The company paid brokers a 4 percent fee up-front, and then attempted to recover these costs from investors through a 1 percent annual charge, or up to 6 percent if they redeemed their shares early.

The company's tax problems stemmed from attempts to increase cash flow to offset these up-front cash payments to brokers. If a fund company recorded commission payments as normal business expenses, they could effectively erase earnings. Although this strategy might prove useful for cutting tax bills, it offered little in attracting new investors. As a result, Eaton Vance and similar firms sought to capitalize and amortize broker payments for reporting purposes, while expensing them for tax purposes. In 1992, the company reported an operating loss to the IRS, adding about $16 million beyond the $63 million in deferred taxes listed as liabilities on its balance sheet. The company then tried to use the $16 million for broker fees, money that otherwise would have gone to the IRS. About 29 other investment firms also offered B shares, nine of which netted more than $1 billion in sales. Along with Eaton Vance, these funds also faced potentially adverse financial consequences from the IRS.

Restructuring and Globalization

In late 1993, Eaton Vance became the first mutual fund company to convert its entire fund family to the ''hub-and-spoke'' structure. Developed by Signature Financial Group, the new structure allowed banks to attach their own names to the funds. The company hoped banks would pursue this option instead of offering their own proprietary products. With the hub-and-spoke structure, the company managed fund assets as a single pool, or hub. Eaton Vance offered shares in funds, or spokes, that invested in the pool at different prices. Although each spoke fund had a board of directors, they shared the investment objectives of the hub. The structure enabled the company to cut expenses by managing assets as a single pool. To direct the hub-and-spoke program, the company appointed William J. Kearns, formerly a senior vice-president of Fidelity Investment's institutional department. Kearns believed the program offered banks private labelling under their own names at low cost, as well as enhanced revenue and distribution. Further, it provided banks a means to enter new market niches that they might not be able to do on their own. Nevertheless, luring banks to place their own names on the funds instead of offering their own proprietary products had disadvantages, particularly the loss of investment management fees.

Under the new plan, in 1995, Eaton Vance began selling new specialty funds through banks, offering two new portfolios that invested in stocks in global information age companies in the entertainment, telecommunications, and personal computers industries. The company managed the funds together with Hong Kong-based Lloyd George Management. Primarily known for its fixed-income portfolios, the company sought to distinguish itself from large fund companies that already dominated the banking arena by selling a variety of new specialty funds. In

addition, Eaton Vance began offering funds that invested in corporate loans or non-investment-grade municipal bonds. The two new funds—Traditional Age Fund and Marathon Information Age Fund—invested primarily in large and small-capitalization companies. Eaton Vance offered these portfolios to the 70 banks that were already selling its other funds. About 25 percent of the company's fund sales through banks came from fixed-income funds, and another 60 percent derived from Eaton Vance's Prime Rate Fund. The company also introduced and marketed to banks a new municipal bond fund, which invested 30 to 40 percent of its portfolio in non-investment grade bonds.

In the same year, Eaton and Vance spun off its 77.3 percent ownership in Investors Bank and Trust Company to the firm's shareholders. The move allowed the company to free its $128 million-asset banking subsidiary from a federal regulation that substantially restricted its growth and compelled it to give more than $400 million in lines of credit to competitors. The divestiture also permitted the bank to earn greater value for Eaton and Vance's shareholders than it otherwise could as a restricted subsidiary. Behind the company's move was a little known federal law, the 1987 Competitive Equality Banking Act, limiting subsidiaries of nonbank holding companies to 7 percent annual growth in balance sheet assets. The law also curbed such banks from providing new products, thus prohibiting Investors Bank and Trust, with $75 billion in assets, from offering commercial banking services.

Despite restructuring under the hub-and-spoke, by 1996 the plan was faltering, and Kearns left Eaton Vance for Boston-based Standish, Ayer & Wood, Inc., an institutional money manager. The company's program suffered from the specialized nature of its assets or portfolios, mostly municipal funds that numerous banks already offered on their own. Nevertheless, other hub-and-spoke plans offered by Citicorp, Chase Manhattan Corp., Bankers Trust New York Corp., and J.P. Morgan succeeded in capturing assets from smaller banks and brokerage firms. On the whole, the hub approach proved enormously profitable for the industry, capturing about $59.4 billion of assets nationwide, or 2 percent of all mutual funds assets in the country. As a result, the company elected to stay with the plan for the foreseeable future.

As 1996 unfolded, the strong American economy presaged impressive investment returns from both the U.S. stock and bond markets. In addition, the company anticipated positive returns from overseas markets, which would benefit Eaton Vance's international equity funds—particularly its Greater China, Greater India, Emerging Markets, and Information Age funds. To expand operations further, the company resurrected a growth and income fund in 1996 after 30 years of dormancy, seeking to capitalize on investor interest in stock funds. The company, managing $14.7 billion in assets, limited portfolio turnover to keep capital gains from eroding returns. By the mid-1990s, equity funds accounted for a growing share of mutual funds sales. As a result, companies specializing in bonds began feeling pressure to diversify their products or be shut out of banks and brokerage firms. Despite reopening its ''tax efficient'' equity fund, the company still maintained about 60 percent of its assets in domestic bond funds versus 17 percent in stock funds.

The company's Northeast Properties, Inc. owned 670,000 square feet of income producing real estate in Massachusetts, New Hampshire, and New York. Revenue from these properties accounted for about 2 percent of the company's total revenue in 1995. In addition, Eaton Vance participated in the development of gold mining properties as a limited partner in two gold mining partnerships, VenturesTrident, L.P. and VenturesTrident II, L.P. The company held a 28 percent interest in Ventures-Trident L.P. and a 19 percent interest in VenturesTrident II, L.P. In 1995, however, the two gold mining partnerships produced losses of $1.4 million, resulting primarily from fluctuations in portfolio valuations.

Through its two principal subsidiaries, Eaton Vance Management and Boston Research Management and Research, the company provided investment advisory and administrative services to 154 funds and more than 953 separately managed accounts. The company's portfolio managers made investment decisions for most of these funds. Lloyd George Management, however, made investment decisions for Eaton Vance's ten global equity funds. The company employed a portfolio management staff consisting of 39 managers and analysts with substantial experience in the securities industry. The company held investment advisory agreements with each of the funds, which provided for fees based on the management services rendered.

The company's success has resulted from its ability to develop and offer new funds, as well as to increase assets of existing funds. Nevertheless, Eaton Vance has faced substantial competition in all aspects of the industry. The company's ability to market investment funds will continue to be critically reliant on access to distribution networks of national and regional securities dealer firms, which also typically provide competing managed investment portfolios. In addition, few obstacles have served to inhibit entry by new investment management firms. As a result, throughout its history Eaton Vance has confronted an ever-increasing number of investment products sold to the public by investment dealers, banks, insurance companies, and others that sell a range of stock, bond, and securities products.

Principal Subsidiaries

Eaton Vance Management; Boston Management and Research; Eaton Vance Distributors, Inc., Northeast Properties, Inc.

Further Reading

"Advance for Eaton Vance?" *Forbes,* February 8, 1988, pp. 176–177.

Eaton, Leslie, "2 Good to B True?" *Barrons,* April 12, 1993, pp. 45–46.

Epstein, Jonathan D., "Eaton Vance Considers Spinoff of Trust Unit," *American Banker,* March 24, 1995, p. 17.

Holliday, Kalen, "Eaton Vance Betting on Hub-and-Spoke," *American Banker,* August 26, 1993, p. 15.

Kapiloff, Howard, "After Misfire, Exec Takes Hub and Spoke Plan to Boston's Stanish Ayer," *American Banker*, June 7, 1996, p. 10.

——, "Bond Fund Specialist Eaton Vance Revives a Stock Fund," *American Banker*, May 21, 1996, p. 20

——, "Eaton Vance to Stick with Hub and Spoke Offering Despite Lack of Interest, *American Banker*, March 5, 1996, p. 7.

Horowitz, Jed, "Eaton Loan-Buying Fund Halts Sales Temporarily," *American Banker,* October 20, 1989, p. 11.

Lipin, Steven, "Eaton Vance's Prime Rate Fund Finds Innovative Way to Boost Yield," *American Banker,* October 5, 1990, p. 18.

Moore, Michael O'D, "Tax-Free Funds Giant Sees Big Sales at Banks," *American Banker,* March 12, 1993, p. 12.

Walbert, Laura, "Damn the Torpedoes," *Forbes,* November 19, 1984, p. 356.

—Bruce P. Montgomery

ECI Telecom Ltd.

30 Hasivim Street
Petah Tikva 49133
Israel
(972) 3-926-6503
Fax: (972) 3-926-6300
Web site: http://www.ecitele.com

Public Company
Incorporated: 1961 as Electronics Corp. of Israel Ltd.
Employees: 2572
Sales: US$451.54 (1995)
Stock Exchanges: NASDAQ
SICs: 3661 Telephone and Telegraph Apparatus

ECI Telecom Ltd. is a leading developer and manufacturer of telephone transmission equipment. Its products provide companies around the world with cost-effective solutions to the ongoing dilemma of ever-increasing demand for transmission capacity. ECI's digital circuit multiplication equipment ("DCME") products increase the efficiency of long-distance telecommunications links via satellite, undersea fiber optic cable, microwave and coaxial cable. These products generated the vast majority of ECI's sales until the early 1990s, when diversifications begun in the 1980s started to constitute a significant proportion of the business. These included access network products, which boost the efficiency and effectiveness of local telephone lines to accommodate integrated services digital network (ISDN) while postponing expensive infrastructure upgrades. In anticipation of a global upgrade to fiber optic cable, ECI prepared an array of specialized equipment, including Syncom and wide area networking products. With a boost from its 1993 acquisition of America's Telematics International Inc., ECI's sales and profit grew dramatically during the first five years of the 1990s. Revenues increased over 500 percent, from $74 million in 1990 to over $450 million in 1995, while net income skyrocketed from $3 million to $87.9 million. ECI is an affiliate of the Clal Group, a top Israeli conglomerate.

Post-World War II Background and Origins

The United Nations' 1947 partition of Palestine into separate Jewish and Arab states and the declaration of an independent Israel in 1948 spawned two trends relevant to the creation and development of ECI. Intermittent military clashes between the two states imbued Israelis with a fierce sense of patriotism and self-preservation, impulses which found partial release in the establishment of many institutions of higher education and research. Israel was soon distinguished by the world's highest ratio of scientists, engineers, and Ph.D.s per capita. Many in the country's "brain trust" were employed by the government to do military research.

Like many of Israel's leading high-tech firms, ECI evolved out of the country's robust defense industry. It was founded as Electronics Corp. of Israel Ltd. in 1961 to manufacture electronic equipment for the Israeli military. ECI developed a specialization in telephone transmission products, which manipulate the signals carried on telephone lines. Military applications of ECI's research included voice-scrambling equipment for the Israeli Air Force.

New management, including many of the company's 1990s-era executives, steered the company away from the defense industry and toward civilian constituencies in the 1970s. This too echoed national trends, which saw high-technology equipment evolve into one of Israel's most important exports. Early product groups focused on long-distance multiplexing: simultaneous transmission of multiple telephone messages over one physical line. One device took advantage of the fact that phone lines were strung in pairs—one line sent signals one way, while the other conducted the return signal—and each was actually only in use about half the time during the course of a typical conversation. ECI developed time assignment speech interpolation (TASI) technology that tracked the beginning and end of each segment of conversation and wedged the elements of a different conversation into the spaces in between. Launched in 1979, this device increased the potential usage of long-distance analog lines by a factor of two. ECI's product beat even Bell Laboratory's (now Lucent Technologies) entry to market.

Company Perspectives:

ECI Telecom Ltd. is dedicated to the business of global networking. Our vision is to provide innovative, managed network solutions that enable network operators and service providers to increase capacity, improve quality, maximize current infrastructure, expand revenues and deliver the services that their customers demand.

Throughout the years we have been the first to deploy commercially powerful new technologies, giving our customers a competitive edge.

ECI Telecom Ltd.'s products are in use in over 110 countries on five continents. Serving most of the major international service providers, our products offer integrated voice, data, fax and video capabilities through four major product groups: Digital Circuit Multiplication Equipment; Access Products; Synchronous Digital Hierarchy; Wide Area Network.

It was used especially on international undersea cables, where efficiency was a paramount concern.

Digitization Spurs Product Development in 1980s

The digitization of telephone switching that began in the 1970s foreshadowed a decline in demand for TASI but challenged telephone equipment manufacturers to develop complimentary devices. Digital telephone switches convert sounds into binary code for more efficient, computer-managed transmission and then translate them back into sounds at the receiving end. Digital circuit multiplexing equipment (DCME) developed by ECI and others bundle these digitized signals for maximum efficiency during transmission, thereby allowing standard long-distance phone lines to carry more information than was originally intended.

As it had in the area of analog multiplexing, ECI faced competition from industry giants like Alcatel of France and American Telephone & Telegraph. But the relatively small size of this niche—US$100 million in a multibillion dollar global market—meant that it was largely overlooked by the top competitors. ECI's ability and inclination to target research and development funds to this sector and its eagerness to embrace international industry standards gave it other competitive advantages over its king-sized rivals. By the end of the decade, ECI had captured over two-thirds of this market. In a 1992 *Money* magazine article, fund manager Robert Zuccaro of Target Investors asserted that "Most global phone companies have become ECI customers in recent years after failing as competitors."

Led by the bellwether DTX-240, which could multiply the capacity of a long-distance channel by up to eight times, DCME operations generated nearly four-fifths of ECI's revenues through the end of the decade. And while they were strictly a niche product in the context of the overall telephone equipment industry, DCME devices commanded an impressive 60 percent gross margin. From 1985—when the company formally short-

ened its name to the acronym ECI Telecom—to 1990, sales increased at an average rate of over 30 percent per year, totalling US$74.5 million in 1990. Net income amounted to $15 million that year.

Although technological progress in the telephone equipment industry continued apace, ECI's DCMEs enjoyed a longer-than-expected run. For while the products' initial target clients were large carriers in developed countries—Deutsche Bundespost Telekom and British Telecom, for example—they found new life in emerging markets like China, the Philippines, and Brazil. In fact, ECI continued to introduce upgrades of this device through the mid-1990s, including the DTX-360, a model that increased circuit capacity tenfold. So while DCME's contribution to ECI's overall sales had shrunk to about one-third by the mid-1990s, it remained the company's most profitable and largest revenue generator.

Access Multiplexers Debut in 1980s

Foreseeing the eventual obsolescence of DCME and seeking to diversify accordingly, ECI teamed up with one of its most important clients, Germany's Deutsche Bundespost Telekom, to develop a device that would increase the efficiency of local telephone lines. Sold by ECI under the trade name DIGILOOP, the resulting "pair gain" devices capacitated the existing copper pairs of wires to emulate digital lines and therefore carry two voice telephone calls on one line. Known in the industry as "access multiplexers," these devices appealed to two different constituencies for different reasons. Common carriers in emerging markets could effectively double the capacity of their local networks, i.e., they could offer service to two separate customers on one physical line. In 1992, ECI won a prestigious contract with Deutsche Telekom to bring the communications infrastructure of the former East Germany up to par with West Germany via DIGILOOP devices.

Telecos in mature markets could offer the increased capacity to their customers as a premium feature—discrete "lines" for faxing or Internet access—without expensive fiber optic upgrades to each customer. When combined with high bit rate digital subscriber line (HDSL) technology also developed and sold by ECI, access multiplexing held out the possibility of allowing phone companies to offer cable television service as well. (In fact, ECI played both sides of this intermedia competition. In 1994, it acquired a 30 percent stake in Israel's Telegate, a startup concerned with the development of technology that would allow cable television companies to offer phone services over coaxial cable lines.)

Access devices grew to become ECI's hottest product line (in terms of sales), with revenues increasing 88 percent from 1993 to 1994 alone. By 1995, they vied DCMEs as the company's largest revenue generator, contributing 32 percent of sales. And notwithstanding this dramatic growth rate, this segment still held out plenty of potential; industry analysts expected the US$4 billion 1994 global market for access products to more than double by 1997. Unlike the DCME segment, however, ECI faced a great deal of competition in the access market, a factor that dampened profit margins in this division.

Meeting the Challenges of the Fiber Optic Era

In partnership with longtime customer Deutsche Telekom, ECI began researching and developing transmission management products for fiber optic networks and their next-generation asynchronous transfer mode (ATM) switches in 1988. The fiber optic cables expanded bandwidth by a ratio of ten-to-one over copper, and the ATM switches merged voice, data, and video transmissions. Products in this new category of equipment used Europe's synchronous digital hierarchy (SDH, also known as synchronous optical network or SONET in the U.S.) standards to enhance the capacity and efficiency of fiber optic lines. SDH/SONET devices maximize the potential of the increased capacity inherent in fiber optic line by assigning bandwidth to customers on an as-needed basis. This differs from the current standard, which assigns a particular amount of bandwidth to each client whether it is being used or not. SDH/SONET therefore holds out the promise of increased usefulness and efficiency for telecos and their customers alike. ECI was among the first companies to achieve a working prototype of an SDH system.

Although the technological refinement of SDH/SONET technologies continued throughout the 1990s, ECI had SDH contracts with customers in Europe, the Middle East, and perhaps most notably China by 1994. By mid-decade SDH products, sold under the trade name Syncom, constituted over 10 percent of ECI's annual sales. With an anticipated annual growth rate of over 60 percent per year, the global SDH market was expected to become one of ECI's key divisions.

In an ongoing effort to diversify its product offerings and geographic reach, ECI acquired Telematics International Inc., an American firm, in 1993. Whereas ECI had long emphasized the voice and video segments of telephone transmission, Telematics specialized in data products, especially those for automatic teller machines (ATMs), local area networks (LANs), and wide area networks (WANs). Telematics developed and manufactured devices that package computer data in the same way that ECI's products package voice and video. And while ECI's geographic strengths lay in Europe and China, Telematics enjoyed a solid reputation in the Americas. Renamed ECI Telematics in 1995, this acquisition added about US$80 million in annual sales to ECI's balance sheet.

ECI's revenues and net income rose in concert with its burgeoning product line and geographic reach in the early 1990s. Sales more than sextupled, from US$74.5 million in 1990 to over US$451 million in 1995. Net earnings nearly kept the pace, multiplying from US$15 million to approximately US$88 million during the same period. These strides are certainly commendable—and have not gone unnoticed by the investment community—but perhaps more importantly, ECI has begun to transform itself from a niche player in the telecommunications equipment industry to a "global integrated network manager." Its strengths in China, where it was first to install SDH equipment should prove vital to this quest.

Principal Subsidiaries

ECI Telesystems Ltd.; Compression Telecommunications Corp. (U.S.A.); Telegate; ECI Telecom Inc. (U.S.A.); ECI Telecom China; ECI Telematics International Inc. (U.S.A.); ECI Telecom (HK) Ltd. (Hong Kong); ECI Telecom GmbH (Germany); ECI Telematics International Ltd. (United Kingdom); ECI Telecom (UK) Ltd. (United Kingdom); ECI Telecom Americas Inc. (U.S.A.); Encoton Ltd. (26%).

Further Reading

Autry, Ret, "ECI Telecom," *Fortune*, August 26, 1991, p. 98.

"Clal Industries, Ltd.: A Universe of Israeli Know-How," *Scientific American*, June 1993, pp. S6–S7.

Ellis, Junius, "A Top Manager Names Stocks Poised to Gain 25% or More," *Money*, July 1992, pp. 161–163.

Mendes, Joshua, "Milk, Honey, and Earnings," *Fortune*, July 12, 1993, p. 20.

Sivy, Michael, "Soaring to Lofty Profits on the Wings of Peace," *Money*, November 1993, pp. 54–56.

Smith Barney, "ECI Telecom Ltd., Company Report," The Investext Group, August 25, 1995.

"Teledata and Fiberoptics," *EC&M Electrical Construction & Maintenance*, November 15, 1991, pp. 129–130.

—April Dougal Gasbarre

Employee Solutions, Inc.

2929 E. Camelback Road, Suite 220
Phoenix, Arizona 85016-4426
U.S.A.
(602) 955-5556
Fax: (602) 955-3311
Web site: http://www.employeesolutions.com

Public Company
Founded: 1991
Employees: 120
Sales: $164.5 million (1995)
Stock Exchanges: NASDAQ
SICs: 7361 Employment Agencies; 6331 Fire, Marine, and Casualty Insurance; 7374 Computer Processing and Data Preparation and Processing Services

Employee Solutions, Inc. is a national professional employer organization (PEO), leasing employees to companies and assuming responsibility for payroll, benefits, and tax administration. Under the "co-employer" contractual arrangement favored by ESI, a client company continues to be responsible for day-to-day management, including determining job descriptions, setting salaries, and hiring and firing employees. ESI is the second largest employee-leasing company in the United States and the largest that is publicly owned. In 1996, the company had co-employer arrangements with more than 1,100 businesses in 46 states covering more than 28,000 leased employees. In addition to its employee leasing services, ESI provides stand-alone risk management services and workers' compensation insurance to clients through its wholly owned subsidiary, Camelback Insurance Ltd. In 1996, approximately 17,000 non-leased employees received these services from ESI. For the nine months ended September 30, 1996, ESI revenues were $290.2 million, triple its revenues for the same period in 1995.

Early History: 1982–91

Employee leasing first became popular in 1982, when a provision in the tax code allowed high-wage professionals such as dentists, doctors, and real estate developers to exclude lower paid, leased workers from company pension plans, saving lots of money in taxes. At the time, Employee Solutions chairman and CEO Marvin Brody was an attorney trying to find tax relief for his clients, and he encouraged them to pay someone else to take over their personnel responsibilities and to administer benefits. By 1984, Brody's clients had nearly 100 employee leasing companies to choose from, with those firms leasing about 10,000 employees to their clients.

When Congress closed the tax loophole as part of the Tax Reform Act of 1986, the future of employee leasing looked uncertain. But Brody discovered that his clients were not eager to take back the payroll and regulatory duties, and the accompanying paperwork, they had turned over to leasing firms. He also recognized that savings could be made in the costs of payroll and benefits by pooling small employers together. "I saw an opportunity for employee leasing to grow because I saw the frustration of my clients," Brody explained in a 1996 article in *Investor's Business Daily*. "I knew that if my clients were worried about costs, plenty of others were, too."

Brody turned to his friend Harvey Belfer, the founder of Arizona-based Contract Personnel Systems, one of the first 30 employee leasing companies in the U.S., to help him. In 1991, Belfer incorporated a new company, Employee Solutions, in Phoenix and became president. Brody, as a director, provided advice and helped in strategic matters.

Early 1990s: Growth of an Industry

Brody's perception of the continuing desire for employee leasing was on target. Small companies turned to Employee Solutions and similar firms to cut benefit costs (while often improving the actual benefits) and to reduce paperwork. Larger companies used leasing as a means to reduce their workforce. "There are fewer legal entanglements, so it's easier to let [workers] go," the senior subcontract administrator at Lawrence Livermore National Laboratory explained in a 1991 *Nation's Business* article.

Leasing companies initially concentrated on small business, generally those with fewer than 110 employees, which could not afford to hire someone to handle just personnel matters. In

---

Company Perspectives:

The Company seeks to strengthen its leadership position in the PEO [professional employer organization] industry by providing client companies with comprehensive and flexible outsourcing services to meet their human resource needs. The Company believes its size, full range of employee outsourcing solutions, nationwide presence, and sophisticated risk management/workers' compensation programs give it a distinct competitive advantage.

---

such organizations, the owner, partners, or other management personnel had to deal with tax reporting, payroll, workers' compensation, unemployment insurance, and whatever benefits the firm offered.

Typically, a small business would fire its employees one day, the employees would go on the payroll of the employee leasing company, and the next day they would be back at the work site as employees of the leasing firm. The leasing firm was responsible for issuing pay checks; providing health insurance and pensions; paying payroll taxes and preparing payroll reports; and handling legal issues related to employment. The client company remained responsible for day-to-day management, including hiring, supervision, salary setting, job descriptions, and firing.

But as the industry grew to over 1,000 firms by 1991, problems began developing. Three areas of concern were evident in the fast-growing industry: financial stability, workers' compensation rates, and company-client relationships. Problems in the first area occurred when so much cash suddenly became available to financially unsound or unscrupulous company officials. Too often they would use the money to pay personal debts and fail to purchase the insurance coverage they promised or deposit the required payroll taxes. To correct this on a voluntary basis, the industry's trade association established strict reporting requirements for its members, including quarterly independent audits to confirm that taxes were deposited on time, that insurance and other benefit programs were funded properly, and that workers' compensation and other required insurance was in force.

The second major issue had to do with the rates paid by leasing companies for workers' compensation premiums. Some newly established leasing companies would use their own flawless experience rating rather than a client's poorer rating to offer lower workers' compensation rates. The insurance industry also accused some firms of misclassifying workers to obtain lower premiums. The insurance industry wanted to prohibit leasing companies from carrying workers' compensation coverage at all, and require the client companies to provide the coverage. The employee leasing industry proposed that leasing companies be required to use the client's experience rating for the first three years, the period at which ratings are adjusted.

Responding to complaints, the U.S. Senate Permanent Subcommittee on Investigations held hearings. The subcommittee found that abuses occurred because no one, neither federal nor state regulators, had clear authority over the industry. For example, many of the leasing companies claimed they were exempt from state insurance regulations under the provisions of the federal Employee Retirement Income Security Act (ERISA).

Between 1991 and 1992, four states passed laws to regulate the industry. Their legislation usually required licensing by a state board and a bond or evidence of a specific net worth, ranging from $50,000 to $100,000. In 1992, Congress considered several bills to clarify who was responsible for regulating the industry but failed to act on any of them.

The third area of concern dealt with the legal relationship between a leasing company and its clients. Initially, leasing companies considered themselves sole employers, assuming legal responsibility for employment matters such as wrongful discharge and employment discrimination, along with payroll taxes and workers' compensation. By the early 1990s, the industry trend began shifting to one of ''co-employer,'' with the leasing company sharing legal responsibility but not assuming it completely.

Magazine articles at the time explained employee leasing and offered examples of successful experiences. But they also outlined the pitfalls and often included questions to ask a leasing company before signing a contract.

ESI Grows: 1991–96

Into this market came Employee Solutions in 1991. Like other employee leasing firms, ESI began as a small, local firm. But Brody and Belfer had a goal of becoming a national, full-service PEO.

Within two years of starting the company, Brody and Belfer took ESI public. In August 1993, the company began trading on the NASDAQ Small Cap Market. That year ESI also began executing an aggressive growth strategy, acquiring the Prescott Group, Inc., an Arizona company, in February, and Pro Pay, Inc. in October. These additions contributed to increased revenues for the year which reached $48.6 million, with net income of $109,550. At the end of 1993, Employee Solutions leased approximately 2,600 employees.

While one of ESI's major attractions to clients was the handling of payroll processing and regulatory compliance, ESI also offered its clients a wide range of employee benefits. Companies could choose from a menu of benefit packages, including major medical, preferred provider organization (PPO), three different health maintenance organizations (HMO); dental care; vision care discounts; group term life insurance; accidental death and dismemberment insurance, pension plans, and 401(k) plans. Because ESI was insuring a large pool of leased employees, it could take advantage of benefits offered to large corporations at a much lower cost than its clients could negotiate individually.

In 1994, internal expansion became a second prominent factor in ESI's growth strategy (in addition to acquisitions). The company moved into the southeastern section of the country, where it operated as Employee Solutions-East, Inc., and opened regional offices in Atlanta; Irvine, California; and Chicago. In

Atlanta, the company's new training facility began preparing a cadre of independent sales representatives.

ESI also expanded its benefit offerings, organizing a workers' compensation program with American International Group and Reliance National Indemnity Company. This meant the company could offer its own workers' compensation coverage to its leasing clients and reduce its exposure to a catastrophic risk. Under this program, ESI was responsible for the first $250,000 on a claim. Any amount above that would be covered by Reliance or AIG under a reinsurance policy. ESI also received approval to form a wholly owned captive insurance company, Camelback Insurance Ltd.

Employee Solutions took a three-step approach to workers' compensation. First, it rigorously screened potential clients, examining a firm's claim history, premium payments, and job classifications, and conducting an on-site inspection. Only about half of all applicants passed this screening. Once a company was accepted as a client, ESI's risk management department designed a safety program for it to educate workers about risks at that particular workplace and to introduce practices or equipment that could reduce injury rates. The final step in the process was to aggressively manage claims once they were filed. In most cases, this involved determining where an injured employee received treatment and bargaining with suppliers to get competitive treatment costs. The company also encouraged workers to take ''light-duty'' jobs until they were able to return to their old job. This strategy helped reduce clients' workers' compensation expenses by more than 50 percent according to an analyst report about the company by Ladenburg, Thalmann & Co. ESI's loss ratio—the cost of claims as a percentage of premiums collected—was less than 30 percent, compared to an industry average of 75 percent.

In November 1994, Marvin Brody was named chief executive officer in addition to serving as chairman of the board. As of the end of the year, ESI had tripled the number of leased employees to approximately 3,600, leased to about 450 clients in 20 states.

In 1995, the company established ESI Risk Management Agency, Inc. (RMA) as a wholly owned subsidiary. RMA made it possible to offer risk management/worker's compensation services to medium-sized companies on a stand-alone basis, without requiring them to lease employees. The company used this option primarily as a marketing tool. ESI's goal was to establish its credibility with stand-alone clients through RMA and then convert risk management clients into full leasing status. By mid-year, Camelback Insurance Ltd. was handling most of ESI's risk management/worker's compensation services program, in coordination with Reliance.

At the beginning of the year the company took over Employment Services of Michigan, Inc., a dormant business that had leased drivers to transportation companies, and renamed it Employee Solutions-Midwest, Inc. This allowed the company to move into Michigan, Ohio, and Minnesota, and it opened a regional office in Detroit.

During the year ESI created ESI America, a wholly owned subsidiary, through which it purchased Hazar, Inc., a national staff leasing company. ESI paid over $7 million for Hazar and several of its subsidiaries, receiving in return approximately 4,100 leased employees and expanding into key markets in California, Illinois, New York, and New England. ''The Hazar acquisition basically doubled our size,'' Brody told Robin Grugal of *Investor's Business Daily*. The growth resulting from these purchases was in addition to internal growth of between 35–40 percent a year anticipated by Brody.

At year's end, ESI's revenues had doubled from the previous year to $164.5 million, and net income stood at $3.8 million, almost ten times that in 1994. The number of employees leased by ESI increased to 11,000, and an additional 3,500 non-leased employees received risk management/worker's compensation services through RMA.

In January 1996, ESI's growth qualified its stock to move from the NASDAQ Small Cap Market to the exchange's National Market. That same month the company had a two-for-one stock split and completed the acquisition of Employee Solutions-East, Inc. and Pokagon Office Services, which was renamed Employee Solutions of Ohio, Inc.

Other major purchases moved the company into a new area, the entertainment industry, and increased its focus on the transportation industry. In March, ESI announced it was buying Aslin Transportation Services, Inc., for which it had been providing risk management/worker's compensation services. Aslin, an employee leasing company based in Indiana, specialized in serving the transportation industry. The company also purchased Penske Truck Leasing Company's Leaseway Personnel Corp., with $100 million in revenue and 1,900 leased employees. The new subsidiary, which was renamed Logistics Personnel Corp., provided permanent and temporary truck drivers, warehouse workers, dispatchers, mechanics, and administrative employees. With the purchase of TEAM Services, which had $65 million in revenue and about 3,000 leased employees, ESI began leasing musicians, recording engineers, and other commercial talent to the music and advertising segments of the entertainment industry. ESI also acquired Employer Sources, Inc., a California-based subsidiary of Hazar. The $400,000 transaction added approximately 1,400 more leased employees to ESI.

In August, Banc One Corp. of Arizona and First Chicago NBD Corp. joined in providing a $35 million revolving credit loan for the company. Banc One increased the credit to $45 million in November, when ESI announced the acquisition of the McCleary-Trapp Companies for approximately $10.7 million. Based in Alabama and South Carolina, McCleary-Trapp leased some 2,000 employees to 125 companies in 15 states, primarily in the southeast. Their clients tended to be light industrial, transportation, and service companies.

The year 1996 also saw the company initiate a third area in its growth strategy, that of joint ventures. In January it entered into a partnership with Tri-City Insurance Brokers, Inc. to sell ESI's stand-alone risk management/workers' compensation services.

In December, the company announced it had signed a two-year contract with U.S. Xpress Enterprises, Inc., one of the largest transportation companies in the U.S. That contract added another 3,800 leased employees to ESI.

But 1996 was not completely smooth for ESI. Some individuals were concerned that ESI was taking on more financial risk than it could cover. In an April 8, 1996, article in *The Wall Street Journal*, John Dorfman cited Peter Kamin and Todd Bourell, money managers with Peak Investment L.P., as fearful that the company did not have sufficient reserves for potential workers' compensation claims, particularly as it took on higher-risk employees such as truck drivers. That article caused ESI's stock to drop, but when the company's 1996 year-end audit by Arthur Andersen said the reserves were adequate, the stocks recovered. Merrill Lynch, for example, upgraded its investment rating for the company in a report on May 21st, saying, "We have yet to see written or hard core evidence of any of the wild and not-so-wild accusations thrown about to date. Most issues have been raised by anonymous individuals. As long as short sellers continue to lose money, the stories will likely be getting worse. We believe those with a long-term view will be rewarded for riding through the storm."

1997 and Beyond

Since the company went public in 1993, ESI had added over 25,000 worksite employees and 1,000 client companies. For ESI itself, success would be dependent on its ability to manage its growth. To increase its revenues in 1997, ESI began offering new services which its leased employees could purchase themselves. These included automobile insurance, prepaid telephone cards, and payroll deduction programs for life, disability, and special health insurance.

Despite the concern reported by *The Wall Street Journal* and a warning in the December 30, 1996, issue of *Business Week* that "a growing army of short-sellers maintain the earnings of this staff-leasing company are destined to fall," the future looked bright for Employee Solutions and the PEO industry. According to the Small Business Administration, 5.2 million businesses had fewer than 500 employees and 98 percent of non-farm companies in the U.S. employed fewer than 100 workers. The National Association of Professional Employer Organizations (NAPEO) estimated that less than 2 percent of small businesses were using PEOs. Although somewhere between 2,300 and 2,500 PEOs operated in the U.S., none had a dominant share of the national market.

Finally, significant regulatory issues, particularly regarding tax matters and liability for employment laws, remained unresolved. For example, the Internal Revenue Service formed a Market Segment Study Group which is examining the tax treatment of benefit plans for leased employees. As stated on its web site, "The Company, and other industry leaders, in concert with and through NAPEO, work with government entities for the establishment of appropriate regulatory frameworks to protect clients and employers and thereby promote the acceptance and further development of the PEO industry."

Principal Subsidiaries

Employee Solutions II, Inc.; ESI America Inc.; Camelback Insurance Ltd.; The Prescott Group, Inc.; Pro Pay, Inc.; Employee Solutions-Midwest, Inc.; Hazar, Inc.; Employee Solutions-East, Inc.; Aslin Transportation Services, Inc.; ESI Risk Management Agency, Inc.; Logistics Personnel Corp.

Further Reading

Bahls, Jane Easter, "Employees For Rent," *Nation's Business*, June 1991, p. 36.

"Banc One, 1st Chicago Join in Lending $35M to Worker-Leasing Firm," *American Banker*, August 5, 1996, p. 40.

Dorfman, John R., "Highflier Employee Solutions Attracts 'Shorts' Who Say It Skimps on Workers' Comp Claims," *The Wall Street Journal*, April 8, 1996, p. C2.

"Employee Solutions—Company Report," Merrill Lynch Capital Markets, May 21, 1996.

"Employee Solutions Inc. Contract with Worldwide Dedicated Services Inc.," *The Wall Street Journal*, September 3, 1996, p. C18.

Grugal, Robin M., "Acting As Client's Shared Personnel Manager," *Investors' Business Daily*, August 16, 1996.

Grugal, Robin M., "Employee Solutions' Marvin Brody: Listening to Clients Paid Off for Lawyer Turned CEO," *Investors' Business Daily*, September 25, 1996.

Holland, Kelley, "Temporary Lull," *Business Week*, April 22, 1996, p. 49.

Maio, Patrick J., "Selling Backshop Services to Small Businesses," *Investors' Business Daily*, October 18, 1995.

National Association of Professional Employee Organizations (NAPEO), http://www.napeo.com/peo.

Resnick, Rosalind, "Leasing Workers," *Nation's Business*, November 1992, p. 20.

"These Highfliers May Be Destined for a Fall," (Table), *Business Week*, December 30, 1996.

—Ellen D. Wernick

Essef Corporation

220 Park Drive
Chardon, Ohio 44024
U.S.A.
(216) 286-2200
Fax: (216) 286-2206

Public Company
Incorporated: 1954 as Structural Fibers, Inc.
Employees: 1,096
Sales: $200.8 million (1996)
Stock Exchanges: NASDAQ
SICs: 3559 Special Industry Machinery, Not Elsewhere
    Classified; 3561 Pumps & Pumping Equipment; 3599
    Industrial Machinery, Not Elsewhere Classified; 8711
    Engineering Services

A market leader and industry innovator, Essef Corporation designs and manufactures components to move, store, and treat water through the use of engineered polymeric materials and proprietary process technologies. Operating on a global scale during the mid-1990s, Essef also relied heavily on the swimming pool and spa business through its Pac-Fab subsidiary, the country's second largest supplier of swimming pool filters, pumps, heaters, controls, and lights. Supported by its involvement in these two industry segments, the company was recording encouraging financial growth during the 1990s after faltering during the 1980s. Internationally, Essef operated manufacturing facilities in Italy, Belgium, and the United Kingdom. In the United States, the company's manufacturing facilities were located primarily in its home state of Ohio and in California.

Origins in the 1950s

Essef began business in 1954 as Structural Fibers, Inc., an Ohio-based company founded by Korean War veteran James Horner. From Structural Fibers' inaugural year forward, the company was focused wholly on developing the use of fiber-glass reinforced plastics as an alternative to steel. Lighter than steel and with greater corrosion-resistant qualities, fiberglass reinforced plastics promised to be the manufacturing material of choice in the decades ahead, but it was up to companies like Structural Fibers to win support for its use in cast, forged, and other formed or fabricated parts. Toward this end, the Ohio-based company scored early success, pioneering the use of fiberglass reinforced plastics in the Polaris and Hercules missiles, jet engines, electrical components, and other national defense-related items. The experience gained through this work steered the company in a new direction, quickly changing its focus after a few short years. While producing fiberglass reinforced plastic components for missiles and jet engines, Structural Fibers developed a proprietary molding technology involving the use of fiberglass reinforced plastics in the mass production of seamless pressure vessels. The technology—a perfection of the internal bag-molding process—represented a turning point in the company's existence, then still in its infancy. By 1959, five years after its formation, Structural Fibers began to specialize in the manufacture of seamless pressure vessels.

Through its proprietary molding process, Structural Fibers was able to carve a solid position in the pressure vessel market, using its internally developed technology to penetrate the market for water treatment equipment. In a little more than a decade, the company established itself as one of the strongest competitors in the country, bolstered by the business developed during the 1960s. By the beginning of the 1970s, Structural Fibers' core business in the pressure vessel market was strong enough to warrant the company's diversification into other business areas and its expansion overseas. Early in the decade, Structural Fibers acquired Pac-Fab, Inc., a manufacturer of iron, brass, and steel pump and filter products, and changed the company's manufacturing capabilities to include polymeric materials, which were used to produce swimming pool filters and pumps. Eventually, Structural Fibers' swimming pool business would account for roughly half of the company's total sales volume.

Before Pac-Fab developed into an integral facet of Structural Fibers' business, the company expanded across the Atlantic. In 1972, Structural Fibers acquired a German company, Nor-Cal

Engineering Co. GmbH, and the following year organized a German subsidiary christened Structural Fibers International, GmbH. As the 1970s progressed, Structural Fibers continued to expand overseas. In 1976, a Belgian subsidiary was formed. Based in Herentals, Belgium, the subsidiary operated as Sa SFC NV and manufactured and distributed fiberglass reinforced plastic pressure vessels and swimming pool filters for European customers.

1981 Acquisition of FAME

By the beginning of the 1980s, Structural Fibers' nearly three decades of involvement with engineered plastics held the company in good stead. Its two business segments, water treatment equipment and swimming pool equipment, were each respected competitors in their respective industries, upheld by the increasing role plastics were playing in the manufacturing world. To increase its exposure to the opportunities offered by plastics, Structural Fibers began to look toward other business areas during the early 1980s, hoping to replicate the success with water treatment equipment and swimming pool equipment in other markets where plastics could be used. This desire to diversify led to the acquisition of FAME Plastics, Inc. in 1981, an acquisition that marked the beginning of an unfortunate chapter in the history of Structural Fibers.

With the acquisition of FAME, Structural Fibers gained entry into a new business area with vast opportunities for growth. FAME manufactured tough plastic cabinetry for the business machine and computer industry, a market that was about to embark on a decade of prolific growth. In the business of manufacturing and marketing computers no company was bigger or more influential during the early 1980s than International Business Machines Corp. (IBM), the behemoth in a burgeoning industry. Through FAME, Structural Fibers tied itself to the fortunes of IBM, obtaining a contract to manufacturer plastic cabinetry for the company known throughout the world as "Big Blue." Structural Fibers' contract with IBM represented what seemed to be a pivotal accord with one the world's largest companies, giving the much smaller Ohio-based company entry into a new market under the auspices of the undisputed market leader. Before the decade was through, however, Structural Fibers' alliance with IBM would saddle the company with burdensome debt and precipitate sweeping changes in management.

As FAME's work with IBM gained momentum during the 1980s, Structural Fibers continued to build on its core businesses of developing and marketing water treatment systems and swimming pool equipment. The accomplishments of the decade were significant, creating a flourishing enterprise that was posting record financial figures at the decade's end; but the growth achieved during the 1980s was not enough to compensate for the losses recorded by FAME. Several months before the acquisition of FAME was completed in September 1981, Structural Fibers purchased Quality Products, Inc. (QPI), then transferred its manufacturing operations to Structural Fibers' Chardon, Ohio facility in 1985 to bolster production of pressure vessels. On the heels of this move, Structural Fibers (renamed Essef Industries in 1982 before adopting Essef Corporation as its corporate title in 1985) completed its initial public offering of stock in June 1987, raising $13.5 million from the offering, which was used to finance coast-to-coast expansion, including the establishment of plants in Daytona Beach, Florida and Ontario, California. Next, in 1988, the company formed ENPAC Corporation, a subsidiary business that designed, manufactured, and marketed proprietary engineered plastic vessels for the containment and transportation of industrial and environmentally hazardous waste materials. The following year another subsidiary operation involved in mitigating the effects of hazardous waste was formed when the company organized Contaminant Recovery Systems, Inc. to develop equipment for limiting hazardous waste generation and recycling process water produced by plating, metal finishing, and other chemical process industries.

By the end of the 1980s, Essef's original businesses were generating record earnings, but the foray into the computer market through FAME was causing the company on the whole to flounder. Sales of IBM's hardware slumped during the decade and the decline had a direct and decided effect on Essef's business. The unanticipated losses incurred by FAME were exacerbated by the increasing reliance placed on the success of FAME to sustain Essef's entire operations. By 1987, sales to IBM accounted for 40 percent of Essef's $102 million in total revenue; in 1988, sales to IBM represented more than 40 percent of Essef's total revenue volume, compounding the effect of anemic computer hardware sales. As a result, Essef's debt rose to $42 million by 1990, when the company took a $20 million charge and discontinued operation of its FAME subsidiary, marking the end of the company's ill-fated relationship with IBM. In the wake of this devastating financial loss, the primary objective was to restore the vitality of the company and close the book on the problems of the 1980s. In reference to the misadventure with IBM, Essef's chairman, James Horner, noted to a reporter from *Crain's Cleveland Business*, "We learned a lot: Don't stick your neck out in business machines."

Recovery in the 1990s

Horner relinquished his post in 1990 after leading the company for 36 years and was replaced by Thomas B. Waldin, former chief executive officer of building products manufacturer, Donn, Inc. Under Waldin's stewardship, Essef mounted a comeback by reducing debt and expanding its mainstay businesses, particularly abroad. The $42 million of debt in 1990 was trimmed nearly in half during the ensuing year, dropping to $22 million by the end of 1991. Sales, meanwhile, rose from $89 million to nearly $96 million, while net income climbed out of the red, increasing from the $500,000 deficit recorded in 1990 to a gain of $2 million. Late in 1991, Sa SFC NA, Essef's Belgium-based subsidiary, formed a new subsidiary in Barcelona, Spain called Structural Iberica S.A., which operated as a distributor of water treatment, well system, and swimming pool products.

By the end of 1992, Essef's debt was whittled down to $16 million and the company was well on its way toward full recovery, having survived the financial ills stemming from what a reporter from *Barron's* termed the company's "FAME fiasco." Poised as a leading maker of plastic pressure vessels for residential, commercial, and residential water treatment systems, Essef once again was exuding the luster of a market leader and was projecting sales gains of between 15 percent and 25 percent a year for the next five years. Equally as important as its water treatment business was Essef's swimming pool equipment business, supported by strong market positions in filters, pumps, and other products that accounted for nearly half of the company's total sales volume. Looking ahead, the company saw tremendous potential for growth in large water-softening and other treatment systems, which were still made primarily with steel. Additional growth potential was seen in Europe, where Essef ranked as a minor player. During the early 1990s, Essef was generating roughly $10 million a year in European sales, but projections for the mid-1990s called for a substantial boost in its European business, perhaps as much as four times the dollar amount collected during the early 1990s.

From the $99.1 million posted in sales in 1992, a modest increase was recorded in 1993, when sales inched upward to $104 million. The string of moderate sales gains was broken in 1994, however, when sales leaped to $134 million. In 1994, Essef made two important moves, acquiring Purex Pool Systems, a manufacturer of swimming pool pumps, filters, and heaters, and forming a joint venture with Germany-based Reflex Winkelmann & Pannhoff GmbH to develop pressure vessels. Following the completion of these two deals, sales surged ahead again, rising to $157.5 million. In 1995, Essef expanded through acquisition for the second straight year, purchasing two pressure vessel manufacturers and a pool and spa valve manufacturer. The two pressure vessel manufacturers, California-based Advanced Structures, Inc., and Italy-based Euroimpex, broadened Essef's water treatment product range and strengthened its market leadership. The addition of Advanced Structures increased Essef's presence in the market for municipal water treatment systems, and the purchase of Euroimpex gave Essef a dominant market position in Italy.

Global Expansion for the Future

After devoting the first three years of the 1990s to consolidating its operations and trimming debt, Essef threw off the shackles prohibiting meaningful financial growth between 1994 and 1995. Acquisitions, innovative product development, and a focus on core businesses contributed to substantial sales gains during the mid-1990s, fueling confidence at the company's executive offices in Chardon. This confidence was manifested in May 1996 when Essef officials announced a global expansion strategy for the company's water treatment business. Essef's board of directors earmarked more than $5 million for the expansion of the company's manufacturing capabilities, including the establishment of facilities in India and the addition of manufacturing operations in Chardon, Ohio and in Herentals, Belgium. While announcing the company's global expansion plans, Essef's chief executive officer and president, Thomas Waldin, remarked, "This program has three clear benefits. First, it builds on our market position in the rapidly growing Far East market; second, it strengthens our local manufacturing capabilities in Europe and North America; and finally, it moves us strongly toward our goal of global cost leadership in water treatment components."

As if to validate the ambitious expansion plans announced in May, sales and earnings rose strongly in 1996. Sales jumped more than 27 percent to a record $200.8 million and net income swelled nearly 25 percent to $9.3 million. As the company moved forward with its global expansion plans, with completion slated for fall 1997, expectations for future success were high, instilling confidence that the market leadership established during Essef's first four decades of existence would lead to continued success during the late 1990s and the beginning of the 21st century.

Principal Subsidiaries

Advanced Structures Inc.; Compool Corp.; Contaminant Recovery Systems; ENPAC Corp.; Essef Manufacturing FSC, Inc. (U.S. Virgin Islands); Euroimpex Spa (Italy); Hobson Brothers Aluminum Foundry & Mould Works, Inc.; Pac-Fab, Inc.; Purex Pool Systems; Reflex-WellMate GmbH (Germany); Structural Europe N.V. (Belgium); Structural North America Water Treatment Systems; Structural North America WellMate Water Systems.

Further Reading

Byrne, Harlan S., "Essef Corp.: It Found That There Is Truly Life After IBM," *Barron's,* December 28, 1992, p. 27.
Casey, Mike, "Essef Hurt by Setback in Its Top Business," *Crain's Cleveland Business,* December 5, 1988, p. 3.
———, "Essef's Nationwide Growth Will Add 25 Jobs in Chardon," *Crain's Cleveland Business,* January 4, 1988, p. 4.

—Jeffrey L. Covell

EXCEL Communications Inc.

9101 LBJ Freeway, #800
Dallas, Texas 75243
U.S.A.
(214) 705-5500
Fax: (214) 664-3615
Web site: http://www.exceltel.com

Public Company
Incorporated: 1988 as EXCEL Telecommunications Inc.
Employees: 1500
Sales: $506.7 million (1995)
Stock Exchanges: New York
SICs: 4813 Telephone Companies Except
    Radiotelephone; 6719 Holding Companies, Not
    Elsewhere Classified

EXCEL Communications Inc. calls itself the fourth largest residential long distance carrier in the United States, although its $506 million in 1995 sales is still dwarfed by leaders AT&T, Sprint, and MCI, which together control roughly 85 percent of the market. Like most of the estimated 1,000 long distance companies started up since the deregulation of the long distance industry, EXCEL does not own its own telephone network; instead it buys the excess switching and transmission facilities of other providers for its own long distance time. EXCEL buys time at wholesale prices, then resells long distance calls to its subscribers at discount prices. Principal suppliers of these blocks of long distance time are Frontier Corp., WorldCom, Inc., and MCI Telecommunications Corp. Subscriber calls are routed through EXCEL's Dallas and Houston call centers; in late 1996, the company added a third call center in Reno, Nevada to service its West Coast subscribers. EXCEL employees track subscribers' long distance usage, and subscribers are billed according to their rate plan. Rate plans vary among subscribers, but include EXCEL's "Simply One" plan, launched in June 1996. Simply One calls are billed at nine cents per minute during evenings and weekends.

EXCEL markets its domestic and international long distance services, which include calling card and 800-number services, primarily to residential customers, but also to commercial and nonprofit subscribers. In October 1996, EXCEL expanded its service offerings by adding paging through PageMart Wireless Inc.'s paging network. The company is also making plans to add services such as Internet access, cellular service, home security monitoring, video services, and local telephone service. By adding these services, EXCEL expects to become less reliant on the volatile, and possibly threatened, long distance telephone industry, while capturing increasing fees from its subscriber base.

EXCEL went public in May 1996, selling ten million shares, or approximately nine percent of the company's stock, on the New York Stock Exchange. Founder and CEO Kenneth Troutt holds approximately 65 percent of the company. With shares trading in late 1996 at around $20 per share (after reaching a high of $47 per share in June 1996) Troutt's worth was estimated at $1.4 billion. EXCEL plans to pump part of the $150 million in proceeds generated by its initial public offering into building the company's own long distance network.

EXCEL has managed to avoid the expensive marketing costs of its competitors; in fact, EXCEL actually makes money from its marketing activities. Rather than pursue the expensive television advertisements, print campaigns, or direct mail efforts of its competitors, EXCEL markets its services solely through a vast network of independent representatives, each of whom receives commissions based on a percentage of the calls made by the subscribers they sign up, as well as on the number of new independent representatives they recruit into the company. Called "multilevel marketing," this technique has been successfully used by companies such as Amway, Mary Kay Cosmetics, and Herbalife to sell products ranging from beauty supplies to vitamins and beyond. In 1996, there were more than one million independent EXCEL representatives. Approximately 25 percent of the company's revenues are generated by signing up new independent representatives, at a rate of about 250,000 per month.

Humble Beginnings for Founder

EXCEL was founded by CEO Kenneth Troutt in 1988 and began operations in 1989. But in his youth, Troutt, who was 48 years old in 1996, probably seemed unlikely to become one of

Company Perspectives:

Excel provides the finest long distance programs in America today. In addition to all the standard services offered by other major long distance companies, Excel offers the opportunity for our customers to save up to 50% on their long distance calls. We also offer a personal 800 service that can't be beat, and all of our customers, just for trying our service, receive the most attractive incentives in the industry.

Texas's, and the United States', wealthiest men. Troutt was born in Mount Vernon, a small town in the south of Illinois. According to Troutt, his father was a bartender and alcoholic who went through a succession of jobs. About his father, Troutt told the *Dallas Morning News,* "We didn't get along." Instead, Troutt and his siblings were raised by his mother, growing up in a Mount Vernon housing project.

Yet, from his earliest years, Troutt, fueled by seeing other children with things his mother could not afford to buy for her family, dreamed of wealth. In fourth grade, when a teacher asked his class what they planned to be when they grew up, Troutt replied, as he told the *Dallas Morning News:* "I want to be rich." Not yet a teenager, Troutt set up a lawn mowing business, hiring his brothers and cousins to do the work. Later, Troutt became quarterback for his high school football team, which in turn led to a partial scholarship at Southern Illinois University.

Initially, Troutt planned to attend law school. But Troutt's ability as a salesman began to show while he was still in college. Working part-time as a life insurance salesman, Troutt became the insurance company's top seller by his senior year. He gave up the idea of law school, telling *Forbes* simply, "[I] found out I was good in sales." From college, Troutt moved to Nebraska, where he started up a real estate and construction business. The business ran into trouble, however, during the recession of the early 1980s. By 1983, with interest rates reaching 20 percent, Troutt dissolved his construction company. His next stop was Dallas, where he started an oil brokerage business. But the Texas oil industry collapsed shortly after, and Troutt once again found himself out of work.

Telecommunications in the 1980s: The Perfect Business

With these experiences behind him, Troutt set out in search of his vision of the perfect business: A product that everyone needs; that requires no inventory and has a distribution structure already in place; that is consumable, thereby creating continual demand; that has relatively low start-up costs and remains, unlike oil, somewhat stable in price; and, last, a product that continues to generate income after the initial sale. Troutt's brother, an accountant, suggested the recently deregulated telecommunications industry.

Troutt soon found inspiration for his future company from telecommunications upstart Sprint. In the mid-1980s, Sprint

was running its own direct marketing venture, called Network 2000, which allowed that company to join AT&T and MCI at the top of the industry. As Troutt told *Success,* one of his former oil company employees brought the idea to him, suggesting, "We could hire these college girls to stand out in front of Safeway and hire college guys to walk up and down residential areas and pay them $2 per application. Then we'd get the commission from Network 2000." But Troutt, reasoning that he would not make his fortune through Sprint, developed a different plan.

Troutt formed his own company, EXCEL Telecommunications, in December 1988, receiving regulatory approval to enter the long distance services industry. The company started operating in 1989, initially serving only the regional Texas market. At first, Troutt acted as his company's own salesman, approaching individuals and, through another company, offering potential customers discount travel packages as an incentive for switching their long distance services to EXCEL. Troutt also attempted to recruit groups such as churches, school bands, and others, offering the group a commission for convincing their members to sign on as subscribers. Then Troutt was introduced to Stephen Smith, who had experience with a company using network marketing techniques in the early part of the decade. Smith suggested that EXCEL create its own network, or multilevel, marketing plan. "Kenny didn't like the idea at first," Smith told the *Detroit News.* "But it started out with so much power." Indeed, as Troutt told the *Dallas Morning News,* "Our cost of sales is almost zero." By April 1989, EXCEL had its own multilevel marketing plan in place.

Companies using multilevel marketing techniques signed up independent representatives, instead of hiring employees. New representatives typically paid the company a fee for joining the network, and networks often had several entry levels, depending on how much the representative paid. The representatives in turn sold the company's products to other individuals, receiving a commission on each order. But a representative's real interest lay in creating a "downline," that is, recruiting other representatives into the network, who in turn would recruit representatives, forming a pyramid-like structure. Moving up the pyramid, a representative would receive a commission and/or percentage for each recruit he or she brought into the network, as well as for recruits signed on as representatives into the first representative's downline. The structure of such organizations were often received critically, however. Although multilevel marketing itself remained legal, these networks often functioned as little more than illegal "pyramid schemes," in which a company generated most or all of its income from recruiting representatives, and not from the sales of any actual product or service.

Troutt and Smith, who joined the company as executive vice-president, at first employed a scattershot strategy, reasoning that since everyone used long distance services, everyone was potentially an EXCEL customer. As its network grew, EXCEL quickly expanded into providing long distance in neighboring states, and soon on a nationwide scale as well. But signing on a customer and keeping that customer proved to be two different animals. "Our philosophy used to be to sign up the cab driver," Troutt told the *Dallas Morning News.* "We had one of the worst attrition rates in the industry and one of the best bad debts." By 1990, despite revenues of more than $6.5

million, the company was losing money. By 1991, the company's losses mounted to $400,000.

Warm Market Strategy for the 1990s

Troutt and Smith changed tactics to a "warm market" strategy. Independent representatives were encouraged to sign on family, friends, co-workers, and others with whom they had personal bonds. As Troutt told *Success,* "If I go out and sign up my mother, my sister, my two brothers, and my two aunts, as long as I don't cost them any money, they will most likely never leave because of our relationship. When AT&T and MCI and Sprint try to get them back with telemarketing or checks, we have a better chance of keeping them."

The warm market proved a successful strategy for EXCEL. Attrition slowed, and the company's fortunes slowly improved, from a loss of $300,000 in 1992 to a gain of $2.4 million in 1993. By that year, too, EXCEL's revenues had begun to take off. Its $30.8 million in 1993 revenues represented a gain of more than 800 percent over the previous year. Part of the company's success resulted from fortunate timing. The early 1990s, with the recession, the Gulf War, and a growing wave of corporate downsizing efforts, was raising job insecurities to a new high. Multilevel marketing plans became increasingly attractive to people seeking additional incomes. Others sought the freedom of becoming a full-time independent agent, which not only made them less dependent on an employer for their job and income security, but also allowed them to go beyond the earnings ceilings in place for most full-time jobs.

And EXCEL's product carried much less risk than the typical multilevel marketing venture. To become a representative authorized to sell EXCEL's services, the prospective representative was required to pay $50. That amount, however, provided for no additional sales training or marketing support from the company. To receive training and sales and marketing materials, a prospective representative paid $195, receiving the title of managing representative. Managing representatives were required to bring in at least 20 new long distance subscribers. Representatives received monthly commissions based on the total of these subscribers' long distance calls. In addition, for $395, a prospective representative could become an area coordinator. Area coordinators were authorized to hold training sessions for the representatives and received a $40 commission for each representative they trained.

One EXCEL representative explained the company's advantage over other multilevel markets to the *Lexington Herald-Leader* in this way: "You pay $195 to start your own business. If you go home and don't do anything, and never even get a customer, you haven't been killed. Whereas if I am in a products business and I ask you to purchase up front $1,500 . . . worth of stuff, you are stuck with whatever it is we're selling if you become unmotivated, get tired or whatever it is."

EXCEL's network of representatives expanded rapidly, with the company adding thousands of new recruits each month. Those who joined early soon began receiving thousands of dollars each month in commissions. By 1994, EXCEL's revenues grew another 419 percent, to $157 million, bringing nearly $16 million in net income. The following year, EXCEL's earn-

ings grew to $44 million, on revenues of $507 million. In that year, the company reorganized under the name EXCEL Communications.

By May 1996, the company went public, selling ten million shares. Founder Troutt, who sold none of his shares in the offering, was now worth more than $1 billion, and earned more than $3 million in salary and bonuses. Co-founder Smith was also doing well: His contract called for him to receive $5 for each new representative joining the network and a commission of 0.5 percent of all long distance charges made through the company.

With this explosive growth, however, came increased scrutiny of the company. EXCEL was forced to revise its training materials after some states charged that they encouraged representatives to recruit more representatives, rather than new long distance subscribers. Because its representatives are independent, the company has also been criticized for being unable to control incidents of "slamming," that is, illegally switching a customer's long distance services. In June 1996, the company was forced to pay an FCC fine of $80,000 for slamming two customers. In September 1996, the Dallas Better Business Bureau revoked EXCEL's membership because of the increasing numbers of complaints that agency had been receiving. Analysts also criticized the company for overstating its earnings, due to EXCEL's practice of spreading out its costs over the full fiscal year. Others complained that the company's promise of discounted service was becoming too difficult to keep as price wars raged throughout the industry.

Present Problems, Future Possibilities

In late 1996, EXCEL, despite a forecasted rise in revenues to more than $1 billion, faced other difficulties. Its attrition rate among representatives hovered around 86 percent, while the number of new representatives applying to join began to slip. Many observers were critical of a person's earning ability as an EXCEL representative. The largest share of the company's more than one million representatives, in fact, received little to no commissions at all. For example, although the company paid out $35.7 million in commissions for the month of April 1996, only about 154,000 representatives received commissions. Of these, more than two-thirds received less than $100 and about 95 percent received less than $1,000. Not all of EXCEL's representatives were happy with the company. In May 1996, a group of representatives, including some of the company's top earners, filed a $400 million lawsuit against the company, charging EXCEL with unfair competition and trade practices, defamation, and interference with their business.

Keeping its long distance customers was also proving more difficult for EXCEL. Attrition rates had grown to four percent per month. The company made a number of moves, including contracting with WorldCom and MCI to expand its long distance capabilities, and also making plans to add new services, such as Internet access, to maintain customer satisfaction as well as to maximize revenues from each customer. In October 1996, the company began offering paging services through PageMart Wireless, Inc. The move to expand its services was hoped to help the company compete in a market soon to become even more competitive with the arrival of perfected internet telephone software. Into the late 1990s, however, EXCEL should be able to continue its evolution into an industry power-house with the help of its legion of representatives.

Principal Subsidiaries

EXCEL Telecommunications, Inc.

Further Reading

Caminiti, Susan, "Troutt Fishing in America," *Fortune,* May 27, 1996, p. 24.

Files, Jennifer, "Going the Distance," *Dallas Morning News,* September 10, 1996, p. 1D.

Finotti, John, "Making Connections," *Florida Times-Union,* May 20, 1996, p. 10.

Fogg, John Milton, "The Ultimate Vehicle?," *Success,* November 1995, p. 18.

Hoffman, Gary, "Network Marketing Strategy Works for Excel," *Detroit News,* July 2, 1996, p. E3.

Kelly, Susan Brown, "Excel's Road to Riches a Winding, Long-Distance One," *Roanoke Times & World News,* September 14, 1994, p. B8.

"Kenneth Troutt," *Forbes,* October 14, 1996, p. 170.

Kirkpatrick, John, and Files, Jennifer, "Looking To Excel," *Dallas Morning News,* October 25, 1995, p. 1D.

McKenzie, Kevin, "Network Marketing Is Excel's Line to Success," *Commercial Appeal,* July 7, 1996, p. 1C.

Marcial, Gene G., "Did Excel Really Excel?," *Business Week,* June 17, 1996, p. 124.

Montgomery, Shep, "Telecommunications Company Excel Making In-road into State," *Mississippi Business Journal,* October 30, 1995.

Tyson, Eric, "Are Multilevels on the Level?," *San Francisco Examiner,* April 9, 1995, p. B1.

—M. L. Cohen

Fair, Isaac and Company

120 N. Redwood Drive
San Rafael, California 94903
U.S.A.
(415) 472-2211
Fax: (415) 492-9381
Website: http://www.fairisaac.com

Public Company
Incorporated: 1960
Employees: 950
Sales: $113.9 million (1995)
Stock Exchanges: NASDAQ
SICs: 7323 Credit Reporting Services; 7372 Prepackaged Software

If you have applied for a new credit card, small business loan, car financing, an insurance policy, or a home mortgage, chances are Fair, Isaac and Company helped decide whether you received it. Headquartered in San Rafael, California, Fair, Isaac is the world's leading developer of computer-based credit scoring and predictive modeling tools, used by credit card companies, insurance firms, and banks and other lenders to measure an applicant's credit risk. In fact, Fair, Isaac is directly responsible for the rise of the credit industry in the last quarter century. Lenders using Fair, Isaac's INFORM, CrediTable, CreditDesk, or other scoring tools are able to make more rapid, and objective, decisions toward the granting or denial of a credit application, enabling millions of consumers to make purchases on hundreds of credit cards, while significantly reducing the lenders' risk. The company's PreScore tools allow lenders to screen out promising candidates for solicitation of the lenders' products. Since the 1970s, Fair, Isaac software has also been used by the Internal Revenue Service for determining which taxpayers should be audited, resulting in fewer, yet higher yielding audits.

With the maturation of the credit scoring industry, Fair, Isaac has begun applying its expertise to new areas. It acquisition of DynaMark, Inc. in 1992 led Fair, Isaac into the direct marketing industry. Combining DynaMark's database and data processing capability with Fair, Isaac predictive modeling tools, the company offers its customers enhanced capacity for targeting their direct mail and marketing campaigns. By identifying the customers most likely to be interested in and to purchase their products, direct mailing firms can significantly reduce the cost of mailing campaigns while increasing the numbers of orders they receive. At the same time, Fair, Isaac has extended its scoring tools to lenders seeking investments in the long-overlooked, and fast-growing, small business community. The company's Small Business Scoring Service (SBSS) has brought similarly rapid credit identification and processing capacity to the making of loans and extension of lines of credit to the small business community. Fair, Isaac has also developed software tools for cross-selling lender services, enabling a bank, for example, to identify which of its borrowers might be interested in opening an account and which of its accountholders might be interested in applying for loans or other products and services offered by the bank. Another Fair, Isaac tool, Fraud Intercept, enables credit card companies to identify real-time purchases made with fraudulent or stolen credit cards.

Fair, Isaac generally receives royalties each time its products are used by lenders and credit reporting agencies. Major clients include 50 of the country's top 100 banks, mortgage lenders like the Federal National Mortgage Association (''Fannie Mae'') and the Federal Home Loan Mortgage Corp. (''Freddie Mac''), General Motors' financing arm, credit card processor Total System Services, and major retailers such as Sears and J.C. Penney. International sales of CrediTable International and other products represent a growing segment of the company's business. Fair, Isaac maintains offices in Germany, France, the United Kingdom, Japan, Canada, Mexico, and South Africa, and the company's products have been used in more than 40 countries, with a focus particularly on Western Europe and the fast-developing Asian region. Although the company is expanding into insurance, small business, and other markets, approximately two-thirds of its revenues continue to come from the credit card industry. In its fiscal year ended in September 1995, Fair, Isaac achieved a net income of nearly $13 million on $114 million in sales. Fair, Isaac is led by President and CEO Larry E. Rosenberger.

Birth of an Industry in the 1950s

The first credit cards began to appear during the 1950s. Credit and loan making procedures were, at the time, almost entirely subjective. Credit analysts followed their own judgments when granting or denying loan or credit requests, a process that required days or weeks. Banks and other lending and financial institutions tended to be locally based, and decisions were likely to be made on a personal basis. This situation led, on the one hand, to retailers and other creditors lending credit to customers at risk for defaulting on their payments. On the other hand, lenders tended to be overly conservative, and discrimination based on age, sex, marital status, and ethnicity was rampant, making credit unavailable to many.

But in the 1950s, William R. Fair, a mathematician with degrees from the California Institution of Technology, Stanford University, and the University of California at Berkeley, began investigating mathematical techniques for use in building models of predictive behavior. Fair was attracted to the relatively unrecognized complexity involved in the credit decision process, finding that the variables typically used in determining credit could produce trillions of possible combinations. Fair determined, however, that by using statistical techniques, such as multivariate analysis to produce scoring algorithms, this complexity could be greatly reduced. Furthermore, recent advances in computer technology, especially the introduction of transistors, allowed calculations to be automated and processed quickly. Joined by Earl Isaac, an electrical engineer, Fair started up a management consultant company as a 50–50 joint venture in 1956. As Rosenberger told *Investor's Business Daily,* "Some firms are founded to create wealth, but this firm was born in 1956 from a desire to do things the partners liked to do."

In 1958, Fair, Isaac introduced their first scoring system, called Credit Application Scoring Algorithms, proving that their system could accurately predict the payment behavior of credit holders, including whether they would pay on time, pay late, or not pay at all. Two years later, Fair, Isaac launched the first version of the company's INFORM product, a process for building scoring algorithms based on a customer's database of past borrowing behavior. In that year, the pair incorporated the company as Fair, Isaac and Company.

Credit lenders were slow to adopt credit scoring, in part because of the slow penetration of computer technology into mainstream commercial use, clinging to traditional judgment-based decision-making methods and relying on credit bureaus, which reported on an individual's past credit behavior. Fair, Isaac received a boost, however, when the Internal Revenue Service (IRS) contracted the company to develop a scoring algorithm that would enable the IRS to locate tax evaders more accurately. That system, put into place in 1972, quickly produced results: The number of audits dropped by a third, and the IRS posted a higher level of uncovered underpayments. During the 1960s, Fair, Isaac attempted to extend their scoring system to employee hiring practices; although this attempt forecasted the flexibility of scoring, the company found little enthusiasm among businesses for such a system. At the end of the decade, however, Fair, Isaac moved to extend credit scoring, beginning research on a behavior scoring system for monitoring credit purchases and payments.

The 1970s proved to be the breakthrough period for credit scoring. The introduction of faster minicomputers led more credit companies to add credit scoring to their application process. In 1972, Fair, Isaac adapted its products for use with minicomputers, allowing credit applications to become fully automated. Credit scoring was also proving flexible enough to meet the variety of lenders' needs. Using data gathered from a lender's own database, credit scoring allowed the lender to build predictive models, and acceptance levels, based on criteria specific to the lender, its customers, and their region. Credit scoring had another advantage in that it was completely objective, and factors such as a person's age, sex, or race held no place in a credit score. Indeed, Fair, Isaac worked hard to prove that these factors held no predictive value in determining an individual's creditworthiness. Lenders were reluctant to set aside their prejudices, however. In 1974, however, they were forced to do so with the passage of the Equal Credit Opportunity Act, which barred such discriminatory factors from the credit equation.

A Risk Management Company for the 1980s

The numbers of credit card holders rose rapidly through the 1970s. Fair, Isaac, now grown to a company with 30 employees, saw its customer base grow as well. Its clients were at first limited to the largest lenders, as smaller lenders balked at the high price of credit scoring products. But credit scoring quickly proved its worth, producing dramatic cuts in companies' bad debt rates. As credit scoring became the industry norm, Fair, Isaac moved to evolve into a new phase of the company's development, that of becoming a risk management company. In 1978, Fair, Isaac launched its first behavior scoring tools, intended to aid credit card companies in managing their existing card holders.

Rising inflation rates and increasing numbers of bad debt rates, coupled with the beginning of a recession, led President Carter to impose temporary credit controls at the end of the 1970s. Fair, Isaac, with more than $6 million in revenues, struggled through the recession, posting a loss of $135,000 in

1981. But its losses proved temporary. The following year, the company was back in the black, and by 1984 the company posted more than $600,000 profit on revenues of nearly $9 million. Earl Isaac died in 1983; William Fair continued to lead the company as chairman, president, and CEO. The company remained equally divided between Fair and Isaac's widow.

Aiding the company's growth was the next in its line of risk management products, its PreScore process, introduced in 1984, for screening direct mail credit solicitations. Companies using PreScore could abandon earlier practices of blanketing entire regions with solicitations for credit cards, only to reject large percentages of those responding. Using PreScore, a credit card company could more accurately target individuals likely to be approved for the credit card. In that year, Fair, Isaac was contracted by an insurance company to extend its scoring algorithms to developing application and risk control processes for that industry. Within the next two years, the company launched two more products, an adaptive control system and its ServiceScore method for screening applicants for public utility services. To keep up the pace of new product development and servicing its clients, the company began to expand, reaching 250 employees by the mid-1980s. Growth was also necessary as the company began to shift from its traditional fixed-price product sales to royalty-producing usage-based sales.

By 1987, the company had doubled its annual sales, to $18 million, earning a profit of more than $2 million. In that year, to fuel research and development and expand employee training facilities, while improving scoring algorithms by acquiring information databases, Fair took the company public. Revenues and earnings rose in the following year. The company, which had been exporting its products to Western Europe since the 1970s, next moved to enter the Japanese market. In 1988, the company reached agreement with Sumitomo Corp. subsidiary Sumisho Electronics Co. Ltd. to develop and market credit scoring services for Japanese Visa card issuers; the company also won a contract to develop a prescoring tool for Sumitomo Credit Services, the credit card subsidiary of Sumitomo Bank Ltd. In the United States, however, the company faced a new national recession.

Evolving in the 1990s

Fair, Isaac saw a decline in its fixed price business in the last years of the 1980s. This decline was offset somewhat by strong growth in sales of the company's usage-based products. But the company failed to match its growth rates of the years before its initial public offering, and income, hampered by increased research and development spending, dropped to a low of $1.6 million on 1990's $25 million. William Fair retired the following year, replaced by Larry E. Rosenberger, who had joined the company in the early 1970s and had held the position of executive vice-president through much of the 1980s. By the time Rosenberger took over, the company had already regained its momentum. Revenues climbed to $31.8 million in 1991, bringing income of nearly $2.8 million.

The company's fortunes were buoyed by changes in the credit card industry itself that led to increased demand for Fair, Isaac's behavior scoring products. As the number of delinquent accounts began to rise during the recession, the percentage of

credit card accounts, which numbered more than 200 million just among Visa, MasterCard, and Discover card accounts, being subjected to behavior scoring rose from 14 percent in 1989 to more than 50 percent by the first years of the 1990s. Fair, Isaac's growth was further stimulated by rising demand for its prescoring products, as credit card companies began the massive mail solicitation campaigns of the mid-1990s. At the same time, more and more smaller banks and lenders were looking outside for scoring services. But Fair, Isaac was itself evolving into a new phase in the company's development.

The company rolled out its USER products, extending its business to the insurance industry, and then moved into the small business loan market with its Small Business Scoring Service, introduced in 1995. Meanwhile, Fannie Mae and Freddie Mac stepped up the use of the company's FICO scoring for home mortgages, despite criticism that credit scoring, which had helped overcome discrimination in the 1970s, now hampered implementation of federal affirmative action policies. International sales also picked up rapidly in the 1990s. In 1992, however, Fair, Isaac made a move that would extend the company's reach into an entirely new market. In that year, Fair, Isaac acquired DynaMark, Inc., a fast-growing marketing services firm, for $5 million, marking the company's first acquisition in its history.

Aided by DynaMark's revenues, Fair, Isaac booked strong gains in annual sales, climbing past $42 million in 1992 and to nearly $67 million in 1993. Joining its scoring expertise with DynaMark's direct marketing and database management strengths, Fair, Isaac began providing cross-selling services that proved attractive to banks and other lenders then undergoing consolidation throughout the industry. Beyond that, the company began to establish itself as a one-stop source for companies seeking greater targeting activities for marketing their products, increasing spending of their customers, and limiting growing attrition rates. Fair, Isaac also began spending heavily on its own sales and marketing activities, achieving gains to $90.3 million in sales in 1994, providing a net income of $10 million. The following year, Fair, Isaac struck agreements with two more database management companies, Acxiom Corp. and Metromail Corp. The company's introduction of its Fraud Intercept product found a number of important early customers, including Total System Services, the world's second largest credit card processor. In September 1996, Fair, Isaac formed a joint venture, called Fair, Isaac/INFORMA, with German firms Schober Direktmarketing and the Struebel Group to offer database management and risk analysis and consulting services. The following month, Fair, Isaac made a second acquisition, of Baltimore-based Credit & Risk Management Associates, Inc., adding consulting capabilities in the United States. William Fair, having founded not merely a company but an entire industry, died in January 1996. By then, Fair, Isaac, with $114 million in 1995 sales, was indeed poised to help the world make "better decisions through data."

Principal Subsidiaries

DynaMark, Inc.; Credit & Risk Management Associates, Inc.; Fair, Isaac/INFORMA.

Further Reading

Garber, Joseph R., ''Deadbeat Repellent,'' *Forbes,* February 14, 1994, p. 164.

Howe, Kenneth, ''San Rafael Firm Will Sell Stock,'' *San Francisco Business Times,* June 1, 1987, p. 1.

Jones, John A., ''Fair, Isaac Growing With Sharper Direct-Marketing Tools,'' *Investors Daily Business,* June 30, 1995, p. B12.

Kutler, Jeffrey, ''Fair, Isaac Does It by the Numbers—And Now They're Starting To Add Up,'' *American Banker,* June 2, 1994, p. 14.

Lucas, Peter, ''Marketing Meets Modeling,'' *Credit Card Management,* January 1995, pp. 77–80.

Pender, Kathleen, ''Rating the Credit Customer,'' *San Francisco Chronicle,* February 17, 1992, p. B1.

Sinton, Peter, ''Fair, Isaac Holds the Cards,'' *San Francisco Chronicle,* June 28, 1996, p. C1.

—M. L. Cohen

Fedders Corp.

505 Martinsville Road
P.O. Box 813
Liberty Corner, New Jersey 07938
U.S.A.
(908) 604-8686
Fax: (908) 604-9715

Public Company
Incorporated: 1913 as Fedders Manufacturing Co., Inc.
Employees: 3,420
Sales: $371.8 million (1996)
Stock Exchanges: New York Boston Philadelphia
    Midwest Pacific
SICs: 3674 Semiconductors & Related Devices; 3585 Air
    Conditioning & Warm Air Heating Equipment &
    Commercial & Industrial Refrigeration Equipment

Fedders Corp. is the largest U.S. manufacturer of room air conditioners, primarily for the residential market. Its sales and earnings in this business have fluctuated considerably, partly because of the unpredictability of North American summer weather and partly because of the cyclical nature of the recession-prone housing market. The company's entry into related businesses in the 1960s was not successful. In the mid-1990s Fedders was basing its hopes for expanded sales on the potential market for air conditioners in Asian countries with reliably steamy summer weather. The company, in 1996, was also manufacturing rotary compressors, principally for room air conditioners, and thermoelectric heating and cooling modules used in a variety of applications.

Before Air Conditioners, 1896–1945

Fedders began as a metalworking shop started by Theodore C. Fedders in 1896 in Buffalo, New York. At first it made milk cans and kerosene tanks for Standard Oil Co. and bread pans for National Biscuit Co. Shortly after the turn of the century Buffalo became the home of such automobile makers as Pierce-Arrow and the Thomas Five. Fedders converted his plant to making radiators for these models and, in time, other automobile makers as well. During World War I the company also made radiators for airplanes, and in addition it manufactured appliances for heating and electrical refrigeration. In 1924 Fedders had net income of $241,000 on sales of $3.2 million. It went public in December 1926, offering 50,000 nonvoting shares at $25 a share.

Fedders's stock was caught in the great 1929 Wall Street crash, sinking to $3 a share from a high that year of $50. The company lost money the following four years, with sales falling by half between 1931 and 1933, when they reached a low of $1.8 million. In 1934, however, sales nearly doubled, and Fedders became profitable again, as it was during the successive years of the decade. Westinghouse Electric Corp. began distributing the company's refrigerator coils and accessories in 1936. Three years later Fedders erected a $200,000 plant in Owosso, Michigan, to produce radiators closer to the auto factories. Net sales reached nearly $6 million in 1940, and net income was $270,000. That year the company had branch offices in seven cities.

Fedders's sales reached $9.1 million, with net income of $386,000, in 1941, but the subsequent halt to automobile manufacturing because of World War II cut deeply into the business, and the company sold the Owosso plant in 1942. Although Fedders received contracts to make links and clips for machine-gun belts and Garand-rifle bullets, in 1944 it earned only $15,498 on sales of $5.7 million. Before the company could retool for the postwar period the Fedders family decided to sell a majority interest in the firm to Frank J. Quigan, Inc. This private company, the world's leading manufacturer of handbag frames, was based in the New York City borough of Queens. Frank J. Quigan, chairman of the board, became board chairman of the renamed Fedders-Quigan Corp., and Salvatore Giordano, president of Quigan, became president of Fedders-Quigan. There was no formal merger of the two companies, however, until 1949.

Air Conditioning Pioneer, 1947–60

Fedders-Quigan, in 1947, moved aggressively into the manufacture of newly introduced room air conditioners and two years later also began to market under its own name the electric water coolers it had been manufacturing for Cordley & Hayes since 1932. Besides Queens and Buffalo, it operated plants in

Trenton and Newark, New Jersey. Sales shot up from $11.6 in 1946 to $33.6 million in 1950, while profits rose from $905,000 to nearly $2 million in this period. The number of employees rose to about 3,000. In 1951, however, Quigan reportedly began speculating in the company's stock and wound up owing Giordano about $500,000. Quigan resigned from the company in order to vacate the court judgments for this amount that Giordano had secured. Giordano, who had joined Quigan as a $16-a-week floor boy in 1927, became chairman as well as president of Fedders-Quigan in 1952.

By the mid-1950s well over a million room air conditioners were being sold each year in the United States. In 1955 Fedders-Quigan sold 120,000 of these units under the Fedders name, far more than any other company, and also made air conditioners for the Whirlpool-Seeger Corp. and the Crosley division of Avco Manufacturing Corp. Almost 15,000 small stores were selling Fedders units in 1956. The company also was making heaters, radiators, and radiator cores for Chrysler Corp. automobiles and home radiators, convectors, and hot-water boilers. In 1956 it began making year-round central air conditioners for five- and six-room ranch-style houses. It also was turning out thousands of women's handbag frames a year, a business it maintained, Giordano said, out of sentiment. He held more than 10 percent of the company's common stock in 1956.

Giordano was a great believer in offering junkets to Fedders-Quigan's dealers and distributors as an incentive to push the product. During the 1950s dealers who had bought 45 Fedders air conditioners were flown by the company for a week-long all-expenses-paid vacation at a Florida beach resort, and those who doubled the number were entitled to take their wives along. A distributor with 10 eligible dealers was entitled to come along himself. In the fall of 1953 more than 500 people made the trip to the Hollywood Beach Hotel. By 1960 some "super" sales representatives were earning enough points for two overseas trips a year. That fall a crowd of 4,000 spent a week at Grand Bahama Island, while nearly 1,000 vacationed in Paris and the "supersalesmen" spent 10 days in Israel.

Fedders-Quigan, which shortened its name to Fedders in 1958, peaked in sales at $70.7 million in fiscal 1957 (the year ended August 31, 1957), when it earned $3.6 million. After two relatively poor years it earned a record $4.5 million on net sales of $68.8 million in fiscal 1960. From 1955 to 1960 the national dollar volume in manufacturing and installing air-conditioning

equipment rose by more than 50 percent, but Fedders had to share the market with a growing number of competitors: more than 50 in all. Increasingly it began to focus its hopes on central residential systems. It also had organized a subsidiary, Fedders Financial Corp., to finance wholesale purchases of Fedders air-conditioning equipment.

Diversification and Expansion, 1964–70

By 1964 Fedders was stagnating, both its sales and profits having slipped from the 1960 levels. On the plus side, finances were sound, despite a long-term debt of $8.6 million, and dividends had been paid each year since 1945. However, management began casting around for additions to its existing products: air conditioners; automobile radiators, heater cores, and oil coolers (still principally for Chrysler); and heat-transfer equipment, including convectors, condensors, evaporators, and dehumidifiers. (The manufacture of frames for women's handbags and pocketbooks was discontinued in 1966.)

A decision was made to diversify into home appliances in 1964, when Fedders signed a five-year contract with the Franklin Appliance division of Studebaker Industries. Under the agreement Studebaker would manufacture a full line of home appliances under the Fedders name, to be sold by Fedders's network of 77 distributors and 15,000 dealers. Fedders introduced a 15-model line of its own manufactured home appliances in 1967. As a result company sales increased from $62.3 million in fiscal 1966 to $88.9 million in fiscal 1967, and net income from $1.2 million to $4.6 million. In 1966 Fedders vacated its leased Newark plant, erecting a large facility for the manufacture of air conditioners at Edison, New Jersey, where it also established corporate headquarters.

Fedders expanded its home-appliance operations by purchasing Borg-Warner Corp.'s Norge division in 1968 for about $45 million in cash, stock, and notes. Chicago-based Norge, which had sales of $114 million in 1967, was making a full line of laundry equipment such as washers and dryers as well as air conditioners and kitchen ranges. Included in its operations were nearly 3,400 franchised "Norge Village" coin-operated, self-service laundry and dry-cleaning units, containing 20 to 50 machines each.

The expanded Fedders was an industry giant with 9,000 employees in fiscal 1970, when it had net sales of $295.8 million and net income of $15.6 million. It was still the largest producer of room air conditioners but saw greater growth potential for engineered central air-conditioning systems, not only in homes but also in industrial plants, hospitals, schools, and mass-transportation systems. Fedders expanded its stake in this business sector by purchasing Climatrol Industries, Inc., a manufacturer of unitary central air-conditioning systems, in 1970 for $27.7 million worth of stock. During this period a share of Fedders stock rose from a low of $3 to as high as $50. To finance its expansion, however, Fedders had raised its long-term debt to $60 million by the end of fiscal 1970.

Nine Consecutive Losses, 1974–82

After a record fiscal 1971, in which it earned nearly $17 million on income of $346.6 million, Fedders fell on hard times. Fiscal 1972 ended with lower earnings and profits due to a seven-and-a-half-month strike at the Edison plant. Business failed to reach the record 1971 level in fiscal 1973. The Arab oil embargo imposed in late 1973 touched off an energy crisis, with consequent sharply higher electricity costs, a national recession, and the collapse of the housing market. In fiscal 1974 Fedders lost $10.5 million and dropped its line of manufactured ranges and refrigerators. The company, in fiscal 1975 (the year ended October 31, 1975), lost nearly $12 million on disastrously low income of $170.2 million—less than half the 1971 total.

Fedders could take some consolation in the fact that it was not the only company in its industry suffering the downturn in market conditions, for between 1970 and 1975 national shipments of room air conditioners fell from nearly six million to fewer than three million. Accordingly, it raised its commitment to central air-conditioning systems by purchasing the domestic assets of Chrysler Corp.'s unprofitable Airtemp division in 1976 for about $58.5 million in cash, notes, and stock. Airtemp was producing air-conditioning systems up to 1,100 tons, compared to Fedders's top limit of 200 tons. Fedders ended the fiscal year with a profit of $249,000 on sales of $291.3 million, but it lost money on continuing operations.

Fedders downsized itself in early 1979 by selling the Norge division, which accounted for 22 percent of its fiscal 1978 sales, to Magic Chef Inc. The very modest purchase price of about $13.3 million in cash and notes indicated that Norge, which had only five percent of the laundry-machine market, was performing poorly. The Norge plant in Effingham, Illinois, was converted to the manufacture of room air conditioners. Fedders ended fiscal 1979 with a catastrophic loss of $36.5 million on income of $176.8 million and lost nearly $29 million more the following year on revenue of only $137.9 million. By the end of fiscal 1980 it had divested itself of the Fedders Refrigeration Co., which made freezers.

The severe recession of the early 1980s compounded Fedders's woes. In 1982 it recorded its ninth consecutive loss (in terms of continuing operations) and, based on its long-term-debenture debt of $66.6 million, had a negative net worth of $42.8 million. In 1983 it put on the market its three central-air-conditioning businesses, which had lost $37.8 million the previous fiscal year, and also placed on the block its 90-acre Edison office and manufacturing complex. There was no buyer for the businesses (which still had sales of $12.4 million in 1984), so their assets had to be sold off piecemeal with the Edison real estate. These properties fetched a total of $42.6 million during 1984 and 1985 and left Fedders with three businesses: room air conditioners under the Airtemp, Climatrol, and Fedders brands, made in Effingham; rotary compressors for powering air conditioners, manufactured in Frederick, Maryland; and replacement radiators, heaters, and additional components for the automotive aftermarket, still being made in Buffalo. Corporate headquarters were moved to Peapack, New Jersey.

Renewed Prosperity in the 1980s

Fedders became profitable again in 1983, when it earned (after discounting extraordinary credits) $1.4 million on drastically reduced income of $80.8 million. The next two years were even better, and in 1985 the company resumed paying dividends, which it had omitted since 1974. Its share of the domes-

tic room air-conditioner market almost doubled between 1984 and 1986, to 16 percent. Fedders also found a profitable market in many parts of the world that wanted air conditioning but where installing central systems with ducts was not easy.

In 1987 Fedders spun off the compressor and automotive-components divisions into a company named NYCOR, Inc. This company remained under Fedders management and was initially located at Fedders's corporate headquarters. In 1989 NYCOR sold its compressor subsidiary, Rotorex Corp., back to Fedders for about $45 million in cash and the assumption of $49.5 million in Rotorex debt. It sold the automotive-components business (FEDCO) in 1990 and became for a time a shell company with a pile of cash. Salvatore Giordano, Jr. succeeded his father as chief executive officer of both Fedders and NYCOR in 1988. His 78-year-old father remained chairman of the board, and was still chairman in 1996.

By the end of the decade Fedders was once again riding high, finishing 1989 with a record $367.6 million in net sales and record net income of $23.7 million. Its share of the North American market for residential room air conditioners had grown from eight percent in 1982 to about 30 percent. To handle its increased business Fedders had acquired additional manufacturing facilities in Tennessee and Ontario, modernized its largest manufacturing plant (at Effingham), and established an international subsidiary. It was marketing its air conditioners under the Tempair name and private labels as well as under the Fedders, Airtemp, and Climatrol brands. The acquisition from General Electric Co. of a Columbia, Tennessee, facility in 1988 for $17.3 million made Fedders the only high-volume producer in the world of plastic-cabinet window air conditioners. Among North American manufacturers of room air conditioners, only Fedders was making its own rotary compressors, which were in short supply. The company's long-term debt had declined to $53.9 million.

Roller-Coaster Ride, 1990–96

However, as the 1990s dawned, Fedders was again headed downward. In fiscal 1990, which ended with a cool summer, it lost $15.6 million—the first of four consecutive years of losses—on net sales of only $241.4 million. Despite this poor year the company, in January 1991, acquired the Emerson Quiet Kool brand from The Jepson Corp. for $56 million in cash plus the assumption of certain liabilities. This left Fedders, according to columnist Dan Dorfman in April 1991, with no cash, a $170-million debt, and the imminent prospect of bankruptcy—all at a time of huge unsold inventories of air conditioners.

The nadir of Fedders's plight was fiscal 1992, when it lost $24.9 million on revenues of $192 million. During that year it sold Rotorex back to NYCOR for $72.8 million and closed the Emerson Quiet Kool plant in Woodbridge, New Jersey, plus another facility in Dover, New Jersey. The company lost another $1.8 million in fiscal 1993 on net sales of $158.6 million. The sale to NYCOR, however, helped Fedders reduce its long-term debt from $173 million to $25 million by May 1993, and it took aim at the international market to decrease its dependence on the vagaries of summer weather in North America.

Exports had made up only 7.6 percent of Fedders's sales in fiscal 1992 and were limited to the Americas. In 1993, however, the company focused on Southeast Asia, the sweltering Middle East, and the southern part of China, notorious for its "Oven Cities." A Fedders Asia subsidiary was created in 1994, and the following year this unit entered into a $24-million, 60–40 percent Fedders Xinle joint venture with China's Ningbo Air Conditioner Factory to manufacture air conditioners at this facility. Initial production was 200,000 units a year, with Fedders hoping to increase the level to 500,000 by 1999. Much of the output was slated to be exported to such countries as Japan and India.

Domestic business also picked up, with three consecutive hot summers, at least in some areas, from 1993 through 1995. Sales were also helped by the company's ability to meet the just-in-time demands of such retailers as Wal-Mart, Best Buy, and Home Depot who were increasingly vital to Fedders's sales. Net sales shot up to $231.5 million in fiscal 1994 and $316.5 million in fiscal 1995, while net income—aided by tax-loss carryovers from previous years—was $21 million and $29.5 million, respectively. In 1995 Fedders paid its first cash dividend since 1991 and, at the end of the year, decided to reintegrate itself with NYCOR, which lost $7.8 million on sales of $32.9 million in 1995. The merger was accomplished in 1996. Fedders ended the fiscal year with record sales of $371.8 million and record net income of $31.2 million.

In 1995 Fedders was manufacturing room air conditioners, primarily for the residential market, in models ranging in capacity from 5,000 to 40,000 BTUs. These were made and marketed under the Fedders, Airtemp, and Emerson Quiet Kool brands and also under private labels. Its manufacturing facilities were in Effingham, Illinois, and Columbia, Tennessee. In 1994 Fedders moved its corporate headquarters to Liberty Corner, New Jersey. Fedders North America had its headquarters in Whitehouse, New Jersey, and a new subsidiary of Fedders International, Inc., Fedders Asia, Pte., moved into Singapore quarters.

Rotorex was manufacturing compressors and pump assemblies, chiefly for Fedders's air conditioners, in Frederick, Maryland. Materials Electronic Products Corp. ("Melcor"), a business acquired by NYCOR in 1992 for $14.9 million, was manufacturing solid-state heat-pump modules performing the same cooling and heating functions as freon-based compressors and absorption refrigerators in Trenton, New Jersey, and near Lawrence Township, New Jersey. These products, sold under the trademark FRIGICHIP, were primarily being used in portable beverage coolers and refrigerators; laboratory, scientific, medical, and restaurant equipment; and telecommunications and computer equipment.

In 1995 the Giordano family owned about 15 percent of Fedders's Class A (nonvoting) common stock and about 95 percent of Class B (nontradable but voting) common stock. The company's long-term debt was $14.4 million in early 1996.

Principal Subsidiaries

Fedders Exporting, Inc. (Barbados); Fedders International, Inc.; Fedders Investment Corp.; Fedders North America, Inc.; NYCOR North America, Inc.

Principal Operating Units

Fedders Asia Pte. Ltd. (Singapore); Emerson Quiet Kool Corp.; Fedders, Inc. (Canada); Fedders De Mexico S.A. de C.V. (Mexico); and RTXX Corp.; Columbia Specialties, Inc.; Fedders Capital, N.V. (Netherlands Antilles); Melcor Corp.; Melcor International Sales Corp.; Rotorex Co., Inc.; Rotorex International, Inc.; Rotorex Technologies, Inc.

Further Reading

Abelson, Reed, "Companies to Watch," *Fortune,* September 11, 1989, p. 152.
Alexander, Louis, "Airlifts for Private Industry," *Flying,* January 1961, pp. 44, 70.
"Chrysler Sells Airtemp Assets to Fedders Corp.," *Wall Street Journal,* February 24, 1976, p. 3.
Cuff, Daniel F., "Fedders Chief Finds Use for Spinoff's Nest Egg," *New York Times,* November 5, 1990, p. D4.
Doherty, Ed, "Welcome to a Long, Hot Summer," *Financial World,* August 31, 1983, pp. 28–29.
Dorfman, Dan, "Fedders Getting Cool Reception," *USA Today,* April 12, 1991, p. B3.
"Fedders," *Wall Street Transcript,* August 12, 1968, pp. 14029-30.
"Fedders Acquires Borg-Warner's Norge Division," *Wall Street Journal,* July 3, 1968, p. 2.
"Fedders Corp.," *Wall Street Transcript,* August 19, 1968, p. 14162.
——, *Wall Street Transcript,* December 28, 1987, p. 87845.
"Fedders Corporation," *Wall Street Transcript,* March 12, 1990, p. 96605.
——, *Wall Street Transcript,* December 4, 1989, p. 95582.
"Fedders Enjoys a Brisk Rebound from Strike-Dampened Showing," *Barron's,* July 20, 1964, p. 18.
"Fedders-Quigan Gets a Break," *Business Week,* December 8, 1951, pp. 114–16.
Kimelman, John, "Company Watch," *Financial World,* November 22, 1994, p. 18.
Lazo, Shirley A., "Payouts Heat Up at Fedders," *Barron's,* July 3, 1995, p. 38.
"Magic Chef Buys Unit of Fedders for $13.3 Million," *Wall Street Journal,* February 13, 1979, p. 17.
"Management Brief: Keeping Cool in China," *Economist,* April 6, 1996, pp. 73–74.
O'Brian, Bridget, "Fedders Insiders Selling Shares This Summer," *Wall Street Journal,* August 9, 1995, pp. C1, C13.
Pine, Michael C., "Fedders: Straw Hats in Summer?" *Financial World,* August 12, 1996, p. 20.
Savona, Dave, "Global Go-Getters," *International Business,* May 1993, p. 22.
Sullivan, Barbara, "Torrid Weather Warmly Received in Effingham," *Chicago Tribune,* July 24, 1995, Sec. IV, pp. 1, 3.
"We Got Razzle-Dazzle," *Forbes,* November 1, 1973, p. 45.
"Why Everybody Likes a Prize Trip," *Business Week,* November 21, 1953, pp. 56–57.
Zipser, Alfred R., "Air Conditioners in Heavy Demand," *New York Times,* June 3, 1956, Sec. 3, pp. 1, 9.

—Robert Halasz

Federal Express

FedEx Corporation

2005 Corporate Avenue
Memphis, Tennessee 38132
U.S.A.
(901) 369-3600
Fax: (901) 346-1013
Web site: http://www.fedex.com

Public Company
Incorporated: 1971 as Federal Express Corporation
Employees: 11,000
Sales: $10.27 billion
Stock Exchanges: New York Toronto Boston Midwest
   Pacific
SICs: 4513 Air Courier Services; 4212 Local Trucking
   Without Storage

FedEx Corporation specializes in overnight delivery of high-priority packages, documents, and heavy freight. The company created the overnight air-express industry virtually single-handedly in the 1970s; its success was such that by the 1990s it faced the sincerest form of flattery: increasing competition from rival carriers. However, FedEx's continued mastery of logistics and its ability to track packages during the shipping process has enabled it to retain its leadership role in the express air cargo industry, as well as act as a moving warehouse for numerous corporate and individual customers. It operates in 211 countries, and serves all of the United States, providing 24-to-48-hour delivery of valuable, time-sensitive cargo to any destination worldwide.

FedEx was founded as Federal Express Corporation in 1971, by 28-year-old Memphis, Tennessee, native Frederick W. Smith. Smith, a former Marine pilot, originally outlined his idea for an overnight delivery service in a term paper he wrote for a Yale University economics class. He felt that air freight had different requirements than air passenger service and that a company specializing in air freight rather than making it an add-on to passenger service would find a lucrative business niche. Speed was more important than cost, in Smith's view,

and access to smaller cities was essential. His strategies included shipping all packages through a single hub and building a private fleet of aircraft. Company-owned planes would free the service from commercial-airline schedules and shipping regulations, while a single hub would permit the tight control that got packages to their destinations overnight. In making his dream a reality, Smith selected Memphis as his hub: it was centrally located and despite inclement weather its modern airport rarely closed.

Term Paper Topic Becomes Reality, 1973

Smith supplemented a $4 million inheritance from his father with $91 million in venture capital to get his idea off the ground. In 1973 FedEx began service in 25 cities with a fleet of 14 Dassault Falcon aircraft and 389 employees. The planes, which were relatively small in size, collected packages from airports every night and brought them to Memphis, where they were immediately sorted. They were then flown to airports close to their destination and delivered by FedEx trucks the following morning.

Smith's idea was costly indeed; it required creating an entire system before the company's first day of business. FedEx added to these start-up costs by beginning expensive advertising and direct-mail campaigns in 1975. The company lost $29 million in its first 26 months of operation: in 1975 alone it gained $43.5 million in sales against an $11.5 million loss. Smith's investors considered removing him from the helm of the fledgling company, but company president Arthur Bass backed the young founder. Bass improved delivery schedules and FedEx's volume climbed to the point where it was profitable: By late 1976 the company was carrying an average of 19,000 packages a night, and by year's end it was $3.6 million in the black.

In 1977 company profits hit $8 million on sales of $110 million. The company had 31,000 regular customers, including such giants as IBM and the U.S. Air Force, which used it to ship spare parts. It also shipped blood, organs for transplant, drugs, and other items requiring swift transport. FedEx serviced 75 airports and 130 cities. While the major airlines gave the company stiff competition on heavily traveled passenger routes, there was virtually no competition on routes between smaller cities. Its principal competitor, Emery Air Freight, used commercial airlines to ship packages, giving FedEx an important time advantage.

Airline Deregulation in 1977 Fuels Growth

Deregulation of the airline industry in 1977 gave the still-struggling company an important boost. At the time of FedEx's startup, the U.S. airline industry had been subject to tight federal regulation. In fact, the company had only managed to get into business through an exemption that allowed any company to enter the common carrier business if its payloads were under 7,500 pounds. These self-same regulations, written in 1938 to protect passenger airlines, would ultimately hold back FedEx's growth. The company was forced to fly up to eight small Falcon jets side-by-side to bigger markets when use of one larger jet would have saved money. Smith led a legislative fight to end regulation, and a bill doing so was passed in 1977. Deregulation meant the company could fly anywhere in the United States anytime, and use larger aircraft like 727s, and later, DC-10s. FedEx bought a fleet of used 727-100Cs, using its Falcons to expand into small- and medium-sized markets.

In 1978, with its prospects looking solid, FedEx went public, selling its first shares on the New York Stock Exchange. The move raised needed capital and gave the company's backers a chance to gain back a portion of their initial investment. Profits for 1979 were $21.4 million on sales of $258.5 million. By late 1980 FedEx was well established and growing at about 40 percent a year. It had 6,700 employees and flew 65,000 packages a night to 89 cities across the United States. Its fleet included 32 Falcons, 15 727s, and five 737s.

Explosive growth continued as a tidal wave of businesses switched to overnight service. Miniaturization of consumer electronics and scientific instruments translated into increasing numbers of small, valuable packages needing express shipment. In addition, many U.S. companies were shifting to just-in-time inventories as a way to keep prices down, lessen quality-control problems, and cut costs. Consequently, these companies often needed emergency shipment of goods and parts, and FedEx was there to provide that much-needed service. It soon began billing itself as a "500-mile-an-hour warehouse."

Competition and Price Wars During the 1980s

A decline in the reliability of the U.S. Postal Service caused even more companies to switch to FedEx for important pack-

ages. Courier-Paks became the fastest growing part of the company's business, accounting for about 40 percent of revenue. In 1980 Courier-Paks—envelopes, boxes, or tubes used for important documents, photographs, blueprints, and other items—cost the consumer $17 but guaranteed overnight delivery. By mid-1980 the company had eight $24 million DC-10s on order or option from Continental Airlines, each capable of carrying 100,000 pounds of small packages. It had also acquired 23 additional used 727s, and operated 2,000 delivery vans.

In mid-1981 FedEx announced a new product that would bring it into direct competition with the U.S. Postal Service (USPS) for the first time: the overnight letter. The document-size cardboard envelope, which could contain up to two ounces, would be delivered overnight for $9.50 at that time.

By 1981 Federal Express had the largest sales of any U.S. air freight company, unseating competitors like Emery, Airborne Freight, and Purolator Courier, which had gone into business about two decades earlier. Unlike FedEx, competitors shipped packages of all sizes using regularly scheduled airlines, and didn't stress speed; FedEx's narrowly focused, speed-oriented service won over many of its competitor's customers. To compete, Emery copied FedEx's strategy, buying its own planes, opening a small-package sorting center, and pushing overnight delivery. Airborne also entered the small-package air express business. United Parcel Service of America (UPS), the leading package-shipper by truck, moved into the air-express business in 1981. The USPS began heavily marketing its own overnight-mail service after FedEx's Courier-Pak began eating into its revenues. The Postal Service's overnight mail was about half the price of FedEx's, but was not as accessible in many locations.

While FedEx was the leader in the U.S. overnight package-delivery industry, DHL Worldwide Courier Express Network built a similar service overseas; the two would become major competitors when FedEx started building its own overseas network. Such increased competition put pressure on FedEx's niche, but its lead was large and its reputation excellent. In 1983 the company reached $1 billion in annual revenues—the first company in the United States to do so within ten years of its start-up without mergers or acquisitions.

Aggressively Pursues International Market Dominance

In 1984 FedEx made its first acquisition, Gelco Express, a Minneapolis-based package courier that served 84 countries. Hoping to recreate its U.S. market dominance overseas, the company made further acquisitions in Britain, the Netherlands, and the United Arab Emirates. Meanwhile, UPS also began building a competing overseas system.

By the late 1970s Smith had realized that up to 15 percent of the company's Courier-Pak business was information that would eventually be digitally transmitted as telephone and computer technology improved. He spent $100 million to develop his own electronic-mail system, which was launched in 1984 as ZapMail. A system for sending letters by fax machine and couriers, ZapMail was plagued by technology problems from the beginning: Fax machines broke down frequently; light-toned originals would not transmit; minor telephone-line disturbances interrupted transmissions. ZapMail cost $35 for documents up to five pages, plus $1.00 for each additional page, and high-volume customers soon discovered it was less expensive to install their own fax machines. The program also faced competition from MCI Communications' electronic-mail system. ZapMail was still losing money in 1986 when FedEx abandoned the system, taking a $340 million charge against earnings. In line with the company's policy of limiting layoffs, the 1,300 employees working on the ZapMail system were absorbed into other FedEx operations.

In 1985 FedEx took a major step in its attempt to expand its services to Europe by opening a European hub at the Brussels airport. Revenue reached $2 billion in 1985. In 1986 the company opened sorting centers in Oakland, California, and Newark, New Jersey, to more quickly handle shipments to nearby high-volume destinations. And FedEx's hubs were being transformed into warehouses for its clients, as parts were stored there until customers needed them, then shipped overnight. For example, IBM used FedEx to store mainframe parts and get them quickly to malfunctioning computer systems. This trend coincided with a decline in FedEx's overnight mail volume, which was hurt by the spread of fax machines and the lower rates charged by competitors. Revenue for 1987 was $3.2 billion, while rival UPS collected about $1.7 billion from overnight delivery.

By 1988 FedEx, with 54,000 employees, was providing service to about 90 countries and claimed to ship about 50 percent of U.S. overnight packages. Mounting competition, however, had led to a price war that eroded company profits from 16.9 percent of revenue in 1981 to 11 percent in 1987. Profits in 1988 were $188 million on revenue of $3.9 billion.

Expanding overseas proved tougher than FedEx had anticipated, and the company's international business lost $74 million between 1985 and 1989. In February 1989, hoping to quickly develop a global delivery system, FedEx bought Tiger International, Inc., for $883 million, thereby acquiring its heavy-cargo airline, Flying Tiger Line. Before the acquisition, FedEx had landing rights in five airports outside the United States: Montreal, Toronto, Brussels, London, and limited rights in Tokyo. The company hoped to supplement these with the delivery routes Tiger had built over its 40-year history, which included landing rights in Paris and Frankfurt, three Japanese airports, and cities through east Asia and South America. FedEx could use its own planes on these routes instead of subcontract to other carriers, which the company had been doing in many countries. Tiger's large fleet of long-range aircraft also gave FedEx an important foothold in the heavy-freight business. In 1988 Tiger had 22 747s, 11 727s, and six DC-8s; 6,500 employees; and revenue of $1.4 billion. Unfortunately, many of Tiger's planes needed quick repairs to meet U.S. government safety deadlines, which led to lower-than-anticipated profits.

The purchase price paid by the company—which several analysts claimed was too much—also increased FedEx's debt by nearly 250 percent to $2.1 billion, and put the company into a market that was more capital-intensive and cyclical than the domestic small-package market. Owning Tiger also put FedEx into an awkward position—many of Tiger's best customers were FedEx's competitors, and the company feared it might lose many of them. Such fears proved unfounded, although Tiger's on-time record temporarily fell to 80 percent after the takeover, climbing to 96 percent by early 1990.

At the same time price wars continued with competitors, some of which made inroads into the overnight market. Earnings from UPS's overnight service rose 63 percent between 1984 and 1988, and its revenues tripled. FedEx had a 55 percent share of the U.S. overnight letter market and shipped 33 percent of U.S. overnight packages. It was clearly the leader in the express-delivery business, but its growth was slowing. FedEx's U.S. shipment volume grew 58 percent in 1984 but declined to 25 percent in 1988. The company compensated by pushing its higher-margin package service, which grew 53 percent from 1987 to 1989. Analysts estimated that packages provided 80 percent of FedEx's revenues and about 90 percent of its profits.

In April 1990 FedEx raised its domestic prices, ending the seven-year price war. The U.S. air-freight industry was consolidating, and rival UPS had heavy capital expenses from its own overnight air service, giving its competitor room to raise its prices. FedEx needed the extra profits—estimated at between $50 million and $75 million a year—to help pay for losses in its international business. Its foreign operations lost $194 million in 1989 as it struggled to integrate Tiger and build a delivery system in Europe. Tiger was unionized but unstructured; FedEx was non-union but bureaucratic. Several uneasy months passed while the two systems were unified and a pilot seniority list was drawn up. To help increase overseas tonnage, the company introduced one-, two-, and three-day service to large shippers between 25 cities worldwide and 85 cities in the United States.

Maintains Market Lead in the 1990s

FedEx entered the 1990s with increasing competition in the U.S. market, but was able to maintain its leading market share. UPS, now its main competitor, continued to slowly woo away some customers by introducing volume discounts, a policy which it had resisted for years. FedEx responded by instituting a customer-by-customer review of its own pricing strategy that resulted in a consolidation of subcontractor trucking routes, the streamlining of pickup and delivery routes, and an increased profitability of certain freight runs; in some cases prices were also adjusted upward. Enhancements were offered to express-service customers, including earlier-in-the day service options, computer software that allowed FedEx clients to electronically prepare all shipping documentation, and Internet tracking of shipments via FedEx's new homepage. And the company's network of retail affiliates was expanded, with new FedEx dropboxes installed in more than 870 office supply superstores nationwide. The results: Despite erosion from aggressive competitors, FedEx's domestic package volume rallied in mid-1992, with revenues growing from $7.6 billion to $7.8 billion over the previous year.

Internally, FedEx began company-wide cost-containment policies to reduce waste and overhead, as well as gain increased efficiency in meeting the needs of its customers. The company's Station Review Process allowed the most effective local policies to be shared by the entire FedEx station network. Despite cost-cutting measures, however, employee-related expenses rose when FedEx became mired in over two years of contract negotiations with the Air Line Pilots Association (ALPA). Despite what Smith had considered generous enough salaries and benefit packages to keep the threat of unionization at bay, heated labor negotiations ultimately resulted in the 1996 unionization of FedEx's 3,100 pilots. However, only a few weeks after the pro-union vote, an organization of company pilots was petitioning the National Labor Mediation Board to call a second vote to oust the union, leading analysts to doubt ALPA's continued influence over FedEx budgetary policy. On the plus side, the expiration of a federal cargo tax during the federal budget impasse of January 1996 would provide FedEx with a fiscal boost as the company maintained prices despite a temporary hiatus in federally directed excise payments.

In the early 1990s FedEx's foreign operations were troubled, and their losses dragged down company earnings. While overall sales rose from $5.2 billion in 1989 to $7.69 billion in fiscal 1991 operating income fell from $424 million to $279 million over the same period, much of it resulting from the costly development of overseas markets. Industry analysts were divided over whether or how soon the company would be able to make its foreign operations profitable. Some analysts questioned how long FedEx could accept international losses while carrying $2.15 billion in long-term debt.

Smith countered such concerns by arguing that when the company's international volume increased, international service would become profitable. In an effort to boost that volume, FedEx traded in its 727s for larger-capacity Airbus Industrie jet aircraft for their three daily European-destination flights, filling extra cargo space with non-express packages to increase per-flight profitability. In 1994 the company became the first international express cargo carrier to receive system-wide ISO 9001 certification; by mid-decade international service accounted for 12 percent of the company's business: FedEx linked over 200 countries and territories worldwide, representing the bulk of global economic transactions. By 1996 the company could boast sales of $10.27 billion against operating income of $624 million.

Further Expansion and a Look to the Future

Aggressive international route expansion included creating divisions in several hemispheres. A Latin America and Caribbean division was created in 1995 to integrate services within the second-fastest world's economic growth area. And in September of that year the company introduced FedEx AsiaOne: a next-business-day service between Asian countries and the United States. Via a hub established at Subic Bay, Philippines, FedEx planned to duplicate its successful hub-and-spoke delivery service within 11 of that continent's commercial and financial centers. Unfortunately, the company's plans were confounded by the Japanese government, which limited FedEx's flying rights from Japan to other Asian countries in mid-1996, after a series of talks between the U.S. and Japan failed to reach a compromise. While the U.S. government contemplated appropriate sanctions against the Japanese government for its failure to honor existing flight privileges with FedEx, Japan viewed the company's growing success in Asia as a threat to its own overseas cargo industry. Despite difficulties with Japan, the extension of its world-renowned service to the Pacific Rim area placed FedEx in a strategic position within one of the fastest-growing economic centers in the world—particularly with regard to China, where the company was the sole U.S.-based cargo service then authorized to do business.

Through 2015 the international express air cargo market was predicted to grow nearly 18 percent per year; FedEx was expected to reap a major portion of that growth as it saw its foreign operations increasing by as much as 25 percent per year. By retaining the confidence of its customers through its logistical capabilities, expanding the carrying capacity of its fleet of over 557 fuel-efficient aircraft and 37,000 vehicles, and a continued dedication to providing cost-effective express service, ''FedEx it'' continued to be the generic way to request express shipment.

Principal Subsidiaries

Federal Express Aviation Services; Federal Express International; Flying Tiger Line Inc.; Tiger Inter Modal Inc.; Tiger Trucking Subsidiary Inc.; Warren Transport Inc.

Further Reading

Flaherty, Robert J., ''Breathing Under Water,'' *Forbes*, March 1, 1977.
——, ''Transportation,'' *Business Week*, March 31, 1980.
Foust, Dean, et al, ''Mr. Smith Goes Global: He's Putting Federal Express' Future on the Line to Expand Overseas,'' *Business Week*, February 13, 1989.
Greising, David, ''Watch Out for Flying Packages,'' *Business Week*, November 14, 1994.
Nomani, Asra Q., ''Sparks Fly over Air-Cargo Agreement,'' *Wall Street Journal*, March 1, 1996.

—Scott M. Lewis
—updated by Pamela L. Shelton

First Pacific Company Limited

24th Floor, Two Exchange Square
8 Connaught Place Central
Hong Kong
(852) 8424388
Fax: (852) 8459243
Web site: http://www.irasia.com/listco/hk/firstpac/
    index.htm

Public Subsidiary
Incorporated: 1981
Employees: 45,000
Sales: HK$54.8 billion (US$7.03 billion) (1996)
Stock Exchanges: Hong Kong Amsterdam NASDAQ
SICs: 6719 Holding Companies; 7300 Business Services;
    6000 Depositary Institutions; 6500 Real Estate; 4810
    Telephone Communication

In the somewhat murky world of Asian conglomerates, First Pacific Company Limited is one of the fastest-growing and most transparent. A publicly traded holding company, First Pacific is majority-owned by Indonesia's powerful Salim Group. First Pacific's portfolio includes 13 companies, operating in 40 countries, with 45,000 employees. The companies, all of which function as independent units, and six of which are publicly traded, are focused on four principal areas: marketing and distribution; telecommunications; property; and banking. Marketing and distribution contribute the largest share—88 percent—of First Pacific's sales, through companies including the Dutch-based international trading giant Hagemeyer; Australian computer and telecom products distributor Tech Pacific International; Metro Pacific, First Pacific's Philippines flagship; Berli Jucker Public Company, a Thailand-based distributor of food and other products; and Indonesia's P.T. Darya-Varia Laboratoria, that country's second-largest pharmaceutical distributor.

While trading continues to be the company's chief revenue generator, telecommunications represents the company's fastest-growing segment. Telecommunications companies in First Pacific's portfolio include Pacific Link Communication, one of Hong Kong's largest mobile phone companies, with 240,000 customers; Smart Communications, which falls under the Metro Pacific arm, and which, with 310,000 customers has captured 39 percent of the Philippines' cellular phone market; and P.T. Metro Selular Nusantara amd P.T. Indolink First Pacific, which provide cellular and paging services to Indonesia. In 1996, First Pacific contracted with Lucent Technologies to build a cellular network in three Indian states for the company's new Escotel Mobile Communications joint-venture with India's Escorts—by early 1997 Escotel had already signed up 5,700 subscribers in a combined population of 126 million. Full implementation of Escotel was slated for mid-1997. First Pacific has also entered joint ventures to provide mobile and paging services in Fujian, Shenzen, Fuzhou, and Xiamen in China, as well as in Taiwan.

First Pacific's vast real estate holdings include, through Metro Pacific, the huge Fort Bonifacio Development Corporation project in metro Manila, Philippines. Plans there include the construction of some 100 50-story buildings, providing space for more than 300,000 residents and more than one million office workers, making the site larger than Hong Kong's entire central business district. Through Metro Pacific, First Pacific also owns Landco, Inc., a high-end residential and resort developer for properties outside of metro Manila. In Hong Kong, First Pacific Davies operates both property and integrated property services (such as security services) companies, managing 110 million square feet of office, residential, and commercial space. Banking, the final and smallest piece in the First Pacific puzzle, is represented primarily by the 27-branch First Pacific Bank network.

Despite the Salim Group's control of First Pacific, the company enjoys an independence that is unusual among companies run by powerful Asian families. First Pacific is led by managing director and founder Manuel Pangilinan, who has been given free rein to build and direct the company. Pangilinan has turned the Salim Group's initial $1.5 million investment into a company that reported a 1996 attributable profit (excluding exceptional gains) of HK$1.57 billion (US$202 million) on turnover of HK$54.8 billion (US$7.03 billion).

Founded in 1981

First Pacific began as a small Hong Kong-based financial services company established to allow four of Indonesia's leading families—the Salim, Sutanto, Sudwikatmono, and Risjad families—to funnel some of their wealth overseas. The Salim family, headed by Soedono Salim (aka Liem Sioe Liong), controlled the largest portion of the new company. Soedono Salim, whose personal worth made him one of the world's wealthiest men, was born in China's Fujian province in 1916. In the 1930s, Liem/Salim moved to Java, in Indonesia, to work for the peanut oil company run by his uncle and brother. In his 20s, Liem struck out on his own, entering the coffee and cloves trade, supplying cloves to the kretek (clove-flavored cigarettes) industry, and soon expanded into other goods. But the key to Liem's fortune lay in the Indonesian war for independence of 1947–49. Liem backed the Indonesian rebels over the Dutch colonial forces, supplying the rebels with food and clothing, and possibly arms as well. During that war, Liem also became acquainted with a young lieutenant colonel by the name of Suharto. With independence, Liem—who adopted the Indonesian-styled name Soedono Salim—branched out into other areas, founding companies selling goods ranging from bicycle parts to noodles to nails. Salim's entry into banking came in 1957, when he acquired Bank Central Asia, which would grow to become Indonesia's largest private bank.

Salim's fortunes rose still higher when Suharto came to power in 1965. Soon after, Salim gained monopolies on the country's clove, cement, and flour markets. Despite his close ties with the Suharto family, however, Salim remained vulnerable in a country that was overwhelmingly Islamic. Only 3 percent of Indonesians were of Chinese origin, yet the Indonesian Chinese controlled some 70 percent of the country's economy. Salim began looking for a way to move some of his profits out of Indonesia. In 1972, Salim and partners (which included Suharto's half-brother Sudwikatmono) set up a small Hong Kong company, First Pacific Finance. In the late 1970s the group stepped up its overseas expansion. The group, popularly known as the Liem Investors, bought a stake in Overseas Union Finance in 1979. Two years later, the group increased its Hong Kong presence. In a move seen as unusual among closely controlled Asian family businesses, Salim directed son Anthony to bring in outside talent to help the group expand. Anthony Salim approached Manuel Pangilinan, a Filipino with an M.B.A. from the Wharton School working as an investment banker for American Express's Hong Kong office, to set up a deposit-taking company in Hong Kong that would enable the Salims to expand into consumer products and finance. With $1.5 million in startup capital, Pangilinan purchased a dormant property company, renamed as First Pacific Holdings, and then a shell company formerly managed by the merchant banking arm of the Jardine hong; that company was renamed First Pacific International.

Missteps in the 1980s

Pangilinan was given complete autonomy to run the three publicly traded First Pacific companies, in part to make the companies more attractive to international investment. The First Pacific group began building a portfolio of acquisitions, beginning with the ailing Hibernia Bank in California. Hibernia, that state's 12th largest bank, had lost $6.7 million in the year before its acquisition. After losing another $13 million in 1982, the bank turned profitable in 1983. Another key acquisition made by First Pacific was a stake in the Dutch trading giant Hagemeyer; First Pacific quickly built up a 67 percent share in that company. Meanwhile, First Pacific began issuing shares in the companies, touting First Pacific as an investment channel into the massive Salim family holdings—principally through the promise of possible ventures between the Liem family and First Pacific's Hagemeyer and Hibernia. Investors became skeptical when this promise failed to come true, in the face of the Liems' reluctance to participate with First Pacific. As Pangilinan himself told *Institutional Investor,* "The Liem pipeline was a pipe dream." In 1984, the company reorganized as First Pacific Group, and began emphasizing itself as a financial services company.

Meanwhile, First Pacific launched an extensive acquisition program that made investors nervous. By the mid-1980s, the company had gathered some 23 companies under its wing, with activities scattered across industries from dry goods (Hong Kong's Dragonseed), to computer products in Australia, to soap and shoe polish distributorships in Thailand, to coffee in Saudi Arabia, to office properties in Hong Kong, as well as a seat on the London Stock Exchange. First Pacific also amassed extensive holdings in the Philippines—although that country had not been among the company's originally planned investment sites. But when a company defaulted on a $1.5 million loan, First Pacific agreed to accept the Manila-based First Philippine Capital Corp. investment bank. That placed First Pacific in the middle of a turbulent political situation in the Philippines following Benigno Acquino's assassination. Other companies were seeking to divest their Philippine holdings and turned to First Pacific. The company gambled, buying up at bargain prices a local subsidiary of Thailand's Berli Jucker and another of the Scott Paper Company, bringing the company into soap and toilet paper. First Pacific's Philippine wing, later renamed Metro Pacific, targeted exclusively companies providing consumer products at first, including First Pacific's largest acquisition, Metro Drug Corporation, the company's leading distributor of pharmaceutical and veterinary products. As a Metro Pacific executive explained to *Business Times*: "Whatever the political situation, there will always be a market for their products so there was more than an even chance that these companies would continue operating well."

The company adopted a policy of identifying undervalued companies in the Pacific Rim (but including the U.S.) and hiring new management to build them. Management of the individual companies were given near-complete autonomy to run the companies. But First Pacific's rapid, seemingly directionless growth soon made it unpopular with investors. Despite the company's strong revenue (to $1.6 billion in 1987) and earnings growth, First Pacific's own stock remained undervalued and raising equity was difficult. The company was criticized for its seemingly chaotic organizational structure. Worse, in 1987 the company was forced to sell off one of its principal assets, Hibernia Bank, after it proved too difficult to make the bank competitive. The company reorganized again, registering in Bermuda, in 1988. By 1990, the company was forced to turn to its parent for financing, giving the Salim Group more equity in First Pacific.

Finding Focus in the 1990s

The company changed direction in 1991. First Pacific was refocused on its four core areas of marketing and distribution, telecommunications, real estate, and banking. The company pared down its holdings, selling off ten companies outside its core areas, and at the same time stopped making acquisitions at the holding company level. With the refocus of the company, investor interest picked up—by 1994, First Pacific barely missed out on being added to Hong Kong's blue-chip Hang Seng Index (HIS). (The company joined the HIS in June 1996.) Meanwhile, its Manila flagship, Metro Pacific, was on a buying spree of its own, purchasing the state-owned Domestic Satellite (Domsat) telecommunications firm in 1994, and that company's 39 percent interest in Smart Communications. Metro Pacific also added Hershey's Filipino franchise, Philippine Cocoa Corp. First Pacific also moved to expand its Berli Jucker conglomerate based in Bangkok, Thailand. By 1992, the company's profits were rebounding, to HK$458 million; in 1993, profits rose to HK$781 million.

While Hagemeyer continued to represent First Pacific's largest holding, the company emphasis shifted to building its position in Asia. By 1994, the company's Asian operations contributed 68 percent of First Pacific's profit for the year. Divisions such as the Tech Pacific computer and software distributorship and the company's interest in Philippine-based Darya-Varia Laboratoria were also growing strongly, more than doubling in size. Meanwhile, Metro Pacific's holdings were bolstered by its winning bid, as part of a consortium of investors, for the 214-hectare Fort Bonifacio, a former undeveloped military reserve in the heart of Manila. First Pacific's early entry into the Asian telecommunications industry, particularly in cellular phones and paging services, helped position the company as those markets prepared to explode. In just a decade and a half, Pangilinan had built First Pacific from a tiny company to one of Asia's largest conglomerates, which posted a profit of HK$1.57

billion (US$202 million) on turnover of HK$54.8 billion (US$7.03 billion) in 1996. The Salim family, which took the daring step of letting an "outsider" control a family business, seemed likely to maintain its hands-off approach to First Pacific. From total investments of only $150 million, the Salim's stake in First Pacific had risen to be worth some $1.2 billion, with no end yet in sight of the Asian economic boom.

Principal Subsidiaries

First Pacific Davies, Ltd. (Hong Kong); FPB Bank Holding Company (Hong Kong) (51%); Hagemeyer N.V. (Netherlands) (50.8%); Metro Pacific Corp. (Philippines) (40%); Pacific Link Communications Ltd. (Hong Kong) (65%); Pacific TeleLink Ltd. (Hong Kong) (64.7%); PT Indolink First Pacific (Indonesia) (60%); Smart Communications, Inc. (Hong Kong) (40%); Tech Pacific Holdings Ltd. (Australia).

Further Reading

Almazan, Alec, "Entering the Land of the Giants," *Business Times*, December 11, 1995, p. 21.

Clifford, Mark L., "The New Asian Manager," *Business Week*, September 2, 1996, p. 22.

Dodwell, David, "First Pacific Tightens Its Grip," *Financial Times*, September 6, 1984, p. 26.

Friedland, Jonathan, "Pacific Overtures," *Institutional Investor*, May 1988, p. 175.

Gopalan, Nisha, "First Pacific Has Fingers in All Pies," *South China Morning Post*, October 13, 1996, p. 4.

Murphy, Kevin, "Horning Into Hong Kong," *International Herald Tribune*, October 7, 1994.

Tanzer, Andrew, "First Pacific's Pearls," *Forbes*, February 13, 1995, p. 48.

"First Pacific: Limbered Up and Raring to Go," *The Economist*, June 16, 1984, p. 57.

—M. L. Cohen

 FUJI PHOTO FILM CO., LTD.

Fuji Photo Film Co., Ltd.

26-30, Nishiazabu 2-chome
Minato-ku, Tokyo 106
Japan
(03) 3406-2111
Fax: (03) 3406-2193
Web site: http://www.fujifilm.co.jp/index_g.html

Public Company
Incorporated: 1934
Employees: 29,903
Sales: ¥1.08 trillion (US$10.20 billion) (1996)
Stock Exchanges: Tokyo Osaka Nagoya Fukuoka Niigata
  Sapporo
SICs: 2796 Platemaking & Related Services; 3695
  Magnetic & Optical Recording Media; 3861
  Photographic Equipment & Supplies; 5043
  Photographic Equipment & Supplies; 5065 Electronic
  Parts & Equipment

Fuji Photo Film Co., Ltd. originated as a cinematic-film producer and has grown into a multidimensional manufacturer and marketer of imaging and information products. Fuji is the second-largest maker of photographic film in the world, trailing only Eastman Kodak, and the largest in Japan. In addition to its wide variety of film for still cameras, Fuji also makes motion picture film, videotape, audiotape, and floppy discs; still cameras—including its highly successful disposable cameras—camcorders, and digital cameras; photofinishing equipment, paper, and chemicals; and various related imaging and information products for office and medical use. The company is also a leading supplier of photofinishing services.

Early History

In 1934 Dainippon Celluloid Company, Japan's first cinematic film manufacturer, spun off its troubled photographic division. Named Fuji Photo Film Co., Ltd., the new company already employed 340 people and named Shuichi Asano as its first president. Its product line included motion picture film, dry plates, and photographic paper. The company struggled for three years, mainly due to the poor quality and high prices of its products relative to imports.

Fuji's first task was to build a reputation in the domestic market. Brand reliability proved critical in the photosensitive-materials industry, since buyers were not willing to risk losing a desired image to inadequate materials, regardless of cost. During its first three years, the company continued to lose sales, increase debt, and struggle to meet research expenses. Fuji could not expand without first addressing quality, so it employed a German specialist to assist in the area of emulsion technology.

The combination of outside consultation and its own research allowed the company to introduce its first film as an independent in 1936, as well as a motion picture negative film. The negative film was much harder to produce, and demonstrated Fuji's new technical competence to Japanese studios.

Fuji built a second factory in Odawara in 1938. Color research began in a new laboratory in 1939, but World War II halted such work. During the war the government set aside all sensitized materials for the military, so consumer-film development had to wait out the war. In 1945 Allied bombing raids partially damaged two Fuji factories, but recovery during the postwar era involved more than infrastructural repair.

The Allied powers allowed civilian trade to resume in 1947, and Fuji immediately began exporting to outlets in South America and Asia. Japanese producers still enjoyed a good reputation in optical products, enabling Fuji to export its cameras and binoculars. In the area of film and other sensitized materials, however, Japanese technology still lagged behind U.S. and European producers.

Although it produced x-ray and cinematic film, Fuji did not produce large amounts of film for the amateur consumer market until the 1950s. In the meantime, it resumed color research and produced its first color film in 1948. In 1949 Indian buyers received a shipment of Fuji motion picture film, the company's first substantial postwar sale.

Company Perspectives:

We will explore the farthest reaches of technology and continue to create a dynamic Imaging and Information culture. This is our corporate philosophy as well as the conceptual foundation of our technological research.

"Imaging" expresses Fujifilm's commitment to design and create new image-recording systems and to research technologies that can continually upgrade the quality of captured images.

"Information" represents a broader challenge of adapting the captured image, via computer technology, to create advanced information systems that can serve a wide variety of filing, presentation, and communication needs.

Today, Fujifilm is more than a photographic enterprise, with growing involvement in the wider realm of Imaging and Information. We, the Fujifilm Group of the world, are about to take a great leap forward into the 21st century.

Domestic and Overseas Growth in the 1960s and 1970s

As the 1940s ended, so did a shortage of raw materials—including silver, paper, and petroleum-based chemicals—that kept Fuji from producing amateur photographic products in large quantities. Licensing agreements between Fuji and Eastman Kodak of the United States allowed Fuji to equal Western producers in terms of black-and-white amateur roll film quality. Fuji, now able to supply its products in large quantities, introduced its first amateur roll film in 1952. By 1958 Fuji had introduced three additional black-and-white roll films.

Fuji enjoyed burgeoning domestic demand for the next 20 years, due in part to tariffs on film imports. During the 1950s Fuji captured the Japanese market for consumer films—a market that would quickly comprise 15 percent of the world's total film sales.

After setting up an export sales division in 1956, Fuji reached 27 export agreements by 1958 in Asia, North America, and Central America. Fuji first entered North America in 1955, and established its U.S. subsidiary ten years later.

As Fuji's international base grew, it still had to fight a perception of poor quality. In order to make a serious drive abroad, the company first had to develop film and paper compatible with the processing systems most commonly used worldwide. In 1966 Fuji introduced its first amateur slide film compatible with overseas processors. By 1969 all its films, photo paper, and chemicals were fully compatible. Employing the sales network it had established in the 1950s, exports began to flow.

In 1970 Fuji had nine overseas offices, and by the end of the decade it had 14 offices and subsidiaries abroad. These subsidiaries then branched out. Fuji's U.S. subsidiary, for instance, opened six offices between 1971 and 1982.

Recognition in these markets proved more difficult. Eastman Kodak's dominance in consumer films forced all producers to make compatible products in the postwar decades. Fuji learned

this after it introduced a cartridge-film eight-millimeter home movie system in 1967. Fuji's product had the support of 14 Japanese and European manufacturers, including AGFA-Gevaert, Europe's largest photographic manufacturer. Kodak introduced its own system shortly after, which quickly gained control of the world market. Fuji had to abandon its system and rushed to develop compatible films. Fuji's overseas growth was slow during the 1970s, adhering to the industry's pace of product development.

In 1970 Kodak held more than 90 percent of the $400 million U.S. market, but Fuji's color films were already faster than Kodak's—meaning they required less light for adequate exposure. In addition, Fuji films were better on warmer tones, including red, orange, and flesh tones. While Kodak pursued the convenience-based mass market, Fuji targeted professionals and serious amateurs. Although it would take several years before Fuji posed a serious threat to Kodak, its quality created a position of strength.

Relative to its competition, Fuji strengthened itself during the 1970s, partially due to the appreciation of the yen between 1971 and 1980. One factor in the growth of Fuji's non-Western markets was its development of manufacturing facilities. Operations in Brazil, Korea, and Indonesia began with Fuji assistance. The operations began with package assembly, but eventually produced presensitized materials, color processing chemicals, and optical products for export. Such manufacturing bases made the company less vulnerable to currency fluctuation and reduced overhead.

Where Fuji saved on manufacturing it spent heavily on research. Fuji began magnetic research in 1954, introduced products by 1960, and in 1963 produced videotape for domestic television. Magnetic products became the key to Fuji's long-term growth. In 1977 this research led to the introduction of Japan's first eight-inch floppy computer discs.

Fuji also developed products related to the photographic process for other industries. In 1967 for instance, Fuji, Mitsubishi Heavy Industries, and Konan Camera Institute developed a system to photographically trace blueprints onto construction materials. In addition to such new applications for heavy industry, Fuji continued to develop new technology for x-rays and other electronic systems for medical technology.

Fuji's core business continued to be film, however, and it pushed for additional access to lucrative Western markets just as Japanese film sale growth began to slow. Fuji had first entered the U.S. market as a private-label film supplier in 1960, and produced its first color film there in 1970. In 1972, it marketed the first film under its own brand name. Fuji went directly to retailers with its new film and received a 2 percent share of the American market, which more than doubled during the 1970s. Fuji's marketing was well-timed, and in 1976 Fuji also caught the attention of professionals and serious amateurs when it beat Kodak with an introduction of faster film (400 ISO speed), something it accomplished in 1984 as well (1600 ISO speed).

Fuji spent heavily to build its U.S. share but had relatively little success. Kodak's research expenditures were still large by comparison, and when Kodak introduced Kodacolor II film in 1972, Japanese companies had to hurry to put comparable films on the market. The recession during the late 1970s complicated Fuji's international drive. Industrywide production overcapacity and price increases for silver and oil-based chemicals cut into earnings.

While silver was still necessary for photographic imaging, its price jump demonstrated the wisdom of Fuji's research into electronic imaging technologies and its mid-1970s hiring campaign for electronics engineers. While many companies posted declines, Fuji's profits were only stagnant for 1977 and 1978.

Fuji was then the third-largest filmmaker behind Kodak and AGFA-Gevaert, but the Japanese companies responded to the setbacks more aggressively. Fuji and its domestic competitor, Konishiroku, raised their film prices only 7 percent—while competitors raised their prices from 10 to 30 percent—despite silver prices skyrocketing from $6 to $49 an ounce in 1979.

Silver inflation alone had cost Fuji ¥15 billion in 1979, and exchange losses on export sales cost an additional ¥4.6 billion. By 1979 consumer demand for magnetic products such as audio- and videotape began to climb dramatically, providing Fuji a faster recovery than its competition. Despite continued increases in raw material costs, Fuji's earnings improved quickly due to escalating demand served by the new magnetic-products division.

Diversification Drive in the Early 1980s

In 1980 earnings jumped 130 percent. Silver prices dropped, and sales for magnetic products still grew. Magnetic products, now 9 percent of sales, pushed exports up to 32 percent, where they remained for the entire decade. Fuji was well poised for a renewed assault on Western film markets.

In the 1980s the U.S. amateur film market changed rapidly. Consumers preferred higher-quality 35-millimeter over Kodak's disc, cartridge, or instant photography. Although the market changed to the advantage of manufacturers like Fuji, who specialized in 35-millimeter films, consumers still demanded convenience. Autofocus cameras and faster film required more sophistication from manufacturers.

Despite this favorable shift in consumer preferences, the photo industry as a whole had matured. Further, while Fuji hoped to gain ground in the U.S. market, that market was only twice as big as the Japanese market in terms of photo sales. Fuji entered the 1980s resolved not only to increase its portion of film sales worldwide, but also to find growth for its products in imaging and electronics.

Minoru Ohnishi replaced Kusuo Hirata and became Fuji's youngest president ever in 1979. Ohnishi had worked for five years in the late 1980s as head of the U.S. subsidiary. His nontraditional appointment overlooked older officers, but he was able to use his experience in the U.S. market to establish a sales network for new products like magnetic tape, optics, and hybrid electronic systems.

Fuji's growth through the early 1980s had come at the expense of smaller film manufacturers such as 3M and AGFA-Gevaert. Now the second-largest firm in the industry, it set its sights on

Kodak's core. By 1982 Fuji's share of the U.S. market had slowly climbed to 5 percent, and Ohnishi set a 10 percent goal.

There were several factors behind Fuji's confidence. First, Kodak's product development in the 1970s was weak. Fuji had kept up with increasingly sophisticated demand by introducing faster and higher resolution films for both cinematic and amateur uses several times. Second, Fuji's research investments had been well placed. Kodak turned from chemical research to electronics late, while Fuji had already recognized the technology's long-term value in processing and imaging. Although Kodak's research expenditures dwarfed Fuji's, Fuji spent a larger share of its earnings on research. In 1979, Kodak applied for 255 patents in the U.S. and Japan, compared to Fuji's 270.

Fuji was the first non-U.S. company to produce videotape. The consumer and trade press praised Fuji tape quality from its introduction. By 1982 magnetic products were already 12 percent of revenues. With broad distribution, a good reputation, and a skyrocketing market, Fuji made large gains.

Magnetic products, like film, provided high margins. Unlike its position in the consumer film market, Fuji enjoyed a prominent role in the magnetic-products marketplace. Between 1978 and 1982 magnetic-division sales increased almost five-fold to $97 million. By 1983 films were only half of Fuji's business.

Newer areas such as biotechnology and office automation had been paid for not with debt but with cash generated from film products and stock sales. Such electronic systems, such as microfilm records for offices and electronic imaging for x-rays, began to contribute to earnings on their own. In addition, Fuji enjoyed high profit margins in all areas. Pretax operating margins increased one-third to 24.4 percent from 1976 to 1981. Fuji's film, tape, and computer-disc manufacturing was highly automated, allowing workers to circulate among factories for increased productivity.

The climate for high-technology industries proved intense in the 1980s, due in part to trade friction and yen appreciation. In addition, Fuji was relatively new to electronic systems, and other companies had a large lead in areas such as medical technology. In order to remain competitive in these new areas, Fuji had to keep cash available and increase momentum in film sales. Fuji steadily increased its U.S. advertising budget, peaking when it outbid Kodak as sponsor to the 1984 Olympics in Los Angeles. Eventually spending $7 million on the campaign, Fuji entered the event with a 6 percent share of the U.S. market. Meanwhile, Fuji had become a sponsor of soccer's World Cup in 1982, and continued to sponsor the event into the mid-1990s.

Simultaneously, the company strengthened distribution. In 1979 Fuji sold film in 30 percent of all film outlets in the United States; by 1984 it sold in 60 percent, expanding beyond specialty photo outlets. By the end of the Olympic year its share jumped to 8 percent, allowing Ohnishi to predict not only a 15 percent share in ten years, but also to carry out a more aggressive approach late in the decade. As Fuji stepped up its efforts to reach the professional market in 1986, its market share approached 10 percent.

Fuji did not face the same battle abroad that it faced in the United States. It already sold over half of the film and photo paper in Southeast Asia, and the 1984 opening of a Chinese office gave it a lucrative foothold in an untapped and huge market. Brand loyalty was not as significant outside the United States, and in 1982 Fuji enjoyed a 10 percent share in Europe, Fuji's second-largest market. One year later it captured 15 percent of that market, prompting the company to construct its first European plant, in the Netherlands, in 1984. Producing selected sensitized materials, the plant paved the way for continued growth on the continent and lessened difficulty with currency fluctuation.

Expanded U.S. Presence in the Late 1980s

By the mid-1980s the U.S. market had begun to open to Fuji. Despite growth, profits there were still elusive. Videotape prices dropped sharply due to overproduction, and advertising costs continued to climb. While a U.S. market that declined overall was bad for Kodak, it helped Fuji, which was not as reliant on photography. Fuji could still pursue market share while continuing to find growth industries for other forms of imaging.

Fuji's renewed drive in the late 1980s came with more confidence. After a surprisingly successful introduction in Japan, Fuji was first on the U.S. market with a disposable camera. In Japan, a market less receptive to instant-photography items, Fuji sold 1.5 million cameras in six months. While the traditional market declined, Fuji managed to discover a completely new segment of consumer photography. By 1992, Fuji was the number one maker of cameras worldwide.

By 1988 Fuji had achieved its 10 percent share and the exchange rate was favorable for building in the United States. It built a plant in Greenwood, South Carolina, to make presensitized plates and related products. In 1989 a factory opened in Bedford, Massachusetts, to manufacture 3.5-inch floppy discs in a joint venture with BASF Corporation (Fuji bought out BASF in 1994 so that the facility was then wholly owned by Fuji). Another factory opened in Greenwood in 1991 to make videotapes. Moving production to the market served by the factory provided faster delivery and immunity from currency exchange losses, and eliminated charges of dumping.

With a double-digit market share firmly in place, Fuji sought to increase use of its processing systems, since Kodak's Colorwatch processing network still provided an obstacle, steadily enlarging its share of the photofinishing market. Launching its own system, Fujicolor Circle, Fuji offered technical support and promotional discounts. For the first time in 15 years of U.S. activity, Fuji put its logo on the back of its paper, no longer fearing consumer preference for Kodak. Fuji's distribution was now strong enough, and it had been successful with its mini photoprocessing labs. Quicker to respond than retailing, processing systems allowed Fuji to capture 16 percent of the U.S. market for photo paper.

Turbulent Times in the 1990s

Fuji entered the 1990s in a very strong position in its home market and enjoying increasing success in foreign markets as well. The company then posted three consecutive years of record sales in the early 1990s, culminating in 1992's ¥1.14 trillion in sales. Net income fell 18.7 percent in 1992 from 1991

levels, however, as Fuji began to feel the combined effects of the prolonged recession in Japan and the sharp appreciation of the yen. Nevertheless, Fuji continued to develop and introduce innovative new products, such as 1991's Fujix Digital Still Camera DS-100, which used a memory card to store images; the Fujix Simple-Hi 8 camcorder, introduced in 1993 as the smallest and lightest camcorder in the world; and the Pictrostat instant color print system, also launched in 1993, which could produce color prints from prints, slides, and objects in one minute without using any processing chemicals.

From 1993 to 1995, Fuji saw its sales stagnate. The company was affected overseas by the continuing strength of the yen and at home by unexpected competition, highlighted in 1994 when the largest Japanese supermarket chain, Daiei, began selling store-brand 35mm film made by AGFA-Gevaert. Fuji's share of the Japanese film market fell from 74 to 69 percent from 1993 to 1994. Meanwhile, Kodak charged Fuji in 1993 with dumping color photographic paper in the U.S. market. To avoid having to pay threatened punitive tariffs, and to counter the effects of the strong yen, Fuji added to its Greenwood facility a factory to make color photo paper. This factory began operation in 1995. The Greenwood complex also saw the addition of a factory to produce Fujicolor QuickSnap disposable cameras that same year and a fifth factory, opening in 1996, for packaging and shipping 35mm Fujicolor film manufactured at its plant in the Netherlands.

The long-term war between Kodak and Fuji was far from over, however. On the U.S. front, Fuji aggressively sought throughout the 1990s to capture more of the wholesale photofinishing market. It was largely successful as its network of U.S. photofinishing labs grew to 21 in 1996 when it spent $464 million to buy six labs from Wal-Mart Stores Inc. The deal also included a ten-year contract through which Fuji was to supply all photofinishing services to the more than 2,250 Wal-Marts nationwide—taking business away from Kodak's photofinishing business, Qualex Inc. Wal-Mart was the leading photofinisher in the country at the time. Later in 1996, Fuji scored another coup when it signed an exclusive agreement with Ritz Camera Centers Inc. to supply paper to Ritz's chain of 550 minilabs, the third largest minilab chain in the country.

On the Japanese front, the battle was being conducted as another trade dispute. This time, Kodak accused the Japanese government and Fuji of illegally restricting access to the Japanese market for film and photographic paper. The U.S. government took the case to the newly formed World Trade Organization (WTO) in 1996, with the European Union soon joining the Kodak side. Fuji contended that Kodak's policies in pricing and marketing its products in Japan were to blame for the company's low market share, and that Kodak faced an environment in Japan similar to what Fuji faced in the United States. In fact, both companies held about 70 percent of their respective home markets, while Kodak held about 12 percent of the Japanese market and Fuji still only 10 percent of the U.S. market. Observers offered no consensus on how the WTO might rule in the case.

Ironically, while these battles were being waged, Fuji had joined the Kodak-led consortium of film and camera companies (the others were Nikon, Minolta, and Canon) to develop the

Advanced Photo System (APS), an effort to revitalize the stagnant still photography market. APS offered easy film loading and the ability to select from three photo sizes (4 inch by 6 inch, 4 inch by 7 inch, and a panoramic 4 inch by 10 inch) as photos are taken. In 1996 Fuji introduced a full range of APS products—films, compact cameras, disposable cameras, photofinishing equipment, a Digital Image Workstation, a Photo Player for displaying images on a television, and an Image Scanner for converting images to their digital equivalent for manipulation on a PC.

In 1996 Fuji enjoyed its best year since 1993, although it still had not recovered to the levels of the early 1990s. Also in 1996, Minoru Ohnishi became chairman and CEO; Masayuki Muneyuki, who had been one of two senior executive managing directors, became president. It would be this new leadership team which would have to deal with the resolution of the WTO suit and the overall battles with Kodak. Having weathered the worst of the difficult economic conditions that faced all Japanese companies in the 1990s, Fuji's future appeared bright. It seemed certain that Kodak would have a serious adversary to contend with for years to come.

Principal Subsidiaries

Fuji Photo Optical Co., Ltd.; Mito Fuji Koki Co., Ltd.; Sano Fuji Koki Co., Ltd.; Okaya Fuji Koki Co., Ltd.; FUJIFILM Microdevices Co., Ltd.; FUJIX Co., Ltd.; FUJIFILM AXIA Co., Ltd.; FUJIFILM Battery Co., Ltd.; F.F.P. Co., Ltd.; Fuji Photo Equipment Co., Ltd.; F.I.T. Co., Ltd.; Fuji Color Trading Co., Ltd.; Fujicolor Service Co., Ltd.; Tochigi Fujicolor Co., Ltd.; Pro-lab Create Tokyo Co., Ltd.; Pro-lab Create Osaka Co., Ltd.; Tokyo Chuoh Genzosho Co., Ltd.; Ibaraki Fujicolor Co., Ltd.; Sanin Fujicolor Co., Ltd.; Hokuriku Fujicolor Co., Ltd.; Fuji Micrographics Co., Ltd.; Fuji Technics Co., Ltd.; Fuji Magne-Disk Co., Ltd; Fuji-Hunt Electronics Technology Co., Ltd.; Fuji X-ray Film Manufacturing Co., Ltd.; FUJIFILM Software Development Center AKITA Co., Ltd.; Fuji Medical Systems Co., Ltd.; Chiyoda Medical Co., Ltd.; FUJIFILM Business Supply Co., Ltd.; FUJIFILM Logistics Co., Ltd.; Fuji Service Co., Ltd.; Fuji Photo Service Co., Ltd.; Fuji Photo Film Canada Inc.; Fuji Graphic Systems Canada Inc.; Fuji Photo Film U.S.A., Inc.; Fuji Photo Film Hawaii, Inc. (U.S.A.); Fuji Medical Systems U.S.A., Inc.; Fuji Photo Film, Inc. (U.S.A.); FUJIFILM Microdisks U.S.A., Inc.; Fuji Hunt Photographic Chemicals, Inc. (U.S.A.); Fuji Photo Film do Brasil Ltda. (Brazil); Fuji Medical Systems Benelux N.V. (Belgium); Fuji Hunt Photographic Chemicals, N.V. (Belgium); Fuji Photo Film (Europe) GmbH (Germany); Fuji Magnetics GmbH (Germany); Fuji Hunt Photographic Chemicals (Deutschland) GmbH (Germany); Fuji Hunt Photographic Chemicals (Italia) Srl (Italy); Fuji Photo Film B.V. (Netherlands); FUJIFILM España, S.A. (Spain); Fuji Hunt Photographic Chemicals (Sverige) A.B. (Sweden); Fuji Photo Film (U.K.) Ltd.; Fuji Hunt Photographic Chemicals (U.K.) Ltd.; Fuji Photo Film (Malaysia) Sdn. Bhd.; Fuji Photo Film (Singapore) Pte Ltd; Fuji Hunt Photographic Chemicals Pte Ltd (Singapore); Fuji Photo Film (Thailand) Ltd.

Further Reading

Bounds, Wendy, ''Fuji, Accused by Kodak of Hogging Markets, Spits Back: 'You Too,' '' *Wall Street Journal*, July 31, 1995, pp. A1, A6.
——, ''Fuji Will Buy Wal-Mart's Photo Business,'' *Wall Street Journal*, July 9, 1996, p. A3.
Eisenstodt, Gale, ''Sharply Focused,'' *Forbes*, December 24, 1990, p. 50.
''50 Years of Fuji Photo Film,'' Tokyo, Fuji Photo Film Company, 1984.
''Fuji Photo: Lower Market Shares Forcing CEO Out,'' *Tokyo Business Today*, May 1995, pp. 18–19.
Hamilton, David P., ''United It Stands: Fuji Xerox Is a Rarity in World Business: A Joint Venture that Works,'' *Wall Street Journal*, September 26, 1996, p. R19.
Rosario, Louise do, and Jonathan Friedland, ''Developing Negatives: Fuji Photo Film Feels the Pressures of Success,'' *Far Eastern Economic Review*, April 14, 1994, pp. 63–64.
''Shuttered: Photo Wars,'' *Economist*, August 5, 1995, pp. 59–60.
Takahashi, Masatake, ''Put the Facts in Focus: Another Look at the Kodak-Fuji Dispute,'' *Tokyo Business Today*, January 1996, pp. 12–15.

—Ray Walsh
—updated by David E. Salamie

Gadzooks, Inc.

4801 Spring Valley Road, Suite 108B
Dallas, Texas 75244
U.S.A.
(214) 991-5500
Fax: (214) 980-8230
Web site: http://www.gadzooks.com

Public Company
Incorporated: 1983
Employees: 1,388 (1995)
Sales: $84.6 million (1995)
Stock Exchanges: NASDAQ
SICs: 5651 Family Clothing Stores

Gadzooks, Inc. is a rapidly growing specialty retailer of casual apparel for teens in metropolitan and middle markets in the southwestern, midwestern, and southeastern United States. The company's goal is to become a national retail chain in major metropolitan areas and small cities.

Gadzooks was founded in 1983 by Jerry Szczepanski and Larry Titus. Szczepanski had no previous background in retail. He had been a university teacher and worked in computers before serving as vice president of T-Shirts Plus, a franchise co-owned by Titus and another partner. When Szczepanski's sons had trouble finding clothes they liked to wear, their dad decided to develop a retail store where teens could buy the clothes they liked, as well as mingle with others their own ages. In the 13 years since that first store opened, Gadzooks grew into a chain of 183 stores in twenty-four states, known for its original merchandising and expansion strategies.

Key Elements of Early Strategy

Gadzooks's unique merchandising strategy involved several key elements. First, Gadzooks stores sought 13- through 19-year-olds from Middle America as customers. Szczepanski recognized that there were a lot of teenagers in America but that they were an underserved segment of the marketplace. Research showed that teens were a significant portion of the population, in fact the fastest-growing segment of the American people. In 1996 the U.S. Census Bureau estimated that there were 25 million teens in the United States, with that number growing to 31 million by year 2010—the most teens in U.S. history. The spending power of teens of course increased with their number. Since teens frequently outgrew their clothes or lost interest in clothes that were out of fashion, they were willing buyers for Gadzooks's merchandise. According to Szczepanski's 1995 letter to shareholders, teens' "annual spending power is estimated at almost $90 billion, while they influence purchases by their parents and others totaling more than twice that amount [about $200 billion]." In addition, the company found that the average spending of teens increased 50 percent in the past five years to about $3,100 per teen in 1995.

Secondly, Gadzooks stores carried "Cool stuff for teens." Basically, Gadzooks sought a broad range of brand-name apparel and accessories for mainstream teens who recognized labels and fashion. The challenge to Gadzooks's corporate buyers was to identify and provide casual apparel and accessories that fit the whims of teen buyers. Gadzooks merchandising emphasized finding the next new trend—such as Jams in the 1980s—and bringing it to the marketplace. Szczepanski told Robertson Stephens & Company conference attendees in 1996 that "teen heroes create demand; it's our job to put it in the stores." Szczepanski noticed that teens liked brand names, which held less risk for the company than Gadzooks manufacturing private-label products for sale in its stores. And brand-name items allowed the store to respond quickly to the demands of teens. Stores stocked a variety of fashionable labels, all easily recognizable by the teen population. Mossimo brand items, for example, accounted for 8 percent of the company's purchases in 1994; No Fear contributed 9 percent that year. Other name brands such as XOXO, Calvin Klein, Dr. Martens, and Oakley were also purchased regularly by Gadzooks's buying staff. As Szczepanski explained in the 1995 annual report: "Gadzooks's success has been built over the years by its proven capability to identify fashionably cool trends and to get into the stores those fashions and labels that teens want to see and be seen wearing."

Unlike many other specialty retailers for teens, Gadzooks carried merchandise for both male and female teens to broaden its customer base. Overall, the stores maintained five categories of merchandise: young men, which accounted for 27.1 percent of sales in 1994; junior women, 24.9 percent of sales that year; unisex apparel, 21.7 percent of sales; accessories, 17.7 percent of sales; and footwear, 8.6 percent of sales. (The junior women, young men, and unisex categories traditionally accounted for three-quarters of the company's sales; footwear and accessories made up the remaining quarter.) Without reliance on a single product category, this dynamic management of merchandise mix maximized sales and profits for the company. Executives also carefully monitored sales, so products matched buying patterns and trends.

All Gadzooks's merchandise reportedly came from U.S. suppliers since overseas sources might take too long to deliver material, thus risking merchandise arriving after trends had passed. The company worked with 450 vendors to maintain 2,000 stock keeping units (SKUs) in its stores, including tops, jeans, shorts, junior dresses, swimwear, t-shirts, shoes, sunglasses, watches, and costume jewelry.

Thirdly, Gadzooks committed itself to outstanding customer service for its teen shoppers. The company developed a "Gaditude" through which a young sales staff created a positive peer environment for teens meeting and shopping. The company insisted on a high level of professional, attentive, and personalized customer service. Sales associates were instructed to greet each customer, inform customers of trends, and suggest merchandise to shoppers. Above all, sales staff treated teens like adult customers, not mall thugs.

Keeping with its youthful orientation, Gadzooks staffed its stores with young sales associates. Generally, sales and assistant store management staff were about 17 or 18 years old. In fact, all of Gadzooks's employees were on the young side. The average age of employees working at the corporate headquarters in Dallas was 28 in 1996. Buyers were about 30 years old and all hired from within the Gadzooks organization except for the company's original buyer. Throughout its history, Gadzooks invested heavily in its personnel and systems, providing career advancement opportunities for its sales staff and management levels. Szczepanski said in the *Daily News Record:* "I'm a firm believer that if you give a 21- or 24-year-old responsibility, they can handle it. They don't have to wait all their lives to have the chance to have responsibility. Give it to them and they'll take it and run with it. We've proven that for many years."

Gadzooks also designed its stores to be interesting, entertaining, and attractive to teens. All stores featured neon lights, television monitors showing music videos, creative signs, and stylish fixtures, including a signature Volkswagen Beetle for displaying merchandise. "Gadzooks has been successful because of its attitude towards serving teenagers," stated the company's first ever annual report. "Our stores are high-energy, fun places to visit and show. We want our customers to feel like Gadzooks stores are theirs, so we give them a store filled with music, excitement, clothing and accessories, and the special service they deserve." Parents liked the stores, too.

Fourthly, Gadzooks concentrated its stores in malls. Stores—each about 2,200 square feet—were opened seven days a week during normal mall hours. Maria Medaris, an analyst for Alex. Brown & Sons, explained the appeal of mall stores for retailers such as Gadzooks. "Malls," she said in *Investor's Business Daily,* "are still the one place where you can drop off your kids at age fourteen, and they won't get into trouble."

The company selected highly visible locations for its mall stores in metropolitan markets, including Dallas, Houston, Atlanta, Cincinnati, and Kansas City. Gadzooks stores also settled in middle markets—notably, Amarillo, Texas; Peoria, Illinois; San Angelo, Texas; Joplin, Missouri; and Tupelo, Mississippi. The company chose new store sites to balance test markets where it had no previous experience, to capitalize on new markets where a store had been tested and showed potential for expansion, and to enlarge mature markets that required additional stores. Because Gadzooks maintained a year-round business with three major selling seasons—spring break, back-to-school, and Christmas—its opening of new stores (and the timing of those openings) became more crucial to its sales activities than the Christmas holiday season. In its whole history, Gadzooks never made an acquisition of a store, except for reclaiming some franchises during the 1980s. It always opened new ones.

Store Expansion, 1980s–90s

Jerry Szczepanski and Larry Titus opened their first store in 1983 in a Mesquite, Texas, mall in a space formerly occupied by a waterbed store. They signed a one-year lease there. In May 1984 the pair launched a second store in a Dallas mall. Their next store opened in Waco a few years later. Said Szczepanski in a *Daily News Record* interview with Julie Vargo: "We knew if we could make the concept work in Waco, we could expand it nationwide." The next store debuted in Wichita Falls, Texas.

Throughout the 1980s Gadzooks enjoyed modest growth as Szczepanski and Titus developed and refined the merchandising concept. They wanted to move into new markets, but needed money to do that. So they tried expanding through franchising. Though they thought it would take two years, they sold 20 franchises in three months in Texas, Oklahoma, Louisiana, and New Mexico. But when the franchisees wanted to change the stores' merchandising strategy to cash in on a skateboarding frenzy, Szczepanski and Titus objected. They wanted their stores back. Throughout 1987 and 1988, the two bought back all 20 franchised stores and started opening other stores.

By January 1992, they operated 33 stores and decided on a more aggressive expansion into new markets, as well as planned to solidify Gadzooks's presence in existing markets. The company's net sales were $18.5 million that year, with average net sales per store of approximately $605,000. A year later Szczepanski and Titus had added 23 new stores and closed one store for a total of 43 Gadzooks outlets. Net sales amounted to $25.4 million. In January 1994 Gadzooks stores numbered 65 and net sales had grown to $38.2 million.

Throughout 1994 Gadzooks enhanced its merchandising strategy in preparation for more store expansion. The company hired a new merchandising manager, improved merchandise allocation and distribution functions, and reviewed merchandise assortment in stores to reduce stock-keeping units in certain categories. The changes resulted in rising inventory turns, improved presentation of merchandise in stores, and increased sales of high-margin merchandise. By January 1995 there were 90 Gadzooks stores, and sales continued to be strong: Net sales totaled $56.5 million, and average net sales per store were $698.1 million. The company achieved comparable-store sales gains every year in its history, so it felt ready to make some bold moves.

Gadzooks further accelerated its store opening program. Then, in October 1995—after 12 years as a progressive, expanding private company—Gadzooks organized the initial public offering of the company's common stock. With IPO shares selling at $12 to $14 per share, the offering raised $18.5 million. Gadzooks used $6.1 million from the sale to repay debt, and $2.1 million to be paid as dividends on preferred stock. Gadzooks employed the rest of the proceeds for store openings, remodeling, and working capital. The year 1995 became the most profitable in the company's history. Net sales equaled $84.6 million; net income more than doubled.

The company again initiated a common stock offering in January 1996. By then Gadzooks comprised 126 stores in 21 states. Average net sales per store were $776,800. By March 1996 the company already opened 20 of the 45 or 50 new stores planned for the year. In September Gadzooks planned for 163 stores to be in operation in 23 states—a plan accelerated to 183 stores in 24 states before the year's end. Instead of the projected 50, Gadzooks stores increased by 57. According to Szczepanski: "Prime store sites with excellent lease terms are more available, and the first group of 20 stores we opened before the spring break season have been performing well above plan. As a result, our board of directors approved moving up the timetable for some stores originally scheduled for opening during the first part of fiscal 1997."

Continued Growth for the Future

In 1997 Gadzooks commissioned a new, 117,000-square-foot distribution facility to service its growing number of stores. Gadzooks anticipated operating hundreds of stores by the year 2000. Kathleen Brown Oher of Dallas-based Southwest Securities, Inc., saw this growth in store numbers as a real possibility for Gadzooks, reporting in *Investor's Business Daily* that she believed the company could grow to 400 stores by then. Szczepanski concurred, "There are significant growth opportunities ahead for Gadzooks as we expand to meet the growing needs of our teenage customers. Our . . . stores, currently serving both metropolitan and middle markets . . . , have barely rippled the surface of the vast potential that lies before us. We are excited by the opportunities that we now have as a public company."

Further Reading

Berry, Kate, "Chain Gearing up for an Adolescent Onslaught," *Investor's Business Daily,* July 12, 1996.

"Ga Ga for Gadzooks," *WWD,* October 10, 1995, p. 13.

"Gadzooks," *WWD,* October 19, 1995, p. 2.

"Gadzooks Files for a Secondary Offering," *WWD,* January 10, 1996, p. 16.

"Gadzooks Has Strong Showing in Its Initial Offering to Public; Raises $18.5 Million," *Daily News Record,* October 17, 1995, p. 10.

"Gadzooks IPO Raises $18.5 Million," *Footwear News,* October 16, 1995, p. 12.

"Gadzooks' Net Skyrockets to $1.9M from $930,000," *Daily News Record,* November 22, 1996, p. 8.

"Gadzooks Raises $36.7 Million from Secondary Offering," *Daily News Record,* February 14, 1996, p. 4.

"Gadzooks: Strong Holiday Sales Boost Plans for Store Openings," *WWD,* January 8, 1996, p. 28.

Kaplan, Don, "Pacific Sunwear, Gadzooks Drive to Nab $2 Billion Void in YM Market," *Daily News Record,* September 12, 1996, p. 3.

Vargo, Julie, "Gadzooks Keeps Making the Grade with Young Shoppers," *Daily News Record,* January 29, 1996, p. 20.

—Charity Anne Dorgan

The Gap, Inc.

One Harrison
San Francisco, California 94105
U.S.A.
(415) 952-4400
Fax: (415) 512-1830
Web site: http://www.gap.com

Public Company
Incorporated: 1969 as The Gap Stores, Inc.
Employees: 60,000
Sales: $4.65 billion (est. 1996)
Stock Exchanges: New York Pacific
SICs: 5651 Family Clothing Stores

With over 1,760 stores, The Gap, Inc. has remained one of the top retailers in the United States by tailoring its clothes to the evolving tastes of the baby-boom generation. As members of this demographic group have shifted from wearing jeans as an expression of rebellion to a more general preference for informality in all modes of dress, The Gap has expanded beyond its original Levi's-only format to the creation of a complete line of apparel suitable for most settings and all ages. This successful corporate transformation was due largely to the ingenuity of Millard "Mickey" Drexler, president since 1983. The company was founded and has remained under the overall control of Donald G. Fisher and his wife Doris F. Fisher.

Capitalizing on the Generation Gap, 1969 to 1975

Donald Fisher was not of the generation to whom The Gap owes its popularity. A member of a family that made its home in California for generations, Fisher was 40 years old and a successful real estate developer in 1969 when he took note of a new trend among the city's increasingly disaffected youth. Blue jeans, for years made chiefly by Levi Strauss & Co. for laborers and outdoorsmen, were suddenly becoming a part of the counterculture's standard costume. Durable, cheap, comfortable, and acceptably offbeat, jeans were the perfect uniform for a genera-

tion of young people anxious to demonstrate its antipathy to corporate America.

Fisher was said to have conceived of The Gap when he was unable to find the right size of Levi's in a department store in Sacramento, California. He realized that jeans had become more popular than current merchandising outlets could accommodate, and like hamburgers, stereo equipment, and gasoline, they could be sold through a chain of small stores devoted solely to that product. With the help of his wife, Doris, Fisher opened a shop near San Francisco State University in one of his own buildings, offering a combination of records and jeans. Their intention was to attract jeans customers by means of the records, but at first no one noticed the jeans, and Fisher was driven close to bankruptcy. In desperation, he placed ads in local newspapers announcing the sale of "four tons" of jeans at rock-bottom prices, and the clothes were soon gone. To emphasize the youthful ambiance of his new store, Fisher named it The Gap, an allusion to a currently hot topic, the Generation Gap.

When Fisher incorporated his business as The Gap Stores, Inc., it was an immediate success. Although the Fishers had no experience in retailing, their stores' combination of jeans, low prices, and wide selection proved irresistible to the huge market of 14- to 25-year-olds. Fisher added new outlets in San Francisco and was soon enjoying the benefits of chain store merchandising: centralized buying and advertising, excellent name recognition, and uniform pricing. Initially, The Gap Stores' buying program was singularly uncomplicated, as the stores carried only one product, jeans by Levi Strauss & Co. The stores were brightly painted, often orange; filled with circular metal display racks known as "rounders"; and usually enlivened by rock and roll music. To keep rents low, the Fishers kept stores small—about 3,000 to 4,000 square feet. They located most of their stores in shopping centers, many of them enclosed in malls.

Two years after opening its first stores, The Gap's sales were running at $2.5 million annually, and the Fishers converted the company into a public corporation, though retained the great majority of stock. With extraordinary celerity, they opened stores across the U.S. while maintaining tight control over the critical accounting, purchasing, and marketing functions of what was soon a sizable corporation. In five years, sales had increased almost 50-fold, to $97 million, and the number of stores had grown to 186, spread over 21 states. Analysts credited the company's success to the Fishers' observance of a few cardinal rules of retailing: Gap stores replaced its stock with maximum speed; its prices were low and stayed that way; big sellers were kept on the rack until they stopped moving, rather than being retired in favor of new styles simply for the sake of novelty; and few items were stocked—jeans, a few shirts, light jackets—each offered in its complete range of colors and sizes, ensuring a minimum of disappointed customers.

The company's growth was also made possible by the extensive national advertising of Levi Strauss, which provided 100 percent of The Gap's merchandise during its early years. Such dependence on a single supplier had obvious dangers, however, and around 1973 The Gap began marketing several labels of its own, as well as national brands other than Levi's. These proved crucial to the company's short- and long-term health; by 1975 Gap stores generated $100 million in net sales.

Ups and Downs, 1976–80

By 1976 the Fishers were ready to make their first substantial public stock offering. The company's spectacular growth had attracted widespread interest, and its offering of 1.2 million shares sold quickly at $18 per share in May. Coincidentally, however, the retail industry went into a steep slide, which, when combined with The Gap's large expenditures for new stores, pushed the company into the red for the final quarter of its fiscal year, ending July 31. The value of the newly issued stock fell to $7.25, prompting nine separate class-action suits from outraged stock purchasers who alleged that the Fishers had tried to dump their holdings before The Gap announced its bad news. These charges came despite the fact that the Fishers sold only about 10 percent of their holdings during the period in question. Rather than wage endless litigation, The Gap settled the suits in 1979 for a total of $5.8 million, or 40¢ per share and did its best to mend its frayed relations with Wall Street.

By the end of the 1970s the company could pay such a figure without undue strain. Adding between 50 and 80 stores annually, The Gap pushed its sales to $307 million in 1980 and was close to achieving nationwide representation. The jeans market was no longer quite so straightforward, however. Members of the great wave of youngsters who had come of age wearing blue jeans in the 1970s were now older, wealthier, and more conservative, and the Fishers were busily attempting to break out of the jeans niche by expanding The Gap's selection of clothing. Several experimental chains featuring upscale fashions were essayed and brought together under the Taggs name but later

liquidated because they were unprofitable. Gap stores were enlarged to handle increasing amounts of what became known as casual wear and were frequently moved outside of shopping centers to freestanding locations, where space was plentiful and rent lower per square foot.

Along with the search for a line of clothes to appeal to an older clientele, the Fishers also faced Levi Strauss & Co.'s decision to supply big mass marketers such as Sears and J.C. Penney with its jeans. Levi's were now sold everywhere, underscoring The Gap's need to develop a label and look of its own. The company's own brands, created during the 1970s, generated about 45 percent of Gap sales in 1980, with Levi's adding an equal amount and other national brands making up the balance. Considering that 10 years earlier essentially all of The Gap's sales were Levi Strauss & Co. products, the 1980 figures represented an achievement, but it was clear that if the company were to avoid inundation by the rising tide of jeans discounters it would have to fashion a new, exclusively Gap image.

Mickey Comes to Town, 1981–86

To accomplish this task, Donald Fisher hired Millard "Mickey" Drexler as president in 1983. Drexler, then 40, had just solved a similar problem with AnnTaylor, creating a more chic image for the chain and quadrupling sales in the bargain. Drexler was born in the Bronx to a family with roots in the garment business and by age 23 was a buyer for Bloomingdale's. After a stint at Macy's, he became president of AnnTaylor in 1980, where his work caught the eye of Donald Fisher, who was contemplating the future of The Gap. Drexler accepted the job as president at the end of 1983 (sales $480 million) and was given a block of stock that would make him one of the country's wealthiest retail executives.

Drexler immediately began The Gap's wholesale transformation, in spite of the company's currently excellent financial status. The new president found little that he liked; proliferating competition in jeans and The Gap's youthful marketing image had forced the company into a price-driven volume business. Its orange-painted stores were cluttered with rounders displaying merchandise of many labels that Drexler later described to the *New York Times* as "trendy but not tasteful. . . well, just plain ugly." Worst of all, most consumers perceived The Gap as strictly for teenagers, at a time when people who grew up in the 1960s were developing more upmarket tastes. It would be difficult to overcome The Gap's 15-year tradition as the place where kids went to pick up a pair of Levi's.

Drexler began by eliminating all private label brands but one: Gap. Levi Strauss products were kept but relegated to the background; henceforth, The Gap would be known not only as a store, but as a line of clothes as well. Drexler created a large in-house design staff to develop clothes that would be casual, simple, made of natural fibers, and more clearly differentiated by gender than were jeans. The look was informal but classic—still denim-based but including a variety of shirts, skirts, blouses, and sweaters in assorted colors and weaves. It was clothing for people who wanted to look and feel young without appearing slovenly or rebellious, a description that fit a vast number of U.S. consumers in the 1980s.

Gap stores were substantially revamped. Neutral grays and white replaced the garish orange, and the ubiquitous rounders gave way to shelves of neatly folded clothing under soft lighting. The company's advertising, as devised by Drexler's longtime colleague, Magdalena (Maggie) Gross, shifted from radio and television to upscale magazines and newspapers and featured older models engaged in familiar, outdoor activities that weren't necessarily connected with the youth culture.

A few years later, Gross launched the "Individuals of Style" campaign, a series of black and white portraits of both famous and unknown subjects by a team of celebrated photographers. The ads stressed style, not The Gap, whose clothes didn't always appear in all of the photos, and they were enormously successful in helping to change the public's perception of the company. The Gap came to mean good taste of an informal variety, and the brand name Gap soon acquired the cachet needed if the company were to compete with other retailers of casual wear such as Benetton and The Limited. In addition, the word "stores" was dropped from the company's name.

Drexler's revolution at The Gap cost a good deal of money, and financial results for 1984 were poor, with profits down 43 percent to $12.2 million. By the middle of the following year, however, it was clear he had pulled off something of a miracle. Gross revenue, profits, and same-store sales were all up; more importantly, the company had fresh energy and a merchandising focus that could carry it for years to come. In the meantime, The Gap had acquired a number of other retail chains, for better and worse. Foremost among these was Banana Republic, founded in 1979 by another California husband and wife team, Melvyn and Patricia Ziegler.

The two-store chain of safari and travel clothing outfits, bought by The Gap in 1983, had a well-established catalogue business. After its acquisition and the introduction of private-label clothing lines, Banana Republic's sales doubled each year through the mid-1980s, but slowed quickly thereafter. Despite the mixed results of the Banana Republic acquisition, the company continued to seek out other chain stores. Pottery Barn was a housewares chain of about 30 stores in New York and California; after several problematic years, it was liquidated in 1986. This same year, Drexler sought to fill another clothing need of the Baby Boomer generation with the debut of GapKids, featuring comfortable, durable clothes for the children of parents who shopped at Gap stores. The concept was a huge success, and along with Banana Republic (which peaked in the late 1980s with revenue of more than $250 million a year) figured largely in The Gap's long-range planning.

There Are No Secrets in Retailing, 1987–95

By 1987 The Gap decided to try its wares outside the U.S., and its first international store was opened in London. Additional stores soon sprang up throughout Great Britain, and in Canada and France. Unfortunately, stateside, Banana Republic's safari gear bubble burst and it became a money-losing liability. The Gap also tested the higher end of the clothing market with Hemisphere, a nine-store chain of upscale U.S. sportswear with European styling. Created in 1987, the same year the company broke $1 billion in sales, Hemisphere offered elegant fashions but soon ran afoul of a severe recession. Disposed of only two years

later, neither the Hemisphere mistake or the demise of Pottery Barn was serious enough to cause more than a few tremors at the parent company, whose spectacular rebirth in the Drexler era left ample room for such experimentation.

In 1990, as Banana Republic searched for secure footing, GapKids prospered and launched a new venture, babyGap. Like its sibling, babyGap was a phenomenal success and became a popular attraction in GapKids stores. For the start of a new decade, The Gap was looking very good indeed: a stock split occurred in September, and at year-end the company's 1,092 stores pulled in $1.9 billion in sales with net earnings of $144.5 million.

In the early 1990s, Banana Republic was busy refocusing its image while GapKids and babyGap flourished. Overall, though, revenue, net income, and return-on-equity were all outstanding ($2.5 billion, $229.8 million, and 40.2 percent respectively due to another stock split in June) in 1991 and virtually every year since Drexler's program had taken effect in 1985. The Gap's transition from a discount jeans warehouse to a sleek fashion arbiter was not altogether painless, yet the result had been more successful than Donald and Doris Fisher ever imagined. In 1991 the Fisher family still held more than 40 percent of the company, which now operated more than 1,216 stores in the U.S., Canada, and the United Kingdom with plans to expand total sales area by 15 percent annually. Not only had The Gap followed its Baby Boomer clientele as they grew older and wealthier, it provided for their children, too. GapKids was the fastest-growing segment of the company as a whole, with most of the more than 223 GapKids stores housing a babyGap department for infants and toddlers.

Though 1992 marked a dip in profits and sales growth due to slower turnover and increased competition, the company addressed these problems by turning away from unisex clothing to more gender-specific items. Along with refurbishing stores and placing more emphasis on women, The Gap came back with record numbers in 1993 and a new franchise, originally called Gap Warehouse, because for some it had become increasingly cool not to spend money on clothes (i.e. the "grunge" and "slacker" looks). Lacking the trademark flare associated with the company, Drexler hired an outside to firm to come up with a new name to no avail. Then when strolling in Paris with colleagues, Drexler saw the perfect moniker for the down-market stores painted on a building: Old Navy. Hence Old Navy Clothing Company, with stores nearly twice as big as other Gap stores, filled with sturdy, value-priced (20–30 percent lower) clothing for the entire family. Despite the circumstances of its birth, Old Navy became another Gap sensation.

Banana Republic, meanwhile, was gaining ground with urbane elegance as a hip alternative to The Gap's casualness. To shore up its product line, the upscale clothier initiated a shop-within-a-shop concept, featuring different collections, jewelry, and leather accessories. By 1994 there were 1,507 Gap-owned stores (188 were Banana Republic) contributing to the company's $3.72 billion in sales. Within a year there were 1,680 stores—210 Banana Republic, 902 Gap, 437 GapKids, and 131 Old Navy. International stores had surged from 1994's 124 (72 in Canada, 49 in the United Kingdom, and 3 in France) to 91 in Canada, 55 in the U.K., 12 in France, 4 in Japan, and 2 in

Germany in 1995. Likewise, The Gap's statistics were robust: a two-for-one stock split paid out dividends in March; sales leapt 18 percent to nearly $4.4 billion; and net earnings rose 11 percent to $354 million over the previous year's $320 million.

Banana Republic, once a blemish on the perfect Gap picture, had blossomed with more new products including footwear, personal care items, a sharper focus on women, and five new stores in Canada. At the same time, Old Navy increased its market share by doubling in size, exceeding the company's hopes for its newest division, while Gap and GapKids lost some of their momentum although babyGap maintained its prominence. New directions for GapKids and babyGap included plush toys, other non-clothing items, and freestanding babyGap stores; The Gap debuted GapScents, and continued to broaden its age range and clothing lines to include work attire. Yet perhaps the biggest news of 1995 was Donald Fisher's decision to relinquish his duties as CEO of The Gap, Inc. His successor, of course, was Mickey Drexler, who added the responsibilities of CEO to those of president. Fisher remained chairman, however, and still kept a hand in running the company he founded nearly 30 years before.

A Fashion Titan, 1996 and Beyond

By 1996 The Gap's dominance of the fashion scene was fixed; consumers of all ages could find something in one of its stores. The industry even honored the company in the April issue of *Elle,* when high-brow designers including Giorgio Armani, Nino Cerruti, Carolina Herrera, Todd Oldham, and Cynthia Rowley paid "tribute to the little company that became master of the universe." Though it began with a singular purpose, The Gap, with its burgeoning cluster of stores and subsidiaries, changed fashion for not only Baby Boomers but for generations to come. The Gap's success was in no small part due to Donald Fisher's and Mickey Drexler's business acuity, especially through vertical integration. By keeping the design, manufacture, inspection, packaging, shipment, display, advertising, and ultimate sale of every item with its name in-house, The Gap maintained exceptional quality and consistency in an increasingly erratic marketplace.

If The Gap's clientele wasn't quite as broad as some department stores or mass marketers, its sophistication and ever-growing consumer base more than made up for it. The Gap—its name formerly a quirky play on generational unrest—came to mean the ultimate in fashion and taste for both younger and older generations. What was next for The Gap? Only Donald and Mickey, who had become as famous in their industry as the other Donald and Mickey were in theirs, knew for sure.

Principal Operating Units

babyGap; Banana Republic; GapKids; Old Navy Clothing Company.

Further Reading

Abend, Jules, "Widening the Gap," *Stores*, November 1985.
Barmash, Isidore, "Gap Finds Middle Road to Success," *New York Times*, June 24, 1991.
Bensimon, Giles, "How They Learned to Stop Worrying and Love The Gap," *Elle,* April 1996.
Caminiti, Susan, "Will Old Navy Fill the Gap?," *Fortune,* March 18, 1996.
"Gap Lands in Japan," *WWD,* November 9, 1995.
Van Meter, Jonathan, "Fast Fashion: Americans Want Clothing That Is Quick and Easy; The Gap Made a Billion Giving It to Them," *Vogue,* May 1990.

—Jonathan Martin
—updated by Taryn Benbow-Pfalzgraf

Genesis Health Ventures, Inc.

148 West State Street
Kennett Square, Pennsylvania 19438
U.S.A.
(610) 444-6350
Fax: (610) 444-3365

Public Company
Incorporated: 1985
Employees: 25,000
Sales: $671.47 million (1996)
Stock Exchanges: New York
SICs: 8051 Skilled Nursing Care Facilities; 8052
Intermediate Care Facilities; 8059 Nursing & Personal
Care, Not Elsewhere Classified; 5912 Drug Stores &
Proprietary Stores

Genesis Health Ventures, Inc. provides integrated health care services for the nation's growing elderly population under the brand name Genesis ElderCare. Genesis has taken an innovative approach to health care delivery, building a comprehensive network of managed care facilities and services designed to help senior citizens maintain their independence and mobility. The Genesis network services offerings include community support programs, physician services, home care support, short-term rehabilitation, out-patient rehabilitation, assisted living communities, retirement communities, pharmacy services and medical equipment, and long-term care. Serving more than 70,000 clients, Genesis has focused its operations on building dominant market share in five regional markets: the Northeast, including Massachusetts, New Hampshire, Connecticut, and Vermont; the Delaware Valley, including Pennsylvania, New Jersey, and northern Delaware; Baltimore/Washington, D.C., including Maryland and northern Virginia; Southern Delaware and Eastern Maryland; and Central Florida.

The Genesis network includes more than 150 owned or leased facilities, including approximately 120 nursing homes and geriatric care facilities, ten primary-care physician clinics, six rehabilitation centers, nine institutional pharmacies, five

home health care agencies, and 16 managed retirement communities, as well as contracts with more than 500 third-party providers. The company's ASCO Healthcare subsidiary provides pharmacy and surgical and medical equipment services for the ElderCare network and other nursing homes throughout the East Coast and Mid-Atlantic region. Genesis's revenues for the year ended September 30, 1996, topped $671 million, with net income of more than $37 million. In 1995 basic health care services accounted for 57 percent of the company's revenues, while specialty medical services generated 37 percent and management services six percent. Genesis is led by chairman and co-CEO Michael R. Walker and president and co-CEO Richard R. Howard, cofounders of the company.

Innovations in Senior Care in the 1980s

Walker and Howard were already veterans of the nursing home industry when they founded Genesis in 1985. They had worked together since the 1970s, building up two $100 million nursing home chains, as well as their own reputations in the industry. When these chains were bought up by industry heavyweights Beverly Enterprises and HCR, Inc., Walker and Howard decided to go into business for themselves. Setting up operations in an old furniture and dry goods store in the small town of Kennett Square outside Philadelphia, their reputations served them well: on the first day of operation, the company was able to arrange some $32 million in loans.

Setting out to build a nursing home chain with a difference, Walker and Howard used these loans to purchase nursing home facilities in Connecticut and southwestern Massachusetts. At the time, the prevailing culture among nursing homes was to provide long-term custodial care, typically on a fee-for-service basis. Walker and Howard, however, looked toward building a health services network, focused on providing geriatric care, that would emphasize rehabilitative services. "No one wants to end up in a nursing home," Walker told *Institutional Investor,* and that belief provided the cornerstone for the company's growth. Through rehabilitative therapy and services, patients were encouraged to return home—or to less care-intensive facilities—and to independent lives. Genesis offered a program of clinical intervention and managed care that emphasized the

Company Perspectives:

Genesis Health Ventures was founded in 1985 on the visionary principal that health care for the elderly was too focused on long-term custodial care. Instead, founder, chairman and chief executive officer Michael R. Walker sought to build a company that worked with each customer to promote independence and the achievement of a full life. To meet that goal, Genesis Health Ventures created a comprehensive network of people, places and programs united by a common philosophy and mission: To listen to what customers want to achieve, to advise them on what's possible, and to work to overcome barriers to living a full life.

restoration of functional ability. This, the company reasoned, would be good for its patients, and for its bottom line. The typical nursing home was expensive to operate, and long-term care provided only low profit margins.

Managed care was still relatively unknown in the health care industry, and nearly unheard of in the geriatric market. However, the projected growth of the elderly population, with forecasts of 35 million by the end of the century and nearly 60 million by the year 2025, signalled the need to control costs among the very population most in need of medical services. From the start, Genesis set out to control its own costs. Rather than contracting out for its network support services, such as pharmacy services, home medical equipment, and rehabilitation therapy, the company instead focused on acquiring these services and their higher profit margins. As clients were discharged from the company's nursing homes, they could be retained within the company's network of other services. In 1986 Genesis made the first of many acquisitions, acquiring the Speech & Hearing Network, which was renamed Team Rehabilitation.

By 1990 the company had more than 30 facilities in its network, with 4,500 long-term beds, generating revenues of nearly $145 million. Genesis continued to expand its services network through carefully planned acquisitions. One important consideration was a proposed acquisition's proximity to other facilities in the company's managed care network. ''If you own a pharmacy in Pennsylvania and a nursing home in North Carolina, you can't share information,'' Walker told the *Baltimore Sun,* ''But if I have a pharmacy, a physical therapist, a physician in the same place, guess what? They can all get together once a week to discuss the patient's health and get that person out of long-term care.''

Genesis next moved to expand into pharmacy and medical supply services—where profit margins ranged from 10 to 15 percent as opposed to the 3 to 5 percent available on nursing homes—acquiring Accredited Surgical Companies, Inc., and Drug Lane Pharmacies, Inc., both of which repackaged and sold drugs. The two companies were combined to form the ASCO Healthcare, Inc., subsidiary, which was expanded into a full-service medical supply company that supplied not only the Genesis network, but outside nursing homes as well. Genesis also expanded its business by entering a management agree-

ment for providing life-care services at continuous-care retirement centers, and by opening a physician-staffed outpatient clinic.

Growth in the 1990s

Genesis went public in 1991, selling 1.8 million shares and raising $13.5 million, which the company used to pay down some $12.6 million in debt. By then, Genesis operated 42 geriatric-care facilities, managed 13 life-care communities, and held service contracts with more than 140 independent health care providers. The company continued to pursue acquisitions, purchasing Concord Healthcare Corp. and Total Care Systems, which helped boost the company's revenues to $171.5 million for its 1991 fiscal year. Genesis, which had been profitable since its formation, posted a net income of nearly $3.3 million for the year. Genesis also took another step toward completing its network by developing a subsidiary called Physician Services. This addition allowed Genesis to become the first and only company in its industry to employ its own primary care physicians for its customers.

The following year, the ASCO subsidiary expanded, acquiring Suburban Medical Services for $9 million. The company opened a second rehabilitative outpatient clinic in order to serve customers discharged from its nursing homes; at the same time, the company moved to extend its services with the construction of an assisted-living facility located next to its geriatric facility in Wilkes-Barre, Pennsylvania. At the end of 1992, Genesis posted a second public offering, of 2.5 million shares at $13 per share, setting the stage for the next phase in the company's growth. By then, the company's revenues neared $200 million, while net profits climbed to $7.4 million.

The next year, 1993, proved to be pivotal in the company's development. Genesis expanded its ASCO subsidiary with the purchase of a home health care company and the acquisition of Health Concepts and Services, Inc., a provider of nursing home staff training and services based in Baltimore. By then, ASCO's revenues had climbed to $80 million, with 80 percent of those sales coming from outside the Genesis network. Within Genesis, the company established its Functional Evaluation & Treatment Unit, later known as the Full Potential process. This unit provided a geriatric assessment program for evaluating and placing patients. Based on physician-directed teams including registered nurses; nurse practitioners; physical, occupational, recreational, and speech therapists; social workers; and dietitians, the unit worked with patients and their families, as well as community and network resources, to develop realistic rehabilitation goals and care plans designed to achieve those goals.

Until 1993, Genesis's emphasis had been on expanding the scope of its network services; however, calls for health care reform from the newly inaugurated Clinton administration led Genesis to shift its focus. One expected consequence of health care reforms in general—and the inevitable reforms to the Medicare/Medicaid system for the company's core geriatric clients—would be abolition of the old fee-for-service health care plans in favor of prepaid, bulk rate plans. With competition for prepayments expected to be intense, Genesis moved to create a critical mass of nursing homes and geriatric facilities that would enable it to compete more strongly for contracts, especially government contracts. In October 1993, the company announced the largest acquisition in its history, with the $205 million purchase of Meridian Healthcare, the largest nursing home operator in Maryland. Genesis added Meridian's 36 geriatric-care facilities to the 58 already in the company's network, nearly doubling its revenues, from $220 million in 1993 to nearly $400 million in 1994. Maryland then became the company's largest market, surpassing Massachusetts. The Meridian acquisition also meant that Genesis would be able to expand its range of services into Maryland, where Genesis was by then the state's largest senior care provider, controlling costs by achieving economies of scale.

The Meridian acquisition was the first in a flurry of new acquisitions. In a move to expand into the burgeoning home health care market, Genesis purchased a 14 percent share in a partnership corporation acquiring Baltimore's Visiting Nurse Association. The company also entered a strategic alliance with Horizon Healthcare to provide pharmacy services in the New England region. By 1995, the company had successfully absorbed Meridian's operations under the Genesis banner, gaining recognition as well for its policy of maintaining both existing management and staff, ensuring continuity of client care. This policy served the company well as it sought further acquisitions.

After acquiring Pennsylvania-based TherapyCare Systems LP for $7 million in April 1995, Genesis, through ASCO, bolstered its home health care business in June of that year with the $2 million acquisition of Baltimore-based Eastern Medical Supplies, Inc., and that company's Eastern Rehab Services, Inc., affiliate. The new acquisitions, which generated about $3.5 million in annual revenues through the sale and rental of home medical equipment and respiratory rehabilitation equipment, provided Genesis with increased access to the home health market through hospital affiliations, hospice contracts, and two retail stores. Helping to fuel the company's expansion was a new public offering that raised nearly $52 million, enabling Genesis to pay down debt associated with the Meridian acquisition.

By August 1995, Genesis announced its next large acquisition, agreeing to pay $82.5 million for McKerley Health Care Centers, the largest nursing home chain in New Hampshire. A principal factor in the family-owned chain's decision to sell to Genesis was the company's treatment of its Meridian employees: all of that company's managers, executives, and staff had kept their jobs, while new jobs had been created, and two of Meridian's executives had been promoted to key executive positions within Genesis itself. The acquisition of McKerley added 15 owned or leased geriatric care facilities, with 1,500 beds and some 1,500 employees.

At the beginning of 1996, with 1995 revenues of $487 million and net income of nearly $24 million, Genesis made plans to build a new, $16 million, 100,000-square-foot headquarters in Kennett Square. At the same time, the company consolidated its operations, bringing its core businesses under the trademarked brand name Genesis ElderCare. Genesis Health Ventures, Inc., was kept on as the company's legal name, and the name under which it traded on the New York Stock Exchange.

Genesis's acquisition drive continued through 1996. In April, the company reached agreement to purchase NeighborCare Pharmacies for $57.25 million. NeighborCare, which supplied drugs to nursing homes, operated pharmacies in physician offices, and provided infusion therapy treatments in homes and nursing homes, was merged into the ASCO subsidiary. The following month, Genesis agreed to pay New York-based National Health Care Affiliates, Inc., $133.6 million to acquire 17 elderly care facilities in Florida, Virginia, and Connecticut, adding more than 2,500 beds, as well as a rehabilitation therapy business and a nutritional therapy business. In keeping with its focus on its core markets, Genesis also agreed to sell several Indiana nursing homes acquired through its Meridian purchase.

Before closing out its 1996 fiscal year, Genesis made its largest acquisition to date, agreeing to pay $223 million to acquire Geriatric & Medical Company, which, with 27 nursing homes, added another 3,500 beds to Genesis's New Jersey and Pennsylvania networks. By the end of its 1996 fiscal year, Genesis had boosted its revenues to $671.5 million and posted net income of more than $37 million. The addition of Geriatric & Medical's revenues to Genesis's 1997 sales was expected to help the company near its goal of $1 billion in revenues, while the Genesis history of carefully managed growth pointed to a continued future along the acquisition trail.

Principal Operating Units

Genesis ElderCare Network Services; Genesis ElderCare Physician Services; Genesis ElderCare Rehabilitation Services; Genesis ElderCare Home Care Services; Genesis ElderCare Centers; ASCO Healthcare-Genesis ElderCare Network; The Tidewater Healthcare Shared Services Group.

Further Reading

Atkinson, Bill, "NeighborCare to Be Bought by Pa. Chain," *Baltimore Sun,* April 23, 1996, Business 1C.

Brooke, Bob, "Genesis Project Marks New Beginning for Downtown," *Philadelphia Business Journal,* January 12, 1996, p. 23.

Fahey, Tom, "McKerley Sought Sale," *Union Leader,* August 23, 1996, Section: Business 1.

"Genesis Health Ventures," *Institutional Investor,* July 1994, p. S22.

Jones, John A., "Genesis Health Is Set up to Manage Care for the Elderly," *Investor's Business Daily,* February 12, 1996, p. A33.

——, "Genesis Expands Geriatric Network by Acquiring Meridian," *Investor's Business Daily,* March 28, 1994, p. 40.

Meisol, Patrick, "With Acquisition of Meridian, Genesis Health Nears Goal of Regional Domination," *Baltimore Sun,* October 3, 1993, Business.

Pallarito, Karen, "CFO's Creative Solutions Win Cain Bros. Award," *Modern Healthcare,* September 9, 1996, p. 44.

Vincent, Dale, "McKerley Health Care Chain Sold for $82.5M," *Union Leader,* August 22, 1995, p. A1.

—M. L. Cohen

We'll Take Good Care of You!

Genovese Drug Stores, Inc.

80 Marcus Drive
Melville, New York 11747
U.S.A.
(516) 420-1900
Fax: (516) 845-8487
Web site: http://www.genovese.com

Public Company
Founded: 1924
Employees: 4,700
Sales: $612.3 million (1996)
Stock Exchanges: American
SICs: 5912 Drug Stores and Proprietary Stores

Genovese Drug Stores, Inc. is a major regional drugstore chain, serving the metropolitan New York area. As of September 1996, the company operated 121 super drugstores: 111 in Long Island and New York City, 4 in New Jersey, and 6 in Connecticut. It also operated two specialty stores—a professional photo store and an arts and craft store. The Genovese family owned 60 percent of the company's stock.

Early History: 1924–78

Joseph Genovese opened his first drugstore in 1924, in Astoria, Queens, New York. A 21-year old graduate of the Columbia College of Pharmacy, Genovese implemented a philosophy of taking care of the customer . . . always.

The early years of the company saw the beginning of trends which would continue to effect the drugstore business through the rest of the century. One such trend was competition from stores outside the drug industry. For example, in the late 1930s, R.H. Macy & Company, New York City's giant department store, began wholesaling its private line of 48 drug and cosmetic items to other stores. Unlike the major national brands, whose prices were fixed under fair trade laws, "Macy's Own" brands could be sold for less. At the same time, on the West Coast, the state pharmacy board in California went to court to try to stop

supermarkets and variety chains such as Woolworth's from selling cosmetics, toothpaste, soaps, and other proprietaries. Druggists were faced not only with competition from department stores and groceries, these retailers were offering less expensive products.

Another trend was the discounts on drugs demanded by hospital associations on the West Coast. These associations, which were privately owned or physician-controlled, had contracts with big companies to sell them drugs, usually at a flat rate. The employees of those big companies no longer had to get their prescriptions filled at the drugstore. Instead they could get them cheaper from the company hospital association.

Finally, the industry had to deal with government regulations, including the Food, Drug and Cosmetic Act of 1938, which, in addition to establishing strong consumer protections such as labeling requirements, also placed the cosmetic industry under the aegis of the Food and Drug Administration.

Despite these external influences, the Astoria drugstore flourished, continuing to concentrate on customer service. In addition to operating his business, the elder Genovese served on the board of trustees of the College of Pharmaceutical Sciences of Columbia University for 11 years, and was a director of the National Association of Chain Drug Stores.

In 1950, the founder's eldest son, Joseph Jr., entered the business full time after graduating from Fordham College of Pharmacy and began to expand the company. In 1955 he introduced self-service to the chain, and began buying other small drugstores and opening new locations. Over the next 20 years, under Joseph Jr.'s leadership, the company grew dramatically. That growth was obvious as, beginning in fiscal 1963, the company began achieving record sales year after year.

In 1968, the Genovese family took the company public, with its stocks trading on the American Stock Exchange. In 1974, they merged the subsidiaries created from the various acquisitions into the parent company.

Joseph Jr. died in 1975, and Leonard Genovese, the youngest son, took over the business. When Joseph Sr. died three years later, in 1978, the company had 50 stores in New York, New Jersey, Connecticut, and Massachusetts.

Marketing Innovations: 1980–92

During this period, the company continued the family tradition of customer service and innovative marketing. Genovese Drugs recognized that drugstores lost a lot of their health and beauty business to supermarkets if customers took the coupons they had clipped from the newspaper with them when they shopped for groceries. Although Genovese used coupons heavily, offering them three times as often as other drugstore chains, the company was not loath to experiment. In 1986, Genovese became the first drugstore chain in the U.S. to make free coupons available to customers at the push of a button.

The company did this as part of a test, introducing Promovision Video Displays Corp.'s Coupon Connection in one of their Long Island stores. The 7½ foot high machine operated like a bank's automated teller machine, with a customer inserting a Coupon Connection card into a slot. Advertising messages flashed across the top screen, and the customer could choose from some 32 coupons, making her coupon selection from the bottom screen. The coupons then slid out of a slot like money would in an ATM.

Later that year, Chairman and CEO Leonard Genovese assumed the position of president. During the end of the decade and the beginning of the 1990s, drugstores were a relatively strong segment in a poor economy. *Forbes* suggested, in an October 14, 1991 article, that investors interested in small-cap stocks should consider Genovese. For the year ended January 31, 1991, the company had annual sales of $465 million, a record for the 28th consecutive year. Earnings doubled to 75¢ a share. This was an improvement on the previous year, in which earnings had declined, and set the stage for five consecutive years of record earnings.

Most of the Genovese stores were located in the suburbs and served relatively large areas. In addition to a prescription drug department staffed by registered pharmacists, the stores offered a wide selection of national brand merchandise, many products selling below the manufacturer's suggested retail price. Cus-

tomers could purchase housewares, toys, books, hardware and small appliances, office supplies and paper goods, greeting cards, film, and tobacco goods as well as name and private label vitamins, cosmetics, toiletries, and health supplies. These products accounted for about 68 percent of company sales in fiscal 1992, with prescription drugs representing the remaining 32 percent. The company also operated a division that provided nursing homes with prescriptions and related medical supplies, and a photo-processing facility for developing and printing film for its customers.

Part of the company's success was due to its marketing, particularly of beauty aids and perfumes. For example, stores maintained a cosmetic profile of customers, borrowing the idea from the pharmacy's patient profiles which recorded medications. The cosmetic files kept track of customers' color and product preferences on profile cards. Employees contacted a customer when her favorite items were on sale. In 1992, the company received a FiFi award from the Fragrance Foundation for its leadership in marketing perfumes.

Moving into Manhattan: 1993–95

In a highly competitive industry, Genovese maintained its position by carefully selecting the location of its stores, by its pricing and merchandising efforts, and by providing quality services.

In 1993, the company began to restructure and expand its 101-store operation. Much of its efforts concentrated on improving purchasing and distribution and on renovating existing locations. But the big news that year was the opening, in November, of the first Genovese drugstore in Manhattan. Genovese brought its super drugstore, suburban layout into the city's lower East Side, providing customers with a brightly lit interior and aisles wide enough for shopping carts. Small by Genovese standards, the 7,500-square-foot store was described as "sprawling" by *WWD*. The store, in a residential location, was open 24 hours a day and featured an upscale cosmetic department which took up 8 percent of the store and was staffed by full-time cosmeticians.

Within a year, the company had expanded to 110 drugstores, with each one ringing up an average of $5 million in sales, or $493 per square foot, according to *WWD*. By that measure of productivity, Genovese ranked sixth among drug chains—ahead of CVS, Walgreen's, or Rite Aid. In terms of volume, the company's $570 million in sales in 1994 made Genovese the 18th largest drugstore chain in the U.S.

Prescription drugs accounted for a growing proportion (35 percent) of those sales. But where Genovese was really beating out its competitors was in the sale of beauty products. Makeup, perfume, nail polish, and related merchandise accounted for almost 9 percent of sales, double the industry average. The company prided itself on the wide selection of products and on its reputation as the place to find the latest, hottest brands. "We always want to be first in our market with new items," Allan Patrick, Genovese's executive vice president, told *WWD* in a 1995 article.

Genovese's performance came amid the growth in alternative sources for prescriptions resulting from the managed care movement. Third-party firms, such as health maintenance organizations, hospitals, and mail-order houses, paid 70 percent of all prescription drug bills in 1995, up from 4 percent in 1960. The trend that began with hospital associations on the West Coast in the late 1930s was now a national reality.

As more employers shifted their employees' health coverage to managed care or health maintenance organizations, drugstores were under great pressure. According to an article in *Investor's Business Daily*, "the name of the game is merchandising and cost-efficiency through technology. You have to have the systems and marketing expertise to attract third-party business."

The year 1994 also saw the company move beyond its traditional merchandise with the opening of The Craft Works, an arts and crafts store, in Connecticut. The 12,000-square-foot store offered more than 35,000 items, including picture frames, materials for making jewelry (including over 3,000 types of beads), water colors and artists' materials, knitting equipment, and children's crafts.

During 1995, Genovese continued to expand, opening new stores, including its second in Manhattan, and buying the pharmacy files and inventory of seven independent drugstores. Towards the end of the year the company introduced a redesigned store logo, adding the corporate tag line, "We'll take good care of you," and a small heart to the Genovese name. Signs inside the stores were updated as well, including department-specific names, such as "small wonders," for baby care. "Genovese was looking to up its recognition with consumers," a spokeswoman explained in an article in *Chain Store Age Executive*. "Research showed that the company was perceived as offering good, caring service. But it didn't fare so well when it came to communicating the contemporary, professional pharmacy image that today's shoppers value."

With its new signs, Genovese continued building a strong presence in the metropolitan New York area. By 1995, the company was the number three drugstore chain in New York City, with a 10 percent share of that $2.8 billion market. Its two major competitors, Duane Reade and Pathmark, each controlled about 14 percent of the drugstore sales in the city. On Long Island, which had a drugstore market of $1.1 billion, Genovese controlled 24 percent of the sales, making it the dominant player.

By the end of the fiscal year, the company had 121 super drugstores, and sales had increased 7.4 percent to a record $612.3 million. Unfortunately, heavy snow storms contributed to a poor fourth quarter and lower reimbursement rates from managed care and third party prescription plans put pressure on profits earned from prescriptions. As a result, earnings fell for the first time in six years.

1996 and Beyond

The year began with a tentative settlement of a class-action lawsuit brought by independent pharmacies challenging the pricing practices of 13 pharmaceutical companies. The drug manufacturers gave health maintenance organizations and hospitals big discounts while charging retail drugstores twice as much. The settlement would give the pharmacists some $400 million to divide among themselves.

During the year, Genovese opened more stores, including a third store in Manhattan. Located in an area that was both commercial and residential, the company showed its ability to respond to neighborhood tastes by providing both a large array of school supplies and a one-hour photo-processing laboratory. Building on the success of its arts and craft store Genovese introduced major arts and crafts departments in many of its stores, with more planned for 1997.

Genovese's commitment to the community was acknowledged by New York City Mayor Rudolph Giuliani as the company was honored for its response to the crash of TWA flight 700 that summer. The company's Howard Beach store in Queens shuttled supplies to the relatives of passengers as they awaited word. The company also provided emergency personnel working at the crash site with assorted paper and plastic products and well as sun block and aspirins.

Following several years of consolidation in the drugstore industry, there were rumors in September that J.C. Penney might buy Genovese, and the drugstore chain's stock rose. Penney's had already bought Thrift Drug Stores and had agreed to purchase Fay's, a 272-store drug chain. While nothing came of the rumors, Genovese did sell its nursing home pharmacy division, for approximately $3 million. Genovese appeared to be responding successfully to competitive pressures from non-drugstore chains as well as managed care.

Further Reading

Brookman, Faye, "Genovese Looks to Beauty for an Edge," *WWD*, June 2, 1995, p. 7.
――, "Staying Flexible Helps Genovese Fly," *WWD*, September 6, 1996, p. 10.
――, "The Suburban Approach in Manhattan," *WWD*, November 5, 1993, p. 8.
"Coupon Machine Makes Cents," *Chain Store Age Executive*, February 1986, p. 49.
"Druggists Eye Perils," *Business Week*, July 1, 1939, p. 28.
"Drugs in Supers," *Business Week*, December 7, 1940, p. 33.
"Drug Store Chains Find the Right Medicine," *Investor's Business Daily*, November 25, 1994.
"Genovese Crafts Store," *HFD—The Weekly Home Furnishings Newspaper*, September 5, 1994, p. 6.
"Genovese Drug Stores, Inc.," *New York Times*, September 15, 1986, p. D2.
"Graphic Makeovers Enhance Retail Image," *Chain Store Age Executive with Shopping Center Age*, July 1996, p. 90.
"Independent Druggists May Settle Pricing Suit," *Investor's Business Daily*, January 19, 1996.
Jaffe, Thomas, "Drug Trade," *Forbes*, October 14, 1991, p. 238.
"Joseph Genovese Jr., 46, Head of Drugstore Chain," *New York Times*, December 16, 1975, p. 42.
"Joseph Genovese, Head of Drugstore Chain, 75," *New York Times*, November 28, 1978, p. D19.
"New Drug Act in Full Effect July 1," *Business Week*, June 29, 1940, p. 28.
"Penney's May Gulp Down Genovese," *Business Week*, September 16, 1996, p. 96.
Reynolds, Mike. "Genovese Chain Goes to the Core of the Big Apple," *Drug Topics*, July 19, 1993, p. 53.
"What's a Drug Store?" *Business Week*, October 1, 1938, p. 41.

—Ellen D. Wernick

The Gorman-Rupp Company

305 Bowman St.
P.O. Box 1217
Mansfield, Ohio 44901-1217
U.S.A.
(419) 755-1011
Fax: (419) 755-1233
Web site: http://www.gormanrupp.com

Public Company
Incorporated: April 18, 1934
Employees: 993
Sales: $149.5 million (1995)
Stock Exchanges: American
SICs: 3562 Pumps & Pumping Equipment; 3594 Fluid
     Power Pumps & Motors

The Gorman-Rupp Company ranks among the ten largest pump manufacturers in the United States. Throughout its more than 60 years in the fluids handling industry, Gorman-Rupp has positioned itself as a niche player, developing a particular emphasis on pumps used in the construction industry. Gorman-Rupp's product line ranges from small pumps for soft drink dispensers and medical devices to massive machines capable of moving up to 200,000 gallons of fluid per minute.

Its core operation, the Mansfield Division, generated 58 percent of total corporate revenues via the design, manufacture, and sale of self-priming centrifugal pumps. Acquired in 1988, the Patterson Pump Subsidiary contributed another 31 percent of sales, but this segment's large volume centrifugal pumps were cited as a drag on Gorman-Rupp's profitability in the mid-1990s. The manufacturer's remaining revenues came from three divisions: Gorman-Rupp Industries, IPT, and Ramparts. These business segments produced small specialty pumps, often for original equipment manufacturers. The corporate credo, "to enter a field of pumping service only when able to provide superior products with better performance," codifies its fairly conservative long-term strategy.

Founded During the Great Depression

Gorman-Rupp's roots stretch back well over half a century to 1933 when two engineers, J. C. Gorman and Herbert E. Rupp, pooled $1,500 and started a pump manufacturing business in a barn outside the small town of Mansfield, Ohio. By that time, pumps had long been integral to many businesses. In fact, pumps remained the second most common machine used in industry into the 1990s. Perceiving an opportunity to carve out a profitable niche in this highly fragmented industry, Gorman and Rupp worked diligently to design pumps with particular features for specific tasks.

They established a long-standing corporate reputation for product development early on, launching "the first simplified self-priming centrifugal pump with no valves or orifices" in 1933. In keeping with its name, a centrifugal pump generates drawing pressure by moving liquids (and in some applications gases) in a circular pattern. The "self-priming" part of the name meant that the machine did not need a consistent flow of fluids in order to maintain its pumping capacity. These relatively quiet, rugged, and inexpensive devices are most often used to remove water (known in industry parlance as "dewatering") at intermittently wet construction sites, sewers, and quarries. Self-priming centrifugal pumps formed the core of Gorman-Rupp's product line.

World War II and Postwar Era

Within six years of its creation, the company was generating about $345,000 in annual sales. In the 1940s, Gorman-Rupp developed a solids handling trash pump that featured a removable endplate for easy maintenance. The company would later call it a "bellwether" product, one often imitated by competitors. Fueled in part by wartime contracts with the U.S. Army and Navy, for which the company was awarded an "E" for excellence, Gorman-Rupp sales multiplied to over $2 million by 1949. Manufacturing capacity grew correspondingly, and the company moved from its rural barn to a factory in town during this decade.

Sales continued to mount rapidly in the postwar era, when Gorman-Rupp's close attention to the dewatering needs of the

Company Perspectives:

Holding to a longstanding commitment to innovation, growth, improvement, and product superiority, Gorman-Rupp has seen its position as a leader in the domestic pump market dramatically expand to incorporate the global market as well. Today, this leadership is reflected in the vital role that Gorman-Rupp pumps are playing in municipal, industrial, and petrochemical operations worldwide.

constriction industry paid off. In 1952, the company re-engineered a diaphragm pump for this market. Diaphragm pumps incorporate a flexible, but impenetrable membrane that prevents the material being pumped from coming in contact with the inner workings of the pump and vice versa. They are designed to pump abrasive or uncontaminated substances, and can also tolerate extended dry runs. Gorman-Rupp improved on the basic diaphragm pump design by decreasing the pump's weight and increasing its capacity. The pump manufacturer benefited indirectly from the residential housing boom of the 1950s. Its revenues tripled over the course of the decade, from $2.25 million in 1949 to $7 million by 1959.

Diversification Begins in 1950s, Accelerates in 1960s and 1970s

But company executives realized that they could not rely on a single market—especially one as cyclical as the construction industry—for consistent sales and earnings growth. The seeds of the diversification process were sown in the early 1950s, when the firm established its Gorman-Rupp Industries Division in nearby Bellville, Ohio. Created to meet the needs of original equipment manufacturers (OEMs), Gorman-Rupp Industries made small, specialized pumps used in larger machines like photocopiers, coffee machines, kidney dialysis machines, and photo-processing equipment. This division's emphasis on research and development helped make it the parent company's highest-margin segment by the mid-1990s.

In 1960, the company went international with the construction of a plant in Ontario, Canada. Gorman-Rupp of Canada Limited mirrored the parent company's main plant in Ohio, and its product line grew accordingly.

Gorman-Rupp also began to diversify within the pump category in earnest in the 1960s. It launched new lines of submersible pumps for mining, centrifugal pumps and fiberglass pumping stations for municipal sewage systems, specialty pumps for moving home heating oil and aircraft fuel quickly and safely, as well as pumps for the consumer market (i.e., the "handy pump") and a backpack pump for firefighters. These technological developments and the new markets they opened helped triple Gorman-Rupp's sales for the second consecutive decade, from $7 million in 1959 to $21 million by 1969.

The company continued to penetrate new niches of the pump industry in the 1970s, launching a magnetic drive pump that could be used to move liquid metals. A key development of this

decade was the creation of the Gorman-Rupp International Division, which marketed the entire line of pumps via overseas distributors. This segment's contribution to sales rose from 7 percent in 1980 to about 11 percent in 1995. Gorman-Rupp hoped to further increase its share of global pump sales by emphasizing the petrochemical, municipal, and industrial markets in the late 1990s. Driven by these developments, total corporate sales doubled over the course of the 1970s, exceeding $50 million in 1978 and reaching more than $58 million by 1979. Having gone public during the previous decade, Gorman-Rupp common stock was listed on the American Stock Exchange in the 1970s, where it continued to trade into the 1990s.

Acquisitions Distinguish Late 1970s and Continue in 1980s

A fairly modest industry contraction saw manufacturers of pumps and pumping equipment shrink from 613 in 1977 to 528 in 1987. Gorman-Rupp played a role in this trend, executing three acquisitions during this period. In 1977, the company acquired its Ramparts Division, which manufactured air-driven diaphragm pumps and replacement parts for the chemical industry. These specialized machines were most often used to move highly corrosive and/or viscous liquids like sulfuric acid and hydrochloric acid. Although the Ramparts Division was still only generating one percent of Gorman-Rupp's annual sales 20 years after its acquisition, the parent company considered its high profit margins an important contributor to long-term growth.

Like many manufacturers, United States pump makers faced heavy competition from foreign producers in the 1980s. To combat this problem, Gorman-Rupp acquired the IPT Pumps Division, a manufacturer of economically-priced, portable, and durable pumps for the construction market, in 1986. Although this division also only contributed 1 percent of annual revenues and scant profits, it helped Gorman-Rupp maintain a presence in this competitive industry segment.

Gorman-Rupp made its largest acquisition to date in 1988, when it paid Banner Industries $14.5 million for control of the Patterson Pump Company. Based in Toccoa, Georgia, Patterson manufactured a comprehensive line of large volume centrifugal pumps used for flood control and irrigation as well as fire pumps for automatic sprinkler systems and fire hydrants. Patterson complemented Gorman-Rupp's existing water, sewer, and fire-fighting lines, enabling the company to offer custom-designed, large-scale fluid transport systems to these key markets.

Although Patterson added $24 million to Gorman-Rupp's sales tally, its returns were less than stellar. Treating its newest affiliate as a turnaround situation, Gorman-Rupp pumped an additional $20 million into plant and office renovations over the ensuing eight years. And while Patterson's profitability remained comparatively low into the mid-1990s, Gorman-Rupp was committed to wringing higher margins from this subsidiary.

The 1990s and Beyond

Several key factors have contributed to Gorman-Rupp's six-decade record of growth. The company has long emphasized innovation and product quality. So confident were Gorman and Rupp in the capabilities of their products that they empowered their distributors "to put a Gorman-Rupp contractor's pump on any pumping job, anytime, anywhere, beside any competitor's pump of comparable size." The company guaranteed that its products would move more volume more efficiently and for a longer time. And "if it wasn't the best all-around pump, our distributors would accept the return and pay the user any installation expense incurred."

Gorman-Rupp's reputation for excellent customer service is predicated on its network of knowledgeable distributors and its thorough inventory of new and replacement products. Gorman-Rupp supported its nearly 1,000 distributors in North America with in-depth product and process training. Sales representatives, distributors, engineers, and customers alike could attend corporate educational programs at one of two permanent training centers. The company also outfitted three recreational vehicles as mobile exhibitions for on-the-spot training and demonstrations. And although many industries and companies made the transition to just-in-time inventory in order to cut costs, Gorman-Rupp perceived its reserve as a key element of customer service. As James C. Gorman, CEO and son of the founder, told *Barron's* magazine in 1982, "Some 20 percent to 30 percent of our business is crisis business. They don't buy anything from us until they are up to their noses in water." A prime example of the wisdom of this strategy came in 1989, when Gorman-Rupp was able to provide an estimated 90 percent of the pumps used to clean up after the Exxon Valdez oil spill. In a brief article for *Fortune* magazine in 1990, CEO Gorman crowed that "Our Alaskan distributor called us on Saturday, and at six Sunday evening we had the first DC-8 load of pumps in Anchorage." In addition to its ready supply of new pumps, Gorman-Rupp estimated its trade in replacement parts was at 20 percent to 25 percent of total revenues. This segment was doubtless another vital factor in the company's customer service equation.

Although Gorman-Rupp is a non-union manufacturer, it has cultivated such a good working environment that one industry observer characterized the company as "paternalistic." It launched hospitalization and profit-sharing programs in the mid-1930s, and carefully avoided layoffs in the recessions of the 1970s and 1980s, a policy that may reflect its Depression-era origins. In return for its fair treatment of employees, Gorman-Rupp enjoyed low turnover and a strike-free history. Healthy labor-management relations also helped give Gorman-Rupp one of the industry's highest productivity rates. In 1996,

the company's volume of sales per employee stood at $153,800, having risen from $120,000 in 1991.

A 1996 analysis of Gorman-Rupp by Robert W. Baird & Co., indicated that the company was ripe for an acquisition. But many of the factors that signaled its readiness to acquire—low debt, good cash flow, and a low stock price—also made it a prime takeover target. Takeover seemed an unlikely outcome, however, given that family and insiders owned a controlling interest in the company. Furthermore, in 1996, 72-year-old James C. Gorman drew the lines of corporate succession, ceding the chief executive office to President John A. Walter, 61. It was expected that Gorman's son, Jeffrey S., 44, who was named executive vice-president at that time, would eventually follow in his father's (and grandfather's) footsteps.

Aside from all their other attributes, Gorman-Rupp products have also proven good at pumping profits for shareholders. The company not only chalked up record sales and operating profits in 1996, but also continued its more than twenty consecutive years of annual dividend increases.

Principal Subsidiaries

Gorman-Rupp of Canada, Limited; The Gorman-Rupp International Company; Patterson Pump Company.

Principal Divisions

Mansfield Division; Gorman-Rupp Industries Division; Ramparts Division; IPT Pumps Division.

Further Reading

Autry, Ret, "Gorman-Rupp," *Fortune*, June 18, 1990, p. 93.

Hillstrom, Kevin, *Encyclopedia of American Industries*, Detroit: Gale Research, 1994, pp. 954–957.

Robert W. Baird & Co., Incorporated, "The Gorman-Rupp Company," The Investext Group, August 26, 1996.

Rosenbaum, Michael, "Pumping Profits: Gorman-Rupp Builds Revenues in a Harsh Climate," *Barron's*, January 4, 1982, pp. 44–45.

Sabath, Donald, "Gorman-Rupp Succession in Place," *The Plain Dealer*, May 29, 1996, p. C1.

Talbott, Stephen, "Gorman-Rupp Seeks OK on Egyptian Plant," *The Plain Dealer*, March 13, 1988, p. C6.

—April Dougal Gasbarre

GOTTSCHALKS
We're Your Store!

Gottschalks, Inc.

7 River Park Place East
Fresno, California 37201-1501
U.S.A.
(209) 434-8000
Fax: (209) 434-4806
Web site: http://www.gotts.com

Public Company
Incorporated: 1904
Employees: 5,181
Sales: $401.04 million (fiscal 1995, ended January 1)
Stock Exchanges: New York Pacific
SICs: 5311 Department Stores

Gottschalks, Inc. is the largest California-based independent department store chain, with 35 namesake department stores and 25 Village East women's large-size apparel specialty stores throughout California, Oregon, Washington, and Nevada. It stood in the mid-1990s as one of America's few independent department store chains. The 90-plus-year-old company has survived the difficult retail environment of the West Coast by leaving larger markets to others and concentrating on smaller, less competitive cities and towns. This and other key strategies helped make the chain of specialty shops and full-line department stores the sales leader of virtually all the markets in which it has chosen to compete. Descendants of the founders continued to hold significant stakes in Gottschalks—as well as four board seats—into the mid-1990s.

After chalking up 20 percent average annual sales increases in the late 1980s, Gottschalks slipped into the malaise that gripped much of the retail industry in the early 1990s. Although its sales increased by almost 40 percent from 1990 to 1995, the company recorded net losses in three out of those six years. Gottschalks hoped to regain profitability in the late 1990s by "increasing same store sales, opening new stores in growing markets, and continued cost containment programs."

Turn-of-the-Century Roots

The chain was founded in 1904 by Emil Gottschalk in Fresno, California. Over half a century passed before the company opened its first branch store in 1961. It was around this time that grand-nephew Irving Levy—whose father had helped found the company—took the helm. In an effort to win over teenage baby-boomers, Gottschalks launched Bobbie West, a chain of junior apparel stores, in the late 1960s. Village East shops, which offered large-sized women's clothing, were launched in 1970.

Irving Levy served as president until his death in 1980 at age 86, guiding Gottschalks' growth into a chain of six department stores and over a dozen specialty boutiques with over $80 million in annual sales. That's when Gerald Blum, whose father was a longtime partner of Irving Levy, assumed the presidency for about two years. Blum advanced to vice-chairman and consultant in 1982, making way for Levy's son, Joseph, to claim his birthright.

Following the lead of other independent, family-owned department store chains like Dayton, Ohio's, Elder-Beerman Stores Corporation (in fact, Elder-Beerman CEO Max Gutmann served on Gottschalks' board of directors in the 1990s), Gottschalks formulated a successful strategy for profitable growth in the highly competitive retail industry. The core of the plan was Gottschalks' concentration on smaller markets in California's central valley, markets dubbed "the other California" by company executives. Gottschalks avoided ruthlessly competitive cities like Los Angeles and San Francisco, which were dominated by national department store chains. It opted instead for overlooked towns with populations of 20,000 to 60,000 people—areas too small to support larger, traditional-sized department stores—and targeted middle-income households. This tactic kept Gottschalks' overhead low by allowing it to build smaller (80,000 to 110,000 square foot), single-level stores with lower real estate costs and cheaper labor. More often than not, it also made Gottschalks "the only game in town," with virtually no competition from other department stores. As one of the state's only major retailers willing to locate in smaller cities and towns, the chain was sought out by developers and

Company Perspectives:

Gottschalks strives to be the home town store in each market and is dedicated to continually providing total customer satisfaction while offering a broad variety of high-quality brand-name merchandise at moderate, competitive prices.

often able to demand ideal anchor locations in the new medium-sized malls and shopping centers that sprang up throughout the 1970s and 1980s.

Moreover, unlike many of its small-town competitors in the retail segment, Gottschalks was often an area's only source of nationally-branded soft goods. In the early 1990s, brand name products generated about 80 percent of total sales, with the remainder being private label or non-branded goods. Prominent brand names included Liz Claiborne, Calvin Klein, Levi Strauss, and Sony. High-end cosmetics from Estée Lauder, Clinique, and Lancome were particularly profitable, ranking as the company's largest-selling product group. Gottschalks' strong customer service quotient has been compared to that of Seattle's Nordstrom. By concentrating on California's inland markets, Gottschalks avoided the dramatic ups and downs endemic to West Coast cities.

Although the chain was relatively small, it was not technologically backwards. In fact, Gottschalks executives often found themselves at the front of the pack in the race to install the most modern equipment. *Chain Store Age Executive's* Susan Warner attributed the chain's progressivism to its private status, writing that "There's no doubt that as an independently held company, Gottschalks enjoys certain freedoms to experiment with more entrepreneurial concepts that often elude publicly held companies that must constantly justify actions to shareholders."

Gottschalks was Fresno's premier retailer to install an air conditioner, and was among the first retailers in the area to accept bank credit cards. According to a 1977 *Chain Store Age Executive* article, in 1976 Gottschalks became America's first department store to totally automate sales transactions. The company installed electronic point-of-sale (POS) "wands" that read bar codes and store credit cards. This technology helped increase efficiency, reduce errors, and keep inventory and customer billing up-to-date. A 1991 profile in *Barron's* magazine noted that Gottschalks' computer information system was capable of hourly monitoring of sales and inventory, giving Gottschalks one of the industry's highest turnover rates. Joe Levy boasted in a 1988 *WWD* article that, "With our computer system we can plunk a new store on the moon if we want."

Mid-1980s IPO Foreshadows Growth

Gottschalks went public in 1986, selling about fifty percent of its equity on the New York Stock Exchange. The proceeds were used to step up the pace of new store acquisition and construction, helping to make Gottschalks California's fastest-growing department store chain in the late 1980s. The number

of Gottschalks units doubled from nine in 1985 to 18 in 1988 and annual revenues increased from $112 million to $196 million in the process. Part of this growth came via the acquisition of two small family-run department store chains in 1987 and 1988. Totaling $11 million, the purchases of the privately-held Malcolm Brock and Samuel Leask & Sons chains added five stores. The chain also refined its specialty store offerings, converting its Bobbie West juniors stores into Petites West boutiques mid-decade in order to attract smaller-sized Asian and Latin women.

This period did not conclude without problems, however. In 1988, Gottschalks decided to close its only money-losing location, ironically the flagship store in downtown Fresno. That October, a devastating earthquake caused "irreparable damage" to a Santa Cruz store, forcing its closure as well. Notwithstanding these hurdles, Gottschalks fared "much better than other companies" in the late 1980s, according to Edward Johnson of Johnson Redbook Service (New York).

Losses Mount in 1990s

Buoyed by almost a decade of successful expansion, in 1990 Joe Levy predicted that Gottschalks would add at least 20 new markets and reach $1 billion in annual sales by 1997. While sticking to its essential strategy, Gottschalks made its first foray outside its home state in 1992, when it opened stores in Washington and Oregon. The company entered the Nevada market in 1995.

But like many of its retail industry rivals, Gottschalks succumbed to internal and external pressures in the early 1990s. A 1992 investigation by the Internal Revenue Service charged that chief financial officer Robert E. Lawson and controller Jack Farnesi had falsified financial records in order to evade federal taxes in the mid-1980s. The company fired the two executives and paid a $1.5 million settlement to the IRS in July 1992. Gottschalks found itself back in court in 1994, when it settled two shareholder lawsuits for a total of $3.5 million.

These issues only exacerbated competitive and economic difficulties that put the squeeze on Gottschalks earnings in the early 1990s. In a 1994 interview with *Daily News Record's* Alexandra Nelson, CEO Joe Levy cited "drought, [military] base closures, cutbacks in aerospace and electronics, and the government cutting back pensions" as fundamental causes of his company's malaise.

Although Gottschalks' sales increased from $287 million in 1990 to over $400 million in 1995, it had a cumulative net loss over those six fiscal years of $4.9 million. Gottschalks planned to employ four basic strategies in an effort to revisit the "glory days" of the 1980s. The company sought improvements in year-over-year store performance, focusing especially on two underperforming stores. Gottschalks also hoped to lessen its overhead through layoffs at administrative levels; outsourcing; contract renegotiations; and paring of some optional expenses. The company planned to increase income by upping finance and service charges on its store credit card and to enhance cash flow by curtailing capital outlays. In fact, Gottschalks suspended previously-laid plans to open three new department stores in 1996, choosing instead to apply those funds to operations.

Whether these measures would enable Gottschalks to resume consistent profitability in the waning years of the 1990s remained to be seen, but one observer voiced doubts. Writing for *Financial World* in 1995, analyst Ed Dravo counseled investors to sell Gottschalks stock, citing competition from category-killer Wal-Mart and middle class wage erosion.

Principal Subsidiaries

Gottschalks Credit Receivables Corp.; Gottschalks Credit Card Master Trust.

Further Reading

Byrne, Harlan S., "Gottschalks Inc.: It Thrives As a Brand-Name Retailer in California's Growth Area," *Barron's*, November 4, 1991, pp. 47–48.

Davey, Tom, "Gottschalks Eagerly Circles Crippled Weinstock's," *The Business Journal Serving Greater Sacramento*, February 18, 1991, p. 11.

Dravo, Ed, "Discount Retail Stocks," *Financial World*, September 12, 1995, p. 77.

Ginsberg, Steve, "Gottschalks: Mining California's Boondocks," *WWD*, April 2, 1990, pp. 6–7.

"Gottschalks CEO a Target of Federal Criminal Probe," *WWD*, December 1, 1992, p. 9.

"Gottschalks Heads to Folsom, Rocklin," *The Business Journal Serving Greater Sacramento*, April 29, 1991, pp. 1–2.

"Gottschalks: New Image for an Old Retailer," *Chain Store Age Executive*, August 1987, pp. 60–62.

"Gottschalks Supplying Data from '85 Requested By IRS," *WWD*, March 9, 1992, p. 15.

"Gottschalks to End Fresno Retail Operation," *Daily News Record*, September 13, 1988, p. 5.

Healea, Tim, "Fickle California Teens Dictate Whether Fashions Fly or Flop," *Discount Store News*, April 3, 1995, pp. 21–22.

Pomice, Eva, "Stores for the 1990s," *U.S. News & World Report*, May 13, 1991, pp. 51–53.

"Two Former Execs of Gottschalks Indicted," *Daily News Record*, June 9, 1992, p. 11.

Walsh, James, "Gottschalks: Looking for Holiday Cheer," *California Business*, October 1991, p. 90.

Warner, Susan, "Does Gottschalks Tell Macy?" *Chain Store Age Executive*, October 1981, pp. 54–58.

"Why Small Chain Uses Wands," *Chain Store Age Executive*, February 1977, p. 23.

Wilner, Rich, "Gottschalks Settles Two Lawsuits, Will Take $3.5M Charge in Period," *Daily News Record*, August 30, 1994, p. 10.

—April Dougal Gasbarre

Grow Biz International, Inc.

4200 Dahlberg Drive
Minneapolis, Minnesota 55422-4837
U.S.A.
(612) 520-8500
Fax: (612) 520-8410
Web site: http://www.growbiz.com

Public Company
Incorporated: 1988 as Play It Again Sports Franchise
   Corp.
Employees: 237
Sales: $100.2 million (1995)
Stock Exchanges: NASDAQ
SICs: 6794 Patent Owners and Lessors

Grow Biz International, Inc. pioneered what the company called the "ultra-high-value" retailing niche. High quality used products are sold alongside new goods in a traditional retail store format. The rapidly growing company began with Play It Again Sports, which was ranked among the largest sporting-goods chains in the United States in 1996. Its other four franchised businesses—all of which buy, sell, trade, and consign used and new merchandise—are: Once Upon A Child, Computer Renaissance, Music Go Round, and Disc Go Round.

Martha Morris was inspired to develop the Play It Again Sports concept in 1983 when she had trouble reselling a nearly new $200 backpack. She borrowed $15,000 from a friend's parents, and the two women started a used sporting equipment store in a vacated tombstone shop near a Minneapolis cemetery. Morris bought out her friend within a few months. Boosted by local television coverage she sold about $120,000 of used equipment during her first year of business. Initially she sold everything on consignment, but she later began buying used equipment outright and selling new goods, such as sales representative samples, last year's models, and retailers' out-of-season equipment.

Morris Meets Dahlberg and Olson, 1988

Financial success and customer feedback told Morris the idea could work elsewhere, so in mid-1988 she went to a franchise development consulting firm for help. K. Jeffrey Dahlberg and Ronald G. Olson, the owners of Franchise Business Systems, Inc. (FBS), had their doubts at first about the potential for a used sporting goods chain. In a 1994 *Fortune* magazine article Olson said, "Her store looked like a garage sale with hours." But, the numbers showed them she was also pulling in a lot of business, so FBS took her on as a client.

Dick Youngblood wrote in March 1992, "Her instinct's were bull's-eye accurate. Despite limited capital, the business grew in 18 months to 19 franchise operations in six states, taking 1989 revenues to more than $800,000 including sales at the two stores Morris owned then, plus the franchise and royalty fees. Sales of the franchised stores alone totaled $1.3 million." Dahlberg and Olson used their combined expertise to polish the entrepreneurial nugget into a gemstone.

Dahlberg acquired his franchising know-how in his family-run hearing-aid business. He began developing the Miracle Ear Centers network when he was named president of Dahlberg, Inc. in 1983. But the combination of uneven earnings and franchise start-up costs of $10–15 million caused friction with his father and a power struggle with a group of California investment firms that held 20 percent of the company stock. In 1986, only a few months after being named CEO of Dahlberg, Inc., he left the company.

A friend introduced Dahlberg to Olson, who had 20 years of retail experience, both with companies such as Dayton Hudson Corporation and on his own. They formed FBS in 1986 as a franchise development, marketing, and investment firm. Among the franchise systems they helped build were a 250-store eye care chain and a 100-store dry cleaning chain. Olson was left to run the day-to-day business of the consulting firm, when Dahlberg reconciled with his father and returned to lead the hearing-aid business in 1988.

Company Perspectives:

Grow Biz International, Inc. develops and franchises value oriented concepts for stores that buy, sell, trade and consign used and new merchandise. Each concept emphasizes consumer value by offering quality used merchandise at substantial savings from the price of new merchandise and by purchasing customers' used goods that have been outgrown or are no longer used. New merchandise is offered to supplement the selection of used goods. The Company franchises its retail concepts nationwide and supports the system with a comprehensive package of centralized services.

1990: Play It Again Sports

In 1990, Dahlberg and Olson bought the franchising operation of Play It Again Sports for more than $1 million plus five years of royalty payments. Dahlberg became chairman and Olson served as president and CEO of the company. The next year, Morris decided to sell them her three retail stores as well, but she signed on as a consultant. By the end of 1991, 134 Play It Again Sports franchise stores were open in 41 states and Canada.

In January 1992, Dahlberg and Olson purchased Sports Traders, Inc., an independent wholesaler owned by Jim Van Buskirk, an early owner of Play It Again Sports. Van Buskirk acquired a 50 percent interest in the first Morris store in 1986, but the next year he left to develop his own Play It Again Sports stores. The wholesale business he started supplied both of his and Morris's stores with new goods to supplement the selection of used sporting equipment purchased from the public. As part of the purchase agreement, Van Buskirk's Play It Again Sports stores continued to operate separately from the growing franchise system.

Play It Again Sports franchises were being sold at a rapid pace. Dahlberg and Olson were able to draw from a pool of middle managers displaced by corporate downsizing. The men believed the Play It Again Sports concept could be translated into other retail areas and began acquiring successfully established businesses in the used goods market. In November 1992, Dahlberg and Olson purchased franchising and royalty rights from Once Upon A Child, Inc., a Columbus, Ohio-based, 22-store chain selling children's clothing, furniture, and toys.

Dahlberg resigned as president and CEO of Dahlberg, Inc. at the end of 1992 in order to devote himself full time to the expanding Play It Again Sports business. Dahlberg, Inc.—sales and earnings boosted by the franchise system Dahlberg built—was sold to Bausch & Lomb in 1993 for $138 million.

Name Changed to Grow Biz, 1993

In February 1993, Olson and Dahlberg opened the first corporate-owned Once Upon A Child store. All of their 16 Twin Cities franchises were sold before mid-year. Also in 1993, the company purchased assets of Hi Tech Consignments, a musical instrument and audio equipment retailer (renamed Music Go

Round) and Computer Renaissance, Inc., a retailer of close-out and used computers. In recognition of the changes, Play It Again Sports Franchise Corp. was renamed Grow Biz International, Inc.

In August 1993, an initial public offering (IPO) was announced: 1.6 million common shares at $10 per share. The Grow Biz stock price jumped to $15 per share during the first trading day. The company raised about $16.7 million from the IPO. Revenues for 1993 increased 89 percent over the previous year to $51.8 million. By the end of the year 490 stores were open in the U.S. and Canada; eight of those stores were owned by the corporation. An additional 282 franchises had been awarded for future opening.

Gillian Judge wrote in 1993, ''The company's recent rapid growth hasn't been without repercussions, and some of the newest franchisees of Once Upon A Child shops grumble that the system has some kinks to work out before it runs as well as Play It Again Sports.'' In order to bolster franchise support Grow Biz began to decentralize operations. During 1994 the company began individualizing concept support and leadership.

Grow Biz's 1994 revenues grew to $83.6 million; net income was $1.4 million, a 300 percent increase over the previous year. The first Canadian Once Upon A Child store was among the record 243 Grow Biz stores opened in 1994. And the company added a fifth business concept that year—compact disc stores. Grow Biz purchased assets, franchising, and royalty rights of CDX Audio Development, Inc., of Green Bay, Wisconsin, which operated 43 CD Exchange stores.

In 1994 the company topped both *Fortune* and *Inc.* magazines' lists of the fastest-growing American public companies. According to *Fortune*, Grow Biz had experienced an annual growth rate of 285 percent in terms of total revenues over the past five years. In an *Investor's Business Daily* article by Claire Mencke, Olson pointed out that initially the company's rapid growth was unexpected. ''But it happened that we brought together a lot of trends: value pricing starting with the used product, the trend in recycling, and the availability of a lot of strip-shopping center real estate.''

Despite the acclaim, 1994 also had its bleaker moments. Grow Biz stock price fell by 15.7 percent in October when lower-than-expected third quarter earnings were announced. According to an October 22, 1994, *Star Tribune* article, the earnings' setback was caused by a reduction in the projected number of store openings for the year, due to a tight strip-mall real estate market, and losses related to foreign investments.

The company had begun to franchise Play It Again Sports stores internationally in 1991. In 1993, Grow Biz entered into joint venture agreements to franchise stores in Europe and Mexico. But toward year-end 1994, Grow Biz withdrew from the Mexican market, closing both of its corporate-owned stores. The company also suffered losses in its corporate-owned German venture, but the franchised stores there continued to operate.

In a 1995 article, Lee Schafer noted that the Play It Again Sports franchises were moneymakers for their owners: a situation that was atypical of the franchise environment at the time. But Schafer pointed out that analysts had some reservations about the other concepts. The computer stores faced uncertainty related to rapidly changing technology, the strength of franchisees among the kids clothes and toys concept was being questioned, and the disc businesses faced stiff competition from new disc sellers. Olson disputed this, and said in the same article that Grow Biz was "concentrating on becoming operationally strong" in all five concept areas.

Grow Biz provided franchisees support and assistance in the following areas: advertising and marketing; centralized buying and warehouse services; point-of-sale computerized information systems; management training; store opening assistance; and periodic field support visits. The franchisees were generally required to comply with guidelines regarding store design, the use of television advertising focusing on the buy/sell concept, and standardized merchandize purchasing processes. An initial franchise fee cost $20,000. Franchisees also paid an annual royalty of three to five percent of gross revenues.

Grow Biz more than doubled the size of its distribution facilities in 1995 and consolidated operations at its headquarters. Revenues for 1995 topped $100 million, while net income climbed 47 percent to $2.0 million. Royalty revenue jumped 51 percent to $11.6 million. By year-end 1995, a total of 1,311 franchises had been awarded: 965 stores were open including 57 stores in Canada, eight in Europe, and one in Australia.

Early in 1995, all the Grow Biz concepts except Music Go Round were ranked first in their categories in *Entrepreneur Magazine's* Annual Franchise 500. Music Go Round, the smallest of the five Grow Biz concepts with 11 U.S. stores in operation, generated $4 million in revenues in 1995. Customers ranged from parents seeking a place to buy or sell musical instruments for their children to professional musicians upgrading their equipment.

Among Computer Renaissance's best customers were first-time computer buyers and sellers and small business owners. The company also purchased used computers from corporations upgrading their systems and from liquidators. Only about 20 percent of store inventory was new. Unlike the other Grow Biz concepts which typically purchased used goods ready for resale, the corporation refurbished used computers and provided franchise operations with technical assistance. Revenues for the 64 U.S. and Canadian stores in operation in 1995 were $23 million.

Compact disc industry sales grew by 33.6 percent in 1994, according to company figures. With Disc Go Round, Grow Biz was positioning itself to capitalize on the strength of the relatively new industry plus the growing CD-Rom market. Disc Go Round 1995 revenues were $17 million; all 99 stores in operation were in the U.S. and Canada. The typical franchisee and customer were younger than those of the other Grow Biz concepts.

Once Upon A Child stores targeted parents with children under 12 years of age. "Gently-used" items—sold for ⅓ to ½ of the new retail price—made up about 80 percent of the Once Upon A Child product mix in 1995; the 164 stores open that year generated $37 million in sales. In contrast, Play It Again Sports had 674 stores in operation in 1995 and generated $255 million in revenues.

Future Possibilities

Grow Biz opened its 1,000th retail store in 1996 and was again included on *Inc.*'s fastest-growing companies list. Stagnant buying power had helped drive the early success of Grow Biz: consumers, especially families with children, were looking for ways to stretch their dollar. But, according to Susan Reda writing for *Store* magazine, economists disagreed about the long-term economic outlook for average Americans.

Grow Biz concepts vied for business with retail stores selling new goods, on one end of the spectrum, to resale, thrift, consignment shops, garage, and rummage sales, on the other. Olson said in the 1996 article by Reda that Grow Biz "raised the bar in terms of consumers' expectations" of used goods. He went on to say, "There's no longer a stigma attached to buying used items."

Grow Biz's success could propel more franchisers to develop competing national used product chains, but the company is banking on its growing name recognition to help it continue to draw consumers to buy and sell merchandise and potential franchisees to choose their concepts over other options.

Further Reading

Apgar, Sally, "Play It Again Owner Buys CD Exchange Company," *Star Tribune* (Minneapolis), July 6, 1994, p. 3D.

Beran, George, "Retail Renegade," *St. Paul Pioneer Press,* January 16, 1994.

DePass, Dee, "Inc. Magazine Selects Grow Biz International As Fastest Growing Small Corporation In Nation," *Star Tribune* (Minneapolis), April 29, 1994, p. 1D.

Iverson, Doug, "Dain Analyst Predicts Growth for Grow Biz," *St. Paul Pioneer Press,* October 11, 1993.

Jossi, Frank, "Inside Small Business," *Minneapolis/St. Paul CityBusiness,* August 19, 1994, p. 13.

Judge, Gillian, "Play It Again," *Twin Cities Business Monthly,* December 1993, pp. 54–58.

Kaeter, Margaret, "Trash for Cash," *Twin Cities Business Monthly,* March 1996, pp. 44–48.

Marcotty, Josephine, "Franchise By Franchise, He's Built His Career," *Star Tribune* (Minneapolis), January 17, 1994.

——, "Jeffrey Dahlberg Resigns Positions at Dahlberg to Devote Full Attention to Play It Again Sports," *Star Tribune* (Minneapolis), December 18, 1992, p. 1D.

——, "Play It Again Sports Franchise Corp. Discussing Public Stock Offering in '93," *Star Tribune* (Minneapolis), May 6, 1993, p. 1D.

McCartney, Jim, "Media Replay Opens Store in Uptown, Minneapolis, Minnesota," *St. Paul Pioneer Press,* December 29, 1994.

——, "Play It Again Sports Franchiser Expands," *St. Paul Pioneer Press,* May 6, 1993.

Mencke, Claire, "Mining an Untapped Market for Used Goods," *Investor's Business Daily,* September 19, 1994.

Pokela, Barbara, "A Used Ski Is Still a Ski That Can Be Sold at Play It Again Sports," *Star Tribune* (Minneapolis), September 15, 1986, p. 8M.

Ratliff, Duke, "Grow Biz: A Recycling Retailer," *Discount Merchandiser,* May 1996, pp. 92–96.

Reda, Susan, "Beyond Discounting," *Stores,* May 1996, pp. 24–26.

Reichard, Kevin, "Used Equipment Has New Life at Computer Renaissance," *Minneapolis/St. Paul CityBusiness,* January 21, 1994, p. 13.

Schafer, Lee, "As the Cookie Crumbles . . . ," *Corporate Report Minnesota,* April 1995, pp. 39–40.

Serwer, Andrew E., "Lessons from America's Fastest-Growing Companies," *Fortune,* August 8, 1994, pp. 42–45.

Singer, Leah, "A Great Vintage," *Success*, June 1994, p. 24.

Steinberg, Susan, "Franchisers of the Future," *Success*, November 1996, p. 92.

Warshaw, Michael, editor, "Renegades," *Success*, January/February 1996, p. 32.

Waters, Jennifer, "Grow Biz to Expand into New Campus," *Minneapolis/St. Paul CityBusiness*, June 2, 1995, p. 6.

Youngblood, Dick, "He Proved California Investors Wrong—And Then Some," *Star Tribune* (Minneapolis), June 29, 1992, p. 2D.

——, "Making the Right Moves Pays Off," *Star Tribune* (Minneapolis), March 8, 1992, p. 2D.

——, "The Play It Again Sports Franchisers Plan to Sell Idea Again and Again . . . " *Star Tribune* (Minneapolis), September 23, 1992, p. 2D.

——, "Jeff Dahlberg Finds That There's No Biz Like Grow Biz," *Star Tribune* (Minneapolis), May 2, 1994, p. 2D.

——, "Seven Twin Cites Firms on Fast-Grower List, *Star Tribune* (Minneapolis), May 3, 1996, p. 3D.

"Shares of Grow Biz International Fall 15.7% After It Reports Lower-Than-Expected Earnings," *Star Tribune* (Minneapolis), October 22, 1994.

—Kathleen Peippo

Grupo Televisa, S.A.

Avenida Chapultepec, 28
06724 Mexico, D.F.
Mexico
52-5-709-33-33
Fax: 52-5-709-04-48
Web site: http://www.televisa.com

Public Company
Incorporated: 1972
Employees: 20,700
Sales: US$1.15 billion (1995)
Stock Exchanges: Mexico City New York London
SICs: 6719 Holding Companies, Not Elsewhere
    Classified; 4832 Radio Broadcasting Stations; 4833
    Television Broadcasting Stations; 2711 Newspapers;
    7812 Motion Picture & Video Production

Grupo Televisa, S.A. has a near-lock on Mexico's popular culture. The company's four Mexican television networks broadcast to more than 300 Mexican television stations, of which Televisa owns more than 240, and reach more than 90 percent of that country's population—for an 85 percent share of Mexico's television viewing audience. But Televisa's reach extends far beyond its home country. The company produces more than 50,000 hours each year of its wildly popular *telenovelas*, entertainment, news, and sports, reaching more than 200 countries, making Televisa the world's largest Spanish-language broadcaster. Televisa's print arm, Editorial Televisa, is the world's largest Spanish-language publisher, with more than 40 magazine titles reaching 17 countries. Televisa's 17 AM and FM radio stations reach more than half of Mexico's population. The company also owns three of Mexico's largest recording companies, the Mexico City-based Cablevision cable television system, film production studios, two professional soccer teams (and the sports arena in which they play); Televisa also offers paging and other services. In the United States, Televisa owns 25 percent of Univision, the country's Spanish-language network. The company also controls some 40 percent of the hugely successful PanAmSat satellite service, which

carries Televisa's direct-to-home satellite television service (a joint-venture with Rupert Murdoch's News Corp., Globo, and Tele-Communications, Inc.). Since late 1996, Televisa has been looking to sell its interest in PanAmSat, which merged with Hughes Communications. In addition, the company has been negotiating a joint-venture with Spain's Television Espanola to launch a DTH satellite service in that country.

Televisa has had its share of difficulties during the Mexican economic crisis of the mid-1990s. The devaluation of the peso has cut heavily into the company's revenues and forced Televisa to undergo a restructuring that has seen it eliminate some of its operations, including part of its cable television interests and a string of "talent" schools with which it had nurtured actors and recording artists for its television and music productions. In response, the company has gone public and achieved full listing on the New York Stock Exchange, and is working to shift its revenues from the peso to the dollar. Long criticized for its intimate relationship with Mexico's ruling PRI party, as well as for its advertising policies, Televisa is facing new challenges to its dominance at home. The privatization of the Mexican economy has reached television, giving rise to Televisa's first serious competitor, Azteca, which has been making strong inroads on the company's share of both the viewing audience and advertising revenues. Televisa's attempts at producing English-language programs has so far proved less than successful; also, in 1996, the company's launch of its DTH service was delayed when a satellite exploded on launching. Televisa is controlled by Emilio Azcarraga Milmo, also known as "El Tigre," (the tiger), who is said to be one of the most powerful—and most secretive—men in Mexico; at the beginning of 1997, Azcarraga, who suffered a heart attack in the early 1980s, took a medical leave of absence. But the Azcarraga family retains control of its multimedia empire, in the form of son Emilio Azcarraga Jean, who already serves as executive vice president and chief operating officer.

Pioneering Mexico's Communications Since the 1920s

The Azcarraga family's dominance of Mexico's airways coincided with the rise to power of the country's ruling Institutional Revolutionary Party (PRI). In the 1920s, Emilio Azcarraga Vidauretta (El Tigre's father) opened one of that country's first radio stations. Azcarraga's strong support of PRI's policies helped him expand his radio network, Radio Programas de Mexico, nationwide by the 1930s. In the 1940s, Azcarraga expanded into films, building the Churubusco Studios into a dominant force in the Mexican film industry. At the end of World War II, Radio Programas de Mexico sealed its lock on the country's radio waves when it absorbed the Mexican radio operations of NBC and CBS.

Television was first transmitted in Mexico in 1942. In 1946, Azcarraga began plans to enter this medium as well, forming Television Asociada, a group of Mexican radio magnates that sought to persuade the government to hand over the television industry to them as well. Azcarraga was not the first to win a television concession from the government, however. That went to *Novedades* publisher Romulo O'Farrill, who formed Television de Mexico, S.A. Azcarraga's move into television came only in 1951, when he formed Televimex, S.A., and won the concession to form the country's second television network. President Miguel Aleman Valdes awarded the third television concession to his own family. The Azcarragas, Alemans, and O'Farrills soon merged their stations into a single network, called Telesistema Mexico. The families retained individual licenses, however, avoiding charges that they were building a monopoly.

Telesistema went international by the early 1960s, forming Teleprogramas Acapulco, which quickly came to dominate much of the Latin American television market. The company also eyed the growing Spanish-language market in the United States. In 1961, the company backed Rene Anselmo in setting up Spanish International Communications Corp. (SICC) and buying KWEX of San Antonio, Texas. Anselmo, born in Massachusetts and a graduate of the University of Chicago (where he helped form the famous Second City improvisational troupe), had worked for Azcarraga since the 1950s. Telesistema supplied SICC with 20 percent of its financing—the legal limit on foreign control of a television station—and all of its programming. The somewhat murky relationship between Telesistema and SICC would eventually lead to a conflict with the Federal Communications Commission. In the meantime, SICC, and its network Spanish International Network (later the SIN Television Network) almost singlehandedly established Spanish-language television in the United States.

Telesistema's growing control of Mexican television faced only minimal interference from the government. In response to public complaints, the government attempted in 1968 to place a 25 percent tax on radio and television broadcasters. When the powerful group of broadcasters protested—in a country where a majority of the population was illiterate, information was gained primarily through radio and television; this gave broadcasters a great deal of power in affecting public opinion, particularly at election time—the tax was quickly abandoned. In its place, broadcasters agreed to give the government 12.5 percent of each station's air time. In 1972, Telesistema achieved complete dominance of the Mexican television market when it merged with Television Independiente de Mexico.

Renamed Grupo Televisa, the company passed into the hands of the second generations of its founding families. But it

was the Azcarraga family, in the form of son Emilio Azcarraga Milmo, that eventually gained complete control of the company. During the 1970s, the company firmly established its hegemony over Mexico's entertainment industry as well. With holdings in television, radio, film, and the recording industry, Televisa was able to achieve synergies that others could not—if, indeed, Televisa would have allowed that: actors and other performers could find themselves blacklisted from Televisa's stations if they performed for one of the government-run stations; advertisers faced a similar fate. Meanwhile, inside the company, Televisa had developed its own "star-making" system, complete with training schools. Apart from its near-monopoly of Mexico's airwaves, much of the company's success with its viewership—which reached more than a 90 percent market share in Mexico—was built around the company's answer to the soap opera, the *telenovela*. These sentimental, melodramatic programs, which the company churned out in what it would proudly refer to as a factory-like assembly line process, proved wildly successful, not merely in Mexico, but throughout the world. Televisa's programming extended far beyond the Spanish-speaking world; dubbed and subtitled versions of its programs became successes in Western and Eastern Europe, Africa, India, and even China. Another fixed part of Televisa's programming offerings were lavish variety-type shows. In 1970, the company's Teleprogrammas Acapulco arm, which had been generating its news reporting from a variety of sources, including the liberal media, launched its own news program, called 24 Horas, which reflected not only Televisa's staunch support of PRI, but also an arch-conservative, anticommunist viewpoint of Latin America during this turbulent political era. The program became the primary news program available in Spanish-language markets under Televisa's control, including the United States.

Challenged in the 1980s

At the start of the 1980s, Televisa faced a threat to its preeminence. President Jose Lopez Portillo had been moving to nationalize Mexico's economy, including the country's banking industry. But Lopez, under pressure to break up Televisa's monopoly, backed down from nationalizing the television industry. In return, Azcarraga reorganized the company, breaking it up into what were, on the surface, independent companies. Included among the tangle of companies was Televisa's relationship with SICC and the SIN network, which brought the company into conflict with the FCC.

By then SIN, which was 75 percent owned by Televisa (the limits on foreign ownership did not extend to television networks), had captured more than 75 percent of the U.S. Spanish-language television market. The SIN network, through SICC, included five owned-and-operated stations; however, SIN and Televisa provided all of the programming for 33 of the country's 35 all-Spanish stations, and 168 part-time Spanish stations. SICC also owned a string of Spanish-language radio stations. The U.S. company was one of the first to use the new satellite transmission technology, forming the Galavision cable network. At the beginning of the 1980s, the Spanish Radio Broadcasters Association, made up of SICC radio competitors, including one of Anselmo's former partners in SICC and SIN, asked the FCC to review the legality of SICC's ownership structure. If the FCC found that SICC exceeded the limits on foreign control, the company would have been stripped of its television stations—and much of its income-producing revenue.

Azcarraga and Anselmo, who owned 25 percent of SIN and 24 percent of SICC, fought to retain SICC's television stations. But the FCC found that Azcarraga and Televisa's de facto control of SICC exceeded the 20 percent limit and ruled that the company would lose its broadcast licenses for its five stations. Anselmo wanted to appeal the decision; however, Azcarraga decided to sell. The FCC agreed to allow the stations to keep their licenses as long as they were sold. The chain of stations was sold to Hallmark Cards Corp. for $300 million in 1987. Azcarraga reorganized SIN as Univision; under terms of the SICC sale, Hallmark was committed to purchasing all of the station's programming from Univision. The following year, Hallmark purchased Univision from Azcarraga for another $300 million. Televisa, however, continued to provide a large part of Univision's programming. Anselmo, meanwhile, had left the company, and began preparations to launch a new company, PanAmSat.

Back in Mexico, Televisa was also receiving flak for its advertising policies. For most of the decade, the company had been selling a majority of advertising space under a so-called "French Plan" (named after a company in-joke). The French plan allowed advertisers to pay for the year's advertising in advance; in return for the advance payment, advertisers received three commercials for the price of one. About 75 percent of Televisa's advertisers fell under the French plan. Smaller advertisers complained that the costs of purchasing a year's advertising in advance was too expensive; buying advertising outside of the French plan also raised the costs of advertising time. Simultaneously, advertisers were limited to Televisa, facing possible blacklisting if they advertised elsewhere.

Televisa was also expanding into new areas. In 1985, it launched its own videocassette distribution arm, Video Visa. In 1989, the company launched the *National*, an English-language daily sports newspaper for the U.S. market. But cracks were beginning to appear in the walls of Televisa's fortress. A similar attempt to launch a Spanish-language sports daily in Mexico had failed. In 1987, the company's radio revenues were dropping, forcing the company to sell off some of its radio stations and lay off some 1,500 employees. Then the *National* proved to be a disaster, losing some $130 million over 18 months and dragging Televisa into the red. On revenues of US$571 million in 1989, the company lost US$25 million. The following year, the company continued to bleed badly, posting a US$163 million loss for the year.

Reorganized and Looking Overseas in the 1990s

A 100 percent increase in Televisa's advertising rates helped bring the company back to profitability. But in order to fuel real growth in the company, Televisa needed to expand more aggressively into the international arena. The company reorganized as a public holding company, while shedding Video Visa and shutting down the *National* in 1991. The company went public in December 1991, selling 20 percent of the company and raising US$807 million. With that money, Televisa went on an international buying spree. The company joined an investor's

group in purchasing Univision from Hallmark; Televisa's stake in the dominant U.S. Spanish-language broadcaster was 25 percent. The $50 million purchase also gained the company a 25-year agreement to provide Univision's programming. Next, the company bought up 49 percent of the only private television network in Chile, then paid $17 million for a 76 percent stake in Peruana de Radiofusion, the second-largest television station in Peru. In 1993, Televisa put up $200 million for 50 percent of PanAmSat, as Anselmo struggled to launch the world's only privately owned satellite network. PanAmSat proved to be a huge success: by 1995, Televisa's stake was worth more than $1 billion.

The company's revenues continued to build, reaching US$1.35 billion in 1992 and US$1.67 billion in 1993. But after posting earnings of more than US$600 million in 1992, the company's net income sagged. By 1993, Televisa netted only US$26 million. By then, the Mexican government was busy privatizing the country's industries. Television's turn came in 1993, when the government sold off two television networks to private bidders. Televisa was barred from bidding for these stations; as a consolation, however, the company was given the right to buy a third government network of 6 stations for $91 million. Televisa also purchased the Editorial America magazine arm of Miami-based America Publishing Company, making Editorial Televisa the world's largest Spanish-language publisher. In 1994, however, Mexico underwent an economic crisis. The subsequent devaluation of the peso forced a sharp drop in Televisa's revenues, down to US$760 million. The company was once again in the red, to the tune of US$54 million.

The company further reorganized, shedding operations including its stakes in the Chilean and Peruvian television networks, 49 percent of its Mexico City Cablevision cable system, and laying off 15 percent of its employees. The company also closed a newspaper, and its three training schools. In 1995, the company moved toward a full listing on the New York Stock Exchange, selling an additional 10 percent stake controlled by the Azcarraga family and raising some $1 billion. Televisa next focused on the direct-to-home satellite market, entering joint-ventures with News Corp., Tele-Communications, Inc., and others. With the public offering of PanAmSat, followed by that company's merger with Hughes Communications, Televisa began looking to sell off its holdings in the satellite company, concentrating instead on providing content to satellite services. The company also began eyeing the English-speaking market; an early attempt at English-language programming, in a joint-venture with News Corp., proved less than successful, however.

In 1995, Televisa managed to eke out an $88 million profit, as revenues rose to $1.15 billion. The company continued to struggle into 1996, however, as it began to face competition for advertising revenues from new Mexican rival Azteca, which had been steadily building market share—and even beating Televisa in some markets. In mid-1996, the company raised $600 million in a private stock placement. Nevertheless, Televisa continued to expand its interests in DTH and other satellite programming ventures, including a 30 percent stake in Sky Entertainment Latin America; it expanded its Television holdings by buying two English-language Mexican television stations on the U.S. border. In January 1997, Azcarraga took a medical leave of absence from the company. But with Azcarraga's son, Emilio Azcarraga Jean, ready to step in, the Grupo Televisa remained firmly in the family's control.

Principal Subsidiaries

Centro Cultural Arte Contemporaneo, A.C.; Empresa Promotora del Valle, S.A. de C.V.; Grupo America; Grupo Radiopolis, S.A. de C.V.; Grupo Telesistema, S.A. de C.V.; Milar, S.A. de C.V.; Radio Comericales, S.C. (99%); Skytel (51%); Telesistema Mexicano, S.A. de C.V.; Televisa S.A. de C.V.; Television Independente de Mexico, S.C.; Univisa, Inc.

Further Reading

Dombey, Daniel, "Hopes Pinned on Mexican Soap," *Financial Times,* May 25, 1995, p. 29.

Fisher, Christy, "Emilio Azcarraga: The Mystery Man Behind 'National,' " *Advertising Age*, December 18, 1989, p. 1.

Johnson, Deborah, "Televisa, a Multimedia Leader," *Broadcasting & Cable*, November 18, 1996, p. 62.

Malkin, Elizabeth, "The Rupert Murdoch of Mexico?" *Business Week*, December 11, 1995, p. 61.

Rozenstiel, Thomas B., "Azcarraga Owns Huge, Secretive Empire," *Los Angeles Times*, June 2, 1989, section 4, p. 4.

Russell, Joel, "The Televisa Empire Keeps Climbing: The Sky's Not the Limit!" *Business Mexico*, January/February 1994.

Silverstein, Jeffrey, "Mexico's Telecommunications Mogul Expanding His Empire," *San Francisco Chronicle*, December 28, 1992, p. B1.

Skinner, Joseph, "Octopus of the Airwaves," *Monthly Review*, September 1987, p. 44.

"Televisa's Grip Hard to Gag," *Video Age International*, September 1993, p. 17.

Torres, Craig, and Joel Millman, "Mexico's Televisa Searches for Global Stardom, "*Wall Street Journal*, May 30, 1996, p. A10.

—M. L. Cohen

Guest Supply, Inc.

720 U.S. Highway One
P.O. Box 6018
North Brunswick, New Jersey 08902
U.S.A.
(908) 246-3011
Fax: (908) 246-3011

Public Company
Incorporated: 1979
Employees: 927
Sales: $159.45 million (1995)
Stock Exchanges: NASDAQ
SICs: 2844 Perfumes Cosmetics; 2676 Sanitary Paper
   Products

Travellers may not recognize the name, but chances are Guest Supply, Inc. has been close to them—very close. Guest Supply is the leading supplier of amenities such as soap, shampoo, and other toiletries and personal accessories, including ice buckets, towels and linens, stationery, and drinking glasses, to the hotel and lodging industry. In 1996, Guest Supply's customers included approximately one-third of the 30,000 hotels in the United States. An increasing number of hotel and motel chains, independent hotels, and cruise ship lines have begun taking advantage of Guest Supply's "One Stop Shopping" concept, contracting with the company to supply all of their facilities' amenities needs. Guest Supply offers packaging design, amenity coordination, production, and distribution through its Rahway, New Jersey manufacturing facility and its network of 14 regional distribution centers. The company manufactures and distributes leading brand name products as well as the company's own products. Guest Supply also offers contract manufacturing services to retail clients including Victoria's Secret and The Limited. Contract manufacturing, which accounted for 14 percent of 1995 annual sales, is a fast-growing segment of Guest Supply's business. The company's $159.5 million in 1995 sales placed it at the top of the highly fragmented, $2.5 billion hotel supply industry.

A Real Cottage Business in 1979

When John J. Todd founded Guest Supply in 1979, he probably did not realize that he would create an entire industry. Indeed, as he told *The New York Times,* "It was a big joke. . . . The industry wasn't there." And, to *Forbes,* Todd added: "I just wanted a few extra things at the end of the month." A year earlier, Todd, 28 years old, was earning some $23,000 per year working as a salesman in the toiletry division of GAF. One night while staying at a Hyatt hotel in Chicago, Todd was forced to wash his hair with soap because he had forgotten to bring along a bottle of shampoo. Remembering a recent article about shampoo manufacturers giving away sample sizes of their new products and spending as much as $30 million to place samples in consumer homes, Todd reasoned that those sample sizes could easily be placed in hotel rooms. "I was traveling and going into hotels all the time," Todd told *Soap, Cosmetics, Chemical Specialties (SCCS),* "when I made the connection that retail companies can take advantage of sampling in hotels and save a significant amount of money."

Todd initially approached the manufacturers. But there he found little interest; manufacturers were more interested in reaching the female consumer, and travelers tended to be male. Todd quickly shifted focus, turning instead to bring his idea to the hotels themselves. His timing was good, as the hotel industry had overbuilt during the 1970s and by the end of the decade hotels were eagerly searching for a competitive edge. Todd quit his salesman's job and took a job as marketing manager with another company. With his wife acting as bookkeeper, Todd took a $2,000 advance on his credit card, arranged a $10,000 line of credit with a local bank, and convinced two friends to join the venture with an added $4,000 investment. Guest Supply debuted in 1979. Headquarters of the new firm was Todd's living room; his basement served as his warehouse and distribution center.

Next, the company began developing a product line. Its first product was shampoo—Gillette's "Ultra Max"—which the company bought in bulk and repackaged into sample sizes. Hotels responded well. "We took a national brand," Todd explained to *SCCS,* "and sold a little sachet for a nickel. For a hotel to spend $200 was not a big expense to try. They found it

215

to be something a guest appreciated . . . [and] gave them a little bit of difference from the guy across the street.'' The company added more amenities to its line, and, in 1980, Guest Supply lined up its first major order, of $100,000 from Marriott Hotels. As a director at that company later told *Forbes,* "We wanted to show our guests we cared about service. A few companies offered customized bars of soap, but no one offered the array that Todd did.''

Todd and his partners left their jobs to begin working full-time with Guest Supply. Sales grew quickly, rising to $1.8 million in 1981, doubling in the following year, and jumping to $7.2 million by 1983. The company was also turning a profit. Net income rose from $88,000 in 1982 to nearly $800,000 in 1984. By then, amenities had become a standard room feature throughout a hotel industry battling not only a glut of hotel rooms but also a national recession. By 1984, some members of the industry had even begun to speak of "over-amenitized" hotel rooms. Other companies were also entering the hotel amenity market. But Guest Supply already went beyond simply supplying amenities. The company offered custom packaging and design, as well as overall amenity coordination. As Todd explained to *Travel Weekly,* "People who are over-amenitizing their hotels haven't properly structured their thought processes. Amenities must be thought of as a marketing tool, a statement of management. When we put together an amenities program for a chain, we ask the hotelier some basic questions. . . . Then we put together an amenities program that makes sense, that incorporates marketing goals, that presents the hotel in a favorable light.''

To further this end, the company formed a subsidiary, Guest Design, Inc., to design, develop, and produce original packaging that featured both the client's name and the product's brand name and coordinated with a hotel room's overall decor. Products offered by Guest Supply featured nationally known and up-and-coming brand names, as manufacturers found this new, revenue-generating sampling program to be a lucrative addition to sample mailing programs. To step up the company's expansion, which included a move to new headquarters, the opening of sales offices in the West Coast, Midwest, and Southeastern markets, as well as in England, and the projected establishment of a network of regional distribution centers, Guest Supply went public in August 1983.

Losing Ground in the Mid-1980s

The Guest Supply formula proved to be a hit. By 1984, the company's customer base had grown to 850, representing nearly 2,500 hotels and other lodging facilities. Marriott continued to be a major client, accounting for some 20 percent of Guest Supply sales. Holiday Inns signed on in 1984, contracting with Guest Supply to supply a line of 20 custom-designed amenities in a mandatory program throughout its nearly 1,200-hotel chain, a contract then worth a minimum of $8 million per year to Guest Supply. The company also moved to increase its own capacity, purchasing bankrupt contract manufacturer Technair Packaging Laboratories and its Rahway, New Jersey factory and adding Miraflores Designs Inc., another large amenities supplier with $7 million in sales, the following year. In 1985, the company posted $18 million in revenues; the amenities industry itself had grown to a $40 million per year business. Customers also included major chains such as Quality Inns,

Best Western, Omni Classics, as well as several cruise lines. The company posted a secondary offering in 1985, raising nearly $9 million to fuel its expansion. By then, Todd's own stock in his "big joke" was worth more than $4 million. Revenues for the following year nearly doubled, to $33 million.

Yet the transition from entrepreneur to head of a rapidly diversifying operation seemed too much for Todd. The purchase of Technair saddled the company with an antiquated, inefficient manufacturing facility. Guest Supply next acquired another large amenity supplier, Breckenridge-Remy, but the company lacked a sufficient distribution network to manage the increase in sales. Todd also attempted to enter the retail licensing market, a venture that was described as "disastrous" for Guest Supply. At the end of 1986, the company posted its first-ever quarterly loss; profit for the entire year was only $812,000. The company's losses deepened over the next year, while the company steadily lost its lead in market share and found itself faced with an ever-increasing number of competitors. Revenues remained stagnant at $33 million in 1987 in an amenities market that by then had reached nearly $400 million in annual sales. Guest Supply's losses for that year fell just under $7 million.

The company rejected an acquisition bid in early 1987 worth more than $53 million. But outside investors were increasing their holdings in, and influence on, the company. In early 1988 Todd proposed to expand the company's operations again, this time to the international market. His proposal was rejected by the board of directors and Todd left the company. Under the terms of his resignation, Todd took with him the company's failing retail unit. Todd was replaced by Clifford W. Stanley, a former vice-president with Johnson & Johnson, who had joined the company in 1985 as chief financial officer. Stanley moved to return the company's focus to its core amenities line and began a $10 million modernization and automating effort in its Rahway plant. In addition to exiting retail, the company abandoned another of its diversification moves, that of selling to distributors. The addition of Breckenridge-Remy doubled Guest Supply's revenues, to nearly $64 million, boosting the company's product line and sales force, while increasing its distribution capacity with a network of seven regional warehouses. Under Stanley, the company began to develop its one-stop shopping concept.

Rebounding in the 1990s

Guest Supply chipped away at its losses over the next years. Its 1988 loss of $3.3 million was reduced to $1.9 million by 1989, and losses were now largely the result of the company's push to modernize its manufacturing and distribution capacity; the company had managed to cut its operating losses from $2.7 million to less than $650,000. Guest Supply's renewed strategy emphasized direct sales and distribution to the hotel industry through a network of distribution centers, including those inherited with the Breckenridge-Remy acquisition. As the company neared the end of its 1989 fiscal year, Guest Supply continued to expand its regional sales and distribution network with a thirteenth center in Atlanta.

Through the 1980s, the hotel industry had once again gone on a building binge, and by the end of the decade that market was oversaturated. The hotel industry was further pummeled by the slide into the recession of the early 1990s, and then the outbreak of the Gulf War. Hotel occupancy rates slipped to 60 percent and lower. The hotel industry's problems cut into Guest Supply's growth, but the company's revenues continued to grow as hotels stepped up their amenity offerings to attract the traveling public. Guest Supply's sales grew to $75 million in 1990. Its upgraded manufacturing facilities were cutting the company's operating costs. Where eight workers once were needed to fill 70 bottles per hour, only five now were needed to fill 300 bottles. The increased capacity enabled Guest Supply to expand into another area of sales. Contract manufacturing began to represent a small but growing portion of Guest Supply's sales. Production of the company's own products provided the overhead for its contract orders; filled largely through excess manufacturing capacity, contract sales for such customers as Proctor & Gamble, Helene Curtis, and The Limited returned some 70 percent of revenues as profit.

The company's losses dropped to $300,000 by 1990. The following year, with revenues growing slowly to $78 million, the company achieved its first profit, of $400,000, since 1986. With its manufacturing capacity and distribution network in place, the company next expanded into a new area, producing trial sizes of other manufacturer's branded products. This was seen as a natural outgrowth of the company's core business, since the company's manufacturing facilities were already geared toward this type of packaging. As Stanley explained to *Portfolio Letter,* "We saw a market which was untouched by everyone else. There are a lot of manufacturers who want to sell trial sizes, but can't because their plant doesn't have those type of facilities, but we do."

Guest Supply regained its industry lead, grabbing an estimated 30 percent of the hotel amenities market. As the recession ended and the hotel industry rebounded, Guest Supply's sales took off, reaching $98 million in 1993 and then $116 million in 1994. In each of these years, net income doubled, to $2.2 million and to $4.1 million. The company stepped up its vertical integration efforts, adding paper products and housekeeping supplies, as well as waste baskets, stationery, and door signs. Hotels commonly purchased these supplies from a variety of vendors. "Our goal," Stanley told *Investor's Daily Business,* "is to get each hotel's entire account." The company added to its product offerings in 1994 with the addition of linens and other textiles produced by other manufacturers; these would quickly add some $20 million in sales in little more than a year.

Guest Supply's contract manufacturing operations, meanwhile, grew by 86 percent in 1995 alone and now represented about 14 percent of the company's total sales. To further fuel this growth, the company invested another $10 million in capital improvements to expand its manufacturing capacity. This in turn led to shortage of warehousing space, forcing the company to build a new 225,000-square-foot warehouse. Originally scheduled to open in September 1996, the warehouse was beset with construction delays. Yet this was a minor and temporary setback to the company, which saw its 1995 revenues rise to $159.5 million. In addition, by developing its infrastructure, Guest Supply was poised to capitalize on yet another burgeoning market. More and more retailers were pursuing plans for entering the huge personal care market. Guest Supply was already positioned to take on this new business. "We have formulating chemists and have literally hundreds of formulas. We customize products and can manufacture quicker," Stanley told *Investor's Business Daily.* Under Stanley, Guest Supply had successfully paved over its past bumps and was now traveling a smooth road to the future.

Principal Subsidiaries

Guest Design, Inc.

Further Reading

Butts, Joan T., "Guest Supply Makes Amenities a Necessity for the Hotel Industry," *Soaps, Cosmetics, Chemical Specialties,* June 1984, p. 31.

Gubernick, Lisa, "The Power of Positive Hairwash," *Forbes,* November 18, 1985, p. 67.

"Guest Supply Fills Trial Size Market," *Portfolio Letter,* July 8, 1991, p. 2.

Horowitz, Carl, "Leader's Success," *Investor's Business Daily,* January 28, 1994, p. 1.

Leo, Darrell, "The Whimsical War of the Soap Dish," *Travel Weekly,* March 31, 1984, p. 88.

Parets, Robyn Taylor, "Guest Supply, Inc.," *Investor's Business Daily,* January 17, 1996, p. A4.

—M. L. Cohen

Hach Co.

**5600 Lindbergh Drive
Loveland, Colorado 80537
U.S.A.
(303) 669-3050
Fax: (303) 669-2932
Web site: http://www.hach.com**

Public Company
Incorporated: 1951
Employees: 865
Sales: $114.3 million (1996)
Stock Exchanges: NASDAQ
SICs: 2819 Industrial Inorganic Chemicals, Not
   Elsewhere Classified; 2869 Industrial Organic
   Chemicals, Not Elsewhere Classified; 3231 Glass
   Products, Mainly of Purchased Glass; 3823 Industrial
   Instruments for Measurement, Display & Control of
   Process Variables & Related Products; 3826
   Laboratory Analytical Instruments

Hach Co. (pronounced "hawk") manufactures laboratory instruments, process analyzers, and test kits that are used to analyze the chemical content and other properties of water and other aqueous solutions. It also manufactures and sells analytical reagents and chemicals to be used in this connection. In addition, the company manufactures and sells a small amount of chemicals for uses not associated with its analytical systems for water analysis. Hach was Colorado's biggest woman-owned business in the mid-1990s. In fiscal 1996 the company enjoyed its 12th consecutive year of record sales and profits.

The Early Years, 1947–70

Clifford and Kathryn Hach founded Hach in Ames, Iowa, in 1947 in a $200 building. The company was originally a partnership. In 1968 it was reincorporated in Delaware as Hach Chemical Co., with Clifford Hach president and treasurer and Kathryn Hach as vice-president. Sales came to about $700,000 and net income to about $80,000 in 1964. Net sales rose from $1.7 million in fiscal 1967 (the year ended April 30, 1967) to $2.7 million in fiscal 1969, while net income rose from $183,344 to $315,684 during this period. Company assets amounted to $2.8 million at the end of fiscal 1969, when there were 137 employees. Later in the calendar year Hach went public, raising $1.7 million by the sale of a small minority of the shares. Most of the money was used to build and equip a new chemical-manufacturing plant in Ames.

Hach went public at an auspicious moment, as concern for the environment had become an issue of international concern. When the first "Earth Day" was observed in 1970, rallies were held in major cities, and an estimated 10 million schoolchildren participated in "teach-in" programs. Utilities and manufacturing companies were being pressed to clean up their activities. Hach launched extensive advertising and sales-promotion programs to publicize what it could do to monitor water purity.

Hach, in 1970, was manufacturing and selling a line of instruments, ranging in price from $200 to $2,000, designed to determine specific water impurities. It was also manufacturing a manometric apparatus that measured the biochemical oxygen demand (BOD) of sewage and industrial wastes in lakes, rivers, and streams—BOD being a measure of water pollution and the most basic analytical measurement in the control of wastewater treatment. Customers for Hach's instruments included municipal water- and sewage-treatment plants, facilities for the treatment of industrial water wastes, and electric-power plants.

Hach was also manufacturing and selling more than 100 different portable water test kits for laboratory and field use. These kits were employed in water and sewage treatment, water conditioning, cooling towers, wildlife conservation, and boiling water. They usually included specially formulated chemical reagents in the form of small powder packets. Test results were achieved by visual comparison of samples against color standards after adding the prescribed reagents, and directions enabled persons without technical backgrounds to conduct tests. The first of Clifford Hach's 10-item criteria for company products was, "Can be used by anyone who can read."

Hach's products were being sold throughout the United States and Canada, primarily by direct mail, with about 45,000 brochures being distributed regularly to attract customers. In addition to its Ames headquarters, the company maintained regional sales offices in California, Connecticut, Illinois, New Jersey, and Texas. New offices were added later in Georgia and Ohio. International marketing had started in 1964, and in 1970 there were 46 independent distributors and sales agents handling Hach's products abroad. In fiscal 1970 instruments accounted for about 56 percent of sales, with chemical reagents and portable test kits splitting the remainder roughly evenly. Foreign countries accounted for approximately 12 percent of sales in fiscal 1969.

Expansion in the 1970s

In 1972 Hach formed an international subsidiary and issued more stock, raising close to $5 million, two-thirds of it for expansion, including a new warehouse and more space for electronic assembly. A company plant was opened in Namur, Belgium, the following year, for the distribution and manufacture of products for Europe and adjacent markets. Sales and profits continued to increase year by year. At the end of fiscal 1975, when Hach had net income of $1.1 million on sales of $9.4 million, the company had achieved compound annual earnings growth averaging 25 percent over five years even though the national economy had fallen into recession during this period.

Hach, in 1975, had a product line of more than 3,500 items, with the instruments now selling for $400 to $4,000. During the fiscal year instruments accounted for 32 percent of sales revenue, test kits for 24 percent, and chemical reagents (in both powder and liquid form) for 44 percent. The drop in instrument sales was attributed to industrial customers saving money by substituting cheaper test kits. Chemical reagents were enjoying the highest profit margins because there were only a few competitors in this field. Industrial and commercial customers accounted for 50 percent of all sales, water and waste-treatment customers for 35 percent, educational customers for 10 percent, and miscellaneous for five percent. The number of customers had grown to 30,000, with the potential customer list exceeding 60,000. Direct-mail marketing in the United States and Canada was being supplemented by advertising in business publications.

In 1977 Hach purchased Carle Instruments, Inc., of Fullerton, California, paying $1.86 million in cash for this manufacturing company, which produced gas chromatography instrumentation used in analyzing a wide range of compounds. D. W. Carle, its president, continued to manage the company, which became a Hach subsidiary. It moved its operations to Anaheim, California, in 1978, and to Loveland, Colorado, in 1984. By 1989, when it was sold to EG&G, Inc., Carle Chromatography was manufacturing and marketing analytical gas chromatographs in a wide range of application-engineered systems designed to meet the needs of natural gas, petroleum, petrochemical, and industrial gas industries. Hach also acquired Fann Instrument Corp. in 1976 for $1.75 million in cash and notes. This Houston-based firm made fluid-analysis products that were used mainly by oil well drillers to analyze and measure the viscosity of drilling muds. It was sold in 1980 to Dresser Industries, Inc. for about $3.2 million.

Clifford Hach took the position of chairman and chief executive officer in 1977, and Kathryn Hach became president and chief operating officer the following year. Water-analysis products accounted for 75 percent of company earnings in fiscal 1978, and steam-generation plants in electric-power installations were its largest industrial customers. In 1978 Hach moved its instrument division and its corporate headquarters to a site next to the airport in Loveland, Colorado. Hach Chemical Co. became Hach Co. in 1980. Net sales reached nearly $20 million in that fiscal year, but net income was only $493,000 after deducting $1 million for depreciation. Long-term debt, nonexistent in the mid-1970s, reached $7.6 million.

Hach in the 1980s

In 1985 the company added a subsidiary called Hach Synthesis that made high-purity chemical compounds in Casper, Wyoming, until 1990. Also in 1985, it leased a Loveland building in an industrial complex to make the plastic components used in its operations. Clifford Hach was chairman in 1985, Kathryn Hach was vice-chairman, and Stelios Papadopoulos president of the company, which had grown to 580 employees. Net sales reached $34.5 million in fiscal 1985, with net income a solid $1.7 million after a $1.7-million charge for depreciation and amortization. The long-term debt had fallen to $4 million.

About this time Hach introduced just-in-time inventory techniques and adopted W. Edward Deming's principles of quality control. Because the former required smaller production lots to be made and delivered quickly, workers had to be capable of performing a number of different jobs. An assembly worker, for example, also had to become knowledgeable in quality control and parts procurement, and to meet Hach's standards this meant keeping sophisticated statistical charts and understanding basic algebra and trigonometry. Many workers could not meet these demands, so in 1989 Hach began offering a basic math course, and it later added a basic writing course. The quality-control campaign, despite its demands, had paid off by 1990, according to a company executive who estimated defects had decreased fourfold since 1985 and who attributed a 70 percent increase in output to the program, with only a 30 percent increase in staff and no increase in floor space.

The late 1980s proved even more profitable for Hach than earlier years. By 1990 it was maintaining 20 sales offices, including one in Belgium and one in Canada. That fiscal year the company enjoyed its sixth consecutive year of record sales and profits, with net sales reaching $63.1 million and net income an impressive $5.1 million. The long-term debt had fallen to $1.9 million. With Clifford Hach's death in 1990, Kathryn Hach became chairman and chief executive officer, while the Hachs' son Bruce became president.

Continued Success in the 1990s

Hach's revenues and profits continued to grow each year, with the former increasing from $72.3 million in fiscal 1991 to $114.3 in fiscal 1996, and the latter from $6 million to $11.3 million over this period. Steam-generation plants were the biggest industrial customers in fiscal 1992. Plant operators were using the company's continuous-reading process analyzers for online monitoring of cooling-tower and boiling-feedwater quality. Hach's turbidimeters were being used widely to assure that water-filtration processes met acceptable standards. Sales abroad accounted for one-third of the total.

By 1993 continuous training was a mandate at Hach, with 150 company-sponsored classes not only in "hard" skills like soldering, blueprint reading, and forklift certification, but also in team building and customer-satisfaction measurement. Steven Farnham, a company executive, explained, for a special report published in the *Denver Business Journal,* that "Something like customer service may seem obvious and generic, but our people in this role have to understand the company's unique commitment to customers, have in-depth familiarity with more than 300 products, possess effective telephone skills and know how to handle 'people problems' so they meet customer needs." With respect to the team-building workshop, typically a class of 20, he said, "For three days you discover how to accomplish 'team' objectives with people very different from yourself. . . . If you can't work well with a team, there's probably no place for you here at Hach." Internal book clubs, a key element of the training program, required members to read a chapter a week and then meet to discuss how the text could help them do their jobs better.

Despite these demands, employees evidently thrived on the regimen, since the worker turnover rate was less than eight percent a year.

Classes on "World Class Manufacturing" were based on Deming's book by the same title. Many of Hach's officers and directors personally met with Deming, and Hach managers created a three-hour course, required for each employee, that included the book's 28 main precepts. Hach also was operating a five-person technical-training center in downtown Loveland that was teaching company employees, customers, and vendors how to use products in a hands-on laboratory setting. The company was refunding employees' tuition for relevant outside courses. Kathryn Hach and Hach Co. were jointly sponsoring seven new college scholarships per year for students majoring in chemistry. She was named 1993's Outstanding Business Woman of the Year by the Colorado Women's Chamber of Commerce.

During the early and mid-1990s Lawter International Inc., an ink and specialty-chemicals manufacturer, made persistent and unwelcome attempts to acquire Hach. Lawter, based in Northbrook, Illinois, first sought to buy Hach in 1983 but was discouraged by the founding family's large holding (about 45 percent) in the company. Nevertheless, in 1985 it bought about 25 percent of the outstanding shares in a privately negotiated transaction. In August 1993 Lawter, which now owned 28 percent of the shares, announced an agreement to acquire the rest for $146 million worth of its own stock. The proposed transaction collapsed three months later, with Kathryn Hach telling reporters it was just too difficult to "blend companies together as different as we are."

Undeterred, Daniel J. Terra, Lawter's chairman and chief executive, made an unsolicited offer in 1995 of $21 a share, or $172 million, for the Hach stock it did not already own. The offer was quickly rejected by Hach's chief executive officer

(now Kathryn Hach-Darrow). Outsiders said a deal never made sense since both Terra and Hach-Darrow were strong-willed executives, and Hach's chief financial officer declared, "From a technological standpoint, there are no synergies between the two companies."

Of Hach's sales in fiscal 1996, analytical reagents and chemicals accounted for 31 percent; laboratory and portable instruments, 30 percent; continuous-reading process analyzers, 17 percent; portable test kits and replacements, 13 percent; and other, nine percent. The instruments continued to be manufactured in Loveland, where Hach also had its corporate headquarters, research, development, and engineering operations, employee training center, and plastic-component manufacturing operation. The chemical manufacturing operations, a chemical research laboratory, and the company warehouse and shipping department were still in Ames. The manufacturing and distribution plant for products sold overseas was still in Namur, Belgium. The company's electromechanical division was discontinued in 1995.

Hach's laboratory and portable instruments were being sold to municipal water and wastewater utilities, chemical manufacturers, industrial water-conditioning firms and organizations, power utilities, commercial analytical laboratories, and government agencies for the testing and monitoring of controlled impurities in water systems. Continuous-reading process analyzers were being sold to municipalities for monitoring and controlling drinking water quality and to ensure that wastewater-treatment procedures complied with government regulations.

Steam-generating plants, petrochemical processors, heavy-industry installations, and pulp-and-paper factories were using process analyzers for online monitoring of cooling-tower and boiling-feedwater quality. The microelectronics industry was using the company's trace-silica analyzers to monitor ultrapure water systems used in processing electronic components.

Hach was offering more than 200 different test kits for 12 different application areas, ranging from agriculture to water quality. They were being sold to municipalities for use in monitoring drinking water distribution systems, to conservation groups for environmental impact studies, to educators for use in testing environmental awareness, to corporate customers for monitoring industrial processes, to the water-conditioning industry for use in testing water quality, and to environmental regulatory authorities for use in checking compliance requirements. Hach was about 42 percent owned by its founding family in 1995. It had no long-term liabilities at the end of the year.

Principal Subsidiaries

Hach Europe, S.A./N.V. (Belgium); Hach FSC, Inc. (Barbados); Hach Sales & Service Canada Ltd. (Canada).

Further Reading

Day, Janet, "Chamber Names Hach Businesswoman of Year," *Denver Post,* November 6, 1993, p. D1.
"Hach Chemical Co.," *Wall Street Transcript,* September 7, 1970, pp. 21671–72.
——, *Wall Street Transcript,* August 11, 1975, pp. 41083–84.

"Hach Chemical Opens European Unit, Expands Its Domestic Facilities," *Investment Dealers' Digest,* January 15, 1974, p. 15.

"Hach Chemical Sees Increasing Demand for Analysis Instruments," *Investment Dealers' Digest,* October 21, 1975, p. 38.

"Hach Company," *Colorado Business,* March 1990, p. 19.

Leib, Jeffrey, "Hach Co., Lawter Scrap Planned Merger," *Denver Post,* November 16, 1993, p. C1.

Machan, Dyan, "Eager Pupils," *Forbes,* September 16, 1991, p. 188.

McGee, Bill, "Hach Soars High with Training Program," *Denver Business Journal,* May 7, 1993, p. 20.

Murphy, H. Lee, "Bungled Deal Leaves Lawter with a $64-Million Question," *Crain's Chicago Business,* September 25, 1995, p. 48.

—Robert Halasz

Hancock Fabrics, Inc.

3406 West Main Street
P.O. Box 2400
Tupelo, Mississippi 38803-2400
U.S.A.
(601) 842-2834
Fax: (601) 842-2834

Public Company
Incorporated: 1957
Employees: 6,996
Sales: $364.2 million (1995)
Stock Exchanges: New York
SICs: 5949 Sewing, Needlework & Piece Goods; 5131
    Piece Goods, Notions & Other Dry Goods

Hancock Fabrics, Inc. is one of the leading fabric chains serving the home sewing market. Known as ''America's fabric store,'' the company retails and wholesales fabric, crafts, and other home sewing accessories in 33 states under the trade names of Hancock Fabrics, Minnesota Fabrics, Fabric Warehouse, and Fabric Market.

The Complete Fabric Store

Founded in 1957, Hancock Fabrics developed the concept of a total fabric retailer. More than just a specialty shop, the first stores opened by Hancock Fabrics were cost-efficient and offered a greater selection of merchandise to consumers at lower prices. ''Long before the 'category killer' catchword was coined and applied to the specialty businesses of toys, office supplies, building materials, and others,'' the company revealed in an annual report, ''Hancock Fabrics pioneered the concept of a *complete* fabric store. As opposed to the high cost and limited selection of a mall location or small specialty shop, Hancock pursued a powerful, cost-efficient store format that permitted consistently lower prices and a greater selection of merchandise for our customer.'' The Tupelo-based company perfected its approach to fabric retailing as years went by, expanding to communities across the United States.

The mid-1970s brought crisis to fabric retailers nationwide when market forces pushed many operators out of business. The excess expansion of previous years, plus inefficient operations and undercapitalization, caused the demise of more than one shop and chain. Hancock Fabrics, however, weathered all this well. Although impacted by excess expansion and the ensuing correction process, Hancock Fabrics nevertheless had earned profits every quarter for 30 consecutive years since the early 1970s.

The next 15 years brought strong sales growth and earning gains for Hancock. Sales in 1985, for example, totaled $281.6 million, with $18.6 million in net earnings. By 1988, sales rose to $315.4 million, and net earnings grew to $22.0 million. Hancock continued opening more new and larger stores and upsizing existing smaller stores throughout the 1980s. The retailer employed 5,265 people in 320 stores during 1985, expanding to 366 stores with 6,051 employees in 1988.

By 1992, Hancock Fabrics was one of seven major retail piece-goods chains, with 482 stores, accounting for approximately 24 percent of the 2,000 full-sized fabric stores in the United States. During this year of peak capacity for the fabric industry, Hancock's sales reached $380.4 million, and net earnings rose to $12.1 million. Employees numbered 7,390.

Industry Reformation in the 1990s

The early 1990s again brought a slowing economy that greatly affected fabric retailers. As Bob Yarbrough explained in the *Mississippi Business Journal,* ''The rugged economy . . . [had] taken the steam out of what was thought to be a recession-proof industry.'' Consumers at this time became cautious buyers, creating a general weakness in both piece-goods and ready-to-wear fashion apparel sales. Store growth throughout the industry exceeded the demands of consumers, so retailers responded with aggressive price promotions that often sacrificed margins. Price discounting was widespread, and market share came second after the conversion of swelling inventories to cash as debt levels grew.

Hancock saw its stock drop from $24¼ in 1991 to $10 in 1992. The stocks of Hancock's competitors, Fabri-Centers of

Company Perspectives:

When Hancock Fabrics was founded in 1957, it marked the introduction of a significant new concept in fabric retailing. With a seemingly endless selection of specialized merchandise displayed in a large-store format, Hancock's supermarket of fabrics and related accessories represented the first real commitment by a retailer to concentrate on one thing and to do it better than anyone else.... Despite the staggering pace of change in today's business environment, the fabric customer continues to be the ultimate reason for everything we do. In that spirit, the people of Hancock Fabrics remain committed to keeping our costs and therefore our prices low as we search the markets of the world for the merchandise values that our customers expect and deserve. You see, even after almost forty years, our mission is still the same—to earn the right to be "America's Fabric Store."

America and House of Fabrics, could not escape the soft economy, either. Fabri-Centers of America, for example, lost nine points in one week during the recession.

Although Hancock was the first stock to reflect the recession, industry analysts remained optimistic about its future. When competitors were first moving from smaller stores to bigger ones, Hancock already was operating larger stores. As Larry Kirk, then Hancock's chief financial officer, explained in the *Mississippi Business Journal,* "We've always operated larger stores, and the others are still making the move from smaller, mall-sized stores to superstores. We have more history with our stores, and changes in sales will show up faster."

Hancock also was the industry's pricing leader. Known for high quality management, Hancock faced the recession with a conservative balance sheet and strong cash flow. At the time, an industry report prepared by Stephens Inc., analysts of the retail fabric industry, noted, "Despite Hancock's recent setbacks, we remain confident in management's ability to successfully execute its long-range growth strategy. We especially like the company's philosophy of running the business for the long haul."

Nevertheless, by 1993, the entire retail fabric industry struggled to survive. The three largest retail fabric chains filed for bankruptcy; many smaller chains and independent shops closed. Hancock's net income more than halved from 1991 to 1992, dropping from $23.0 million to $12.1 million. Net income was down to $5.4 million by 1993. Hancock's earnings per share (before the cumulative effect of changes in accounting methods) also fell, from $1.03 in 1991 to $0.57 in 1992. By 1993 earnings decreased to $0.26 per share.

From 1992 through 1994, Hancock also endured a decrease in sales. Sales in 1992 totaled $380.4 million; they dropped to $367.7 million in 1993 and $366.8 million in 1994. In addition, expenses as a percentage of those lower sales increased. Average stock prices also decreased, from $13.57 in 1992 to $11.00 in 1993 to $8.38 in 1994. Gross margins fell as well. In 1992

Hancock Fabrics reported a gross margin of $173.0 million, a decrease of $11 million from the preceding year. This dipped again to $161.5 million for 1993. Though its debt level was somewhat higher than in the past, Hancock nevertheless remained in sound financial condition and earned profits each quarter.

Those companies remaining in operation in 1993 initiated a correction process. These retailers, including Hancock Fabrics, greatly reduced their store concentrations and prepared for changes in the competitive structure of the industry. They closed stores, reduced square footage, and liquidated inventories. Retailers adopted different strategies that affected all areas: product mix, marketing, expansion, even financial risk.

Hancock Responds to Change

Hancock's response to industry changes were calculated and effective. The company worked to improve the efficiency of its merchandise mix by adding complementary products to its stores and by discontinuing unproductive items. The retailer downplayed fashion apparel in favor of more popular merchandise categories such as home decorations, quilting, specialty fabrics, and seasonal goods.

Hancock began to promote its stores as complete fabric retailers with the largest selections of merchandise at the best prices and with the best service. Other marketing efforts emphasized the pleasures of sewing, quilting, and home decorating.

To reach new customers and excite existing ones, in 1995 Hancock Fabrics developed a half-hour sewing show, "Sew Perfect," for the Home & Garden Television Network (HGTV). A charter advertising partnership with the network allowed Hancock to maintain a consistent advertising presence on the network throughout the broadcast schedule. For more print-oriented consumers, Hancock introduced a sewing and decorating magazine. The first issue of *Home Expressions* debuted in October that same year.

Hancock also co-branded a MasterCard, the "Fabric Card," in 1995. The card offered a low interest rate, as well as rebates on purchases and special monthly incentives such as coupons and discounts for use at Hancock stores.

Moreover, the company reevaluated its place in the fabric industry. In the 1995 annual report, Hancock Fabrics revealed to its shareholders: "Perhaps the most fundamental action that resulted from the challenges of the last few years was the company's renewed commitment to its roots. While many of our competitors were dividing their resources and attention among a variety of ventures, Hancock intensified its focus on the business of fabric retailing. Believing that better opportunities were available in a business that was approaching competitive balance than in segments where competition was destined to become increasingly intense, the company determined to improve and expand its operations in the business that we understand best." So, in addition to its marketing efforts, Hancock revised its operational strategies to improve the company's performance. Hancock closed 22 underperforming stores and opened 20 new ones in 1995. The company even discussed (but abandoned) the acquisition of its competitor House of Fabrics that year. At the end of 1995, the company was in the best financial condition in seven years, and operational and financial performances continued to improve. "Our concentrated effort to stock the right goods in the correct allocations at the optimum time is resulting in improved sales, better inventory productivity, and reduced markdowns," explained Chief Executive Officer Larry G. Kirk in 1996.

The Future

Although most of the changes caused by excess capacity are believed to be in the past for fabric retailers, the industry still must contend with the effects of expansion in the future. According to the company's 1995 annual report, "In the coming quarters, Hancock too will participate in the industry's purging of unproductive stores and the reallocation of inventory. Excluding acquisition possibilities, we expect to close more stores than we open. . . . However, in doing so, we will increase the productivity of our assets and improve returns to our shareholders."

The prolonged weakness in the demand for apparel goods was expected to remain as well. The pressure on retailers no doubt will continue as the relationship between their supplies and consumer demands is restored. As in the 1970s, some retailers will disappear; some will consolidate and combine, and others, like Hancock, will survive by virtue of their financial soundness and stability. In fact, the company anticipates strong growth in sales and in earnings in the years ahead. As Kirk explained in a November 1996 press release, "Fabric retailing is heading into another phase of the shakeout and consolidation that has been under way for the last three years. The restoration of competitive balance and the recovery in apparel demand are providing greater opportunities for stable, well capitalized operators. We will continue to make revenue growth a major priority emphasizing new concepts and products, natural expansion into underserved markets, and strategic acquisitions that would be additive to earnings. We are off to a good start . . . , and we look forward to a strong finish."

Further Reading

"Big Three Decorative Fabric Chains Post Results," *HFD—The Weekly Home Furnishings Newspaper,* December 9, 1991, p. 28.

"Hancock Fabrics Discontinues Acquisition Talks with House of Fabrics," *Business Wire,* December 29, 1995, p. 12291126.

"Hancock Fabrics in Acquisition Talks with House of Fabrics," *Business Wire,* November 1, 1995, p. 11011421.

"Hancock Fabrics, Inc.," *HFD—The Weekly Home Furnishings Newspaper,* August 30, 1993, p. 30.

"Hancock Fabrics, Inc.," *Memphis Business Journal,* December 9, 1991, p. 7.

Yarbrough, Bob, "Hancock Fabric Stock in Freefall," *Mississippi Business Journal,* June 15, 1992, p. 1.

—Charity Anne Dorgan

Heartland Express, Inc.

2777 Heartland Drive
Coralville, Iowa 52241
U.S.A.
(319) 645-2728
Fax: (319)645-2338

Public Company
Incorporated: 1978
Employees: 2,000
Sales: $191.5 million (1995)
Stock Exchanges: NASDAQ
SICs: 4213 Trucking, Except Local; 6719 Holding
    Companies, Not Elsewhere Classified

Heartland Express, Inc. is one of the leading trucking companies serving the short-to-medium haul truckload market in the United States. Based outside of Iowa City, Iowa, Heartland's operations are primarily concentrated within the region east of the Rockies and west of the New York/Pennsylvania border. The company focuses especially on the Midwest and Southeast regions; the company also offers limited but expanding service to the West and East Coast regions, however, and serves all 48 states in the continental United States. Heartland trucks generally travel the north-south traffic lanes, avoiding the more intense competition along the east-west traffic lanes, which are dominated on the one hand by the country's major trucking lines and on the other by the railroads.

The average haul of a Heartland Express truck covered 625 miles in 1995. The company owns about half of its fleet of more than 2,000 tractors; historically, the company has contracted with owner-operators to fill out its fleet of tractors. The company also owns a fleet of trailers, generally on a two-to-one trailer-to-tractor ratio, allowing Heartland to station many of its trailers at the facilities of its major customers. Heartland owns and operates one of the youngest fleets in its industry. The average age of its tractors is 17 months, and the average age of its trailers is 30 months. All of Heartland's trailers are of the 53-foot, aluminum plate type.

In addition to its headquarters facility in Coralville, Iowa, the company operates regional distribution facilities in Iowa City; Columbus, Ohio; St. Louis, Missouri; and Atlanta, Georgia. Service from these regional centers focuses on 400-mile short haul freight runs for its major customers in each region. The company's major customers include Sears Logistics Services, which accounted for nearly 15 percent of Heartland's revenues in 1995, and the Kellogg Company, which accounted for nearly 11 percent of Heartland's revenues in 1995. Other major customers include General Mills and Whirlpool Corp. Overall, the company's top five customers accounted for nearly half of its 1995 revenues. In addition, 75 percent of Heartland's 1995 revenues came from just 25 customers. With the exception of Sears Logistics Services and Kellogg, none of the company's customers account for more than ten percent of the company's sales.

Heartland's long-standing reputation for quality service and dependability allows it to charge premium prices in the highly competitive trucking industry. The company operates no scheduled runs, enabling it to provide its customers with the flexibility to ship as suits their needs. Heartland also boasts high employee retention rates in an industry beset with high driver turnover. The company encourages driver loyalty by maintaining short-distance runs and regularly scheduling drivers to return home; Heartland drivers tend to return home weekly, compared with industrywide returns of up to six weeks. Heartland drivers, almost all of whom are nonunion, are also compensated for "deadhead" or empty miles. In addition, the company provides college scholarships to the children of all of its employees based on their length of service with the company. After five years, employee children receive half the cost of college education, based on the annual tuition at the University of Iowa; after ten years, employee children receive full tuition scholarships.

New Beginning in 1978

The origins of Heartland Express can be traced to 1955, when it was started out as a hauler for the recently launched Whirlpool line of washing machines. The company remained small for the next two decades, growing to a fleet of 16 trucks by the late 1970s. It was only in 1978, when Russell A. Gerdin bought the company, that Heartland's evolution into a leading trucking company began. By then, Gerdin, whose father had owned a small trucking company, already had more than a dozen years of experience in the trucking industry.

Gerdin graduated from Moorhead State University in Minnesota in 1965 and went to work for his father's company. Gerdin and his father, however, could not agree on the best way to run the family's business. Their conflict centered especially on the best way to increase the company's fleet of trucks. As Gerdin told *Investor's Business Daily,* "I watched Dad work on those trucks and pay interest all his life. As soon as he got a dollar, he would buy a new one and take on more interest. I said: 'I'll buy one truck and, when I get that paid off, I'll buy another one'—exactly different from Dad."

Gerdin and his father were unable to resolve their different visions for the company. After only six months, Gerdin left his father's business to go into business for himself. He bought his own trucking line, Great Plains Transportation, a small company based in Nebraska, in 1966. Over the next decade, Gerdin would own or partly own five more trucking companies, all of which were based in the Midwest. At the time, however, federal regulations severely restricted the routes available to trucking companies. Because most routes were already controlled by larger, established trucking companies, newer and smaller trucking companies found it difficult, if not impossible, to achieve any real internal expansion. Union control over the trucking industry was also a factor in limiting companies' growth.

Toward the end of the 1970s, Gerdin moved to Iowa and, together with several others, bought the assets of the predecessor company to Heartland Express, incorporating the company under that name in 1978. Gerdin was named chairman, chief executive officer, president, and secretary of the company. Heartland, too, might have remained a small, regional company. But, in 1979, the trucking industry was deregulated, opening new opportunities for the smaller companies in the industry. And few companies were able to take advantage of the changes in the industry as well as Heartland.

Gerdin set to work building the company's fleet, following his own ideas and adding one truck at a time. Another company policy set early in Heartland's history was that of maintaining a relatively young fleet, thereby limiting costly maintenance, while improving the company's dependability for its customers. As one company official later told the *Des Moines Register,* "We have a three-year cycle with our tractors—350,000 miles and they are out of here. We want to run trucks. We don't want to repair them. We want to change the oil and do small repairs. We are not doing real major repairs. We want to keep quality pieces of equipment on the road . . . that we feel are more dependable." The relative youth of its fleet also allowed Heartland to maintain a low service employee to tractor ratio of one employee for every seven tractors, compared with the industry average of one to 3.5.

Heartland quickly established a reputation for reliable service among the industry. While keeping early major customers like Whirlpool and Amana, Heartland added others, including Sears and Kellogg, that would also maintain long-term relationships with the company. By 1982, the company was bringing in nearly $11 million in annual sales, and, by keeping its costs low, the company managed to achieve net income of more than $1 million.

Going Public in the 1980s

The company continued to grow slowly but steadily through the first half of the 1980s, despite the nationwide recession of the period. In fact, the new realities of doing business during this time actually helped Heartland grow. More and more manufacturers began to automate production and turn to "just in time" inventory systems, supplying production lines with materials and parts only at the time they were actually needed, which enabled manufacturers to decrease their reliance on costly warehousing. In turn, the manufacturers became more reliant on short-haul shippers to meet their inventory needs. With reliability now more than ever a critical factor in a manufacturer's shipping needs, Heartland's reputation for dependability helped the company secure its growing position in the trucking industry. Yet another factor in Heartland's success was its high trailer to tractor ratio. By maintaining on average twice as many trailers to its tractors, Heartland was able to station some of its trailers at its customers' plants. This had two benefits. Trailers could be loaded and unloaded by the manufacturers, cutting down on time between shipments. Meanwhile, Heartland's tractors were free to haul other loads.

By 1986, Heartland had doubled its revenues, to nearly $22 million. The company's string of profits also continued, reaching $3 million in that year. By November 1986, Heartland was prepared to step up its expansion. Gerdin took the company public, selling 1.5 million shares at $10 per share. Most of the shares sold were Gerdin's, reducing his control of the company to about 65 percent. Portions of the proceeds from its initial public offering (IPO) went to expanding the company's fleet. By 1987, after posting profits of $3.5 million on revenues of $26 million, the company's fleet had reached 126 company-owned tractors and 125 owner-operator tractors. After purchasing 59 drop deck dry vans from a Missouri-based trucking company, Heartland's fleet included more than 600 trailers, more than half of which were less than a year old. The new acquisition led Heartland to expand its operations as well, as the company added a service center in LaMonte, Missouri to support the new additions to its fleet.

In 1988, with a tractor fleet numbering more than 300, almost half of which were company owned, and the number of trailers at 715, Heartland posted a net income of more than $5 million on $34.6 million in sales. The following year, Heartland stepped up its expansion, purchasing the assets (including 120 dry van trailers) from PDQ Transportation Inc., a Tennessee-based trucking line. This move enabled Heartland to extend its trucking services beyond the Midwest region into the Southeast. Taking over PDQ's customers proved to be a challenge for the company, however. After a drop in earnings early in 1989, the company moved to shed the less profitable of its new customers. Late that year, Heartland opened a second regional service facility in Dyersburg, Tennessee and committed to expanding its service in the Southeast region.

Profiting from the Recession, the Early 1990s

By late 1989, the economy was in a downturn as the country entered the recession that stretched into the early 1990s. But under Gerdin's guidance, Heartland had consistently avoided taking on long-term debt; in fact, the company claimed that it still had not spent all of the money raised in its IPO. As Gerdin told *Forbes,* "In good times, maybe we don't look so smart. But now we do." Gerdin's conservative leadership paid off as Heartland moved to take up business from competitors struggling to survive in the poor economic climate. Gerdin made a new move in 1989 to solidify the company's standing when it began converting its entire fleet to new 53-foot trailers, the first in the industry to do so. The new trailers, longer than the typical 48-foot trailer found in the industry, provided the company, and its customers, with 11 percent more freight space, with little difference in operating costs. Heartland also moved to convert its company-owned tractor fleet to the more fuel-efficient cabover design.

The conversion of the company's nearly 1,500 trailers was completed in 1990. By that year, the company's fleet had grown to 525 tractors, including 235 new cabover tractors, an increase of nearly 100 over the previous year. Despite the conversion of the fleet, Heartland stayed true to Gerdin's original conviction and managed to remain debt free. "Not only do we have no debt, but we are dealing from a base of business decisions, rather than on whether we have enough cash flow," John Cosaert, Heartland's chief financial officer and co-founder told *Investor's Daily.* "A lot of people are putting themselves in a bad position because of leverage." By the end of 1990, the company's fleet had grown to nearly 300 company-owned tractors. Revenues grew to $63 million, providing a net income of more than $7.3 million.

Early in 1991, Gerdin reduced his control of the company, putting up 650,000 of his own shares in a secondary offering, leaving him with 51 percent of the company's stock. By the end of that year, Heartland doubled the size of its company-owned tractor fleet as it continued to expand, especially in the Southeast. To further expansion in that region, Heartland started up Heartland Distribution Services (HDS), a subsidiary concentrating on short-haul traffic, in 1992, and opened a distribution center in Atlanta, Georgia to service the new subsidiary. By the end of that year, HDS had already outgrown that facility, and the company bought a new, larger center in Atlanta. Also in 1992, Heartland combined its LaMonte, Missouri and Dyersburg, Tennessee centers into a new terminal located in St. Louis, Missouri designed to accommodate the company's short-haul growth in the region. Meanwhile, the company's trailer fleet underwent a new conversion, now to aluminum plate trailers. The new trailers were wider by more than three inches than conventional trailers, further increasing load capacity; the aluminum plate was also stronger, lowering maintenance costs, and the new trailers were expected to last ten years instead of the seven years that conventional trailers usually lasted.

Poised for the Future

By 1993, Heartland revenues had jumped to $115 million. The following year, however, Heartland moved to double the size of the company by acquiring Munson Transportation Inc., a struggling trucking company based in Monmouth, Illinois. Under the conditions of the acquisition, Munson received shares of Heartland stock, then worth $73 million, while Heartland assumed Munson's $55 million debt. In addition to acquiring Munson's aging fleet and facilities, Heartland gained access to Munson's Northeast and West Coast markets, expanding Heartland to a national trucking line. After attempting to merge Munson's operation into the company, Heartland finally consolidated both companies, closing Munson's Illinois facilities and moving its operations to Heartland's Coralville, Iowa headquarters. The company also sold off most of Munson's aging, diversified trailer fleet, returning the company to its uniform, 53-foot aluminum plate fleet of trailers.

A booming year for trucking in 1994 helped Heartland overcome the challenges of the Munson acquisition. By the end of 1995, in addition, Heartland had wiped out its entire debt. As a company posting nearly $200 million in sales, with a net income of more than $20.5 million, Heartland had taken its place as one of the top ten truckload carriers in the United States.

Principal Subsidiaries

Heartland Express Inc. of Iowa; Heartland Distribution Services; Heartland Equipment, Inc.; Heartland Monmouth Warehouse Corporation; Munson Transportation, Inc.; Munson Transport Services, Inc.; Munson Equipment, Inc.

Further Reading

Ford, George C., "Heartland Express Growing, Adding Jobs, Customers," *Cedar Rapids Gazette,* July 28, 1996.

Jones, John A., "Heartland Express Back on Track After Major Overhaul," *Investor's Business Daily,* February 15, 1996, p. B12.

——, "Heartland Express Focuses Growth on Regional Markets," *Investor's Business Daily,* December 18, 1992, p. 30.

Kramer, Farrell, "Heartland Express," *Investor's Daily,* March 11, 1992, p. 1.

Lawless, Jim, "Obscure Heartland Rockets into Limelight," *Des Moines Register,* June 21, 1993, Bus. Sec., p. 7.

Meeks, Fleming, "Bring on the Flood," *Forbes,* November 12, 1990.

Padley, Karen, "Heartland Express Grows with Service to Big Companies," *Investor's Business Daily,* December 16, 1991, p. 34.

Petroski, William, "Powerful Acceleration," *Des Moines Register,* February 4, 1996, Bus. Outlook Sec., p. 14.

Rogers, Doug, "Heartland Express Stays in Center of Nation's Road Map," *Investor's Daily,* February 13, 1991, p. 32.

—M. L. Cohen

Helen of Troy

Helen of Troy Corporation

6827 Market Avenue
El Paso, Texas 79915
U.S.A.
(915) 779-6363
Fax: (915) 774-4795

Public Company
Incorporated: 1968
Employees: 285
Sales: $167.1 million (fiscal 1996, ended last day of
    February)
Stock Exchanges: NASDAQ
SICs: 3999 Manufacturing Industries, Not Elsewhere
    Classified; 3634 Electric Housewares & Fans

Named for the most beautiful woman in classical mythology, Helen of Troy Corporation commands an industry-leading 35 percent share of the retail hair appliance market via its Vidal Sassoon and Revlon brand names. The company's transformation from a struggling chain of wig shops into an industry leader is primarily credited to shrewd and timely licensing, from its purchase of limited rights to the Vidal Sassoon name in 1980 to the 1996 acquisition of rights to use the Dazey, Carel, and Dr. Scholl's brands. Line extensions and geographic diversification helped Helen of Troy enjoy a growth rate of 15 percent from 1986 to 1996 in spite of its concentration in a generally low-growth industry. By the early 1990s, the company sold brushes, combs, hair accessories, shavers, and massagers as well as its core electric and battery operated hair care appliances. Its distribution arms reached from the United States to Europe, Australia, South America, South Africa, and Asia.

Late 1960s Origins

The company was founded in 1969 by Louis Rubin, a Chicago native who had moved to El Paso, Texas, to enjoy the weather. A 32-year veteran of the wholesale and retail cosmetics business, Rubin and his 25-year-old son Gerald launched Helen of Troy to sell wigs, then a mainstream fashion acces-

sory. Wigs were so hot that the father-son team soon had six boutiques in El Paso and their company was ranked among the top firms in the industry. In the early 1970s, however, wigs fell out of fashion. In the middle years of the decade, the Rubins phased out their wig business in favor of professional-quality styling tools like blow dryers and curling irons. By 1978, Helen of Troy had cultivated a 25 percent niche in that market and Louis sold the company to Gerald. Although his $6-million-selling firm was marginally profitable, it was clear to the young entrepreneur that Helen of Troy faced scant prospects for growth in the salon market.

Rubin wanted to penetrate the high-growth consumer hair appliance market, but faced several obstacles. Competition from industry giants like General Electric and Gillette would require massive cash outlays to advertise the Helen of Troy brand. In fact, those entrenched companies' yearly advertising and promotion budgets surpassed the Texas firm's annual sales. With its comparatively meager cash flow, Helen of Troy would be hard-pressed just to penetrate the consumer market, let alone bring the brand to profitability. Rubin also worried that a mass launch of the nameplate would alienate its core hairdresser clients.

Acquisition of Vidal Sassoon Brand Jump-Starts Company in 1980s

Louis Rubin alerted his son to a possible solution in 1980, when he discovered that British hairstylist-to-the-stars Vidal Sassoon was seeking licensees for his famous name. As *Inc.* magazine's Paul B. Brown put it in his 1988 article, "it was as if God had decided to speak directly to [Gerald Rubin]." But it was by no means a miracle. When Rubin approached Sassoon about the license, he found himself in a bidding war with none other than Gillette and General Electric. Rubin mustered all his powers of persuasion—not to mention a lucrative 10 percent royalty deal on a guaranteed $25 million in sales plus a $100,000 signing bonus—to win his company's first five-year contract. The license covered "all of Sassoon's electric- or battery-powered personal care appliances in the United States and Canada."

The name proved a talisman for Helen of Troy, whose net income rebounded from a loss of $1.1 million in 1980 to a profit of about $1.8 million by 1983 on back-to-back doublings of unit sales in 1981 and 1982. Rubin had to swallow his pride and face the fact that his company's name was becoming a "Trojan brand," hidden behind the well-known Sassoon trademark. Sassoon products quickly grew to account for 80 percent of sales, but the company did not abandon its Helen of Troy name, maintaining that brand for its professional line. The company went public in 1981, raising $1 million to help pay off its licensing fees. The Rubin family retained about a 20 percent stake in Helen of Troy.

Helen of Troy wasn't the only company to benefit from the Sassoon name's cachet. In the early 1980s, Sassoon sold his licensing business to Richardson-Vicks, which was in turn acquired by mega-marketer Proctor & Gamble Co. in 1985. When Helen of Troy's licensing contract came up for renewal in that same year, Rubin negotiated a reduction of the royalty to 7 percent. Helen of Troy's relationship with Proctor & Gamble would prove highly beneficial. For example, the hair dryer company enjoyed "fallout" promotion from every one of the tens of millions of dollars P&G spent on advertising its Vidal Sassoon shampoo. P&G's commercials featured Vidal Sassoon himself assuring consumers, "If you don't look good, we don't look good." Although he was specifically promoting the shampoo, Helen of Troy's hair appliances undoubtedly benefitted from the campaign. In a 1991 *Forbes* magazine article, Southwest Securities analyst Richard Edelman went so far as to assert that "they've really ridden the coattails of P&G."

Helen of Troy didn't rely solely on the Sassoon name for its success; Rubin and his employees also worked hard to cultivate a reputation for attentive customer service and timely delivery. Although it did not manufacture its own goods, its well-chosen Asian suppliers enabled the company to boast "the lowest defect rate in the industry" in its 1996 annual report.

By the mid-1980s Helen of Troy led most of its main product categories, with 35 percent of the market for hatchet-style hair dryers, 29 percent of curling irons, 23 percent of brush irons, and 30 percent of combination curling iron/curling brush appliances. Helen of Troy's sales multiplied more than tenfold, from an estimated $6 million in 1978 to about $90 million in 1987, and net income grew to $8.5 million.

Having consolidated its position in these core markets, Helen of Troy sought to expand its product line into newer hairstyling devices—crimping irons, hot air styling brushes and hairsetters—as well as other segments of the hair care and beauty markets like brushes and combs, hair accessories, lighted mirrors, and shavers. While still only a small fraction of its total business, the firm's continuing interaction with professional stylists via its original Helen of Troy brand proved pivotal to this effort. Input from these clients fostered the development of new features like automatic shut-off, diffusers, the "cold shot" style setter, dual and adjustable handles, variable heat settings, increased wattage, new controls, and a removable filter, among other options. Late in the decade, Helen of Troy launched the "Sable" line of hair care appliances designed especially for African-Americans' typically thicker, less manageable hair. The company also diversified its distribution channels from its traditional emphasis on department stores to include mass merchants, discounters, and supermarkets during this period. As a result of its ongoing diversifications, Helen of Troy's revenues neared $120 million and its net profit exceeded $10.5 million by 1990.

Geographic Diversification and New Licensing Emphasized in Early 1990s

While the company continued to refine and expand its product line in the early 1990s, it also focused on two new growth strategies: geographic diversification and additional licensing. As it had in the United States, Helen of Troy followed Proctor & Gamble to Europe, purchasing the right to sell Vidal Sassoon hair appliances in nine European countries in 1990. The company expanded its international licensing agreement to include 12 other European nations, including France and Germany, in 1993. By the end of fiscal 1996, overseas sales accounted for nearly one-third of Helen of Troy's annual revenues.

Seeking a repeat of its success with the Vidal Sassoon brand, in 1992 Helen of Troy licensed global rights (excluding Mexico and parts of Europe) to apply the Revlon label to its hair care appliances. Contrary to some observers' warnings, the Revlon line did not cannibalize sales from the Vidal Sassoon products. In fact, analysts with Dillon, Read & Co. observed that "Retailers like the ability to purchase two distinct brands from one manufacturer, allowing them to offer customers enhanced assortments while leveraging purchases against a single supplier." And like its Sassoon arrangement, Helen of Troy profited from Revlon's marketing efforts. By the mid-1990s, industry analysts estimated that the combined yearly advertising expenditures of the Revlon and Sassoon parent companies totaled $300 million, dwarfing Helen of Troy's less than $10 million annual ad budget. Helen of Troy expanded its rights to the Revlon brand to include ladies' shavers and artificial nails in 1996. That fall, the company made its first forays outside the hair care business with the acquisition of North American rights to Dr. Scholl's brand foot baths, foot massagers, and body massagers, as well as Dazey, Lady Dazey, and Lady Carel brand "hard hat" salon-style hair dryers and Turbo Spa products.

Helen of Troy suffered a fairly serious setback in 1991, when the bankruptcies of three major customers, the poor performance of a subsidiary chain of beauty supply stores, and recession conspired to reduce net income by more than 55 percent from the previous year. Helen of Troy sold its faltering Beauty Biz Inc. chain of 35 stores in Oklahoma, Texas, and Kansas to Sally Beauty Supply in 1993. The company reincorporated in Bermuda in 1994, creating a holding company structure and taking advantage of tax and financing benefits in the process. Sales increased by 41 percent from $118.8 in fiscal 1990 to $167.1 million in fiscal 1996 and profits increased by 21 percent, from $10.8 million to $13.1 million.

Industry analysts were unified in their optimism about Helen of Troy's future prospects. Both M.H. Meyerson & Co. and Dillon, Read & Co. Inc. cited the company's negligible debt, healthy cash flow, highly recognized brand names, and record of growth in a stagnant industry in their predictions for 20 percent growth through the turn of the century. Dillon, Reed projected that Helen of Troy's sales would near a quarter of a billion dollars by 1998 and profits would total close to $20 million.

Principal Subsidiaries

International Appliances Ltd. (Hong Kong); Helen of Troy (Far East) Ltd. (Hong Kong); Helen of Troy (Cayman) Ltd. (Cayman Islands); Helen of Troy International, BV (Amsterdam); Helen of Troy Ltd. (Barbados); Helen of Troy Services Ltd. (Hong Kong); Helen of Troy Corp.; Helen of Troy International Marketing Ltd. (Barbados); HOT (UK) Ltd. (United Kingdom; 50%).

Further Reading

Bernard, Sharyn, "Large Curls Seen Drawing Big Sales," *HFN: The Weekly Newspaper for the Home Furnishing Network,* September 23, 1996, p. 38.

Brown, Paul B., "License to Steal," *Inc.,* December 1988, pp. 141–142.

Byrne, Harlan S., "Helen of Troy," *Barron's,* September 28, 1992, pp. 35–36.

——, "Helen of Troy: Handsome Gains from Hair-Care Products," *Barron's,* August 7, 1989, pp. 37–38.

——, "Lovely Prospects," *Barron's,* January 23, 1995, p. 18.

Carr, Carol, "Helen of Troy," *HFD: The Weekly Home Furnishings Newspaper,* December 18, 1989, pp. 59–60.

Cochran, Thomas N., "Helen of Troy Corp.," *Barron's,* November 14, 1988, pp. 60–62.

Ellis, Beth R., "Helen of Troy Sails into Expanded Horizon," *HFD: The Weekly Home Furnishings Newspaper,* October 19, 1987, pp. 56.

Giges, Nancy, "Big Hair Inspires '96 Offerings," *HFD: The Weekly Home Furnishings Newspaper,* December 18, 1995, pp. 66–67.

Greenbaum, Jessica, "Hair Today, but Where Tomorrow?," *Forbes,* December 19, 1983, pp. 98–99.

"Helen of Troy Corp.: Care Products Firm's Profit Jumped in Its Third Period," *Wall Street Journal,* January 9, 1992, p. 3B.

"Helen of Troy Record Sales," *HFD: The Weekly Home Furnishings Newspaper,* January 22, 1996, p. 68.

Jaffe, Thomas, "Trojan Hair Dryer," *Forbes,* March 20, 1989, p. 221.

Jancsurak, Joe, "Two Handles Are Better Than One: Vidal Sassoon," *Appliance Manufacturer,* August 1994, pp. 72–73.

Marcial, Gene G., "Will Helen Launch 1,000 Buy Orders?," *Business Week,* April 25, 1988, p. 114.

Poole, Claire, "Marketing Moocher," *Forbes,* September 16, 1991, pp. 144–145.

Purpura, Linda M., "Helen of Troy Adding Line," *HFD: The Weekly Home Furnishings Newspaper,* February 5, 1990, p. 70.

Ratliff, Duke, "Helen of Troy: 'The Right Stuff,' " *HFD: The Weekly Home Furnishings Newspaper,* February 21, 1994, p. 47.

"Record Results for Helen of Troy," *HFN: The Weekly Newspaper of the Home Furnishing network,* July 22, 1966, p. 46.

Sloane, Leonard, "Black Women's Hair Care: Market's There, and Now so Are the Appliances," *New York Times,* August 15, 1992, p. 46.

Stouffer, Paul W., "Vidal Signs; New Sassoon Pact Aids Earnings Pickup at Helen of Troy," *Barron's,* July 20, 1987, pp. 53–54.

Troxell, Thomas N., Jr., "Selling Sassoon: His Label Is a Boon to Helen of Troy's Line," *Barron's,* August 27, 1984, p. 37.

—April Dougal Gasbarre

Helmerich & Payne, Inc.

Utica & 21st Streets
Tulsa, Oklahoma 74114
U.S.A.
(918) 742-5531
Fax: (918) 742-0237

Public Company
Incorporated: 1926
Employees: 2,500
Sales: $393.2 million (1996)
Stock Exchanges: New York
SICs: 1381 Drilling Oil & Gas Wells; 1382 Oil & Gas
Field Exploration Services; 6552 Land Subdividers &
Developers, Not Elsewhere Classified

Helmerich & Payne, Inc. (H&P) is a survivor in the volatile world of oil and gas exploration, contract drilling, and production, and when the company marked its 75th year in 1995, it was believed to be the oldest contract driller in the United States. Part of H&P's success has come from its long-time commitment to diversified operations: the company owns more than 1.6 million square feet of commercial and industrial real estate, including Tulsa, Oklahoma's landmark Utica Square Shopping Center. The company has also long held a strong investment portfolio, which contributed more than $10 million to its pre-tax income in 1995. Until that year, H&P also operated Natural Gas Odorizing, Inc., a world leader in mercaptan-based natural gas odorizing agents; the sale of that subsidiary in 1996 added $24 million to the company's $72.6 million net income for the year ended September 30, 1996.

H&P's core business is in oil and natural gas. The company is engaged in the exploration for and development and acquisition of oil and natural gas reserves in its home state of Oklahoma, as well as in Louisiana, Kansas, and Texas. H&P's 1995 reserves of some 280 billion cubic feet of natural gas and more than six million barrels of oil made it the 52nd-largest oil company in the world. H&P's contract drilling subsidiary, Helmerich & Payne International Drilling Co., owns and oper-

ates more than 30 land rigs and 11 offshore drilling platforms in the United States. Internationally, H&P owns and operates another 35 land rigs, chiefly in South America, with a primary focus on Venezuela and Colombia. Utilization rates for the company's rigs hovers around 90 percent both domestically and internationally. H&P is led by president and CEO Hans Helmerich, grandson of company founder Walt Helmerich. In 1996 the company posted revenues of $393.2 million.

Barnstorming the Oil Boom in the 1920s

H&P was founded in 1920 by Walt Helmerich and William Payne. Helmerich was born in 1895 in Chicago. In 1914, bored with academic life at the University of Chicago, Helmerich left school to work in New Orleans and Beaumont, Texas, and eventually at Western Electric Company in Chicago. When the United States entered World War I in 1917, Helmerich enlisted in the Army Signal Corps and became a pioneer member of the country's newly forming air force, where he quickly rose to become a test pilot and flight instructor for the famous Curtis JN-4 ''Flying Jenny,'' and a member one of the military's first ''aerobatic'' flying teams. After the war, Helmerich took his piloting skills on the road, buying three planes and forming a barnstorming stunt flying team with two friends. Shortly before the troupe's first performance in 1919, both of Helmerich's partners were killed in a test flight. By then, Helmerich was married to Cadijah Colcord, daughter of Oklahoma oil pioneer Charles F. Colcord. Offered a job with brother-in-law Ray Colcord, Helmerich went to work overseeing the drilling of a well in Ossawatomie, Kansas, then helped relocate Colcord's rig to South Bend, Texas.

The pair quickly struck oil with Colcord's rig, pumping 300 barrels a day; Helmerich purchased a share of the rig—and the profits—for $9,000. In 1920 Helmerich raised enough money, in part by selling the scrap metal from his airplanes, to buy his own drilling rig. Helmerich was joined by William Payne, who had worked as an oil scout for Charles Colcord. Payne's background was in bacteriology and chemistry, with an undergraduate degree from Oklahoma A&M, and graduate work in microbiology at Massachusetts A&M and Amherst. Payne gained practical experience working for a pharmaceutical company in Detroit and later

---

Company Perspectives:

Honesty. Commitment. Integrity. Our pledge is to approach the next 75 years with these time-tested values etched clearly in our minds, remaining forever indebted to the thousands of loyal Helmerich & Payne, Inc., co-workers who have gone before us and kept the faith.

---

as a bacteriologist for that city; during World War I, Payne joined the Army Sanitation Corps and helped isolate the influenza virus that had caused an outbreak in 1918. After the war, Payne went to work for Colcord's North American Oil and Refining, then helped form Helmerich & Payne in 1920.

The partners originally plied the South Bend oil fields and carted their rig as far as New Mexico. In 1923 Helmerich sent his wife and newborn son, Walt Helmerich III, to live with her family in Tulsa, Oklahoma. By then H&P owned three rigs, and in 1926 the partners moved two of their rigs to Oklahoma in order to tap into the oil-rich Osage County field. Their first strike, a 2,350-foot wildcat producing 5,000 barrels per day in Braman, Oklahoma, led the partners to formally incorporate as Helmerich & Payne, Inc. Payne supervised the company's drilling activities, while Helmerich took charge of financing.

The young company soon faced the Depression and an oil glut that saw the price of a barrel of oil fall from $1.43 per barrel to just ten cents per barrel at the depth of the Depression. H&P began selling down its oil leases, while continuing to operate drilling rigs under contract. At the time, locating oil was as much based on luck as on science, with rates of around one producing well for every 50 drilled. Eventually, the company focused its operations on contract drilling. The company nevertheless continued its own exploration and drilling efforts, and in 1936 H&P made a major strike in the Hugoton natural gas fields in southeastern Kansas. Starting with four wells, H&P's Hugoton strike would provide a backbone for the company's growth; sixty years later, the Hugoton field still accounted for two-thirds of H&P's natural gas reserves. The company established another landmark in 1936, constructing a working rig on the lawn in front of Oklahoma's State Capital building. That well would continue producing until it was finally plugged in 1976.

William Payne left H&P in 1936, founding the Big Chief Drilling Company in Oklahoma City, and in 1965 Payne's success in the industry led him to be named Oklahoma's "Oil Man of the Year." Meanwhile, Helmerich struggled to obtain financing for H&P during the Depression. By 1939, H&P owed some $1 million in debt, and the company verged on bankruptcy. Helmerich refused to declare bankruptcy and managed to secure the loans to rescue the company. As part of the financing agreement, the company reorganized as a Delaware Corporation, and Helmerich was forced to relinquish partial control of H&P.

Postwar Growth

Demand for oil and gas had plummeted during the Depression, while overproduction had kept prices low. With the

outbreak of World War II, demand again surged. Yet contract drilling rates were low, especially for the highly competitive shallow drilling market, and H&P stepped up its own exploration efforts, turning now to deep drilling projects. Toward the end of the war, the company scored successes with three deep wildcat wells in the Texas Panhandle, and several other 5,000-foot wells were also producing in the range of 300 to 500 barrels a day. In order to make the company more attractive to lenders, H&P reorganized in 1944 as the White Eagle Oil Company, which would be chiefly engaged in exploration and production. H&P was organized as the company's contract drilling subsidiary. The following year, the company made its first acquisition, of Cardinal Oil Company, which had more than 240 producing wells and an average daily production of over 5,000 barrels. By 1949, the company was posting revenues of $6.7 million.

The company prospered in the postwar years. Automobile use was on the rise, sparking a huge demand for oil products. By 1952, the company was operating 17 deep-drilling rigs in six states. At the same time, the rise in demand brought on increased competition, and by the early 1950s the oil industry was entering a new slump. Drilling contracts fell, and H&P saw its profits threatened. By the mid-1950s H&P was ripe for new management, and the company did not have to look far. In 1954 Helmerich's son, Walt Helmerich III, was named executive vice-president. The younger Helmerich, a graduate of Harvard Business School—and one of the company's first college graduates—quickly assembled a new management team and set to work improving the company's operating efficiency. The company also began hiring its first drilling engineers, who introduced new technology to the company's exploration and drilling operations, particularly in secondary recovery techniques that would extend each well's production output. Secondary recovery output reached 80,000 barrels per year in 1954 and rose to 250,000 per year by 1958. Meanwhile the company was expanding its operations, entering the international market with lease-partnerships in Venezuela in 1957. The company soon entered the Philippines, Bolivia, and Cuba. H&P also acquired Engineering Construction Company (ECCO), a pipeline construction company. In 1959 the company reorganized again, dropping the White Eagle name and going public. H&P's revenues by then were $14.2 million. The following year, Walt Helmerich III replaced his father as the company's president.

Diversification in the 1960s

With a fresh slump in the oil industry at the start of the 1960s, H&P began a new program of diversification to enable it better to weather the industry's traditionally cyclical nature. The company acquired Natural Gas Odorizing, Inc., (NGO) of Houston in 1960. NGO manufactured chemicals that added odor and taste to natural gas, which were necessary for detecting the presence of the volatile material. Over the years, NGO would become an industry leader, capturing as much as a 50 percent share of the gas odorant market. In 1962 H&P acquired Horton Company, a specialist in laying cable for the telephone industry. Horton's patented cable-laying plow was soon adapted for ECCO's pipeline work. The acquisition of Houston-based F. H. Maloney Company in 1964 brought H&P into manufacturing, with the production of molded rubber, machined metal, and other products for oil and pipeline companies. That same year saw H&P enter the commercial real estate market with the purchase of the Utica Square shopping center in Tulsa.

Throughout this period of diversification, H&P continued to expand its presence in the oil industry. Land-based drilling continued to decline during the 1960s, forcing the company to look in a new direction. Preparations for entering the burgeoning off-shore drilling market began in 1964, with the construction of the company's own off-shore rig. Launched in 1968, the rig was severely damaged during a storm the following year, and the company's drilling contract was canceled. In response, H&P traded the rig to offshore driller Atwood Oceanics, Inc., in exchange for a 28 percent interest in that company. Next, H&P, with sales passing $27 million by 1965, attempted a new acquisition, this time of a company larger than itself. By 1968, H&P had bought up enough stock to make itself the largest single investor in Sunray DX, an oil and gas company. H&P and Sunray began merger discussions, but before these were completed, Sun Oil stepped in with an offer to purchase Sunray. H&P attempted to block the acquisition, but failed. Nevertheless, H&P retained a significant share of Sun/Sunray stock and realized a handsome profit through the merger. The company retained that investment, which helped increase revenues to $38 million by the end of the decade, while continuing to expand its stock portfolio with investments in other public companies.

With drilling contracts continuing to suffer in the early 1970s, H&P accelerated its exploration activity, but the company had not kept pace with advances in technology made by the larger oil companies and needed to aggressively recruit geologists and other engineers. This effort soon paid off with the opening of three wells in Buffalo Wallow Field in Texas, which combined for a potential output of 75 billion cubic feet of natural gas. By the late 1970s, the company's gas output topped its oil production for the first time. The company—along with the entire oil industry—was given a fresh boost by the oil crisis of 1973. With oil prices rising, and the search intensifying for alternative sources of oil reserves, H&P's international operation grew. By the end of the decade, H&P was operating 12 of its own rigs in Venezuela alone, while drilling under contract for another nine rigs. The company's rigs were also drilling wells in Colombia, Ecuador, Peru, Belize, Guatemala, and Bolivia. H&P's revenues climbed to $77.5 million in 1976 and neared $150 million by 1979. As the decade closed, the total number of H&P-owned rigs topped 50, with utilization rates of 99 percent. Deregulation of the oil industry stimulated a boom in the search for oil. Meanwhile, oil prices were skyrocketing, reaching as high as $50 per barrel. As more and more sources of oil were developed, OPEC, watching its share of the oil market dwindle from 70 to 30 percent, reacted in panic. Quickly, the market was flooded with oil.

Surviving the Bust in the 1980s

By the end of the 1980s, nearly 80 percent of the oil industry had gone bankrupt. For H&P, which saw its 1982 revenues climb to $338 million and net profits soar to $75.6 million, the tide began to turn by 1983. Revenues began to drop, to $208 million in 1984, down to $160.5 million by 1988. The company struggled to retain profits: net income slid to $48 million in 1983 and to $7 million in 1986. But in 1989, with revenues of $171 million, H&P was the only drilling company in the world to post a profit, of $22.7 million.

The company could credit its survival to a conservative fiscal policy set in place during the late 1970s. Where other drilling companies attempted to cash in on the oil boom with rapid expansion, Helmerich focused instead on increasing its production of natural gas. Meanwhile, the company's stock portfolio, its real estate investments, and its NGO and other subsidiaries, helped cushion the company's bottom line and allowed it to continue investing in upgrading and building state-of-the-art drilling rigs, and to step up its presence in off-shore drilling. By 1991, the company had spent some $112 million in upgrading and expanding its equipment, while managing to pay for its new rigs by securing long-term contracts with the major oil companies. By then, the third generation of Helmerichs took over the company's leadership with the appointment of Hans Helmerich as president and CEO. Walt Helmerich III remained as company chairman.

With so much of its competition out of business, H&P could now compete for some of the industry's largest drilling contracts, including a contract with BP Exploration for the vast Cusiana Field discovered in Colombia at the start of the decade. H&P became a leader in international drilling, particularly in South America. During the first half of the 1990s the company continued to expand, raising its total number of operating rigs to more than 75 by 1996. The company's revenues also made a strong return, reaching $239 million in 1992, climbing to $329 million in 1994, and jumping to $393 million by 1996. The sale of its NGO subsidiary helped boost the company's profits to nearly $73 million in that year. Entering the remaining years of the century with no long-term debt, and with new long-term drilling contracts for its cutting-edge technology, H&P was poised to continue its legacy as an industry barnstormer.

Principal Subsidiaries

Helmerich & Payne International Drilling Co.; Helmerich & Payne Properties Inc.

Further Reading

Flanigan, James, "Helmerich & Payne versus Parker Drilling," *Forbes,* October 30, 1978, p. 54.
Jones, James A., "Helmerich & Payne Hikes Oil Drilling as Gas Prices Rise," *Investor's Business Daily,* April 29, 1996, p. A35.
Krauss, Alan, "Helmerich & Payne Scores Even During Oil Industry Slump, *Investor's Daily,* January 11, 1990, p. 30.
Percefull, Gary, "Helmerich & Payne Knows It's a Jungle out There," *Tulsa World,* October 1, 1989, p. G1.
Roberts, James, and Chris Hernandez, *Helmerich & Payne, Inc.: The First 75 Years,* Tulsa: Helmerich & Payne, Inc., 1995.
Rutherford, Dan, "Stock of Tulsa's Helmerich & Payne Skyrocketing," *Tulsa World,* October 18, 1996, p. E1.
Schafer, Shaun, "Focused on the Family," *Tulsa World,* May 20, 1996, p. A9.
Schein, Chris, "H & P Continues Rig Upgrades," *Tulsa World,* March 10, 1991, p. G5.
——, "Decade of Work Pays off for Driller," *Tulsa World,* January 26, 1992, p. G1.
Tuttle, Ray, "Seen Worst, Done Best," *Tulsa World,* July 29, 1996, p. A7.

—M. L. Cohen

Hoechst

Hoechst A.G.

65926 Frankfurt am Main
Federal Republic of Germany
(49) 69 3050
Fax: (49) 69 305 17082
Web site: http://www.hoechst.com

Public Company
Incorporated: 1952 as Farbwerke Hoechst A.G.
Employees: 169,760
Sales: DM52.18 billion (US$36.5 billion) (1995)
Stock Exchanges: Munich Hanover Bonn Frankfurt
    Hamburg Basle Zurich Brussels London Paris
    Antwerp Amsterdam Vienna
SICs: 2865 Cyclic Crudes and Intermediates; 2841 Soap
    and Other Detergents; 2851 Paints and Allied
    Products; 2830 Drugs; 2280 Yarn and Thread Mills

With operations in 120 nations around the globe, Hoechst (pronounced "herckst") A.G. is the world's largest chemical manufacturer. By the mid-1990s, less than 25 percent of its annual revenues were generated in its home country of Germany. From its roots as a dyestuffs producer, the company grew to become one of that nation's top three chemical firms. It was a key component of the IG Farben chemical cartel, and emerged from the post-World War II breakup of that conglomerate as a strong and growing entity. Hoechst developed a particular focus on pharmaceuticals in the ensuing decades, but its diverse product line—including agricultural and industrial chemicals, fibers, polymers, and engineering services—helped to shelter it from vacillations in any one market. In 1996 the Kuwaiti government, through Kuwait Petroleum Corporation, continued to hold the 25 percent stake in Hoechst that it had first acquired over a decade before.

19th-Century Origins

Founded by Eugen Lucius in 1863, the company takes its name from the village of Hochst am Main near Frankfurt. At the time its entire capital consisted of a three horsepower steam engine and a small boiler in which anilin oil and arsenic acid, boiling together, produced a synthetic fuschia dye. By 1874 this primitive machine gave way to a new chemical plant. In a period of 20 years the Hoechst workforce grew from 5 to 1900 employees. By the end of the century, Hoechst had several thousand workers and a good reputation as an employer. The company reduced the traditional 12-hour day to 8 hours, and provided its employees with athletic facilities, midwives, and prenatal care.

Throughout the late 19th and early 20th centuries, dyestuffs accounted for 90 percent of Hoechst's sales. Although an 1883 brochure allotted the company's work in pharmaceuticals only one sentence, this work was, in retrospect, significant for both Hoechst and the history of pharmacology. At first glance, a dye company like Hoechst might seem an unusual setting for pioneering work in drugs, but it must be remembered that the German dye industry, with its ties to major universities, had a degree of technical expertise unrivaled in the world. Furthermore, many dyes and drugs shared a similar chemical composition.

In 1883 a Hoechst chemist working with quinine discovered Antipyrin, one of the first analgesics. The company cooperated with leading researchers Koch and Erlich to produce the Novocaine familiar to dental patients, and also Salvarsan, the first effective treatment for syphilis. Salvarsan was one of the first disease-specific medicines. Most 19th-century drug discoveries were, like aspirin, general remedies. The list of Hoechst's achievements in pharmacology includes the 1906 synthesis of adrenaline and the 1923 isolation of insulin.

Despite its contributions to medicine, Hoechst was not popular with American chemical manufacturers. Along with other German companies, including Bayer and BASF, Hoechst waged an intense price war against its U.S. rivals in the dye industry. One tactic of the German dye trust was "dumping"—selling chemicals below cost in order to eliminate indigenous competitors in the American dye market.

Global Conflict Spurs Creation of IG Farben

Although the American chemical companies fought back, the German chemical trusts, of which Hoechst was a leading member, did impede the growth of the U.S. chemical industry.

The political implications of the German trade wars became apparent during World War I when the Americans found themselves at a technical and productive disadvantage for waging war. Before the advent of nuclear weapons, chemical companies played a leading role in arming a country. Not only did they produce gunpowder and mustard gas, but they made hundreds of synthetic substitutes for organic materials that were in short supply due to war needs or embargoes. After the outbreak of World War I the German chemical industry rushed to fill military requests for inorganic chemicals, pharmaceuticals, explosives, and photographic chemicals. While domestic business increased Hoechst, along with the others, lost its share of the American market and all its U.S. assets. After the war laws were passed to protect the American dye and drug industry from the aggressive policies of the German chemical companies. England, France, the United States, and Germany had all developed elaborate organizations to coordinate chemical production during the war. When peace came, however, all of the countries except Germany quickly dismantled these organizations. The survival of these organizations in Germany, coupled with American protectionism, encouraged the formation of the IG Farben in 1925.

Early in the century two large chemical cartels had been formed within Germany, one of which was centered around Hoechst. In 1925 it was decided by the leaders of the chemical industry that the two cartels should merge into a single company called the Interessen Gemeinschaft Farbenwerke, or IG Farben. From an early date the IG Farben was active in politics, especially in urging that Germany re-arm itself.

That such a large cartel should wield political power comes as no surprise, but the extent of the IG Farben's influence and the nature of its activities gives it a special distinction. After developing its own spy network and placing its directors in the German senate or Reichstag the IG Farben, as the representative of Germany's most important industry, was very influential in the 1933 elections. The man the IG Farben supported was Hitler.

The IG Farben profited greatly from Nazi Germany's political policies. Hitler's plans for world domination coincided neatly with the IG Farben's plans to monopolize the international chemical industry. After the fall of France the Nazis requested that the IG Farben formulate plans for managing the chemical industries in conquered lands, and the cartel complied.

Postwar Breakup of IG Farben

After the war the directors of the IG Farben were charged with war crimes. Their indictment at the Nuremberg trials stated that due to the activities of the IG Farben "the life and happiness of all peoples in the world were adversely affected." This was a serious charge, to which charges of fomenting war and killing slave laborers were added. Despite the gravity of the accusations and the large amount of evidence taken from the IG Farben's own records, no director received more than a four-year prison sentence. A few even returned to sit on the board of directors at Bayer and Hoechst.

Since the German cartel was closely connected to the Nazi regime, the Allies wanted the IG Farben broken up into smaller and less influential companies. The plan for dismantling the IG Farben into three large and nine small companies was less radical than the original plan proposed by the U.S., but by the year of the plan's implementation, 1952, the focus of U.S. foreign policy had shifted away from Germany and toward Russia. Enmeshed in the Cold War, a distracted U.S. finally agreed with France and England not to break the IG Farben into smaller pieces.

The companies absorbed into the IG Farben had lost their corporate identity and this posed a problem for the Allied bureaucrats charged with the task of dividing up the cartel. In general, the largest three companies were given back their pre-1925 holdings. This meant that Hoechst inherited its original Frankfurt works. Over the objections of some Allies, Hoechst also managed to obtain Bobingen AG, a fiber manufacturer.

The newly organized Hoechst grew quickly. The German economy, rebounding from the war, needed chemicals, and Hoechst's factories had survived the Allied bombing attempts. In its first year of independence from the IG Farben, Hoechst had sales of DM211 million. The next year, 1953, Hoechst obtained world rights (exclusive of the U.S.) to manufacture polyester. In 1954 the company began work with polyethylene and polyolefins; in 1956 it began to manufacture petrochemicals. By 1960 the company was clearly on its way to regaining its stature as one of the world's leading chemical companies. By the end of the decade, Hoechst achieved a compounded growth rate of 15.4 percent a year. To put this figure in perspective, one of the fastest-growing American chemical companies during the 1960s, Union Carbide, had a compounded growth rate of 6.8 percent.

Hoechst's growth was much quicker than that of Bayer and BASF, because, unlike the other two companies, Hoechst did not invest in expensive petroleum projects; instead it purchased oil and gas through large term contracts. Hoechst also had a well-diversified product line that protected it from the volatility of the marketplace. Its largest division, paints and plastics, represented only 22 percent of sales. Plastics, fibers, agricultural chemicals, and pharmaceuticals completed the product line. In 1963 Hoechst acquired a Dutch company that made plastic moldings. In 1965 the company built a Trevira polyester plant in neighboring Austria. In France that same year a venture in oxo-alcohols was started. In addition, Hoechst began manufacturing polystyrene in Spain.

Diversification into Pharmaceuticals Marks 1970s

With sales of well over two million marks, Hoechst had by 1970 surpassed the IG Farben from which it sprang. On paper, the company's profit margin had decreased 9 percent, which would have been quite a decrease for an American firm. German businesses, however, have different bookkeeping procedures. They tend to minimize profits where American companies tend to inflate them. The decrease in profits did not stop Hoechst's program of international expansion. Berger, Jenson and Nicholson, Britain's largest paint maker, was on the Hoechst shopping list, along with France's Roussel Uclaf, in which Hoechst took a majority equity position.

Moreover, the United States, with its lower labor costs, was also an attraction. Germany was in the midst of a labor shortage, and the presence of Arabic and Mediterranean guestworkers was becoming a sensitive issue. American workers accepted lower salaries, were entitled to fewer fringe benefits, and were more amenable to layoffs than German workers. Hoechst's acquisition of Hystron Fibers Incorporated in South Carolina made a quick amendment to its U.S. operations.

In the midst of Hoechst's foreign expansion, pharmaceuticals emerged as a significant market. Hoechst had almost gained control of the entire diuretic market, and was a leader in oral medication for diabetics. During this time problems emerged with the maturation of some established drugs and also with drug pirating in Italy. However, pharmaceutical sales still managed to grow at a rate of 13 percent a year despite these setbacks. The growth was fueled by a production of antibiotics, serum, and steroids, as well as a new hookworm medicine popular in Asia and Latin America. By 1978 Hoechst was fortunate to possess a large line of pharmacological products because the company suffered losses in the fibers market. *Forbes* magazine estimated that in a period of three years Hoechst lost one billion marks. Feedstock costs were rising, prices were down, and patents had expired. Company executives took solace in the knowledge that their company's diverse product line would shield it from long-term harm, and that pharmaceuticals would eventually repay their high up-front costs with equally fat profits.

Emphasis on U.S. Market in 1980s

Hoping to increase its global market share from three-and-a-half to five percent, Hoechst focused on the world's largest nation of consumers, the U.S. In 1980 Hoechst built a $100 million plant in Freeport, Texas, the largest single investment it had made. With the addition of this plant Hoechst became larger than Du Pont. John Brookhuis, president of the company's American subsidiary, was proud of Hoechst's growth. "When our parent company celebrated its centennial there was especial joy that Hoechst world-wide had just passed Celanese Corporation in sales."

Encouraged by its 20 years of growth, the management of Hoechst became determined to secure a larger share of the U.S. drug market. This would not be an easy task, even for Hoechst. Up to this point a single drug, the diuretic Lasix, accounted for 80 percent of U.S. sales. The first plan of action was to double the U.S. sales force, and also to target hospitals, the major customers for ethical drugs. Early in the decade, Hoechst presented Harvard's teaching hospital, Massachusetts General, with a history-making US$70 million grant to fund cooperative genetic research. Hoechst acquired New Jersey-based Celanese in 1987. By the mid-1990s, this subsidiary (renamed Hoechst

Celanese Corporation) was generating nearly 25 percent of the group's annual sales. Hoechst capped its North American push with the 1990 purchase of a majority stake in Celanese Mexicana.

Efforts during the 1980s were not, of course, limited to North American pharmaceuticals. In an ambitious move, Hoechst purchased the industrial ceramics division of Germany's largest fine china maker, Rosenthal. At the time, the Japanese controlled 90 percent of the market for semi-conductor ceramics, but Hoechst was determined to take away some of Japan's share. Hoechst faced a substantial capital investment in the business to attain competitiveness, but with profits increasing markedly, company management did not anticipate a cash flow problem.

The 1990s and Beyond

As the twin demons of recession and drug industry consolidation bedeviled Hoechst in the early to mid-1990s, the company devised new strategies. Key among them was the joint venture, wherein two or more companies share the costs and benefits of researching, developing, and marketing new products. Joint ventures with Courtaulds in fibers, Schering in pesticides, and Wacker in plastics were expected to boost productivity in these lagging sectors. Cooperative projects such as these also helped forge vital relationships in new and emerging markets. In 1990, for example, the company signed an agreement with Japan's Teijin to manufacture flame-retardant fibers.

Ironically, acquisitions were also used as economizing measures, as Hoechst executives expected to squeeze economies of scale from new affiliates. Accordingly, the company acquired three European powder coatings operations, a German fibers producer, and a controlling stake in an American manufacturer of generic drugs. In a 1995 bid to re-establish itself as a leading player in the drug business, the company acquired Marion Merrell Dow for US$7.1 billion. The merger moved Hoechst into third place in the continuously consolidating pharmaceutical industry.

But in spite of these efforts, Hoechst's sales wavered in the early 1990s and its profits declined in four consecutive years from 1990 to 1993. To make matters worse, the company was found responsible for several chemical spills in 1993. Chairman Wolfgang Hilger retired early the following year, and was succeeded by 30-year Hoechst veteran and Chief Financial Officer Jurgen Dormann. Faced with a difficult trading environment and a multitude of internal inefficiencies, the new CEO vowed to increase profitability.

His first move was to appoint an eight-member task force composed of executives from Hoechst's global operations. The new leadership took a number of downsizing measures. Massive layoffs trimmed total group employment from over 179,000 in 1991 to just under 166,000 in 1995. A global rationalization of operations also helped cut costs. Dormann's plan appeared to be working in the mid-1990s. Sales increased by over 10 percent from DM46.05 billion in 1993 to DM52.18 billion in 1995, and profits multiplied from less than DM1 billion to a record DM2.25 billion during the same period.

Principal Subsidiaries

Behringwerke AG; DyStar Textilfarben (50%); Herberts; Hoechst Schering AgrEvo (60%); Hoechst Trevira GmbH& Co. KG; Messer Griesheim (66%); SGL Carbon (50.1%); Roussel Uclaf (France; 56.6%); Hoechst UK; Société Français Hoechst SA (France; 99.9%); Hoechst Marion Roussel S.p.A. (Italy); Hoechst Italia S.p.A.; Hoechst Holland; Hoechst Austria; Hoechst Ibérica (Spain); Hoechst do Brasil S.A.; Hoechst Celanese (U.S.A.); Hoechst Marion Roussel Inc. (U.S.A.); Hoechst Japan; Hoechst South Africa (75%); Hoechst Australia.

Further Reading

Alperowicz, Natasha, "Dormann Leads a Revolution at Hoechst," *Chemical Week*, June 15, 1994, pp. 38–41.

Around the World with Chemistry by Kurt Lanz, New York: McGraw Hill, 1980.

Bdumler, Ernst, *A Century of Chemistry*, Dusseldorf: Econ, 1968.

Hayes, Peter, *Industry and Ideology: IG Farben in the Nazi Era,* London: Cambridge University Press, 1987.

"Pharma: German Majors Compared," *ECN-European Chemical News*, September 4, 1995, p. 24.

Williams, Dede, "Hoechst Ponders Polymers Future," *ECN-European Chemical News*, September 25, 1995, p. 31.

—updated by April Dougal Gasbarre

The Home Depot, Inc.

2727 Paces Ferry Road
Atlanta, Georgia 30339
U.S.A.
(770) 433-8211
Fax: (770) 431-2739
Web site: http://www.homedepot.com

Public Company
Incorporated: 1978
Employees: 95,000
Sales: $15.47 billion
Stock Exchanges: New York
SICs: 5211 Lumber and Other Building Materials; 5251
Hardware Stores; 5231 Paint, Glass, and Wallpaper
Stores

The Home Depot, Inc. the largest home center retailer in the United States, operates 478 warehouse stores and sells more than 40,000 items to both the rapidly growing do-it-yourself home improvement market and construction professionals. The company's stores are located in 19 states, on the West Coast as well as in the southwestern, northeastern, and southeastern regions of the United States. California and Florida are the states containing the most Home Depot outlets, most of which are clustered around urban areas. A typical Home Depot warehouse—more than twice the industry norm at an average of 105,000 square feet—stocks building materials, wall and floor coverings, paint, plumbing supplies, hardware, tools, electrical supplies, and supplies for landscaping and gardening.

Roots in Handy Dan

The company was incorporated in June 1978 as a result of a corporate management shake-up by new ownership of the Handy Dan home center chain. As a result of the managerial shuffle, Bernard Marcus, Arthur Blank, and Ronald Brill found themselves out of work. With backing from a New York venture capital firm, Marcus and his two associates formed The Home Depot and opened the company's first outlets in the Atlanta, Georgia, area. The concept that had helped secure financing for the project was that when the price of merchandise was marked down, sales increased while the cost of making those sales decreased. The major problem that had plagued most cut-rate retail operations, however, was poor service at the operations level, which hired unskilled, low-paid employees to keep costs down.

Marcus and his partners realized that recognizing customers' needs was one of the most important elements in a company's growth. They were aware that at the time do-it-yourselfers made up more than 60 percent of the building supply industry's sales volume, but the majority of them did not have the technical knowledge or expertise to accomplish most home repair or improvement projects.

The Home Depot management team set about to solve this problem in two ways. First, they made sure that all Home Depot stores were large enough to stock at least 25,000 different items. Their competitor locations normally had room for only 10,000. The second solution was to train the sales staff in each store to help remove much of the mystery attached to home improvement projects from the minds of consumers. Marcus and his partners believed that, with the education provided by knowledgeable sales staffers, Home Depot customers would gain the confidence to take on more projects at home, coming back to Home Depot outlets to purchase what was needed and get additional advice from sales staff.

Home Depot built its sales staff from both dedicated do-it-yourselfers and professional tradespeople, hiring most employees in full-time capacities. Only 10 percent of Home Depot's sales personnel were part-time. Whenever possible, each store had a licensed plumber and electrician on staff, and customers were urged to call the Home Depot store in their area if they had any problem or questions while they were doing their home repair or improvement projects. The company also scheduled in-store instructional workshops for its customers and in some cases brought in local contractors as teachers.

This approach paid off. By 1984 the company was operating 19 stores and reported sales of $256 million, a 118 percent increase over 1983. In 1986 Home Depot's sales reached the $1 billion mark, and the company was operating 50 retail outlets.

Troubles During the Mid-1980s

The company's growth was not without its problems, however. In 1984 Home Depot paid $38.4 million for the nine-store Bowater warehouse chain, with outlets in Texas, Louisiana, and Alabama. The acquisition created immediate difficulties. Bowater's reputation with consumers was shoddy, and the merchandise in its stores did not match what Home Depot carried in its other outlets. In addition, Bowater's employees did not meet Home Depot's standards; Home Depot would eventually be forced to dismiss almost all of them.

During these years Home Depot's sales continued to climb, but for the first time in the company's history the cost of sales also increased. In 1985 the company's earnings fell 42 percent, and with the ever-increasing costs of opening new outlets—at that time it was more than $8 million per store—the company's long-term debt rose from $4 million to $200 million in just two years. By the end of 1985, the company's stock price had plummeted. It was clear that changes were needed if Home Depot was to continue to grow and prosper.

The company slowed down its expansion. In 1986 Home Depot only opened ten new stores, all in existing, established markets. A stock offering of 2.99 million shares at $17 per share helped reduce and restructure the company debt. Marcus also installed a computerized inventory control system and upgraded the company's management training programs. In keeping with Marcus's commitment to slower, more conservative growth, the company continued opening new stores to completely capture existing markets instead of striking out into new regions of the country.

1989: A Breakthrough Year

By 1989 Home Depot had surpassed Lowe's Companies in sales, becoming the largest home-repair chain in the United States. By year's end almost all outlets were using the company's new satellite data communications network. The fast and accurate exchange of information now linking stores permitted continued growth by enhancing the company's responsiveness to market changes. The satellite also served as a foundation for the Home Depot television network, a system that produces and transmits live programming by top management to each outlet. The company's net earnings increased 46 percent in 1990, and Home Depot effected a three-for-two stock split that same year. Sales increased 38 percent over 1989. With the trend for continued growth in the do-it-yourself market shown by a 33 percent increase in the number of customer transactions logged by the company in 1990, along with an increase of 4 percent for the average customer sale, Home Depot seemed to be an emerging giant in the U.S. retail marketplace.

The company began the 1990s with the goal of doing more than $10 billion in sales from 350 locations by 1995. Part of this plan included a 75-store expansion into the northeastern United States, one of Home Depot's strongest markets despite the region's economic setbacks. Company officials believed the area's dense population and large number of older homes would generate impressive results. Expansion plans also included the state of Washington.

Despite the continued health of the home remodeling market, the company's stock flattened out in 1993, as the firm began to saturate its market. Along with superstores like Bed Bath & Beyond, Home Depot suffered from consumer reaction to the proliferation of large warehouse megastores. In reaction, the company began to search for ways to redefine its marketplace, as well as developing enhancements to its three-tiered "price, assortment, and service" strategies.

Continued Growth During the 1990s

Throughout the 1990s Home Depot tested out several programs designed to determine where business could grow next. In 1991 it sampled customer interest in an installation program for items like carpets, doors, and windows. The program met with success and was adopted throughout Home Depot stores. A bridal registry was tested, as well as a drive-in lumberyard and a delivery service. Home Depot also established an environmental marketing department to help educate consumers about what product choices are more environmentally friendly. Over 70 hardware products—from light bulbs to paint—were identified for customers via in-store flyers and posters. Customer satisfaction again came under consideration in a program called S.P.I—store productivity improvement—in which cleaning, restocking, and other routine tasks are scheduled after store hours. In 1995 Home Depot opened its first 24-hour store and published a book on home repair, the 480-page *Home Improvement 1-2-3*, compiled with *Better Homes and Gardens* magazine publisher Meredith Corporation.

In addition to entering new U.S. markets, Home Depot began to examine other options. In 1994 the company spent $150 million on a 75 percent share of Aikenhead's Home

Improvement Warehouse, a Canadian hardware chain. While Home Depot examined the possibility of expansion both north and south of the border, by the following year plans to open outlets in Mexico had been put on hold, and the number of planned Canadian openings had been reduced to 25 through 1996. Instead, the company added to the number of its EXPO Design Centers, bringing the total to five. Begun in 1991 and located throughout the U.S., these stores have captured the upscale interior design market and further expanded the company's sales base. In addition, efforts to court the commercial market also began to reap profits; overall, Home Depot net earnings achieved a 5-year compound growth rate of 35 percent over the first half of the 1990s.

In addition to its dual concerns of maintaining both the bottom line *and* customer satisfaction, Home Depot has continued to take a leadership role in many of the communities that its stores have entered. Under the leadership of Blank, who contends that corporate America has a responsibility to give back to the society within which it flourishes, Home Depot's Team Depot has become involved in humanitarian causes ranging from local welfare organizations to Habitat for Humanity and the Boys and Girls Clubs of Canada and the United States. In addition to encouraging the continuous volunteer efforts of its employees, the company also employed 1996 Olympic hopeful athletes, paying them competitive wages as part-time employees during their training for the Atlanta-based games, of which Home Depot was a corporate sponsor.

Although some forecasters continued to shed doubt upon the company's ability to maintain its phenomenal level of growth through the year 2000, company management has remained confident. By 3rd-quarter 1996 Home Depot had reported earnings of $221—up 26 percent from the previous year—and was ranked among the ten largest retailers in the United States. Despite the losses posted to competitors in the do-it-yourself retail market, Home Depot's 9 percent increase in same-store sales in 1996 showed that, within the $90 billion consumer home improvement market, orange had become the color of choice.

Further Reading

''The Home Depot,'' *Management Horizons*, July 1990.
''Home Depot and the Home Center Industry,'' *Mid-Atlantic Journal of Business*, December 1994.
''The 'How' in Home Improvement,'' *New York Times*, June 14, 1992.
''Shelter from the Recession,'' *Time*, June 10, 1991.
''Will Home Depot Be 'The Wal-Mart of the '90s?' '' *Business Week*, March 19, 1990.
Zemke, Ron, *The Service Edge*, New York: NAL Books, 1986.

—William R. Grossman
—updated by Pamela L. Shelton

Hooters of America, Inc.

1815 The Exchange
Atlanta, Georgia 30339
U.S.A.
(770) 951-2040
Fax: (770) 618-7032
Web site: http://www.hooters.com

Private company
Incorporated: 1984
Employees: 1,300
Sales: $300 million (1995)
SICs: 5813 Drinking Places, Alcoholic Beverages; 5812
    Eating Places

Hooters of America, Inc. operates and franchises a chain of casual restaurants that feature waitresses known as Hooters Girls. The first Hooters Restaurant opened in Clearwater, Florida, in 1983. The concept was licensed in 1984 to Hooters of America, and by 1996, there were nearly 200 Hooters restaurants nationwide and systemwide sales had reached more than $300 million.

The first Hooters restaurant was opened on April Fools' Day in 1983 in Clearwater, Florida, by six friends and businessmen, none of whom had any experience in the restaurant industry. As Gil DiGiannantonio, one of the partners, told *Florida Trend* magazine three years later, after Hooters had become a roaring success, they were "a bunch of guys who got tired of going to fern bars." Apocryphally, the six combed Clearwater Beach searching for attractive young women who were interested in becoming the first Hooters Girls.

In addition to DiGiannantonio, a sales representative for a liquor distributor, the other founding partners were: L.D. Stewart and Dennis Johnson, also partners in a general contracting business; Kenneth Wimmer, who had worked for Stewart and Johnson before starting his own paint business; Ed Droste, owner and chief executive of a resort development business, and William Ranieri, a former service-station owner who had retired to Florida. Stewart was the majority owner.

Free Publicity Launches the Concept, 1984

The restaurant struggled for almost a year before receiving a fortuitous break in the form of free publicity. In January 1984, Tampa hosted the National Football League Super Bowl between the Los Angeles Raiders and the Washington Redskins. John Riggens, then a star running back for the Redskins, ate lunch at Hooters the day before the game. After the Super Bowl, he returned with several teammates for a midnight snack. With the resulting media attention, Hooters quickly went from grossing $2,000 a night to nearly $4,000.

In 1984 the original owners, who had formed Hooters of Clearwater, Inc., sold expansion and franchise rights to Neighborhood Restaurants of America, a group of Atlanta investors, who formed Hooters of America, Inc. Hooters of Clearwater received 10 percent of Hooters of America and 3 percent royalties on all Hooters sales. Hooters of Clearwater also retained the final say on restaurant design and menu, and the right to build Hooters restaurants in Pinellas and Hillsborough counties in Florida.

Within two years, Hooters had become a $16 million chain with nine restaurants in Florida and two in Atlanta. By 1991, there were more than 50 Hooters restaurants and Hooters of America had revenues of more than $100 million. The chain had reached more than 100 restaurants and $200 million in revenues by the end of 1993.

Hooters continued to thrive on free publicity. When the Soviet national boxing team was in Tampa to fight the Americans in the summer of 1986, the Soviets ate dinner at Hooters. The next day, the *Tampa Tribune* ran a full color picture of a Russian boxer eating chicken wings with a Hooters Girl, wearing a tight-fitting Hooters T-shirt, standing next to him. In July 1986, the first Hooters girl, Lynne Austin, was *Playboy* magazine's Playmate of the Month. The men's magazine also included a small article about Hooters and some of the pictures showed Austin in a Hooters outfit. Droste told *Florida Trend,* "We were already doing well at that point, but (the *Playboy* article) was important because it gave us our first national exposure."

But probably the greatest marketing coup came in 1995 when Hooters of America hired a hairy male actor and dressed him in a Hooters waitress outfit to poke fun at allegations that Hooters restaurants discriminated against men. Hooters of America ran full-page advertisements showing ''Vince'' in *USA Today* and the *Washington Post*. But more importantly, according to then vice president of marketing Michael McNeil, television camera crews showed up at every Hooters restaurant in the U.S. the same day to do local stories.

Hooters Girls: The Real Secret to Success

Hooters of America liked to boast that ''Hooters is to chicken wings what McDonald's is to hamburgers.'' But the Hooters Girls, not the restaurants' food or drink, were always the essence of the Hooters concept. Hooters restaurants hired young, attractive women as waitresses and dressed them in orange running shorts—''sized to fix comfortably,'' according to corporate literature—and white tank tops or T-shirts. Hooters of America readily acknowledged that ''the concept relies on natural female sex appeal'' and the waitresses were encouraged to sit down and chat with the predominately male clientele.

Hooters Girls also made celebrity appearances at sporting events and charity functions, and were pictured on billboards, trading cards, and calendars. Hooters of America published a glossy *Hooters Magazine* that featured Hooters Girls in everything from swimsuits to evening wear. According to the corporate literature, Hooters Girls were expected to ''always maintain a prom-like appearance with hair, make-up and nails done neatly. Hooters Girls should project a positive attitude with a bubbling personality and the prettiest smile in the world.''

Although the founders of the original Hooters in Clearwater always insisted the name referred to an owl in the restaurant's logo, they did so tongue-in-cheek, and it was a claim that few people accepted. ''Obviously the name is a double entendre,'' McNeil told *Business First,* a Columbus, Ohio, business newspaper in 1994. ''Hooters is an innocuous slang expression for a part of the female anatomy. We don't deny that. We also realize that most people believe that that is the case.'' Critics of the name and concept dubbed Hooters the nation's first ''breastaurant.''

The 1990s and Battles with the EEOC

In 1996, the *American Spectator* noted that Hooters featured ''socially adept and lightly dressed young women who delight a generally beefier crowd of male patrons by simply feeding them from a reasonably priced menu. It is a simple but successful concept, one that would offend only the worst sort of prig.'' But offend it did.

Women's groups expressed outrage at the skimpy Hooters Girls uniforms. Hooters restaurants were also forced with some regularity to defend themselves against allegations of sexual harassment. In the most high profile case, three former waitresses at a Hooters franchise operated by Bloomington Hooters Inc. at the Mall of America in Minnesota filed suit in 1993, claiming they had been fondled and verbally abused by male employees at the restaurant. Representing the waitresses, attorney Lori C. Peterson, who also sued the Stroh Brewery Co. over its controversial Swedish Bikini Team commercials, went on television talk shows to denounce the Hooters concept. Among her demands were that Hooters change its name and uniforms.

But in an interview with *Corporate Report Minnesota,* attorney Lisa A. Gray, hired by the restaurant, countered, ''For me to deny that sex appeal is part of the concept, part of what's happening at Hooters, would be ludicrous. But I've always thought feminism is all about choice. If people are offended by Hooters, they should vote with their feet. Don't go to the restaurant to eat. Don't apply to work at it.'' Hooters of America also denied that Hooters restaurants fostered a ''hostile environment'' for women and publicly stressed a strict corporate policy against any form of sexual harassment. The suit was eventually settled out of court.

Hooters restaurants also attracted the attention of the Equal Employment Opportunity Commission (EEOC), which launched an investigation in 1991 into alleged discrimination because Hooters refused to hire male waiters. In an 80-page finding released in 1994, the EEOC determined that ''no physical trait unique to women is required to service food and drink to customers in a restaurant.'' The EEOC demanded that Hooters of America pay $22 million to men who could show they had been denied jobs because of their gender. The agency also demanded that Hooters establish a scholastic fund ''to enhance the skills, employment opportunities or education of males.''

The EEOC findings were generally ridiculed by the news media and a public that had grown skeptical of government interference, especially since the EEOC had a backlog of seemingly more serious cases. Bureaucracy watchdog James Bovard, writing in the *Washington Post,* responded, ''What sort of education program did the EEOC have in mind? Teaching the new male hirees how to flirt with burly construction workers without getting punched in the nose?''

Hooters of America argued that Hooters Girls, in addition to food service, provided entertainment, which entitled the restaurants to an exemption from equal employment laws under the ''Bona Fide Occupational Qualification'' section of the Civil Rights Act. Forcing Hooters to hire men as waiters, the restaurant chain said, would be like forcing Radio City Music Hall to hire male Rockettes for its famed chorus line.

In a more serious vein, McNeil explained that ''Hooters Girls have been the essence of our business since the first store opened in 1983,'' and pointed out that Hooters employed men as cooks and in management positions. Hooters fought back with a $1 million publicity campaign, featuring ''Vince,'' the hirsute waiter in a skimpy Hooter's outfit, designed to ridicule the EEOC. Under the headline ''What's wrong with this picture,'' the newspaper ads complained, ''The Equal Employment Opportunity Commission is wasting taxpayers dollars, ignoring its mission, and setting aside the interests of individuals with real discrimination claims in an effort to force Hooters Restaurants to hire men to be Hooters Girls. This excessive government interference threatens Hooters business and the jobs of more that 13,000 employees. Taking away jobs from Hooters gals to hire men is unfair and it's just plain ridiculous.''

Tad Dixon, then public relations manager for Hooters of America, told *Nation's Restaurant News* that his office received more than 500 telephone calls the day the campaign broke.

Hooters of America also coordinated a "March on Washington" with a rally at Freedom Park in Washington, D.C., where more than a hundred Hooters Girls carried placards with such slogans as "Men as Hooter Guys—What a Drag."

In addition to the newspaper ads, Hooters used "Vince" on billboards, other print materials, and even on its radio commercials. In a brief statement, the EEOC called the public relations campaign an effort "to intimidate a federal law enforcement agency, and, more importantly, individuals whose rights may have been violated." But, eventually, the EEOC dropped its demands and the investigation. In 1996 Gilbert F. Casellas, then chairman of the EEOC, sent a letter to the U.S. House subcommittee on employment in which he concluded "it is wiser for the EEOC to devote its scarce litigation resources to other cases."

In 1996 the privately owned Hooters of America operated 57 Hooters restaurants and franchised 135. Of the more than $300 million in revenue generated systemwide, Hooters of America said 65 percent came from the sale of food, 30 percent from the sale of beer and wine, and 5 percent from Hooters merchandise, including Hooters Girls trading cards. *Restaurant & Institutions* ranked Hooters as the 75th largest food-service chain in the United States, and 11th among casual, dinner-house restaurant concepts.

Further Reading

Brovard, James, "The EEOC's War on Hooters," *Wall Street Journal,* November 17, 1995, p. A18.

"EEOC's Politically Correct Crusade Against Hooters a Wasted Effort," *Nation's Restaurant News,* December 4, 1995, p. x.

Grimsley, Kristin Downey, "Hooters Plays Hardball with the EEOC," *Washington Post,* December 10, 1995, p. H1.

Hagy, James, "How Big Can Hooters Get?" *Florida Trend,* September 1987, p. 80.

Hayes, Jack, "Hooters Comes Out Against EEOC's Sex-Bias Suit," *Nation's Restaurant News,* November 27, 1995, p. 3.

"Hooters Vs. the EEOC, *Seattle Times,* May 6, 1996, p. B4.

Prewitt, Milford, "Hooters Unit Sued for Harassment," *Nation's Restaurant News,* May 3, 1993, p. 3.

Segal, David, "Hooters Vows to Decide Where the Boys Aren't," *Washington Post,* November 16, 1995, p. B11.

Shiflett, Dave, "Hooters Gals," *American Spectator,* July 1996, p. 48.

Wieffering, Eric J., "Defending Hooters," *Corporate Report Minnesota,* September 1991, p. 52.

Wright, J. Nils, "Hooters Eatery is Coming to Town with Controversial Fare," *Business Journal* (Sacramento, California), April 25, 1994, p. 8.

—Dean Boyer

Hormel Foods Corporation

1 Hormel Place
Austin, Minnesota 55912-3680
U.S.A.
(507) 437-5611
Fax: (507) 437-5489
Web site: http://www.hormel.com

Public Company
Incorporated: 1901 as George A. Hormel and Company
Employees: 10,600
Sales: $3.05 billion (1995)
Stock Exchanges: New York
SICs: 2099 Food Preparations, Not Elsewhere Classified;
    5147 Meats & Meat Products

Hormel Foods Corporation is a diversified producer of packaged-food products, emphasizing quality, convenience, nutrition, and ethnic foods. Hormel has successfully evolved over its more than a century in business from meatpacker to value-added food manufacturer. In addition to its flagship SPAM brand, Hormel also produces and sells products under such brands as Chi-Chi's, Dinty Moore, Dubuque, Farm Fresh, House of Tsang, Jennie-O, Light & Lean 97, Marrakesh Express, Mary Kitchen, Peloponnese, Po River Valley, Top Shelf, and, of course, Hormel.

Meatpacking Business Founded in Late 19th Century

Hormel's history began when the company's founder, George A. Hormel, borrowed $500 in 1887 to form a retail meat market and pork packing business with his partner, Albrect Friedrich. Hormel established a powerful precedent when he refused to be complacent about their early success and pushed ahead with his plans to set up and operate a packing house. He and Friedrich agreed to disband their partnership in September 1891, and in November of that same year Hormel and employee George Petersen had transformed a small, abandoned creamery into a meatpacking plant complete with smokehouse and slaughterhouse, operating under the name George A. Hormel

and Company. In addition, he opened the Hormel Provision Market to sell his products; it quickly became the town's largest and most successful retail meat business.

Faced with low profit margins and competition from large meatpackers who could afford state-of-the-art refrigeration facilities, Hormel made expansion his first priority. Within the first few years his two brothers and other members of his family had joined the business, allowing George Hormel to put down his cleaver and devote himself exclusively to management. In 1899 Hormel spent $40,000 to upgrade his facilities, building a new refrigeration facility, new pumps and engines, an electric elevator, smokehouses, and a hog kill. In 1901 the company acquired several acres of adjacent land, and two years later it constructed additional facilities such as a casing processing room and a machine shop. In 1908 it also opened a new office facility, which the company used for more than 60 years.

During this period of expansion Hormel also worked to refine and improve its products. In 1903 it registered its first patent, "Dairy Brand," with the U.S. Patent Office. In 1915 Hormel began to produce several lines of dry sausage, a product that proved particularly popular with ethnic consumers.

In an effort to increase sales volume, Hormel sent salesmen outside of Austin to set up branches and distribution centers. By 1920 the company operated branches in Minneapolis, Duluth, St. Paul, San Antonio, Dallas, Atlanta, Birmingham, and Chicago. In 1905 George Hormel traveled to England to establish the foundation for an export business. Between 1905 and the end of World War I, exports grew to constitute about a third of the company's yearly volume.

Hormel and Company participated fully in America's World War I effort. To control the price and supply of meats, the government regulated the meatpacking industry. Hormel expanded its labor force and the hours they worked to help satisfy the increased demand for meat both at home and abroad. With so many American men, including George Hormel's son Jay, away at war, the company employed women for the first time in its history. In addition to producing meat for the war effort, Hormel employees bought Liberty bonds and donated an hour's wages per day to the Red Cross.

Company Perspectives:

Company Mission: To be a leader in the food field with highly differentiated quality products that attain optimum share of market while meeting established profit objectives.

Quality Policy: We will supply defect-free products and services which conform to clearly defined requirements to meet the needs of our customers, employees, and others we serve.

The five principles of quality management form the foundation of this policy. They are: the definition of quality is conformance to customer requirements; the system of quality is prevention and continuous improvement; the performance standard is zero defects; the measurement of quality is the price of nonconformance; all work is a process.

Survived Scandal Following World War I

When Jay Hormel returned from the war, he rejoined the company and uncovered a scandal that very nearly put Hormel out of business. The company's assistant controller, "Cy" Thomson, had embezzled more than $1 million from the company and had channeled it into several poultry farms. The company had borrowed $3 million that year for operating expenses and hoped to repay the sum at the end of the year. At year end, however, they were unable to do so, and George Hormel had to confront his bankers and convince them to extend the loan.

The embezzlement scandal provided George Hormel with additional incentive to fortify his company. He did so by arranging for more reliable capital management, by dismissing unproductive employees, and by continuing to develop new products. In 1926, after years of research, Hormel introduced "Hormel Flavor-Sealed Ham," America's first canned ham.

In 1929 Jay C. Hormel became the company's second president, and his father, George, became chairman of the board. Under the new president the company continued to expand its product line: some of the company's best-known products—Dinty Moore beef stew (1935), Hormel chili (1936), and SPAM luncheon meat (1937)—entered the market and became extremely popular.

The company survived a bitter labor strike in 1933, during which disgruntled union employees, armed with clubs, physically removed Jay Hormel from the company's general offices and shut off the plant's refrigeration system. The two parties reached a compromise within three days. Soon, the company gained recognition for its innovative labor relations policies. Jay Hormel developed the "Annual Wage Plan," under which employees were paid weekly, their working hours fluctuated according to need; employment was considered permanent and workers were guaranteed a year's notice before they could be terminated. In addition, the company introduced profit sharing, merit pay, a pension plan, and a joint earnings plan. Under this plan, in 1983 Hormel employees received more than $4 million.

During his tenure Jay Hormel cofounded the Hormel Foundation, which controlled the company through holdings of its capital stock, and which served "religious, charitable, scientific, literary, or educational purposes." This foundation funds the Hormel Institute, a research facility located at the University of Minnesota which conducts highly respected research on fats and other lipids and how they affect human life.

SPAM Became Staple During World War II

During World War II, Hormel and Company became a "war facility" and once again increased its meat production. By 1945 Hormel was selling 65 percent of its total production to the U.S. Government. SPAM, Hormel's canned spiced ham and ground pork product, became the staple of U.S. servicemen throughout the world; in 1941 Hormel was producing 15 million cans a week, and the government was distributing it under the lend-lease program. Overfamiliarity bred substantial contempt and ridicule during and after the war, but the product demonstrated uncanny resilience: by 1959, Hormel had sold over 1 billion cans of SPAM.

When George Hormel died in 1946, Jay Hormel took his place as chairman of the board of directors and H. H. Corey became Hormel's third president. During the eight years of his presidency, the company continued to renovate and upgrade its existing plants and acquire new facilities. It purchased several new packing operations—in Mitchell, South Dakota; Fort Dodge, Iowa; and Fremont, Nebraska. With the wartime restrictions on tin now lifted and with a tremendous demand for Hormel's canned meat products, the company improved its canning facilities in its Dallas and Houston plants and arranged for independent canning companies to manufacture Hormel products. In addition, Hormel made a concerted effort to make better use of its raw material, and in 1947 the company began to produce gelatin from pork skins.

Hormel's product line expanded along with the company's facilities. Mary Kitchen Roast Beef Hash, Corned Beef Hash, and Spaghetti and Beef in Sauce appeared in 1949, along with a new line of meat spreads.

With its constant expansion, the company had to consider how to dispose of its increased waste material. Hormel researchers developed an anaerobic digestive system that removed waste cleanly and efficiently. In 1946 the company financed a $2.25 million sewage system that it shared with the Austin community.

In 1954 Jay Hormel died, and Corey assumed his chair on the board of directors, while R. F. Gray succeeded Corey as president. He held this position for ten years, during which the company continued to pursue quality and efficiency. Hormel added several more slaughtering, processing, and packing facilities throughout the country, and in 1965 it added a new 75,000-square-foot, automated sausage manufacturing building to its Austin plant.

Several new products appeared in this decade as well. In 1960 the company introduced its "Famous Foods of the World" line. The following year Little Sizzlers' sausage entered the market, followed two years later by a fully-cooked sausage product, Brown'n Serve. The largest success of the decade, however, was the Hormel Cure 81 Ham, a skinless, boneless, trim, cured ham with the shank removed.

After another decade of progressive growth under two different presidents, M. B. Thompson and I. J. Holton, the directors realized that in order to remain competitive in the industry, Hormel needed to undertake a wholesale renovation of its Austin plant. In 1975 the company began planning this $100 million, state-of-the-art facility, which opened in 1982. At more than a million square feet, it was among the largest and most productive in the industry, and featured robotic technology and automatic ham deboners. Hormel continued to diversify its product lines as well, introducing precooked bacon and three new varieties of Perma Fresh luncheon meats. By 1980 Hormel was producing over 700 different products.

Bitter Strike and Move Away from Meatpacking in the 1980s

Though this new facility was capable of processing more than two million hogs a year and producing more than 200 million pounds of products annually, the industry began to shrink in the 1980s and Hormel began to feel the effects. In the 1980s consumers began to eat less meat and meat producers for the first time had to struggle to make their products appealing. With a 40 percent increase in the price of hogs, Hormel was pinched. It asked employees to accept wage cuts in Austin of more than $2 an hour. In 1985, the union decided to strike. Fifteen hundred workers left their jobs. Under the glare of national publicity, striking workers harassed the 700 scabs whom Hormel hired five months later. Five hundred union workers eventually returned to work—under lower pay scales—but the others were either dismissed or were forced into early retirement.

The wounds from this bitter strike were slow to heal, but Hormel moved ahead, and under president, chairman, and CEO Richard L. Knowlton (who had accepted a $236,000 raise in the midst of the strike), it adjusted to a rapidly changing market by moving away from the traditional meatpacking business and its many problems and concentrating on satisfying consumers' appetites for processed foods.

In an 18-month period in the late 1980s, Hormel introduced 134 new products, including Top Shelf vacuum-packed unrefrigerated meals with a shelf life of 18 months. Knowlton considered this "one of the most important products ever introduced by Hormel. It represents a revolutionary breakthrough in packaging technology and offers consumers a new level of convenience." After acquiring Jennie-O Foods, a turkey-processing company, in late 1986, Hormel went on to acquire a small producer of fresh marinated chicken-breast entrees in 1988 and targeted its fish operations for expansion in an effort to exploit the more health-conscious market. With these new and acquired products, Hormel overcame a period of sluggish sales and earnings between 1979 and 1984 to record net earnings of $60.1 million in 1988, up from $29.4 million in 1984.

Focus on Healthful, Convenient, Ethnic Foods in the 1990s

In the 1990s, Hormel worked hard to react quickly to consumers' increasing appetite for more healthful and more convenient foods as well as ethnic foods. It did so by seeking out targeted acquisitions and through new products and line extensions. The company also sought out additional opportunities for international expansion.

Hormel's continuing move away from meatpacking and toward value-added food production was highlighted by the 1992 appointment of Joel W. Johnson as president. Johnson became the first president not to have risen through the Hormel ranks, having been hired away from rival Kraft General Foods. Johnson added the CEO title in 1993, then became chairman of the Hormel board as well upon Knowlton's retirement in 1995.

In 1991 Hormel celebrated 100 years in business. The following year, the three grandsons of George Hormel—George Hormel II, James Hormel, and Thomas Hormel—who held control of the company through the Hormel Foundation, filed suit to attempt to force the foundation to diversify its holdings, which consisted almost entirely of Hormel stock. After an initially favorable ruling, the Hormel heirs eventually lost the suit in 1994. By 1996, the company's decision to repurchase as many as 5 million shares of Hormel stock was destined to further increase the foundation's Hormel holdings, possibly setting the stage for future litigation.

Meanwhile, in 1993 the company's own diversification efforts precipitated the first name change in company history: George A. Hormel and Company became Hormel Foods Corporation, a name more reflective of Hormel's food products orientation of the 1980s and 1990s. At the same time, however, the company did not abandon long-time mainstays such as SPAM. Johnson was credited with reviving SPAM sales by repositioning the canned pork mix as a quick and easy base for a "SPAMburger." He called it the "only hamburger made out of ham." The SPAM line was also successfully expanded with low-sodium and light extensions. In 1993 SPAM maintained a stunning 80 percent market share of its sales category.

Hormel aggressively went after the leaner food products category in the early 1990s. In 1992 the company introduced Light & Lean 97 hot dogs, which were 97 percent fat free and were praised for their taste by the likes of *Eaters Digest*, a consumer magazine. Additional Light & Lean 97 products were soon introduced, including all-beef hot dogs, boneless ham, turkey breasts, smoked sausages, and packaged luncheon meats.

The ethnic foods category was an area targeted for expansion in the 1990s primarily through acquisitions. In 1992 the House of Tsang and Oriental Deli brands were acquired, with Dubuque meats and Herb-Ox instant broths and seasonings added the following year. In mid-1995, Hormel purchased from Rockridge Trading Company the Peloponnese brand, a line of Mediterranean-based specialty foods including olives, olive oil, peppers, stuffed grape leaves, and salad dressings. Later that same year, the assets of Melting Pot Foods were acquired, which featured Po River Valley risotto rice, Marrakesh Express couscous, and Terrazza pasta and beans.

Another acquisition—that of American Institutional Products, Inc. (AIP) in 1994—brought Hormel a presence in the distribution of food products to hospitals, nursing homes, and other health care facilities. AIP made instant food thickeners and pureed food products.

Hormel also spent heavily to add to and upgrade its facilities in the early to mid-1990s. In 1993 it bought from Rochelle Foods a 1.8-million head hog processing plant located in Rochelle, Illinois, then spent $4 million in renovating the site. Hormel also spent $15 million to upgrade its Davenport, Iowa, gelatin/proteins plant, and $20 million to expand and renovate its Fremont, Nebraska, hog processing plant. In 1995 alone, the company spent $97.18 million in capital additions and improvements, the most ever in company history. Meanwhile, in fiscal 1994, Hormel Foods exceeded the $3 billion revenue level for the first time.

Mid-1990s and Beyond

A couple of lawsuits involving Hormel made headlines in 1995. Hormel sued Jim Henson Productions over a wild boar named Spa'am that appeared in the movie *Muppet Treasure Island*. Although Hormel contended the character tarnished its SPAM trademark, a circuit judge rejected the argument and said it was legitimate satire. Hormel settled a more serious case out of court when it agreed to pay $7.5 million to settle a class-action suit brought by fish distributors and processors who claimed that Hormel's Farm Fresh Catfish Company and six other catfish wholesalers conspired to fix prices for nearly a decade. While some of the smaller defendants had admitted guilt, neither Hormel nor the other major defendants—ConAgra Inc. and Delta Pride Catfish Inc.—admitted responsibility.

In the mid-1990s, Hormel increasingly looked overseas for growth opportunities, and often turned to joint ventures to pursue foreign revenue as well as domestic sales. After opening sales offices in Hong Kong and Mexico earlier in 1994, Hormel in December of that year joined with Beijing Agriculture Industry and Commerce to form Beijing Hormel Foods Co. This venture began constructing a hog processing plant in 1996 to be completed in 1997, which will be able to process 300,000 hogs each year and produce pork products under the Hormel brand for sale in China. In Mexico, Hormel Alimentos S.A., a joint venture with Grupo Herdez S.A. of Mexico, was formed in 1995 to market U.S.-manufactured Hormel products in Mexico. Another 1995 joint venture was with Darling Downs Bacon Cooperative Association Limited of Australia.

The following year saw additional joint ventures. In January 1996 Hormel and the U.K.-based Patak Spices Ltd. formed Patak's Foods USA to import and market Indian sauces, pastes, pickles, and chutneys in the United States. In July Hormel and Grupo Herdez formed a second joint venture—Herdez Corp.—which will distribute Mexican foods products in the United States. Then in December Hormel spent $64.3 million to purchase a 21.4 percent interest in Campofrio Alimentacion, S.A., a Spanish food company based in Madrid. All of these 1996 activities expanded Hormel's already extensive presence in the ethnic foods category.

Although Hormel Foods continued to suffer in the mid-1990s from the adverse affects of its still heavy reliance on pork as raw material for its products, the company overall was stronger than ever. In 1995 Hormel posted its 11th straight year of increased net earnings. More importantly, Hormel's profitability continued to grow, reaching nearly 4 percent in 1995, almost double the levels of the mid-1980s. It was clear that Hormel's diversification was paying off and boded well for the future. The company also maintained a very low debt load, positioning it to continue to make targeted acquisitions or perhaps even make a blockbuster deal that would break it free of its traditional conservative style.

Principal Subsidiaries

Dan's Prize, Inc.; Dubuque Foods, Inc.; Farm Fresh Catfish Company; Hormel Foods International Corporation; Jennie-O Foods, Inc.; Beijing Hormel Foods Co. Ltd. (China); Hormel Alimentos, S.A. de C.V. (Mexico); Campofrio Alimentacion, S.A. (Spain; 21.4%).

Principal Divisions

Meat Products Division; Deli Division; Grocery Products Division; Frozen Foods Division; Specialty Products Division.

Principal Operating Units

Meat Products Group; Foodservice Group; Prepared Foods Group.

Further Reading

Berss, Marcia, " 'This Isn't Ross Perot and GM,' " *Forbes*, June 8, 1992, p. 103.

Dougherty, Richard. *In Quest of Quality: Hormel's First 75 Years*, Austin, Minnesota: George A. Hormel Company, 1966.

Gibson, Richard, "Any Way You Slice It, Johnson's Hormel Isn't Just Spam: Cautious Processed-Food Company's New Chief May Add to Mature Line," *Wall Street Journal*, November 23, 1993, p. B4.

——, "ConAgra, Hormel Pay a Pretty Penny in an Ugly Catfish Price-Fixing Case," *Wall Street Journal*, December 29, 1995, p. A3.

Lund, Doniver Adolph, *The Hormel Legacy: 100 Years of Quality*, Austin, Minnesota: George A. Hormel and Company, 1991, p. 231.

Mill on the Willow: A History of Mower County, Minnesota, Lake Mills, Iowa: Graphic Publishing, 1984.

Smith, Rod, "Geo. A. Hormel & Co. Begins Second Century 'At Ravine's Edge' Making Food Products to Sustain Modern Consumer Lifestyles," *Feedstuffs*, May 27, 1991, pp. 28, 30, 31.

——, "Hormel Builds to $3 Billion, Citing Its 'On-Trend' Products," *Feedstuffs*, January 30, 1995, pp. 6–7.

——, "Hormel Nears $3-Billion Sales, Reconfirms Century of Values," *Feedstuffs*, March 30, 1992, pp. 6, 26.

—updated by David E. Salamie

Hutchinson Technology Incorporated

40 West Highland Park
Hutchinson, Minnesota 55350-9784
U.S.A.
(320) 587-3797
Fax: (320) 587-1810

Public Company
Incorporated: 1965 as Hutchinson Industrial Corporation
Employees: 4,880
Sales: $300 million (1995)
Stock Exchanges: NASDAQ
SICs: 3572 Computer Storage Devices; 3679 Electronic
  Components, Not Elsewhere Classified

Hutchinson Technology Incorporated (HTI), a high-tech firm located in the middle of rich farmland just west of Minneapolis, Minnesota, holds 70 percent of the world wide-market for rigid disk drive suspension assemblies. Most personal computers contain its primary product, a thin metal spring which holds the recording head in position a few millionths of an inch from the disk. HTI designs and manufactures the close-tolerance components by using chemical, mechanical, and electronic technologies. Increased sales of personal and portable computers and the enhanced role of suspension assemblies in the disk-drive industry in relationship to storage capacity, speed of access to data, and reliability, have been important factors in the HTI's rapid growth.

Early Years as a Custom Component Maker

HTI developed out of the collaboration between John Geiss and Jeffrey Green. The men met in the early 1960s; they were neighbors in a Minneapolis apartment building. Geiss, an engineer for Minnco Products, asked Green, a Sperry technical writer, to help with a manual for a photo-etching process. The men became friends and shared an interest in the photo-etching process. So when Geiss later suggested they develop a manufacturing business using the technology, Green agreed.

The men looked for a suitable, low-rent building in the metropolitan area of Minneapolis-St. Paul, but instead their first site became a chicken coop in Geiss's hometown of Hutchinson, 60 miles west of the Twin Cities. In 1965, the men established Hutchinson Industrial Corporation. Low on personal funds, they depended largely on private investors for financial backing, and paid rent and some other bills with company stock. Geiss moved to Hutchinson but Green stayed on at Sperry.

Their original idea was to use the photoetching technology to manufacture a lower-cost heater for gyroscopes in rocket guidance systems. That first venture failed to get off the ground, but they continued to look for new product ideas and business opportunities. A set of events opened up a door for the fledgling business, and they found their first customer: Green's employer, Sperry. By sending specifications and materials back and forth by bus between Hutchinson and Minneapolis, they put their photo-etching and laminating equipment to its first real test. But the company's first big break came when Geiss convinced a Control Data Corporation (CDC) buyer to allow the Hutchinson company to make a sample disk drive component. CDC liked what they saw, and Geiss and Green began manufacturing ferrite tracks. The down side of the deal was that CDC's disk drive manufacturing process was unique and therefore not marketable to other disk drive makers.

During the first decade of its existence HTI produced a variety of components—mainly in small lots—for computer, satellite, medical, and even fake fur manufacturers. In 1972 the company began construction on a new building, eventually converting the chicken coop into a maintenance and equipment fabrication shop. The company continually reworked its photo-etching processes: by the mid-1970s the company was using fourth generation equipment. They also added tool and die capabilities and laser welding. The upgraded facilities and technology helped the company finally land work with IBM.

HTI Catches the Early-1980s Wave of Personal Computer Production

The late 1970s brought an end to the majority of HTI's small quantity production runs. The company refocused its energy on

Company Perspectives:

We will be the leader among all suppliers serving the disk drive market. As a leader we recognize that our people are the source of our strength and we will treat them with the highest regard. We will promote creativity, efficiency and vitality by encouraging involvement, teamwork and the development of our people.

We will maintain our market share by aggressively developing products and services which offer timely solutions that enable disk drive manufacturers to advance their technology and capability.

We will fundamentally understand, develop, improve and leverage our competencies and technologies through product, process and system design to set the industry standard of performance and quality excellence.

We will aggressively pursue new levels of quality, productivity, flexibility and reliability in order to deliver products and services that provide the most value at the lowest total cost in the least amount of time.

We will assure that the value delivered to our customers will be reflected in the return to our shareholders.

the disk drive market and brought on more technical people. Growth magnified the differences between founders Geiss and Green. In the early 1980s Geiss, who was CEO, tried and failed to convince the board of directors to accelerate business diversification in order to increase revenues. In 1982, Geiss decided to leave the company and sought a buyout for his 35 percent of the company stock. A struggle ensued between a Geiss faction and a newly organized Green faction. A resulting lawsuit was decided in Green's favor. Eventually, Geiss and other original shareholders accepted a buyout offer. Green became CEO, and Wayne Fortun took over as company president. The business was renamed Hutchinson Technology Incorporated (HTI).

The early 1980s personal computer boom sent disk drive manufacturing into high gear. HTI grew rapidly, adapting and adding equipment, and hiring new employees to meet the demand for rigid disk drive components. HTI delivered their first thin-film suspension assemblies in 1983. High start-up costs and delays related to fine-tuning the new manufacturing processes kept profit margins low, but HTI proceeded to work on another new product, flexible circuits. The company ended the 1983 fiscal year with a net loss. Increased thin-film suspension assembly sales and revived suspension component shipments to a major customer pushed net sales for 1984 to $31.4 million, 95 percent higher than the previous year; net income was $3.2 million.

The addition of complex assembly manufacturing in 1985 helped boost net sales another 68 percent, to $52.7 million. Fifty-five percent of that year's sales were in a volatile segment of the computer market. The components and assemblies HTI manufactured for the makers of small-and medium-sized computer systems were subject to rapid price and technology changes. The majority of HTI's remaining sales were in the large computer market, which was more stable. HTI also sold

some flexible circuits to Honeywell, Teledyne, Hewlett Packard, and Textronix for use in military applications.

HTI offered its stock to the public for the first time in August 1985 for $10 per share. The newly-issued stock lost as much as half of its value shortly after its offering. In February 1986, Clinton H. Morrison of Dain Bosworth said the drop resulted from of the combination of IBM order cutbacks and "an unfavorable recommendation by one of the underwriters." But Morrison pointed out that HTI had developed and implemented difficult to duplicate manufacturing technologies, which were well respected by the industry, as evidenced by its market share. In spite of the set back, HTI remained profitable by implementing a production slow-down and employee layoffs.

Focus on Engineering and Expansion in the Late 1980s

The vertically integrated HTI adapted and combined high-tech processes including photo-etching, laminating, and laser welding in order to keep pace with the rapidly changing disk drive industry. The company also implemented quality control programs and management systems designed to meet the expectations of its biggest customer. According to a September 1986 *Corporate Report Minnesota* article, direct sales to IBM accounted for about 50 percent of HTI revenues, and indirect sales by way of original equipment manufacturers boosted the figure even higher. In the same article an IBM procurement manager, Hud Sherlock, said of HTI, "They continue to have a good record in terms of reliability, quality, and durability. We demand zero defects from our vendors, and Hutchinson Technology has done a lot to achieve that goal." And Steve Marshall of Seagate said, "Their reliability and pricing can't be beat. We had our own flexure assembly plant, but shut it down. We found we couldn't put them together for what they can do it for."

In 1988 HTI's Green sparked a public controversy when he announced that the Minnesota business climate was a factor in the decision to open a plant in South Dakota. Newspaper columnists and editors, officials of the State of Minnesota, and other business leaders exchanged public barbs regarding the contention that workers' compensation laws, taxes, and the propensity of state government to involve itself in business matters were driving employers from the state. Regardless of the reason for choosing Sioux Falls, South Dakota, HTI needed the new facilities. The company turned out 1.9 million suspension assemblies a week, while the demand was for 2.2 million. In another move to increase available capacity, HTI began to phase out its low-margin complex assemblies.

The small-town company had expanded its horizons considerably under Green's leadership. In May 1988, Dave Peters described the company as being "in the forefront of high-tech manufacturing techniques," which involved such things as maintaining low inventory, using worker clusters rather than assembly lines, and sharing volume and quality statistics with employees on a daily basis. In 1988, HTI opened sales and technical support offices in Singapore and Seoul, South Korea; at that point, 40 percent of HTI products were sent to the Far East by either direct or indirect sales. The company also looked to the future by delving into production of detector cells for nuclear research and cancer treatment.

HTI began its 1989 fiscal year with its first quarterly loss since becoming a publicly-held company; employee layoffs and cost-cutting measures were implemented. The company had just experienced an interval of heavy start-up expenditures and high employment and overtime costs, while the disk drive market weakened. In addition, consumers were showing a strong preference for 3.5-inch rather than 5.25-inch disk drive computer systems. Consequently, HTI was left with an inventory of the larger format components and retooling costs.

In February of 1989 the company announced that it was holding acquisition talks with a Japanese company, Minebea Co. Ltd. HTI stock climbed to $15 per share, but fell to $9 after the company rejected the Minebea purchase bid as "grossly inadequate." In the second quarter of 1989, HTI was hit by more big losses and the criticism of financial analysts, some of whom maintained that with its dominance over its much smaller competitors, the company should be able to control pricing and be less susceptible to industry downturns. Fortun, HTI president, countered that their prices were already higher than competitors, and the trend in the disk drive market was for falling, not rising, prices. HTI ended 1989 with a loss of $5.7 million.

Fluctuations in the 1990s

HTI acted quickly to stop its downslide and entered the 1990s on an upswing. The disk drive industry backlog of inventory was down; orders for the smaller disk format were rising; and the low-profit complex assemblies were phased out of HTI's product mix. And although the company had lost some of its market share, it still held 60 percent of the suspension assembly market. Technology stocks as a whole were gaining strength, and HTI price per share rose 42 percent within the first three months of 1990. Analyst Clinton Morrison noted in *Corporate Report Minnesota* that HTI's slump the previous year had pushed management to improve efficiencies and implement cost-cutting measures that had a positive effect on its profit margins. The company ended fiscal 1990 with profits of $5.3 million.

HTI stock price remained linked to the ups-and-downs of the industry and its own profit margins throughout the next year. Then, in spite of a decline in yearly profits, HTI stock skyrocketed. Dick Youngblood asserted in the *Star Tribune* that a number of long term changes in the market and the company were behind the newly found investor confidence: the disk drive market was more stable due to a drop in the number of manufacturers; a line of HTI-designed suspension assemblies was well-received by the market; and the company was automating its manufacturing processes, spending $35 million over the previous three years and planning to spend additional $18 million.

But HTI stock fell to less than half its 52-week high following a projected drop in third-quarter revenues and earnings. Technical problems had slowed production just as demand was rising, and efficiency and productivity had been hampered by a move to around-the-clock production. The bad news came on the heels of a $27.75 per share secondary stock offering in March. Morrison noted in the *Star Tribune* that some of the slide was due to the reaction of new investors who were unfamiliar with HTI's history of ups-and-downs. HTI stock recovered and climbed above the $40 mark in December, when the company announced expansion plans for both its Hutchinson and Sioux Falls plants.

Stock price volatility continued to hound HTI in 1993 as familiar problems related to growth and demand drove down earnings. Once again, HTI had to make rapid manufacturing adjustments as disk drive manufacturers flocked to buy the newly developed nano-sized suspension assembly. HTI was the only producer of suspension assemblies for the smaller, cheaper heads.

The company caught up with the demand for its nano-sized suspension assemblies by the end of the second quarter of its 1994 fiscal year. Suspension assemblies accounted for 97 percent of HTI's business in 1994; the remaining three percent was from etched and stamped components, welded assemblies, and laminated components. Eighty-five percent of all business came from its largest customers: Seagate Technology, Read-Rite Corp., Yamaha Corp., IBM, and SAE Magnetics Ltd.

In 1995, HTI began work on a new plant in Eau Claire, Wisconsin, and entered into a technology-sharing agreement with IBM. The company shipped nine million suspension assemblies a week in the final quarter of the year. The nano-sized suspension assemblies accounted for nearly 90 percent of HTI suspension production for fiscal 1995. In addition, an even smaller suspension assembly—pico-sized—was put into production, and a suspension assembly with embedded leads was being developed; both anticipated future trends in the disk-drive industry. Stock prices ranged from $27 to $91 in 1995. Net sales were $300 million, with net income of $21.1 million.

HTI stock continued to ride the highs and lows of the technology sector in 1996. And once again, company earnings were subject to production problems related to growth. HTI had nearly doubled its total number of employees during the most recent expansion drive. Wayne Fortun succeeded Jeffrey Green as CEO in 1996, but Green stayed on as chairman of the board. Historically, HTI sacrificed short-term gain in order to meet the needs of the marketplace; disk drive manufacturers worldwide grew to depend on the Hutchinson, Minnesota, business. According to the *1996 Corporate Report Fact Book,* "nearly all significant drive producers use the company's products, which range from sub-2.5-inch drives for laptop and notebook computers to 10.5-inch drives for mainframe systems." HTI found success by keeping pace with the rapidly changing technology of the computer industry. And the company continued to provide new solutions to the problems the disk drive industry presented as it moved toward the next century.

Further Reading

"Briefs," *Star Tribune* (Minneapolis), May 17, 1996, p. 3D.

Broderick, Richard, "Big Hutch on the Prairie," *Corporate Report Minnesota,* September 1986, p. 60.

Carideo, Anthony, "Computer Parts Maker Expects a Turnaround," *Star Tribune* (Minneapolis), January 22, 1990, p. 1D.

——, "Hutchinson Sees 2nd-Quarter Loss," *Star Tribune* (Minneapolis), April 24, 1989, p. 10D.

——, "Hutch Tech Revenue Swells While Profits Continue to Shrink," *Star Tribune* (Minneapolis), April 25, 1988, p. 6D.

——, "If You're Thinking of Investing in Secondary Offerings, Do Your Homework," *Star Tribune* (Minneapolis), June 13, 1992, p. 2D.

——, "Local Computer-Related Firms Getting Deserved Recognition," *Star Tribune* (Minneapolis), December 31, 1990, p. 1D.

——,"Stock of Hutchinson Technology Hurt by Slowdown in Disk Drive Market," *Star Tribune* (Minneapolis), April 3, 1993, p. 2D.

——, "Technology Stocks Rebounding Strongly," *Star Tribune* (Minneapolis), March 19, 1990, p. 1D.

DeSilver, Drew, "Computer Adapters," *Minneapolis/St. Paul CityBusiness,* June 7, 1996.

——, "Computers," *Minneapolis/St. Paul CityBusiness,* June 28, 1996.

"Company News," *Star Tribune* (Minneapolis), May 24, 1988, p. 4D.

"Corporate Capsule," *Minneapolis/St. Paul City Business,* July 8, 1994, p. 25.

"Corporate Capsule," *Minneapolis/St. Paul City Business,* August 18, 1995, p. 25.

Feyder, Susan, "Riding Roller Coaster on Way to Top," *Star Tribune* (Minneapolis), December 11, 1995, p. 1D.

Fredrickson, Tom, "Hutchinson in Overdrive as Staff, Plants Expand," *Minneapolis/St. Paul CityBusiness,* January 21, 1994, p. 6.

——, "Hutchinson Spends $2 Million to Build New Training Center," *Minneapolis/St. Paul CityBusiness,* October 7, 1994, p. 2.

——, "Minnesota Growth 40," *Minneapolis/St. Paul CityBusiness,* July 21, 1995, p. 7.

"Hutchinson Technology Inc.," *1996 Corporate Report Fact Book,* p. 291.

"Hutchinson Technology Inc.," *Corporate Report Minnesota,* May 1990, p. 92 and February 1991, p. 83.

McCartney, Jim, "Acquisition Offer Is Rejected by Hutchinson Technology," *St. Paul Pioneer Press Dispatch,* March 23, 1989.

——, "Hutchinson Technology Reports Heavy Losses," *St. Paul Pioneer Press Dispatch,* March 21, 1989.

Meyers, Mike, "Hutchinson Technology Selects Eau Claire," *Star Tribune* (Minneapolis), March 21, 1995, p. 1.

Morrison, Clinton H., "Periscope—Hutchinson Technology, Inc.," *Corporate Report Minnesota,* February 1986, p. 111.

Novak, Jay, "Editor's Note," *Corporate Report Minnesota,* November 1988, p. 6.

Past . . . Present . . . Future. . . , Hutchinson Technology Incorporated, July 1994.

Peters, Dave, "He Makes Business Climate His Business," *St. Paul Pioneer Press Dispatch,* May 9, 1988, p. 1.

——, "Tech Firm Picks S.D. Site," *St. Paul Pioneer Press Dispatch,* March 10, 1988.

Peterson, Susan E., "Hutchinson Says It's Talking with Suitor," *Star Tribune* (Minneapolis), February 1, 1989, p. 2D.

——, "Hutchinson Technology Plans to Expand 2 Plants," *Star Tribune* (Minneapolis), December 10, 1992, p. 3D.

——, "Hutch Tech Says 3rd-Quarter Numbers Will Be Down," *Star Tribune* (Minneapolis), June 10, 1992, p. 3D;

Phelps, David, "Hutchinson Technology Confidence Crisis Called Blip," *Star Tribune* (Minneapolis), March 4, 1996, p. 1D.

Youngblood, Dick, "CERN Buys Hutchinson Firm's Cells," *Star Tribune* (Minneapolis), August 22, 1988, p. 1D

——, "What's Behind Big Run-up in Hutch Tech's Stock?" *Star Tribune* (Minneapolis), February 10, 1992, p. 2D.

—Kathleen Peippo

Hutchison Whampoa Limited

Hutchison Whampoa Ltd.

Hutchison House, 22nd Floor
10 Harcourt Road
Hong Kong
(852) 8121 0161
Fax: (852) 8121 0705

Public Company (majority-owned by Cheung Kong
 Holdings)
Founded: 1880
Sales: HK35 billion (US$4.5 billion) (1995)
Employees: 26,855
Stock Exchanges: New York
SICs: 4731 Transportation of Freight and Cargo; 4899
 Communications Services; 6552 Land Subdividers and
 Developers; 6719 Offices of Holding Companies;
 7011 Hotels and Motels

Hutchison Whampoa Ltd., a vast conglomerate based in Hong Kong, has become a force to be reckoned with in real estate, ports, retailing, manufacturing, telecommunications, and energy. As one of Hong Kong's most venerable hongs (colonial trading houses, Hutchison began as an importer and wholesaler before diversifying in the 1960s. Bloated and unwieldy in the 1970s, Hutchison unloaded dozens of companies, strengthened its bottom line, and merged with Whampoa. Taken over by Li Ka-shing's Cheung Kong Holdings, Hutchison Whampoa soon dominated the world's second busiest East-West trading and shipment ports system; owned substantial property in Hong Kong's pricey real estate market; and held major shares of top performing energy, investment, retailing, and telecommunications companies. With Hong Kong's return to Chinese ownership in July 1997, Hutchison Whampoa, along with other colony companies, were poised for a new generation of corporate life.

Colonial Roots, 1800s to Mid-1900s

Hutchison Whampoa's immense success was in great part due to the Opium Wars between the British and the Chinese.

The first round, fought from 1839 to 1842 and easily won by the British, secured the use of Hong Kong and five ports for open trade through the Treaty of Nanking. The second round, from 1856 to 1858, was resolved through the Tientsin treaties that gave Great Britain, France, Russia, and the United States further access to Asian trade through 11 additional ports. Although the resolution of opium conflicts spawned many companies responding to free trade, the two companies that later became Hutchison Whampoa Ltd. were directly influenced by the Second Opium War and its consequences.

Hutchison Whampoa's roots lay in two of Hong Kong's earliest colonial trading companies. The first, Hutchison International, was established as an importer and wholesaler of consumer products by John Hutchison in 1880. The second company, Hongkong and Whampoa Dock, preceded Hutchison by nearly two decades. Founded in 1861, a year after the Kowloon peninsula was added to China's Treaty of Nanking secessions of 1842, Hongkong and Whampoa Dock was the crown colony's first registered company. In the beginning the company's future was somewhat uncertain; its owner, John Couper, had disappeared during the second opium conflict and was presumed kidnapped and dead.

Whampoa carried on, under new management, with its dry dock operations located on the deepwater port of Canton, one of China's largest and busiest cities and the first Chinese port frequented by Europeans. Four years after its charter, Whampoa purchased its first Hong Kong docks. Linked by the Canton-Kowloon railroad, Whampoa expanded its prominence as a transshipment gateway between Hong Kong, China, and the world. By 1898 when the New Territories (the mainland area joining Kowloon, along with Deep Bay, Mirs Bay, and well over 200 offshore islands) were leased to the British for the next 99 years, both Whampoa and Hutchison International were well established in the area.

Hong Kong, though separated from its erstwhile parent country both geographically and politically, was affected by China's upheavals over the next several decades. The Boxer Uprising (1898–90), the end of the Manchu dynasty in 1912, and the advent of World War I sent ripples through Hong Kong's trading, yet World War II by far did the most damage

Company Perspectives:

Hutchison Whampoa, based in Hong Kong, is a diversified corporation. Its business success is derived from four core divisions: property development and holdings; ports and related services; retail, manufacturing, and other services; and telecommunications. The Group is committed to the controlled growth of its existing businesses in Hong Kong and overseas, and to long-term investment opportunities presented by the economic growth taking place in China.

when the Japanese occupied the colony. Throughout these tumultuous years, both Hutchison International and Whampoa continued their businesses and managed to grow.

A Jewel of the Crown, 1950–79

In the 1950s Hutchison International and Hongkong and Whampoa Dock thrived independently. Hong Kong became an increasingly busy worldwide port despite its small (just shy of 399 square miles) land mass. By the mid-1960s Hutchison International was being run by Sir Douglas Clague, who had big plans for the 85-year-old company. Clague began a far-flung diversification program by buying controlling interest in A.S. Watson and Hongkong and Whampoa Dock. The former retailed soft drinks, drugs, and food through supermarkets and drugstores, while Whampoa's dry dock operations had expanded throughout the Hong Kong area. After Watson and Whampoa, Clague caught acquisition fever and gobbled up a myriad of companies in the following years.

By the mid-1970s most of Clague's kingdom was crumbling around him, which forced the Hongkong & Shanghai Bank to step in and rescue Hutchison. Pouring money into the company (for what amounted to more than a 20 percent stake), the Bank sent Clague packing and brought in Australian spinmaster ''Dollar'' Bill Wyllie to turn Hutchison around.

Wyllie lived up to his name and reputation during his tenure and markedly reduced expenses in a few short years. In 1976 he sold off 103 companies; a year later he acquired the remaining interest of Hongkong and Whampoa Dock and merged it with Hutchison. The rechristened company, Hutchison Whampoa, was in good financial shape and controlled much of Hong Kong's dock activity through its shipyards and container terminals. In 1978 the company went public, listing on the Hong Kong stock exchange under the ticker symbol HUTH. To Wyllie and Hutchison Whampoa's management, the sky was the limit for the revitalized company. Yet despite his profound impact, Wyllie would have a short tenure at Hutchison.

A mere two years after the merger and one year after going public, the Hongkong & Shanghai Bank unexpectedly sold its 22.8 percent interest in Hutchison Whampoa for half of its worth. The new owner, Cheung Kong Holdings, was run by the legendary Li Ka-shing, one of Hong Kong's richest men.

Hutchison Whampoa's acquisition thwarted any plans Wyllie may have had of his own and he left the company in 1981. Li Ka-shing came to his power and prominence the hard way—in fact, his childhood and youth purportedly read like a novel. Soon after fleeing China in 1940, Li's father died and the 13-year-old was faced with supporting his family. Working for a manufacturer of plastics and watchbands, Li sold plastic flowers on the street. By the time he was 23, he had saved a few thousand dollars, which he invested in his own plastics company. This company, eventually named Cheung Kong (Holdings) Ltd., became the colony's largest private property developer and was responsible for building about 25 percent of Hong Kong's new apartments annually.

As the 1980s progressed and the Hong Kong-China reunification drew closer (in July 1997), many residents and businesses began to fret about the changes of reverting to Beijing's control. When the Chinese government remained adamant about their sovereignty rights, leaving little room for negotiation, the resulting economic slump affected both Hong Kong and the mainland. To all appearances, however, Hutchison Whampoa was doing exceedingly well with revenue (or ''turnover'' as the company called it), reaching just over $671 million (HK$5.2 billion) in 1984. That same year China and Great Britain announced a new agreement over the colony's status to quell mounting uneasiness and stop the flight of some 50,000 business professionals per year. Although Hong Kong would be allowed to keep its own legal system and capitalist economy, China, nevertheless, would retain ultimate control of the land mass and its surrounding bays and islands.

Another mitigating factor of the 1980s was the ongoing problem of losing precious land to the sea, making Hong Kong real estate increasingly valuable. In response to the shrinking marketplace, Whampoa's former dockyards at Hung Hom were razed to make way for the Whampoa Garden complex. Mid-decade brought Simon Murray, a former French paratrooper and Foreign Legionnaire, to Hutchison Whampoa's helm as managing director. By the time Murray arrived, the company's Hongkong International Terminals (HIT) unit had become the world's largest privately-owned container terminal operator, helping pump turnover to nearly $705.4 million and income to $154 million in 1985 into the company.

Hutchison began diversifying again in the late 1980s, this time into utilities (Hongkong Electric, with a complete monopoly on Hong Kong's electric service), mining (the UK's Cluff Resources), oil (Canada's Husky Oil), and telecommunications (in the UK and Australia). In two short years from 1985 to '87, revenue had almost doubled from $705 million to $1.36 billion and income rose from $154 million to $240 million. By 1989 income had grown to $391 million on turnover of $2.3 billion.

A World Leader, 1990–97

Hutchison Whampoa extended its telecommunications network through a three-way joint venture with Cable & Wireless and the China International Trust & Investment Corporation in 1990, sending the AsiaSat I (a 2,750-lb. refurbished Hughes satellite), into space. The next year Hutchison Whampoa was on a roll: the AsiaSat I was put to use for STAR TV, broadcasting to 38 Asian countries (or roughly 52 percent of the world's population) through another three-way joint venture between Hutchison (18 percent), News Corp. (63 percent), and Li (19 percent); Millicom, a UK cellular phone company, was added to Hutchison's telecommunications unit (making it the largest cellular provider in the UK); and nearly all of Whampoa Garden had been sold by year's end.

The company's HIT unit augmented its operations with 75 percent of Felixstowe Ltd., the UK's leading container port, in 1991 and a half-interest in Shanghai's container port in '92, furthering its dominance as the world's largest privately-owned container terminal operator with 65 percent of Hong Kong's container traffic (over 200 container trucks passed through its gates every hour). On the heels of these accomplishments came 1992 figures of $2.7 billion in turnover and an income dip from 1991's $428 million to just under $393.6 million due to a weak year for Husky Oil (whose shares the company had unsuccessfully tried to sell) and continuing setup costs for telecommunications expansion.

With Hong Kong's 99-year lease nearly over and Communist rule looming on the horizon, Hutchison Whampoa, like many companies based in the colony, hoped a solid footing with Beijing would ensure a smooth transition. To this end Hutchison continued to develop joint ventures for mutual advantage, because, as Li diplomatically told *Financial World*, "economic pluses outweigh political minuses." In 1993, amidst a flurry of new agreements with the mainland, Simon Murray left Hutchison due to disagreement over the company's future. Yet it was business as usual, when Chinese officials announced their intention to build the country's largest commercial store ever, with the bulk of its financing (95 percent) coming from Hutchison. When year-end figures were released, the company had ample reason to celebrate: income rose 107 percent from 1992's $393.6 million to $813 million on turnover of $3.2 billion.

The next year, 1994, Hutchison bought the remaining interest in Felixstowe Ltd., after paying Orient Overseas a reported $75 million for its 25 percent share. Additionally, Hutchison entered into another deal involving several Hong Kong and Chinese partners investing $120 million in Shanghai property. As Hong Kong real estate reached a critically limited state, Hutchison increasingly turned to China for lucrative property transactions. Hutchison finished the year with slightly less than $3.9 billion in revenue and broke the $1-billion-mark for income, the majority coming from Hong Kong businesses, 5 percent from Asia, 2 percent from the United States, and a loss from the European group due to the costs of setting up its new telecommunications ventures.

The telecommunications unit got a boost in 1995 with the coming expiration of Hongkong Telecom's monopoly on domestic fixed service networks. Along with two other competitors, Hutchison received approval to develop its own services. In real estate, Hutchison paid $125 million to buy out the Hong Kong Hilton's lease to tear down the hotel in favor of more marketable developments. Though the recently refurbished hotel was quite profitable, the value of its land parcel far exceeded its worth.

Hutchison turnover for '95 was $4.5 billion, up 16 percent from 1994, and income rose 19 percent to $1.2 billion.

In 1996 Hutchison announced plans for a new company, Hutchison Telecommunications Ltd., to consolidate its telecommunications interests, which included mobile phones, fixed lines, and paging systems. Hutchison also bought back a 25 percent share of its domestic paging business from Motorola. As the company's last year under British rule, 1996 brought downturns in both Hutchison's container terminals and real estate units. Yet by the end of the year ports and real estate were recovering and expected to post satisfactory gains. Hutchison's 168-year-old retailing and manufacturing division, A.S. Watson & Company, continued to thrive in 1996 with a virtual monopoly of supermarket and drugstores in Hong Kong and more in China, Taiwan, and Singapore; and Orange plc, Hutchison's European telecommunications gamble, was taking hold in its market while a similar service in Hong Kong was expected to rival Hongkong Telecom.

Though few doubted Hutchison Whampoa's future was anything but secure, the weight of several factors loomed great. Li, who owned 44 percent of the company and was past the age of traditional retirement at 69, had often said he'd retire after Hong Kong reverted to Beijing's control. With Murray gone, who would succeed him? For years, rumors swirled about an internal power struggle between Li's two sons, Victor (31) and Richard (29), who were both executive directors, deputy chairmen, and held a host of other posts. Yet regardless of who controlled Hutchison Whampoa and its four core businesses, more significant was the coming political climate: the eyes of the world gazed intently upon Hong Kong as Beijing came calling.

Principal Subsidiaries

Aberdeen Commercial Investments Limited; Binion Investment Holdings Limited; Cavendish Hotels (Holdings) Limited; Cavendish International Holdings Limited; Chung Kiu Telecommunications (China) Limited; Darwin Investments Limited; Elbe Office Investments Limited; Fortress Limited; Foxton Investments Limited; Glenfuir Investments Limited; Grafton Properties Limited; Harley Development Inc.; Hey Wealth Limited; Hongkong and Whampoa Dock Company Limited; Hongkong International Terminals Limited (HIT); Hongville Limited; Hunghom Bay Commercial Investments Limited; Hutchison Communications Limited; Hutchison Delta Finance Limited; Hutchison Delta Ports Limited; Hutchison Estate Agents Limited; Hutchison Freeport Harbour Limited; Hutchison Hotel Hong Kong Limited; Hutchison International Limited; Hutchison International Hotels Limited; Hutchison Mobilefunk GmbH; Hutchison Paging Limited; Hutchison Power Development Company Limited; Hutchison Properties Limited; Hutchison Telecommunications Limited; Hutchison Telecommunications Technology Investments Limited; Hutchison Telecommunications (Australia) Limited; Hutchison Telecommunications (France) S.A.; Hutchison Telephone Company Limited; Hutchison Whampoa (China) Limited; Hutchison Whampoa (Europe) Limited; Hutchison Properties Limited; Lunogo Limited; Mountain Cream (International) Limited; Mossburn Investments Limited; Omaha Investments Limited; Orange plc; Oregon Investments Limited; Palliser Investments Limited; Pan Asian Systems Limited; Park 'N Shop

Limited; Port of Felixstowe Limited; Provident Commercial Investments Limited; Rhine Office Investments Limited; Richmond Investments Limited; Shanghai A.S. Watson Yimim Food Company, Limited; Shanghai Park 'N Shop Supermarket Company Limited; Strategic Investments International Limited; Tremayne Investments Limited; Trillium Investments Limited; Turbo Top Limited; Union Faith Energy (HK) Limited; United Soft Drinks Limited; Vember Lord Limited; A.S. Watson & Company Limited; A.S. Watson Industries Limited; Watson's The Chemist Limited; Watson Park 'N Shop Taiwan Limited; Watson's Personal Care Stores Pte Limited; Watson WhaKwong (Hong Kong) Food Company Limited; Whampoa Investments Limited; Yantian International Container Terminals Limited; Zeedane Investments Limited.

Principal Operating Units

Property Development & Holdings; Ports & Related Services; Retail, Manufacturing & Other Services; and Telecommunications.

Further Reading

Canna, Elizabeth, "Deal Links Hong Kong Giants," *American Shipper,* April 1992, p. 67.

Chowdhury, Neel, "Hong Kong's Looking Good," *Fortune,* December 9, 1996.

DuBashi, Jagannath, "Changing the Guard," *Financial World,* April 2, 1991, p. 56.

Goldstein, Carl, "Stranglehold Loosens," *Far Eastern Economic Review,* October 15, 1992, p. 60.

Morton, Peter, "Husky Oil Put on Sale Block," *The Oil Daily,* April 4, 1991, p. 1.

"Preparing for China," *The Economist,* January 11, 1997, p. 58.

Sender, Henny, "Boardroom Tangle: Hong Kong's Hutchison in Disarray Over Strategy," *Far Eastern Review,* November 5, 1992, p. 63.

Tanzer, Andrew, "Li Breaks Out," *Forbes,* November 25, 1991, p. 100.

—Taryn Benbow-Pfalzgraf

Natuzzi

Industrie Natuzzi S.p.A.

Via Iazzitiello, 47
70029 Santeramo in Colle (Bari)
Italy
(39) 80 8820111
Fax: (39) 80 837637

Public Company
Founded: 1956
Employees: 2,631
Sales: L839.3 billion (US$529.7 million) (1995)
Stock Exchanges: New York
SICs: 2512 Upholstered Frames; 6719 Holding
    Companies, Not Elsewhere Classified; 6722
    Management Investment

With an estimated two percent of the global market for leather furniture, Industrie Natuzzi S.p.A. is a trend-setter in this highly-fragmented industry. Noting the fragmentation of the industry, the company calls itself "the only truly global furniture manufacturer." Although it is headquartered in a small southern Italian town in an area better known as an agricultural center, only seven percent of its sales are generated in its homeland. The remainder comes from exports, with its largest markets in the United States, Europe, and Asia. The vertically-integrated company boasts more than a dozen Italian plants and was poised to open its first American production facility in the late 1990s. It was also one of Italy's largest non-governmental employers.

Post-World War II Origins

The origins of the company can be traced to post-World War II Italy, where young Pasquale Natuzzi, son of a cabinetmaker, began an apprenticeship with a local furniture maker. Natuzzi designed and assembled his first solo project in 1956 at the age of 16, and was manufacturing competitively-priced, fabric-upholstered furniture on his own by the end of the decade. It was in these early years that Natuzzi nurtured a strong work ethic, learned the principles of furniture design, and gained an appreciation for quality craftsmanship.

In 1962, the young entrepreneur moved his 12-employee factory from Taranto, Italy, to his hometown of Matera, where he was soon manufacturing more than 2,500 furniture groups per year. He doubled production over the next year, adding 38 workers to the roster in the process. Tragedy brought a brief but significant halt to the growing business's progress, when the factory was destroyed by fire in August of 1973. In a company history, Pasquale Natuzzi cited this event as a catalyst for change; he not only rebuilt the facility by the year's end, but also began to seek out new lines of business.

He soon settled on diversification into leather-upholstered furniture, which commanded much higher profit margins. As he would later reflect in an interview with *Forbes* magazine's Peter Fuhrman, "[The price difference] had nothing to do with the cost of leather, which was only slightly higher than good fabrics. But there was this idea that a leather sofa was something that could only be sold in small volumes for high prices."

Natuzzi turned that equation on its ear, electing to trim fat margins and make up for the loss with high volume. Focusing especially on contemporary-styled sofas, Natuzzi brought leather to an unprecedentedly wide market by offering comparable quality at an incomparable price. He took this marketing concept throughout Europe and across the Atlantic to Canada by the end of the decade. By the early 1980s, Natuzzi had accumulated annual sales of about $10 million.

Laying the Foundation for Success

Several key factors contributed to the steady, profitable growth of Natuzzi. Dividend reinvestment was a core value, as Natuzzi explained in a 1989 interview with *HFD's* Christie Adams: "We reinvest all of our profits in the company to create new facilities, to purchase new equipment, to make product better, and to make the work of our employees easier." Adams asserted that "the backbone of the Natuzzi Group is design." In 1989, the company was investing more than U.S.$2 million annually in design, engineering, and prototyping. The company carried out these designs with an exacting regard for detail. In the process, Natuzzi grew so successful that suppliers started setting up production near the corporate headquarters. Natuzzi's quest for quality control led inexorably to the acquisition of these upline suppliers, including tanneries, foam block factories, and cushion plants. By the mid-1990s, Natuzzi managed the production of roughly 93 percent of the raw materials it needed. As the company grew to international magnitude, Natuzzi used his buying power to demand "the absolute lowest price possible" from his remaining suppliers.

Employee welfare, efficiency, and customer service have been the cornerstones of Natuzzi's success. Employee welfare has been a high priority for Pasquale Natuzzi, who often referred to them not as employees but as "collaboratori," or co-workers. Due to the natural variability of leather hides, manual labor consumed three-fourths of the value of a Natuzzi piece. The CEO told Adams that "since we make our product by hand, and the attitude of our workers has impact on the finished product, we work very hard to keep their motivation high."

Improving conditions for his "co-workers," combined with the CEO's desire for cost controls, drove the company's steady improvements in manufacturing automation. The company married old-world craftsmanship and attention to detail to cutting-edge technology. Computers increased the company's efficiency; Natuzzi's more than one dozen factories were networked to coordinate production of the hundreds of models in more than 150 colors and two dozen grades of leather. There were computers on every desk, and even sales representatives used laptop computers to illustrate styles and trends to buyers instead of schlepping heavy catalogues from store to store. In addition Natuzzi used a "just-in-time" operating schedule since before there was a name for this highly-efficient (and widely emulated) production schedule.

Natuzzi's attention to customer service has been another vital factor in its success. At the heart of the company's popularity with retailers were its low wholesale prices, which resulted in high inventory turnover and subsequently "higher payback per square foot." Natuzzi carefully scrutinized currency markets and bought futures in order to insulate his company from the damaging effects of global currency fluctuations. His discretion in this area kept prices to retailers and the end customer stable, further cementing Natuzzi's client relationships. The company was also renowned for its timely deliveries. These business strategies would become ever more critical as the

company moved into overseas markets, especially the United States. But together, Natuzzi's qualities formed a compelling package to furniture retailers in Europe and around the world. A top executive with America's Levitz chain praised Natuzzi's prescience in a 1989 *HFD* article: "Natuzzi is definitely a step ahead all the time in price, styling, and quality."

Natuzzi Leads "Italian Invasion" of U.S. Furniture Market in 1980s

Like a modern-day Christopher Columbus, the Italian furniture maker discovered America's largely untapped leather sofa market on a trip to New York in 1982. Even accounting for import duties and overseas shipping, Natuzzi found that he could undercut U.S. wholesaler's prices by more than 50 percent. His competitively-priced bids won accounts large and small, from major national department stores like Macy's, Bloomingdale's, and Dillard's, to specialty furniture retailers and so-called "promotional powerhouses" like Seaman's and Levitz. *HFD* characterized the concept as "Class Meets Mass" in a 1988 piece.

But price and service were not the only things that drew clients to Natuzzi; with his clean shaven head and chic silk and leather duds, the Italian furniture magnate had an undeniable charisma. An awestruck employee called him "the heart, the engine [of] Natuzzi" in a 1992 *HFD* profile. In spite of his broken English, Natuzzi was able to express his enthusiasm for the business to potential clients and the American business press. *Forbes'* Peter Fuhrman described him as a "sober and disciplined businessman" who looked like "Mr. Clean in a Versace outfit" in a 1994 profile.

Natuzzi was hailed as "one of the most outstanding success stories of the Italian invasion" by *HFD's* Liz Seymour in 1987. By the end of the decade, Natuzzi alone was supplying one-fifth of the leather furniture sold in the United States and that single market generated more than 80 percent of the company's annual revenues. Natuzzi spearheaded the "invasion," which saw Italian furniture grow to encompass more than 10 percent of all furniture imported to America. A 1988 company profile in *HFD* credited Pasquale Natuzzi with making leather "one of the hottest furniture categories for volume furniture retailers in the United States. [He] has breathed new life into the upholstered business as a whole." From 1980 to 1985, the company's sales increased more than six fold, from L6 billion to L45 billion (over U.S.$30 million) on production of about 1,700 seating units per day.

IPO, Global Strategy Mark Early 1990s

In the early 1990s, Natuzzi added three new strategies to his core formula. In order to garner more of the U.S. furniture market, he concentrated on adding new markets across the country and consuming more display area in existing venues by expanding his company's product offerings. From its bulkhead in North Carolina, the company sought clients in the Midwest and on the West Coast, adding a California office.

Natuzzi expanded its leather furniture offerings from the core sofas to include "motion" models like sleep sofas, rockers, swivel occasional chairs, and recliners. The CEO also reached back into his company's history, revisiting the market for fabric-upholstered furniture he had abandoned in the late 1970s. Noting that the market for sofas upholstered with cloth was four times larger than the leather market, he hailed it as "the best opportunity to grow." In order "to fill the historical gap in the craftsmanship sphere," Natuzzi acquired a controlling interest in Spagnesi, a manufacturer of "traditional European upholstered furniture with exposed wood frames" with sales of U.S.$29 million based in Tuscany. The company also added a line of slipcovered furniture in 1996.

Having achieved virtually complete vertical integration of production, Natuzzi turned downstream, to retailing, for increased profit retention. In 1990 he launched the Divani & Divani chain of franchised furniture stores. Within five years, the company boasted 73 stores in Italy, Portugal, and Venezuela. Natuzzi launched a second chain under the NOVUM name in 1996, hoping eventually to have 120 of these specialty shops. The CEO also sought to expand his geographic reach to Asia, especially Japan but also Taiwan, Singapore, the Philippines and Korea, as well as Australia, Mexico, and Canada.

Pasquale Natuzzi took his company public in May 1993 on the New York Stock Exchange, selling about $77 million worth of his own stake. He continued to hold about 49 percent of the company's equity in 1994, while daughters Anna, a manager of product development, and Nunzia, a personnel manager, owned a combined six percent. Industrie Natuzzi shares, which started at $15, had reached $27 by August 1994 and were projected by Allan Raphael and Arthur Lerner of First Eagle International Fund to reach $60 by 1996, according to an August 1994 *Business Week* brief.

In April of 1994, Natuzzi told *HFD's* Alessandra Ilari that "Our mission is to grow and offer new employment." In 1992, he unveiled plans to bring that ideal to the United States with construction of a plant in Texas. This would put the company close to both cattle producers and American furniture retailers, thereby reducing freight and duty charges as well as shorten delivery time to what had become Natuzzi's biggest market. In 1994, the furniture maker fulfilled a long-held dream with the launch of "Natuzzi 2000," a six-year building program budgeted at half a billion U.S. dollars. The plan was to consolidate 20 production centers as well as distribution in four buildings at one location. When finished, Natuzzi expected to expand domestic employment by three times.

Natuzzi's ongoing performance did not suffer under the weight of these capital requirements, however. In spite of flat upholstery marketing in the mid-1990s, sales nearly doubled from L465.7 billion in 1993 to L839 billion (U.S.$529.7 million) in 1995, while net income increased from L63.4 billion to L95.9 billion (U.S.$60.5 million). As the company sailed into the waning years of the 20th century, there was every indication that this excellent record of profitable growth would continue.

Principal Subsidiaries

Natuzzi Americas, Inc. (U.S.A.); Natuzzi Pacific Pty Ltd. (Australia).

Further Reading

Adams, Christie, "Nobody Does It Bolder: Natuzzi Styles the Market with Innovation," *HFD: The Weekly Home Furnishings Newspaper,* October 9, 1989, pp. 36–37.

Brin, Geri, "Natuzzi's Next Move," *HFD: The Weekly Home Furnishings Newspaper,* September 14, 1992, pp. 22–23.

Colangelo, Michael, "Natuzzi: Class Meets Mass," *HFD: The Weekly Home Furnishings Newspaper,* February 15, 1988, pp. 1–3.

Fuhrman, Peter, "Leather Man," *Forbes,* November 7, 1994, pp. 296–297.

Ilari, Alessandra, "Natuzzi: Fabric-Covered Furniture," *HFD: The Weekly Home Furnishings Newspaper,* April 18, 1994, p. 6.

Marcial, Gene G., "Natuzzi: An Undiscovered Italian Gem," *Business Week,* August 8, 1994, p. 65.

Norton, Leslie P., "Seeking High Profits and Straight Talk," *Barron's,* May 2, 1994, pp. 43–44.

Seymour, Liz, "That's Italian!," *HFD: The Weekly Home Furnishings Newspaper,* April 13, 1987, pp. 33–38.

—April Dougal Gasbarre

Insight Enterprises, Inc.

1912 West Fourth St.
Tempe, Arizona 85281
U.S.A.
(602) 902-1001
Fax: (602) 902-1141
Web site: http://www.insight.com

Public Company
Incorporated: 1988
Employees: 695
Sales: $342.8 million (1996)
Stock Exchanges: NASDAQ
SICs: 5961 Mail Order Houses

Insight Enterprises, Inc. specializes in the direct marketing of brand-name microcomputers, peripherals, and software through catalog, phone, and Internet sales. The company's customer-focused account executives sell to price-conscious, computer-literate end users in U.S. and Canadian home, business, government, and education markets. Insight also offers services to manufacturers who outsource their marketing, sales, or distribution activities.

Insight seeks to provide customers—motivated by convenience, choice, and price—with a computer superstore delivered to their mailboxes. Its goal is to be the best direct marketer in the world through broad product selection and value pricing, one-stop shopping for customers, readily available products, expert technical advice before sales, speedy delivery, and support after sales with a continuing relationship between account executives and customers.

Entrepreneurial Beginnings, the 1980s

Eric Crown was working as a retail computer sales person when, moved by the entrepreneurial spirit, he decided to earn more money for himself instead of someone else. Perhaps recalling a college paper he wrote, he started to act on his idea for a computer mail order company. Despite the paper's ''C''

grade, he went on to create a multimillion dollar direct mail business—no small thing given the challenges of direct marketing computers. As one industry executive told *Direct:* ''Anybody can start a computer catalog—that's not difficult. What is difficult is to succeed against the inherent odds.'' To prosper as a direct marketer, Crown would need to overcome the notoriously small profit margins in computer catalogs and fierce competition from other catalogs, discount retailers, superstores, and resellers. Each of his direct marketing efforts would require a high response level and significant sales. Yet he succeeded brilliantly.

Eric Crown and his brother Tim established Hard Drives International in 1986 and began selling mass storage computer products. They borrowed $2000 on a credit card, rented 100 square feet of office space, and bought an ad in *Computer Shopper* magazine selling hard drives. Their advertised price was less than the brothers could buy the hard drives for, but the Crowns calculated that prices would drop between the time of buying the ad and its actual appearance. The result was $20,000 in hard drive sales and a better profit than even they expected.

In 1988 Hard Drives International evolved into Insight Direct. Insight marketed mass storage products through ads in computer magazines and inbound toll-free telephone lines. In 1991 the company added product lines, including name-brand personal computers, software, and peripherals. By 1992, Insight spent $1.5 million each month on ads in print media.

Growth Years During the 1990s

In 1993 the company added catalogs to market more than 20,000 computer-related products, including hard drives, CD-ROM drives, and software. At this time, the company also began using outbound telephone account executives who focused on larger, corporate customers.

Insight's account executives became one of the hallmarks of the company. They worked for volume sales and customer loyalty, hoping to establish long-term relationships with their customers. As Eric Crown explained: ''We're not so much after market share as we are after customer share.'' Typically, two out of every three sales went to existing customers.

Company Perspectives:

Insight exists to satisfy its customers and is committed to total customer satisfaction. With commitment comes a keen awareness that creating satisfied customers involves every aspect of the operation, from understanding their needs and providing the products and services they demand, to ensuring that every policy, procedure, and operation is customer focused. With all this in place, Insight still believes that the most critical cornerstone of customer satisfaction is creating strong relationships.

Experienced account executives cultivated strong relationships with their clients so that Insight would become the primary source for their computer-related purchases. Eric Crown termed the overriding principle of the sales force "solution selling." Insight routinely extended weekly training to its already knowledgeable account executives. Corporate goals for profitability were shared freely—and were well known—among sales staff. As Diane Cyr explained in *Direct,* "The sales model here is all Crown . . . if you're good you get rich, and if you're not you get out. Miss your goal by one cent, no bonus. Exceed your goal, and you might go on a Caribbean cruise, take a trip to New Orleans, or personally get handed 500 bucks by Eric Crown himself. The more you sell, the bigger the rewards, the bonuses, the commission percentage. Reps are even empowered to offer volume discounts, cut deals, do whatever it takes to get the customer." The result was an 8 percent call response rate to catalogs in 1995, with one-third converted to sales.

Insight's 800-number system contributed to establishing strong relationships between its 300 account representatives and customers. The company maintained more than 1,000 toll-free telephone numbers linked with specific catalogs and promotions. Each catalog or promotion was assigned an individual 800 number, which connected to specific account executives. So account representatives were linked by their areas of expertise—whether small business, geographic area, or whatever—to a given catalog or promotion. This system made targeting and tracking customers easy. Account executives also had individual toll-free telephone numbers, so they could be contacted repeatedly, giving customers the opportunity to speak with an individual who was familiar with them instead of whichever representative just happened to answer the phone.

Another innovation—Insight's own brand of computer—debuted in 1993. Insight combined Intel Corporation's Pentium microprocessor and cutting-edge bus technology to create a state-of-the-art machine. The Pentium microprocessor provided the capabilities needed for three-dimensional graphics, calculating, and video applications, and the bus technology interfaced add-on cards (for example, graphics, networking, or modems) with the microprocessor. Priced lower than competitors' models, Insight's system offered high-speed graphics workstation applications, as well as use as a server for computer networks. As time went on, Insight downplayed its own products. Sales of its computers eventually shrank from 30 percent of the company's total sales to less than 10 percent. The company discontinued the sale of Insight brand computers in 1996, opting to concentrate on its strengths in marketing and fulfillment instead of developing its own products.

Insight also first offered outsourcing services to leading manufacturers such as Toshiba, AST, Samsung, Conner Peripherals, and Motorola in 1993. Essentially, Insight assumed marketing, sales, accounting, and/or distribution functions for these manufacturers. Insight might create catalogs or process orders from those catalogs for major industry players—with remarkable results. Toshiba Accessories' sales, for example, increased tenfold after Insight took over some of its marketing operations. By 1995, 12.2 percent of Insight's sales came from its outsourcing activity.

In 1994 Insight instituted Air Insight—a shipping service that provided hardware and software to customers on the same day that they placed orders. In doing so, the company provided its customers with a streamlined distribution system. Previously, most of the company's orders were delivered overnight.

By 1995 Insight reduced its monthly spending on print ads to $150,000. The company introduced its home page on the World Wide Web and issued the first ever Real Audio Talking Advertisement on the Internet. Insight's Internet marketing efforts drew thousands of hits and elicited about 500 catalog requests every day.

Insight also became a publicly traded company on NASDAQ in 1995. It offered 1.5 million shares of common stock at $9.00 per share and closed at $10.37½ on the first day of trading. Insight accrued $245 million in sales that year, plus $6.1 million in operating earnings. Employees numbered more than 500, and the catalog house file held 1 million names.

Insight also signed a letter of intent to purchase AN-DATACO, a San Diego-based system and network marketer for the UNIX client/server market, for approximately $16.8 million in late 1995. The acquisition did not materialize, however, because benefits of the move were determined to be less than anticipated. "Insight will continue to consider potential acquisitions of complementary or additional businesses even though the ANDATACO acquisition will not be completed," Tim Crown said in January 1996.

Insight broke ground for a new headquarters for its corporate and sales staff in Tempe, Arizona, in January 1996. The 103,000-square foot facility features "bullpen" sales areas with training centers. At the groundbreaking, Eric Crown said: "This building will be a state-of-the-art facility. We expect to see higher sales productivity as a result of the move, as members of our sales force are motivated by the successes of other members of the team."

Strategies for the Future

In 1996 Dataquest, a research firm, predicted that the demand for home personal computers would slow while the small and mid-size business computer market would grow. Since these are typically large repeat customers from corporations, government, and education, Insight initiated *The Business Computing Source Book,* a spinoff of its catalogue aimed directly at the business-to-business market. Featuring products exclusively for office applications and use, the catalog's average order was $1000, more than $300 greater than orders from Insight's consumer-oriented catalog. Dan Sager, senior vice-president of marketing for Insight, revealed: "Most computer catalogs are segmented by product category, such as Apple, PCs or UNIX. But this spin-off focuses on the target customer rather than the product." Insight expected to mail up to 12 million catalogs in 1996.

The company also instituted a networking catalog and a network manager Web site targeted for local-area network managers. According to Insight's president Tim Crown, "As with the consumer catalog, we will use extensive targeting to reduce the number of 'cold' mailings necessary to meet our goals. This strategy ensures increased response rates at a lower cost. Our networking book will further pinpoint our business catalog offerings, reaching an elite group of network product buyers." Insight's business-to-business sales grew from 33 percent of total sales to 67 percent by the end of 1995 to 80 percent by the fourth quarter of 1996. Insight also offered a leasing program in 1996 through PFO Capital Leasing of Newbury Park, California, to provide corporate customers with leasing options. Eric Crown noted: "Offering these aggressive leasing options through PFO will allow us to better meet the financing needs of business customers."

Business customers are the target market of the future, specifically corporate, government, and educational enterprises with 10 to 1000 employees. According to the 1996 annual report, "Historically, these have been Insight's best customers, and they represent the largest, most attractive segment of the computer direct marketing industry. They are computer literate, value conscious, volume buyers who purchase frequently and require little technical support. Research shows this segment also has the most potential for growth over the next few decades." Insight expects to see some rapid growth in this area, hiring more employees for outbound business-to-business telemarketing operations. Said president Tim Crown: "We continue to strengthen our position as a leading source for business buyers through increased marketing activities and outbound telemarketing. . . . [W]e anticipate a large percentage of our future sales growth to be affected by enhanced outbound telemarketing efforts and alternative marketing methods."

The company also envisions an increase in Internet-generated sales. Eric Crown told *Success* magazine in November 1996 that "we're up to 50,000 accesses per day on our Web site. We do a couple of million in annual sales on the Internet. Our goal there is $20 million in annual sales. It helps to have the newest gee-whiz displays. We have rotational pictures—you look at a product and spin it. We'll ship you 3-D glasses. We've added real-time audio: As soon as you click on it, it talks to you."

Though catalog circulation doubled in 1996, Insight expects that it will decrease in coming years as the company begins to target its best prospective customers and focus on existing customers. According to Dan Sager, senior vice-president of marketing, "The future of direct marketing is in supplanting the face-to-face selling approach."

Principal Subsidiaries

Insight Direct, Inc.; Intech Direct Company; ITA, Inc.; Direct Alliance Corporation (formerly IA Direct, Inc.); Insight Credit Corporation; Insight Distribution Network International, Inc.

Further Reading

Cyr, Diane, "Thirtysomething Else," *Direct,* October 1995, p. 1.

Deck, Stewart, "Interactive 3-D Bows on the 'Net," *Computerworld,* August 12, 1996.

Dvorak, John, "Making Money on the Internet—Some Thoughts," *Boardwatch Magazine,* August 1996.

Gilbertson, Dawn, "Arizona Stocks Dazzling, Jump 8 Percent in Third Quarter," *Arizona Republic,* October 2, 1996.

" 'Green' PCs Conserve Power, But Make Some Compromises," *PC Week,* October 4, 1993, p. 109.

"Insight Adds New Catalog Targeting Business Customers," *Business Wire,* March 18, 1996, p. 3180208.

"Insight Computer Trims 386, 486 PC Prices," *PC Week,* December 2, 1991, p. 27.

"Insight Direct, Zenon Unveil Pentium PCs with PCI Slots," *PC Week,* November 8, 1993, p. 30.

"Insight Gives Them the Business," *Direct,* April 15, 1996, p. 15.

"Insight Uses Virtual Reality in $1 Million Sweepstakes," *Business Wire,* April 4, 1996, p. 4040135.

Lanctot, Roger, "Catalogs Multiply as Category Grows," *Computer Retail Week,* August 5, 1996.

"Notes 'n Quotes," *Computer Shopper,* January 1995, p. 801.

Oberndorf, Shannon, "Insight Takes on B-to-B," *Catalog Age,* May 1996, p. 15.

Poor, Alfred, "Best Overall Suppliers," *Computer Shopper,* December 1995.

Riggs, Larry, "Multiple Zones Hit the Phones," *Direct,* September 1, 1996.

"Valley Firms Design Hot-Rod Systems," *The Business Journal— Serving Phoenix and the Valley of the Sun,* November 5, 1993, p. 25.

"Winning Systems," *Success,* November 1996, p. 10.

—Charity Anne Dorgan

IMG

International Management Group

One Erieview Plaza, Suite 1300
Cleveland, Ohio 44114
U.S.A.
(216) 522-1200
Fax: (216) 522-1145
Web site: http://www.imgworld.com

Private Company
Incorporated: 1960
Employees: 1,500
Sales: $1 billion (1995 est.)
SICs: 7941 Professional Sports Clubs & Promoters; 7812
Motion Picture & Video Tape Production; 6794
Patent Owners & Leasors; 8742 Management
Consulting Services

Headquartered in Cleveland, Ohio, International Management Group is the world's largest and most influential sports marketing agency, ranking among *Forbes* magazine's top 200 private companies in the mid-1990s. From its roots as a one-man-show representing professional golfers, International Management Group (IMG) has expanded its scope to include athletes in virtually every professional sport, including team sports. Well-known athletes in the IMG stable include football's Joe Montana, hockey's Wayne Gretzky, skier Alberto Tomba, and tennis player Andre Agassi. The company has not limited itself to the realm of sports, however; it also represents entertainers like Itzhak Perlman and fashion models like Niki Taylor and Lauren Hutton. The company has even managed a papal tour. IMG has a hand in an average of six events each day, ranging from athletic contests to arts and entertainment festivals. It also produces television programming through subsidiary Trans World International. With offices in 26 countries worldwide, IMG is geographically diverse. In fact, Asia was considered the firm's key area of expansion in the waning years of the 20th century.

Sports Illustrated's E. M. Swift characterized IMG as "quite simply, the most powerful, farsighted, far-reaching (some would say grabby) corporation in the world of sport" in a thorough treatment of the subject published in 1990. Its founder, chairman, and chief executive officer, Mark Hume McCormack, has been hailed as "The Most Powerful Man in Sports" by *Sports Illustrated* (1990), "King of the Courts" by *Tennis* magazine (1995), "The Most Powerful Man in Golf" by *Golf Digest,* and one of the *London Sunday Times'* most influential people of the 20th century. In a profile naming him the tenth most important sports figure of the postwar era, *Sports Illustrated*'s Swift asserted, "Virtually everything being done today in the management and corporate sponsorship of athletic events, in merchandise licensing and in made-for-TV sports started with McCormack." Without a doubt, McCormack represented the essence not only of the company, which he continued to own outright through the late 1990s, but also of the sports marketing industry.

Origins in the 1960s

Born in the early 1930s and raised in Chicago, McCormack first became involved in sports as a teen. Since a childhood head injury prevented him from participating in contact sports, he took up golf. McCormack went on to become an accomplished amateur golfer, earning top regional honors and leading the team at the College of William and Mary. Notwithstanding his early success, McCormack eschewed professional golf for Yale Law School, eventually joining the Cleveland law firm of Arter & Hadden. But he by no means abandoned the sport; in his spare time, McCormack arranged paid exhibition outings for the professional golfers with whom he maintained contact. Key among these was Arnold Palmer, a former competitor from college days.

As McCormack told the story to *People Weekly*'s Jack Friedman, in 1960 Arnold Palmer asked his attorney friend to take charge of his financial interests so that Palmer could focus on refining his golf game. McCormack did far more than just accounting and reviewing contracts; the attorney-turned-agent was convinced that "sports was an ideal marketing vehicle—high in visibility, positive in image and international in scope." Confident that businesses of all sizes and types would pay handsomely for the opportunity to affiliate themselves with professional athletes, McCormack set out to make his idea pay.

He arranged appearances, endorsements, and licensing of Palmer's name and image. Within just two short years, the pro golfer's annual income increased from $60,000 to more than half a million dollars. McCormack retained 25 percent of those earnings as his fee. Palmer's success soon drew golfers Gary Player and Jack Nicklaus into the fold, and the attorney found himself representing the golf world's "Big Three." (Nicklaus would later quit IMG.) Palmer was the agent's biggest individual success; over the course of his career, his appearance and endorsement income would far exceed his golf winnings. In fact, Arnold Palmer would for the next 30 years garner more endorsement income than any other professional athlete. He was unseated from that throne by pro basketball's Michael Jordan in 1991.

McCormack's move into sports management was excellently timed. He created the industry just as Palmer's career, televised sports, and commercial air transportation were beginning to take off, literally and figuratively. Palmer's unquestionable talent provided a quality foundation upon which McCormack built a marketable image. Television supplied the venue and drew the all-important advertising dollars, and airlines enabled the agent and his clients to arrange and travel to high-paying events around the world.

But it obviously took more than timing to build a multimillion-dollar sports management agency. McCormack also had an innate business sense and was not adverse to hard work. He's been called "the absolute personification of the aggressive, hard-driving American," and a look at the sexagenarian's exhausting routine illustrated that assertion. During the work week, he woke at 4:30 a.m., devoting two hours in the morning to phone and written correspondence. Each day was tightly scheduled, dictating letters and making overseas phone calls from 5:00 a.m. to 7:00 a.m. on weekdays and then proceeding in half-hour periods, even scheduling breaks and sleep down to the minute and racking up hundreds of thousands of air miles in the process. In addition to running a multimillion dollar operation, McCormack (who, incidentally, had no formal business training) authored two bestselling management guides and a periodical newsletter.

Diversification Begins in the Late 1960s

McCormack began to diversify into new sports and concurrently take his business international when he contracted with South African golfer Gary Player. The pace of globalization began to quicken in the late 1960s, when he signed British golfer Tony Jacklin; Olympic gold medalist Jean-Claude Killy, a French skier; and Scottish race car driver Jackie Stewart. McCormack used big-name international sports figures such as these to insinuate IMG into new markets, and then established international offices staffed with nationals who could recognize and take advantage of country-specific trends.

By the late 1980s, IMG had expanded into several sports and entertainment fields, including classical and operatic music, figure skating, and gymnastics. But its most important area of expertise, next to golf, of course, was tennis. By the end of the decade, the firm represented one-third of the sport's top 30 male players, including Ivan Lendl, Andre Agassi, and Mats Wilander, as well as four of the top ten women, making players like Arantxa Sanchez Vicario and Martina Navratilova household names in the process. IMG expanded its relatively small presence in the field of team sports through the acquisition of top agencies like Reich, Landman and Berry, a baseball players' agency acquired in 1987; National Basketball Association agent Larry Fleisher; and National Football League representative Ralph Cindrich in 1988. By 1990, IMG managed the careers of 25 professional basketball players, 40 pro football players, 75 Major Leaguers, and three National Hockey Leaguers.

McCormack did not limit himself to representing individual celebrities, however. In 1968 IMG inked a contract with the organizers of the Wimbledon tennis tournament to coordinate television and video licensing. In the ensuing years, IMG affiliated itself with golf's U.S. and British Opens and the European PGA Tour, as well as tennis's U.S., Australian, and Italian Opens. McCormack did for these competitions what he had done for their competitors: increased income. For example, the Royal and Ancient Golf Club of St. Andrews's British Open had been earning about $100,000 in annual licensing fees from U.S. broadcast television networks in the mid-1970s. After the organization signed with IMG in 1977, McCormack negotiated a new, $1 million agreement for television rights. The superagent also began advising companies on appropriate events and athletes to sponsor, linking multinational food conglomerate Nestle with the PGA Tour and Federal Express with college football's Orange Bowl, for example.

In 1967 McCormack organized a television production company, Trans World International (TWI), to film his company's growing stable of sporting events and produce them for distribution on broadcast television, cable TV, and video. The production division's hallmark was its Trans World Sports show, which featured sports news and highlights from around the globe and was dubbed into more than a dozen languages for broadcast in 60-plus countries. By the mid-1990s, this operation was producing thousands of hours of original programming. TWI eventually became IMG's largest division, generating more than one-third of the corporation's annual revenues by 1996. By that time, it ranked as the most prolific originator of sports programming outside of the major broadcast television networks.

Event Management Highlights the 1980s

IMG also began to develop its own celebrity athlete showcases independent of the events sanctioned by professional sports associations. The "Skins Game" is a prime example of this concept. Inaugurated in 1983, this annual made-for-television golf invitational features four of the year's top players in a hole-by-hole shoot-out. The winner of each of the first six holes won $10,000, $20,000 apiece for each of the next six holes, and $30,000 for each of the last six holes. Participants in what *Sports Illustrated*'s John Garrity called "television's richest game show" donated 20 percent of their earnings to charity. It was a win-win situation for all: players won cash (or at least received some publicity), sponsors got hours of air time, and IMG banked 25 percent of the whole.

Although contrived competitions like the Skins Game were an unquestionable success (William Symonds of *Business Week* dubbed it "the hottest game in golf" in 1988) the Skins Game was not without critics. Jack Craig of *The Sporting News* was particularly biting, saying that the "success of the Skins Game is a tribute to greed" in a December 1986 column. In 1993, *Sports Illustrated* characterized the so-called competition as "the most objectionable of golf's trashsport events."

McCormack even wielded influence over amateur sports. For example, he was a leading proponent of the movement to extend the Olympic Games over three weekends to garner more television viewers and generate increased licensing fees. But even as he appealed to the highest achievements of athletes and aspirations of sports fans, he also catered to its lowest common denominator with the creation of televised "trashsport" programs like The Superstars, The Battle of the Network Stars, and American Gladiators.

Diversifications soon made IMG a vertically integrated sports management behemoth. At a single event, it was not unusual for the company to represent the sponsors, negotiate appearance fees for the key participants, organize the competition itself, and film it for distribution on broadcast television and video. IMG's all-encompassing influence inevitably inspired criticism from some sports journalists and competing agencies, who felt that the company's overlapping interests—not to mention its virtual monopoly on the top players in several professional sports—made it most effective at representing its own interests, sometimes to the detriment of its clients. Predictably, McCormack disagreed, asserting that he was just trying to give all of his clients "more bang for the buck."

In 1990, McCormack told *Sports Illustrated*'s Swift, "An Olympic athlete running in a Hertz uniform is a generation away." Unabashedly capitalistic statements such as this drew criticism that IMG-style promotion impugned the integrity of sport, but that was a question best debated by athletic ethicists. As a business, IMG was an undeniable success. Revenues increased from $25 million in 1970 to an estimated $320 million in 1985 and more than $700 million by 1990, creating a rampaging growth record of which even Mark McCormack was wary.

The 1990s and Beyond

Although IMG had been on the international scene virtually since its inception, multinational activities were at the core of the firm's growth plans in the 1990s. In Swift's 1990 *Sports Illustrated* article, McCormack predicted: "Southeast Asia is going to be the growth area for all sports. South America, the decade after that. And Africa the decade after that." IMG acted accordingly. In the early 1990s, it undertook golf course design and development, concentrating especially on Europe and Asia. IMG often kept an equity position in the course, adding yet another layer of influence to its already thorough grip on the sport.

The agency was soon managing Indian cricket tournaments and Indonesian badminton. In 1993, IMG played a role in the creation of official soccer and basketball leagues in China, acquiring majority stakes in two of the basketball teams in 1996. In an interview with *The (Cleveland) Plain Dealer*'s Terrence Johnson, IMG Senior Executive Vice-President Robert Kain said, "The potential is absolutely breathtaking."

Given its indisputable dominance of the sports management industry, perhaps the biggest question facing IMG was its post-Mark McCormack fate. Although the founder and CEO, older than 65 years of age, has vowed never to sell the company to the public, he has reportedly discussed possible buyout plans with Nike's Philip Knight and media moguls Rupert Murdoch and Kerry Packer. And while McCormack continued to exercise a great deal of control over IMG, he had by 1996 delegated most of the routine operations to senior managers. As a result, some analysts considered a management buyout a strong possibility. Of course, McCormack could also transfer the business to the three children who were involved in the business, including sons Breck, 32, and Todd, 29, who guided the increasingly important Hong Kong operations and daughter Leslie, 24, of the Paris office. In his seminal article of 1990, E. M. Swift of *Sports Illustrated* quoted McCormack saying, "I have a lot of intricate plans about what happens to the company when I die. I think I've got a plan that would keep the key people in place after I'm gone, but no one will know what that plan is until something does happen." By the mid-1990s, that "something" had not yet come to pass.

Principal Subsidiaries

David Leadbetter Golf Academy (United States and Austria); Evert Enterprises/IMG; Nick Bollettieri Tennis Academy; Gary Player Enterprises; IMG Resort Services.

Principal Divisions

Client Management; Event Management; Corporate Marketing; Televisions and Film Production; Financial Management.

Further Reading

Braham, James, "From Tee to Green ($), Mark McCormack Shares His 'Street Smarts,'" *Industry Week,* November 12, 1984, pp. 30–31.
"Closed Game," *Sports Illustrated,* December 6, 1993, p. 14.
Craig, Jack, "Success of 'Skins Game' Is a Tribute to Greed," *Sporting News,* December 15, 1986, p. 8.
Friedman, Jack, "Dealsman Mark McCormack Has Some Business Advice They Don't Offer at Harvard," *People Weekly,* October 8, 1984, pp. 119–121.
Garrity, John, "Cash Cow," *Sports Illustrated,* December 9, 1991, pp. 46–49.

Johnson, Terrence L., "Playing for Gold," *Cleveland Plain Dealer,* October 1, 1996, pp. 1C, 2C.

Keeton, Ann, "Sports Marketing: McCormack Scores Big," *Daily News Record,* November 11, 1985, p. 25.

Schmuckler, Eric, "Still the One," *Brandweek,* March 11, 1996, pp. 28–29.

Swift, E.M., "Forty for the Ages: No. 10, Mark McCormack," *Sports Illustrated,* September 19, 1994, pp. 72–73.

——, "The Most Powerful Man in Sports," *Sports Illustrated,* May 21, 1990, pp. 98–111.

Symonds, William, "Masters Shmasters," *Business Week,* November 21, 1988, p. 68.

—April Dougal Gasbarre

Jack Schwartz Shoes, Inc.

155 Sixth St.
New York, New York 10013
U.S.A.
(212) 691-4700
Fax: (212) 691-5350

Private Company
Incorporated: 1936
Employees: 90
Sales: $175 million (1996 est.)
SICs: 5139 Shoes & Footwear, Wholesalers &
    Manufacturers

Although Jack Schwartz Shoes, Inc. ranks among America's largest privately-held shoe manufacturers, sales of its flagship British Knights athletic shoe brand pale in comparison to high profile competitors like Nike and Reebok. The company evolved from a stodgy manufacturer of men's dress shoes into a marketer of hip, urban-styled athletic footwear in the 1980s. After riding its British Knights brand to a cresting wave of popularity in the late 1980s, the company's four Schwartzes—CEO Bernard, his nephews Jack and Larry, and his niece, Janet Schwartz Feldman—sought to reinvigorate their brand and company.

Roots in Men's Dress Shoes: The 1930s–60s

The company was founded in Manhattan's Tribeca district in 1936 by corporate namesake Jack Schwartz. Over the course of its first 50 years in business, Jack Schwartz Shoes Inc. (JSSI) concentrated exclusively on men's dress shoes, selling them under the Charles Walker and Kent & Howard brands. Schwartz ran the company until his death in 1944, when son Donald advanced to the chief executive office. Another son, Bernard, joined the company two years later, and Donald's sons Jack and Larry joined the family firm in 1972 and 1985, respectively. Bernard succeeded his brother as CEO upon the latter's death in 1975.

JSSI broke into the burgeoning athletic shoe market in 1975 with the Pro Players brand, which soon earned a fairly strong following in the Midwest and on the East Coast. But it wasn't until the 1983 inauguration of the British Knights brand that the company gained a national presence and enjoyed sustained growth. Named to reflect the United Kingdom's influence on the athletic shoe market and to portray an image of quality, the British Knights line started with a rather simple canvas boat shoe. Although the style wasn't particularly well-received, the brand name caused quite a stir. Recognizing the potential of their new brand, the Schwartzes started phasing out Pro Players and the older dress shoe lines in 1985 to concentrate on designing sports shoes that befit the British Knights moniker. Unlike its dress shoes, which were made in the United States, JSSI's BKs were manufactured by unaffiliated companies. Most were sourced from Asia, where labor and other overhead costs were significantly lower than in the United States.

Chief marketing executive Larry Schwartz quickly realized that New York was a great launchpad for urban styles that appealed to trend-seeking and trend-setting teens. Not coincidentally, British Knights' daring designs and flamboyant colors appealed to inner city black and Hispanic males. As Schwartz later commented in a corporate press release, "The inner city is the key to many industries, but it is the lifeblood of the sneaker industry. . . . [T]hese days the only way to get a middle-class suburban high school kid to buy your product is to have an inner city kid wear it." Luckily for JSSI, inner city kids *did* start wearing the shoes they called "BKs," and it wasn't long before suburbanites picked up on the trend. The branded shoes enjoyed (and later actively cultivated) a streetwise reputation that strengthened their appeal to rebellious teens and young adults.

British Knights and the 1980s

JSSI's sales skyrocketed in the late 1980s, from just $8 million in 1986 to $136 million in 1989. The British Knights brand garnered three percent of the United States athletic shoe market by 1988, ranking it seventh among the leading footwear brands. *Footwear News*'s Rich Wilner acknowledged BK as "one of the hottest young athletic footwear companies in the country" in a 1992 company profile. In fact, the shoes became so popular that in 1990 Larry Schwartz told *Fortune* magazine's Alan Deutschman that "We've held back and controlled growth

266

because we wanted to maintain a mystique for the brand.'' The company tried to manage its exclusivity, for example, by limiting distribution to specialty athletic shoe stores like Foot Locker and eschewing mass merchandisers.

But just as the fashion appeal of Keds, Doc Martens, Birkenstocks, and Hush Puppies have waxed and waned over the years, the fervor for British Knights began to subside in the early 1990s. It became clear that the Schwartzes had failed to sufficiently reign in the brand. As sales growth started to slow, Larry Schwartz acknowledged that ''Our success in the late 1980s was clearly a fad. Our challenge is to turn a fad into a brand.'' British Knights slid out of the top ten brands by 1992, and its market share fell to less than 2 percent. In 1996, annual sales of BKs were estimated at $125 million.

Strategies for the 1990s

In an effort to recapture some of the success it had enjoyed in the mid- to late 1980s, Jack Schwartz Shoes began to adopt the marketing methods used by ''establishment'' shoe makers. Following the lead of Oregon-based Nike, Inc.—albeit on a much smaller scale—the Schwartzes mounted ever-larger marketing campaigns featuring celebrity endorsers and emphasized technology in addition to fashion.

Advertising was a particular emphasis. Jack Schwartz had not aired television ads until 1988, relying instead on print ads, billboards, radio spots, and especially word-of-mouth to promote British Knights. The marketing budget increased from $2 million in 1988 (about two percent of JSSI sales), to an estimated $15 million in 1991, well over ten percent of revenues. Production expenses and the increased purchase of television and cable air time, especially MTV, combined with the high cost of celebrity endorsements, were the primary forces behind this increase. Although it was using mainstream methods to reach its audience, JSSI continued to cultivate a rebellious image, both through the spokesmen it employed and the messages they portrayed.

In 1991, JSSI hired rap and dance artist MC Hammer to represent British Knights. The company co-opted the entertainer's number-one hit ''You Can't Touch This'' as a marketing theme and sponsored his concert tour. Another commercial featuring Hammer ''dissed'' Nikes as shoes for the older generation with the tagline ''Your mother wears Nikes.'' The ads encouraged the audience to ''Choose Change,'' presumably to switch to BKs. But JSSI's Hammer campaign ran into what had become a familiar problem for British Knights: overexposure. Hammer, who also represented Pepsi and its affiliate Taco Bell, was derisively called a ''spokes-machine'' in a 1991 *ADWEEK* article. As Hammer's turn in the spotlight ended, JSSI sought new endorsement candidates.

By the end of the year, JSSI had already begun to pursue a different advertising approach, this one focusing on the technological attributes of the shoes as well as the attitude behind them. In 1991 the company launched Dymacel, a shock-absorbing system based in part on the diamond in the British Knights logo. The marketing firm soon sought out young, talented, but often quirky professional basketball players to represent this footwear.

Lloyd ''Sweet Pea'' Daniels, then a member of the San Antonio Spurs, was a prime example; he had a personal history marred by drug abuse and violence. But according to JSSI, Daniels' reformation made him an excellent role model for inner city youths faced with the same dilemmas he had overcome. Derrick Coleman of the New Jersey Nets was another professional athlete with a ''bad boy'' reputation chosen to represent British Knights. Although the former ''rookie-of-the-year'' skipped out of a three-day advertising shoot after the first day, JSSI managed to get three television commercials out of him before his contract ended. JSSI hoped that these streetwise characters would appeal to the rebellious nature of their target audience.

The company also tried several promotional stunts in the early 1990s. Some were well-meaning, while others ranged from gimmicky to downright tasteless. In the first category was a series of ''Scared Clean'' anti-drug seminars sponsored by British Knights and featuring Lloyd Daniels. Participants were eligible to receive a free pair of BKs. A 1994 stunt parodied gun buyback programs by enticing high school students to exchange apparel featuring the Joe Camel cigarette logo for free sneakers. While these activities purported to promote a social welfare agenda, others made no pretense of good intentions. A ''World's Smelliest Socks Contest,'' for example, encouraged people to mail their stinkiest sweat socks to JSSI. The prize? A three-year supply of British Knights Predators, a resurrected canvas basketball shoe. Although not a promotional stunt per se, a 1989 shoe model—dubbed the ''Top Gold''—that featured a gold chain was criticized as ''the epitome of empty and non-functional materialism luring the black community'' in the *Michigan Chronicle.*

In addition to its advertising and promotional campaigns, JSSI hoped to achieve ''controlled expansion'' in the 1990s via several marketing strategies. The company sought to increase its penetration of the women's shoe market—which constituted only 20 percent of JSSI's annual sales in 1989—by launching new styles of athletic and casual shoes. But men's and boys' shoes remained the firm's primary focus. Key among these was the debut of the ''LUGZ'' line in 1993. The line was expanded from a base in boots—the LUGZ name was a play on the lug sole popular in the mid-1990s—to include coordinated jeans, casual apparel, and outerwear as well as casual and athletic footwear. By 1996, this line was generating about $50 million in annual revenues.

Geographic expansion also held out potential for growth, as international sales in 15 countries stood at $5 million in 1989. The company formalized its overseas business as the British Knights International division in 1991, by which time these revenues constituted over nine percent of annual sales, or about $13 million. Sixty percent of foreign sales were generated in Europe. BK also sought to offer products at lower price points without sacrificing profit margins. As a privately-held company, Jack Schwartz Shoes Inc. has enjoyed the luxury of concentrating on long-term growth and profitability. It remained to be seen in early 1997 whether the Schwartzes' strategies of product diversification and geographic expansion would pay off with rejuvenated sales growth as the 21st century approached.

Further Reading

"Advertising: Shoes for Camel Clothes," *Wall Street Journal,* April 6, 1994, p. 8b.

Berton, Lee, "Smelly Socks and Other Tricks from the Public-Relations Trade," *Wall Street Journal,* November 30, 1993, p. 1b.

"BK Expands Space, Retail Lines, Brand," *Footwear News,* November 27, 1989, p. 50.

Burns, Phyllis-Lynne, "Parents, Educators Criticize 'Top Gold' Athletic Shoes," *Michigan Chronicle,* January 28, 1989, p. 1.

Cooper, Ann, "Sneakers: Running a High-Stakes Footrace," *ADWEEK Eastern Edition,* February 1, 1993, pp. 30–33.

Deutschman, Alan, "Sneaky Business," *Fortune,* April 9, 1990, p. 109.

Foltz, Kim, "Campaign for British Knights to Escalate Sneaker Wars," *New York Times,* February 20, 1991, p. 17D.

Jorgensen, Janice, ed., *Encyclopedia of Consumer Brands,* Vol. 2, Detroit: Gale Research, Inc., 1992, pp. 79–80.

Lee, Sharon, "British Knights' Double-Edged Designs," *Footwear News,* March 21, 1988, p. 26.

——, "British Knights Quadruples Ad $," *Footwear News,* March 13, 1989, p. 28.

——, "British Knights Slashes Prices with Dymacel," *Footwear News,* February 18, 1991, p. 48.

——, "British Knights Wants to Be No. 4," *Footwear News,* June 25, 1990, p. 30.

Lippert, Barbara, "British Knights Kick Dirt on America's Mom Image," *ADWEEK Eastern Edition,* March 11, 1991, p. 21.

Selinger, Iris Cohen, "Celebrity Overexposure," *ADWEEK Eastern Edition,* March 4, 1991, pp. 12–13.

Wilner, Rich, "Anatomy of an Ad Campaign," *Footwear News,* October 12, 1992, pp. 6–7FN.

—April Dougal Gasbarre

JCPenney

J.C. Penney Company, Inc.

6501 Legacy Drive
Plano, Texas 75024-1000
U.S.A.
(972) 431-1000
Fax: (972) 431-1455
Web site: www.jcpenney.com

Public Company
Incorporated: 1913
Employees: 205,000 (1995)
Sales: $21.4 billion (1995)
Stock Exchanges: New York Antwerp Brussels
SICs: 5311 Department Stores; 5961 Mail Order Houses

With over 1,200 stores in all 50 states as well as Puerto Rico, Mexico, and Chile, J.C. Penney Company, Inc. (JCPenney) is the largest department-store retailer and catalog merchant in the United States, with licensing agreements for its products throughout the world. The company boomed in its early days in Western mining towns because it offered all goods at "one fair price" and brought fashionable goods from the East to remote towns. The company struggled through the 1970s, as upstart companies like Wal-Mart began selling goods at discount prices and long-time rivals like Sears gave JCPenney tough competition in the hardware and appliance departments. A major reorganization of the company from a mass marketer into a fashion-oriented national department store during the 1980s, along with the relocation of its corporate headquarters from New York to less expensive Texas, put JCPenney in a strong position to compete in the tough retailing climate of the 1990s.

The Golden Rule, 1900 to 1919

James Cash Penney started his first retail store in 1902 in Kemmerer, Wyoming, a small mining town. He was 26 years old and had grown up on a farm near Hamilton, Missouri. Two years after graduating from high school, Penney went to work for a local retailer, J.M. Hale. Penney's health suffered while he was in the Midwest, and his doctor advised him to move to the cooler climate of Colorado. After several ups and downs in Longmont, Colorado, Penney started working for the Golden Rule Mercantile Company, a dry goods retailer founded by T. M. Callahan. Callahan soon promoted young Penney to his Evanston, Wyoming, store to work with one of his partners, Guy Johnson.

Penney put in three years as a salesman, and Callahan and Johnson decided to make him a manager and partner. Penney chose to open his first Golden Rule store in Kemmerer because many of his Evanston customers lived there. The local banker cautioned Penney against opening a "cash only" store, as three others had failed in Kemmerer, but Penney didn't want to accept mining company scrip or credit. Penney invested his whole savings—$500—and had to borrow $1,500 to be the third partner, with Callahan and Johnson, in the Kemmerer store. Penney's instinct proved correct; the store had $28,898 in sales its first year.

In 1907 Callahan and Johnson dissolved their partnership, and Penney bought them out, taking over three stores. He implemented the principles of his former partners and expanded the chain throughout the Rocky Mountains by allowing his store managers to buy a one-third partnership in new stores, provided they had a trained salesperson to take their place as manager at the old store. He established a central buying and accounting office in Salt Lake City, Utah, in 1909, and had 34 stores with more than $2 million in sales by 1912. In 1913, Penney incorporated the company as J.C. Penney Company, Inc. and moved the corporate headquarters to New York City to be closer to manufacturers and suppliers.

By 1915 the company had 83 stores and the next year ventured east of the Mississippi River for the first time with stores in Wausau and Watertown, Wisconsin. Penney became chairman of the board in 1917, when the company had 175 stores, and Earl Sams became president. The company continued to open stores at a fast clip. Private label brands were a major reason for the success of the company. Customers liked them because of controlled quality and cheaper prices than brand names; Penney liked them because he could control the price and make a higher profit margin. Belle Isle, Ramona, Honor Brand, and Nation Wide were private label names for piece goods, and Big Mac, Waverly, and Lady Lyke were labels on work shirts, men's caps, and lingerie, respectively.

Rapid Growth and Expansion, 1920s–50s

During the next several years, the company's growth was explosive. As Penney's personal wealth increased, so did his charity. Though he had quietly been giving thousands of dollars to local churches and organizations, in 1923 he founded Penney Farms, a 120,000-acre experimental farming area in northern Florida for down-on-their-luck farmers. In 1925 when the company's 674 stores generated sales of $91 million, Penney was again giving some of his good fortune back, this time in establishing the J.C. Penney Foundation to fund a myriad of family-related agencies. The next year, when the company opened an 18-story office and warehouse building in New York, Penney went back to Florida and built the Memorial Home Community, a 60-acre residential tract for retired ministers, church workers, and missionaries, adjacent to Penney Farms.

The 25th anniversary was celebrated in 1927, and founder James Cash Penney declared that the company had a good shot at achieving sales of $1 billion by its 50th anniversary in 1952. The company's managers and executives, who had equity in individual stores they ran or oversaw, traded their ownership for a stake in the company as a whole. In 1929 the company was listed on the New York Stock Exchange. When the Great Depression hit, the company coped by cutting back its inventory and trying to purchase goods at lower prices so it could pass the price cuts on to customers. The company survived the hard times largely because it had become known for its high quality goods and service, and people turned to JCPenney for the basic items they needed. The company's profits even increased during the Depression, and by 1936 sales rose to $250 million, and the number of stores grew to 1,496.

During World War II, the company sold a record number of war bonds through its stores. Materials and merchandise were scarce, yet the company increased its sales to $500 million in 1945. In 1946 Earl Sams was promoted to chairman, with Penney as honorary chairman, and Albert Hughes, a former Utah store manager, was elevated to the presidency. The company—now with 1,602 stores—opened a store in Hampton Village, Missouri, in 1949 in a "drive-in shopping district," a precursor to suburban malls. After only four years as chairman, Earl Sams died in 1950. In an unusual corporate move, J. C. Penney resumed the chairmanship instead of promoting Albert

Hughes. A year before its 50th anniversary, the company reached its goal of $1 billion in sales.

In 1954 Penney created the James C. Penney Foundation (its predecessor, the J.C. Penney Foundation, went under during the Depression) to continue his philanthropy, and in 1957 he served as a charter member of the Distributive Education Clubs of America, helped create the Junior Achievement Clubs, and endowed a chair at Westminster College. At the same time, William Batten, a vice-president, conducted a study in 1957; the results indicated the company should adapt to changing consumer spending habits, especially by beginning to sell on credit instead of for cash only. The next year, Hughes became chairman and Batten became president. The company issued its first JCPenney card and instituted other changes as a result of the study, including the introduction of major appliances, home electronics, furniture, and sporting goods.

A New Era, 1960–75

In 1962 JCPenney got into the mail-order business for the first time by buying General Merchandise Company, a Wisconsin firm with a discount store operation as well. JCPenney was different from many of its competitors with its late entry into the catalog mail-order business. Other big retailers started in mail-order and then launched into retail stores. JCPenney created the Treasury discount stores from the General Merchandise discount operation. The next year, it mailed its first JCPenney catalog. In eight states, customers could order from the catalog from inside JCPenney stores; a Milwaukee distribution center supplied the goods. The company's first full-line stores, with all the new merchandise lines instituted by President Batten, opened in 1963 in Audubon, New Jersey, and King of Prussia, Pennsylvania. They were prototypes for the JCPenney stores of the next two decades.

The company needed bigger headquarters because it had grown significantly in 38 years; it built a 45-story office in New York in 1964, where the company stayed until its later move to Dallas. At the same time, Batten became the company's fourth chairman and beauty salons, portrait studios, food facilities, and auto service centers were added to full-line stores. Sales topped $3 billion in 1968; in 1969 the company added an Atlanta, Georgia, catalog distribution center and purchased Thrift Drug Company.

Two years later, when James Cash Penney died at age 95, sales for the company he founded hit $5 billion and the catalog business made a profit for the first time. Able to take advantage of the fact that disposable income in the U.S. was rising faster than inflation, JCPenney reached its highest number of stores in 1973, with 2,053 stores, 300 of which were full-line establishments. Donald Seibert was elected fifth chairman of the board and CEO in 1974, the same year a third catalog distribution center was opened in Columbus, Ohio. The company offered, and sold, three million shares of common stock in 1975, and Sesame Street joined JCPenney's fold by signing an exclusive licensing agreement for children's wear.

While the company was riding high on these achievements, the recession that began in 1974 took its toll. JCPenney's stock plunged from a high of $51 a share to $17. Earnings dropped from $185.8 million to $125.1 million. Investors believed low-margin items like appliances were squeezing profits, and that discount and self-service home-center stores were doing a better job than JCPenney in the hardware business. The advent and strong growth of the specialty apparel store also meant tough competition for JCPenney. Like other businesses, JCPenney rebounded and had good growth in 1975, but its executives began to suspect the company needed to be restructured.

1976–85: Mass Merchandiser or Department Store?

Walter Neppl became president in 1976 (Siebert was still chairman), and the company launched its women's fashion program in five markets, designed to help the company compete against specialty stores cropping up in malls. A fourth catalog distribution center, in Lenexa, Kansas, was added in 1978. By then, sales had grown to $10.8 billion, the women's fashion program was introduced in new markets, and a home furnishings line was added. As a fifth distribution center was added in 1979, in Reno, Nevada, the catalog service went nationwide. Sales of the service surpassed $1 billion, making the company the second-largest catalog merchandiser in the United States.

To continue expanding the credit policies of the company, JCPenney began accepting Visa in 1979; MasterCard was accepted the next year. The company closed the Treasury discount stores in 1980 because they were unprofitable and decided to focus resources on its JCPenney stores. In 1981 when the company's sales totaled $11.9 billion, JCPenney was the first to sell zero-coupon bonds in domestic public markets. It also reorganized its executive structure around the office of the chairman. Seibert remained chairman, Neppl moved to the new vice chairmanship, and William Howell was made an executive vice president. With these officers in place, the company launched a massive reorganization to transform the company from a mass merchant into a national department store. It would take almost a decade to achieve the goals outlined in the JCPenney stores positioning statement, issued in 1982.

The company's first order of business was to expand the fashion programs in men's, women's and children's departments, and the company divided its stores into two categories, metropolitan (based in regional shopping centers) and geographic (based in smaller communities). A sixth catalog distribution center was also opened in 1982, in Manchester, Connecticut. With the $14 million remodeling of its key store in Atlanta, JCPenney rolled out the prototype of its latest store design. Atlanta was only the beginning. In 1983 JCPenney announced a $1 billion program to give its stores facelifts and rearrange merchandise. Apparel, home furnishings, and leisure lines would be emphasized, and auto service, hard line appliances, paint, hardware, lawn and garden merchandise, and fabrics were phased out. Its big mass merchant competitors, Montgomery Ward and Sears, continued in these lines.

Retail analysts who followed JCPenney called the company's decision difficult but necessary. These lines provided $1.5 billion in annual sales, but were keeping the company from positioning itself as a true department store. In addition, low-margin goods were preventing the company from making its profit potential. In 1983 Howell, who most recently held a vice chairmanship (along with David R. Gill, who'd started with the

company back in 1953), was elected the sixth chairman of the board, and David Miller was named president. The company also introduced a communications system for broadcasting directly to its stores using satellite transmissions from headquarters. Merchandise buyers from the home office could show store managers, salespeople, and local buyers what merchandise was available, and the local employees could help select what goods would likely sell in their stores. This gave the company the cost-saving advantages of being centralized, but also allowed it to be sensitive to fashion and seasonal preferences in local markets.

Thrift Drug, long dormant since JCPenney purchased it, scored some big points in 1984, when several major industrial companies became mail-order pharmacy customers. Also in 1984, JCPenney purchased the First National Bank of Harrington, Delaware, and renamed it J.C. Penney National Bank, to assist in credit and financial services. The company began accepting American Express cards as well as Visa, MasterCard, and JCPenney credit cards, and the bank was issuing its own Visas and MasterCards. Thrift Drug celebrated its 50th anniversary in 1985; JCPenney's total year-end sales hit $13.6 billion.

A Dramatic Turnaround, 1986–95

In 1986 JCPenney acquired Units, a chain of stores selling contemporary knitwear and by the next year the company was well on its way to achieving the goals it set forth in 1982. Moving its corporate headquarters to just outside Dallas, Texas, JCPenney was able to cut $60 million from its annual budget although about 1,250 New Yorkers lost their jobs. JCPenney's president, David Miller, added vice chairman and COO to his titles, and the company began focusing on four major merchandising groups by dividing them into separate business divisions: women's, men's, children's, and home and leisure. By the end of 1986, there were 1,482 JCPenney stores dotting the country, about to undergo a major change. In 1987 the company discontinued sales of home electronics, hard sporting goods, and photo equipment in its stores. The space that became available was then used for women's apparel. Also in the late 1980s, JCPenney opened freestanding furniture stores, called Portfolio, on an experimental basis.

The company's five regional operations were narrowed to four in 1988 to make communication between merchandising divisions and stores easier. The company also launched a massive leveraged employee stock ownership plan (LESOP) in 1988. With its new stance as a national department store focusing on apparel, the company had benefitted from its prime regional shopping center space, the most such space of all U.S. retailers. Shoppers at regional malls were there to buy clothes and accessories, not washing machines and paint, and JCPenney was poised to take better advantage of these spending habits. Earnings rebounded as a result, rising from $4.11 per share in 1987 to $5.92 in 1988 from total sales of $14.8 billion.

In 1989 JCPenney was named the U.S.'s exclusive distributor for Olympic apparel, sold its JCPenney Casualty Insurance Company, and debuted the JCPenney Television Shopping Channel. The company was not, however, immune to the intense competition and promotional atmosphere of late 1989 and early 1990, and earnings slipped slightly to $5.86 per share on sales of $16.1 billion in 1989. In 1990 Miller retired and vice chairman Gill took on the former's responsibilities as COO of JCPenney stores and catalog service. The company also broke ground for its new corporate headquarters in Plano, Texas, just north of Dallas; winnowed its stores down to 1,328 by closing underperforming outlets; and moved away from some of its private labels, focusing instead on major brand names like Haggar, Healthtex, Jockey, Levi Strauss & Company, Maidenform, Ocean Pacific, Oshkosh, Reebok, Van Heusen, and Warner's. Earnings for 1990 fell to $4.33 per share from overall revenue of nearly $17.4 billion, slowed by the uncertainty over the Persian Gulf and the coming recession.

The next year, the full brunt of the recession and the Gulf War hit consumers and JCPenney rather hard. Retail sales fell from 1990's nearly $16.4 billion to $16.2 billion, but income and per share earnings nosedived (from $577 million to $80 million and from $4.33 to .39 respectively). While the company responded to a shaky economy and adjusted its retail businesses accordingly, its insurance division far outshined other operations with a pre-tax income surge of 44 percent from 1990's $55 million to $79 million in 1991. To the relief of shareholders and management alike, JCPenney rebounded in 1992 while celebrating its 90th anniversary. After relocating to its new headquarters in Plano, the company was rewarded with replenished catalog sales; record performances from JCPenney Insurance and JCPenney National Bank; retail sales of $18 billion, and a net income hike of $777 million with an ROE leap of 18.6 percent over 1991. Further, James E. Oesterreicher was named president and Gill retired after 39 years with the company.

JCPenney's continued concentration on women—who accounted for 80 percent of apparel sales and on whose behalf each store now allocated up to 41 percent of its space—was paying off. Coupled with a ''contemporary and fashion-forward environment,'' sales rose substantially in 1992 and 1993, due to a revitalized Worthington career collection and the debut and ongoing success of new bath and body products. Another proprietary brand, the Original Arizona Jean Company (begun in 1990), soared in earnings to $400 million from the previous year's $90 million. A hip redesign of the Plain Pockets line, Arizona quickly eclipsed JCPenney's expectations, prompting a slew of additional designs in different sizes and colors. On the heels of these triumphs came a two-for-one stock split in March 1993; a new advertising campaign reflecting the company's invigorated stance (JCPenney—Doing It Right); year-end retail sales just shy of $19 billion (up 5.4 percent); and income of $940 million (up 21 percent) due in part to stronger catalog sales of $3.5 billion (an 11 percent increase).

The next year, 1994, JCPenney was still riding the crest of its Arizona wave and introduced Little Arizona denimwear for toddlers. The continued hoopla over the brand's success had even prompted longtime rival Sears to jump into the proprietary denim fray with its own line, Canyon River Blues. Everyone, by now, from consumers to analysts, took note of JCPenney's extraordinary turnaround. Figures for 1994 further demonstrated the company's achievement, with $20.4 billion in retail sales ($800 million from Arizona brandwear), a 6.8 percent comparative store sales increase, and net income topping $1 billion. This year also found Oesterreicher promoted to vice chairman and CEO, W. Barger Tygart named president, and Howell in his 11th year as chairman.

Doing it Right, 1995 and Beyond

In 1995 JCPenney's recovery lost its momentum, falling short of both its own and analysts' expectations. Retail sales increased only 0.9 percent for the year ($20.6 billion vs. $20.4 billion), income fell from 1994's outstanding $1 billion to $838 million, and comparative store sales experienced a 1.4 percent drop. Accentuating the positive, the company announced that its Gift Registry (introduced in 1994) had already signed up 125,000 registrants (100,000 brides and 25,000 newborns) and planned to hit 250,000 by the end of 1996, while another new venture in home furnishings opened four new stores in 1995 (a Las Vegas store attracted 10,000 patrons on its first day alone) with plans for another 20 locations on the drawing board.

Yet regardless of JCPenney's retail store performance, its lesser known businesses, comprised of its drugstore chain, insurance, and banking services divisions, scored rather well for the year. Thrift Drug, the 10th largest drugstore chain in the nation with 645 stores in 12 states, had sales of nearly $1.9 billion in '95 (a 20.2 percent increase) and plans for new outlets in North Carolina and New Jersey. The Insurance group, which began reciprocal businesses services in 1990 and moved into Canada in 1992, ran up revenues of $697 million, a 22.1 percent leap from 1994's $571 million; while JCPenney National Bank's revenues grew 21.7 percent from $131 million to $160 million with 470,000 active Visa and MasterCard accounts and receivables of $823 million.

In 1996 the company moved in several directions to regain the footing lost in 1995: allocated $2.1 billion in capital expenditures over the next three years to open 100 new domestic stores and refurbish 500; expanded its international presence through varied licensing agreements; and announced plans to acquire the Eckerd drugstore chain for a combination of cash ($1.3 billion) and stock. To retain its claim as the U.S.'s largest department store, especially with old foe Sears pounding on the door, JCPenney's executives turned up the heat with more private label brands and, oddly enough, coffee. The former included Zonz, an Arizona offshoot for teens, and new additions to its menswear collection; the latter concerned a joint venture with the Coffee Group of Costa Mesa to install ''JC Java'' coffee bars in 800 of its stores, beginning with a handful in Orange Country, California in the fall of 1997. Although Bloomingdale's has had restaurants in their stores for decades and upstart Nordstrom had coffee bars, was the concept still new enough to attract more customers to JCPenney? Oesterreicher and his management team certainly hoped so, because after all—JCPenney was supposed to be ''Doing it Right.''

Principal Subsidiaries

JCPenney Collections Stores; JCPenney Home Stores; JCPenney Life Insurance Co.; JCPenney National Bank; JCPenney Specialty Stores; Thrift Drug Inc.

Principal Operating Units

JCPenney Stores; JCPenney Catalog; Thrift Drug; JCPenney Insurance; JCPenney National Bank.

Further Reading

Barron, Kelly, "JCPenney Hopes Its Coffee Bars Will Cater to Average Consumers," *Knight-Ridder/Tribune Business News* (originally from *Orange County Register*), January 21, 1997, p. 121B1108.

Bradford, Stacey L., "Eckerd: Pennies from Hell?," *Financial World,* December 16, 1996, p. 24.

Kelly, Mary Ellen, "NAFTA Broadens the Field; Retailers Look Toward Mexico," *Discount Store News,* December 6, 1993, p. 3.

Lettich, Jill, "JCPenney Struggles to Maintain Upscale Image," *Discount Store News,* October 7, 1991, p. 34.

McLoughlin, Bill, "National Chains Build Housewares: Sears, Penney, Ward Mixing in Better Goods," *HFN (The Weekly Newspaper for Home Furnishing Network),* November 18, 1996, p. 1.

Palmieri, Jean E., "JCPenney, Sears Shoot it Out," *Daily News Record,* January 27, 1997, p. 6.

Picard, Diane E., and Zissu, Alexandra, "More Signs Christmas Not So Hot as Penney's, Carson's, DH Report Sales," *WWD (Women's Wear Daily),* January 3, 1997, p. 2.

Vargo, Julie, and Palmierei, Jean, "A Private Label War Grows More Public," *Daily News Record,* February 10, 1997, p. 4.

—Lisa Collins
—updated by Taryn Benbow-Pfalzgraf

Kaydon Corporation

Arbor Shoreline Office Park
Suite 500
19345 U.S. Hwy. 19 N
Clearwater, Florida 34624-3148
U.S.A.
(813) 531-1101
Fax: (813) 530-9247
Web site: http://207.49.155.80/kaydon

Public Company
Incorporated: 1941 as The Kaydon Engineering
    Company
Employees: 2,015
Sales: $290.7 million (1996)
Stock Exchanges: New York
SICs: 3562 Ball And Roller Bearings; 3569 General
    Industrial Machinery, Not Elsewhere Classified; 3592
    Carburetors, Pistons, Rings, Valves

With more than a decade of nearly unbroken sales and earnings growth, Kaydon Corporation has been quietly building an empire of custom-designed engineering solutions. Kaydon and its subsidiaries design, manufacture, and market products such as antifriction bearings, bearing systems and components, filtration systems, metal castings, shaft seals, slip rings, and other custom, specialty, and high-technology products. The company's products are sold to four primary market sectors. Special Industrial Machinery, which accounted for nearly 28 percent of sales in 1995, includes components such as compressor filters, robotic manipulator bearings, medical scanner bearing systems, and printing machine roll bearings for machine tools, material handling equipment, medical diagnostic equipment, large air and gas compressors, robots, and other specialized machinery. Replacement Parts and Exports, at 38.5 percent the largest of Kaydon's market sectors, includes replacement parts, such as railroad diesel piston ring sets, filter elements and shaft seals, space bearings, and slip rings and assemblies, for major equipment users and government and military agencies.

Heavy Industrial equipment represented more than 17 percent of sales in 1995, providing hydraulic excavator swing bearings, power generation lubrication oil filter units, road grader hydraulic filter elements, and sealing rings, piston rings, slip-rings, and assemblies, to the construction, mining, oil, and power industries. Kaydon's Aerospace and Military Equipment sector, representing the remaining 16.5 percent, has long supplied aircraft and military vehicle components such as jet engine shaft seals and sealing rings, landing wheel brake bearings, radar and fire control custom bearings, tank turbine engine shaft seals, and descendants of the product on which the company was founded, military turret bearings.

Since going public in 1984, Kaydon has built itself into one of the world's leaders in specialty bearings. Growth has come both internally through expanding sales of its core products and through a series of carefully planned acquisitions adding new specialty and high-technology products. Kaydon, which for more than ten years was a protégé company of Bairnco's Glen Bailey, has carved out a niche for itself by providing solutions to difficult and high-technology engineering problems. Kaydon operates 12 manufacturing facilities in seven states, as well as plants in Mexico and the United Kingdom. The company is led by chairman and CEO Lawrence Cawley and president and COO Stephen Clough. In 1996, the company posted net income of $50.5 million on revenues of $290.7 million.

Launched in World War II

The Kaydon Engineering Company was founded in 1941 in Muskegon, Michigan, in order to support the United States entry into World War II. Kaydon originally provided a specially designed thin-section bearing for the gun mounts on the Navy's ships. By the end of the war, Kaydon had expanded its bearings line beyond military applications. A hallmark of the company's products, however, was that they were custom-designed, specially engineered, and difficult to manufacture solutions for customer equipment problems. The company's dedication to such specialty products would continue to guide Kaydon throughout its history.

Kaydon clung to its bearings, growing to three manufacturing plants through the 1960s. That was when the company attracted the attention of Glen Bailey. Bailey had spent much of the decade working as a mid-level manager for ITT Corp. under Harold Geneen; Bailey's job was to take Geneen's acquisitions in the wire and cable industry and turn them around to profitability. In 1967, Bailey decided to go into the turnaround business for himself, acquiring New Jersey-based Keene Packaging Associates for $1.7 million. With $65 million in loans, Bailey set out to build his own $1 billion conglomerate—through the 1970s Bailey acquired some 20 small companies, which together neared $300 million in revenues by the beginning of the 1980s.

Bailey's second acquisition was Kaydon, which he bought in 1969. Over the next decade, Bailey pumped some $50 million into Kaydon, upgrading its plants to state-of-the-art equipment, adding specialty filtration products to its line, and expanding Kaydon's facilities to seven plants for a total of 900,000 square feet of manufacturing space. At the same time, Bailey guided Kaydon toward new customers in its core markets and brought the company into new markets, including the robotics industry and the developing market for CAT scanners. Bailey's strategy for Kaydon was working: by 1975, the company was posting nearly $36 million in revenues; four years later, the company topped $65.5 million in sales. By 1981, Kaydon's sales had risen to $85 million. The company's operating profits also saw steady growth, from $3.8 million in 1975 to $22.4 million in 1981.

Reborn in the 1980s

By then, however, Bailey had soured on the conglomerate concept. Instead, Bailey sought to build a different type of corporate empire. He restructured his collection of companies, combining them into separate divisions, and renamed the parent corporation as Bairnco ("bairn" was a Scottish word for child). Bailey's idea was to nurture the separate divisions until they could be spun off as independent companies. As Bailey, who would appoint himself chairman of each new spinoff, told *Business Week*, "Big companies kill the entrepreneurial spirit. I'd much rather have five $200 million companies with highly motivated management than a single, institutionalized $1 billion one." Bailey sought to nurture the entrepreneurial spirit in his management as well. Managers of the Bairnco divisions were given ample incentive to build the division—in the form of being offered the opportunity to take over the leadership of a

newly spun off company. Further incentive was added in the form of performance bonuses: all employees could double the salaries with bonuses linked to the division's net income. Lastly, while Bailey would himself take a share of stock in a new spinoff, management of the newly independent company would also receive a large share of the company's stock.

Despite the recession of the early 1980s, which saw Kaydon's sales drop to $80 million in 1982 and then to $72 million in 1983, Bailey was ready to give birth to Bairnco's first "child" by 1984. In April of that year, Bairnco spun off Kaydon Corporation to stockholders. Bailey was named chairman of the new public entity, and received 9 percent of the company's stock, while Kaydon's management, including president Richard Shantz, received a total of 20 percent of the stock, at $2 per share. The new Kaydon debuted at $3.50 per share, and within five years its stock price would climb to $30 per share. But Kaydon also began its return to independence with a heavy debt load: some $60 million in cash debt against $10 million in equity. Yet, as the market for the company's bearings and filtration products began to recover, Kaydon's revenues rebounded, climbing to a new high of $86 million, for net earnings of $5.7 million.

Under Shantz, Kaydon adopted the growth strategies of its former parent, and began extending into new product areas. Kaydon sought to redefine itself from a producer of specialty bearings to a manufacturer of custom-designed and engineered product solutions. By 1984, the company had added bearings for jet engine components and an antifriction roller lift valve assembly for the automotive market. The latter product, which helped to reduce engine exhaust emissions, quickly proved successful among automobile makers rushing to meet new federal emissions restrictions.

Kaydon looked beyond internal expansion to fuel the company's growth. Taking another lesson from its former parent, the company set out on the acquisition trail. Its first acquisition came in 1986, with the $29.6 million cash purchase of Koppers Company's Ring and Seal division. Ring and Seal, located in Baltimore, Maryland, had originally produced cast iron stoves as far back as 1832, then made cannon balls during the Civil War, but by the 1980s had matured into a specialized producer of sealing rings and shaft seals for a customer base similar to Kaydon's bearings and other products. The acquisition quickly lifted Kaydon's revenues, to $112.5 million in 1986 and to $133.5 million the following year. Earnings were also strong, reaching $17 million for 1987. By then, Kaydon had already made its second acquisition, a $5.1 million cash purchase of the Spirolox specialty retaining ring division of TRW Inc. In 1987, Shantz took over the chairmanship of the company from Bailey, who remained on the board of directors. In November of that year, Lawrence Cawley, who had joined the company in 1985, was named president and chief executive officer. The company's market focus was also undergoing a shift. While Aerospace and Military continued as the company's primary market segment, replacement parts and export had grown to nearly one-third of company sales; at the same time, the company was rolling back sales to the automotive and agricultural markets—in the face of shrinking profit margins—to represent only 6 percent of sales.

In 1988, Kaydon made its first international move, building a plant for its newly formed Maquiladora, Mexico, subsidiary in order to produce large bearings—up to 120 inches in diameter—for the construction industry. The following year, Kaydon went international again, this time with the acquisition of IDM of Reading, England. At the same time, Kaydon acquired Electro-Tec Corp. of Blacksburg, Virginia. The two acquisitions, made for $22 million in cash, brought the company into the slip ring business. Used for transmitting electrical signals or power between rotating and stationary members of electromechanical devices, slip rings fit well into Kaydon's portfolio of highly engineered, customized specialty products. The IDM acquisition also gave Kaydon an important foothold for expanding into the European market. Together the acquisitions helped boost the company's revenues to $151 million. Inside Kaydon management, Lawrence Cawley succeeded Richard Schantz as company chairman, while Stephen Clough, who had been serving as vice-president, was named the company's president.

New Acquisitions for the 1990s

As Kaydon entered the new decade, it continued on its expansion through acquisition strategy. Next up was the $40 million cash purchase of Cooper Bearings, based in King's Lynn in the United Kingdom, and its Cooper U.S.A. subsidiary. The Cooper acquisition further enhanced Kaydon's status in the specialty bearing market, adding Cooper's line of highly specialized split roller bearings, further strengthening Kaydon's European position and placing the company among the world leaders of the specialty bearing market. Meanwhile, the company had been working to refocus the company's market emphasis, boosting the revenue share of replacement parts and exports to nearly 40 percent of sales, while lessening its reliance on the weakening military and aerospace markets, and phasing out of the automotive market (which the company left in 1995). Despite an upsurge in military orders surrounding the Persian Gulf War, the company's growth was hampered by the recession of the early 1990s; in 1991, Kaydon posted its first and only revenue decline since its spinoff in 1984. In that year, also,

Kaydon moved its corporate headquarters from Muskegon to Clearwater, Florida.

By 1992, however, the Cooper acquisition allowed Kaydon to post a rebound, gaining some $23 million in sales to end the year with $183 million. Over the next three years, Kaydon continued to add to its stable of subsidiaries—and its revenues—with four acquisitions, including Kenyon Corp., Industrial Tectonics Corp., DJ Moldings Corp., and, in 1995, the $22 million cash purchase of Seabee Corp., a privately held designer and producer of custom-engineered machinery components. By then, Kaydon's strong record of successful acquisitions was helping Kaydon build its revenues to nearly $300 million, with net earnings of more than $50 million, by year-end 1996. Glen Bailey, who stepped down from Kaydon's board of directors to concentrate on his own corporate empire, must certainly be proud of his "child."

Principal Subsidiaries

Cooper Bearings (United Kingdom); Cooper Bearing, U.S.A.; Electro-Tec Corp.; IDM Electronics (United Kingdom); Industrial Tectonics Inc.; Kaydon Corp. Filtration Division; Kaydon Corp. Sumter Division; Kaydon Mexico; Kaydon Ring and Seal, Inc.; Seabee Corp.; Victor Fluid Power Inc.

Further Reading

"Bairnco: An Empire That Spins Off Companies to Grow," *Business Week*, April 30, 1984, p. 68.

Kingman, Nancy "Bairnco Spins Off Kaydon, Plans More Similar Ventures," *American Metal Market*, April 30, 1984, p. 15.

——, "Kaydon, Free but Debt Laden, on Move," *American Metal Market*, June 18, 1984, p. 12.

Kramer, Farrell, "Kaydon Finds Success by Offering Hard-To-Make Goods," *Investor's Daily*, October 19, 1990, p. 30.

Weil, Henry "'We Grow Companies': So Says Glen Bailey of Bairnco Corp.," *New York CityBusiness*, June 3, 1985, p. 23.

—M. L. Cohen

Kirby Corporation

1775 St. James Place. Suite 300
Houston, Texas 77056-3453
U.S.A.
(713) 829-9370
Fax: (713) 964-2200

Public Company
Incorporated: 1969 as Kirby Jamaica, Inc.
Employees: 1,925
Sales: $386.79 million (1996)
Stock Exchanges: New York
SICs: 4449 Water Transportation of Freight, Not
    Elsewhere Classified; 6331 Fire, Marine and Casualty
    Insurance; 7538 General Automotive Repair Shops

Kirby Corporation is the largest marine transportation company in the United States, and the country's leading transporter of bulk liquid products. Through its subsidiaries, including Dixie Carriers, Inc., Kirby's Inland Division provides inland tank barge transportation in four major areas: industrial chemicals, petrochemical feedstocks, agricultural chemicals, and refined petroleum products. Kirby's expanding inland fleet includes 513 tank barges, 124 towboats, and six bowboats. The Inland Division provides the bulk of the company's revenues, and the Kirby fleet has captured 20 percent of the total domestic tank barge transportation market. Kirby's Offshore Division, with seven offshore tankers, two offshore tank barges, six offshore dry cargo barges, two offshore break-bulk ships, nine offshore tugboats and seven harbor tugboats, transports refined petroleum products, and dry-bulk, container and palletized cargoes, along the Gulf Coast and to foreign ports in South America, Africa, and Europe. Expansion of Kirby's fleet has come primarily through acquisition. Since 1989 the company has actively engaged in consolidating the domestic marine transportation industry, acquiring a number of competing companies, including Brent Towing Co., Sabine Towing & Transportation, Alamo Inland Marine Co., Ole Man River Towing, Inc., Scott Chotin, Inc., TPT Transportation Co., and AFRAM

Lines (USA) Co., Ltd. Kirby has also converted nearly all of its domestic barge fleet to the double-hull type required by federal environmental law; by 1996, of the company's 513 inland tank barges, only 90 were still of the single-skin variety.

While marine transportation provides the largest portion of Kirby's revenues, the company's Diesel Repair operations contribute some $70 million in annual sales. Through that division's three operating subsidiaries, Marine Systems, Inc., Engine Systems, Inc., and Rail Systems, Inc., the company sells, overhauls, and repairs medium-speed large diesel engines and related parts. The company's five service centers help maintain the entire domestic power marine and industrial industry. The company also is a major distributor of diesel engines and parts to the marine and power generator markets, and the railroad and nuclear power industry. In addition, Kirby has been involved in the insurance business, primarily in Puerto Rico, through its Universal Insurance Co. subsidiary; since 1992, however, after merging Universal with Eastern America Insurance Company, Kirby has been exiting the insurance industry. In 1996, after reducing its holdings in Universal to 47 percent, Kirby deconsolidated Universal from its financial statements. Terms of the Eastern merger call for Kirby to reduce its Universal holdings to zero at the turn of the century.

Kirby is led by chairman George Peterkin, who has been with the company since the 1950s, and president and CEO Joseph H. Pyne, Jr. In October 1996 Kirby, which had listed on the American Stock Exchange since 1957, began trading on the New York Stock Exchange.

A Petroleum Spinoff of the 1970s

Kirby started out as a subsidiary of Kirby Industries, Inc.; incorporated as Kirby Jamaica in 1969, the company was formed as part of an oil and gas concession in Jamaica. In the early 1970s, the company's name was changed to Kirby Petroleum Co. But in 1974, despite earnings of $6.5 million on revenues of $85 million, Kirby Industries liquidated its activities, because, as then-president Peterkin told *Newsweek*, "the market did not value [Kirby's] assets at the proper price." As part of the liquidation, Kirby Petroleum was spun off as a public

Company Perspectives:

Kirby's strategy is to enhance shareholders' value by growth through acquisitions in a consolidating industry where attractive industry fundamentals and opportunities to differentiate by providing value added services exist. Since 1989, when Kirby Corporation began a program of consolidation through acquisitions within the marine transportation industry, its total return to shareholders has outperformed the S&P 500 and the Dow Jones Marine Transportation Index. Kirby's acquisitions and internal growth have expanded revenues (excluding insurance) at a compounded 25 percent rate since 1989. Through cost reduction efforts and operating efficiencies generated by its integrated distribution network, Kirby expects continued improvement in operating results. Future acquisitions, be they shipper fleets, independent fleets, or new builds, will present incremental additions to Kirby's fleet. Kirby is not limited to earnings improvement through acquisitions or new construction. In the future, as in the past, Kirby will entertain opportunities to increase shareholder value through stock repurchases.

company, renamed Kirby Exploration Company. The new company brought with it two former Kirby Industries subsidiaries, Dixie Carriers, acquired in 1968, and Universal Insurance, started in 1972. Revenues for the new company were $51 million in 1976.

The company's sales reached $58 million by 1978, and $73 million by 1980, driven largely by a boom in the marine transportation market. But the company's oil and gas business was sagging; in 1980, the company agreed to merge with a company to be formed by the New York investment firm Kohlberg, Kravis, Roberts & Company. That merger was called off in 1981, after the parties could not reach agreement on the distribution of shares in the company to be formed. As the economy slid into the recession of the early 1980s, Kirby's oil and gas business began dragging down the company's profits, producing an operating loss of $118,000 in 1981. But in 1982, the oil and gas units operating loss jumped to $29 million, sinking Kirby into the red by $15 million on $102 million in revenues. In 1983, the company acquired General Energy Corp. in a stock-swap merger, and the following year formed a new subsidiary, Kirby Exploration Co. of Texas.

Kirby also made attempts to diversify its operations, moving into data processing, through an interest in Davenport Data Processors, Inc., and into semiconductor services, through a 97.7 percent ownership position in Materials Technology Corporation. The Davenport interest was sold to Bank of America in 1984. The company sold off the semiconductor business the following year. More successful was the 1982 acquisition of Marine Systems, bringing the company into diesel repair. Meanwhile, Kirby's oil and gas segment continued to falter. When the oil industry collapsed in the second half of the 1980s, Kirby discontinued its oil and gas operations. That portion of the business was sold to American Exploration Company for

$62 million in cash in 1988. About half of that went to retiring debt and covering costs of the sale. With the rest, the company began weighing its options for the future, including investing in other industries, or returning to the oil and gas industry. Instead, Kirby turned to its marine transportation unit.

Sailing into the 1990s

Peterkin's involvement in the barge business reached back to 1948, when his father and uncle, who also controlled Kirby, invested in Dixie Carriers. Peterkin, who had graduated from the University of Texas, joined the company that year. Dixie by then operated a 20-barge fleet. Five years later, Peterkin became president of the family-owned company. In 1968, Dixie was acquired as a subsidiary to Kirby Industries. When Kirby Petroleum was spun off after the Kirby Industries liquidation, Dixie was included as a subsidiary to the new public company.

The marine transportation unit already formed a major part of Kirby's operations. By 1981, over half of the company's revenues came from its barge business, which also produced nearly two-thirds of the company's operating income. But that business, too, was under pressure throughout the 1980s. Several factors combined to turn the once-solid marine transportation industry into a financial minefield. Chief among these was rampant overbuilding of barges during an industrywide boom in the 1970s. With demand rising and hauling rates high, companies rapidly began expanding their fleets—by 1981 there were some 28,000 barges, including a historic high of 4,900 tank barges, working the country's waterways. Investment interest from Wall Street helped fuel the expansion of fleets, as investors sought out barges as attractive tax shelters.

In 1980, however, President Carter declared a grain embargo against the Soviet Union—until then the country's biggest grain buyer. At the same time, new federal regulations imposed waterway user fees for the first time in the industry's 200-year history. (Waterways had been decreed free in the Northwest Ordinance of 1787.) The user fee, meant ultimately to recover 100 percent of the cost of waterway improvement and maintenance, which cost taxpayers some $300 million in the early 1980s, started at six cents per gallon of fuel, then rose to 10 cents per gallon. With fuel consumption reaching some 11,000 gallons or more for a single barge's return trip, coupled with a flattening of the market, the marine transportation industry underwent a shakeout, with many smaller—and larger—companies failing. By 1983, 20 percent of the country's barge fleet were idled. Then new environmental regulations, imposed in the wake of such major oil disasters as the Exxon Valdez spill, demanded that companies carrying petroleum and other chemical products convert their fleets from single-skin hulls to more disaster-resistant double-skin hulls. The cost of converting a barge, as well as building new double-skin barges, finally proved too much for many of the companies that had survived the shakeout of the early 1980s.

Kirby's barge subsidiary struggled along with the rest of the industry, with revenues falling in the first half of the 1980s. But Kirby had resisted the urge to expand its fleet during the 1970s boom, building new barges only when they were under contract. At the same time, the company focused on winning primarily long-term, fixed-rate contracts, which served the company well as the bottom dropped out of the spot contract market and rates plunged. By the end of the 1980s, Kirby emerged as one of only a handful of surviving independent barge lines.

Kirby, by then exiting the oil and gas business, recognized an opportunity to expand its marine transportation unit. With many of its competitors floundering, Kirby began adding to its fleet by acquiring other companies, starting with the $25 million cash acquisition of Brent Towing Co. in 1989. That acquisition was followed less than two weeks later by the acquisition of Alamo Inland Marine Co. for another $27 million in cash. The two acquisitions doubled Kirby's fleet, to 164 tank barges and 64 towboats. The expanded operations helped raise Kirby's revenues from $98 million in 1988 to $141 million in 1989. The company also added to its diesel repair operations, opening a fourth service facility, located in St. Louis, Missouri. The following year, the company added nine new double-skin tank barges to its fleet, purchased four used double-skin tank barges and five towboats, and placed an order for the construction of six new double-skin tank barges. Then, in a stock and cash deal worth $145 million, Kirby acquired Western Pioneer, Inc., and its Delta Western subsidiary, bringing Kirby into the Pacific Northwest and Alaskan markets. The company also acquired the assets of International Barges, Inc., which included three cryogenic tank barges serving the anhydrous ammonia market, for $2.6 million.

Kirby changed its name to Kirby Corporation in 1990 to reflect the company's new direction. In 1992, Kirby was back on the acquisition path, purchasing in that year Sabine Towing & Transportation Co., a subsidiary of Sequa Corporation, for $36.9 million in cash; the assets of Ole Man River Towing, including that company's tank barges, towboats, and property holdings, for $25.6 million; and Scott Chotin, Inc., based in Louisiana, and that company's 29 inland tank barges and 10 dry cargo barges, for stock and cash worth $34.9 million. In its diesel repair arm, Kirby opened a fifth service facility, located in Louisiana. The company then made the first step toward exiting the insurance market, merging its Universal insurance arm with Eastern America Insurance Company, with Universal as the surviving entity. Terms of that deal called for Eastern/Universal to redeem Kirby's stock—75 percent after the merger—in the company over the next 12 years.

Kirby's expansion drive continued. In 1993, the company's fleet grew to 468 barges and towboats, and an additional 16 offshore vessels, with the $24 million purchase of 72 inland tank barges from Ashland Oil Co. subsidiary TPT Transportation, and the $25.5 million acquisition of AFRAM Lines. Co., a worldwide shipper of dry bulk and container cargo, primarily for the U.S. government. The company completed the year with the $15 million purchase of 53 inland tank barges from Midland

Enterprises, Inc. Revenues for 1993 reached $378 million, providing a net income of $22.8 million.

While not all of Kirby's endeavors were equally successful—in January 1994 the company attempted to open a new shipping line between Memphis and Mexico and South America; the company aborted that line in August 1994 in the face of stiff competition; in 1996, Kirby was forced to idle its AFRAM fleet and began to look into exiting the government/military transport market—Kirby continued to post impressive gains into the mid-1990s as demand for barge transportation underwent a new surge. The company added to its fleet with the purchase of 65 inland tank barges and leases on an addition 31 inland tank barges from Dow Chemical Company for $24 million in cash; at the beginning of 1995, the company placed an order for construction of 12 new double-skin inland take barges. The company's 1995 revenues surged to $440 million, including $45 million from the company's insurance operations. Kirby de-consolidated Universal from its revenue statement for 1996. In that year, the company faced a weaker market for its marine transportation. However, its diesel repair arm posted strong growth, boosting the company's profits to $27 million on revenues of $386 million for the year.

Principal Subsidiaries

Brent Transportation Corporation; Chotin Carriers, Inc.; Dixie Carriers, Inc.; Dixie Marine, Inc.; OMR Transportation Company; Sabine Transportation Company; TPT Transportation Company; Western Towing Company; AFRAM Carriers, Inc.; Dixie Carriers, Inc.; Dixie Fuels Limited; Kirby Tankships, Inc.; Sabine Transportation Company; Marine Systems, Inc.; Rail Systems, Inc.

Principal Divisions

Inland Marine Transportation; Offshore Marine Transportation; Diesel Repair.

Further Reading

Jones, John A., "Kirby Adds to Its Barge Fleet as Need for Carriers Grows," *Investor's Business Daily*, September 2, 1993, p. 34.
——, "Kirby Expands Tank Barge Fleet While Demand Is Strong," *Investor's Daily*, July 30, 1991, p. 32.
"Kirby Sells Off," *Business Week*, June 9, 1975, p. 30.
O'Donnell, Thomas, "Waiting for Ivan," *Forbes*, November 22, 1982, p. 50.
Palmeri, Christopher, "Barging Ahead," *Forbes*, August 30, 1993, p. 80.

—M. L. Cohen

Kit Manufacturing Co.

530 East Wardlow Road
P.O. Box 848
Long Beach, California 90801
U.S.A.
(310) 594-7451
Fax: (310) 426-8463
Web site: http://rvusa.com/manufact/kit/kithome.html

Public Company
Incorporated: 1947
Employees: 967
Sales: $101.5 million (1995)
Stock Exchanges: American
SICs: 2451 Mobile Homes; 3792 Travel Trailers &
    Campers

Kit Manufacturing Co. designs, manufactures, and sells manufactured housing (mobile homes)—relocatable, factory-built dwellings constructed on wheel undercarriages—and recreational vehicles (RVs) designed as short-period accommodations for vacationers and travelers. The company ranked eighth in sales in 1994 among leading U.S. manufacturers of recreational trailers. Kit celebrated its 50th anniversary in 1995, with cofounder Dan Pocapalia still at the helm.

Trailers Only, 1945–58

Kit was founded in October 1945 in Long Beach, California. Its first product was a small "teardrop" trailer, so-called for its shape. It was to be sold as a kit, with its components assembled by buyers and attached to the rear of a motor vehicle. The manufacturing "plant" was a latticed-front fruit stand in Pico Rivera, and the original plan called for building 60 units. However, the kit proposal was soon dropped, and the company began manufacturing prefabricated but fully assembled trailers.

The company's initial model, the Kit Kamper, made its debut in February 1946 at a trade show in Hollywood's Gilmore Stadium. Because of a shortage of materials so soon after the end of World War II, the 12 show models had an unusual exterior combination of war-surplus aluminum and fiberglass fenders. Inside, the trailer included all the comforts of home, including an innerspring mattress and an all-aluminum kitchen with butane stove and icebox. The response exceeded all expectations, with nearly 500 orders booked. About 3,500 Kit Kampers were produced and delivered in 1946.

In January 1947 Kit moved to a 100,000-square-foot manufacturing facility in the harbor area of Long Beach. Shortly after, production began on a larger, 8-by-14-foot travel trailer. Demand for the two models exceeded production. Kit trailers were popularized through department stores and new and used car dealers and also received publicity as prizes in the annual Soap Box Derby and the "Queen for a Day" radio program. A number of units were flown into Buffalo and Detroit in the dead of winter.

By the end of 1947 production had jumped from the original two per week to 120, and sales had climbed from $1,000 to $50,000 weekly. A few years later Kit secured an order from the federal government, which needed trailers as temporary housing.

Expanding Operations, 1958–73

Pocapalia became president of Kit in 1956, and the company began producing mobile homes at a plant in Caldwell, Idaho, in 1958. A second Caldwell plant, for RVs, was opened in 1964. In fiscal 1968 (ending October 31, 1968), the last year before Kit became a public company, it earned net income of $688,000 on net sales of $22 million. Common stock was initially offered at $14.50 a share, but the majority of the outstanding shares remained in the hands of existing holders. Pocapalia, who assumed the position of chairman as well as president in 1971, retained about 30 percent of the stock. Arnold J. Romeyn, who joined the company in 1946 and was serving as secretary and treasurer, retained about 25 percent. The company's long-term debt was $1.8 million in 1970.

Kit, at this time, was building mobile homes that retailed between $4,300 and $7,500, and manufactured housing from $8,150 and $12,000. Recreation vehicles offered were the truck-mounted Kit Kamper and Road Ranger models; the Kit Companion Vacation Trailer, top seller in the Pacific Northwest; and the recently introduced Sportsmaster travel trailer. Mobile homes and manufactured housing were accounting for about 70 percent of sales; recreational vehicles for the remainder. The company was selling its products through a network of 700 dealers in 30 states.

The early 1970s were a period of great expansion for the company. In fiscal 1972, when sales reached $47 million, Kit opened plants to manufacture Road Rangers in Chino, California, and in McPherson, Kansas; and a mobile-home facility in Duncanville, Texas. Kit was continuing to produce both mobile homes and RVs in Caldwell, and mobile homes in McPherson; Mount Vernon, Ohio; Forest Grove, Oregon; and Long Beach, Riverside, and Vacaville, California.

Surviving the Energy Crisis, 1973–81

The 1973 Arab oil embargo and consequent economic recession struck a heavy blow to Kit's business, with sales dropping from $54.2 million in fiscal 1973 to $32.5 million in fiscal 1974. The company lost $2.2 million in 1974 and $465,000 in 1975. Its stock, once trading as high as $25 a share, fell as low as $1 a share in 1974 and never topped $2.75 a share in 1975. The long-term debt widened to $3.2 million at the end of fiscal 1975. The company soon turned the corner, however, and earned $1.6 million in fiscal 1978 on record revenues of $61.9 million. Recreational vehicles now accounted for about 60 percent of sales.

Kit sold its Riverside and Duncanville plants in 1976. The following year it sold its idle Mount Vernon facility and opened a third McPherson plant. In 1979 the company was producing mobile homes in single, double, and triple width, ranging in length from 36 to 70 feet and in width from 14 to 40 feet, with floor area from less than 1,000 to more than 2,300 square feet. They retailed from under $15,000 to over $40,000. Travel trailers were designed to be towed behind passenger vehicles and campers to fit in pickup-truck beds. Fifth-wheel travel trailers, introduced in 1972 under the Mark V name, were intended to be towed behind and attached to special couplers in the beds of pickup trucks. Mini-motor homes, built on van truck chassis, were introduced in 1976. Kit products were being sold by 394 dealers in 25 states and three Canadian provinces.

The second energy crisis that followed the Iranian revolution of 1978 ended this brief period of prosperity. Net sales plummeted all the way to $28.8 million in fiscal 1980, during which the company, following a loss of $741,000 in fiscal 1979, incurred a deficit of $1.5 million. RV sales, badly hurt by gasoline shortages, fell to only 37 percent of the company total in 1980 from 60 percent in 1978. Mini-motor homes and Kit Kampers were discontinued, and the number of Kit dealers dropped to 208 in 22 states and two Canadian provinces. The company closed its RV plant in Chino and its mobile-home plant in Forest Grove. A Caldwell plant was converted from RVs to mobile homes, and in 1981 the company was operating facilities only in Caldwell and McPherson.

Gradual Recovery, 1981–88

Kit returned to profitability in fiscal 1981. Recreational vehicles once again topped mobile homes in sales the following

year. The company introduced a new line of lightweight travel trailers suitable for hauling by the current models of smaller, more fuel-efficient motor vehicles. Brand names for its RVs during this period included Royal Oaks, Oak Crest, Oak View, Fairview, Sea Crest, Golden Sunrise, Chateau, and Regal.

Kit's sales, however, did not approach the record 1978 figure during the early 1980s. Profits were modest, and in fiscal 1983 the company actually lost $740,000. The culprit was the mobile-home business, which fell into deficit in fiscal 1982 and did not return to profitability until five years later. In January 1983 Kit announced that the manufactured-housing product line was being overhauled, aimed at accommodating demand for units that were lower priced and constructed more like site-built homes. During fiscal 1984 mobile homes accounted for only 27 percent of company sales.

In fiscal 1987 Kit topped its 1978 highs with sales of $68.1 million and net income of $1.8 million. Increased interest rates on conventional, site-built housing were said to have given manufactured houses a competitive advantage, resulting in an upturn of sales. The RV business was also doing well that year, with Royal Oaks, Oak Crest, Golden State, and Limited models selling for between $19,000 and $45,000.

Slump, Then Resurgence, 1989–95

After Kit reached a new sales record of $73.8 million in fiscal 1988, the mediocre economic climate of the following years took a toll on its business. Revenues declined each successive year through fiscal 1992, when they fell to $55.5 million. Although the company remained in the black, the RV sector lost money in 1991 and 1992, when a new management team was brought in. Its deficit widened in fiscal 1993, despite a sales gain of 11 percent to 3,335 units. The company as a whole lost $33,000 on sales of $59.1 million that year.

Kit's McPherson manufactured-home plant was destroyed in a 1992 tornado. Production continued at Caldwell, where about 500 homes were produced in 1993, along with RVs. In 1993 the company began work on a second Caldwell facility—opened in 1994—behind the main building, in order to double its production of manufactured homes, most of which were being placed in the western states. In making the announcement, Kit spokesman Ed Tucker declared that "Public awareness and acceptance have increased year by year. ... The majority of homes we sell go on private property available for 30-year land-home financing. The homes we build are an affordable value." In 1994 they ranged in floor area from 1,100 to 2,500 square feet and were selling at $28,000 to $90,000.

Kit expanded its sales network for manufactured housing in 1995 to take in three more Western states: Wyoming, Colorado, and parts of northern Arizona. The company had been selling its homes in Idaho, Washington, Oregon, Utah, Nevada, and Montana, with Utah and Idaho the biggest markets. About 1,400 manufactured homes were produced in 1994. Approximately 91 percent were double- and triple-wide homes, with the remaining nine percent single-wide models starting in size at about 700 square feet.

The company's RV business turned around in 1994, when sales rose more than 50 percent, to 5,009 units, moving Kit into the top 10 in this field. Produced in Caldwell, the 35-foot-long Companion Cordova was its largest model, with living-room and bedroom walls that slid out by pressing a button. Produced in McPherson and selling for $21,000, the 33-foot-long Sportsmaster fifth-wheeler was a "toy hauler for the guys" with a 10-foot rear patio that could carry snow machines, golf carts, bicycles, motorcycles, Sea Doo watercraft, or all-terrain vehicles. A Kit executive said the market consisted of people age 45 to 65 who "sell their home and want to travel." Selling for between $9,000 and $32,000, the company's RV models had carpeted hardwood floors, kitchen skylights, solar panels, electric brakes, deluxe range/ovens, enlarged galleys, and power roof vents.

Kit opened a new RV manufacturing facility in Caldwell in 1995, about three miles from the plant producing manufactured homes and the Road Ranger and Companion RVs. This new plant, aimed at meeting demand in the Northwest and Canada, initially produced the 33-foot Sportsman fifth-wheeler but eventually was to manufacture all 21 models in the Sportsmaster line, ranging up from a 19-foot trailer selling for $8,000. About 2,800 Sportsmasters a year were being produced in McPherson at this time. Kit's RV production reached 5,516 in 1995.

Kit's sales rose by about 50 percent to $89.7 million in fiscal 1994, and its net income reached a record $1.9 million. Sales increased to $101.5 million in fiscal 1995, but net income was only $1.3 million due to new-production and plant expansions and consolidations, and the company lost $53,000 on manufactured housing. There was no long-term debt in January 1996. Pocapalia increased his stake in Kit from 30 to 46 percent in 1994, when Romeyn sold his 25-percent holding back to the company, which retired the shares.

Kit's Operations in the Mid-1990s

Recreational vehicles accounted for 73 percent of Kit's sales in 1995. They measured from 16 to 36 feet in length and provided sleeping accommodations for two to 10 people, with over 50 different floor plans offered. Components and accessories included name-brand appliances, radial tires, rubber roofs, and fiberglass insulation throughout. Interior features included an entertainment center with AM/FM cassette stereo, skylights in the bath and living areas, queen-size bed, microwave oven, and ducted air conditioning and heating system. Several models had slide-out features for interior expansion of the living room and master bedroom. Awnings were available and could be converted into an enclosed patio.

The company's RV product lines included Sportsmaster, Road Ranger, Companion, and Patio Hauler. Retail prices ranged between $9,500 and $45,000. Some 239 independent dealers were distributing the company's RVs throughout the United States, 32 in Canada, and five in Japan.

Kit's Manufactured Housing Division was producing homes in 40 available floor plans ranging from 750 to over 2,500 square feet, towed by truck to locations where they were set up and connected to utilities. Retail prices, exclusive of land costs, ranged from $25,000 to $115,000. Distribution was through a network of approximately 50 dealers in nine western states.

Most models included walk-in closets, spacious open areas, and Roman tubs with special showers. The Sea Crest was the smallest. Sierra models were double- and triple-wide, with an array of styles and custom features. The spacious Kit Special home was offered in a popular double-section configuration. The Golden State line was described as outstanding value for individuals placing a premium on comfort and luxury. Designed specifically with subdivision application in mind, the Briercrest came ready to attach a site-built garage.

Kit, at the end of fiscal 1995, owned production facilities in McPherson and Caldwell, where it also owned a warehouse and leased a production facility. It also owned an idle plant in Chino, available for lease, and was leasing its executive and administrative offices in Long Beach.

Further Reading

Baumel, Carol, "Kit Manufacturing Co.," *Wall Street Transcript,* April 26, 1971, p. 23927.
Canorpis, Mark, "New Manufacturing Plant Will Build RVs in Caldwell," *Idaho Business Review,* May 1, 1995, p. 1.
——, "Sales Offices Set Up in Three States As More Homes Roll Out of Kit Plant," *Idaho Business Review,* April 3, 1995, p. 12.
Carlson, Brad, "Kit Manufacturing Plans Major Expansion," *Idaho Business Review,* June 28, 1993, p. A1.
The Kit Story. Long Beach, Calif.: Kit Manufacturing Co., 1990.
Rose, Peter, "Kit Sees Revenues Soar, Expects More in Future," *Idaho Business Review,* September 18, 1994, p. 1.

—Robert Halasz

Kmart Corporation

3100 W. Big Beaver Road
Troy, Michigan 48084
U.S.A.
(313) 643-1000
Fax: (313) 643-5398
Web site: http://www.kmart.com

Public Company
Incorporated: 1912 as S.S. Kresge Company
Employees: 307,000
Sales: $34.4 billion (1996)
Stock Exchanges: New York
SICs: 5211 Lumber and Other Building Materials; 5331
   Variety Stores; 5411 Grocery Stores; 5651 Family
   Clothing Stores

Kmart Corporation, the second largest U.S. retailer (behind Wal-Mart) with over 2,100 outlets in 50 states, Guam, Mexico, Puerto Rico, and the Virgin Islands, once so dominated the discount store marketplace few believed any competitor could shake its mighty grip. Yet too much diversification and too little attention to its core business took its toll in the early 1990s, knocking an increasingly bloated and diffuse Kmart off its pedestal. By divesting its noncore assets, refinancing, and slashing costs by $900 million, Kmart returned to buoyancy in 1996 going head-to-head with Wal-Mart, Target, and a similarly revitalized Sears.

Kresge Red Fronts and Green Fronts, 1899 to 1929

The giant Kmart Corporation grew from a Detroit five-and-dime store opened in 1899. Its proprietor was Sebastian Spering Kresge, a former Pennsylvania tinware salesman, who along with a partner, John McCrory, adopted the chain-store idea first used by Frank W. Woolworth. When Kresge and McCrory dissolved their partnership, McCrory took over the stores in Memphis, and Kresge maintained those in Detroit. Kresge's eponymous outlet sold costume jewelry, housewares, and personal grooming aids. Its success encouraged him to open a second store in Port Huron, Michigan, the same year; others followed in rapid succession. By 1912, when Kresge incorporated his company in Delaware with a capitalization of $7 million, there were 85 stores producing annual sales of $10.3 million. Four years later he reincorporated in Michigan, this time with a $12 million capitalization.

Always in high-traffic, convenient locations, Kresge Red Front stores featured open displays of merchandise with items systèmatically associated. Following their founder's abhorrence of credit, they kept their prices to thrifty nickel and dime limits, until inflation after World War I made the cost of many items too high. Undaunted, Kresge opened a chain of Green Front units in 1920, all selling merchandise at prices ranging between 25¢ and $1. He also acquired Mount Clemens Pottery, to supply the stores with ever-popular inexpensive dinnerware.

In 1924 the company's 257 stores generated annual sales of $90 million. Convinced this success should go hand in hand with corporate responsibility toward the less fortunate, the company founder established the Kresge Foundation, making an initial contribution of $1.3 million plus securities worth $65 million.

The following year Kresge resigned the presidency he'd held since 1907 to concentrate on long-range goal-setting as company chairman. His planning bore fruit in January 1929, when a Kresge store opened in the United States' first suburban shopping center, Country Club Plaza, in Kansas City, Missouri, thereby anticipating a shift in shopping patterns by some 15 years.

Another long-range goal crystallized in September 1928, with the formation of a Canadian subsidiary that opened the country's first Kresge store the following May. Based in Kitchener, Ontario, the initial venture was so successful that the company's $5 million investment financed another 18 stores in locations from Winnipeg to Montreal by the end of 1929. These brought the total number of Kresge stores to 597, together yielding sales of $156.3 million.

Kresge Weathers the Depression, 1930 to 1940

The company's orderly expansion changed after 1929, when the Depression-era stock market plunged the price of Kresge stock from $57.50 per share to an eventual low of $5.50. This was a severe blow to company management, which had pledged its support by taking turns to buy the deflated stock, gambling on its bottoming out at $26. Kresge found himself at a loss, having promised to buy 100,000 shares he could no longer afford, and the company took them off his hands. By 1936, however, the chairman had bought back at cost his own shares plus the 251,306 others owned by the management.

The Depression also brought falling sales as well as inventory losses through the failure of suppliers' businesses. Competition also increased; the scramble for the retail dollar fueled rivalry from Sears, Roebuck and prompted other chains to open department store "bargain basements." Forced to broaden its inventory to meet this threat, Kresge had to raise its prices, so that Green Front stores had many items selling for up to $3 despite their former $1 ceiling.

With the Depression over by 1940, there were 682 stores in 27 U.S. states, plus 61 in Canada. Together, the stores produced 1940 sales of $158.7 million. As the decade advanced, many homeowners moved out to the suburbs from inner city locations; the retailers followed. Kresge management cautiously opened one suburban shopping center store in 1947, adding to the first one that had opened in 1929. Three more followed in 1948. By 1953 there were about 40 suburban stores in the United States, plus one in Canada.

Massive Expansion, the 1950s

By the mid-1950s chairman Sebastian Kresge was long retired from active company management. An operating committee of 16 executives appointed by the board of directors steered the corporate strategy. Although the committee frequently combined smaller stores in high-volume areas to provide better selection and more efficient service, there were 616 U.S. stores by 1954, plus 74 in Canada. Many of the units featured modern conveniences like air conditioning, self-service displays, and shopping baskets. All these operations combined to reach sales figures totaling $337.9 million in 1954—up from $223.2 million in 1945.

Although the variety store image still guided company activities during the 1950s, pricing limits were fading away, with the concept of discount retailing coming to the fore in its stead. Kresge offered economical private-label products ranging from clothing to house paint. The variety of brand name offerings also broadened to include electric appliances, radios, and lawn mowers.

In the late 1950s food grew into the largest single department, warranting training in food management for all store managers. Many stores had delicatessens, and Kresge in-store luncheonettes provided shoppers with a large assortment of snacks, lunches, and dinners devised by the test kitchen at the company's Detroit headquarters. By 1958 these mini-restaurants were so popular that at least one new or remodeled facility opened alongside a delicatessen counter in some Kresge store each week.

A wider variety of merchandise plus higher pricing brought a need for a layaway plan allowing customers to save for expensive items. It was, however, still against company policy to offer credit, although competitors were luring customers in this way.

In 1959, coinciding with the opening of the first Kresge store in Puerto Rico, Harry Blair Cunningham succeeded to the presidency of S.S. Kresge Company. Cunningham, aged 58, had been with Kresge since 1928. A former newspaper reporter, he had worked his way up from trainee status through the store manager ranks, eventually becoming general vice-president. Twin assignments went with this position: one was to tour all of Kresge's U.S. stores, assessing the future position of the company and its competitors in the variety store industry; the other was to prepare himself for the company presidency, when Franklin Williams would retire in two years' time.

Cunningham's travels convinced him that Kresge's competitors were not other variety chains, but the new discounters aiming for fast inventory turnover, which they could achieve by lower markups on a large assortment of small items. Discounting, in fact, was a return to Sebastian Kresge's basic merchandising philosophy, which would be a bulwark against competition in the future, just as it had been in the past. Cunningham, after a period of testing, concluded that higher sales volume, rather than higher markups, would boost the company's profits, which had dropped during the 1950s.

The Birth of Kmart, the 1960s

In 1962 the company opened its first discount store in a suburb of Detroit, calling it Kmart. Within a year, there were 17 others. Unlike Kresge stores, Kmarts were not placed in shopping centers but were built in plazas by themselves, to avoid internal competition and also to provide ample parking. To ensure a 25 percent annual pretax return on investment, each store featured decor that was pleasant, though not extravagant, and each aimed for eight inventory turnovers per year. The Kmart stores were an instant success; by 1963, there were 63 facilities, 51 of which provided repair and maintenance service for automobiles. Three years later, the number of Kmarts had swelled to 122.

The Kmart introduction still left the company with a number of older Kresge stores, still on long leases, which were too small to display Kmart's expanded merchandise lines. Numerous Kresge stores, mostly in deteriorating business areas, were renamed Jupiter Discount Stores and converted to facilities offering a limited variety of low markup, fast-moving merchandise like clothes, drugstore items, and housewares. By 1966 there were almost 100 Jupiter stores in operation.

In 1965 the company underwent several changes. One involved the sale of long-time subsidiary Mount Clemens Pottery. Another was the acquisition of Holly Stores, a retailer of women's and children's clothing that had been a Kmart licensee since 1962, and was operating clothing departments in 124 Kmarts, Kresges, and Jupiters at the time of the acquisition. The same year, the company acquired Dunhams Stores Corporation, a sporting goods supplier already operating under license in 42 Kmarts. Dunhams then became Kmart Sporting Goods, Inc.

S.S. Kresge Company's sales for 1965 reached a record $851 million, representing a 23.6 percent gain from 1964. There were 895 stores, of which 108 were in Canada. Although discount retailing had gained momentum somewhat later in Canada than in the U.S., the Canadian subsidiary had opened its first Kmart in London, Ontario, in 1963. At the same time, while inner-city deterioration in Canada had not reached the same level as in U.S. cities, the company turned some of its smaller, older Canadian stores into Jupiters.

The successful Canadian operations made a large contribution to the total sales figures for 1966, which topped $1 billion for the first time, reflecting a 28 percent rise over 1965. Company founder Sebastian Kresge did not live to see this triumph. He died in September 1966 at the age of 99, having retired from the company chairmanship only three months earlier. Spurred by its Canadian success, the company found another international opportunity in Australia, via a joint venture: Kmart (Australia) Limited, with retailer G.J. Coles & Coy, Limited. The 1968 undertaking, in which Kmart held 51 percent of the shares, produced five Australian Kmarts by 1970.

By 1969 S.S. Kresge Company had decided against purchasing the licensee of its automotive departments, instead opening another subsidiary called Kmart Enterprises, Inc., to operate the departments, now so popular that 56 had opened in that year alone. That year the number of company stores stood at 1,022, sales at $4.6 billion, and average profit per store at $42,358.

Further Diversification, the 1970s

As the 1960s ended, an economic slowdown posed challenges for S.S. Kresge. The company resorted to heavier-than-usual promotional markdowns in December 1969 and January 1970 that shaved profit margins. Other problems included the difficulty of keeping to a 25 percent annual rate of sales gain for an ever-expanding number of stores; the fact that the rate of sales growth in a store slowed as the store aged; and the increase in inventory that came from formerly licensed in-store departments. All these factors led to an earnings slowdown in 1970's first quarter, bringing company stock down 11.5 points in one day. Still, sales for 1970 reached almost $2.2 billion.

In 1972 Cunningham was succeeded as chief executive by Robert E. Dewar, a former company lawyer and president since 1970. The presidency was filled by Ervin Wardlow, whose forte was merchandising.

The three upper managers hurdled these challenges with strategies forged under Cunningham's tenure, like the central-

ized buying for both Kresge and Kmart stores that reduced possible in-house conflict between variety store and discount divisions. The company also expanded its management training program, so variety store managers could switch to discount facilities with ease. Meticulous crafting of the training program guaranteed each store manager could make decisions about products, promotions, pricing, and locations to ensure the store's competitiveness. Other policies included limiting each store to one entrance and exit, thus reducing staff needs and escalating sales per employee, and designing smaller stores of 65,000 to 70,000 square feet, adequate for smaller, more affluent shopping communities. All of these changes gave the company a chance to upgrade merchandise while phasing out leased departments on all items except shoes.

The course charted for the 1970s brought Kresge an annual sales growth of 22 percent from 1972 to 1976, with 1976 sales totaling $8.4 billion. The company, however, was not without its failures. A fast-food drive-in chain called Kmart Chef, set up in 1967, closed in 1974 after having peaked at just 11 units. The costly credit card operation, used by only 9 percent of Kmart's customers, was withdrawn the same year, while a $65 million purchase of Planned Marketing Associates, an insurance company renamed Kmart Insurance Services Inc., brought a loss of $8 million in 1975, although a modest profit of $344,000 was recorded for 1976. By this time the company's 1,206 Kmarts were accounting for almost 95 percent of sales. For this reason, shareholders changed the company name to Kmart Corporation in 1977.

Bolstering a Faded Image, 1978–89

The late 1970s saw changes in Kmart's seemingly impregnable position. New competitors with more inviting stores made company facilities seem shoddy, and specialty stores began to stock Kmart staples like sports equipment, drugs, and personal grooming aids. Changes in public taste showed up in lagging profits, which sank 27 percent in 1980 on record sales reaching $14.2 billion. Other warning signals showed in plunging inventory turnover, which dropped from the 8-times-annually level of the 1960s to 3.8 times by 1979. Utility bills, wages, and other overhead costs soared because of inflation, but fierce competition prevented the company from raising its discount prices.

Kmart responded by cutting the number of scheduled new stores in favor of remodeling existing units and restocking them with more fashionable merchandise. It also installed a computer system to handle inventories, orders, shipments, and other procedures that could speed up delivery times to each store. Other changes included the 1978 sale of the company's 51 percent interest in Kmart (Australia) Limited to Coles Myer for new Coles Myer shares, thus closing out Kmart's ownership of the Australian Kmart stores.

Bernard M. Fauber succeeded Dewar as chairman and chief executive in 1980. Fauber steered the company through an economic slowdown and into diversification that year, with purchase of a 44 percent interest in a Mexican discount chain, as well as a joint venture into Japanese mass-merchandising with Japan's biggest retailer, The Daiei, Inc. Kmart also bought Texas-based Furr's Cafeterias Inc., a 76-unit chain that was a natural outgrowth of the cafeterias in Kmart stores.

In 1984 Kmart expanded its acquisition program and diversified into specialty markets. Because Kmart had already been experimenting with its home improvement departments, a logical move was the $88.2 million purchase of a nine-unit Texas chain called Home Centers of America, Inc. Kmart made Home Centers' operations into warehouse-type stores, changing the name to Builders Square. Next came the Walden Book Company (Waldenbooks), costing $300 million for 845 stores that had produced sales of $417 million in 1983. An Oregon-based chain of 164 drugstores called PayLess joined the growing lineup in 1985.

There was another change in 1984—this one in Kmart strategy when apparel division president Joseph Antonini launched a new line of clothes named for actress Jaclyn Smith that helped turn apparel into the company's fastest-growing business. By the time he succeeded to the company chairmanship in 1987, Antonini's strategy had added racing driver Mario Andretti to the list for automotive accessories promotions, Fuzzy Zoeller for golf products, and caterer Martha Stewart for kitchen and housewares support. The celebrities helped the bottom line—profits for 1987 rose 19 percent, to reach $692 million on total sales of $25.6 billion. Other factors in year-end figures were the sale of all U.S. Kresge and Jupiter stores to McCrory's, the $238 million sale of Furr's Cafeterias and another cafeteria chain called Bishop Buffets, Inc., to Cavalcade Foods, Inc., and the disposal of Mexican interests.

New ventures in 1988 included a partnership with Bruno's Inc., a food retailer, which generated the American Fare hypermarket near Atlanta in 1989; purchase of a 51 percent ownership interest in Makro Inc., which operated membership warehouses; and launch of Office Square, a discount office supply chain. In 1989 Kmart acquired PACE Membership Warehouse Inc. and the remaining 49 percent of Makro, converting Makro stores to PACE formats. It also opened Sports Giant, a group of sporting goods stores, and finished the year with sales of $27.7 billion and income of $800 million.

Beleaguered But Not Beaten, 1990s

The company changed its logo from red and turquoise to red and white, with "mart" written within the larger "K" in 1990. Next came the acquisition of The Sports Authority into which it rolled the Sports Giant stores. Kmart also began a long overdue six-year overhaul of its stores (including openings, closings, enlargements, and refurbishings) to help shore up its image. The following year, 1991, as the company opened its first Super Kmart Center, Wal-Mart emerged as a credible threat and soon overtook Kmart in sales and market share. Still believing diversification was a good investment, the company purchased a 21.6 percent interest in OfficeMax, an office supply chain, with intent to acquire the remaining shares later in the year. By 1992 Kmart was still in an acquisition mode, buying 13 stores in the Czech Republic and Slovakia's Maj department store chain; Borders book superstores as a complement to Waldenbooks; and Intelligent Electronic's Bizmart chain. Sales for 1992 hit $34.6 million, a healthy notch above 1991's $32.5 billion, and Kmart's workforce hit an all-time high of 373,000.

Realizing that Kmart's future lay in its core retail business, the company began shedding noncore assets and sprucing up its

stores. In 1993 Kmart sold 91 of its 113 PACE membership Warehouses to Wal-Mart. In 1994 came the spinoff of Office-Max and the Sports Authority (keeping a quarter interest in the former and 30 percent of the latter); the sale of PayLess Drug Stores (retaining 46 percent interest) and its 22 percent interest in Coles Myer Ltd.; an alliance to open stores in Mexico and Singapore; and the launch of Kathy Ireland's apparel line. Sales for 1993 had hit a high of $37.7 billion with income of $941 million; sales for 1994 fell to $34.6 billion but the big news was a staggering loss of $940 million.

More serious than ever in its reorganization, Kmart's newest journey began with the appointment of Floyd Hall, former chairman of Target stores, as president, CEO, and chairman of the board in June 1995. Next came the spinoff of the Borders Group (Borders and Waldenbooks' combined corporate name), the sale of its remaining interest in OfficeMax and the Sports Authority, and the divestment of 860 auto service centers to the Penske Corp. With widespread rumors of bankruptcy, the downgrading of its rating, and analysts predicting Kmart's demise, many wondered if the nearly 100-year-old retailer could survive increased competition from both Wal-Mart's and Target's newer, snazzier stores. Hall set out to prove Kmart not only wasn't going under—but had just begun to fight.

Leaner and Meaner, 1996 and Beyond

After closing 214 stores, disposing of its Czech, Slovak, and Singapore properties, and pledging to reduce expenses by $600–800 million, Kmart was ready to prove its retail mettle. Its new merchandising credo centered around four simple words: brands, consumables, convenience, and culture. To help achieve its goals came a new advertising campaign featuring comedian Rosie O'Donnell and director Penny Marshall, popular brand name expansion (especially the Martha Stewart line, which was absorbing Kmart's home textiles), and a massive shakeup in upper management. The company then announced the sale of its remaining interest in Thrifty PayLess to Rite Aid, refinanced its debtload, started leasing out hundreds of its largest parking lots, and built a hip new three-story Kmart in Manhattan near Greenwich Village.

Kmart's recovery began to show in its 1996 numbers—for the first three quarters of the year it reported sales of $23.7 billion with a loss of $56 million, while the previous year's figures were sales of just under $24 billion and a much heftier loss of $151 million. Costs for 1995 and 1996 were reduced by $900 million, and management gave the Kmart credit card (first introduced in the 1970s) another try—but there was still much more to be done. Could Floyd Hall could do for Kmart what Arthur Martinez did for Sears? Was Kmart the new comeback kid on the block? Only time would tell.

Principal Subsidiaries

Builders Square Inc.; Kmart Canada Limited; Kmart Fashions; Super Kmart Centers.

Further Reading

Brauer, Molly, "Kmart Posts Profit, Denies Buyout Rumor," *Knight-Ridder/Tribune Business News,* November 21, 1996.

Halverson, Richard, "Leaner, Meaner, Cleaner: Nearly $1 billion in Cost Cutting Has Goosed Earnings and Improved Efficiencies," *Discount Store News,* December 9, 1996, p. 27.

"Kmart Rises from Would-Be Fall, But Others Not So Lucky," *Discount Store News,* July 1, 1996, p. 59.

"Kresge's," *Fortune,* June 1, 1940.

"Kresge's Triple-Threat Retailing," *Business Week,* January 29, 1966.

Main, Jeremy, "Kmart's Plan to Be Born Again, Again," *Fortune,* September 21, 1981.

Mammarella, James, "The Martha-ization of Kmart's Home," *Discount Store News,* December 9, 1996, p. H3.

Sellers, Patricia, "Attention, Kmart Shoppers," *Fortune,* January 2, 1989.

"S.S. Kresge Expansion Is Costly," *Barron's,* September 7, 1936.

"When 2 Cents = $380 Million," *Forbes,* April 1, 1970.

—Gillian Wolf
—updated by Taryn Benbow-Pfalzgraf

Knott's Berry Farm

8039 Beach Boulevard
Buena Park, California 90620
U.S.A.
(714) 220-5200
Fax: (714) 220-5150
Web site: http://www.knotts.com

Private Company
Founded: 1920
Employees: 6,300
Revenues: $230 million (1995)
SICs: 7996 Amusement Parks; 5812 Eating Places; 5399
   Miscellaneous General Merchandise Store; 2033
   Canned Fruits & Vegetables

Knott's Berry Farm grew from a small roadside berry stand 22 miles south of Los Angeles into one of the most popular amusement parks in the United States, attracting more than 3.5 million visitors in 1996. It was privately owned by the family of Walter Knott, who started the berry farm in 1920.

Berry Beginnings, 1920

In 1911, Walter Knott, then 22 and recently married, gave up his job as a bookkeeper in Pomona, California and bought 106 acres of land in the Mojave Desert to homestead. He later told interviewers, ''With all that land, I thought we'd get rich.'' Instead, the land proved too poor to farm and Knott was forced to find other jobs, such as working in mining and highway construction, while his wife, Cordelia, stayed behind to raise their three young children, later to become four. Then in 1915, Knott learned about a cattle rancher in San Luis Obispo County who was looking for someone to sharecrop a few acres to provide the ranch with vegetables. The Knotts moved to the ranch and raised vegetables for the next three years, selling at market what they or the ranch hands did not eat. When they had saved $2,500, the Knotts moved again, to Buena Park, south of Los Angeles, where Knott and a cousin, J.L. Preston, leased ten acres of untilled land to start a berry farm.

Knott produced his first crop for market in 1920, a year that saw wholesale berry prices in California fall by 50 percent. In desperation, the Knotts put up a small roadside stand to sell what berries they could. So did a lot of other farmers. ''We had to do something to make our berries stand out,'' Cordelia Knott told *The Saturday Evening Post* more than 20 years later. ''But we didn't cut prices. All we did was wrap our baskets in plain, clean store wrapping paper and put rubber bands around them. Others were using newspapers and twine.'' The attention to marketing paid off and the Knott's berry farm survived its first challenge. By 1927, the Knotts had added a coffee shop and a small store for jams, jellies, juices, and pies.

That same year, they contracted to buy the ten acres they had been farming for $1,500 an acre, and they leased ten more acres. Two years later, in 1929, the stock market collapsed and land values in southern California fell to $300 an acre. Nevertheless, Knott continued to make payments on his original ten acres of land and bought an additional ten acres at the lowered price.

Not long afterwards, in 1932, Knott heard a rumor that someone had crossed loganberries, blackberries, and raspberries to produce a new, much larger fruit. He traced the rumor to Rudolph Boysen, city parks superintendent in nearby Anaheim, California, who had experimented with cross-pollinating the berries several years before. Boysen had abandoned his experiments, but showed Knott six scraggly plants growing near a ditch. Knott transplanted them to his farm, where they flourished. Within a few years, the oversized berries, which Knott sold in one-pound baskets because they did not look right in the usual half-pound baskets, were returning more than $1,700 an acre. In tribute to Boysen, Knott named them boysenberries.

Dawn of the Amusement Park, 1940s

In 1941, an article in *Farm Journal and Farmer's Wife* noted: ''Over a hundred thousand cars stopped last year at a roadside farm known as Knott's Berry Place. . . . In exchange for country fried chicken, berry pies, fresh produce, nursery stock and cut flowers, the occupants of these cars left $509,031 with Farmer Knott.'' At the time, Knott's berry farm had grown to more than 120 acres and employed as many as 400 people in peak season.

The Knotts had also added a small dining room to the original coffee shop and began serving fried chicken in 1934. On opening day, Cordelia Knott served eight chicken dinners at 65 cents apiece. By 1941, when *Farm Journal* visited, the restaurant, called the Chicken Dinner, had been enlarged to seat 600, and the neighboring farmers' wives and children hired by Cordelia Knott were serving an average of 10,000 dinners a week. On a banner day in 1941, they served nearly 6,000 chicken dinners.

By then, the Knotts had also added a gift shop and several "attractions," including a room of rare music boxes from France, Switzerland, and Germany; son Russell's personal collection of rocks that glowed under ultraviolet light; several rock gardens with miniature waterfalls, water wheels, and wishing wells; a replica of George Washington's Mount Vernon fireplace, which the Knotts had admired while on vacation; and a 12-foot-tall volcano built of lava rock trucked in from the Pisgah Mountain and equipped with a boiler that rumbled, hissed, and spit steam at the push of a button. "It's not half as fool a thing as it seems," Knott told the *Farm Journal.* "When the customers pile up so we can't seat them, the girls send them out to . . . play with the volcano. They get so interested that I've had to install a loud speaker system to call them to their meals when the tables are ready." The volcano cost $600, and Knott figured it paid for itself the first month.

In 1940, Knott had also started work on what would become the centerpiece of the developing amusement park—an abandoned, two-acre Old West mining town that he was moving board by board from the desert. In 1942, *The Saturday Evening Post* noted that the 1860s ghost town was "authentic to the last misspelled sign, and original bullets in some of the doors."

Like many of the projects at Knott's Berry Place, the ghost town began modestly enough. Knott's grandparents had come West from Texas in a covered wagon and Knott commissioned an artist to commemorate the experience. The result was "The Covered Wagon Show," a cyclorama showing a wagon train struggling across alkali flats. A narrator would describe the hardships faced by the early settlers while a girl's voice could be heard in the background whimpering for water.

Knott decided it was not sufficient to display such a spectacle in a modern building, so he found an abandoned hotel near Prescott, Arizona, the Old Trails Hotel, built in 1868. He had it dismantled and shipped to Buena Park and reassembled on the berry farm. Before long, he had added several other abandoned, frontier buildings, including the Calico Saloon, serving sarsaparilla and boysenberry punch, and the Bottle House, built from more than 3,000 empty wine and whiskey bottles turned inward so they would not whistle in the wind.

He also added live Wild West shows, a Boot Hill cemetery with many authentic headstones, and the mile-long Ghost Town and Calico Railway, salvaged from the old Denver and Rio Grande rolling stock. In 1956, more than 625,000 passengers paid to ride the narrow-gauge railway and Knott's Berry Farm, renamed in 1947, brought in $9.8 million.

In the 1950s, Knott also bought and restored Calico, a 70-acre, abandoned silver mining town east of Barstow, California, which he later donated to San Bernadino County. It was still in operation as a tourist attraction in the mid-1990s.

The Disney Influence, 1950s–70s

In 1955, the Knott family attended a pre-opening tour of Disneyland, just a few miles away in Anaheim. As they left, Knott glumly asked his youngest daughter, Marion, if she thought anybody would ever visit Knott's Berry Farm again. They did, and in record numbers, but Disneyland had a definite impact on the development of Knott's Berry Farm.

Soon after Disneyland opened, Knott added a cable-car ride, a "mine" where youngsters could pan for gold, and an electronic shooting gallery. In 1960, Knott's Berry Farm added the Calico Mine Ride, described at the time as the park's "most adventurous undertaking." Six years later, Knott completed construction of a brick-by-brick replica of Philadelphia's Independence Hall, including a one-ton, cracked Liberty Bell. The structure was so realistic that the Philadelphia Bicentennial Reconstruction Committee later borrowed Knott's building plans when it could not locate the original blueprints for the historic landmark.

But perhaps the most significant change for Knott's Berry Farm came in 1968, when vandalism forced the Knotts to erect a fence around their 200-acre amusement park and, for the first time, begin charging a general admission. Until then, visitors had come primarily for the chicken dinners and shopped or viewed the attractions while they waited to be served. But once the restaurant patrons had to pay an admission fee, they expected to be entertained the way they were at Disneyland.

Under the guidance of Marion Knott Anderson, who had assumed creative control of the family business, Knott's Berry Farm launched a $17 million expansion. Between 1968 and 1975, the park added the Calico Logging Co., one of the country's first flume rides, to the Old West Ghost Town, and developed two new themed areas, the Fiesta Village, which portrayed Spanish California, and the Roaring 20s, which featured more traditional amusement park rides, including the Corkscrew, the world's first 360-degree roller coaster. The popularity of the Corkscrew propelled Knott's Berry Farm to the third most popular amusement park in the United States behind Disneyland and Disney World.

In 1976, Knott's Berry Farm added a 20-story Sky Jump, patterned after the famous parachute drop at New York's Coney

Island, to the Roaring 20s theme area, and in 1978, the park added a second roller coaster, Montezooma's Revenge, which took riders from 0 mph to 55 mph in five seconds. Throughout the 1970s, Knott's Berry Farm consistently drew about three million visitors a year, making it the most successful, family-owned amusement park in the United States.

By 1979, however, attendance at Knott's Berry Farm had started to slip, dropping the park into sixth place behind Disney World, Disneyland, Universal Studios Hollywood Tour, Six Flags Great America in Chicago, and Busch Gardens Dark Continent in Tampa.

To shore up its position, Knott's Berry Farm began a $100 million expansion that culminated with the opening of the Kingdom of the Dinosaurs in 1987 and Wild Water Wilderness in 1988. In 1989, an estimated five million people visited Knott's Berry Farm, up from 2.8 million in 1979. Only Disney World, Disneyland, and Universal Studios Hollywood drew more visitors. Walter Knott, however, did not live to see the revival. He died in 1981, at the age of 91. That same year, Terry E. Van Gorder became the first non-family member to take the helm as president and CEO of the company.

In 1996, the trade publication *Amusement Business* ranked Knott's Berry Farm, with 3.55 million visitors, as the thirteenth most popular amusement park in the United States. Disneyland, with 15 million visitors, was number one.

Amusement Business considered Walt Disney World as three separate parks: The Magic Kingdom (13.80 million), Epcot Center (11.24 million), and Disney-MGM Studios (9.98 million). Rounding out the top parks were Universal Studios Florida in Orlando (8.4 million); Universal Studios Hollywood (5.4 million); Sea World of Florida in Orlando (5.1 million); Busch Gardens Dark Continent, Tampa, Florida (4.17 million); Six Flags Great Adventure, Jackson, New Jersey (4 million); Sea World of California, Orlando, Florida (3.89 million); and Paramount's Kings Island, Kings Island, Ohio (3.6 million).

Camp Snoopy Debuts in 1983

In 1983, Knott's Berry Farm had signed an exclusive agreement with Charles Schultz, creator of the Peanuts cartoon characters, for the theme park to be the official home of Snoopy and the Peanuts Gang. The six-acre Camp Snoopy, the first themed park area designed solely for children under 12, opened in 1983.

Then in 1991, Knott's Berry Farm announced that it would develop a 300,000-square-foot, indoor theme park, called

Knott's Camp Snoopy, at the Mall of America in Bloomington, Minnesota. The Mall of America was the largest shopping mall in the United States. Opened in 1992, the mall's Camp Snoopy, operated by Knott's Berry Farm, featured a flume ride, roller coaster, and Snoopy Fountain, the largest attraction, where visitors could shoot coin-operated water cannons at moving targets.

Knott's Berry Farm Foods

Knott's Berry Farm's foods division, selling jams, jellies, pies and fruit syrups, remained strong even while the family-owned business concentrated on developing the amusement park.

In 1991, the company bought the PeggyJane's brand of salad dressings, creating PeggyJanes from Knott's Berry Farm, and introduced Knott's Berry Farm Premium Ice Cream and Nonfat Yogurt. The division had sales of $60 million in 1994. The following year, Knott's Berry Farm sold its packaged foods divisions to ConAgra Inc., in Omaha, Nebraska.

Knott's Berry Farm also continued to sell fried chicken at the amusement park, serving about 1.5 million chicken dinners a year. In 1991, Knott's Berry Farm formed a restaurant division and opened the first offsite Mrs. Knott's Chicken Restaurant in Irvine, California. A year later, restaurants were opened in Moreno Valley and Mission Viejo, California. In 1992, Knott's Berry Farm reported that the offsite restaurants were struggling, in part because people perceived them as extensions of the chicken-only Mrs. Knott's at the amusement park. Within a couple years, only the restaurant in Moreno Valley survived.

Further Reading

Coffey, Gary, "Camp Snoopy on Target for August 11 Opening," *Amusement Business,* May 11, 1992, p. 42.

Dyslin, John, "Life Is Berry, Berry Good," *Prepared Foods,* September 1993, p. 36.

O'Brien, Robert, "Walter Knott's Berry Farm and Ghost Town," *Reader's Digest,* October 1957, p. 178.

O'Brien, Tim, "Mrs. Knott's Restaurants Living Up to Expectations," *Amusement Business,* February 10, 1992, p. 15.

Risto, Pauline, and White, Magner "—Then We Could Lick Anything," *The Saturday Evening Post,* May 2, 1942, p. 38.

Rowe, Jeff, "A Less Than Entertaining Year in Buena Park," *Knight-Ridder Business News,* July 27, 1993.

Taylor, Frank J., "I Never Saw Such an Establishment!," *Reader's Digest,* October 1941, p. 88.

—Dean Boyer

KOLLMORGEN

Kollmorgen Corporation

1601 Trapelo Road
Waltham, Massachusetts 02154
U.S.A.
(617) 890-5655
Fax: (617) 890-7150
Web site: hhtp//www.kollmorgen.com

Public Company
Incorporated: 1916
Employees: 1,700
Sales: $228.7 million (1995)
Stock Exchanges: New York
SICs: 3621 Motors & Generators; 3625 Relays &
Industrial Controls; 3826 Laboratory Analytical
Instruments

Kollmorgen Corporation has had its share of ups and downs. Kollmorgen, which has been a primary supplier of periscopes and related equipment to the U.S. Navy and its allies since 1916, is a leading manufacturer of high-performance motion control systems and electro-optical equipment. The company is organized along these two primary business segments. Kollmorgen Motion Technology Group includes the operating units Kollmorgen Motion Technologies US and its divisions; Kollmorgen Artus, based in Avrille, France; and Kollmorgen VMG, with facilities in Blacksburg, Virginia and Bombay, India. The Motion Technology Group designs and produces servo motors and drive electronics for commercial, aerospace, defense, and industrial customers, with applications such as electronic assembly, machine tools, materials handling, robotics, and semiconductor processing serving industries ranging from office equipment and printers to heart pumps, respirators, and other medical and therapeutic systems. Defense and aerospace production includes actuators, drive electronics, power converters, tachometers, and torque motors for military and commercial aircraft, flight controls, space and underwater vehicles and systems. The Motion Technologies Group generally provides the largest share of Kollmorgen's revenues. In 1995, the Motion

Technologies Group accounted for 57 percent of the company's sales.

Kollmorgen Electro-Optical includes the company's periscopes, optronic mast systems, weapons directors and stabilized weapon control systems, military optics, such as infrared imaging systems, and vehicle sights. The company's defense customers include the U.S. military services and their allies. Electro-Optical, which produced 43 percent of Kollmorgen's sales in 1995, also serves the electric power generation industry with plant-specific and system modeling software. In 1997, the company, in a joint venture with Gretag AG of Switzerland, announced plans to spin off its Macbeth unit, which provided color measurement, color matching, and related technologies, as GretagMacbeth Holdings AG. Kollmorgen retains a 48 percent interest in the new company, which is expected to go public on its own.

Periscope Designer Meets Printed Circuit Maker in 1970

Kollmorgen was founded by Otto Kollmorgen in Northampton, Massachusetts in 1916 to design and make periscopes for the U.S. Navy's young submarine division. Throughout the company's history, Kollmorgen remained the Navy's primary designer and supplier of periscopes, and it quickly began selling these systems to allied navies. The company remained largely a single-product business until the early 1960s, when it began diversifying through a series of acquisitions, including the purchase of Inland Motors Corporation and Photocircuits Corp., bringing the company into the motion technologies, semiconductor, and other fields. By 1970, before the merger with Photocircuits, Kollmorgen had annual sales of $23 million. Photocircuits, which by then had sales of $15 million, became Kollmorgen's largest operating unit and introduced a radical restructuring of the company.

Founded by John D. Maxwell in Glen Cove, New York in 1951, Photocircuits, under the leadership of Robert Swiggett, was a pioneer in the emerging printed circuit technology, which would soon revolutionize the electronics industry. In 1953 Photocircuits received a contract to provide half of the circuit

---

Company Perspectives:

Kollmorgen is a global leader in providing technology-based industrial products in the fields of high performance motion control, analytical instruments and advanced electro-optical systems. Our mission is to profitably grow our businesses by providing superior quality, value and service to our customers. By contributing to our customers' success, we will forge sustainable competitive advantages in our own markets. We believe that accomplishing this mission will position each of our businesses as a consistent and growing contributor to Kollmorgen and provide superior returns to our shareholders.

---

boards needed for the installation of the military's continental air defense system, a contract that would provide some $1 million per year to the company for the next 14 years. Until that point, Photocircuits had been a loosely organized company, operating from a garage, then a cellar, then a basement below a bar. With the company's first large contract, however, the company hired a business consultant to help form a more traditional, centrally managed structure.

Photocircuits pursued an aggressive research and development program seeking to diversify the company beyond printed circuit boards. By the late 1950s, however, the company faced increased competition for its printed circuit board business, especially for customized orders requiring quick design-to-delivery turnaround times. In response, Photocircuits began organizing small task forces charged with processing customized orders. By 1960, the company institutionalized the task force concept, creating a separate Proto department, which operated independently of the rest of the company's rapidly expanding operations. The Proto department, with only 35 people, quickly became a profit engine for the company.

Photocircuits' research and development drive produced a number of new technologies. By 1967, Photocircuits was approaching $10 million in sales, but the company was staggering under the weight of its own growth. As Swiggett told *Inc.,* "Rarely did we meet promised deliveries. Quality problems were enormous; profit performance was erratic; morale was poor. Production managers burned out quickly, functional departments fought with one another. Only the rapid growth of the market and the even more disorganized condition of our large competitors sustained us."

Swiggett, together with younger brother James Swiggett, who had joined the company in 1953, at first clung to traditional management techniques and looked to the novel computer systems technology to sort out the company's production scheduling and management difficulties. Photocircuits spent some $500,000 developing a customized version of System 70, produced by IBM, which was installed in 1969. "The complexity of our production routine was so mind-blowing that we thought something like the IBM process control system was what we needed," Swiggett told *Inc.* But the effort failed. "Statistically, we got everything we wanted. The computer worked beauti-

fully, but company performance, if anything, got worse. Foremen were preoccupied with printouts instead of people. Managers spent time worrying about internal systems instead of our customers." Finally, a recession at the start of the 1970s forced Photocircuits to a decision: either slash its research and development spending, crucial for maintaining the company's edge in the fast-evolving printed circuit board industry, or junk System 70. The company chose the latter course; in the process of abandoning System 70, however, Swiggett abandoned the company's traditional, central management organization structure as well.

Meanwhile, Photocircuits had been seeking capital to fund its further expansion. The company looked into going public, but found itself valued at only $9 million in a public offering. Then Dick Rachals, president of Kollmorgen, offered to purchase Photocircuits' printed motor operations. Instead, talks between Rachals and Swiggett led to a merger of the two companies. Terms of the merger valued Photocircuits at $14 million. It was during the merger, however, that Swiggett moved to get rid of Photocircuits' System 70 system and set to work reformulating the company's management structure.

"Productization" for the 1970s

Swiggett was inspired by *The Human Side of Enterprise,* a book published by Douglas McGregor in 1960 that challenged traditional, top-down management techniques. Swiggett also found inspiration in the success of the company's Proto department. At the start of the 1970s, Swiggett, by then one of three group vice-presidents after the merger with Kollmorgen, set out to reorganize the former Photocircuits operations along the Proto model. He broke up operations into six teams, each with its own manager and responsibility for the team's production, profits, and losses. Each team dealt directly with its own customers, set its own prices, controlled its own inventory, and negotiated with other team managers for production capacity. The company would eventually label this structure "productization." But the new structure produced dramatic performance improvements. Within six months, per-employee production had doubled, on-time delivery rates rose from 60 percent to 90 percent, and Photocircuits' profits were rising. "In the middle of a depression," Swiggett told *Inc.,* "what could've been a disaster turned into a real good moneymaker. So we really had it burned in our souls that small teams could be terribly effective."

Productization arrived just at the right time. By 1971, the newly merged Kollmorgen, hit by the recession, was posting an operating loss and revenues were stuck at around $40 million. Kollmorgen, itself divided into eight divisions, was suffering the same production problems as its Photocircuits unit. Management, shared among Maxwell, Rachals, and Norman Macbeth, whose own company had been acquired by Kollmorgen, was riddled with conflicting styles. In 1972, top management met for a weekend conference to sort out the company's difficulties. Swiggett, who was fired and rehired during that weekend, convinced management to let him try productization on the entire Kollmorgen operation. Swiggett divided the company's eight divisions into autonomous teams. Then the company set growth objectives for itself, including the doubling of revenues every four years and a goal of a 20 percent rate of return on equity. As an added incentive, Swiggett introduced a bonus plan in 1975, based on what he called a "return on net assets," or RONA, which would reward all levels of employees with as much as a 20 percent gain on their annual salaries. This incentive spurred the company to make drastic inventory reductions.

Swiggett, who became Kollmorgen's president and CEO, quickly proved that his management philosophy could work for the company. By 1976, revenues had jumped to $82 million, providing net earnings of nearly $4.5 million. By the end of the decade, sales had nearly doubled again, to $154.5 million, more than doubling net earnings to nearly $10 million. In 1980, Swiggett published a seven-page pamphlet, titled *The Kollmorgen Philosophy,* emphasizing the company's commitment to the team management approach.

Takeover Scare in the 1980s

That commitment to the team management approach, however, would eventually lead the company into trouble in the next decade. The slide into the national recession of the early 1980s reached the company by 1982, and the company saw its earnings begin to drop. Despite doubling sales again, to $326 million in 1984, the company was struggling to remain profitable. But then, as the country was climbing out of the recession, the bottom fell out of the electronics industry—in what was called the industry's worst depression in two decades—and Kollmorgen's profits fell, too. The company began posting losses in 1985 and, by 1986, the company was in the red, dragged down in part by its Multiwire division. The team management approach was faulted for some of the company's difficulties. During the first half of the decade, the company had allowed the Multiwire division to more than double its capacity, building new plants and leasing new facilities, despite signs of the coming slump in the electronics industry. Robert Swiggett, then 68 years old, stepped down as president and CEO, replaced by his younger brother, James Swiggett.

Compounding the company's losses was the sale, in 1986, of its consistently profitable Photocircuits division, which had accounted for $75 million of the company's annual sales, to that division's management. By 1987, Kollmorgen's sales had slumped to $301 million. The company managed to post a meager profit that year, of $285,000, but by then its stock had fallen from a level in the mid-30s to just $13 per share. The company now found itself vulnerable to the takeover craze of the mid-1980s.

In 1988, Kollmorgen was approached by Vernitron Corporation, a Long Island-based industrial electronics company, which had been taken private two years earlier in a leverage buyout, to merge the two firms. Kollmorgen declined the offer, and Vernitron, which, with approximately $100 million in sales, was only one-third the size of Kollmorgen, went public with a $20 per share takeover bid. Kollmorgen introduced a shareholder's rights plan as a "poison-pill defense," leading the two companies into a legal and corporate takeover battle that would last for nearly two years, and rejected the bid. Vernitron countered with a $23 per share offer, then threatened a proxy battle, offering to raise the purchase price to $25 per share if the proxy fight were successful. Meanwhile, Kollmorgen had managed to turn the company around during 1988, raising revenues to $344 million and posting a profit of more than $14 million.

By April 1989, however, Kollmorgen gave in to Vernitron and offered to negotiate a merger of the two companies. Vernitron stayed with its $23 per share offer, and the companies agreed to merge at that price. But, over the next several months, Kollmorgen, which had seen the costs of the takeover battle compound a renewed struggle for profitability, began a restructuring of the company, which included selling off part of its troubled Multiwire division and then combining Multiwire's leftovers with another division and selling off the newly formed division as well. The costs of discontinuing these operations forced the company into a third-quarter loss of nearly $10 million. In response to Kollmorgen's mounting losses, Vernitron broke off its merger with Kollmorgen. By the end of the year, Kollmorgen's revenues had fallen to just below $228 million and the company's loss for the year neared $19 million. Kollmorgen's stock, which had neared $24 per share during the takeover battle, crashed to $12 per share. By then, James Swiggett turned over the presidency of the company to John L. Youngblood.

Rebuilding in the 1990s

Vernitron, however, was not quite finished with Kollmorgen. As soon as a standstill agreement between the companies expired in May 1990, Vernitron renewed its bid for Kollmorgen, organizing a proxy fight to replace Kollmorgen's board of directors and offering to purchase Kollmorgen for $15 per share. This time, however, Vernitron, weakened by the battle (its own sales had slumped to $80 million and its losses from the takeover attempt mounted to $20 million), proved to be easier to resist. As Vernitron owner Stephen W. Bershad told the *New York Times,* "I don't think anyone is a winner here. This is a disaster."

As Kollmorgen emerged from its two-year battle, it was confronted with a new reality: the ending of the Cold War spelled trouble for the company's critical defense-related business. The company continued to slim down its operations, shedding the rest of its interconnections business, worth nearly $100 million in 1988, and restructuring around its two remaining core businesses, electro-optical instruments and motion control. Youngblood left the company in early 1991, replaced by Israeli-born, Harvard-educated Gideon Argov. As the new decade got under way, Kollmorgen ran first into the global recession and then into the economic uncertainty surrounding the Persian Gulf War. By the end of 1991, the company's revenues barely cleared $200 million and its losses, compounded by restructuring costs, sank to $36 million.

The company's losses continued into 1992, as its revenues continued to slide, to $195 million. By 1993, however, Kollmorgen was back in the black, posting a net profit of $4.8 million on $185.5 million in sales, helped by new defense contract awards totaling some $50 million. Toward the mid-1990s, the company continued to rebuild, and it began steering operations toward the commercial sector. In 1995, after its Electro-Optical division received a $35 million contract to build the U.S. Navy's "photonic" mast system, a type of periscope system that does not penetrate a submarine's hull, Kollmorgen's revenues began to climb again, reaching $228 million. After the ups and downs of the past decade, Kollmorgen could still look forward to the company's future survival and growth.

Principal Operating Units

Kollmorgen Motion Technologies; Industrial Drives; PMI Motion Technologies; Inland Motor Corporation; Artus (France); Virtual Motion Group; SMG (U.S.A.; India); Kollmorgen Electro-Optical; Proto Power Corporation; Kollmorgen Instruments Corporation.

Further Reading

DeYoung, Garrett H., "A Battered Kollmorgen Takes the Big Fall," *Electronic Business,* July 23, 1990, p. 92.

Jordan, John, "Kollmorgen Gives Ground in Battle To Avoid Takeover," *Fairfield County Business Journal,* April 17, 1989, p. 1.

Levine, Bernard, "Kollmorgen Losses End Vernitron Deal, Acquisition," *Electronic News,* September 25, 1989, p. 1.

Moran, Kay J., "Kollmorgen Nets $35M Navy Deal," *Daily Hampshire Gazette,* February 9, 1995, p. 3.

" 'New Management' Pioneer Jim Swiggett," *Inc.,* February 1987, p. 34.

Norris, Floyd, "The Bitter Fight for Kollmorgen," *New York Times,* May 16, 1990, p. D10.

Rhodes, Lucien, "The Passion of Robert Swiggett," *Inc.,* April 1984, p. 121.

Santo, Brian, "Photocircuits Sold to Mgmt. in $25M Leveraged Buyout," *Electronic News,* October 6, 1986, p. 1.

Wax, Alan J., "Cornered Kollmorgen Fights To Remain Free," *Newsday,* January 16, 1989, p. 4.

—M. L. Cohen

Kronos, Inc.

400 Fifth Avenue
Waltham, Massachusetts 02154
U.S.A.
(617) 890-3232
Fax: (617) 890-8758
Web site: http://www.kronos.com

Public Company
Incorporated: 1977
Employees: 1,044
Sales: $148 million (1996)
Stock Exchanges: NASDAQ
SICs: 3579 Office Machines, Not Elsewhere Classified

Kronos, Inc. is the leading manufacturer of work place time-keeping systems and also produces similar data-collection systems. The integrated hardware and software systems that it engineers, manufactures, and distributes collect and process information designed to increase productivity in the work place. The company also maintains an extensive service and support organization for its customers. Kronos enjoyed uninterrupted revenue growth throughout the 1980s and into the mid-1990s, with profits increasing every year since 1988.

Development and Early Years, 1977–84

Kronos (the Greek word for time) was founded in 1977 by Mark S. Ain, a computer science and engineering graduate of the Massachusetts Institute of Technology with an M.B.A. from the University of Rochester whose work experience consisted of stints at Esso International, Digital Equipment Corp., and a Concord, New Hampshire, consulting firm. Working out of his home in Newton, Massachusetts, Ain and inventor Larry Baxter had been planning since 1974 to introduce a microprocessor-based product for a technologically backward industry. Ain and his partner considered 150 possible products and narrowed this field to 12 before choosing the time-clock business, which had remained essentially unchanged since 1888. In place of the standard electromechanical time clock, used for payroll pur-poses, Baxter devised an electronic time clock. The year 1978 was devoted to funding the endeavor, and the Kronos electronic time clock was introduced in December 1979. The first one in the United States, it sold for under $1,000, compared to about $400 for electromechanical time clocks.

Electromechanical time clocks, some still in operation after 40 years, recorded only the hour and minute that workers punched in and out, leaving to clerks the tedious and error-prone task of totaling the numbers every week or two. By contrast, electronic clocks delivered a total each day, printed on the time card, and could be linked to other computers to total the numbers for the payroll period electronically. Nevertheless, developing their clock took Ain and Baxter nearly three years instead of the six months they expected, mainly because the software had to accommodate hundreds of different corporate policies on such matters as how overtime was calculated and how late a worker would be permitted to punch in before being docked.

Kronos's first customer was a small copy shop on Broadway in New York City, so small, Ain recalled to a *Boston Globe* reporter, "that the only place for the clock was in the rest-room." Another early customer, he added, was a frustrated convenience dairy owner in a tough section of Brooklyn who "called and said that he was about to use an ax on 'the clock' or on one of our servicemen" and whose second clock caught on fire. Business was so poor that on three occasions Ain told his employees not to cash the paychecks he distributed. In the fall of 1980, however, the company received $500,000 in venture-capital investment. By 1981 Kronos had sales of about $2 million a year, and in 1984, when sales reached $9 million, the company was making a modest profit and was able to move to Waltham from leased quarters in Cambridge near Harvard University's business school.

Growth But No Profits, 1985–87

By mid-1985 Kronos's models had advanced considerably in sophistication. They could be programmed to keep workers from clocking in (now by magnetic ID card) too early or out too late and thus earning unauthorized overtime. They could break

Company Perspectives:

Our mission is to lead the data collection systems industry by delivering high quality, cost-effective products and services that exceed the expectations of our customers.

down labor costs by worker, department, overtime hours, and shifts and calculate labor costs every day to keep them from outstripping sales. The company's clientele included restaurants, retailers like Montgomery Ward (its biggest customer in 1986), hospitals, factories, and even brokerage houses and law firms. The Marriott hotel chain was installing $4 million worth of Kronos's most advanced system, one linked to an IBM computer, in all 150 of its hotels and was expecting to save at least $6.5 million a year, mostly in labor expenses.

In 1987 Kronos introduced its Jobkeeper Central system, which automated a company's production data, recording such items as billable time, job status, and production efficiency. Another system introduced in this period was Timekeeper Central, which fed the data from time clocks to a mainframe computer that calculated a company's pay rates and work rules for the payroll program. This enabled managers to track their employees at any moment and avoid overtime by scheduling first the ones who had not worked a full week. By early 1987 Kronos had installed nearly 30,000 time clocks in about 25,000 companies.

Company revenue came to $17 million in fiscal 1986 (the year ended September 30, 1986). This represented a compounded annual growth rate of more than 60 percent since the first 1979 shipment. However, Ain pointed out that Kronos had received $6 million in venture capital and $1.5 million and $2.5 million from a private equity placement. The company, he told the *Boston Globe*, "has only been at the break-even point for the last three years or so. We're now transitioning to profitability, looking to go public a year from now."

This assessment was rather optimistic if, as a *Forbes* article reported, Kronos had accumulated losses of $2 million by 1987. During that year Ain raised $3 million more by another private stock placement but chose not to take the company public. When the stock market crashed in October 1987, Ain's irritated backers believed the company had missed its chance to raise as much as $50 million from the sale of stock.

During fiscal 1987 Kronos's revenues grew to $20.3 million, but the company lost $176,000. At this point disgruntled board members, who included investors from Drexel Burnham's venture-capital unit and New England Capital, pressured Ain into hiring Yagiv Kadar, a Boston paper-company executive, as chief operating officer. Kadar immediately fired 15 longtime employees hired by Ain and made the underperforming sales staff meet quotas 60 percent higher than before.

The Path to Public Ownership, 1988–92

Kronos had net income of $316,000 on revenues of $25.9 million in fiscal 1988; net income of $1.4 million on revenues of $32.9 million in 1989; net income of $1.5 million on revenues of $39.6 million in 1990; and net income of $2.3 million on revenues of $47.8 million in 1991. In June 1992 the company made its initial public stock offering, raising $9.9 million. Ain again was in full control of his company as president, chairman, and chief executive officer. Clients included such corporate giants as General Motors, Nabisco Brands, American Express, Coca-Cola, and Sony Pictures. One customer said Kronos products had paid for themselves within six months. About 25,000 units were being shipped a year.

Originally offered for $12 a share, Kronos stock traded as high as $24 in 1992. The underwriter estimated that Kronos had great potential for growth because only an estimated 15 percent of the 650,000 U.S. businesses with 25 or more hourly employees were operating with computerized time clocks. The company posted revenues of $58.1 million (about 10 percent from international operations) and net income of $3.6 million in fiscal 1992. Ain told a *Wall Street Journal* reporter that sales had remained strong despite the recession of the early 1990s because "We tend to get big orders when a company gets in trouble, because that's when they want to control costs. We received four or five big orders the last two years from companies that had just filed bankruptcy."

Growing Sales and Profits, 1993–96

During fiscal 1993 Kronos earned $4.1 million on net revenues of $67.1 million. Its biggest client at this time was Nations-Bank, with whom it had signed a multi-year deal worth $5 million to $6 million. Kronos also had won a $3.2-million contract in 1992 with Chicago's Board of Education to install equipment tracking staff attendance, labor costs, and bus movements. Its Timekeeper systems were selling for between $1,300 and $250,000, depending on how many employees a company had and the type of operating system being used. Applying similar technology, new company products also were tracking inventories and managing shipping and receiving. Customers now included General Electric, Pillsbury, and Sears stores.

Kronos made several acquisitions in 1993 and 1994. These were the technology and certain assets of Computer Recovery, Inc. a time-accounting software-development concern; Shop-Trac Data Collection Systems, a manufacturer of software; all the territories covered by Bay Area Realtime Systems, Inc.; all the territories covered by Midwest Time Accounting Systems, Inc.; certain territories covered by Interboro Systems Corp.; and all of the southern California territories covered by Compu-Cash Corp. Kronos moved its manufacturing facility from Lowell, Massachusetts, to Chelmsford, Massachusetts in 1994.

Kronos had net revenues of $92.9 million in fiscal 1994 and $120.4 million in fiscal 1995. Net income came to $4.9 million and $8.4 million, respectively. In fiscal 1996 the results were even better: $148 million and $11.4 million, respectively. In January 1995 the company adopted a shareholder-rights plan to defend against a hostile takeover. Shares of its common stock traded for as high as $50 during the year. Ain held 6.4 percent of the stock in 1995; institutions held 83 percent of the company's common stock in 1996. Kronos had no long-term debt in June 1996.

Kronos Products in the Mid-1990s

Among the major systems offered by Kronos in 1995 were Timekeeper Central, Timekeeper/AS, ShopTrac Data Collection, and Workforce Management. The Timekeeper systems automatically calculated employee hours data and then consolidated information into a number of standard labor management reports. The ShopTrac Data Collection System captured labor and material data for manufacturers to provide real-time information on cost, location, and completion time. This included time and attendance data to provide information for the basis of managing labor resources. The Workforce Management System, developed for the retail and hospitality markets, consisted of several integrated modules that generated the correct staffing level required for the expected level of business, then combined this data with detailed employee information to produce a complete, detailed work schedule. This information was then integrated with the Timekeeper Central System to enable management to compare actual labor costs to budgeted costs.

Optional software modules offered by Kronos included Scheduling, which assisted in creating employee schedules; CardSaver, which recorded employees' in-and-out data for wage and hour inquiries; Accruals, which calculated each employee's available benefit time; and Attendance Tracker, which recorded and documented employee absences. It also offered the Archive Program, automatically performing long-term record keeping. These modules and the program were all designed to expand and enhance the range of functions performed by Kronos's time-and-attendance and shop-floor data-collections systems. The company also was marketing standard, "off-the-shelf" interface software, including Time Bank (purchased from a third party), Kronos Database Poster (an interface from Timekeeper Central to industry-standard X-Base databases), and DKC/Datalink, an interface between Datakeeper Central and popular MRP systems.

Kronos's Datakeeper Central System was collecting and formatting data and transmitting it to MRP and other related applications or host systems. Its TimeMaker System was designed to give smaller businesses the advantage of automated time and attendance. Gatekeeper was being used to control employee access to a facility. Kronos TeleTime System allowed customer telephones to serve as data input devices. The company also was marketing ACES and ACES PLUS, obtained from a third party, to read data from forms and transmit that data to a time-and-attendance database.

Kronos also was manufacturing a complete family of intelligent data-collection terminals to collect and verify data and communicate this data to a computer for use with the company's application software. Some of these terminals—wall-mounted, desk-mounted, and hand-held—were designed to operate in harsh environments. It was also marketing a number of accessories to its products, including badges, badge-making equipment, time cards, bar-code labels, and modems.

Kronos's extensive service and support organization accounted for 27 percent of its net revenues in fiscal 1995. This organization relocated from corporate headquarters in Waltham to a new Customer Support Center in Chelmsford during 1996. The company had 21 direct sales and support offices in the United States in 1995. It also had two such offices in Canada, one in Great Britain, and one in Mexico. In addition to about 50 independent dealers in the United States actively selling and supporting Kronos's products, the company also had such dealers in Argentina, Australia, Canada, Guam, Guatemala, Hong Kong, Jamaica, Mexico, Netherlands Antilles, Panama, Puerto Rico, Singapore, South Africa, Venezuela, and the West Indies. In 1996 it opened subsidiaries in Australia and South Africa. Kronos also had a joint-marketing agreement, established in 1993, with ADP, Inc., under which this company marketed "Total Time," a proprietary version of Kronos's PC-based time-and-attendance software, together with data-collection terminals manufactured by Kronos.

Kronos was leasing its headquarters in Waltham and its manufacturing facility in Chelmsford in fiscal 1995. In November of the calendar year the company signed a 10-year agreement allowing it to lease another facility in Chelmsford and simultaneously relocated its manufacturing operations to the new facility. Kronos also was leasing 46 sales and support offices in North America and Europe during 1995.

Principal Subsidiaries

Kronos Computerized Time Systems, Inc. (Canada); Kronos de Mexico, S.A. de C.V. (Mexico); Kronos International Sales Corp. (U.S. Virgin Islands); Kronos Securities Corporation; Kronos S/T Corporation; Kronos Systems Limited (United Kingdom).

Further Reading

Bulkeley, William M., "Kronos Corp. Expects to Report Decline in Net for Quarter, Rise for Full Year," *Wall Street Journal,* October 23, 1992.
Bushnell, Davis, "Your Time, His Clock," *Boston Globe,* March 23, 1987, pp. 37–38.
Jereski, Laura, " 'I'm a Bad Manager,' " *Forbes,* February 8, 1988, pp. 134–35.
Newport, John Paul, Jr., "Timing Is All," *Fortune,* June 24, 1985, pp. 67–68.
Oliveri, David, "Kronos Carries the Time Clock into the Future," *Boston Business Journal,* September 21, 1992, p. 7.
Strohler, Steven R., "City Payroll Unit Will Get Privatized," *Crain's Chicago Business,* June 14, 1993, p. 35.
Weiner, Elizabeth, "Time Clocks Catch Up with the Computer Age," *Business Week,* November 26, 1984, p. 178H.

—Robert Halasz

LaCrosse Footwear, Inc.

1407 St. Andrew St.
La Crosse, Wisconsin 54603
U.S.A.
(608) 782-3020
Fax: (608) 782-3025
Web site: http://www.lacrosse-outdoors.com

Public Company
Incorporated: 1983
Employees: 1,432
Sales: $122 million (1996)
Stock Exchanges: NASDAQ
SICs: 3021 Rubber & Plastics Footwear; 3143 Men's
     Footwear Except Athletic; 3144 Women's Footwear
     Except Athletic; 6719 Holding Companies, Not
     Elsewhere Classified

Celebrating its 100th anniversary in 1997, LaCrosse Footwear, Inc. is the largest manufacturer of rubber, leather, and vinyl footwear in the United States. It specializes in premium-quality protective footwear for the sporting, occupational, and recreational markets. It has four major brands: the original LaCrosse brand; the Danner brand, established in 1932 and acquired by LaCrosse in 1994; the Red Ball brand, acquired in 1996; and the Rainfair brand, marketed through a joint venture established in 1996 between LaCrosse Footwear and Rainfair, Inc., of Racine, Wisconsin. The company has about 1,400 employees in six production facilities, and all of its products are assembled by hand in the United States. Sales for 1997 are projected to reach $150 million.

The company was first established in 1897 as La Crosse Rubber Mills Company, a manufacturer of rubber horseshoes, by a group of local citizens in La Crosse, Wisconsin. Led by Albert Hirshheimer, Michael Funk, and George Zeisler, the company started with 25 employees working on 160 steam-powered sewing machines. It originally planned to manufacture rubber goods of every description, with the notable exception of footwear. It soon switched from producing horseshoes to making rubber-coated fabrics and raincoats. From the beginning, La Crosse stressed "quality goods, workmanship, and honest values."

Business was good for the La Crosse Rubber Mills in the late 1890s, and by the turn of the century the company had expanded its facilities and increased its workforce to 400 people. It was producing about 850 rubber-coated garments a day. To reduce the risk of fire, it installed the city's first sprinkler system in its factory, which was reportedly located on land once owned by Buffalo Bill Cody. In 1898 the opening of a new addition was celebrated by a "rubber ball" for employees, complete with orchestral music. In 1899 Albert Hirshheimer took over as president of the Rubber Mills, as it was known locally.

Capitalizing on the popularity of a nonrubber rain garment called Laxette, the La Crosse Rubber Mills launched a national magazine advertising campaign in 1904 to market its clothing under the "Indian Hill Brand." Within a few years, however, the company discontinued making rubber-coated fabrics and raincoats and started producing canvas and rubber footwear. Its workforce was reduced to 150 employees, who could produce about 1,200 pairs of footwear a day. It adopted a new slogan, "Everything in Rubber Footwear," in 1908 and produced a line of 1,000 different styles of shoes. Among its most popular offerings were the Red Fibre Heel Brand of rubbers and overshoes built for long-lasting wear and the first buckle overshoes ever made. Showrooms were opened in a leased building on South Front Street in La Crosse, showing the company's line of clothing as well as its popular footwear.

In 1912 two of the company's founders, Michael Funk and Albert Hirshheimer, purchased controlling interest in the La Crosse Rubber Mills. They put Michael Funk's two sons, Albert P. Funk and Arthur S. Funk, in charge of management and operations. Arthur S. Funk had recently returned to La Crosse from studying at the University of Notre Dame in South Bend, Indiana, where he had pioneered the development of synthetic rubber, also known as neoprene.

New Concrete Facility Built in 1913

Until 1913 the company's manufacturing operations were housed in a wooden structure. That year the first of several concrete buildings was constructed on St. Andrew Street, directly north of the old facility. Originally three stories high and later expanded to four, the new building had twice as much space devoted to manufacturing, and the 350-member workforce began to produce 6,000 pairs of footwear a day. In 1916 a second concrete building was built, adding 75,000 square feet and doubling capacity yet again. The workforce grew to about 1,000 employees and was producing about 15,000 pairs of footwear a day. The company started its own bus line to transport workers, who had difficulty getting to work because of inadequate roads and too-short streetcar lines. With business booming, another "rubber ball" was held, with attendance reaching 5,000 people.

By 1921 production had leveled off to about 13,000 pairs per day, with a "rush" capacity of about 20,000 pairs. In the early 1920s the Funk family bought out Albert Hirshheimer, who retired as president in 1922. He was succeeded by Albert P. Funk. Soon the company started an aggressive building campaign, adding a one-story fireproof warehouse and cafeteria as well as research and test facilities. In 1923 a third four-story concrete building, plus powerhouse, warehouse, and laboratory buildings, added another 75,000 square feet. In 1927 a single-story building with a new mill room and storage areas added another 85,000 square feet. By this time the company was truly national, with a retail presence in every state. It also did a healthy export business under the direction of a New York City-based export manager.

Still growing in 1929, the company announced a 100,000-square-foot expansion that would add factory and office space as well as a new machine shop and vulcanizing area. Company president Albert P. Funk said at the time, "We are undoubtedly facing one of the brightest years in our history, with every department operating at full capacity." He noted that sales in tennis footwear were an especially bright spot for the company. With 2,000 employees on the payroll, La Crosse Rubber Mills was named the largest employer in La Crosse in 1930.

La Crosse Rubber Mills Awarded First Army Contract in 1941

The company weathered the economic depression of the 1930s, and at the end of the decade it installed the latest conveyorized assembly-line equipment and shoe-making machinery. In 1941 it received a contract from the U.S. Army to produce 43,200 pairs of Arctic, rubbertop overshoes. It was the first of several government contracts that La Crosse Rubber Mills would fulfill over the coming years. During World War II it produced jungle rubber footwear, hip boots, four-buckle overshoes, tennis shoes, and rubbers for use by military personnel. When the war ended in 1945, the company promised all returning veterans who had worked for the company that they would either get their old jobs back or be hired for even better

ones. The company also streamlined its manufacturing and fabricating processes by eliminating all bench work. Albert P. Funk died in 1945, and his brother, Arthur S. Funk, succeeded him as president of the company.

La Crosse Rubber Mills began the 1950s marketing a full line of rubber footwear, including sporting boots, tennis and basketball shoes, and novelty shoes. In 1951 it introduced the Big Chief hip boot and the Duluth work overshoe. In 1954 Albert P. Funk, Jr., became the company president, and annual sales totaled $4.5 million. Under a newly negotiated pension plan with the United Rubber Workers-CIO, 65-year-old workers with at least 25 years of service were given full payments. As the 1950s drew to a close, La Crosse Rubber Mills was offering 192 different products in eight product groups: insulated footwear, sporting boots and pacs, industrial and general business boots, farm and work overshoes, family fashion overshoes, rubber-soled canvas shoes, and vinyl plastic protective boots.

La Crosse Rubber Mills continued to grow steadily during the 1960s and 1970s at a rate of about 10 percent annually. The modern "Burly" knee-high rubber boot was introduced in 1963 and featured an innovative ankle-gripping design. During the mid-1960s the company maintained a production capacity of 20,000 pairs of footwear a day at its 350,000-square-foot facility in La Crosse and a workforce of 700 to 750 people. It advertised 31 styles of canvas shoes. By 1972 sales reached $10.5 million. The company's workforce grew to an average of 850 during the 1970s. In 1978 Frank J. Uhler, Jr., became president, and the company stopped manufacturing and started importing athletic footwear. By the end of the decade sales reached the $20 million mark, with 80 percent of sales from rubber footwear and 20 percent from canvas footwear.

Sale to New Owners Ended Hostile Takeover Bid in 1982

In 1980 sales of canvas footwear decreased to 10 percent of sales, with 90 percent attributed to rubber footwear. With 800 employees, La Crosse Rubber Mills was the third largest employer in La Crosse. In 1982 the company had to fight off a hostile takeover bid from Endicott Johnson Co., of Endicott, New York. To avoid a takeover, George Schneider and president and chief operating officer Frank J. Uhler, Jr., purchased the company from the heirs of the founding family and other shareholders in a leveraged buyout. Schneider was a member of the company's board of directors and husband of Virginia Funk, granddaughter of founder Michael Funk. He became chairman and Uhler remained president. As of March 1996, the Schneider Family Voting Trust owned 52.8 percent of the company's outstanding common stock.

In 1983 the company acquired an injection molding plant in Claremont, New Hampshire, that allowed it to produce low-priced boots to complement its higher-priced products made in La Crosse. Annual sales rose that year to $27 million, and the company was producing about 8,800 pairs of footwear per day, or 2.2 million pairs annually. The next year sales rose more than 10 percent to $30 million, and company employees enjoyed their first checks under a new profit-sharing plan. La Crosse also introduced the first waterproof boot with a removable liner for kids in 1984.

Adopted New Corporate Name for 1986

On December 26, 1985, the company adopted a new name, LaCrosse Footwear, Inc., eliminating the space between ''La'' and ''Crosse'' in its new logo. Under its LaCrosse label the company introduced the Iceman boot, which pioneered the use of double-insulation construction in rubber footwear. The popular Iceman boot would be worn by Iditarod dogsled winners and be used on an expedition in China that explored the frigid upper reaches of the Yangtze River. Five years later the company expanded the line with the Ice King, a triple-insulated boot rated to −100 degrees Fahrenheit. That was later followed by the LaCrosse Footwear ''boot system,'' a line of rubber bottom performance footwear with interchangeable liners that was designed for use in hunting, fishing, and other rugged outdoor activities.

Toward the end of the decade LaCrosse stopped importing athletic shoes from the Far East. Sales continued to grow steadily and by 1989 had reached $50 million, boosted in part by a $4.7 million contract—the company's largest ever—with the U.S. government to produce more than 682,000 vinyl overshoes for U.S. military personnel. The company's three-hundred-item product line reflected a shift in marketing strategy, as LaCrosse sought to offer products less dependent on weather conditions. Mild winters usually had a negative effect on LaCrosse's sales. As a result, the company tried to place greater emphasis on its industrial and sporting footwear as it entered the 1990s.

As the 1990s began, LaCrosse continued to enjoy good relations with the U.S. military. In 1990 it received a $3 million defense contract to manufacture 300,000 pairs of mustard gas-proof boots for the Persian Gulf conflict. A second defense contract was awarded in 1991 to produce an additional 700,000 pairs of the mustard gas-proof boots. As a result of its new marketing focus, LaCrosse achieved a leadership position in the sporting goods apparel industry by 1993. It had 1,465 full-time employees, who were producing 21,000 pairs of footwear a day. Sales reached $85 million, and the company was manufacturing more than 400 types of boots and rubber footwear from 170 compound formulas.

LaCrosse Acquired Danner in 1994

In March 1994 LaCrosse acquired the Danner Shoe Manufacturing Co., located in Portland, Oregon, which specialized in leather footwear for hiking, hunting, fishing, and cross-training. Danner was originally founded in 1932 in Chippewa Falls, Wisconsin, by Charles Danner and his father-in-law, William Weyenberg, as a small family factory that handcrafted work shoes. After Weyenberg passed away in 1933, Danner relocated his family and business to Portland in 1936. By the end of World War II, Danner had become established as a high-quality manufacturer of popular logger-style work boots. During the 1960s Danner produced leather hiking boots that were light and flexible, yet sturdy and comfortable. In the 1970s Danner designed and patented a unique way of making a waterproof boot using the first free-hanging Gore-Tex inner bootie.

LaCrosse acquired Danner for $13.5 million in cash, 277,778 shares of common stock ($13 per share market value), and the assumption of approximately $4.4 million in liabilities.

In April LaCrosse completed its initial public offering (IPO), resulting in net proceeds to the company of $17.6 million, plus an additional $2.7 million the next month in connection with the exercise of an over-allotment option granted to the underwriters. LaCrosse used the proceeds from the IPO to reduce short-term debt taken on to finance the Danner acquisition, pay off $3.4 million of long-term debt, and plow into working capital. Sales for 1994 reached an all-time high of $108.3 million. New product introductions included the Firetech line, firefighting footwear that fit like a shoe and had a patented steel arch guard that offered greater protection against punctures. Frank J. Uhler, Jr., retired as president and chief executive officer and was succeeded by Patrick K. Gantert.

Sales for 1995 were down about 9 percent to $98.6 million. Even though LaCrosse had been focusing on making its products less weather-dependent, sales were affected by the mild winter weather during the first quarter of the year. Sales were also affected by softening in the retail market during the fourth quarter of 1995. However, the harsher winter weather had a favorable impact on first quarter earnings in 1996. It had the effect of helping to clear retailers' shelves, resulting in larger advance orders for the fall.

Major Acquisitions in 1996

LaCrosse made two major acquisitions in the first half of 1996. The first was the acquisition of Red Ball, Inc., a leading designer, manufacturer, and marketer of branded outdoor sporting and protective footwear used in hunting, fishing, and other outdoor activities. Red Ball, with 1995 revenues of $5.8 million, had been operating under the protection of Chapter 11 of the Federal bankruptcy code since February 1996. The acquisition of Red Ball for approximately $6 million in cash provided LaCrosse with the opportunity to expand the distribution of the Red Ball brand to mass merchants as well as to introduce new products to the LaCrosse line. In July LaCrosse began manufacturing Red Ball products at its Claremont, New Hampshire, facility.

The second major acquisition involved establishing a joint venture in May 1996 with Rainfair, Inc., a leading designer, manufacturer, and marketer of protective clothing and footwear for the safety, industrial, and uniform markets. The company was based in Racine, Wisconsin, for more than 100 years. The joint venture between the two companies assumed the old Rainfair name and purchased the assets of the old Rainfair, Inc. Rainfair's owner and CEO, Craig L. Leipold, continued as CEO of the joint venture. The joint venture brought together complementary product lines and brand names, providing significant cross-selling opportunities, especially in the industrial market.

With LaCrosse set to celebrate its 100th anniversary in 1997, it occupied a leadership position in its established markets. Recent acquisitions have increased its product offerings and provided it with an even stronger position in the sporting and outdoor, farm and general utility, and occupational and children's markets for rubber, leather, and vinyl footwear and rainwear. After retiring all of its preferred stock in 1996 to lower its borrowing costs, LaCrosse was in excellent financial condition to pursue even higher levels of sales in the coming years.

Further Reading

''LaCrosse Footwear, Inc. Set to Purchase Assets of Red Ball, Inc.,'' press release, May 8, 1996.

''LaCrosse Footwear, Inc. to Form Joint Venture with Rainfair, Inc.,'' press release, May 17, 1996.

''LaCrosse Footwear Reports First Quarter Results,'' press release, April 19, 1996.

''LaCrosse Footwear Reports Second Quarter Results,'' press release, July 26, 1996.

''LaCrosse Footwear Today Reported Increased Net Income for the Third Quarter,'' *PR Newswire,* October 18, 1996.

—David P. Bianco

Leslie's Poolmart, Inc.

20222 Plummer Street
Chatsworth, California 91311
U.S.A.
(818) 993-4212
Fax: (818) 349-1059

Public Company
Incorporated: 1963 as Leslie's Poolmart, Inc.
Employees: 780
Sales: $162.4 million (1995)
Stock Exchanges: NASDAQ
SICs: 5999 Miscellaneous Retail Stores, Not Elsewhere Classified; 5961 Catalog & Mail-Order Houses; 3086 Plastic Foam Products; 7389 Business Services, Not Elsewhere Classified

The world's largest specialty retailer of swimming pool supplies, Leslie's Poolmart, Inc. operates a chain of full-service retail outlets and markets its products through a nationwide mail-order catalog business. During the mid-1990s, Leslie's Poolmart operated more than 250 stores in 27 states. Each of the company's stores were staffed by employees trained in water chemistry and pool equipment maintenance.

Origins

In 1963, Philip Leslie and his partner, Raymond Cesmat, opened a chain of swimming pool supply stores in the Los Angeles area. The two colleagues spent the ensuing quarter century building Leslie's Poolmart into a thriving chain, establishing 65 stores during their first two decades together and creating an enterprise that generated nearly $60 million in yearly sales. By all accounts, the chain of Leslie's Poolmart stores stood as a healthy, vibrant, and profitable business by the late 1980s, its development representing the exemplary story of two entrepreneurs who had carved a lasting niche in their industry and succeeded where others had failed. Together, Leslie and Cesmat had achieved much.

But in terms of Leslie's Poolmart's corporate history the bulk of the company's financial and physical growth, and all of the drama surrounding such growth, occurred after Leslie and Cesmat went their separate ways. Their separation marked the beginning of Leslie's Poolmart's prolific development into the nation's dominant pool-supply retailer, an era in the company's history that began in 1987 when Cesmat decided he wanted to leave the business. His decision touched off a feud and, unwittingly, sparked the remarkable rise of Leslie's Poolmart.

When Cesmat informed Leslie in 1987 that he wanted to sell his stake in the privately-owned company, trouble started brewing. Leslie offered to buy Cesmat's stock, but at a price Cesmat felt was grossly inadequate. Cesmat wanted more—a lot more—and a rift developed quickly between the two founders, a rift that would prove to be Leslie's undoing. Cesmat filed to have the corporation dissolved, a move that put the fate of the company into the hands of the courts and paved the way for new ownership. In the spring of 1988, a California Superior Court judge resolved the issue, ordering that ownership of the company would go to the highest bidder. The winning bid, a $23-million offer, was submitted by an investor group led by Hancock Park Associates, a Los Angeles-based venture capital firm that represented neither Leslie nor Cesmat. After 25 years spent building the business into a $57-million-a-year company, Phil Leslie was decidedly angry about the ruling and later expressed as much when he told a *Forbes* reporter, "They sold it out from under me."

1987: A New Beginning

Leslie pocketed $10 million from the deal, but lost stewardship of the company he had co-founded. Hancock Park Associates, the new owners of Leslie's Poolmart, took over after Leslie's departure and replaced the company's co-founder with someone with far less experienced in the business world, 31-year-old Brian McDermott. At the time, McDermott knew little about the business world and even less about assuming the duties of a top executive, but he had spent his life around swimming pools. A competitive swimmer since age six, McDermott spent his early adulthood starring on Williams College's varsity swim team and paying his way through col-

Company Perspectives:

As the world's largest specialty retailer of swimming pool supplies and related items, Leslie's Poolmart enjoys the considerable benefits of leadership in a highly recession-resistant, solidly growing business. Approximately 75 percent of the company's sales pertain to the on-going maintenance and care of pools, making a vast majority of Leslie's products non-discretionary and regularly purchased in nature. These products range from consumables such as chlorine, brushes, skimmers, and other cleaning accessories to high ticket, less frequently purchased items such as pumps, filters, and automatic pool cleaners. We also provide a wide selection of recreational products, resulting in a store that can provide virtually everything pool owners need to maintain and enjoy their pools.

lege by managing pools during the summers. Whether or not this life-long yet tangential association with the swimming pool business would prove sufficient to successfully guide McDermott in his new role as Leslie's Poolmart's chief operating officer was questionable at the time, but after a rocky beginning the self-described "chlorine head" proved himself entirely capable.

For McDermott, the first few months at his new job were particularly rough. In May 1988, just as he was adjusting to his new executive position and just as the pool season got underway, 61 of the chain's 66 store managers refused to open their shops, deciding collectively to express their loyalty to Phil Leslie by ignoring the company's new management. McDermott immediately found himself in a precarious position, but responded with prompt action. He reopened the shops with new managers and was granted a restraining order against anyone who conspired to sabotage the future course of Leslie's Poolmart, whether such activity was lead by Phil Leslie or any of his supporters.

Surviving the May revolt was only one of the problems facing McDermott and Leslie's Poolmart's new management. Hobbled by nearly $20 million in acquisition debt, Leslie's Poolmart lost money until 1990, but by the following year the chain began to turn its fortunes around. The burdensome debt, which had precluded significant expansion since 1988, was removed in April 1991 when Montgomery Securities sold 47 percent of the company to the public. The company's initial public offering raised $28 million, which McDermott used to pay off debt and to implement his strategy for the company's future. McDermott's strategy was simple yet ambitious: expansion from California to New York, with the ultimate goal of creating what retailers referred to as a "category killer," or a company whose market dominance precludes the development of any serious competition.

As McDermott set his sights on expansion, there was much to be gained in the swimming pool-supply industry by a retailer intent on blanketing the country with new stores. Although Leslie's Poolmart already ranked as the world's largest swim-

ming pool-supply retailer at the time of the 1991 initial public offering, it controlled less than three percent of the U.S. market, which generated more than $3 billion in sales each year. Highly fragmented, the industry offered tremendous room for growth for a nationwide chain, and as the 1990s began no company occupied a better position to seize the opportunity and put a stranglehold on the U.S. market than Leslie's Poolmart. Aside from the myriad small, independent retailers, Leslie's Poolmart's only serious competition came from large, discount chains such as Home Depot. But chains like Home Depot could hardly be considered an equal match for Leslie's Poolmart. Home Depot, whose merchandise mix embraced a variety of retail categories, stocked 75 swimming pool-supply products. Leslie's Poolmart, by contrast, stocked 2,800 products, offering a wide variety of merchandise that ranged from chemicals such as chlorine, algicide, and soda ash, to leaf skimmers and pool-cleaning machines. Equally important as the company's superior product selection was the superior service offered at Leslie's Poolmart's stores. Each store was staffed by employees trained in water chemistry and pool equipment maintenance. Each store offered free water analysis, giving customers the opportunity to bring in a water sample and have a Leslie's Poolmart employee prescribe a solution for whatever the problem might be. Although McDermott was determined to build on Leslie's Poolmart's stalwart market position to create an enterprise without rival, the company already was without rival as it entered the 1990s. One industry analyst succinctly described the company's enviable position to queries from a *Los Angeles Business Journal* reporter, "There's nobody else doing what they're doing."

The analysts' words characterized a retail "category killer," but despite Leslie's Poolmart's advantages over competitors the company's future growth and profitability were not guaranteed as expansion began in earnest following the 1991 initial public offering. The company was subject to the vagaries of weather and the cyclical nature of its business year, and could not ignore the competition mounted by large, discount chains. Historically, Leslie's Poolmart posted all of its profits during the second and third fiscal quarters, which were contemporaneous with the duration of the swimming pool season, April through September. During the first and fourth fiscal quarters, the primary objective was to minimize losses. To offset the company's vulnerability to the seasonality of its business, Leslie's Poolmart had entered the commercial swimming pool market in 1989, when the company began serving year-round swimming pool customers such as health clubs, hotels, and municipalities. Further penetration of the commercial market would occur during the early 1990s, as the company looked to build upon its 1989 foray and develop a diversified clientele capable of generating year-round sales and profits.

1990s Expansion

Moving forward from 1991, McDermott's primary objective was the expansion of the chain, with further development of the commercial business ranking as a subsidiary yet important goal. As aggressive expansion began, pursuit of the company's primary objective was made easier by a flourishing side business that served as a valuable marketing tool. In addition to the scores of full-service stores composing Leslie's Poolmart's operations, the company also distributed a nationwide mail-order catalogue of swimming pool products to more than two million households, or 65 percent the country's residential, in-ground swimming pool owners. With the support provided by its catalogue sales, the company began expanding vigorously in 1991, opening 19 stores during the year to lift its store count to 102. The store openings extended the company's presence into Maryland and Michigan, two new markets for the chain, and represented one of several key achievements during the year. Aside from the spate of store openings and the April public offering, Leslie's Poolmart posted record mail-order catalogue sales and opened a second distribution center during the year, making for a highly successful beginning to the company's ascendancy to the ranks of retail category killers.

Although the summer of 1992 was the coolest in the United States in 77 years, the weather did not keep Leslie's Poolmart from recording a very active year. In February, the company announced its strategic entry into warehouse-style discount merchandising by articulating plans to open discount facilities in Texas and Southern California. Five stores were subsequently opened, featuring the same breadth of merchandise as the company's full-service outlets but at discount prices. The warehouse-style stores, which operated as Pool Club-USA, did not offer the services, repairs, and level of customer service that the company's full-service stores did and quickly proved to be a great disappointment. Before the year was through, four of the five Pool Club-USA stores were converted to the full-service format and the fifth was closed.

Despite the failure of Leslie's Poolmart's discount concept, great strides were gained on several fronts during 1992. The company opened 26 stores during the year, recorded its 29th consecutive year of record sales, and completed a pivotal acquisition that strengthened its presence in the commercial market. During a year in which the company would register a 75 percent increase in commercial sales, Leslie's Poolmart acquired North Hollywood-based Sandy's Pool Supply, Inc., a 22-store chain and national mail-order operation recording burgeoning growth in the commercial segment of the swimming pool business. With the addition of the Sandy's Pool Supply units and the outlets opened through internal means, the number of stores composing the chain grew to 143 by year's end, or more than two-and-a-half times the number of stores in operation when McDermott first joined Leslie's Poolmart.

The substantial gain in stores registered during 1992 helped lift sales to $96.3 million, up from the $82.6 million generated the year before, but the severity of the climate in 1992 could not be brushed aside and profits fell during the year from $5.1

million to $4.1 million. To stimulate earnings growth, McDermott slated only 15 store openings for 1993, deciding to devote more of the company's resources to increasing per store sales and integrating the outlets gained from the Sandy's Pool Supply acquisition. Additionally, McDermott increased the company's direct-mail advertising and adopted a low-everyday-price policy instead of routinely putting specific items on sale to better compete with large discount chains like Home Depot.

By the end of 1993, when the number of stores had risen to 158 and sales had climbed nearly 25 percent to $120 million, Leslie's Poolmart had captured four percent of the U.S. swimming pool market, which by this point eclipsed $3.5 billion in annual revenue volume. To increase the company's share of the market, McDermott engineered the most prodigious expansion in Leslie's Poolmart's history in 1994. During the company's first fiscal quarter alone, 25 new stores were opened. In response, annual sales and net income marched upward, helping make Leslie's Poolmart one of the "best small companies in America" according to *Forbes'* annual rankings.

As Leslie's Poolmart entered the mid-1990s and formulated plans for the remainder of the decade, ambitious expansion continued be the mantra repeated at company headquarters in Chatsworth, California. Forty-four new stores were opened during 1995, giving the company a total of 224 stores by the end of the year. In the years ahead, further expansion was anticipated, as the company pursued its objective of operating 500 stores and generating $500 million in annual sales by 2000. By the end of 1995, Leslie's Poolmart was nearly half-way toward its objective in terms of physical size, but the potential for its financial growth offered considerably more room for progress during the remainder of the 1990s.

Principal Subsidiaries

Sandy's Pool Supply, Inc.

Further Reading

Byrne, Harlan S., "Leslie's Poolmart," *Barron's,* August 30, 1993, p. 44.
Feldman, Amy, "Beggar Thy Partner," *Forbes,* June 6, 1994, p. 85.
Glover, Kara, "Leslie's Poolmart Plans to Build on Its Success in Pool Supplies Industry," *Los Angeles Business Journal,* November 14, 1994, p. 29.
Trief, Jaymes, "Four Small L.A. Companies Positioned for Stardom," *Los Angeles Business Journal,* June 27, 1994, p. S2.

—Jeffrey L. Covell

LEXMARK

Lexmark International, Inc.

55 Railroad Avenue
Greenwich, Connecticut 06836
U.S.A.
(606) 232-2000
Fax: (606) 232-2300
Web site: http://www.lexmark.com

Public Company
Incorporated: 1991
Sales: $2.16 billion (1995)
Employees: 5,000
Stock Exchanges: New York
SICs: 3579 Office Machines; 3577 Computer Peripheral
   Equipment

Lexmark International, Inc. is one of the world's fastest-growing designers, manufacturers, and suppliers of laser and inkjet printers and related supplies for both the office and home markets. The company has quickly become a leader in the development and production of an extremely broad line of office imaging items, such as color inkjet printers, dot-matrix printers, inkjet cartridges, wheelwriter typewriters, coated paper, cables and adapters, memory chips, computer keyboards, and supplies for original equipment manufacturers (OEMs). Lexmark has manufacturing operations in Lexington, Kentucky; Boulder, Colorado; Orleans, France; Sydney, Australia; Rosyth, Scotland; and Juarez, Mexico. As a spinoff from IBM, the company inherited a worldwide distribution network which management has built upon and expanded dramatically to include sales offices throughout the United States and Canada, and in such far away locations as The Netherlands, Denmark, Belgium, England, France, Italy, Spain, Norway, Austria, Hong Kong, Singapore, Taiwan, Japan, Argentina, Mexico, and Brazil. With such a strong demand for its products, and an aggressive international sales force, it is not surprising that Lexmark's revenues have catapulted to $2.2 billion in just five years.

Early History

The birth of Lexmark International was a result of IBM's attempt to remain competitive in the intense atmosphere of the late 1980s, when so many smaller firms began chipping away at Big Blue's market share in the computer industry. When IBM initiated a strategic downsizing campaign to cut its workforce by selling or spinning off its peripheral businesses, the Information Products Division was designated as one of the targets. In the early part of 1991, IBM completed a deal to sell Lexmark ("Lex" stands for "lexicon" and "mark" stands for "marks on paper"), its newly renamed Information Products Division, to the private investment group of Clayton, Dubillier, and Rice for approximately $1.5 billion. The leveraged buyout, arranged largely by Martin Dubillier, one of the founders of the investment firm, was financed mostly through bank loans which left the newly created company $1 billion in debt. Dubillier, knowing that Lexmark required astute and aggressive management if it was to survive and prosper with such a heavy debt load, hired Marvin Mann, an IBM vice-president with 32 years of experience, to serve as Lexmark's chairman, president, and chief executive officer.

Intimately knowledgeable about the successes and failures of IBM's business, Mann jumped into his new position with unbridled enthusiasm. Working 18-hour days, and starting with the outline of an organization, he began to reinvent a $2 billion operation. The leveraged buyout included the transfer of IBM's Lexington, Kentucky plant to Lexmark. Mann made the plant the focus of the company's production facilities and immediately implemented a strategy to streamline its workforce. By means of generous benefits for voluntary retirements, transfers, or separations, including one-time assistance payments of $25,000, and one-time career retraining payments of $2,500 (also part of the agreement with IBM), Mann was able to reduce the plant's workforce from over 5,000 to only 1,200 employees. This downsizing significantly reduced Lexmark's operating costs.

At the same time, Mann began to hire virtually all of his management team from IBM. Part of the deal with IBM gave Mann the authority to approach IBM employees to work for Lexmark, and the new president had absolutely no qualms about bringing in experienced managers who were willing to reshape the business. Ultimately, Mann managed to recruit the heads of IBM's research and development, sales, marketing, production, and human resources departments. In order to increase efficiency and smooth the workflow, Mann decided not to establish

305

Company Perspectives:

Lexmark's laser printer strategy is to target fast-growing segments of the network printer market and to increase market share by providing high quality, technologically advanced products at competitive prices. To enhance Lexmark brand awareness and market penetration, Lexmark will continue to identify and focus on customer segments where Lexmark can differentiate itself by supplying laser printers with features to meet specific customer needs.

---

the traditional "contention system," where staff members from different departments within the company challenge each others' proposals, a primary management strategy at IBM and its subsidiaries. Instead, Mann wanted his managers to focus their energies on positive suggestions that would keep Lexmark ahead of its competition.

Perhaps the most innovative management restructuring occurred in the area of manufacturing operations. Initially, small teams of employees were formed in order to make the production lines more efficient and to eliminate problems related to quality control. However, the process of transferring responsibility for decision making from management to workers was not always a smooth one. In one instance, early on in the reorganization, a team of employees redesigned the laser printer production process and then presented their recommendations to management who asked the group to sign an approval form for the design. Realizing that the decision making process, and all the responsibility that goes with it, was completely in their own hands, the group of workers shied away and refused to sign the document that would change the production process. One month later, the same group of workers returned with a more detailed redesign of the laser printer production process, and immediately supported it with their signatures. The two lessons Mann and his management team learned from this experience were that, first, empowerment doesn't work until workers believe that they can actually take ownership of the production process and, second, that involving employees in decisions that affect the production process takes time. These fundamental changes in management-employee relations went a long way toward establishing a highly motivated and effective workforce at Lexmark.

Growth and Development

After having reduced numerous layers of management, created highly independent product development teams, organized a brand new, extremely aggressive sales force, and discarded IBM's traditional appraisal and suggestion program, Mann was ready to take Lexmark to new heights. In 1992, as the company improved its product development time cycles and made its manufacturing processes more and more efficient, a new dot matrix printer was introduced for use at both work and home, along with an extremely lightweight battery-powered printer for portable personal computer users. Later that year, Lexmark introduced a PostScript-compatible inkjet printer, and also began to make a mark in the field of laser network printing. These laser

printers were manufactured for Macintosh and were the first products bearing the Lexmark, rather than the IBM, name. At the same time, however, Lexmark retained its right under a licensing agreement to manufacture printers under the IBM logo.

In addition to expanding its product line with such items as color printers, Lexmark significantly increased the number of its original equipment manufacturer (OEM) printer customers, and was well on the road to doubling that number within its projected timetable of one year. Lexmark also aggressively expanded its IBM PC-compatible keyboard business, which, by the end of fiscal 1992, had grown to include over 40 original equipment manufacturers besides IBM. Lexmark was able to double its operating profits after only two years of operation. The company produced $1.8 billion in revenues during fiscal 1992 and, with a good cash flow and astute management of its financial resources, Lexmark was able to dramatically reduce its debt from $1.15 billion to approximately $700 million, an impressive accomplishment within such a competitive industry.

In 1993, Lexmark significantly enhanced its presence in the Pacific Rim with the acquisition of Gestetner Lasers. Arranged through its subsidiary, Lexmark Australia, the print maker Gestetner was the company's first acquisition and, like all subsequent purchases, was fully incorporated into the company's manufacturing operations. At this time, the company made a commitment to increase its business operations in the international sector and, after a restructuring plan implemented in 1992, improved manufacturing operations in France and built up distribution, marketing, and administrative operations throughout Europe. As a result of these measures, sales from the company's European business shot up to approximately $500 million. Through astute pricing and product sourcing decisions, management was able to minimize the effects of exchange rate fluctuations on the company's European revenues. Other major events during 1993 included the introduction of a new series of network laser printers, and a licensing agreement with Interlink Electronics to develop joystick technologies for a burgeoning market.

By the beginning of 1994, Lexmark had made its name in the laser printer industry. The sale of inkjet printers increased 27 percent over the previous year, much of this due to the entry of the company into the low-end color inkjet market. Associated printer supplies increased by 28 percent, attributed primarily to the continued growth of the company's installed printer base. Keyboard revenues increased only six percent, but the company's notebook computer line proved to be one of its most popular products in the retail market. In fact, Lexmark's presence in retail stores was growing at an astounding rate, with over 20 percent of the company's total revenues generated from retail sales. By the end of the year, Lexmark was ranked fourth in the retail market, closing in on such giants as Hewlett-Packard, Epson, and Canon Computer in inkjet sales. A study conducted during this time indicated that consumer recognition of Lexmark and its products had grown from 36 percent to 41 percent in just three months.

In addition to the increase in revenues, Lexmark received a major endorsement from Microsoft when the software titan picked the company as its first partner for the WindowsAtWork printing environment. Pleased with Lexmark's innovative and aggressive style, Microsoft subsequently chose the company to work on a second generation of products which would be optimized to run in a Windows environment. The close of 1994 marked a milestone in Lexmark history as the IBM logo was finally removed from all company products to be replaced by the Lexmark name. Perhaps the most satisfying moment for Mann, however, arrived when Lexmark was able to reduce its debt to a mere fraction of the total amount by the end of 1994.

Into the Future

In 1995, Lexmark introduced one of its most successful products, MarkVision, the most thorough and comprehensive printer management system designed up to that time. Local Area Network (LAN) users within large corporations significantly increased their efficiency by installing MarkVision, which allowed staff to view all the available printers and check the print job status of each of them without leaving their desk. Another feature of MarkVision provided network administrators with access to the same information so that printer settings could be easily changed through a unique remote operator panel. The click of a mouse gave individuals the ability to remotely perform multiple tasks from their desktop, and simultaneously control and manage all printers across the entire network, regardless of whether the printer was on another floor in the building or across the country. Within a very short time, MarkVision had developed into one of the most popular network and systems management applications, used by many of the leaders in the network industry. With the success of Mark-Vision, Lexmark was able to introduce related applications such as the MarkNet IR, or infrared adapter. This highly compact product enabled a mobile printer to print, synchronize, and transfer files from an infrared-equipped notebook or laptop computer without the use of switch boxes or cables that required extensive hook-up procedures.

By the end of fiscal 1995, Lexmark was able to report nearly $2.2 billion in revenues, with approximately 70 percent of sales generated from printers and associated supplies. Nearly 40 percent of Lexmark revenues came from sales outside the continental United States, mostly derived from countries in Europe and around the Pacific Rim. With international sales up 25 percent over 1994, the company planned to continue expanding its presence overseas through a strategic effort to manufacture more competitive products, improve marketing and intensify sales efforts.

According to the trends within the industry, Lexmark management was confident that most of the company's revenues through the end of the 90s would be generated from its consumable supplies business, especially in the area of replaceable cartridges for printers. Because cartridges must be replaced two to three times per year, the demand for laser and inkjet cartridges increased at a much higher rate than initially expected. Lexmark planned to meet this need into the next decade by increasing its production facilities in the United States, Europe and Latin America. During the mid-1990s Lexmark management decided that, for the foreseeable future, the company would be the only supplier for new print cartridges of its laser and inkjet printers, thus contributing to the stability of Lexmark's earnings.

Principal Subsidiaries

Lexmark Australia.

Further Reading

Brown, Bruce, ''An Ink Jet In Every Pot,'' *PC Magazine,* May 28, 1996, p. 301.

Flanagan, Patrick, ''IBM One Day, Lexmark The Next,'' *Management Review,* January 1994, p. 38.

Lavilla, Stacy, ''Lexmark Makes Printers Manageable Through DMI,'' *PC Week,* March 4, 1996, p. 30.

——, ''Lexmark Takes Aim At Low-end Printer,'' *PC Week,* January 29, 1966, p. 30.

——, ''Lexmark Unleashes High-End Optra,'' *PC Week,* April 8, 1996, p. 31.

——, ''Low-end Releases Pick Up Printer Pace,'' *PC Week,* July 29, 1996, p. 28.

Perenson, Melissa J., ''It's All In The Speed,'' *PC Magazine,* May 14, 1996, p. 74.

Pinella, Paul, ''Lexmark International Inc.,'' *Datamation,* June 15, 1993, p. 65.

Ryan, Ken, ''Making A Mark: Lexmark Nipping At Heels of Major Printer Vendors,'' *HFN The Weekly Newspaper For The Home Furnishing Network,* May 15, 1995, p. 75.

''Scotland Plant Planned,'' *The New York Times,* October 4, 1995, p. C3(N).

—Thomas Derdak

Linamar Corporation

301 Massey Road
Guelph, Ontario
Canada
N1K 1B2
(519) 836-7550
Fax: (519) 824-8479

Public Company
Incorporated: 1966 as Linamar Machine Ltd.
Employees: 3,500
Sales: C$545 million (1995)
Stock Exchanges: Toronto
SICs: 3462 Iron & Steel Forgings; 3531 Construction
    Machinery; 3714 Motor Vehicle Parts & Accessories;
    6710 Holding Offices; 7300 Business Services; 3728
    Aircraft Parts & Equipment

Canadian-based Linamar Corporation is one of the fastest-growing manufacturers of high precision machined and assembled components in the world. Approximately 80 percent of the company's business comes from the automotive industry, including large contracts for the production of steering, engine, transmission, and braking system components. With an impressive customer base of General Motors, Chrysler, Detroit Diesel Corporation, and Ford, company revenues increased over C$100 million from 1994 to 1995. The remaining 20 percent of the company's business is in the manufacture of farm equipment. Headquartered in Guelph, Ontario, Linamar operates through 17 autonomous companies located in such diverse countries as Hungary, Russia, and Kazakhstan.

Early History

The driving force behind Linamar Corporation is its founder and principal owner, Frank Hasenfratz. A native of Hungary, Hasenfratz emigrated from the land of his birth in 1956 during the chaotic and violent Soviet invasion and occupation. Arriving in Austria as a refugee, he served as a translator for his fellow Hungarians who also fled after the Soviet invasion. Working his way to France, he met some Italian crewmen who allowed him to travel free to Canada on their freighter. Met by immigration officials when the ship docked in Quebec City, Hasenfratz was interviewed, given immigration status, and provided with a total amount of C$5.00 to start a new life. Not knowing where to go, the young man of 22 years remained a few days in the railway station in Quebec City, and then traveled to Guelph when he heard of an employment opportunity. He was hired by W.C. Woods Company as a machinist, but was laid off after a short stint of six months.

Undismayed, and full of confidence in himself, Hasenfratz soon found another job as a machinist. From 1958 to 1964, he worked diligently in order to save his money for the right entrepreneurial opportunity. In 1964, the time was right. With $600 he had saved from his six years of work, he opened a one-man machine shop in his own garage. His first contract was for the manufacture of automotive oil pumps. By 1966, Hasenfratz's firm was incorporated as Linamar Machine Ltd., and had grown large enough to employ five people at the Linamar Ariss Plant in Guelph. During the same year, the ambitious businessman received his big break—a contract to manufacture automotive oil pumps for Ford Motor Company of Canada.

Throughout the late 1960s and the decade of the 1970s, Hasenfratz worked hard to expand the customer base of Linamar. Gradually, not only did the company garner larger and larger contracts for component parts from Ford Motor Company of Canada, but also from defense industry firms located in both the United States and Canada. As his customer base grew, so did revenues and the number of employees. By the end of the 1970s, Linamar's revenues totaled C$7 million and over 80 people were employed at the company's Ariss Plant in Guelph.

Growth and Expansion During the 1980s

By 1980, sales at Linamar had increased to C$10 million, and Hasenfratz was ready to implement an aggressive acquisitions strategy to quicken the pace of his company's growth. One of the first purchases made during the 1980s was White Farm Equipment of Canada, Ltd. Having previously engaged in sub-

Company Perspectives:

As we continue to move toward the year 2000, we will maintain our high level of capital investment to equip our management team and manufacturing operations with the latest in highly productive technology and equipment. We will not waiver from our drive to constantly improve and to identify those market areas that will give the company the ability to sustain long-term growth.

contract work for the company, Hasenfratz jumped at the opportunity to acquire White Farm which, in spite of its annual sales base of approximately $280 million, had filed for bankruptcy under chapter 11. The first year after White Farm's acquisition, Linamar made a handsome profit, but shortly thereafter a minority partner in the transaction activated a provision in a shareholder agreement and Hasenfratz was forced to sell his interest in the company. Nonetheless, Linamar had greatly benefitted from the acquisition, since the company had gained expertise in the design and manufacture of farm equipment.

Like many other companies during the 1980s, Linamar's growth was due to its acquisition policy. But the difference between Linamar and other larger corporations at the time was that Linamar integrated acquisitions quickly into its manufacturing operations, rather than breaking up its acquisition into divisions or component parts and then selling them to the highest bidder. Major acquisitions during this period included Bata Engineering (renamed Invar Manufacturing Ltd.), located in Batawa, Ontario. The rationale behind the acquisition was to take advantage of the company's expertise in the production of sophisticated components for defense and commercial applications. Perhaps the most important acquisition during the 1980s, however, was Western Combine Corporation. Western manufactured the Rotary Combine model 8570 for Massey Ferguson in North America, and was soon selling it globally under the auspices of Linamar.

The strategic acquisitions of Bata Engineering and Western Combine were augmented by Linamar's policy of developing its own semi-autonomous subsidiaries. Located mostly in Guelph, the first of these subsidiaries was Linex, created to provide more high precision metal component parts for the automotive and defense industries, and office equipment manufacturers. Hastech was initially formed to manufacture aerospace and defense components, while Spinic manufactured high-volume brackets, spindles, and water pumps for the automotive industry. Emtol was established to provide Linamar with a new facility able to produce large component parts for the defense, agricultural, and automotive industries, including such items as engine blocks, injector bodies, and anti-lock braking system valve housings. Similarly, both Roctel and Transgear were created to provide highly specialized machined components for the automotive industry.

The impetus behind Linamar's formation of its own network of subsidiaries was the changing scene of the North American automotive industry during the early and mid-1980s. As the

foreign car companies captured more of the automobile market during the entire decade of the 1970s, the American car manufacturers began to fight back. The 1980s saw a renewed commitment to higher quality and more durable automobiles by the Big Three manufacturers, including Ford, Chrysler, and General Motors. In order to achieve the goal of consumer satisfaction and, consequently, a larger share of the car market, the Big Three companies began a comprehensive policy to reduce the number of suppliers, and increase the outsourcing of components rather than individual automotive parts. As a result, Ford, Chrysler, and General Motors took extreme measures to evaluate all their suppliers, and awarded long-term contracts to those who had a passing grade. If supplier firms did not receive a passing grade, their contracts were not renewed or they were asked to upgrade their manufacturing facilities.

Linamar management recognized that the Big Three intended to reduce the number of their suppliers, and immediately established a pilot program at the Transgear subsidiary to meet the newly formulated expectations. Linamar reduced costs, began taking time studies of value-added activities, converted its production lines to the new Japanese Kaisen system (which reduced inventories up to 40 percent), clustered its machinery in team groupings that manufactured an entire component, and retrained its employees to work as a team rather than as individuals on an assembly line. With all of its effort to satisfy the demands of the Big Three, Linamar was justly rewarded. By the end of the 1980s, the company had won major contracts from Ford, Chrysler, and General Motors. Most importantly, however, in a complete turnaround from just 10 years earlier, nearly 80 percent of all the company's business came from the automotive industry.

The 1990s and Beyond

With an established reputation for reliability, meticulous accuracy, and low manufacturing costs, Linamar began to reap the benefits of its hard work. In 1992 alone, the company's Spinic subsidiary won the Ford Quality 1 Preferred Customer Award, its Linex subsidiary won the Saco Defense Supplier of the Year Award, and parent Linamar received the extremely prestigious Canada Award for Business Excellence in the Quality Category. When any customer visited one of the company plants located in Guelph, one saw streaming flags indicating Ford's Quality 1, Chrysler's Pentastar, and General Motors' Mark of Excellence Awards.

Hasenfratz, of course, was not the kind of entrepreneur to rest on his laurels. During the 1980s, a state-owned firm located in Hungary, Mezogep, had improved upon a component made for combines by a German corporation. Linamar had been importing the component, called a "cornhead," since 1989. Recognizing the potential market for the component, Hasenfratz returned to his native land and purchased Mezogep in 1992. Industry analysts initially criticized the purchase as misguided, since Hungary had developed a notorious reputation as an unproductive labor market. But Hasenfratz thought this criticism itself was mistaken, especially since the industry held the traditional attitude of most foreign firms working in Eastern Europe—namely, that an American or Canadian manufacturing firm should take advantage of the cheap labor force to lower its own manufacturing costs.

Defying traditional attitudes, Hasenfratz decided to take the opposite approach toward the labor market. He strongly believed that, if the management was good, then the assembly line workforce would be equally as good. Hasenfratz proceeded to hire hard-working, corruption-free managers who, in turn, hired people like themselves. He also reached a unique agreement with his Hungarian management team, including ownership and profit incentives if certain manufacturing goals were met. By 1995, results from the Mezogep operation had even outstripped Hasenfratz's own expectations. Growing into one of Linamar's most successful businesses, Mezogep recorded profits of more than US$3 million, reported efficiency levels between 80 percent and 90 percent, and had added two divisions while employing 560 people. Recently, Mezogep has widened its manufacturing base to include an automotive division which makes component parts for the international automotive market.

Hasenfratz didn't stop with the purchase of Mezogep, which merely seemed to whet his appetite for overseas expansion. In 1992, in conjunction with its Western Combine Corporation subsidiary, Linamar airlifted over 100 tons of farm equipment to Russia by employing the world's second largest airplane. Although there had been a long history of failed dealings between Russian farmers and other North American and German combine manufacturers, Hasenfratz was confident that his company wouldn't make the same mistakes. Consequently, Hasenfratz sent along three Russian-speaking farmers from Canada, along with a comprehensive system that not only included combines, but also large drying machines and huge storage bins for grain. Again, Hasenfratz had anticipated what was needed to create a successful project. Working closely with their Russian counterparts in the city of Chelybinsk, the Canadian farmers helped collect one of the largest harvests ever in the area.

Insisting on supervising the harvest of grain for a period of three years, and implementing both a training program and a repair program for the equipment, the experience soon became a showcase for international cooperation. Proving that grain-handling equipment and methods used in North American could be adapted to regions in Russia with the same production of high-quality grain at lower costs, additional pilot programs were quickly established. Equipment and technical assistance from Canada were used in Kazakhstan and Ukraine, and Linamar also set up a joint venture plant in Russia to manufacture combine equipment. Interestingly, the plant chosen for the operation was a former military plant used by the Russian army but closed due to lack of funds.

In addition to expanding the company's activities in Eastern Europe and Russia, Hasenfratz positioned Linamar to take advantage of the burgeoning North American market. Hasenfratz sees the North American Free Trade Agreement (NAFTA), which combines the U.S., Canada, and Mexico in a free trade agreement, as the counterpart and answer to the European Common Market. A strong advocate of a thoroughgoing, unregulated free trade among the United States, Canada, and Mexico, in 1993 Hasenfratz negotiated a five-year contract with Volkswagen of Mexico to manufacture automobile components for the Golf and Jetta models.

In the summer of 1996, Linamar was listed as one of the 200 fastest-growing companies in the world by the Deloitte & Touche Consulting Group/Braxton Associates. With the hiring of over 400 workers in 1996 alone, Linamar has become Guelph's largest industrial employer. The growing contracts for machine parts to the Big Three American automotive companies—Ford, Chrysler, and General Motors—puts Linamar in position to break the C$1 billion mark by the year 2000.

Principal Subsidiaries

Linamar Transportation, Inc.; Linex Manufacturing, Inc.; Hastech Inc.; Spinic Manufacturing Company, Ltd.; Emtol Manufacturing, Ltd.; Invar Manufacturing, Ltd.; Roctel Manufacturing, Ltd.; Autocom Manufacturing; Vehcom Manufacturing; Transgear Manufacturing, Inc.; Ouadrad Manufacturing, Ltd.; Comtech Mfg., Ltd.; Traxle Mfg., Ltd.; Portage Manufacturing, Inc.; Western Combine Corporation; Mezogep Incorporated; Linamar U.S.A., Inc.

Further Reading

"Canada's Top Manufacturer Takes Aim," *Prospective Business Magazine,* Volume 3, Number 4, pp. 35–40.
"Confessions of an Automotive Supplier," *Canadian Industrial Machinery,* March 1994, pp. 16–44.
Hutchison, John, "Thinking Big About Small Business Exports," *Canadian Business Review,* Autumn 1996, pp. 18–20.
Lindsay, Wendy, "Precision Plus," *Trade and Commerce Magazine* (Supplement), 1993, pp. 3–15.
Nadler, John, "Double Agent," *Canadian Business,* January 1995, pp. 37–40.
Nottingham, Lucy, "Integrated Risk Management," *Canadian Business Review,* Summer 1996, pp. 26–28.
Nunn, Tom, "Linamar Leaps on to List," *The Record,* June 21, 1996, p. A3.

—Thomas Derdak

LOWRANCE ELECTRONICS

Lowrance Electronics, Inc.

12000 E. Skelly Drive
Tulsa, Oklahoma 74128-2486
U.S.A.
(918) 437-6881
Fax: (918) 234-1702
Web site: http://www.lowrance.com

Public Company
Incorporated: 1958
Employees: 970
Sales: $94.58 million (1996)
Stock Exchanges: NASDAQ
SICs: 3812 Search Navigation & Aeronautical Systems

Since the late 1950s Lowrance Electronics, Inc. has been helping serious sports fishermen find fish. Lowrance, based in Tulsa, Oklahoma, designs, manufactures, and markets a range of sonar equipment, also known as depth finders, under the Lowrance, Eagle, and Sea brand names. Lowrance sonars provide visual readouts of underwater information, including geologic structure (bottom contour and consistency, depth of water, presence of underwater objects) and the presence, depth, amount, and even type of fish, improving not only the sports fisherman's catch, but also providing navigational assistance and enhanced safety for the recreational boater. Many of the company's sonar units also provide information on water temperature, traveling speed, and distance traveled. Lowrance sonar units house a transmitter, receiver, transducer, and a flasher, paper graph, or liquid crystal display; are waterproof or weatherproof and shock resistant; and are capable of providing accurate information in salt and fresh water, at speeds up to and beyond 70 miles per hour and at maximum depths up to 2,000 feet.

The company's high-end Lowrance brand sonars, which typically retail from $350 to $550, are marketed at more sophisticated users and are sold primarily through original equipment manufacturers (OEMs) and at boating showrooms. The Lowrance brand includes advanced features, such as Advanced Signal Processing (ASP) and Loran-C circuitry, as well as 18

interchangeable transducers. These transducers are selected and mounted according to the size and type of boat and are available in a range of frequencies and angles for the variety of sport fishing interests, from deep sea fishing to shallow water fishing.

At the lower end, the company's Eagle brand sonars are sold primarily through wholesalers, mail order, and mass merchandisers such as Wal-Mart stores, which account for about 14 percent of the company's annual sales. Eagle sonars offer fewer features than the Lowrance brand, and the prices of these units range between $99 and $300. Because the Eagle brand sonars generally are mounted by the consumer, they are usually outfitted with universal transducers suitable to a wider range of boat hulls and fishing areas. The company's Sea brand sonars, introduced in 1995, are distributed through coastal dealers and are targeted primarily at oceangoing sports fishermen and recreational boaters.

Lowrance also designs, manufactures, and markets Loran-C receivers and sonar accessories, such as mountings. Since 1991, the company has also produced Global Positioning Satellite (GPS) receivers, including the company's hand-held Global Map series, that provide highly accurate navigational assistance to boaters, hikers, hunters, recreational aviators, and others. GPS receivers represent the fastest growing portion of Lowrance's annual sales, accounting for 23 percent of the company's nearly $95 million in sales in 1996, compared with sonar products' 63 percent. The company operates manufacturing facilities in Tulsa and in Ensenada, Mexico. Darrell Lowrance, a co-founder of the company, remains president and CEO and holds 50.3 percent of the company's stock.

The "Little Green" Revolution of the 1950s

Fishing may be as old as humankind, but in the late 1950s the sport remained a largely hit-and-miss proposition. Advances in rod and reel technology, as well as in understanding such factors as thermoclines, or the temperature levels preferable to specific species of fish, had done much to improve a fisherman's chances. But "the one that got away" continued to be a popular fishing refrain, until, that is, Carl Lowrance and sons Darrell and Arlen introduced portable sonar to the sport.

Born in Cushing, Oklahoma, Carl Lowrance moved with his family to Claremore, Oklahoma in the 1930s, where the family operated a fruit and vegetable farm. In 1935, Lowrance, just out of high school, started up his own business with $123, hauling produce in an old pickup truck along a route stretching from the Gulf Coast to Oklahoma. After serving a stint as a flight instructor in the military during World War II, Lowrance and wife Thelma started up a banana ripening and distribution business, called the Banana House, that by the end of the 1950s grew to a 15-semitrailer operation. During these years, Lowrance also started up a side business raising quail for the Ralston Purina Co. Lowrance farm, which raised as many as 40,000 quail per year, was among the world's largest.

Lowrance had long been an avid fisherman, and sons Darrell and Arlen inherited their father's enthusiasm for the sport. It was during the 1950s, on a family fishing trip to Canada, that the Lowrance family hit upon the idea that would revolutionize sports fishing. Darrell and his father, apart from their enthusiasm for fishing, were also among the first inland skin divers in the country. Their experience under the surface of the water, particularly in Oklahoma's Great Lake, taught them several important facts about fish: That fish generally lived in schools; that species tended to inhabit specific areas in a body of water; and that, of great importance, one could not know from the surface where those areas were likely to be. The family sought a means for locating the fish.

As a flight instructor, Carl Lowrance had gained knowledge of sonar, an abbreviation of sound, navigation, and ranging, developed by the U.S. Navy during World War II as a means of tracking enemy submarine movements. After the war, fishermen attempted to adapt sonar to commercial use; these units were bulky and fairly primitive. The pulse length, that is, the ultrasonic signal sent and received by the transducer, for early sonar devices was four to eight feet long, making it suitable for locating large objects, such as a submarine or extremely large schools of fish. But these devices were not at all suited for the fishermen operating small craft and interested in individual fish.

Lowrance's idea was to adapt sonar for sports fishing, using the newly developed transistor technology. Transistors enabled Lowrance to reduce the size of a sonar unit so that not only could it be mounted even in a small skiff, it could also be operated on batteries. The next step was to reduce the unit's pulse length. Darrell Lowrance, then a freshman at the University of Arkansas studying math and physics, managed to reduce the pulse length to one foot, small enough to identify larger fish. By 1956, the Lowrances were ready with their first unit, dubbed the Fish Lo-K-Tor. In 1958, the family incorporated their business as Lowrance Electronics, Inc.

The company first contracted with a West Coast manufacturer to produce 2,000 units of their device. But the results were unsatisfactory. The family contracted with a second, larger West Coast manufacturer, but again the family was dissatisfied with the quality and quantity of what that company produced. Finally, in 1959, the Lowrances decided that the only way to control the quality and quantity of their invention, as well as ensuring its prompt delivery, was to go into manufacturing themselves. The family started up a factory and began producing the Lowrance

Fish Lo-K-Tor. Their first step was to replace, free of charge, 700 of the earlier units that had already been sold.

Improvements and Competition, 1960s–80s

The "little green box," as the Fish Lo-K-Tor became known, soon revolutionized sports fishing. The first devices featured a small rotating neon light, or flasher, that lit up when the sonar pulse reached the waterbed, surface, or registered objects in between. The company worked to improve the product, reducing the pulse length to under one foot, while adding other features. The first of these was the technology to shoot the transducer's pulse through the hull of a boat. Next, the company developed a temperature-stable transducer that could also be used for ice-fishing. The unit's display was improved, adding a measurement dial to give accurate, visual readouts of the depth of the waterbed, and the depth and size of fish. The readout enabled the fisherman to determine the type of bottom as well: The neon flasher provided different readings for gravel, grass, or mud bottoms—important information for determining the type of fish likely to inhabit these environments. Another refinement, introduced in 1960, was a back-lighted faceplate, that allowed the Lo-K-Tor to be used in the pre-dawn darkness, a time of day favored by the serious fisherman.

The Lowrances began traveling across the country, giving demonstrations of their product. The company received a boost in 1964 when their product was featured in *Field and Stream,* the bible of the sports fisherman. Other improvements to the product followed rapidly. In the mid-1960s, the company developed interference suppression systems, improving the unit's accuracy; patented time-varying gain control circuits; and introduced the first transducers that could be used at speeds ranging from 15 to 65 miles an hour or more. At the end of the decade, the company unveiled other improvements, such as its patented system for variable pulse length suppression, ending electrical and acoustical interference, and a new patent for electronic speed control circuitry. Another important addition to the Fish Lo-K-Tor line was a paper printer, which provided printouts of the sonar findings. A fisherman could reuse the printout, enabling him to return to proven fishing locations during the same or subsequent fishing trips.

By the 1970s, the company faced intense competition in the recreational sonar market. At one point, more than 300 companies were marketing fish finders. Lowrance managed to survive by continuing to introduce innovative technology to their products. Among the company's important additions to its product line during the 1970s were the industry's first fully interchangeable selection of transducers, allowing their products to be used across a wide range of boat types and fishing interests. In 1979, Lowrance was the first to introduce microprocessors and keyboard entry into their sonar products. At the beginning of the 1980s, however, the industry at last underwent a shakeout, reducing the number of sonar manufacturers to less than 25. Lowrance maintained its industry lead, and by 1983 the company's sales neared $28.5 million, providing a net income of $1.4 million. By then, Carl Lowrance, who had retired from the company in 1975, was already making a mark in a new endeavor—raising salamanders, at first as bait, and then to supply the optical research community. (Salamander retinas were similar to human retinas, but larger, making them easier to use in research; Lowrance operated the only salamander farm in the country.)

Growth into the 1990s

In the early 1980s, Lowrance Electronics further refined its technology, introducing high resolution transmitters and receivers that now made it possible to identify an individual fish only an inch above or below another fish. Until the mid-1980s, Lowrance's dominance of the market was based principally on its paper graph displays, as well as on flashers. But in 1981, another company, Vexlar, introduced the first liquid crystal display (LCD) device. That product's poor resolution resulted in poor sales. Two years later, however, another company, Hummingbird, introduced the first true LCD sonar. With only 30 pixels, it came nowhere near the resolution of Lowrance's 1,000-line paper graph printers. But intense marketing and low prices, often subsidized, enabled the new LCD devices to challenge Lowrance's leadership position. Lowrance suffered a loss in 1985, of $2.2 million. Its revenues also dropped, to $33.7 million from $37.5 the year before.

Lowrance, which continued to hold the edge on shortness of pulse length, entered the LCD market, producing, in 1986, the industry's first true high resolution LCD displays. The company then followed that development with Super Twist LCD displays providing greater readout visibility. To fuel product development, which included the introduction of Loran-C navigational aids, the company went public in December 1986. By then, the company had regained its momentum, raising sales to $36 million and posting a net profit of $2 million.

Sales leaped to $45 million the following year, and the company again posted more than $2 million in net profits. After another bumpy year in 1988, which saw the company losing nearly $2.5 million on $42 million in sales, the company's sales, aided especially by increasing sales of its low-end products, climbed past $60 million by 1990. But by then the entire marine industry was in a slump. Boat sales were slipping and, with them, sales of Lowrance products. The company struggled to remain profitable, with net income hovering around $250,000 in 1989 and 1990. Then, in 1991, with the outbreak of the Persian Gulf War during the company's peak sales period, coupled with the ongoing recession and what was described as a nine-year "low" in the marine industry, Lowrance again stumbled, dropping revenues to $53.5 million and losing $2.4 million. Adding to the company's difficulties was rival Hummingbird's claims (accompanied by a massive advertising campaign) of having introduced a long-coveted three-dimensional fish finder. Lowrance responded by challenging that products actual 3D ability. The two companies filed lawsuits and eventually reached a settlement, with both sides claiming victory.

Lowrance's difficulties again proved temporary, however; by 1992, sales of Lowrance's newest addition to its product line—GPS receivers, first added in 1991—were beginning to have an impact on its bottom line. The GPS receivers, which used the military's network of 24 satellites locked in geosynchronous orbits, extended the appeal of Lowrance products beyond the sports fisherman, to hikers, hunters, and recreational aviators. Lowrance's Global Map products, which featured a built-in background map of the entire world, used a series of 64 cartridges providing detailed charts and maps, down to one-tenth of a mile, of every region in the United States, as well as much of the world. Among early users of the Global Map series were drivers in the grueling Baja 1000 off-road race. The next step in the Global Map series was the introduction of the Global Map 2000. Bundling GPS, sonar, and Loran-C receivers into one unit, the Global Map 2000 offered a powerful navigational tool. Its ability to record a history, enabling the user easily to retrace his path, set a new standard in the industry.

In 1993, to control costs, Lowrance started up a production facility in Ensenada, Mexico, moving parts of its transducer and cabling production there. The company continued to enhance its sonar line. Its BroadView sonars offered another feature long sought by sports fishermen, that is, the ability to provide readouts not only of depth but out to the sides. These readings could then be displayed in a truer 3D graphic. The company, however, was forced to settle a patent infringement suit brought against it by another company; under terms of the settlement, Lowrance paid $1 million and made a one-time payment of $100,000 to license the technology. The lawsuit, and a market crippled first by an extended winter and then by flooding throughout large regions of the country, took the company into the red again, for a loss of $700,000 despite a rise in revenues to $81.3 million in 1994. Carl Lowrance, retired from salamander farming in 1986, died in 1995.

In 1994, Lowrance had introduced another landmark product, the Eagle AccuNav Sport, a battery-powered, hand-held GPS receiver. The company quickly extended the Sports series, unveiling the Lowrance GlobalNav Sport in 1995 and the Lowrance GlobalMap Sport in 1996. This last, a hand-held version of the Global Map 2000, offered all of the larger unit's features, but in a size small enough to be easily carried by hikers, hunters, and others. Battery powered, the portable unit also featured a lithium ion backup battery capable of retaining large amounts of information in memory. In 1996, the company also introduced the AirMap GPS receiver, designed specifically for aviators.

GPS sales rose quickly, from 13 percent of the company's revenues to nearly one-fourth of sales by 1996, boosting total sales to nearly $95 million. In an effort to control costs and boost margins further, the company announced plans to expand its Mexico facility in 1997. This move appeared necessary as the company attempted to gain a larger share of the booming GPS market, 90 percent of which was already controlled by just two companies. Lowrance's strong record of technological innovation, its reputation for quality, and its history as a true fisherman's friend, made the company a strong challenger for future market share.

Principal Subsidiaries

LEI Extras, Inc.; Lowrance Avionics, Inc.

Further Reading

Gianturco, Michael, "Submarine Stocks To Buy," *Forbes,* April 27, 1992, p. 168.
Gibbs, Jerry, "Lowrance Global Map 2000: Marine Mapping Moves Inland," *Outdoor Life,* May 1996, p. 80.

"Inventor of Sonar Lo-K-Tor Dead at 82," *Tulsa World,* July 13, 1995, p. N12.

Karas, Nick, "Fishing for Savings But Losing Quality," *Newsday,* January 21, 1992, Sports Sec., p. 104.

Lowrance Electronics, Inc., "Company History," http://www.lowrance.com/lowrance/corp/corp3.htm.

——, "Decades of Innovation," http://www.lowrance.com/lowrance/corp/corp2.htm.

Maurer, Mitch, "Lowrance Slates Mexico Facility," *Tulsa World,* August 28, 1993, p. B8.

Powell, Sam, "Lowrance Leading Anglers into Space Age," *Tulsa World,* March 24, 1996, Sports Sec., p. B10.

Sasser, Ray, "Sonar Technology Still Takes Fishing to New Depths," *Dallas Morning News,* April 4, 1996, Sports Sec., p. 15B.

West, Gordon, "Small Is Better: A Look at Inland Maps on Lowrance Portable GPS Receivers," *Trailer Boats,* July 1996, p. 80.

—M. L. Cohen

Mail Boxes Etc.

6060 Cornerstone Court West
San Diego, California 92121-3795
U.S.A.
(619) 455-8800
Fax: (619) 455-8961
Web site: http://www.mbe.com

Public Company
Incorporated: 1980
Employees: 185
Sales: $59.1 million (1996)
Stock Exchanges: NASDAQ
SICs: 6749 Franchises, Selling or Licensing

Mail Boxes Etc. is the world's largest franchise network of postal, business, and communications retail service centers. Nearly eight times larger than its nearest competitor, the Mail Boxes Etc. (MBE) system consists of about 2,600 U.S. outlets (as of 1996) and another 449 units in 51 foreign countries. The chain continues to grow at the brisk pace it established almost from its birth in 1980. From its origins as an alternative to the U.S. postal system for both sending and receiving, MBE has expanded its line of services to include copying, faxing, passport photos, office supplies, and a wide range of other conveniences. The bulk of MBE's revenue comes from franchise royalties and marketing fees, as well as from sales of new franchises.

MBE was founded in 1980 by Anthony DeSio, a former aerospace executive whose résumé included stints with Lockheed, General Electric, and Western Union. Desiring a business of his own, DeSio and three partners envisioned an establishment at which people could conduct their postal business in an environment somewhat more agreeable than that of the typical U.S. Post Office—for a premium price, of course. They opened the first MBE store in Carlsbad, California, with an initial investment of $25,000 from each partner. Initially, the company's core business was mail box rental with 24-hour access. Among the other services offered were sales of postage stamps and wrapping and shipping of packages via independent delivery services such as Federal Express and United Parcel Service (UPS).

Franchising Sparks Growth in Early 1980s

Within a short time, there were three MBE outlets in operation. Funds for further expansion proved hard to come by, however. Since banks and venture capitalists failed to grasp the potential of the concept, DeSio and his partners turned to franchising in order to finance their company's expansion. The first MBE franchises were sold during the company's first year of operation, and by 1982 MBE was selling area franchises for multiple outlets. Despite the company's quick growth, squabbles arose between the partners. As a result, DeSio paid about $900,000 for controlling interest in the company in 1983. He has remained at MBE's helm ever since.

It was not long before MBE began to evolve from a chain of surrogate post offices into a chain of surrogate offices for small business operators. Early on, DeSio realized that mail boxes and shipping made a pretty small hook on which to hang an entire franchise network. One of the first new services he added was sending and receiving faxes. From the beginning, an individual could pass an MBE postal box off as an office suite number on a business card or letterhead. Now that person was able to list the fax number of an MBE location as his or her own number. In addition, MBE could provide the cards, stationary, rubber stamps, and other business identification items that contained those numbers.

As the 1980s continued, MBE was able to take advantage of the explosion of home-based businesses in the United States. MBE outlets were able to provide tiny firms that could not afford their own support staffs or equipment with the kinds of services that larger companies had in-house. In 1986 DeSio took the company public, selling most of the 51 percent of company stock he then owned, and raising about $5 million in capital to fuel further expansion. That year, MBE earned $900,000 on sales of $4.6 million.

By 1987 there were more than 400 MBE franchise locations in 37 states. Service continued to be the company's main competitive edge over the U.S. Post Office. For one thing, MBE

Company Perspectives:

To develop an international distribution system for providing postal, business, and communication services to consumers and businesses of all sizes.

To make this distribution system available to governments and private sector businesses seeking a cost-effective alternative to the establishment of their own chain of retail outlets.

To manage the operation of the MBE network to provide the highest quality of service to our customers and an excellent return on investment for MBE franchisees and shareholders.

could receive packages for rental box customers, a service regular post office boxes did not provide. And in addition to simply providing a wider array of services, MBE outlets were likely to be staffed by the franchisor, whose very livelihood depended on getting customers to come back. To do that, many operators offered such conveniences as allowing customers to check on their rental boxes by telephone. By 1988 MBE stores were in 43 states, and numbered more than 700. It was one of the fastest-growing franchisors in the United States, and nearing the head of the pack among non-food franchisors. Company revenue had grown to $12.4 million by this time, with after-tax earnings reaching $1.85 million.

Late 1980s Bring International Expansion

MBE went international in 1988 as well. This was done by selling a master franchise for all of Canada to a company called Can-Mail Inc. for a licensing fee of $500,000, plus a share of the royalties it received from its Canadian franchisees. MBE was not the first American mail center chain to cross the border, however. A year earlier, Colorado-based Pak Mail Centers had opened a store in Canada. The fact that MBE was beaten into Canada by Pak Mail—a chain a fraction of MBE's size— reflected DeSio's conservative approach to financing. His aim was to expand quickly without sinking deeply into debt and without overburdening the parent company's management or corporate structure.

By 1990 the MBE chain was over 1,200 outlets strong, compared to only about 230 for its nearest competitor, Pak Mail. Stores were located in Mexico and Japan by this time. The company continued to add new services to its line, including electronic tax filing at many locations. As the popularity of MBE and other retail postal centers grew, the company began to agitate for a better deal from the Postal Service and private carriers such as UPS and Federal Express based on the volume of business the centers were generating for the carriers. MBE finally broke through in 1990 with an overnight carrier called DHL Worldwide. In exchange for a discount that allowed MBE to charge customers the same rate as if they had gone to DHL directly, MBE began serving as official drop-off sites for DHL.

The addition of secretarial, answering, and other services made MBE even more of a one-stop business services center by

the early 1990s. The company's success spawned a wave of new competitors, with names like Postal Annex Plus, The Packaging Store, and Mail 'N More, but MBE remained the clear leader in this emerging industry, with several times as many outlets as the next largest chain. As the national "downsizing" trend among corporations heated up, MBE was able to take advantage of the growing SOHO (small office/home office) market, which was composed to a large extent of former professional employees of shrinking companies.

Despite the growing range of services being offered at MBE stores, shipping services remained the company's core business. While each outlet was able to emphasize its own strengths, it was its connection to the big shippers, especially UPS, that made MBE attractive to many potential franchisees, and franchise fees remained by far the most important source of revenue for the company. In 1991 franchise fees made up 27 percent of MBE's $25.7 million in revenue. That year the company's ongoing alliance with UPS was cemented when UPS purchased 9.5 percent of MBE's stock, with warrants that gave UPS the option of increasing its holdings to more than 17 percent over the following three years. The transaction was mutually beneficial. For MBE, it ensured that UPS would not set up its own retail network, as Federal Express had done, thereby depriving the chain of one of its biggest revenue sources. And for UPS it provided a low-cost, wide-ranging distribution system that was already intact and fully operational.

As the 1990s continued, MBE took on even more roles in its attempt to become a provider of every business service imaginable. The MBE network soon began functioning as customer service or distribution centers for a wide variety of business equipment companies, which found it more economical to use MBE than to set up their own outlet systems. Among the companies that used the MBE chain in this way have been Nintendo, Acer Computers, Xerox, Panasonic, Toshiba, and Hewlett-Packard. Another service the company began to experiment with around this time was airline ticket distribution. For fiscal 1992, MBE's revenue grew to $36 million, with the majority again coming from franchise fees, royalties, and the sale of supplies and equipment to franchisees. The franchises themselves, by this time numbering nearly 2,000, were generating a total of about $570 million in sales.

Toward 5,000 by the Year 2,000

By 1993 MBE was well-enough established on both the national and international levels that it was able to introduce its "Big or Small. We Ship It All" program, in which participating MBE stores had the capacity to ship just about any item to just about any destination in the world. MBE also forged an alliance with the Staples chain of office supply superstores, giving rise to the appearance of MBE "boutique" stores inside of Staples outlets. Before the end of that year, there were more than 2,100 MBE Centers throughout the world, over 130 of them outside the United States. The chain was growing at the rate of about one store a day. Italy, France, the United Kingdom, Spain, Greece, and Turkey, to name just a few, were all home to MBE stores by the mid-1990s. MBE's international expansion was accomplished through the sale of master licenses, which gave a company the rights to subfranchise MBE stores for a whole country. The MBE concept was particularly appealing in countries with historically poor mail service, since customers there were generally eager to skirt the existing national postal monopolies.

MBE reported revenue of $43.7 million for fiscal 1994, a moderate increase over the previous year. Around that time, the company launched its first-ever national advertising campaign. The campaign was supported by the creation on a trial basis of a National Media Fund, which derived its money from an additional 1.5 percent monthly charge to participating MBE Centers. Because of the program's success, the fund was made permanent in 1996, and MBE has maintained a strong national advertising presence since that initial campaign.

The company's international expansion continued to move quickly during the next couple years. In June 1995 MBE's 100th European location was opened in Paris, and by the year's end there were 327 centers operating outside the United States. By that time, the company had sold a total of 47 national licenses for foreign countries. Development remained strong in 1996 as well. Among the international areas for which master licenses were sold that year were Israel and South Africa. Italy became the second country outside the United States (following Canada) to open its 100th center. Domestically, 287 new MBE Centers were sold in 1996, as the company surged toward its goal of 5,000 centers by the turn of the century.

Market research indicated that one in five U.S. households had used MBE by 1996. By this time, the success of the MBE concept was clear even to the U.S. Post Office, which sought to win back some of its lost business by offering its own version of "pack and ship" service. This attempt at vertical integration by the Post Office met with resistance on the part of the private postal service industry, which felt that the Post Office was competing unfairly by using money from its first-class mail monopoly to subsidize its Pack and Ship operation. In addition, shippers UPS—which by this time owned 15 percent of MBE—and Federal Express, both major allies of the mail centers, were infuriated by the Post Office's use of their logos and images in ads that they called misleading. In spite of the Post Office's counterattack, MBE seems poised for several more years of growth, especially in Asia and other areas where wheeling and dealing are common and methods of sending and receiving packages quickly and securely are hard to come by.

Further Reading

Benford, Noonie, and Diane Gage, "Out of the Woods, into the Forest," *Venture,* August 1988, pp. 24–25.

Byrne, Harlan S., "Mail Boxes Etc.: It Builds Earnings through Rapid, Global Growth," *Barron's,* April 5, 1993, pp. 50–52.

"Call Me Usmail," *Economist,* August 20, 1988, p. 59.

Gendron, George, "A Sweet Deal," *Inc.,* March 1991, p. 12.

McLeod, John A., "Consumers Pay More but Get More at Private Postal Centers," *Marketing News,* October 1, 1990, p. 8.

Page, Paul, "Retail Delivery Outlets Decry New Move by 'Customer-Friendly' Postal Service," *Traffic World,* June 3, 1996, p. 26.

"Reinventing the Post Office," *Fortune,* January 19, 1987, p. 8.

Schlax, Julie, "Rain, Sleet, Snow and Franchising," *Forbes,* November 26, 1990, p. 224.

Tannenbaum, Jeffrey A., "Mail Boxes Etc. Delivers Profits but Not to Everyone," *Wall Street Journal,* October 13, 1993, p. B2.

—Robert R. Jacobson

Manitowoc Company, Inc.

---

500 S. 16th Street
P.O. Box 66
Manitowoc, Wisconsin 54221-0066
U.S.A.
(414) 684-4410
Fax: (414) 683-6277
Web site: http://www.manitowoc.com

Public Company
Incorporated: 1902 as Manitowoc Dry Dock Company
Employees: 3,200
Sales: $313 million (1995)
Stock Exchanges: New York
SICs: 3531 Construction Machinery; 3585 Refrigeration
& Heating Equipment; 3731 Ship Building & Repair

Manitowoc Company, Inc. is a diversified manufacturer of ice machines and large commercial refrigeration equipment for the hotel, health care, food service, and convenience store industries, and of lattice boom cranes and crane rentals for heavy industry construction, as well as being one of the only three remaining repair and maintenance shipyards for both freshwater and saltwater vessels operating in the Great Lakes Region. The company's facilities are located in Wisconsin, Tennessee, Iowa, Ohio, Texas, Florida, and Pennsylvania, with additional sales and distribution offices in Europe. In 1995, with the acquisition of The Shannon Group, Inc., a large manufacturer of commercial refrigerators and freezers, Manitowoc became one of the leaders in the food service equipment industry.

Early History

The founders of Manitowoc Company, Charles C. West and Elias Gunnell, originally worked for Chicago Shipbuilding Company in Chicago, Illinois. However, in 1899, when Chicago Shipbuilding was purchased by American Shipbuilding based in Cleveland, Ohio, the former firm was subsumed under the latter and lost its decision-making authority and engineering autonomy. Disappointed with the results of the purchase, West and Gunnell decided to buy a shipyard of their own. West, a marine engineer and naval architect, and Gunnell, an experienced shipbuilder, designer, and mechanic, reached the conclusion that their shipyard would build steel ships rather than the wooden ships commonly built at the turn of the century. Yet after consulting their acquaintances within the shipbuilding industry, the two entrepreneurs were convinced that the best plan of action was first to purchase a yard where wooden ship repairs could be done, since this would provide them with financial stability, and then, in due time, buy and install the necessary equipment for building steel ships.

The only shipyard for sale on the shores of Lake Michigan was located in Manitowoc, Wisconsin. Owned by brothers Henry and George Burger, the Manitowoc operation had grown large and lucrative from its extensive wooden ship repair business. Having found an acquisition that ideally suited their purposes, West and Gunnell bought the Burger and Burger shipyard in 1902 for $110,000. Gunnell assumed the position of president and West became the general manager of the new Manitowoc Dry Dock Company. The first vessel launched by Manitowoc Dry Dock was the *Cheguamegon,* a wooden passenger steamer already under construction at the time of the purchase. By 1903, however, the company had contracted its first steel ship repair job, and by 1905 the firm had launched the passenger steamer *Maywood,* the first steel vessel built in the Manitowoc shipyard.

In 1904, Gunnell, West, and L. E. Geer, the secretary and treasurer of Manitowoc, had created a separate tool company to manufacture marine engines and other types of machinery necessary to outfit a ship. In 1905, Manitowoc purchased this company and incorporated it within its shipbuilding operations. In 1908, Manitowoc purchased the Steam Boiler Works, a major manufacturer of marine boilers, pulp digesters, dryers, furnaces, ladles, vulcanizers, kilns, buoys, buckets, creosoting retorts, and tanks. These two acquisitions gave Manitowoc the ability not only to build new steel vessels, but the capability to completely equip them for operational service. With sales increasing and financial stability assured, to reflect a more modern image management decided to change the name of the firm to Manitowoc Shipbuilding Company in 1916.

Manitowoc Shipbuilding Company grew dramatically during World War I. Although the war had started in 1914, the United States did not enter the hostilities in Europe until 1917. When Congress declared war on Germany in April of 1917, however, the entire operations of Manitowoc were subsumed under the authority of the U.S. Shipping Board Emergency Fleet. The Board immediately placed a large contract with Manitowoc for 3,500-ton freighters, and the company embarked on an extensive expansion program to fill this order. During the course of the war, Charles West was recruited by the U.S. Navy Bureau of Construction to supervise the construction of a shipbuilding plant at Ford Motor Company near the firm's headquarters in Michigan. For more than 18 months, West commuted from Manitowoc to Detroit and then back again to fulfill his duties to both companies. Before the war, Manitowoc turned out an average of six ships per year. By the time the war ended in 1918, the company was capable of turning out 18 ships annually and had already made 33 3,500-ton freighters used during the war effort.

Unfortunately, when World War I ended the U.S. government cancelled the remaining freighter contracts with Manitowoc. This loss of wartime revenue led to a postwar depression, not only for Manitowoc but for the entire shipbuilding industry in the Great Lakes region. With its expanded capacity for shipbuilding, and numerous employees hired for the wartime production effort, West and Gunnell searched for new business that would compensate for the disappearance of government contracts. Luckily, the two men arranged for the company's shipbuilding plant to be converted into a railroad locomotive maintenance and repair shop. This kept the company barely solvent, and with funds enough to pay employee wages, but it was clear that Manitowoc would have to undergo a transformation to survive.

In 1920, West and Gunnell came to a sharp disagreement as to the direction of the company. West was convinced that Manitowoc could only survive by implementing a broadly based diversification strategy. Gunnell, on the other hand, maintained that the company should continue to emphasize its shipbuilding capacity. Unable to reach a point of mutual agreement, the company was put up for sale. Interestingly enough, West made the only offer to purchase the firm. For a total of $410,000, West and Geer bought the company and renamed it the Manitowoc Shipbuilding Corporation. An immediate policy of diversification was established, including an expansion of the boiler works and new products for the machine shop. Since marine boilers were losing their popularity, the boiler works diversified into the manufacture of paper mill equipment, dryers

for coal, rock, and clay, brewery tanks, air nozzles, and heating boilers. The machine shop reached an agreement to manufacture Moore Speedcranes under the Moore patents. By 1927, Manitowoc had taken over the manufacture and sale of all of the crane models produced by the Roy and Charles Moore Crane Company. Of course, the diversification program did not mean that shipbuilding at the company was interrupted. During the 1920s, Manitowoc constructed its first self-unloading vessel, two carferries, five tugboats, four deck barges, two dipper dredges, two dump scows, two derrick scows, a floating dry dock, and the largest suction dredge in the world.

The Great Depression and World War II

With the stock market crash of 1929, the era of the Great Depression began in the United States. Manitowoc was, like many other businesses during the time, hard hit by the downward trend in business. Sales dropped precipitously from more than $4 million in 1931 to less than $500,000 by 1933. During the middle of the decade, the company operated at a net loss for four years in a row. Many employees were laid off, and those that remained were forced to take a reduction in their salaries. The company's shipbuilding business was severely affected by the Depression, and management was forced to rely more heavily on the crane business. During the 1930s, Manitowoc introduced an improved version of the Moore Speedcrane and began a maintenance service to repair and keep cranes in first-class condition. Manitowoc cranes soon garnered a reputation for high quality within the industry and were purchased to help construct the Senate Office Building, the National Gallery of Art, the National Archives, and the Jefferson Memorial, all located in Washington, D.C.

In 1940, as the start of another world war became more evident to U.S. government officials, the Navy contracted Manitowoc to build ten submarines and provided the company with funds to make the necessary plant improvements and expansion. Although West hesitated because of his previous experience with U.S. government contracts, which left the company in dire financial straits after World War I, he reluctantly decided to engage in a comprehensive plant conversion. The increased capacity soon proved itself useful. Just one week after Pearl Harbor had been attacked by the Japanese, which initiated the American involvement in World War II, the company received an order from the U.S. Navy for immediate delivery of six cranes for use in salvaging operations in the harbor. More than 58 cranes were made by the company for the Navy's Floating Dry Docks during the war, and 79 cranes and shovels were delivered to the U.S. Army.

Besides a huge order for submarine construction during the war, Manitowoc also built landing craft for use in both the Pacific and European theaters of operation. Extensive testing was conducted along the shores of Lake Michigan by company engineers, and design changes were made before actual production was begun. Manitowoc built a total of 1,465 landing craft, and received a Presidential Citation for the vehicle's performance during the Normandy landing in June of 1944. In addition, by the end of the war the company had constructed 28 submarines for the U.S. Navy and had received the Navy "E" for excellence in production five times.

The Postwar Years

The immediate period after War World II brought the same problems that confronted the company after World War I: the necessary reorganization of the company and its manufacturing facilities to a peacetime economy. Unlike what happened the previous time, however, the U.S. Navy reimbursed Manitowoc for its wartime expenses and helped it to dismantle the Navy's portion of its shipbuilding operations. West, still in control of the company's direction, decided once again that diversification was the answer. Looking for products to manufacture that did not require significant capital investment, Manitowoc started making dry cleaning units and, in addition, freezers for Firestone and Westinghouse. Soon the firm was making commercial frozen food cabinets used in supermarkets and restaurants and, by 1950, more than 50 percent of Manitowoc's equipment works was devoted to this business.

Manitowoc's shipbuilding operation was plagued by union strikes throughout the late 1940s but, with the end of the postwar recession in the marine industry, the firm reclaimed its role as a major shipbuilder and repair facility in the Great Lakes region. During the early 1950s, the company constructed the prototype of *Nautilus*, the country's first nuclear submarine. In addition, numerous commercial vessels were built during the decade, including the largest self-unloader on the Great Lakes, a coal hauler, the first diesel-powered carferry, and five crane barges. Charles West was particularly pleased to see his company survive the difficulties of the postwar period and, when he died in 1957, left behind what he considered to be a thriving firm with great potential for the future.

During the 1960s, Manitowoc continued to grow. The manufacture of dry cleaning units was expanded, as well as the production of freezers and frozen food cabinets. In 1967, the company introduced The Manitowoc Ice Dispenser, which quickly became very popular in both the hospital and lodging industries. Since shipbuilding at the time consisted mostly of smaller vessels such as dump scows and crane barges, management decided to combine its operations with another Great Lakes shipbuilding firm and relocate to Sturgeon Bay, Wisconsin. In 1968, Manitowoc purchased all of the assets of the Sturgeon Bay Shipbuilding and DryDock Company and subsequently renamed its reorganized business the Bay Shipbuilding Corporation. This combination of both resources and facilities resulted in major contracts during the 1970s, including the first 1,000-foot ship, built to haul coal for Detroit Edison.

Growth and Transformation During the 1970s and 1980s

In addition to relocating and reorganizing its shipbuilding operation during the early 1970s, the company divested its dry cleaning operation and sold off its freezer and frozen food cabinet business. The most successful and profitable product made by the company after World War II was its custom-built cranes. From the mid-1920s to 1945, management regarded the sale of its cranes as a fortuitous product of a necessary diversification program started after World War I. But after World War II, the demand for the company's cranes began to increase dramatically. In fact, during the 1950s and 1960s, Manitowoc was at the forefront of developing technological innovations to increase the quality of its cranes. The company was the first manufacturer to use T-1 high-strength steel in booms, design a controlled-torque converter for crane applications, and develop extendible crawlers. In 1967, Manitowoc engineers designed an assembly that doubled the lift capacity of any basic crane. By 1977, sales for Manitowoc cranes were reported at $146.5 million, whereas shipbuilding and repair revenues amounted to $73 million and ice cube maker sales totaled $14.4 million.

During the 1980s, Manitowoc rode an economic roller coaster. The recession of the early 1980s, and the collapse of the petroleum boom, led to a dramatic plunge in Manitowoc's sales. The company's crane business fell flat, especially in the areas of large lift cranes used in the construction and offshore oil industries. The company's manufacture of ice-making machines for the foodservice, health care, and convenience store markets also took a nose dive, and shipbuilding at the Sturgeon Bay facility had to be abandoned altogether. By the end of the decade, conditions at Manitowoc had improved slightly. Manitowoc's crane business had benefited from the revival of offshore drilling in the Gulf of Mexico, and the company claimed that it was the only manufacturer of large lift cranes left in the United States; all of the firm's competitors had either sold their holdings to foreign interests or gone out of business. The company's ice machine business replaced the crane business as Manitowoc's most profitable operation during the middle and late 1980s, and the Sturgeon Bay facility reported that it was one of only three remaining Great Lakes shipping repair and maintenance shops for the country's largest iron-ore carriers.

The 1990s and Beyond

During the early 1990s, management at Manitowoc implemented a comprehensive cost-cutting and reorganization strategy, including a revamped marketing program that significantly enhanced the company's presence across the United States and in Europe. Modernization at the firm's large crane and boom-truck facilities increased production, and the introduction of new crane designs, especially the Model 888 crane with a 220-ton lift capacity, gained immediate market acceptance. At the same time, Manitowoc expanded its ship repair business to include two additional locations in the Great Lakes Region and, by the mid-1990s, operated more than 60 percent of all drydock footage on the Great Lakes. Most important of all, however, was the acquisition in 1995 of The Shannon Group, Inc., a major manufacturer of commercial refrigeration equipment. The purchase of Shannon turned Manitowoc into the largest supplier of commercial ice-cube machines and walk-in refrigerators in the world.

By the mid-1990s, Manitowoc had recovered from its losses during the late 1980s. Approximately 39 percent of all sales was from cranes and related products, whereas food service equipment accounted for 54 percent of total sales and shipyard repairs reported seven percent of all sales. In 1995, sales had increased 16 percent over the previous year, and all of the company's indicators pointed toward an ever-increasing sales volume in the years ahead. With the world's bestselling heavy-lift lattice boom crane and the addition of The Shannon Group to its commercial refrigeration equipment, Manitowoc is looking forward to larger and larger profits in the years that lead up to the 21st century.

Principal Subsidiaries

Femco Machine Co.; Kolpak Manufacturing Company; Manitex, Inc.; Manitowoc Engineering, Inc.; Manitowoc Engineering Works PTE, Ltd.; Manitowoc Equipment Works, Inc.; Manitowoc Europe B.V.; Manitowoc Europe Holdings, Ltd.; Manitowoc Europe Limited; Manitowoc International Sales Corp.; Manitowoc Korea Company, Ltd.; Manitowoc Nevada, Inc.; Manitowoc Re-Manufacturing, Inc.; Manitowoc Western Company, Inc.; North Central Crane & Excavator Sales Corp.; The Shannon Group, Inc.; West Manitowoc, Inc.

Further Reading

Byrne, Harlan S., "Manitowoc Company: Cost-Cutting Lays Ground for Earnings Rebound," *Barrons,* January 6, 1992, pp. 39–40.

——, "Manitowoc Company: From Cranes to Cold Cash, It Bucks Capital-Goods Trend," *Barrons,* November 12, 1990, pp. 41–42.

Conley, Paul F., "Barge Rates Likely To Fall," *Journal of Commerce,* January 8, 1996, p. S49(1).

Krapf, David, "Inland Barge Construction Is Booming," *Journal of Commerce,* August 26, 1996, p. 8B(1).

Manitowoc: 75 Years of Growth and Diversification, 1902–1977, Manitowoc, Wisconsin: The Manitowoc Company, 1977.

Moore, Walt, "New Company, New Crane," *Construction Equipment,* October, 1994, p. 81(1).

Phalon, Richard, "Back in the Game," *Forbes,* December 5, 1994, pp. 58–60.

"U.S., Other Nations To Meet on Shipbuilding Subsidiaries," *The Wall Street Journal,* October 4, 1996, p. A8(E).

—Thomas Derdak

ⓂMARUZEN

Maruzen Co., Limited

3-10 Nihonbashi 2-Chome
Chou-ku, Tokyo 103
Japan
(81) 3 3272-7211
Fax: (81) 3 3274-3238
Web site: http://www.maruzen.co.jp

Public Company
Incorporated: 1869 as Maruya Shosha
Employees: 2,111
Sales: ¥132.3 billion (US$1.3 billion) (fiscal year ended March 31, 1996)
Stock Exchanges: Tokyo
SICs: 5942 Book Stores; 5943 Stationery Stores; 5611 Men's & Boys' Clothing Stores; 5621 Women's Clothing Stores; 5730 Radio, Television & Computer Stores

With a ranking among *AsiaWeek* magazine's top 1000 companies of 1996, Maruzen Co., Limited is one of Japan's largest and best-known booksellers. From its initial concentration in the importation and sale of books and journals, the company has expanded into consumer merchandise and information systems. In the mid-1990s, over 60 percent of the firm's sales went to public institutions like schools and universities, with the remainder generated via retail book stores and other goods and services. While sales of monographs and periodicals are the bedrock of Maruzen's activities, the company also sells computers and proprietary software, stationary and office supplies, clothing and art. The company's activities in the service sector include providing access to electronic databases, preservation and conservation of rare books, and computer network development. According to Maruzen, the unifying theme of these diverse activities is "Creating Intellectual Environments."

Nineteenth-Century Origins

Maruzen's roots stretch back into the late 1860s, an era when Japan was evolving out of a 200-year period of feudal government under the Tokugawa shogunate. After years of isolation ended by the arrival of American Commodore Matthew Perry in 1853, Japan entered a period of rapid modernization that brought about sweeping social, economic, and political change. Established in 1869, Maruzen straddled the cusp of this cultural shift. Maruzen founder Yuteki Hayashi was urged to establish a bookstore by Yukichi Fukuzawa, an educator and stalwart proponent of Westernization. Hayashi sought out, translated, published, and sold seminal works of the Western world. The company's first store, located in Yokohama, was joined by an outlet in Tokyo's Nihonbashi section in 1870.

Originally known as Maruya Shosha, the business not only brought the concept of the joint stock corporation to Japan, but also began translating and publishing Western encyclopedias and other reference works for Japanese distribution. The company started publishing *Hyakka Zensho,* a 12-volume summary of European knowledge, in 1883. It also released a Japanese version of *Chamber's Information for the People,* another highly-regarded encyclopedia. In 1902, Maruzen added the *Encyclopaedia Britannica* to its list of imported publications.

Hayashi's relationship with Fukuzawa, who founded Japan's first private system of elementary and secondary schools as well as Keio University in Tokyo, formed the basis of Maruzen's strong sales to educational institutions. Over its decades of service to schools and universities, the company developed a comprehensive array of scholarly periodicals. By the mid-1890s, sales to these markets constituted more than half of the company's annual revenues. As Japan's own educational and research institutions developed, Maruzen was also well-prepared to print and distribute Japanese journals overseas.

Dawn of the 20th Century Brings Diversification

Maruzen did not limit its imports to intellectual properties. After the turn of the 20th century, it began to import contemporary business machines from the United States and Europe. The company got a foothold in the fledgling information technology industry in 1900, when it started importing and selling Wellington typewriters and American-made Monroe calculators. These early activities laid the foundation for Maruzen's later involvement in computerized databases and networks.

Company Perspectives:

Maruzen Company, Limited, was established in 1869 as Japan's first joint stock corporation. By importing Western publications and other goods, Maruzen took the lead in introducing to Japan information about overseas cultures. Today, Maruzen has earned a solid position as one of Japan's leading booksellers, and the company has also diversified into other areas. In information-related fields, Maruzen's business activities include providing multimedia information services, developing networks, marketing office automation equipment, and offering facilities development services. In addition, the company has a strong presence in lifestyle and culture fields, such as stationery and fashion apparel. Through its domestic network of 39 stores, 29 sale offices, and more than 70 sales outlets in universities and colleges and its overseas network of 4 offices, Maruzen is developing a diversified portfolio of business activities around its core operations in books and journals.

Maruzen also began trading in consumer goods early in the 20th century. The company started in this vein with domestic and imported stationery and office supplies. The firm expanded into clothing with an emphasis on brand-name, mostly British, apparel. In 1915 it received the country's first shipment of world-famous Burberrys raincoats. Maruzen later manufactured its own clothing, which was sold in company-owned stores and independent department stores as well as by mail order. Western-style liquor, eye wear, and even golf equipment and accessories were later added to the merchandise mix. By the mid-1990s, Maruzen was importing furniture and supplies for offices and libraries, computers, office automation equipment, educational equipment, and teaching materials.

Diversification Continues in 1960s and 1970s

During the 1960s and 1970s, Maruzen began to broaden its activities into the fields of arts and electronic information services. The company's involvement in the arts began in the early 1960s, when it hosted an exhibit of international art books. From this rather meager effort evolved the country's biggest art book fair. As it had in the past, Maruzen focused on making Western art and cultural institutions accessible to the citizens of Japan. Maruzen encouraged and assisted major museums from around the world in building Japanese annexes to their institutions. The Japanese retailer parlayed its relationships with the world's museums into a new profit center by reproducing and selling works of art. A 1990 agreement with the British Museum exemplified these efforts.

Maruzen established itself as an innovator in Japan's electronic information services industry in the late 1970s when it teamed up with Knight-Ridder Information Inc. to offer Japanese citizens their first opportunity for online access to an overseas database, specifically Knight-Ridder's DIALOG database of scientific documents. Maruzen enhanced its service to libraries with the development of the Computer Assisted Library Information System (CALIS), launched in 1985. CALIS provided library purchasing and cataloging departments with the information they needed to select, order, and catalog books and journals. This service made it easy for libraries to choose Maruzen as their book supplier. A selection of about 1,100 CD-ROMs and electronic books rounded out Maruzen's computer hardware and software offerings.

By combining its vast data resources with its computer networking expertise, Maruzen was able to design, install, and support local access networks (LANs) and other information management systems for its existing pool of library and museum clients. But it didn't stop there. By the early 1990s, the company was designing the physical environs as well, offering an integrated package including design, furnishings, computer hardware and software, and audiovisual equipment. The company later tailored these services for businesses and even competing publishers. In fact, Maruzen claims that its computer division "has been offering an MIS (management information systems) package for publishers for nearly 30 years."

The 1990s and Beyond

Maruzen expanded its operations into the preservation and conservation of rare books and documents, many of which were printed on rapidly-deteriorating acidic paper, in the late 1980s. The company started a microfilming program in 1989, and had duplicated some 160,000 volumes by 1993. Maruzen completed the filming of the National Diet Library Collection (comparable to America's Library of Congress) in 1991, thus preserving over 150,000 Meji Era books. Maruzen, which characterized this project as "a feat as yet unmatched by any other library around the world," also won a contract with the National Diet Library to sell the film collection to other libraries. The union of Maruzen's computer know-how and preservation expertise facilitated the development of a sophisticated storage and retrieval system that allowed "multiple access to up to 200 reels of microfilm in a LAN environment."

In order to highlight its preservation program and commemorate its 120th anniversary, Maruzen spent more than $5.39 million to buy one of the fewer than 50 Gutenberg Bibles in existence. Maruzen's acquisitions of other rare books—including the Hyakumantoh Dharani ("Buddhist incantations to ward off disasters") and the Rosetta Stone—saluted the company's blending of Eastern and Western cultures. The company said that these books "are representative of Maruzen's commitment to the dissemination of knowledge and are lasting symbols of the key role that the printed word has played in the development of cultures around the world."

From its earliest days, Maruzen has strived to keep pace with the ever-changing field of information dissemination. This effort has helped the company evolve from a retail bookseller into a provider of very advanced information services. Moreover, the company's creation of a retail outlet in Singapore addressed one of its most apparent weaknesses, a lack of internationalization. If Maruzen can keep up with the rapid technological changes and the growing need for international markets inherent in the modern information service business, it is well positioned to continue into the 21st century.

Principal Subsidiaries

Maruzen International Co., Ltd. (U.S.A.); Maruzen Singapore Takashimaya; Maruzen Kyoei Prince (Indonesia); Maruzen Pasaraya Sultan Agung (Indonesia); Maruzen Mega Pasaraya (Indonesia); Maruzen Jaya Jusco Bandar Utama (Malaysia).

Principal Divisions

Book Division; Journal Division; International Division.

Further Reading

"Corporate Profile: Maruzen," Tokyo: Maruzen Co., Ltd., 1993.

"English Books in Japan," *Publishers Weekly,* June 3, 1988, pp. 50–51.

Gorsline, George, and Wyley L. Powell, "UTLAS-Japan Communications Link," *Information Technology and Libraries,* March 1983, pp. 33–34.

"How Distribution Works; Japanese Distributors and Importers Are Fast, Efficient, and Perform a Multitude of Tasks for Their Money," *Publishers Weekly,* January 12, 1990, pp. S27–S31.

Taylor, Sally A., "Asia: The Now & Future Book Market," *Publishers Weekly,* March 14, 1994, p. 34.

——, "Book Fairs Are a Growth Market in Asia This Year," *Publishers Weekly,* March 11, 1996, p. 18.

—April Dougal Gasbarre

The McGraw·Hill Companies

The McGraw-Hill Companies, Inc.

1221 Avenue of the Americas
New York, New York 10020-1095
U.S.A.
(212) 512-2000
Fax: (212) 512-3514
Web site: http://www.mcgraw-hill.com

Public Company
Incorporated: 1909 as McGraw-Hill Book Company
Employees: 15,004
Sales: $3.3 billion (1996)
Stock Exchanges: New York Pacific
SICs: 2721 Periodicals Publishing and Printing; 2731
    Book Publishing and Printing; 7375 Information
    Retrieval Services; 4833 Television Broadcasting

The McGraw-Hill Companies, Inc., a leading international multimedia publishing and information company, caters to the education, business, industrial, professional, and government markets through books, magazines, film, and a myriad of worldwide electronic networks. Formed initially from the merger of McGraw Publishing Company and Hill Publishing Company, the business always aimed to provide technicians, scientists, and business people complete, accurate, and up-to-date information of both specialized and general interest. Almost from its beginning the company pursued acquisitions and mergers that would increase market share, reach new markets, and expand its global reach.

The Early Written Word, 1860s to 1915

Born in 1858, John A. Hill—typesetter, silver prospector, newspaper publisher, and railroad engineer—came to the attention of the publisher of *American Machinist* with his contribution of letters and articles on practical aspects of railroading. When the publisher began *Locomotive Engineering* in 1888, Hill was his choice for editor. By 1869 Hill had become part owner of both magazines and in 1897, divesting his interest in

Locomotive Engineering, Hill took over full ownership of *American Machinist*, and established the American Machinist Press in 1898. In 1902 he incorporated Hill Publishing Company, going on to acquire *Power, Engineering and Mining Journal*, and *Engineering News*. By 1909, Hill was a leading trade publisher of not just magazines but of books such as *Colvin and Stanley's American Machinist's Handbook* (1908) and Herbert Hoover's *Principles of Mining* (1909).

Hill's chief competitor was onetime teacher and subscription salesman James H. McGraw. McGraw was an advertising salesman for the American Railway Publishing Company in 1884, where he rose to vice president by 1886. On resigning from American Railway, McGraw began to acquire magazines that reported on technological progress. Titles included the *American Journal of Railway Appliances; Electrical Industries* (later retitled *American Electrician); Electrical World; Electrical Engineer; Electrochemical Industry;* and *Engineering Record*. In 1899 McGraw incorporated McGraw Publishing Company; its first engineering handbook, the *Standard Handbook for Electrical Engineers*, was published in 1907.

In the years following the Civil War, the United States changed from an agrarian to an industrial society. Both McGraw and Hill found a growing market of technicians concerned with the practical applications of science to transportation, lighting, and engineering, among other facets of daily life. In 1909 Edward Caldwell and Martin M. Foss, the respective heads of the book departments of the two firms, agreed that a merger of the two book departments would serve both companies well. After the two men persuaded their bosses, a coin toss decided whose name would come first in naming the new company, the loser becoming president. The McGraw-Hill Book Company, with John A. Hill as president, was thus born, locating itself in McGraw Publishing's building in New York City.

The two companies, however, were still distinct, different entities: the magazines that formed the chief interests of both and supplied articles for many of the books remained separate concerns. In 1914, as World War I broke out in Europe, Hill moved his company into an air-conditioned building in New York City, one specially constructed to house his publications and their printing facilities. By 1910 the McGraw-Hill Book

Company had established itself with its first publication, *The Art of Engineering*, and its first series, Electrical Engineering Texts. This series marked the beginning of a company trend toward publishing series of books by multiple authors covering an entire range of knowledge in a specific field.

A New Era, 1916–28

A more complete merger of the McGraw and Hill interests came in 1916 when John A. Hill died at the age of 57. Arthur Baldwin, Hill's attorney, led Hill Publishing for a brief time following Hill's death. McGraw became president of the book company; the two established the McGraw-Hill Publishing Company in 1917, with its offices located in the Hill Building, publishing *Electrical World, Electric Railway Journal, Electrical Merchandising, Engineering Record, Metallurgical and Chemical Engineering, The Contractor, American Machinist, Power, Engineering and Mining Journal, Coal Age,* and *Engineering News*. This concentration of interests, along with the enlargement of the book company, now a subsidiary of McGraw-Hill Publishing, made McGraw-Hill the largest technical publisher in the world at that time.

The U.S. entered World War I in 1917, and this was a particularly good time for technical publishers including McGraw-Hill. The first title to benefit from increased wartime demand was the *American Machinists' Handbook*, originally published before the war. There was also increased demand for engineering books in radio communication, aviation, construction and maintenance, chemical warfare, trench construction, automotive transportation, aerial photography, and antisubmarine tactics. McGraw-Hill responded quickly to this market; an example was its record response to the U.S. Army Educational Commission's order for 150,000 technical books, which were printed, bound, specially packed, and shipped to France in a matter of days.

After World War I, McGraw-Hill expanded rapidly. With Foss in charge of editorial and sales activities and Caldwell heading up finances and production, the book company had grown by establishing close contacts with the faculties of various universities and engineering schools, not only to make sales, but also to find new authors. With the addition of a series designed for educational use, McGraw-Hill formed a college department in 1927, thus establishing a lasting emphasis on textbooks. Foss was equally innovative in finding new ways to market the technical books that seldom found space in general bookstores. By both advertising at cost in the parent firm's magazines and sending letters and circulars to subscribers, Foss offered interested parties a chance to examine a book for 10 days without payment, an approach that quickly resulted in increased book sales.

During the 1920s James McGraw began to shift some of his authority in the company to other people. The first shift came when he named himself, his son James McGraw Jr., and Malcolm Muir to a governing board of trustees. Then in 1925, McGraw turned over the presidency of the book company to Edward Caldwell, who was succeeded by Martin M. Foss the next year. In 1928 Malcolm Muir became president of the publishing company; James McGraw remained chairman of the board.

With the purchase of the A.W. Shaw Company of Chicago in 1928, McGraw-Hill extended its reach into the field of business books and magazines. The editorial staff turned one of Shaw's monthlies, the *Magazine of Business*, into a weekly, covering and interpreting news of specific interest to business people. Now named *Business Week*, it has become the best known of all McGraw-Hill publications.

New Ventures, 1929–45

Just after the stock market crash of 1929, *The Business Week* (as it was then known) predicted, in its November 2, 1929 issue, that "Business will gradually and steadily recover as businessmen regain their perspective and go back to work." Following this optimistic line of thought McGraw-Hill established four new magazines in 1930, opened a West Coast office and book depository in San Francisco, and under the imprint of Whittlesey House, named after James McGraw's father-in-law, entered the trade book field for the first time. The first title under the new imprint, selected to distinguish this division from trade publications, was Ernest Minor Patterson's *The World's Economic Dilemma*.

McGraw-Hill commissioned a new office building designed by Raymond Hood and located on West 42nd Street in New York City. Nicknamed "Big Green" because of the blue-green cast of its Art Deco exterior, the new McGraw-Hill building aroused controversy because of the horizontal banding of its windows, now a standard feature of many modern office buildings. When first occupied in 1931, Big Green included a complete production plant taking up four floors. The increasing severity of the economic depression during the early 1930s, however, forced McGraw-Hill not only to make deep cuts in personnel and salaries but to sell its press machinery and equipment in 1933. In 1932, the parent company's deficit ran to $239,137.

That same year Whittlesey House had its first bestseller, *Life Begins at Forty*, by Walter B. Pitkin. The company's other publications made themselves useful sources of information for business people by providing hard facts and analysis of the economic situation. The vocational-education department of the book company helped those seeking new skills. Established in 1930, it concentrated on mechanical arts, agriculture, and home economics. The 1930s also saw major shifts at the executive level of McGraw-Hill; in 1935 James H. McGraw handed the chairmanship over to James McGraw Jr. During the next two years Malcolm Muir failed to get along with the McGraw family; in 1937 he left to run *Newsweek*, and James H. McGraw Jr. became both president and chairman of the board. By 1937 the company had an annual profit of more than $1 million.

With the coming of World War II in the 1940s McGraw-Hill was in an advantageous position. Because its technical publications were especially important to the war effort, its paper requirements received special priority. The company's magazines began to cover a range of relevant wartime topics from accelerated training in the use of metalworking power tools to dehydrated foods. In addition the company began to publish special wartime titles, such as *En Guardia*, a Spanish-language paper promoting Latin American relations; and *Overseas Digest*, excerpting articles from other McGraw-Hill titles for distribution to military personnel posted abroad.

It was in the area of special training manuals, however, that McGraw-Hill was to make a special effort. As untrained men and women poured into industry and the armed services, accelerated technical training became increasingly important to the war effort. By 1943 the book company had published 231 titles for the Engineering and Science Management War Training Program. Of the 304 books published by 1944 to further the war effort, many dealt with radio and electronics, a newly important part of warfare. One title, *Mathematics for Electricians and Radiomen*, by Nelson M. Cooke, first published in 1942, continued to be successful after the war, and by 1964, under the new title of *Basic Mathematics for Electronics*, had total sales in excess of 485,000 copies.

Although McGraw-Hill had been present in the United Kingdom and Germany as well as other countries since before World War I, the company made use of the opportunities World War II offered to increase its foreign activities. In 1943 the book company opened a book-export department, which by 1944 had a foreign-language translation office. The same year, McGraw-Hill acquired the Embassy Book Company Ltd. of Toronto, which was later renamed to the McGraw-Hill Company of Canada, Ltd. and then again to McGraw Ryerson. In 1945, to provide its magazines with international coverage, the company started the World News Service.

After World War II, 1946–59

After the war the book company prospered under the presidency of Curtis G. Benjamin, who succeeded James S. Thompson, president for only two years. Benjamin developed a text-film department, a venture inspired by the use of educational films during World War II to supplement textbook materials. As teachers discovered the value of motion pictures and film strips in the classroom, the market expanded, and by 1965 McGraw-Hill was the leader in the field. Another wartime dividend for the company was the 13-volume U.S. Navy Flight Preparation Training series printed for the Bureau of Aeronautics during the war.

With the growth of commercial aviation in the postwar period, McGraw-Hill found a large market for civilian editions of the series. Building on the close contacts with governmental agencies in research and development made during World War II, the company contracted to publish the Radiation Laboratory series, 27 volumes concentrating on the results of wartime research into radar. According to Charles A. Madison's 1966 *Book Publishing in America*, this series, published in 1949 and costing more than $1.2 million, "set a precedent for the commercial publication of government-financed projects." Although McGraw-Hill lost money on another project, the National Nuclear series, the company made an arrangement with the U.S. Atomic Energy Commission to produce an eight-volume compilation of scientific reference materials that was presented at the first International Conference on the Peaceful Uses of Atomic Energy at Geneva in August 1955.

Another project started in the late 1940s was the publication of James Boswell's manuscripts. Consisting of the voluminous collection of original manuscripts of the 18th-century Scottish author collected by Colonel Ralph H. Isham, the project was guided through negotiations with its purchaser, Yale University, by Edward Aswell, Whittlesey House's editor-in-chief since 1947. Publication of a projected 40 volumes began in 1950. It was not to be under the Whittlesey imprint, however, as Yale preferred to have the McGraw-Hill name on the books. Thus began the relegation of Whittlesey House to juvenile titles. Another milestone, this one commercial, proved to be the publication in 1950 of *Betty Crocker's Picture Cook Book*, which achieved sales of more than 235,000 copies in its first two years.

When its cofounder, James H. McGraw, died in 1948 at age 87, McGraw-Hill Publishing was well on its way to developing a departmentalized organizational structure. An independent technical-education department had been established in 1941, then a text-film department in 1945. The acquisition of the Gregg Publishing Company in 1949 transformed the company's business-education department into the Gregg division. In response to the need for training literature during the Korean War, beginning in 1950, the book company established a technical-writing division to produce specialized materials for both government and industry. The next year, following a reorganization of the handbook, technical, and professional publishing department, the industrial- and business-book department was born, and the medical publishing department was formed in 1945. It was not until 1954, when it acquired Blakiston Company from Doubleday, which specialized in medical titles, that McGraw-Hill began to have a major share of the medical market under the newly named Blakiston division.

What proved by far to be the most important division for company progress in the postwar period was the international division, established in 1946. In less than 15 years, book exports trebled, with a profitable business in text-films, filmstrips, and the sale of foreign-language rights. A major force in the international growth of the company was Curtis Benjamin, who proceeded along lines mapped out by James Thompson. Benjamin succeeded, along with B. G. Dandison, head of the international division, in making the company successful in foreign countries; in 1962 McGraw-Hill was presented by President John F. Kennedy with a presidential E-for-Export award, making McGraw-Hill the first commercial publishing firm to be so honored.

During the 1950s, James McGraw Jr., who had headed up the company since 1935, was replaced by another son of the first

McGraw, Curtis. He was followed by Donald C. McGraw, yet another son.

Just before the death of Curtis, the company purchased the National Petroleum Publishing Company, the W.C. Platt Company, and Platt's Price Service, Inc., all from Warren C. Platt. The book company then began three major encyclopedia projects in the late 1950s, each continuing on into the 1960s: *The McGraw-Hill Encyclopedia of Science and Technology*, *The Encyclopedia of World Art*, and the *New Catholic Encyclopedia*. When in 1959 the publishing company commemorated its 50th year, revenues exceeded $100 million.

Growth and Diversification, 1960–79

While Curtis Benjamin remained chairman of the board and CEO of the book company, Edward Booher, who had joined the company in 1936, became president in 1960. They doubled overall sales within five years, contributing 39 percent of the total income of the parent company in 1965. The F.W. Dodge Corporation, information provider to the construction industry, was purchased in 1961. The following year the general book division was formed by merging the industrial-and-business-book department with the trade department. The purchase of Webster Publishing Company in 1963 marked the company's entry into the elementary school and high school textbook markets.

In 1964 the book company and the F.W. Dodge Corporation merged with McGraw-Hill Publishing Company to form McGraw-Hill, Inc. The reorganization created a single corporation, the parent company, with three operating divisions: book publishing, the Dodge complex, and magazines and news services. The company established an Australian publishing unit the same year. With the acquisition of the California Test Bureau in 1965, McGraw-Hill strengthened its educational services. The company moved into two new fields in '66: one was legal publishing with the purchase of Shepard's Citations, Inc.; the other was financial information services through the acquisition of Standard & Poor's Corporation. Other acquisitions were Schaum Publishing Company, Capitol Radio Engineering Institute, and *Postgraduate Medicine* magazine, all in 1967. The company also expanded into Mexico in '67 and into Japan in 1969.

A key figure in this expansion was Shelton Fisher. Beginning as promotion manager for *Business Week* in 1940, by 1968 Fisher had succeeded Donald McGraw as president and CEO of McGraw-Hill. His goal was to change the perception of McGraw-Hill as an old-fashioned publisher of trade magazines into that of a dynamic media giant. Fisher further extended the company's reach into Canada, Brazil, and India, bought four televisions stations from Time Inc., and moved the company out of Big Green and into its present, new 50-story international headquarters in 1972. While increasing the company's prestige, the large capital outlay came at a time when a recession caused a loss in revenues for the McGraw-Hill magazines. After a period of uncertainty during which the McGraw family worked out a succession, Harold McGraw Jr. became president of the parent company and Fisher assumed the chairmanship. This changed within a year when Fisher retired and Harold McGraw Jr. became chairman in addition to his other positions.

The picture of McGraw-Hill, Inc. at the end of the 1970s, according to John Tebbel's *History of Book Publishing in America*, was of "an extremely healthy, well-managed conglomerate, composed of several operating divisions." Along with the book and publications companies, there was the information system company, composed of the F.W. Dodge division, Sweet's division, and Datapro Research Corporation. Two other divisions were Standard & Poor's Corporation and the McGraw-Hill Broadcasting Company. In 1978 total operating revenues amounted to more than $761 million.

Its very success made McGraw-Hill the target of a takeover attempt by the American Express Company in 1979. The chairman of American Express, James D. Robinson III, and its president, Roger H. Morley, were shocked by the ferocity with which Harold McGraw fought the attempted stock buyout. Concerted action by the McGraw family, along with various legal actions, defeated the bid for ownership. Although American Express had failed, McGraw-Hill remained a prime target for a takeover. Harold McGraw was planning to retire in four years and while another generation of McGraws waited in the wings, none were as yet ready to run the corporation. By appointing Joseph L. Dionne, who had been in charge of planning, to the newly created position of vice president of operations, McGraw sought to improve management organization and put someone in charge who could generate the fast growth needed to discourage further takeover attempts.

Dawn of the Electronic Age, 1980–90

Dionne became president and CEO in 1983, while McGraw remained chairman. Although still committed to print publishing, Dionne planned to reduce the 80 percent of the business that was print-oriented in 1983 to 65 percent or 70 percent over several years. One part of this goal had been achieved years earlier when the company acquired Data Resources, Inc., which held a vast share of the world's business and economic data. As McGraw-Hill moved into the electronic information marketplace, much of the information supplied by the news service, magazines, Standard & Poor's, Dodge, Platt, and Shepard's was made available in computerized form and in various configurations.

Another move was to enter the computer publishing field by acquiring *BYTE, Unixworld*, and *LAN Times* magazines, as well as Osborne Books, all of which provided support information to computer users. Another part of Dionne's plan for revitalizing the company was shifting from media-based planning to market-focused business units; 20 such units were created in 1985. Although harboring some reservations, Harold McGraw approved of the direction in which Dionne was taking the company; in 1988 he became chairman emeritus and Dionne added the title of chairman to those of president and CEO. In its attempt to weather the communications revolution, McGraw-Hill had undergone three major reorganizations in four years, resulting in an organization centered around 14 market-focus groups. These reorganizations, the automation of F.W. Dodge, and the shutdown of the general-book division, ending the company's involvement in the trade book market, caused a layoff of more then 1,000 workers.

The company expanded globally and had success with the Standard & Poor's Marketscope, and with other online, real-time services. Early in 1990, however, two online services, McGraw-Hill News and Standard & Poor's News, were discontinued. Some acquisitions resulted in costly writeoffs, notably Numerax Inc., an electronic data and services operation. Yet McGraw Hill continued to invest in strong growth markets and divest itself of publications and units connecting it with its past. *American Machinist & Automated Manufacturing, Coal Age,* and *Engineering & Mining Journal* were sold in 1987. To master the new information superhighway meant a continuation of the acquisition strategies, mergers, and innovations that marked the company's birth.

In 1988 McGraw-Hill celebrated its centennial, acquired Random House's college division for over $200 million; and created the Harold W. McGraw Jr. Prize in Education to honor the chairman emeritus's efforts on behalf of education and literacy. Operating revenues for the year were just shy of $1.7 billion. The next year, 1989, McGraw-Hill entered into a 50–50 joint venture with Macmillan combining the elementary, secondary, and vocational education businesses of both companies. In 1990 a new electronic textbook publishing system was implemented, allowing teachers to custom design textbooks with the results printed, bound, and shipped within 48 hours.

Keeping the World Up to Speed, 1991 and Beyond

The early 1990s found McGraw-Hill growing steadily in its quest to provide information in a wide range of formats for persons of all ages. In 1993 the company bought out Macmillan's half of the Macmillan/McGraw-Hill School Publishing Company for $160.8 million and by the following year, McGraw-Hill's three business segments—Educational and Professional Publishing, Financial Services, and Information and Media Services—helped the company rake in almost $2.8 billion in revenue, a sizeable leap from the previous year's $2.2 billion. The Educational/Professional unit accounted for the most revenue (42 percent) while Financial Services dominated income with over 48 percent (despite the worst bond market since 1927 and rising interest rates).

For McGraw-Hill, Inc., 1995 proved a pivotal year, a year in which the company ceased to exist—at least in its current form. To reflect its ongoing diversity, the company changed its name from McGraw-Hill, Inc. to The McGraw Hill Companies, Inc. followed by a broadcast media campaign showcasing how the company was "keeping the world up to speed." Other milestones for 1995 were an all-time high stock price and two-for-one stock split; additional ratings services and new alliances for Standard & Poor's; a myriad of new CD-ROM products including *Harrison's Principals of Internal Medicine* (the world's best-selling medical textbook); a joint venture between the company's secondary school publisher, Glencoe/McGraw-Hill, *National Geographic,* and Capital Cities/ABC; the acquisition of UCB Canada and *Hospital Practice;* and new offices in Asia, Europe, and the Middle East.

McGraw-Hill's most famous periodical, *Business Week,* experienced a phenomenal year in 1995 with exceptional circulation (one million-plus with a readership of nearly seven million) and pumped up advertising volume and revenue. Additionally, *Business Week Online* gained in popularity and *Business Week Enterprise,* a magazine for small-business executives, pub-

lished international editions in Asia, Europe, Latin America, and the Middle East. With so many new opportunities swirling about, McGraw-Hill, inevitably, let others go: Shepard's publishing operations and SRA Technology were sold, while *Open Computing* ceased publication. And despite a disastrous showing in Mexico after the peso's collapse, McGraw-Hill still managed to increase overall earnings by nearly 12 percent to $227.1 million and revenue topped $2.9 billion, a 6.3 percent increase over 1994's stellar performance.

In 1996 McGraw-Hill continued to expand its operations globally, with several high profile acquisitions, including Open Court Publishing Company for its K-8 elementary education division; *Healthcare Informatics* and *InfoCare* magazines from Wiesner Publishing for its Healthcare Information unit; and the Times Mirror Higher Education Group, which prompted the formation of the Higher Education and Consumer Group to house it and McGraw-Hill's well established college division. Next came another name change, as the Financial Information Services unit was renamed to reflect its most important asset, Standard & Poor's, to Standard & Poor's Financial Information Services. For the first nine months of 1996, McGraw-Hill was looking good as net income grew by 8.8 percent and overall revenue increased by 2.7 percent to $2.2 billion, making it an easy assumption that the conglomerate would top $3 billion by year's end.

As the world's largest educational publisher in addition to its financial, business, governmental and professional services, the McGraw-Hill Companies' reach is far and vast. Its informational media services, second to none in many disciplines, touches millions every hour and has truly accomplished what the company envisioned as "keeping the world up to speed."

Principal Subsidiaries

CM Research Inc.; Calificadora de Valores, S.A. de C.V.; Capitol Radio Engineering Institute, Inc.; Columbia Administration Software Publishing Corporation; Computer and Communications Information Group, Inc.; DRI Europe, Inc.; DRI/McGraw-Hill; Editora McGraw-hill de Portugal, Ltda.; Editorial Interamericana, S.A.; Editoriales Pedagogicals Associadas, S.A.; International Advertising/McGraw-Hill Inc.; J.J. Kenney Company, Inc.; Liberty Brokerage Investment Corp.; MHFSCO, Ltd.; MMS International; McGraw-Hill Broadcasting Company, Inc.; McGraw-Hill Capital Corporation; McGraw-Hill Capital, Inc.; McGraw-Hill Data Services-Ireland, Ltd.; McGraw-Hill Financial Publications, Inc.; McGraw-Hill Holdings (U.K.) Limited; McGraw-Hill Information Systems Company of Canada Limited; McGraw-Hill Interamericana, Inc.; McGraw-Hill/Interamericana de Chile Limitada; McGraw-Hill/Interamericana de Espana, S.A.; McGraw-Hill/Interamericana de Mexico, S.A. de C.V.; McGraw-Hill/Interamericana de Venezuela S.A.; McGraw-Hill/Interamericana, S.A.; Inc.; McGraw-Hill International Enterprises, Inc.; McGraw-Hill Libri Italia; McGraw-Hill News Bureaus, Inc.; McGraw-Hill Publications Overseas, Inc.; McGraw-Hill Ryerson Limited; Medical China Publishing Limited; Money Market Directories, Inc.; Nueva Editorial Interamericana, S.A. de C.V.; Rock/McGraw, Inc.; Standard & Poor's Compustat; S&P's ComStock; Standard & Poor's-ADEF; Standard & Poor's Consumer Investor Network; Standard & Poor's Equity Investor Services; Standard & Poor's

Index Services; Standard & Poor's International Ratings, Inc.; Standard & Poor's International, S.A.; Standard & Poor's Investment Advisory Services, Inc.; Standard & Poor's Ltd.; Standard & Poor's-Nordisk Rating AB; Standard & Poor's Securities, Inc.; Tata McGraw-Hill Publishing Company Private Limited; Tower Group International, Inc.

Principal Operating Units

Educational and Professional Publishing (Higher Education and Consumer Group, Legal Information Group, Professional Publishing Group, School Publishing Group, McGraw-Hill Software); Standard & Poor's Financial Information Services (Corporate, Institutional, International, Municipal, and Retail Sectors); Information and Media Services (Broadcasting Group, *Business Week* Group, Construction Information Group, Publication Services Group, Tower Group International).

Further Reading

Burlingame, Roger, *Endless Frontiers: The Story of McGraw-Hill,* New York, McGraw-Hill, 1959.

Holt, Donald D., "The Unlikely Hero of McGraw-Hill," *Fortune,* May 21, 1979.

Imprint on an Era: The Story of the McGraw-Hill Book Company, New York: McGraw-Hill, [n.d.].

Madison, Charles A., *Book Publishing in America,* New York, McGraw-Hill, 1966.

Milliot, Jim, "New Media Helps Spur Sales at McGraw-Hill Cos.," *Publishers Weekly,* April 15, 1996, p. 20.

Tebbel, John, *A History of Book Publishing in the United States,* 4 vols., New York: R.R. Bowker Company, 1972–1981.

Waters, Richard, "McGraw Hill Margins Improve," *Financial Times,* February 3, 1995, p. 22.

—Wilson B. Lindauer
—updated by Taryn Benbow-Pfalzgraf

Merrill Corporation

1 Merrill Circle
St. Paul, Minnesota 55108
U.S.A.
(612) 646-4501
Fax: (612) 649-1348
Web Site: www.merrillcorp.com

Public Company
Incorporated: 1968 as K. F. Merrill Corporation
Employees: 2,253
Sales: $245.31 million (1996)
Stock Exchanges: NASDAQ
SICs: 2791 Typesetting; 2752 Commercial Printing
Lithographic; 2741 Miscellaneous Publishing

Merrill Corporation delivers diverse document management services to the worldwide financial, legal, and corporate communities. Merrill, based in St. Paul, Minnesota, is the number three financial printer in the world, behind industry mainstay Bowne & Co. and printing powerhouse R. R. Donnelly. While financial printing remains a core market, and top revenue producer, for the company, Merrill has steadily reduced its reliance on that volatile market. In 1996 financial printing provided slightly more than 36 percent of the company's revenues, corporate printing nearly 30 percent, commercial clients 21.5 percent, and document management services nearly 13 percent.

Merrill's services include typesetting, printing, reproduction, electronic filing, custom communications design, and publishing. The company prints prospectuses and other timely, transaction-based and compliance documents for the worldwide financial community. Mutual funds and other investment vehicles are another important source of company revenue. The company's Merrill/May subsidiary is a leading provider of customized marketing, corporate identity, and franchise products. Document management services include document reproduction, litigation support, imaging, scanning, storage and retrieval, electronic SEC filing, and other document reproduction

services. Merrill has been at the technological forefront of the printing industry, using high-speed telephone-based data transmission to serve its clients through an innovative "hub and spoke" system, with typesetting and other services centralized at its St. Paul headquarters, and sales and service centers operating in 22 North American cities. The company also operates five regional printing facilities, which handle approximately half of the company's printing needs. The remainder is contracted out to a network of printer "partners." Most of Merrill's revenues are domestic; however, Merrill has achieved a significant international presence through a series of joint ventures in Europe, Asia, and South America, principally with Burrups Ltd. of the United Kingdom. Merrill founder Kenneth F. Merrill retired as chairman in 1996. John W. Castro, principal architect of Merrill's growth, continues to lead the company as president and CEO.

Founded in 1968

Merrill and his wife, Lorraine, started their typesetting business in their home in St. Paul in 1968. Called K. F. Merrill, the company soon began serving the financial printing needs of the Twin Cities market. For most of the next decade, Merrill acted as the company's sole salesman, while also assisting in all phases of the business, from proofreading to delivering the final product. By the end of the 1970s, the company had grown to regional status and dominance of the St. Paul/Minneapolis market—without owning a single printing press. Toward the end of the decade, the company had about $1 million in sales and some 30 employees. Yet years of working 18-hour days had begun to take its toll on Merrill, by then in his 60s. After three heart attacks, he began looking for someone to take over the day-to-day operations of the company.

Merrill chose Chicago native John W. Castro, who joined the company in 1978 as production manager. Only 29 years old at the time, Castro's printing experience already stretched back to the mid-1960s. After graduating from high school, Castro had taken a construction job in order to earn money for college. Laid off from that job after six months, Castro took a friend's advice and applied for a pressman's job in a local manufacturer's print shop. There he developed a keen interest in graphic arts and printing, and particularly the newly developing application of electronics technology to the still-traditional printing industry. While working full time at the print shop, Castro managed to complete three years of college at Chicago's DePaul University. An offer of a job with a Chicago printing company, however, convinced Castro to leave college without a degree. The printing company placed Castro at the forefront of the still-nascent computerized typesetting applications. As Castro's expertise grew, he began consulting for other printing companies looking to use the new technology, and in this role he met Kenneth Merrill.

Merrill offered Castro the job as Merrill's production manager. But, as Castro told *Minnesota Ventures,* Merrill "was really looking for a partner. And the thing I always thank him for is that he gave me a lot of immediate authority in the business, from day one." Castro, with Merrill's encouragement, worked to transform the company, which, despite sales of more than $1 million, was struggling to break even. And the company, although dominant in its market, was faced with a new challenge. By the late 1970s, the financial printing industry's larger firms were beginning to expand nationally. Competitors such as industry leader Bowne & Co. were establishing printing operations in the Twin Cities area, responding to a similar expansion by their mainstay law firm and underwriter clients. Merrill, which relied on a single client for some 30 percent of its sales, soon faced a choice: to expand the company nationally or sell it to a competitor.

Named president of the company in 1981, Castro and a team of top executives weighed their options. They decided to build Merrill into a national printing operation, with an eye on breaking into the New York market, the heart of the financial printing business. "[W]e started to figure out where to grow this business," Castro told *Minnesota Ventures,* "We didn't have cash so we had to figure out a way to grow it that was different and less expensive than our competitors did it." What Castro came up with was a "hub-and-spoke" system based on that being deployed by the airline industry. Rather than imitate its competitors, which typically moved into a new market by establishing complete printing operations, Castro turned to his background in computerized typesetting and the developing technology in telephone data transmission.

Castro's approach would tackle two significant problems. Establishing printing operations in other regions required a great deal of capital. Printing, however, tended to be a volatile business, with demand for services following a peak and valley activity cycle. Building its own printing facilities would require

Merrill not only to raise more cash than it had, but also to be able to absorb the costs of operating during low demand periods, while being able to supply clients during times of high demand. Castro determined that the company would avoid owning its own printing presses, a policy the company followed through much of the 1980s. Instead, Merrill's typesetting and related operations were centralized at its St. Paul headquarters.

Expansion was driven by setting up far less capital-intensive sales and service centers in target markets. Customer orders were taken by a sales office, beginning in Chicago, and the project would be sent to the St. Paul headquarters using a dedicated analog phone line capable of transmissions of about 48 characters per minute. The finished product would be transmitted back to Chicago, where it was brought to a printer "partner," one of several local printing firms contracted to complete Merrill's orders. Successful expansion of the company, however, depended on overcoming still another obstacle. The financial printing industry remained somewhat of an "old boys club," with relationships between printers and clients stretching back decades or more. Bowne & Co., for example, had been in operation since 1775. Castro overcame this obstacle by aggressively recruiting the top salespeople in each market, paying top salaries and relying on their ties with clients to bring Merrill business. In this way Merrill essentially bought into the 'buddy' system of the financial printing market.

Rising to the Top in the 1980s

Castro established Merrill as a lean, price-competitive organization, plowing earnings into enhancing its technology—particularly its data transmission capacity—instead of building printing presses. In contrast, its competitors were saddled with heavily unionized, capital intensive printing operations. Yet, as Castro pointed out to *Inc.,* "The term 'financial printing' is kind of a misnomer. Three-quarters of the work performed is typesetting, not printing. How can others possibly keep up with us?" Printing often represented the largest cost associated with an initial public offering or merger agreement. Unburdened by the need for large cash outlays, Merrill was able to provide its services at lower cost. The company quickly moved to enter the crucial New York market, which accounted for nearly 40 percent of the industry's $630 million in yearly sales, facing some initial resistance. "They used to laugh at us," Castro, who was named CEO in 1984, told *Minneapolis-St. Paul CityBusiness.* "Here's a company in Minnesota trying to compete with Wall Street and the deal doers."

Merrill caught the wave of the bull market of the 1980s, capturing clients among that period's flood of mergers, acquisitions, hostile takeovers, and initial public offerings. Sales grew quickly, reaching $8.3 million in 1983, and climbing to $25 million by 1985, as the company established sales offices in seven major markets. Much of its success lay in its use of technology, while its competitors struggled to convert their typesetting operations, hampered by union contracts requiring retraining of their employees. Merrill's employee base, which grew to 400 by the mid-1980s, remained non-union, while the company's employee-friendly policies kept them loyal to Merrill. By 1986 Merrill was printing a new prospectus—its own, as it went public, offering 1.7 million shares. The company was also moving to hedge its operations against a downturn in the financial market, expanding its commercial printing operations. Early in 1987, the company added advertising typography capacity to its Chicago office, and acquired Financial Publishers, a company that produced newsletters for banks. Sales continued to rise, to $38.5 million and net income of $1.6 million in 1986, and to just under $50 million, with earnings of nearly $3 million the following year. In less than a decade, Merrill had risen to become the industry's sixth-largest financial printer.

1987: Profiting from 'Black Monday'

The so-called 'Black Monday' stock market crash of October 1987 claimed the financial printing industry as one of its additional victims. Almost overnight financial printing sales, which had grown to an estimated $800 million per year, shriveled to around $600 million. Merrill's stock slid from $14 per share to $4.25 per share, prompting the company to buy back a large chunk of its shares the following year. But Merrill, which still had about $9 million in cash from its IPO, was in better shape than its industry rivals. Within three years, three of its chief competitors-Sorg, Charles P. Young, and Pandick, Inc.—ranked fifth, fourth, and second, respectively—would declare bankruptcy and go out of business entirely.

Merrill, too, was hit hard by the collapse of the financial printing market. But it had successfully expanded its corporate printing services, including products such as 10-Ks, 10-Qs, and annual reports, to account for about 60 percent of revenues by the end of the decade. The company's revenues grew, to $55 million in 1988 and to $63 million in 1989, returning profits of $4.5 million and $3.8 million, respectively. Then Merrill was forced to take a temporary earnings hit, after writing off stock it had purchased in rival Sorg when that company declared bankruptcy. Nonetheless, the company continued to expand, opening new sales offices, including one in Atlanta, and purchasing for around $3 million the Chicago, Los Angeles, and San Francisco offices of then-struggling Charles P. Young. That purchase also included printing presses in Chicago and Los Angeles, marking Merrill's first company-owned presses. The cost of the acquisition, coupled with the writeoff of the Sorg stock, however, produced the company's first loss in ten years, of nearly $1.25 million on revenues of $69 million.

Growth During the 1990s

In the aftermath of the stock market crash, the printing industry quickly began to consolidate. When Pandick declared bankruptcy in 1990, Merrill negotiated an agreement to take over Pandick's Dallas printing facilities, allowing Merrill to expand its capacity at virtually no cost. The collapse of its competitors, as Castro told Corporate Report Minnesota, was "the easiest way to go from No. 6 in the market to No. 3." By then, however, Castro had skillfully led the company into diversifying its services, expanding its commercial printing capacity while adding new services such as reproduction and custom design. In this way, Merrill was well positioned for the next blow to the barely recovering financial printing industry. The recession of 1990 and the outbreak of the Gulf War combined to put a near halt on the transactions upon which financial printers depended.

Merrill acquired two small printing companies, Southeastern Financial Printing Corp. of Atlanta, and Group Web, Inc., of St. Paul, in February 1990. The Group Web acquisition also included printing and binding equipment. By then, Merrill was handling approximately 25 percent of its own printing needs. Merrill was also moving into a new direction, legal publishing, through its Merrill/Magnus Publishing Corp. subsidiary, hoping to build on its knowledge of the legal community. Meanwhile, the company continued to expand its business by making acquisitions. In July 1990, Merrill acquired Sorg's former Illinois operation, S Printing Co., adding still more printing equipment to the company's in-house capacity. In that same month, the company also purchased Group Printing California, based in Los Angeles. These acquisitions, and Merrill's expanding share of the financial and corporate printing markets, which was reaching 14 percent, helped propel the company's sales past the $100 million mark for its 1991 fiscal year.

Another factor in Merrill's favor was the printing industry's practice of awarding contracts on a bid basis, generally from among three competing bids. With three of its principal competitors out of business, Merrill found itself receiving a greater number of invitations to bid on contracts. And the end of the recession meant also that there were many more contracts upon which to bid. Financial printing once again began to supply a primary source of Merrill's revenues, soon accounting for more than a third of annual sales, up from a low of 21 percent of revenues at the beginning of the decade.

The company steadily gained ground in the first half of the 1990s. Its growth was further aided by a joint venture agreement made in 1992 with London-based Burrups Ltd., the leading European financial printer. Another acquisition, of May Printing Company for $25 million in 1993, also boosted revenues and strengthened the company's commercial printing business, by then the fastest-growing segment of company sales. Merrill's sales neared $150 million in 1993, bringing a net profit of nearly $9 million; by 1994, sales rose to $182 million, for a net income of over $13 million. The following year, with sales growing to $237 million, Merrill was again preparing new acquisitions, and in 1996 the company paid $33 million for the purchase of assets of Corporate Printing Co. of New York, and an additional $7.4 million in cash and notes for FMC Resource Management Corp. based in Seattle. These purchases helped raise Merrill's revenues to nearly $250 million for its 1996 fiscal year. And with its combination of strategic insight, technological savvy, excellent service, and luck, Merrill seemed certain to grow further into its relatively new role as a printing industry powerhouse.

Principal Subsidiaries

Merrill/May; Merrill Burrups Worldwide (50%); Quebecor Merrill Canada Inc. (49%).

Further Reading

Berry, Kathleen M., "Merrill Grows Fast as a Survivor among Wall St. Printers," Investor's Business Daily, July 22, 1993, p. 36.
Biemesderfer, S. C., "Merrill Gets Streetwise," Corporate Report Minnesota, January 1992, p. 59.

Micros Systems, Inc.

12000 Baltimore Avenue
Beltsville, Maryland 20705-1291
U.S.A.
(301) 210-6000
Fax: (301) 490-7077
Web site: http://www.micros.com

Public Company
Incorporated: 1977 as Picos Manufacturing, Inc.
Employees: 653
Sales: $178 million (1996)
Stock Exchanges: NASDAQ
SICs: 3578 Calculating & Accounting Machines, Except
    Electronic Computers; 7372 Prepackaged Software

Micros Systems, Inc. is a leading worldwide designer, manufacturer, supplier, and servicer of point-of-sale (POS) computer systems for hospitality providers, principally full-service and fast-food restaurants, including restaurants located in hotels and other lodging establishments. In 1995 the company's POS systems were in more than 35,000 restaurants. Micros also was marketing and distributing property-management information systems (PMS) products, supplied by a German subsidiary, Fidelio Software GmbH, to hotels and other lodging establishments. These systems had been installed in more than 4,200 sites. Both companies also were producing the software for these systems. In 1996 Micros was one of 14 companies recognized by *Forbes* as among "the world's best small companies" for five consecutive years, each year ranking higher than the previous year.

The Start-Up Years, 1977–81

Micros Systems was founded by Louis Brown, Jr. The son and grandson of Maryland dairy farmers, he recalled sweltering on a summer day in his childhood and wishing he could be in the air-conditioned Westinghouse Electric Corp. building not far away. Brown attended Johns Hopkins University on a scholarship and earned an engineering degree. "I knew right out of college that three geeks in a basement with a silicon chip could create some very dangerous products," he told a *Forbes* interviewer in 1994. "I don't mind being a geek. It's easier than farming."

With $20,000 in savings Brown, then 26, started a company called IDEAS, Inc. to design computers for the government. He was acting as a consultant for MKD, an electronic cash-register company, when its vice-president, Bernie Silverman, suggested there was a future in making "smart" cash registers, that is, point-of-sale terminals. Brown founded PICOS Manufacturing in 1977 to produce these machines for restaurants; the company was renamed Micros Systems the following year. Located in Beltsville, Maryland, in the Washington-Baltimore corridor, Micros found it relatively easy to recruit the needed software engineers. Revenues rose from $1.4 million in fiscal 1978 (the year ended July 1, 1978) to $4.2 million in fiscal 1979 and $6.7 million in fiscal 1980. The company lost $88,000 and $109,000 in its first two years, respectively, but had net income of $142,000 in 1980.

Making Progress, 1981–85

Micros Systems made its initial public offering in February 1981, raising nearly $7 million. Information Development & Applications, Inc. (the successor to IDEAS) retained 35 percent of the stock. The company ended the fiscal year with a solid $9.1 million in sales and net income of $303,000. The following year, however, Micros's opening of district offices in five new metropolitan markets failed to pan out. Caught in a national recession, the company recorded an $868,000 loss on sales of $12.6 million and sustained a 78 percent increase in debt. Some $300,000 of the loss was due to a technical problem in the company's 400-series terminals. A $1.25-million loan from a Baltimore bank was placed in jeopardy as Micros's net worth fell below the stipulated $3.7 million.

Undiscouraged, the company's management, headed by Jeffrey Rice, introduced a series of POS and electronic cash-register products aimed at the lower end of the hospitality and food-service markets in 1982. This line combined two remote order-entry integral printers and an alpha numeric display made by a Japanese manufacturer with Micros's own software. For full-service restaurants, Micros offered a system providing daily food-cost percentages and inventory information, payroll processing, and the management of accounts-payable functions. For the fast-food industry, Micros was offering fully interactive terminals that processed customer orders and provided comprehensive information to management. In fiscal 1983 the company earned $470,000 on revenues of $15.3 million.

By the end of the calendar year Micros was supplying more than 2,000 front-desk accounting systems to lodging properties throughout the world, connecting a hotel's front desk with POS terminals in food and beverage areas and providing instant authentication and electronic transfer of charges to guests' bills. These systems also communicated with Micros call-accounting systems, which recorded and instantly entered a guest's telephone charges on the bill. In October 1983 the company introduced a Petroleum Management System, activated by credit card, for retail and convenience stores that also sold gasoline. Toward the close of the year it acquired ASTEC, Inc., a leading producer of microcomputer software specializing in back-office accounting programs tailored to the needs of the restaurant industry.

Major Food-Service Player, 1985–93

After eight years of administration by its founding engineers, Micros came under the management of Reay Sterling, Jr., an experienced corporate executive who was named president and chief executive officer in 1985. The following year the company introduced its 4700, the first system for food-service operations based on an industry-standard personal computer: IBM's landmark PC. POS terminals, keyboards, remote printers, video display units, and guest-check printers were configured to each customer's specifications. Sterling later called the Micros 4700 "the product that saved the company."

The bottom line did not immediately support this assessment, however. After net income passed $1 million for the first time in fiscal 1985, revenues plummeted, and Micros lost money in the next two fiscal years. A small profit was recorded in fiscal 1988, largely due to growing overseas sales, but company assets fell to a four-year low of $14.3 million. Nevertheless, Micros found a backer in Westinghouse Electric, which was on the lookout for small technology companies. It bought 19 percent of Micros's shares in 1986 for $2.8 million, shoring up the firm's credibility, and acquired another 2.3 million shares in 1988 from two major stockholders for $5.3 million, raising its stake to 58 percent. By this time Micros had installed more than 50,000 terminals in more than 40 countries.

During fiscal 1989 Micros Systems raised its revenues to $25.5 million and its net income to $1.3 million. It introduced the 2700 Hospitality Management System, a new terminal for use in table-service restaurants rather than fast-food outlets, opened a dealership in Germany in July 1989, and another in Great Britain in November 1989. Overseas sales now accounted for 25 percent of the total, up from eight percent in three years. Westinghouse raised its stake in the company to 66 percent in October 1989.

The figures were even sweeter in fiscal 1990: $2.6 million profit on revenues of $35.2 million: a return on equity of 27.6 percent. In January 1990 Micros added a lower-cost 1700 system for small restaurants. The company earned $3.3 million on revenue of $39.6 million in fiscal 1991, acquired a 15 percent interest in its French distributor, opened an office in Boston, and introduced a new touch-screen product. *Financial World* ranked it number one among the 500 fastest-growing publicly traded companies in the United States, based on growth in earnings per share over the past five years. During fiscal 1992 Micros introduced an advanced touch-screen system for the 2700 and a 2400 fast-food system, featuring a remote printer and video-screen subsystem accommodating a wide variety of kitchen-production and order-routing schemes. The company earned $4 million on revenue of $44.3 million. Overseas sales reached about one-third of the total, with operations in Europe, Asia, and Mexico.

The Micros machines were being designed for a hostile food-preparation environment, with no flat surfaces on which to sit a drink and few seams or openings, if any, in order to protect against potential disasters like a spilled soft drink. Software had dozens of features that could be turned on and off to meet a broad range of service and order requirements. The company's packages were designed to limit training time, since typical fast-food restaurant chains could experience an employee turnover rate of 200 to 300 percent a year. Most of Micros's orders were in the $20,000 range, with some large hotels running to $60,000. A high-quality system to a restaurant needing perhaps only one terminal and one kitchen printer could be delivered for about $5,000.

During 1993 Micros launched a new generation of software and equipment, including an 8700 system smaller, cheaper, and easier to use than the 4700 and a Manager Workstation for management analysis of sales and operational trends at fast-food restaurants. By the fall of 1994 it had an installed base of 4,000 terminals at 750 sites, with major clients including Circus Enterprises, Planet Hollywood, and MGM Grand Hotel's Las Vegas casino. It also introduced a new version of the 2700 and a hand-held terminal, integrated with the 4700, that waiters could use to send a diner's order via radio from the table to the kitchen. This device found application in many sports arenas as well as pool-side restaurants.

Reaching the Hotel and Casino Market, 1993–96

Revenues reached $55.3 million in fiscal 1993, with net income rising to $5.8 million. Sterling died suddenly in July 1993, and Brown, the chairman, temporarily assumed his duties as president and chief executive officer. Subsequently the post went to A. L. Giannopoulos, a Westinghouse executive who was a member of Micros's board of directors. Also in 1993,

Micros took a 15-percent stake in Fidelio Software GmbH of Munich, Germany, with an option to acquire all of the company by 2000. The share in this supplier of property-management systems (PMSs) and the world's leading developer of hotel computer information systems included majority interests in three subsidiaries responsible for the distribution and service of Fidelio products in the United States and Europe. A Micros manager said the acquisition provided "seamless integration"; when interfaced with a Fidelio system, the 8700 would be able to notify the front desk when a guest was dining, making it possible for the guest to receive messages or calls in the hotel's restaurant.

The Fidelio partnership also gave Micros some of the tools it needed to enter the lucrative gambling industry. At MGM Grand, it was offering, in addition to POS and PMS services, interfaces to liquor-dispensing systems, credit authorization and—most important—the casino-management system. In place of the tedious but vital chore of tracking complimentary items manually, the 8700 was capturing this data electronically and sending it via an interface through a chosen identification number to a tracking system, for verification with casino management and posting as such on a guest's folio at the hotel's front desk.

During 1995 Micros installed about 300 cash-register work stations in the restaurants, bars, and shops of MGM Grand and the Luxor Hotel in Las Vegas. Part of Micros's rapid revenue and profit growth in the second half of 1993 was attributed to sales of its touch-screen terminals to casinos.

Restaurateurs were grateful to Micros for enabling them to compare profit margins on every item on the menu, allowing them to decide which ones to promote and which to drop, and also to track the sale of every item and cross-check that record against the system's inventory-tracking system. "You must remember one thing," the operator of the "44" restaurant in New York City's fashionable Royalton Hotel told a *Forbes* reporter. "Every single person in your restaurant is trying to steal from you. These machines make that nearly impossible."

Micros had net income of $8.7 million on revenues of $79.3 million in fiscal 1994, both records. In fiscal 1995 these figures surged again, to $11.6 million and $112 million, respectively. In September 1995 Westinghouse sold its stake in Micros, which it had acquired for $11 million to $12 million, for $161.9 million. (Its stock, selling for $2.08 a share when Westinghouse acquired most of its holdings in 1988, reached an all-time high of $41.25 in December 1994.) Micros bought the remaining 70 percent of Fidelio, which had estimated revenues of $57 million in 1995, for about $28.8 million in December 1995.

Micros stock reached $50.75 a share before suddenly dropping to $25 on Monday, March 25, 1996, after the company announced that it "anticipated significantly lower earnings" in the third quarter of fiscal 1996, which was coming to a close. A broker said the firm had infuriated investors by making the announcement on the previous Friday evening. The company's stock was trading in the range of $30–$35 a share during the fall of 1996. Final figures for fiscal 1996 reported revenues of more than $178 million—a 59-percent gain over the previous year—but net income of $10.5 million, a nine-percent drop that the

company attributed to the acquisition of Fidelio and other key distribution channel locations it believed would have a favorable financial impact in the future. Long-term debt rose nearly $10 million, to $15.5 million.

In 1995 Micros was distributing the ProHost Table Service Management System, designed by Rock Systems Inc. ProHost, which interacted with the 8700 and 2700 systems, had a touch-screen terminal enabling the host or hostess to stay informed on the status of all tables. An optional page ranger allowed waiting customers to wander as far as two miles until the pager alerted them that their table was ready and allowed both guests and the kitchen staff to page servers.

In 1996 MasterCard International announced it had teamed with Micros to develop an integrated-systems solution enabling full-service restaurants to accept automated teller machine cards enhanced with Maestro, its global on-line POS debit program, for payment directly at the table. As a result, Micros was developing a driver within the 8700 system and planned to integrate the driver with the systems of other payment-industry hardware providers. Micros introduced, in May 1996, its new 3700 POS, which it said combined the most advanced POS capabilities for table-service restaurants with management tools like labor and inventory management and guest-services applications in one system.

Micros in the Mid-1990s

In mid-1995 Micros POS systems were in more than 32,000 full-service restaurants or operators of restaurants, including T.G.I. Friday's, Family Restaurants, Perkins, Planet Hollywood, Ruby Tuesday's, and Whitbread, and in full-service restaurants in hotel chains, such as Hilton, Hilton International, Hyatt, Inter-Continental, Marriott, Radisson, and Ritz-Carlton. Its more than 3,000 fast-food customers included Arby's, Burger King, and Woody's. The 600 Fidelio PMS systems had been installed in lodging establishments that included various Radisson Hotels, Red Roof Inns, and Wyndham Hotels and Resorts. Fidelio products were in more than 3,600 sites worldwide, including certain Ciuga, Fote, Hilton International, Inter-Continental, Movenpick, Peninsula, and Ramada Europe locations.

Micros also was offering service and support for its POS and PMS products, including installation, training, hardware and software maintenance, spare parts, media supplies, and consulting services. Service revenue accounted for about 23 percent of the company's total revenue in fiscal 1995.

Micros's chief base of operations was in Beltsville, Maryland, where it owned one building and leased two others. The company's administrative, manufacturing, sales, marketing, customer-service, and product-development facilities were all located here. Manufacturing at Beltsville consisted primarily of assembly and testing of various purchased components, parts, and subassemblies. The company was leasing nine domestic and seven foreign sales, service, and support offices: in Boston, Chicago, Dallas, Denver, Las Vegas, Los Angeles, Miami, Portland (Oregon), and San Francisco in the United States, and in Dusseldorf and Frankfurt, Germany; London; Madrid; Paris; Singapore; and Zurich, Switzerland.

Principal Subsidiaries

Fidelio France S.A. (France); Fidelio Software Corp.; Fidelio Software U.K. Limited; Micros of Delaware, Inc.; Micros Foreign Sales Corp. (Barbados); Micros of South Florida, Inc.; Micros Systems AG (Ltd.) (Switzerland); Micros Systems Deutschland GmbH (Germany); Micros Systems Hispania (Spain); Micros Systems Holdings GmbH (Germany); Micros Systems (U.K.) Ltd.; Micros Systems Services GmbH (Germany); MSI Delaware, Inc.

Principal Operating Units

Hotel Systems Business Group; Leisure & Entertainment Business Group; Quick Service Business Group; Table Service Business Group.

Further Reading

Hinden, Stan, "Electronic Registers Help Micros Systems Ring Up Profits," *Washington Post,* Washington Business section, December 21, 1992, p. 31.

——, "Westinghouse, Micros Systems Come Up Winners," *Washington Post,* Washington Business section, September 25, 1995, p. 29.

Knight, Jerry, "Micros Stock Drops Following Weak Earnings Forecast," *Washington Post,* March 26, 1996, pp. C1, C3.

Lewis, Kate Bohner, "Thou Better Not Steal," *Forbes,* September 7, 1994, pp. 216–17.

Marcial, Gene G., "Why This Tech Stock Didn't Tank," *Business Week,* January 15, 1996, p. 80.

Prakash, Snigdha, "Micros Takes Its Future in Hand with Smaller Systems," *Washington Post,* Washington Business section, April 5, 1993, p. 9.

Shaffer, Gail, "Ringing Up Increased Sales," *Warfield's,* October 2, 1991, p. 40.

Troy, Timothy N., "Acquisitions, Alliances Highlight IAHA HITEC Show," *Hotel & Motel Management,* July 26, 1993, p. 20.

——, "Flexibility a Key for Vendors Betting on Casinos," *Hotel & Motel Management,* September 19, 1994, p. 27.

——, "Servicing with Software," *Hotel & Motel Management,* September 20, 1993, pp. 28, 30.

Tyner, Joan, "Micros' Computerized Cash Registers Now Ringing Up Profits," *Washington Post,* Washington Business section, April 18, 1993, pp. 3, 28.

Young, Eleanor, "Micros Systems, Inc.," *Wall Street Transcript,* February 27, 1984, p. 72958.

—Robert Halasz

Minolta Co., Ltd.

3-13, Azuchi-machi 2-chome
Chuo-ku, Osaka 541
Japan
(06) 271-2251
Fax: (06) 266-1010
Web site: http://www.minolta.com

Public Company
Incorporated: 1937 as Chiyoda Kogaku Seiko Kabushiki Kaisha
Employees: 4,821
Sales: ¥365.75 billion (US$3.66 billion) (1996)
Stock Exchanges: Tokyo Osaka Nagoya Frankfurt Düsseldorf
SICs: 3651 Household Audio & Video Equipment; 3661 Telephone & Telegraph Apparatus; 3827 Optical Instruments & Lenses; 3861 Photographic Equipment & Supplies

Since Kazuo Tashima began using German technology to produce one camera a day in 1928, Minolta Co., Ltd. has gone on to become one of Japan's Big Five camera makers. Although Minolta initially did so by copying German technology, it then developed new products on its own, and marketed them successfully in Europe and the United States. As the market for camera equipment matured in Japan, Europe, and the United States, the firm diversified into a number of related areas. Minolta is a major producer of cameras, photocopiers and other imaging products, radiometric instruments, and planetariums, with production facilities in Japan, the United States, Germany, France, Malaysia, China, Hong Kong, and Brazil, and a worldwide marketing network.

Founded in 1928 to Build Cameras in Japan

Minolta began modestly in 1928 when 28-year-old Kazuo Tashima agreed to represent his father's import-export company, Tashima Shoten, on a government-backed trade mission to Paris to promote Japanese silk. In Paris Tashima toured a factory that specialized in high-grade optics, and decided he could produce similar equipment in Japan profitably. Japanese businessmen, including Tashima's father, opposed the idea of producing optical equipment domestically. Unable to start his new venture as a part of Tashima Shoten, Tashima borrowed money from his father's chief clerk and went into business on his own.

Tashima opened shop on November 11, 1928, calling his venture Nichi-Doku Shashinki Shoten (Japan-Germany Camera Company). The name reflected the company's reliance on German technology and expertise. Partners Willy Heilemann, an importer of German items in Kobe, and Billy Neumann, a German engineer with a background in optical instruments, brought state-of-the-art German technology to the new firm. By March 1929 the staff of about 30 was producing each day one bellows camera, called the Nifcalette—with imported lens and shutter. Within three months, production had grown to 100 cameras a month.

A year later the Great Depression hit Japan hard, bringing labor strife and strikes. Tashima later referred to his company as ''a small boat which set sail right into the storm.'' Nevertheless, Tashima promoted development of new camera models as the Depression intensified, and introduced several models in 1930 and 1931.

A new model introduced in 1933 first carried the Minolta brand name, which Tashima created. The name sounds like the Japanese word *minoru-ta*, which means ripening rice field. The term reminded Tashima of a proverb his mother frequently used, ''The ripest ears of rice bow their heads lowest,'' meaning that the more successful one becomes, the more humble one must be. The name, however, also has a Western meaning, as an acronym for Machinery and Instruments Optical by Tashima.

In 1934 the company began to sell the Minolta Vest, the product that made its reputation. Like other camera companies, Minolta used sheepskin to make a flexible camera bellows. When a shortage of imported sheepskin threatened production, the company developed the first rigid bellows of synthetic resin for the Minolta Vest. The innovation made the Vest easier to focus and less expensive. For the first time, a Minolta product was successful outside of Japan.

339

Company Perspectives:

Founded in 1928, Minolta Co., Ltd. is a leading manufacturer of photocopiers and other image information products, cameras and other optical products, radiometric instruments, and planetariums. As Minolta has steadily cultivated new technologies and extended its established strengths into related areas, its operations have become increasingly diverse. Recently, the Company has been emphasizing the expansion of business in equipment and systems for inputting, outputting, and processing image-related information.

The Vest's success made expansion possible. Tashima built new production facilities, including a factory devoted to lens production at Sakai. His emphasis on innovation led to the development of the first twin-lens reflex camera in Japan, the Minolta Flex, in 1937. That same year, Tashima reorganized and incorporated the company and renamed it Chiyoda Kogaku Seiko Kabushiki Kaisha (Chiyoda Optics and Fine Engineering Limited) to reflect its broader focus.

Produced Binoculars and Other Optical Products During World War II

In September 1940 Japan joined Germany and Italy in the Tripartite Pact, which divided Asia and Africa into spheres of influence. Japan's was to be Southeast Asia. As it became clear that war was ahead, Japanese military planners determined to develop precision optical equipment for range-finding, navigation, and bombing aids.

During World War II, when the U.S. military used electronics to track enemy ships and aircraft, the Japanese chose optics. Chiyoda Kogaku Seiko produced high-powered binoculars and other optical instruments with wartime uses. Demand was so high that it opened the Itami plant in 1942 solely to manufacture optical glass.

Japan ultimately was devastated by the war. One of the primary goals of the Allied occupation forces was the restoration of Japan's economy. That helped Tashima, who was just as determined to put Minolta back on its feet. Employees dug through the company's bombed-out factories to salvage parts. In 1946 the company produced Japan's first postwar camera, the Semi III.

Since the Japanese camera industry's major prewar competitors, the Germans, had been ruined during wartime bombing—while the Japanese developed their own optical industry—worldwide markets first opened to the Japanese in the postwar years. The Minolta Semi III was the first camera to be exported after the war, with a shipment of 170 cameras in 1947.

Also that year, Chiyoda Kogaku Seiko became the first company to produce coated lenses in Japan, and in 1948 it began to design and produce a camera to compete with the industry standard, the Leica 35 millimeter. Chiyoda Kogaku Seiko designed a new sand-cast body in which lenses could be changed, with a hinged back cover to make film loading easier.

The new Minolta 35 included a faster f2.8 lens and more-dependable flash photography.

Expanded Exports Starting in Mid-1950s

The company still had to contend with its poor image in overseas markets. Japan had copied German lens technology, and the made-in-Japan label still implied goods of inferior quality. Other Japanese camera firms changed that perception. Takeshi Mitarai of Canon—then known as Precision Optical—persuaded U.S. occupation forces to stock his cameras in military stores. U.S. servicemen stationed in the East took their cameras home, and Japanese-made cameras soon came to stand for high-quality lenses. That new reputation was reinforced industrywide when U.S. photographers assigned to the Korean War began to use Nikon cameras; they claimed that their Nikon lenses were superior to the Leicas they were accustomed to using. Chiyoda Kogaku Seiko began exporting to the United States in 1955 through an agreement with the American firm FR Corp. The company introduced another breakthrough, the achromatic double-coated lens, in 1956, giving the company entry into the European market beginning late in 1957.

In 1958 Chiyoda Kogaku Seiko put its optical experience to a new use by building its first planetarium. The timing was propitious—the Soviet Union had launched Sputnik I, the first earth-orbiting artificial satellite, the year before, sparking new interest in space.

Also in 1958, Chiyoda Kogaku Seiko introduced its first single-lens reflex (SLR) camera. The SLR allowed a photographer to see exactly what was being shot through the camera lens by using an angled mirror that reflected the image to the viewer. Previous cameras—called rangefinder cameras—used two lenses, one to take the photo and one for the photographer to look through. When interchangeable lenses came into use in the early 1950s, the rangefinder posed problems: the photographer saw the same image no matter what lens was used, instead of seeing what the camera would actually photograph. The difference between the two images could be substantial. By the mid-1950s the major Japanese camera companies were developing the more convenient SLRs, and Chiyoda Kogaku Seiko introduced its version, the SR-2, in 1958. Its major competitor was Nikon's SLR, also introduced in 1958, which was recognized as the best of the SLRs at the high end of the market.

Chiyoda Kogaku Seiko opened its first overseas subsidiary, Minolta Corporation, in New York City in 1959. The company chose to name the subsidiary Minolta because of the popularity of its Minolta brand name. Shortly thereafter, in mid-1962, Chiyoda Kogaku Seiko changed its own name to Minolta Camera Co., Ltd. In the 1960s the company continued improving its camera line. It introduced the Uniomat, with a programmed shutter, in 1960, which led to fully programmed autoexposure in the Hi-Matic. In 1962 John Glenn chose the Hi-Matic to take the first photos of earth from space. In 1966 Minolta introduced its longest-running camera line, the SR-T series, which was produced continuously until 1981. These cameras featured through-the-lens light metering, using a patented light compensator to improve exposure in backlit photos. These new products made Minolta more competitive in Europe, so Minolta opened a European subsidiary, Minolta Camera Handelsgesell-schaft, in Hamburg in 1965.

Diversification in the 1960s and 1970s

More importantly Minolta diversified. In 1960 the company entered the office copying market—an area that would prove as successful as cameras—when it produced the Copymaster. In 1962 it expanded into the data-retrieval field with the Minolta 401S microfilm reader-printer; and in 1965 the company opened its Mikawa plant, which produced the Minoltafax 41, the first copier that could reduce document size.

Minolta continued to develop its links with the U.S. space program, developing the Minolta Space Meter, a state-of-the-art technology for measuring exposures, for the first manned orbit of the moon, the 1968 Apollo 8 mission. The meter was used on nine more Apollo missions, including the mission that landed a man on the moon in 1969.

Minolta developed digital watches, video recorders, and pocket calculators in the 1970s, although not all the company's innovations were successful. In 1975 a Minolta-developed of-fice copier that used a complex, high-resolution technology was launched just as plain-paper copiers took over the industry. The company introduced a single-lens reflex camera using cartridge film in 1976, but despite a $2 million U.S. advertising campaign the product was unsuccessful.

Other camera developments were more successful. In 1977 Minolta produced one of the first ''smart'' cameras. Its XD Series cameras had the first system to override user aperture settings in poor lighting.

Minolta also advanced in other areas. The company entered the field of medical instruments in 1977 with the development of a fingertip pulse oximeter. Its MS-18 Planetarium, built in Tokyo, contained the first fully automated planetarium system, and its new photocopiers produced higher-quality images and included both enlarging and reducing capabilities. Those suc-cesses were particularly important because the camera market was saturated in Japan, Europe, and the United States.

Redefined Corporate Image in the 1980s

Minolta responded by redefining itself. It adopted a new logo in 1981 to reflect its broader purpose, and redefined its mission as processing light and images in all types of environ-ments.

In 1983 Tashima, who had run the company since he founded it, left active management. Tashima relinquished the presidency to his son, Hideo Tashima, and became chairman of the board, the position he held when he died in 1985.

In the 1980s Minolta made advances in office-automation products, including copiers and a new word processor, but new camera technology brought the company the most attention. In 1985 Minolta unveiled its Maxxum, a SLR 35-millimeter cam-era with an autofocusing system. The Maxxum became a suc-cessful competitor to the less-expensive non-SLR cameras, such as Canon's Snappy and AE-1. A U.S. advertising cam-paign costing over $15 million and technological advances that

made the Maxxum the European Camera of the Year for 1985 aided its success. The Maxxum challenged Canon's preemi-nence in the 35-millimeter market, but it was not long before Minolta's Japanese competitors struck back with autofocus cameras of their own. Canon improved on the Maxxum by building the focusing system into the lens itself instead of housing it in the camera body with a mechanical link to the lens, as Minolta had done. Canon's advance made focusing faster, but its camera was more expensive than the Maxxum.

Minolta entered the facsimile machine market with the intro-duction of several models in 1986. Meanwhile, the company's planetariums became more sophisticated, first in 1984 with the launch of the Infinium—the first single sphere model that used lens projection—then in 1989 with the introduction of the In-finium, the first planetarium with a swing-type structure. Also developed by Minolta during this period were the first binocu-lars to offer continuous autofocusing, launched in 1990.

Difficult Times in the Early 1990s

Minolta suffered through a prolonged downturn in the early 1990s, with a number of developments contributing to the malaise. First, the camera market had become even more com-petitive in the late 1980s with the introduction of the first 35mm disposable camera, the QuickSnap from Fuji Photo Film, in 1987 and the first super-compact camera, Konica's Big Mini, in 1989. More convenient and less expensive than the bulky, feature-packed cameras offered by Minolta, Canon, and the other major camera makers, the new smaller models quickly caught on—with Fuji seemingly coming out of nowhere to attain the top spot in cameras by 1992. During the same period, video cameras—or camcorders—became increasingly afford-able and further eroded the sales of the traditional cameras Minolta specialized in.

A second factor in Minolta's difficulties—although it affec-ted the company's financial results in only one year, 1992—was the lawsuit filed by Honeywell Inc. in 1987 against Minolta. Honeywell had won approval for several patents relating to autofocus technology, which it had intended to use in its own 35mm camera but eventually abandoned the effort in the mid-1970s. When autofocus SLR cameras gained great popu-larity in the mid-1980s, Honeywell prepared lawsuits against nearly all the major camera makers. Minolta eventually settled with Honeywell out of court in 1992, agreeing to pay ¥16.9 billion (U.S.$125.1 million) for infringing patent rights. After posting a net loss of ¥2 billion in 1991, Minolta lost ¥36.1 billion in 1992 thanks in part to the settlement.

The third factor in the overall decline was the prolonged Japanese recession of the early 1990s, which hurt domestic sales, and the appreciation of the yen, which hurt exports—about three-quarters of total sales in the early 1990s. Minolta's net sales declined for three straight years, starting in 1992. Although the company's losses narrowed each year, Minolta would not return to profitability until 1996. In the midst of these troubled years, in 1993 Hideo Tashima became chairman and Osamu Kanaya, who had served as president and COO of Minolta Corp., replaced Tashima as president.

Comeback Appeared Complete by 1996

To turn the company around, Tashima and Kanaya pursued three main objectives: moving production out of Japan to lessen the effects of the strong yen, developing a camera to compete in the compact category, and continuing to diversify the Minolta product line and derive a smaller percentage of revenues from cameras. The first objective of moving production overseas began to be implemented in 1992 with the establishment of Minolta Lorraine S.A., based in France. This facility was set up to make toner, lenses, and other components for imaging products; low-end copiers were then added to its assembly lines, with these products sold mostly in the European market. In 1994 production of plain-paper copiers and laser printers began in China through the Shilong Business Equipment Corporation subsidiary. That same year, Minolta entered into two joint ventures in China for the manufacture and sale of cameras and copiers.

In early 1995 Minolta successfully entered the compact camera category with the launch of the Riva Zoom 70W (known in Japan as the CAPIOS and in North America as the Freedom). Minolta also joined the cooperative development effort brought together by Eastman Kodak Co.—the others were Fuji, Canon, and Nikon—which created the Advanced Photo System (APS), an effort to revitalize the stagnant still photography market. APS offered easy loading and the ability to select from three photo sizes (4 inch by 6 inch, 4 inch by 7 inch, and a panoramic 4 inch by 10 inch) as pictures are taken. Minolta introduced a full line of APS cameras in early 1996 under the VECTIS brand. The VECTIS line included five compact models and a high-end SLR version that featured five interchangeable lenses. Later in 1996, Minolta launched a children's camera tied to a new animated series.

The company's desire for further diversification was highlighted in mid-1994 by the decision to change the company name to Minolta Co., Ltd., dropping ''Camera.'' The company soon showed a renewed commitment to innovative new product development. In 1995 Minolta launched the BC 3000 book copying system, the first product able to produce high quality copies of bound books. Also in 1995, digital cameras were added to the Minolta product family with the marketing of the RD-175, touted as ''one of the smallest and lightest SLR-type digital cameras in the world.'' Highlighting 1996 introductions were the CF 900 multifunction machine, able to copy, scan, and print in full color; and the Infinium 11, 11, and 11 planetariums, extensions of the Infinium line and ''the world's first projectors to enable planetarium visitors to experience virtual worlds.''

By 1996, Minolta had certainly begun to turn its fortunes around, although its profit margin of 1.2 percent was significantly lower than that of the mid-1980s. The diversification program seemed to be working; camera sales made up 44 percent of overall sales in 1991, but only 29.4 percent in 1996. Along with its revitalized reputation for innovation, Minolta appeared ready to be a major player in the high tech world of the 21st century.

Principal Subsidiaries

Minolta Camera Sales Co., Ltd.; Minolta Business Equipment Trading Co., Ltd.; Minolta Planetarium Co., Ltd.; Tokai Minolta Co., Ltd.; Kinki Minolta Co., Ltd.; Minolta Media Works Co., Ltd.; Aoi Camera Co., Ltd.; Sankei Seimitsu Kikai Co., Ltd.; Toyohashi Seimitsu Kogyo Co., Ltd.; Nara Minolta Seiko Co., Ltd.; Nankai Kougaku Kogyo Co., Ltd.; Okayama Minolta Seimitsu Co., Ltd.; Miki Minolta Kogyo Co., Ltd.; Fujikasei Co., Ltd.; Tokyo Minolta Camera Service Co., Ltd.; Minolta Hoken Daiko Co., Ltd.; Minolta Digital Studio Co., Ltd.; Dynax Trading Co., Ltd.; Minolta Logistics Co., Ltd.; Minolta Quality Service Co., Ltd.; Minolta Corporation (U.S.A.); Minolta Business Systems, Inc. (U.S.A.); Mohawk Marketing Corporation (U.S.A.); Astro-Tec. Mfg., Inc. (U.S.A.); Minolta Advance Technology Inc. (U.S.A.); Minolta Canada Inc.; Minolta Business Equipment (Canada), Ltd.; Minolta Copiadora do Amazonas Ltda. (Brazil); Minolta GmbH (Germany); Plankopie Vertriebsgesellschaft für Kopiersysteme GmbH (Germany); Minolta Bürosysteme GmbH Nürnberg (Germany); Minolta Bürosysteme GmbH München (Germany); Minolta Bürosysteme GmbH Frankfurt (Germany); Minolta Bürosysteme GmbH Berlin (Germany); Minolta France S.A.; Repro Conseil S.A. (France); Minolta Lorraine S.A. (France); Minolta (UK) Limited; Minolta (Schweiz) AG (Switzerland); Minolta Austria Gesellschaft mbH; Hernitz Bürosysteme Gesellschaft mbH (Austria); Minolta Camera Benelux B.V. (Netherlands); Minolta Europe Finance B.V. (Netherlands); Minolta Business Equipment (Belgium) N.V.; Minolta Svenska AB (Sweden); Minolta Business Equipment Sweden AB; Minolta Italia S.r.l. (Italy); Minolta Portugal Limitada; Minolta Business Equipment Spain S.A.; Minolta Denmark A/S; Minolta Magyarorszag Kft. (Hungary); Minolta Polska Sp. zo. o. (Poland); Minolta spol. sr. o. (Czech Republic); Minolta Slovakia spol. sr. o.; Minolta Romania s.r.l.; Minolta Baltia (Lithuania); Minolta Bulgaria o.o.d.; Minolta Ljubljana d.o.o. (Slovenia); Minolta Zagreb d.o.o. (Croatia); Minolta Beograd d.o.o. (Serbia); Minolta Ukraine; Shanghai Minolta Optical Products Co., Ltd. (China); Wuhan Minolta Wiaic Office Automation Equipments Co., Ltd. (China); Minolta Hong Kong Limited; Minolta Industries (HK) Limited (Hong Kong); Minolta Singapore (PTE) Limited; Minolta Marketing (M) Sdn. Bhd. (Malaysia); Minolta Malaysia Sdn. Bhd.; Minolta Precision Engineering (M) Sdn. Bhd. (Malaysia); Minolta New Zealand Limited; Minolta Business Equipment Australia Pty. Ltd.

Further Reading

Bremner, Brian, ''From the Mind of Minolta—Oops, Make that 'Honeywell,' '' *Business Week*, February 24, 1992, p. 34.

Hammonds, Keith H., ''Polaroid and Minolta: More Developments Ahead?,'' *Business Week*, July 16, 1990, p. 32.

Kusumoto, Sam, and Edmund P. Murray, *My Bridge to America: Discovering the New World for Minolta*, New York: Dutton, 1989.

''Minolta Through Six Decades,'' *Minolta Messenger*, Number 7, 1988.

Prud'homme, Alex, ''New Believer,'' *Business Month*, August 1990, pp. 44–45.

—Ginger G. Rodriguez
—updated by David E. Salamie

Mitel Corporation

350 Legget Drive
Kanata, Ontario K2K 1Y6
Canada
(613) 592-2122
Fax: (613) 592-4170
Web site: http://www.mitel.com

Public Company
Incorporated: 1971
Employees: 3,867
Sales: C$576 million (fiscal year ending March 1996)
Stock Exchanges: New York Toronto
SICs: 3661 Phone/Telephone Equipment; 3674
  Semiconductors

Mitel Corporation is an international supplier of telecommunications products and solutions and a pioneer in integrating telephones and computers. Best known for its switching systems which enable small companies to route calls, Mitel is also the only Canadian manufacturer of custom-designed microchips. Through its business communications systems and semiconductor divisions, Mitel designs, manufactures, and markets business telephone systems and peripherals, computer-telephony integration (CTI) products, and microelectronic components. Mitel's operations are located primarily in Canada, the United States, the United Kingdom, and Sweden. Ranked among the top 100 companies on the Toronto Stock Exchange, Mitel had revenues of C$576 million for the fiscal year ending March 1996.

Early History

In 1971, Michael Cowpland and Terence Matthews, two British-born engineers, incorporated Mitel Corporation in Ontario, Canada. Two years later, the duo left their jobs with Microsystems International Ltd., a subsidiary of Northern Telecom, and Mitel commenced its high-tech operations, putting together printed circuit boards for telephone switches. Their timing was excellent. The 1968 deregulation of U.S. giant American Telephone and Telegraph (AT&T) created a demand for telephone equipment, and Cowpland and Matthews responded.

1973–81: A High Flying High-Tech Company

Mitel carved out a niche for itself producing high-quality, economically priced telephone switching equipment. Mitel's first big winner was a tone receiver that converted the "beep" from a touch telephone to regular telephone signals. This made it possible for central telephone switching offices to decode the signals from push-button telephones. Two years after starting operations, Cowpland and Matthews' tiny two-person company had transformed into a business employing 30 people with annual sales of C$300,000. In 1975, Mitel introduced a more sophisticated tone-to-pulse converter that made touch telephones compatible with any telephone system. In 1976, the company set up a semiconductor division so that Mitel engineers could design their own integrated circuits. In 1979, the year AT&T began allowing its 23 Bell System companies to buy Mitel telecommunications equipment, Cowpland and Matthews introduced the device Mitel was to become famous for—an electronic public branch exchange (PBX) for small companies.

PBX was an internal switching system that routed calls within an organization and to the outside world. It allowed people within a company to make interior or exterior calls, and for incoming calls to be directed to the correct party, without having to go through telephone company wires. When U.S. regulators said that private companies had to be allowed to buy their own switching systems and plug them into existing telephone lines, the demand for PBXs exploded. Within three years, Mitel's PBX products, for companies with 10-160 lines, were the hottest-selling telephone systems in the United States, taking 14 percent of the fast growing PBX market.

Mitel was flying high, with sales doubling each year. As Pauline O'Connor of *Canadian Business* wrote in 1982, "Their ability to do this, year after year for almost a decade, earned them both the awe of their colleagues and the adulation of investors whose huge cash infusions were critical to keep the company growing. Stock market investors pumped $250 million into the firm since 1979 in hopes of getting a ride on that

---

Company Perspectives:

The Company's mission is to be a world leader in creating communications solutions that provide exceptional value to its customers. Our leadership strategy is centred on advancing people-to-people communications in an open, distributed and standards-based environment.

---

endlessly soaring growth curve.'' Mitel had become a huge operation, with 13 plants and 4,200 employees around the world. In mid-1981, the company's stock was selling at $48. But then the company was hit with a double whammy: the biggest recession in 30 years and a slowing in the United States' PBX market.

1981–84: Trying to Make It in the Big Leagues

As Mitel president and chairman respectively, Cowpland and Matthews now faced a challenge common to successful entrepreneurs. Could they survive their rapid growth and keep Mitel in the big leagues? The answer depended on how they dealt with three factors: the company's financial base, markets, and management.

First, Mitel needed to consolidate its financial base. Since 1977, Cowpland and Matthews had paid for Mitel's growth by selling stock, with less than 30 percent of the company's expansion financed by its own revenues. With the market down, that option was no longer available. Mitel had to turn to banks to borrow the $200 million it needed for expansion between 1982–1984. That was a big jump from the $47 million in bank debt it had been carrying.

Second, Mitel needed to expand its markets, since sales to the maturing U.S. market accounted for 90 percent of the company's revenues. Mitel chairman Matthews, began marketing Mitel's products to Europe and the Third World, setting a sales goal of $100 million by 1985. His efforts resulted in an $80 million, 4-year sale to Mexico's government-owned telephone company, a $22 million sale to British Telecommunications, and a $10 million contract to upgrade hotel switchboards in Italy. In France, he won an agreement to build a plant free of government ownership ties. When the Socialists won in national elections, that plan was put on hold and eventually scrapped.

Mitel chose a good time to diversify its markets. In Britain, where Mitel had opened a sales office in the mid-70s, British Telecom was about to lose its monopoly and needed to upgrade its equipment to be able to compete. Mitel's British manufacturing plants, licensing agreements with British manufacturers, and network of private distributers placed the company in an excellent position to serve the British telephone equipment industry. Other European countries were also beginning a major overhaul of their archaic telephone systems and Third World countries wanted to build their telephone infrastructure. In 1981, there were approximately 43 phones for every 100 people in Western Europe, compared to 70 for every 100 Canadians and 73 for every 100 Americans.

The third factor Mitel needed to address was its management. As O'Connor explained in her *Canadian Business* article, ''Of the handful of high-tech firms to survive such rapid growth without either running out of cash or losing financial control, all have had to restructure from top to bottom.'' With only minor reorganization, however, Cowpland and Matthews continued to operate through a ''team approach,'' building consensus throughout the organization, and giving existing personnel major responsibilities. By the end of the fiscal year, in March 1982, company revenues had risen 85 percent to C$204 million and profits were up 99 percent to C$34 million. Sales to international markets reached C$50 million, from only C$6 million two years earlier.

The year 1982 saw two major developments which kept Mitel in a strong competitive position. The first was the anticipated completion of the company's new SX-2000, a digital switch able to handle voice, data, and video signals over as many as 10,000 lines. With this new technology, companies could use PBXs to direct electronic mail, telexes, computer data, and video images. The second development was the signing of an agreement in principle with IBM to co-develop a family of switching systems that would link IBM mainframe computers to the office of the future. But the year saw profits cut in half and revenue growth slowed to only 25 percent.

Cowpland and Matthews initiated an austerity program. Mitel closed its Burlington, Vermont plant and laid off the 150 workers there as well as 346 more people at three other U.S. plants. It also halted construction of a new facility in New Brunswick. But problems continued. Because of design issues with its software program, the SX-2000, due out early in 1983, fell behind schedule. Mitel's attempt to produce a big PBX required it to shift from the analog technology used in its smaller switching systems to digital technology, and that development cost the company a lot of money.

To add to its frustrations, the PBX market in the U.S. was heating up again as AT&T's local subsidiaries were spun off into seven regional companies, the ''Baby Bells.'' These companies were free to buy and sell telephone equipment as they pleased. With 22 companies manufacturing PBX systems, the $1 billion market was ripe for a shake-out, and the delay in shipping the SX-2000 put Mitel in danger of losing some of its customers.

Then in June, IBM announced it was buying a 15 percent share of the California-based Rolm Corp., which manufactured a rival of the SX-2000. That move ended the agreement between Mitel and IBM, and the stock market reacted strongly, with Mitel's share price falling to a low of C$14. The company was in the red for fiscal 1984, its first loss in the ten years it had been doing business. Part of the deficit could be explained by the drop in Mitel's share of the U.S. market, down to 11.6 percent, and the costs of closing the Burlington facility. The primary factor, however, was the amount of research money spent on the SX 2000.

Finally, in early 1984, Mitel began shipping its large PBX systems. At the same time, the company continued its austerity measures, selling its Irish subsidiary, Mitel International, as well as a C$10 million plant under construction in Buctouche,

New Brunswick to another high-tech company. The company also cut back on its approximately C$65 million in R&D spending, laid off staff, and reorganized its planning operations. To help get costs under control, Cowpland and Matthews brought in a management consulting firm. Despite these efforts, Mitel lost money for the second year in a row.

1985–92: Ownership Turmoil

British Telecommunications plc came to the rescue of the nearly bankrupt company in 1985, paying about $217 million for a controlling 51 percent of Mitel stock. The purchase gave British Telecom entry into the North American market through both Mitel's manufacturing and international distribution activities. Matthews and Cowpland both left the company that they had founded 14 years earlier.

Initially, investors were hopeful that the capital from the sale and British Telecom's involvement would restore Mitel's financial health. But in 1990, after five years, British Telecom went looking for a buyer for the company. In 1992, the British firm sold its Mitel holdings to Schroders Ventures, an international venture capital and management buyout group, for a total of C$66 million (US$55 million).

1993–95: Alliances and CTI

The purchase by Schroders Ventures marked the beginning of a turnaround for Mitel. Early in 1993, Dr. John B. Millard, who had run his own consulting company before moving to Nippon Electric Co. of America, was appointed president and CEO of Mitel. Soon afterward, Dr. Henry Simon, chairman of Schroder Venture Life Sciences Advisors, was named chairman of the board at Mitel.

From the start of his tenure, Millard talked about linking telephone systems with computers to make a single network for transmitting voice along with text, video, and images. The company quickly began research and development activities into this new technology called computer telephony integration (CTI). According to a corporate White Paper, Mitel believed that "the real potential of CTI lies in the value that is created by the integration of the people and relationship aspects of business with [an organization's] business processes and technology infrastructure." One of its first steps, therefore, was to examine the different requirements needed by users at the desktop, workgroup, and enterprise levels.

Over the next few years, Mitel took two approaches to implementing CTI. First, the company built on its PBX systems, moving that technology toward the world of computing by opening its architecture to third-party developers and interfacing to the computer network. With this approach, as Mitel's Annual Report explains, "a telephone switch passes certain call information to a computer, allowing the computer to manage the call based on a command from a software application." Using the Mitel Telephony Applications Interface (MITAI), a toolkit, developers designed products such as FastCall software to automate incoming and outgoing calls on a personal computer, the CallProducer server to add telephony to a local area network, and Phoneware software that could manage e-mail, contact databases, personal information managers, and voice

and fax mail managers. Mitel also produced the Superset console series of video display terminals. These CTI products worked with Mitel's LIGHT series of PBX switching systems.

Mitel's second approach to CTI was through its Client Server Telecom (CST) division. Here, the company started with the computer and added telephony functions directly to it, creating a single platform for computing and telecommunications. This approach did not use the PBX as its platform, developing instead an open architecture communications system that could be used alone, as a workgroup server, or in conjunction with a PBX. As Joanne Chianello explained in an article in the *Ottawa Citizen*, "With only one server, users will be able to manage their voice mail, e-mail, faxes and printing. When on the road, workers will be able to call into headquarters and, using the buttons on a phone pad, order e-mail and faxes to be sent to a new fax number. They can even have the computer system read messages to them using text-to-voice technology." The new server-based platform, called MediaPath, was developed in alliance with Digital Equipment Corporation and Microsoft Corp.. Mitel also signed an agreement with Lannet Data Communications Ltd to develop a new switching module to connect Media-Path with a local area network (LAN).

But the company's Business Communications Services included more than CTI. The LIGHT series of PBX switches used fiber-optic cables to send signals made up of pulses of light rather than pulses of electricity, as occurred with digital switches. The company formed a "Multimedia Alliance" with Unisys to manufacture and distribute equipment that allowed cable operators to offer telephony. In 1995 Mitel introduced a new calling number identification chip (caller ID) that made it possible to identify a calling number on Call Waiting. The chip was to be used in advanced fax machines and intelligent answering machines to screen out "junk" transmissions.

Mitel's other major area of business was in semiconductors. The development of CTI and other telephony devices required custom-designed microchips. With its 20 years experience creating integrated circuits, Mitel was the only company in Canada with the facilities to manufacture such microchips. The company's semiconductor business grew from $51 million in 1992 to $120 million in 1995.

1996 and Beyond: Semiconductors and CTI

The year 1996 saw Mitel continue its turnaround, with record sales in the first two quarters. "We have a race between two growing divisions—semiconductors and the computer-telephony products which are really coming on," Millard told the *Ottawa Citizen* in October.

Early in the year, Mitel completed the purchase of ABB Hafo AB of Sweden, a Swedish semiconductor plant. That acquisition increased Mitel's production capacity, which had become backlogged with orders at its semiconductor manufacturing facilities in Caldicot, Wales and Bromont, Quebec. Mitel Semiconductor AB was also expected to develop its own line of integrated circuits for the medical, industrial, and space markets. By October 1996, semiconductors accounted for 31 percent of Mitel's revenues, up from 20 percent the year before.

In the CTI area, the company introduced several new products, including its prototype telephone that plugged directly into a personal computer. Mitel was the first telecommunications company in the world to take the Universal Serial Bus (USB) concept and use it for a plug-in telephone. As Tom Davis described it in his article in *PC Week*, "When the phone starts to ring, components that link the PC to caller ID instantly place an image or icon representing the caller in a corner of the recipient's monitor. The user can choose to answer it in the traditional manner or take advantage of several call-routing options." Because it took advantage of the Universal Serial Bus in plugging into the PC, the phone still worked while the computer was turned off, and the computer continued to handle other tasks while processing calls.

In June 1996, field trials began of NeVaDa (Networked Voice and Data), the latest step in the on-going evolution of Mitel's PBX systems. NeVaDa allowed customers to run voice as well as video and data over a single fiber-optic line in an enterprise-wide local area network. NeVaDa, uses a switching mechanism developed in alliance with Madge Networks Inc. of The Netherlands, which bought Lannet Data Communications. The device was selected Voice Integration Product of the Year at the 1996 Networking Industry Awards in Birmingham, England.

The NeVaDa network was expected to create more interest in the SX-2000 LIGHT PBX system. That could only help Mitel's core PBX sales which had decreasing revenues because of competition and a maturing market. By the end of 1996, CTI products were only about five percent of sales in the company's business communication systems division, but the market for CTI was expected to reach $8 billion by the end of the century.

After three years of talking about CTI, Millard was able to tell his shareholders, "Now we actually have the products getting ready to generate significant revenue. That's a good feeling." With its semiconductor business growing so strongly, the company appeared able to weather the period it would take for its CTI products to make a major contribution to Mitel's revenues, assuming that the CTI market lived up to its promise. Mitel was optimistic that CTI would carry the company into the end of the century.

Principal Subsidiaries

Mitel, Inc. (U.S.A.); Mitel Telecommunications Systems, Inc. (U.S.A.); Mitel Telecom Limited (United Kingdom); Mitel (Far East) Limited (Hong Kong); Mitel Semiconductor AB; Mitel de Mexico S.A. de C.V. (Mexico; 49%); Tianchi-Mitel Telecommunications Corporation (China; 50%).

Further Reading

Anderson, Ian, "Switching Allegiances: Why The Breakup of US Telephone Markets is Wiring Up Canadians," *Canadian Business*, October 1983, p. 15.

Bagnall, James, "Mitel Gets Back on Profit Bandwagon Through New Products," *Ottawa Citizen*, October 31, 1996, p. D12.

Bernard, Viki, "Mitel, Lannet Join Forces on ATM Switch," *PC Week*, July 31, 1995, p. 45.

Blackie, Bruce, "Mitel Powers Up For CTI Charge," *Ottawa Sun*, July 26, 1996, p. 31.

Borrus, Amy and Edith Terry, "British Telecom: What's Behind the Mitel Buy," *Business Week*, May 27, 1985, p. 57.

"BT Drops Mitel Stake, Reports $223 Mil Loss," *Telephone-Engineer-and-Management*, August 1, 1992, p. 41.

Chianello, Joanne, "Future Looks Rosy for Mitel Corp.," *Ottawa Citizen*, July 26, 1996, p. E1.

Cowpland, Michael, "Mitel: Awakening the European Telecommunications Industry," *Canadian Business Review*, Summer 1983, p. 30.

Daly, John, "The Color of Money," *Maclean's*, July 20, 1992, p. 40.

Davey, Tom, "PC/Telephone Integration Answers the Call of USB," *PC Week*, February 19, 1996, p. 32.

——, "Mitel Moves to NeVaDa: SONET Card Lets Users Run Voice, Video and Data over ATM," *PC Week*, September 2, 1996, p. 106.

Diebel, Linda, "A Waning High-Tech Star," *Maclean's*, June 20, 1983, p. 37.

Fallon, James, "British Telecom Buys 51% of Mitel," *Electronic News*, May 13, 1985, p. 1.

Fennell, Tom, "Digital Visions: The Race Is On To Marry Computers With the Telephone and TV," *Maclean's*, April 22, 1996, p. 34.

Feschuk, Scott, "Mitel Pegs Growth on Making Semiconductors," *Globe and Mail*, July 26, 1996, p. B10.

Finlayson, Ann, "The Fall of a High-Tech Star," *Maclean's*, May 14, 1984, p. 30.

Hostetler, Michele, "Sharing the Network Pipe: Voice and Data Make Peace," *Investor's Business Daily*, November 20, 1996.

"How Mitel Plans To Regain Its Momentum," *Business Week*, March 5, 1984, p. 42.

McCarthy, Stuart, "Future 'Is Here Today' For Mitel," *Ottawa Sun*, September 25, 1996, http://canoe2.canoe.ca/cit-bin/bolder/Ottawa HiTech/920_comp1.html/mitel.

"Mitel Soaring With Record Sales," *Ottawa Sun*, October 31, 1996, p. 52.

O'Connor, Pauline, "Now Comes The Hard Part," *Canadian Business*, October 1982, p. 74.

Perrin, Sterling, "Mitel Debuts New Merged Architecture," *Telecommunication*, June 1996, p. 18.

Schroeder, Erica, "Telephony Services Will Be the Talk of Las Vegas," *PC Week*, April 1, 1996.

Semiloff, Margie, "Switched Voice Apps Demo'd At CTI Booth," *Communications Week*, April 1, 1996, p. 45.

"Software Hardship at Mitel," *The Economist*, November 12, 1983, p. 82.

Strauss, Paul R., "Mitel After the Fall: A Big Board Loser Dusts Itself Off and Tries Again," *Data Communications*, May 1984, p. 85.

Symonds, William C., "Newbridge's Joyride on the Info Highway," *Business Week*, March 28, 1994.

"Unisys and Mitel," *Television Digest*, October 17, 1994, p. 6.

Vardy, Jill, "Mitel Aims For Big Piece of Computer-Telephone Integration," *Financial Post*, July 26, 1996, p. 7.

——, "Analysts Predict Mitel Shares Will Rise After Improved Results," *Financial Post*, October 31, 1996, p. 29.

—Ellen D. Wernick

Mobile Telecommunication Technologies

Mobile Telecommunications Technologies Corp.

200 South Lamar Street
Mtel Center, South Building
Jackson, Mississippi 39201
U.S.A.
(601) 944-1300
Fax: (601) 944-7194

Public Company
Incorporated: 1988 as Mobile Telecommunications
    Technologies Corp.
Employees: 2,650
Sales: $245.9 million (1995)
Stock Exchanges: NASDAQ
SICs: 4812 Radiotelephone Communications

A pioneer in wireless communications, Mobile Telecommunications Technologies Corp. offers paging and messaging services to U.S. and international customers. Known to pager customers in the United States through its SkyTel subsidiary, Mobile Telecommunications (MTel) served customers in more than 19 countries during the mid-1990s through its SkyTel system, which transmitted messages to more than one million pagers in North America, Latin America, and the Pacific Rim. During the first half of the 1990s, the company recorded robust financial growth, more than doubling its annual revenue volume, and increasing the number of paging units in service nearly tenfold. On September 19, 1995, Mtel made wireless communications history by launching the world's first two-way narrowband wireless messaging service dubbed "SkyTel 2-Way," enabling customers to respond to messages from their two-way messaging units. Already a flourishing enterprise before the introduction of SkyTel 2-Way, Mtel was expected to record more prolific growth during the late 1990s after its two-way messaging service began contributing to the company's revenue volume.

Mtel's Predecessor and Its Founder

Acquaintances of John N. Palmer described the founder of MTel as gracious, aggressive, cosmopolitan, and deeply tied to his home state of Mississippi. They might have added a strong pioneering spirit to Palmer's list of personality traits, particularly when explaining the six-foot, five-inch Mississippian's role in bringing paging and cellular technology to the masses. Palmer's aggressiveness and ability to foresee the monetary benefits of emerging technologies served him well in the business world, enabling him to establish two well-respected companies and to point to himself as one of the instrumental driving forces behind the explosive growth of pager and cellular service in the United States. MTel was Palmer's second creation, but its formation was closely linked to the establishment of his first technology-based company, Mobile Communications Corporation of America, with one giving birth to the other. In the development of both of these businesses, Palmer demonstrated a foresightedness that distinguished him from rivals. When this innovative prescience was combined with his aggressiveness, the result was the flourishing business describing MTel during the 1990s.

By the time Palmer started MTel, the legacy of Palmers in Mississippi stretched back seven generations, charting a family tree that included his great-great-grandfather John D. Palmer, who once sold a small railroad to author William Faulkner's father. Decades after the Palmer family name became part of an obscure footnote in the Faulkner family's history, John N. Palmer embarked on a professional career that wedded his name to the history of commercial wireless communications in the United States. After graduating with undergraduate and M.B.A. degrees from the University of Mississippi in 1960, Palmer established a one-man accounting firm in a hotel in Jackson, Mississippi. Twenty-five years old at the time, Palmer occupied modest quarters on the hotel's fourth floor, paying for his small office space by auditing the hotel's books. Five years later, he made his pivotal first move. In 1965, Palmer purchased a local telephone answering service that served 300 customers and gave him a Federal Communications Commission (FCC) license to operate a primitive radio paging service. Palmer had a good feeling about his first FCC license, the first of many to come. "I said," Palmer reflected to a *Forbes* reporter years later, " 'You know, that license is probably going to be valuable one day.' " The decades ahead validated Palmer's intuition.

By 1973, Palmer had acquired nine more paging companies and won FCC licenses to operate paging services within and surrounding a three-state territory comprising Mississippi, Alabama, and Louisiana. These properties were then merged with a regional paging firm in western New York State, creating a company Palmer christened Mobile Communications Corporation of America. By the time Palmer took Mobile Communications public in 1981, he was keenly aware of the value of telecommunications licenses. In the decade ahead, he began displaying the aggressiveness that would earn him distinction in the wireless communication industry by pursuing FCC licenses in earnest.

When the first independent cellular telephone licenses were offered, Palmer was there, eager to gain a foothold in what he believed would be a lucrative business. In 1983 and 1984, Palmer accomplished his objective, winning licenses to operate cellular telephone systems in five U.S. cities, including the coveted Houston and Los Angeles markets. At roughly the same time he was bidding for cellular telephone licenses, Palmer's efforts in another area were finally paying dividends, creating what would prove to be MTel's foundation. In 1978, Palmer began lobbying the FCC to set aside frequencies for nationwide paging networks, pleading his case at a time when local paging services were still in their infancy. Six years later, when Palmer was swooping up the first of his five cellular telephone licenses, the FCC did what Palmer had hoped for by offering the opportunity to obtain nationwide paging licenses. Not surprisingly, Palmer seized the opportunity, forming a Mobile Communications-led joint venture to obtain one of the first three national paging licenses issued in 1984. Three years later, Mobile Communication's national paging license manifested itself as National Satellite Paging, a subsidiary company that later was renamed SkyTel Corp., the heart of MTel's business during its fledgling years and into the 1990s.

Mtel Is Formed

As efforts were underway to get Mobile Communication's national paging service up and running, Palmer turned his attention to his recently acquired cellular telephone properties. In 1985, he sold 50 percent interest in Mobile Communication's cellular properties to BellSouth, marking the beginning of a business relationship that three years later engendered the formation of MTel. Palmer received $67 million from BellSouth for the 50 percent stake, as well as a guarantee from BellSouth that the telecommunications giant would finance the acquisition of additional cellular properties and absorb 99 percent of the losses incurred by the BellSouth-Mobile Communications partnership. Three years after this deal was struck, however, Palmer decided cellular properties had become overpriced, prompting

him to make a move that paved the way for MTel's debut as an independent corporate entity.

In February 1988, Palmer agreed to merge Mobile Communications into BellSouth in exchange for stock worth $710 million. As part of the transaction, Palmer walked away with 1.2 million shares of a new company called Mobile Telecommunications Technologies Corp, or MTel, as the company would become known. Essentially the offspring of Mobile Communications, MTel comprised a collection of telecommunications-related businesses and investments that BellSouth either chose not to absorb or was precluded from acquiring under the terms of the Bell system breakup, but Palmer's new company was more than just the dregs of Mobile Communications. Despite the company's 1988 pro forma operating losses of $12 million on $21 million in revenue, MTel was drawing the attention of industry observers who were attracted by the company's 90 percent stake in National Satellite Paging, which had been operating for a year. The first national paging service in the United States, National Satellite Paging was MTel's primary asset, a paging network with 178 transmitters in 100 metropolitan areas that enabled MTel to provide service to 85 percent of the nation's population. It was with this paging network that Palmer would build his second business and create one of the pioneering forces in the paging industry.

In 1989, Palmer endeavored to expand MTel's customers' ability to reach one another, not only nationally but internationally as well. A joint venture agreement was reached with Telesat Canada, extending National Paging's presence in Canada. A joint venture with Singapore Telecom was formed to develop satellite paging for the Pacific Rim. As the company prepared to enter the 1990s, all hopes were pinned on SkyTel, the former National Satellite Paging, to invigorate MTel's profitability. Toward this end, Mtel's executives were not alone in expecting robust growth in the paging industry. Industry analysts were projecting at the end of the 1980s that the nationwide paging industry would grow from the 100,000 subscribers signed on in 1989 to 1.5 million by 1995, with nationwide revenues approaching $1 billion. On the international front, where MTel was already establishing a presence, encouraging growth was being recorded as well. In 1988, when MTel was spun off from the Mobile Communications-BellSouth combination, there were 18,000 subscribers; by 1990, as MTel moved toward years of prolific growth, the number of worldwide subscribers had grown to 75,000.

Early 1990s Genesis of SkyTel 2-Way

To a large extent, the expectations of the late 1980s were realized during the early 1990s. The number of SkyTel's subscribers swelled from 30,000 in 1989 to 220,000 by 1993, Mtel's market value tripled during the period, reaching $860 million, and annual sales marched steadily upward from $37 million to $133 million by 1992. On the heels of this promising growth, however, even greater rewards were in the offing as Palmer steered MTel in a new direction that once again made the man and the company pioneers in the paging industry. In July 1992, the FCC awarded MTel a nationwide license to operate a two-way, wireless messaging system, granting it "pioneer preference," the first time the FCC awarded the preference to a commercial project. Receiving the unprecedented nod from the FCC represented a windfall, virtually guaranteeing that MTel would receive an operating license as soon as the FCC cleared a frequency in 1994 and assuring that the company would be well on its way toward building a national network while competitors were stepping over each other in pursuit of licenses.

Realizing the opportunity that lay before him, Palmer set aside $100 million to be spent in 1993 to get his two-way, wireless messaging network up and running, aiming to establish the service in 300 major U.S. markets by mid-1995. Palmer also began actively searching for partners to provide financial and technological assistance in developing the new business, which was initially named Nationwide Wireless Network but eventually became known as SkyTel 2-Way. Confident that the new subsidiary could be turned into a lucrative facet of MTel's business, Jai Bhagat, executive vice-president of MTel and the president of the nascent two-way messaging venture, noted to a reporter from *PC Week,* "We're a small company, but nobody thought we could make SkyTel work, and look what happened. We're confident we can repeat history."

If history was going to repeat itself, then MTel executives could look forward to animated growth from its two-way messaging service because SkyTel had proven to be remarkably successful. While work was underway to launch two-way messaging service by mid-1995, SkyTel was growing by leaps and bounds, controlling 75 percent of the national market. Ranked as the largest paging service in the United States, SkyTel had benefitted from the exponential growth of pagers during the first half of the 1990s, enriched by the swarms of new subscribers to paging services. The projections made in 1989 for industry-wide revenues to approach $1 billion by 1995 had been eclipsed dramatically. By 1994, paging revenues were up to $3 billion and expected to grow vigorously for the remainder of the decade, validating the prudence of Palmer's business decisions for the previous two decades. Although some industry pundits had disparaged Palmer for divesting his cellular telephone properties during the 1980s, Palmer's commitment to investing in the paging business tempered any regrets stemming from the decision to exit the cellular business. Pagers were smaller than cellular telephones, their batteries lasted longer, and pager service was substantially cheaper than cellular service, with the monthly cost for local pager service averaging $10 compared to $67 for cellular service.

The introduction of two-way pager service was expected to increase the advantages of pagers over cellular telephones to particular customers, enabling pager carriers to return acknowledgment messages and allowing senders and receivers to transmit electronic mail and full text back and forth without using a telephone line. Palmer's search for a partner to help with the development of SkyTel 2-Way netted Microsoft Corp., which initially committed $30 million to the project on top of MTel's $100 million. After a $300 million investment on Mtel's part, the long-awaited launch date of the two-way service arrived on

September 19, 1995, marking the debut of a service that was expected to generate roughly 25 percent of MTel's total sales by 1997.

The establishment of SkyTel 2-Way represented a milestone in the history of wireless communications, a historic achievement that Palmer hoped would lead to a lucrative future for Mtel. As corporate executives celebrated the launch date of SkyTel 2-Way, however, there were justifiable reasons to celebrate the progress of the company's mainstay SkyTel business. In 1995, Mtel placed more pager units in service than it had during the previous seven years combined, more than doubling its customer base during the year from 450,000 to more than one million subscribers. Revenues increased significantly as well, jumping from 1994's $163 million to $246 million in 1995, fueling confidence that the addition of the SkyTel 2-Way business would provide a dramatic boost to the company's business during the late 1990s. As the company headed toward the late 1990s, its legacy of pioneering work in wireless communications held it in good stead, convincing many that Mtel's future would be as successful as its past.

Principal Subsidiaries

MTel International, Inc.; MTel Latin America, Inc.; MTel Puerto Rico, Inc.; Mtel Paging, Inc.; United States Paging Corporation; Destineer Corporation; Mobilecomm Europe Inc.; MTel Space Technologies Corporation; MTel Technologies, Inc.; MTel Maine, Inc.; Com/Nav Realty Corp.; Intelligent Investment Partners, Inc.

Further Reading

Bhargava, Sunita Wadekar, "Many Were Paged but Which Will Be Chosen?," *Business Week,* June 22, 1992, p. 122J.
Hamm, Steve, "Mississippi Megahertz," *PC Week,* July 26, 1993, p. 8.
Krapf, Eric, "Paging Goes Two-Way, but Data Applications Delayed," *America's Network,* March 1, 1995, p. 32.
Meeks, Fleming, "Why New Beepers Vibrate," *Forbes,* August 21, 1989, p. 72.
——, "John Palmer Goofs Off (or Tries to)," *Forbes,* June 21, 1993, p. 12.
"MobileComm Seeking OK for System," *HFD: The Weekly Home Furnishings Newspaper,* July 13, 1992, p. 83.
Moeller, Michael, "SkyTel Zeros in on Two-Way Service: Provider Poised to Bid for NB-PCS," *PC Week,* August 7, 1995, p. 37.
Moore, Mark, "MTel CEO Counts on 2-Way Paging," *PC Week,* September 30, 1996, p. 39.
Ryan, Ken, "MobileComm Slates New Pager for Retail," *HFD: The Weekly Home Furnishings Newspaper,* October 12, 1992, p. 250.
"Senior Vice President Leaves SBC Inc., Accepts Position with Mtel," *Knight-Ridder/Tribune Business News,* July 16, 1996, p. 7.
Sprout, Alison, "Space Age Pager," *Fortune,* November 18, 1991, p. 188.
Teitelbaum, Richard S., "Robert Fugate, 29," *Fortune,* May 21, 1990, p. 158.
Walsh, Matt, "Beep! Beep!," *Forbes,* August 15, 1994, p. 66.

—Jeffrey L. Covell

Mothers Work, Inc.

1309 Noble Street
Philadelphia, Pennsylvania 19123
U.S.A.
(215) 625-9259
Fax: (215) 440-9845
Web site: http://www.motherswork.com

Public Company
Incorporated: 1981
Employees: 2,600
Sales: $199.2 million (1996)
Stock Exchanges: NASDAQ
SICs: 5621 Women's Clothing Stores; 2339 Women's
and Misses' Outerwear, Not Elsewhere Classified

Mothers Work, Inc. is the largest specialty retailer of career-oriented and high-end maternity clothing in the United States. After cornering and developing the market for career apparel targeted at moms-to-be, Mothers Work has expanded to include casual and special-occasion maternity wear as well. Mothers Work operates over 450 stores throughout the United States, under the names Mothers Work, A Pea in the Pod, Motherhood Maternity, Mimi Maternity, and Motherhood Works. The company also owns and operates the Episode U.S.A. clothing chain, which deals in non-maternity women's clothing.

The Early Years

Mothers Work, Inc. was founded in 1981 when Rebecca Matthias, pregnant with her first child, experienced an almost impossible time locating career-oriented maternity clothing. While she had no difficulty finding an abundance of casual wear, Matthias could not find anything that she felt was appropriate to wear to her job at a Boston computer company. She believed that other mothers-to-be were surely having similar problems, and realized that the market for career apparel for pregnant women was a virtually untapped segment of the clothing industry. At the time, most other maternity clothing stores specialized in casual styles—comfort at an affordable price, since the clothes were needed for only a short time.

Soon after her first son was born, Matthias quit her job and decided to find career-oriented maternity apparel and sell it through a mail-order catalog. At the time, Matthias had $10,000 in her savings account, of which she used almost half to purchase maternity outfits she felt were representative of the clothing that women would wear to work. The rest of the money was used to create, print, and distribute a black-and-white catalog to a few hundred prospective customers. In early 1982, the first edition of a catalog that she called "Mothers Work" was shipped out, containing photos of herself and her son, and an extremely limited selection of clothing at prices that averaged between $50 to $100.

The first catalog generated approximately $3,500 in sales, which unfortunately did not even cover Matthias's original expenses. Feeling deflated, she might have given up if it had not been for the fact that she still possessed a good deal of the inventory she had purchased. Thus, she decided to try one more catalog. The second catalog, however, was the result of extensive market research and preparation, which brought about some dramatic changes. For example, she learned that consumers typically did not respond favorably to black-and-white catalogs. Therefore, the second edition contained more color photographs of the available clothing items.

When customers received the second catalog in late 1982, the response was immediate interest in a conservative matching blazer and jumpsuit that Matthias had added to the collection as an experiment. Although she was pleased with the positive response, this actually posed great problems for her because she had dyed the blazer herself to match the jumpsuit, which she had purchased at a different store. Essentially, orders were pouring in for an item of which only one was in existence. So Matthias quickly searched and found a sample maker who agreed to cut and sew the suit for her if she provided the material. She did, and the outfit was the second catalog's biggest hit. Matthias now knew that her customers were interested in items that fell on the more conservative end of the spectrum. With the money she earned from the second catalog, she altered her product line slightly and began preparing for a third edition.

Rapid Expansion in the 1980s

In 1983, after giving birth to her second child, Matthias and her husband moved their family to Philadelphia. Once there, she obtained access to space in a local manufacturing plant where she set up a production and shipping facility for Mothers Work. Matthias had decided that she needed to find a way to rely less on purchasing items from other stores, due to the fact that availability was always uncertain at best. Therefore, she wooed an experienced designer from Albert Nippon named Beate Hemman to come to work for her, and then hired her own sewing crew to staff the new facility. Together, the group set out to create and produce sophisticated clothing items for the third catalog.

The following year, sales continued to increase and Matthias began to toy with the concept of opening retail stores to sell the Mothers Work product line. Because she did not possess the capital to open her own store, she decided to try franchising the concept to someone else, who could then test Mothers Work's ability to sell in a retail setting. By 1985, Mothers Work had opened six franchises around the United States, all of which were performing beautifully. Matthias was pulling in approximately five percent of those stores' profits, but wanted to open one of her own and fully reap the benefits. Late that year, she obtained a $150,000 loan and used the money to open her own Mothers Work store in Boston, Massachusetts.

One of the problems that often plagues retail clothing chains is the loss of profit when merchandise must eventually be marked down in order to sell. Because Mothers Work actually produced a majority of the items that it sold, Matthias felt that the company should be well-equipped to diminish such problems. She requisitioned the help of her husband, Dan, who was highly talented and experienced in computer database and software programming. He designed an information system for the Mothers Work chain that connected each individual store with the production headquarters in Philadelphia. The system, called Trend Track, enabled each store to keep on hand only one or two of each piece of merchandise at a time. Every night, each store's computer connected with the database at headquarters and reported the previous day's sales. New stock was then produced and sent out from headquarters on a daily basis to replenish the missing items from each store. Mothers Work soon became so efficient that its stores were actually constructed without back rooms.

Meanwhile, Rebecca Matthias was attempting to locate interested parties to invest in the expansion of the Mothers Work chain. Due to the fact that she had identified and cornered a segment of the clothing market in which there was not any true competition, it was not a difficult sell. By the end of 1986, she had secured over $1 million in venture capital and began using it to open new stores nationwide. This process continued throughout the rest of the decade, and by 1990 Mothers Work was composed of 40 stores across the United States, and annual sales were hovering around $10 million.

Diversification into the 1990s and Beyond

In the early 1990s, the company continued to distribute its catalog and sell its product through the mail-order channel, but was focusing the majority of its attention on the retail aspect of the business. Catalogs were now dubbed "Mothers Work and Play," reflecting a shift in demand toward casual dress as well as conservative office apparel. Due to her knack for following market trends, noting her customers' demands, and then responding accordingly, in 1992 Matthias received the Ernst & Young Entrepreneur of the Year Award.

Still, Matthias refused to rest on that achievement and instead pushed for further expansion. In 1993, the company went public, offering stock to the general population and earning about $16 million from the sale. This was a considerable accomplishment, given that the company's total sales for that year were just over $30 million. With the added capital, Mothers Work immediately began to expand, adding approximately 50 new stores in 1994 alone. Sales nearly doubled in the space of one year, topping off at $59 million.

In 1995, Mothers Work began to diversify its holdings through a number of acquisitions. First came the purchase of over 60 "A Pea in the Pod" stores, a competitor specializing in maternity clothing that was somewhat more casual than the Mothers Work line. Later that year, Mothers Work also acquired 217 "Motherhood Maternity" retail units, which brought the company's total number of retail locations to almost 400. Once again, yearly sales jumped forward dramatically, leveling off at $106 million.

The following year, as Mothers Work celebrated its 15th anniversary, it made another interesting acquisition when it purchased over 20 "Episode U.S.A." stores throughout the country. The addition of Episode U.S.A. marked a solid entrance for Mothers Work into the non-maternity women's career apparel market. At the time of the acquisition, Episode U.S.A. was involved in bankruptcy proceedings, but Mothers Work management believed that a shift into casual and dressy apparel would help revive the chain. In mid-1996, the company began signing leases for new store locations and worked to redevelop the chain's product line. Matthias projected that the chain would grow gradually throughout the rest of the decade, eventually including around 100 stores.

Entering the end of the century, Mothers Work was well-positioned for continued future growth. In the process of growing from a $3,500 mail-order business to a multimillion-dollar enterprise composed of almost 500 store locations, Mothers Work had achieved steady increases in both sales and profits throughout its 15 years of operation. The company was continuing to expand its maternity-wear holdings, while also entering itself into the general women's apparel arena. Based on its past successes and flexible management style, Mothers Work seemed capable of easily handling the demands it would face in the coming century.

Principal Subsidiaries

Cave Springs, Inc.; Mothers Work (RE), Inc.; Motherhood Maternity Shops, Inc.; Motherhood Maternity International,

Inc.; The Page Boy Company, Inc.; Episode U.S.A.; Maternity Works; Mimi Maternity; A Pea in the Pod.

Further Reading

Dumaine, Brian, ''America's Smart Young Entrepreneurs,'' *Fortune,* March 21, 1994, p. 34.

Edelson, Sharon, ''Episode USA Gets New Lease on Life,'' *WWD,* June 19, 1996, p. 4.

Fox, Bruce, ''Tight Inventory, Quick Turns: MIS Bolsters Success of Mothers Work,'' *Chain Store Age Executive,* December 1992, p. 103.

Oberbeck, Elizabeth Birkelund, ''The Start-Up: Treading Water Until Your Ship Comes In,'' *Working Woman,* April 1990, p. 41.

—Laura E. Whiteley

Muzak, Inc.

2901 Third Avenue, Suite 400
Seattle, Washington 98121
U.S.A.
(206) 633-6210
Fax: (206) 633-6210
Web site: http://www.muzak.com/muzak.html

Private Company
Incorporated: 1934 as Muzak Corporation
Employees: 715
Sales: $86.9 million (1995)
SICs: 4832 Radio Broadcasting Stations; 3651 Household
Audio & Video Equipment; 3652 Prerecorded
Records & Tapes; 7389 Business Services, Not
Elsewhere Classified; 4841 Cable & Other Pay
Television Services

A fixture of the American soundscape, Muzak, Inc. offers a full range of service to businesses across the globe, including 60 channels of music, in-store audio and visual advertising, music videos, and one-way satellite communications systems that enable customers to transmit voice, data, and video to multiple receivers. For half a century, Muzak was the purveyor of what was commonly referred to as "elevator music," the watered-down instrumental renditions of easy-listening compositions that were piped into scores of retail locations and workplaces for their purported influence on worker productivity and consumer spending. A 1987 merger with Seattle-based Yesco Audio Environments, however, moved the company away from background music into the market for foreground music, or music selections consisting of compositions performed by the original artists. Over the course of the ensuing decade, Muzak evolved into a sophisticated and diverse marketer of a host of data, voice, and video services for more than 175,000 businesses in the United States and abroad.

Muzak's Technological Birth

Few people associate his name with the birth and ubiquitous presence of "elevator music," but despite his anonymity George Owen Squier left an indelible imprint on American society. A graduate of West Point in 1887, Squier rose to the rank of a two-star general in the U.S. Army during his 36-year military career, but scored his greatest success as an inventor, establishing himself as a pioneer in the history of science in the United States. As a young artilleryman, Squier made a significant contribution to the development of high-speed telegraphy when he invented the polarizing photochronograph, an instrument capable of measuring the speed of a projectile. Charged with determining the military potential in the experiments of the Wright brothers, Squier became the first airplane passenger in the world when he hopped aboard a Wright-constructed aircraft for a nine-minute flight in 1908. Squier's legacy to the world, however, was something capable of sparking far more tumult than a historic airplane flight or a groundbreaking high-speed measuring device could arouse. His lasting contribution was once characterized as "metastisizing," described by novelist Vladimir Nabokov as "abominably offensive," and referred to in *Smithsonian* magazine as "a stupefyingly bland, toxically pervasive form of unregulated air pollution, about as calming as the drone of a garbage compactor." Squier's gift to the world was Muzak, a commercial product that irritated some, soothed others, and reigned for generations as a household name.

Roughly a decade after his pioneering flight, Squier was tapped as the head of the U.S. Signal Corps, a promotion concurrent with the United States' entry into World War I. While superintending the Signal Corps, Squier developed a way to play a phonograph over electric power lines that served as the technological foundation for Muzak. Squier patented the invention in 1922 and later in the year sold the patent to a massive utilities combine called North American Company, which backed Major General Squier in launching Wired Radio, Inc. It took another 12 years, however, before North American first essayed Squier's technology on the market. The year the technology was first tested—in 1934—also marked the year Squier came up with a new name for the company that would employ his patented technology. Squier combined the name of the widely popular Kodak camera and the sound of music, ending up with Muzak. The year the Squier technology first was used and the year the Muzak name was born also marked the year of Major General Squier's death, but the name and the concept he created would flourish for the remainder of the century, becoming a pervasive presence both in the United States and abroad for generations to come.

Muzak's first customers were residents in the Lakeland section of Cleveland, Ohio, who paid $1.50 a month for three channels of audio entertainment ranging from dance music to news. The first Muzak recording, also completed in 1934, was performed by Sam Lanin's orchestra, which recorded a medley of "Whispering," Do You Ever Think of Me?," and "Here in My Arms." Shortly after the service debuted in Cleveland, Muzak's leaders realized the company could not compete against commercial radio, so they altered their focus and began marketing the audio service to hotels and restaurants in New York City before 1934 was through. Two years later, Muzak's management made a signal move that would steer the company toward greater heights when they began marketing Muzak service to factories and other work areas. Shortly after the introduction of Muzak into work areas, the company benefitted enormously from a windfall study. The reaction to the study would fuel Muzak's growth for decades to come.

In 1937, the theory that music increased efficiency and reduced absenteeism in the workplace was substantiated by a team of industrial psychologists in Britain. On the heels of this disclosure, a study conducted at the Stevens Institute of Technology in New Jersey showed that "functional music" in the workplace reduced absenteeism by 88 percent and early departures by 53 percent. Additional studies demonstrated equally impressive results, convincing many that there was a direct correlation between the sound of music and higher productivity. At a dairy in McKeesport, Pennsylvania, a recording of "The Blue Danube" was played, inducing the cows to produce more milk. Elsewhere, recordings reportedly inspired chickens to lay more eggs. As news of these studies spread, a more receptive audience for Muzak's unique services was created, giving the company a viable customer base to target.

Driven by the strong, positive reaction to the scholarly studies, Muzak expanded geographically to take advantage of the burgeoning demand for "functional music" in the workplace. To execute its expansion plan, Muzak developed a franchise system in 1938, enabling it to establish a presence in major U.S. cities such as Boston, Washington, D.C., Philadelphia, Detroit, and Los Angeles. The company's coast-to-coast expansion quickly attracted the attention of a corporate suitor, the first of many to come in Muzak's history. In 1938, Warner Brothers purchased Muzak Corporation and the publishing rights for the volumes of classical and semi-classical compositions North American had acquired by the end of the 1930s. Warner Brothers' tenure of ownership was brief, however, lasting roughly a year. In 1939, Warner Brothers sold Muzak to a triumvirate comprising Waddill Catchings, Allen Miller, and William Benton, founder of Benton & Bowles Advertising Agency, publisher of the *Encyclopedia Britannica,* and a U.S. Senator from Connecticut.

World War II and Postwar Growth

Of the three owners, Benton wielded the most influence, and eventually bought out his two partners to gain full control in 1941, when the theory that music in the workplace increased productivity was put to its first great test. The United States' entry into World War II proved to be a crucible for Muzak's "environmental music," as the need for heightened production on nearly all industrial fronts offered the opportunity to use the power of Muzak on a mammoth scale. Thousands of factories, arsenals, and shipyards were wired for music during the war, and production, as a result, increased 11 percent at those facilities that aired hits such as "Victory Polka," "Deep in the Heart of Texas," and "Swinging on a Star." By the war's conclusion, Muzak's effectiveness had convinced corporate America that background music was a valuable aid in the workplace, and large corporations signed on for Muzak's service, including companies such as Prudential Life Insurance Company, Bell Telephone, and McGraw-Hill Publishing Company.

By the beginning of the 1950s, Muzak's position in the business world was secure. Less than two decades after being introduced as a unique and novel service, Muzak was not only being piped into several of the nation's largest corporations but also into hundreds of smaller businesses as well. As the roster of Muzak clients expanded, the company funnelled money into research to develop technological improvements and to scientifically refine the music itself. Muzak's engineers developed something the company called "Stimulus Progression," a process of programming music at faster tempos to counteract the tendency of the human mind and body to slow down during the late morning and mid-afternoon. According to various studies conducted by Muzak, Stimulus Progression increased concentration, lowered blood pressure, and heightened productivity by gradually raising the intensity level of music in 15-minute cycles, with the relative level of each 15-minute cycle escalating during the late morning and mid-afternoon. On the technological front, no invention ranked higher during the immediate postwar years than the 1953 development of "M8R," an electronic tape playback system that enabled Muzak to switch its recordings from phonograph to audio tape. The development of M8R brought full automation to the Muzak network, making it economically viable for the first time for franchises to operate in communities with populations under 25,000.

By the end of the 1950s, after Muzak began switching from telephone lines to FM subcarriers, hundreds of thousands of employees and consumers across the U.S. were either consciously or subconsciously listening to the emotion-tamed strains of Muzak. Muzak was being played in a wide spectrum of businesses, aboard trains and airplanes, and, beginning with the Eisenhower Administration, in the White House. New ownership arrived late in the decade when Muzak, with 150 franchisees in the United States, Canada, and abroad, was sold to Wrather Corporation in 1957. Under the auspices of Wrather Corporation, Muzak grew robustly. The company's franchise network expanded substantially and the number of recordings in Muzak's library proliferated during a 15-year span that included, among other highlights, the inclusion of Muzak aboard the Apollo XI spaceship that carried Neil Armstrong to the moon.

In 1972, Muzak was passed to the hands of another corporate parent when Teleprompter Corporation purchased the company from Wrather Corporation. The expansion of Muzak's music library picked up pace during Teleprompter's period of control, with as many as 600 compositions being added each year to the company's collection of easy-listening hits, as the new management strove to develop a broader palette of contemporary melodies. Midway through the 1970s, the company's vast musical selection was entered into a computer, enabling engineers to locate compositions with great speed and precision. Additional progress on the technological front during the 1970s saw the launching of Muzak's own broadcast satellite late in the decade, signalling the beginning of the conversion from FM transmission to satellite broadcast.

Muzak Moves to Foreground in the 1980s

As Muzak neared its 50th year of business, yet another ownership change was set to take place. In 1981, Westinghouse Corporation purchased Teleprompter and, reportedly, only learned later that it had acquired Muzak Corporation as part of the deal. It was while under Westinghouse's control that one of the most significant developments in Muzak's history occurred, one that pointed the way toward the company's future and distanced it from its past. In 1984, the company struck a private-label agreement with one of its few competitors, Seattle-based Yesco Audio Environments. Founded in 1968, Yesco pioneered the foreground music concept, carving a niche for itself by playing the popular recordings of hits by the original artists rather than instrumental renditions of those hits. Muzak had achieved much in the background music industry during its five decades of market domination—80 million people listened to Muzak every day during the early 1980s and its programs were syndicated in 19 countries—but the wave of the future was in the foreground music industry. The 1984 deal with Yesco represented Muzak's first move into this market, adding foreground music selections to Muzak's library that were then provided to Muzak customers under the TONES name. The following year, Muzak began broadcasting its own original artist program called Foreground Music One.

In 1986, Muzak was acquired by The Field Corporation, a Chicago-based holding company owned by department store heir Marshall Field V, who oversaw Muzak's 1987 merger with rival Yesco. The merger completely reshaped Muzak for the future, precipitating what *Billboard* magazine would later describe as Muzak's transformation from a "passé 'elevator music' specialist to a dynamic, multi-faceted communications company." The merger also brought an end to Muzak's heavy involvement in the background music industry and greatly strengthened its presence in the foreground music industry. Muzak's vice president of programming and licensing would later note as much when he remarked, "There are still a couple of companies out there doing that kind of old-style, 1,001-strings, ruin-your-favorite-song kind of thing, but we dropped all that in 1987."

Muzak, which had been headquartered in New York since 1936, relocated its corporate offices to Seattle after the signal merger with Yesco and began developing into the sophisticated, diverse communications company that earned *Billboard*'s esteem. One year after the merger, Muzak, then known officially as Muzak Limited Partnership, debuted Music Plus, which consisted of five channels of music, audio marketing messages, data messaging, and business television delivered via satellite. Additional services to businesses were offered in 1991 when the company launched its ZTV video network, which offered six channels and 11 music formats to night clubs, restaurants, and bars. The following year, as the pace of new product introductions intensified, Muzak launched SuperLink, a retail advertising service that connected large grocery wholesalers with large groups of retailers, and added seven more channels to its Music Plus service.

Mid-1990s Diversification

Sales by the end of 1992 had climbed to $54.2 million, a total that would increase strongly in the coming years as Muzak broadened its range of services to businesses. New ownership took control in 1992 when management and Centre Partners, a money pool administered by Lazard Freres & Co., acquired Muzak from The Field Corporation. At the time, Muzak's operations comprised 176 franchisees and 16 company-owned outlets that sold "environmental music," satellite-delivered video, data communications, and other products in the United States and in two dozen foreign countries. Building on this base, the company's new owners spearheaded the development of several new programming services during their first years of control, introducing informational programming services, Muzak Newscast and DTN Wall Street, in 1993 and forming Muzak Special Products Division in 1994 to provide a broader range of services to the company's business clients.

The creation of Muzak Special Products Division, which positioned the company as an alternative marketing service for record labels, helped push sales in 1994 up to $83.4 million, a substantial increase over 1993's total of $58.5 million. In 1995, the company bolstered its Music Plus service by adding four channels for a total of 16 channels, and increased its presence in Europe through a joint venture with a Dutch company named Alcas Achtergrondmuziek. The partnership with Alcas gave Muzak the capability to market business music, advertising, business television, visual merchandising, and data communication services throughout much of Europe.

As Muzak prepared for the late 1990s and the beginning of the 21st century, it stood strongly poised to take advantage of emerging technologies in the arena of business communications. A business arrangement with EchoStar Communications Corporation in 1996 enabled Muzak to expand its music selection to 60 channels by the end of the year, further strengthening its resources for the years ahead. Less than a decade after its merger with Yesco, the company had completely revamped and diversified its services to meet the variegated demands of business clients across the globe, evolving into much more than Major General Squier first envisaged in 1922. As the company forged ahead, a conversion to public ownership was in the offing.

Further Reading

Baker, M. Sharon, "Muzak's New Tune Echoes a Drop in IPOs," *Puget Sound Business Journal,* September 6, 1996, p.1.

Borzillo, Carrie, "Many Sides of Muzak Elevate Seattle Co. to New Status," *Billboard,* February 20, 1993, p. 1.

nautica

Nautica Enterprises, Inc.

40 West 57th Street
New York, New York 10019
U.S.A.
(212) 541-5757
Fax: (212) 977-4348

Public Company
Incorporated: 1966 as Pacific Coast Knitting Mills, Inc.
Employees: 1,000
Sales: $302.5 million (1996)
Stock Exchanges: NASDAQ
SICs: 5023 Homefurnishings; 5136 Men's & Boys'
Clothing & Furnishings; 5137 Women's, Children's &
Infants' Clothing & Accessories; 5611 Men's &
Boys' Clothing & Accessory Stores; 6794 Patent
Owners & Lessors

Nautica Enterprises, Inc. was, in the mid-1990s, designing, sourcing, and marketing men's apparel, some of which appeared in Nautica Shops in leading department stores. The company also was licensing the Nautica name for a range of products, including men's cologne and skin-care products, watches, eyewear, and footwear. It also was operating factory outlet stores for its products. Nautica was ranked first (along with two others) by *Forbes* among 200 small companies by return on equity between 1989 and 1994. For most of that period its corporate name was State-o-Maine.

California-Based Company, 1966–75

Nautica originated in 1966 as Pacific Coast Knitting Mills, a firm engaged in manufacturing and distributing double-knit natural and synthetic fabrics in Vernon, California. This company had net sales of $2.1 million and net income of $55,533 in fiscal 1968 (the year ended February 29, 1968). It went public in 1971, offering a minority of its outstanding shares for $8 a share. The company ended fiscal 1972 with $4.1 million in sales but only $44,340 in net income.

In 1972 Pacific Coast Knitting Mills acquired, for $850,000 in cash and notes, almost all the stock of Van Baalen Heilburn & Co., a Rockland, Maine, firm engaged in manufacturing and distributing men's sportswear, swimwear, and robes, generally under the trade name State-o-Maine. Van Baalen, which originated in 1921 in New York, had moved to Maine in the late 1930s to lower its labor costs. At the time of its purchase it was making robes under the Christian Dior name and had long-term contracts with designers John Weitz and Pierre Cardin. The company had net sales of $3 million and net income of $51,880 in fiscal 1971. It was renamed Van Baalen Pacific Corp. after its acquisition.

With Van Baalen in tow, Pacific Coast Knitting Mills raised its sales, but its earnings remained modest. In fiscal 1974 it had record sales of $5.3 million but net income of only $22,000, a circumstance attributed by management to substantial knitting-mill losses. Sales grew to $5.9 million in fiscal 1975, but the company took a $1.5–million loss because of discontinued operations. Its stock quickly fell out of favor with investors, dropping as low as 12 cents a share in 1973 and two cents a share in 1975.

New York–Based State-o-Maine, 1975–83

In June 1975 the knitting-mill business was sold to Stanley Flaster, the president of Pacific Coast Knitting Mills, who renamed it Flastex, Inc. Flaster's wife, who owned the biggest block of Pacific Coast stock, and Myron Herschler, its vice-president and another big investor, sold their shares to Harvey Sanders, the company's chairman, secretary, and treasurer, and Milton Weinick, a director. Sanders and Weinick were partners in a New York City accounting firm that bore their names. Sanders emerged with 41 percent of the stock, and Weinick, named vice-president and treasurer, with 31 percent. The company, renamed State-o-Maine, moved its headquarters to New York and won a $725,000 loan from the National Bank of North America, but only on the condition that Sanders also loan the company $225,000. In 1979 Weinick became chairman as well as treasurer, with Sanders as vice-president and secretary. Sanders's rank rose to president in 1983, and he added the title of chief executive officer in 1992.

Company Perspectives:

Our company continues to evolve as we strive to improve our business. We reaffirm our commitment to value, quality and product integrity. We pledge to continue to work with our retail partners in implementing our strategies and developing new ways in which to serve our customers. Our creed of controlled growth remains intact as we move toward the end of the century.

State-o-Maine made modest profits in the late 1970s but was still shunned by investors. In fiscal 1980 it earned $245,000 on net sales of $12.7 million but ended the fiscal year with a long-term debt of nearly $1 million. Three years later the company had upped its sales to $19.2 million and its net income to $509,000: steady if unspectacular figures. Customers for its robes and its jogging suits included Bloomingdale's, Nordstrom, and Saks. The firm's fortunes advanced that year when a department-store executive introduced Sanders to David Chu, a young, Taiwanese-born clothing designer. Chu and a partner had started a company called Nautica in 1981 and had introduced a collection of brightly colored men's outdoor jackets. They sold well, but the partner did not want to invest the necessary funds for expansion. For a small amount of cash and the assumption of about $1 million in liabilities, State-o-Maine bought out Chu's partner in 1984. Chu later traded his 20-percent interest in the company for State-o-Maine stock.

Nautica's Rise to Prominence, 1984–91

Sanders and Chu devised an expansion plan combining Nautica's products and maritime-based image with State-o-Maine's production and distribution network. This plan entailed selling only to carefully selected high-end stores—only one or two department stores in each market outside New York City—and showcasing Nautica's products as a collection rather than splitting them by categories. These products grew to include men's dress shirts, neckwear, hosiery, belts, suspenders, small leather goods, jewelry, watches, gloves, hats, sunglasses, fragrances, and skin care. Nautica's growth was spectacular, its sales increasing from about $1 million in fiscal 1985 to about $20 million in fiscal 1988, about half-and-half to department and specialty stores. Outerwear accounted for about 45 percent, "activewear" for another 40 percent, and casual sportswear, a line introduced in 1987, for 15 percent. A full collection of women's products was introduced in fall 1988.

Fueled by Nautica's popularity, State-o-Maine became a hot company in the late 1980s. Sales soared from $28.9 million in fiscal 1986 to $75 million in fiscal 1989, and net income shot up from $1.6 million to $5.4 million. The company's market capitalization grew from $2 million in 1983 to $74 million before the end of 1991. At first about half the company's production was manufactured in Rockland, but this proportion fell to one-third as Nautica established a Hong Kong subsidiary and increasingly outsourced its needs to Far East suppliers. In 1990 State-o-Maine halted production at its Van Baalen subsidiary, restricting the operation to distribution and importing all of its

clothing. State-o-Maine opened retail stores in New York City and Newport Beach, California, in 1987 and a Rockland factory-outlet store in 1988.

By the end of fiscal 1991, in which Nautica accounted for $63 million of State-o-Maine's $95 million in sales, Chu was a major presence in his field. He maintained total command over the Nautica image, with design control over every style in both the men's and women's clothing lines—now totaling nearly 500 pieces—and also over the licensed products, such as watches and fragrances. He even designed many of Nautica's fabrics. In an interview for a cover story by *Bobbin*, Chu said the Nautica image represented the "relationship of people to nature. What we try to do is provide functional apparel that is stylish—apparel that can be worn in all kinds of weather and all kinds of nature patterns. . . . The beauty about the textile industry today is the new technologies featuring new fabrics, waterproof fabrics and microfibers, which make the final product more functional.''

By the spring of 1991 Nautica had established nearly 100 in-store shops, with distinctive deck flooring in certain areas. Its high-end image was fiercely protected by Sanders; when a department store marked down its goods mid-season, the account was dropped. Nautica's carefully crafted marketing plan included advertisements in such magazines as *GQ, Esquire, Sports Illustrated, Vanity Fair,* and *Vogue,* and also sponsorship of sailing competitions, including the U.S. and international Youth Sailing Championships. For 1992 it created its very own championship in Portugal: the Nautica Cup. That year State-o-Maine opened an expensive new showroom on Manhattan's elegant 57th Street and hired 10 additional designers and merchandising coordinators. However, Nautica's money-losing women's division, which never accounted for more than 15 percent of sales, was discontinued in May 1991.

Continued Expansion and Growth, 1992–96

State-o-Maine added another arrow to its quiver in 1992, when it acquired Bayou Sport for an undisclosed sum. With annual sales volume of about $5 million, this company was manufacturing and marketing men's moderately priced cotton woven and knit shirts, swimwear, slacks, and shorts under its own name.

Reflecting the overwhelming presence of the biggest sector of its business, State-o-Maine was renamed Nautica Enterprises in 1993. That year the number of Nautica shops within department stores reached 428. Nautica also had 543 specialty accounts and 18 factory outlet stores. The far-flung number of retail stores licensed abroad under the Nautica name included 10 in South Korea and nine each in Mexico and Japan. Licensed products—including boys' and girls' wear, luggage, and even Lincoln-Mercury Villager vans—now made up about 25 percent of sales, which totaled $151 million in the fiscal year.

Fiscal 1994 was better yet, with net sales reaching $192.9 million and net income $16.8 million. Sanders—who owned about 11.5 percent of the company—took $6.6 million in salary, according to a trade publication. During the calendar year the number of in-store shops rose to 548. They were averaging 800 square feet in size and $400 in sales per square foot. The number of outlet stores increased to 31; they averaged about 3,000 square feet and $375 per square foot.

In fiscal 1995 Nautica Enterprises advanced once more, its net sales reaching $247.6 million and its net income nearly $24 million. For the 1991 to 1995 period it posted an average annual gain of 24 percent in sales and 54 percent in net income. The 1995 profit margin of 10.5 percent was the third-highest among the apparel industry's mid- and large-size public firms. That year the company's accounts grew to 1,100 department stores and more than 500 specialty stores. Sanders announced that he planned to double the size of some of its new in-store shops to an average of 2,200 to 3,000 square feet, compared to the 800- to 1,800-square-foot range of the current ones. Also in 1995, the company continued its aggressive outlet-store expansion, presented a new Nautica Competition activewear label, announced a licensing deal to sell women's wear under the Nautica label in August 1996, and announced a licensing agreement to market Charles Goodnight robes and loungewear.

Fiscal 1996 was another record-busting year for Nautica Enterprises, its net sales reaching $302.5 million and its net income just short of $32 million. The company opened 146 new shops and expanded 122. In September 1996 it announced its entry into the home-furnishings market with three home-textile licensees: Dan River for sheets and bedroom ensembles; Ex-Cell Home Fashions for shower curtains, bath accessories, and table linens; and Leshner Corp. for bath and beach towels. Company executives estimated Nautica Home would register about $50 million in retail sales by the end of its first year. The women's line, produced through a licensing agreement with Bernard Chaus, opened in more than 100 new in-store shops. Men's tailored-clothing and infants'/toddlers' lines were scheduled to reach stores in spring 1997. Also in 1996, the company announced a joint venture with Financo to distribute the Nautica men's collection throughout Europe, where it would open a showroom in January 1997, a license agreement with Unionbay to design and market a men's denim collection, and a license agreement with Kellwood Co. for dress shirts.

Nautica Enterprises ended fiscal 1996 with 885 in-store shops but expected to have 1,077 by the end of fiscal 1997 (February 28, 1997). It saw potential for an eventual 1,500 such shops. It was also planning to expand the size of 159 of its stores in 1996, of which at least 46 would feature a separate area for the Nautica Competition line. The company was planning to add five to 10 outlet stores per year for the next five years. Nautica ended fiscal 1996 with 58 freestanding stores and 145 in-store shops in 30 foreign countries. New openings scheduled for 1996 included Argentina, Brazil, and Beijing, China. Nautica Enterprises had virtually no long-term debt in 1995.

Nautica Enterprises in the Mid-1990s

In fiscal 1996 Nautica International, Inc., a wholly owned subsidiary of Nautica Enterprises, was offering an array of men's sportswear, outerwear, and activewear, primarily targeted to the 25-to-54-year-old age group. Sportswear included sweaters, woven and knit shirts, rugby shirts, pants, and shorts. Outerwear included parkas, bomber jackets, and foul-weather gear. Activewear included fleece and french terry tops, french terry pants and shorts, T-shirts, and swimwear. This clothing came in three principal groups: Anchor, Crew, and Fashion.

State-o-Maine, also a wholly owned subsidiary, was offering Nautica-brand robes and loungewear, sportswear, and swimwear under the Bayou Sports label, apparel designed and sourced for private-label programs (which were first introduced in 1993), and robes and loungewear under the Charles Goodnight label. Except for the Nautica-brand furnishings, these products were more competitively priced and more broadly distributed than the company's other offerings.

Nautica products were being sold primarily to leading department and specialty stores. Its principal customers included Dillard's, May Company Department Stores, Dayton's-Hudson's-Marshall Field's, Federated Department Stores, Bloomingdale's, Lazarus/Rich's, and Nordstrom. State-o-Maine was selling primarily to department stores, including the first four above, and such national chain-store operators as J.C. Penney and Sears, Roebuck.

Nautica Enterprises was maintaining a high profile for its products by advertisements in national and regional magazines and through a cooperative advertising program with its retail customers. This effort was being augmented by a series of special events and sponsorships. In fiscal 1996 the company was the official clothing sponsor for the U.S. Sailing Team and the official apparel sponsor for two events on the Senior Professional Golfers' Association tour.

Nautica Enterprises' products were being designed by the company's own staff and manufactured chiefly in Hong Kong, China, the Philippines, Malaysia, Singapore, Saipan, Thailand, India, and Turkey. The Nautica name and related trademarks were being licensed for sale abroad—both wholesale and through a number of retail stores—by Nautica Apparel, a wholly owned subsidiary.

Nautica Enterprises operated 38 factory outlet stores in fiscal 1996 through another wholly owned subsidiary, Nautica Retail USA, and it maintained flagship stores on Manhattan's Upper West Side and in Newport Beach, California. It was operating three warehouse and distribution facilities in Rockland, Maine, two of which were owned by the company and the third leased. It was leasing administrative and sales offices and a design studio in Manhattan and was also leasing sales offices in Dallas.

Principal Subsidiaries

Nautica Apparel, Inc.; Nautica International, Inc.; Nautica Retail USA, Inc.; State-o-Maine, Inc.

Further Reading

Austin, Phyllis, "Taking Care of Business," *Maine Times,* June 3, 1994, p. 2.

Black, Susan S., "Nautica: Its Ship Has Come In," *Bobbin,* May 1991, pp. 52, 54–56.

Brady, Jennifer L., "Nautica to Keep Launching In-Store Shops," *Daily News Record,* October 4, 1996, p. 14.

Esquivel, Josephine R., "Bobbin's Top 40," *Bobbin,* June 1996, pp. 53–54, 63, 68.

"Featuring the Future," *Daily News Record,* February 7, 1994, p. 48.

Furman, Phyllis, "Sailing Ahead in Choppy Apparel Seas," *Crain's New York Business,* November 13, 1984, pp. 3, 46.

Johnson, Sarah, "Nautica Adding Home," *HFN,* September 2, 1996, p. 1.

Lockwood, Lisa, "State-o-Maine Buys Nautica for Undisclosed Amount," *Daily News Record,* August 8, 1984, p. 6.

"Nautica Licenses Chaus to Make Women's Wear," *Daily News Record,* September 18, 1995, p. 2.

Ryan, Thomas J., "It's Full Steam Ahead for Nautica's Course," *Daily News Record,* May 16, 1996, p. 5.

——, "Nautica Ent. Planning Major Push in In-Store Shops, Outlet Stores," *Daily News Record,* September 30, 1994, p. 2.

——, "Nautica Enterprises to Double Size of Some In-Store Shop Formats," *Daily News Record,* September 14, 1995, p. 2.

——, "Nautica to More Than Triple Number of In-Store Shops," *Daily News Record,* September 30, 1993, pp. 3, 11.

Temes, Judy, "Creating an Image Chops State-o-Maine's Earnings, *Crain's New York Business,* October 22, 1992, p. 46.

Weisman, Katherine, "Kismet on Seventh Avenue," *Forbes,* November 25, 1991, pp. 152–53.

—Robert Halasz

New England Business Services, Inc.

500 Main Street
Groton, Massachusetts 01471
U.S.A.
(508) 448-6111
Fax: (508) 486-0738
Web site: http://www.nebs.com

Public Company
Incorporated: 1952
Employees: 2,014
Sales: $254 million (1996)
Stock Exchanges: New York
SICs: 2761 Manifold Business Forms

As small offices across North America become increasingly automated because of the advances in computer software and other technology, Groton, Massachusetts-based New England Business Services, Inc. (NEBS) keeps pace. Since 1952 the company has become a leader in supplying small business owners with customized and custom-designed business forms, checks, business cards, and other office needs. Selling its business forms, checkwriting systems, customized promotional materials, and related office supplies primarily by mail-order catalog, NEBS has continued to expand and modernize its product line, earning the goodwill of growing numbers of entrepreneurs by responding to their unique needs. Recent years have witnessed the inclusion of computer software, specialized desktop publishing materials, and other electronic services to NEBS's product line. In addition to being a distributor of *One-Write Plus,* the accounting system most widely used by small businesses nationwide, NEBS markets a complete line of paper products for use with *Page Magic* business-oriented desktop publishing software.

The NEBS product line consists mainly of manual and computer business forms, as well as preprinted items such as time cards, mailing and display labels, bags, signage, and tags. Forms—invoices, statements, receipts, purchase orders, and the like, available as carbonless or carbon multipart sets—are either of the all-purpose variety or are designed to meet the specific needs of a particular business. Such specific forms would include trade-specific construction estimates, jewelry appraisal forms, service station repair forms, restaurant guest checks, and retailer lay-away forms. Additional products include form holders, pricing systems, and other form-related or preprinted products. As a consumable part of the day-to-day operations of small business firms, reorders provide NEBS with its greatest profitability.

Catalog Sales Reach More Customers, 1950s and 60s

NEBS had its start in 1952, when Al Anderson, a forms salesman based in Cleveland, Ohio, became aware of the lack of customized forms in the small quantity and reasonable price range that would make them accessible to the average small business. Instead, small retailers, beauty salons and barber shops, electricians and plumbers, and other small service businesses often used their rubber stamps on generic carboned forms. Anderson decided to fill this business niche. Because of the scattered nature of the small business market, he decided that direct mail marketing would be the most efficient and least costly way to build his company. Moving to Townsend, Massachusetts, he assembled a selection of business forms manufactured by a variety of outside printing companies, put together a brochure, and mailed it out. He focused his sales efforts on smaller companies with 20 or fewer employees, that is, customers for whom buying custom-printed business forms was usually unrealistic because of the large print-runs per form required from most printed form suppliers. The idea was a success; orders came pouring in and by 1955 Anderson had moved NEBS out of his backyard barn into real office space. He also hired Jay R. Rhoads, Jr. to help handle the business side of his growing forms business. By 1968 NEBS was posting $3.5 million in net sales. The 90,000 active customers for its products were serviced by 163 full- and part-time employees.

Printing Capabilities Provide Key to Expansion, the 1970s

In 1970 Anderson retired, leaving CEO Rhoads to expand NEBS's marketplace. Working closely with his brother, Richard H. Rhoads, now company president and director, Rhoads

Company Perspectives:

NEBS has established and retained its market leadership by providing the high-quality products a small business needs at affordable prices and with outstanding customer service.

planned for an ambitious expansion of the company. Realizing that the average customer purchased only a limited quantity of any one form during a given year, NEBS concentrated on the efficient management of large volumes of small orders. The company could soon pride itself on a six-day forms turnaround schedule. Because of its ability to respond quickly to customers depending on it for the forms they used in their day-to-day operations, reorders quickly reached a rate of more than 70 percent of sales volume.

A crucial element of any major growth, Rhoads realized, was ending NEBS's reliance on outside vendors to provide its base forms. With printing capabilities of its own, the company would be able to capture wholesaler profits as well as the retail markup it currently earned. By 1973, with 315 employees and net sales of $11 million, NEBS expanded its customer base to 258,000, thereby reaching the point where it could absorb the overhead of its first large-run high-speed printing press. With the addition of the press, NEBS expanded its Townsend office and warehouse facilities, upgraded its computer system, and began expanding its product line. Over the next few years Rhoads would also set up printing plants in Peterborough, New Hampshire and Maryville, Missouri to better serve NEBS customers on a regional level. In addition, through the 1976 establishment of office and production facilities for NEBS Business Forms, Ltd., in Midland, Ontario, the company expanded its sales territory into the English-speaking regions of Canada (bilingual forms would be marketed beginning in 1985). This expanded sales territory, growing far outside the New England region to encompass both the United States and Canada, was aided by the introduction of a toll-free 800 number for phone sales. By 1981, 40 percent of the orders for NEBS products were received by phone.

In October 1977 NEBS went public with an offering of 50,000 shares of common stock; the company would be listed in the NASDAQ beginning in December 1980. With sales now passing $30 million and a customer base that included more than 411,000 small businesses in both the United States and Canada, 1977 would be a banner year for the company. But it was only the beginning of a major growth spurt. As its customer base grew by 41 percent to 700,000 very small business firms by 1981, net sales followed suit, reaching $79 million by the end of fiscal 1981. Although the inflationary national economy had impacted these sales figures, NEBS's actual growth could be measured by the 1,300 employees now promoting and producing its products. Company estimates, which put "real" growth in 1981 at 9.7 percent, reflected the company's corporate restructuring activities and capital expenditures in anticipation of further expansion. The NEBS Forms Division, which accounted for the largest percentage of both sales and profit, had become an independent operating entity in 1980. Corporate offices, in search of more space, were

relocated to Groton, and plans were implemented for the construction of a manufacturing plant in Flagstaff, Arizona to better service customers in the Western states. In 1981, NEBS also made a three-for-two split of its common stock to encourage additional investment in the company.

Changes and New Markets, the 1980s

As the company progressed through the sluggish 1980s, its project development program remained its primary focus. Alerted early on to the possible proliferation of computers in small businesses, NEBS began serving the needs of those firms investing in first-generation computer technology. Custom-printed continuous forms, perforated into pages and lined by "pin" holes for use with dot matrix printers, became a top seller for NEBS, which offered small companies competitive prices and fast service. In addition, the 1984 acquisition of the Santa Clara, California-based Devoke Company allowed NEBS to offer its customers special-purpose computer furniture as well.

The market for computer-related products would begin to level off in mid-decade, a lull after the storm of PC installations in the small business market. This slowdown caused NEBS to divest itself of its Devoke subsidiary by the end of the decade. In addition, the company worked to restructure and adjust its product mix in an effort to battle the increasingly stagnant office supply market that characterized the late 1980s. In 1986, for instance, after a year of relatively flat earnings, NEBS implemented several programs to make its order entry and production processes more efficient. An automated order entry system was initialized, thereby decreasing the turnaround time for customer orders. Combining this with other restructuring and cost-containment measures and a seven percent reduction in staff, the company was able to report another banner year, increasing earnings by 30 percent to $16.89 million.

In addition to expanding its product line, the company continued to expand its market. Its Canadian subsidiary entered the French-speaking Quebec market in 1985, offering a line of bilingual forms modeled on the traditional NEBS line. And in 1988 NEBS opened an overseas division, entering the office forms market in the United Kingdom as NEBS Business Stationery. Headquartered in Chester, England, this division marketed a complete selection of forms and other office products throughout Great Britain and Northern Ireland. Domestically, DFS Business Forms, a network of independent dealers, was implemented as a means to further increase visibility and market share among very small businesses.

Small retail operations proved to be an especially lucrative niche for NEBS, which provided everything from bags, tags, and signage to preprinted sales slips, company check systems, and labels. Products were also made available on recycled paper. Another cause for optimism was the continuous increase in government-imposed regulations of small business enterprises in both the United States and Canada. An increasing bureaucracy would generate increasing numbers of forms, some of which NEBS could provide. As accounting software systems began to be adopted by small firms, NEBS created and marketed compatible forms under its NEBS Computer Forms division. Checks, invoices, statements, and purchase orders were designed for compatibility with such software vendors as

Quicken, Peachtree Accounting, Open Systems, and *DacEasy.* Estimating its potential customer base at approximately five million small businesses in 1980, NEBS would see its share of that base grow to almost 25 percent by the end of the decade.

Personal Computers Pose Threat to Future, the 1990s

Ironically, the computer technology that had sparked NEBS's expansion in the early 1980s was threatening to undermine it by the 1990s. The proliferation of desktop publishing software, color laser printers, and "designer" papers allowed even simple home-office businesses to produce sophisticated letterheads, forms, business cards, and labels on a PC, bypassing the need for the custom printing services that NEBS provided.

In response, the company began to enter the software market in the 1990s. In addition to continuing to offer forms compatible with the major accounting software packages then on the market, NEBS developed *Form Filling,* a software package designed to eliminate tedious setup of computer-generated forms. *Form Filling* was competitively priced and marketed along with a broad range of forms that included payroll check systems with detailed stubs, all of which were available as laser or dot-matrix forms.

Early in the decade, NEBS acquired SYCOM, Inc., a Madison, Wisconsin-based marketer of custom business forms to professional offices. Marketed both by mail and phone, SYCOM forms provided the company with a specialized product geared for accountants, attorneys, dentists, and other professionals in the health care field. In January 1993 it would also acquire rights to the *One-Write Plus* software developed by MECA Software, Inc. Through this acquisition the company gained both a distributor network and a skilled sales and service staff for the popular, easy-to-use general ledger software package. *One-Write Plus* would be managed through NEBS Software, Inc.

Fluctuations in the nationwide small business economy, which had boomed during the 1980s, would tend downward in the early 1990s. During 1991 alone a Dun & Bradstreet report showed that small business failures had reached 43 percent, and the number of new small firms opened during the year rose only three percent from 1990. In 1990 NEBS reported net income of $20.6 million; only two years later it would see that figure shrink to $15.47 million. By 1993 net income reached a record low: $14.2 million on sales of $237.1 million to more than one million small businesses.

In an attempt to combat such lackluster sales and dropping earnings, NEBS developed a new product line, aggressively pursued its custom forms market, and reorganized its distribution network. Although the market for manual forms had begun to contract, due in part to both the adoption of computerized accounting systems and the proliferation of technologically enhanced electronic point-of-sale equipment, management also recognized the need to more actively promote these forms, which they viewed as a "point of entry" into the NEBS product line. The DFS Business Forms dealer base, expanded to include the growing number of office supply "superstores," renewed their efforts to market NEBS software to computer peripherals retailers. The company also began a telemarketing program, combining catalog mailings with customer contact by phone. In 1993 the company's 2,217 employees were able to serve the needs of more than 1.2 million small business customers, with a 48-hour turnaround time between order receipt and shipment.

More Colorful Palette Revitalizes Lackluster Sales

NEBS achieved banner success in 1995, with sales for the company's domestic operations alone reaching $241.8 million. Net income for 1995, which had begun a slow rebound from its 1993 low, reached $16.3 million on total sales of $263.7 million. Part of the reason for the turnaround was a cost-reduction program implemented by the company that resulted in the layoff of 100 employees. In addition, the company decided to close its SYCOM subsidiary, integrating that company's operations into their NEBS counterparts.

Much of the credit for the company's financial turnaround was also given to the introduction of "Company Colors" forms and stationery. Responding to customer demand for more image-conscious printed products without the expense of custom printing, NEBS created desktop papers, as well as coordinating letterhead, business cards, and forms, all using a palette of the five most popular two-toned color combinations. This program would be modified into NEBS Colors in 1996. Another factor contributing to overall growth in 1995 was the introduction of the *Page Magic* desktop software package, along with a line of coordinating paper products. In addition, many of NEBS's most popular manual forms were redesigned to achieve a more contemporary look.

During 1995 the company also formed an alliance with Kinko's, Inc., a successful photocopy center with more than 750 branches located throughout the United States. In an effort to generate new forms business for the company, NEBS placed custom printing consultants into 22 selected Kinko's copy center locations, where they could help customers design custom business forms, brochures, and other stationery items. These orders could be immediately modemed to company printing plants for quick production and delivery. Unfortunately, the partnership did not produce the desired results and the company closed these custom-printing desks in September of 1996.

Looking to the Future of Small Businesses

From its beginnings as a producer of preprinted business forms, NEBS has continually transformed itself to meet future challenges. Rededicating itself as "The Small Business Resource" in 1996, the company released several CD-ROM products designed to help entrepreneurs plan, structure, and finance their fledgling business operations. Increased resources were channeled into the expansion of mailing lists and development of *Success Reference Guides,* an enlarged catalog and small business resource system that includes the company's complete product line. Reengineering was begun on NEBSnet, a computer graphics workstation that enhanced retail customer orders. And the company furthered its future focus by introducing www.nebs.com, a website organized around business advice and product promotion.

During fiscal 1996 NEBS would continue its efforts to adapt to a changing small business climate. Meanwhile, the December 1995 retirement of CEO Richard H. Rhoads ended a combined 25 years of leadership by the Rhoads brothers. Under the new leadership of incoming CEO and President Robert J. Murray the company effected a new organizational structure and rededicated itself to the direct marketing of forms and related office products for small businesses. Such refocusing efforts included directing NEBS resources toward software distribution rather than more costly software development. Selling its *One-Write Plus* software to Peachtree Software Inc. in early 1996, NEBS retained distribution rights and an exclusive marketing agreement for *One-Write Plus*-compatible forms.

The company's organizational restructuring would prove costly in the short run. By the close of its fiscal year in June 1996, NEBS reported net income of $11.929 million; further setbacks were suffered after the company was ordered to pay a pre-tax charge of $5.2 million after closing its satellite sales desks in Kinko's retail copy centers. But the establishment of a Business Management group to engage in strategic policy and product development and an increased level of operating efficiency boded well for the future. By 1996 the company had a working relationship with more than 25,000 retail dealers, representing only ten percent of the total private label business forms reseller's market. NEBS's decision to grow retail outlets through its DFS units marked this market as the focus of future growth for the company.

NEBS has continued to be aware that its overall performance is directly related to the health of the small business community, both in the United States and elsewhere. And that community has been changing. The ubiquitous PC has streamlined accounting methods, while shifting consumables have caused NEBS to refine its product mix continuously. The increasing sophistication with which small business owners have planned their promotional strategies—through creativity, professionalism, and the development of a striking and unique image—has directed the company's efforts in promoting its forms business. Continuing to market its products to the ten million small businesses and more than 20 million in-home offices throughout the United States, Canada, and the United Kingdom, NEBS has increasingly focused its marketing efforts on retail, although the direct mail of repeat orders continues to be the company's primary area of profitability. With almost five decades of experience within this expanding market, NEBS remains uniquely qualified to profit from the long-term trend toward increased small business ownership.

Principal Subsidiaries

NEBS Business Forms, Ltd. (Canada); NEBS Business Stationery (United Kingdom); Shirlite, Ltd. (United Kingdom).

—Pamela L. Shelton

NGC Corporation

13430 Northwest Freeway
Houston, Texas 77040
U.S.A.
(713) 507-6400
Fax: (713) 507-3871
Web site: http://www.ngccorp.com

Public Company
Incorporated: 1984 as Natural Gas Clearinghouse
Employees: 1,185
Sales: $3.66 billion (1995)
Stock Exchanges: New York
SICs: 1921 Natural Gas Liquids; 4923 Gas Transmission
& Distribution; 6719 Holding Companies, Not
Elsewhere Classified

NGC Corporation is North America's leading energy commodity and service provider, offering ''one-stop'' gathering, processing, marketing, and transportation of natural gas, natural gas liquids, crude oil, and electricity. Led almost since its formation by Chairman and CEO Charles L. (Chuck) Watson, NGC has achieved its market dominance through two major mergers: the 1995 merger of Natural Gas Clearinghouse with Trident NGL Holdings Inc.; and the 1996 merger of all of NGC with most of Chevron Corporation's natural gas and gas liquids businesses, including its Warren Petroleum Company subsidiary. NGC acts as a holding company conducting its activities through two primary subsidiaries: Natural Gas Clearinghouse, which, with its subsidiaries, handles the company's natural gas and electric power marketing activities; and Warren Petroleum, formerly Trident NGL, under which NGC conducts its natural gas liquids (NGL), crude oil, and natural gas transmission business. NGC is also active in Canada, through its joint venture with Nova Corporation, and in Europe, through its joint venture with British Gas plc. The company has made plans to expand operations into Mexico. NGC is owned by Nova Corporation, British Gas, and Chevron, each of which controls approxi-

mately 25 percent of the company; NGC management and other shareholders control the remaining shares of the company. Watson himself holds nearly seven percent of NGC.

NGC's marketing arm essentially acts as an energy services middleman. NGC arranges for the purchase of natural gas supplies from as many as 600 different suppliers ranging from major natural gas producers to small independents. The company generally purchases or negotiates for the purchase of specific volumes of natural gas through fixed short-term and long-term contracts and arranges for their transmission or transportation through company-owned and third-party pipeline systems. Supplies purchased are aggregated by the company and resold to the company's customers, including local distribution companies, energy utility companies, power plants, and retail and industrial end-users. Through NGC's Electric Clearinghouse, Inc. subsidiary, the company has also entered the emerging electric services market. NGC complements its marketing activities with the gathering, processing, fractionation (that is, separation into component parts), and transmission of natural gas liquids, crude oil, and other petroleum and gas-based products, such as butane. The company's growing assets include ownership or operating interests in 33 gas processing plants and nearly 11,000 miles of natural gas gathering pipeline systems, located primarily in Kansas, Louisiana, Oklahoma, and Texas.

The Chevron merger has allowed NGC to increase its share of the natural gas marketing market from a six percent share to an industry-dominant 14 percent share. The company's daily volume is expected to rise from approximately seven billion cubic feet to more than 11 billion cubic feet, placing NGC ahead of close competitors Enron Corporation and Amoco Corporation, which handle approximately nine billion cubic feet per day and six billion cubic feet per day, respectively. The Chevron merger also makes NGC the continent's second largest natural gas liquids producer and is expected to double the company's 1995 two billion cubic feet per day natural gas processing volume and 84,000 barrels per day natural gas liquids volume. The merger of Chevron's $3 billion natural gas revenues into NGC should also double the company's revenues, which neared $3.7 billion in 1995.

Negotiating the Deregulation of the 1980s

The natural gas industry was tightly regulated until the late 1970s, with the gathering, transportation, and marketing of natural gas dominated by a few companies and pricing restrictions that kept gas prices below market value. Prior to deregulation, natural gas was typically sold on a flat-rate, long-term contract basis. Gas producers sold to interstate pipeline companies, which sold the gas to distributors, which in turn marketed the gas to end-users. The National Gas Policy Act (NGPA) of 1978 began the process of deregulation, loosening restrictions on the transmission, marketing, and production of natural gas, and establishing new pricing layers, which removed price controls from new gas production. Over the next decade and a half the NGPA would be implemented by a series of orders promulgated by the Federal Energy Regulatory Commission (FERC), beginning with Order 380, introduced in 1984, which allowed third-party marketers to sell gas at prices competitive with the gas producers. This was followed by Order 436, which allowed transportation of natural gas over interstate pipelines and opened the way for market-responsive pricing.

The immediate effect of the NGPA was to increase drilling activities, as producers sought to develop gas resources that could be sold without pricing restrictions. But, in 1982, with the onset of a national recession, demand for natural gas collapsed. This situation opened the way for a new method of selling gas, spot pricing, and, with the deregulation of the industry, gave rise to an industry of third-party marketers. The Natural Gas Clearinghouse was set up in June 1984 as a broker for negotiating spot market transactions between producers and end-users. The Clearinghouse itself would not take title to the gas it brokered. The Clearinghouse was formed as a joint venture by investment banker Morgan Stanley, New York law firm Akin, Gump, Strauss, Hauer & Feld, and Transco Energy Company, an interstate natural gas pipeline company with a 10,000-mile system reaching an 11-state market. By October 1984, the Clearinghouse was in business, arranging its first spot market sale of 200 million daily cubic feet of natural gas. The company also negotiated with other pipeline systems to link up with the Clearinghouse.

The venture struggled in its first year. Then Transco and other pipeline companies defected, believing they could negotiate better pricing on their own. Morgan Stanley bought out Transco and Akin, Gump in 1985 for $24 million and recruited Chuck Watson to head up the company. Watson, then 35 years old, had gained 13 years of experience in the energy industry at Conoco Oil. Born at the Great Lakes Naval Academy in Illinois, Watson graduated with a business degree from Oklahoma State University and went to work for Conoco. Considered a rising star at the company, Watson received a series of promotions around the company, giving him a wide range of exposure to pipeline transportation and operations and to the marketing of natural gas and natural gas liquids. When Morgan Stanley hired him as president and CEO of the Natural Gas Clearinghouse, Watson set out to change the company's focus. Instead of merely acting as a broker, Watson used Morgan Stanley's financial backing to buy and then resell gas, while also beginning to build the company's own transmission, distribution, and processing infrastructure through a series of acquisitions. Meanwhile, new orders promulgated by FERC began to in-

crease the volumes of gas the independent marketers were allowed to handle. The Clearinghouse quickly gained a leadership position in the gas marketing field, seeing sales rise to 1.3 billion daily cubic feet by 1988 and top two billion daily cubic feet the following year, making the Clearinghouse the country's largest independent natural gas marketer.

The Bill Gates of Gas in the 1990s

Watson sought further growth for the company. In 1989, he arranged to sell the Clearinghouse to two oil and gas exploration and production companies, Apache Corporation and Noble Affiliates, Inc., gaining those companies' financial backing to fuel expansion. Watson remained as president, CEO, and now chairman of the Clearinghouse. At the end of 1989, he arranged for the Clearinghouse to acquire Apache's Nagasco, Inc. gas gathering system, boosting the Clearinghouse's natural gas volume to 2.55 billion daily cubic feet. The following year, the Clearinghouse, which had been developing natural gas futures, began trading gas futures at the New York Mercantile Exchange. By 1990, the Clearinghouse was posting annual revenues of $1.7 billion.

By the beginning of the 1990s, however, margins on sales of natural gas were dropping from a high of 25 cents per 1,000 cubic feet to the single-digit range in the 1990s, reaching a low of two to three cents per 1,000 cubic feet in the 1990s. Watson responded by expanding the Clearinghouse beyond natural gas marketing into gathering, processing, and marketing natural gas, as well as other fuel oils, building the Clearinghouse into a "one-stop energy store." The company formed its NGC Oil Trading and Transportation subsidiary and began expanding its gathering and processing capacity through acquisitions and contracts of facilities. Between 1990 and early 1994 the company spent some $150 million buying gathering systems and processing and storage facilities. Financing the company's expansion came from selling it, adding Dekalb Energy Company to the list of owners. Then, in 1992, the company, which had revenues of nearly $2.1 billion in 1991, with an operating profit of $78.5 million, was sold to Louisville Gas & Electric Company and British Gas, each of which controlled a one-third share of the company; management retained control of the remaining one-third. In that year, FERC Order 636 took away the last of the regulatory restrictions on the natural gas industry. In response, the Clearinghouse, through a new subsidiary, Hub Services, Inc., joined with three gas utility companies to form Enerchange LLC, which would own and operate three natural gas marketing hubs. The hubs, which were located at the intersection of interstate pipelines, offered various transaction services to customers, including taking deliveries from multiple suppliers and arranging sales to a range of distributors and end-users.

The company's revenues, aided by growing sales of natural gas liquids and crude oil, neared $2.5 billion in 1992 and $2.8 billion in 1993. The company's operating profit, a key industry indicator, also remained strong, at $96.8 million in 1992 and $92 million in 1993. Net profits for these years were $44 and $46 million, respectively, highlighting the tight margins available in the industry. These margins were also leading to an industry shakeout, as the field of marketers began to narrow, and mergers and acquisitions among industry giants marked the industry's consolidation. Canada's Nova Corporation entered the U.S. field in 1994, paying $170 million for Louisville Gas & Electric's share in the Clearinghouse; ownership was now split at 36.5 percent held by both Nova and British Gas and 17 percent held by Clearinghouse management. Terms of the Nova acquisition also brought the Clearinghouse into Canada, through a 50 percent joint venture in Novagas Clearinghouse Ltd., based in Calgary. Also in 1994, the Clearinghouse moved to enter the European market, then beginning its own deregulation, forming the Accord Energy joint venture with British Gas.

Watson, however, continued to steer the Clearinghouse toward his "energy store" concept. In 1995, the company took an important step toward increasing its capacity in products other than natural gas when it merged with publicly held Trident NGL Holdings Inc. The deal, worth more than $750 million in cash, stock, and the assumption of Trident's debt, more than doubled the company's natural gas liquids capacity. The merger also took the company public. The company's name was changed to NGC Corporation, reflecting the company's diversification from its natural gas marketing base. By 1995, natural gas marketing contributed only 65 percent of the company's $3.7 billion in revenues. By then, Watson was already preparing to complete the company's energy store concept, bringing NGC into selling electricity. Setting up its Electric Clearinghouse subsidiary in 1994, NGC was poised to take advantage of the coming deregulation of the electricity marketing industry, which, at an estimated $200 billion per year, was some three times larger than the natural gas market.

The energy store concept was not unique to NGC. The importance of being able to offer customers a full range of energy services was recognized throughout the industry. A new wave of mergers and acquisitions swept the industry. With the Trident merger, NGC's share of the market had grown to eight percent, and the company began to forecast capturing as much as 12 percent during the second half of the decade. By the end of 1996, however, the company had easily surpassed its own forecast. In January 1996, NGC entered talks with industry giant Chevron Corporation to merge Chevron's gas gathering, processing, and marketing operations with NGC. By June of that year the companies had reached agreement and, by September 1996, the merger was completed. NGC acquired Chevron's Natural Gas Business unit and parts of its Warren Petroleum subsidiary; Chevron joined British Gas and Nova as owners of NGC, with each controlling approximately 25 percent of the company. NGC's Trident subsidiary was renamed Warren Pe-

troleum, and Chevron's natural gas marketing activities were merged under the Natural Gas Clearinghouse subsidiary. The Chevron merger also added to the company's electricity capacity, making NGC the country's third largest independent power marketer.

With the merger, NGC also became the industry's largest gas marketer, with daily volumes of ten billion cubic feet and daily sales of some 470,000 barrels of natural gas liquids taking a 14 percent share of the market. Analysts began comparing Watson, who had steered NGC to become one of the top 150 businesses in the country, with Microsoft's Bill Gates. Watson stepped down as president in November 1996, but retained his chairman and CEO titles, promising to continue controlling day-to-day activities and continuing to identify the electricity industry as the key to NGC's future growth. In January 1997, the company announced its intention to spend $650 million on capital improvements, investments, and acquisitions. NGC was well positioned to take a leadership share in the impending deregulation of the electricity industry.

Principal Subsidiaries

Accord Energy, Ltd. (United Kingdom; 50%); Electric Clearinghouse; Hub Services, Inc.; Natural Gas Clearinghouse; NGC Oil Trading and Transportation; Nova Gas Clearinghouse, Ltd. (Canada; 50%); Ozark Gas Pipeline; Warren Petroleum.

Further Reading

"Central Unit Set Up for Spot Sales," *Oil & Gas Journal,* June 25, 1984, p. 32.

Durgin, Hillary, "Energy Firms See Future Role as Multi-Service 'Stores,' " *Houston Chronicle,* September 5, 1995, Bus. Sec., p. 1.

Grugal, Robin M., "NGC Corp.," *Investor's Business Daily,* August 5, 1996, p. A4.

McWilliams, Gary, "Chuck Watson's Power Play," *Business Week,* April 8, 1996, p. 98.

Palmeri, Christopher, "Power Broker," *Forbes,* November 6, 1995, p. 60.

Toal, Brian A., "Not So Fanciful Pipe Dreams," *Oil & Gas Investor,* October 1995, p. 59.

Williams, John, "Business Powers Locked in Feud over Summit: Watson's Laid-Back Style Hides Intensity," *Houston Chronicle,* December 22, 1996, p. A1.

—M. L. Cohen

Nichols Research Corporation

4040 S. Memorial Parkway
P.O. Box 400002
Huntsville, Alabama 35802-1326
U.S.A.
(205) 883-1140
Fax: (205) 895-2525
Web site: http://www.nichols.com

Public Company
Incorporated: 1976
Employees: 2,000
Sales: $242.3 million (1996)
Stock Exchanges: NASDAQ
SICs: 8731 Commercial Physical & Bio Research

Nichols Research Corporation has diversified beyond its core business of providing technology services to the defense industry and to U.S. military and government agencies, including the Department of Defense (DoD) and intelligence agencies. With the slowdown on defense spending in the 1990s, Nichols has expanded its business to include commercial and civilian clients such as Federal Express, AT&T, and the Centers for Disease Control in Atlanta. Through a series of acquisitions, Nichols has also applied its technology expertise to the burgeoning information technology (I/T) needs of the health care market. Nichols's emphasis on systems technology, however, has enabled the company to continue to improve its defense-related revenues, despite defense-spending slowdowns, and build a more than $1 billion backlog by 1996. In that year, Nichols surprised the defense community by winning two of four DoD High Performance Computing Modernization major shared resource center contracts, together worth more than $300 million over eight years. Nevertheless, increases in Nichols's commercial business has enabled the company to decrease its reliance on defense spending. Of the company's $242 million in 1996 revenues, defense work accounted for some 55 percent, down from more than 90 percent in the mid-1980s. The company's health care business already accounts for seven percent of revenues, with that segment

expected to grow by 30 percent before the turn of the century. Founders Chris Horgen and Roy Nichols continue to play active roles in the company's leadership. Horgen is chairman and chief executive officer; Nichols is vice-chairman, senior vice-president, and chief technical officer. Michael Mruz, with a background in computer services, joined the company as president and chief operating officer in 1994.

In keeping with its diversification, Nichols operates under four business units. Nichols Federal oversees the company's defense contracts, including sensor systems and technology; missile and air defense systems and technologies; space surveillance and avionics; army tactical systems and technologies; and intelligence programs. Major clients include the U.S. Army, Air Force, and Navy and NASA, as well as the Australian Defense Force. Nichols guidance systems, for example, could be seen in action during the Persian Gulf War, controlling the Patriot air defense missile system. Nichols is also actively involved in upgrading the Patriot system. The other Nichols units are involved in I/T work. Nichols InfoFed works with nondefense government agencies at the federal and state levels. Nichols InfoTec pursues contracts from commercial telecommunications and transportation firms. Nichols Select specializes in the health care and insurance industries.

Star Wars Success in the 1980s

Nichols Research Corporation was founded by former McDonnel Douglas employees Chris Horgen and Roy Nichols in 1976. The pair set up shop in a 1,200-square-foot office in Huntsville, Alabama, the site of the Army Strategic Defense Command and the Army's Redstone Arsenal, and a city with a history as a defense center going back to World War I. Starting with about $30,000 in capital (most of which went to purchasing a desktop computer), the company's initial focus was on providing research and development of optical technology and sensor systems for the military and for the space program. With the signing of the Anti-Ballistic Missile treaty in the early 1970s, the country's defense initiatives turned toward a greater reliance on surveillance systems. Nichols's optical technology expertise quickly enabled the company to win contracts. In 1976, Nichols won its first DoD contract, as well as subcontracts with six prime defense contractors engaged in the growing strategic defense area. The company's first-year revenues were $300,000.

Nichols's optical expertise positioned the company for steady growth into the 1980s. By then, with the inauguration of President Ronald Reagan, the DoD's thrust turned to the Strategic Defense Initiative (SDI), also known as the Star Wars program. This effort, which called for the deployment of a space-based surveillance and weapons system, was part of an overall acceleration of defense spending designed to secure the United States' lead in the long-standing Cold War. Hundreds of companies, large and small, lined up to participate in the initial development phase of the SDI program, which was budgeted at $19 billion for its first five years, with full deployment eventually expected to be worth more than $1 trillion. Nichols's optical sensor expertise placed it in a prime position to take part in the SDI "gold rush."

In 1983, when SDI funding began, the company won a contract to study the use of optical sensors for tracking missile launchings and for determining whether a missile actually carried an armed warhead or was merely launched as a decoy. SDI helped launch Nichols's revenues into orbit: In 1983, the company posted slightly less than $7 million in sales and a net profit of $315,000. By 1986, the company's revenues had grown to $28 million, and Nichols posted net earnings of $1.34 million. As Roy Nichols told *Newsweek*, "Our growth would be 10 to 15 percent less without SDI." By then, SDI contracts and subcontracts with other SDI contractors, such as Sparta, Inc., a Huntsville neighbor competing to become principal architect of the SDI system, contributed about 86 percent to Nichols's annual sales.

Nichols went public in 1987 after a year that saw the company's revenues jump by 38 percent. Nominal contract awards reached $38 million, with options worth $55 million, raising the company's backlog to $78 million with options. Three new SDI contracts with the U.S. Army contributed to the company's growth that year. Nichols was awarded prime contractor status for the Defense System Survivability Analysis contract, worth $7.8

million with options; prime contractor for the $6.3 million Wide Field of View Optical Technology Program; and subcontractor for Teledyne Brown Engineering for a Systems Engineering and Technical Assistance contract worth $9 million with options. By then, however, Nichols began to take its first steps to lessen its reliance on SDI, which was coming under increasing attack by a skeptical Congress. Beyond Star Wars, the company was also gaining new customers among the government's defense agencies, with tactical business contracts with White Sands Missile Range in New Mexico and Eglin Air Force Base in Florida. In addition, the company was profiting from the Small Business Innovative Research (SBIR) program, which directed crucial defense dollars to smaller companies while also introducing these companies to new customers among government agencies, winning 15 contract awards in 1987.

The following year, Nichols recorded still stronger growth. Contract awards totaled $118 million, and its backlog reached $136 million with options. By then, the company's staff had grown to 500, and the company had moved to new headquarters in Huntsville. Nichols also made its first acquisition, of Radiometrics, Inc., which added prototype development and measurement capacity to the company's base of expertise, as well as new customers, including the Army Missile Command and NASA. SDI continued to play a major role in the company's growth and included subcontractor awards with Martin Marietta and General Electric worth more than $28 million.

The company's revenues neared $43 million in 1988 and continued the company's unbroken string of profitability, with a net income of $2.3 million. Nichols's growth was also enabling it to bid on, and win, larger contracts, both as prime contractor and as subcontractor. The company expanded its conventional defense business, with the U.S. Army providing four major contracts in tactical and theater weapons. Nichols's contributions included work on the Fiber Optic Guided Missile Program; Foreign Missile Subsystems and Technology Analysis; Guidance and Control Support; and a contract under the Combined Allied Defense Experiment. Three years later the company's work would gain worldwide recognition with the outbreak of the Persian Gulf War, as Patriot missiles, controlled by Nichols's guidance systems, took out Iraqi Scud missiles.

Post-Cold War Growth

The acceleration of U.S. defense spending in the 1980s was responsible, directly or indirectly, for the collapse of the Soviet Union and the Communist Era in 1989. Although SDI itself became a casualty of the ending of the Cold War, its threat or promise, although never actually fulfilled, spurred the Eastern Bloc on its own spending program, bankrupting the Soviet economy and opening the way to demands for greater freedoms and free market systems. The spending spree had also taken its toll on the U.S. economy, pushing the country into the red to the tune of more than $1 trillion. With the collapse of the Cold War, the DoD came under increasing budget pressures and the 1990s presented a picture of massive cuts in defense spending.

By the start of the 1990s, however, Nichols's diversification efforts were well under way. Unlike larger companies such as Rockwell and Martin Marietta, Nichols's emphasis was on software, over hardware, and the company was taking a leading role in setting many technical standards in the defense market. The company had successfully extended its business beyond SDI into the tactical arena, with contracts with the Army, Air Force, Navy, NASA, and the intelligence agencies providing more than one-third of the company's $54 million in 1989 revenues; by 1990, the company's tactical contract awards totaled more than its strategic awards for the first time in Nichols's history. The company was also winning larger awards than ever before, including $63 million in intelligence contracts, an area of DoD spending that was less likely to become a victim of the budget cuts. Nichols also enjoyed success in picking up options on its existing contracts. In 1990, the company placed nearly $500 million in contract bids, and its revenues swelled to $75 million, providing a net income of $3.8 million. Adding to the company's stability as the defense industry faced the uncertainty of the new decade was Nichols's strong backlog of nearly $270 million in contracts in 1990.

That backlog grew to $467 million by 1992, including the company's largest contract award in its history, of $66 million to provide systems engineering and technical support to the SDI Organization's Ground-Based Interceptor program. Defense spending continued to form 95 percent of the company's revenues, which topped $90 million in 1991. Already, however, SDI contracts formed only 50 percent of Nichols's total revenues, which climbed past $117 million in 1992. Net income neared $6 million. The company made a new acquisition that year, of Utah-based Astech, which boosted the company's intelligence software capability. Nichols was poised for even stronger growth. As one analyst told *Defense News,* "This is one of the few defense companies out there for whom you could say business is booming."

Despite its strong defense performance, boosting revenues to $159 million in 1993, Nichols was already making plans to move the company into the civilian and commercial arena, particularly by leveraging its I/T experience into contracts for commercial computer services. Toward this end, the company eyed the health care industry, which, in terms of information technology, lagged some 20 years behind the banking and finance industries, offering Nichols the opportunity to gain strong market share in what would inevitably become a multibillion dollar business. Information technology was also seen as an important factor in Nichols's defense growth, as I/T was becoming an increasingly significant factor in government defense spending.

The company's diversification moves came at the right time. In 1994, Nichols recorded its first declines in its history, with revenues dropping to $143 million and net income falling to $6.5 million. To step up its I/T growth, Nichols set out to expand the company with a series of acquisitions that would bring additional, and crucial, I/T capacity. In July 1994, the company announced its intention to acquire Communications and Systems Specialists, a $6 million company based in Maryland that specialized in computer simulations and I/T services for NASA and the intelligence agencies. Nichols followed that acquisition with that of Computer Services Corporation, based in Birmingham, Alabama, in 1995, adding that company's base of health care information services. A third acquisition followed soon after, when the company picked up another Alabama firm,

Conway Computer Group, which provided software and I/T services to the insurance industry, including workers' compensation cases, risk management, underwriting, and other insurance areas. These acquisitions helped raised Nichols's revenues to $170 million in 1995; they also helped the company secure prime commercial contracts, including a more than $10 million contract with Federal Express for multimedia training services and a $35.8 million contract with the Centers for Disease Control in Atlanta for computer support services.

Entering its 1996 fiscal year, Nichols had already raised its I/T capacity to 35 percent of the company's revenues. Its defense work, however, continued to be strong: In April 1996, the company won the first of four DoD contracts for upgrading the agency's consolidated supercomputing centers. One month later, the company surprised the defense industry by winning the second of the four contracts. Together, the two contracts were worth more than $300 million over eight years. Meanwhile, Nichols was continuing to expand through acquisitions. In June 1996, the company purchased Advanced Marine Enterprises, Inc., a maker of advanced simulation and virtual reality technology for naval and marine applications. The company also picked up 20 percent of TXEN, Inc., a database management provider for the health care, insurance, and third-party administrator markets. Nichols announced its intention to purchase the rest of TXEN in June 1997. Nichols also teamed with Medifinancial Solutions, Inc. of New Jersey to form Healthshares L.L.C, a joint venture engaged in providing integrated information systems and support services to the health care industry.

Nichols's expansion efforts quickly proved profitable. The company ended its 1996 fiscal year with $242.3 million, up 42 percent over the year before, generating $9.4 million in net income. And, with a backlog of $1 billion in contracts and another $500 million in options as well as plans to make more than $1 billion in new bids in its 1997 fiscal year, Nichols's growth seemed certain to continue beyond the turn of the century.

Principal Subsidiaries

Communications & Systems Specialists, Inc.; Conway Computer Group; Computer Services Corporation; TXEN, Inc. (19.9%); Healthshares L.L.C (50%).

Further Reading

Finegan, Jay, "Star Wars, Inc.," *Inc.,* April 1987, p. 68.
Finnegan, Philip, "Nichols Research Eyes Acquisitions To Rekindle Growth," *Defense News,* July 25/July 31, 1994, p. 24.
——, "Nichols Research Knows Only Growth in Eroding Market," *Defense News,* September 21/September 27, 1992, p. 32.
Hubbard, Russell, "Nichols Research Poised for Healthcare Tech Boom," *Birmingham Business Journal,* September 2, 1996, p. 23.
Jones, John A., "Nichols Research Gets Rush of Defense Systems Contracts," *Investor's Business Daily,* November 5, 1996, p. B14.
McKillop, Peter, "Star Wars Fell on Alabama," *Newsweek,* July 14, 1986, p. 56.
"Nichols Research Sweeps DoD Computer Awards," *Defense Week,* May 13, 1996.

—M. L. Cohen

NORDSTROM

Nordstrom, Inc.

1501 Fifth Avenue
Seattle, Washington 98101-1603
U.S.A.
(206) 628-2111
Fax: (206) 628-1795

Public Company
Incorporated: 1901 as Wallin & Nordstrom
Employees: 37,000
Sales: $4.11 billion (1995)
Stock Exchanges: NASDAQ
SICs: 5311 Department Stores; 5651 Family Clothing
Stores; 5661 Shoe Stores

Nordstrom, Inc. was started in 1901 as a single shoe store in Seattle, Washington, that was opened by two Swedish immigrants. From those origins, the family-owned enterprise expanded into a 90-outlet, 18-state chain, which tallied $4.11 billion in sales in 1995. Carefully supervised expansion, tight family management, wide selection, and attentive customer service have long been the hallmarks of Seattle-based Nordstrom, the largest independent fashion specialty retailer in the United States.

Small Shoe Store Opened in 1901

John Nordstrom, a 16-year-old Swede, arrived in Minnesota in 1887 with $5 to his name and, after working his way across the United States, settled briefly in Seattle. In 1897 he headed north to Alaska in search of gold. He found it. In 1899, $13,000 richer, Nordstrom moved back to Seattle, where he opened a shoe store with Carl Wallin, a shoemaker he had met in Alaska. On its first day of business in 1901, Wallin & Nordstrom, sold $12.50 in shoes.

Business quickly picked up. By 1905 sales increased to $80,000. The business continued to grow, and in 1923 the partners opened a second store in Seattle. By 1928, however, 57-year-old John Nordstrom had decided to retire from the shoe

business, and passed on his share to his sons Everett and Elmer. Carl Wallin retired soon after and likewise sold his share to the next generation of Nordstroms. In 1933 John Nordstrom's youngest son, Lloyd, joined the partnership.

The business that John Nordstrom left was substantially larger than the one he started back in 1901. It was up to the next generation of Nordstroms, however, to build on their father's success. In 1929 the Nordstrom brothers doubled the size of their downtown Seattle store. In 1930, despite the onset of the Great Depression, the two stores made $250,000 in sales. The shoe stores survived the Depression, but faced another severe threat during World War II, when leather rationing prohibited U.S. consumers from buying more than three pairs of shoes per year. The Nordstrom brothers had to search nationwide for supplies of shoes.

Expansion and Diversification in the 1950s and 1960s

In the postwar decades, the Nordstrom brothers built the company into the largest independent shoe chain in the United States. In 1950 the Nordstroms opened two new shoe stores: one in Portland, Oregon, and one in a Seattle suburb. Nine years later, Nordstrom remodeled its Seattle flagship store, and stocked it with 100,000 pairs of shoes—the biggest inventory in the country. By 1961 Nordstrom operated 8 shoe stores and 13 leased shoe departments in Washington, Oregon, and California. That year, the firm grossed $12 million in sales and had 600 employees on its payroll.

In the early 1960s, the Nordstrom brothers came to a crossroads of sorts. Spurred by their success, they were convinced that their business could expand. The brothers were unsure whether they should simply expand their shoe business to the East and South or branch out into other areas of retailing. The brothers chose to diversify, and purchased Best Apparel, a Seattle-based women's clothing store. With the addition of apparel outlets, the company expanded rapidly. In 1965 the Nordstroms opened a new Best Apparel store adjacent to a Nordstrom shoe store in suburban Seattle. In 1966 the company acquired a Portland retail fashion outlet, Nicholas Ungar, and merged it with the Nordstrom shoe store in Portland.

In the late 1960s, the modern Nordstrom department store began to take shape. Between 1965 and 1968, the company opened five stores that combined apparel and shoes. In 1967, when annual sales had reached $40 million, the chain's name was changed to Nordstrom Best. The firm diversified further in these years, as Nordstrom Best began to sell men's and children's clothing as well.

Third Generation Took Control in 1970

In 1968 Everett Nordstrom turned 65, and he and his two brothers decided to turn over the reins of the company to the next generation of Nordstroms. Five men—Everett's son Bruce, Elmer's sons James and John, Lloyd's son-in-law John A. McMillan, and family friend Robert E. Bender—took control of the company in 1970.

In August 1971 the company went public, offering Nordstrom Best stock on the over-the-counter market. Family members retained a majority of the stock, however, and as of the mid-1990s they continued to hold a significant interest. In 1971 Nordstrom earned $3.5 million on sales of $80 million. In 1973, when sales first topped $100 million, the company changed its name to Nordstrom, Inc.

The firm continued to grow steadily throughout the 1970s by opening new stores, increasing volume in existing stores, and diversifying. In 1974 annual sales hit $130 million. The following year, Nordstrom bought three stores in Alaska. In 1976 the firm launched a new division, Place Two, which featured, in smaller stores, a selected offering of men's and women's apparel and shoes. By 1977 Nordstrom operated 24 stores, which generated sales of $246 million.

In 1978 Nordstrom expanded into the southern California market, opening an outlet in Orange County. That year, the firm reaped $13.5 million in earnings on nearly $300 million in sales. Buoyed by the success, Nordstrom's executives charted an aggressive expansion program, and began to open bigger stores in California. Their late-1970s confidence presaged a decade of phenomenal, but controlled, growth.

Rapid Growth in Early 1980s
Fueled by Legendary Customer Service

By 1980 Nordstrom was the third-largest specialty retailer in the country, ranking behind only Saks Fifth Avenue and Lord & Taylor. That year, the firm operated 31 stores in California, Washington, Oregon, Utah, Montana, and Alaska. In 1980 a new expansion plan called for 25 new stores to be added in the

1980s, and the Nordstroms projected that both earnings and total square footage would double by 1985.

The projection was not sufficiently optimistic. In 1980 sales hit $407 million, and in the next few years, sales and earnings continued to rise substantially. Between 1980 and 1983, when sales jumped to $787 million, earnings more than doubled, going from $19.7 million to $40.2 million. In 1982 Nordstrom launched a third division, Nordstrom Rack—a string of outlet stores that the firm used to move old inventories at discount prices. The chain's biggest growth area, however, was in the huge California market. By 1984 there were seven Nordstrom stores in that state. Five years later, Nordstrom had 22 full-size stores in California.

Nordstrom increasingly came to be recognized as an efficient, upscale, full-service department store. Its aggressive customer service plainly brought results. The firm consistently maintained the highest sales per square foot of retail space ratios in the industry, nearly twice those of other department stores.

Nordstrom's success was due to a variety of factors. Throughout its existence, shoes accounted for a good deal of the firm's sales—about 18 percent in 1989. In most fashion and apparel stores, shoes constitute a smaller percentage of sales. In addition Nordstrom consistently maintained huge inventories and selection, which were usually twice the size of other department stores. In the mid-1980s, a typical outlet stocked 75,000 pairs of shoes, 5,000 men's dress shirts, and 7,000 ties. Moreover, a decentralized corporate structure allowed local buyers, who knew their customers' needs, to make inventory selections.

Most significantly, though, Nordstrom's management encouraged the development of an aggressive sales force. The vast majority of Nordstrom clerks worked on commission, and the average salesperson earned $24,000 annually. Managers generally promoted from within the ranks of salespeople, which intensified the desire to sell.

In the 1980s the firm's customer service became legendary, as tales of heroic efforts by salespeople became legion: clerks were known to pay shoppers' parking tickets, rush deliveries to offices, unquestioningly accept returns, lend cash to strapped customers, and to send tailors to customers' homes. Salespeople received constant pep talks from management, and motivational exercises were a routine part of life at Nordstrom. Nordstrom also created an extremely customer-friendly environment. Many stores had free coat check service, concierges, and piano players who serenaded shoppers.

As the economy boomed in the 1980s, Nordstrom's figures climbed apace. In 1985 sales first topped $1 billion, as they jumped to $1.3 billion. In 1987 the firm reaped profits of $92.7 million on sales of $1.92 billion.

Began Eastward Expansion in the Mid-1980s

Nordstrom's growth in the latter half of the 1980s stemmed from a combination of expansion into new territories and the creation of larger stores in existing Nordstrom territory. In 1986, when the firm operated 53 stores in six western states, Nordstrom began to turn its sights to the East. In March 1988, Nordstrom opened its first store on the East Coast, a 238,000-

square-foot facility in McLean, Virginia, just outside Washington, D.C. On its first day, the store racked up more than $1 million in sales. Over the first year, the store brought in $100 million in sales.

The same year, Nordstrom expanded on the West Coast as well, opening its biggest store, a 350,000-square-foot facility in downtown San Francisco. The lavish San Francisco store featured 103 different brands of champagne, 16 varieties of chilled vodka, and a health spa, among other luxurious amenities.

By the end of 1988, Nordstrom had 21,000 employees toiling in its 58 stores. Together they convinced customers to buy $2.3 billion worth of goods in 1988, and earned profits of $123 million for the corporation.

Expansion in other areas of the East continued in the late 1980s. In 1989 Nordstrom opened a second store in the Washington, D.C., area—in the Pentagon City Mall. That same year the firm also opened outlets in Sacramento and Brea, California. Capping the decade, the company won the National Retail Merchants Association's Gold Medal. Clearly, Nordstrom had become a paragon of retailing success. Envious of its market share and sales figures, many competitors began to imitate its strategies of large inventory and lavish customer service.

Nordstrom continued to rely on its aggressive sales staff, but the corporate policy of encouraging clerks to go out of their way to make sales caused the company some grief. The employees' union (which was later decertified) complained about the pressure on employees to sell. In late 1989 a group of unionized employees charged that they were not being paid for performing extra services to customers.

In February 1990, after a three-month investigation, the Washington State Department of Labor & Industries alleged that the company had systematically violated state laws by failing to pay employees for a variety of duties, such as delivering merchandise and doing inventory work. The agency ordered Nordstrom to change its compensation and record-keeping procedures, and to pay back wages to some of Nordstrom's 30,000 employees. Soon after, the firm created a $15-million reserve to pay back-wage claims. The company, however, remained a target of class-action lawsuits on these matters, which were finally settled out of court in early 1993 when Nordstrom agreed to pay a set percentage of compensation to employees who worked at Nordstrom from 1987 to 1990. The settlement cost the company between $20 and $30 million.

Other unforeseen events in 1989 and 1990 hit the company as well. The San Francisco earthquake of 1989 took a significant bite out of retail sales in the San Francisco Bay area. The general nationwide downturn in retailing hurt the company more, however. In September 1990, Nordstrom, then a 61-store company, announced it would cut costs by 3 to 12 percent and laid off some personnel. In the fourth quarter of 1989, Nordstrom's earnings dropped 34 percent from the previous year. Earnings fell about 7 percent for the entire year, from $123.3 million in 1988 to $115 million in 1989; sales, however, increased nearly 15 percent in that year, from $2.33 billion to $2.67 billion.

Slower Growth in the 1990s

In the early 1990s, Bruce, James, and John Nordstrom, John McMillan, and Robert Bender collectively still owned a 40 percent stock interest and continued to maintain tight control of the company. Although Nordstrom suffered from the recession of the early 1990s, it continued to expand and open new stores in the East and Midwest. In September 1990, Nordstrom launched its first store in the metropolitan New York area, in Paramus, New Jersey. In April 1991 Nordstrom debuted its first Midwest store—in Oak Brook, Illinois, a Chicago suburb. In typical Nordstrom style, the store unveiled featuring 125,000 pairs of shoes, a concierge, an espresso bar, and a wood-paneled English-style pub. In 1991 the company also opened stores in Riverside, California; Edison, New Jersey; and Bethesda, Maryland.

Sales and earnings rebounded a fraction in 1990. Sales rose 8 percent to $2.89 billion, and profits rose a miniscule 0.7 percent to $115.8 million. In 1990 women's apparel and accessories accounted for 59 percent of Nordstrom's total sales; men's apparel accounted for 16 percent; and shoes—still a company mainstay—constituted 19 percent of all sales.

Such single-digit growth became the norm for Nordstrom throughout the early and mid-1990s, as sales grew sluggish thanks in large part to fluctuations in demand for women's apparel and the severe recession in southern California, where more than half of the company's total store square footage was located in the early years of the decade. The double-digit growth of the 1980s was gone—in fact, the sales increases of the 1990s were largely attributable to new store openings, with same-store sales flat.

Largely shying away from the troubled California market, Nordstrom increasingly sought out new territory for expansion, particularly in the Midwest, South, and Northeast. In 1996 alone, the Philadelphia, Dallas, Denver, and Detroit metropolitan areas were added to the Nordstrom empire through new store openings. From 1996 to 1999, the company planned to open 15 Nordstrom stores, adding 3.6 million square feet to the chain total, an increase of one-third. Connecticut, Ohio, Georgia, and Kansas were among the states slated to receive their first Nordstrom store.

While it continued its steady expansion, Nordstrom also made a number of moves indicative of a company in something of a transition. Nordstrom produced its first mail-order catalog in the early 1990s, opened the first Nordstrom Factory Direct store near Philadelphia in 1993, and launched a proprietary Visa card in 1994. Also in 1994, Nordstrom began testing an interactive home shopping channel, in partnership with US West Inc. and J.C. Penney Co. In keeping with its reputation for customer service, Nordstrom envisioned a system in which a customer could not only view merchandise but also interact with a sales clerk who would be visible on the screen. Such high-tech marketing fit well with the profile of a typical Nordstrom customer, generally considered to be early adopters when it came to new technology.

Meanwhile, with net earnings slipping somewhat (from 5.3 percent in 1988 to 3.91 percent in 1993), Nordstrom sought to cut costs, in particular its selling, general, and administrative costs, which accounted for 26.4 percent of sales in 1992. This relatively high figure resulted from Nordstrom's generous employee incentive program that fueled the company's reputation for customer service. By 1995, however, these costs had actually increased to 27.2 percent of sales, while net earnings improved only slightly to 4.01 percent.

Although considered innovative in many areas, Nordstrom had stayed away from large investments in systems technology prior to the mid-1990s. In 1995 a new information system was installed, along with a new system for personnel, payroll, and benefits processing. Most importantly, Nordstrom's first inventory control system rolled out that same year in southern California, with companywide rollout the following year. Although the status of an item throughout all stores could be checked using the system, Nordstrom maintained its traditional decentralized buying, bucking an industry trend toward centralization.

Perhaps the most significant transition took place in the management arena late in 1995, when Nordstrom's four co-chairmen—Bruce, James, and John Nordstrom and John McMillan—retired. This third generation of Nordstroms to lead the company were replaced by former co-presidents Ray Johnson and John Whitacre, who became the new co-chairmen (although Johnson subsequently retired in September 1996), and were in turn replaced in the co-presidency by six fourth-generation family members—Bill, Blake, Dan, Erik, Jim A., and Pete Nordstrom—all in their early thirties. The new management team faced the difficult task of taking over in the hypercompetitive and sluggish sales environment of the mid-1990s as well as attempting to maintain Nordstrom's position as one of the top upscale retailers in the country.

Principal Subsidiaries

Nordstrom Credit, Inc.; Nordstrom Distribution, Inc.; Nordstrom National Credit Bank.

Further Reading

Bergmann, Joan, "Nordstrom Gets the Gold," *Stores*, January, 1990.

De Voss, David, "The Rise and Rise of Nordstrom," *Lear's*, October 1989.

"Down the Tube: Nordstrom," *Economist*, June 5, 1993, p. 80.

Falum, Susan C., "At Nordstrom Stores, Service Comes First—But at a Big Price," *Wall Street Journal*, February 20, 1990.

Lubove, Seth, "Don't Listen to the Boss, Listen to the Customer," *Forbes*, December 4, 1995, p. 45.

McAllister, Robert, "Nordstrom Tightens Its Belt for the Long Haul," *Footwear News*, September 6, 1993, p. 1.

Nordstrom, John W., *The Immigrant in America*, Seattle: Dogwood Press, 1950.

Schwadel, Francine, "Nordstrom's Push East Will Test Its Renown for the Best in Service," *The Wall Street Journal*, August 1, 1989.

Solomon, Charlene Marmer, "Nightmare at Nordstrom," *Personnel Journal*, September 1990.

Spector, Robert, and Patrick D. McCarthy, *The Nordstrom Way: The Inside Story of America's #1 Customer Service Company*, New York: Wiley, 1995.

Stevenson, Richard W., "Watch Out Macy's, Here Comes Nordstrom," *New York Times Magazine*, August 27, 1989.

Yang, Dori Jones, "Nordstrom's Gang of Four," *Business Week*, June 15, 1992, pp. 122–23.

Yang, Dori Jones, and Laura Zinn, "Will 'the Nordstrom Way' Travel Well?," *Business Week*, September 3, 1990, p. 82.

—Daniel Gross
—updated by David E. Salamie

The North Face, Inc.

2013 Farallon Drive
San Leandro, California 94577
U.S.A.
(510) 618-3500
Fax: (510) 618-3531

Public Company
Incorporated: 1994 as The North Face, Inc.
Employees: 518
Sales: $158.23 million (1996)
Stock Exchanges: NASDAQ
SICs: 5699 Miscellaneous Apparel & Accessory Stores;
2399 Fabricated Textile Products, Not Elsewhere
Classified

The North Face, Inc. is a manufacturer and distributor of high-grade equipment and apparel used in mountaineering, skiing, and backpacking. While the reputation of North Face was built on outfitting expeditions, the company's later growth has come through the introduction of high-tech apparel in upscale retail stores. With Summit Shops, North Face has established its use of a ''store within a store'' concept. Summit Shops are located within the company's wholesale customer's stores. As of 1996 there were 25 Summit Shops, with another 100 planned for opening sometime in 1997. The company also operated nine retail stores, two distribution centers, and three outlets in the U.S., with domestic distribution to approximately 840 wholesalers representing nearly 1,200 storefronts. Virtually all of the company's goods are manufactured, to North Face's specifications, by some 50 unaffiliated contractors located in North America and Asia.

The Early Years: 1965–73

According to the 1996 company prospectus, the name North Face originated with the company's founders and comes from the fact that the north face of a mountain in the northern hemisphere is usually the most formidable and challenging for mountain climbers. North Face was founded in 1965 by outdoor enthusiasts retailing premium-grade backpacking and climbing equipment. North Face began to wholesale and manufacture backpacking equipment in 1968. The business continued to grow and expand. In the early 1970s North Face added outerwear to its product line.

Innovation in Product Design: 1975–90

Innovative product design and consistent development and introduction of new products have always been North Face's greatest strengths. In 1975 North Face introduced a benchmark in the outdoor equipment industry with its geodesic dome tent. This design became the standard for lightweight, high-performance tents used in high-altitude and polar expeditions. The geodesic dome also became very popular for general backpacking and camping as well. The same year North Face also introduced another original, sleeping bags incorporating shingled construction of synthetic insulation. Like the dome tent, these sleeping bags have become the industry standard.

In the early 1980s the company launched its ''extreme skiwear'' line. Another addition to the North Face product line came in 1988, when the Expedition System was introduced. A complete line of severe cold weather clothing consisting of integrated components, the Expedition System was designed to be used together in various combinations. According to the company, there is wide use of this clothing system by world-class mountain climbers. By the late 1980s North Face was the only manufacturer and distributor in the United States of a comprehensive line of premium-grade, high-performance equipment and apparel used in mountaineering, skiing, and backpacking.

Shaky Ground for North Face

While the reputation of North Face products has remained sound, internal decision-making has occasionally been questioned. During the growth phase of the 1980s, the company attempted to manufacture all of its own products. This led to problems of obsolete materials, large amounts of capital invested in an inventory of finished goods, and late delivery of high-demand products. However, these were not the only detri-

Company Perspectives:

The North Face has developed a superior reputation for quality, performance and authenticity by providing technically advanced products capable of withstanding the most extreme conditions. For nearly 30 years, the Company's outdoor apparel and outdoor equipment have been the brand of choice for numerous high altitude and polar expeditions. These products are used extensively by world-class climbers, explorers and extreme skiers, whose lives depend on the performance of their apparel and equipment. To maintain and further enhance this unique legacy, the Company continuously develops and introduces innovative products that are functional and are designed to be both technically superior and, in many instances, to set the industry standard in each product category. The Company cultivates its extreme image through its targeted marketing efforts and its teams of world-class climbers, explorers and skiers.

ments to the financial health of North Face. In the late 1980s, North Face opened outlet stores to sell lower-priced products in an effort to dispose of obsolete materials. The product reputation of North Face was based on a high-end, or expensive, association with the inherent product quality. The lower-priced products confused or missed the intended consumers and did not help the company's overall image. Also, these outlets were not well received by North Face's wholesale customers and were eventually closed. All of these business activities had a negative effect on North Face's finances and launched the company into the next phase of its history.

In May 1988, Odyssey Holdings, Inc. (OHI) acquired the company, known at that time as North Face Corporation. OHI owned about 30 companies in the outdoor and brand-name apparel industry and was at that time headed by William N. Simon, now president of North Face.

In January 1993, a new executive staff was recruited to make needed changes in North Face's operations. Among those newly recruited was Marsden S. Cason, who was at that time the president of North Face and a director and executive officer of OHI. Some of the significant changes initiated by the new management team included hiring experienced executives and operating managers, establishing a focus on sales and gross margin, expanding contracted sources of goods and materials, closing discount outlets, and discontinuing unprofitable product lines. Eventually, as a result of these initiatives, the company would realize a significant increase in sales and profits. However, in 1993 the parent company, OHI, filed for protection under Chapter 11 of the U.S. Bankruptcy Code.

A Dramatic Turnaround Beginning in 1994

North Face continued to operate at a loss until 1994, when the strategic changes mentioned began to take a positive effect; 1994 was a year of significant transitions for North Face. On June 7 the company was purchased at public auction for $62 million by a group consisting of J. H. Whitney & Co., Cason,

and William S. McFarlane. On June 8, 1994, TNF Holdings changed its name to The North Face, Inc. Also in June 1994 Cason was appointed CEO of North Face.

The 1990s: Opportunities, Threats, and a Look to the Future

One of the inherent weaknesses of being in a focused, niche industry, according to experts, is attempting to sustain growth in a field with a limited number of customers. This is what necessitated the introduction of Summit Shops selling Tekware as North Face attempted during the 1990s to obtain a share of the leisure apparel industry. Such a shift represented a major departure from traditional North Face territories. North Face's success in this new venture depended, in part, upon the buyers of casual wear, a market that can be fickle. For North Face, entering this market could be seen by industry observers as either a weakness or an opportunity. In addition, another possible weakness that presented itself was overdependence on contracted vendors to supply the majority of the company's manufactured goods.

The largest area of opportunity that North Face was involved in was the expansion into the casual apparel industry with the introduction of "Summit Shops." Another area of opportunity for North Face was the possibility of future government contracts for tent sales, given the company's longtime association as a supplier to the U.S. Marines Corps. Finally, further development and introduction of new and innovative designs of products in the future seemed to be a likely avenue for North Face to gain or retain market share.

Nonetheless, North Face faced very real threats to its future growth. While the company remained subject to the same kinds of business threats that any business faced, such as major shifts in consumer tastes and preferences, its most prevalent threat was competition. Archrival Patagonia, for example, had historically carried a very similar product line. And there always loomed the threat of new competition because of relatively low barriers to entry and the possibility of a breakthrough in product design.

While North Face had weathered some rough and challenging times, the company seemed by the mid-1990s to be on firm footing and ready to begin another new phase. North Face recommended itself as a company poised for future growth by building on its strengths: brand-name recognition, product reputation and differentiation, innovative product design and diversity, aggressive entry into the casual wear market, and, as attested to by company profits and increases in the value of the company's stock, the decisive and able senior-level management that will continue to drive North Face's climb to success.

Principal Divisions

A5 Adventures, Inc.

Further Reading

Cohen, Bud, "Management Teams Buys North Face for $59M," *Daily News Record,* June 2, 1994, p. 11.
Lubove, Seth, "Katmandu Comes to Neiman Marcus," *Forbes,* October 21, 1996, p. 42.

Maycumber, S. Gray, ''Performing on a Broader Stage; Performance Fibers and Fabrics Moving into Mainstream Apparel,'' *Daily News Record,* September 16, 1996, p. 4.

''North Face Inc. (New Securities Issues),'' *The Wall Street Journal,* July 2, 1996, p. C18(E).

''North Face IPO Is a Hit on First Day,'' *WWD,* July 3, 1996, p. 10.

''North Face Posts 62.4% Net Rise, Plans Secondary Offering,'' *WWD,* October 30, 1996, p. 14.

Oring, Sheryl, ''$200M Bankruptcy Snags Local Retailers; North Face, Sierra Designs Hit,'' *San Francisco Business Times,* January 29, 1993, p. 1.

''Outerwear Firm North Face Plans to Raise $30M in IPO; Expects to Use Proceeds to Cut Debt,'' *Daily News Record,* June 21, 1996, p. 22.

Scott, Mary, ''North Face Dismisses 7 of 10 Reps,'' *STN,* November 1994, p. 3.

Socha, Miles, ''The North Face (Plans to Open 25 In-Store Shops),'' *Daily News Record,* May 29, 1996, p. 3.

''The North Face, Inc. Upgrades Sales Force,'' *PR Newswire,* November 27, 1996, p. 1127SFW017.

White, Constance C. R. ''North Face's Tekware,'' *New York Times,* April 16, 1996, p. B14.

—Karen Leslie Boyd

North Star Steel Company

15407 McGinty Road, Dept. 51
Wayzata, Minnesota 55391
U.S.A.
(612) 742-7575
Fax: (612) 742-6687
Web site: http://www.cargill.com

Wholly Owned Subsidiary of Cargill, Inc.
Founded: 1965
Sales: $570.00 million (1993)
Employees: 3,200 (1993)
SICs: 3312 Blast Furnaces and Steel Mills

As the core business of Cargill, Inc.'s worldwide steel operations, North Star Steel Company has exploited its early expertise in minimill steel production, its ability to stay ahead of the curve of new steelmaking technology, and its long history of expansion and acquisition to become, by 1996, the second-largest minimill steel producer in the United States and the eighth-largest U.S. steelmaker overall.

With scrap recycling and steelmaking facilities in eight states, North Star in 1997 claimed an annual capacity of roughly 5 million tons of steel and overseas customers in 30 countries. North Star's major products include special bar quality steel for use in automotive applications, deck furniture, and machinery manufacture; merchant bar quality steel—such as rounds, flats, and angles—used in construction and steel fabrication; wire rod used in such diverse products as chain link fences, bed springs, flyswatters, and nuts, nails, and screws; seamless pipe used in the oil and gas well drilling industry; reinforcing bar (or rebar) used in building and highway construction; and grinding balls used to crush ores in the cement, fertilizer, and mining industries. North Star steel has been used in the manufacture of auto parts for Chrysler, engine parts for Boeing, and construction materials for Minnesota's Mall of America, the largest indoor shopping mall in the world, and the Arizona Diamondback's major league baseball stadium in Phoenix.

The Rise of a Minimill: 1965–74

North Star Steel was founded in October 1965 for the purpose of constructing a single-plant steel mill in St. Paul, Minnesota. Within two years of its birth, however, North Star's management had adopted the new "minimill" approach to steelmaking pioneered in the early 1960s. By 1967 the plant was in operation, recycling scrap and turning out basic commodity steel products for the steel products industry. Traditional steelmaking techniques produced steel from raw iron ore, coke, and limestone melted in coke oven blast furnaces. Using clean and efficient electric arc furnaces (EAFs) minimills (so named because they were originally smaller than Big Steel plants in size and capacity) like North Star, however, melted scrap metal from recycled factory clippings and discarded autos and home appliances at a fraction of the cost of the big "integrated" mills.

Besides the 40 percent energy savings derived from the EAF process, minimills were also often strategically located near their customers, usually in nonurban areas; employed nonunion labor; cost half as much to build as typical large blast furnace plants; and boasted substantially superior productivity levels. Because the steel produced by the early minimills was initially inferior in quality to the steel of the big integrated producers, however, North Star, like other minimill producers, at first limited itself to producing wire rods, rebars, angles, flats, and other basic commodity steel products.

Within two years of North Star's first minimill production in 1967, the Nuclear Corporation of America of Charlotte, North Carolina, opened a $6 million minimill in Darlington, South Carolina. The event was historically significant, for Nucor (as Nuclear was renamed) quickly became the nation's most profitable minimill steelmaker, a darling of Wall Street, and a synonym for the new focused and efficient steel firms destined to give Big Steel a run for its money. In the 1970s, the rise in foreign, and especially Japanese, steel imports, the debilitating costs of a heavily unionized workforce, and the inherent efficiencies of the minimill's use of scrap and EAFs took their toll on such big steel producers as U.S. Steel, Bethlehem Steel, and LTV. North Star and its competitors rushed to fill the void, and the so-called golden age of minimills began. In 1970 North Star had increased its St. Paul capacity by adding a second furnace,

378

and by 1974 its annual steel capacity had risen from 125,000 to 300,000 tons. With employees now numbering 600, North Star had begun to establish itself as one of the largest producers of construction industry rebars in the country.

Cargill, Inc.: 1974–83

In the early 1970s, Cargill, Inc., a privately held Minnesota-based giant in the agricultural products and food processing industries, began to diversify into new fields. Besides a new presence in the waste disposal, metals processing, and beef and salt production markets, Cargill also sought a place in the steel industry, and in February 1974 it acquired North Star and its thriving minimill business. Flush with its new access to Cargill's deep corporate pockets, North Star acquired a new mill being built in Wilton, Iowa, in 1974 and in February 1976 broke ground on a grinding ball plant in Duluth. The Wilton mill came on line in 1976 and was soon producing 150,000 tons of rebars and structural flats annually and employing 250. In 1977 the Duluth grinding ball plant began operations.

The energy crisis of the mid-1970s conspired with the inefficiencies and bloated costs of the integrated steelmakers as well as overcapacity and sluggish demand in the worldwide steel industry to send Big Steel into a tailspin from which it never completely recovered. As the integrated steelmakers closed plants, laid off workers, and outsourced production, Nucor, North Star, and new minimill operators like Birmingham Steel and Chaparral Steel began to make inroads into Big Steel's higher-quality products. Having definitively proved that scrap-based EAF mills could produce basic steel products, North Star and its competitors began adopting improved technologies such as continuous casting, which saved money by enabling molten steel to be shaped into solid shapes without intermediate steps.

With Nucor blazing the trail, North Star and the other minimills moved from commodity rebars, rods, and merchant bars to galvanized steel (i.e., zinc-coated steel with greater corrosion resistance) and structural beams and girders for the heavy construction industry. By 1977, Nucor had expanded into the production of steel decking for floors and roofs and in 1979 began producing cold-finished bars for use in the manufacture of shafts and precision parts. In 1978, North Star also began

moving up the quality-steel ladder, breaking ground for a special bar quality steel mill in Monroe, Michigan, to service the auto, petroleum, mining, forging, and cold-drawing industries. Strategically located near the headquarters of the Big Three auto plants, the steel from the Monroe mill would be made into engine parts, suspension components, and power transmission gears.

As employment in the U.S. steel industry peaked at 399,000 in 1980, North Star began full production at the Monroe, Michigan, mill and acquired the Magnimet Corporation (renamed North Star Recycling in 1990) to expand its scrap metal trading and processing operation. Through its network of metal traders, North Star was now buying and processing 10 to 15 different grades of scrap, which could be shredded, sheared, sorted, and cleaned before shipment to its mills. By the mid-1990s, North Star's scrap recycling operations were producing so much scrap (over 3 million tons a year) that it was selling it off to other steelmakers. In 1982 U.S. steelmakers fell victim to a punishing industrywide depression that raked corporate profits for four years. North Star nevertheless acquired a wire rod steel mill in Beaumont, Texas, from Korf Industries in 1983 and announced the appointment of a new executive vice president, Robert A. Garvey, a fast-rising manager who had begun his North Star career as the St. Paul plant's melt shop superintendent.

The Garvey Years: 1984–96

A metallurgical engineer who began working in steel mills at age 18, Garvey gave fair warning of his career's promise in 1978 when he was promoted to general manager of North Star's St. Paul mill less than a year after joining the company. In 1984, within a year of his promotion to executive vice president, Garvey was lifted to the presidency of North Star and continued the breakneck acquisition program he had begun the year before. His first addition was the rolling mill of the bankrupt Ohio River Steel in Calvert City, Ohio, which he followed in April 1985 with the acquisition of the inactive Hunt Steel Co. minimill of Youngstown, Ohio. North Star began retooling the former Hunt Steel plant to manufacture steel billets and blooms (basic types of semifinished steel) as feeder stock for the Calvert City mill, whose acquisition was finally completed in December 1985. After an aborted move to Phoenix Steel in 1986, Garvey returned to North Star in time to see the newly retooled Youngstown facility come on line in November and to lead the acquisition of Universal Tubular Services of Houston, Texas, which was promptly renamed North Star Steel Houston.

In January 1987, Garvey invited North Star's plant managers and corporate staff to a Florida business retreat where they were introduced to the tenets of the "total quality management" (TQM) movement then sweeping corporate America. North Star's corporate meetings were soon leading off with discussions of safety and quality, with finances and production relegated to second place on the agenda. As a result of this new emphasis, North Star's safety record became among the industry's best, and its quality program was enabling it, through its Youngstown and Houston mills, to become the first U.S. minimill to produce seamless tubing and casing. In 1987 North Star established a minimill industry precedent when it began to recycle so-called white goods (refrigerators, washers and dryers, and the like) for its scrap needs, and in 1989 it began evaluating sites for a new recycling minimill in the West or Southwest to tap that underexploited market.

While North Star was securing its niche in the minimill industry, Nucor was introducing another major weapon in the minimills' quest for Big Steel's market share. In 1989 it installed a new thin-slab steel caster made in Germany at its new Crawfordsville, Indiana, plant. The technology would finally enable minimills to produce the high-quality flat-rolled sheet steel used in the automotive and appliance manufacturing industries. Nucor's smaller minimill competitors were slow to follow its lead, however. North Star, for example, did not announce plans to build its own thin-slab mill until 1994 when it found a partner for the venture in the form of Australia's BHP Steel. As prices for scrap threatened to rise so high that the minimills' cost advantage over Big Steel disappeared, North Star and Nucor turned to scrap substitutes to regain their edge. In 1990 North Star and Cleveland Cliffs Inc. of Ohio formed a joint venture to explore the technical and commercial feasibility of producing iron carbide to replace scrap in the steelmaking process. By late 1994 Nucor had completed construction of its own iron carbide plant in Trinidad.

Another slump descended on the steel industry in 1990, and in 1991 North Star was forced to close its Milton, Pennsylvania, rebar/merchant products plant. But North Star and the other minimills had made their mark: by the early 1990s the U.S. steel industry was recycling more cars for scrap than the U.S. auto industry was producing, and fully 70 percent of all steel produced in the United States was being manufactured from scrap. In 1992, the steel industry began to recover, and North Star announced an agreement to sell oil industry tubular steel to a new customer in Russia. On the labor front, North Star was heartened by the decision of its Monroe, Michigan, employees to reject union representation, but late in the year the U.S. Court of Appeals ruled that North Star owed compensation to some of its Minneapolis clerical workers for unilaterally raising their health insurance rates while they were engaged in contract negotiations—a violation of federal law. In 1993, North Star announced it would double the production capacity of its St. Paul mill to 650,000 tons and won Cargill's final approval for the construction of a new $140 million minimill in Kingman, Arizona. The new plant—North Star's seventh—would add another 500,000 tons to North Star's capacity and exploit the 500,000- to 600,000-ton wire rod market on the West Coast. At an industry conference, Garvey explained that "our strategy for a West Coast mill is simple: the Southwest is one of the few regions where scrap is in surplus supply and steelmaking capacity is down. . . . we will create jobs and capture West Coast and Southwest market share from imports."

After Garvey won an unprecedented concession from Arizona power utilities in early 1994 to allow North Star to buy electricity from any utility it chose, construction of the new plant began in May. The $40 million expansion of the St. Paul mill was completed the same year, and in November Garvey announced a joint venture with the world's 13th largest steelmaker, BHP Steel of Australia, for a thin-slab flat-rolled steel minimill in the Midwest to rival Nucor's revolutionary Crawfordsville, Indiana, facility. The venture would be named North Star BHP Steel and would turn out 1.5 million metric tons of

steel when operational. North Star too now seemed poised to invade Big Steel's high-quality sheet steel business.

By 1995 it was becoming clear that the original minimills would face competition in their ongoing quest to unseat the big integrated producers' dominance of U.S. steel; ironically, it would come from a new generation of minimills. Although Nucor was on a pace to become the largest U.S. steelmaker by the turn of the century—and could therefore only loosely be described as a "minimill"—a host of new minimills under construction were threatening to flood the U.S. steel market with flat-rolled steel by the end of the 1990s. Such upstarts as Gallatin Steel and Steel Dynamics (led by a team of former Nucor executives) were expected to quadruple U.S. minimill production in the space of only three years, and North Star's venture with BHP in northwestern Ohio was only one of at least ten new plants whose output was expected to drive up scrap prices and lead to a "death spiral" price war among the less stable U.S. producers. In June 1995, North Star finally broke ground for its Ohio mill, and in September Garvey announced North Star would infuse another $1.3 million into its St. Paul mill to optimize its ability to generate scrap from car bodies and appliances. North Star also placed orders for the bar and rod rolling bar for its new Kingman, Arizona, plant and signed a ten-year contract with BOC Gases who would provide the oxygen, nitrogen, and argon as well as some of the equipment for North Star's pollution-control systems. With its new Arizona and Ohio plants under way, North Star seemed to have secured its place among the leaders of the growing minimill crowd.

New Leadership, New Markets: 1996–97

North Star's optimism was dealt an unexpected blow in January 1996 when Garvey shocked the industry by announcing he was moving to North Star's closest competitor, Birmingham Steel, as its new CEO. The departure surprised everyone and left Cargill, one industry expert guessed, "just a little bit ticked." While Garvey noted the many similarities between Birmingham and North Star as a factor in his decision to leave, some suggested that the real reason North Star's "moneymaker" had switched ships was the freedom Birmingham had offered him—at North Star Garvey's decisions were always subject to Cargill's approval. Within days, Cargill named James T. Thompson, a former vice president of Cargill Steel, as Garvey's successor and promoted two other North Star executives to senior positions.

Despite Garvey's abrupt departure, his two key projects—the Ohio flat-rolled steel mill and the new Arizona wire rod and bar mill—moved toward completion in 1996. North Star began commissioning the Kingman, Arizona, site in March and it came on line in September. North Star officials boasted that the minimill was "a quantum leap forward in steelmaking" and as evidence cited its continuous shaft furnace, the first in the United States; a fully automated production process that enabled the entire plant to be run by only 180 employees; a state-of-the-art emissions control system; and an efficiency level that allowed a truck delivering scrap in the morning to leave five hours later with steel made from the same scrap.

In October North Star's scheduled startup of its $400 million joint venture with BHP Steel hit a snag when some supplies failed to meet specifications, and full production at the plant was put off until the first quarter of 1997. When operational, North Star's eighth plant would add 1.5 million tons to North Star's capacity and bolster its position in the automotive, original equipment, and industrial manufacturing markets.

Principal Subsidiaries

North Star Steel Kentucky; North Star Steel Minnesota; North Star Steel Duluth; North Star Steel Iowa; North Star Steel Michigan; North Star Steel Texas; North Star Steel Arizona; North Star Steel Ohio; North Star Steel Houston; North Star Recycling Co. (Eagan, Minnesota); North Star Recycling (Monroe, Michigan); North Star Recycling (Tampa, Florida); North Star Recycling (Toledo, Ohio).

Further Reading

Baker, Stephen, ''Big Steel's Big Opportunity,'' *Business Week*, January 10, 1994.

——, ''Why Steel Is Looking Sexy, '' *Business Week,* April 4, 1994.

——, ''The Brutal Brawl Ahead in Steel,'' *Business Week*, March 13, 1995.

Beirne, Mike, ''Garvey Keeps North Star on the Quality Path,'' *American Metal Market*, February 18, 1993, p. 14A.

——, ''New Mill Gets $20M Boost,'' *American Metal Market*, February 28, 1995, p. 2.

Garvey, Robert A., ''Why the Sun Shines Along the Belt,'' *American Metal Market*, February 18, 1994, p. 14.

Henkoff, Ronald, ''Inside America's Biggest Private Company,'' *Fortune*, July 13, 1992, pp. 83–90.

''North Star Planning $1.3-Million Upgrade,'' *American Metal Market*, September 4, 1995, p. 4.

Petry, Corinna C., ''Garvey to Manage Birmingham Steel,'' *American Metal Market*, January 8, 1996, p. 1.

Sacco, John E., ''Ohio Mill's Start Stalled for 3 Months,'' *American Metal Market*, September 9, 1996, p. 2.

—Paul S. Bodine

NOVELLUS

Novellus Systems, Inc.

3970 North First Street
San Jose, California 95134
U.S.A.
(408) 943-9700
Fax: (408) 943-3422

Public Company
Incorporated: 1984
Employees: 1100
Sales: $373.7 million (1995)
Stock Exchanges: NASDAQ
SICs: 3559 Machinery, Special Industry, Not Elsewhere
Classified

Based in San Jose, California, Novellus Systems, Inc. is a leading semiconductor capital equipment manufacturer of chemical vapor deposition (CVD) systems. The CVD process places a layer of either conductive or insulative material on a silicon wafer in order to connect two or more levels of circuitry in the process of manufacturing semiconductors. CVD technology, which developed around 1982, improves upon the problems of antiquated furnace diffusion and sputtering techniques. Novellus designs, manufactures, markets, and services CVD systems. One of Novellus's strengths is that its machines process 5 to 7 wafers at a time, while most CVD systems can only process one at a time. Novellus' machines cost up to $1 million, and the company's customers include most of the world's major semiconductor producers: NEC, Motorola, Advanced Micro Devices, and LSI Logic.

Founded in 1984

A relatively young company, Novellus had a precarious start in 1984. The company, founded by Brad Mattson and other former employees of Applied Materials, built a prototype CVD system, but ran out of money to continue operations. Robert Graham, then senior vice president of Applied Materials, tried to persuade his company to purchase Novellus, but Applied

Materials declined. In 1986, Graham resigned from Applied Materials and joined Novellus at the helm, as president and CEO. With experience beginning Intel's Japanese operations, Graham began at Novellus by seeking Japanese distributors. In 1987, Novellus shipped its first product: Concept One. Concept One is a two-part system, consisting of a machine that positions wafers for handling, and a processing chamber, where insulating or dielectric chemical films are deposited on the wafers.

Novellus went public in 1988, at $8 a share. At that time, the chemical vapor deposition market was dominated by U.S. companies, and was growing rapidly, attracting the interest of overseas competitors. Between 1987 and 1988 (paralleling Novellus's sales burst from $3.2 million to $23.2 million) the market grew 88 percent, from $278.5 million to $523.2 million. This growth is even more astonishing when compared to the company's earlier compound annual growth rate of 28 percent between 1984 and 1987. Such demand for CVD technology was fueled, in part, by the rising demand for facsimile machines and car phones, and the advent of high definition television. These products utilize the CVD process because their complex structures use several levels of interconnecting circuits.

A potential long-range problem for those active in the CVD market was the cyclical nature of such technologies. In 1989, Novellus CEO Robert Graham told *Electronic Business* that he anticipated another three to four years of spectacular growth for the CVD market before it would inevitably be supplanted by a newly developed technology. Four segments define the CVD market: atmospheric, low pressure, plasma-enhanced, and photo. At this time, Novellus focused entirely on the largest of the four segments—the plasma-enhanced segment—which comprised over 50 percent of the entire CVD market. Competitor Applied Materials, on the other hand, worked toward the creation of a machine that could handle multiple segments.

In 1989, a small number of companies dominated the U.S.-controlled, burgeoning CVD market. The top players included Novellus, Applied Materials, Inc., and Genus. With 158 employees, Novellus's 1989 sales reached $51 million, with net income of $11.2 million. A 1989 stock sale helped Novellus retain a healthy amount of cash and an impressive balance sheet.

In 1990, the key to control of the CVD market was tungsten. Previously, aluminum was used to connect transistors on each layer of a device, as well as between layers. However, with geometrics becoming narrower in modern devices, the sputtering technique used with aluminum became inadequate. Tungsten, on the other hand, fills the holes between layers (or vias) more uniformly. Taking advantage of this new technology to edge ahead of Applied Materials and Genus, Novellus broadened its offerings in 1990, addressing the tungsten CVD market with its new Concept One-W. This new system combined batch and wafer-at-a-time processing, creating uniform wafers in six-wafer chambers, where five were used for deposition and one for loading. By handling five wafers at a time, the chip-making cost was reduced. A previous problem of tungsten deposit backslides was also solved with a combination of vacuum-clamping and gas-exclusion techniques. Stock prices leapt from $11 to $18 between January and April of that year, reflecting an earnings increase of 50 percent in the first quarter, and revenues 45 percent higher than those of the previous year's first quarter. However, later in the year the company was hurt when the overall market fell.

International Expansion During the 1990s

To make up for the domestic recession, Novellus became active in the international market, expanding into Japan—where 45 percent of the world's chips were now manufactured—and Europe. The Japanese market paid off, helping to boost Novellus's sales in the first half of 1991. In fact, Japanese bookings accounted for over one-third of 1991 revenues, and total international business supplied well over 50 percent of the company's sales. Novellus's biggest Japanese customer was NEC Corp.

Thanks primarily to Japanese business in 1991, sales increased to $80 million, with net income of $16.8 million, and stock prices reached a high of $27¼. The company expanded to employ 265 people, but continued to keep profit margins at 21 percent with a 29 percent return on shareholders' equity. Moreover, Novellus had no debt to speak of and cash had grown to a

reserve of $44 million. Stock prices tripled to $27 between January and April of 1991, sinking again to $22 by August.

Competition with Applied Materials continued to be a priority, with Novellus still ranking number 2 behind Applied for domestic business. To gain an edge over Applied Materials, Novellus launched an innovative partnership with Lam Research Corp. Novellus and Lam joined together to secure an offer from Cypress Semiconductor's fabrication facility for a tungsten deposition system (Concept One-W, supplied by Novellus) and metal etcher (supplied by Lam). This order was the first sale of Concept One-W since the product was introduced in September, 1990 (later that year Novellus installed a second Concept One-W machine at Signetics Co.'s fabrication plant in Albuquerque, New Mexico). The partnership set a precedent in the industry, where teamwork had been an anomaly. Novellus also continued to claim a competitive advantage due to the efficiency of its machines, which completed 50 percent more wafers per hour than those of the closest rival, and sold for 25 percent less. At the beginning of 1992, *Business Week* called Novellus "the industry's fastest-growing and most profitable public company."

Novellus achieved strong sales and a near-sparkling balance sheet through its ongoing implementation of an outsourcing strategy. The company works closely with a handful of trusted suppliers, outsourcing the manufacture of major subassemblies and thereby minimizing costs and capital expenditures. The only manufacturing performed by the company itself is final assembly and testing, with this work performed by only 12 shop-floor employees. Thus, Novellus is free to concentrate its efforts on product design, and staff costs are held low. In 1991, the company's sales per employee figure exceeded $350,000, almost twice the industry average. Developing strong relationships with vendors, Novellus has on several occasions purchased parts for them when they lacked cash-on-hand. Such investments pay off in the long term, fueling lasting and lucrative partnerships. Another advantage offered by Novellus is its clean room, where a customer's process can be run on the machine before it is installed. Start-up time was improved by depositing on the wafers before shipping units.

A major change in leadership occurred in two phases, beginning in 1992. Novellus president and CEO Robert Graham stepped up to the chairman position, and Daniel Queyssac became president/CEO of Novellus. Queyssac was previously chief operating officer of SGS-Thomson Microelectronics N.V., a significantly larger company. After only six months, Queyssac left the company due to differences over managerial style, and was replaced by former senior vice president and chief financial officer Joseph Dox, who had been semi-retired.

In 1992, the worldwide chip-making machinery market was valued at $9.9 billion, and Japanese companies had cornered a 47 percent share. Novellus was a serious competitor for Hitachi Ltd. (with $54.8 billion in sales) and Canon Electronics (with $538 million). Weak economic conditions in Japan caused Novellus's earnings to fall from 87 cents a share to 34 cents in the first nine months of 1992. Novellus had been profitable since 1988. However, by the end of 1992, sales declined to $69.8 million (a 12.7 percent decline over 1991 sales) with net income of $6.2 million. International sales had slid from 55 percent to 44 percent of revenues between 1991 and 1992. In addition, low sales may partially have been due to the lack of expected orders for Concept One-W machines, as well as the slowness of interest in Concept Two (a cluster machine, combining deposition equipment with modules that fulfill other aspects of chip-making). Stock prices fell from a 52-week high of $26.50 to $8, then rose again in the end of 1992. On the bright side, despite the 1991–92 recession, Novellus's profits grew 20 percent, with sales of $350,000 per employee.

In 1993, the leadership transition was completed when Rick Hill became the new company CEO. That year, the company combined the modular architecture of the Concept Two and the tungsten CVD process chamber, resulting in another new product—Concept Two-ALTUS. Helping to undo the damage of decreased business in Japan, Novellus demonstrated strong penetration into Korea, with a $14 million order from Hyundai Electronics for Concept One-200 plasma-enhanced CVD systems. After ten years in business, the Concept One line still accounted for substantially all of the company's sales. In 1993, Concept One-W received the seal of approval from Sematech, certifying the machine to produce devices with the appropriately sized geometries. Sematech tested the machines in a 21-day, 24-hour-per-day trial. Novellus was able to use this certification to solicit additional accounts for its main product line. Sales in 1993 surged to $113.5 million (a 63 percent increase), with income at $16.1 million (triple the previous year). Primarily responsible for this extraordinary recovery were higher unit shipments of Concept One-Dielectric and Concept One-W systems, and initial shipments of Concept Two-Altus systems.

Even more impressive were the figures the following year, in 1994, when sales nearly doubled, reaching $224.7 million, with an incredible net income of $44.9 percent. Novellus benefited greatly from the worldwide shortage of chip-making capacity and the 1994 expansion of chip-making factories. In addition, the fact that semiconductor technology had changed from six-inch to eight-inch wafers caused worldwide chip-makers to seek out newer, more precise equipment. To meet increased order demands, Novellus's employee workforce now numbered 530—exactly twice that of 1991. However, to ensure against overhiring, Novellus strictly adhered to its rule that revenue per employee must not sink below $300,000. Cash holdings continued to be strong, with 1994 cash around $105 million and no long-term debt. With stock trading at around $40 a share, Novellus made a secondary offering of 1.5 million shares to offset the 1992 sales decline, caused by the downturn in Japanese business.

One of the challenges Novellus met in retaining strong financials while working with Japanese customers (who still made up 25 percent of sales) was the slow payment habits of the Japanese (120-day cycles being common) and the rising value of the yen against the dollar. To alleviate these problems, Novellus established a $7 million line of credit in yen at Sanwa Bank and Bank of America in Japan. Upon billing of Japanese customers, Novellus drew yen from its accounts and sent dollars back through intracompany payments. Then, when invoices were paid, Novellus immediately replaced the money in the accounts. In this way, yen-dollar fluctuations presented no prob-

lem to previously completed sales transactions. In other countries with comparatively slow paying habits (including Korea, Taiwan, and Singapore), Novellus utilized confirmed letters of credit, guaranteeing payment within 30 days.

Applied Materials—the company that declined to buy Novellus in its faltering early years—filed a patent infringement lawsuit against the company in 1995. The lawsuit charged patent violation associated with the use, in Novellus's Concept One and Concept Two systems, of plasma-enhanced tetraethylorthosilicate (TEOS), a silicon-containing source gas used in dielectric CVD. In the $704 million CVD market, Applied continued to be the leading company in the dielectric segment. However, Novellus demonstrated higher growth than Applied in 1994, challenging Applied's market share. The case became more complicated, with two additional patent infringement suits, related to metal CVD technology, filed in association with the initial dielectric CVD technology suit. Novellus claimed that Applied's WxZ tungsten CVD system infringed on a Novellus patent, and Applied counterclaimed that Novellus systems infringed on a separate Applied patent.

Strongly Positioned for the Future

By 1995, Novellus systems were used by all of the world's largest semiconductor device manufacturers. The company received the Texas Instruments' Supplier Excellence Award, and was named among the Ten Best Process Equipment Companies in the VLSI Research annual survey. Sales in 1995 were $373.73 million (a 66 percent increase over 1994), with net income of $82.5 million (an 83.7 percent income increase). A new product, Speed, was completed that year. Speed is a high-density plasma system with simpler, more cost-effective solutions for inter-metal dielectric films. Novellus's entire product line now consisted of dielectric solutions (Concept One, Concept One Maxus, Concept Two Sequel, Concept Two Dual Sequel, Concept Two Sequel-S), dielectric HDP solutions (Speed and Speed/Sequel), and metal solutions (Concept One-W) and Concept Two-Altus, and Concept Two-Dual Altus). To service its expanded international markets and product lines, Novellus now employed over 800 people.

Market conditions were difficult throughout 1996, with lowered bookings and higher expenses affecting net income. Stocks of manufacturers and suppliers in the $150 billion worldwide semiconductor industry took a downturn, with Novellus handling the downturn better than others. A new product—a plasma-enhanced anti-reflection layer system—was introduced at Semicon Japan. Novellus was rated the favorite large supplier of wafer processing equipment in VLSI Research's 1996 Customer Satisfaction Survey.

According to Novellus, the total available dielectric and metal CVD market is expected to grow to $2 billion by 1998. The company's name, "Novellus," is derived from the Latin word for "unique," and the company has carved a unique market niche for itself since it began in 1984, keeping labor costs low and profits high while maintaining a presence in new technological developments. While the nature of the semiconductor market leads to fast growth and easy failure, Novellus has managed to weather storms including economic recession and the weakening of Japanese business, remaining near, if not at, the top of the market.

Principal Subsidiaries

Novellus Asia (China); Novellus Systems, Ltd. (United Kingdom); Nippon Novellus, KK (Japan); Novellus Korea; Novellus Systems, V.V. (The Netherlands); Novellus Singapore Pte LTD; Novellus Taiwan.

Further Reading

Carwell, Tim, "Ten Hot Stocks Take the Test," *Fortune*, October 14, 1996, pp. 86–87.

"Chip Makers Zilog, Xicor, Novellus Post Strong 1st Period Net," *Wall Street Journal*, April 19, 1994, p. B4.

Connelley, Joyce A., "Fast-Blooming CVD Market: Equipment Makers' Bright Spot," *Electronic Business*, August 21, 1989, pp. 69–70.

Dorsch, Jeff, "Applied in Legal Fight vs. Novellus," *Electronic News*, January 30, 1995, pp. 1–2.

Dorsch, Jeff, "Hyundai Fab Shopping Spree Runs up Another Tab: $91M," *Electronic News*, December 13, 1993, pp. 1–2.

Hof, Robert D., "Novellus: Thriving—With a Little Help From Its Friends," *Business Week*, January 27, 1992, p. 60.

Holden, Daniel, "Lam, Novellus Will 'Cluster,'" *Electronic News*, August 10, 1992, p. 19.

Marcial, Gene G., "This Chip Baby Is Growing Fast," *Business Week,* April 30, 1990, p. 105.

"Novellus Announces Cost-Effective ARL Solution at Semicon Japan," The Weber Group, December 4, 1996.

Pitta, Julie, "Vapor Ware," *Forbes*, May 25, 1992, pp. 254–255.

Quinn, James Brian, "The Intelligent Enterprise a New Paradigm," *Academy of Management Executive*, November, 1992, pp. 48–63.

Serwer, Andrew Evan, "A High-Tech Stock The Big Boys Like," *Fortune*, April 8, 1991, p. 28.

—Heidi Feldman

Nu-kote Holding, Inc.

17950 Preston Rd., Suite 690
Dallas, Texas 75252
U.S.A.
(214) 250-2785
Fax: (214) 250-4097
Web site: http://www.nukote.com

Public Company
Incorporated: 1987 as Nu-kote Corporation
Employees: 3,300
Sales: $424 million (1996)
Stock Exchanges: NASDAQ
SICs: 3955 Carbon Paper & Inked Ribbons; 3861
Photographic Equipment & Supplies; 6719 Holding
Companies, Not Elsewhere Classified

Based in Dallas, Texas, Nu-kote Holding, Inc. is the largest independent imaging-supply company in the world, manufacturing a complete line of printing products that include typewriter, impact printer, and thermal fax ribbons; magnetic ink character recognition (MICR) ribbons for check encoding printers; ink rollers; carbon and facsimile paper; and re-manufactured—and even refillable—inkjet and laser printer cartridges, which it markets under both the Nu-kote and Pelikan brand names. Some would argue that the company's product line is a little too complete; of the more than 1,700 replacement products that Nu-kote manufactures and distributes for use in copiers, printers, and other imaging equipment, the majority are high-quality, low-cost versions of products boasting such brand names as Hewlett-Packard, Ricoh, Epson, and Canon. By company estimates, Nu-kote's product line satisfies owners of 22,000 different models of duplicating equipment, almost 90 percent of all the laser and inkjet printers on the market.

Not surprisingly, the inroads Nu-kote has made into the market for these consumable replacement products with their high profit margins has not gone unnoticed by the giants of the imaging equipment business. As of 1996 four suits for patent infringement had been filed against Nu-kote, although none had resulted in significant constraints on the company's business. Determined to build its niche within the burgeoning imaging supplies market, the independent Nu-kote continues to offer consumers equivalent products at between 20 to 60 percent less than those of major imaging hardware manufacturers.

Nu-kote was not always the office supply giant that it is today. Originally established as a manufacturer and supplier of carbon paper popular because it didn't leave a black residue on one's hands, Nu-kote by the mid-1980s had evolved into a modest division of the Burroughs Corporation. The company's business had expanded into manufacturing and marketing ribbons for typewriters and impact printers. In the age of office automation and advances in computer technology, these were two items that were quickly being eclipsed by more high-resolution, non-impact printing and duplicating equipment. By 1986, when the Rochester, New York-based Burroughs merged with Sperry Corporation to form Unisys, tiny Nu-kote was watching orders for its products recede against the rising tide of a technology in which laser, inkjet, and thermal technologies dominated. In 1987 Unisys decided to divest itself of several small supply businesses, among them, Nu-kote.

A Changing Corporate Culture

Enter David Brigante. A former film major at Los Angeles's Loyola Marymount University and an employee of Nu-kote since 1980, he teamed up with several of his fellow managers and, with the backing of the New York-based Clayton, Dubilier & Rice investment group, led a leveraged buyout of the ex-Burroughs division. Soon-to-be CEO Brigante began to transform the tiny company from an atrophying arm of Unisys to a viable independent firm. But this meant more than just juggling management; it meant downsizing, running leaner, loosing the extra "weight" so characteristic of larger businesses. Brigante relocated the company from Rochester to Dallas at the end of 1989, while at the same time cutting top-level corporate staff from 42 to 4, with just one secretary between them. "We're all operating people, not corporate boardroom types," Brigante told Steward B. Leavitt in *Office Products International.* "And, we've surrounded ourselves with people who know how to go into a factory and make it work better, and who know how to stand before a customer and make commitments we will meet.''

In 1992 Nu-kote was ready to go public. By October of that year its initial offering was being traded on the NASDAQ exchange at $6 per share. As a manufacturer of products that have already been designed, the small but growing company was able to offer customers lower prices than its competition—original equipment manufacturers (OEMs) like Hewlett-Packard and Canon—due to the fact that it did not have to carry substantial R&D or design overhead for its products. Like David pitting himself against Goliath, the company's ability to gain increasing market share was a direct result of its agility and marketing savvy.

The 1990s: Growth Through Acquisition

In February 1992 Nu-kote also began a policy of acquisition by welcoming International Communication Materials, Inc. (ICMI) into its corporate family. One of the largest U.S. manufacturers of toner for laser printers and copiers, ICMI would change the future of Nu-kote, bringing its product line technologically up-to-date through the introduction of non-impact technology and positioning the company for future growth. The combined efforts of the company's 962 employees grossed sales of $95.4 million, largely through Nu-kote's introduction of toner cartridges to its product line. The resulting net earnings for 1992 were $1.5 million.

In early 1993 the company acquired Future Graphics. Based in California, Future Graphics was an international leader in the business of recycling—remanufacturing plastic laser printer cartridges—as well as a distributor of cartridge components and other supplies. Remanufactured laser cartridges sell at between 30 and 50 percent less than OEM products, providing retailers with a more attractive profit margin. Another plus is the reduction in the number of used cartridges that end up in landfills each year, a fact that would prove to enhance the product's value still further in the environmentally conscious 1990s. Nu-kote's acquisition of Future Graphics expanded its technology base through the addition of remanufacture and inkjet technologies, while also boosting its work force to 1,100 people. Nu-kote's 1993 sales rose to $120 million. Net income for the year was posted at $7.5 million; this figure would climb even higher—to almost $8 million—by the close of fiscal 1994.

Imaging Giants Wage Duplicate Legal Battles

Characteristic of other technological advancements, the retail prices associated with printers, fax machines, personal copiers, and other imaging hardware have dropped relative to their level when first introduced to the consumer market. OEMs including Hewlett-Packard and Ricoh counted on profit margins of up to 70 percent on sales of their own brand-name replacement cartridges and ribbons to offset these falling hardware prices. Like the pricing relationship between razors and razor blades, the repeat costs associated with replacement parts far outstrips the cost of the actual imaging device over the equipment's lifetime. And in the case of laser toner cartridges (each one which can set the consumer back up to 10 percent of the cost of the printer itself), the ink supply accounts for a fraction of the total cost. The bulk of the manufacturing costs go to producing the electronic print head that dispenses toner evenly. Although the print head has a life-span that far outlasts the ink supply, consumers have no way of refilling the cartridges and so discard the whole assembly. ''It's a little like gluing the gas tank of your car onto the engine, so that every time you run out of gas you have to get a new engine,'' Brigante maintained in *Forbes*.

By extending the life of OEM cartridge assemblies, Nu-kote had become the top independent in the replacement product industry. It purchased new cartridges from OEM suppliers and modified them with a replaceable ink supply, or collected used ones from office supply stores, then refilled them with toner and sold them as remanufactured cartridges. The company would also develop a two-piece, refillable cartridge that dramatically cuts printing costs for the consumer. Not surprisingly, OEMs were not content to watch Nu-kote benefit from their technology and expand its 15 to 20 percent share of this lucrative market any further. In 1993 Ricoh filed a trademark infringement suit against its ambitious and multifaceted rival. The suit was partially settled in 1994, after Nu-kote/ICMI redesigned its Ricoh-compatible replacement toner cartridges.

Meanwhile, PC-giant Hewlett-Packard decided to test its own case against the company, accusing Nu-kote of patent and trademark infringement in September 1994. Not to be left out, Japanese computer giants Canon and Epson joined with Ricoh and Hewlett-Packard in 1995, accusing the Dallas-based independent of patent infringement on their inkjet technologies. ''It's a joke,'' Brigante declared to Teresa Riordan of the *Wall Street Journal* in late 1995. ''They flood the Patent Office with dubious applications until some poor examiner finally grants a patent for something as obvious as a round edge on a vial. It's clearly a way to obstruct competition. It doesn't have anything to do with creating new science.'' Nu-kote responded to the suit by filing counterclaims against Hewlett-Packard, Canon, and Epson, citing trademark misuse and antitrust violations. ''We're going to be seeing more and more cases like this because aftermarkets have become so valuable,'' a lawyer for Nu-kote was quoted as saying in the *Wall Street Journal*. ''Our society needs to decide how much protection it wants to give patent holders at the expense of consumers.'' Although litigation was expected to last several years, the suit with Epson was resolved in 1996, in large part in favor of Nu-kote.

While OEMs contend that Nu-kote's cartridges are inferior in quality and potentially damaging to their hardware when used by consumers, company products have been found to be of equal quality to those of the OEMs—by both consumer end users and the OEM's themselves. In its European plants, contracts to produce replacement imaging supplies under the OEM brand names accounts for 25 percent of Nu-kote's business. After all, Brigante would argue, OEM's are like any other customer—they want high quality at a competitive price: which is what Nu-kote offers.

Expands Share of European Market Via Pelikan

In the imaging supplies market, one of the biggest growth centers was in the office superstore arena, where Office Depot, Office Max, and Staples were battling for control of the ever-growing small business/home office market. Nu-kote's chief competitor in the superstore arena was Pelikan Holding AG, a $658 million producer of pens, inks, stationary, and typewriter and printer ribbons located in Zug, Switzerland. With a home-court advantage, Nu-kote was steadily making inroads into Pelikan's U.S. customer base, reversing the loyalties of former Pelikan customer Office Depot in early 1994. However, the campaign was becoming costly for both companies. Instead of continuing a pricey advertising campaign to compete for superstore loyalties, Brigante orchestrated a unique agreement that avoided an imminent price war and sharpened both companies' competitive edges. In mid-July 1994 Pelikan signed a letter of intent agreeing to sell its Hardcopy (imaging products) division to its U.S. rival for $100 million. In exchange, Nu-kote would transfer between 20 to 30 percent of its stock and a percentage of its corporate debt to the Swiss manufacturer.

Under the arrangement with Pelikan, Nu-kote expanded its inkjet technology and made inroads into Europe, leveraging its own products within an expanded customer base under the Pelikan brand, a household word throughout the continent. Pelikan, which had been operating at a loss due to the European recession, was now finally able to concentrate its energies on its core business—a quality line of writing instruments and stationary—and reap the profits of owning a percentage of its former competitor. Nu-kote's absorption of Pelikan's strong R&D and manufacturing divisions—in the acquisition it gained hundreds of patents and potential new products, as well as plants in Switzerland, Germany, Columbia, Mexico, China, and Scotland—meant that both companies could now reduce both manufacturing and administrative overheads by condensing duplicate marketing and production operations within their new network of manufacturing plants and offices.

The acquisition of Pelikan Hardcopy effectively tripled Nu-kote's size; sales for fiscal 1995 would jump from $151 million to $193 million, although net earnings reflected over $14.5 million in restructuring expenses associated with the company's expansion with a loss of $12.4 million. Despite this temporary setback, the growing company expanded its sales force to 3,100 during the year.

The Pelikan merger also freed up capital within Nu-kote, allowing it to expand its own production of non-impact replacement products. The market for laser and inkjet printer and copier toner cartridges effectively doubled during the latter half of the 1990s; the replacement ink market alone was worth approximately $9.5 million by 1996. Meanwhile, sales of rib-

bons for typewriters and first-generation printers like the daisy wheel still generated sales of $1.6 billion in the United States— and accounted for 55 percent of company revenues in 1994. While the demand for this outdated technology was declining relative to the more advanced laser imaging systems, by the late 1990s many smaller firms were not ready to leave their noisy, but less-costly-to-operate daisy-wheel printers out at the curb. Sales of impact-related Nu-kote products in the international market actually doubled between fiscal 1995 and 1996, partially as a result of the Pelikan Hardcopy acquisition. Indeed, 1996 would be a banner year for the company, as it posted net earnings of $13.1 million on sales of over $424 million.

In addition to laser and inkjet technology, Nu-kote was able to make inroads into the replacement market for bubble-jet printers, ordinarily a market where Canon has had exclusive domain as the holder of numerous patents. In July 1994, through its newly acquired Modular Ink Technology AB (MIT) subsidiary, Nu-kote gained strategic patent rights of Jarfalla Industry Competence Centre, a Swedish-based technological innovator in the area of printer technology. A former R&D subdivision of IBM, Jarfalla/MIT had engineered "piezoelectric" ink jet technology, which was expected to crack the bubble-jet market due to its speed, versatility, and reduced costs. Nu-kote was quick to begin marketing their proprietary inkjet technology to the OEMs, entering into several relationships with hardware manufacturers in the months that followed.

By early 1996 Nu-kote could boast manufacturing plants in five states, as well as in Colombia, South America, the United Kingdom, Germany, and Switzerland. Administrative offices are also positioned in these locations, allowing the company to facilitate orders between its manufacturing centers and its network of distributors and wholesalers worldwide. First-quarter earnings for 1996 posted at $4.9 million, with sales of $104 million as a result of the influx of Pelikan-generated European business.

Looking Ahead

With its strong position in numerous markets around the world, Nu-kote was now in a position to benefit from the dynamic growth within the global imaging supplies marketplace. China and India were two markets that the company was aggressively pursuing by the end of the 1990s. Its ability to offer quality products at competitive prices, which gained it such lucrative accounts as the Sears department store chain, promised to make Nu-kote's products increasingly attractive as the office supply industry continued its competitive momentum. And the steady increase in the retail price of replacement parts—especially for popular color print technologies that multiply the cost-per-page fivefold—were expected to grow the imaging supply market, with much of the growth going to suppliers like Nu-kote, which could provide quality products at a substantial savings to consumers.

Nu-kote has also begun to look beyond re-producing products based on those of the OEMs; with its enhanced R&D capabilities and its emphasis on developing reusable and recyclable products, the company would expend over $12 million in the area of development in fiscal 1997 alone. Among its most popular company-developed products have been the Pelikan

"Easy Click" and Nu-kote "Cartridge Plus" inkjet systems, both compatible with Hewlett-Packard's Deskjet printer models. Nu-kote expects the gross profit margin for these and other company-developed products to increase with sales volume and as these products are integrated into the company's cartridge recovery and remanufacture program. Increasingly consolidating its manufacturing and distribution operations, Nu-kote has carried its global vision to the supply side of the business equation, seeking out suppliers from all corners of the globe that can best fulfil the raw-material requirements of its plants.

As imaging technology continues to advance, new product lines will continue to open up. Nu-kote remains particularly focused upon becoming a vertically integrated supplier of ink jet cartridges, which are among the fastest-growing segment of the imaging supply market due to their proliferation among home computer users. In 1996 alone, of the 210 new products introduced by the company, 62 were ink jet supplies. Nu-kote has utilized the technological advances of its MIT subsidiary to position it as a leader in this lucrative market. In the duplicating business, Nu-kote's success has yet to be duplicated.

Principal Subsidiaries

Nu-kote International, Inc.; Nu-kote Imperial, Ltd.; International Communications Materials, Inc.; Viro-kote, Inc.; Nu-kote Imaging International, Inc.; Future Graphics, Inc.; Nu-kote Latin America, Inc.; Interfas Holding, S.A. (France); Greif-Werke GmbH (Germany); Pelikan Scotland, Ltd.; Pelikan Produktions AG (Switzerland); Modular Ink Technology AB (Sweden); Nu-kote Italia s.r.l. (Italy).

Further Reading

Berry, Kathleen M., "Clear Image: Nu-kote Holdings Sets Tone Selling Toner," *Investor's Business Daily,* October 16, 1995.
Leavitt, Stewart B., "Entrepreneurial Nu-kote: The Cinderella of Imaging Supplies," *Office Products International*, March 1995.
Palmeri, Christopher, "Copycat," *Forbes*, January 22, 1996.
Riordan, Teresa, "Patents: The Battle for Office Machines," *Wall Street Journal*, October 30, 1995.
Silverman, Susan D., "All's Fair in Business," *International Business*, October 1994.

—Pamela L. Shelton

Oakley, Inc.

10 Holland St.
Irvine, California 92718
U.S.A.
(714) 951-0991
Fax: (714) 454-1071
Web site: http://www.oakley.com

Public Company
Incorporated: 1975
Employees: 700
Sales: $218.6 million (1996)
Stock Exchanges: New York
SICs: 3851 Ophthalmic Goods; 3089 Plastics Products,
    Not Elsewhere Classified; 3229 Pressed and Blown
    Glass and Glassware, Not Elsewhere Classified; 3827
    Optical Instruments and Lenses

Oakley, Inc. is an innovation-driven designer, manufacturer, and distributor of high-performance eyewear, including sunglasses and goggles. Oakley sunglasses sell for anywhere from $40 to $225 a pair. Key aspects of Oakley's success include celebrity endorsements, especially by athletes, together with high-tech designs that include interchangeable lenses, high optical clarity, and damage resistance, and selective distribution through high-end retailers and specialty stores. These elements of Oakley's brand-building strategy work together to increase the perceived value of the company's products. Its products are not available from mass market retailers, and Oakley vigorously litigates any unauthorized distribution of its products as well as patent infringements to keep competitors out of its lucrative business. With net margins for the company hovering around 25 percent, *Forbes* estimated that it cost Oakley about $15 to manufacture a $100 pair of sunglasses out of plastic, carbon fibre, and other new materials.

Oakley was founded by Jim Jannard in 1975 when he began selling handgrips for motocross motorcycles from the back of his car. Something of a motorcycle enthusiast, Jannard attended the University of Southern California in 1970. The long-haired student dropped out, reportedly because the Irish setter he brought to class irritated his professors. He spent about a year driving around the Southwest on his motorcycle. When he returned to Los Angeles, he traded in his motorcycle for a small Honda and began selling motorcycle parts out of his trunk to shops that serviced motorcycles. In 1975 he designed a rubber grip for off-road motorcycles and began selling it along with the motorcycle parts. That was the beginning of Oakley, a company he named after one of his dogs.

Jannard was about 35 when he began Oakley in 1975. Toward the end of the decade he began selling motocross goggles. Featuring his own designs, the goggles were made of high-impact plastic that was lighter and stronger than the glass goggles then in use. With the help of some young salespeople, Jannard began handing them out at motocross competitions and selling them through Oakley's motorcycle parts accounts.

When the motorcycle goggles became a hot item, Jannard began developing eyewear that was part goggles and part sunglasses for skiers and bicyclists. In 1983 Oakley began selling ski goggles. Next year the company moved into the sunglasses market. Cyclist Greg Le Mond wore Oakley sunglasses in 1986 on his way to winning the Tour de France, becoming the first of many star athletes to be associated with marketing Oakley sunglasses. Jannard was encouraged to develop new sunglass models. One was the company's trademark Blades model, which featured interchangeable wraparound lenses that slipped into a simple carbon-fibre frame.

To market his new sunglasses, Jannard and his salespeople handed out many pairs to top athletes in the late 1980s and early 1990s. At one golf tournament, they gave a pair to basketball star (and golfer) Michael Jordan, and Jordan has been wearing Oakley sunglasses ever since. Other celebrities who have been associated with Oakley sunglasses include Philip Knight, head of Nike, tennis star Andre Agassi, skater Bonnie Blair, and baseball great Cal Ripken, Jr.

A key element of Oakley's distinctive marketing approach has been the use of influential athletes. Relying primarily on the "editorial" endorsement of influential athletes, Oakley was able to increase consumer awareness of the company's product performance and overall brand image. Oakley believed serious athletes were quick to recognize the superior technology and performance of its products.

Many of Oakley's endorsements have been obtained at little or no cost. In 1994 Oakley paid about $4 million to its endorsers, or about three cents per sales dollar. Andre Agassi, for example, didn't charge his friend Jim Jannard for his endorsement, even though he used to have an endorsement contract with Bausch & Lomb's Ray Ban brand of sunglasses. By comparison, it cost Phil Knight of Nike $10 million per year to sign Agassi to an endorsement contract for ten years. Michael Jordan, who first wore Oakley sunglasses while playing golf, then while playing baseball for the Birmingham Barons, negotiated a stock package with Jannard when Oakley went public in 1995 that included a position on the company's board of directors.

The use of influential athletes to endorse its products helped make Oakley the acknowledged leader in the sports sunglasses market. Its high-performance sunglasses and goggles were worn by professional baseball and basketball players, skaters, skiers, cyclists, golfers, tennis players, and others. In 1990 the company had net income of $7.7 million on sales of $68.6 million. Sales were off slightly in 1991, then rebounded in 1992 to $76.4 million, with net income increasing to $9.1 million.

In the early 1990s Oakley's products were becoming popular in the nonsports fashion segment of the market. Sales and net income rose significantly in 1993 and 1994, to $92.7 million and then $124.0 million. By the end of 1994, the company made eight lines of sunglasses and three lines of goggles, accounting for a 13 percent market share of the U.S. premium (over $30 retail) sunglasses business. Its products were distributed in more than 60 countries.

Throughout its history Oakley has been selective about introducing new products. Starting with the basic Blades brand, which retailed for around $110 plus $60 for each additional coated lens in 1995, the company developed other product lines. The cheapest pair were a $40 pair of Frogskins. Agassi has worn Oakley's eye jackets brand, which were introduced in December 1994. The M-Frame, a high-impact line that features superhard polycarbonate lenses, can withstand a blast from a 12-gauge shotgun at 15 yards, or the force of a one-pound pointed weight dropped from a height of four feet. They sold for about $130 a pair in 1995. Trenchcoats, a line of camouflage eyewear, were introduced in October 1995, followed by Straight Jackets in May 1996. The much-anticipated X-Frames, originally announced for 1996, were put on hold until 1997. Oakley also made three lines of goggles: H2O, Motocross, and Ski.

Oakley Went Public in 1995

As Oakley prepared to go public in 1995, Jannard gave himself a $21 million bonus at the end of 1994. He owned 64.8 percent of the company, and his net worth was estimated to be $750 million. His chief executive officer, Mike Parnell, who was 42 in 1995, received about $4.8 million in 1994. They each owned jet planes that they leased back to the company after it went public. Parnell owned about 7 percent of Oakley. Overall, the company was valued at about $820 million.

The year 1995 began well. Sales for the first half were 37 percent above sales for the first half of 1994. In August, 10 million shares were offered to the public at $23 per share, some $4–$6 higher than the range of $17–$19 per share originally envisioned by the underwriters. The initial public offering (IPO) raised $230 million, with $154 million going to insiders. Jannard made nearly $139 million. His holdings in the company were valued at $627 million after the stock rose to $27.125 a share on the day after the IPO, making him the second richest Orange County resident behind billionaire Donald Bren. The remaining $76 million for Oakley was earmarked to build a new corporate headquarters and pay off debt.

Litigating Infringements and Unauthorized Distribution in the 1990s

In December 1995, Oakley won two patent infringement suits against Bausch & Lomb Inc. and Lombardie Booster. The Court of Commerce in Paris ruled that some models of Bausch & Lomb's Killer Loop sunglasses infringed on two of Oakley's design patents. In a separate judgment, the same court ruled that Lombardie Booster's Infrared and Morpho sunglasses infringed on three of Oakley's design patents. Although Oakley was awarded less than $50,000 in damages in each case, the rulings served to help Oakley keep its competitors from copying its trendy glasses. Earlier in the year, the company was able to halt the sale of fake Oakleys delivered to Big 5 Sporting Goods, which the retailer had heavily advertised. The retailer agreed to cooperate with Oakley in tracking down the distributor of the fake sunglasses, all of which were ordered destroyed by the court. In April 1996 Oakley filed suit against The Clubhouse, a sporting goods store located in Thousand Oaks, California, charging that it resold Oakley sunglasses to an unfashionable discount warehouse. The discounter, Price/Costco, apparently offered Oakley's e Wire brand sunglasses in its mail-order catalog.

Historically, Oakley has vigorously litigated any unauthorized distribution of its products as well as patent infringements. This helps keep competitors out of such a lucrative business. One attorney told *Forbes* that Oakley "uses litigation as a marketing tool." He estimated he had spent 2,000 hours helping ten sunglass makers fight Oakley in court in the early 1990s.

Oakley had some 320 patents issued or pending worldwide, plus 249 registered trademarks, as of 1995. Jannard's chief legal advisor, boyhood friend Gregory Weeks, has spent much of his career enforcing Oakley's patents and trademarks, starting with Jannard's first motorcycle handlebar grip. Oakley has zero tolerance for counterfeiters and uses its sales force, concerned consumers, and hired investigators to seek out counterfeiters and sue them.

Plans for New Corporate Headquarters in 1996

In January 1996 Oakley unveiled plans for its new "interplanetary corporate headquarters," to be located on 40 acres in Foothill Ranch in Orange County. The $35-million facility had "the look and feel of a post-industrial age gone awry," according to the *Orange County Register*. "Steel beams, oversized rivets, and galvanized metallic surfaces give the structure—dubbed 'Technical Center'—a dark, intimidating presence." The company's founder and chairman, Jim Jannard, reportedly wanted the facility to "look as if it were the sole survivor in a 'post-nuclear kill zone'."

A sense of privacy was achieved by setting the facility back from the main entrance, where a winding road takes visitors past rock formations. The dark-shaded, two-story building comes into view only after the final turn of the road.

Over the main doorway, plans called for a 40-foot high metal ring with a convex stainless steel center, similar to Oakley's trademark ellipsis. Inside are the corporate offices, an auditorium, a boutique, and a museum. The adjacent warehouse is the size of four football fields and contains a basketball court. Other features of the Oakley campus included a helicopter landing pad, a small park for employees, a jogging track that circles the area, and an amphitheater. Much of the corporate campus appeared to reflect Jannard's personal style and take into account the youth of the company's workforce, whose average age is under 30.

As for landscaping, an architect who had done work for Great Britain's royal family designed prehistoric-looking rockwork to surround the campus. Native plants and trees were to be used around the grounds instead of manicured lawns, and the parking lot would be lighted by heavy-duty airport landing discs instead of traditional parking-lot lights.

First-Ever Annual Meeting Held in 1996

Oakley held its first-ever annual meeting for shareholders at El Toro, California, in June 1996. Jannard presided over the meeting, which was attended by basketball star Dennis Rodman and was held at the Command Museum at El Toro Marine Corps Air Station. Soldiers wearing Oakley camouflage Trenchcoat sunglasses directed shareholders at the base. Jannard, refusing as usual to allow his photograph to be taken, was wearing black M-Frames sunglasses during the meeting.

The company reported to shareholders on 1995 earnings, which grew 49 percent to $39.6 million. Sales rose nearly 40 percent to $173 million. The company's stock had nearly doubled to $45.25 per share since its IPO in August of the previous year. Jannard gave a speech to the shareholders in which he emphasized Oakley's high-tech abilities and competitive strength. "We solve problems with inventions and then we wrap those inventions in art," he said about the company's products. The next line of sunglasses that Oakley planned to introduce were X-Metals. The company also planned to introduce sunglasses especially for cricket players in the international market.

A secondary offering of stock, underwritten by Merrill Lynch & Co. and Alex Brown & Sons Inc., also took place in June. Jannard and Parnell were planning to sell about 5 million shares, worth about $220 million at current market prices. After the sale, Jannard would still own at least 45 percent of the company. Jannard's compensation for 1995 consisted of a $380,697 salary and a $9.3 million bonus, earned in part for exceeding financial performance targets.

In July the company reported that first half 1996 financial results were good. Profits climbed 32.5 percent to $26.7 million, compared to $20.2 million a year ago. Sales were up 35.4 percent to $111.5 million from $82.3 million the previous year.

In August Oakley entered into an agreement with Essilor International and its U.S. subsidiary Gentex Optics, makers of prescription lenses. The deal gave Oakley access to prescription lens laboratories and lens-making capabilities. Oakley planned to make its e Wire frames ($130) available in prescription sunglasses within a month. Previously, prescription lenses had accounted for less than one percent of the company's sales and were limited to only two of its sports sunglasses. Oakley's agreement with Essilor International and Gentex Optics was expected to cut the time for obtaining prescription lenses for Oakley sunglasses from three weeks to just one week.

In addition, Oakley was granted an option to purchase Essilor and Gentex's nonprescription-lens unit within four years. At the time Gentex was the world's leading producer of advanced-technology polycarbonate lenses and was Oakley's sole supplier of polycarbonate lenses. As part of the deal, Oakley also obtained an exclusive right to purchase a new scratch-resistant coating and decentered sunglass lens blanks, which would enable it to create optically superior dual lens sunglasses.

Nike to Compete in Premium Sunglasses Market

In October, Nike announced it would enter the $1.5 billion premium sunglasses market. It planned to focus on sports performance sunglasses, the same niche occupied by Oakley. Interestingly, basketball superstar Michael Jordan was under a ten-year contract with Oakley and was also a member of its board of directors. He was also signed with Nike to endorse its products. With Nike entering the sports performance sunglasses market, it was unclear how he would handle his dual obligations.

Nike began with two styles of sunglasses designed specifically for track and field, the V12 ($160) and the V8 ($145). Nike spent a year developing them with the help of a visual sports expert and tested them on top-flight track athletes. Among the eyewear's special features were small vents on the sides to eliminate fogging and nose bridges that adapted to facial contours.

Nike also announced it would introduce the Magneto brand of glasses in the winter of 1996–97. The unusually designed Magnetos have no temples; they adhere to the face of the wearer with two small, semi-sticky round discs called AMPs that are placed on the wearer's temples. The AMPs hold the sunglasses to the face with tiny magnets. The advantage, according to Nike: the glasses are lighter and won't bounce when you run.

After effecting a two-for-one stock split in early October, problems with one of its principal distributors, Sunglass Hut International Inc., began to show with lower-than-expected sales in September, causing Oakley's stock price to drop by 16.9 percent. Sales to Sunglass Hut accounted for approximately one-third of Oakley's total volume in the first half of 1996. Oakley reported a strong third quarter, with profits up 53 percent to $15.7 million versus $10.2 million a year ago. U.S. sales increased 44 percent to $47.4 million and international sales gained 39 percent to $20.3 million. On December 5, Oakley announced that Sunglass Hut had cancelled all purchase orders through January 1997. Oakley delayed the launch of its new X-Metal brand of sunglasses, and its stock lost 33 percent of its value, falling to $10.625 a share.

Acquired U.K. Distributor in 1996

In November Oakley announced it had reached an agreement to acquire Serval Marketing, its exclusive distributor in the United Kingdom and Ireland. The distributor would be renamed Oakley U.K. Financial terms of the agreement were not disclosed. Based outside London, England, Serval Marketing was Oakley's exclusive UK and Irish distributor for 15 years, since 1981. It employed about 35 individuals, and its chairman, Carl Ward, and managing director, Ray Tilbrook, were signed to five-year employment contracts to ensure they would continue in the same roles for Oakley U.K.

Michael Parnell noted that "the U.K. and Irish markets continue to be one of our strongest and most important regions overseas. This acquisition will enable us to integrate one of our most profitable distributors, improve productivity, and better respond to the increasing demand in this growing market."

Closing out a very eventful year, three shareholders filed a class action suit in December against Jim Jannard and Michael Parnell, Oakley's two top executives, charging they misrepresented the state of the company's operations to take advantage of Oakley's secondary stock offering in June 1996. The two underwriting firms and Oakley were also named in the suit. According to the suit, Jannard sold 9 million shares at $23.81 per share (adjusted for October's stock split) for $205.2 million, and Parnell sold 1 million shares for $22.8 million. Six weeks later, Oakley's stock dropped to $15.375 on news that Sunglass Hut was experiencing weak sales. The lawsuit charged that company executives artificially inflated Oakley's stock by claiming that business with Sunglass Hut was strong and that the X-Metal line would be introduced by the end of 1996.

Sales in the fourth quarter of 1996 declined sharply, due to the loss of orders from Sunglass Hut and sluggish European sales. For the year, sales were up 27 percent to $218.6 million from $172.5 million in 1995. Net income for the fourth quarter was only $3.6 million versus $9.2 million the previous year. For the year, net income increased 16 percent to $46.0 million from $39.6 million a year ago. The X-Metal line was expected to be introduced later in 1997 along with other new products currently under development.

Pursuing an aggressive strategy to achieve direct distribution in its international markets, Oakley announced it would begin a direct distribution operation in Japan starting in May. Oakley canceled its contract with one of two authorized distributors in Japan that had sold to the snow ski, motorcycle, sunglass specialty, and sporting goods markets. Oakley hoped that establishing direct distribution in Japan would better position the company for long-term growth and increased market share in the country. Its other distributor, which focused on the surf and snowboard markets in Japan, was retained for the time being.

Perhaps indicating the company's strong commitment to superior design, Oakley established a new position, vice president of design, to which Colin Baden was promoted in February. Baden joined Oakley in February 1996 as director of design and advised Oakley on company image issues since 1993. He was formerly a partner at Lewis Architects of Seattle, Washington.

Oakley Geared for New Challenges

At its annual meeting in 1996, Oakley proclaimed its goal was "world domination." To achieve that goal and keep its sales and earnings growth on track, Oakley must deal with several problems that cropped up during 1996 and 1997. Its earnings were severely affected by the performance of its key distributor, Sunglass Hut, toward the end of 1996. That situation may force Oakley to reevaluate its selective distribution strategy. Another challenge may come from a new competitor, Nike, who entered the premium sportswear sunglasses market in 1996. As the future plays out for Oakley, Jannard and his associates will be formulating strategies from their newly built corporate headquarters.

Further Reading

Aaron, M. L. et al., "Oakley Inc.—Company Report," Alex, Brown & Sons, Inc., August 27, 1996.

"California's Oakley Inc. Builds 'Interplanetary' Headquarters," *Knight-Ridder/Tribune Business News*, January 18, 1996.

"Chief of Sunglass Company Makes $139 Million Overnight in Public Offering," *Knight-Ridder/Tribune Business News*, August 10, 1995.

"Irvine, Calif.-Based Oakley Pairs Up With Top Prescription-Lens Maker," *Knight-Ridder/Tribune Business News*, August 28, 1996.

McHugh, Josh, "Who's Hiding Behind Those Shades?," *Forbes*, October 23, 1995, p. 66.

Mehta, Stephanie N., "For Everything Under the Sun, Specialized Sunglasses," *Wall Street Journal*, February 5, 1996, p. B1.

"Nike to Enter Premium Sunglasses Market," *Knight-Ridder/Tribune Business News*, October 14, 1996.

"Oakley Bullish on Future with Rodman's Appearance at El Toro, Calif.," *Knight-Ridder/Tribune Business News*, June 30, 1996.

"Oakley Net Gains 53 Percent in 3rd Quarter," *WWD*, October 21, 1996.

"Oakley Says Sales Strong After Stock Price Drops," *WWD*, October 14, 1996.

"Oakley Sees 4th-Period Net Trailing Estimates," *WWD*, January 27, 1997.

"Sunglasses Maker Oakley Scores Two More Victories Against Design Copycats," *Knight-Ridder/Tribune Business News*, December 14, 1995.

"3 Oakley Holders File Suit Against Two Executives; Class Action Charges Insider Trading," *Daily News Record*, December 31, 1996.

—David P. Bianco

Orkla A/S

P.O. Box 308
N-1324 Lysaker
Norway
(47) 22-50-10-80
Fax: (47) 22-50-16-91
Web site: http://hugin.sn.no/ork

Public Company
Incorporated: 1991
Sales: NKr21.53 billion (US$3.43 billion) (1995)
Employees: 18,353
Stock Exchanges: Oslo
SICs: 2033 Jams, Jellies, Juices, Ketchup, Sauces; 2038
Frozen Pizza, Frozen Dinners; 2043 Cereal
Preparations and Breakfast Foods; 205 Bakery
Products; 2082 Breweries, Beer Manufacturing; 2086
Soft Drinks, Bottled or Canned; 2092 Seafoods, Fresh
and Frozen; 2099 Yeast Manufacturing; 2711
Newspapers, Publishing and Printing; 2721
Magazines, Publishing and Printing; 2821 Lignin and
Diphenol Manufacturing; 2841 Detergents,
Manufacturing; 2844 Cosmetics Manufacturing; 2869
Vanillin and Ethanol Manufacturing; 4911 Electric
Power, Generation and Transmission; 5461 Retail
Bakeries; 6282 Investment Counselors, Advice

Orkla A/S is the largest branded consumer goods group and food and beverage producer in Scandinavia and one of the five largest companies in Norway. It operates in three major business areas: brand name consumer goods (80 percent of its 1995 operating revenues), chemicals (17 percent), and financial investments (3 percent). Orkla's US$3 billion branded goods segment contains its food products, beverage, confectionary, snack, biscuit, detergent, cosmetic, personal products, and newspaper/magazine operations and is divided into four segments: Orkla Foods, Orkla Brands, Orkla Beverages, and Orkla Media. Orkla is the Nordic region's largest supplier of biscuits, Nor-

way's largest supplier of groceries and its second-largest producer of chocolate and snacks, and Denmark's market leader in snacks. Moreover, Orkla Foods is the Nordic region's leading producer of preserved vegetables, ketchup, frozen pizza, juice, jam, fruit soups, and marzipan and is a major producer of frozen dinners, caviar, fresh and chilled meats, cereals, bread and yeast, and seafood.

Orkla Beverages consists of Orkla's 45 percent interest in Pripps Ringnes (in association with the Swedish car maker Volvo), the leading producer of carbonated soft drinks and water products in Norway and Sweden. Orkla Media, the second-largest private media firm in Norway, owned 17 Norwegian newspapers in 1994 and was one of the four major owners of Norway's newspaper circulation market. It also owns 50 percent of Norwegian magazine publisher Hjemmet Mortensen, and operates several local newspapers, magazines, and printing plants in Poland.

Orkla's chemicals segment is run by its Borregaard division, which specializes in the development, production, and marketing of lignin-based binding and dispersing agents for applications in animal feeds, agrochemicals, oil drilling mud, cement, and dyes; fine chemicals products like intermediates (used as a contrast agent in X-ray photography) and vanillin (used in flavoring and perfume); and specialty pulp (used in textiles, photographic paper, and the manufacture of thickening agents in foods). In 1995 Borregaard had sales of US$800 million, employed 2,500, and maintained production plants in 11 countries and sales operations throughout the world.

Although a small part of Orkla's overall operations, its financial investments division, Orkla Finans A/S, owns one of Norway's largest securities portfolios (primarily in large Norwegian companies), which on August 31, 1996 had a market value of NKr9.72 billion, representing about one-quarter of Orkla's combined balance sheet. In addition to portfolio management, Orkla Finans offers capital management, stockbroking, project financing, and international financial consultancy services.

In 1995 Orkla's sales within Norway accounted for 52 percent of its operating revenues, sales to Scandinavia (excluding

Norway) accounted for another 27 percent, and sales to the rest of Europe totaled 16 percent of total revenues. The United States and other non-European markets accounted for only 5 percent of Orkla's 1995 revenues. Orkla maintained production and other facilities in mainland China, Iceland, Singapore, Japan, the United States, and several European countries.

Orkla Industrier A/S: 1904–85

The original firm of the present-day Orkla A/S conglomerate traces its roots back to the first pyrite mining operations conducted at Løkken Verk, Norway (south of Trondheim near the Orkla River), which began in 1654. In the succeeding years, a smelting industry grew up around the mines in the area, and after a period of disuse, in 1904 the Løkken Verk mines were reopened by the newly formed Orkla Industrier. For the next 40-plus years, Orkla focused on developing its mining businesses. In the years following World War II, however, Orkla Industrier began building up an ever widening investment portfolio of other companies and in 1958 established an important joint venture with the Unilever Group (makers of "All" detergent, among other products) to manufacture detergents and personal products—a relationship that was still in place in 1997. In 1981, Orkla extended its strategy to diversify beyond its original mining businesses by purchasing its first newspaper publisher.

Borregaard A/S: 1918–85

In 1986 Orkla agreed to merge with Borregaard A/S, a major Norwegian chemicals company, to form a new entity, Orkla Borregaard A/S. Borregaard traced its roots back to 1918, when a partnership of Norwegian business interests had acquired the British firm The Kellner Partington Paper Pulp Co., Ltd., itself founded in 1889. A manufacturer of pulp and paper in Norway, Sweden, and Austria, Kellner Partington had fueled its growth through a combination of British capital and Austrian technology. Rechristened Borregaard, the new firm began establishing a reputation as one of the world's foremost producers of pulp and paper, with production facilities in several countries and international sales.

In 1938, Borregaard entered the chemicals business when it began using sugar compounds found in the byproducts of wood pulp production as the raw material for the production of ethanol (used in alcohol and as a solvent). In 1960, it began

expanding its chemicals and consumer products, and in 1962 and 1967 it extended its pulp byproduct chemicals manufacturing applications from ethanol to vanillin and lignin, respectively. Although by the mid-1970s Borregaard still owned one of the two largest wood pulp mills in Norway, in the early 1980s it made the radical leap from using pulp as its primary raw material to the production of fine chemicals that used nonpulp-based applications from the specialized fields of advanced chemicals manufacture.

The reason for the shift was plain: demand for Borregaard's traditional wood processing products had begun to fade, and it was forced to begin unloading its international production facilities. In 1979, for example, it sold off its Borregaard Osterreich AG subsidiary for NKr84 million; then in 1983 it sold a 6 percent interest in its stock to food and beverages group Nora Industrier A/S, only to purchase back a 42 percent interest in Nora a year later. In 1985, Borregaard and Nora turned to each other's shares again: in a so-called demerger, Borregaard gained a 45 percent share in Stabburet-Nora—a Norwegian fresh and wholesale grocery company—in exchange for half a million shares of its own stock. Borregaard's overhaul of its historical identity as an old-line paper and pulp producer was about to enter a new phase.

Orkla Borregaard A/S: 1986–91

Borregaard's merger with Orkla in 1986 began the most important stage in its transformation into a high-tech global chemicals maker. As Borregaard's businesses were integrated into Orkla's corporate structure, Orkla's management undertook a major restructuring of the Borregaard fold to bring it in line with the new global markets for advanced chemicals products. Meanwhile, Orkla could now add to its traditional brand-name consumer goods, media, and investments businesses Borregaard's wood processing, chemical products, hydroelectric power generation, forestry, and engineering operations.

In 1987, Orkla Borregaard closed its Løkken Gruber mining operations and a year later merged with four Norwegian firms: Johan Norlie A/S, Berskaug A/S, parsley producer Persilfabriken A/S, and real estate firm Orkla Eiendom A/S. To further bolster its new consumer and media orientation, it acquired Ostlandske Fryserier A/S's cold storage plant in Brummunddal, Norway, in 1988 and map publisher Planforlaget in early 1989. During 1989 and 1990 Orkla Borregaard enhanced its position in the chemicals industry with the purchase of increased interests in the chemicals firms Elkem and Dyno Industrier, the acquisition of a Swedish firm's international lignin operations, and the formation of a joint venture with the Eni Group of Italy to produce vanillin, synthetic vanillin, raw materials, and derivative products.

Nora Industrier A/S: 1969–91

Less than five years after Orkla's monumental merger with Borregaard, the company moved again to expand its product lines and market share through a major acquisition: on January 1, 1991, Orkla Borregaard and Nora Industrier were united through an exchange of stock to form Orkla A/S. Nora Industrier had been formed in 1978 from the consolidation of several Oslo breweries with roots going back to the 1820s. Within a few years, it had become Norway's leading supplier of beer and carbonated soft drinks, fortified by holdings in the Norwegian food market.

Within five years of its founding Nora had acquired holdings in a brewery, a mineral water producer, and a glassmaker and merged operations with a fourth firm. In 1984 alone it bought another brewery (A/S Lillehammer Bryggeri) and a health drink maker (Vitaminveien 6), established a real estate firm, and began acquiring a 47 percent interest in Helly-Hansen A/S, a major Norwegian manufacturer of men's and women's clothing founded in 1877. Between 1986 and 1988 Nora merged with yeast makers Gjaer A/S and Idu Gjarfabrikken A/S, chemicals producer Oslo Kjemiske Industri A/S, seed supplier Norsk Froforsyning A/S, flour mill Bjolsen Valsemolle A/S, and beverage maker Hamar Bryggeri, among others. In 1987 Nora moved closer to Orkla's product sphere by gaining a substantial ownership stake in six Nordic industrial bakeries and becoming a majority shareholder in the new bakery industry group Bakers A/S. By 1995 the Nora unit within Orkla A/S would be one of the largest suppliers of foods and ingredients to the Norwegian grocery trade, catering, bakery, and food manufacturing industries. In 1988 it merged its breweries and mineral water companies with beverage maker Ringnes Frydenlund, creating a single beverage division and a major new force in the Norwegian beverage market.

Ringnes had been founded as Ringnes Bryggeri (brewery) by Amund and Ellef Ringnes in 1876. Among its landmark products were Vørterol (1903), "recommended by 400 doctors"; the first bottles of a popular new soft drink named Solo (1934); the first Coca-Cola sold in Norway (1938), the first Heineken beer produced in Norway (1975), and the introduction of the market-leading Ringnes brand of beer itself. With Ringnes leading its beverage markets, Nora let Hamar Bryggeri's bottling pact with Pepsi expire in 1987, and in 1989 and 1990 acquired ten companies, from mineral water producer Narvik Minneralvann A/S and food producer Danish Fancy Food A/S to brewer Tou A/S and health food producer Elfas Helsekost A/S.

Orkla A/S: 1991–94

Until the Nora merger, Orkla Borregaard for all its rapid growth had remained primarily a Norwegian company with scattered businesses in Denmark. Its holdings in Sweden—the largest segment of the Scandinavian market—were almost non-existent. With Nora now anchoring Orkla's industry-leading consumer brands group, however, Orkla A/S entered the 1990s poised to become a broadly positioned *Scandinavian* firm ready to expand into Europe and beyond. Its specific long-term goal was to reduce its dependence on Norwegian sales to less than half of annual revenues, and toward that end in 1991 Orkla Beverage joined in a Polish joint venture to gain a foothold in the newly opened Iron Curtain market and two years later established Ringnes Beer Ltd. of Poland.

Orkla's late 1980s campaign to restructure Borregaard into a global high-tech chemicals firm continued in the early 1990s with the erection of a new fine chemicals plant in Norway and the acquisition of Daishowa Chemicals of the United States and industrial ethanol producer Kemetyl AB of Sweden in 1991. In 1993, it added the lignin operations of Finland's Metsä-Serla

and the Italian and Chinese diphenol (used in the production of vanillin) plants of Italy's EniChem Synthesis in 1994. In addition, the EniChem deal—which was expected to net Orkla NKr500 million in 1995—gave Orkla's new Borregaard Synthesis unit control of the Norwegian firm EuroVanillin, the second-largest vanillin producer in the world.

Orkla also focused intently on its media empire. In 1991 Orkla Media bought three Norwegian newspapers, and in November the Norwegian government awarded Netcom GSM A/S, a mobile telecommunications company owned by Orkla Communications, the go-ahead to provide cell phone services to Norway's central region beginning in late 1992. Then in 1993, in a joint venture with Norske Egmont Orkla, the company acquired a 50 percent stake in Hjemmet Mortensen group, the market leader in the Norwegian magazine business. It followed this with the purchase of interests in the Norwegian newspaper *Bergens Tidende* and six Polish newspapers in 1993. In 1994, Orkla Media acquired the newspapers *Drammens Tidende og Buskeruds Blad* and *Varden* and gained a stake in the newspaper *Fjordenes Tidende*. Finally, in its critical food segment, Orkla scooped up Swedish biscuit maker Gøteborgs Kex AB, Finnish biscuit maker Kantolan, and grocery wholesaler R.N. Grossist of Sweden. Concentrating on the consumer food market, it bought out the remainder of Bakers A/S and sold half its interest in clothier Helly-Hansen before repositioning its household products, biscuits/snacks, and chocolate/confectionary units under one roof: Orkla Brands.

Procordia, Abba, Pripps, Ringnes—
and Coca-Cola: 1995–96

Orkla's activities in the food industry in the early 1990s paled in comparison to its third major acquisition in a decade: the purchase in April 1995 of Procordia Foods and Abba Seafood AB from Swedish car maker Volvo for US$578 million. The deal, however, would not only make Orkla a US$1.6 billion corporate colossus with annual food sales twice the size of current levels. Volvo also agreed to enter into a joint venture with Orkla to create a new beverage industry leader out of the two companies' flagship bottlers, Pripps (Sweden's largest brewery) and Ringnes (Coca-Cola's largest Norwegian bottler), respectively. The new Pripps Ringnes AB would make Orkla the number one beer, carbonated soft drink, and water products company in Norway and Sweden and, through Pripps Ringnes's stake in Oy Hartwall Ab and Baltic Beverage Holdings, the market leader in beer sales in, respectively, Finland and the Baltic/St. Petersburg, Russia.

Orkla's CEO Jens P. Heyerdahl told interviewers that the magnitude of the Volvo acquisition/merger would improve Orkla's ability to stave off foreign competition for its nearby markets. Although Heyerdahl had helped to defeat Norway's proposed membership in the European Union (EU) in 1994, the Procordia/Abba/Pripps Ringnes deal demonstrated that he now wanted to position Orkla to enter the European market he had once scorned by way of Sweden, an EU member since 1994. Because the new venture, Pripps Ringnes, would effectively control 82 percent of the Norwegian beer market, 60 percent of the Swedish soft drink market, and 95 percent of Norway's market for bottled water, however, the second phase of the Volvo-Orkla deal had to wait upon the approval of both the EU and Norway and Sweden's antitrust agencies. The anchor of the Volvo-Orkla food deal, Procordia AB, had been formed by the Swedish government in 1969 as Statsforetag, and in its two-decade-plus existence had branched from beverage sales into foods, pharmaceuticals, media services, hotels, tobacco, engineering, and development. By the end of 1990 it had sales of SKr36.6 billion and 45,000 employees and maintained subsidiaries and affiliated companies in Denmark, Spain, the United Kingdom, Japan, the Netherlands, France, the United States, and Switzerland. By the time Volvo assumed direction of the company, however, Procordia was, as the *Wall Street Journal* characterized it, "only moderately profitable," and thus Volvo was unable to get prospective international buyers outside of Scandinavia to make compelling bids.

By September 1995, the EU and the Swedish government's antitrust agency had granted Orkla permission to absorb Procordia and Abba in exchange for several concessions: Orkla could no longer prevent the Swedish food company ICA from marketing its own private-label juices and jams, and Orkla itself would refrain from producing private-label juices and jams in Sweden for three years. More importantly, Orkla agreed to sell off its Hansa Bryggeri, the second-largest brewer in Norway, in 1996 to ease competitors' antitrust anxieties.

Almost as soon as the deal was finalized, however, Orkla faced a major obstacle. As part of its 42-year-old bottling and distribution contract with Pripps, the Coca-Cola Company—whose products accounted for 35 percent of Pripps Ringnes's total sales—was entitled to renegotiate its Pripps contract, and it quickly submitted a new contract in which Pripps would not only be required to focus exclusively on Coke's products but also sell Coke the Pripps line of soft drinks that it marketed along with Coke's products. Pripps's management rejected Coke's demands, calling them "corporate imperialism," and in December 1995 Coke dropped Pripps as its sole supplier for the Swedish market, citing Pripps's new management (i.e., Orkla) and the company's "weak" performance. Pripps countered that its Swedish sales had grown 10 percent annually in each of the past eight years, but the damage was already done. In December, union members of a Pripps bottler in Norway stopped production of Coke products in sympathetic protest even though Pripps's Norwegian operations were unaffected by the terminated Swedish contract.

Unaccustomed to such unrest in its foreign operations, in July 1996 Coca-Cola terminated its *Norwegian* bottling and sales agreements as well, forcing Orkla's new Pripps Ringnes venture to lay off 1,400 workers. With Coke now determined to set up its own bottling and sales operations in Scandinavia, Coke and Orkla agreed on a $166 million severance package that would temporarily extend the historic Coke-Pripps collaboration until the beginning of 1999. Orkla was now free to promote its own soft drink products (such as Mozell and Farris) over Coca-Cola's, and with 60 to 65 percent market share in the Swedish and Norwegian soft drinks market it hoped to be able to compete against Coke's new Scandinavian soft drink machine.

Global at Last: 1996–97

If Orkla's new beverage operations were in tumult, the expansion of its chemicals businesses proceeded at a more orderly pace. By the mid-1990s, an ever more substantial portion of Borregaard's sales were coming from Asia. It was the majority owner of a fine chemicals company for the manufacture of crop pesticide products in China's Jiangsu province, had established a laboratory for technical customer support in Singapore, and maintained sales offices in Singapore, Japan, and mainland China. In May 1996, Borregaard LignoTech and China's Kaishantun Chemical Fibre Pulp Mill signed an agreement to jointly produce lignin-based products (primarily for additives to concrete) through a new joint venture in northeast China, and a year earlier Orkla had opened a new lignin plant outside Seattle. As the century drew to a close, Borregaard had successfully made the transition from a basic paper and pulp supplier to a niche producer of vanillin and intermediates to a diversified global producer of a full range of chemicals for the construction, agricultural, and pharmaceuticals industries.

Orkla's campaign to become an even larger presence in the European media market also advanced in the mid-1990s. In mid-1996, for example, Orkla Media signed a letter of intent with the Hersant Group, a French media giant, to take over Hersant's controlling interest in the Polish newspaper publishing company Presspublica, which owned the national daily *Rzeczpospolita* and the newspaper's printing company Warszawa Print. The deal brought to nine the number of local and regional Polish dailies owned by Orkla Media, not counting its printing facilities in northern and southern Poland. With the Presspublica acquisition, improved advertising revenues in its Norwegian newspaper businesses, and cost reductions in its magazine segment, Orkla Media's profits edged upward in mid-1996.

Throughout 1995–97, Orkla wrestled with the problems and opportunities presented by the Procordia/Abba/Pripps Ringnes merger of 1995. In early 1996 beer and soft drink sales in Sweden fell in part because of high Swedish alcohol taxes, which drove consumers to buy private beer imports. Under a European Union deadline, Orkla finally sold brewery Hansa Bryggeri to a group of investors in December 1996 to meet the terms of the 1995 Pripps Ringnes merger, and to consolidate its new Abba Seafood business in September 1996 Orkla sold its German seafood operations and mackerel and shrimp factories in Sweden and reduced its interest in Abba's Danish mussel factory. By intentionally focusing on fewer products and markets, a leaner Abba Seafood promised to offer Orkla increased longterm profitability.

Productivity improvements, a new 20-year extension of its detergent/personal products agreement with Unilever, Sweden's reduction of its value-added tax (VAT) on food, price increases for Orkla's Swedish grocery products, the reorganization of its Swedish fruit and berry production operations, and improved versions of its Omo and Blenda detergent brands—all contributed to an increase in Orkla's consumer-branded products segments in 1996. From operating revenues of NKr15.47 billion in 1990, Orkla's revenues had risen to NKr21.53 billion by 1995. As the day drew near when identical, truly "Nordic" brands could be marketed in every Scandinavian country, in 1996 Orkla reached its long-sought goal of 50 percent or more non-Norwegian sales.

Principal Subsidiaries

Orkla Foods A.S.; Stabburet A/S; Procordia Food AB; Abba Seafood AB; Regal Mølle A.S.; Idun Industri A.S.; Bakers AS; Pripps Ringnes AB; Ringes A.S.; Lilleborg A.S.; Göteborgs Kex AB; Saetre AS; Nidar AS; Orkla Media A.S.; Orkla Commnication A.S.; Hjemmet Mortensen AS; Orkla DM AS; Borregaard; Borregaard Industries Limited; Orkla ASA; Orkla Finans A.S.

Further Reading

Alperowicz, Natasha, "Nordic Chemical Sector Reshuffles," *Chemical Week*, June 21, 1995, p. 25.

"Beer Maker Is Sold to a Group of Investors," *New York Times*, December 31, 1996.

Carnegy, Hugh, "Hansa Bryggeri Sold," *Financial Times*, December 31, 1996.

——, "Investment Gains Lift Orkla at Eight Months," *Financial Times*, October 4, 1996.

Frank, Robert, and Stephen D. Moore, "Coca-Cola Seen Resuming Talks over Bottler," *Wall Street Journal*, December 11, 1995.

Johnson, Greg, "World Watch," *Los Angeles Times*, June 20, 1996, p. D4.

Markiewicz, Tadeusz, "Orkla to Snap Up *Rzeczpospolita*," *The Warsaw Voice*, June 2, 1996.

McIver, Greg, "Coca-Cola Sets Scandinavia's Drinks Market Fizzing," *Financial Times*, June 25, 1996.

Moore, Stephen, "Volvo to Sell Food Unit to Orkla, Set up Beverage Joint Venture," *Wall Street Journal*, April 4, 1995, p. A16.

Nordli, Jan-Frode, "NetCom Gets Norway's 2nd GSM Mobile Phone Franchise," *Newsbytes News Network*, November 8, 1991.

"Norway Orkla Unit, Coca Cola to End Cooperation," *Wall Street Journal*, January 28, 1997, http://www.wsj.com

"Orkla Pre-Tax Up 18.6%," *Financial Times*, June 7, 1996.

"Pacts Will Be Terminated with Unit of Volvo, Orkla," *Wall Street Journal*, June 20, 1996.

"Sino-Norwegian Joint Venture to Produce Lignin-Based Products," *AsiaInfor Services*, 1996, Electric Library, http://www.elibrary.com

"Sweden Approves Orkla Purchase," *Wall Street Journal*, September 15, 1995.

"Sweden's Pripps Loses Coca-Cola Franchise, Dealing Blow to Orkla," *Dow Jones Publication Library*, Wall Street Journal Interactive, December 1, 1995, http://www.wsj.com.

"Union at Norwegian Bottler Threatens Production Halt," *Wall Street Journal*, December 5, 1995.

"Volvo Sells Food Firms," *Automotive News*, April 10, 1995.

"Volvo to Sell Food Unit to Orkla, Set Up Beverage Joint Venture," *Wall Street Journal*, April 4, 1995.

—Paul S. Bodine

OSMONICS
Osmonics, Inc.

5951 Clearwater Drive
Minnetonka, Minnesota 55343-8995
U.S.A.
(613) 933-2277
Fax: (612) 933-6141
Web site: www.osmonics.com

Public Company
Incorporated: 1969
Employees: 1,017
Sales: $111.61 million (1995)
Stock Exchanges: New York
SICs: 3569 General Industrial Machinery, Not Elsewhere
Classified; 3589 Service Industry Machinery, Not
Elsewhere Classified; 3492 Fluid Power Valves &
Hose Fittings

Osmonics, Inc. is helping to purify the world. Based in Minnetonka, Minnesota, Osmonics is the world's largest vertically integrated supplier of reverse osmosis and ultrafiltration equipment, components, and controls, and the world's second-largest maker of crossflow membrane elements, behind Dow FilmTec. Osmonics manufactures equipment and components used in water purification, fluids separation and handling, removing solids, and concentrating wastes, allowing water to be recycled or returned to the environment. This company pioneered the commercial use of crossflow membranes—and purification processes such as reverse osmosis, nanofiltration, and ultrafiltration—but has avoided the end-use market in favor of either directly supplying customers with complete filtration solutions or supplying the components and supplies for original equipment manufacturers (OEMs).

Osmonics operates manufacturing facilities in Texas, Colorado, Iowa, California, New York, Wisconsin, Arizona, and Paris, as well as its 300,000-square-foot plant in Minnetonka. The company also operates sales offices throughout the United States and in Switzerland, Singapore, Bangkok, and other countries, serving much of the world. Osmonics' product lines fall into six categories: replaceable filters; crossflow membranes; pumps and fluid handling components; laboratory products; controls and instruments; and water treatment equipment. Osmonics' products serve six primary markets, including the electronics industry, specifically in the manufacture and production of semiconductors and printed circuit boards. Industrial processing applications generate a large portion of Osmonics' sales: the company's equipment and components serve the automotive and finished metals markets; chemical processing, pharmaceutical, cosmetics, and bioengineering industries; photographic and printing processes; pulp and paper manufacturing; and the textile, inks, and dyes processing markets. In potable water markets, Osmonics provides solutions for drinking water, desalination, laundry and car wash facilities, aquariums, pools, and spas. Other applications of Osmonics products are in medical laboratories; petroleum, gas, and mining industries; and food, beverage, and dairy processing.

In 1995, after a decade of growth fueled by acquisition, Osmonics restructured the company and placed all of its subsidiaries under the Osmonics brand name. In that year the company posted revenues of nearly $112 million and net income of $11.2 million. The company, which continues to be led by founder D. Dean Spatz, has been consistently profitable since going public in 1971.

Founded as a Class Project in 1969

D. Dean Spatz, a native of Albuquerque, New Mexico, attended Dartmouth in the early 1960s as an undergraduate studying engineering. Spatz originally intended to continue his education at Dartmouth's Tuck Thayer business school. As an undergraduate, however, Spatz was involved in researching reverse osmosis techniques, a then-revolutionary technology for purifying water and other fluids. Spatz was given a class assignment to find a way to supply drinkable water, leading him to study osmosis, nanofiltration, and ultrafiltration techniques as part of a government-funded research program. The program included a grant for Spatz of $200 per week, encouraging him to drop his business school plans.

After graduating, Spatz went to work for a company in Minneapolis that hoped to commercialize the reverse osmosis

Company Perspectives:

Osmonics develops, manufactures, markets, and supports quality products used in high technology water purification, fluid handling, filtration, and separation applications by a broad range of industrial, commercial, and institutional customers. We will be recognized throughout the world as the best single source of these products, because we understand users' needs, offer them integrated solutions, and provide expert service and support.

process. Under terms of his contract, the company was supposed to provide Spatz with money to start his own company. "In the first year, I realized they didn't know how to run a business," Spatz told *Corporate Report Minnesota,* "There were no controls, and at the end of the year they admitted they didn't have the $75,000 they'd promised to stake in my own business." Spatz next turned to connections at Dartmouth, finding an investor to put up the money he needed. In 1969 Spatz and Ralph E. Crump founded Osmonics in Spatz's garage.

The founding of Osmonics, and its reverse osmosis technology, came at the right time. By the late 1960s, increasing awareness of the environment was fueling growing demands for environmental responsibility. Calls were made to clean up polluted waters and to develop processes that would safeguard the world's water supply from further pollution. Reverse osmosis offered promising advantages over such traditional water purification techniques as charcoal filtration.

Osmosis is a natural process in which a fluid (or gas) passes through a porous membrane. Osmosis occurs randomly: fluids in high concentration on one side of a membrane will pass through to the side with lower concentration until an equilibrium on both sides has been reached. Reverse osmosis is a method for overcoming the naturally occurring osmosis process and its tendency to reach equilibrium. In reverse osmosis, pressure is applied on the fluid, or feed, to force it to pass through a membrane. The membrane contains openings large enough for the water to pass through, but larger solids in the fluid—for example, salt in salt water—become trapped by the membrane. The membranes, housed in disposable elements called sepralators, can be designed, through the use of electron microscopes and other equipment, to select which components of the fluid will be allowed to pass through the membrane. The resulting purified fluid, called the permeate, is then collected. Adapting reverse osmosis to practical and industrial applications also required a method for removing the solids, called the concentrate, so that the membrane could be reused. Crossflow membranes allowed a portion of the feed to be used for flushing the membrane.

Reverse osmosis and the related ultrafiltration techniques offered a superior method for purifying water and other fluids. Osmonics' first step in developing its business was to design and build equipment based on reverse osmosis techniques with practical industrial applications. In 1969 the company began production of equipment for purifying car wash rinse, removing the harsh detergents from the water. This equipment marked one of the first commercial applications of reverse osmosis technology. By the end of the year, sales of its equipment allowed the company to leave Spatz's Minneapolis garage and set up shop in a leased, 5,000-square-foot plant in St. Louis Park, Minnesota. The following year, Osmonics extended the reverse osmosis process to other applications. The company installed the first medical pure water system, for the kidney dialysis department of the Mayo Clinic, and developed the first laboratory and electronics-grade reverse osmosis systems. Ultrapure water was especially necessary for the development of the microprocessor. In 1970 Osmonics also introduced the first spiral wound membrane sepralators, establishing an industry standard.

In the next year, Osmonics moved toward greater vertical integration by setting up its own facilities for manufacturing crossflow membranes. In order to finance the move, Osmonics went public, selling 100,000 shares for $5 per share. The company extended its technology into two new industrial applications: industrial waste oil reclamation and food processing. The following year the company moved to a new 15,000-square-foot leased space in Minnetonka. Through the 1970s, the company obtained several patents, including a basic patent on standard reverse osmosis/ultrafiltration systems. The company introduced its own OSMO sepralators, using membranes supplied by Eastman Kodak, and acquired TJ Engineering, Inc., based in California, which also used the Kodak membranes to manufacture sepralators. In 1973 the company began manufacturing its own SEPA membranes, and would soon manufacture all of the membranes used for its products.

Osmonics continued to introduce new reverse osmosis applications. Among the new applications of the company's technology were a patented metal reclamation process; the first commercial whey fractionation process, as well as a method for separating milk proteins from whey for the cheese industry; zero-discharge systems for cleaning metal-finishing wastes and recycling the water used in that process; pretreatment systems for boiler feed; the first photography waste recovery system; and procedures for producing ultrapure water usable for injections by the pharmaceutical industry.

Throughout the 1970s, Osmonics' revenues also grew steadily. In 1974 the company neared $1 million in sales, with net income of $81,000. In 1977 sales neared $2.5 million, with net income of nearly $300,000, and by 1980 the company's sales topped $5.5 million, with net income of more than $600,000. The company's production facilities were also growing, to 20,000 square feet in 1973 and to 40,000 square feet in 1978. In that year, the company also purchased a 44-acre plot in Minnetonka in order to build the company's future headquarters. The company also made a secondary offering of shares in 1976, declared a two-for-one stock split in 1977, and declared a three-for-two stock split in 1980.

Restructuring for the 1980s

By the beginning of the 1980s, Osmonics had expanded into the 16 markets that would form the company's core. The recession of the early 1980s, however, cut into the company's growth. As purchases of capital equipment dried up, Osmonics' sales faltered. Spatz was forced to scale back the company, from 100 to 80 employees. Spatz also determined to restructure the nature of Osmonics itself. "Even though it was great fun to be personally involved in projects and closing deals, I knew I had to put more effort into growing sales," he told *Corporate Report Minnesota.* Spatz set out to restructure the company from one that relied entirely on sales of capital equipment. Instead, he led Osmonics toward achieving a 50 percent split between capital equipment sales and the more predictable sales of components and supplies. Osmonics also built a 100,000-square-foot facility, consolidating its research, engineering, manufacturing, and administrative operations. Then Spatz led the company on a course of acquisition that would boost Osmonics' product offerings and the company's revenues from $5.6 million in 1982 to nearly $47 million by 1991.

The company's new direction helped to re-energize its sales. By 1983, the company's revenues jumped to $8 million. Osmonics made the first of its acquisitions that year, acquiring Hytrex and that company's disposable cartridge filter product lines in an exchange of stock from Hoechst Celanese Corporation. The following year, Osmonics acquired a company called Flotronics, which made coalescers and metallic and ceramic microfiltration filters, allowing Osmonics to expand its laboratory business. The company's next acquisitions, of Aqua Media International Inc. and Aqua Media of Asia, Ltd, in 1985, brought the company into international sales, particularly in the rapidly developing economies of Asia. Osmonics broadened its line of pump products by acquiring American Pump Company and its air diaphragm pumps. The company also purchased a stake in Poretics Corporation, bringing in that company's track-etch microfiltration membrane. The 1987 acquisition of Boston-based Vaponics, and its Bangkok sales office, helped Osmonics expand its distillation business in the medical, laboratory, and pharmaceutical markets.

Osmonics also established offices in Switzerland and Singapore to broaden its share of the global market. Rounding out the 1980s were two more acquisitions, of Orec, based in Phoenix, Arizona, and that company's ozonation product line; and Mace Corp., based in Upland, California, from Michigan-based Humphrey Products Co., complementing the company's line of Teflon pumps and flow control components. Amid these acquisitions, Osmonics continued pursuing technological advances internally, patenting its sepralator housing and cap, a flow control manifold, the Spiraflex crossflow sepralator, and the SEPA CF test cell.

Building the Osmonics Brand in the 1990s

In 1990 Osmonics announced its largest-ever contract, for $3 million with Boeing Corp. Osmonics continued its acquisition drive with the 1991 purchase of Eastman Kodak's Fastek division, which produced rolled filters, membranes, and other filtration and purification products. The Fastek product lines, similar to Osmonics' own lines, were sold primarily to Kodak, and under terms of the acquisition, Osmonics would continue to supply Kodak. By 1992 Osmonics' sales broke the $50 million mark, and the company prepared a major acquisition. In 1993 Osmonics acquired Milwaukee-based Autotrol Corp. for $45.5 million in a stock-swap merger, helping to raise Osmonics' 1993 sales to $89 million, with net income of $7.9 million.

Between 1994 and 1996, the company announced several new acquisitions, including Lakewood Instruments, based in Phoenix Arizona; Desalination Systems, Inc., of Vista, California, in a stock swap worth some $30 million; Western Filter Co., of Denver, Colorado, for approximately $7 million; the remaining 18 percent of Poretics, giving the company 100 percent control of that subsidiary; and, finally, Aquamatic, Inc., a $12 million maker of water treatment equipment specialty valves and controls based in Rockford, Illinois.

Osmonics' program of acquiring developing companies, developing new technology, and expanding its capabilities into new markets had raised the company's revenues to $112 million by 1995. In that year, the company moved to enhance its image by consolidating its subsidiaries under the Osmonics name—a move designed to enhance its recognition as a company that had grown from an exotic pioneer to a vertically integrated supplier of mainstream technology.

Further Reading

David Brauer, "Starting up and Managing in Minnesota: Osmonics and the Evolution of an Engineer," *Corporate Report Minnesota,* November 1994, p. 18.

"Osmonics President Named Top Entrepreneur in Minnesota," *Cheese Market News,* August 30, 1991, p. 10.

—M. L. Cohen

Otter Tail Power Company

215 South Cascade Street
P.O. Box 496
Fergus Falls, Minnesota 56538-0496
U.S.A.
(218) 739-8200
Fax: 218-739-8218
Web site: http://www.otpco.com

Public Company
Incorporated: 1907
Employees: 798
Sales: $328.6 million (1995)
Stock Exchanges: NASDAQ
SICs: 4911 Electric Services; 6719 Holding Companies,
   Not Elsewhere Classified

Otter Tail Power Company, an investor-owned electric utility, serves a 50,000-square-mile territory in western Minnesota, eastern North Dakota, and northeastern South Dakota. Operating in a highly regulated electric industry and in an extreme climate, Otter Tail Power has built a reputation of being a well-run company and a good investment. Management historically has had strong ties to its operating region. The company launched a successful diversification program into nonregulated businesses in the late 1980s.

The Frontier Days

Vermont native George Burdict Wright arrived in Minnesota in 1855 and worked as a surveyor, civil engineer, and land examiner. In 1867 he took ownership of 160 acres of riverfront land about 170 miles northwest of what is now Minneapolis. Wright added adjacent land to his holdings and began looking for ways to develop the property. Wright and the owner of the property on the other side of the Otter Tail River struck an agreement and began construction of a dam, sawmill, and gristmill in 1870. The property changed hands shortly after completion of the project, but Wright resumed ownership toward the end of the decade. Wright, an enthusiastic promoter of the area, was instrumental in founding the city of Fergus Falls.

Just prior to his death in 1882, Wright and two other men launched the Fergus Brush Electric Company (named for Charles F. Brush, inventor of the electric arc light) and provided nighttime lighting service to local businesses until a competing technology entered the scene in 1884. George Wright's widow and son, Vernon Ames Wright, inherited the Fergus Falls holdings. The Boston architect later purchased his stepmother's share of the property and became directly involved in its development.

The Founding of Otter Tail Power in 1907

By the turn of the century, the city of Fergus Falls had taken over a privately held plant and was providing electricity to residential and commercial customers. The Wright Dam, also known as the Central Dam, served industrial customers through direct drive power. Beginning in 1902 Vernon Wright began to shift his customers to electricity. Improvements in electric transmission had opened the way for development of more remotely located dams, and just downstream from Fergus Falls was a site with both good water flow and room for a holding pond. But Wright needed investors for the $100,000 dam project.

Frederick G. Barrows, one of the original developers of the city's power plant, invested in the Dayton Hollow Dam project and convinced other Fergus Falls businessmen to do so as well, thus paving the way for the incorporation of Otter Tail Power Company in 1907. Wright led planning and operations, while Barrows managed the financial aspects of the business.

Dam construction was difficult, dangerous work. Ralph S. Johnson wrote, ''The men wore felt hats or caps, not hard hats. With derring-do that was typical of the times, they lugged heavy rocks across twelve-inch planks stretched high above the raging torrent of the river. But they got the job done.'' Otter Tail Power's first hydroelectric station at the Dayton Hollow Dam began operation in 1909.

Northern Light Electric Company, operated by C. B. Kidder in Wahpeton, North Dakota, was Otter Tail Power's first customer. Kidder's power source was a steam engine: it was now cheaper to purchase rather than generate electricity. Otter Tail Power hired three brothers to build a 25-mile low-voltage transmission line connecting the power plant to Northern Light Electric.

Company Perspectives:

Our vision is one of: being the energy supplier of choice by providing quality service with low, stable rates; improving sales, earnings and performance annually, to the balanced benefit of customers, shareholders and employees; being instrumental in creating jobs and improving the economy and quality of life in the area in which we do business; being an industry leader with successful involvements in other ventures that can enhance both our service area and bottom line.

A few months following the start-up of the Dayton Hollow Dam, the new city dam, which was located upstream from Fergus Falls, failed. Wright's Central Dam and the other dams just downstream were badly damaged by the rush of water. The Dayton Hollow Dam was protected by its distance from the city dam and the capacity of its holding pond. In spite of rumors of sabotage and community interest in rebuilding the city dam, Fergus Falls and Otter Tail Power Company successfully negotiated terms for an electric service contract. The company now served the two largest communities in the region. Wright sold the damaged Central Dam to the company, and Kidder, who had agreed to supply steam-generated power when water levels were low at the hydroelectric plant, was hired as Otter Tail Power's general manager.

Expansion Begins in 1913

Otter Tail Power Company's first major expansion began in 1913: Ten Minnesota towns were hooked up with electric service; Northern Light Electric Company was acquired; and construction commenced on a river diversion project. Plant and equipment costs from 1913 to 1917 exceeded $1 million. Labor to construct miles of new transmission line was done largely by hand. Crews of linemen worked seven days a week to connect new towns to the system.

Fred Barrows, who had been drawn away from the business by opportunities in mining, lumber, and land speculation, sold his share of Otter Tail Power Company in 1921. Another significant personnel change occurred when general manager C. B. Kidder died in 1920 and was succeeded by Clifford S. Kennedy. "A legendary figure in the company, Kennedy could best be described as a benevolent autocrat," wrote Ralph S. Johnson.

The construction boom quieted in the early 1920s with the addition of two steam-generating plants at the Hoot Lake river diversion site; the new plants burned eastern bituminous coal shipped in by train from Duluth. With competing companies serving surrounding areas in Minnesota, Otter Tail Power moved west. By 1926, the company's territory reached Washburn, North Dakota, on the Missouri River, and more generating capacity was needed. Otter Tail Power pioneered the use of North Dakota lignite coal in large-scale power production. The new lignite plants, along with the dams and the Hoot Lake plants, served as the backbone of the company for more than 20 years.

The Depression Years

The droughts of the 1930s hit Otter Tail Power Company hard. Its source of hydroelectric power dwindled, and the agricultural economy of the region it served faltered. Although he was the largest shareholder, Wright stopped dividend payments. Kennedy aggressively cut costs and pursued new business. In 1934 electric rates were cut. Ralph Johnson noted that the action created a long-lasting bond between the company and the people it served.

The 1930s also were marked by the passage of leadership from Vernon Wright to his two sons. Both of the men were educated in eastern universities and had worked in various departments in the company. Thomas C. Wright succeeded Vernon as president in 1933, and Cyrus G. Wright was named vice-president in 1936. Vernon continued on as chairman of the board until his death in 1938.

The National Rural Electrification Act of 1936 instituted government-financed electric cooperatives in underserved areas. Although Otter Tail Power had built its first power line to farm customers in 1919, it was an investor-owner company and added lines based on economic factors. Even though the company objected to the existence of federally subsidized competition, Otter Tail Power had to find a way to coexist. Ultimately, the company sold the cooperatives electricity at wholesale prices and, according to Johnson, went on to establish a relationship with the cooperatives that was unique for its time.

Otter Tail Power ended the 1930s under improved conditions. When rainfall increased, the agricultural economy improved, and business recovery followed. Electric consumption climbed. A second major expansion period began in 1940. Otter Tail Power gained service territory to its south, east, and north and by the end of 1944 served about 500 communities in an area of about 50,000 square miles.

World War II and Postwar Modernization

World War II left Otter Tail Power shorthanded. About 20 percent of company employees served in the military even though they could have claimed a "strategic" industry exemption. With factories committed to the war effort, materials, tools, and equipment were also in short supply. Construction and maintenance work was restricted. C. S. Kennedy left the company just before the war ended. His resignation marked the beginning of a trend toward the decentralization of Otter Tail Power Company.

When World War II ended in 1945, ration-weary Americans went on a consumption binge. The rapid increase in demand for electric power strained Otter Tail Power's neglected plants and electric lines while personnel and parts were still in short supply. While the nation's manufacturing industry made the shift from war to peace-time production, Otter Tail Power had to make due: A railroad locomotive was used to boost output at a Bemidji, Minnesota plant, and elsewhere every available piece of equipment was put into service. The first new pieces of equipment available were diesel generators. They helped mitigate the capacity problem, but operating Vice-President Cyrus Wright was still forced to ask customers to scale back on peak-hour electric use during the winter of 1947–1948 while construction on new steam-generating plants was being completed.

The decentralization process resulted in a doubling of the number of district offices by 1948. In 1949, the districts were divided into five divisions, which were led by electrical engineers. Otter Tail Power had become an increasingly specialized company. Business professionals entered the middle-management ranks and technical school graduates filled many nonmanagement positions. Joining Otter Tail Power at this time were two men who would later lead the company: Albert V. Hartl and Robert M. Bigwood.

Federal Influence in the 1950s

By 1948 electric loads to rural cooperatives accounted for 18.9 percent of Otter Tail Power's system peak. That year, the Bureau of Reclamation (later renamed the Western Area Power Administration) announced plans to market power generated by new federal dams to municipalities, public entities, and cooperatives. Otter Tail Power stopped building new capacity for the Garrison Dam region in North Dakota, but worked with the cooperatives during the transition period. In Minnesota, Otter Tail Power, together with Northern States Power Company and Interstate Power Company, made rate agreements to ensure the continued business of the cooperatives there.

The prospect of cheap power lured some local governments to set up municipal power agencies; the city of Fergus Falls was contemplating the idea in the early 1950s. Faced with the possibility of losing its home town as a customer, Otter Tail Power offered to purchase and operate the city's electric system; if a deal could not be made the company would build a new office building elsewhere. The issue was hotly debated, but a majority of the citizens of Fergus Falls voted for the proposed purchase deal.

Otter Tail Power faced production overcapacity when service to rural electric cooperatives began declining in 1952. To capture more retail electric sales the company accelerated retail marketing efforts: Associations with electric appliance dealers were cultivated; use of electric heat was promoted; special rates for ''total electric'' homes and businesses were offered; and the right to use Reddy Kilowatt, an investor-owned electric utility symbol, was secured. Retail sales increased, and Otter Tail Power began a plant building program that lasted from the late 1950s into the 1960s.

Building Interconnections: The Late 1950s–60s

Otter Tail Power extended its 115,000-volt transmission grid in the late 1950s. Subsequent interconnections with adjacent electric systems set the stage for sharing electric power. In 1961 the company became a charter member of the Upper Mississippi Valley Power Pool. Benefits included a reduction of individual generating capacity requirements, decreased operating costs through using the most economical units in the pool, and greater reliability of service to customers.

Thomas Wright retired in 1961; Cyrus Wright succeeded him as chairman of the board. Albert Hartl moved up to the post of president and became the first nonfamily member to lead the company.

In 1963 Otter Tail Power joined with other investor-owned companies, cooperatives, and electric agencies to form the Mid-Continent Area Power Planners (MAPP) to coordinate future facility and transmission development in a region including ten states and part of Canada. The company entered into joint agreements for the construction of a 230,000-volt transmission line and a 410,000-kilowatt lignite-burning power plant in 1967.

Otter Tail Power formalized its own internal planning system in 1967 with the appointment of a vice-president of planning and a planning council assigned to investigate investment opportunities. In 1969, the company and a group of Fergus Falls businessmen agreed to build a total electric motel in the city. When costs became prohibitive for the business group, the company bought them out and established the Otter Tail Management Corporation. A second subsidiary, Otter Tail Realty Company, was formed to manage the land acquired for the motel project. The motel was sold in 1973. Another diversification about the same time, in the mobile home business, was a costly failure.

Big Expenditures: The 1970s–80s

The rapid increase of residential and industrial electric loads of the late 1960s and early 1970s again drove the need for increased electric capacity. Even while the Big Stone Plant near Milbank, South Dakota, was under construction, another jointly owned lignite-burning plant was being planned. In 1975, the company began developing comprehensive load-control management systems and offered rate reductions to customers who would restrict peak-time electric use.

CEO Al Hartl retired in 1975. Otter Tail Power's annual revenues climbed from approximately $21 million to $71 million over the 15 years he led the company. Bob Bigwood, Hartl's successor, rose to the top of the company at a time when many of the top managers were approaching retirement; the company's leadership team was rebuilt over the next few years.

Electric rates had generally fallen until the late 1950s, when customers began to experience incremental increases. But the immense costs associated with the Big Stone and then the Coyote plant construction forced Otter Tail Power to ask the regulatory commissions for substantial rate hikes. The company faced objections from customers, but the regulators granted the increases.

A lingering dispute was settled out of court in 1981, when Otter Tail Power agreed to pay the city of Elbow Lake $1.3 million over a period of 14 years. When the two parties could not come to an agreement over the renewal of electric service in the early 1960s, the city formed a municipal electric company. Otter Tail Power refused to use their lines to transmit electricity from the U.S. Bureau of Reclamation to the city. In 1967, Elbow Lake filed a suit for $3.5 million in damages against the company for delaying establishment of the business. The U.S. Justice Department followed up with an antitrust suit against the company in 1969. The U.S. District Court decided in favor of Elbow Lake. When the U.S. Supreme Court upheld the ruling in 1973, Otter Tail Power began transmitting power to the city.

A Mixed Bag in the 1980s and 1990s

Otter Tail Power had financed its large jointly owned generating plants through first-mortgage bonds, pollution control bonds, and preferred and common stock offerings. After the Coyote plant was completed in 1981, the company was able to begin using internally generated funds for its smaller scale construction and capital expenses. A period of rate stability began as did the passage to new leadership: John C. MacFarlane, with the company since 1961, was next in line to serve as president.

A National Association of Regulatory Utility Commissioners survey released in 1985 ranked Otter Tail Power first in increased productivity for the period between 1972 and 1983. In 1981, James P. Shannon wrote, ''Well before productivity became a buzzword in American industry, Otter Tail Power cultivated among its employees the kind of cohesiveness and company pride which, translated into efficiency of operation, have helped this small rural utility achieve a record of productivity which shareholders and customers have come to appreciate—for different reasons.''

According to an article by George Beran, Otter Tail Power Company long-term investors earned an average annual return of 23 cents per dollar during the ten-year period from 1981 to 1991. And when the agricultural downturn of the 1980s resulted in job loss and population decline in Otter Tail Power's service area, the company fostered an economic development program to gather together financial and human resources to help create and keep jobs in the region.

The 1990 amendments to the Clean Air Act set new emission reduction standards. Sulfur dioxide and nitrogen oxides, which are released when coal is burned, combine with water in the atmosphere to form an acid, which falls back to earth via precipitation. To meet the new guidelines, Otter Tail Power either had to switch to coal containing a lower level of sulfur or install additional pollution-control equipment. In 1995 the company began burning subbituminous coal in its Big Stone plant. In 1994 the Minnesota Public Utilities Commission (PUC) directed electric utilities to include environmental costs related to fossil fuel emissions when submitting plans for future generating plants.

Diversification for the Future

Otter Tail Power incorporated a holding company, Mid-States Development, Inc., in 1989. According to Joel Hoekstra, John MacFarlane had begun ''crafting his diversification plan shortly after he took the helm in 1982.'' Kilowatt-hour sales, which experienced annual growth of seven percent in the 1960s and 1970s, had fallen to one to two percent and remained flat. Earlier ventures into nonregulated businesses prompted the company to bring in an experienced investment specialist this time around. Mid-States' first business venture, a suit manufacturer, failed, but its second purchase, a machining company, was a success. Another subsidiary, North Central Utilities, Inc., was established in 1992 to purchase regulated businesses.

By 1995, Otter Tail Power held radio stations, a telephone utility, manufacturing operations, electrical and telephone construction contractors, and a medical imaging equipment supplier. The low-profile Otter Tail Power gained some media attention in 1995 when Mid-States Development, Inc. purchased an 85 percent interest in a Northern League baseball franchise, the Fargo-Moorhead Red Hawks, for about $1.2 million. Mid-States initially offered to buy a minority interest in the team to assure radio broadcast rights of the games, but other investors pulled out of the deal.

In the 1995 annual report John MacFarlane attributed the current success of the electric utility to downsizing—the number of employees was reduced from 850 in 1985 to 800 in 1987—while increasing electric sales, revenues, and the number of customers.

Subsidiary growth also improved the company's outlook. About 38 percent of total revenues came from subsidiaries in 1995. Hoekstra said Otter Tail Power CEO and Chairman MacFarlane was modest about his successful diversification program, saying, ''I'm like a baseball player: I have to get my job back every spring.'' The future success of Otter Tail Power would be influenced by not only the health of its diversified businesses but also proposed changes in the electric industry itself and continuing environmental concerns.

Principal Subsidiaries

Mid-States Development, Inc.; Midwest Information Systems, Inc.

Further Reading

Beran, George, ''Electrics May Be Short on Dazzle, But Not on Rewards To Investors,'' *St. Paul Pioneer Press,* May 4, 1992.

Carideo, Tony, ''Life USA Holding Inc. Reported Considering an Initial Public Offering,'' *Star Tribune* (Minneapolis), February 27, 1992, p. 2D.

Hoekstra, Joel, ''Utility Player,'' *Twin Cities Business Monthly,* April 1996, pp. 51–53.

Johnson, Ralph S., *The Power People: The Story of Otter Tail Power Company,* Fergus Falls, MN: Otter Tail Power Company, 1986.

Meersman, Tom, ''PUC Says Utilities Must Start Tallying Ecological Costs of Power Plants,'' *Star Tribune* (Minneapolis), February 5, 1994, p. 1B.

''Minnesotans Will Flock to Water—For Cleanup Duty,'' *Star Tribune* (Minneapolis), May 31, 1990, p. 2B.

''Otter Tail Power Company,'' *Corporate Report Minnesota*, March 1990, p. 62.

''Otter Tail Power Co. Agrees To Pay $1.3 Million to City of Elbow Lake,'' *Minneapolis Tribune,* February 7, 1981.

Otter Tail Power Company: 75th Anniversary, Fergus Falls, Minn.: Otter Tail Power Company, August 1984.

''Otter Tail Power Ranks First in Productivity Increase,'' *Star Tribune* (Minneapolis), March 5, 1985.

''A Power Lineup,'' *Minneapolis/St. Paul CityBusiness,* December 15, 1995, p. 5.

''Profile: Otter Tail Power Company,'' *The Daily Journal* (Fergus Falls, Minnesota), February 25, 1995.

Peterson, Susan E., ''Moving Beyond Kilowatts,'' *Star Tribune* (Minneapolis), July 31, 1995, p. 1D.

——, ''Playing Ball,'' *Star Tribune* (Minneapolis), August 20, 1996, p. 1D.

Shannon, James P., ''Well Thought of Where They Come From,'' *Corporate Report Minnesota,* October 1981, p. 54.

Von Sternberg, Bob, ''Cleaner Coal, Cleaner Air,'' *Star Tribune* (Minneapolis), December 29, 1991, p. 1B.

—Kathleen Peippo

The Pampered Chef, Ltd.

350 S. Rte. 53
Addison, Illinois 60101
U.S.A.
(630) 261-8900
Fax: (630) 261-8586
Web site: http://www.pamperedchef.com

Private Company
Incorporated: 1980
Employees: 600
Sales: $300 million (1996 est.)
SICs: 5999 Miscellaneous Retail Stores, Not Elsewhere
Classified

Classified among *Inc.* magazine's 500 fastest-growing privately-held businesses, The Pampered Chef, Ltd. is one of America's top direct-selling organizations. Over the course of its less than two decades in business, the operation has grown from a one-woman show in a suburban Chicago kitchen to a staff of 600 in a 200,000-plus square-foot headquarters building with sales of over $200 million. The Pampered Chef's army of over 25,000 "kitchen consultants" across the United States sells a line of about 150 professional-quality kitchen tools through more than 30,000 at-home "kitchen shows" every week. The stunning growth of "The Kitchen Store That Comes to Your Door" mirrors two important trends of the 1980s and early 1990s: the proliferation of home-based businesses and "cocooning."

Founded in 1980

The Pampered Chef was founded in 1980 by Doris Christopher, who like many women in her generation sought to balance a vital professional career with a fulfilling home life. Having interrupted her career as a home economics teacher with the University of Illinois Cooperative Extension Service to raise her two daughters from birth to school age in the late 1970s, the 35-year-old Christopher found herself at a crossroads. As she described it in an April 1996 interview for the *Chicago Tribune,*

Christopher began to seek "a part-time job that would allow me to be a mom too." Quickly narrowing her focus to self-employment opportunities that capitalized on her interests and experience in the kitchen, she investigated catering and retail sales of cooking utensils. But she eliminated both these options because catering demanded long, odd hours, and retailing required a high capital investment. Husband Jay urged her to launch a party-plan, direct-selling operation á la Tupperware, but Doris balked, recalling in a November 1996 *Success* piece that "I thought home parties were a waste of time, that perhaps the products were overpriced."

But with the continuing support of her spouse, who reminded her that *her* business could be set up in any way she wished, Christopher began to realize that her cooking and teaching expertise was perfectly suited to the demonstration techniques often used in direct selling, and that there was an untapped market for professional-quality, multi-use kitchen gadgets. Armed with this core concept and a $3,000 cash-out from a life insurance policy, the mom-turned-entrepreneur bought a dozen each of about 70 kitchen gadgets from Chicago's wholesale Merchandise Mart. The Pampered Chef would not require one more dime of additional financing over the course of its first decade-and-a-half in business, funding all its growth from cash flow.

Christopher set her home-selling events apart from their predecessors by calling them "kitchen shows" and naming her sales representatives "kitchen consultants." She scheduled her first kitchen show for October 1980, avoiding what she called the "silly games" that characterized other home selling parties and opting instead for an entertaining evening of cooking demonstrations, eating the fruits of the demo, and some low-pressure selling. That first night's recipe was leavened with trepidation: Christopher later recalled that "during the entire drive to my first show, I vowed that I would never, ever do this again. My stomach was in knots. Of course, on the drive home, I knew differently."

Exponential Growth in 1980s and Early 1990s

This modest beginning belied the phenomenal growth to come; Christopher sold $10,000 worth of kitchen gadgets in her first quarter in business. She brought in a friend as a part-time sales representative in May 1981, and had recruited a total of 12 kitchen consultants by the end of the year. Sales passed $200,000 by 1983, and more than doubled in 1984. Warehousing of the burgeoning business's products outgrew the Christopher family's household basement that year, when TPC's headquarters were moved to a 2,500 square-foot building. By 1987, the business generated by the company's more than 200 sales representatives demanded a full-time purchasing, warehousing, and distribution staff. Husband Jay quit his job as a marketing executive that year to join his wife's company as executive vice-president of operations. By the end of the decade, TPC boasted 700 kitchen consultants. Coverage in nationally-circulated magazines in the early 1990s brought another wave of consultants on board, and by 1993 the company had sales representatives in all fifty states.

While direct, demonstrative selling has proven a powerful marketing method for TPC, its sourcing of unique and useful kitchen tools was also vitally important. In 1995 Christopher told *Inc.* magazine's Robert A. Mamis that "People I knew didn't like to cook, because it wasn't easy for them. Part of me said, 'Maybe I can never convert them.' But another part said, 'They're using knives that aren't sharp and forks with missing tines. If they had the right tools, it would be fun.' " But finding the right tools wasn't easy for the average cook; they were expensive rarities in retail stores, and even if a budding chef found them, she'd likely have an even harder time figuring out how to use and care for them properly.

Christopher sought to fill this market void with a line of high-quality, multi-purpose wares. She assembled an array of about 150 products ranging from peelers and juicers to bakeware and cookware, about one-third of which were exclusive to TPC. Although TPC often has a hand in the development and refinement of the products it carries—making them more ergonomic or combining several functions in a single tool, for example—it does not manufacture them. Many are emblazoned with their makers' names and marks, then packaged in TPC boxes with the marketer's use-and-care information. Believing that the origin of the utensils was far less important to her customers than knowing how to use them, Christopher created an in-house test kitchen to develop simple yet innovative recipes and menus that used TPC products. While many of the company's gadgets have more than one use—the "Bar-B-Boss," for example, incorporated a bottle-opener, fork, and knife in one grill tool—TPC's creatively-written recipes often require more than one TPC tool. Something as simple as a tray

of crudités can call for three separate TPC tools: a v-shaped cutter, lemon zester, and "garnisher" (a wavy cutter). A plan for a whole meal might specify more than a dozen different products. When compiled in a company cookbook and used in kitchen shows, these recipes became powerful selling tools.

Years of trial and error resulted in fairly simple pricing and commission plans. Christopher arrives at an individual item's retail price by multiplying its wholesale cost by two. An initial investment of $100 buys a new kitchen consultant a set of about two dozen kitchen gadgets to use in demonstrations. As new utensils are introduced (two or three times each year), sales reps are required to purchase samples for demonstration purposes. Christopher "keeps faith" with her sales reps by keeping all new introductions—even obvious dogs—on the line for at least one year.

Following recipes written with TPC tools in mind, kitchen consultants guide kitchen show attendees in the use and care of the equipment. The consultants—99 percent of them women—start out earning a 20 percent commission on gross sales and earn an extra 2 percent after exceeding $15,000 in sales. The chief executive who had started out seeking a part-time job didn't expect her recruits to commit to a 40-hour (or more) week; instead, she required a meager $200 bimonthly sales quota. On top of commissions, incentives for prolific sellers included all-expenses-paid family vacations to Disney World. TPC literature emphasized that a career in direct sales "is considered by many to be a ground-floor opportunity with no glass ceiling."

The Mid-1990s and Beyond

That assertion was perhaps best exemplified by Doris Christopher herself, for what started out as a part-time job had turned into the chief executiveship of a multi-million-dollar nationwide venture by the mid-1990s. Although the founder has commented only half-jokingly that she might not have launched TPC had she known what she was getting into, the effort has made her a millionaire many times over. When growth began to spiral out of the entrepreneur's control, she was compelled to hire outsiders with expertise in the management of large, growing businesses.

Aside from her millions, The Pampered Chef has also earned Christopher national recognition. In 1992 the School of Human Resources and Family Studies Home Economics Alumni Association at her alma mater, the University of Illinois, recognized her with an Award of Merit. Ernst & Young, *Inc.*, and Merrill Lynch named her a regional National Entrepreneur of the Year in 1994, and *Inc.* gave her a tongue-in-cheek MBA—a "Master of Bootstrapping Administration"—in 1995.

TPC's charitable activities were in keeping with the company's food orientation. Launched in 1991, its "Round-Up from the Heart" promotion set aside $1 for every kitchen show hosted by its representatives between September 1 and December 31 of each year, and encourages customers to round their orders up to the nearest dollar. The firm donated these extra funds—a total of over $1.3 million in its first five years—to Second Harvest food banks across the country.

Americans spent increasing amounts of their free time, not to mention disposable income, on entertaining at home in the late 1980s and early 1990s. Kitchens were recognized as the "heart and hearth" of the household. Many categories of consumer goods—including cookware—were buoyed by this strong and ongoing trend known as "nesting" or "cocooning." Given retail analysts' predictions that this homeward movement would continue for decades, The Pampered Chef appeared poised to build on its success. Although Christopher had grown rather tight-lipped about her privately-owned company's financial status by the early 1990s, she did reveal that she expected the firm to generate $300 million in revenues in 1996. Furthermore, the businesswoman predicted that "a billion dollars isn't far in our future."

Further Reading

Fitzpatrick, Michele L., "Recipe for Success," *Chicago Tribune,* April 14, 1996, Section 17, pp. 1, 7.

Mamis, Robert A., "Master of Bootstrapping Administration," *Inc.,* August 1995, pp. 40–43.

"The Pampered Chef Story," *Food, Family & Friends: Quick & Easy Recipes For Everyday Occasions,* New York: Time-Life Custom Publishing, 1995, pp. 5–9.

Piccininni, Ann, "Home Parties: Mixing Selling with Socializing— There's Also a Future in Management," *Chicago Tribune,* July 26, 1992, p. 18SW.

Rodkin, Dennis, "Up the Down Economy," *Chicago,* May 1992, pp. 85–91.

Warshaw, Michael, "Home-Based $300 Million," *Success,* November 1996, p. 23.

—April Dougal Gasbarre

Paul Harris Stores, Inc.

6003 Guion Rd.
Indianapolis, Indiana 46254
U.S.A.
(317) 293-3900
Fax: (317) 298-6940
Web site: http://www.paulharrisstores.com

Public Company
Incorporated: 1952
Employees: 2,200
Sales: $167.5 million
Stock Exchanges: NASDAQ
SICs: 5621 Women's Clothing Stores

Paul Harris Stores, Inc. was incorporated on April 8, 1952. The company's cofounders, Gerald Paul and Earl Harris, began the operation by selling prepackaged apparel in supermarkets under the name Packaged Apparel. In 1954 Gerald Paul, age 30, and Earl Harris, age 37, established the company's first store in a strip mall on U.S. 40 in Plainfield, Indiana, just outside of Indianapolis. The store sold clothing for the whole family and featured late hours (open until nine) and air conditioning, unusual for the time. With a good location on the only east-west route into Indianapolis, the store did well and expanded in the same location, which was anchored by a supermarket and a drugstore. Soon a second location was opened, again in a strip mall with a drugstore and supermarket, in Indianapolis. Gradually the firm expanded to include more locations in Indiana, then it opened stores in adjacent states.

In the early 1960s the company decided to move from strip malls to covered shopping centers. Even though the strip mall stores were doing well, Paul and Harris felt that the future of retailing would be in the indoor shopping centers. Moving into covered malls meant higher rents, and the company had to become more focused. The transition included narrowing the store's product line to women's clothing only. The first Paul Harris Store located in a mall was in Akron, Ohio. The expansion was fueled by funds raised when the company went public

in 1960. Its stores featured flashy displays that created a lot of attention and media coverage in leading trade publications. Later in the decade the company turned its old strip mall locations into Paul Harris Discount Stores, which later became Clothes Out Junction and eventually The $5–$10–$15–$20 Place.

In the 1970s Paul Harris Stores wanted to be known as a store for "young swingers." They carried trendy styles of the day, from disco to psychedelic. Things were going well when disaster struck. On June 18, 1978, a tornado hit Indianapolis, smashing the company's distribution center and shutting down the company's headquarters. The company had to find temporary warehouses and replace all of its lost stock. It took about two years to fully settle with the company's insurers. The storm caused a shortage of merchandise throughout the chain, and shelves and racks remained unreplenished for some time.

Offered Clothes for Working Women in the 1980s

The 1980s saw tastes in women's clothing become more subdued. As more and more women went to work, Paul Harris moved toward clothes for working women, offering suits and dresses. In 1985 Earl Harris retired and established his own consulting business, leaving Gerald Paul in charge of the company.

As Paul Harris focused on working women, it found that it needed to address women's needs for more casual wear. It started the casual line of Pasta brand clothing and displayed it in its own section within existing Paul Harris stores. Pasta offered "colorful, casual, comfortable street clothing." Pasta caught on, and Paul Harris opened some freestanding Pasta stores in the mid-1980s. Eventually Pasta stores carried both Paul Harris and Pasta clothing.

The company was rapidly expanding. In 1986 it opened 68 stores. In 1987 it opened new discount stores under the name, The $5–$10–$15–$20 Place. These new format discount stores sold apparel priced at $5, $10, $15, or $20. While they carried some Paul Harris apparel, they also sold overruns and off-price merchandise from other retailers and manufacturers. Paul Harris first got into discount stores in the late 1960s. As the

Company Perspectives:

Paul Harris is a unique specialty retailer of women's cloth-ing, selling the Paul Harris Design private label brand. We offer a distinctive color-coordinated selection of casual clothing and accent pieces, such as embroidered vests, and accessories to women whose wardrobe is an important part of her life. Our target customer is a woman who goes to Paul Harris to buy complete outfits and mix-and-match separates.

Our customer wants "current styles," but she is not "trendy." She demands comfortable, casual, color-related, versatile apparel that moves from work to casual activities simply by dressing it up or down. She demands easy wear and easy care (washable) merchandise like cotton knits, woven novelties and soft related separates. This customer wants to get the "most" from her fashion dollars and de-mands value.

Paul Harris meets the demands of this traditional, 'mid-dle American' customer with sportswear separates and ac-cessories specifically developed for her lifestyle and clothing needs.

company moved from strip malls into regional malls it turned its old strip mall locations into Paul Harris Discount Stores, which later became Clothes Out Junction. Clothes Out Junction stores would be converted to the new $5–$20 format over the next few years. Overall earnings for 1987 were $4.74 million on sales of $190 million.

1988: A Bad Year for Specialty Stores

The year 1988 was the worst to date in the company's history. It was also a bad year for many specialty retailers. Paul Harris reported a loss of $5.6 million for the year on sales of $195 million. The company's earnings in the second half of the year were not enough to overcome losses in the first and second quarters. In 1987 and 1988 the company had adopted a sportier look, including miniskirts and other trendy items, that failed to score with Paul Harris's career-oriented customer base. Conse-quently, Paul Harris was forced to heavily mark down its unsold trendy items.

Paul Harris rebounded in 1989 and reported a healthy profit of $1.9 million on sales of $235.9 million. The turnaround from losses in 1988 was attributed to a better balance between inventory and demand. The company was able to sell more merchandise closer to full price. Other improvements included a new point-of-sale terminal system that made it easier to track merchandise sales and consumer trends. The company also be-gan experimenting with a new air-freight system to speed up deliveries from overseas. Gerald Paul became more involved with merchandising and purchasing, a function he had previ-ously delegated with poor results.

In 1989 the company returned to its historically more tradi-tional line of clothing aimed at working women. The company also made a point to differentiate its Paul Harris line from its Pasta fashion line, which was targeted to teens and young adults. The company was focusing on a strategy of increasing sales per square foot, part of which involved store closings. Less productive stores were closed, and new-store openings were scaled back.

1990: Good Start, Then Disaster

The year 1990 began as a high point for the company. There were 377 stores in 37 states, and sales volume was around $240 million. The company planned to open about 10 new stores and close the same number. Sales per square foot averaged around $200, while other highly successful specialty retailers such as The Limited and Limited Express averaged $400 or more per square foot. Based on its $1.9 million profit for 1989, the company was judged to have returned to profitability, although it posted a first quarter loss in 1990 of $371,000.

Then the stores had a crisis when business conditions turned sour. All the company's stores had a terrible Christmas season, a time when retailers expected to do as much as 40 percent of their year's business. It became clear that Paul Harris had expanded too quickly, opening 76 stores in one year. It also turned out that the change in focus on working women was made too abruptly, causing Paul to comment that the stores went from "too young and junior" to "too dull and classic."

One problem was merchandising. For a long time, Gerald Paul had done the merchandising himself, putting together the product every season. As his duties as CEO became more demanding, he found he couldn't handle merchandising, too. With nobody in the company to handle merchandising, he looked outside the company. Two outside merchandisers failed to satisfy Paul, and the third tried to change Paul Harris into an upscale retailer. When that failed, the company was forced into reorganization under the protection of U.S. bankruptcy laws in 1991.

For 1990, Paul Harris reported losses of $30.5 million for the fiscal year ending February 2, 1991. Losses in the fourth quarter alone were approximately $28.6 million. Sales for the year were $230.5 million, down 2.3 percent from 1989's sales of $235.9 million.

Company Files for Bankruptcy in 1991

On February 27, 1991, Paul Harris filed for Chapter 11 protection in the U.S. Bankruptcy Court. The company cited problems in obtaining short-term financing, due primarily to its substantial losses in the fourth quarter of 1990. As a result, vendors stopped shipments to the company. Paul Harris listed liabilities of $54.3 million, including $50.6 million in unsecured claims, and assets of $91.4 million. Three banks agreed to provide $19 million in letter of credit financing to be used for the purchase of goods for operations while the company was in Chapter 11.

In 1991 and 1992, Paul Harris closed 175 stores and kept 201 open. Its workforce was cut almost in half, to 2,600. For fiscal 1991 it reported losses of $22.4 million on sales of $197.2 million.

Emerges from Chapter 11 After 18 Months

On August 31, 1992, Paul Harris emerged from operating under Chapter 11 upon confirmation of its Second Amended Plan of Reorganization. The company's liabilities were to be settled through a combination of initial and deferred cash payments plus the issuance of new stock and long-term notes. Unsecured creditors received 25 percent cash, a pro rata share of $24 million in notes, and 5.7 million shares in the reorganized company. After the stock distribution, unsecured creditors held 71 percent of the company's common stock, with existing shareholders having 17 percent and management 11.5 percent. For the 26 weeks prior to August 2, operating under the protection of Chapter 11 the company had sales of $60.6 million, with net income of $6.8 million.

The reorganized Paul Harris offered moderately priced casual apparel that could be worn either at work or at play. It also explored alternatives to regional malls and worked out less costly formats for new stores. It was able to cut its $150,000 construction cost in half by trimming such elements as hardwood floors, paneled-wood treatments, and expensive paint and lighting. It began experimenting with locations in strip malls, opening two locations in the fall of 1992. Half of its 15 planned new stores for 1993 were slated for strip malls.

While in Chapter 11, additional research was undertaken to find out more about the company's customer base. It set up toll-free numbers to allow shoppers to chat with Gerald Paul. Focus groups were set up. The results of its customer research told Paul Harris that its target customer was a working woman, aged 18 to 35, earning under $30,000 a year and living mainly in Midwestern and Southern suburbs. About half were married, usually with children, and the other half were single and tended to spend more on fashion. Gerald Paul told *WWD* that the most important finding from the company's customer research was that women want "casual wear and what we call 'versatile clothing' that can go to work and also be used in off-hours." That meant replacing navy suits with blazers and silk shirts.

The reorganized company also changed its merchandising approach. Previously, the company had two merchandising staffs, one for the career clothes offered by Paul Harris and one for the casual line marketed as Pasta. In 1992 the company merged the two divisions under one general merchandise manager, Eloise Paul, Gerald Paul's daughter. She became the company's senior vice president of merchandise.

The new merchandising program focused on providing deep selections of mix-and-match separates. Buying deep also gave Paul Harris more leverage to make deals on fabrics and manufacturing. Nearly all of the company's Paul Harris and Pasta brand merchandise was private label, supplied by 15 to 20 key vendors. To improve its merchandise mix, the company set up test programs to test apparel for silhouette, color, and fabric. Six to 12 units of a style and color would be sent to designated test stores and prominently displayed, with feedback coming within three weeks.

Testing led to another change. The firm had previously relied on overseas manufacturers for about three-fourths of its goods. Since testing in-season required faster turnaround times,

Paul Harris began to forge more ties with U.S. vendors, who now supplied more than half of the company's merchandise.

As a result of these changes, the newly reorganized Paul Harris turned a profit for the last half of 1992. Sales for the last half of fiscal 1992 (26 weeks ending January 30, 1993) were $85 million, with net income of $5.7 million.

Fischer Joins Paul Harris in 1993

In August 1993 Charlotte Fischer was named to the company's board of directors. She had been consulting for the firm since 1992 and was a major contributor to its reorganization. Her track record in retailing was remarkable. From 1986 to 1991 she was president and CEO of Claire's Boutiques and a member of the board of its parent company, Claire's Store Inc. While with Claire's, she took the company from 300 stores and $74 million in sales to 1,100 stores with $257 million in sales in just five years. Then, she was abruptly fired from her position, reportedly because of a personality conflict with someone in the parent company's management. In 1991 she started her own consulting firm, C.G.F. Inc. She was also briefly hired as CEO of failing Parklane Hosiery in early 1992, but couldn't rescue the company from Chapter 11. Paul Harris reported that sales for fiscal 1993 were $154.3 million and net income was $5.8 million.

In April 1994 Charlotte Fischer was named CEO-designate to succeed Gerald Paul at the end of the fiscal year in January 1995, when Paul was to retire. In August the company introduced the Paul Harris private label credit card. By 1995, the card accounted for some 8 percent of the company's sales. Transactions involving the card had an average of 91 percent more sales dollars than the company's average sales dollars per transaction.

In October 1994 the company opened its first Paul Harris Direct at the Franklin Mills outlet mall outside Philadelphia, Pennsylvania. The Paul Harris Direct concept, which allowed the company to introduce its brand merchandise to people who liked to shop at outlet malls but visited malls less frequently, was expanded in 1995 and 1996. A second Paul Harris Direct was opened in April 1995 at the Horizon Outlet Center near Indianapolis, with favorable results.

In December Gerald Paul, 70, was named "CEO of the Year" by *Indiana Business Magazine*. Sales for the year were $167.8 million, with net income of $3.1 million. The company's stock traded in the $2.50 to $7.25 range.

Charlotte Fischer became chairman, president, and CEO in 1995

As planned, Charlotte G. Fischer took over as CEO, chairman, and president upon the retirement of Gerald Paul at the end of January 1995. Paul remained on the board as chairman emeritus. Her first full year as chairman, president, and CEO of Paul Harris was a good one. The company enjoyed a strong Christmas and holiday season. Fourth quarter earnings were $4.2 million, up from 1994's fourth quarter earnings of $4.1 million. Comparable store sales were down three percent, due mainly to bad weather in January 1996. Sales for the year were

$167.5 million, with net income of $1.6 million. The company's stock traded in the $1.06 to $3.13 range.

During 1995 the company closed 13 of the $5–$20 stores as part of its strategy to phase out the division. Another 15 stores were converted. The $5–$20 stores were fully phased out by September 1996, allowing the company to focus its resources on building the Paul Harris name and reputation for affordable, quality casual wear.

The company took significant steps in 1995 to improve the look of its stores and "allow prompt buying ideas by grouping merchandise together as outfits, and to ensure that our sales people provide friendly, knowledgeable buying and fashion assistance," according to the company's annual report. Plans were developed for 1996 for "customer friendly" upgrades, described in the company's annual report as "spacious, well-lit dressing rooms with ample mirrors; seating areas with comfortable sofas and chairs; moveable racking systems that make it easier to rotate merchandise to offer our customers a 'new look' every few weeks; new lighting systems; improved general appearance; and expansion of our accessory area."

New customer service programs introduced in 1995 included more training for retail associates, district managers, and store managers. New district managers began attending the Paul Harris University for four days of training, then they in turn trained and supervised store managers. The company also instituted a liberal "no questions asked" returns policy. A toll-free hotline was set up that allowed customers to leave personal messages for Fischer, who received an average of 75 calls per month.

In merchandising, new items were added to the mix, including denim pants, skirts, and jumpers, and popular lines such as vests and turtlenecks were expanded. Clear price points were established, and virtually all items in Paul Harris stores were priced under $59.

At the start of 1996 the company operated 235 stores in 26 states and the District of Columbia, with the heaviest concentration of stores in Indiana (44 stores), Ohio (32 stores), Illinois (27 stores), Pennsylvania (23 stores), and North Carolina (12 stores). Of the 235 stores, 217 were Paul Harris fashion division stores located principally in regional enclosed shopping malls. The remaining 18 stores were The $5–$10–$15–$20 Place division stores, most of which were located in strip shopping centers. The phase-out of the $5–$20 stores was completed in September 1996.

A prototype store was opened in April 1996 in Indianapolis. According to the company's annual report, the prototype store "incorporated the ambiance and layout we believe most effectively appeals to our customers." The store was to be used as a guidepost for developing new stores, with the help of ongoing customer surveys and focus groups.

By January 1997 the company's stock was trading around the $20 per share range, due in part to strong earnings throughout the year. Analysts were beginning to perceive Paul Harris as a growth company, not one that was simply downsizing in response to its emergence from Chapter 11. January sales were up 30 percent from the previous year, based on a comparable number of stores, and increased 2 percent overall to $7.7 million from $7.6 million in January 1996, which included five weeks of operations. Net sales in December increased 16 percent to $39.9 million from $34.4 million the previous year, and comparable store sales for December were up a record 23 percent. That followed the highest third quarter net income in the company's history, $.17 per share or $1.8 million.

Under the leadership of Charlotte Fischer and her customer-focused management team, Paul Harris appeared to be well positioned to move ahead. The company's merchandising focus was centered on affordable outfits for women that could be easily mixed and matched to create a distinctive "Paul Harris look." Some analysts believed that Fischer would significantly expand Paul Harris in the coming years into a national chain.

Further Reading

Belcove, Julie L., and Jonathan Auerbach, "Turnaround Time," *WWD,* April 28, 1993, p. 8.

"Fischer to Succeed Paul Harris's Paul," *WWD,* April 20, 1994, p. 15.

Johnson, Douglas, "CEO of the Year: Leadership of Style," *Indiana Business Magazine,* December 1994, p. 8.

Marson, Carla, "How Does Paul Harris Stack Up? Analysts Await Permanent Turnaround," *Indianapolis Business Journal,* September 24, 1990, p. 1A.

Marson, Carla, "Paul Harris Expects Slow Growth After Reversing 1988 Losses," *Indianapolis Business Journal,* July 2, 1990, p. 13.

Marson, Carla, "Paul Harris Stores Rebounds from 1988 Losses with Strong 1989 Performance," *Indianapolis Business Journal,* March 12, 1990, p. 13A.

"Paul Harris Stores, Inc.," *The Brous Report,* October 30, 1996.

"Paul Harris Stores, Inc. Reports January Comp Store Sales Up 30 Percent," *PR Newswire,* February 6, 1997.

Sturgeon, Julie, "Lady in Waiting," *Indianapolis CEO,* August 1994, p. 16.

—David P. Bianco

Payless ShoeSource®

Payless ShoeSource, Inc.

3232 East Sixth Street
Topeka, Kansas 66607-2207
U.S.A.
(913) 233-5171
Fax: (913) 295-6220
Web site: http//www.paylessshoesource.com

Public Company
Founded: 1956 as Pay-less National
Employees: 25,000
Sales: $2.33 billion (1995)
Stock Exchanges: New York
SICs: 5661 Shoe Stores

Payless ShoeSource, Inc. is the largest footwear retailer in the United States. The company's 4,261 stores operate in all 50 states as well as Puerto Rico and the U.S. Virgin Islands. Payless has built its success by offering a large selection of shoes at very low prices. In 1996 the average cost of a pair of Payless shoes was only $11.00. The company has been able to maintain its affordable prices by sticking exclusively to a self-service format, keeping a tight rein on cost structure, and insisting on efficient sourcing and inventory controls. Founded in Topeka, Kansas, in the mid-1950s by cousins Louis and Shaol Pozez, Payless was acquired by May Department stores in 1979. The company remained a May subsidiary until 1996, when it was spun off to May shareholders. Payless ShoeSource had become such an American institution by 1996 that, during that year alone, over 40 percent of women in the United States purchased at least one pair of shoes from a Payless store.

Company Origins in the 1950s

Payless ShoeSource was founded as Pay-Less National in Topeka, Kansas, in 1956 by two cousins, Louis and Shaol Pozez. Three ''Pay-Less'' stores were opened in Topeka within a year of the company's founding. The company then expanded into Oklahoma, Texas, and Nebraska, opening 12 new outlets by the end of the decade. From the start, Payless stores were designed to maintain low prices by keeping overhead to a minimum. The first outlets were located in former supermarkets with the original fixtures replaced by simple, unpainted, wooden shelving, constructed in large part by store managers. The self-service format of the stores allowed Payless to limit staff, which usually consisted only of a manager and one or two clerks. This no-frills approach to operations kept the average price for a pair of shoes at the original Payless stores below $3.00.

Payless was not alone in offering budget footwear in a self-service format to American consumers. The self-service shoe industry emerged soon after World War II when cheap imported shoes began to be available on a widespread basis. Growth was fuelled by changes in fashion that emphasized a looser fitting, more casual shoe as well as more variety in footwear. The 1950s baby boom also contributed to the rise in large discount shoe stores which catered primarily to middle income families with children. Like most of these low-end shoe stores, Payless's major market was in women's and children's shoes which constituted about 60 and 30 percent of sales, respectively. By the early 60s, the $6 million sales rung up in Payless's 38 stores represented only a small fraction of the estimated $270 million volume of the self-service retail shoe industry.

Growth and Acquisitions in the 1960s

In the early 60s, Pay-Less National, which had been operating retail stores under various names, including Pay-Less Self Service, National Self Service, Gambles Discount Shoes, and Shopper's City, changed its corporate name to ''Volume Distributors'' in order to reflect the company's diverse operations more closely. In 1962 Volume Distributors went public to raise capital for further growth. The influx of cash from the IPO allowed the company to open an average of 12 new stores annually in the early 60s. In order to cope with the increased inventory, in 1966 Volume Distributors adopted a new computerized inventory system that used stock-keeping units (SKUs) to keep track of the large number of shoe styles and sizes that were stocked in the company's 50 stores. The new system was temporarily sidetracked when a tornado completely destroyed the company headquarters and warehouse in Topeka on the very

413

evening that the first computer-generated inventory report was to be produced. Volume Distributors quickly picked up the pieces from this natural disaster and built new corporate offices at another location in Topeka.

In 1967 "Volume Distributors" was renamed "Volume Shoe Corporation" in order to identify it more closely with the footwear industry. In the same year the company launched an accelerated expansion program that saw the number of stores top 100 and annual sales rise to over $10 million by the end of the decade. In addition to new store openings in the late 1960s and early 70s, Volume Shoe implemented a program of acquisitions to accelerate growth further. From 1968 through 1973 Volume Shoe purchased eight smaller retail shoe companies, adding a total of 145 stores to the growing chain. The prosperity of the company during the inflation-plagued early 70s actually led to a conflict with the Nixon administration in 1971 when Volume Shoe raised its dividend in spite of a government imposed wage-price freeze. Company president Louis Pozez was summoned to Washington to justify the dividend hike in a meeting with the President's "Cost of Living Council," but ultimately no further action was taken against the firm.

Accelerated Expansion in the 1970s

The rate of new store openings continued to accelerate through the mid-1970s. By 1975 Volume Shoe was operating 486 retail units in 31 states with total net sales of almost $75 million, making it the largest chain of family shoe stores in the United States. The Payless ShoeSource name was adopted in 1978 for the bulk of Volume Shoe retail outlets and the company logo was changed to the now familiar yellow, orange, and brown. The success of Volume Shoe and its Payless Shoe-Source outlets was due in part to the company's skill at choosing locations for its stores. Although early stores were primarily freestanding, in the late 70s Payless outlets also opened in major malls across the country. By 1979, 40 percent of all Payless stores were mall-based. The distribution of Payless units in a variety of real estate locales including suburban strip developments, central business districts, shopping centers, and shopping malls, promoted the visibility and consumer recognition of the bold yellow logo as well as increasing the range of customers who would feel comfortable shopping at Payless stores.

From the start, Payless's relationship with its suppliers was key to the company's success. In the early years, the company bought their shoes "off the shelf" from American as well as foreign manufacturers, protecting themselves from shortages

and sudden price increases by utilizing a large number of suppliers. In the early 60s no single manufacturer supplied more than six percent of Payless's merchandise. By the mid-60s Payless was having shoes made to their own specifications to ensure that the shoe styles available in their stores matched the expectations of increasingly demanding consumers. These company specific shoe styles would eventually evolve into private label brands that would become the staple of Payless Shoe-Source outlets from the mid-70s. The development of in-house brands allowed Payless to maintain tight control over style and quality, the two issues that had driven customers away from many discount chains in the 70s.

Acquired by May Department Stores

In 1979 Volume Shoe, with its 739 Payless ShoeSource stores generating annual sales of $191 million, was acquired by May Department Stores in a $160 million stock swap. May was one of the leading retailers in the United States, with annual sales near $3 billion. The retail giant owned 11 department and discount store chains but Volume Shoe was May's first entry into the discount shoe business. Volume Shoe was considered an excellent acquisition by analysts. The self-service shoe chain was earning operating profits of $28 million or almost 15 percent of sales, one of the best performances in the retail sector. May's capital allowed the Payless chain to expand at an accelerated pace and by 1981 there were 1,089 Payless outlets in 34 states. More than half of these stores were located in the Sunbelt states, where an influx of population was creating record retail growth. In the early 80s, the Payless chain included 246 outlets in Texas and California alone. In 1983 Payless's presence in California was further strengthened by the acquisition of 66 Koby Shoe Stores, a California-based chain formerly owned by Kobacker Co.

In order to accommodate the growing number of Payless stores, Volume Shoe constructed a new 300,000-square-foot distribution center in Topeka. The new center, which would be expanded twice over the course of the following decade, became the heart of the Payless network of stores as its computerized inventory and picking system insured the delivery of the 20,000 pairs of shoes sold annually by the average Payless store in the early 80s. With changes in the worldwide economy, Volume Shoe began to rely more heavily on Asian manufacturers to supply these shoes and in 1983 the company opened an international office in Taipei, Taiwan, to coordinate overseas production. By the beginning of the next decade, factories in China were producing 80 percent of Payless's merchandise and the Taipei office became the center of the company's sourcing subsidiary, Payless ShoeSource International.

Louis and Shaol Pozez, the cousins who founded Payless, stayed on to facilitate the transition to the new ownership but retired in the early 80s to be succeeded by former executive vice president Harry Berger. In 1985, Berger was in turn replaced as president by Richard Jolosky, who ran the company through 1988. After an eight-year hiatus Jolosky returned to Payless as president in 1996. Jolosky's distinctive management style, which on one memorable occasion included dressing up as General Patton to rally the sales troops, was instrumental in the development of the aggressive competitiveness that marked Payless's approach to business through the 80s and 90s. Jolosky had spent a number of years as a senior vice president of Wal-Mart, the giant discount chain that dominated the industry in the 80s and 90s, and says he learned a lot from founder Sam Walton. "When I visited stores with Sam, he never looked to see the things that we were doing better than the competition," Jolosky recalled in a 1996 interview with *Forbes.* "He always looked for the things that the competition was doing better than us." As president of Payless, Jolosky turned this lesson against Wal-Mart as he made certain that Payless always remained competitive in both price and product with the huge discounter.

May continued the vigorous expansion of the Payless Shoe-Source chain through the late 80s and early 90s, opening about 200 new stores each year. With almost all of these stores now known under the Payless name, in 1991 the corporate name was also changed from Volume Shoe to Payless ShoeSource. During the early 90s, Payless also introduced Payless Kids stores, which were added adjacent to existing Payless ShoeSource outlets. In 1985 there were 1,662 Payless stores. By 1991 this number had almost doubled to 3,295. Sales during the same period rose from near $700 million to $1.5 billion.

Independent Again in the 1990s

Although Payless's earnings also increased through the late 80s, return on sales failed to keep pace with the company's earlier performance or with May's core department store holdings. Earnings as a percentage of sales had been about 15 percent when May purchased Volume Shoe, but flat sales in the discount shoe sector saw this figure fall to about 11 percent in the late 80s and then tumble again to less than 8 percent in 1995. Growing competition from such giant discount chains as Wal-Mart and Kmart as well as an overall decline in the off-price apparel market contributed to this downturn. In addition, the consolidation and conversion of 679 shoe stores acquired from Kobacker Co. and Shoe Works Inc. in 1994 added substantially to operating costs. Payless, whose contribution to May's overall sales shrank from 20 to 14 percent from 1993 to 1996, was no longer considered a key part of May's long-term strategy for growth and in 1996 May spun off Payless Shoe-Source to shareholders.

As Payless ShoeSource embarked on its new life as an independent publicly traded company, the company operated 4,270 stores including 775 Payless Kids outlets. Plans were quickly implemented to close or relocate about 500 of the less profitable locations and to continue opening new stores. While overall sales declined during the first half of 1996, store-for-store sales as well as profit margins were up from the same period in 1995. Payless CEO Steven J. Douglass was optimistic that the implementation of new promotional strategies would see improved earnings through the end of the decade.

Principal Subsidiaries

Payless ShoeSource International (Taiwan).

Further Reading

Grove, Mary Beth, "The Odd Couple," *Forbes,* November 18, 1996, p. 178–180.

Houser, Douglas, "Volume Shoe Maintains Program to Expand Shoe Store Network," *Investment Dealers' Digest,* February 15, 1972, p. 30.

La Monica, Paul, "May Department Stores: The Shoe Doesn't Fit," *Financial World,* April 8, 1996, pp. 16, 18.

"May Department Stores Agrees to Buy Volume Shoe Corp.," *Wall Street Journal,* July 24, 1979, p. 2.

"May's Return to Its Roots," *Business Week,* October 19, 1981, pp. 89–92.

Patterson, Gregory, "May Stores Buys Shoe Outlets from Two Stores," *Wall Street Journal,* July 28, 1994, p. 8B.

Quintanilla, Carl, "May to Spin Off Payless to Holders, Close or Move Stores," *Wall Street Journal,* January 18, 1996, 4B.

Sanger, Elizabeth, "Productivity by the Square Foot," *Barron's,* January 13, 1986, pp. 41–42.

Solomon, Goody, "Best Foot Forward: Self-Service Shoe Stores Are Growing by Leaps and Bounds," *Barron's,* February 22, 1965, pp. 11–12, 15.

"Volume Distributors Walk Profit March on Self-Service Sales," *Investment Dealers' Digest,* December 30, 1963, pp. 19–20.

"Volume Shoe Building Sole Base for Extensive Expansion Effort," *Investment Dealers' Digest,* December 25, 1967, pp. 37–38.

"White House Talks with Six Firms on Payout Rises Are Inconclusive," *Wall Street Journal,* September 8, 1971, p. 3.

—Hilary Gopnik

Philip Morris Companies Inc.

120 Park Avenue
New York, New York 10017
U.S.A.
(212) 880-5000
Fax: (212) 907-5502

Public Company
Incorporated: 1919 as Philip Morris & Company Ltd.,
    Inc.
Employees: 168,000
Sales: $51.17 billion
Stock Exchanges: New York Amsterdam Antwerp Basel
    Brussels Frankfurt Geneva Lausanne London
    Luxembourg Paris Tokyo Zürich
SICs: 2000 Food & Kindred Products; 5140 Groceries &
    Related Products; 2111 Cigarettes; 2082 Malt
    Beverages; 6552 Subdividers & Developers, Not
    Elsewhere Classified; 6150 Business Credit Institutions

As a major player in an industry dogged by health concerns, a shrinking domestic market, and widespread investor fears about its future, Philip Morris Companies Inc. (Morris) continues year after year to achieve record-breaking sales and profits, most of them thanks to the enduring appeal of the Marlboro Man. From a position of relative obscurity in the cigarette business in the early 1960s Philip Morris has ridden Marlboro's success to leadership of the world tobacco market, and in the process accumulated enough cash to finance a series of enormous acquisitions in the food industry. Annexing both Kraft and General Foods Corporation, the company is now the world's second-largest food concern as well as the largest cigarette maker; and there is little doubt that Morris will continue to wean itself of over-dependence on its lucrative but increasingly embattled tobacco trade.

The Early Years: 1847–1920s

In 1847 an Englishman named Philip Morris opened a tobacco shop in London's fashionable Bond Street area. When British soldiers returning from the Crimean War made the smoking of Turkish-style cigarettes—until then exclusively a habit of the poor—*de rigueur,* Morris was soon busy as a manufacturer as well as merchant of the newly popular product. He introduced a number of successful cigarette brands, including English Ovals, Cambridge, and Oxford Blues, and continued as one of the leading British tobacconists for many years. Morris's company eventually built a small but stable business in the United States, where its brands sold primarily on the strength of their British cachet. The U.S. market, however, was until 1911 all but owned by the American Tobacco trust, which enjoyed a monopoly in cigarettes comparable to that of John D. Rockefeller's Standard Oil in the oil business.

When the tobacco cartel was dissolved by court order in 1911, a U.S. financier named George J. Whelan formed Tobacco Products Corporation to absorb a few of the splinter companies not already organized into the new Big Four of tobacco—American Tobacco, R.J. Reynolds, Lorillard, and Liggett & Meyers. His first manufacturing acquisition was the maker of Melachrino cigarettes, a company at which Reuben M. Ellis and Leonard B. McKitterick had made names for themselves as outstanding salesmen. Ellis and McKitterick became vice-presidents and stockholders of Tobacco Products Corporation as Whelan considered their amicable relationships with the thousands of tobacco retailers in the New York area an invaluable asset. Whelan purchased the U.S. business of Philip Morris Company in 1919 and formed a new company to manage its assets: Philip Morris & Company Ltd., Inc., owned by the shareholders of Tobacco Products Corporation. Ellis and McKitterick thus became part owners and managers of the new Philip Morris brands.

Marlboro Debuts, 1925

While Whelan wheeled and dealed his way toward a financial collapse in 1929, Ellis assumed control of Morris in 1923, at which time the company posted a net income of about $100,000. Ellis's first important move as president was the 1925 introduction of a new premium—20¢ a pack—cigarette called Marlboro, which did well from the beginning and leveled off at steady sales of 500 million cigarettes a year. Industry leaders such as Camel and Lucky Strike sold more than 25 billion a year. Marlboro was originally marketed to women, the wealthy, and the sophisticated, in complete contrast to its 1955 cowboy-image reincarnation. After a seven-year absence, McKitterick rejoined Ellis in 1930 and the two men set about buying Morris's stock from their former employer, now in retreat from the tobacco business. Whelan sold off all of his tobacco interests, allowing Ellis and McKitterick to gain control of Morris by 1931. The company marketed cigarettes mainly under the names of English Ovals, Marlboro, and Paul Jones; handled a modest amount of pipe tobacco as well; and owned a single manufacturing facility in Richmond, Virginia. By any measure, it was a minor competitor in an industry dominated by the remaining pieces of the former American Tobacco trust.

Ellis and McKitterick were both veteran salesmen in the tobacco business, however, which in the 1930s meant that they personally had done business with many thousands of the tobacco jobbers and retailers up and down the East Coast. In a field not yet controlled by the rising mass marketers, such as supermarket chains, those years of handshaking had built for both men a powerful store of goodwill among those who would determine which cigarettes would be pushed at the retail level and which would be allowed to languish. When Ellis and McKitterick launched a new mid-priced cigarette called Philip Morris English Blend in 1933, they could count on the strong support of their jobber network to help them through the difficult introductory period. To further cement their alliance with jobbers, Morris executives let it be known that the company would refrain from selling to the new mass marketers directly, preventing the latter from retailing English Blend at less than the price of 15¢ set by the jobbers and dealers. The jobbers, already beginning to suffer from price competition with the big chains, readily agreed to Morris's plan—they pushed English Blend at 15¢ after Morris guaranteed that the same package would not end up on supermarket shelves at 10¢.

As experienced marketers, Ellis and McKitterick came up with several novel advertising gambits as additional support for their new product. Morris introduced the use of diethylene glycol as a moisture retentive in its cigarettes, adducing as proof of glycol's milder effect on the human throat a host of more or less scientific evidence gathered by bona fide researchers who were, however, paid for their work by the company. Ellis and McKitterick circulated results of the research among physicians, while settling in their advertisements for the general claim that ''scientific tests have proven Philip Morris a milder cigarette.'' The company kept up this advertising slant for many years despite skepticism voiced by the Federal Trade Commission, among others. Morris's second advertising strategy was the revival of an earlier campaign in which a bellhop was told to fetch a pack of Morris cigarettes. The ''call for Philip Morris,''

slogan used on posters as early as 1919, was updated for radio in 1933 with the recruitment of a bellhop named John Roventini to serve as a living representation of the ad. Roventini, under the name of Johnnie Morris, enjoyed many prosperous years putting in countless appearances in New York and other major cities, while his strident call could be heard every week on radio broadcasts.

Roventini soon earned himself a large fortune, by bellhop standards, and Morris began its long climb to the top of the cigarette world. Sales of English Blend were strong from its introduction in January of 1933, helping Morris to triple its net income—to $1.5 million—in a single year and by 1935 to challenge Lorillard as the fourth-largest cigarette maker in the United States. Ellis and McKitterick were both deceased by 1936, but under new chairman Alfred Lyon the company continued its rise, in that year selling 7.5 billion cigarettes and laying firm hold on the industry's number four spot. Morris was viewed as something of a phenomenon, its combination of marketing expertise and jobber loyalty enabling it to take market share from much larger and wealthier cigarette leaders such as American Tobacco and Reynolds. Lyon personally directed the construction of what quickly became the industry's largest and most effective sales force; although Morris's special relationship with jobbers did not last long—supermarkets proving to be the wave of the future—it remained a company fueled by its expertise in sales and marketing.

By 1939 sales had reached $64 million, and World War II soon put even more pressure on cigarette production. When Morris's sales doubled by 1942, Lyon and company president Otway Chalkey began casting about for some means to expand capacity, especially difficult given the fact that tobacco needed to be cured several years before its use in cigarette production. When Axton-Fisher Tobacco Company of Louisville, Kentucky, was put up for sale in 1945, Morris paid a premium price—$20 million—to win its large stores of tobacco and a second manufacturing plant. The move looked good until the war's end in August of that year precipitated a huge drop in cigarette consumption, a cut in sales made more painful by Morris's overestimation of peacetime demand. Many of the company's biggest orders in the fall of 1945 were left to grow stale on retail racks, and net income plummeted just as Morris was attempting to float a new bond issue at the end of the year. The company withdrew the offering and suffered a certain amount of embarrassment, but its underlying business was sound and Morris soon bounced back. A massive 1948 advertising campaign claiming that English Blend did not cause ''cigarette hangover,'' a previously unknown disorder, led to a fresh gain in market share and profit.

Repositioning During the 1950s

Despite Morris's success with such advertising claims, the company somehow failed to foresee the most important new development in the cigarette business in many years: the introduction of milder and less harmful filtered cigarettes. Unlike Morris's version of mildness, filtered cigarettes were indisputably less damaging to the throat, and increased public awareness of smoking's real health dangers spurred a rapid shift to filters in the 1950s. Morris was slow to recognize the importance of this innovation, and it was not until 1955 that the company repositioned its old filter entry, Marlboro, as a cigarette with broad appeal by working the myth of the American cowboy into the product's marketing strategy. It took time, however, for the new Marlboro image to take hold, and by 1960 Morris had slipped to sixth and last place among major U.S. tobacco companies, its bestselling entry able to do no better than tenth among the leading brands. It appeared that changing consumer preference had left Morris well out of the new era in tobacco.

Morris had at least three cards yet to play, however. One was the emergence in 1957 of a marketing tactician capable of resurrecting the glory days of Alfred Lyon. Joseph Cullman III took over management of the company in 1957 and guided its amazing growth over the course of the following two decades, much of it earned in the international market. Morris was perhaps the earliest, and ultimately the most successful, U.S. tobacco company to foresee the potential sales growth in the worldwide cigarette business. In 1960 Cullman appointed George Weissman as director of international operations; the company's second greatest resource, Weissman is generally credited with making Morris the United States' leading exporter of tobacco products. The company's ace in the hole was the Marlboro Man, who would prove in the long run to be one of the most successful advertising icons ever created. For whatever combination of reasons—nostalgia for the Old West, clever packaging, tobacco taste—Marlboro almost singlehandedly raised Morris from also-ran to industrial leader during the next quarter century.

While Cullman attended to Morris's resurgence in the tobacco business, he also began the first of many attempts to diversify the company's assets, thereby rendering it less dependent on a product that was gradually becoming known as a serious health hazard. In the mid-1950s Morris bought into the flexible packaging and paper manufacturing trades, and in the early 1960s it added American Safety Razor, Burma Shave, and Clark chewing gum, hoping in each case to use Morris's existing distributor network and marketing experience to sell a wider variety of consumer products. None of these early acquisitions proved to be of great value, with the possible exception of its packaging division, not sold until the mid-1980s. Then, in 1970 the company added Miller Brewing to its holdings. Miller was then only the seventh-largest brewer in the United States, but the combination of a repositioned High Life beer and the introduction of the United States' first low-calorie beer, Miller Lite, brought the company all the way up to number two by 1980. On the other hand, Morris's 1978 purchase of the Seven-Up Company for $520 million was little more than a disaster: after several failed advertising campaigns the soft drink manufacturer was sold in the mid-1980s.

Marlboro's Rise to Superbrand Status, 1960s–70s

In the meantime, the Marlboro Man was running wild, carrying Morris up the ranks of cigarette makers with astonishing speed. Throughout the 1960s Marlboro registered yearly leaps in popularity, especially among the growing segment of younger smokers. By 1973 it was the second most popular cigarette brand in the United States and accounted for roughly two-thirds of Morris's tobacco business. In 1976 it moved past Reynolds's Winston as the leader with 94 billion cigarettes sold that year,

helping Morris to become the United States' and the world's second-largest seller of tobacco. In 1961 Morris had controlled 9.4 percent of the market; in 1976 that figure topped 25 percent and continued to rise. With all other competitors in a slump, Morris and Reynolds together controlled well more than half the market. The two leaders thus found themselves in a very comfortable position: growing health concerns about smoking made it unlikely that any new competitor would join the tobacco business, and the need for massive, effective advertising made it difficult for the current competition to maintain its position. The net result was abnormally large profits for the two leaders, especially as their dominance of the market really took hold in the 1980s and they were able to raise prices frequently without fear of being undercut.

Complementing Marlboro's success was the emergence of new fields for Morris. The 1975 introduction of Merit brand signaled Morris's entry into the new low-tar market, a category that would mushroom as U.S. smokers became increasingly concerned with the deleterious effects of inhaling cigarette smoke. The company also began to focus increased marketing dollars on its premium brands, which produced greater profits per pack sold. Meanwhile, under the guidance of Weissman, the company's international business greatly expanded. While the U.S. cigarette market was flat in the 1970s and in retreat by the mid-1980s, international business continued to grow rapidly, and Marlboro soon ranked as the world's bestselling cigarette. That trend would continue through the following decade under the leadership of worldwide tobacco vice president Geoffrey C. Bible.

Morris's response to increasing U.S. controversy over smoking was to sell cigarettes with lower tar, meanwhile promoting all of its brands overseas where relatively less sophisticated consumers cared little about the health risks involved. In 1993 it cut the price of its Marlboro brand in an effort to gain an increased share of a sluggish market. Unfortunately none of these strategies went to the heart of the company's fundamental problem: the association of tobacco with lung disease. By the mid-1990s Morris had become embroiled in the rash of product liability lawsuits spawned by fifth-ranked Liggett's settlement of a class-action legal action in March 1996. The company was plagued by allegations that it had knowingly suppressed the harmful side-effects of smoking from consumers, and repeatedly made headlines as several former employees—some of them scientists—accused Morris of suppressing knowledge of the addictive quality of nicotine, manipulating levels of the drug in its Marlboro brand, and deliberately courting teenage smokers. In 1996, amid reports of Morris's 3rd-quarter combined tobacco earnings of $2.23 billion and the announcement of a 20 percent increase in its annual stock dividend rate, came the announcement that the FDA planned to regulate the tobacco industry and restrict tobacco-related advertising. While Morris responded with a countersuit in an attempt to block the FDA ruling, many analysts believed that the company faced a tough uphill battle.

1985: The General Foods Acquisition

Meanwhile, to ensure its own safety, Morris had begun to diversify its holdings away from tobacco. In 1985, even as it passed Reynolds to become the largest domestic cigarette manufacturer, the company paid $5.75 billion for General Foods Corporation, the diversified food products giant. General Foods was large enough to offer Morris a significant source of revenue apart from the tobacco industry, and its reliance on advertising and an intricate distribution system was similar to Morris's core business; but General Foods was a rather lackluster company in a mature industry, and the acquisition did not kindle great enthusiasm among business analysts. They compared it unfavorably to Reynolds's purchase of Nabisco Brands at about the same time, and predicted that the move would not be sufficient to free Morris of its tobacco habit. In 1987, for example, two years after the General Foods purchase, Morris's total revenue had reached $27.7 billion and its operating income $4.1 billion. The lion's share of that income—$2.7 billion—was earned by the domestic tobacco division, where the slackening of competition allowed a luxurious rate of return on its $7.6 billion in sales. By contrast, General Foods's $10 billion contribution to revenue netted only $700 million in operating income, meaning that it was fully five times as profitable to sell a pack of Marlboros as a box of Jell-O or a jar of coffee from General Foods. Indeed, 60 percent of Morris's total profit for 1987 was generated by Marlboro's popularity both at home and abroad.

In 1988 the company took a more decisive step toward reshaping its corporate profile. For $12.9 billion it acquired Kraft, Inc., an even larger and more dynamic food products corporation. Morris chairman Hamish Maxwell merged his company's two food divisions into Kraft Foods, Inc. Under its chief executive officer, Michael Miles, Kraft underwent a successful program of labor cuts and efficiency measures designed to raise its earnings level to something approaching that of the tobacco division. With $27 billion in sales by 1995, and more than 2,800 different product offerings, Kraft ranked as the world's second-largest food company. Within this conglomeration was Post which, as the third-ranking U.S. producer of breakfast cereal, instigated a cereal price war in mid-1996. In a bold attempt to gain market share and stay the rising consumer boycott of pricey breakfast cereals, prices on Post brands were slashed across the board in April, pushing number one producer Kellogg to reluctantly follow suit.

A low inflation rate coupled with an increasing consumer demand for low prices characterized the first half of the 1990s. Such a combination prompted downsizing, loss of jobs, and a search for new markets on the part of many in the food industry. Paralleling its success in expanding its tobacco market, Morris extended its food merchandising infrastructure worldwide. Under its Kraft Foods International division, new markets were established in Europe, South America, and the Asia/Pacific region. Morris also expanded its holdings overseas, buying Jacobs Suchard, a Swiss maker of coffee and chocolate for $4.1 billion in 1990; four years later it purchased confectionery companies in Russia and the Ukraine, as well as making inroads into the Chinese market through several joint ventures.

A World Leader in Packaged Consumer Goods, the 1990s

The success of Kraft and Miller, coupled with Morris's still highly profitable tobacco market, has made Morris the world's largest producer and marketer—as well as the largest U.S. exporter—of packaged consumer goods. In fact, by the early 1990s substantially more than half of the company's revenue was generated by non-tobacco products. One of the contributors was Miller Brewing's $3.5 billion in sales. Retaining its spot as the second-largest competitor in its field, Miller has managed to successfully hold its market share in the face of a changing beer market and a 100 percent increase in the beer tax levied by the U.S. government in 1991. The rise in the number of small-scale "craft" breweries and changing demographics caused a slump in the beer market nationwide; along with number-one ranked Anheuser-Busch and number three-ranked Coors, Miller responded by entering the microbrewery market with its Red Dog and Icehouse brands, as well as by purchasing shares in small breweries in Maine and Texas. Despite heavily marketing its "lite" beers to the Baby Boomer market, Miller's 3rd quarter 1996 income fell 1.7 percent and the company responded by cutting operating costs.

By the close of 1995 Morris's portfolio of brands included 68 that reported sales of over $100 million. Of those 68, six non-tobacco products—Kraft, Miller, Jacobs, Oscar Mayer, Maxwell House, and Post—passed the $1 billion mark. New marketing efforts included revised Marlboro and Virginia Slims merchandise catalogs and a sweepstakes for trips on the "Marlboro Unlimited," a luxury train scheduled to tour Marlboro country in 1998. Although the company's leadership continued to reject plans to divest Morris of its tobacco holdings, because of such successful diversification efforts, Morris planned to continue using the extraordinary cash flow generated by its domestic tobacco sales to finance further moves into the food industry, where the relatively low rate of return can be eventually compensated by means of sheer size.

Principal Subsidiaries

Philip Morris U.S.A.; Philip Morris International Inc.; Kraft Foods, Inc.; Kraft Canada Inc.; Kraft Foods International, Inc.; Miller Brewing Company; Philip Morris Capital Corporation; Mission Viejo Company.

Further Reading

"Philip Morris & Co.," *Fortune*, March 1936.
"Philip Morris Comeback," *Fortune*, October 1949.
Nulty, Peter, "Living with the Limits of Marlboro Magic," *Fortune*, March 18, 1985.
"Philip Morris to Put Its Ad Money Where Its Marlboro Price Cuts Are," *Wall Street Journal*, April 6, 1993.
"Philip Morris Proposes Curbs on Sales to Kids," *Wall Street Journal*, May 16, 1996.

—Jonathan Martin
—updated by Pamela L. Shelton

Physio-Control International Corp.

11811 Willows Road N.E.
Redmond, Washington 98052
U.S.A.
(206) 867-4000
Fax: (206) 885-6507

Public company:
Incorporated: 1955 as Physio-Control Co.
Employees: 905
Sales: $173.16 million (1996)
Stock Exchanges: NASDAQ
SICs: 3845 Electromedical Apparatus; 7372 Prepackaged
    Software

Physio-Control International Corp. is the world's leading manufacturer of external defibrillators, medical devices that apply an electrical shock to victims of sudden cardiac arrest or ventricular fibrillation, in which the heart begins to flutter or beat irregularly, to restore a normal heart rhythm.

Physio-Control defibrillators account for half of all those sold to hospitals in the United States. In addition, the company has a commanding 85 percent to 90 percent share of the advanced life support market in the United States, consisting primarily of paramedic and fire-rescue vehicles, and was an early leader in the developing "first-responder" market for automatic external defibrillators (AEDs). AEDs were designed to be used by police officers, firefighters, security guards, and others with limited medical training who often arrive first at the scene of an emergency.

Physio-Control, which went public in 1995 after being sold to an investment group by Eli Lily & Co. the year before, had sales of $173.16 million for fiscal 1996. The company, whose products are sold in 70 countries, was traded on the NASDAQ exchange under the symbol PHYS.

The 1950s–60s and Dr. Karl Edmark

Dr. Karl William Edmark (1924–94) was in his last year of residency at Lahey Clinic in Boston in 1954 when he built his first electronic monitor, a boxy-looking device with a light that flashed every time a patient's heart beat and set off an alarm if the beat faltered during surgery. He patented the device, which he called a Heartbeat Indicator, and in 1955, set up a corporation, the Physio-Control Co., to handle any income from his invention.

Later that year, Edmark moved to Seattle, where he became one of the city's leading cardiovascular surgeons, performing the first open-heart surgery at Swedish Hospital and, later, establishing the Cardiovascular Associates Laboratory at Providence Hospital. He also continued to experiment with electronics, developing the Pressure Pulsometer, which monitored a patient's blood pressure during surgery.

In 1961, Edmark unveiled a defibrillator that operated on direct current. When a heart goes into fibrillation, it begins to flutter and is unable to pump blood through the body. Defibrillators administer an electrical shock, which momentarily stuns the heart and allows it to return to a regular heartbeat. Until Edmark introduced his DC Pulse Defibrillator, medical defibrillators used AC, or alternating current, which caused patients to spasm violently because of the high voltage. The DC defibrillator allowed surgeons to administer a more-controlled, low-voltage shock that restored the heartbeat without causing additional trauma.

Edmark licensed manufacturing and distribution rights to the DC Pulse Defibrillator and the Pressure Pulsometer to American Optical, one of the first big companies to enter the electronic medical-instruments industry. Over the next few years, Physio-Control, which had been bankrolled by Edmark and a few personal friends, received about $10,000 annually in royalties, which was plowed back into research.

Then in 1965, American Optical announced that it had refined Edmark's inventions to the point where it no longer felt it needed a licensing agreement with Physio-Control to manufacture and sell the devices. Without a source of revenue, Edmark faced a decision: either he could shut down Physio-Control or begin running it as a business instead of a research laboratory. He chose the later. He also asked W. Hunter Simpson, then Northwest district manager for IBM Corp. in Seattle, if he was interested in becoming Physio-Control's first full-time president.

Simpson had known Edmark since 1963, when he had hired the cardiologist as a consultant. At the time, IBM, which designed the first heart-lung machine for the Mayo Clinic, had been interested in further exploring the medical instruments industry. Although it meant giving up a secure position and taking a cut in pay, Simpson accepted Edmark's offer, starting his new job in January 1966.

A graduate of the School of Business at the University of Washington, who also had studied pre-med, Simpson spent his first year at Physio-Control raising $300,000 in venture capital, attracting local investors such as Bagley Wright, whose company, Pentagram Corp., built the Space Needle for the Seattle World's Fair. He also changed the name of the company to Physio-Control Corporation, and more narrowly defined the company's market niche. According to Harriet and Terry King in *The Team*, a book published by Physio-Control detailing its first 25 years, Simpson told the company's five employees, "Our immediate goal is to install coronary care systems in Puget Sound hospitals and smother them with love, attention and service. After that, when the time is right, we can think about marketing nationally."

Lifepak/33, 1968

It did not take long. Physio-Control manufactured its 100th patient monitor and defibrillator in the fall of 1967, and reported revenues that year of more than $500,000. Financially, Physio-Control was near the break-even point, and Simpson told stockholders at the annual meeting in the spring of 1968, "The name of the game is now marketing." About the same time, Physio-Control learned that Zenith Corp. was developing a bulky—but portable—56-pound monitor/defibrillator. Simpson faced the challenge head-on, assigning Stanley Seiffert, Physio-Control's manager of technical operations, the task of designing a portable monitor-defibrillator that would be more than 20 pounds lighter. Physio-Control named the yet-to-be-built device the Lifepak/33.

Physio-Control introduced the Lifepak/33—which ended up weighing 34 pounds—at the annual American Heart Association meeting in November 1968, but not without some last-minute difficulty. The night before the show opened, someone tried to smash two of the units. The devices were also left on, draining the batteries. But if a competitor was behind the vandalism, as many believed at the time, the publicity surrounding the "sabotage" made the Lifepak/33 the star of the show.

Soon afterwards, Physio-Control was able to raise another $600,000 in venture capital, and commercial production of the Lifepak/33 began in February 1969. The 15th and 45th units were sold to the U.S. Navy, which installed them aboard Air Force One and Air Force Two, the aircraft assigned to carry the president and vice president of the United States. That same year, Jacksonville, Florida, became the first city to install portable defibrillators in all 10 of its fire department emergency vehicles. Physio-Control closed out its fiscal year, at the end of September 1969, with more than $1 million in sales for the first time, although still posting a loss for the year of $35,000 because of production start-up costs.

Physio-Control went public in 1971, selling 20,000 shares of stock at $25 each. All but 7,000 shares were purchased by original investors in the company. Physio-Control also launched a national advertising program built around the success of innovative Seattle's Medic 1 program, which equipped emergency vehicles with sophisticated medical equipment, including a Lifepak/33. Sales increased that year to $2.4 million, with net earnings of $266,000.

Two years later, in 1973, Physio-Control introduced the Lifepak 3, a third generation of its portable external defibrillator. The company also began construction of a $2 million headquarters and research center on 11 acres overlooking the Sammamish River in rural Redmond, Washington, later to become the home of Microsoft Corp. In 1974, Physio-Control added the Lifepak 4, which featured an electrocardiogram strip-chart recorder to provide a permanent record of a patient's heartbeat, to its growing family of portable Lifepak defibrillators. Revenues that year topped $10 million, and Physio-Control posted earnings of $1.05 million.

For several years, Physio-Control products had been distributed primarily by Minneapolis-based Medtronic, Inc. But in 1975, inventory began to accumulate in Medtronic's warehouses. Physio-Control was worried that Medtronic eventually would be forced to slash prices on more than $5 million worth of defibrillators and dialysis machines, seriously upsetting the company's long-term marketing plans, When Medtronic suggested that it might be interested in acquiring the much smaller Physio-Control, Simpson turned the offer around. Betting that he would be able to sell the stockpiled inventory in an orderly manner—and finance the acquisition with the proceeds—Simpson offered instead to purchase Medtronic's instrument-sales division. The gamble paid off with Physio-Control posting records sales that year of $12.9 million, although earnings were down.

Meanwhile, the company was also facing another challenge. Physio-Control learned that a United Kingdom company was developing a defibrillator designed specifically to be used by paramedics in the fast-growing emergency medical market. The small, portable units were expected to weigh half as much as Physio-Control's newest model, the Lifepak 4. John Gallagher, then vice president of engineering at Physio-Control, was assigned the task of pulling together a design team to rebuff the challenge with a radically different Lifepak 5.

Initially, the design team considered packing the components of the defibrillator into a bright orange belt that could be worn by the paramedics. But feedback from Seattle's Medic 1 staff indicated that was unworkable because the bulky belt design would interfere with wearing seat belts in the emergency-response van. Physio-Control eventually settled on a more conventional design, and the Lifepak 5—weighing just 18 pounds—was introduced at the annual meeting of the American College of Cardiology in February 1976.

Physio-Control's sales that year rose by more than 20 percent, to $15.7 million, although net income, still affected by the Medtronic acquisition and inventory glut, remained below $1 million. The following year, 1977, sales topped $21 million and net income almost doubled to $1.7 million. Physio-Control, which received a Presidential "E" Award from the U.S. Department of Commerce, had become the largest manufacturer of defibrillator/monitors in the world, exporting medical devices to 33 countries.

Acquisition by Eli Lilly, 1980

In 1979, Physio-Control acquired Biomega Corp., in Gainesville, Florida, which made semi-automatic blood-pressure monitors for use in emergency vehicles. The company also formed a joint venture with Valleylab Inc. in Boulder, Colorado, to develop and market pacemakers and other implantable medical devices. Revenues continued to grow, surpassing $41 million, while net income that year was more than $3.9 million. Physio-Control had also grown to more than 700 employees.

In addition, the company had begun attracting considerable interest from much larger corporations looking to expand their medical-device divisions. In early 1980, Physio-Control announced that it was being acquired by pharmaceutical giant Eli Lilly & Co. in a stock deal worth about $145 million, returning $170,000 for every $1,000 the original investors had put into the company in 1966. At Physio-Control's annual meeting, Hunter told shareholders, "The fit is quite magnificent, almost designed, because of the attitudes and philosophies of the two companies." In prescient fashion, Simpson also noted, "The stability of size (offered by Eli Lilly) is also important. I don't care how good a company is in this day and age, there is always the possibility of recall (of a product). It could be disastrous for a small company."

In 1985, Physio-Control introduced the world's first automatic external defibrillator. The Lifepak 300, designed for use by police, firefighters, security guards, and other "first responders," was a battery-powered defibrillator about the size of a shoe box and weighing just six pounds. The computer-controlled defibrillator automatically interpreted a victim's heartbeat and determined if a defibrillating shock was indicated. The device also was designed not to allow a shock to be administered if it was not indicated.

The same year, Physio-Control, which had pioneered profit-sharing and the 10-hour, four-day work week for its employees, was included in an annual listing of "The 100 best companies to work for in America." Simpson also retired at the end of 1985,

ending 20 years at the helm of Physio-Control. He was succeeded as president and chief executive by Gilbert W. Anderson, then 57, Physio-Control's executive vice president. A graduate of the University of Washington, Anderson previously had been chief executive at Stetson-Ross, a manufacturer of heavy equipment and electronics products.

Sales of the Lifepak 300—despite its innovative design—were sluggish until 1988, when researchers from the University of Washington published a report in the *Journal of the American Medical Association* that documented in-flight deaths of airline passengers and called for airlines to carry automatic defibrillators on board. The university study—funded by Physio-Control, the Laerdal Medical Group, a Swedish competitor, and the National Center for Health Services Research, a federal agency—found that 60 percent of nearly 600 in-flight deaths reported during the period, were related to heart attacks. The American Heart Association later endorsed the study in calling for automatic defibrillators to be carried aboard commercial passenger flights. In 1990, Virgin Atlantic Airways became the first airline to carry automatic defibrillators aboard its overseas flights, purchasing them from Physio-Control.

FDA Shutdown in 1992

In 1992, Physio-Control voluntarily shut down production of its defibrillators and patient monitors after a review by the U.S. Food and Drug Administration found the company had failed to follow "good manufacturing practices," including inadequate failure investigations, not properly inspecting critical components of its products, and failing to adequately document manufacturing and testing procedures in writing.

Although the FDA never claimed that patients had been harmed by malfunctions of the medical equipment, and no recalls were ordered, Physio-Control signed a consent decree outlining steps it would take before resuming production. Richard O. Martin, former vice president of business development who had succeeded Anderson as president and chief executive in 1991, later told the *Puget Sound Business Journal* that Physio-Control "truly, fundamentally believed" that it was in compliance with all FDA requirements. He blamed the sanctions on political pressure then being brought to bear on the FDA to become more forceful in its interpretation of the rules.

In a newspaper column, Martin would later write, "Perhaps the FDA needed to flex some muscle; the agency's reputation was besmirched due to the controversy over its generic drug scandal, the recall of the Dalkon shield IUD, and silicone gel breast implants. If that is the case, then it seems to me the FDA is guilty of shooting itself in the foot. Our government is not only crippling the medical community but maiming the entrepreneurial companies that are the backbone of American business."

Whatever the reason for the FDA's action, the shutdown contributed to the first-ever loss reported by Eli Lilly, for the third quarter of 1992. Eli Lilly did not disclose how much of its $268 million loss stemmed from the problems at Physio-Control, which kept all 1,000 employees on the payroll. But the company's Medical Devices and Diagnostics Division, which included Physio-Control, took a pretax charge of $180 million "responding to regulatory initiatives, including actions to strengthen . . . good manufacturing practices and procedures.'' Sales at Physio-Control fell from a high of $158 million in 1991 to less than $80 million in 1992.

The shutdown, which only affected production for domestic sales, also lasted much longer than anyone expected. Physio-Control, which predicted it would resume full production within six months, finally was allowed to resume production of the Lifepak 10, an in-field model representing about 40 percent of the company's pre-shutdown revenues, 12 months later. The company was not allowed to resume full production of all lines until June 1994, 753 days after the shutdown began.

By then, Eli Lilly & Co. had pumped an estimated $140 million into Physio-Control to keep it going. Simpson, then retired, told the *Journal American,* ''Physio is a precious thing, and if it hadn't been for Lilly, it would have disappeared a year ago.'' Although Eli Lilly said it was unrelated to the difficulties at Physio-Control, the pharmaceutical company also announced at the start of the year that it would sell three of the companies in its medical devices division, including Physio-Control, and spin off the others in a public offering. In July, Physio-Control was sold to Bain Capital Corp., a Boston investment group, for $23.3 million. Steve Pagliuca, managing director at Bain Capital, was named chairman of Physio-Control.

Recovery and Outlook

Despite the long shutdown, Physio-Control recovered quickly because of its strong market presence. During the shutdown, the company had developed a backlog of more than $70 million in orders from hospitals and emergency medical services. Incredibly, the company eventually filled more than 80 percent of those orders. Martin told the *Puget Sound Business Journal,* ''That, more than anything else, speaks to what the customer thought of Physio-Control. People actually waited until they could get the Physio product.''

In December 1995, less than 18 months after buying Physio-Control, Bain Capital sold 90 percent of the company in an initial public offering for $172 million. That year, the company reported sales of $148.7 million, nearly 95 percent of its pre-shutdown sales. In 1996, sales reached a record high $173.16 million.

Capping its comeback, in 1996 Physio-Control was named one of the best manufacturing facilities in the United States by *Industry Week,* which noted that the company's portable defibrillators ''have to be particularly rugged to withstand the harsh treatment they are often subjected to in the field. In product demonstrations (sales representatives) have been known to pick up the instruments and heave them onto the floor as if they were bowling balls—a maneuver known as 'the salesmen's toss.' As in the old Timex watch commercials, they then proceed to show that the products still work.''

In 1996, Physio-Control also received FDA approval to market the Lifepak 500, a lightweight, automatic external defibrillator (AED) designed for use by ''first responders,'' who often arrive first at the scene of an accident or medical emergency. The battery-operated, computer-controlled Lifepak 500, which sold for less than $4,000, automatically analyzed a victim's heartbeat and indicated, through voice prompts and visual readouts, whether a defibrillating shock was necessary. The shock was applied by pushing a button.

One of Physio-Control's competitors in the first-responder market was Heartstream Inc., a company formed in 1992 by five former Physio-Control employees, which also introduced a lightweight AED in 1996. Physio-Control sued Heartstream in 1995, alleging the theft of trade secrets, and Heartstream countersued, alleging unfair business practices. The lawsuits were still pending in early 1997. Other competitors in the emerging market included Zoll Medical, SurVivaLink, and Laerdal Medical.

Analysts indicated there was an enormous, potential market for AEDs, including sports stadia, high-rise office buildings, doctors' offices, public swimming pools and beaches, health clubs, retirement homes, and community centers. An estimated half million Americans suffer sudden cardiac arrest every year and only about 5 percent survive, in part because defibrillation needs to be administered within the first 10 minutes to be most effective. In the mid-1990s, the American Heart Association, the American College of Cardiology, and the International Association of Fire Chiefs were among the organizations calling for widespread access to early defibrillation. At Physio-Control, Martin, who was elected chairman in 1997, liked to say that one day AEDs would be as common as fire extinguishers.

Further Reading

Andrews, Paul, and Polly Lane, ''Physio-Control Halts Output; Company Stands by Reliability Record,'' *Seattle Times,* July 8, 1992, p. C8.
Buck, Richard, ''Physio-Control Sold to Boston Company,'' *Seattle Times,* July 22, 1994, p. F1.
''FDA: Physio's Production Still Has Problems,'' *Seattle Times,* September 15, 1993, p. D3.
Grunbaum, Rami, ''Physio-Control Pushes to Revive Itself,'' *Puget Sound Business Journal,* October 23, 1992, p. 1.
Grunbaum, Rami, ''Vital Signs Turn Robust for Physio-Control,'' *Puget Sound Business Journal,* March 8, 1996, p. 3A.
Heberlein, Greg, ''Physio in Second Incarnation as Public Company,'' *Seattle Times,* December 12, 1995, p. C1.
''His Turn: An Interview with Dick Martin,'' *Byline,* August 1993, p. 1.
Liebman, Larry, ''Eastside Firms Get Jump on Jump-Starting Hearts,'' *Puget Sound Business Journal,* October 24, 1988, p. 20.
Sheridan, John H., ''America's Best Plants: Physio-Control Corp.,'' *Industry Week,* October 21, 1996, p. 46.
Swenson, John, ''Getting on a First-Name Basis with Redmond's Physio-Control,'' *Journal American,* April 5, 1992, p. D1.
Williams, Scott, ''Lilly Plans to Sell Physio-Control,'' *Seattle Times,* Jan. 18, 1994, p. D1.
Williams, Scott, ''Physio-Control Aims to Boost Staff, Regain Market Share,'' *Seattle Times,* May 20, 1993, p. D1.
——, ''Physio-Control Faces an Uncertain Future: Production Resumes, but Parent May Decide to Sell Redmond Firm,'' *Seattle Times,* January 7, 1994, p. E1.

—Dean Boyer

Planet Hollywood International, Inc.

Suite 600
7380 Sand Lake Road
Orlando, Florida 32819
U.S.A.
(407) 363-7827
Fax: (407) 363-4862

Public Company
Incorporated: 1991
Employees: 6,500
Sales: $270.6 million (1995)
Stock Exchanges: NASDAQ
SICs: 5812 Eating Places; 5399 Miscellaneous
    Merchandise Stores; 6794 Patent Owners and Lessors

Planet Hollywood International, Inc. is the controlling body for a number of different entertainment-based theme restaurants located throughout the world. The company's name reflects its most well-known venture, a chain of approximately 50 "Planet Hollywood" restaurants that offer patrons a chance to dine in the midst of various film and television props and memorabilia. Another restaurant concept controlled by Planet Hollywood International is the more recent "Official All Star Cafe" chain, which centers on professional sports and follows a sports-bar theme. The company also runs the "Marvel Mania" and "Chefs of the World" restaurants. A unique aspect of most Planet Hollywood International ventures is that the investors and owners are typically celebrities, many of whom actually frequent the restaurants and mingle with the customers.

Theme Restaurant Concept Originates in 1972

The first Planet Hollywood restaurant opened in New York City in 1991, but the events leading up to its inception can be traced back almost 20 years earlier. In 1972, a young man by the name of Robert Earl opened a dinner-theater in London called "The Beefeater," which offered customers (mainly tourists) a medieval-themed dining experience. Earl, who had graduated with a degree in hotel and restaurant management from the University of Surrey, possessed a talent for creating entertain-ment-based restaurant concepts that drew large numbers of customers. He soon developed The Beefeater into a popular local success, which prompted him to open other similar restaurant concepts nearby. In the late-1970s, he created "Talk of London," "Shakespeare's Tavern," and "The Cockney Club," all of which remain operational today.

Although successful in London, Earl saw greater growth potential in the American market, and therefore came to the U.S. in the early-1980s to sell his concepts to the developers of a then-new Disney World attraction called Epcot Center. The deal fell through, but Earl decided to stay in Florida anyway and try his luck in the Orlando restaurant business. He opened a number of theme-restaurants using medieval and Wild West ideas, nurturing his new restaurant group until it was sold to a larger holding company in the mid-1980s.

After changing hands again numerous times, his enterprise landed in the lap of Mecca Leisure, who had just purchased rights to Hard Rock International's eastern region. Hard Rock International was the controlling body for the "Hard Rock Cafe" chain of music-industry-based theme restaurants. In 1989, Mecca appointed Earl as the new chief executive of their portion of the Hard Rock operation, and put him in charge of expanding the chain in the eastern United States.

Within two years, Earl had helped the eastern-region Hard Rock Cafe chain grow from 7 units to 20. It was during that time that Earl met film producer Keith Barish, who would soon become his business partner and the cofounder of Planet Hollywood International, Inc. Earl and Barish shared a belief that music, movies, and sports were capable of transcending all barriers, language and otherwise, between the people of the world. The two men decided to capitalize on the worldwide appeal of the film and television entertainment industry by opening a restaurant based on that theme. Dubbing their creation "Planet Hollywood," Earl and Barish opened the restaurant in New York City in late 1991.

Quick Success in the Early 1990s

Planet Hollywood was immediately successful, drawing crowds that often lined up outside the restaurant for hours in order to get tables. Part of the restaurant's appeal lay in its museum-like quality; a multitude of real film and television costumes, props, and memorabilia made up its decor. The rest of the attraction was attributed to a genius marketing strategy used by the restaurant's founders. They asked celebrities such as Arnold Schwarzenegger, Sylvester Stallone, Bruce Willis, Demi Moore, and Whoopi Goldberg to act as the restaurant's investor/owners. Every once in a while, these celebrities would stop by "their restaurant" to check in and mingle briefly with their fans. Although this was a somewhat rare occurrence, customers still flocked to the restaurant in hopes that they would be one of the lucky few to dine with the stars.

A year after launching Planet Hollywood, Earl left behind his post at Hard Rock and also severed ties to his original theme-restaurant group in Orlando. He and Barish began planning the worldwide introduction of additional Planet Hollywood restaurants, and started by recruiting more celebrity investors for the new locations. Climbing on board were film actors Don Johnson and then-wife Melanie Griffith, director John Hughes, comedienne Roseanne, and actors Tom Arnold, Wesley Snipes, and Danny Glover. By mid-1993, Planet Hollywood International had opened new restaurants in London and southern California, and was completing the construction of a fourth unit in Chicago.

New York City architect David Rockwell was hired by Earl and Barish to design the new units, each of which typically seated over 200 people and contained film props and floor layouts that were unique to their locations. Different items on display throughout the chain included Dorothy's dress from "The Wizard of Oz," the pottery wheel used by Demi Moore and Patrick Swayze in "Ghost," a replica of the castle from "Dracula," the Batmobile, the Flintstone buggy, and a plastic model of the meat slab that was pulverized by Stallone in the film "Rocky." Customers were also treated to celebrity hand print walls and big-screen televisions which played promotional clips for upcoming movies.

Meanwhile, a Hard Rock International executive by the name of Peter Morton filed suit against Earl and Planet Hollywood, alleging that Earl had engaged in the appropriation of trade secrets. Morton, a cofounder of Hard Rock International and the CEO of its western region, believed that Earl's Planet Hollywood chain was a ripoff of the Hard Rock concept. Earl nonchalantly dismissed the charges, however, and the case against Planet Hollywood never amounted to much in court. Furthermore, Morton's complaint did little to deter Planet Hollywood from expanding further, nor did it curb the public's desire to patronize the new and rapidly blossoming chain. Soon Planet Hollywood was known as a worldwide leader in the theme restaurant business.

By the end of 1993, Planet Hollywood had not only opened two new restaurants in Washington, D.C., and Cancun, Mexico, but it had also signed leases for 5 new units in Phoenix, New Orleans, Aspen, Maui, and Minneapolis's "Mall of America" (the largest shopping mall in the United States). Each opening was a gala event, drawing enormous crowds of people to catch a glimpse of the many media personalities who made appearances and celebrated the new successes. But the true test of a new location occurred the day after the "official" opening, at which time a restaurant actually opened its doors to the general public. Without fail, each new Planet Hollywood passed these "tests"

with ease, and in the first year of operation most were generating revenues of almost $15 million per unit.

A strong asset of the Planet Hollywood concept was that each unit sold licensed Planet Hollywood merchandise in addition to serving food and drinks. Items of all kinds were sold, from key rings and T-shirts, to sweatshirts, watches, and leather coats. Sales of this merchandise helped boost Planet Hollywood's profit margins considerably above those achieved at other restaurants that relied solely on food items to bring in profits. Merchandise became so popular that within a few years, the company began to open separate retail stores called "Planet Hollywood Superstores," a move which even further increased yearly profits.

The End of the Century and Beyond

In 1994, Planet Hollywood continued its aggressive expansion program, and units continued to open worldwide. The company also began developing additional theme-restaurant ideas, including the concept for the Official All Star Cafe. Acknowledging the success that Planet Hollywood had achieved from drawing upon the public's interest in celebrity life, Earl and Barish decided that the Official All Star Cafe would be the perfect sports-based equivalent. They began recruiting professional sports figures to invest in the concept, drawing in people such as hockey great Wayne Gretzky, football icon Joe Montana, and basketball superstar Shaquille O'Neal. Plans for the new restaurants included a menu of "stadium cuisine" supplemented by home cooking, and sales of professional sports merchandise and souvenirs.

Also in 1994, the company opened what would soon become its highest-grossing Planet Hollywood unit, in Las Vegas. Unlike most previous units, which seated approximately 250 people, the Las Vegas restaurant was designed to seat 500 and was planned by Rockwell so that there would be no "bad" seats. The unit's opening rivaled a sporting event or the Academy Awards in magnitude, in that it drew a crowd of over ten thousand people who packed themselves into stadium-like bleachers nearby to witness the stars' arrivals at the event. Even former President and First Lady George and Barbara Bush were on hand to celebrate. Later that year another 500-seater was opened in Orlando's Disney World, which gave Earl and Barish ownership of the two highest-grossing restaurants in the United States.

At that point, Planet Hollywood was composed of 18 units around the world, and the company was projecting the addition of 17 more during 1995. The Planet Hollywood chain was expanding almost on its own, so Earl decided to begin focusing his attention and energy on other avenues of growth while the chain took care of itself. In August 1995, ground was broken in New York City nearby the original Planet Hollywood, and construction of the first Official All Star Cafe began. Meanwhile, plans were in the works to develop a theme-restaurant chain based on characters from the Marvel Comics series. Also, television game-show producer King World began working with Roseanne Barr's production company on a "Planet Hollywood Squares" television game show, which was to be a revival of the original "Hollywood Squares" from decades past with a new Planet Hollywood twist.

With Planet Hollywood quickly becoming a household name, the company decided to go public in 1996. Not only was stock offered to the public, but the company also convinced MBNA to issue Planet Hollywood VISA credit cards, which gave cardholders priority seating at the restaurants. A joint venture with ITT Corporation was also formed to develop Planet Hollywood casinos in Las Vegas and Atlantic City in the future. Furthermore, Marvel Entertainment Group, Inc. and Planet Hollywood International decided to move ahead with the comic book character-based restaurant concept, calling it ''Marvel Mania.'' Ideas for a new concept called ''Chefs of the World,'' which was to feature a ''star-studded'' culinary staff, also began to arise.

Some began to wonder whether Planet Hollywood was spreading its resources too thin, and speculations surfaced as to whether the company would be able to continue the growth trend that it had been experiencing for the past five years. Earl maintained ambitious goals to keep the company expanding by 30 to 40 percent each year, in both the number of restaurant locations and in annual revenues. Criticisms of that plan, however, centered on the idea that the more units that were opened, the less unique a customer's experience in patronizing the restaurant chain, which could lead to a drop in sales. Furthermore, theme restaurants were popping up all over the country, providing Earl and Barish with intense competition. The Harley-Davidson Cafe was gaining popularity, as were other concepts such as Robert DeNiro's Tribeca Grill, the Country Star chain (backed by Wynonna Judd, Vince Gill, and Reba McEntire), and the Thunder Roadhouse (backed by Dennis Hopper, Dwight Yoakam, and Peter Fonda).

But Planet Hollywood and the Official All Star Cafe did possess one major advantage over their competition, which was the celebrity endorsement received through stars' ownership and investment in the chains. Many customers thus viewed these restaurants as the ''originals.'' As for continued growth potential, Earl dismissed skepticism with easy confidence. Given that in only 5 years the company had grown from one $3.5 million restaurant in New York to an almost $300 million operation with approximately 50 units spread throughout the world, it seemed to be a safe bet that Planet Hollywood possessed the ability to continue the trend of success into the coming century.

Principal Operating Units

Planet Hollywood Restaurants; Official All Star Cafe; Marvel Mania; Chefs of the World.

Further Reading

Ball, Aimee Lee, ''Mr. Universe,'' *New York,* July 15, 1991, p. 38.

Greenberg, Herb, ''Earth to Planet Hollywood,'' *Fortune,* December 23, 1996.

Guttman, Monika, ''Why the Stars Orbit Planet Hollywood: With Meteoric Growth, the Eateries May Go Public,'' *U.S. News & World Report,* November 27, 1995, p. 60.

Hayes, Jack, ''Robert Earl: The King of Planet Hollywood Promises the Stars—and He Delivers,'' *Nation's Restaurant News,* October 9, 1995, p. 164.

Kapner, Suzanne, '' 'Starry' Vegas Night Shines on New Planet,'' *Nation's Restaurant News,* August 8, 1994, p. 7.

Levine, Joshua, ''Hamburgers and Tennis Socks,'' *Forbes,* November 20, 1995, p. 184.

Martin, Richard, ''Hard Rock Hits Planet Hollywood with Copycat Suit,'' *Nation's Restaurant News,* March 16, 1992, p. 3.

McClellan, Steve, ''King World Developing 'Planet Hollywood Squares,' '' *Broadcasting & Cable,* September 25, 1995, p. 11.

Miracle, Barbara, ''Beyond Planet Hollywood,'' *Florida Trend,* December 1993, p. 10.

Papiernik, Richard L., ''All Quiet on the Hollywood Front After 'Picture Perfect' IPO,'' *Nation's Restaurant News,* May 13, 1996, p. 11.

''Planet Hollywood, Marvel Comics Team for Themer,'' *Nation's Restaurant News,* June 6, 1994, p. 2.

Prewitt, Milford, ''Robert Earl: CEO Planet Hollywood Inc., Orlando, Florida,'' *Nation's Restaurant News,* January 1995, p. 54.

Selinger, Iris Cohen, ''Lights! Camera! But Can We Get a Table?'' *Advertising Age,* April 17, 1995, p. 48.

Walkup, Carolyn, ''Planet Hollywood Gears to Launch Unit in Chicago,'' *Nation's Restaurant News,* July 15, 1993, p. 94.

—Laura E. Whiteley

Playboy Enterprises, Inc.

680 N. Lake Shore Drive
Chicago, Illinois 60611
U.S.A.
(312) 751-8000
Fax: (312) 751-2818
Web site: http://www.playboy.com

Public Company
Incorporated: 1953
Employees: 583
Sales: $247.2 million (1995)
Stock Exchanges: New York
SICs: 2721 Periodicals Publishing & Printing; 4841
   Cable & Other Pay Television Services; 6794 Patent
   Owners and Lessors

Playboy Enterprises, Inc. is an international powerhouse in the publishing, entertainment, and licensing industries. The company was established through the publication of *Playboy* magazine in 1953, and became known throughout the world for its centerfold pictures of well-built nude women. During the 1990s, however, the company transformed itself into a diverse operation which included pay-per-view television, weekly TV programming, movies, videos and video catalogs, a cable TV network, and the marketing and selling of name-brand retail products (including clothing, liquor, sound systems, and condoms). In spite of this diversification strategy, the company has always been and will continue to be identified with *Playboy* magazine which is published in an American edition and 16 foreign editions. Well down from its peak circulation during the late 1960s and early 1970s, the company's flagship publication still has the highest circulation among men's magazines with approximately 3 million readers.

Born in the 1950s

Hugh Hefner, the founder of the "*Playboy* empire," was born in 1927 in Chicago, Illinois. Raised in the strict religious tradition of German-Swedish Protestantism, Hefner and his younger brother were forbidden to drink, smoke, swear, and, particularly distressing to the two boys, attend movies on Sunday. Hefner's father, an accountant for an aluminum company, was almost never home, and his mother, an austere and imposing women, was the dominant personality in raising the children. Within such a family setting sex was regarded as horrid, something never to be discussed or even mentioned. Young Hugh developed into an introverted young man, escaping into a fantasy world of writing, drawing cartoons, and collecting butterflies.

Upon graduating from high school in 1944, Hefner served as a clerk in military installations throughout the United States for the remainder of World War II, and then was discharged in the summer of 1946. He followed his high school sweetheart, Millie Williams, to the University of Illinois at Champaign-Urbana, and attended classes as a psychology major, and gained renown as a contributor of cartoons to the campus humor magazine. After graduating in 1949, Hefner married Millie, moved back to Chicago and, in order to support his family, worked in the personnel department of a cartoon manufacturing company. Hating the job, Hefner decided to quit and attend classes in psychology at Northwestern University. He soon dropped out, however, and took a position as a copywriter in the advertising department of *Esquire* magazine. When his boss refused to give him a five dollar raise, Hefner suddenly quit his job. In 1952, Hefner found himself without steady employment. At the same time, his marriage to Millie, which was rocky from the beginning, fell apart.

Although Hefner hated his job at *Esquire,* it was while working at the publication's office in Chicago that he came up with his idea for a new product. *Esquire* had been successful in creating an image of what it meant to be an urbane young man, sophisticated and worldly, and interested in fancy sports cars, good food, expensive clothing, exotic wine, hi-fi equipment, and women. Hefner grabbed this idea and decided to take the formula one step further—by including photographed female nudes in the magazine. He approached a freelance art director, Art Paul, and asked him to help design his magazine in exchange for private shares of stock in the product. Pawning his

---

Company Perspectives:

Playboy *magazine and the Company's powerful brand have been fixtures in popular culture for more than four decades. As we approach the millenium, emerging communications technologies such as DTH, the Internet and digital compression will provide us with even more exciting new opportunities for growth, both domestically and in new overseas markets. Playboy will continue to represent a high-quality adult lifestyle. We look to the future with confidence that the power of the Playboy brand will drive the continued profitable worldwide expansion of our entertainment empire.*

---

possessions to support himself, Hefner worked odd jobs during the daytime. But through the evenings of 1952, with Paul's help, Hefner assembled the first issue of *Playboy* magazine on his kitchen table in a small Chicago apartment. Hefner purchased the famous nude calendar picture of Marilyn Monroe for $200 from the calendar company, inserted some risque cartoons and jokes of his own, rounded up a few literary pieces that had previously been published in other magazines, and in November 1953 went to press. With $600 of his own money, and $10,000 raised through the sale of private stock to friends and supporters, Hefner published the first issue of *Playboy* magazine. It carried no date, since Hefner didn't know when he'd have the money to publish a second issue, or even if there would be one.

The bold and brash new publication sold 55,000 copies at 50 cents apiece, and Hefner was on his way to establishing the Playboy empire. By the publication of the fourth issue, Hefner had made enough money to rent an office in downtown Chicago and begin hiring a staff. Still, he retained firm control of all aspects of the magazine's publication. Unknown to most people, however, was the initial difficulty Hefner had in convincing women to strip for his cameras. In fact, at one point Hefner was unable to find any women who wanted to pose nude for his magazine. When an attractive female subscription manager at the magazine came to ask him for an addressograph machine, Hefner responded that she could have her machine if she would pose as the Playmate of the Month. The beautiful subscription manager agreed, and word got around that the photo sessions were conducted with respect, good humor, and consummate professionalism. From that time onward Hefner was deluged with photos from women working at the Playboy office in Chicago and from models throughout the United States.

Growth During the 1960s

By 1960, Hefner had created one of the most successful publishing empires in the United States: circulation had surpassed the one million mark, and advertising revenues had skyrocketed to $2.3 million. Buoyed by his achievement, in the early 1960s Hefner decided to open what he called Playboy Clubs, where any tired businessman could eat good food, drink, and be entertained, all the while being waited on by Playboy ''Bunnies,'' as he called the waitresses and hostesses who wore nothing more than rabbit ears and a one-piece corset with a cottontail fixed to the bottom. Riding on the wave of the sexual

revolution of the 1960s, Hefner opened numerous Playboy Clubs across the United States. At the same time, he began to diversify into more standard clubs, casinos, and resorts. In Chicago, Hefner purchased the old Knickerbocker Hotel and transformed it into the posh and elegant Playboy Towers. Beginning in 1965, Hefner invested over $55 million to develop resort hotels in Jamaica, Miami, Great Gorge, New Jersey, and Lake Geneva, Wisconsin. The Lake Geneva resort, the company's flagship hotel complex, cost $18 million. Other diversification strategies included the construction of Playboy apartment complexes, an agreement with Columbia Pictures to make first-run movies, the production of television shows and records, and the publication of sheet music. From 1965 to 1970, sales at Playboy Enterprises jumped dramatically, from $48 million to just over $127 million.

Throughout the 1960s, Hefner carefully created his own Playboy myth. He purchased a huge Victorian estate in the heart of the most fashionable Gold Coast area on Chicago's near North Side, and proceeded to decorate it with a combination of Renaissance and contemporary furnishings. Hefner lived in a room off the great hall, complete with a $5 million circular bed, while bunnies and former playmates of the month occupied other rooms on the upper two floors of the mansion. The swimming pool in the backyard was decorated with the trappings of a Roman temple; so many late night parties were held there that neighbors began to file complaints. In fact, the Friday Night Party at the Playboy Mansion, as Hefner dubbed it, was part of what fostered the man's growing legend. Hefner was the master of ceremonies that included swimming, drinking, eating, dancing, and, of course, lots of voyeurism. Having invited as many bunnies, playmates, casts of stage plays, movie stars, and celebrities in Chicago that he could find, Hefner would strut among his guests with pipe in mouth looking quite similar to a reincarnation of the Great Gatsby.

The Bunny Comes of Age

The early 1970s were the best years to date for Hefner's Playboy empire. The circulation of *Playboy* magazine reached its height in 1972 with 7.2 million readers. Pretax profits in 1973 amounted to $20 million, and the company was quickly approaching the 1000 mark for advertising pages. Yet Hefner, growing more dissatisfied with the lack of celebrity access and general conservatism in Chicago, decided to move his residence from the Windy City to the sunshine and glitz of Beverly Hills, California. In the process, he hired Derick Daniels to take charge of managing Playboy's day-to-day operations and its growing business interests. However when Daniels, who had been instrumental in the develop of Knight-Ridder Newspapers, arrived on the scene in the mid-1970s, he found an empire in disarray. Pretax profits had shrunk to $2 million in 1975, and barely topped $5 million in 1976. The entertainment division, including movies, television, records, and sheet music, was generating terrible losses.

With the full support of Hefner, who was no longer interested in managing the company, Daniels implemented a comprehensive reorganization strategy. The new head of Playboy made a clean sweep of management at all levels, getting rid of over 100 employees ranging from vice-presidents to assistant publicists. The most important retrenchment came in the entertainment division. Daniels withdrew the company from producing movies and television shows, discontinued its record and sheet music business, except for licensing arrangements, and began to reassess the kind of advertisements run in the pages of its flagship magazine. To compensate for the losses incurred from its foray into entertainment, Daniels decided to develop the company's gambling operations. Although Playboy's nightclub and resort division was losing money, its London-based casinos were generating the majority of the company's cash flow. Daniels upgraded the London casinos, opened a new casino in Cable Beach, the Bahamas, and made plans for a hotel-casino in Atlantic City, New Jersey.

Yet even under the steady leadership and management of Daniels, the Playboy empire continued to languish during the early 1980s. The number of Playboy clubs dropped precipitously, from a high of 22 to only 3. In 1982, because of licensing and legal problems, the company was forced to divest the one bright spot in its financial firmament, the gambling business. All of its casinos in the United States and British territories, including those in Atlantic City, London, and the Bahamas, were sold off to other firms. With a resulting loss of over 50 percent in sales for the company in 1982, compounding a loss of over $69 million during the previous two years, Hefner decided to replace Daniels with someone he knew more intimately and trusted more thoroughly: his own daughter.

Reorganization and Reorientation during the 1980s

Christie Hefner, a Phi Beta Kappa and summa cum laude graduate of Brandeis University in 1974, joined her father's company one year later. In 1985, she was promoted to the position of president, while Hugh Hefner continued as editor-in-chief and majority stockholder in the company. Projecting a highly professional image of the businesswoman of the 1980s, Christie Hefner made a conscious decision to remain far away from the libertine excesses of her father's lifestyle. Dressed in elegant but demure Gucci business suits, the new president quickly installed a talented management team with extensive corporate experience to help her revitalize the fortunes of Playboy. Her most daunting challenge, however, was how to deal with the dramatic changes in the public's attitudes toward sex that had occurred over the last 30 years. During the 1950s, the idea of guiltless sex and naughty nudity had catapulted Hugh Hefner to his success, but in the 1980s, where everything seemed tolerated (if not completely accepted) in the sexual arena, Christie's task was not only to turn the company around but redefine the Playboy credo of "Entertainment For Men."

With Christie at the helm, Playboy began to create an image for itself as the champion of free speech and first amendment rights. Contracting more and more authors to write about social issues, the company publicly supported gay rights, AIDS research, and the plight of battered women. With its growing overseas presence, *Playboy* magazine became a forum for dissidents from developing countries to write about abuses of power and government corruption. In the first issue of the company's Taiwan publication of *Playboy,* an interview with one of the leaders of the Tiananmen Square student uprising in China received a large amount of space. Although the magazine still reveled in its pictorials of busty women, Christie was hard at work transforming the image of the company in order to attract a more diverse audience.

Still, competition during the 1980s was intense. *Penthouse, Hustler,* and *Oui* magazines provided more graphic nude pictures than Playboy. Perhaps worst of all was the decision by the Meese Commission in 1986 to describe the magazine as pornographic. After this decision became public, major vendors such as 7-Eleven and newsstands around the country refused to sell the magazine. Traditionally, 75 percent of all sales of *Playboy* magazine had come from full-price newsstand sales. When this source of revenue suddenly vanished, Playboy quickly changed course and implemented a highly successful subscription campaign. By the end of the decade, circulation had leveled off at approximately 3.4 million readers, with over 75 percent coming from subscription sales, but the change in direction took time and profits remained stagnant.

One of the bright spots in the Playboy empire was the re-creation of the entertainment division. The company had formed a Playboy Channel during the early 1980s in order to take advantage of the burgeoning cable television market. With television subscribers decreasing from a high of 750,000 in 1985 to 430,000 by 1989, Christie and her staff decided to replace the Playboy Channel with a pay-per-view service named Playboy At Night. With soft core movies and Playmate videos, the new cable operation gained access into over 4 million homes and suddenly became the third largest pay-per-view service in the United States. At the same time, the company started putting more money into producing videos, and by the end of the decade Playboy was ranked the third largest nontheatrical distributor of videos, just behind Walt Disney and Jane Fonda. The "For Couples Only" collection, including the highly regarded couples oriented massage video, was one of Playboy's best selling series of videos.

The 1990s and Beyond

The 1990s started auspiciously for Playboy, especially in the overseas markets: overseas circulation jumped from 500,000 during the mid-1980s to over 1.5 million; 14 foreign editions were being published under license; the company began developing TV programming for Western Europe, where a greater degree of tolerance for nudity made Playboy television more acceptable; and a Playboy licensee opened 20 sportswear boutiques selling jogging suits, jeans, dress shirts, and attache cases with the Playboy logo on each item. The company also initiated a Playboy Channel in Japan, arranged in partnership with Tohokushinsha Film Corporation. In another new development, Playboy revived its gaming interests by taking a 15 percent stake in a casino located on the Greek Island of Rhodes.

During the mid-1990s, *Playboy* magazine was still edited by Hugh Hefner, with many of the magazine's signature features, graphics, and cartoons. Advertising pages had dropped to 595 for the year 1995, but circulation was holding at a steady 3.5 million, in spite of the stiff competition from other magazines with more explicit nude centerfold pictures. Christie Hefner succeeded in reducing overhead costs for running the magazine, but Hugh Hefner maintained that he needed a staff of 60 and a budget of approximately $4 million to edit *Playboy* from his Beverly Hills mansion. Still the majority owner of stock in the company, Hugh Hefner had forsaken his pipe and silk pajamas in order to settle down and marry the 1989 Playmate of the Year, Kimberley Conrad. Hefner and Conrad's son, Marston, played amid the unused Jacuzzis around the mansion.

In the time since Hugh Hefner started *Playboy* magazine, American attitudes towards sex have undergone enormous changes. This change in perception has left the second generation of management without a clear course to follow. Yet Christie Hefner is committed to developing the Playboy empire, and to making its products more attractive to the tastes and proclivities of a wider, more mature, and sophisticated audience.

Further Reading

"An Ailing Playboy Gets a New Manager," *Business Week,* September 27, 1976, p. 30.

Beyond Illustration: The Art of Playboy, Chicago: Playboy Enterprises, 1971.

"The Bunny Battles Back," *Forbes,* June 26, 1978, p. 17.

Byer, Stephen, *Hefner's Gonna Kill Me When He Reads This . . . ,* Chicago: Allen-Bennett, 1972.

"Can You Bare It?," *Forbes,* March 1, 1971, pp. 17–20.

Davidson, Bill, "Czar of the Bunny Empire," *Saturday Evening Post,* April 28, 1962, pp. 34–38.

Ellis, James, "Now Even Playboy Is Bracing for a Midlife Crisis," *Business Week,* April 15, 1985, pp. 66–68.

Kelly, Keith J., "Playboy's Fortunes Tied to the Bunny," *Advertising Age,* October 24, 1994, p. 45.

Kindel, Stephen, "Sex, Truth and Videotapes," *Financial World,* March 19, 1991, pp. 38–40.

Levine, Joshua, "The Rabbit Grows Up," *Forbes,* February 17, 1992, pp. 122–127.

Machan, Dyan, "The Hef and Christie Saga," *Forbes,* August 28, 1995, p. 89.

Miller, Russell, *Bunny: The Real Story of Playboy,* New York: Holt, Rinehart and Winston, 1985.

Murphy, H. Lee, "Playboy's Roving Eye: Wall Street Likes Looks of Its New Ventures," *Crain's Chicago Business,* November 1995, p. 33.

"No Dice," *Economist,* October 10, 1981, pp. 33–34.

"Playboy Puts a Glint in the Adman's Eyes," *Business Week,* June 28, 1969, pp. 142–146.

Sparks, Debra, "Playboy Turned On," *Financial World,* October 21, 1996, p. 28.

Weyr, Thomas, *Reaching for Paradise: The Playboy Vision of America,* New York: New York Times Books, 1978.

"Why Bulls Shun Bunnies," *Forbes,* March 1, 1973, p. 40.

—Thomas Derdak

Potash Corporation of Saskatchewan Inc.

Potash Corporation
of Saskatchewan Inc.

Suite 500
122 - 1st Avenue South
Saskatoon, Saskatchewan
Canada S7K 7G3
(306) 933-8500
Fax: (306) 652-2699

Public Company
Incorporated: 1975
Employees: 4,600
Sales: US$906.9 million (1995)
Stock Exchanges: Toronto
SICs: 3295 Minerals-Ground or Treated; 5052 Coal,
    Other Minerals & Ores; 1474 Potash, Soda & Borate
    Minerals

Potash Corporation of Saskatchewan Inc. is the world's largest producer of potash and the third largest producer of phosphate. Potash and phosphate are mined for their essential nutrients, potassium and phosphorus, which are used in making fertilizer. Potassium is used to increase crop yields, raise the food value of certain plants, and aids in resisting diseases leading to crop failure. Phosphorus, which is instrumental in the process of plant photosynthesis, is necessary for the normal growth of either an animal or plant, and is an essential ingredient for its maintenance and repair. Through an aggressive acquisition policy, the company has been able to make its presence felt throughout the world. Two of the most important acquisitions, Texasgulf and White Springs Agricultural Chemicals, manufacturers of animal feed products, have enabled Potash Corporation of Saskatchewan to dominate the North American phosphate fertilizer market. In addition to its stable sales base in Canada and the United States, the company has sold large amounts of its products to China, Taiwan, South Korea, Japan, and Brazil.

Early History

Potash Corporation of Saskatchewan Inc. (PCS) was established on February 4, 1975, by what is called an Order-In-Council of the Canadian Government. Private potash companies had been operating in Saskatchewan since the mid-1950s, but the federal government of Canada had failed to reach any agreement with those companies that would not only guarantee increased production capacity of potash but a greater degree of benefit and ownership for the people living in Saskatchewan province. Created to function as a commercial provincial crown corporation to produce and market potash, the firm actually began its life as a functioning producer during the 1976–77 fiscal year. By the end of that time, the company had acquired two mines, the Duval Mine and the Sylvite Mine, renamed the Cory Division and Rocanville Division, respectively, and had increased its production capacity from zero to the second largest producer in the North American market with over 540,000 tons. The corporation had established a network of 16 distribution warehouses, 15 of which were located in the United States, and had started to market all its foreign sales through Canpotex, a marketing agency set up in Toronto by all the potash firms operating in Saskatchewan for the sole purpose of promoting the sale of potash outside the North American market. Profits of US$890,000 were made on sales of just over US$22 million, and more than 1,100 people were employed by the company.

PCS initially started its operations in five geographically distinct areas within the province of Saskatchewan, which possess approximately 40 percent of the world's known reserves of potash. In addition to the Cory Division and the Rocanville Division, the company purchased the Alwinsal mine, the Allan mine, and the large potash reserves at Esterhazy, which significantly increased its holdings. The raw ore of potash, comprising 50 percent sodium chloride, 45 percent potassium chloride, and 5 percent clay, is found in naturally occurring potash beds about 25 feet thick in Saskatchewan. Discovered during the early 1940s as the Canadian government drilled for oil to fuel the Allied War effort against Germany and Japan, the potash beds are located between 3,000 and 7,000 feet below the earth's surface. Found to be a highly effective ingredient to enhance crop yields, potash was soon used in fertilizer products. By the late 1970s, PCS had grown so large that it controlled 40 percent of Saskatchewan's total production capacity. Most impressively, company sales had skyrocketed from US$22 million in 1977 to over US$312 million by the end of fiscal 1979–80.

The Economic Downturn of the Early and Mid-1980s

Unfortunately, during the early 1980s PCS confronted one of the most difficult periods in its short history. Company sales had plummeted to US$188 million in 1982, due largely to the deteriorated conditions of the North American market. The U.S. Government initiated a comprehensive program to reduce grain inventories across the country by reducing the total amount of planted acreage and, when combined with a lengthy drought, sharply reduced the application of potash products. Fertilizer consumption within the U.S. dropped 23 percent from 1980, while other fertilizer producers managed to capitalize on PCS's lost market share by taking advantage of American freight deregulation and lower levels of oceangoing freight. At the same time, foreign markets such as Brazil and Indonesia were oversupplied with potash products, thus lowering prices and revenues for the company.

Management at PCS responded by implementing a major cost reduction program, which included production reductions, inventory reductions, intermittent shutdowns, and employee layoffs. In addition, management reduced the amount of capital budgeted for lower-priority programs and research and development activities. Yet by the end of fiscal 1985, sales had increased only slightly to US$197 million, and net income for the company was reported at a loss of US$49 million.

The bad news for PCS continued into 1986. The slight increase in sales, initially interpreted as a sign of more promising economic indicators by company management, was misleading. In 1986, sales fell to US$155 million, and losses were reported at US$103 million, the worst financial record in the company's history. In contrast to the period between 1975–81, when planted acres, prices, and agricultural land values were on the rise and potash consumption was growing at an average rate of 6.3 percent in the United States alone, the period between 1982–85 brought with it falling prices, land values, and a reduction in planted acreage, resulting in a drop of potash consumption that totaled 2.5 percent per year. Compounding the company's problems was the United States farm policy which withdrew over 75 million acres out of production. The use of potash-based fertilizers for corn and soybean, the two most essential crops for potash consumption, decreased dramatically across the United States due to its farm policy. Thus, in the U.S. market, potash prices fell to an all-time low.

There was a bright light on the horizon for the company, however. Through its association with Canpotex Ltd., the marketing agency selling potash to overseas customers, offshore sales of 4.2 million tons surpassed the previous record of 2 million tons set in 1980. Markets in Asia and Oceania were growing at a quick pace, and exceptionally strong sales records were being set in China, Japan, Korea, Indonesia, Malaysia, and Australia. In fact, PCS signed a contract with the Chinese government to deliver over 550,000 tons of potash, the largest contract arranged through Canpotex for a single customer.

Growth and Resurgence During the Late 1980s and Early 1990s

A dramatic reversal of PCS's fortunes occurred during the late 1980s. By 1988, revenues increased to US$368 million, while net income was reported at US$106 million. The cost-cutting measures initiated by company management during the early and mid-1980s began to show their rewards. Daily, monthly, and yearly production records were broken at the company's five facilities in Saskatchewan, while production costs were held to a minimum. Record tonnage was sold to China, Korea, Malaysia, Taiwan, Argentina, Chile, and Italy, and prices began to improve over the levels of the mid-1980s. The use of potash began to increase within the United States market, largely due to the fact that more acreage was used for planting than in the previous four years.

In 1989, the decision was made to privatize PCS. The most significant event in the company's history came when the Province of Saskatchewan sold approximately 13 million shares in an initial public offering of company stock on the Toronto exchange. Over 11 million of the shares sold went to residents of Saskatchewan. The capital raised from the public offering helped the company upgrade its mining operations and expand its presence in foreign markets, especially Asia and Oceania.

By 1991, PCS reported an increased net income of 78 percent over the previous year, while revenue from overseas sales jumped 18 percent during the same time. In September 1991, the company purchased Florida Favorite Fertilizer, Inc., an American-based full-range fertilizer company with facilities in Florida, Georgia, and Alabama. Florida Favorite's production of blended, granulated, and solution-mixed fertilizers significantly improved PCS's presence in the United States fertilizer market. In addition, the company acquired Horizon Potash, a potash producer based in Carlsbad, New Mexico, for the purpose of strengthening its market share as the world's leading potash supplier.

During the early 1990s, PCS was affected by the march of international events. The Gulf War, and the subsequent elimination of Iraq as a threat to peace in the Middle East, led to an increased demand for potash in the region. Jordan and Israel, two of the world's leading suppliers of potash, increased their production. Yet PCS was able to make significant inroads into the regional market as the demand for its fertilizer products increased.

More importantly, however, to the worldwide demand for potash was the fall and dissolution of the USSR in the latter part of 1991. As the various republics within the former Soviet Union became politically independent, a new Commonwealth of Independent States was established. Two of these newly independent republics, Russia and Belarus, included the most important potash-producing regions in the world. As the Russian economy made the transition from state-owned companies to private businesses, which involved a major decrease in the production of potash, the difficulties that ensued included a dramatic drop in potash consumption throughout Eastern Europe, especially those countries formerly associated with the Soviet bloc. Russia and Belarus, traditional suppliers to all of Eastern Europe, attempted to shift more of their sales to markets located in Latin America and Asia, which were normally supplied by other producers, such as PCS. But the loss of captive markets, the difficulties involved in the change to a market economy, and the lack of an efficient infrastructure (such as useable railroad lines), hampered companies in Russia and Belarus from effectively competing with PCS at the time. Consequently, PCS's global market share remained stable, but management recognized the need for expanding its product line.

The Mid-1990s and Beyond

By 1993, under the direction of C. E. Childers, who had been hired by the Saskatchewan provincial government in 1987 to help improve the fortunes of PCS, the company began to reap rewards from a carefully conceived strategic plan. Childers was the driving force behind an aggressive acquisitions policy that expanded PCS's market share. One of the most important of these purchases was the Potash Company of America, which gave PCS the ability to ship its products from both the West and East Coasts of Canada. In addition, the company began to develop and market more intensely its industrial applications for potash, including the manufacture of detergents, soaps, glass and ceramics, textiles and dyes, chemicals and drugs, and recycling materials. Some of the more innovative industrial potash products were an ice melt, lawn and garden products, and a water softener named 1 Softtouch which, rather than using a sodium-based mix, were made with potassium. Sales for 1993 were reported at US$374.3 million.

In 1994, PCS's sales jumped an amazing 59 percent, to a record of US$597 million. For the first time since 1988, the worldwide consumption of potash had increased over the previous year. Part of this increased demand resulted from the consolidation and closure of numerous inefficient mines in Eastern Europe, Belarus, and Russia, and the growing disruption of supply and consumption patterns in those countries caused by the continuing social, political, and economic upheaval. At the same time, as income levels began to rise in Asia and Latin America, the demand for more and better food, and more fertilizer, also increased. As the world's largest potash producer, PCS increased its production facilities to send record amounts of tonnage to Malaysia, Thailand, New Zealand, Argentina, Russia, and India. Stronger markets and more stable prices in both Europe and Brazil helped add to the company's increased sales volume.

With the acquisition of Texasgulf, Inc. in early 1995, PCS engaged in a major product shift. Texasgulf, a leader in the production of phosphate rock and phosphate chemicals, conducted its operations in Aurora, North Carolina, and owned the largest vertically integrated phosphate mine and chemical processing facility in the world. While most of its sales came from phosphate fertilizer, the company also produced a large line of phosphate-based products such as animal feed supplements and purified phosphate acid for industrial use. Attracted by Texasgulf's stability during downturns in the fertilizer market, management at PCS saw the acquisition as an important step in mitigating the harmful effects on the company due to the volatility of the worldwide potash market. The purchase of Texasgulf doubled PCS's assets, and its number of employees. White Springs Agricultural Chemicals was also purchased at approximately the same time, thus making PCS the third largest producer of phosphate fertilizer in the world. By the end of fiscal 1995, sales at PCS dramatically increased to US$906.9 million.

As the economies of Russia and Eastern European nations began to stabilize, and the political and social tumult subsided, the republics of Russia and Belarus improved their infrastructures and increased potash production and sales to the worldwide markets. In order to protect itself from future reductions in demand and prices due to Russian competition, PCS decided to purchase Canadian-based Arcadian Corporation, the largest producer of nitrogen fertilizer products in the world. The acquisition increased the importance of PCS as a world fertilizer supplier, since the company completed its consolidation of the three primary fertilizer nutrients, potash, phosphate, and nitrogen.

Potash Corporation of Saskatchewan has grown into one of the world's most important suppliers of fertilizers. With talented management, headed by C. E. Childers, and ever-increasing demands for its products from developing countries around the globe, the company is in the position that most other firms within the fertilizer industry envy.

Principal Divisions

PCS Sales; PCS Phosphate-Raleigh; PCS Phosphate-Aurora; PCS Phosphate-White Springs; Florida Favorite Fertilizer; PCS Potash-Allan; PCS Potash-Cory; PCS Potash-Esterhazy; PCS Potash-Lanigan; PCS Potash-Moab; PCS Potash-New Brunswick; PCS Potash-Patience Lake; PCS Potash-Rocanville; Davenport Feed Plant; Kinston Feed Plant; Marseilles Feed Plant; Saltville Feed Plant; Weeping Water Feed Plant.

Further Reading

Elliot, Ian, "Agriculture Hit Hard As Budget Is Slashed in Canada," *Feedstuffs,* March 13, 1995, pp. 3–7.
Geer, John, F., "Mixed Marriage," *Financial World,* October 21, 1996, pp. 46–47.
Greenshields, Vern, and Mortin, Jenni, "Crown Corporation Series," *Star-Phoenix Newspaper* (Saskatoon, Saskatchewan), February 24, 1982, Section C, p. 1.
Henry, Brian, "Potash Corporation Emerges As a Fertilizer Major," *Chemical Marketing Reporter,* September 9, 1996, pp. 3–36.
Kirschner, Elisabeth, "Elf Aquitaine to Sell Stake in Phosphate Firm," *Chemical & Engineering News,* March 13, 1995, p. 8.
Lazo, Shirley, A., "Riding High Profits, Potash Lifts Dividends," *Barron's,* August 15, 1994, p. 37.
Muirhead, Sarah, "Potash Corporation Announces It Will Buy Texasgulf," *Feedstuffs,* March 13, 1995, p. 3.

—Thomas Derdak

PRINTRONIX

Printronix, Inc.

17500 Cartwright Road
P.O. Box 19559
Irvine, California 92713
U.S.A.
(714) 893-1900
Fax: (714) 660-8682

Public Company
Incorporated: 1974
Employees: 800
Sales: $159.26 million (1996)
Stock Exchanges: NASDAQ
SICs: 3577 Computer Peripheral Equipment, Not
    Elsewhere Classified

Irvine, California-based Printronix, Inc. designs, manufactures, and markets a leading line of midrange, high-speed printers and printing software applications used with PC network, minicomputer, and mainframe computing systems. Printronix produces three families of heavy-duty printer systems. The five-member family of ProLine Series 5 line matrix printers, based on patented technology developed by Printronix, offers print speeds ranging from 150 lines per minute up to 1,200 lines per minute. The company's line matrix printers are especially suited to industrial graphics applications, such as onsite bar coding and order routing, as well as multipart form printing. Printronix's LaserLine product family hits both the entry-level and top-of-the-line medium-to-high-volume continuous form laser printing markets, producing high quality graphics output at speeds ranging from 24 to 31 pages per minute, or from 50,000 to 250,000 pages per month. The LaserLine printers, which can print on plastics and synthetic materials, as well as any type of paper, use Printronix's DuraFusion toner process, providing greater document durability. The third family in the Printronix line is its ThermaLine thermal transfer printers, providing on-demand or high-volume label printing at speeds ranging from five to ten inches per second. Printronix also manufactures private-label printers under contract with companies including IBM, Unisys, and Hewlett Packard.

Printronix supports its printers with its Printronix System Architecture (PSA). By unifying the hardware and software base of its printer families, PSA allows application programs to work with any of Printronix's own printer systems, while providing compatibility with other printer systems. PSA also includes international font packages including Arabic, Hebrew, Greek, Cyrillic, Turkish, and four Kanji fonts for the Japanese, Chinese, Taiwanese, and Korean markets. The company maintains production facilities in Irvine, the Netherlands, and Singapore. In 1996, the company stepped up its focus on the Asian market with construction of a new state-of-the-art facility in Singapore. International sales, which accounted for ten percent of the company's $159 million in revenues for the year ended March 31, 1996, are expected to drive Printronix's future growth. Printronix is led by founder, President, and CEO Robert A. Kleist.

From a Garage to Industry Leader in the 1970s

Robert A. Kleist, an electrical engineer who began his career with Ampex, had already co-founded two successful companies—Dartex, a maker of tape transport systems later acquired by Tally Corp.; and Peripheral Business Equipment, later merged with Peripheral Equipment Corp. to form computer-maker Pertec Computer Corp.—before joining with friends and fellow engineers Gordon Barrus, Leo Emenaker, David Mayne, Ray Melissa, and Mel Posin to form Printronix. At the time, minicomputers were the fastest growing computing segment, and increasing numbers of small businesses were integrating computer systems into their operations. The Printronix group recognized a need for a new type of printer that could accompany the minicomputer into the variety of industrial environments while providing high-speed, high-volume print capacity. The team developed a new printer technology that could produce multipart printouts, such as invoices, purchase orders, and paychecks, as well as the recently introduced bar coding systems. Based in Emenaker's garage, the new company built its first printer, the P300, in 1974.

The P300, which introduced "dot matrix" technology, differed markedly from the printers in use at the time. These were on the whole serial printers, meaning they printed documents one character at a time, much like typewriters. Serial printers presented a number of limitations to manufacturers demanding increasing industrial printing capacity. Serial printers could not be used for multipart forms, could not produce graphics, depended on special paper, and were not suited to the dust, temperature extremes, and other environmental hardships of the typical industrial setting. The P300 abandoned serial printing for Printronix's line matrix printing. The P300 translated electronic documents into commands driving a bank of tiny hammers to print small, overlapping dots across an entire line. Merging the dots allowed the P300 to print not only letters and numerals, but also lines, charts, and other graphics. The P300 was able to print on a variety of paper types; because it used far fewer moving parts than serial printers, it was especially suited to the industrial environment and offered greater durability, easier repair, and high volume capacity. Priced at $5,000, the P300 was, as Kleist told *Dun's Review,* "The closest thing to a universal printer for the minicomputer industry."

But starting up a new company in the midst of the 1970s recession was risky, and the company struggled for its first two years. Printronix was unable to find investors; instead, venture capitalists, wary of investing in a one-product company, suggested that Printronix needed to develop more variety of printer types to attract large customers. Yet Printronix stood by the P300, convinced that its wide range of features and its suitability to a variety of tasks would make it appealing to a wide range of customers. "A little company," Kleist told *Fortune,* "can't succeed by doing many different things." To get the company going, the partners raised nearly $700,000 among them, and then later sold two licenses overseas, adding another $500,000.

The next step was finding customers. Unable to afford to hire and train its own sales staff, Printronix instead turned to distributors to sell its products—an unusual move for the computer industry at the time. "We effectively created our own class of large customers by aggregating a lot of little customers under a regional distributor," Kleist told *Fortune.* And to *Dun's Review,* he added, "It put more salesmen in the field talking to customers than we could have done ourselves, and it not only helped preserve vital capital, but gained us the acceptance our product deserved." The strategy worked. By 1976 the company was in the black, and by 1977 sales of the P300 had reached 300 units per month, generating revenues of $4.3 million and a $270,000 profit. With this growth, Printronix was able to begin marketing directly to large customers, while maintaining its distributor network for sales to smaller clients. In 1978, Printronix added a second printer, the P600, a line matrix printer capable of doubling the P300 print speed. The company also established a reputation for quality, offering a one-year guarantee instead of the then industry standard 90 days. But the P

series proved to be up to the high volume demands placed upon them. Indeed, many of Printronix's printers would remain in operation for more than 20 years.

Going public in 1979, Printronix quickly built itself into one of the top ten printer makers, taking 15 percent of the market for medium-speed printers by the beginning of the next decade. By then, the company had stepped up its direct sales force, which now accounted for more than half of printer sales. The company also moved to vertical integration, leasing a manufacturing plant in Irvine to build its hammer banks. In March 1981, the company, which already saw foreign sales accounting for nearly 30 percent of total sales, formed a subsidiary in the Netherlands and began manufacturing printers there. Sales by then had nearly tripled, to nearly $37 million. The following year, with sales topping $52 million and with profits nearing $12 million, Printronix moved to expand its product line.

In 1982, the company unveiled two new products, the multifunction Taskmaster MVP2 printer and the Intelligent Graphics Processor (IGP). The MVP, targeted at the small business and office markets, filled in the low-end of the printer line, printing at 150 lines per minute and offering the then-unique ability to switch among word processing, data processing, graphics, and plotting applications. The IGP system, which could be retrofitted to the P series installed base and factory-installed on new units, offered enhancing graphics processing/printing capacity. The following year, Printronix acquired Massachusetts-based Data Printer, Inc., manufacturer of high-speed band printers, adding first a high-end, 1,200 lines per minute printer and then a 2,000 lines per minute model to the company's product line. The acquisition helped boost Printronix sales, from $78 million in 1983 to more than $116 million in 1984. By then, Printronix controlled between 60 and 88 percent of the low-, medium-, and high-speed line printer markets.

Hammered in the 1980s

But new computer technologies began to emerge in the early 1980s. IBM introduced its first personal computer in 1983, sparking demands for new types of smaller, consumer-oriented, serial matrix printers. This market, which sold primarily through the retail channel, was quickly exploited by Japanese manufacturers, including Epson and Okidata. With the rise of the PC, sales in the minicomputer and microcomputer markets began to stagnate. In 1984, Printronix attempted to enter the new personal printer market with the acquisition, for $8.7 million in stock, of Anadex, Inc., a California manufacturer of serial matrix printers with about $30 million in sales. Within a year of the acquisition, however, Anadex's sales dropped by some 70 percent, as the entire computer industry, buffeted by a new recession, collapsed in the middle of the 1980s.

Having grown to 1,200 employees, Printronix was forced to lay off more than 250 people in 1985. The Anadex acquisition helped the company's revenues near $150 million that year. But, unable to penetrate the retail market dominated by Japanese printer makers, and missing the newly emerging laser printer market, the company's sales of PC-oriented printers dropped. Coupled with stagnation in the line printer market, Printronix began facing losses. To shore up operations, the company moved some of its manufacturing to Mexico and opened a production facility in Singapore. The following year, the company consolidated its Anadex subsidiary, closing its plant and forcing Printronix to take a nearly $7 million writeoff. As sales slipped to $132 million, the company's losses, further deepened by the costs of moving its manufacturing operations overseas, reached $11.7 million for 1986, marking the company's first-ever annual loss.

The company moved to counter its losses by diversifying its product line. In July 1986, Printronix introduced its first laser printers, a high-volume printer and a lower-priced desktop printer. The company also unveiled a new generation of line printers, with speeds ranging from 200 lines per minute up to 1,200 lines per minute. Printronix also attempted to enter the band printer market with a printer capable of speeds up to 2,000 lines per minute. But the company failed in that attempt; taking a $5.1 million inventory and equipment writedown, the company's revenues continued to sag, to $123.6 million, and Printronix again posted a loss in 1987, of $4.9 million.

By the end of the decade, sales of personal computers had overtaken the rest of the computer market. With sales of mainframe and minicomputers shrinking, Printronix restructured the company to enable Printronix, as Kleist wrote in the company's 1989 annual report, "to become profitable at a lower level of sales." Printronix abandoned its diversification effort, focusing instead on the company's core midrange printer market. Two California manufacturing plants were closed and the Dutch subsidiary was converted from manufacturing to providing distribution facilities for the European market. With lower production costs, Printronix was able to climb back into the black. After posting a new $4.4 million loss on 1989's $135 million in sales, the company managed a profit of more than $3.5 million in 1990, despite a drop in sales to $125 million. The dawn of a new recession, however, quickly dashed Printronix's hopes for sustaining its profitability.

Retooled for the 1990s

The recession cut deeply into Printronix. Sales dropped to $107 million in 1991 and bottomed out at $88.5 million in 1992. Losses also mounted, from $1.8 million in 1991 to nearly $8.5 million in 1992. But by then the company had already initiated a series of steps designed to retool the company and return it to profitability. The first of these involved shifting its laser technology back to the midrange market, with the launch of a continuous-form laser in 1991 and cut-sheet laser in 1992. In that year, also, the company extended its industry-leading barcoding capacity into thermal printing, adding the first in a line of label printers. At the same time, Printronix began development of its PSA technology, including an emphasis on developing font sets for the Asian market. By 1993, the company launched the fourth generation of its line matrix technology, allowing the company to seize back that market; over the next three years, its share of the market grew from 25 to 40 percent.

Next, Printronix moved to control costs by outsourcing some of its manufacturing operations to other companies, including hiring Texas Instruments to provide printed circuit boards. By 1994, sales were on the rise again, reaching $107.4 million, and the company showed a profit of $2.3 million. But Printronix was not the only manufacturer in the computer industry beginning to see the value of outsourcing. In 1994, IBM abandoned its own printer manufacturing efforts and instead signed a three-year contract with Printronix to provide private label printers bearing the IBM name. A second contract that year added the Printronix line of printers under the Unisys brand name. The following year, Printronix signed a three-year contract with Hewlett Packard to provide that company's line of matrix printers. These contracts helped boost Printronix's sales to $146.6 million in 1995 and $159 million in 1996, with net profits of around $7 million for both years.

Printronix's future looked bright for the remaining years of the century. The launch of the company's Chinese font set scheduled for 1997 was expected to tap strongly into a potentially huge market. Font sets for Vietnamese and Hindi language printers were also being prepared, as the company forecasted sales in Asia, then accounting for ten percent of the company's sales, to grow by 300 percent within the year. Unveiling its latest generation of printer families in 1996, and predicting that these new products would account for 75 percent of the company's 1997 revenues, Printronix seemed likely to maintain its position at the top of the midrange printer market.

Further Reading

Brown, Julia G., "Lineup: Printronix Broadens Its Base," *Electronic Business,* June 1983, p. 116.

Bylinsky, Gene, "New Companies That Beat the Odds," *Fortune,* December 1977, p. 76.

Jones, John A., "Printronix Drives Up Sales of Rugged Computer Printers," *Investor's Business Daily,* July 14, 1995, p. B12.

Lazzareschi, Carla, "Printronix Hopes To Rebound with a Diversified Line," *Los Angeles Times,* July 13, 1986, part 4, p. 1.

McKendrick, Joseph E., "Making an Impact: Printronix Sticks with Midrange Printer Market through Thick and Thin," *Midrange Systems,* October 1, 1991, p. 15.

"Printronix, Inc.: Reaping the Rewards of Innovation," *Dun's Review,* March 1981, p. 44.

Tan, Audrey, "Printronix Expects Huge Jump in Asia-Pac Sales," *Business Times (Singapore),* November 13, 1996, p. 2.

—M. L. Cohen

Quality Dining, Inc.

3820 Edison Lakes Pkwy.
Mishawaka, Indiana 46545
U.S.A.
(219) 271-4600
Fax: (219) 271-4610

Public Company
Incorporated: 1981
Employees: 11,000
Sales: $237.6 million (1996)
Stock Exchanges: NASDAQ
SICs: 5812 Eating Places

Quality Dining, Inc. is a holding company for a growing number of fast-food and casual dining restaurants. A multi-concept franchisee and franchiser (or "concept owner"), Quality Dining operates over 500 restaurants in 20 states. As franchisee, their operations include Burger King and Chili's Grill and Bar Restaurants. As franchiser they have ownership of Grady's American Grill, Spageddies Italian Kitchen Restaurants, and Bruegger's Bagel Bakeries. Restaurant industry analysts have identified Quality Dining as one of the best-performing franchisers in the country. In 1995 the company was ranked sixth in *Forbes* magazine's "200 Best Small Companies" in America.

Survival in the Early 1980s

Quality Dining owes its origins to chairman and chief executive officer Daniel B. Fitzpatrick and his brother John D. Fitzpatrick (since retired from the company), who learned the restaurant business from the ground up. Daniel Fitzpatrick—one of seven children—was just 14 years old when his father, a steelworker, suffered a debilitating stroke. It was important to the family that they all help in caring for their father at home rather than institutionalizing him. Fitzpatrick told Jan O. Spalding of *Indiana Business Magazine,* "We were faced with a pretty daunting task. In my neighborhood it was either starve, steal or go to work. My mother said 'work.'" Daniel Fitzpat-

rick began by delivering newspapers, then moved to bussing tables at an Italian restaurant. Before long he changed jobs to work for his brother at a Burger Chef restaurant as an entry-level manager. After high school he switched to Burger King while earning his degree in business administration from the University of Toledo, Ohio. His talents earned him a promotion to director of operations for several Burger King restaurants in Kalamazoo, Michigan. By 1981 he and brother John decided to put their entrepreneurial skills to the test and acquired a franchise for two struggling Burger Kings in suburban Detroit.

As the second largest fast-food chain in America, the superbly-managed Burger King Corporation has franchised Burger King restaurants since 1954. Their "Have It Your Way" philosophy emphasizes quality service, generous portions, and competitive prices. As of January 1996, Burger King was comprised of 8,194 company-owned and franchised restaurants worldwide, making it one of the most recognized names in the industry—and a smart franchise choice for the enterprising brothers.

In the 1970s fast-food chains, particularly McDonald's and Burger King, had successfully penetrated inner-city markets, proving most successful as lunch-time servers. Name and product recognition, reasonable pricing, special appeal to children, and convenience contributed to rapid growth in sales for most franchisers. Families living in the suburbs traveled more, and more women were working away from home, chauffeuring children and appreciating the ease of eating "on the road." Burger King's flagship sandwich, "The Whopper," competed with its rival, the McDonald's "Big Mac," and featured what Burger King considered a competitive advantage with their "flame-broiled" burgers. By the early 1980s vigorous competition between fast-food chains warranted that more than a "concept" was needed to ensure franchise profitability.

In an interview with Richard L. Papiernik of *Nation's Restaurant News,* Fitzpatrick recalled that he and his brother "scrubbed floors, cleaned the kitchens, did rescheduling and in-house training, and jumped into cooking and serving lines," which soon paid off through a positive turnaround in profits. Joined by brothers Gerald O. Fitzpatrick and James K. Fitzpatrick, in 1983 and 1984 respectively, the company soon moved

Company Perspectives:

Critical to the long-term success of our business is the Company's ongoing commitment to exceeding guests' expectations. Quality Dining is led by an experienced and focused management team with a passionate approach to serving our guests. We recognize that "hands-on" management style is crucial to maintaining the current service level which our guests count on. In order to strengthen our position, we added experienced management professionals throughout the organization. We are committed in the years ahead to invest in people, systems, and facilities necessary to maintain the highest level of service to our guests.

into Burger King's South Bend, Indiana, market. Despite double-digit unemployment and inflation, and an 18 percent prime rate, they continued to develop under-performing units. Daniel Fitzpatrick told Marilyn Alva of *Restaurant Business* that "from May 1983 to November 1991 we opened one new Burger King restaurant every 85 days." The Burger King Corporation recognized Daniel Fitzpatrick's entrepreneurial leadership by naming him best operator of a multi-unit Burger King franchise in 1985.

From Fast-Food to Casual Dining in the 1990s

Increasingly throughout the 1980s and into the next decade, Americans became concerned about the nutritional quality of fast food. Changing consumer tastes, and the recognition of a ripe market in the Midwest's casual dining (i.e. table service, as opposed to counter service) segment, prompted Fitzpatrick's decision to expand. In 1991, after persistently pursuing Dallas-based Brinker International, Inc., Fitzpatrick's company was finally granted the rights to develop Chili's Grill & Bar restaurants in Indiana, Michigan, and Ohio, a geographical market Fitzpatrick was familiar with. Fitzpatick recognized the ingredients of a successful franchiser. Chili's restaurants featured a casual atmosphere and a broadly-appealing menu including a variety of hamburgers, fajitas, chicken and seafood entrees, barbecued ribs, salads, sandwiches—and modest pricing. Fitzpatrick reported to Marilyn Alva of *Restaurant Business*, "We utilize the same principles we learned at Burger King: Pay attention to costs and put money back into the business." The company soon made a move to the East Coast when it purchased the stock of Grayling Corporation, the operator of eight Chili's restaurants in greater Philadelphia, and agreed to develop 24 new Chili's restaurants in the Midwest and Philadelphia markets over the next seven years.

By this time Quality Dining executive John D. Fitzpatrick, original co-franchisee with brother Daniel, paid $600,000 in cash and 20,000 shares of common stock for two Burger King Restaurants in the Detroit, Michigan, market. In 1994 the two restaurants reported combined sales of $2.25 million. Agreeing not to compete with the company for a period of five years, John resigned from all positions he held with Quality Dining.

During this period Burger King increased portion sizes on several of their products while simultaneously cutting prices. Burger King advertising was spotlighted in conjunction with Walt Disney's blockbuster movie "The Lion King." Due to the success of their own efforts combined with the Burger King Corporation's promotional and advertising expenditures, cooperative purchasing arrangements, and other goodwill efforts with its franchisees, Quality Dining decided to further develop their Burger King division. In an effort to expand its territories through its wholly owned subsidiary Bravokilo, Inc., Quality Dining acquired all of the issued and outstanding common stock and/or assets of Shonco, Inc., which owned and operated eight Burger King restaurants in the Detroit, Michigan, metropolitan area, and also owned the rights to construct four additional restaurants. William R. Schonsheck, previous owner of Shonco, Inc., became an executive officer of Quality Dining and the chief operating officer of their Burger King Division.

Rapid Expansion in the Mid-1990s

Fitzpatrick was determined to raise the capital needed to remain competitive, and to challenge his management team and offer stock options and rewards to employees. He had concluded that the time had come for listing his company, then Burger Services, Inc., on the NASDAQ. The stock offering had raised over $25.5 million in March 1994, following a company reorganization that made Quality Dining a management holding company with four wholly-owned subsidiaries. In October 1995, Quality Dining completed a second public stock offering, raising more than $31.5 million. Fitzpatrick told *Indiana Business Magazine's* Jan O. Spalding, that "Growth should be focused, never preceding the company's resources or the capability of the management team," and further advised, "as you grow a company like this, one of the challenges is to make sure you have management strength at every level of the organization."

Fortified by sales and stock revenues, Quality Dining acquired ownership of the Spageddies Italian Restaurant concept from Brinker International, Inc., releasing Quality Dining from previous franchise and development fees, royalties, and other expenses previously paid to the franchiser. Spageddies are promoted as midscale Italian casual dining restaurants, with a festive appeal, conforming to the fundamental Quality Dining ideal of large-portioned, quality, value-priced food. Spageddies' sales for fiscal 1995 totaled $4.7 million. Further negotiations with Brinker International, Inc. resulted in the company's end-of-1995 purchase of the Grady's American Grill restaurant concept for $74.4 million, which included ownership of 42 Grady's American Grill Restaurants in 16 states.

Dave Findlay, Quality Dining's vice president of strategic planning and investor relations, told *Nation's Restaurant News* that "With respect to Grady's, it changes the profile of our company pretty dramatically. We go from a company with a majority of its revenues deriving from the Burger King business to one where the Grady's business becomes No. 1 in revenue generation. We also have a concept that we can develop nationally, which we haven't been able to do in the past," he added. By the final quarter of 1995, overall restaurant sales had increased 63.6 percent from the previous year, to over $105 million earned from the operation of 59 Burger King restaurants, 18 casual dining restaurants under the trade name of

Chili's Grill & Bar, 12 bakeries under the trade name of Bruegger's Bagel Bakery (Quality Dining franchised its first Bruegger's Bakery in September 1994), and five casual dining restaurants under the trade name of Spageddies.

Pursuing its aggressive growth strategy, Fitzpatrick's team soon identified bagel chains as the fastest-growing segment of the restaurant industry. As the nation's top bagel operators, competitors Bruegel's Bagel Bakeries, a privately owned company based in Burlington, Vermont, and Einstein Bros. Bagels Inc., of Golden, Colorado, raced to saturate the most viable markets. Established since 1983, Bruegger's accumulated 425 retail stores in 26 states by 1996, with average per unit sales of $800,000 annually. Following Bruegger's 1995 sales, which topped $220 million, Quality Dining moved into the arena and acquired the company for approximately 5.1 million shares of common stock, plus up to 141,450 shares of convertible preferred stock. Analysts speculated that Bruegger's was in need of additional capital in order to meet competitive expansion strategies and decided the Quality Dining offer was better than what the open market would have provided. Relevant to their decision was the value placed on Quality Dining's impressive operational record.

Under the new organization, Bruegger's operates as a wholly owned, freestanding subsidiary of Quality Dining. Of the 454 Bruegger's restaurants, 203 are company-owned as opposed to franchised, reinforcing a dual-distribution policy practiced by savvy franchisers who benefit from higher profits and increased control. Consistent with Fitzpatrick's strategy of buying exceptional management skill along with each company purchase, Steven Finn, former Bruegger's president and chief executive officer, was given leadership of the division. A working rapport had originated between Finn and Fitzpatrick back in the early 1980s when Finn was a senior vice president at Burger King and Fitzpatrick was a beginning franchisee. More than a decade later Finn convinced Fitzpatrick to join him in becoming a member of Bruegger's board of directors, and soon convinced Fitzpartick of the profit potential a company like Bruegger's had to offer. After the acquisition, the company added Nord Brue and Michael Dressel, Bruegger's cofounders, and Steve Finn, to Quality Dining's board.

To help expedite its Bruegger's expansion, Quality Dining offered a $25-a-share stock issue in July of 1996, raising net proceeds of approximately $60 million on 2.5 million shares of common stock. Considered the new driving force for Quality Dining, Bruegger's finished fiscal 1996 as the largest chain of fresh bagel bakeries in the United States. The company attributes its popularity to traditionally prepared kettle-boiled bagels which are then hearth-baked daily, producing a notably superior product. In addition to freshly baked bagels, they offer 10 varieties of branded cream cheese, deli-style bagel sandwiches, soups and other food and beverage items, including freshly roasted coffees.

Looking ahead into the late 1990s, restaurant analysts expect the bagel franchise wars to intensify. With an estimated $2.6 billion bagel-shop market to infiltrate, the country's number two chain, Einstein Bros. Bagels, is stepping up efforts to establish the most units in the best markets. Adding more than 100 units in 10 states, Einstein Bros. bought Noah's New York Bagels Inc., of San Leandro, California, and plans to continue opening about 300 stores per year. In January 1997, Einstein's announced its intention to buy Fanagle A Bagel, out of Boston, Massachusetts, owners of three high-volume stores, with several more openings scheduled in New England. Also performing well is another competitor, the 265-unit Manhattan Bagel Co., from Eatontown, New Jersey, with a strong presence on both coasts. The Bruegger's plan is to have nearly 500 stores established by the end of 1997, and some 1,000 units by 1999.

Interpreting nationwide demographic studies, San Francisco-based analyst, John W. Weiss of Montgomery Securities stated that "Bruegger's will generate 45 percent of Quality Dining's revenues by fiscal 1998," according to Richard L. Papiernik of *Nation's Restaurant News*. A new corporate headquarters, in Mishawaka's Edison Lakes Corporate Park was begun in 1996 to house the increased staff, which has more than doubled since the Bruegger's acquisition.

Overall, the restaurant industry is intensely competitive and Quality Dining is all too aware of the many well-established competitors with substantially greater financial and territorial resources, including McDonald's, Wendy's, Hardee's, T.G.I Friday's, Applebee's, Bennigan's, Olive Garden, Red Lobster, Chi Chi's, Dunkin' Donuts, the bagel chains previously mentioned, as well as a number of locally-owned, non-chain restaurants. Despite 1996 first-quarter decreased earnings—down 40 percent from the first quarter of 1994—blamed partly on restructuring charges and unusually bad weather, growing pains throughout this period are to be expected. While some critics have questioned the rapid expansion strategies of Quality Dining, Fitzpatrick, who owns 25.6 percent of his company's common stock, has consistently relied on good management, a well-focused business plan, and quality products. He told Peter Key of *The Indianapolis Star and News* that "Achieving growth, requires leadership. And that means getting a company's employees to buy into its leader's goals. Rarely do they believe in a company per se, they believe in you; they believe in the leader or they believe in nothing at all."

Principal Subsidiaries

Bravokilo, Inc.; Southwest Dining, Inc.; Full Service Dining, Inc.; Best Bagels, Inc.; Grayling Corporation.

Further Reading

"After Profits Grow 72% in 1995, Quality Dining Takes in Grady's," *Nation's Restaurant News*, January 8, 1996, p. 12.
Alva, Marilyn, "All in the Family," *Restaurant Business*, November 1, 1995, pp. 62–64.
"The Best Small Companies in America Directory", *Forbes*, November 4, 1996.
"BK Franchisee Releases 1st Post-IPO Results," *Nation's Restaurant News*, April 11, 1994, p. 14.
"Brinker Selling Two Restaurants to Quality Dining," *New York Times*, November 3, 1995, p. C3 (N).
"Bruegger's, Einstein Bros. Fuel Bagel Race," [http: // www. bakery-net. com/rdocs/nbbrueg. html.;mt.
Howard, Theresa, "Quality Dining's Net Income Jumps 36% in 2nd Quarter," *Nation's Restaurant News*, September 26, 1994, p. 14.

Key, Peter, "Indiana's Quality Dining, Inc. 'Very Well Run,' Analyst Says," *Knight/Ridder/Tribune Business News,* April 5, 1996, p. 4050051.

Papiernik, Richard L., "Expansionary Chains Pull Investors at Piper Conference," *Nation's Restaurant News,* June 24, 1996 pp. 11–12.

Papiernik, Richard L., "Daniel Fitzpatrick: Persistence Pays Off: Quality Dining Baron Knows What He Wants and Won't Take No for an Answer," *Nation's Restaurant News,* October 14, 1996, pp. 160–164.

——, "Quality Dining Bids For Top Bagel Spot; Bruegger's Acquisition Heats up Battle for Segment Dominance," *Nation's Restaurant News,* March 4, 1996, pp. 1–2.

"Quality Brakes Grady's Growth During Fiscal '96," *Nation's Restaurant News,* February 19, 1996, p. 78.

"Quality Dining Acquires Chili's Franchisee," *Nation's Restaurant News,* December 19, 1994, p. 14.

"Quality Dining's Gross Portfolio in $70 M Deal with Brinker Intl.," *Nation's Restaurant News,* Nov. 13, 1995, p.2.

"Quality Dining, Inc., Completes Bruegger's Buy," *Nation's Restaurant News,* June 17, 1996, p. 58.

"Quality Dining, Inc. Signs Deal to Acquire Grayling Stock," *Nation's Restaurant News,* November 28, 1994, p. 55.

"Restaurants are Acquired from Brinker Int'l," *Wall Street Journal,* December 26, 1995, p. B4.

Spalding, Jan O., "A Whopper of a Company," *Indiana Business Magazine,* July 1996. pp. 8–13.

"Weather and Restructuring Bite Quality Dining in 1st Quarter," *Nation's Restaurant News,* April 1, 1996, p. 12.

—Terri L. Burgman

Quiksilver, Inc.

1740 Monrovia Avenue
Costa Mesa, California 92627
U.S.A.
(714) 645-1395
Fax: (714) 722-4261
Web site: http://www.quiksilver.com

Public Company
Incorporated: 1976 as Quiksilver U.S.A.
Employees: 454
Sales: $172.7 million (1995)
Stock Exchanges: NASDAQ
SICs: 2321 Men's/Boys' Shirts; 2331 Women's/Misses'
   Blouses & Shirts; 2329 Men's/Boys' Clothing, Not
   Elsewhere Classified; 2339 Women's/Misses'
   Outerwear, Not Elsewhere Classified

A celebrated name among surfers across the globe, Quiksilver, Inc. designs and distributes casual sportswear, beachwear, and snowboard wear, marketing its apparel under the Quiksilver, Roxy, Private Surf, Que, and Raisin labels. Although Quiksilver produced a broad range of apparel items for several distinct types of customers during the mid-1990s, the company's chief focus has been setting fashion trends for surfers. Founded by two young American surfers in 1976, Quicksilver recorded enviable success with its boardshorts, swimsuits, and other surfing apparel and accessories during its first decade of business. Encouraged by this success, the company's management diversified into other types of active wear during the 1980s and began selling merchandise through department stores, rather than dealing exclusively with smaller specialty shops. The maturation of the narrowly focused start-up company developed it into a multi-faceted corporation that reigned as a market leader during the 1990s.

Origins

The Quiksilver name first appeared in the United States thanks to the entrepreneurial efforts of two inveterate surfers, Robert B. McKnight and Jeffrey Hakman. Hakman was the more accomplished surfer of the two, having won several international surfing championships, but McKnight shared an equal passion for the sport and its attendant lifestyle. Born and raised in Pasadena, California, McKnight graduated from the University of Southern California with a degree in business in 1976, the year he decided to move to Oahu, Hawaii, and spend his days surfing on the island's world renowned north shore. While on Oahu McKnight renewed his friendship with Hakman and together the two surfing addicts discussed their desire to start a business that could finance their days on the beach. They decided to try to get the licensing rights for Quiksilver, a six year-old company based in Torquay, Australia, where it was founded by two surfers, Alan Greene and John Law.

For McKnight and Hakman, obtaining the licensing rights to Quiksilver represented a perfect opportunity to turn their favorite pastime into a vocation. The company's boardshorts and swimsuits, which were tight-fitting and outfitted with velcro straps, were quickly becoming the rage among surfers in Australia, turning the Quiksilver brand name into a highly coveted, trendy label. McKnight and Hakman hoped to achieve commensurate success with the Quiksilver name in the United States, but neither of the two aspiring entrepreneurs thought of creating a beach wear apparel empire, particularly McKnight, whose business intentions were modest. Reflecting on his entry into the business world, McKnight explained, "I thought I could make a few shorts and stay near the beach and party." Despite his less than grandiose plans, McKnight soon found himself guiding the fortunes of a rapidly growing, flourishing enterprise. "I never thought the business would fail," McKnight remembered, "I just didn't expect it to get so big so quickly."

McKnight and Hakman's surprising success with the Quiksilver brand name began in April of 1976, when Hakman entered a surfing competition in Australia. Hakman won the event, and as luck would have it, he met Greene and Law and sat up all night with Quiksilver's owners eating, drinking champagne, and discussing the possibility of securing the U.S. licensing rights to the Quicksilver name. After plates of food and bottles of champagne, Greene and Law agreed to sell Quiksilver's U.S. rights to McKnight and Hakman on one condition, a unique proviso that became the first obstacle the two Americans had to hurdle in order to launch themselves into business. The duty of fulfilling

Company Perspectives:

"The Quiksilver logo, a cresting wave and snowcapped mountain, represents active sports and global excellence. Our heritage comes from the beach and the sport of surfing and extends out to include other lifestyles where the dictates for fashion and function come from active people with high standards. Since its birth over 20 years ago, Quiksilver has maintained its commitment to performance, style, and endurance and has taken the message around the world. The company credo is built upon our premier brand, Quiksilver. Quiksilver is a worldwide surf/board-riding lifestyle label based on authenticity and reputation for excellence. Our goal is to provide the market with purity of concept and provide our customers product they can wear with pride since it represents quality and value from a solid foundation. Quiksilver's substance lies in its history, its product quality and innovation and its authentic connection to the extreme sports culture. In addition to Quiksilver, Pirate Surf, Que, Roxy, and Raisins represents our complete dedication to the outdoor lifestyle. This dedication has made Quiksilver a world standard."

Greene and Law's demand fell solely to Hakman; McKnight, back in Hawaii, could be of no assistance. Greene and Law informed Hakman that they would agree to the proposal provided Hakman ate the large paper doily under his plate, which Hakman promptly did. After swallowing the plate-sized piece of paper, Hakman shook hands with Greene and Law and placed a call to Oahu to tell McKnight of the good news.

McKnight, who spearheaded the business end of the venture, offered the specifics of the proposal to Greene and Law. McKnight and Hakman invested no money, but agreed to pay a royalty of one percent of sales for three years, which jumped to three percent after three years, and an additional one percent of sales to support international promotions. Next, McKnight hurried to secure the capital required to launch the business. He returned to California and asked his father, who was a sporting goods importer, to lend him $20,000 to finance a production run of Quicksilver apparel. McKnight's father agreed, and a few months after Hakman's all-nighter with Quicksilver's Australian owners, the two young Americans were ready to start production for their new company, Quiksilver U.S.A.

McKnight and Hakman debuted their first line of apparel in the summer of 1976. They bought some fabric on credit and manufactured 600 pairs of boardshorts, featuring six separate designs, for their first season. The two entrepreneurs then took their boardshorts, which were priced higher but were more colorful than similar merchandise produced by established rivals Ocean Pacific and Hang Ten, and peddled them to three surf shops in Southern California. With their product distributed, all McKnight and Hakman could do was wait and see if they had made a prudent move. In nine days, the 600 pairs of boardshorts were nowhere to be found on the shelves and racks of the three surf shops, having sold out with encouraging speed.

Several years after their remarkably successful inaugural year of business, McKnight and Hakman found themselves surrounded by a wealth of new competitors, as start-up company after start-up company entered the active beach wear industry. The influx of new competition created a contentious marketing environment for companies like Quiksilver, but McKnight and Hakman kept their operation lean, eschewing debt, and remained tightly focused on producing the type of merchandise that first launched them toward success. Describing this period in the company's history, McKnight noted, "While everyone else was making swimwear, we were setting the standard for surfwear," an approach that would hold Quiksilver in good stead in the decades ahead. "We've been successful," McKnight went on to explain, "because our philosophy has always been to bring the image off the beach and into the stores. Since we were all surfers, we knew what kids wanted."

1980s Expansion

McKnight's commitment to his business strategy successfully carried Quiksilver through its fledgling years, creating a firmly established company by the beginning of the 1980s. The 1980s witnessed a host of sweeping changes that reshaped Quiksilver as it maneuvered through its corporate adolescence, beginning in 1981 when Hakman exited the business, leaving on amicable terms with McKnight to return to Australia and surf. Four years later, a turning point in Quiksilver's history occurred when McKnight took Quiksilver to the next plateau of the retail apparel business and began distributing Quiksilver merchandise to department stores.

The foray into the retail mainstream began gradually and conservatively, manifesting two defining characteristics of Quicksilver's development during its first decade. The move into department stores marked the beginning of the company's evolution into a more sophisticated enterprise. As the 1980s progressed, Quiksilver became more than a business whose chief objective was to finance McKnight's surfing and partying at the beach. A full-fledged corporation was in the making, propelling Quiksilver's growth forward at a substantially faster pace and engendering the attendant pitfalls of rapid growth.

Following McKnight's decision to expand Quicksilver, the company celebrated the conclusion of its first decade of business by completing its initial public offering of stock in December 1986, when annual sales were up to $19 million and the stock market was receptive to small-sized companies like Quiksilver. McKnight and his minority partners sold 50 percent of the company to the public, raising $16 million to bolster Quiksilver's financial foundation as it developed its department store business. With the proceeds gained from the public offering, McKnight bought the Quiksilver trademark for the United States and Mexico, paid off all the company's short- and long-term debts, and expanded Quiksilver's line of production runs in preparation for greater department store business. From 1986 the company operated under the name Quiksilver, Inc.

As Quiksilver intensified its involvement with department stores, eventually distributing its merchandise to retailers such as Macy's, Marshall Fields, Dayton Hudson, and the Dillard Group, McKnight decided to a bring in someone with greater experience in dealing with department stores. In July of 1987, McKnight hired John C. Warner, who at the time was senior vice-president and general merchandising manager of Macy's Department Stores' Denver operation. Initially, Warner was hired as head of sales, but he quickly proved to be a tremendous asset and seven months after joining the company was named chairman and chief executive officer of Quiksilver.

With Warner occupying the two top managerial posts and McKnight serving as president, Quicksilver moved headlong into fostering the growth of its department store business. Sales in 1987 amounted to $30 million and shot up the following year to $48.3 million, while earnings rose to $3.7 million. Sales to department stores made up 40 percent of Quiksilver's $48.3 million in sales in 1988, and offered tangible evidence that the company had made commendable progress into the retail mainstream. The company's range of merchandise had expanded substantially as well, growing well beyond the original line of six styles of boardshorts. Once the sole source of revenue for the company, boardshorts by the late 1980s accounted for only 18 percent of total annual sales, while the balance was derived from a host of different apparel items. T-shirts accounted for 15 percent of total sales, shirts 11 percent, pants 12 percent, fleece wear 9 percent, walking shorts 27 percent, jackets 4 percent, and surfing accessories another 4 percent.

In addition to these products, the company was also moving beyond purely surfing-related merchandise, diversifying its business as the strength of the Quiksilver brand name increased. In 1988, the company introduced six skiwear designs, offering the same number of styles as it had 12 years earlier with boardshorts. The initial success of the skiwear line nearly matched the initial success of the boardshort line, selling out in five weeks and grossing $500,000.

The growing spectrum of Quiksilver products appeared in roughly 2,000 stores nationwide during the late 1980s, including in the original three surf shops that purchased the company's first line of boardshorts in 1976. Fueled by this vast distribution system, annual sales leaped from the $48 million registered in 1989 to more than $70 million in 1989. By this point, when sales to department stores accounted for nearly 50 percent of total sales, some industry observers predicted that the company would become too big and low-price retailers would begin selling their merchandise, a development that would erode profitability and potentially tarnish the appeal of the Quiksilver name to the hard-core surfing set. Aware of the problem, Warner confided to a *California Business* reporter in 1989, "We have no illusions that our growth as Quiksilver in our existing businesses is limited somewhat down the road, but we want to continue growing and will do so by acquisition, start-up, or licensing."

1990s Diversification

As the company entered the 1990s, it continued to record robust sales gains. Sales in 1990 neared the $100 million mark, fueled by the continued success of the company's traditional line of surfing apparel, but the early years of the decade signalled a disruption in Quiksilver's rousing 1980s rise. Two trends emerged during the early 1990s, both of which negatively affected Quiksilver. First, a nationwide economic recession developed, sending many retailers reeling, particularly the large department stores that accounted for the bulk of Quiksilver's business. To combat the recession, department stores reduced the amount of square footage devoted to selling young men's apparel among other things, which caused Quiksilver's sales to dip.

Exacerbating this development was the growing popularity of the "grunge" look during the early 1990s, a fashion style that embraced muted, earthy hues rather than the flashy, colorful styles that had predicated Quiksilver's popularity during the 1980s. As a result, Quiksilver's neon boardshorts were no longer the rage of the day, and the company began to suffer.

To beat back the effects of the recession and changing fashion tastes, Quiksilver diversified its apparel lines and refocused its efforts toward selling to specialty stores. In 1991, the company acquired Na Pali, S.A., the European licensee of the Quiksilver brand in Europe, and established a subsidiary headquartered in France to design and produce Quiksilver apparel for all countries in Western Europe. By the mid-1990s, Quiksilver was collecting more than 30 percent of its total annual revenues from its European operation, a definite contribution to the company's resurgence by the middle part of the decade. Help came from elsewhere as well, including the company's foray into producing snowboard clothing and its entrance into the market for women's sportswear. Women's sportswear became a key facet of Quiksilver's business following the company's November 1993 acquisition of The Raisin Company, Inc., a manufacturer of women's swimwear and sportswear. Aided by the addition of a strong European business, a return to the specialty and surf shops, and the expansion of its apparel lines, Quiksilver survived the recession and stood firmly positioned as a market leader by the mid-1990s.

During the mid-1990s, Quiksilver derived roughly 40 percent of total revenues from surf shops and nearly 45 percent from specialty shops. After building its department store business significantly during the latter half of the 1980s, the company had largely abandoned these retailers by the mid-1990s, deriving less than 15 percent of total sales from department stores. This shift back to the company's roots was perceived as a positive step by a number of industry analysts, as was the company's encouraging financial growth. Between 1992 and 1995, annual net income rose from $371,000 to more than $10 million, while sales leaped from $89 million to $172 million. As the company prepared for the late 1990s in the wake of this robust growth, expectations were high, fueling confidence that years ahead would strengthen Quiksilver's market position as a dominant force.

Principal Subsidiaries

Quiksilver Europe; The Raisin Company, Inc.; ATI Apparel Trade International; QS International, Inc.

Further Reading

Barron, Kelly, "Quiksilver Surfwear Explains Its Third-Quarter," *Knight-Ridder/Tribune Business News,* September 13, 1996, p. 9.

Buchalter, Gail, "Fun, Fun, Fun," *California Business,* July 1989, p. 16.

——, "Do What You Wanna Do," *Forbes,* October 3, 1988, p. 82.

David, Gregory E., "Quiksilver: Don't Catch this Wave," *Financial World,* January 17, 1995, p. 18.

Nelson, Alexandra, "Sadeghi Exits Post at Quiksilver, Inc.," *Daily News Record,* July 21, 1992, p. 2.

"Quiksilver Earnings Up 10 Percent, Sales Jump 15 Percent in 2nd Quarter," *Daily News Record,* September 26, 1996, p. 5.

Slovak, Julianne, "Quiksilver," *Fortune,* February 26, 1990, p. 90.

—Jeffrey L. Covell

Quality Outdoor Gear and Clothing Since 1938

Recreational Equipment, Inc.

1700 45th Street East
Sumner, Washington 98390
U.S.A.
(206) 395-3780
Fax: (206) 395-3108
Web site: http//www.rei.com

Member-Owned Cooperative
Incorporated: 1938
Employees: 2,500
Sales: $447.6 million (1995)
SICs: 5941 Sporting Goods & Bicycle Shops; 5699
   Miscellaneous Apparel & Accessory Stores; 5961
   Catalog & Mail Order Houses; 2399 Fabricated
   Textile Products, Not Elsewhere Classified

The nation's largest consumer cooperative, Recreational Equipment, Inc. (REI), operates a chain of retail outlets and a mail-order catalogue business that market sports apparel, outdoor sporting equipment, and mountain climbing gear. During the mid-1990s, REI operated roughly 46 stores that stretched from coast to coast. The cooperative was owned by its 1.4 million member-customers who received annual patronage dividends in proportion to their spending. In addition to its involvement with outdoor clothing and equipment, REI operated a full-service adventure travel company named REI Adventures.

Early History

When a group of Pacific Northwest mountain climbers searched for a way to get their hands on highly coveted Swiss ice axes, their solution was the formation of REI, an enterprise destined to become the largest consumer cooperative in the United States. At the time of REI's formation in 1938, serious mountain climbers in the Pacific Northwest were in need of quality, European-manufactured mountaineering equipment, but there was little they could do individually to bridge the 5,000-mile gap separating Seattle and the epicenter of European mountaineering manufacturing. Swiss ice axes and other European-manufactured, mountain climbing equipment were unavailable in Seattle during the 1930s, forcing climbers in the Pacific Northwest to use inferior mountaineering equipment while their European counterparts enjoyed the advantages of quality equipment designed for serious use. To open up a distribution conduit from Europe to the northwest corner of the United States a group of 23 Seattle, Washington climbers led by Lloyd Anderson took collective action and turned to the roots of the modern cooperative movement for the philosophical backbone to support their group effort.

Anderson, an engineer who served as REI's president during the cooperative's first three decades of existence, looked to England for a way to import Swiss ice axes to the United States. His research uncovered the Rochdale Equitable Partners Society, an organization established in Rochdale, England, during the 19th century that was widely regarded as the progenitor of the modern cooperative movement. From the Rochdale Cooperative, Anderson adopted the principles that would guide REI during its inaugural year and into the 1990s, creating a cooperative whose membership was open to all, with each active member receiving one vote and annual dividends in proportion to patronage. After paying a modest, one-time membership fee, customers became owners of the cooperative and received a percentage of the amount they spent on merchandise each year, a percentage that was determined by the cooperative's annual profit total. Organized as such, REI represented a bold experiment in the retail industry, an enterprise with an egalitarian perspective pursuing socialist, utopian objectives that were conspicuously out of place in the fast-paced, profit-crazed retail world. The concept worked, however, succeeding in an industry littered with failed businesses whose strategies were more in line with capitalist ideals.

Not surprisingly, REI's development into the country's largest consumer cooperative and into one of the nation's largest retailers was a slow, gradual process. The object was not to create a flourishing chain of retail outlets, but to create a way for Seattle climbers to obtain state-of-the-art European climbing equipment at the best prices possible. The cooperative, in fact, did not operate a retail location until six years after its formation. Initially, REI operated out of Lloyd Anderson's house in West Seattle, but public demand for mountaineering hardware led to the establishment of the cooperative's first store in 1944, a modest operation comprising three shelves situated in the back of a gas station in downtown Seattle.

From this milestone in the company's history, the arrival of the next turning point was nine years away, occurring in 1953 when REI hired its first full-time employee to manage the cooperative's sole store. The store by this point was collecting $72,000 a year in sales, and its stewardship fell to a young local climbing enthusiast named Jim Whittaker, who, along with his twin brother, Lou, had spent his life scaling the myriad mountains dotting the Pacific Northwest. Whittaker joined REI a decade before he became the first American to reach the summit of Mt. Everest, an achievement that earned the inveterate mountain man worldwide fame and local acclaim and drew attention to REI, Whittaker's place of employment (off the mountains) for a quarter of a century. Whittaker's involvement with REI led to the beginning of a new era in the cooperative's history, bringing to a close the decades of Anderson's presidency and marking the beginning of REI's development into a retail giant.

Expansion Begins in the 1970s

Anderson served as REI's president from its founding year to 1971, overseeing the establishment of the company's first store in 1944 and its relocation to Seattle's Capitol Hill neighborhood in 1962. His departure in 1971 paved the way for Whittaker's ascendancy to the cooperative's presidency and years of unprecedented growth for the sleepy, one-store enterprise. Under Whittaker's leadership, the cooperative diversified and expanded. A product-testing subsidiary named THAW, which was formed in 1967, was built into a clothing manufacturing subsidiary during Whittaker's tenure in the 1970s. A second store was established in Berkeley, California, in 1975, making its debut 31 years after the first store opened its doors. After this lengthy gap separating store openings, Whittaker waited a mere year before opening REI's third store, establishing it in Jantzen Beach, Oregon. Quickly, REI was transforming into a regional retail powerhouse under Whittaker's directorship, executing a common evolutionary leap expected of many retail corporations but not necessarily of a consumer-owned cooperative. For years, certain members of REI's board of directors (elected by active customer-owners) had been growing alarmed at the changes taking place, changes that, according to some, were altering the philosophical foundation upon which REI had been created. As the 1970s progressed, the rancor

intensified, pitting a faction of rebellious board members against their president, Jim Whittaker. The resolution of this dispute set the stage for the most prolific growth in REI's history, marking a definitive juncture in the story of the cooperative's life.

Essentially, the philosophical battle waged during the 1970s hinged on the central issue of growth, on whether REI would follow Whittaker's ambitious expansion plans or the desires of those board members who wanted to preserve the cooperative's more simplistic roots. It was a struggle in which Whittaker did not want to participate. Whittaker quit in 1979, later telling a *Forbes* reporter, "A lot of board members were against growth; they wanted it to be the same little store." Whittaker went on to found a new manufacturer of mountain gear, a company whose merchandise was marketed under the "Because It's There" label, but his departure did not signal a return to the more supine years of REI's past. Instead, the cooperative entered the 1980s fully committed to the scale of expansion proposed by Whittaker.

In the election to decide Whittaker's successor, the proponents of no growth lost out to those who clamored for expansion, paving the way for a new president whose professional background determined REI's future. Elected to replace Whittaker was Jerry Horn, a former merchandise executive for Sears who joined REI and immediately began preaching strategic planning. The focus on strategic planning worked wonders for REI's profitability, boosting annual patronage dividends considerably. Horn added a line of children's apparel, replaced the cooperative's full-time clerks with more inexpensive seasonal workers, and in 1981 acquired Mountain Safety Research (MSR), a manufacturer of backpacking stoves, helmets, carabiners, and other mountaineering equipment. In a few short years Horn could point to tangible evidence in support of his work. Patronage dividends increased from a depressed five percent when he joined the company to 12 percent by the early 1980s, an increase that validated the shouts for growth during Whittaker's tenure.

Horn resigned from REI in June 1983, opting to leave the cooperative to run a stockholder-owned campsite company. Horn left a rapidly growing company supported by seven stores and a mail-order catalog business that generated roughly 25 percent of the cooperative's annual revenue volume. Annual sales, by this point, had marched upward at a 26 percent annual pace for the past three decades, rising to $72 million by 1982, while annual profits neared $9 million, the bulk of which was divided among the cooperative's 465,000 customer-owners. To take charge of this flourishing retail enterprise, the cooperative's board elected 36-year-old Wally Smith to replace Horn, a selection that augured more growth for REI. Smith, whose childhood dream was to become a stockbroker, first joined REI as a summer worker in 1965, becoming the first manager of the cooperative's Berkeley store when it opened a decade later. Before being elected as the cooperative's fourth president, Smith earned a business degree from the University of Washington. He then proceeded to use his educational training to orchestrate REI's expansion.

By the time Smith was settling into his new position at REI, the cooperative was selling not only a variety of climbing equipment, apparel items, and sleeping bags, but also items that had little to do with the objectives first articulated by Lloyd Anderson during the 1930s. REI, through its seven retail outlets and the more than five million catalogs it distributed each year, was a purveyor of signed and numbered art reproductions and gourmet popcorn by the time Smith took the helm. To charges that REI was developing into an organization that bore little resemblance to the cooperative formed nearly a half century earlier, Smith expressed no remorse. "The demand for backpacking goods peaked in the 1970s," he explained to a reporter from *Forbes* just after assuming REI's presidential duties. "What responsible company doesn't change with the times?"

Four years after being elected president, Smith had quickly established a legacy of expansion at REI. In 1987, the cooperative operated 17 stores, up substantially from the seven stores Smith inherited in 1983. Expansion on the East Coast was started during the year with the establishment of a store in Reading, Massachusetts, and ambitious expansion scheduled for the immediate future promised to strengthen the cooperative's national presence significantly. Sites selected for REI stores in 1988 (the cooperative's 50th anniversary year) included San Francisco, San Diego, Atlanta, Philadelphia, and California's San Fernando Valley, part of a five-year plan that called for the opening of between 15 and 20 25,000-square-foot stores.

1990s: Growth and a New Flagship Store

Fueled by this prodigious expansion, annual sales swelled to more than $200 million by the end of the decade, reaching $231 million by the beginning of the 1990s. The cooperative's subsidiary operations, THAW and MSR, had also recorded encouraging growth during the 1980s, adding to the luster of the REI organization as it prepared for the decade ahead. THAW's sales volume increased 166 percent during the 1980s, while MSR, one-quarter the size of THAW, registered more prolific growth, increasing its sales volume an astounding 453 percent. By 1990, there were 22 stores spread across 13 states; a year later there were 27 stores scattered throughout 16 states extending from Alaska to New York. Eight years after Smith's election, REI's membership rolls included more than two million registered members, more than 900,000 of whom were designated as active members—twice the number during Smith's inaugural year.

Growth on all fronts necessitated the construction of a state-of-the-art 400,000-square-foot distribution center in Sumner, Washington in 1991, evidence that the onset of a national economic recession was having little effect on REI. The cooperative, in fact, performed admirably during an economic downturn that devastated many retailers throughout the country. In 1992, when REI operated 32 stores in 18 states and announced plans to double in size by the end of the decade, the cooperative posted record sales, a feat duplicated in 1993, when REI acquired tent manufacturer Walrus, Inc., and again in 1994. The most remarkable news of the early 1990s, however, was the cooperative's announcement in 1993 that it would relocate its flagship Capitol Hill store and construct a modern store more suited to the needs of the company during the 1990s and the decades ahead.

Since its establishment in 1962, the Capitol Hill store had grown along with the cooperative, but in helter-skelter fashion.

As the cooperative grew, the flagship store expanded, swallowing up adjoining buildings along Pike Street and eventually snaking its way through five levels of retail space measuring 37,000 square feet. By the early 1990s, Smith and REI's board had decided the time had come for a new store, a store that would put an end to the nightmares of parking near Pike Street and make a bold statement about the future of REI.

As designs were being developed for the new store, REI continued to experience heartening growth. In 1994, REI operated 40 stores in 18 states, generated $432 million in sales, and ranked as the sixth largest sports apparel retailer in the United States. After two years of registering record sales and averaging 16 percent annual growth during the worst of economic times for retailers, projections for 1995 were justifiably optimistic. In 1995, however, expectations collided with reality. Anticipating growth during the year in excess of 15 percent, Smith was chagrined to record a modest gain in sales of 2.8 percent. Any disappointment stemming from 1995's lackluster sales performance was swept away the following fall when REI celebrated the grand opening of its new flagship store among throngs of disbelieving customers.

REI's new Seattle store opened in September 1996 after more than three years of planning. Measuring nearly 100,000 square feet, the new store contained 80,000 square feet of retail space, or more than twice the space of the cooperative's old and shuttered Capitol Hill store. Aside from increased retail space and an onsite, multilevel parking garage, there were numerous features that put the store in a class of its own and quickly made it a destination point for tourists visiting the Pacific Northwest. On the 1.2-acre site occupied by the flagship store, 21,000 square feet was set aside for native Northwest flora and a pond and waterfall charged with recirculated rainwater. Winding its way through the REI park was a 470-foot outdoor mountain-bike trail for customers to test bikes before purchase. Inside, the store featured a Rain Room that showered water on customers trying on waterproof clothing, a camp-stove-testing and water-filter-testing area next to the store's campsite and stream, and the most eye-catching of all the new features and interactive displays gracing the store, the 110-ton, 65-foot REI Pinnacle, the tallest free-standing indoor climbing structure in the world. Housed in a glass enclosure that offered summit views of the Puget Sound, the Olympic Mountains, and downtown Seattle, the indoor climbing rock accommodated as many as 15 climbers at a time and represented one of the most effective marketing tools for the store.

As REI prepared for the late 1990s, there was much to be celebrated. The opening of the new flagship store proved to be a rousing success, fueling confidence that the years ahead would bring commensurate success. Although some charged that the cooperative had strayed from its roots by opening a store of such scale and grandiosity, others maintained that REI had merely built upon the foundation created by Lloyd Anderson to produce an enterprise capable of competing and growing during the 1990s and the century ahead. Whatever the feelings of the nearly 1.4 million customer-owners composing the cooperative's membership during the mid-1990s, the spectacle of the new flagship store pointed to the continued evolution of the principles first established by Anderson in 1938.

Principal Subsidiaries

Mountain Safety Research; THAW; Walrus, Inc.; REI Adventures.

Further Reading

Baldwin, William, "The Money-Minded Mountaineers," *Forbes,* October 24, 1983, p. 73.

Button, Graham, "Still Climbing," *Forbes,* May 25, 1992, p. 12.

Green, Frank, "Concept of Cooperatives Gains Popularity in the Grocery Fields," *Knight-Ridder/Tribune Business News,* August 30, 1994, p. 8.

Flash, Cynthia, "REI Co-Op Opens Flagship Store in Seattle," *Knight-Ridder/Tribune Business News,* September 11, 1996, p. 9.

Kim, Nancy J., "Signs, Material Convey a Message at New REI," *Puget Sound Business Journal,* September 11, 1996, p. 4.

Nogaki, Sylvia Wieland, "Seattle's Outdoor Gear Cooperative REI To Move," *Knight-Ridder/Tribune Business News,* December 6, 1993, p. 12.

Prinzing, Debra, "REI Subsidiary: Grown Up and Standing Alone," *Puget Sound Business Journal,* September 2, 1991, p. 2.

Spector, Robert, "A Steady Climb," *Sporting Goods Business,* July 1991, p. 98.

Volk, David, "Muscle-Powered But Not Muscle-Bound," *Puget Sound Business Journal,* June 24, 1991, p. 39.

—Jeffrey L. Covell

Red Roof Inns, Inc.

4355 Davidson Road
Hilliard, Ohio 73026-2491
U.S.A.
(614) 876-3200
Fax: (614) 771-7838
Web site: http://www.redroof.com

Public Company
Incorporated: 1972
Employees: 5,200
Sales: $291.44 million (1995)
Stock Exchanges: New York
SICs: 7011 Hotels, Motels

Red Roof Inns, Inc., controlled by the Morgan Stanley Real Estate Fund, was the third largest budget lodging chain in the United States. In 1996, the "rooms only" motel chain owned and operated more than 230 inns in 33 states. Except in a few locations where zoning or building codes interfered, all the motels featured the chain's signature red roofs.

The Trueman Years: 1972–86

Red Roof Inns was founded in 1972 by James R. Trueman, a native of Cleveland and a developer of apartments, office buildings, and mobile home parks, who anticipated a growing market for budget travel lodging—quality rooms without costly amenities. Trueman opened his first Red Roof Inn in Grove City, a suburb of Columbus, Ohio, in February 1973. The motel was named for the Red Roof Tavern, a steakhouse in Kalamazoo, Michigan.

Trueman, a sportsman who also owned the TrueSports auto racing team, guided Red Roof Inns Inc. for the next 14 years, until his death in 1986, following a two-year battle with cancer. By then, Red Roof Inns, which promoted its motels with the simple slogan "Sleep Cheap," had become the largest privately owned and operated chain of budget motels in the United States, with 180 motels in 30 states and $148 million in annual revenues. Eleven days before his death, Trueman also saw Bobby Rahal drive the TrueSports/Red Roof Inn car to victory in the Indianapolis 500.

Less than a week before he died, Trueman announced a company reorganization that called for William J. Denk, then head of the company's development division and a longtime friend who had helped Trueman found Red Roof Inns, to succeed him as president. He named Richard Bibart, who had joined the company in 1984 as general counsel and vice president of planning, to head the Red Roof Inns Management Co., the new operating arm of the Red Roof Inns. When Trueman died, ownership of the company passed to a trust with his widow, Barbara, as chairman.

Without Trueman at the helm, Red Roof Inns lost its aggressiveness and expansion slowed. In 1987, Denk acknowledged to *Ohio Business* that life at Red Roof Inns was different without Trueman. "What we lost—and we lost a hell of a lot—was the entrepreneurial spirit that Jim gave to this company. I think it's a classic case of the difference between entrepreneurial management and systems management. Jim owned the majority of this company, and could pretty much do what he wanted with it. My style is, I report to the company's board, and I have to manage with that in mind. As a result, I think I'm more bottom-line oriented than Jim was."

1988: "Hit the Roof" Debuts

When Denk, at the age of 65, retired as planned in 1988, Bibart was named to head the corporation. That same year Red Roof Inns, targeting the business traveler, became the first budget motel chain to offer copy machines and fax services at all its properties.

The company also hired W.B. Donar & Co., a Detroit-based advertising firm, to create a more sophisticated, aggressive advertising campaign. The result was "Hit the Roof," a series of television commercials featuring actor Martin Mull, who ridiculed high-priced extras at other motels, such as a supposed $27 chocolate mint on the pillow at night and off-key lounge entertainment. The motel chain's first television advertising campaign, "Hit the Roof" received a silver Effie Award from the American Marketing Association.

The following year, Red Roof Inns opened its 200th motel, in Orlando, Florida, which was also the first Red Roof Inn with a swimming pool. Red Roof Inns also broke with its no-frills

---

Company Perspectives:

We place great emphasis on the three components that create strong customer value in our segment—price, location, and consistent quality.

We know that many of the guests who travel in the economy segment do so to save money. Price is paramount and we strive to keep our prices down. We have been successful. Our average daily rate is well below our economy segment competitors.

We enjoy premier sites in many of our markets. As a testimony to our superior locations, we achieve higher occupancy levels than our competitors at nine out of 10 Red Roof Inns.

Our rigorous operating standards help ensure that we deliver a consistent guest experience throughout our chain.

---

tradition to add swimming pools to its motels in Tampa and Kissimmee. Although business travelers continued to be the mainstay for Red Roof Inns, management felt swimming pools were critical to compete for families vacationing at the nearby destination resorts, including Disney World. Still, Bibert told *Lodging Hospitality,* "We must be careful about adding amenities that will increase room rates."

In 1989, Red Roof Inn also announced a major renovation program, updating its guest rooms and lobbies in older motels, many of which had not changed since 1976. The lobbies were expanded to add "warmth," while some rooms were enlarged to offer business travelers more work space. "Business King" rooms were also outfitted with telephone modem jacks for computer hook-ups. Targeting about a dozen motels per year, Red Roof spent an estimated $15 million on renovations between 1989 and 1991.

Early in 1990, Red Roof Inns surprised the industry by announcing that it would develop its first full-service hotel—including restaurant, indoor swimming pool, health club, and conference center—in Columbus, Ohio, near company headquarters. The upscale, 182-room hotel was named the Trueman Club, after the company founder.

New Life with Morgan Stanley in the 1990s

Late in 1993, the Morgan Stanley Real Estate Fund, a division of investment banker Morgan Stanley Inc., bought Red Roof Inns for $600 million. The *Wall Street Journal* reported that Morgan Stanley, known for buying distressed properties, initially approached Red Roof Inns about acquiring a minority interest in the chain, with the infusion of cash fueling long-delayed plans for expansion. After the purchase, analysts following the hospitality industry pointed to the acquisition as evidence that the investment value of hotels and motels, stagnant for several years, was once again on the rise.

Under Morgan Stanley, Red Roof Inns, which had added only The Trueman Club to its list of properties since 1990, acquired more than a motel a month for the next year and a half. Morgan Stanley also brought in a new management team and

named Jack Van Fossen, a longtime director, as president and chief executive.

In 1995, Red Roof Inns also added its first new-construction motels in five years, in El Paso, Laredo, Houston, and San Antonio, Texas. The new motels came with a redesigned floor plan, with exterior room entrances in the ground floor, but still avoided costly extras. John Campbell, then chief operating officer, told *Hotel & Motel Management* that Red Roof Inns would continue to fight "amenity creep," something he said the motel chain had lost sight of in the 1980s. "We don't spend an extra penny if it doesn't add value for guests," Campbell said. "We have to make sure we stay in our niche."

Late in 1995, Morgan Stanley took Red Roof Inns public with a $160 million initial public offering, the 10 million shares representing about 35 percent of all stock in the company. Soon afterwards, Francis "Butch" Cash, a longtime Marriott Corp. executive who had succeeded Van Fossen as president and chief executive, announced that Red Roof Inns would begin a franchising program for the first time in its 23-year history.

Trueman, the entrepreneur, had established the policy against franchising. As Bibart told *Lodging Hospitality* in 1989, "It was clear to Jim Trueman that Red Roof could grow rapidly. [But he] felt strongly about the ability to control the product and to operate it in a first-class manner." Morgan Stanley had restated that policy and concern about control when it acquired Red Roof Inns in 1993. Peter Krause, then head of Morgan Stanley's lodging and leisure division, told *Hotel & Motel Management,* "While we have no opposition to franchising, we don't see ourselves getting into that. We like to own and we like to control. You lose control when some third party owns and operates the property."

However, in an interview with the *Wall Street Transcript* in late 1996, Cash explained, "We think that [Red Roof Inns] should be opening 45 or 50 properties per year and in order to do that, we need to have a very active franchising program." He predicted Red Roof Inns would award about 25 franchises per year. Cash also said the company was looking for joint-venture partners for motels that Red Roof Inns would manage. He told the *Columbus Dispatch Business Reporter,* "How many inns should we have? A lot closer to 1,000 than 300."

Further Reading

Coulton, Anne, "Red Roof: Beyond Sleep Cheap," *Lodging Hospitality,* September 1989, p. 26.

Hall, Matthew, "Trueman's Legacy Lives on at Red Roof Inns Inc." *Ohio Business,* June 1987, p. 11.

Lilly, Stephen, "Red Roof Launching First Upscale Hotel," *Business First-Columbus,* January 15, 1990, p. 1.

Nozar, Robert A., "Red Roof Plugged Back in for Growth," *Hotel & Motel Management,* June 5, 1995, p. 1.

Pachelle, Mitchell, and Pauline Yoshihashi, "Morgan Stanley to Buy Red Roof Inns, A Sign 'Vulture Funds' Seek Survivors," *Wall Street Journal,* November 17, 1993, p. A3.

Troy, Timothy N., "Red Roof Buy Signals Return of Big Money," *Hotel & Motel Management,* December 13, 1993, p. 1.

—Dean Boyer

Regal-Beloit Corporation

200 State Street
Beloit, Wisconsin 53511-9940
U.S.A.
(608) 364-8800
Fax: (608) 365-2182

Public Company
Incorporated: 1955 as Beloit Tool Company
Sales: $295.9 million (1995)
Employees: 2,600
Stock Exchanges: American
SICs: 3694 Electrical Equipment for Internal Combustion
Engines; 3541 Machine Tools—Metal Cutting Types

Regal-Beloit Corporation is the fifth-largest firm in the U.S. engine electrical equipment industry and a major manufacturer of power transmission systems and commercial cutting tools. Its products are used in the manufacture of everything from X-ray machine parts and amusement park rides to Boeing 747s and Daytona 500 racing cars. In 1995, it ranked as the 47th largest public company in the state of Wisconsin and the 55th largest company by market value on the American Stock Exchange (according to *Equities* magazine).

Regal-Beloit's largest segment, the Power Transmission Group, manufactures gear boxes, transmissions, forklift axles, ring and pinion gears, mini-gear motors, and manual valve actuators used in such products as conveyor belts, packaging equipment, street pavers, graders, irrigation systems, grocery checkout equipment, paper-making machinery, ice cream vending machines, rescue equipment, farm equipment, gas flow control systems, and precision medical equipment. Through its nine divisions, Regal-Beloit sells its power transmission products to distributors, original equipment manufacturers, and end users in the dairy, farming, and construction industries, among many other sectors. As one stock market analyst put it, Regal-Beloit "manufacture[s] gears and mechanical parts that aren't very exciting, but you can't run the world without them."

Although Regal-Beloit's Cutting Tools Group accounted for only 13 percent of the company's sales in 1995 it was the second-largest full-line manufacturer (in dollar value) of drills, end mills, gages, taps (a tool for forming a screw thread), and reamers (a tool for enlarging holes). Its Beloit-based Regal Cutting Tools operation alone ranked as the 36th largest company in the U.S. metal cutting machine tools industry in 1995. The thousands of steel and carbide rotary cutting tools Regal-Beloit produces are used as essential product-making tools across a wide swathe of metalworking applications in the U.S. economy, including the aerospace, automaking, and petroleum industries among others. Seventy percent of the company's cutting tool sales are sold on a nonexclusive, "open line" basis through independent industrial distributors, and the remainder are sold to select customers through Regal-Beloit's National Twist Drill and New York Twist Drill divisions. Because cutting tools are expendable, or "perishable," Regal-Beloit derives significant revenue from the sale of replacement drills and cutting tools to its customers.

In 1996, Regal-Beloit serviced the $1.5 billion market for power transmission equipment and commercial cutting tools through several divisions (each offering complete product lines for their individual markets) and operated 17 domestic and three overseas plants/service/distribution centers.

Beloit Tool Company: 1955–72

Regal-Beloit Corporation was founded in 1955 by entrepreneur Kenyon Y. Taylor as the Beloit Tool Company in the southeastern Wisconsin community of Beloit. Working from his home with three friends, three desks, and three telephones, Taylor manufactured specially designed metric and decimal-dimensioned cutting tools from a "plant" in his garage. Emphasizing superior customer service from the start, Taylor offered 24-hour delivery of his special taps to his mostly local customers. Within six months of the company's inception, orders were multiplying, and Taylor hired more workers to expand his production capacity. Quickly running short of space, he moved Beloit Tool to an old abandoned roller-skating rink east of downtown Beloit. By the end of its first full year in

450

Company Perspectives:

Regal-Beloit Corporation is a leading producer of power transmission systems and perishable high speed steel rotary cutting tools. The Company prides itself on consistent, fast delivery of quality products which meet the customers' specific needs.

business, Beloit Tool had posted losses of $40,000, the first and only time it registered an unprofitable year.

In 1957 Taylor acquired Crest Tool Industries, a cutting tool company that specialized in providing tools to U.S. government purchasing agencies, and two years later Beloit Tool had passed the $100 million sales level. The same year, it demonstrated its early commitment to employee-sensitive management by establishing a profit-sharing plan, a byproduct of Taylor's reaction to the treatment of workers as "commodities and clock numbers" that he had experienced firsthand during the Depression. With sales soaring, in 1963 Taylor moved his corporate headquarters to a new location in an old farmhouse in nearby South Beloit, Illinois, and in 1965 acquired the historic Durst Foundry and Machine Works of nearby Shopiere, Wisconsin. That company's founder, Walter Durst, had founded Durst in 1932 and built a significant niche manufacturing equipment for the farming industry, mostly in the form of pump drives, large specially designed transmissions, forklift axles, and a variety of standard and custom gear boxes. Taylor kept Durst on as a consultant and renamed the new operation Durst Power Transmission Division.

Regal-Beloit Corporation: 1973–90

In 1973 Taylor officially changed Beloit Tool's name to Regal-Beloit (after, some said, a type of flower) and continued his strategy of expanding its market share and diversifying its business niche by acquiring promising companies in its basic power transmission and cutting tools lines. The U.S. power transmission market had traditionally been fragmented among dozens of smaller manufacturers, and the pickings for an acquisition-minded, cash-heavy firm like Regal-Beloit seemed ripe. In its cutting tool segment alone, Regal-Beloit had already absorbed such small players as Empire Gage, Walter T. Cole, Waukegan Quality Tool Works, Q.T. Tool, Stanworth Tool, M.E.C. Corporation, Caledec Gage, Premium Cutting Tools, and Glenbard Manufacturers. Turning to the power transmission segment, in mid-1978, Taylor purchased Orbmark Company, the developer of a high-torque, low-speed hydraulic motor, and a year later he brought James Packard, a seasoned corporate manager from PepsiCo's Frito-Lay division, on board Regal-Beloit's management team. In expectation of the huge sales potential of foreign markets, in 1979 Taylor also unveiled Regal-Beloit International Sales Corporation, which he headquartered in the firm's Beloit offices.

Early in the 1980s Regal-Beloit began a program of plowing $7 to $8 million annually into new equipment to ensure that its manufacturing processes were as efficient and modern as possible. At the same time, it was also earning a reputation as the

only firm in the industry that purchased *used* equipment from machinery dealers and auctioneers—at a 30 percent savings—to keep operating costs down. Buying only bug-free products from reliable dealers, Regal-Beloit by 1996 was saving $3 million annually on equipment purchases. It also began adopting the low-inventory technique later known as "just-in-time delivery" several years before it became de rigueur among America's corporations.

Taylor's ambitious acquisition program continued in the 1980s. Twelve firms were purchased and absorbed during the decade, substantially expanding the firm's market share, manufacturing capability, and profitability. As James Packard later commented, "by quickly instituting effective cost controls, more efficient manufacturing methods and our strong customer service philosophy, these new divisions became strong contributors to the company's overall performance." Moreover, by holding out for a reasonable selling price, paying only cash (rather than stock), and considering only firms that could generate earnings in the first year following acquisition, Regal-Beloit recuperated its acquisitions costs quickly and kept its debt low. Finally, by preserving the identity of the acquired company's product line and assiduously applying "lean" manufacturing techniques (such as "just-in-time"), its new acquisitions could grow rapidly once in the corporate fold.

Regal-Beloit's 1980s buying spree commenced in 1981 with the acquisition of Grove Gear of Union Grove, Wisconsin, a manufacturer of standard and special worm gear speed-reducing gear boxes, adaptors, and accessories, founded in 1947. In 1984, however, Taylor stepped down as CEO while remaining chairman of the board, and turned Regal-Beloit's reins over to Packard, who continued the company's grand acquisition strategy as sales broke the $57 million mark, a company record. In mid-decade, Regal-Beloit's Durst Power Transmission Division began expanding to cater to large manufacturers of off-highway vehicles, and construction and industrial equipment. Packard returned to the acquisition waters again in 1985 with the purchase of Noster Industries Inc. of Michigan and National Twist Drill of Columbia, South Carolina, a producer of large-volume drills, taps, end mills, gages, and reamers.

By its 30th anniversary year, Regal-Beloit was employing 1,250 people working out of 18 manufacturing and customer service facilities nationwide. Packard led its large facilities through a major improvement program, incorporated new products and related manufacturing equipment into the company's plants, and began a systematic workforce flexibility program in which nearly a third of Regal-Beloit's employees were training for new positions at any given time. After three decades at Regal-Beloit's helm, Taylor finally relinquished the chairmanship to Packard in 1986. As sales reached $78 million, Packard installed the first U.S. computer-controlled manufacturing process for grinding threaded tools in 1986, and the Power Transmission Group won several major contracts, including a $5.5 million agreement with the federal government to design and test transmissions for refueling vehicles.

Beginning in the early 1980s, the power transmission equipment industry had become mature—growth was slow, sales were declining, and the profusion of industry firms led to excess manufacturing capacity. The industry, which had long been dominated by old line and "captive" manufacturers (companies manufacturing equipment exclusively for their parent firm), began to undergo a radical transformation in which foreign and domestic competition intensified and new specialized product niches began to emerge. In this new competitive environment, some smaller companies failed because they were unable to afford new equipment, and some larger firms began to outsource their work to cut costs. Regal-Beloit exploited both opportunities: the failing smaller firms made attractive acquisition targets, and Regal-Beloit's experience with diverse product lines enabled it to claim the outsourced work of the larger firms. Packard led it into a wider and wider series of product markets in which, though it often was not the largest firm, its flexibility, customer service performance, and streamlined manufacturing processes could find a very profitable niche. The power transmission equipment industry was inexorably contracting, but Regal-Beloit seemed to face only opportunity.

As the company adjusted to its 1985 acquisition of National Twist and Noster's product lines, in 1986 it began a string of five plant expansions in five years and a year later acquired four more firms: Paterson Gear Motor of Roscoe, Illinois; Illinois Gear of Chicago, a manufacturer of fractional horsepower gearmotors; Ohio Gear of South Carolina, a manufacturer of standard and special worm gear and concentric shaft speed reducers; and Richmond Gear of South Carolina, a producer of high-performance ring and pinion gear sets and transmissions. The additions broadened Regal-Beloit's product line, pumped up its financials, and enabled it to minimize its dependence on any single one of its markets.

Surveying his firm's new profile, Packard commented to the *Beloit Daily News*, "all things considered, we think we're going to be an exciting company." As if to drive home the point, he had added three more companies by decade's end: New York Twist Drill (1988), Foote-Jones Gear (1989), and Electra-Gear (1989). Founded in 1949, New York Twist Drill (Ronkonkoma, New York) manufactured drills, taps, end mills, reamers, and gages for high-volume applications and filled out Regal-Beloit's Cutting Tool Group. Electra-Gear, of Anaheim, California, and Foote-Jones Gear, of Chicago, Illinois, expanded the Power Transmission Group product lines. By 1991, Regal-Beloit's growth-through-acquisition strategy had amounted to 20 individual acquisitions, and in August 1989 it was named to *Financial World* magazine's "Growth 500," finishing 261st on the strength of its 23 percent five-year annual earnings-per-share growth rate.

Powering to the Top: 1990–97

In May 1990, Regal-Beloit broke ground on a new $2.4 million world headquarters building in downtown Beloit, signaling its aim to return to its original Wisconsin roots after 27 years on the other side of the Illinois border. When it opened in March 1991, the 24,000-square-foot building housed Regal-Beloit's corporate offices, data processing center, and advertising, accounting, and personnel departments in a light-flooded design intended to avoid a "factory" feel. The much-ballyhooed move, however, was clouded by uncertainty. Regal-Beloit's capital expenditures for 1990 were expected to hit $8 to $10 million, a ten-year high, and amid rumors of a potential takeover bid, management could only confirm that 30 percent of

company stock was in "friendly" hands. Moreover, a contract to build replacement transmissions for the U.S. Army had been poorly bid, and Regal-Beloit was forced to swallow the loss. Finally, because of its broad product diversification, the recession of the early 1990s dragged at Regal-Beloit's profits, and corporate sales were off by as much as 20 percent according to some projections.

Nevertheless, the company's fundamental financial conditions remained positive. It had achieved an average annual return on investment of 17.2 percent (despite little use of debt) between 1955 and the move to the new building, had raised cash dividends 26 times in those 31 years, and had declared 123 consecutive quarterly payments without a dividend reduction. Although Packard was forced to admit that because of the recession Regal-Beloit's sales volumes were "significantly reduced," it had done better than many of its smaller competitors, which now presented themselves as attractive acquisition targets. Moreover, with healthy operations in Illinois, New Jersey, Texas, California, South Carolina, North Carolina, and New York, its long-pursued acquisition strategy seemed as viable as ever. "We are still looking at companies to purchase," Packard told an interviewer in 1991. "Our ability to grow will come through acquisitions. Right now we have a strong cash position, virtually no debt, and we are pretty well poised to be aggressively seeking out acquisitions at this point."

Consequently, in July 1991 Packard completed Regal-Beloit's first European acquisition with the purchase of Opperman Mastergear Ltd. of Newbury, England. The acquisition added 220 employees (most in England, the rest at Opperman's German operation) to the company's ranks. With sales arcing past $152 million, two more acquisitions—hydraulic pump drive manufacturers Hub City, Inc. of Aberdeen, South Dakota, in April 1992 and Terrell Gear Drives, Inc. of Charlotte, North Carolina, in November—boosted Regal-Beloit's sales to $199.8 million by year-end. In 1993 price increases in the used metal-cutting machine tools industry were offset by increased sales figures for the Power Transmission Group, all of whose units posted improved numbers. With exports accounting for roughly 3 percent of company sales and rising, Packard began casting about for another likely acquisition target in Europe, where the power transmission market was scattered among several small firms. By the end of 1993 Regal-Beloit's total sales had edged up to $220 million.

Packard strengthened Regal-Beloit's profit margins throughout the 1990s by continuing to install computer-aided manufacturing systems, dropping nonperforming products and unveiling new ones, and restructuring facilities. He also began implementing "cell" manufacturing techniques in which a wider variety of products could be manufactured by abandoning the traditional practice of committing entire plants to the production of a single product in favor of divvying up each facility into flexible manufacturing cells to produce multiple products as needed. As Regal-Beloit's sales jumped to $242.6 million in 1994, Packard found another market share-broadening target in the marine and industrial transmission operations of Borg-Warner Automotive and Engine Components Corporation, which unit Regal-Beloit acquired in January 1995. Christened the Velvet Drive Transmission Division, the operation contributed mightily to Regal-Beloit's 21.9 percent increase in sales for 1995, which was further boosted by the progress of Regal-Beloit's new Italian operation, Costruzioni Meccaniche Legnanesi, acquired in late 1994.

Aborted merger talks with Brad Foote Gear Works of Illinois, material and labor shortages, power outages and extreme heat, and slowing sales of Regal-Beloit's agricultural power transmission products all seemed to doom management's optimistic sales forecasts for 1995. Nevertheless, by the close of the year strong demand from virtually all industrial customers and the increasing progress of Regal-Beloit's foreign subsidiaries (which were closing in on 10 percent of all power transmission sales) had produced new records for sales, net income, and earnings per share.

If anthropologist Margaret Mead was correct in describing the city of Beloit as a "microcosm" of American society, Regal-Beloit had served as a kind of microcosmic barometer of the U.S. industrial economy throughout its history. Its markets were so diverse and its products so essential and varied that its quarter-by-quarter performance could reliably be used as an index of the condition of American industry. By the 1990s, it had become a Wall Street darling (since 1992 its stock had been significantly outstripping the Dow Jones factory equipment index), and in 1996 *Forbes* magazine named it among the "200 Best Small Companies in America." Moreover, more than one industry analyst shared the opinion that Regal-Beloit was an "extremely well-run company . . . a low-cost, efficient manufacturer" managed by "capable" executives with an eye toward the "long haul." In a 1996 interview, chief financial officer Kenneth Kaplan described Regal-Beloit's prospects in more cautious terms: "Obviously there are markets we haven't gotten into, customers we haven't reached. You are always looking for ways to improve designs, cut costs, to get more price-competitive." Packard echoed the bottom-line focus of Regal-Beloit's corporate culture: "We watch all of our costs, all of our expenses very, very closely, and we make our capital expenditures go a long, long way."

Principal Subsidiaries

New York Twist Drill Inc.; Opperman Mastergear Limited (United Kingdom); Mastergear GmbH (Germany); Hub City, Inc.; Costruzioni Meccaniche Legnanesi S.r.L.; Regal-Beloit International Sales Corporation; Regal-Beloit Corporation FSC.

Further Reading

Doherty, Chuck, "Regal-Beloit Plans Purchase," *Milwaukee Sentinel*, February 25, 1992.

Hajewski, Doris, "Firm's Frugality Pays Off," *Milwaukee Journal Sentinel*, October 8, 1995.

Jones, John A., "Regal-Beloit Keeps Profits Up As Heavy Industry Rolls On," *Investor's Business Daily*, January 2, 1996, p. A33.

Krantz, Matt, "How One Firm Saves a Third by Buying Used," *Investor's Business Daily*, October 15, 1996, p. A4.

"Newest 'Kid' on a Super Block," *Beloit Daily News*, April 24, 1991, special issue on Regal-Beloit Corporation.

Osenga, Mike, "Pump Drives Key to Expanding Off-Road Program," *Diesel Progress*, September 1993, pp. 52–55.

Ostrander, Kathleen, "The Big Move," *Milwaukee Sentinel*, March 28, 1991.

——, "Regal Dips, but Seeks Acquisition," *Milwaukee Sentinel*, April 25, 1991, p. 3.

"Regal-Beloit Corporation," *Wall Street Journal Interactive Edition*, http://www.wsj.com.

Romell, Rick, "Fit for *Forbes*: Bottom Line Helps Regal-Beloit Make List," *Milwaukee Journal Sentinel*, October 25, 1996, p. 9D.

Rondy, John, "Regal-Beloit Corporation," *Business Journal of Milwaukee*, July 31, 1993, p. 17.

Sandler, Larry, "Regal-Beloit Eyes Growth in Europe," *Milwaukee Sentinel*, March 18, 1993.

Savage, Mark, "Regal-Beloit Plans Acquisitions," *Milwaukee Sentinel*, December 16, 1994, p.

"The CEOs of Wisconsin: James Packard," *The Business Journal of Milwaukee*, March 27, 1993.

—Paul S. Bodine

Regis Corporation

7201 Metro Boulevard
Minneapolis, Minnesota 55439
U.S.A.
(612) 947-7777
Fax: (612) 947-7600

Public Company
Incorporated: 1954
Employees: 25,000
Sales: $499.4 million (fiscal year ended June 30, 1996)
Stock Exchanges: NASDAQ
SICs: 7231 Beauty Shops

Regis Corporation is the world's largest owner and operator of mall-based hair and retail salons. Atypical of the industry, the company owns, rather than franchises, the vast majority of its salons which are operated under five divisions: Regis Hairstylists, MasterCuts, Trade Secret, Wal-Mart Salons, and International. The 1996 purchase of the popular franchise chain Supercuts, Inc. boosted Regis's share of the highly fragmented hair salon market 2.5 percent.

Family Business Roots

Regis Corporation's history began with Russian-born barber Paul Kunin, who set up business in 1922. He built a chain of about 60 shops located in leased space in smaller-city department stores. "My father was never in the top department stores in Minneapolis. He was in the good places in Fargo," said Myron Kunin in a November 1985 *Corporate Report* article. Although Kunin had grown up working in the shops, it was his father's real estate ventures that he found intriguing.

Myron Kunin and his sister Diana bought the business in 1954. But their father kept the real estate holdings, and Kunin had to settle for being in the hair care business. Kunin eventually bought his sister's share of Regis Corporation and began trimming back the number of downtown department salons. In the mid-1960s, he began opening salons in the enclosed malls that were beginning to spring up in the suburbs of middle-sized and small-sized cities around the country. The new salons had an upscale image and upscale prices. By 1975 Regis Corporation owned 161 salons, and sales for the fiscal year were $10.6 million.

Regis was an anomaly in an industry which was, according to William Swanson, "better known for its small-time mom-and-pop operations, managerial unevenness and generally meager earnings." While the other hair care chains were generally franchised, Regis owned and operated its salons, which allowed for more control over the business. Compound annual sales grew by 29 percent and earnings per share grew by 32 percent for the period between 1978 and 1983.

Move to Public Ownership

Regis became publicly owned in April 1983. The company held about ½ percent of the $13.5 billion U.S. salon market and operated more than 300 salons at the time. Piper, Jaffray & Hopwood analyst Dick Pyle, cited by Swanson, said Regis's success as a salon owner and operator was most likely due to factors such as knowledge of the business, good site selection, favorable leases, steady growth, fair treatment of employees, and consistency of image. Its Regis Hairstylists salons catered to a largely female clientele: women who were willing to pay upper-end prices for trend-setting services and products.

In 1984, Regis bought a chain of about 60 shops which targeted male customers. But, according to a 1989 *Fortune* magazine article by Julianne Slovak, write-offs related to the Your Fathers Mustache purchase cut into earnings for two years, and Regis converted the salons to other concepts.

Executive vice president Peter Fudurich—who joined the company in the 1960s when the California chain he worked for was purchased by Kunin—was in line to succeed Kunin as president. Kunin trusted Fudurich and the management team to oversee daily operation of the company. Kunin, already in 1985, had a number of interests outside of Regis Corporation, including television stations and real estate holdings and developments. He was also well-known as an art collector, having spent millions on works by 20th-century American painters. But Fudurich's illness and death forced Kunin back into the day-to-day involvement in the business.

Company Perspectives:

Our objective is to continue double-digit growth in sales and profits. We plan to enter the twenty-first century as a billion-dollar company. Our locations are prime. Our associates are the best trained in the industry. Continuing strong results reflect both sound strategy and good execution.
We are fashioned for profitable growth.

In 1987, Kunin brought on board Paul Finkelstein, who had worked for both his family's Glemby International Hairstyling Salons and their chief rival, Seligman & Latz. Anthony Carideo wrote in 1988, ''Paul Finkelstein, Regis' savvy new president, is adding profits to the bottom line after several years of rapid expansion but erratic earnings comparisons.'' Finkelstein helped profits by restructuring commissions and emphasizing product sales. Sales for fiscal year 1988 were $192 million. Net income was $7.9 million, up 42 percent from the previous year.

Regis purchased the assets of more than 500 Seligman & Latz salons in August 1988. The nation's second largest department-store beauty chain had Essanelle Salons in about 60 stores, including Saks Fifth Avenue and Neiman Marcus. Regis was granted exclusive rights to run the beauty salons in Saks stores.

Back to Private Ownership

Regis owned about 700 salons when the company returned to private ownership in October 1988—Wall Street's expectations regarding their short-term performance, and the company's desire to reward new company managers through equity ownership were among the reasons cited for the change. Public shareholders held 30 percent of stock and received $17.70 per share—a price driven up by protests that the initial offering was too low.

Regis Corp. was merged into Regis Acquisition Corp., a subsidiary of Curtis Squire Inc., a venture-capital firm controlled by the Myron Kunin family. The company incurred $113 million in debt to finance the buyout, pay a $33 million cash dividend to Curtis Squire, and purchase the Essanelle Salons. Unfortunately, the highly leveraged financing quickly became a huge stumbling block.

Kunin and Finkelstein had planned a big expansion into the department-store salon business. But because of the debt load and changing financial climate, the company was refused new loans. Kunin personally funded the 1989 purchase of Maxim's Beauty Salons, a chain started by his uncle. Regis intended to purchase Glemby, which produced about $260 million in annual revenues, but could not do so without outside financing.

Banker and Minnesota Twins owner Carl Pohlad was introduced to the scenario. Pohlad and financier Irwin Jacobs were among the owners of MEI Diversified Inc.—a company which, according to Eric J. Wieffering, ''made a lot of investors wealthy'' in a 1986 bottling company sale to PepsiCo but had been less than successful in subsequent deals. Kunin and Pohlad began discussions regarding an MEI ownership stake in Regis in 1989, but failed to reach an agreement.

A Bad Hair Deal

Operating income had been improving, but Regis failed to make some of its loan payments, and the terms were renegotiated at much higher interest rates. The hair salon company needed to reduce its debt, so Kunin returned to Pohlad. A deal with MEI was finally struck early in 1990. MEI agreed to purchase the New York-based Glemby Co. Inc., the nation's largest department-store hair salon chain, and Regis's Maxim's Beauty Salons Inc. and Essanelle Salon Co. for a total of about $50 million.

MEI held an 80 percent share of the newly-formed MEI-Regis Salon Corporation. Kunin and Regis owned the remaining 20 percent, and the company received a contract to manage the salons. More than 2000 salons were included in the joint venture and had combined annual sales of about $400 million. Regis retained sole ownership of its Regis Hairstylists and MasterCuts salons.

Analysts and investors reacted positively when the MEI-Regis pairing was announced. Wieffering wrote in *Corporate Report Minnesota*, ''Here, they said, was the perfect match: a company with a lot of cash to invest and a business being run by one of the best operators in the industry.'' But, the deal went sour when the department-store salons' performance failed to meet MEI's expectations.

In May 1991, MEI filed a lawsuit against Glemby Co. Inc. claiming in U.S. District Court that the financial conditions and prospects of the business had been misrepresented. MEI had paid about $30 million for Glemby. Finkelstein, as a member of the founding family, was initially named in the suit but was later dropped from the list of defendants. Seeking to reduce its own debt further, Regis had been making plans to return to public ownership. That action was jeopardized when MEI announced that it also paid too much for the Regis salon chains it had purchased.

Despite building friction, the dispute between MEI and Regis was settled. The two companies agreed on a lower purchase price, and the MEI-Regis hair salons management contract was extended. But, MEI continued to pursue the suit against Glemby.

Return to Public Ownership

The plan to go public proceeded after Regis found debt financing for $92 million in bank loans remaining from the buyout. But the June 1991 public offering fell short of expectations: the 3.2 million shares sold for $2 off the asking price of $15, and the company raised only about $42 million. The sale reduced Kunin's share of Regis to 56 percent. Regis ended fiscal year 1991 with revenues of $307.7 million and net losses of $3.2 million.

The Regis and MEI partnership continued to deteriorate: MEI took over the management of the joint venture salons early in 1992 and changed the name of the operation to MEI Salon Corporation. MEI claimed Regis had mismanaged the stores, but Regis said the poorer than expected financial showing of the joint venture was due to the Gulf War and the economic recession. The hair business had been considered recession proof, but sales were sharply down, especially in department stores where most of the MEI-Regis salons were located. A rash of department store bankruptcies forced the closure of 150 to 200 of the MEI-Regis salons. In May 1992, Regis sued MEI for expenses related to the management of the MEI-Regis salons. MEI countered with a $150 million suit against Regis alleging fraud, racketeering, and contract violations.

As the legal battle raged on, Regis continued to grow. In December 1992, the company purchased Consumer Beauty Supply, a mall-based beauty product retailer which complemented their service-oriented chains. Regis purchased a similar concept from Trade Secret Development Corp. the next year. Both the chains sold brand-named products such as Nexxus and Redken as well as the Regis line. Jennifer Waters wrote, ''Both Trade Secret and Beauty Express are considered cash cows of the hair salon industry because of the growth in retail sales in recent years.'' The Trade Secret purchase put Regis into the franchising business for the first time.

In the meantime, MEI's series of losses had forced the company to file for Chapter 11 bankruptcy protection; their dispute with Regis was settled through the U.S. Bankruptcy Court in December 1993. Regis agreed to loan Toronto-based Magicuts Inc. $5.9 million for the purchase of the MEI salons. The settlement, which also included the transfer of Regis stock to MEI, cost Regis about $15 million. The legal battle hit the company's stock price as well. Regis stock fell from the $13 public offering price to the $6–$9 range and stayed there until the suit was settled. The stock was trading in the mid-teens in the beginning of 1995.

Changes had been taking place in the hair salon industry. ''To stave off competitors such as the publicly traded Supercuts, which has aggressively franchised its way to 850 salons, Regis has been building its own discount chain by adding 35 to 40 stores to its MasterCuts Division for the last two years,'' wrote Jagannath Dubashi in a 1994 *Financial World* article. MasterCuts—established in 1985 to cater to men, young adults, and children—had grown to 257 salons by the end of fiscal 1994 and contributed 16 percent of total revenues. In comparison, the company owned about 800 Regis Hairstylist salons which generated over half of total revenues.

Regis had begun operating haircare salons in Mexico in 1988 and in the United Kingdom in 1990. In 1993, the company held 260 international salons: 217 in its United Kingdom (U.K.) subsidiary, 35 in Canada, and 8 in Mexico. Sales from the U.K. subsidiary, which also included salons in South Africa, contributed 9.4 percent of total company sales for the 1993 fiscal year. In 1995, Regis acquired Essanelle Ltd., which operated 79 upscale salons located in British department stores such as Harrods; the purchase also included some salons in Switzerland. The addition of 91 salons in the next year made Regis the U.K.'s dominant hairstyling firm.

Building for the Future

In May 1996, Regis created a fifth leg of operation with the purchase of 154 National Hair Care Centers LLC salons operating in Wal-Mart stores. The salons had total annual revenues of about $28 million. Susan Feyder wrote that according to Piper Jaffray Inc. analyst Saul Yaari, ''the deal is significant because of the relationship Regis will have with Wal-Mart as it puts hair salons into new stores.'' The giant retailer expected to build 100 supercenters in 1996. Regis hoped to land spots in 30 to 50 of them.

Regis spent $30 million on acquisitions in fiscal 1996. Company revenues climbed to $499 million; net income was $19 million, up 31 percent from the previous year. The company also brought its debt to capitalization ratio down to 37 percent—it had been hovering around 60 percent four years earlier. Kunin retired as chief executive office at the end of the fiscal year, but retained his position as chairman of the board. Regis president and chief operating officer Finkelstein succeeded him.

In July 1996, Regis announced plans to purchase SuperCuts, Inc., a pioneer in the discount haircut market, in a deal which exceeded $100 million. Founded in 1975, the franchiser was purchased by an investor group in 1987 and taken public in 1991. Revenues tripled between 1991 and 1995. But, a rapid expansion of corporate-owned stores resulted in a $7.1 million loss in 1995. Regis stock fell 20 percent to around $26 per share, when news of the purchase was made public. Piper Jaffray analyst Yaari said in a July 1996 article by Sally Apgar, ''I think the merger is a good fit, but the price was rich and, therefore, the risk is higher.'' Yaari also thought Wall Street might view the company—now with six business areas—as spreading itself too thin.

Further Reading

Apgar, Sally, ''Salon Chain Regis Corp. to Buy Products Retailer,'' *Star Tribune* (Minneapolis), December 8, 1992, p. 3D.
——, ''Regis Plans to Acquire Supercuts,'' *Star Tribune* (Minneapolis), July 16, 1996, p. 1D.
Brook, Steve, ''MEI Settles with Regis in Hair Salon Dispute,'' *St. Paul Pioneer Press*, May 24, 1991.
Carideo, Anthony, ''MEI Diversified, Regis On Brink Of A Split,'' *Star Tribune* (Minneapolis), March 7, 1992, p. 3D.
——, ''Some See Regis Buyback Offer As Low,'' *Star Tribune* (Minneapolis), March 28, 1988, p. 8D.
Dubashi, Jagannath, ''Myron's Makeovers,'' *Financial World*, April 26, 1994, pp. 48–49.
Feyder, Susan, ''Edina-Based Regis Corp. Is Planning To Buy 154 Wal-Mart Hair Salons,'' *Star Tribune* (Minneapolis), May 10, 1996, p. 3D.
Jones, Jim, ''Tress Chic—The Twin Cities Hair-Care Industry Regis,'' *Star Tribune* (Minneapolis), February 17, 1991, p. 3D.
Jones, John A., ''Regis Expands It Hair Salon Empire in U.S. and Europe,'' *Investor's Business Daily*, June 5, 1996.
Marcotty, Josephine, ''Edina-Based Regis Corp. Plans to Acquire European Hair-Salon Operator for $6 Million,'' *Star Tribune* (Minneapolis), August 17, 1995, p. 1D.
Nettleton, Pamela Hill, ''Hair Today,'' *Twin Cities Business Monthly*, September 1995, pp. 68–73.
Peltz, James F., ''Combing For Cash,'' *Los Angeles Times*, July 16, 1996.
Pyle, Richard E., ''Periscope: Regis Corporation,'' *Corporate Report Minnesota*, October 1983, p. 118.
Slovak, Julianne, ''Companies to Watch: Regis Corp.,'' *Fortune*, January 2, 1989, p. 96.
Swanson, William, ''Beauty and the Business,'' *Corporate Report Minnesota*, November 1985, pp. 92–96.
Waters, Jennifer, ''Regis Cuts Deal to Buy Trade Secret,'' *Minneapolis/St. Paul CityBusiness*, November 12, 1993, p. 3.
Wieffering, Eric J., ''Two Sharks in a Bathtub,'' *Corporate Report Minnesota*, August 1992, pp. 57–62.
Youngblood, Dick, ''Regis Looks Like Winner, By Well More Than a Hair,'' *Star Tribune* (Minneapolis), January 30, 1995, p. 2D.

—Kathleen Peippo

Rhino Entertainment Company

10635 Santa Monica Boulevard
Los Angeles, California 90025
U.S.A.
(310) 474-4778
Fax: (408) 441-6575
Web site: http://www.rhino.com

Private Company
Incorporated: 1977
Employees: 140
Sales: $70 million (1996 est.)
SICs: 5735 Record & Prerecorded Tape Stores; 7922
    Theatrical Producers & Services; 2731 Book
    Publishing

Rhino Entertainment Company produces novelty records, archival reissues, definitive musical anthologies, and various artists series. The company also operates Rhino Home Video and Kid Rhino (a children's line of entertainment products). Rhino considers itself to be a pop culture archive company, proclaiming that ''Rhino Records is the label that collects records so that you don't have to.''

The story of Rhino Entertainment is largely the story of its president, Richard Foos, and managing director, Harold Bronson. Avid music listeners and collectors, Foos was a sociology student at the University of Southern California in the late 1960s, when Bronson worked at the University of California, Los Angeles (UCLA) as a student representative for Columbia Records. Attending a local swap meet, Foos was inspired when he met a dealer who had purchased hundreds of records at a used record store for $3. The vendor was selling each LP for a dollar, turning a healthy profit. Foos went to the same record store—Aaron's—and bought his own $3 pile of records. His entrepreneurial venture began out of the trunk of his car, driving to flea markets to try to sell the old jazz and blues recordings. Then, Rhino Records was born in October 1973, when Richard Foos opened a store on Westwood Boulevard, a few blocks south of UCLA. Harold Bronson eventually was hired to work in the store.

The store, at that time, was filled with used tables and chairs and crazy ideas. The lack of customers in the early days gave Foos and Bronson extra time to brainstorm about promotions. Bronson began to implement customer-attraction events exhibiting the slightly offbeat Rhino flair, such as Polka Day, Redneck Day, and Hassle the Salesman Day. Two years later, as a 1975 promotion, the first actual Rhino record—a vinyl 45 rpm release entitled ''Go to Rhino Records'' sung by a local eccentric street singer named Wild Man Fischer—was issued and given away for free in the store. When local radio stations began to play the record, Rhino earned an underground following, and business picked up.

By 1978, the Rhino label was officially launched by Fischer, with a full-length album, *Wildmania*, recorded partially at Dodger Stadium and produced by Harold Bronson for $500. In November 1978, Rhino carved a niche for itself with its first reissue: a picture disc by the 1960s pop band The Turtles. This disc was the first step in plans to reissue the entire Turtles catalog. The philosophy behind re-releases of novelty tunes and past hits was to create records which did not yet exist that partners Foos and Bronson would want to buy. Reissues were to be a goldmine for Rhino, and the company was off to a good start; the label grossed nearly $60,000 in its first year. Although financial success was upon them, Foos and Bronson maintained a low-budget environment, retaining the thrift shop furniture, taking small salaries, using the copy machine at a local stationery store rather than buying one, and even instituting an employee schedule for cleaning the bathrooms.

Growth continued, and in 1983 Rhino was a $2 million company. Foos was persuaded to purchase an old copy machine, but the homespun character of the offices continued to prevail. Employees have always been an integral part of Rhino's philosophy and operations, representing Rhino's unique ''take'' on popular culture and music to the customer. Foos and Bronson ensure that employees share their passion for popular culture, and meet with them every six months in order to run the company democratically. Employees are encouraged to develop product ideas based on their own musical tastes, and

---

Company Perspectives:

Rhino Entertainment is the music industry's pop culture archival company, predicting, nurturing, and creating musical trends. In addition to Rhino Records, Rhino Entertainment has home video, family (children's), mail order, film, and book divisions. Maintaining a privately owned company, Rhino's co-founders, Richard Foos and Harold Bronson, strive to implement pro-employee, pro-community, and pro-environmental practices. The company preserves and makes widely available original recordings of the best popular music in every genre: nostalgia, pop, rock 'n' roll, blues, jazz, R&B, disco, hip-hop, country, folk, Cajun, Latin, and more, as well as spoken word, comedy, and video.

---

the Big Ideas program offers a bonus to employees who present innovative ideas. Over the years, employee-centered rituals such as Open Forum meetings would be instituted. A portion of all employees' salaries would be tied to company performance, and credits on Rhino products list employees who worked directly on that release. Thus, invested in a number of ways in the company's future, employees play a uniquely involved role in the success story of Rhino.

Another unique aspect of Rhino's corporate identity is its emphasis on social responsibility. Back covers of releases are often devoted to information on issues ranging from AIDS to homelessness to animal overpopulation. Further, Rhino's merchandising of reissues is placed in the context of social consciousness, using commercial release of cultural icons as a tool for understanding the not-so-distant past. Proceeds from album sales are often donated to relevant charities, and Rhino has been involved over the years with national causes (such as the Rock the Vote campaign and the "ban the box" campaign for CDs) as well as the local community (specifically the Wooten Center, a Los Angeles inner-city recreation and education center).

Rhino stepped out on another limb in April 1984, releasing the first spoken-word/comedy CD in history: The Firesign Theatre's *Three Faces of Al*. The company also released *The Turtles' Greatest Hits* and *Jerry Lee Lewis' Greatest Hits*. The next year marked the debut of Rhino Home Video, with the release of *My Breakfast With Blassie*, a satire of the Louis Malle film *My Dinner with Andre*, featuring comedian Andy Kaufman and wrestler Freddie Blassie. By fall of 1985, Rhino was ready to end its independent distribution, signing with Capitol Records for distribution through CEMA.

In 1987, Rhino had its first #1 hit when Billy Vera's pop-soul ballad "At This Moment" reached the top of the *Billboard* Hot 100 singles chart. By February, the song was Rhino's first RIAA gold single, and by March, the entire album (*By Request: The Best of Billy Vera & The Beaters*) became Rhino's first gold album. The company was selling 50,000 copies of the album each day, and its success almost became a recipe for disaster. Foos and Bronson spent a year trying to come up with another gold single, only stopping themselves after wasting significant earnings.

Reissues continued to serve Rhino's consumer market, and Rhino went back to focusing on what had made the company successful in the first place. In 1990, the company took advantage of—or perhaps fueled—the 1970s nostalgia sweeping the nation. Rhino released the first five volumes of a 1970s retrospective entitled *Have a Nice Day: Super Hits of the '70s*. This series was so popular that, by 1996, it would contain 25 volumes. Another landmark issue that year looked further back in time to the beat generation. Launching Rhino Word Beat, a spoken-word label, *The Jack Kerouac Collection* was a three-volume box set which earned Rhino Grammy nominations for Best Historical Album and Best Liner Notes. Expanding to reach the country music audience, Rhino also released vintage material by country artists Johnny Cash, Willie Nelson, Merle Haggard, and Buck Owens in 1990.

Children became a new market for Rhino in 1991. Aiming to please the children of America and their music-shopping parents, the Kid Rhino label was launched in February of that year, licensing classic songs from Hanna-Barbera.

A worldwide distribution agreement was entered with Atlantic Records (distributed by WEA) in 1992, entailing cooperative reissues of Atlantic's releases, especially from the 1950s through the 1970s. The "Atlantic Launch" was Rhino's biggest undertaking to date, in terms of promotions and releases. The company also entered into an agreement to distribute Avenue Records, including seven albums by the 1960s group War that had been out of print for a decade. That year, the company earned its second RIAA gold album, with *The Righteous Brothers Anthology (1962–1974)*, a two-volume retrospective. Two Rhino releases earned places in the Library of Congress' American Folk Life list of recommended 1992 titles: *Jubilation! Great Gospel Performances* and *Blues Masters: The Essential Blues Collection Vols. 1–5*. Revenues were boosted in the fourth quarter by bestselling box sets including *Aretha Franklin, Queen of Soul: The Atlantic Recordings* and *Monterey International Pop Festival*. The Aretha Franklin set earned the company its first Grammy, capturing the 1992 award for liner notes. The *Monterey* boxed set contained previously unpublished photos, interviews with festival participants, performance notes, and background on the festival. Net proceeds were donated to charitable organizations. Overall, 1992 was Rhino's most successful year to date, grossing over $55 million for the company.

One reason for Rhino's 1992 success may have been its unprecedented act of going on the road without its artists. Strictly as a name-recognition maneuver, Rhino took a 19-city tour of summer music festivals, investing somewhere from $60,000 to $100,000 to sell the idea of Rhino's institutional identity. Booths were set up at festivals in Austin, Texas; Telluride, Colorado; Boston; Philadelphia; Yosemite Park, California; and elsewhere, with each booth offering catalogs and promotional material and mailing list sign-up sheets. Rhino followed up the festival, sending prize packages of Rhino samplers, merchandise, and fliers to the new mailing list.

Several partnerships brought Rhino's product to larger audiences in 1993. The company took on a line of spoken word tapes from apparel manufacturer Esprit, featuring recordings from social issues lecturers such as Gloria Steinem and Jeremy

Rifkin. With the clothing, craft, and accessories chain Putmayo, Rhino released a series of world music albums which were sold in Putmayo retail outlets. Kid Rhino and McDonald's embarked upon a new partnership in 1993, working together to create recordings starring McDonaldland characters such as Ronald McDonald. *Ronald Makes It Magic*, the first product of the partnership, was released the next year. A megalicensing deal was made with Warner Bros. Animation, securing the rights for Kid Rhino to release audio titles using voices of the classic Looney Tunes characters as well as three new kids on the block (Yakko, Wakko, and Dot). This deal resulted in a highly successful first album which included wacky songs from Steven Spielberg's *Animaniacs* (a Fox Children's Network TV Show).

Reviving the folk festival tradition, Rhino joined Ben & Jerry's and Concert Associates to present a two-day "Troubadours of Folk Festival" at UCLA in the summer of 1993, inspired by Rhino's anthology of the same name and featuring performances by over 30 folk artists of the past, present and future. The festival later became a PBS special and was released by Rhino Home Video in 1994 and 1995. Marking the first folk festival of its magnitude in the Los Angeles area in 25 years, the event featured folk artists of the past and present along with a crafts festival and 200 vendors.

The company was lauded as a serious film producer in 1993, when *The Panama Deception*, a Rhino Home Video coproduction, received an Academy Award for Best Documentary. Adding to the laurels, Rhino International received its first gold record, the French release of *Aretha Franklin's 20 Greatest Hits*. Other new steps were the FORWARD label—which focused on new music by established contemporary artists such as BeauSoleil, Todd Rundgren, Richie Havens, and NRBQ—and the restoration of the Atlantic Records jazz catalog. The company also released the first major retrospective on late 1970s and early 1980s punk, powerpop, and new wave music, a nine-volume set called "DIY" (Do it Yourself). This set was targeted at both older fans who remembered the songs and younger consumers aged 16 to 30 who were part of the punk revival that spawned the Seattle grunge sound, with groups like Nirvana, Pearl Jam, and Soundgarden.

Rhino turned Sweet 16 in 1994, and the company threw a birthday party in the form of a national identity-promoting tour. Accolades for Rhino releases were plentiful in 1994. A third RIAA gold album was certified: *Billboard's Greatest Christmas Hits (1955–resent)*. Two Grammy nominations were received that year: BeauSoleil's *La Danse de la Vie* was nominated for the Best Contemporary Folk Grammy and the *Monterey International Pop Festival* box set earned a nomination for Best Historical Album. Finally, *The Best of War ... And More* received RIAA gold certification.

In the spring of 1994, Rhino and the Library of Congress signed a deal enabling Rhino to compile and release anthologies of historic recordings from the national archive, with the first slated project a box of presidential speeches. This agreement was the first large-scale licensing and production deal between a label and the Library of Congress. Rhino also acquired the rights to the Monkees catalog, and subsequently videos of their TV series and specials were released, along with the movie *Head*, a new Monkees feature film, and reissues of all nine

original Monkees albums with previously unreleased bonus tracks and new liner notes. Two new divisions were established—Rhino Films and Rhino Books. As the 1970s receded further into the distance, Rhino unveiled the first five volumes of *Just Can't Get Enough: New Wave Hits of the '80s*. Looking to the future as well as the past, Rhino went on-line in October of 1994, on CompuServe. Sales for the year were record-breaking, surpassing $65 million.

New ventures continued in 1995, when Rhino launched its partnership with Turner Entertainment Co., releasing classic movie soundtrack albums from M-G-M films. Rhino Movie Music would release soundtracks in conjunction with the Turner Classic Movies cable television network, including *Doctor Zhivago, Show Boat, Meet Me In St. Louis, Easter Parade, North By Northwest, That's Entertainment! The Ultimate Anthology of M-G-M Musicals*, and *Lullaby of Broadway: The Best of Busby Berkeley at Warner Bros*. Turner/Rhino's *The Wizard of Oz* soundtrack collection was a big seller for the company, and the box set release of John Coltrane recordings in *The Heavyweight Champion: The Complete Atlantic Recordings* was a highly acclaimed jazz event. A new catalog arrangement with Elektra Entertainment resulted in the release of *Love Story, 1966–1972*, a double-CD anthology of the 1960s psychedelic band Love. Making its debut in the movies, Rhino Films was expected to complete shooting of its first original production, *Plump Fiction*, featuring Julie Brown, Sandra Bernhard, Tommy Davidson, Paul Dinello, Dan Castellaneta, Paul Provenza, and Colleen Camp.

Having achieved a high level of success with its longstanding pop culture audience, Rhino began to tap other markets for its existing releases in 1995. The company directed attention to developing its market in the black community, launching the "Deep in the Groove" campaign to emphasize existing releases and new various-artists series such as *Phat Trax* and *Smooth Grooves*. The latter, a four-volume classic romantic rhythm-and-blues series, reached gold status by Rhino standards through the sale of over 500,000 units in 1995. The company also debuted an urban marketing campaign, dubbed "Rhino, Baby! You Didn't Know? Now You Know!", to familiarize young urban music fans with Rhino's already-existing catalog of R&B, soul, funk, and early hip-hop.

Rhino Home Video had a landmark year in 1995, with its first gold certification, earned for the classic Jimi Hendrix film *Rainbow Bridge*. The company also earned its fifth RIAA gold album certification for *Billboard's Greatest Christmas Hits (1935–1954)*. Overwhelming advance orders for Rhino Home Video's *The Monkees Deluxe Limited-Edition Box Set* caused the item to sell out before the end of the year. The Word Beat label, Rhino's Library of Congress partnership, releases its first box set, *The Library of Congress Presents: Historic Presidential Speeches (1908–1993)*. Revenues surged again, with more than $70 million in 1995 sales, and the company still had no major debt. The company played an active role in royalty reforms, joining Sony, Atlantic, MCA, EWMI, and Denon to urge a fair share for older artists whose catalog material is reissued.

In 1996, Rhino Home Video began to be distributed by WEA. The company continued to explore new technology, placing a Rocky Rhino site on the World Wide Web. New releases of a Curtis Mayfield retrospective, a *National Lampoon Radio Hour* box set, *Youth Gone Wild: Heavy Metal Hits of the '80s*, and *John Wesley Harding's New Deal* were accompanied by the 23rd through 25th volumes of the *Have a Nice Day: Super Hits of the '70s* series. Partnership with Starbucks coffee chain resulted in the production of two special CDs for its caffeinated customers.

U.S. Secretary of Labor Robert Reich visited Rhino's Los Angeles headquarters in 1996, and praised its continuing democratic attitude toward employee involvement, bestowing Rhino with a corporate citizenship award. Ironically, Foos simultaneously sent a letter to Bob Dole, who had recently criticized rap music, offering him a copy of Rhino's *White Men Can't Wrap*, a compilation of pop hits spoken by actors of the 1950s and 1960s.

The name "Rhino" was selected by Richard Foos when he opened that original record store on Westwood Boulevard in Los Angeles, to signify the way in which he opened the doors and blindly charged ahead. In 1996, according to *Success*, only 10 percent of the records produced in the United States are profitable, while 90 percent of Rhino's products earn profits. This track record has placed Rhino in the rare position of having no debt and no history of significant earnings loss over the years. With spirit, daring, and unique flair, Rhino has continued to charge ahead—with a finely focused vision of how to succeed in the entertainment industry.

Further Reading

Bessman, Jim, "Rhino Compilation Recalls Monterey Fest," *Billboard*, August 29, 1992, pp. 10–11.

Bessman, Jim, "Rhino Rolls Out Major Atlantic Catalog Push," *Billboard*, July 18, 1992, pp. 8–9.

Borzillo, Carrie, "Labels Mate Music, Crafts, Cosmetics," *Billboard*, May 15, 1993, pp. 10–11.

"Consumer Friendly, the Rhino Chain Succeeds," *Billboard*, July 3, 1993, pp. 45–46.

Davies, Barbara, "Rhino Takes Its Name on Tour; Info Booth Rides 19-City Fests Schedule," *Billboard*, August 1, 1992, p. 40.

"Eighteen Excellent Reasons to Feature Rhino Entertainment," Los Angeles: Rhino Entertainment Company, 1996.

Friend, Tad, "Rhinophilia: Consumed," *New Republic*, August 17, 1992, p. 9.

"Great Moments in Rhino History," Los Angeles: Rhino Entertainment Company, 1996.

Holland, Bill, "Rhino Enters Label Venture with Library of Congress," *Billboard*, November 5, 1994, pp. 14–15.

Holland, Bill, "Sony, Rhino Plan Royalty Reforms for Older Artists," *Billboard*, March 4, 1995, pp. 10–11.

Nathan, David, "Rhino Looks to Bring Home Higher Visibility to R&B Releases," *Billboard*, December 17, 1994, pp. 14–15.

Paige, Earl, "Rhino, Esprit Team for Spoken Tapes," *Billboard*, April 24, 1993, p. 23.

Rosen, Craig, "Avenue/Rhino Deal Good for War Reissues," *Billboard*, September 5, 1992, pp. 10–11.

Rosen, Craig, "Rhino Spearheads Multiple-Act L.A. Summer Folk Fest," *Billboard*, May 22, 1993, pp. 12–13.

Russell, Deborah, "Rhino Series Harks Back to the Punk Era," *Billboard*, January 23, 1993, pp. 1–2.

Warshaw, Michael, "How the Rhino Brothers Trained Their Instincts and Turned $3 into $70 Million," *Success*, October 1996, pp. 28–30.

—Heidi Feldman

Robert Half International Inc.

2884 Sand Hill Road
Menlo Park, California 94025
U.S.A.
(415) 854-9700
Fax: (415) 954-9735
Web site: http://www.rhii.com

Public Company
Incorporated: 1948 as Robert Half Inc.
Employees: 2,100
Sales: $898.63 million (1996)
Stock Exchanges: New York
SICs: 7300 Business Services; 7361 Employment
   Agencies

Robert Half International Inc. (RHI) is a leading provider of temporary, full-time, and contract employees, and is the oldest and largest specialist placing accounting, finance, and information technology professionals. RHI operates five divisions. Accountemps places accountants and other financial professionals in temporary positions; Robert Half provides permanent personnel in the fields of accounting, banking, and finance; RHI Consulting supplies contract information technology professionals; OfficeTeam specializes in high-end temporary administrative personnel; and The Affiliates supplies paralegal and support personnel for temporary positions in the legal field. At the end of 1996, the company had more than 190 offices in 38 states, Canada, the United Kingdom, Belgium, France, and the Netherlands. RHI also has independently owned and operated franchises in Kansas City, New Orleans, and Israel. Revenues for 1996 totaled $898.6 million.

Early History

Robert Half was a pioneer in the employment services industry, founding Robert Half Inc. in 1948 as an employment agency for accountants. He eventually created Accountemps to supply accountants and other financial professionals to firms needing those skills on a temporary basis, while continuing to place permanent employees through his Robert Half offices. Following the success of his business in California, Half began franchising the concept around the country. The temporary personnel industry grew slowly during the 1960s and 1970s, then began to expand rapidly during the 1980s. By 1985, there were 150 independent Robert Half and Accountemps franchises.

1985–90: New Management

The second half of the decade saw major changes in the company. In 1985 Harold M. "Max" Messmer, Jr. assumed the presidency of Robert Half Inc. In July 1986, Boothe Financial Corporation acquired all the outstanding stock of the company and Messmer almost immediately began a program to buy all the franchises in the Robert Half system. In 1987, after being divested by Boothe, Robert Half International Inc. went public, and Messmer became chief executive officer as well as president. The following year, he added chairman of the board to his duties.

During 1989, the company began opening new offices, and Gibbons, Breen, Van Amerongen, L.P., a merchant banking concern, bought 3.1 million shares of the company, approximately 27 percent of the outstanding common shares. As the decade ended, RHI had revenues of $234.5 million, a 29 percent increase from 1988.

The temporary staffing industry experienced double-digit expansion during the 1980s, and many people believed temporary employment firms would survive any national recession. As a result of rapid consolidation, the number of larger, national firms increased, and competition for contracts was intense. This led to a price war which began in the general clerical segment of the industry but soon spread to the specialized areas such as accounting.

1990–93: Recession and Recovery

In 1990, RHI's concentration on the niche of accounting and financial temporary placements helped avoid much of the price war, and the company could afford to acquire Wayne S. Mello & Associates, a financial recruiting firm in Florida. Robert Half, the permanent placement operations, reached a peak in its revenues of $450 million. However the employment recession which began that year did have an effect on the company, with revenues growing by only 9 percent, a big drop from 1989.

In a normal year, the Robert Half permanent placement activity accounted for 15 to 20 percent of the company's total revenues. This meant that RHI was more dependent on permanent placements than most temporary staffing firms, and as the demand for permanent employees fell as a result of corporate downsizing and restructuring, RHI's business began to weaken.

Management's reaction to the situation was a ''go slow'' strategy. They reduced overhead, cut and focused the advertising budget, and improved cash management. The poor economy also made it easier for the company to acquire Robert Half and Accountemps franchises, which were suffering, and to buy a Seattle-based temporary employment firm, which placed accounting and data-processing employees.

Management also decided the time was right to test a move away from their traditional financial placements. Late in 1991 they started a new division, OfficeTeam, placing temporary high-end, office administrative personnel. This start-up business was in response to requests from longtime clients for help when they needed temporary employees with administrative, word processing, and office management skills. To keep overhead low, RHI placed an OfficeTeam salesperson in a few Accountemps offices. That year the new division brought in $2 million in revenues. That was a bright spot in a year in which revenues dropped by 16 percent and earnings per share by more than 50 percent.

In 1992, its second year, OfficeTeam revenues increased to $12 million, and accounted for nearly 5 percent of the company's total bookings. The permanent placement business, however, brought in only $22 million, less than half the amount it generated in 1990. The company responded by merging most Robert Half offices with Accountemps facilities or combining satellite offices into a single hub office to serve an area.

Company revenues began to turn up towards the end of 1992 as employers felt confident enough to add temporary employees to their workforces. Having expanded into administrative placements through Office Team, the company decided to explore making placements in the legal field, and acquired The Affiliates, a firm in Southern California that placed temporary and permanent paralegal, legal administrative, and other legal support personnel.

During 1993, RHI expanded to the East Coast with the purchase of Key Financial, a Washington, D.C., firm that placed accountants, and opened offices in France, Belgium, and the United Kingdom. The company also completed placing an OfficeTeam salesperson in each of its 135 domestic offices. The temporary administrative placement service had turned into a very successful undertaking as it brought in nearly $41 million that year, more than 13 percent of total revenue. RHI found it had little competition in this area from the national giants such as Kelly or Manpower since most OfficeTemp placements were with longstanding clients who needed only a few workers at a time. Company revenues for the year reached $306.2 million.

Total employment in the U.S. began to grow in the last half of 1993 and RHI's permanent placement business finally started to improve as a result. As the economy strengthened and corporate downsizing and restructuring slowed, the temporary staffing industry found itself thriving. Employers wanted the flexibility to respond quickly to changing market conditions and to avoid overstaffing. Where traditionally employers hired temporary workers primarily to fill in during busy periods, now there was a growing demand for professionals with skills not usually associated with temporary work—home health care, prison management, and scientists and technicians.

1994–96: New Directions

RHI responded to the demand for additional specialized placements by creating RHI Consulting, a new division providing systems analysts, computer engineers, and other information technology specialists to clients on a contract basis. Specialized staffing in the IT area became very popular among temporary employee firms during the mid-90s. Not only was the demand there, but the assignments were for longer durations than many other types of placements and, perhaps most importantly, the margins were higher.

As RHI was branching into other areas, it continued to pull together its core business. By March 1994, the company had acquired all but four of the original 150 Robert Half and Accountemps franchises. According to a Kidder Peabody analyst's report that month, ''Management believed that centralized ownership would help reduce costs, aid the funding and implementation of advanced data processing systems, and bring more sophisticated marketing, accounting and legal practices to former stand-alone operations.'' By the end of 1996, only two franchise offices remained in the United States.

The temporary help industry continued its explosive growth. According to the National Association of Temporary Staffing Services (NATSS), in 1995, 2.16 million people worked as temporary employees each day, up from 185,000 in 1970. They represented 1.78 percent of total employment, holding one out of every 56 jobs, compared to one out of every 100 jobs in 1990 and one out of every 384 jobs in 1970.

Furthermore, NATSS estimated that nearly a quarter (24.2 percent) of the total temporary personnel payroll was made up of specialized professionals, including accountants and information technology specialists. The industry itself generated $39.2 billion in 1995, almost twice as much as it had five years before, when receipts were $20.5 billion.

For RHI, 1995 was an outstanding year. Revenues increased by 41 percent to $628.5 million, all through internal growth. OfficeTeam had revenues of $147 million, and the two-year old

RHI Consulting brought in $39 million through its 38 locations. The company was ranked 18th among all NYSE companies based on total return to investors for the 1993–95 period.

The industry credited its growth to several factors, benefiting both employers and employees. The primary advantage to both parties was greater flexibility. Employers were able to manage their work flow and workforce more effectively—using temporary help to complete special projects, fill short-term vacancies, and avoid overstaffing. For the employees themselves, taking temporary assignments afforded, according to Edward Lenz, "flexibility, independence, supplemental income, skills training, 'safety-net' protection while between permanent jobs, and the opportunity to find permanent work." RHI also offered its temporary employees a competitive benefit package.

In addition to its employment activities, RHI was a recognized research authority. Its annual national and regional salary guides were used by the U.S. Department of Labor in the preparation of the *Occupational Outlook Handbook*, and the company's accounting and information technology *Hiring Indexes* provided important hiring projections. A variety of surveys kept executives, managers, and temporary employees informed about issues as diverse as why companies hire temporary help to the length of the average executive's workday.

Both Max Messmer and the company's founder, Robert Half, published books and articles on hiring and job search practices. Half's books included *The Right Way to Get Hired in Today's Job Market, Making It Big in Data Processing, How to Get a Better Job in This Crazy World,* and *Finding, Hiring and Keeping the Best Employees.* In 1995, Messmer wrote *Job Hunting for Dummies,* part of the . . . *For Dummies* series published by IDG Books. He also wrote *50 Ways to Get Hired* and *Staffing Europe.*

The company's reputation also was enhanced by endorsements from leading professional associations, including the American Payroll Association, National Association of Credit Management, the American Institute of Professional Bookkeepers, and Professional Secretaries International. It also had worldwide marketing alliances with major accounting and word processing software publishers and major CPA review course companies.

Business continued to be good for the company through 1996, as it had a two-for-one stock split and reported record revenues of nearly $900 million and income of over $61 million.

1997 and Beyond

The temporary staffing industry was a growing segment of the economy. But with some 7,000 firms supplying their clients with temporary help, big national or international companies had the edge. As CEO Messmer explained in a 1996 *Barron's* article, "Smaller outfits don't have the clout to attract professionals—accountants, medical workers, technicians, programmers—who can deliver the highest margins for the temp company, because the smaller firms don't offer jobs across the country."

In just over 10 years, Robert Half International had grown from a small franchiser to a leading international company in this market. It had created successful specialized niches that connect with its longtime core business of accounting and financial placements, and had paid for its expansion through internal growth. The demand for accountants and auditors remained high, as the Bureau of Labor Statistics projected a 32 percent increase in those jobs over the next decade. The number of computer and information technology jobs was expected to double over the same period, many of which could be expected to be filled by contract staffers. All of these factors made the future look good for RHI.

Principal Subsidiaries

Norman Parsons (France).

Further Reading

Arthur, Douglas, "Robert Half International Inc.," Company Report, Kidder, Peabody & Co.: New York, March 29, 1994.

Brandstrader, J. R. "It's an Ill Wind," *Barron's*, March 25, 1996, p. 18.

Lenz, Edward. "Flexible Employment: Positive Work Strategies for the 21st Century," *Journal of Labor Research*, 1996, http://www.natss.org.

Siwolop, Sana. "Renting the Workers, but Buying the Stock," *The New York Times*, December 15, 1996.

"Temporary Help Services Continue Growth; Several Factors Cited," Alexandria, VA: National Association of Temporary Staffing Services, June 17, 1996, http://www.natss.org.

—Ellen D. Wernick

ruby tuesday, inc.

Ruby Tuesday, Inc.

**4721 Morrison Drive
Mobile, Alabama 36609
U.S.A.
(334) 344-3000
Fax: (334) 344-4998**

Public Company
Incorporated: 1972
Employees: 36,000
Sales: $620.13 million (1996)
Stock Exchanges: New York
SICs: 5812 Eating Places

Ruby Tuesday, Inc. is a leading company in the casual-dining restaurant industry in the United States, specializing in the under-$10 per person category. Its flagship Ruby Tuesday chain has grown to 314 units from its original location in Knoxville. The company also runs two other major chains, both featuring ethnic specialties—Mozzarella's Cafe, an Italian style restaurant with 47 locations, and the 20-unit Tia's Tex-Mex. Ruby Tuesday was founded in 1972 with the opening of the Knoxville outlet, enjoyed ten years of expansion as an independent company, then spent 14 years as part of Morrison Inc. (later known as Morrison Restaurants Inc.) from 1982 to 1996, and finally became independent again in 1996 when Morrison split up into three separate publicly traded companies, one of which was Ruby Tuesday, Inc.

Origins in Knoxville

That original Knoxville location had its beginnings in a Hollywood-like deathbed scene. In 1972 Samuel E. (Sandy) Beall was a 22-year-old University of Tennessee, Knoxville, student majoring in finance, who on the side helped William Kholmia manage a group of Pizza Hut restaurants. Kholmia suffered a massive heart attack that year. On his deathbed, Kholmia—wanting his protégé to be his own boss—offered Beall $10,000 to open a restaurant.

Beall took up the offer, and together with four of his college buddies scraped together another $10,000 to open the first Ruby Tuesday, which was located near the university campus in Knoxville. Beall named the restaurant after the then-ubiquitous Rolling Stones' song "Ruby Tuesday," which he kept hearing on the jukebox. The restaurant itself, which was a converted old house, featured barn wood walls, fake Tiffany lamps over the tables, and a $1.45 hamburger served on an English muffin. Beall also secured the first liquor-by-drink license in Knoxville, which enhanced the restaurant's popularity with students. Ruby Tuesday's subsequent success made Beall too busy for school, so he dropped out to devote himself full-time to his venture.

Over the next several years, Ruby Tuesday grew slowly, adding a new outlet about every nine months. As the chain expanded, the rustic decor and inexpensive fare proved popular with not only college students but also young couples. By 1982, ten years after founding, Ruby Tuesday was a chain of 15—nearly all of which were located in regional shopping malls—and Beall had begun to develop a second concept called L&N Seafood Grill.

Sold to Morrison in 1982

As Ruby Tuesday's rate of growth began to increase in the early 1980s, Beall realized he needed more capital to expand the flagship chain and develop other concepts. He considered taking the company public, entering the franchising game, or selling the company. It was the last option that he eventually took, following a real estate agent/acquaintance's suggestion that Morrison Inc. might be a likely buyer.

Morrison was a cafeteria and contract food service chain founded in 1920 and headquartered in Mobile. An ill-conceived diversification in the 1960s into motels, china and small wares, insurance, and other disparate areas led to confusion and reduced profit margins by the late 1970s. Morrison's fortunes were turned around following the appointment of Ernest Eugene Bishop as CEO in 1980. Bishop quickly divested the company of all its non-restaurant and food-service businesses, and then, in April 1982, enhanced Morrison's restaurant sector by buying Ruby Tuesday for $15 million in cash and stock. At the time, Ruby Tuesday revenue averaged about $1 million a year per restaurant.

Bishop left Beall in control of the day-to-day operations of Ruby Tuesday, making Beall president of the newly created Specialty Restaurant Division of Morrison. Beall soon opened the first L&N Seafood Grill, located in Knoxville, then developed the Silver Spoon Cafe concept, a New York City delicatessen-style restaurant. The first Silver Spoon opened in 1984, also in Knoxville.

Rapid Growth in the Mid- and Late 1980s

By 1985 it was clear that the sale of Ruby Tuesday to Morrison had indeed enabled the restaurant chain to markedly increase its growth rate. At fiscal year-end 1985, there were 35 Ruby Tuesdays in business, more than double the number at the time of the sale, along with seven L&N restaurants. The Specialty Restaurant Division as a whole brought in $70 million in revenue, 11 percent of Morrison's total. More importantly, the Ruby Tuesday restaurants were improving Morrison's overall profitability since the Specialty Restaurant Division's $7.5 million in profits represented 18 percent of the parent company's total.

The increasing importance of the specialty restaurants to Morrison's future was quite evident when Bishop decided in 1985 that Beall should be his successor. That year Bishop made Beall executive vice president of Morrison's specialty restaurants and cafeteria operations. Since before Ruby Tuesday was sold to Morrison, Beall lived in the resort town of Hilton Head, South Carolina, and commuted to Knoxville, where Ruby Tuesday was still based. In 1986 Bishop asked Beall to relocate to Mobile to become president and COO of Morrison, and Beall agreed, proving his dedication and his desire to succeed Bishop by leaving his beloved Hilton Head.

Meanwhile, the specialty restaurants continued to grow at a rapid pace in the late 1980s, nearing the 200-unit mark by decade-end, with more than 125 Ruby Tuesdays among them. All of this growth was achieved through company-owned units, keeping Morrison in total control of operations, control that would have been impossible if the company had decided to franchise. And as Morrison's cafeteria operations suffered from a general category-wide decline, the specialty restaurants be-

came even more important, accounting for half of Morrison's profits by decade-end.

Revamped Restaurant Lineup in the Early 1990s

In the early 1990s, in order to provide more growth opportunities and to guard against the fluctuations of the retail market, the Ruby Tuesday chain was shifted from an emphasis on shopping mall locations to a longer-term 50–50 mix of mall and free-standing locations. In conjunction with this shift came Ruby Tuesday's inclusion in so-called restaurant parks, clusters of dinner houses that share some development and ongoing operational costs and that provide customers a range of restaurant choices in a small area—even the easy ability to switch their restaurant choice if the wait at one restaurant is too long. One of the first restaurant parks featuring a Ruby Tuesday was located in the Denver suburb of Englewood—with the other dinner houses being Chevys, Grisanti's, and Stanford's.

In 1992 Morrison restructured itself, emphasizing restaurants over cafeterias by changing its name to Morrison Restaurants Inc. The dinner house restaurants—Ruby Tuesday, L&N, and Silver Spoon—were positioned within Morrison Restaurants as the Casual Dining Group, later known as the Ruby Tuesday Group. The year 1992 also saw Beall become CEO of Morrison, and Morrison posted its first $1 billion revenue year.

In the early 1990s, Beall was beginning to become disenchanted with the L&N Seafood concept. Ruby Tuesday's success was largely attributed to its per-person check average of $8.75, and Beall was finding it nearly impossible to get L&N's average even under $10. At the same time, the Silver Spoon concept was not overly successful either, and was considered too similar to Ruby Tuesday itself. Meanwhile, Beall was strongly interested in entering the burgeoning Italian restaurant sector, and signed a letter of intent late in 1992 to acquire Uno Restaurants Corporation and its chain of 110 Italian restaurants. Early the following year, however, Uno pulled out of the deal after a disagreement over the purchase price.

Left without this prize acquisition, Beall decided it was time to abandon Silver Spoon and create a new casual Italian restaurant, to be called Mozzarella's Cafe. In 1993 Silver Spoon units began to be converted to Mozzarella's, which featured a variety of pasta dishes and pizzas, as well as fresh seafood, steak, and grilled chicken selections. The check average—$9.50—was higher than Ruby Tuesday's, but still under the $10 mark; the under-$10 category was where Beall wished to position all of the Ruby Tuesday Group concepts.

Beall continued to revamp the Ruby Tuesday Group later in 1993 and in the following two years. The group entered into a joint venture in mid-1993 with the Dallas-based 12-unit Tia's Tex-Mex, founded by Larry Lavine (founder of the highly successful Chili's chain), who needed financing to fund further expansion. As part of the joint venture agreement, the Ruby Tuesday Group was given a five-year option to acquire Tia's, which it did in January 1995 for $9 million in common stock. Tia's restaurants were conceived to be "reminiscent of a grand old Mexican restaurant," featured display kitchens and outdoor patios, and offered various Tex-Mex dishes with a $9 check average.

The year 1993 also saw the debut of Sweetpea's, a Southern-style dinner house, in suburban Atlanta. Featuring such home-style and comfort-type meals as country-fried steak and chicken pot pie and a check average in the $7 range, Sweetpea's was positioned to compete with such stalwarts as Cracker Barrel and Shoney's. In 1994, having already grown to four units, the Sweetpea's name was changed to Snapp's because the Ruby Tuesday Group could not secure legal rights to the name and because the Dallas-based Black-eyed Pea (another Southern-style restaurant) raised objections to the name, fearing customer confusion.

In mid-1994, the Ruby Tuesday Group announced that it would phase out the L&N Seafood Grill concept, given that L&N could not conform to the Ruby Tuesday under-$10 check average. Most of the L&Ns were subsequently converted to either Ruby Tuesdays or Mozzarella's Cafes, although several were simply closed. $19.7 million was set aside to implement the phase-out.

Mid-1990s and Beyond

In May 1995, Ruby Tuesday entered into a license agreement with Jardine Pacific to develop Ruby Tuesday restaurants in the Asia-Pacific region. The first Ruby Tuesday located outside the United States opened in Hong Kong in July 1995, with additional units planned for mainland China, Singapore, Malaysia, and Australia.

Ruby Tuesday came full circle in 1996 when Morrison was split into three separate public companies: Ruby Tuesday, Inc., the former Ruby Tuesday Group; Morrison Fresh Cooking Inc., comprised of Morrison's cafeterias and quick-service restaurants; and Morrison Health Care Inc., the health care food service business of Morrison. Of the spinoffs, Beall said, "Now that our businesses have matured, we no longer need a layer of administrative management between these self-supporting independent operations and the shareholders." Legally, Ruby Tuesday, Inc. was the successor company to Morrison Restaurants Inc.; Beall retained his position as president and CEO of Ruby Tuesday.

Ruby Tuesday's first year of its second period as an independent company was a rough one. Although revenues increased 20.3 percent to $620.13 million in fiscal 1996, the company posted a net loss of $2.88 million due in part to increased competition in its restaurant sector and in part to $25.9 million in asset impairment and restructuring charges that were posted during the third quarter. First-half 1997 figures showed modest profits but at levels lower than the first half of 1996.

Although off to a rocky start, Ruby Tuesday, Inc.'s potential as an independent company was great. Beall planned to open 35–40 new restaurants each year, and set a goal of having 500 Ruby Tuesdays in place by 1999. He also planned to start offering franchises to help achieve these goals, with the western United States—largely untapped territory—slated for franchised growth. There also was the potential to develop another hot concept, and Beall had mentioned an under-$10 Asian restaurant as a possibility. Overall, Beall set an ambitious goal of growing Ruby Tuesday, Inc. into one of the top restaurant chain groups by the turn of the century.

Principal Operating Units

Ruby Tuesday; Mozzarella's Cafe; Tia's Tex-Mex.

Further Reading

Bernstein, Charles, "Beall Puts the 'More' in Morrison: Samuel E. 'Sandy' Beall III Is Determined to Make Morrison Inc. a Casual-Restaurant Chain Empire Every Bit as Strong as Brinker and General Mills Restaurants," *Restaurants & Institutions*, July 1, 1994, pp. 20–22, 26, 30, 34.
——, "Morrison: Hello, Ruby Tuesday," *Restaurants & Institutions*, August 26, 1992, pp. 27–28.
Carlino, Bill, "Forging a New Identity," *Nation's Restaurant News*, March 28, 1994, p. 66.
——, "Morrison Splits into 3 Companies," *Nation's Restaurant News*, October 9, 1995, p. 1.
——, "Ruby Tuesday Tunes Trio, Adds Sweetpea's to Stable," *Nation's Restaurant News*, May 24, 1993, p. 5.
Gordon, Mitchell, "Morrison's Moves: Cafeteria Operator Profiting from Full-Serve Eateries," *Barron's*, September 30, 1985, pp. 50–51.
Greenwald, Judy, "Profitable Recipe: Morrison Finds Few Things Beat the Cafeteria Trade," *Barron's*, September 13, 1982, pp. 52–53.
King, Paul, "Divided They Fall: Former Morrison Cos. Face Drop in Profits," *Nation's Restaurant News*, May 6, 1996, p. 11.
Palmeri, Christopher, "Hello, Ruby Tuesday," *Forbes*, December 20, 1993, p. 194.

—David E. Salamie

Safeskin Corporation

12671 High Bluff Drive
San Diego, California 92130
U.S.A.
(619) 794-8111
Fax: (619) 350-2378
Web site: http://www.safeskin.com

Public Company
Incorporated: 1985
Employees: 2,500
Sales: $150 million (1996 est.)
Stock Exchanges: NASDAQ
SICs: 3069 Fabricated Rubber Products, Not Elsewhere
     Classified

Safeskin Corporation is the leading manufacturer of latex gloves for the U.S. health care market. Safeskin pioneered the hypoallergenic latex examination glove market, having developed a proprietary manufacturing process that removes much of the allergen-producing proteins found in natural latex. Safeskin has taken the lead in the fast-growing nonpowdered segment of the examination glove market and has made strong inroads in the market for surgical gloves as well. Safeskin gloves are used in a variety of health care and medical settings, including the dental and veterinarian fields, and for nonmedical uses such as in the clean rooms for semiconductor manufacturing and other high technology industries requiring sterile manufacturing environments. Safeskin management, administration, sales and marketing, and product development functions are located at its San Diego headquarters. Manufacturing, including latex processing, takes place at the company's Thailand and Malaysia plants. The company is led by President, CEO, and Co-chairman Richard J. Jaffe, a founder of the company. Safeskin co-founder Neil Braverman, until 1996 a co-CEO of the company and who also owns Paramount Oil Company based in Florida, remains a co-chairman of the company. Safeskin's growth parallels the rise of the AIDS scare; the company has assumed a leadership role in producing high-quality gloves for the medical community

and has also been instrumental in setting FDA standards for latex gloves.

A Better Glove for the 1980s

Both Braverman and Jaffe had already proved their entrepreneurial mettle when they joined together to build Safeskin in 1987. Braverman's career began with an engineering degree from Georgia Institute of Technology in 1960 but would take him to the Far East, where he would spend some 25 years building Flair Corporation, an electronics manufacturer, before selling his company to U.S. Industries in 1985. In that year, Braverman incorporated Safeskin, but the company would remain inactive for the next two years.

Meanwhile, the younger Jaffe had been attending Cornell University's business school. Jaffe ended his studies in 1977, however, when he joined his brother in setting up Nutri-Foods International to make Italian ices and other frozen snacks. Operating at first from a rented garage in Long Island, New York, Nutri-Foods sold their products to hotels, camps, stores, and especially at area elementary schools. The company did well, until government regulations forced schools to drop junk foods, including Italian ices, from their school lunch programs.

Jaffe was forced to rethink his company's focus. "We had the choice of going out of business or coming up with something new," Jaffe told *Investor's Business Daily*. "We knew kids would continue to eat (Italian ices); now it was up to us to find a product that the schools would let them eat." At this point, Jaffe deployed a tactic that would come to serve Safeskin well: he talked to his customers. Jaffe discovered that by altering Nutri-Foods' Italian ice recipe, specifically by removing the sugar and adding two ounces of real fruit juice, he could get the company's products back into the schools. The new ices, dubbed Guido's Ice Juicy, were a big hit with the company's young customers. "It came down to listening to the customer, to going out there and saying, 'Hey, what do you need?' " Jaffe continued. "And once we developed what they needed, the business took off."

Nutri-Foods' success attracted the attention of the Coca-Cola Company, which paid the Jaffe family some $50 million to

467

acquire Nutri-Foods as part of Coca-Cola's foods division in 1985. Jaffe himself was part of the package, and for the next two years he served as the foods division's president. Jaffe left Coca-Cola in 1987, intending to take a year off to write poetry and play golf. But within two months, Jaffe met Neil Braverman, and he was back in the entrepreneurial world.

By then, Braverman had decided on Safeskin's direction. The AIDS outbreak among the homosexual population in the early 1980s was threatening to spread to the general population, a threat dramatized by the media attention surrounding actor Rock Hudson's death from AIDS. Then the medical community was shaken by a well-publicized claim that a patient had contracted the HIV virus from her dentist. The rising incidence of HIV infection, and the parallel rise in Hepatitis B incidence, prompted recommendations from the Centers for Disease Control that health care providers and anyone who came in contact with bodily fluids wear latex gloves, a recommendation that would later be passed into law. Manufacturers rushed to fill the demand for latex gloves, flooding the market with inexpensive latex gloves; many of these gloves were soon faulted for their low quality, often revealing flaws such as pin-prick holes, which eliminated their ability to protect against virus transmission.

Braverman brought Safeskin into the latex glove market. His years in the Far East had enabled him to develop strong manufacturing contacts in Malaysia, the world's prime source for natural latex. Safeskin at first manufactured regular latex gloves, beginning in 1987. But Braverman quickly recognized an opening in the market. "A friend of mine who is a dentist told me that there was a need for a good quality glove," Braverman told the *South Florida Business Journal,* "but I knew that I would need money to begin manufacturing." The money would come from Jaffe, whom Braverman met in 1987. More important, Jaffe brought his sales and marketing experience to complement Braverman's background in engineering and manufacturing. The pair became co-CEOs of the company, with Jaffe working from the company's San Diego headquarters and Braverman working from Safeskin's Boca Raton, Florida headquarters. Safeskin opened its first manufacturing plant in Malaysia.

Safeskin faced a glutted market already dominated by major producers. But Braverman and Jaffe recognized a new opportunity in latex gloves. "At the time, manufacturers were making gloves to protect doctors from the AIDS patient. To me, that was a requirement. I said, 'You have to do that or you can't be in business,' " Jaffe told *Investor's Business Daily.* "What we

decided to do was protect the health-care worker from the glove itself." Safeskin had recognized a new need in the health care community. "Behavior was changing. Doctors were starting to wear gloves 10 hours a day, not just 10 minutes a day. The way we saw it was that anything you put up against your skin for 10 hours a day is going to cause a rash."

Indeed, health care providers faced two problems from the latex gloves. Cornstarch and other powders were added on the inside of the gloves to aid in putting on and taking off the gloves. But with extended wear, the powders were causing irritations to the wearer's skin, and many providers were developing contact dermatitis, a condition that could become debilitating, from the gloves. The powders also carried the risk of contaminating the patient and acting as impurities to skew lab results. At the same time, the powders were known to draw out the proteins from the latex, leading to a second, still more debilitating threat from prolonged contact with latex gloves. Latex, a natural product from rubber trees, contained a number of natural proteins that acted as allergens in people. Prolonged contact with latex products was found to increase allergic sensitivity to latex, a condition that would affect a growing percentage of the health care community. Extreme allergic reactions to latex presented the risk of life-threatening anaphylactic shock; sufferers faced this risk even from breathing the air in which powdered latex gloves had been used. Safeskin turned its attention to developing a hypoallergenic latex glove. Using a proprietary process, the company succeeded in leeching out most of the natural proteins found in latex. After six months of development, the company was ready to launch its first latex glove product, winning FDA approval to label the glove as hypoallergenic.

Winning credibility and convincing customers proved another hurdle for the company, which bucked the industry's low-price, commodity trend by insisting on premium prices for Safeskin gloves. By the time the company introduced its first glove, the market was already flooded with latex gloves. As Jaffe told *Forbes,* "We had manufactured 200 million gloves, but we had no customers, no distribution, and there was a two-year glut on hand. We dug a pretty deep hole for ourselves." Safeskin next set out to build a distribution network. Facing stiff competition from established glove makers for the attention of purchasing agents, Safeskin took the company's gloves on a different route, working with a network of manufacturers' representatives to reach customers directly. "We bypassed purchasing agents and went to the end users—the docs and nurses—to educate them on the benefits," Jaffe told the *San Diego Union Tribune.* Safeskin hoped that these users, impressed by the quality and greater comfort of the Safeskin glove, would pressure their purchasing departments to buy the Safeskin product. The strategy worked. Sales, which were less than $1 million in 1988, climbed to $4 million in 1989, then to $9.5 million in 1990.

A Market Leader for the 1990s

The company, meanwhile, had been preparing to expand its product line. As complaints about the problems associated with the powders used in latex gloves began to rise throughout the health care industry, Safeskin had been listening closely. But instead of launching a reduced-powder glove, the company again took a different approach. Although powders remained a necessary part of the manufacturing process, Safeskin developed a proprietary technique for removing all of the powder from their gloves after production. Demand for the powder-free hypoallergenic glove, introduced in 1991, was overwhelming. By the end of the year, Safeskin's sales had doubled again, to $17 million, and the company posted its first-ever profit of $1.2 million.

Turning profitable gave the company the ability to develop its own sales and marketing staff and, in 1992, the company began direct marketing, hiring experienced salesmen for the new department. "We got those with five years of experience and a record of successful sales because we couldn't afford to train them," Jaffe told the *San Diego Union Tribune*. With the new strength in sales and the launch of Safeskin's HypoClean powder-free hypoallergenic glove, Safeskin's revenues doubled yet again, nearing $34 million, for a net profit of $6 million in 1992. The sales staff was encouraged to follow the company's founders' policy of asking customers what they wanted from their gloves. The company responded by extending its range of glove sizes, adding extra-small and extra-large sizes to the industry's three-size standard. The company's sales and marketing activities also were gaining success in convincing purchasers that higher-priced Safeskin gloves were also more cost-effective than their low-priced competitors.

The company's share of the total latex glove market was on the rise, growing from one percent in 1991 to 14 percent by the end of 1993. Within the hypoallergenic and powder-free categories, however, Safeskin was already the clear market leader, with 49 percent and 96 percent shares, respectively. By then the company, already turning out some 1.2 billion gloves per year, was having difficulty meeting demand at its two Malaysian plants. Safeskin set out to expand its manufacturing base. To finance this expansion, and to pay down debt, the company went public in December 1993, selling 2.9 million shares at $12 per share, for $30 million. The company, with sales rising to $57.3 million for net earnings of $11.7 million, paid off its debt and purchased land for a new production operation in Thailand, which began operation at the end of 1994.

Safeskin also looked to expand its product offerings by entering the surgical glove market, which, at some $400 million in yearly sales, represented the largest of the medical glove markets. At the same time, Safeskin was promoting its products beyond the health care industry to the pharmaceutical industry, veterinarians, and workers in semi-conductors, computer processors, and other clean rooms, as well as tollbooth operators and police officers. Another potential growth area was in food processing and handling. Meanwhile, powder-free gloves were becoming the fastest growing category of the latex glove market, growing by 200 percent between 1993 and 1994 alone.

In 1994, the company introduced two new products, the Dura-Fit and Satin Plus gloves, both aimed at the examination glove market. Safeskin was also making plans to expand its presence in the $500 million European market, opening two new sales offices in the United Kingdom and Germany, complementing a sales and warehouse operation already in place in the Netherlands. European sales were expected eventually to reach as much as 25 percent of Safeskin's annual sales. The company's sales continued their strong growth, reaching $84 million.

In March 1995, the company entered the surgical glove market with the launch of its Supra line of latex surgical gloves. The glove featured a unique textured surface and an ergonomic design to minimize fatigue and the risk of carpal tunnel syndrome and other repetitive stress injuries to surgeons' hands. In that same month, Safeskin received a major revenue boost: an agreement to form a distribution alliance with General Medical Corp., a medical and surgical products distributor. The alliance, which called for General Medical to distribute Safeskin's gloves under General Medical's private label, would add a minimum of $75 million to Safeskin's revenues over the initial three-year life of the agreement. Toward the middle of the year, however, Safeskin hit a bump: heavy rains in the rubber-producing region had reduced the supply of latex, while increased automobile sales were driving up the demand for rubber, resulting in latex prices reaching their highest levels in 60 years. Safeskin's strong relationship with its customers enabled the company to raise its glove prices for the second half of the year, helping to offset the higher costs of raw latex. During the year, Safeskin introduced its first nonlatex glove, made of nitrile, a petroleum derivative, for the laboratory and scientific markets, and the company also moved to reduce its overhead by opening a latex processing plant at its Thailand site. Nevertheless, pricing pressures dampened the company's income growth, which posted a slight four percent increase to $14.9 million, despite the company's jump in revenues to $117 million. The company began a restructuring effort, consolidating its headquarters at its San Diego location, as Safeskin prepared to expand the company beyond its core glove product lines. Braverman, however, remained behind at an office in Boca Raton and in the following year reduced his participation in the company, stepping down from his position as co-chief executive, but remaining co-chairman of the company.

By the beginning of 1996, however, Safeskin was the clear leader in the glove market, reaching a 24 percent share to top chief competitor Baxter Health Care Corporation's 18 percent share. In the following year, the company continued its expansion, adding new production lines at its Thailand site to increase capacity and preparing to launch new products, including a new surgical glove using NASA design technology. The company also responded to the growing number of health care workers and others afflicted by the rise in latex allergies by introducing a nitrile glove for the examination glove market.

Throughout 1996, the company continued to make strong gains. In July of that year, the company negotiated an extension of its agreement with General Medical, boosting revenues from that alliance to at least $100 million. By the end of the year, after posting a two-for-one stock split, the company announced two new contracts worth as much as $110 million combined. The first contract named the company one of two suppliers for the 1,800-facility hospital alliance of Premier Purchasing Partners, worth from $80 million to $90 million over five years. The second contract was with Catholic Materials Management Alliance, with 230 health care facilities, worth $21 million over three years. Safeskin, which was estimating more than $150 million in revenues for 1996, closed out the year with a new boost to its image, when it was named to Standard & Poor's

SmallCap 600 Index. The company continued seeking to expand its product line beyond gloves. With Jaffe's knack for anticipating markets, Safeskin's future ventures should fit the company well.

Further Reading

Benko, Laura B., "Gloves That Give Protection Minus Irritation," *Investor's Business Daily,* April 4, 1996, p. A6.

——, "Safeskin's Richard Jaffe: Setting Industry Standards by Seeing Change on the Horizon," *Investor's Business Daily,* August 23, 1996, p. A1.

Lau, Gloria, "Safeskin Corp.," *Investor's Business Daily,* August 2, 1994, p. A6.

Nesse, Leslie Kraft, "Safeskin's Strategy Fits Like a Glove," *South Florida Business Journal,* July 15, 1994, p. B1.

Riggs, Rod, "Safeskin's Owners Find Business Fits Like a Glove," *San Diego Union Tribune,* April 19, 1994, p. C16.

"Safeskin Tried Hand at Powder-Free Hypoallergenic Latex Surgical Gloves," *Health Industry Today,* March 1995, p. 3.

Schifrin, Matthew, "I Happen To Be Very Lucky," *Forbes,* November 4, 1996, p. 176.

Vogel, Mike, "Stock Sale May Hand Glove Maker $30 Million," *Miami Daily Business Review,* November 3, 1993, p. A1.

—M. L. Cohen

GROUPE SCHNEIDER

Schneider S.A.

64-70 avenue Jean-Baptiste Clément
92646 Boulogne-Billancourt Cedex
France
(1) 4699-7000
Fax: (1) 4699-7100
Web site: http://www.schneiderelectric.com/html/gb/
hom.htm

Public Company
Incorporated: 1966
Employees: 92,700
Sales: FFr59.42 billion (US$12.1 billion) (1995)
Stock Exchanges: Paris
SICs: 1731 Electrical Work Contractors; 3571 Electronic
  Computers; 3612 Power, Distribution & Specialty
  Transformers; 3613 Switchgear & Switchboard
  Apparatus; 3625 Relays & Industrial Controls; 3629
  Electrical Industrial Apparatus, Not Elsewhere
  Classified; 3643 Current-Carrying Wiring Devices;
  3644 Noncurrent-Carrying Wiring Devices; 3669
  Communications Equipment, Not Elsewhere
  Classified; 3674 Semiconductors & Related Devices;
  3678 Electronic Connectors; 3679 Electronic
  Components, Not Elsewhere Classified; 3699
  Electrical Machinery, Equipment & Supplies, Not
  Elsewhere Classified; 3823 Industrial Instruments for
  Measurement, Display & Control of Process Variables
  & Related Products; 3824 Totalizing Fluid Meters &
  Counting Devices; 3825 Instruments for Measuring &
  Testing of Electricity & Electrical Signals; 5063
  Electrical Apparatus & Equipment; 6719 Offices of
  Holding Companies, Not Elsewhere Classified; 8711
  Engineering Services

After a dizzying series of complicated restructurings, acquisitions, and divestments that began in 1980 when the company was a conglomerate, Schneider S.A. has emerged in the late 20th century reduced, almost, to a position of global leadership in just one area—the electrical industry. Almost, because Schneider has not yet divested its troubled Spie Batignolles electrical contracting and construction subsidiary, which it intends to do. Its other main subsidiary, Schneider Electric S.A.— the core of the new Schneider—specializes in electrical distribution, industrial control, and automation and serves the electrical power, industrial, infrastructure, and building markets. Truly international in operation, Schneider derives only about 37 percent of its sales from its domestic market, with the rest of Europe accounting for about 25 percent, North America for about 21 percent, and the remainder of the world, most notably Asia, for about 17 percent.

Early History

Schneider was originally founded in 1782 to manufacture industrial machinery at Le Creusot. The company was taken over by two Schneider brothers—Adolphe and Eugène—in 1836, at the dawn of the industrial age in France. By 1838 Schneider had built the first French steam locomotive and it later expanded into building other large, complex mechanical devices. By the late 1800s it had become involved in a wide variety of heavy industries, including steel manufacturing.

Schneider gained recognition as a major French company during World War I. It survived nationalization efforts during France's three-year popular-front government of 1936–39 and was called upon to help mobilize French forces in the months before World War II. Overrun during the war by German troops, Schneider's factories were either closed or redirected to support the German war effort.

By the time the war ended in 1945, many of Schneider's factories had been bombed or were obsolete. Charles Schneider undertook a recovery effort in which the company was reorganized into a holding company. In 1949 Schneider's industrial interests were transferred to three operating subsidiaries in civil and electrical engineering, manufacturing, and construction. The following year Charles Schneider was killed in an accident; he was the last member of the founding family to head the company.

Empain-Schneider Era, 1963–80

With the benefit of government direction and regulation, Schneider entered the 1960s fully recovered from war damage and well established in its various operations. In 1963, however, another family industrial group called Empain acquired a large financial stake in Schneider. Empain, founded in 1881 by Edouard Empain, was a pioneer in rail transit. The company installed the Paris Metro system in 1900 and later formed a successful rail-construction firm called Electrorail.

While the Empain and Schneider operating companies remained largely separate, the holding company conducted a series of further acquisitions that greatly expanded the subsidiaries' involvement in basic industries. The two operating companies grew increasingly close between 1966 and 1969, when they were merged into a single group called Empain-Schneider.

The new company's assets remained divided between Schneider S.A. (incorporated in France) and Electrorail (incorporated in Belgium), but they shared the same management structure and president, Baron Edouard Empain. By 1971 Empain-Schneider had become one of the most important industrial groups in the world, with interests in virtually every sector of heavy industry and infrastructure.

In 1972 Empain-Schneider took over the civil- and electrical-engineering group Spie-Batignolles. With interests in nuclear power, construction, and oil platforms, Spie Batignolles was formed in 1968 by the merger of the Société de Construction des Batignolles (SCB; founded in 1846 by Ernest Gouin) and the Société Parisienne pour l'Industrie Electrique (SPIE; founded in 1902).

Three years later Empain-Schneider acquired control of another vital French company, the industrial electrical products supplier Merlin Gerin. Founded in Grenoble in 1920 by Paul-Louis Merlin and Gaston Gerin, the company was a leader in industrial circuit breakers and switching gear.

A third major industrial group controlled by Empain-Schneider was Creusot-Loire, a heavy-equipment and special-steels manufacturer. It was also a leading builder of nuclear power stations through its subsidiaries Framatome and Novatome, and was heavily involved in turnkey projects abroad. By the late 1970s Empain-Schneider had developed a fourth major subsidiary, an energy and communications products group called Jeumont-Schneider. This company consisted of existing Schneider enterprises and several others controlled by the Jeumont-Industrie industrial group.

Restructuring, 1980–87

In 1980, however, the Empain family divested itself of its interest in Empain-Schneider, forcing the reorganization of the company and reducing Empain's involvement in the group from 45 percent to about 5 percent of turnover. As a result, the company also changed its name back to Schneider S.A. A more serious restructuring took place the following year when a Socialist government under President François Mitterand came to power.

The government sought to nationalize major companies in an effort to better coordinate industry with its national objectives. Under the new program the first sector to be nationalized was banking; the state took control of all banks with more than $220 million in assets. This included Schneider's banking subsidiary, the Banque de l'Union Européénne.

Between 1981 and 1987 Schneider undertook a restructuring program whose objective was to transform the company from a complex family financial trust with many diverse interests into a leading international industrial group. As part of this effort, Schneider divested its machine-tool, heavy-equipment, shipbuilding, and steel operations, and later sold its lower-margin rail transport, nuclear-power, and private-telecommunications businesses.

The sectors that remained under the new simplified structure included construction of electric-power plants and power-distribution systems, building and civil-engineering projects, industrial infrastructure, and a wide variety of industrial electronics systems. Schneider's primary operating subsidiaries remained Spie Batignolles, with 55 percent of total revenue; Merlin Gerin, with 31 percent; and Jeumont-Schneider Industries, with 14 percent in 1987. Reflecting Schneider's position in international markets, 41 percent of the company's revenues were generated through foreign projects.

The person who spearheaded the restructuring effort was Didier Pineau-Valencienne, who was appointed vice-chairman and CEO late in 1980, then became chairman and CEO the following year. Pineau-Valencienne built his reputation by turning around a small French chemical company, then found further success at the French chemical giant Rhone-Poulenc before being asked to take command of Schneider.

During the difficult restructuring process, Pineau-Valencienne gained a reputation for waging controversial corporate battles, even earning the nickname "Dr. Attila." In 1984 he failed to win government support for his plan to restructure Schneider's troubled capital-goods subsidiary, Creusot-Loire. After declaring the subsidiary bankrupt, Pineau-Valencienne was roundly accused of mismanagement and incompetence.

Undaunted, Pineau-Valencienne continued with his restructuring plan and sold off those parts of the company he considered unrelated to Schneider's core operations. In the process, Schneider accumulated a large cash reserve that Pineau-Valencienne earmarked for strategic acquisitions.

Major Acquisitions and Further Restructuring, 1988 Through the Mid-1990s

The first of these was for the industrial-automation company Telemecanique, which Pineau-Valencienne had hoped to merge with Merlin-Gerin. The takeover battle, launched in February 1988, involved many bitter and complicated legal and labor disputes, and finally government intervention. By July Schneider had won permission to acquire Telemecanique, but in the process had inspired a national debate on hostile takeovers.

Pineau-Valencienne next turned his attention to the United States. In 1990 Federal Power, a maker of low-voltage distribution equipment and medium-voltage switchgear, was acquired. That same year, Schneider acquired EPE Technologies, a world leader in uninterruptible power supplies (UPS), although Schneider subsequently, in 1996, sold most of its interest in EPE in a leveraged buyout after deeming UPS outside its core businesses. Schneider's U.S. spending spree reached a peak, however, in 1991 when it acquired Square D Company, based in Palatine, Illinois, for US$2.23 billion in another hostile takeover. Square D—founded in 1902 and with sales of US$1.65 billion and operations in 23 countries—was a market leader in electrical distribution, industrial control, and automation products, systems, and services. It became the flagship for Schneider's North American division, which was headed up by Charles W. Denny, who had spent more than 30 years at Square D before being placed in charge of Schneider North America as well as gaining a spot on the Schneider executive committee.

The acquisition of Square D led to the further restructuring of Schneider's industrial operations. In 1991 Schneider increased its interest in Merlin Gerin, and also formed an industrial sector called Schneider Industrie which pulled Schneider's major industrial subsidiaries—Square D, Merlin Gerin, Telemecanique, and Jeumont-Schneider Industries—into an umbrella group. The following year, Schneider divested itself of Jeumont-Schneider, leaving Schneider Industrie with purely electrical industry operations. From that point forward it was clear that Pineau-Valencienne intended for Schneider to eventually reduce itself to its electrical holdings alone.

Further moves over the succeeding years bore this out. In 1992 Schneider gained full control of Merlin Gerin through a merger. The next year the operations of Merlin Gerin, Square D, and Telemecanique were brought together under an overall global management structure where, for example, Schneider North America included the operations of all three companies within North America. Then in 1994, Schneider's corporate structure was further rationalized when a new Schneider Electric S.A. subsidiary, based in France, was created and both Merlin Gerin S.A. and Telemecanique S.A. were merged into the new subsidiary and ceased to exist as separate companies. Although Square D Company technically remained a subsidiary, Schneider essentially positioned Square D, Merlin Gerin, and Telemecanique as its major brands within Schneider Electric.

On the heels of this flurry of activity, Pineau-Valencienne made world headlines when he was arrested in Belgium in May 1994 and jailed for 11 days pending trial in a complex criminal-fraud investigation that involved Schneider's takeover of two Belgian subsidiaries that were remnants of the Empain-Schnei-der era. After Pineau-Valencienne returned to France following his release on bail, an international warrant was issued for his arrest in early 1995, effectively barring him from leaving France for several months until Belgian authorities finally rescinded the arrest warrant. The case seemed to have made little progress even into early 1997, and Pineau-Valencienne, who stayed in charge of the company throughout the episode, and other Schneider officials continued to insist that the case was entirely groundless.

Meanwhile, Pineau-Valencienne was struggling to deal with Schneider's last remaining non-electrical holding, Spie Batignolles. Spie was active in two main areas: electrical contracting and construction. While the former was related to the activities of Schneider Electric, the latter was not. Furthermore, because of difficult conditions in the French real estate market, Spie's construction sector was performing poorly, posting losses of FFr2.25 billion from 1991 to 1994. Wishing eventually to divest itself of its Spie holding—which was about a 59 percent stake—or at least Spie's construction sector, Pineau-Valencienne decided to first gain full control of the troublesome unit. He did so by engineering a merger between the companies in July 1995, which also had the side benefit of garnering Schneider a large tax credit. Possible buyers of Spie included Candover, a U.K. venture capital group; the French construction group Eiffage; Sweden's Skanska AB; and Amec, a U.K. building group.

Although the acquisition of Square D had significantly increased Schneider's overseas holdings—more than 62 percent of overall revenue was derived from outside of France by 1995—Schneider had in the process saddled itself with a heavy debt burden. Pineau-Valencienne thus identified debt reduction as a key to Schneider's future. The much-anticipated divestment of Spie Batignolles would of course help him do just that, although the company's debt-to-equity ratio had already been reduced to 46 percent by 1995. Schneider's chairman also wished to reduce the percentage of shareholdings held by other French firms; such cross holdings were typical of public companies in France, but Pineau-Valencienne wanted to create a shareholding structure along Anglo-American lines. He also sought to increase the percentage of international investors in Schneider and eventually have Schneider listed on the New York, London, Frankfurt, Munich, and Tokyo exchanges—goals in keeping with the company's global nature. Assuming the company's Belgian difficulties have been laid to rest and Spie can be successfully divested, at the dawn of the new century Schneider appeared to have a very bright future as a global power in the electrical industry.

Principal Subsidiaries

Schneider Electric S.A.; Spie Batignolles; Square D Company (U.S.A.).

Principal Divisions

European Division; French Division; International Division; North American Division.

Further Reading

Day, Charles R. Jr., "The Ecstasy Is Worth the Agony," *Industry Week*, November 15, 1993, p. 20.

Donlon, J. P., "Groupe Dynamic," *Chief Executive*, March 1994, p. 26.

Du Bois, Martin, "Claims Against Schneider SA Total Over $53.9 Million in Probe of Fraud," *Wall Street Journal*, May 19, 1995, p. B5D.

——, "Judge Affirms Schneider Head to Stay in Jail: Alleged Misappropriation or Embezzlement Put at Up to $141.6 Million," *Wall Street Journal*, June 2, 1994, p. A11.

——, "Schneider's Chairman Steers Globally While He's a 'Prisoner' in His Country," *Wall Street Journal*, February 2, 1995, p. A14.

Kamm, Thomas, "Schneider Weighs Merger with Unit, Spie Batignolles," *Wall Street Journal*, March 7, 1995, p. A15.

Miller, James P., "Square D Accepts Sweetened Bid of $2.23 Billion from Schneider," *Wall Street Journal*, May 31, 1991, p. A3.

Moskal, Brian S., "After the Battle, Square D Works the Peace," *Industry Week*, December 2, 1991, p. 45.

Murdoch, Adrian, "The Strange Case of Didier Pineau-Valencienne," *Chief Executive*, October 1995, p. 24.

Yates, Ronald E., "Profits Come Around After Square D Deal," *Chicago Tribune*, December 3, 1996, pp. 1, 4.

—updated by David E. Salamie

SEARS

Sears, Roebuck and Co.

3333 Beverly Road
Hoffman Estates, Illinois 60179
U.S.A.
(847) 286-2500
Fax: (800) 427-3049
Web site: http://www.sears.com

Public Company
Incorporated: 1906
Employees: 275,000 (1995)
Sales: $34.9 billion (1995)
Stock Exchanges: New York
SICs: 5311 Department Stores; 5961 Catalogue and Mail
Order; 7629 Electrical Repair

Sears, Roebuck and Co. is one of the few U.S. corporations whose name is virtually synonymous with an entire business segment: retail. Although Sears formerly sold insurance (Allstate), real estate (Coldwell Banker), and financial services (Dean Witter), the company sold or spun off its nonretail assets (including the famed Sears Tower) in the 1990s to concentrate on the original source of its fame. For decades, Sears prided itself on being the U.S. middle class's primary general goods merchant, the place where average people bought everything from clothes and auto supplies to sporting goods and refrigerators at an affordable price. This changed forever during Sears's overhaul, as hard goods were moved from mall-based stores to free-standing facilities, and the "softer side" of Sears was pumped up with better women's clothing, a new line of cosmetics and beauty products, and family denimwear under the Canyon River Blues label.

Humble Beginnings, Late 1800s to 1914

Sears bears the name of Richard W. Sears, who was working as a North Redwood, Minnesota, freight agent for the Minneapolis and St. Louis Railroad in 1886 when a local jeweler gave him an unwanted shipment of pocket watches rather than return them to the manufacturer. Sears sold them to agents down the line, who resold them at the retail level. He ordered and sold more watches, and within six months made $5,000. He quit the railroad and founded the R.W. Sears Watch Company in Minneapolis.

Sears's business expanded so quickly that he moved to Chicago in 1887 to be in a more convenient communications and shipping center. Soon customers began to bring in watches for repairs. Since he knew nothing about fixing them, Sears hired Alvah Roebuck, a watch repairman from Indiana, in 1887. A shrewd and aggressive salesman—a colleague once said of him, "He could probably sell a breath of air"—Sears undersold his competition by buying up discontinued lines from manufacturers and passing on the discounts to customers. At various times from 1888 to 1891, thinking himself bored with the business, he sold out to Roebuck, but came back each time.

In 1888 Sears published the first of its famous mail-order catalogues. It was 80 pages long and advertised watches and jewelry. Thanks to Richard Sears's restless search for new merchandise, within two years the catalogue had grown to 322 pages, selling clothes, jewelry, and such durable goods as sewing machines, bicycles, and even keyboard instruments. In 1894 the catalogue cover proclaimed that Sears was the "Cheapest Supply House on Earth."

The company changed its name to its current form in 1893, but Alvah Roebuck, uncomfortable with Sears's financial gambles, sold out his share two years later and remained with the firm as a repairman. Sears promptly found two new partners to replace him: local entrepreneur Aaron Nusbaum and Nusbaum's brother-in-law, haberdasher Julius Rosenwald. The company recapitalized at $150,000, with each man taking a one-third share. The company continued to prosper, so much so that when the cantankerous Nusbaum was forced to sell out in 1901 after clashing with Sears, his interest was worth $1.25 million.

There was little harmony between the two remaining partners, however. Sears believed in continuous expansion and risk-taking, while Rosenwald advocated consolidation and caution. He also objected to Sears's fondness for the hard sell in his catalogue and advertising copy. Had the Federal Trade Commission existed then, some of Sears's advertising practices probably would not have passed muster; it should be said in Sears's defense, however, that he invented the unconditional money-back guarantee and stood by it.

In 1905 construction began on a new headquarters plant on Chicago's west side to consolidate all of the company's functions. To help raise the necessary capital, Sears went public in 1906. Yet Wall Street was leery of the incautious Richard Sears, and he resigned as president in 1908 when it became clear that he was obstructing the company's way in the capital markets. He was appointed chairman, but his heart was never in that job. He retired in 1913, never having presided over a board meeting and died the following year at the age of 50. Near the end of his life, he summarized his career as a merchant: "Honesty is the best policy. I know, I've tried it both ways."

New Leadership and Growth, 1915 to the Late 1920s

Sears was now Julius Rosenwald's company to run, and he did it with such skill and success he became one of the richest men in the world. Sales rose sixfold between 1908 and 1920, and in 1911 Sears began offering credit to its customers at a time when banks wouldn't even consider lending to consumers. During this time the company grew to the point where its network of suppliers, combined with its own financing and distribution operations, constituted a full-fledged economic system in itself. Rosenwald's personal fortune allowed him to become a noted philanthropist—he gave away $63 million over the course of his life, much of it to Jewish causes and to improve the education of Southern blacks. As a result of the latter, he became a trustee of the Tuskegee Institute and a good friend of its founder, Booker T. Washington.

The depression of the early 1920s dealt Sears a sharp blow. In 1921 the company posted a loss of $16.4 million and omitted its quarterly dividend for the first time. Rosenwald responded by slashing executive salaries and even eliminated his own. He was also persuaded to donate 50,000 shares from his personal holdings to the company treasury to reduce outstanding capital stock and restore Sears's standing with its creditors. Sears thus weathered the crisis and benefited from the general prosperity that followed.

Rosenwald retired as president in 1924, retaining the chairmanship he had inherited from Richard Sears. He was succeeded by Charles Kittle, a former Illinois Central Railroad executive. In 1925 Sears began to take on its current shape when it opened its first retail outlet in Chicago. Seven more stores

followed that year, and by the end of the decade 324 outlets were in operation. Retailing became so successful for Sears that by 1931, the stores topped the catalogue in sales. Sears's entry into retailing was the brainchild of vice president Robert Wood, who was an executive at archrival Montgomery Ward before Rosenwald hired him in 1924. Wood was always known as "the General" after serving as the U.S. Army's Quartermaster General during World War I. He had also been chief quartermaster for the construction of the Panama Canal. He much preferred business to the military, however, and his long career in merchandising earned him a reputation for genius.

For its first 40 years, Sears had targeted the U.S. farmer as its main customer, luring him with a combination of down-home earthiness and the tantalizing prospect of material luxury. Two postal service innovations—the rural free delivery system in 1891 and the parcel post rate in 1913—had helped target this consumer by making it affordable to reach remote locations by mail. Sears quickly became parcel post's largest single customer. Then Wood saw that automobiles would soon make urban centers more accessible to outlying areas, broadening the customer base for retail outlets. Thwarted by the conservative top management at Ward's, he wasted no time in implementing his vision at Sears. At first, the stores simply absorbed surpluses from the catalogue, but they soon began to offer a full range of goods. Sears also became the first chain to put free parking lots next to its stores. More than anyone else, it was Robert Wood who turned Sears into a leviathan.

Robert Wood Takes the Helm, 1929 to the Mid-1940s

Charles Kittle died suddenly in 1928, and Wood succeeded him. In 1929 Sears arranged a merger between two of its suppliers, Upton Machine and Nineteen Hundred Washer Company, to form Nineteen Hundred Corporation, which changed its name to Whirlpool in 1950. Somewhat against its intentions, Sears became increasingly involved in the affairs of its suppliers, many of which were small companies whose outputs were almost entirely geared to its needs. Another leadership change occurred in 1932, when Julius Rosenwald died at the age of 69 and was succeeded as chairman by his son Lessing.

The onset of the Great Depression hurt sales badly from 1930 to 1934, but thanks to cost-cutting measures, Sears posted a loss only in 1932. The company, in fact, diversified in 1931 when it created its Allstate subsidiary (named after the company's own Allstate tires) to sell auto insurance. Wood saw it as another way to capitalize on the growing popularity of the automobile. He installed as general manager insurance agent Carl Odell, an acquaintance who had suggested the idea as they commuted to work one day.

Lessing Rosenwald retired in 1939. Preoccupied with running his father's estate, he had never attended a board meeting. Wood succeeded him, and the power of chief executive passed from the presidency to the chairmanship. At about this time, however, Wood also became controversial because of his prominent support for America First, an isolationist organization that was the vehicle through which Charles Lindbergh made his notorious anti-Semitic speeches. Wood dropped his backing once the U.S. entered World War II and publicly supported the war effort, but remained a strong critic in private ever after.

As war loomed, Sears benefitted from increases in military spending and a consumer buying panic. In 1941 sales reached an all-time high of $975 million, a 30 percent increase over the previous year. Sales then leveled off, however, and raw material shortages made durable goods hard to come by. Even as late as 1946, it had to refund $250 million in orders that couldn't be filled. Military procurement helped make up for the shortfall. During the war, Sears supplied the Armed Forces with just about everything that didn't need gunpowder to make it work, and even a few things that did—as some factories belonging to Sears suppliers were converted into munitions plants by the War Department. Sears also began its first foreign ventures during and immediately after the war. In 1942 a store opened in Havana (later nationalized by the Castro government in 1960), and several opened in Mexico in 1947.

Wood's Postwar Expansion, Mid-1940s to 1960s

Once the war ended, Sears flourished with sales up to $1 billion in 1945, and doubled the next year. Anticipating an economic boom, Wood launched an aggressive expansion program. Concentrating on the Sun Belt states, he located many of the new stores in the path of suburban expansion before the areas built up. One store in California was established on a dairy farm and had cows roaming around the parking lot when it opened. Thanks to the General's prescience, Sears left its rivals in its wake. In 1946 it held a small sales advantage over Montgomery Ward, but in 1954 posted sales of $3 billion while Ward, which had been slower to anticipate postwar trends, mustered only $1 billion. Sears also became a symbol of U.S. prosperity. In the late 1940s the Associated Press's Moscow bureau chief reported that the most effective piece of foreign propaganda in the Soviet Union was the Sears catalogue.

At the same time, Sears became a widely hailed living experiment in corporate management. Wood had long wanted to decentralize the company, and its postwar success gave him the luxury to remold it in his image of "corporate democracy." The merchandising operations were carved up into five regional "territories," with each given a high degree of autonomy. Although buying operations remained centralized in theory, buyers were in fact allowed substantial independence. To its employees, many of them returned veterans (the company hired 50,000 people between 1946 and 1949 alone), Sears became, as author Donald Katz put it in *The Big Store*, "a place where country boys and infantrymen could speak their minds and still roam free."

During the early 1950s, Sears began to stock more clothing as durable goods sales slackened. The new postwar suburbanites who bought their first homes had already filled them with all the Sears appliances they needed. At about this time, the company strengthened its ties with its suppliers even further. Between 1951 and 1960, it acquired virtually complete control of Warwick Electronics, which made Sears televisions, radios, phonographs, and tape players. In 1961 it effected a merger between 15 of its soft goods suppliers and created the Kellwood Company.

Robert Wood retired in 1954 at the age of 75, but retained power over appointment of his successors until shortly before his death (in 1969). A series of caretaker chairmen followed

him, all of whom were favorites of his. None of them served more than six years. The first was Theodore Houser, who retired in 1958 and was succeeded by Fowler McConnell. McConnell was followed in 1960 by Charles Kellstadt, who served for two years and after whom the Kellwood Company was named. Austin Cushman succeeded Kellstadt and served until 1967.

In 1963 the company posted sales of $5.1 billion, and an executive with the discount chain Korvette quipped that Sears was not only the No. 1 retailer in the U.S., but also numbers two, three, four, and five. Surveys showed that one in five U.S. consumers shopped at Sears regularly; its sales volume was greater than that of some entire industries. The company had become big enough to justify its own shopping center development subsidiary, Homart Development, which had been formed in 1960.

The Retailing Giant Begins to Falter, Late 1960s to 1980

In 1967 Sears posted $1 billion in monthly sales for the first time. Gordon Metcalf succeeded Cushman as chairman that year. In 1970 Allstate Enterprises, a subsidiary formed in 1960, acquired Metropolitan Savings and Loan Association, the first of several savings and loans it purchased over the next two decades. Also in 1970, construction began in Chicago on the 110-story Sears Tower. Completed in 1974, the Sears Tower was the tallest building in the world for many years and a symbol of corporate pride at a time when Sears's dominance of U.S. retailing was unchallenged.

That era was fading, however, even as its monument rose above the Chicago skyline. Arthur Wood (no relation to Robert Wood) succeeded Metcalf in 1973, and he was the last of the General's protégés to serve as chairman. Recession caused by skyrocketing oil prices led to a $170 million drop in profits in 1974 on only a modest sales increase, and financial performance remained flat through the middle of the decade. It became apparent to Wood and others that success had made Sears complacent and the company had long ignored some real problems.

Competition was getting serious. Specialty shops that filled the very malls anchored by Sears stores were cutting into market share, as were discounters like the resurgent S.S. Kresge Co., which changed its name to Kmart Corporation in 1977. Robert Wood's vaunted corporate democracy had turned into an ungainly feudal state. The buyers, given complete freedom, operated an internal economy of their own. Terrible inefficiencies and intramural rivalries resulted. Yet this system had become enshrined as the "Sears way," and those who had flocked to the General's banner believed in it. Decentralization peaked under Gordon Metcalf; he was known to consult with his territorial chiefs on problems, then leave the solution to them, saying, "You boys just work it out."

Hard times meant these shortcomings could no longer be obscured by success or justified in the name of tradition. Sears had to be shaken up, and it fell to Edward Telling, a company veteran who succeeded Arthur Wood in 1978, to do it. As head of the eastern territory, Telling had smashed local concentrations of power in the name of efficiency and proceeded to do the same for the parent company, centralizing all buying and merchandising operations. Territorial bureaucracies were slowly eliminated.

The General's ghost took a while to exorcise. Income declined from 1978 to 1980 and was subjected to intense scrutiny by Wall Street. Outsiders weren't always impressed by Telling, a downstate Illinois native whose homespun manner tended to conceal—often by choice—his erudition and keen intellect. It was through his guidance that Sears undertook a major corporate reorganization in 1981. This involved the formation of an overall holding company for its three business groups: the buying and merchandising operations, Allstate, and Seraco Group (which included Homart and other commercial real estate and residential real estate finance units).

Diversification and Its Consequences, 1981–91

Telling also saw the burgeoning financial services industry as one in which Sears should get involved. In 1981 Sears acquired the Los Angeles-based Coldwell Banker Company, the nation's largest real estate brokerage, and securities firm Dean Witter Reynolds Inc. Three years later, Sears launched Prodigy, an online service, with IBM and CBS. At the end of 1985, Telling retired and left a radically different company from the one he had inherited. He had reined in Sears's sprawling bureaucracy and taken the first steps toward complementing the company's store with a diversified financial services company having the size and capital to take on the industry's leaders.

Telling was succeeded by Edward Brennan, who, as chairman of the Merchandise Group under Telling, liked to preach that Sears was "one big store" and had labored tirelessly to centralize merchandising operations. In 1985 Sears unveiled its Discover Card, a combined credit and financial services card that also offered savings accounts through Greenwood Trust Company, a bank Allstate Enterprises had acquired earlier that year. By this time it was estimated that one in every 30 living Americans had worked for the company in some way at some time. In 1987, perhaps conceding that the era of the big general merchant was over, the Merchandise Group launched a new strategy to turn Sears into a collection of specialty superstores. The next year Sears acquired Eye Care Centers of America, Pinstripes Petites, and Western Auto Supply as its workforce reached an all-time high of 520,000. Yet the surge of adrenaline anticipated by Coldwell Banker and Dean Witter failed to materialize.

As Sears's stock price lagged, takeover rumors circulated and management pondered ways to increase shareholder value and stave off possible attempts. In late 1988 Sears announced plans to sell Coldwell Banker's commercial real estate unit, the Sears Tower, and a 10 percent buyback of its own stock. Further, Brennan, who had become company chairman in 1986, announced a new retail strategy of "everyday low prices" to reduce the number of sales and promotions. These new moves, however, provided unsatisfactory solutions. The Sears Tower went on the block during a commercial real estate glut in Chicago and no buyer was found. Lower prices squeezed profit margins because of the company's still-bloated cost structure. Merchandise Group profits fell from more than $700 million in 1986 to $257 million in 1990, as overall profits slid from over $1.3 billion to $892 million during the same period.

In 1990 the financial services divisions contributed the bulk of earnings, with Dean Witter posting its best year ever. By the first quarter of 1991, layoffs and other cost-cutting measures had begun to take hold and at year's end overall profit was back up to nearly $1.3 billion.

A Slimmer, Resurgent Sears, 1992 to Late 1990s

Whether or not Sears could sustain financial improvement through growing sales remained to be seen in the early 1990s. Brennan, representing the third generation of his family to work for Sears, was under considerable pressure from investors and the financial press to turn the company around and increase outsider representation on the board of directors. In 1992 the company slashed 47,000 jobs and suffered a shocking year-end loss of almost $2.3 billion on sales of $53.1 billion.

To stave further losses and concentrate on Sears's department store roots, Brennan began what became the largest restructuring ever: he sold the Eye Care Centers, the remainder of Coldwell Banker (residential real estate), and spun off Dean Witter and the Discover card services. The Automotive Group, under siege after a service fraud scandal and 20 percent sales dive, quit repairs to concentrate on selling tires and batteries, then filled vacant bays through a deal with Pennzoil's Jiffy Lube. Over in Merchandise, Brennan's new hand-picked successor, Arthur C. Martinez, moved quickly and decisively to put a shine to Sears's tarnished image. Catering to the company's female consumers (estimated at 70 percent of sales), Martinez launched a far-reaching advertising campaign on the "softer side of Sears," brought in more famous-name clothing items, and put the company's former mainstay—the 101-year-old catalogue—out to pasture (smaller, specialized catalogues were revived in 1994).

Year-end figures for 1993 supported the streamlining efforts and a $4 billion renovation program with lesser sales ($30.4 billion) but a return to profitability at $2.4 billion. By 1994 Sears's half-million-plus workforce had been whittled to less than 361,000, underperforming stores were closed, and others enlarged by a total of 3.4 million square feet to include national brand names other than its own eponymous label. The company was also finally relieved of the Sears Tower (put in trust for transfer in 2003) and freed of $850 million of debt. The next 12 months marked a year filled with more immense change— Brennan retired and was succeeded by Martinez, the Homart division was sold, and Allstate, the country's largest publicly-held property and casualty insurance carrier with over $20 billion in sales, was spun off.

In 1995 Martinez added further feminine touches to Sears with 152 Circle of Beauty cosmetics boutiques, a joint venture providing skin care, fragrance, bath, makeup, and stress-relieving products. To make way for the beauty lines, appliances, hardware and furniture were moved out of mall-based stores and into their own free-standing buildings (as Sears Hardware, Sears HomeLife and Sears franchise stores) to help serve the rural segment previously handled by the catalogue. Additionally, Sears followed rival J.C. Penney's lead and introduced its own line of denim sportswear under the Canyon River Blues label. Although Lee and Levi's jeans were big sellers at Sears, the private label ran about $10 less and debuted with a splashy media campaign in late 1995.

Sears's ongoing turnaround was a rousing success. Canyon River Blues rang up $100 million in just seven months, newly upgraded jewelry and shoe departments perked up 28 percent and 13 percent respectively, and Western Auto, the company's stalwart auto titan, spawned a line of aftermarket merchandise stores called Parts America, opening 30 stores in 1995 and 60 in 1996. When 1995 closed, Sears had bounced back with a vengeance: sales climbed a notch to $34.9 billion but net income was a sturdy $1.8 billion, with retail profits hitting $1 billion for the first time.

Another secret of Sears's success, its credit card, had contributed mightily to the company's revenue by signing up 6.4 million new cardholders in 1996 alone. With over 55 million cardholders nationwide, Sears's credit services pumped in mounds of profit (most recent figures were from 1993, with income of $706 million). Wall Street had also taken notice, as stock rose from $15 in 1992 to $51 in early 1996, about the time Martinez was named *Financial World's* 22nd annual CEO of the Year. But Martinez had yet to slow down, and plans for the future were already firmly in place: adding another 285 to 350 mall-based department stores during the remainder of 1996, while 500 Sears Hardware stores, 250 HomeLife stores, and 800 independently-owned Sears dealers were planned by the year 2000.

As Sears headed into the next century its founders would undoubtedly have been proud of the company bearing their names. Though it slipped into an identity crisis (was it a department store, a discounter, a specialty store, or a bizarre combination of one or more?) and corporate disarray, perhaps the outcry over Sears's decline was so sharp because the company had carved out a special niche in both U.S. retailing and life in general. Called the "ultimate Sears repairman" by *Financial World*, Martinez's efforts have been lauded worldwide—but most especially by U.S. consumers who hoped his efforts wouldn't be the last on behalf of this American icon.

Principal Divisions

Sears; Sears Auto Centers; Sears Brand Central; Sears Canada; Sears Consumer Financial Corp.; Sears Hardware; Sears HomeLife; Sears Mexico; Sears Overseas Finance N.V. (Netherlands); Sears Roebuck Acceptance Corp.; National Tire Wholesale (NTW); Parts America; Tire America; Western Auto.

Further Reading

Berlinski, Peter, and Pierce, J. J., "Circle of Beauty Program Makes Over Sears Image," *Private Label,* November/December 1995, pp. 1–6.

Bremner, Brian, and Michael Oneal, "The Big Store's Big Trauma," *Business Week,* July 10, 1989.

Byrne, John A., "Strategic Planning," *Business Week,* August 26, 1996, pp. 46–52.

Chandler, Susan, "Where Sears Wants America to Shop Now," *Business Week,* June 12, 1995.

Emmet, Boris, and John E. Jeuck, *Catalogues & Counters: A History of Sears, Roebuck & Company,* Chicago: University of Chicago Press, 1965.

Katz, Donald R., *The Big Store,* New York: Viking, 1987.

Loomis, Carol J., "The Leaning Tower of Sears," *Fortune,* July 2, 1979.

McDonald, John, "Sears Makes It Look Easy," *Fortune,* May 1964.

McMurray, Scott, "Sears Fashions a New Future for Itself," *U.S. News & World Report,* May 13, 1996.

Omelia, Johanna, "Circle of Beauty Squares Off at Sears," *Drug & Cosmetic Industry,* November 1995.

Oneal, Michael, "Sears Faces a Tall Task," *Business Week,* November 14, 1988.

Pierce, J. J., "Designer Jeans at Sears, Kmart Textiles in Tiers," *Private Label,* November/December 1995, p. 7.

"Sears's War," *Fortune,* September, 1942.

Siler, Julia Flynn, Laura Zinn, and John Finotti, "Are the Lights Dimming for Ed Brennan?" *Business Week,* February 11, 1991.

Sparks, Debra, "Arthur Martinez: *Financial World's* CEO of the Year," *Financial World,* March 25, 1996.

Underwood, Elaine, "Jean-Etic License," *Brandweek,* May 29, 1995, pp. 1,6.

Veverka, Mark, "That Softer Side of Sears Still Has Taste for Auto Grit," *Crain's Chicago Business,* May 29, 1995.

Weil, Gordon L., *Sears, Roebuck, U.S.A.,* New York: Stein and Day, 1977.

—Douglas Sun
—updated by Taryn Benbow-Pfalzgraf

Semitool, Inc.

655 West Reserve Drive
Kalispell, Montana 59901
U.S.A.
(406) 752-2107
Fax: (406) 752-5522
Web site: http://www.streetlink.com/sl/fin/smtl.htm

Public Company
Incorporated: 1979
Employees: 1,350
Sales: $174.2 million (1996)
Stock Exchanges: NASDAQ
SICs: 3559 Special Industry Machinery, Not Elsewhere
　　　Classified; 3567 Industrial Process Furnaces & Ovens

Semitool, Inc. designs, manufactures, markets, and services equipment used in the fabrication of semiconductors. Its products include batch and single-substrate spray chemical processing tools, thermal processing equipment, and wafer-carrier cleaning systems. These products provide improved yields (the number of good die per wafer) through higher uniformity of production and reduced contamination levels, and increased throughput (the number of wafers processed by a particular tool in a given period) through advanced processes that reduce cycle times. They are also used to manufacture other materials and devices, including thin film heads, compact-disc masters, flat-panel displays, hard-disk media, and ink-jet print heads. Semitool's customers in 1995 included Advanced Micro Devices, Fujitsu, GEC Plessey, IBM, Intel, Motorola, National Semiconductor, Seagate, Siemens, and SGS-Thomson.

Private Company, 1978–94

Raymon Thompson, a mechanical engineer with a background in semi-conductor equipment, purchased a machine shop in Orange County, California, in the 1970s and founded Semitool there in 1978. The company's first product was a horizontal on-axis spin rinser/dryer that removed chemicals from the surfaces of silicon wafers being imprinted with computer chips. In 1979 Thompson moved the fledgling company to his hometown of Kalispell, Montana.

Semitool introduced the company's spray-solvent and spray-acid tools in the early 1980s and its first automated tool in 1984. Thompson then founded Semitherm, a partnership with a group of former Texas Instruments engineers, to develop vertical furnace systems for "baking" silicon wafers. This company was merged with Semitool in 1994. During the 1980s Semitool introduced several generations of its spray-solvent and spray-acid tools for chemical processing and its vertical furnaces for thermal processing and began to market its products to manufacturers outside the semiconductor industry. Exporting abroad began in 1981.

In fiscal 1991 (the year ended September 30, 1991) Semitool, together with Semitherm, had net sales of $25.1 million and total assets of $15.1 million but a net loss of more than $1.1 million and a debt of $3.1 million. There were approximately 200 employees. For a 1991 survey Thompson told *D&B Reports*, "I have an absolutely outstanding work force, from software engineers right down to the gal who cleans the floor. I think it's largely an ethic of our area here in this part of Montana. People love living here, and they come to work with an internal peace of mind. They're ready to participate as a creative human being, not as a monkey." In 1995 Semitool employees were working weekly 4-day, 10-hour work shifts; the third weekend shift was putting in a three-day work week.

Semitool lost $303,000 on nearly $28 million of net sales in fiscal 1992 and $447,000 on net sales of $42.8 million in fiscal 1993. The company's first profitable year was fiscal 1994, in which it had net income of $2.1 million on net sales of $55.8 million. Total assets reached $37.1 million. That year Semitool doubled the size of its plant and introduced three new products: Equinox, Magnum, and Storm.

Public Company, 1995–96

Semitool's debt, however, reached $13.5 million at the end of fiscal 1994, so Thompson decided to take the company public. About 30 percent of the outstanding common stock was

Company Perspectives:

The Company is committed to developing new products, new applications for existing products and enhancing existing products to address evolving process requirements. Accordingly, the Company devotes substantial resources to product innovation and collaborative development efforts.

offered to the public in February 1995 at $13 a share, with 60 percent of the money raised to be used for debt reduction.

Although a *Barron's* analysis indicated that the offering was pricey, Semitool's stock reached $36.75 a share—nearly triple the offering price—in July. With nine-month sales in fiscal 1995 double that of the same period in the previous year, Semitool announced a three-for-two stock split on July 24. Demand for Equinox, Magnum, and Storm had contributed heavily to a $63-million backlog of orders. Also in 1995, the company won a contract from the research-and-development consortium Sematech for the creation of a new furnace to cook batches of silicon-chip wafers and a $7.7-million contract to supply furnaces to a domestic manufacturer. It also agreed to acquire Semy Engineering, Inc., in 1996 and opened offices in Oregon, Italy, and Japan. During the year Semitool's factory was expanded again.

Semitool recorded net income of $14.9 million on sales of $128.3 million in fiscal 1995. With a five-year average annual return on equity of 42.6 percent, it placed ninth on *Forbes'* 1995 list of the 200 best small companies in America. Company debt had dropped to $4.9 million by the end of the fiscal year.

Semitool's stock plummeted, however, in September 1995 and was trading at only $11.50 a share one year after reaching its peak. In a class-action suit filed in March 1996, a stockholder charged that the company's executives had issued false and misleading information while unloading their own shares, thereby enabling themselves to pocket $8.3 million before the stock fell in value. Thompson, who had been chairman, president, and chief executive officer of Semitool since its inception, held, with his wife, Leila, 51.2 percent of the stock at the end of fiscal 1995.

In February 1996 Thompson announced the largest sale in Semitool's history, a $23-million multi-year order for the VTP 1500 vertical furnace from a domestic semiconductor manufacturer. The company ended fiscal 1996 with net income of $15.1 million on sales of $174.2 million, both figures topping the previous year's totals. In October, however, Semitool announced it was reducing its work force by about 10 percent because of soft demand in the semi-conductor-equipment industry.

Semitool's Products in the Mid-1990s

Semitool's batch chemical processing tools were incorporating centrifugal spray technology to process wafers and substrates by exposing them to a user-programmable, sequenced spray of chemicals inside an enclosed chamber. The wafers, and the cassette and chamber in which they were loaded, were dried by centrifugal spinning coupled with a flow of warm nitrogen. Semitool's batch chemical processing products included the spray-acid and spray-solvent tools. They were also being used in the manufacture of a variety of products other than wafers. The purchase price of these tools ranged from $150,000 to $700,000, with prices (as for other Semitool products) depending on configuration.

The spin rinser/dryer was being used primarily for removing chemical residues from substrate surfaces with deionized water and utilized the same enclosed-chamber, spray-processing, and centrifugal-drying technologies employed by the spray-acid and spray-solvent tools. More than 20,000 of Semitool's spin rinser/dryers had been sold since the company's inception. The purchase price ranged from $10,000 to $150,000 in 1995.

The Magnum was a multi-module chemical processing tool that clustered the company's solvent, acid, and spin rinser/dryer capabilities into a single automated unit. It incorporated a company-designed advanced robot that employed fiber-optic communications, absolute positioning, and a linear motor track to ensure precise, reliable, and particle-free automated wafer handling. The purchase price ranged from $900,000 to more than $2 million.

The Equinox was being employed for substrate processing. Its capabilities included immersion, spray, ultrasonics, hydrofluoric vapor, and infrared heating, to address cleaning, stripping, etching, developing, and gold-plating applications. In addition to its customary silicon-wafer applications, the Equinox was being used to process ceramic substrates, thin film heads, and photo masks. It was selling for between $175,000 and $730,000.

The Storm wafer carrier-cleaning system was being used to clean and dry the cassettes and plastic boxes in which the wafers were being transported and stored. It employed a unique rinsing/spinning process that occurred inside an enclosed chamber. The price ranged from $190,000 to $400,000.

Semitool's VTP 1500 vertical furnace was designed to avoid variances in the process exposure times of individual wafers, thereby avoiding the nonuniformity inherent in traditional vertical furnace processing. Semitool's patented double-lift chamber design also permitted the heating element to be lifted away from the sealed process chamber, allowing wafers to cool more rapidly in a controlled environment and thereby saving time. The VTP 1500 also had the flexibility to be quickly reconfigured for varying processes and to be easily upgraded to accommodate larger wafer sizes. The price ranged from $550,000 to $950,000.

Semitool also was fabricating frames, consoles, and the components to fill them itself, rather than subcontracting for these materials. "All this is engineered here, and it's all built here," Thompson told a Montana newspaper. "It's very unusual for a company like ours to actually build the robots [but] we don't hesitate to design products and build products that require workmanship. We know it's tough for the other guys to do that."

Semitool's Properties in the Mid-1990s

At the end of 1995 Semitool had U.S. sales offices in Arizona, California, Colorado, New Hampshire, New York, North Carolina, Oregon, Pennsylvania, and Texas. There were also offices in France, Germany, Great Britain, Ireland, Israel, Italy, and Japan. (Customers outside the United States accounted for about 43.5 percent of sales in fiscal 1995.) The company's chief property was a 170,000-square-foot facility on a 110-acre site in Kalispell. It planned to build a facility in Cambridge, England, in 1996 for its European sales, service, and customer-demonstration operations.

Principal Subsidiaries

Semitool Europe Ltd. (United Kingdom); Semitool France SARL (France); Semitool Halbleitertechik Vertriebs GmbH (Germany); Semitool KK (Japan).

Further Reading

Malo, Patrick J., ''New Chip-Furnace Deal Will Fuel Growth,'' *Investor's Business Daily,* July 11, 1995, p. A6.

''Montana Manufacturer Takes Dim View of U.S. Leadership,'' *D&B Reports,* November/December 1991, p. 30.

Schwennesen, Don, ''A Sweet 16: The Years Have Been Good to Ray Thompson and Semitool Inc.,'' *Missoulian,* June 18, 1995, p. F1.

——, ''Semitool Brass Accused of Lying, Insider Trading,'' *Missoulian,* March 9, 1996, p. B1.

''Semitool,'' *Barron's,* January 9, 1995, p. 29.

''Semitool Begins Work Reduction,'' *PR Newswire,* October 2, 1996, p. 1002CLW028.

''Semitool Stokes 3Q Sales; Stock Split Is Planned,'' *Electronic News,* August 14, 1995, p. 14.

—Robert Halasz

Shanghai Petrochemical Co., Ltd.

Jinshanwei
Shanghai 200540
China
(86) 21 794-1941
Fax: (86) 21 794-2267

*Public Company (majority-owned by China National
    Petroleum Corp.)*
Founded: 1972
Employees: 60,000
Sales: RMB12.3 billion (US$1.5 billion) (1995)
Stock Exchanges: Hong Kong New York Shanghai
SICs: 2824 Organic Fibers, Noncellulosic; 2911
    Petroleum Refining; 1321 Natural Gas Liquids

With more than 55 plants, Shanghai Petrochemical Co., Ltd. (SPC) is China's largest and most diverse petrochemical enterprise, ranking among the country's biggest corporations. By the early 1990s, the firm was China's only petrochemical entity to combine petroleum, chemicals, chemical fibers, and plastics operations at one site. Its complex included: one ethylene plant, two chemical intermediates units, two polyester units, an aromatics plant, a polyvinyl alcohol plant, a polyacrylic fiber plant, and a plastics factory. SPC's hundreds of petrochemical products have applications in many industries, including: agriculture, pharmaceutical, automotive, aviation, appliance, and textile. In 1996, the company set new production records, refining 4.85 million metric tons (mt) of crude oil (on a capacity of 5.3 million mt) into premium gasoline, diesel fuel, asphalt, and other petroleum products. The by-products of these processes were used to produce 465,000 mt of ethylene; 701,000 mt of synthetic fibers; and 344,000 mt of synthetic plastics. *Asian Monetary Magazine* named SPC China's Best Managed Company that same year.

SPC's size is not the only factor that sets it apart from the majority of Chinese companies. The firm's development can serve as a study in the post-World War II modernization of industry and trade in the People's Republic of China. SPC's creation corresponded with the reopening of the country to foreign diplomacy. As China warmed to international relations—both diplomatic and economic—SPC evolved from a dependence on rather backwards domestic technology to a preference for purchasing advanced plant and process from foreign firms. With the government's approval, the company eventually sought development loans from foreign banks. In 1993, this trend reached an important stage when SPC became one of a limited number of Chinese firms to have equity traded on international stock exchanges.

Background and Foundation in 1972

Like all major Chinese enterprises, Shanghai Petrochemical Company's history is intimately linked to China's communist government. In fact, the impetus behind the 1972 creation of this petrochemical company can be traced to the ascendance of political leaders Zhou Enlai and Deng Xiaoping in the waning years of Mao Zedong's life.

In the early 1970s, the People's Republic of China was beginning to emerge from a chaotic period known as the "Cultural Revolution" (1966–76), when Chairman Mao encouraged anti-intellectualism and isolationism while largely neglecting economic development. The social and political upheaval that resulted from this movement hampered the country's budding industrial efforts, reducing overall industrial production by 12 percent from 1966 to 1968.

With the approval of Mao, who experienced a debilitating stroke in 1972, Zhou began a series of reforms, including the gradual reopening of international relations. After a 20-year hiatus of official Sino-American relations, he hosted a clandestine meeting with U.S. national security advisor Henry Kissinger in 1971, and supported President Richard Nixon's historic visit the following year. This relaxation of tensions between the two nations was an important step toward opening the door to importations of the petrochemical processing equipment that was vital to the successful development of the Shanghai Petrochemical Complex.

SPC was organized in 1972 as a wholly-owned subsidiary of China National Petroleum Corp. (SINOPEC), the government-controlled arbiter of the nation's petroleum industry. The plant was built on Hangzhou Bay in Jinshanwei, about two hours outside Shanghai. One of about a dozen "special economic zones" created in the late 1970s and early 1980s to draw international investment and trade, Shanghai would grow to become China's premier industrial and manufacturing center. The first phase of SPC's development lasted four years and cost the Chinese government an estimated US$800 million. Although the plant used some imported technology, most of its equipment and processes were developed domestically.

In 1978, after a period of political turmoil surrounding Mao's and Zhou's deaths in 1976, Deng Xiaoping and the Chinese Communist Party (CCP) formulated a rigorous ten-year plan for economic growth. This program placed utmost emphasis on "Four Modernizations": industry, defense, agriculture, and science and technology. And in a dramatic reversal of previous policy, the country began to solicit capital from overseas sources to help finance these modernizations.

Basic chemicals, including petrochemicals, were among the highest priority industries, because they constituted the basic building blocks of many modern consumer goods. Petrochemicals are used in such widely varied products as drugs, fabrics, fertilizers, paints, and plastics of all types. As a result, SPC enjoyed a great deal of support from the government. For example, SINOPEC—which soon grew to rank among the world's top five petroleum producers—sold crude oil to SPC at a 40 percent discount to world market prices.

But with such rewards came heavy responsibilities. In order for the Chinese government to maintain full employment, many of the nation's largest firms were obliged to take on upwards of 50 percent more workers than necessary. Furthermore, they had no authority to use incentive or punishment to motivate workers. SPC also had heavy social obligations, including construction and maintenance of its own utilities (power and water plants) and transportation network (a wharf, railroad hub, and highways), not to mention primary and secondary schools and universities, hospitals, movie houses, and shopping centers. By the early 1990s, the complex employed over 60,000 and supported at least 40,000 more. For most of its history, SPC concentrated more on increasing its production levels and meeting its social obligations than making a profit. In fact, the company was compelled to forward any annual financial surplus to the government, which rationed out the funds according to national economic plans.

Economic Reforms Continue Apace in the 1980s

While China often fell short of its stated goals, it did make progress toward economic liberalization in the 1980s. Increasing openness to external influence was evidenced at SPC in the purchase of technology from companies outside the People's Republic of China. In fact, the petrochemical company contracted most of the construction and purchased much of its equipment from foreign firms for its subsequent expansion programs. By the early 1990s, over 80 percent of its production facilities were based on imported technology. The Chinese government lent SPC the US$850 million needed to finance this program, which lasted from 1980 to 1985. The debts were paid by 1988.

In 1987, SPC embarked on a third stage of capacity expansion. This three-year program borrowed US$920 million from domestic sources and tapped international lenders for another $350 million. The subsequent addition of an imported 450,000 mt/year ethylene unit ranked SPC number one among China's ethylene plants and pushed the nation into the world's top ten ethylene producers. Ethylene is one of the organic chemical industry's most important feedstocks. It can be polymerized to create polyethylene plastic for packaging; combined with sulfuric acid and hydrolyzed to make gasoline additives; or combined with oxygen to create an ingredient for antifreeze and soaps.

SPC had for most of its first two decades in business concentrated on meeting seemingly insatiable domestic petrochemical demand. The company took its first tentative step toward the export markets with the 1984 creation of Shanghai Jinshan Associated Trading Corp. (SJATC), an overseas trading office. Corporate export volume constituted less than 4 percent of annual sales by 1991, but the company had forged vital ties to customers in 20 different countries. These international contacts would become increasingly important as SPC sought joint venture partners in the early 1990s.

Internationalism Dominates 1990s

China accelerated its "economic liberalization program" in September 1992. With an eye on increasing efficiency and becoming more involved in the global economy, it gave company managers more authority to allocate resources, both human and material, and slowly began to ease wage, distribution, and price controls to correspond slightly more closely to market levels. Along with this freedom came increased accountability for fiscal performance.

As China's domestic petrochemical industry grew close to meeting internal demand, petrochemical ministers began to turn their attention to international export and downstream diversification in the early 1990s. Joint ventures were key to SPC's overseas strategy. Joint venture and patent laws adopted in the late 1970s helped reassure foreign entrepreneurs that their assets and ideas would not be stolen. Furthermore, China made efforts to reduce bureaucratic "red tape" and relax tax codes to entice outside investors. Realizing the largely untapped potential of the Chinese consumer market, the usually wary leaders of the global chemical industry snapped up joint venture opportunities. From 1993 to 1996, SPC signed cooperative agreements with at least nine foreign firms, including BP Chemicals, Phillips Petroleum Co., Mitsubishi Corp., and Union Carbide.

Economic liberalization also meant that the Chinese government was willing to sell minority stakes in some of its most capital-intensive businesses to reduce outright borrowing. But in order to make the shares attractive to bottom-line-minded investors, the companies had to "spin-off" their social welfare components as separate entities. Before SPC could make its mid-1993 flotation, it separated into Shanghai Petrochemical Company, Ltd., which got all the production units, and Jinshan Industrial, which oversaw other interests like schools and hospitals. SPC also had to adopt international accounting principles including stating its after-tax profit as opposed to the traditional standard of "tax plus profit."

Having cleared these and other hurdles, SPC became one of China's first and largest companies to make an initial public stock offering in July 1993, when the government sold 29.6 percent of its equity via H shares traded on the Hong Kong stock exchange and American Depository Receipts (ADRs) offered on the New York stock market. The H shares debuted at about HK$1.40, while each ADR represented 100 class H shares, and was initially priced at US$20.39 apiece. Seeking ground-floor equities in the so-called ''market of one billion,'' investors quickly oversubscribed the offering. SPC planned to use the proceeds to pay down about US$123 million in foreign debts and fund new capital projects.

Considerations for the 1990s and Beyond

SPC's stock performed well in the mid-1990s, as its net income multiplied from RMB443.1 million in 1992 to over RMB2 billion by 1995. *Far Eastern Economic Review's* Henny Sender warned that ''[the stock] was blessed less by its own strength than by the fact that demand for China shares far exceeded supply'' in those heady days.

Sender was by no means the only analyst to sound the alarm with regard to SPC and its securities. For notwithstanding the company and country's admirable strides toward economic liberalism, several areas of concern remained. For example, although SPC was relieved of the majority of its social welfare responsibilities prior to its initial stock offering, it was still required to ''allocate a portion of its profits to its public-welfare fund,'' according to a July 1993 brief in the *Far Eastern Economic Review*. Furthermore, SPC's reliance on SINOPEC for subsidized crude oil, which constituted over half of its production expenses, undermined its entire balance sheet. For while SPC proved profitable in the early 1990s, some of that prosperity was clearly due to the steep discount on crude it received from SINOPEC. Just as the government relaxed controls on the price of SPC's products (a benefit), it could easily rescind its discounts on crude (a detriment). As the *Far Eastern Economic Review's* Ivan Png and Changqui Wu pointed out in October 1995, ''a company like Shanghai Petrochemical may be making millions of dollars without really succeeding in market terms.'' Issues such as these must have weighed heavily on the minds of any SPC investor.

In 1995, Wu Yixin succeeded Wang Jiming, who moved on to the presidency of SINOPEC, as SPC President. Soon after taking office, Wu Yixin revealed that the company would require US$9.3 billion to pay for the next three years' expansion programs. In light of the scarcity of government funds for these projects, SPC issued 500 million new H shares on the Hong Kong stock exchange to generate over RMB4 billion (about US$500 million) in mid-1996. The floatation reduced SINOPEC's share of SPC to 64 percent. The capital investment program included capacity increases of both ethylene and synthetic fibers to 1 million t/y by 2005. By the year 2000, SPC forecast sales of RMB20 billion and income before taxes of RMB5 million.

Further Reading

''Chemical Industry Launches Growth Scheme,'' *China Chemical Reporter*, January 10, 1994, p. 1.
''China Petrochemical Expansion Progressing,'' *The Oil and Gas Journal*, August 5, 1991, pp. 28–30.
''China's Polyvinyl Alcohol Output Holding the World's First Place,'' *China Chemical Reporter*, October 6, 1996, p. 4.
''Development of China's Ethylene Industry,'' *China Chemical Reporter*, May 16, 1996, p. 10.
''Development of China's Ethylene Industry,'' *China Chemical Reporter*, August 16, 1996, p. 15.
''Expansion Projects to Cost $9.3 B,'' *HK Standard*, May 11, 1996, p. 3.
Hendry, Sandy, ''Shanghai Petrochemical to Raise Equity Capital,'' *Chemical Week*, March 3, 1993, p. 24.
McElligott, Suzanne, ''China's H Share Chemical Quartet,'' *Chemical Week*, August 30/September 6, 1995, pp. S31, S33.
Peaff, George, ''Shanghai Petrochemical Is Free Market Proving Ground,'' *Chemical Marketing Reporter*, September 6, 1993, p. 3.
Png, Ivan, and Changqi Wu, ''A Tale of Two Companies,'' *Far Eastern Economic Review*, October 12, 1995, p. 39.
Sender, Henny, ''Ready for Action,'' *Far Eastern Economic Review*, 15 July 1993, p. 82.
——, ''Industrial Revolution: Shanghai Petrochemical Is Reforming, But Slowly,'' *Far Eastern Economic Review*, April 28, 1994, p. 74.
''Shanghai Ethylene Project Completes,'' *China Chemical Reporter*, Number 9, 1992, p. 3.
''Shanghai Petrochemical Adds New Investments,'' *Chemical Marketing Reporter*, January 17, 1994, p. 8.
''Shanghai Petrochemical Is in the Black,'' *chemical Marketing Reporter*, May 2, 1994, p. 8.
''Shanghai Petrochemical Faces Challenges of Reform,'' *Wall Street Journal*, January 19, 1994, p. B4.
''SPC Sets Its Strategies for Future Growth,'' *ECN-European Chemical News*, May 16, 1994, p. 5.
Twaronite, Lisa, ''Shanghai Petrochemical Co. Awaits China Oil Price Reform,'' *Journal of Commerce and Commercial*, December 3, 1993, p. 11A.
Wood, Andrew, ''Shanghai: Surprise Number of Ventures,'' *Chemical Week*, March 23, 1994, pp. 40–42.
Wood, Andrew and Lyn Tattum, ''Ringing in the Changes at Chinese Firms,'' *Chemical Week*, August 31, 1994, p. S38.
Wood, Andrew, and Ian Young, ''Foreign Companies Rush to Invest,'' *Chemical Week*, August 31, 1994, p. S4.

—April Dougal Gasbarre

Skadden, Arps, Slate, Meagher & Flom

919 Third Avenue
New York, New York 10022
U.S.A.
(212) 735-3000
Fax: (212) 735-2001

Private Company
Founded: 1948 as Skadden, Arps & Slate
Employees: 3,000
Sales: $635 million (est.)
SICs: 8111 Legal Services

Skadden, Arps, Slate, Meagher & Flom stands as a monolith in the corporate environment, one of the two largest law firms in the world. The firm built upon its status as the most sought-after mergers-and-acquisitions (M&A) firm in the country to ride the surge of corporate-takeover activity in the 1970s and 80s. As a result of this demand, the firm stood in a position to charge its clients unprecedented fees and grow at an astonishing pace. In the process, Skadden, Arps changed the practice of law into an aggressively competitive business, by handling new kinds of business and increasing the lengths to which its lawyers would go to provide client service. The firm's grand scale has provoked its fair share of media attention, including numerous features in the national business press and its own biography.

Origin and Founders, 1940s-50s

According to Lincoln Caplan, in *Skadden: Power, Money, and the Rise of a Legal Empire*, the firm was founded on April Fools' Day in 1948 as an informal partnership with $12,000 of start-up capital. The firm's first fee was a modest $532.50. Joe Flom, a graduate of Harvard Law School, joined the firm as an associate in 1948, and eventually influenced the firm's growth more than any founding partner.

Flom served as the visionary architect of Skadden, Arps's growth. According to *Institutional Investor*, "Flom built Skadden, Arps, Slate, Meagher & Flom into one of the largest, most profitable law firms in America, while ... redefining the use of

the law in M&A.... Flom was the epitome of the market warrior, and he brought the Darwinian ethos of the marketplace into the world of corporate law." Flom's early expertise centered around shareholder's derivative actions. Such actions are devices for the owners of a company to bring suit against its board of directors and management for failing to uphold their duties in running a company. In a typical corporation, the owners/shareholders elect the board of directors, who in turn selects management to run the company. If the board enters into a buyout in a way that does not give maximum value to the shareholders, a derivative action is likely.

Growth, 1960s-80s

The growth of the firm was remarkable: In the mid-1960s, the firm grew to 20 lawyers and had more work than it could handle. According to Caplan, Skadden, Arps started by making $37,660 in revenue and $6,510 in profits its first year; however, "by the late seventies, intense demand allowed Skadden to raise its hourly billing rates to as high a level as any firm's in New York City." Those rates allowed Skadden, Arps to bring in $225 million a year in revenue by the end of 1986. A decade later, Skadden, Arps made $210 million profits on $635 revenues, according to recent estimates by *Fortune* magazine. The firm is not totally peerless in terms of generating revenue; for example, in 1992, Baker & McKenzie surpassed Skadden, Arps in terms of revenue. More than large revenues are required to build a lasting firm. As a reminder that not all megafirms managed to survive intact, Skadden, Arps was hired by bankruptcy creditors of one of its former competitors, Finley Kumble.

The growth in the firm's revenues is due in part to growth in its physical size and reach. Skadden, Arps has over 3000 employees, including 1000 attorneys, and hires up to 700 new employees every year. In 1976, Skadden, Arps opened a Washington office, and it opened a Chicago office in 1984. Skadden, Arps had 13 offices in 1990, with half of its attorneys in its New York office. Currently, the firm claims nine domestic offices, in New York; Boston; Washington, D.C.; Wilmington, Delaware; Los Angeles; San Francisco; and, Newark, New Jersey. The firm also keeps foreign offices in Beijing, Brussels, Budapest, Frankfurt, Hong Kong, London, Moscow, Paris, Prague, Sydney, Tokyo, and Toronto.

Company Perspectives:

With approximately 1,000 attorneys in 21 offices, Skadden, Arps, Slate, Meagher & Flom is one of the largest law firms in the world. We provide a wide array of legal services domestically and internationally to the corporate, financial, industrial and governmental communities. In the United States, we represent a broad spectrum of clients, from small high-technology start-up companies to more than one-third of the Fortune *250 industrial corporations, as well as many financial and governmental entities.*

Since our first non-U.S. office opened in 1987, Skadden, Arps has expanded into major financial centers, as well as emerging market economies, around the globe. International matters constitute a growing percentage of the firm's business, as U.S. companies seek new investment opportunities abroad and governments worldwide move to privatize state-owned industries. As a reflection of this new global marketplace for legal services, we now have a total of 12 offices in Asia, Australia, Canada, and Western and Central Europe, in addition to our nine U.S. offices, and substantial practices in areas such as Israel and Latin America.

Law Firm Marketing

Notably, the ethical canons and codes of the legal profession, in particular rules restricting solicitation of clients, have limited the ways in which law firms can attract new business. The last half of this century, however, has seen a shift in law firm marketing. Clients have become more sophisticated, and law firms operate more like other businesses, trends that correspond to a lessening of ethical restrictions on law firm marketing. According to a 1982 memorandum, Skadden, Arps's goal was to "enhance the reputation of the firm and insure its continued viability and its ability to earn substantial income for its partners . . . ." Skadden, Arps did this by aggressively developing new business.

According to Caplan's book, Joseph Flom has described the takeover movement positively: "Merger and acquisition activity has performed a critically important function. Companies have become leaner and meaner." As a key feature of its marketing strategy, Skadden, Arps cunningly analyzed the business environment for opportunities that could gain advantages for its clients.

Skadden, Arps went beyond the services offered by typical firms, aiming to work harder and longer at solutions to their clients' broader problems. Skadden, Arps seems to have filled a hole left by the "white shoe" law firms of Wall Street: Many more established firms would not handle takeovers for fear of upsetting their longstanding corporate clientele. Beyond innovations in client development, Skadden, Arps pioneered new fee structures. For example, the firm instituted a revenue-generating practice of charging corporate clients retainers. In return for paying a sizable retainer, the client could expect to have Skadden, Arps available as counsel in the event of a hostile takeover. This also prevented potential acquiring companies from using Skadden, Arps against a client on retainer.

Trends in the American business climate contributed in part to the amazing revenues gathered by the firm. Takeovers, the field in which Skadden, Arps gained its greatest dominance, became an increasingly popular option in corporate America for several reasons. Individuals, who represented an increasing segment of post-World War II investors, demanded shorter-term returns on investment than had earlier investors. With such pressures on the annual bottom line, corporate management needed to find ways to sustain growth in the face of increasing global competition. Further, takeovers grew in fiscal size as well as in number in the 1980s as the price of stocks rose.

In the 80s, companies were offered new vehicles to raise large amounts of capital, such as leveraged buyouts (LBOs) and junk bonds. In an LBO, a buyer could acquire a target by getting a loan secured by the target's assets. If the ratio of secured assets to outstanding debt was high, the bonds used to leverage the takeover were known as junk bonds. In other words, junk bonds basically represented high-risk, unratable debt. Companies attempted to use junk bonds to acquire larger ones, increasing the demand for law firms with significant mergers-and-acquisitions experience.

Law Firm Governance

Since its inception as a partnership with no formal agreement, the firm has changed into a limited liability company (LLC), a hybrid juridical form. LLCs were created by state legislatures as ways of infusing partnerships with the corporate feature of limited liability, while allowing them to retain their partnership characteristics. According to Caplan, profits in Skadden, Arps, Slate, Meagher & Flom, LLC, are split between members by an eight-member committee. The committee looks at the members' quality of work, their hours billed, profitability of their respective practice areas, and their contributions to firm management. Since the late 1970s, Skadden, Arps partners (now, members) have been some of the highest paid attorneys in the country.

Skadden, Arps has taken novel steps in law firm governance. In 1990, the firm changed its management structure to operate less like a partnership and more like a typical American corporation, emulating a board of directors. The firm also developed the Rainy Day Fund, for a law firm a financially ultra-conservative measure, which provides a means of leaving the firm with enough money to carry all expenses for six months in case of emergency, as explained by Caplan.

Lawyer Compensation

Traditionally, Skadden, Arps has hired and promoted based on merit, progressively recognizing employees, including legal secretaries, paralegals, and clerks, from all segments of society. For example, Skadden, Arps promoted its first female partner in 1981. For the long hours and stress, employees at the firm are well compensated. At rates competitive with any law firm in the world, first-year Skadden, Arps associates make $85,000 per year and can increase their earnings to $178,000 annually after seven years. Those levels of compensation are earned by long hours: Lawyers at Skadden, Arps have been known to bill over 2,000 hours per year, as well as doing an average of 42 hours per year on free legal services for the poor.

The employees working in the Skadden, Arps Manhattan office are afforded all the implements required for a modern-day corporate meritocracy. The office has been designed as a large 24-hour work station. The facility includes state-of-the-art office equipment, all-night telephone receptionists, a fitness center, and law library that never closes.

Skadden, Arps handled its first tender offer in 1964, and Flom worked on a number of deals in the 1970s that defined the firm's reputation as a leader in corporate takeovers. ''The firm's turning point occurred in 1974 when Flom represented International Nickel Corporation and successfully won control of a target company, ESB Inc.,'' according to Caplan. Flom saved Chicago's Marshall Field from a takeover attempt by Carter Hawley Hale in 1975, by delivering a clever piece of advice. The firm advised takeover target Marshall Field to build stores where Carter Hawley Hale already had outlets. This potential saturation of any particular market could be seen to have anti-competitive effects under the Sherman Act, thereby inviting the possibility of Federal Trade Commission scrutiny of the merger. The antitrust aspects of the takeover overly complicated the deal. As a result of this advice, Marshall Field made itself an extremely unattractive takeover target. Flom's reputation for aggressively defending corporate-takeover clients in ways such as in the Marshall Field deal solidified his firm's reputation in mergers and acquisitions. In the late 1970s and through the 1980s, Skadden, Arps was involved in almost every major merger and acquisition in the United States.

Its reputation as the nonpareil law firm in an exciting field brought attention to Skadden, Arps. While law firms typically were reserved and press-wary, Skadden, Arps has regularly garnered the type of media attention previously reserved for the most public of corporations. For example, journalist Steve Brill featured the firm in a major *Esquire* article as well as in the first issue of *American Lawyer*. The firm also attracted its share of glamour in other ways. In the early 1980s, the former president of MGM, Frank Rothman, became a partner in the Los Angeles office of Skadden, Arps.

Setbacks, Lessons for the Future

Despite its reputation as a competent and respected corporate firm, Skadden, Arps has stumbled at times. Pennzoil v. Texaco serves as a textbook example, literally, of a spectacular defeat for the firm on an unprecedented scale. As told by Caplan, the firm's client, Texaco, acquired Getty Oil, a prudent move, according to many legal experts at the time. Unfortunately, in so doing, Texaco was found to have interfered with prior contractual relations for the sale of Getty Oil to Pennzoil. As a result of that tort, Pennzoil was awarded the largest judgment in history—$10.5 billion. A procedural error on the part of Skadden, Arps may have contributed to the high award. Skadden, Arps passed up the opportunity to have the case tried in Delaware where juries, reportedly, do not favor granting such high awards.

Skadden, Arps also failed in preventing a book about the *Mossad*, the Israeli intelligence agency, from being published.

The firm had been engaged by the government of Israel to keep the book off the shelves because it contained information that could threaten the lives of *Mossad* agents. Although the book was published, the commotion raised by the firm's efforts served as free publicity, piquing interest in the book from the public and multiplying the book's sales.

Skadden, Arps, Slate, Meagher & Flom successfully read major shifts in the business environment and made a series of noteworthy innovations, particularly in mergers and acquisitions. In so doing, the firm irreversibly changed the practice of corporate law and the environment of Corporate America. Skadden, Arps has risen to the pinnacle of global American law firms.

Further Reading

Caplan, Lincoln, *Skadden: Power, Money, and the Rise of a Legal Empire*, New York: Farrar Straus Giroux, 1993.

Erdman, Andrew, ''Say It Ain't So, Joe,'' *Fortune*, September 9, 1991, p. 185.

Eisler, Kim Isaac, *Shark Tank: Greed, Politics, and the Collapse of Finley, Kumble, One of America's Largest Law Firms*, New York: St. Martin's Press, 1990.

Flom, Joseph, ''Joseph Flom,'' *Institutional Investor*, June 1987, pp. 392–94.

Henriques, Diana B., ''Top Court Under Fire: Critics Say Politics Is Hurting Delaware Judiciary,'' *New York Times*, May 23, 1995, p. D1.

Kumble, Steven J., and Lahart, Kevin J., *Conduct Unbecoming: The Rise and Ruin of Finley, Kumble*, New York: Carroll & Graf, 1990.

Lambert, Wade, ''Skadden Arps Alleges Theft of Records (Libel Case Involving R. Fuisz and TEREX Corp.),'' *Wall Street Journal (Eastern Edition)*, June 25, 1993, p. B7.

''Lawson Software Provides Improved Employee Productivity and Cost Savings at Skadden, Arps,'' http://www.lawson.com:80/6success/service/default.htm, February 14, 1997.

Lezner, Robert, ''In Grandpa's Footsteps (Skadden, Arps' I. Shapiro Helps Structure Russian Privatization),'' *Forbes*, May 11, 1992, p. 104.

Pogrebin, Robin, ''The Best Lawyers in New York,'' *New York*, March 20, 1995, pp. 32–46.

Serwer, Andrew, ''Lawyers, Fun, and Money,'' *Fortune*, December 13, 1993, p. 190.

''Skadden, Arps, Slate, Meagher & Flom,'' *Martindale-Hubbel Online Directory*, http://www.martindale.com, February 14, 1997.

Skadden, Arps, Slate, Meagher & Flom: An Overview, New York: Skadden, Arps, Slate, Meagher & Flom, 1994.

''Skadden, Arps, Slate, Meagher & Flom,'' *Forbes 500 Largest Private Companies*, http://www.forbes.com:80/privates/1418.htm, February 14, 1997.

Smith, Randall, and Stevens, Amy, ''Skadden Pays Stiff Price for Expansion,'' *Wall Street Journal (Eastern Edition)*, May 15, 1995, p. B1.

Stevens, Amy, ''Is Insider Trading Back at Law Firms?,'' *Wall Street Journal (Eastern Edition)*, May 1, 1995, p. B1.

Stevens, Amy, ''Skadden Wins Contest for Bell Atlantic, But It Wasn't Easy,'' *Wall Street Journal (Eastern Edition)*, October 15, 1995, p. B5.

Teitelman, Robert, ''Flom's Way,'' *Institutional Investor*, February 30, 1994.

—Edward C. Ingram

Slim-Fast Nutritional Foods International, Inc.

777 S. Flagler Drive
West Tower, Suite 1400
West Palm Beach, Florida 33401
U.S.A.
(407) 833-9920
Fax: (407) 822-2876

Private Company
Incorporated: 1945 as Thompson Medical Company
Employees: 75
Sales: $600 million (1995)
SICs: 2099 Food Preparations, Not Elsewhere Classified

Slim-Fast Nutritional Foods International, Inc. is a leading producer of weight management and health food products. Its best known product, thanks to an advertising campaign featuring charismatic Los Angeles Dodgers manager Tommy Lasorda, is Ultra Slim-Fast, a meal-replacement product which takes on the appearance and texture of a milkshake. Other products include frozen entrees and desserts, snack items, and hot chocolate mix. Slim-Fast's products are marketed through retail outlets such as supermarkets and drugstores.

The Early Years

What would become Slim-Fast Nutritional Foods International, Inc. began with S. Daniel Abraham's ability to sell itch relief cream. Abraham exited the U.S. Army in 1945 at age 21 and went to work at his uncle's small drug company in New York. While working there, he read an advertisement in a trade journal for an itch-relief cream, and decided to purchase the product and its maker for $5,000. Abraham left his uncle's company, and began traveling throughout neighboring states to offer doctors and pharmacists samples of his product while distributing his advertisement posters. Abraham's fledgling enterprise soon became known as the Thompson Medical Company.

Abraham used his profits to hire chemists and pharmacologists to modify other manufacturers' existing products. In addition, he purchased the rights to other pharmaceutical companies' smaller and less-successful product lines, which he then revamped and marketed as Thompson Medical products. In 1956, Abraham unveiled his first diet product, called Slim-Mint gum, which contained a hunger suppressant called benzocaine. By 1960, his company had also added a line of diet pills called Figure-Aid.

It was not until 1976, with the introduction of Dexatrim, that Abraham's experimentation in the diet-control market began to pay off big. Dexatrim was a diet pill containing the appetite suppressant phenylpropanolamine (PPA). Although the use of PPA was somewhat controversial at the time, Dexatrim soon became the best-selling diet pill on the market, and helped Thompson Medical's sales surpass $50 million by the end of the decade.

The 1970s and 1980s: Slim-Fast Is Born

Thompson Medical introduced Slim-Fast in 1977. When mixed with low-fat milk the powdered formula took on the taste and texture of a milkshake. Marketed as a 1,200-calorie-per-day meal-replacement product, Slim-Fast was engineered to be used at both breakfast and lunch, and then supplemented with a sensible and healthy dinner. Unfortunately, during its first year on the market, Slim-Fast was pulled from circulation along with all other fluid meal-replacement products after almost sixty dieters died while using 300-calorie-per-day liquid diets made by other manufacturers. To counter the loss of earnings that had been generated and then lost by the Slim-Fast product, Abraham engineered a public offering in 1979 of approximately 4 million shares of Thompson Medical stock. The offering brought in $8.4 million in earnings, most of which was spent on advertising and promotion of the company's products.

Luckily, Abraham was able to reintroduce his Slim-Fast product in the early 1980s, at the same time that Dexatrim sales began to decline due to the Food & Drug Administration's growing concerns regarding the use of PPA in consumer products. The re-admittance of Slim-Fast to the diet control market helped Thompson Medical achieve sales of approximately $197 million in 1984, and laid the foundation for the product's future success.

Throughout the mid-1980s, Thompson Medical's sales fluctuated as more manufacturers entered the diet-control market and competed for market share. In late 1987, just after the October stock market crash, Abraham decided to make the company private once again, and began repurchasing shares of Thompson's stock. A year later, he had acquired 33 percent of the company's stock, a controlling interest that he maintains to this day. At this time, he also stumbled upon what would become the most successful advertising tool used by Slim-Fast in the coming years: televised celebrity endorsements.

In 1988, Los Angeles Dodgers manager Tommy Lasorda needed to lose 20 pounds, and Slim-Fast was in need of a celebrity to promote its product in the same way that Oprah Winfrey was promoting competitor Opti-Fast. The company signed Lasorda as its spokesman, and offered to contribute $20,000 to his favorite charity if he would stick to the diet plan. Within months, Lasorda had lost almost 30 pounds, and a Nashville-based group of nuns received a new convent in his name. Research showed Lasorda to be an especially effective spokesman with female consumers, who found him to be credible because he was a man admitting to a weight problem on national television, and he was seeing successful results due to his use of the Slim-Fast product.

The 1990s and Beyond

Throughout the 1980s, Thompson Medical had diversified its product offerings and had begun to market such over-the-counter remedies as Aspercreme, Sportscreme, and Cortizone-5. By 1991, in response to Slim-Fast's rapid growth in the diet and nutritional foods segment, Abraham spun-off the division to become its own company, although he retained his position as chairman and majority-stockholder.

Just after the split, Slim-Fast began to experience a decrease in sales, due in part to Oprah Winfrey's highly-publicized weight gain after discontinuing use of a fluid meal-replacement product. Without Thompson Medical's diverse portfolio to back it, Slim-Fast had to find a way to support itself through this time period. Thus, the company began planning the introduction of a variety of new products under the Slim-Fast brand name, and Slim-Fast Nutritional Foods International, Inc. was born.

The new Slim-Fast offerings were accompanied by a broadening of the company's focus to combine weight loss with a stress on the importance of a healthy lifestyle and the nutritional benefits of Slim-Fast products. A new slogan was introduced, advertising the company's products as a part of the "Slim-Fast way of life." New product offerings emphasized convenience, and included pre-mixed Slim-Fast in cans and refrigerated cartons, hot chocolate mix, frozen entrees and desserts, and snacks such as cheese curls and popcorn. ConAgra, a leading force in the health and diet business with its Healthy Choice product line, manufactured and distributed the frozen foods. The pre-mixed Slim-Fast was manufactured by Farmland

Dairies, and the snack items were made in partnership with Borden.

In another effort to move the company beyond its typical weight-loss products, Slim-Fast produced new television advertisements featuring celebrity testimonials to the health benefits derived from the "Slim-Fast way of life." While many people questioned Slim-Fast's ability to compete in the health-food arena against giants such as Weight Watchers and Lean Cuisine, Slim-Fast hoped its new advertising campaign would generate increased sales. A new spot featuring Lasorda was aired, as were other spots containing media personalities Frank and Kathie Lee Gifford, actor Peter DeLuise (Dom's son), ex-New York Mayor Ed Koch, and singer Mel Torme.

In 1992, about a year after Slim-Fast separated from Thompson Medical, Ron Stern was promoted to the position of president of Slim-Fast. Stern had previously been with the company in a vice-presidential role, and was instrumental in the signing of Lasorda as spokesman three years earlier. Although Slim-Fast held a 70 percent share of the meal-replacement market at that time, Stern noted that a rapidly increasing amount of competition threatened the company's market share. Slim-Fast decided to lower the wholesale price of its products by an average of 55 cents, thereby making its competitors' products more expensive to stock.

The following year, Slim-Fast began airing a talk-show style infomercial in an attempt to counter the growing segment of companies that were offering mail-order diet products. Interestingly, Slim-Fast did not actually sell its products through the infomercial. Instead, the television spot tried to persuade consumers to go to retail stores for weight control products, rather than purchase such items through the mail. Using this method, Slim-Fast made efforts to retain its market share without having to enter the mail-order arena to compete effectively.

Slim-Fast Nutritional Foods International, Inc. entered the mid-1990s in a position of dominance in the weight management and health-food industry. With a controlling share of the market, Slim-Fast was beginning to receive accolades for its performance. "No single brand has demonstrated the vitality, marketing savvy and well-timed ability to tie into Americans' desire for weight management and proper nutrition as has Slim-Fast," according to *Supermarket Business*. As one of the few brands that follows the Surgeon General's recommendations on diet and health and as a recipient of the Good Housekeeping Seal of Approval, Slim-Fast was well equipped to handle the pressures of an increasingly cautious consumer society. With an expanding array of product offerings and a seemingly endless base of customers interested in better health, Slim-Fast was well positioned for future growth in the late 1990s.

Further Reading

Berman, Phyllis, and Amy Feldman, "An Extraordinary Peddler," *Forbes*, December 9, 1991, p. 136.

Dagnoli, Judann, "Heavying Up on Diet Ads," *Advertising Age*, December 23, 1991, p. 3.

———, "Slim-Fast Beefs Up Menu of Food Items," *Advertising Age*, May 27, 1991, p. 33.

Doherty, Katherine, "Farmland Carton-Packages Slim-Fast," *U.S. Distribution Journal,* May 15, 1991, p. 40.

Freeman, Laurie, "Ultra Slim-Fast: Ron Stern," *Advertising Age,* July 6, 1992, p. S8.

Levin, Gary, "Infomercials Take a Different Spin," *Advertising Age,* September 20, 1993, p. 8.

Liesse, Julie, "Frozen Novelties Look for Hot Summer," *Advertising Age,* May 13, 1991, p. 6.

"Meal Replacements," *Supermarket Business,* April 1991, p. G22.

Rigg, Cynthia, "After Binge, Slim-Fast Is Thinning," *Crain's New York Business,* March 18, 1991, p. 3.

Winters, Patricia, "Slim-Fast Dishes Up New Foods," *Advertising Age,* January 7, 1991, p. 38.

—Laura E. Whiteley

SPARTON CORPORATION

Sparton Corporation

2400 E. Ganson St.
Jackson, Michigan 49202
U.S.A.
(517) 787-8600
Fax: 517 787-1822

Public Company
Incorporated: 1916 as Sparks-Withington Company
Employees: 1,500
Sales: $102.82 million (1996)
Stock Exchanges: New York
SICs: 3812 Search and Navigation Equipment; 3679
    Electronic Components, Not Elsewhere Classified;
    3714 Motor Vehicle Parts and Accessories; 3465
    Automotive Stampings

Sparton Corporation has a century long history of manufacturing technologically advanced equipment for the transportation, electronics, communication, and defense industries. Founded at the turn of the century, Sparton has participated in many of the technological milestones of the 20th century, including the introduction of the automobile, fully electric radios, refrigeration, and television. Although since the 1960s Sparton was known primarily as a defense contractor, cuts in defense spending in the 1990s saw the company redirecting its target markets towards the commercial electronics industry.

Turn-of-the-Century Origins

The Sparton Corporation was founded as the Withington Company in 1900 in Jackson, Michigan, by Philip and Winthrop Withington. William Sparks became the third partner in the business a few years later and the company name was changed to the Sparks-Withington Company. Sparks-Withington began as a small manufacturer of steel parts for agricultural implements but as the automobile revolution began to sweep through Michigan in the early part of the century, Sparks-

Withington added steel automotive stampings like hub caps and brake drums to their product line. By 1909, the company was manufacturing car radiator cooling fan assemblies, which quickly became a major part of the company's production output, reaching 275,000 units by 1917. It was during this period that Sparks-Withington began to make use of the trade name "Sparton," a contraction of the company name and an evocation of the disciplined Spartans of Ancient Greece. The company's first major product innovation came in 1911 when the all-electric car horn was developed by Sparks-Withington engineers. The Hudson Automobile Company soon adopted the Sparton electric horn as standard equipment for its automobiles, replacing the optional bulb horns that had characterized the early era of the automobile. The electric horn has remained a staple product for Sparton since its introduction.

Radio and Television Production in the 1930s and 1940s

The Sparks-Withington Company was officially incorporated in Ohio in 1916 and then reincorporated in 1919 when shares in the company began to be sold on the New York Stock Exchange. After a brief period of military production during World War I, Sparks-Withington used its growing expertise in the electronics field to bring out a line of battery powered radios, followed in 1926 by production of the country's first all-electric radio, promoted as "Radio's Richest Voice." While many American companies suffered during the Great Depression, Sparks-Withington expanded. In 1930, the company formed a wholly-owned Canadian subsidiary, Sparton of Canada, Ltd., to introduce the Sparton radio line in Canada. In the same year, the company acquired the Cardon-Phonocraft Company of Jackson, Michigan, and integrated their radio tubes and combination radio-phonograph products into the Sparton line. Sparks-Withington further expanded their radio accessory business with the purchase of Home Products Corp. of Michigan. In 1932, the company entered a new market with the introduction of the Sparton electric refrigerator. The intense competition in this industry was largely responsible for the company's 1938 net loss of $60,000, however, and the company dropped the product line by the end of the decade.

Company Perspectives:

Sparton Corporation is dedicated to: the conduct of our business at the highest ethical level; the manufacture of superior quality products in the most efficient manner possible at the lowest possible cost; loyally serving each customer to the utmost of our ability by making continuing contributions that support his progress; constantly improving our company's technological base to better serve our customers; the creation of new ideas, new products and new processes in order to remain the low cost producer in our chosen marketplaces; making our company grow faster than the economy; the maximization of shareowner value; providing a work environment that is safe, modern and clean and one where our employees can achieve their highest potential.

By the beginning of the 1940s, Sparks-Withington was operating five factories in Jackson, Michigan, in addition to their Canadian subsidiary's facility in London, Ontario. Annual sales topped $5 million. Like most American manufacturers, Sparks-Withington switched to military production during World War II, manufacturing bomb hoists, communications equipment, magazine clips, and a wide variety of other military products for the war effort. With a return to peace, Sparks-Withington set out once again to expand its range of products. In 1945, the company acquired the Illinois-based Steger Furniture Manufacturing Co. to manufacture cabinets for the radio and radio-phonographs that had become the mainstay of the Sparton product line.

Before the war Sparks-Withington engineers had experimented with the development of television receivers, and had even field tested an early model, but disagreements in implementing industry-wide standards for television compounded with the outbreak of World War II to delay the widespread introduction of television to the American public until 1948. With its electronic expertise and established brand recognition in Sparton brand radios, the company was in a good position to enter this new and potentially lucrative market. Under the Sparton trade name, Sparks-Withington began full scale production of black and white television receivers in 1948 and then introduced a color model some five years later. In 1954 the company further expanded into the communications industry by founding WWTV, a local television station in Cadillac, Michigan.

Entry into Defense Technology in the 1950s

Through the first 50 years of Sparks-Withington's operations, management of the firm had remained firmly in control of the Sparks and Withington families. However, in 1950, a proxy fight led by shareholder John J. Smith culminated in the takeover of the board of directors by a new group of investors. Smith was elected president and within two years the founding families had resigned their leadership positions with the company. In keeping with the change in management and in recognition of the strength of the 30 year old trade name, in 1956 the

Sparks-Withington company name was officially changed to the Sparton Corporation.

By the early 1950s, radio and television sets accounted for two-thirds of Sparton sales, which had reached almost $24 million by the opening of the decade. In spite of strong sales, intense competition in the electronics industry increasingly reduced profit margins until, in 1954, Sparton was faced with a $300,000 net loss. During this same period Sparton had been slowly building up its automotive and electronic divisions through acquisitions and new product development. Most notably, Sparton engineers began a program to use the company's expertise in radio technology to develop a sonobuoy system for the American navy. Sonobuoys—small, air-dropped listening devices used to detect and locate submarines—would prove to be one of the company's most lucrative product lines through the following three decades. By 1956, it had become clear that the defense industry could provide better growth and higher profit margins than the highly competitive radio and television industries. Sparton made the dramatic and risky decision to discontinue all American production of the radios, televisions, and stereos, which had been the company's largest product categories, in order to concentrate on the growing military electronics business.

After posting an initial loss in the first year after the decision to drop TV and radio production, Sparton rebounded to record profit levels by the end of the decade. In addition to the expansion of the company's military electronics division, a number of acquisitions brought Sparton into new markets. The purchase of Allied Steel and Conveyors of Detroit, Michigan, saw the company's entry into the materials handling industry and the acquisition of the Flori and Houston Pipe Companies spelled a brief foray into steel pipe manufacturing. During the late 1950s and 1960s, Sparton also experimented with a Railway Equipment Division as well as a Controls Systems Division but both operations were discontinued after a few years of operation. Sparton's long history in the automotive industry was consolidated in 1959 with the founding of the Sparton Manufacturing Company, which operated out of a new plant in Flora, Illinois. Sparton Manufacturing primarily produced automotive and marine horns and buzzers. By 1960 the 6,600 horns manufactured each day at the plant provided all of the horns for Studebaker cars, 65 percent of Chrysler's, and 75 percent of American Motors'.

Growth and Diversification in the 1960s and 1970s

During the 1960s and 1970s Sparton's Military Electronics Division became the company's largest income producer, generating over 60 percent of the company's approximately $40 million in sales by the end of the 1960s. The division's primary product continued to be the submarine seeking sonobuoys that had launched the company's entry into the defense industry. Sonobuoy components were manufactured at a number of facilities across the country, including plants in Grand Junction, Colorado, DeLeon Springs, Florida, and Brownstown, Indiana. Sparton's original manufacturing plant in Jackson, Michigan, was converted into a state-of-the-art engineering research and design facility, providing complete support services for all satellite plants. In addition to the company's Military Electronics

Division, Sparton Southwest, Inc., a division based in Albuquerque, New Mexico, was founded in 1961 to produce weapon control equipment and precision instruments for the aerospace industry. Sparton of Canada, which had continued its production of radio and televisions into the mid-1960s, now also converted to military electronics manufacturing.

In 1970, Sparton was faced with a hostile takeover bid from Servotronics, Inc., a maker of airplane parts. Partly in an attempt to raise the number of shares controlled by Sparton management and thereby elude the takeover, Sparton acquired Lake Odessa Machine Products, an auto parts firm privately owned by Sparton president John J. Smith and his family. After a lengthy legal battle, Servotronics and Sparton reached a settlement and the takeover was abandoned. The Lake Odessa acquisition strengthened Sparton's presence in the automotive equipment industry by adding wire parts and assemblies to Sparton's line of horns and electronic components. The Sparton Manufacturing Company, the company's automotive products division, also expanded its facilities and product lines through the 1960s and 1970s. New plants were built in Grayville, Illinois, and Blytheville, Arkansas, and the administrative and engineering offices in Flora, Illinois, were more than doubled.

Sparton made a significant move toward further diversification in 1972 with the purchase of Michigan Oil Company and the simultaneous acquisition of over 100,000 acres of oil leases in the Michigan oil basin from McClure Oil. Michigan Oil was an oil and gas exploration company with operations in Michigan, Louisiana, North Dakota, and offshore Australia. Sparton management felt that investing in oil and gas exploration would allow the company to convert money earned through its manufacturing activities into capital values. In the long run, however, the company's Michigan Oil subsidiary was unable to generate a profit. The consistent annual drain on Sparton's bottom line caused by the costs of maintaining exploration eventually forced the company to seek a buyer for Michigan Oil and, after 18 consecutive years of losses, the subsidiary was ultimately sold in 1990.

Decline of the Defense Industry in the 1980s and 1990s

The 1980s saw further growth in Sparton's automotive divisions as a number of acquisitions and plant expansions increased manufacturing capacity and further diversified product lines. In 1986 Sparton purchased Kent Products, Inc. and White Cloud Products, Inc., automotive stampings manufacturers previously owned by Sparton chairman John J. Smith and his brother Lawson Smith. Sparton automotive divisions were subsequently consolidated to form three operating units; Sparton Engineered Products-Flora Group, Sparton Engineered Products, Inc.-Lake Odessa Group, and Sparton Engineered Products, Inc.-KPI Group. After achieving record sales of $118 million in 1981, Sparton faltered in the mid-1980s due to cost overruns in the company's military electronics division. A number of new design specifications for the Navy's sonobuoy program ended up costing far more than anticipated in Sparton's contract bid and, in spite of $158 million in sales, the company recorded a net loss of over $3 million in 1985. Through the 1980s, Sparton Southwest, renamed Sparton Technology, Inc. in 1983, began to concentrate its engineering

efforts on commercial/industrial electronics. New monitoring and communications systems developed by the division generated sales that would prove significant as the company entered the 1990s.

The 1990s were a time of transition for the 90-year-old firm. The fall of the Soviet Union inevitably led to massive cuts in American defense spending and Sparton was forced to reposition itself away from the defense industry and towards the commercial marketplace. From 1992 to 1994 Sparton's government related sales declined $115 million and the company was unable to compensate for this loss with increases in its other areas of expertise. Sparton Electronics, long the center of Sparton's defense industry with its sonobuoy product line, implemented a transition plan that would convert the division from a defense contractor to a commercial engineering and manufacturing firm. The newly designed division was to offer customers in the electronic industry full service contract manufacturing support including design services and technical resources, as well as manufacturing and marketing services. Although by 1996 this new group of services represented more than one half of total revenues for Spartan Electronics, costs incurred in the development of this business led to operating losses for the division for most of the early 1990s. The Sparton Technology division was to survive the loss of defense-related business by building on its base of proprietary communications and monitoring products. With its already established line of industrial electronics, STI was in a better position to adjust to cuts in defense spending than other Sparton divisions and by the mid-1990s both revenues and profits for the New Mexico-based unit were steadily rising.

While pressures from cuts in defense spending were seriously undermining Sparton's electronic units, the restructuring of the American automobile industry was eating away at profit margins in the company's automotive divisions. Although all three of Sparton's automotive groups (KPI, Flora, and Lake Odessa) had significant increases in sales during the first half of the 1990s, price restrictions on the part of the big three automakers cut profits to increasingly slim margins. Sparton was forced to increase debt in order to finance the expansion needed to accommodate higher sales. In 1996, the company made the critical decision to get out of the automotive supply business rather than invest in the massive growth needed to remain profitable in the increasingly competitive environment. In October of that year, Sparton Engineered Products Inc.-KPI Group, which had previously been merged with the Lake Odessa Group, was sold to Dura Automotive Systems for $80.5 million. Sparton's remaining automotive unit, Sparton Engineered Products-Flora Group, was also put on the market in 1996.

The combined difficulties in Sparton's electronics and automotive units led to three consecutive unprofitable years for Sparton in 1994, 1995 and 1996, with annual net losses of about $5 million. The shedding of the company's automotive divisions also reduced revenues to only $103 million. Ultimately, it was hoped that the additional capital generated by the sale would enable Sparton to invest more heavily in its growing electronic contract manufacturing business and return the nearly century old firm to profitability.

Principal Subsidiaries

Sparton Electronics, Inc.; Sparton of Canada, Ltd.; Sparton Technology, Inc.; Sparton Engineered Products, Inc.-Flora Group.

Further Reading

"Auto Horns by Sparton," *Investment Dealers' Digest,* November 7, 1960, p. 80.

Cahill, William R., "Buoyed by Sonobuoys," *Barron's,* November 25, 1985, pp. 51–52.

"Sparton Corporation Expects to Post Operating Loss for December 31 Fiscal Half," *Wall Street Journal,* December 28, 1970, p. 6.

"Sparton Corporation Puts Off Its Annual Meeting; SEC Probe Is Cited," *Wall Street Journal,* October 7, 1977, p. 23.

"Sparton's President and Brother Buy 12 Percent in Tender of Shares," *Wall Street Journal,* January 21, 1971, p. 10.

—Hilary Gopnik

Sterling Electronics Corp.

4201 Southwest Freeway
P.O. Box 1229
Houston, Texas 77251-1229
U.S.A.
(713) 627-9800
Fax: (713) 629-3939
Web site: http://www.sterlink.com

Public Company
Incorporated: 1956 as Sterling Radio Products, Inc.
Employees: 655
Sales: $322.1 million (1996)
Stock Exchanges: New York
SICs: 5065 Electronic Parts & Equipment, Not Elsewhere
  Classified

Sterling Electronics Corp. distributes electronic components and subsystems. Its principal customers, in the mid-1990s, were manufacturers who purchased the company's parts in order to make such products as personal computers, computer workstations, and computer peripherals; electronic measurement devices; process control systems; medical monitoring equipment; and telecommunications devices. Sterling Electronics was distributing about 80,000 items from about 40 vendors in 1996 and also was custom-assembling some products. It was among the 10 largest publicly owned electronic distributors in the United States.

The Early Years, 1939–66

The company's forerunner, Sterling Radio Products, was founded in 1939 as a radio-parts wholesaler by Henry M. Spolane. Spolane, who had previously sold radio tubes in Chicago, initially sold tubes and other parts out of the trunk of his car to repair shops in the Houston area and elsewhere in East Texas. Sales were slightly less than $100,000 in 1940. The company thrived during World War II, when such parts were in short supply. By 1950 it had about 10 employees. Henry's son

Michael, a World War II veteran, joined the company in 1946 and became president in 1956, when it was incorporated. Under his direction the product line broadened to include components used in computers and telecommunications equipment. The company name was changed to Sterling Electronics, Inc. in 1959.

Sterling Electronics' net sales rose from $2.2 million in fiscal 1956 (the year ending October 31, 1956) to $3.9 million in fiscal 1961. Net income grew from $29,157 to $128,066 during this period. In October 1961 the company went public, offering a minority of the outstanding common stock for $5 a share. By then it was also distributing television replacement parts and accessories; designing, engineering, and assembling sound systems for commercial and home use; and selling high-fidelity sound-reproduction equipment and components. Sterling Electronics had more than 3,000 customers in Texas and Louisiana. Headquarters were in Houston.

In the next four years Sterling Electronics acquired four companies, extended its sales area to New Mexico and Arizona, and took up the manufacture of printed circuit boards. By 1964 the company was a retail as well as a wholesale distributor. Its net sales reached $10.2 million in fiscal 1966 (the year ended April 2, 1966), when its net income was $309,219.

Headlong Expansion, 1967–69

Sterling Electronics, Inc. was reorganized as a holding company, Sterling Electronics Corp., in 1967, and Spolane became its chairman the following year. It acquired at least 20, and perhaps more than 35, companies from 1967 through 1969. These acquisitions not only greatly extended Sterling's distribution business, including taking on machine tools and metals, but also added the manufacture of electronic and electromechanical systems, subsystems, and components as well as electronic data processing and seismic and marine services. Net sales jumped more than sixfold in three years, to $66.6 million in fiscal 1969. To finance its headlong expansion the company offered 375,000 shares of stock at $46.25 a share in 1968 and had assumed long-term debt of $11.8 million by the end of fiscal 1970. Revenues rose to $85.7 million in fiscal 1970.

The Electronics Marketing Group was the biggest segment of the company at the end of fiscal 1969, selling a broad line of parts and components to manufacturers for industrial use, to dealers for resale, and to consumers at retail through company-owned stores. This group—the distribution arm of the company—accounted for 69 percent of total sales and had a nationwide network of 68 distribution points. It was stocking more than 40,000 items. The 32 retail stores stocked such products as radios, stereos, tape recorders, and high-fidelity music systems, as well as accessories, components, and repair parts.

The Components & Systems Technology Group, consisting of 15 manufacturing divisions in many areas of electronics, accounted for 22 percent of sales. Some of the products of this division had vital roles in the manned missions to the moon of the Apollo project. The balance of the company's revenues was derived from three other groups: Seismic & Marine Services, providing geophysical seismic services in connection with the exploration for oil and other hydrocarbons; Computer Services, providing electronic data-processing services; and Metals & Machinery, selling metals (primarily stainless steel) and new and used machine tools to industrial users and distributors. During the year Sterling Electronics spun off the Computer Systems Group, which became publicly owned Sterling Computer Systems, with the parent company initially holding about 69 percent of the shares.

The 1970s: A Decade of Retrenchment

Sterling Electronics' growth came to an ugly end in fiscal 1971, when it lost $7.6 million on sales of $65.5 million. It lost another $3.6 million in fiscal 1972. By then the company had begun a long process of selling off subsidiaries, and it did not top the 1969 revenue peak for 20 years. Its stock, trading as high as $55 a share in 1968 after a three-for-two split, dropped as low as 50 cents a share in 1974. Sterling Electronics lost nearly $3.8 million in fiscal 1975 and, after small profits in 1976 and 1977 and a small loss in 1978, fell $2.5 million in the red in fiscal 1979. Its assets dropped from $29.9 million in 1972 to $13 million in 1983.

By the end of fiscal 1973 the wholesaling of electronic parts and equipment to dealers, once Sterling Electronics' core business, was accounting for only five percent of sales. In that year it sold the major part of this distribution system—the Texas and Louisiana territories—to two of its executives, who founded a company named Kent Electronics Corp. Its West Chester Electric Supply Co. subsidiary, representing about 13 percent of sales, was sold to the unit's president in 1975 for cash and stock. E & M Laboratories, an unprofitable subsidiary, was sold to TRAK Microwave Corp. in 1976.

In fiscal 1976 the Industrial Electronic Marketing Group accounted for 53 percent of Sterling Electronics' sales. Customers were principally manufacturers of capital goods containing electronic circuitry such as electronic measurement devices, computer mainframe and peripheral equipment, process control systems, medical monitoring equipment, and communications devices. Product lines consisted of about 40,000 items. Twenty-four percent of sales (but only eight percent of income) came from the Retail Electronic Manufacturing Group, which sold consumer electronic devices, principally for entertainment purposes, through 24 company-owned stores in Texas and Louisiana.

The Component Manufacturing Group was making and marketing a variety of electronic components and subsystems through such subsidiaries as Airmark Plastics Corp., Phaostron Instruments and Electronic Co., and Sterling Electronics and Instruments Co. This group accounted for 19 percent of sales and 27 percent of income in fiscal 1976. The Computer Systems Group was providing data-processing and data-preparation services in Houston through Sterling Computer Systems. It accounted for only four percent of sales in fiscal 1976 but 14 percent of income.

Sterling Electronics sold its chain of retail stores in 1978. The outside businesses and certain assets of Sterling Computer Systems were sold in 1980, and its remaining assets were liquidated in 1984. Also in 1980, the company sold three West Coast distribution branches and the Magnetic Windings division, manufacturer of electronic transformers, power supplies, and coils, of its Sterling Electronics and Instruments Co. subsidiary. This reduced the Component Manufacturers Group to two subsidiary units: Airmark Plastics Corp., manufacturer of precision edge-lighted plastic panels and knobs used in instrumentation displays, principally for aircraft; and Phaostron Instruments and Electronic Co., producer of an extensive line of analog panel meters, avionic mechanisms, and prime flight instruments.

Struggling Through the 1980s

As a result of these divestments and the severe economic recession of the early 1980s, Sterling Electronics' revenues fell to a 16-year low of $40.2 million in fiscal 1983. It lost money in both the 1982 and 1983 fiscal years. Manufacturing had long been more profitable to the company than distributing and in fiscal 1983 accounted for 64 percent of operating income, although only 16 percent of sales. That year the company added a new subsidiary to sell, install, and service microwave communications, electronic security, fire alarms, and other components to industrial and institutional users in the Houston area. This business was disposed of in 1988.

After two improved years Sterling Electronics lost money again in fiscal 1986, when its sales dipped from $57.6 million to $49.4 million. Prosperity was just around the corner, however, for after netting only $54,686 the following year, the company registered a $1.9-million profit in fiscal 1988—the first time since 1980 it had topped the million-dollar mark. That year, when Sterling Electronics was distributing from only 13 locations, it began an expansion program to place its wholesaling operations in additional geographic markets. It purchased Industrial Components, Inc., a Minneapolis-based electronics distributor, for $1.7 million, and Image Electronics International, Inc. for $4.6 million. But Airmark's panels failed to pass military tests, so this company was downgraded from a subsidiary to a division of Phaostron.

After a strong fiscal 1989, in which it had net income of $2.8 million on record revenues of $90.7 million, Sterling Electronics saw sales slump because of a glut in computer memory chips. The company, a major distributor of Japanese-made memory circuits, was facing competition from the popular, Korean-made one-megabit Dynamic Random Access Memory (DRAM) chip, found in everything from personal computers and copiers to electronic printers and certain consumer electronics. Sterling Electronics made only $46,000 in fiscal 1990 on sales of $88 million, and its stock plunged to $1.50 a share from as high as $7.50 in 1988, when it was being touted as a takeover target.

Unprecedented Prosperity in the 1990s

During the next two years Sterling Electronics sold unprofitable subsidiaries and focused on its core business—wholesale electronic-parts distribution. A middle-tier distributor, it was specializing in selling to small- to medium-sized electronics firms, especially computer manufacturers. Sales grew nearly 40 percent between fiscal 1990 and 1992, although profits remained modest.

In fiscal 1993 Sterling Electronics raised its revenues to $150.2 million, a 26-percent gain from the previous year, and its net income up 83 percent to $2.2 million. Spread around the country, its 23 warehouses used computerized ordering systems and offered just-in-time delivery. Sales were evenly split among connectors, passive and electromechanical devices, and both memory and nonmemory semiconductors. A popular item was the flat-panel displays used on digital readouts of gasoline pumps. "We don't want to have all our eggs in any one basket, like semiconductors," a company executive told a *Houston Post* reporter. Sterling Electronics' long-term debt had passed $21 million in 1992, but the soaring price of its shares enabled it to redeem $11.5-million worth of its convertible debentures in October 1993.

Ronald Spolane, one of Michael Spolane's twin sons, succeeded his father as chairman and chief executive officer of Sterling Electronics in 1993. Michael Spolane died in January 1994. Company revenues climbed 33 percent to $200.6 million in fiscal 1994 and net income 159 percent, to $5.7 million. Spolane attributed his company's surge to price cuts for personal computers and successful acquisitions. Prominent among these was Passive Technology Sales, Inc., a $7-million-a-year California distributor purchased in 1990 for stock and $900,000 in cash. While expanding its distribution network, Sterling Electronics decided to get out of manufacturing, selling Phaostron Instruments in 1995 to the subsidiary's president.

Fiscal 1995 was another recordbreaking year for Sterling Electronics, with revenues reaching $242.3 million and net income $7.8 million. In September 1995 Bell Industries, the seventh-largest publicly owned electronics distributor, made a $143-million bid for Sterling Electronics, the 10th-largest. Ster-

ling, distributing Japanese semiconductors, was outperforming Bell, which was distributing U.S.-made semiconductors. Sterling Electronics, which had taken several steps to ward off a takeover attempt, rejected the unsolicited offer.

Sterling Electronics had more good news for its shareholders in fiscal 1996. Revenues soared by one third, to $322.1 million, and net income also increased one third, to $10.4 million. The company's long-term debt, however, rose to $33.7 billion from $13 billion at the end of the previous fiscal year.

In September 1996 Sterling Electronics announced it would purchase Marsh Electronics Inc., a Wisconsin distributor of electronic parts to industrial customers. Earlier, during 1995, the company had acquired the Samad division of DGW Electronics Corp. Samad was a Toronto-based electronic-components distributor with branch locations throughout Canada.

By mid-1996 Sterling Electronics' distribution network had increased to 33 locations, covering more than 75 percent of the geographic markets in the United States for electronic components. Five of these locations were in Canada. All were connected by a data-communications network to a computerized, on-line, real-time, order-entry, inventory-management system. The company was selling about 80,000 items, including connectors, integrated circuits, microprocessors, power supplies, resistors, capacitors, relays, switches, and liquid-crystal displays. Semiconductors accounted for 47 percent of sales in 1995; passive and electromechanical products for 31 percent; connector products for 21 percent; and manufacturing-group products for one percent. They were being purchased from about 40 vendors, including Toshiba, Hitachi, and Sharp. Sterling Electronics' 14,000 customers were mostly small manufacturers of telephone equipment and personal computers. It was leasing properties in Houston, Dallas, Minneapolis, Phoenix, San Jose, California, and Woburn, Massachusetts.

Principal Subsidiaries

Sterling Electronics (Canada) Corp.; Sterling Partners, Inc.

Further Reading

Antosh, Nelson, "Sterling Saying No Deal—For Now," *Houston Chronicle,* September 1, 1995, pp. C1, C8.

Bris, Alfred, "Sterling Electronics, Inc. (SEC)," *Wall Street Transcript,* July 8, 1968, pp. 13799–800.

Fisher, Daniel, "Sterling Focusing on What It Knows," *Houston Post,* April 25, 1993, p. T-9.

Greer, Jim, "Sterling's Stock Really Humming," *Houston Post,* May 1, 1994, p. T-12.

Labate, John, "Sterling Electronics," *Fortune,* November 28, 1994, p. 189.

Levine, Bernard, "Sterling Finally Rejects Bell Takeover," *Electronic News,* September 25, 1995, p. 1.

Seay, Gregory, "Chip Glut Takes Byte," *Houston Post,* November 19, 1989, p. D1.

Silverman, Dwight, "Bell Industries' Bid for Sterling Ended," *Houston Chronicle,* September 20, 1995, p. C2.

"Spotlight on Sterling Electronics," *Journal of Commerce,* September 7, 1973, pp. 3, 5.

—Robert Halasz

The Stroh Brewery Company

100 River Place
Detroit, Michigan 48207-4291
U.S.A.
(313) 446-2000
Fax: (313) 446-2206

Private Company
Incorporated: 1909
Employees: 4,000
Sales: $1 billion (1995 est.)
SICs: 2082 Malt Beverages

The Stroh family began brewing beer in a family-owned inn during the 18th century in Germany. In 1848, during the German Revolution, Bernhard Stroh, who had learned the brewing trade from his father, emigrated to the United States. In 1850 he founded a brewery which has been owned and operated by the family for more than 145 years. While the company has expanded considerably in recent decades, it is still directed by a Stroh, and all of its stock shares are in the hands of Stroh family members.

Founded as Lion's Head Brewery in 1850

Bernhard Stroh established his brewery in Detroit in 1850 when he was 28 and immediately started producing Bohemian-style beer, which had been developed at the municipal brewery of Pilsen, Bohemia, in 1840. In 1865 he purchased additional land and expanded his business. He adopted the Lion's Crest from the Kyrburg Castle in Germany and named his operation the Lion's Head Brewery. The company still uses the crest in its advertising.

Bernhard Stroh Jr. took charge of the brewery on the death of his father, the founder. He changed the brewery's name to the B. Stroh Brewing Company. With the introduction of pasteurization and refrigerated rail cars, Stroh was able to ship some of his beer to Florida and Massachusetts. In 1893 Stroh Bohemian Beer won a blue ribbon at the Columbian Exposition. The company's name was changed to The Stroh Brewery Company in 1902. In 1908 Bernhard Stroh's brother Julius took over the

brewery. After a tour of famous European breweries, he introduced the European fire-brewing method in the Stroh brewery. Today Stroh's is the only fire-brewed beer on the American market. Common in Europe before World War I, the fire-brewing process uses a direct flame rather than steam to heat beer-filled copper kettles. The company claims that the resulting higher temperatures bring out more of the beer's flavor.

During Prohibition Julius Stroh operated the business under the name The Stroh Products Company, producing near beer (beer with its alcohol extracted), birch beer, soft drinks, malt products, ice cream, and ice. Though production of most of these items ceased when Prohibition ended in 1933, a special unit of the brewery still makes Stroh Ice Cream. The product is sold in retail groceries and independent ice-cream parlors in Michigan.

Upon Julius Stroh's death in 1939, his son Gari assumed the presidency. Gari's brother John succeeded him in 1950 and became Stroh's chairman in 1967. Gari's son Peter, who had joined the company following his graduation from Princeton in 1951, became president in 1968. He is now chairman of the board.

Expanded Market Area Significantly in the 1960s and 1970s

In 1964 the company made its first move toward expansion from its traditional position as a small but successful producer of one brand of beer and ice cream when it bought the Goebel Brewing Company across the street, adding about 200,000 barrels of volume. At the same time, Peter Stroh directed the company into a period of large-scale changes motivated principally by two causes: the 1958 Michigan beer strike, and the emergence of the Anheuser-Busch and Miller brewing companies as corporate leaders in the beer industry.

In 1956 Stroh sold 2.7 million barrels of beer. A long statewide beer strike two years later enabled out-of-state beers to capture larger shares of the Michigan market, and while Stroh remained the largest brewer in the state in 1968, it still had not fully recovered the ground lost in the strike. Sales were low in Michigan that year and far behind the sales of 12 years earlier. Recognizing that half the company's production was sold outside Michigan, Peter Stroh ended a 40-year relationship with

---

Company Perspectives:

As a company, The Stroh Brewery Company faces formidable competition in a world and industry that are ever-changing, yet one fact is for certain. Stroh is a dedicated family brewing company who's quest is to continue the fine art of quality craft brewing.

Stroh's advertising agency to search for a large national agency that would help develop the company's growing business on a national scale.

By 1971 the Stroh Brewery Company had moved from 15th to 13th place in the national beer market. In 1972 it entered the top ten for the first time and had a market area of nine states. A year later it was the eighth-largest brewery in the United States, selling four million barrels of beer per year in 17 states.

At the same time Miller and Anheuser-Busch entered into intense competition; Anheuser wanted to maintain its position as America's dominant brewer, while Miller attempted to rise from its seventh-place rank to overtake Anheuser's position. The large advertising budgets, wide distribution areas, and efficient production methods used by the two breweries through the 1970s proved impossible for many regional breweries to match. Peter Stroh's willingness to depart from years of tradition enabled Stroh to survive, though his family's pride in the brewery's heritage made many of his revolutionary changes difficult to implement. It was not surprising that Peter's decisions would have seemed radical to many in a company that had produced only one brand for nearly 130 years. Stroh himself had previously seen his role as "more a braumeister than a promoter," but the soft-spoken man now remarked that "as the industry changed I've had to become more marketing oriented. Deep in my heart I know it's either grow or go."

Peter Stroh broke the company's old-world management tradition by recruiting outside experts from such companies as Pepsico and Procter & Gamble to manage the brewery's affairs. He also expanded the product line by introducing Stroh's second brand, Stroh Light, in 1978 (changed to Stroh's Light in 1989). Adamant in the conviction that his brewery should not sacrifice its product's taste, however, Stroh insisted that the light version be held to 115 calories rather than being cut to the 96 calories of most other light beers. At 115, Stroh Light was 25 percent lower in calories than Stroh's regular beer.

The 1973 increase of market area to 17 states had caused the brewery nearly to outgrow its production capacity by 1978, when it produced 6.4 million barrels of beer. The Detroit facility was 66 years old and had a capacity of seven million barrels annually. As it became difficult to make efficient shipments to new markets in the East, the company recognized that it required a new brewery.

Acquired Schaefer and Schlitz in the Early 1980s

A solution presented itself in the form of New York's F&M Schaefer Brewing Corporation, one of the regional breweries that had been a victim of Miller's growing market share. Stroh, planning to purchase all of Schaefer's stock to gain control of the brewery, paid an initial $800,000 for 8.5 percent of the total shares. After the takeover was complete in 1981, the combined breweries ranked seventh in beer sales. Under the terms of the deal, Stroh gained access to Schaefer's Allentown, Pennsylvania, brewery. With its capacity of a million gallons, the Allentown brewery was one of the industry's most efficient U.S. operations. In addition, Stroh was able to take advantage of Schaefer's distributors in the northeastern part of the country. The acquisition also brought Stroh three new brands: Schaefer and Piels beers, and Schaefer's Cream Ale. The company now had a volume of over 40 million barrels and 400 distributors in 28 states, Washington, D.C., Puerto Rico, and other Caribbean islands. The Stroh Brewery Company began to take the form of a smaller version of the industry leaders.

Early in 1982 Peter Stroh made a bid on 67 percent of the Schlitz Brewing Company, the first step in acquiring the third-largest brewery in the United States. By April of that year, Stroh had purchased the entire company for $17 a share. Schlitz became a wholly owned subsidiary of the Stroh Brewing Company, making Stroh the third-largest brewery in the United States. The acquisition was by no means simple. Schlitz resisted the takeover by taking Stroh to court. Schlitz finally accepted the takeover when Stroh raised its offer from an initial $16 per share to $17, and the U.S. Justice Department approved the acquisition once Stroh agreed to sell either Schlitz's Memphis or Winston-Salem breweries.

Along with the expansion of Stroh's brewery came a departure from the company's traditional marketing approach. Stroh had always been marketed as a popularly priced "blue-collar" beer, with a six-pack selling at 25¢ less than national premium brands. Commercials noted the fire-brewed flavor of the beer. A large part of Stroh's national market, however, began to find it difficult to reconcile the brew's low price with its advertised quality. The new premium beers recently introduced by Miller and Anheuser became more popular with the working class that had previously purchased Stroh beer. In order to revive blue-collar sales, Stroh reduced the price of Schlitz to below the premium level.

Stroh divested itself of the Schlitz-run Geyser Peak Winery in order to concentrate on beer products. Despite the success of its light beer, Stroh initially moved with typical caution in introducing new products. Because of its two major acquisitions the company now marketed regular and light versions of Schlitz, Stroh, and Old Milwaukee, as well as Goebel, Piels, and Schlitz Malt Liquor. Even so, it was not until four years after the introduction of Stroh Light that the company introduced another new product of its own. In 1982, Stroh entered the premium market with the introduction of its super-premium brand, Signature, after a two-year R&D process involving 100 recipe tests.

The move from a regional market into the national arena was especially challenging for Stroh's advertising and promotional efforts. As mentioned above, the company did away with the emphasis on its fire-brewing process when consumers seemed unable to reconcile Stroh's reputed high quality with its relatively low price. Ad campaigns became more upbeat, first using an "Alex the Dog" commercial where Alex would fetch, buy, or pour beer for his owner. The company then turned to the "From One Beer Lover to Another" campaign that had science fiction and phantasmagorical themes. The brewery won two awards for its "Beer Lover" ads. In 1985 Stroh moved to the good times-good friends-good beer theme popular in the beer industry. Its slogan was "Stroh's Is Spoken Here." The company felt the theme was more relevant to the all-American beer drinker and showed more confidence in the beer, rather than being merely entertaining.

In the 1980s the company also turned to corporate sponsorship to gain needed national publicity. In 1982 Stroh was a sponsor of the World's Fair in Knoxville, Tennessee, an event that strengthened Stroh's new national standing considerably. For many years Stroh had received little television exposure because of an agreement between the major networks and Anheuser and Miller which allowed the two top brewers exclusive advertising rights. Stroh fought the agreement and in 1983 was allotted advertising time on ABC's Monday Night Baseball, on two NBC boxing events, and on other popular U.S. television sports shows. Confronted with nearly prohibitive network costs, the company began "The Stroh Circle of Sports" on cable television and independent stations. The program featured live events with reporting and analysis. For increased publicity opportunities, Stroh also turned to such sports as hockey—which had been overlooked by Anheuser and Miller—and sponsored broadcasts of National Hockey League games on the USA cable network. The company also sponsored the Formula One stock car race with Valvoline Motor Oil, an event considered an important boost for Stroh's international name recognition. "High Rollers," a contest for amateur bowlers, was also developed and sponsored by the company. Stroh's most popular nonsports promotion during this period was the "Schlitz Rocks America" concert series.

Declining Fortunes in the Late 1980s

In 1985, Stroh claimed 12 percent of the U.S. beer market and maintained its third place position behind Anheuser-Busch and Miller. By 1990, Stroh's market share would be cut nearly in half and it would fall into fourth place; it would in fact barely escape the 1980s as an independent company.

The roots of these difficulties lay in the heavy debt load—$500 million—the brewer took on to finance its acquisition of Schlitz. The debt weakened the company's financial position just as the U.S. beer market was reaching a plateau. With sales stagnating industrywide, competition increased. Stroh spent heavily in an attempt to transform the Stroh brand into a premium national brand, but the deeper pockets of Anheuser-Busch and Miller prevailed and the effort failed. Stroh had already lost $100 million when it waited too long to close its aging Detroit brewery—finally shuttered in 1985. Later in the decade Stroh was hurt by rising raw material costs, forcing the company to cut its advertising and promotion. This angered wholesalers who switched to rival brands.

In 1989 the beleaguered brewer appeared to be on the verge of selling out to rival Adolph Coors, but the two companies failed to reach an agreement. Later that same year, Stroh sought to bolster its position by purchasing the then number five U.S. brewer, G. Heileman Brewing Company, but again no agreement could be reached. Meanwhile, Stroh's attempts in the mid- and late 1980s to diversify into other beverages—such as White Mountain Cooler, a fruit-flavored drink with 5 percent alcohol, and Sundance sparkling-water fruit drinks—met with little success.

Turnaround in the Early 1990s

In 1990 Coors moved past Stroh into third place among U.S. brewers. After the Coors and Heileman deals failed to materialize, Stroh had to sell assets to reduce its debt load simply to survive. In 1989 Sundance was sold to a partnership, of which Stroh held a partial interest. Three years later, Stroh sold this partial interest as well. Stroh also gradually jettisoned its packaging business, selling its last packaging plant in 1993. It was in 1991, however, that Stroh was able to retire its Schlitz debt when it sold its 31.6 percent interest in the Spanish brewer Cruzcampo to Guinness for $335 million. That same year, William L. Henry was appointed president and COO, after having set up the company's first financial planning department and then serving as vice-president of marketing planning.

Henry and Stroh chairman and CEO Peter Stroh then implemented a three-pronged strategy to revitalize the company—developing new products, brewing beer under contract for other brewers, and expanding overseas. The new product area was critical because the explosion in beer brand and types of beer in the 1990s undermined the market share for all established brands. Stroh's strategy when seeking to enter the market for a new type of beer was to extend one or more of its existing brands. In the increasingly popular non-alcoholic beer segment, for example, Old Milwaukee NA was introduced in 1991, while Stroh's Non Alcoholic debuted in 1993. Old Milwaukee NA quickly became one of the top three selling non-alcoholic brews. In the ice beer category, Stroh launched Old Milwaukee Ice, Schlitz Ice, Schlitz Ice Light, Bull Ice, and Schaefer Ice, all in 1994. Another hot category in the early and mid-1990s was the packaged draft beer; Stroh made its presence felt in this category as well with Stroh's Draft Light, Old Milwaukee Genuine Draft, and Schlitz Genuine Draft.

Another important new product area was specialty beer, the hottest beer category of the 1990s and led by the hundreds of microbreweries that arose to craft them, not by the industry leaders. Stroh and the other leaders, however, were not shut out of this category; in some cases they purchased all or part of microbreweries, in others they formed units to produce specialty beers. Stroh did both. It purchased the Augsburger brand in 1989 and over the next several years developed and introduced both specialty and seasonal brews under the Augsburger name. The company also purchased Ontario's Sleeman Brewing & Malting and a second, undisclosed, small brewer. In 1994 Stroh launched Red River Valley Select Red Lager, a regional premium specialty beer produced by a division of the company's St. Paul, Minnesota, brewery called Northern Plains Brewing Company. Two years later, Red River Honey Brown Ale was introduced.

The international market provided growth opportunities for Stroh that were very limited in the stagnant, hypercompetitive U.S. market. In 1986 Stroh International, Inc. was created to begin to tap into these markets. Canada, India, Japan, Mexico, and Russia were the main targets of Stroh's overseas push.

From 1992 through 1995, Stroh's international sales grew each year at rates exceeding 50 percent. In 1994, the company entered into a licensing agreement with Rajastan Breweries, Ltd. (located outside Delhi) to produce, distribute, and market Stroh's and Stroh's Super Strong beers in India. The following year, an agreement was reached with Sapporo Breweries Ltd. of Tokyo whereby Sapporo began distributing Stroh's beer nationwide in Japan. By 1995, exports comprised more than 10 percent of overall Stroh sales.

The explosion in microbreweries provided Stroh (and the top three U.S. brewers) with another growth opportunity, contract brewing, whereby a microbrewery used one of Stroh's breweries to produce their beer using their own brewmaster and their own recipes. In return, Stroh received a percentage of the resulting revenue. Contract brewing thus provided another revenue source for Stroh as well as keeping its breweries running at higher utilization rates. By 1995, about 30 percent of Stroh's total output was for contract production for such stellar micro brands as Samuel Adams for the Boston Brewing Company and Pete's Wicked Ale for Pete's Brewing Company, as well as several brands for Portland Brewing Company.

In early 1995 Henry assumed Peter Stroh's CEO position to become the first non-Stroh family member to hold that position for the company. The following year Stroh finally landed a long-sought-after target when it acquired Heileman for about $290 million. Over the preceding decade, Heileman had been bought by the Bond Corp. of Australia for $1.3 billion (in 1987), then purchased out of bankruptcy court by the Dallas buyout firm Hicks Muse Tate & Furst Co. for $390 million (in 1993). The Heileman purchase brought more than 30 brands to the Stroh family, many of which Heileman had itself acquired since its founding in LaCrosse, Wisconsin, in 1858. Among the more important brands were Colt 45, which when combined with Schlitz Malt Liquor, gave Stroh more than half of the malt liquor market, and Henry Weinhard's, a regional specialty brand whose market Stroh hoped to expand. Other Heileman brands included Special Export, Old Style, Rainier, Schmidt's, Lone Star, Champale, and Mickey's.

Heileman also brought Stroh greater capacity for its contract brewing through its five breweries (one of these—the San Antonio brewery—was closed following the acquisition because of its proximity to Stroh's Longview, Texas, facility). Thanks to Heileman's West Coast breweries—in Portland and Seattle—Stroh had a much better geographic spread of facilities. The company viewed this as aiding not only U.S. distribu-tion but also exports, especially in the Far East; for example, beer previously made in Texas for the Japanese market could now be made in Seattle with resulting transportation savings and fresher product.

Stroh neared the turn of the century in a much stronger position than it had entered the 1990s. The company held a 9.6 percent share of the U.S. beer market following the Heileman acquisition, still in fourth place but closing in on Coors. The possibility of a further acquisition or two was quite real, with Pabst—the new fifth place brewer—the most likely target (in 1996 Pabst was Stroh's largest contract customer, after Stroh had assumed Heileman's contract with Pabst). In mid-1995, the European market became much more attractive to Stroh and other U.S. brewers when the 24 percent European tariff on imported beer was eliminated in an agreement between the United States and the European Community. In addition to increasing exports, Stroh was also seeking to add to its nonbeer revenues, as evidenced by the 1996 agreement with the Joseph Cerniglia Winery of Vermont to establish Green Mountain Cidery, which would produce and distribute draft cider products. All of these developments added up to a bright future for The Stroh Brewery Company.

Principal Subsidiaries

Captiva Beverage Co.; Northern Plains Brewing Co.; Stroh International, Inc.; Stroh Properties Inc.

Further Reading

Baron, Stanley Wade, *Brewed in America: A History of Beer and Ale in the U.S.*, New York: Arno Press, 1972.

Child, Charles, "New Brews on Tap as Stroh Tries to Cure Sales Hangover," *Crain's Detroit Business*, March 29, 1993, pp. 3, 28.

Kelley, Kristine Portnoy, "Fuel for the Fire," *Beverage Industry*, February 1995, p. 26.

Norman, James R., "Back from the Brink," *Forbes*, June 22, 1992, p. 74.

Roush, Matt, "Will Buyout Brew Jobs?: Stroh-Heileman Link Looks Good," *Crain's Detroit Business*, March 4, 1996, pp. 3, 30.

Sfiligoj, Eric, "Back from the Brink and Looking Ahead," *Beverage World*, May 1994, p. 22.

Stopa, Marsha, "New Name on the Door: Stroh CEO Henry Faces Heady Challenges," *Crain's Detroit Business*, December 12, 1994, pp. 3, 15.

"Stroh's Acquisition of Heileman: A Mid-Tier Player Gains Critical Mass," *Impact*, September 15/October 1, 1996, pp. 1–6.

—updated by David E. Salamie

SUPERVALU

Supervalu Inc.

11840 Valley View Road
Eden Prairie, Minnesota 55344
U.S.A.
(612) 828-4000
Fax: (612) 828-8998

Public Company
Incorporated: 1926 as Winston & Newell Company
Employees: 43,000
Sales: $16.49 billion (1996)
Stock Exchanges: New York
SICs: 5141 Groceries, General Line; 5399 Miscellaneous
    General Merchandise Stores; 5411 Grocery Stores;
    5912 Drug Stores & Proprietary Stores

Supervalu Inc. was born of a merger, and a pattern of mergers, acquisitions, and divestitures has marked its rise to eminence in the food wholesale and distribution industry. Minnesota-based Supervalu—which was called Super Valu Stores, Inc. from 1954 to 1992—is the second-largest wholesaler and distributor in the United States, with retail support and distribution centers nationwide which supply products to more than 4,100 stores in 48 states. The company operates nearly 300 franchises and more than 500 retail stores in 29 states primarily under the names of Cub Foods, Shop 'n Save, bigg's, Save-A-Lot, Laneco, Scott's Foods, and Hornbachers—making Supervalu the 14th largest U.S. food retailer—and provides highly developed retail support for the independent grocery store operators who belong to its network of subsidiaries, franchises, and customers. Supervalu also holds a 6 percent stake in Cabot Noble Inc., a holding company for the Phar-Mor chain of deep-discount drug stores and the ShopKo discount department chain.

Roots in Series of Minneapolis Wholesalers of the Late 1800s and Early 1900s

Supervalu's origins lie in the 1871 merger of the Minneapolis wholesale grocery firms B.S. Bull and Company and Newell and Harrison Company. The new Newell and Harrison existed for only three years; in 1874 George R. Newell bought out his partners and renamed the company George R. Newell Company.

Meanwhile, one of Newell's former partners, Hugh G. Harrison, formed a wholesaling venture called H. G. Harrison Company in 1879. After a series of reorganizations (including Harrison's sale of his interest), this company became Winston, Harper, Fisher Company in 1903, headed by F. G. Winston, a Minneapolis railroad contractor; J. L. Harper, a merchandiser; and E. J. Fisher, a financier. In 1916, Harrison's grandson, Perry Harrison, joined Winston, Harper, Fisher as vice-president and co-owner.

In 1926, George R. Newell Company and Winston, Harper, Fisher Company merged to form Winston & Newell Company, with Perry Harrison and L. B. Newell, Winston's son-in-law, as principle shareholders. Winston & Newell was incorporated in 1926 in response to the threat that independent retailers faced from the emerging grocery store chains that began developing in the 1920s. Winston & Newell hoped to improve services to these independent retailers so they could withstand the competitive impact of the chain stores. At the time of its creation, Winston & Newell was serving some 5,000 small grocery stores and had sales of $6 million—making it the largest grocery wholesaler in the Midwest.

With Minnesotan Thomas G. Harrison at its helm, Winston & Newell became one of the first wholesale distributors in the nation to join the new Independent Grocers Alliance (IGA). Harrison, the son of Perry Harrison, had joined Winston, Harper, Fisher Company in 1919 as an assistant sales manager. He successively became assistant treasurer and executive vice-president, directing the operations of Winston & Newell and later Super Valu in a variety of executive positions from 1926 until his retirement as CEO in 1958.

Harrison, in guiding the company through the Great Depression, was primarily responsible for introducing many practices that changed the way in which grocery stores conducted business. Cash-and-carry and self-service shopping, almost unheard of at the time, were two of his innovations at Winston & Newell. He broke with tradition again when he stopped using a pricing structure with an arbitrary markup and began charging instead

---

Company Perspectives:

The philosophy of SUPERVALU companies will always be a "total commitment to serving customers more effectively than anyone else could serve them." We believe the pursuit of this meaningful goal is the continuing and overriding responsibility from which every corporate activity must evolve. We value today's success as merely the beginning of a constantly expanding level of achievement.

We believe that customers are most knowledgeable, skilled, and capable buyers who will always seek out and do business with that supplier which most effectively serves their wants and needs.

Therefore, by serving our customers more effectively than anyone else could serve them, and by efficiently managing our business with highly skilled and dedicated people, we are confident that we shall continue to increase SUPERVALU's sales and share of market. We believe that this philosophy and practice will result in continuing profitable growth for SUPERVALU and provide security and opportunity for our many thousands of loyal employees.

---

the manufacturer's price plus a percentage fee that declined with volume. This practice gave the company impressive cumulative profits. During the 20-year period from 1942 to 1962, *Fortune* reported that the company's sales volume increased from about $10 million to more than $300 million.

Broke with IGA and Formed Own Associations in Early 1940s

It was during World War II that Winston & Newell began the march to becoming Supervalu and attaining its position as the world's largest food wholesaler and distributor, a position it held until the late 1980s. Although no acquisitions were made during the 1940s, in 1942 the company ended its affiliation with IGA and formed its own association, known in the industry as a "voluntary." Winston & Newell offered independent retailers services such as food processing and packaging, preparation of advertising for individual store use in local newspaper advertising, and store planning assistance, in addition to supplying most of the merchandise sold. This voluntary association introduced the Super Valu name and operated independently from the wholesale business. Super Valu and another voluntary association called U-Save (which was also formed under the auspices of Winston & Newell) were familiar to grocers in Iowa, Minnesota, and North Dakota. By 1942 the company had wholesale sales of $10 million and some 400 stores belonged to its wholesale-retail team.

In 1954 Winston & Newell Company changed its name to Super Valu Stores Inc. in order to clarify the connection between itself and the voluntary association. During the 1950s Super Valu began to grow by acquiring other voluntary associations. In 1955 it purchased Joannes Brothers of Green Bay, Wisconsin, a firm which had begun serving stores in northern Michigan and northeastern Wisconsin in the 1870s. Joannes Brothers became Super Valu's Green Bay Division. In 1958

Russell W. Byerly became president of Super Valu. Byerly, a North Dakota native who joined Winston & Newell in 1932 as a bookkeeper, served as president until 1964 and later was chairman of the board and chief executive officer.

Series of Acquisitions in the 1960s

Acquisition followed acquisition during the 1960s as Super Valu expanded throughout the Midwest. In 1961 Super Valu moved into the Ohio Valley with the purchase of the Eavey Company, one of the nation's oldest food wholesale distributors. In 1963 the company acquired the J.M. Jones Company of Champaign-Urbana, Illinois, and the Food Marketing Corporation of Fort Wayne, Indiana. Each of these companies could trace its beginnings to the early days of the grocery business. Jones began as a general store and developed into a large wholesale business; Food Marketing dated back to the early 1800s, as Bursley & Company and the Bluffton Grocery Company. The Food Marketing acquisition also brought Super Valu into the institutional market. After acquisition, these two companies were operated as autonomous divisions in a company that historically gave its divisions and stores as much free rein as possible.

In 1964 Super Valu expanded its area of operation outside the Midwest by acquiring Chastain-Roberts Company, which had begun in 1933 as a wholesale flour and feed company, and the McDonald Glass Grocery Company, Inc. of Anniston, Alabama. These acquisitions formed the basis for Super Valu's Anniston Division.

In 1965 Super Valu acquired the Lewis Grocer Company of Indianola, Mississippi. The Lewis Grocer Company was founded by Morris Lewis Sr. in 1895 and eventually became a multimillion dollar wholesale grocer, branching out later into the retail grocery business.

The 1960s were a growth period for Super Valu in ways other than acquisition. The company expanded its retail support services to include accounting, efficiency studies, budget counseling, and store format and design advice. In 1962 Super Valu established Planmark, a department that offered engineering, architectural, and design services to independent retailers, subsidiaries, and corporate stores. Planmark became a division in 1975; with Studio 70, its commercial design arm, Planmark used computer-assisted design to analyze and develop plans for construction, expansion, or remodeling. This innovation, implemented in the recessionary years of the late 1970s, allowed Super Valu retailers to take a project from planning to opening faster than their competition. Super Valu also began providing financial assistance for retailers building new stores, bankrolling some 500 stores in a three-year period in the 1960s. Super Valu also signed leases on its retailers' behalf, allowing them to locate in prime space in shopping centers and other locations.

In 1968 Preferred Products, Inc. (PPI) was incorporated as a subsidiary of Super Valu to develop its private label program. A food packaging and processing division, it was started in the 1920s as a department of Winston & Newell.

Super Valu also formed an insurance agency—Risk Planners, Inc.—in 1969. This wholly owned subsidiary began by providing insurance on retail property for the company and its retail affiliates. Tailored specifically to the needs of retailers, its products have expanded to include all types of insurance for Super Valu and its stores and franchisees, as well as independent retailers' employees and families.

Diversified Operations in the 1970s

Diversification was the moving force at Super Valu in the 1970s, in part because the U.S. government in the late 1960s made it clear that it was not going to allow further consolidation of the food industry. Beginning with the 1971 acquisition of ShopKo, a general merchandise discount chain, Super Valu began what proved to be a highly profitable program of nonfood marketing operations. ShopKo, founded by James Ruben in Chicago in 1961, opened its first store in Green Bay, Wisconsin, in 1962. In 1971 Super Valu acquired Daytex, Inc., a textile goods company, but the venture proved unsuccessful and its assets were liquidated in 1976. Meanwhile, Super Valu sales surpassed $1 billion for the first time in 1972.

When Jack J. Crocker became chairman and CEO of Super Valu in 1973, he initiated another diversification venture, County Seat. A success story in its own right, County Seat opened its first store in 1973 selling casual apparel, including the complete Levi's jeans line. By 1977 there were 183 County Seat stores, and the chain's earnings were $8 million in that fiscal year. When it was sold for $71 million to Carson Pirie Scott and Company of Chicago in 1983, there were 269 stores in 33 states.

Crocker, a CPA who came to Super Valu from the presidency of the Oregon-based grocery and pharmacy chain Fred Meyer, Inc., also directed the company's continuing acquisition and expansion program. Very much a part of the trend toward consolidation in the food wholesale industry, Super Valu continued to purchase smaller food wholesalers, acquiring Pennsylvania-based Charley Brothers Company in 1977. Charley Brothers, which began as a retail grocery store in 1902 and moved into wholesaling in 1918, served Shop 'n Save stores and other independent retailers in Pennsylvania.

The advent of universal price codes and scanning equipment in the grocery business led to the introduction, in the mid-1970s, of Testmark, an independent research center providing store measurement data. This data had been available from Super Valu stores since 1965 and, during the period before Testmark was established, had been handled by Super Valu merchandising research, an internal department for clients who preferred not to use commercial research companies. In direct competition with these commercial research companies, Testmark, with Super Valu's backing, offered its customers the advantage of cooperation within the Super Valu network and with major chains and independents nationwide. Testmark's autonomy was enhanced by its Hopkins, Minnesota, location, separate from Super Valu's corporate headquarters.

Crocker's tenure at Super Valu was characterized by his success in running what was one of the better-capitalized and stronger wholesalers in the country and by the casual no-frills operation he ran. Company headquarters were in a warehouse, not a plush office. Crocker personally founded a professional

soccer team, the Minnesota Kicks, in 1976. They, too, were a Crocker success story, becoming popular in their home territory.

Crocker's successes were apparent on the bottom line, as well. By fiscal 1978 earnings per share had increased approximately 50 percent since Crocker's first year with Super Valu, but, Crocker explained to *Financial World* in 1977, "I don't think about profits very much. If you're doing things right, profits always follow." By the end of the 1970s Super Valu's sales were $2.9 billion.

Moved into Retail Grocering with Acquisition of Cub Foods in 1980

Super Valu ushered in the 1980s with the acquisition of Cub Foods, a discount grocery store operation. Warehouse stores, with bare bones facilities and prices, were a phenomenon of the 1970s. Cub Foods was founded by the Hooley family, grocers since 1876 in Stillwater, Minnesota. The Hooleys opened their first warehouse store with the Cub name in a Minneapolis suburb in 1968. When Super Valu purchased the chain in 1980, there were five Cub stores and a Hooley supermarket in Stillwater. Culver M. Davis was appointed president and chief executive officer of Cub Foods in 1985. Davis had joined the Hooley organization in 1960 and was a founder, with the Hooley family, of the discount stores.

Super Valu originally acquired the Cub chain to boost its wholesale sales, but, *Business Week* reported in 1984, soon realized it had a "tiger by the tail," and that Cub had "taken on a (retailing) life of its own." The company improved the atmosphere of Cub Foods stores by using attractive decor, keeping the stores clean, and increasing product offerings, including perishables, which the early warehouse stores did not offer. As a result, Cub Foods evolved into a combination of the conventional grocery store and the warehouse store, known in the industry by the late 1980s as a "super warehouse."

Although Cub Foods competes directly with a number of Super Valu's customers' stores and its own corporate stores, the company saw a benefit in the opportunity Cub offered its retailers to learn about warehouse-store operations from the inside. Several of its retailers did not totally agree, citing a 10 to 15 percent reduction in business when a Cub Foods store opened in their market area. To address this complaint, Super Valu started franchising its Cub stores and also developed County Market, a downsized version of Cub with the same low prices, but aimed at smaller communities and at independent retailers who could not meet the financial commitment that buying a Cub franchise required. By 1989, 74 Cub Foods stores (of which Super Valu owned 34) were in nine states and had sales of approximately $3 billion.

By 1986 Super Valu had introduced another variation on the Cub theme. Developed for retailers who needed to improve their stores' look and style to meet competition, the Newmarket format combined warehouse pricing with an upscale product line and services such as video rental, check cashing counters, and baggers. The first Newmarket store opened in the St. Paul-Minneapolis area, and has been so successful that the company is offering it in other locations.

In June 1981 Jack Crocker, at age 57, stepped down from his position as CEO. Crocker, who headed Super Valu for nine years, brought the company to just over $4 billion in sales. He is reported to have handpicked Michael W. Wright, who had joined Super Valu as an executive vice-president in 1977 and become president in 1978, to be the next CEO. Wright had first come to Crocker's attention when he handled some legal matters for the company in Minneapolis. Wright, a former captain of the University of Minnesota football team, had put himself through law school by playing professional football with the Canadian Football League.

Expansions West and South in the 1980s

Super Valu took its expansion west in 1982 when it acquired Western Grocers, Inc. Western had distribution centers in Denver, Colorado, and Albuquerque, New Mexico; in 1984 these two centers became separate divisions. Super Valu also moved into Nebraska in 1982 by acquiring the Hinky Dinky distribution center near Omaha from American Community Grocers, a subsidiary of Texas-based Cullum Companies. In 1984 Super Valu sold the center back to Cullum.

With intentions of gaining a strong market presence in Florida, in 1983 and 1984, respectively, Super Valu purchased Pantry Pride's Miami and Jacksonville distribution centers. In what Super Valu considered a breach of their agreement, Pantry Pride began selling off its stores. With this and the fact that the Florida market had historically been dominated by the chains, Super Valu, claiming that the Florida market would take a large amount of capital to develop, sold the Miami center to Malone & Hyde in 1985, and the Jacksonville center to Winn-Dixie in 1986.

In 1985, Super Valu created its Atlanta Division when it acquired the warehouse and distribution facilities of Food Giant. Through this division the company supplied Food Giant, Big Apple, Cub Foods, and independent stores. Food Giant, according to a 1988 *Financial World* report, "refused to implement Super Valu's turnaround plan for store upgrading," and the retail stores that Super Valu owned through the original transaction and a later acquisition of stock lost money for the company. By 1988 the company had divested itself of these stores, but operated or franchised seven Cub stores in the Atlanta area.

Also in 1985, Super Valu acquired West Coast Grocery Company (Wesco) of Tacoma, Washington. Wesco, founded by the Charles H. Hyde family in 1891, was Super Valu's largest acquisition to that time. Wesco had distribution centers in two Washington cities and Salem, Oregon, and a freezer facility in another Washington city. Super Valu's West Coast operations were hurt when the Albertson's chain opened a distribution center to supply its own stores in Washington.

In 1986 and 1987 Super Valu acquired two more distribution centers in Albuquerque and Denver, respectively. These centers were owned by Associated Grocers of Colorado which, at the time of the Denver purchase, was in Chapter 11 bankruptcy proceedings. In December 1988, Super Valu acquired the Minneapolis; Fargo, North Dakota; and Green Bay, Wisconsin, distribution centers of Red Owl Stores, Inc. The former Denver

and Albuquerque divisions of Western Grocers were moved into these new facilities.

By the mid-1980s Super Valu had developed a substantial presence in the military-commissary marketplace. The company had been supplying both product and retail support to military commissaries in the United States and abroad and, in 1986, demonstrated its commitment to international operations by appointing a military and export product director. Super Valu International had its beginnings with the Caribbean and Far East markets and eventually supplied fresh goods and private label canned goods, general merchandise, and health and beauty aids to most countries of the world.

During the 1980s ShopKo continued to expand and to turn in substantial profits for the company. At the end of fiscal 1989 ShopKo operated 87 stores in 11 states from the Midwest to the Pacific Northwest and had sales of $1.28 billion. Super Valu's only nonfood retail operation at the time, ShopKo had its headquarters and distribution center in Green Bay, Wisconsin, and distribution centers in Omaha, Nebraska, and Boise, Idaho.

It was perhaps the successes of ShopKo and of Cub Foods that led Super Valu to its biggest venture in retailing in the 1980s—the "hypermarket," a retailing concept that originated in Europe after World War II. The first hypermarkets introduced in America in the early 1970s were not successful, but in the mid-1980s Hyper Shoppes, Inc., a predominantly French consortium, reintroduced the hypermarket in the United States. Super Valu was a 10 percent investor in the venture, which opened bigg's, a 200,000-square-foot food and general merchandise store in the Cincinnati, Ohio, area.

With the experience of this venture under its belt, Super Valu created its own version of the hypermarket, Twin Valu. A combination of a Cub Foods and a ShopKo, this 180,000-square-foot store opened in early 1989 in Cleveland. A second Twin Valu opened in Cleveland in 1990. The hypermarket concept as executed by Super Valu emphasized low prices, good selection, and brand-name merchandise.

In 1988 Super Valu lost its position as the world's largest wholesaler when Oklahoma City-based Fleming Companies bought Malone & Hyde, a purchase Super Valu declined to make. At the end of the 1980s, Super Valu served some 3,000 independent retailers in 33 states. The company still owned and operated 70 conventional grocery stores and some Cub Foods stores and served its corporate stores and customers from 18 retail support and distribution centers.

Acquisition of Wetterau Inc. and Other Purchases Highlight Early 1990s

Super Valu entered the 1990s having to contend with the loss of $220 million in business from the sale or closing of three major customers in 1989: Red Owl stores in Minneapolis, Skaggs Alpha Beta stores in Albuquerque, and two Cub Foods stores in Nashville. The loss of business through acquisition of its independent retail customers by major chains—nearly all of whom were self-distributing—would continue to pose a threat to Super Valu and other wholesalers throughout the 1990s. Part of Super Valu's response to this threat was to further bolster its own retail operations.

Meanwhile, Super Valu's ShopKo subsidiary had grown so rapidly it was beginning to be too large for Super Valu to manage. The company decided to divest itself of part of ShopKo through an initial public offering (IPO). In October 1991 the IPO resulted in the sale of 54 percent of ShopKo to the public, netting Super Valu $420 million. Wright told *Grocery Marketing* that if Super Valu had not taken this step, "it was a case where we would have ended up with the tail wagging the dog."

The very next month Wright began to reinvest the cash, and to boost the company's retail sector, through the purchase of Scott's Food Stores, a 13-store chain based in Fort Wayne, Indiana. With the addition of Scott's, Super Valu became the 25th largest retailer in the United States.

In early 1992, Super Valu Stores Inc. changed its name to Supervalu Inc. Later that year, the company made its largest acquisition to date when it acquired Wetterau Inc., the fourth largest wholesaler in the country, in a $1.1 billion deal. The addition of Wetterau's $5.7 billion in sales volume to Supervalu's $10.6 billion leapfrogged Supervalu over Fleming and back into the top spot in U.S. grocery wholesaling. Wetterau, founded in 1869 and based in Hazelwood, Missouri, was led at the time of the merger by Ted C. Wetterau, a member of the fourth generation of Wetteraus to run the company. Wetterau became vice chairman (with Wright) of Supervalu and a company director. Wetterau retired late in 1993, leaving Wright in sole control of Supervalu once again.

In addition to bolstering Supervalu's wholesaling operation, Wetterau brought Supervalu a significant retail operation—180 stores in 12 states (added to Supervalu's stable of 105 stores in 11 states). Most significantly, Wetterau's stores included the Save-A-Lot chain of limited-assortment stores, a format new to the Supervalu fold and one that would expand under Supervalu's supervision. The newly combined retail operations moved Supervalu into 14th place among U.S. food retailers. The company set a long-term goal of being one of the top ten retailers by the end of the 1990s.

The Wetterau acquisition was soon followed by additional acquisitions, several in retail. Late in 1993 Supervalu acquired Sweet Life Foods Inc., a wholesaler—based in Suffield, Connecticut, with $650 million in revenues—which had a few retail operations in New England, one of Supervalu's weaker regions. In March 1994, the 30-store Texas T Discount Grocery Stores chain was acquired. Then in July, Supervalu bought Cincinnati-based Hyper Shoppes, Inc., which ran 7 bigg's stores in Cincinnati, Denver, and Louisville, Kentucky, and had more than $500 million in annual revenues. Meanwhile, in June 1994, Fleming leapfrogged back over Supervalu into the number one wholesaling position when it acquired Scrivner Inc., then number three. At that time, Fleming claimed $19 billion in revenue to Supervalu's $16 billion.

Restructuring in Mid-1990s

Supervalu announced in late 1994 that it would begin to implement a restructuring program called Advantage in early 1995. Over a two-year period, the company eliminated about 4,300 jobs (10 percent of the total workforce) and divested itself of about 30 underperforming retail stores. The Advantage pro-

gram also centered around three chief aims: revamping the distribution system into a two-tiered system in order to lower the costs to retailers; creating a new approach to pricing called Activity Based Sell; and developing "market-driving capabilities" that would increase sales for Supervalu's retail customers, chiefly through category management. The last of these goals also involved the realignment of the company's wholesale food divisions into seven marketing regions: Central Region, based in Xenia, Ohio; Midwest Region, Pleasant Prairie, Wisconsin; New England Region, Andover, Massachusetts; Northeast Region, Belle Vernon, Pennsylvania; Northern Region, Hopkins, Minnesota; Northwest Region, Tacoma, Washington; and Southeast Region, Atlanta, Georgia. Supervalu took a $244 million charge in 1995 to implement the Advantage program, which was the company's response to increasing market pressures—low inflation, industry consolidation, a slowdown in growth, and changes in the promotional practices of manufacturers—which had yet to hurt the company's earnings but were certain to begin to do so if the company took no action.

In late 1996 Supervalu bought the 21-store Sav-U Foods chain of limited assortment stores from its rival, Fleming Companies. The purchase provided Supervalu its first southern California retail presence. The stores were to be converted to Save-A-Lot stores, and the company made plans to eventually run 200 to 300 Save-A-Lot stores in the area.

Also in late 1996, ShopKo and Phar-Mor Inc., a chain of more than 100 deep-discount drug stores, merged under the umbrella of a new holding company called Cabot Noble Inc. Although initially Supervalu was to have no stake in the new company, the final agreement gave Supervalu 6 percent of Cabot Noble in order to reduce the amount of financing needed for the merger. Supervalu also gained about $200 million as a result of the purchase of most of its shares in ShopKo.

Supervalu neared the 21st century continuing to contend with the volatility of wholesaling. A major customer in the northeast closed in 1995, while another in the southeast was lost the following year. Still, the company's Advantage program showed that Supervalu was proactively taking major steps to protect its position near the top of the industry. Supervalu had also started to take some tentative steps toward expanding its presence overseas, through a 20 percent stake it held in an Australian wholesaler and its agreement to supply products to a new supermarket in Moscow. The retail side also clearly figured large in future plans, with already in 1996 more than one-quarter of revenue resulting from retail. Adding up to a bright future was Supervalu's continuing focus on helping its retailers stay competitive as well as keeping Supervalu competitive in the cutthroat food industry.

Principal Subsidiaries

Cabot Noble Inc. (6%); Cub Foods Stores; Foodland Distributors; Hazelwood Farms Bakeries, Inc.; Hornbachers; Hyper Shoppes, Inc.; Laneco, Inc.; Moran Foods Inc./Save-A-Lot Ltd.; Planmark, Inc.; Preferred Products, Inc.; Risk Planners, Inc.; Scott's Foods Stores, Inc.; Shop 'n Save Warehouse Foods, Inc.; Studio 70; Supervalu International; USCP-WESCO, Inc.

Further Reading

Byrne, Harlan S., "Super Valu Stores: Food Wholesaler Gives Thanks for Its Retail Operations," *Barron's*, November 19, 1990, p. 51.

——, "Super Valu Stores Inc.: It Looks to the Unconventional for Growth in Retailing," *Barron's*, April 24, 1989, p. 49.

Merrefield, David, "The New Super Valu," *Supermarket News*, June 22, 1992, p. 1.

Morris, Kathleen, "Beyond Jurassic Park: Meet the First Big Company Likely to Make It Out of 'Dinosaur-Hood,'" *Financial World*, June 22, 1993, p. 28.

Parr, Jan, "Leader of the Pack," *Forbes*, February 8, 1988, p. 35.

Schifrin, Matthew, "Middleman's Dilemma," *Forbes*, May 23, 1994, p. 67.

"Supervalu: 50 Years on the Road to Excellence," special section of *Grocery Marketing*, 1992.

Weinstein, Steve, "The Reinvention of Supervalu," *Progressive Grocer*, January 1996, p. 26.

——, "Tomorrow the World," *Progressive Grocer*, October 1992, p. 58.

Zwiebach, Elliot, "Super Valu to Buy Wetterau," *Supermarket News*, June 15, 1992, p. 1.

—Nina Wendt
—updated by David E. Salamie

SyQuest Technology, Inc.

47071 Bayside Pkwy.
Fremont, California 94538
U.S.A.
(510) 226-4000
Fax: (510) 226-4108
Web site: http://www.syquest.com

Public Company
Incorporated: 1982
Employees: 1,541
Sales: $200.4 million (1996)
Stock Exchanges: NASDAQ
SICs: 3572 Computer Storage Devices

In an industry where obsolescence is often only months away and a single misstep can sink a company, SyQuest Technology, Inc. has emerged—bruised and battered—a survivor. SyQuest is a pioneer and worldwide leader in removable cartridge computer storage systems using the industry-standard Winchester hard drive technology. After sustaining two years of losses, including more than $136 million in 1996 alone, SyQuest is on the rebound. Leading the way is the company's new product line, including the industry-leading 1.5 gigabyte Syjet drive, and the 230 and 270 megabyte EZ Flyer drives. SyQuest drives, unlike the wildly successful Zip and Jaz drives of archrival Iomega Corp., use Winchester technology to offer access speeds and data transfer rates that rival fixed-disk hard drive systems. Targeted especially at high-end and professional users, but also at an increasingly storage-sensitive consumer market, SyQuest drives combine unlimited storage capacity with near-real-time access for megabyte-hungry graphics, music, and video files and applications. SyQuest's headquarters are in Fremont, California, with a product development plant in Boulder, Colorado, and main manufacturing facilities in Penang, Malaysia. After a restructuring of the company in 1996, which saw the ouster of company founder Syed Iftikar, SyQuest is led by computer industry veterans Ed Marinaro, as chairman, and Edwin Harper, as chief executive officer.

The Storage Revolution of the 1980s

Winchester hard drive technology, created in the 1970s by IBM, was a primary factor in the personal computer explosion of the 1980s. Winchester technology (so-called because, like the famous 30–30 repeating rifle, the original Winchester hard drive featured dual 30-megabyte disks) represented a breakthrough in data storage. The Winchester drive made possible not only large data storage, but also fast access to that data as well as the ability to access data randomly. The Winchester drive was also more durable and more reliable than previous storage systems. The new Winchester drives, which used 14-inch disks, were, however, initially suited only to large computer environments.

Enter Syed Iftikar. A native of India and a graduate of the University of Madras, Iftikar's involvement in the computer industry began in the 1960s. An engineering student, Iftikar went to his professor for advice on where to direct his future. As Iftikar told *The Business Journal*: "I asked him whether I should pursue mechanical, electrical or industrial engineering. He said, 'Son, get into the computer industry. Take all the computer classes you can. It's the wave of the future.' " Iftikar took his professor's advice to heart, leading him to leave India. "All the exciting things in innovation were happening in America," Iftikar continued, "So I came."

Iftikar joined Memorex Corp., where he worked for some 10 years as a part of that company's think tank. But it was his next move that would revolutionize the computer industry. In 1979, Iftikar left Memorex to cofound (with Al Shugart, Finis Conner, later of Conner Peripherals, Inc., and Tom Mitchell) industry powerhouse Seagate Technology. Named vice-president of mechanical engineering, Iftikar led the development team that created the first 5.25-inch hard disk drive using Winchester technology. That drive quickly became the de facto standard of the computer industry, and especially the nascent personal computer market—indeed, that market was only made possible by the development of the smaller hard drive.

By the start of the 1980s, Iftikar had identified a new potential for the Winchester technology: removable storage. In 1982 Iftikar left Seagate to found SyQuest (short for "Syed's

509

Company Perspectives:

The goal: To maintain world leadership in removable Winchester technology. The new SyQuest is focused, refueled and racing toward the goal. Your company's customer-focused strategy centers on bringing to market the most highly compatible, price competitive, high capacity product lines while upholding the quality standard that is synonymous with the SyQuest name.

quest'') and develop the first removable storage system. Such a system offered a number of advantages over fixed drives, including an expandable storage solution, and greater data security—data cartridges could be removed and locked away. Funding for the company came from Iftikar's Seagate stock. By December 1982, SyQuest was ready to launch its first product, the SQ306, a 3.9-inch removable cartridge drive with a 6.38-megabyte storage capacity. SyQuest manufactured the drive, then sold it to original equipment manufacturers, which would package the drive for sale to end users.

SyQuest floundered in its first years. The removable storage market inspired a host of competitors, including Iomega, DMA, Eastman Kodak, and Data Technology Corp. By 1984, SyQuest was already facing failure. Its hopes were hinged on a contract to supply storage systems to the U.S. Army. But rival DMA appeared to have the lead in winning the contract. As a former SyQuest executive explained to *The Business Journal*, ''It was well known in the disk drive industry that whoever got that contract survived. [Iftikar] had read in the paper that we had lost it. Who knows, we might have. But it was [Iftikar's] chutzpah that turned it around. He personally met with the military, persuaded them and won the contract. DMA went out of business shortly afterward.''

Desktop Publishing's Choice in the Late 1980s

By 1986, SyQuest had raised its storage capacity to 15 megabytes; the following year, the company debuted a 44.5-megabyte cartridge system. At the same time, the computer also produced tape-based backup systems. The personal computing revolution was, by then, well underway. SyQuest's original focus had been on the booming IBM-compatible market. But the company's success came from a different direction. The rise of the Apple computer and its graphical Macintosh line spawned an entirely new industry: desktop publishing. Desktop publishing, which would remain for years an Apple specialty, made heavy use of graphics, creating large, multi-megabyte files that demanded extensive storage capacity (a typical fixed-disk hard drive at the time barely exceeded 80 megabytes). SyQuest's drives quickly became the choice of the desktop publishing industry.

SyQuest's popularity among desktop publishers quickly propelled the company into the forefront of removable storage systems makers. Revenues reached $20 million by 1988, more than doubled to $50 million the following year, and topped $80 million in 1990. By that year, the company had sold more than

150,000 of its systems. Sales of cartridges for its drives were also becoming a primary revenue-driver for the company, with some 700,000 cartridges sold by 1990. Claiming as much as a 90 percent share of the removable storage market, the company expanded its Fremont headquarters, opened an engineering and product development arm in Boulder, Colorado, and built a 40,000-square-foot manufacturing plant in Singapore. Some 75 percent of the company's sales were to Macintosh users. By 1991, SyQuest had topped $115 million in sales, posting a net income of more than $6 million. An ebullient Iftikar, predicting $1 billion in sales by 1995, told *The Business Journal*, ''We are in just the first phase of growth.''

Missing the Beat of the 1990s

Already in the early 1990s, SyQuest's control of the Apple market was reaching saturation. In order to fuel future growth, the company needed to expand its share of the booming (and far larger) IBM-compatible market, which, with the introduction of the new Windows operating system, was preparing to enter a new growth phase. In 1991, SyQuest opened a subsidiary, Sydos Inc., in Boca Raton, Florida, charged with developing SyQuest systems for the IBM PCs and challenging rival Iomega's Bernouilli Box for control of that market.

SyQuest hit the 1990s on a roll. But it was already feeling the effects of its rivalry with Iomega. A price war between the two companies had forced a 17 percent drop in SyQuest's 1991 net earnings. And the coming years would see a new set of challenges that nearly bankrupted the company.

Nevertheless, SyQuest's revenues continued to build strongly. Fueled by an initial public offering in December 1991, which raised some $23 million, SyQuest's sale climbed to $174 million in 1992, and topped $206 million in 1993. Earnings were strong, rising from $13.5 million in 1992 to $15.2 million in 1993. But some 55 percent of sales, and an even larger percentage of earnings, came from sales of additional cartridges for SyQuest systems. This left SyQuest vulnerable to a challenge from an unexpected source. Since 1992, a French company, Nomai Inc., with assistance from the French government, had been developing and distributing its own cartridges for SyQuest systems. Then in 1993, Iomega announced an agreement with Nomai to distribute that company's SyQuest-compatible cartridges on a worldwide basis. SyQuest launched a bitter legal battle with the two companies, but was unable to secure an injunction against sales of the Nomai cartridges. The company warned its customers that the Nomai cartridges could damage the SyQuest drivers; and further attempts to prevent sales of the cartridges by threatening to void the warranty on SyQuest systems if they were damaged by the Nomai cartridges also proved less than successful.

The following year highlighted another vulnerability for the company. A market glut of fixed-disk drives caused a collapse in prices, which fell some 25 percent in the first half of 1994. The lowered hard drive prices tugged away customers who might otherwise have purchased a SyQuest drive. SyQuest was forced to respond with its own price cuts. But the announcement of a new generation of larger and more powerful SyQuest drives caused customers to postpone their purchases—a common difficulty in the ever-evolving computer industry. SyQuest was forced to write down inventory on its discontinued line of 2.5 inch drives, causing the company to post its first quarterly loss in five years. Nevertheless, SyQuest's problems seemed only temporary. In May 1994, it launched its new line of 110- and 270-megabyte cartridge drives in the 3.5-inch size that had become the standard of the PC market. The company's marketing strategy for the new drives emphasized their usefulness as a backup device—over other features, such as expandability, security, transportability, and, importantly, their high-speed access capability. By June 1994, the company was also able to end its dispute with Nomai and Iomega, reaching a licensing agreement that would give SyQuest royalties on sales of the rival cartridges.

The effects of the lower prices in the hard drive market showed in the company's balance sheet for 1994. The company had raised sales to $221 million, fueled by acceptance of its 3.5-inch PC-compatible drives; yet net earnings had slumped to $5.4 million. And the computer industry was undergoing a sea-change that caught SyQuest by surprise. For one, the IBM PC/ Windows system was finally maturing into the desktop publishing market. Despite its efforts to enter the PC market, SyQuest's fortunes were still very much hitched to Apple, which was having its own problems. Then a new force entered the computing world. ''Multimedia'' became the buzzword for 1995— and, as personal computer use finally shifted massively into the home, Iomega stood ready with a product, and a savvy marketing strategy, that would offer home computer users a place to store a sudden proliferation of graphics, music, video, and other files, as well as the steadily swelling applications to create and view them. That product was the Zip drive.

In fact, in 1992 SyQuest had been offered the technology behind the Zip, which had been developed by Fuji, but turned it down. Lighter than SyQuest's Winchester-based drives, the Zip drives were also slower. But they were easier to use, more reliable for the home consumer, and, importantly, much cheaper to produce. The introduction of the Zip drive in 1995 took the removable cartridge market by storm. The Zip's ease of use, and a brilliant marketing drive that promised users a place to hold all the ''stuff'' that was suddenly filling up their hard drives, attracted the attention even of SyQuest's core Macintosh base. Sales skyrocketed, reaching some 2 million units within a year. SyQuest responded to the challenge with a misstep.

Months after the Zip drive had captured the attention of the computer industry, SyQuest rushed out the EZ135, which was designed to appeal to the home computer user. Based on Winchester technology, the EZ135 offered marked advantages over the Zip drive, including much faster access and transfer rates, and a 35 megabyte-per cartridge advantage. But the unit was heavier, and also more expensive, and SyQuest quickly learned that price was often the deciding specification for the home user. When Iomega dropped its price on the Zip drives, SyQuest was forced to respond, cutting prices to below manufacturing costs. This meant that SyQuest lost money for each EZ135 it sold; while the company hoped to make up the difference with sales of cartridges for the new machine, the Zip drive had already captured the market, and sales of the EZ135 lagged.

In September, the end of its 1995 fiscal year, SyQuest posted a net loss of $11.2 million, despite a revenue gain to $299.5

million. The company's losses continued to mount: in the first quarter of its 1996 fiscal year, SyQuest posted a net loss of $33 million on revenues of $78 million. The company's sales had still been gaining, but the success of the Zip drive began to cut into the company's core product line, the high-end SQ5200 and SQ3270 cartridge drives. In February 1996, the company was forced to restructure, moving its manufacturing operations from its long-time Singapore base to Malaysia, where the company had completed construction on a modernized, automated plant. The restructuring caused the company to slash its payroll by some 1,500 employees; charges for the restructuring, including closing its Singapore operations, resulted in the company posting a new, $51 million loss for its second 1996 quarter.

Analysts were sounding the death knell for the company. SyQuest's restructuring continued: in May 1996, its board of directors replaced the company's senior management, installing Ed Marinaro as chairman, and Edwin Harper as president and chief operating officer. The company also replaced its chief financial officer and senior vice-president. Iftikar maintained his position as chief executive officer, but was now placed within the sphere of the office of the president, and lost day-to-day control of the company he had founded. Iftikar stepped down from the company in September 1996. With the company's stock price tumbling to just $5 per share, SyQuest became the target of a class-action suit brought by shareholders, who charged management with security law violations. By the following month, however, the company faced a new crisis: its net tangible assets had fallen into the negative, and its NASDAQ listing, predicated upon a company holding more than $1 million in net tangible assets (assets, excluding goodwill, minus liabilities), was under threat. The company hurriedly made a placement of stock to raise $20 million. Analysts began predicting that the company would soon be sold—or declare bankruptcy.

An Uncertain Future

SyQuest did neither. As Iomega announced its forthcoming 1-megabyte Jaz drive, SyQuest was preparing the launch of two new products that would regain its leadership in the removable storage market. The first, the EZFlyer 230 (later expanded to 270 megabytes) featured a 3.5-inch, 230-megabyte removable cartridge based on Winchester technology. The second, the SyJet, featured a 1.3 gigabyte (later 1.5 gigabyte) disk platter system. At the same time, SyQuest cut the price of the EZ135 in half in order to dump its inventory, forcing Iomega to make its own price cuts on the Zip drive. SyQuest also reoriented its marketing position, returning to its focus on the high-performance customers that had always formed its base. The company also stepped up its entry into the retail channel, expanding sales into some 1,800 chains.

The strategy appeared to be working. While the company continued to post losses through 1996—the final tally was some $136 million in net losses on revenues of only $200 million— losses finally began to slow as it entered the next fiscal year. The company's fortunes were buoyed by the announcement of an exclusive manufacturing and distribution partnership with Legend Group, the largest manufacturer and distributor of computers in the booming Chinese market. Yet SyQuest's position in the storage market was not yet secure. New technologies, including recordable CD-ROM drives, DVD (digital video disk), and others expected to expand in the coming years may yet threaten SyQuest—and arch-rival Iomega—as the storage solution kings.

Further Reading

Abate, Tom, "SyQuest Seeking to Fund Rebound," *San Francisco Examiner*, June 7, 1996, p. E1.

Biggs, Brooke Shelby, "Iomega Rise Means Fall for Fremont Firm," *Business Journal—San Jose*, May 27, 1996, p. 1.

Hachman, Mark, "SyQuest Searches for an Answer," *Electronic Buyers' News*, June 10, 1996, p. 8.

Jameson, Barbara, "SyQuest Drive Hits Market Late, Competition Erodes '95 Profits," *Boulder County Business Report*, June 1996, p. 15.

Khermouch, Gerry, "Removable Disk Drive Price War Anticipated," *Chilton's Electronic News*, July 15, 1991, p. 12.

Levine, Doug S., "Plug-In Profits: SyQuest Poised to Bounce Back," *San Francisco Business Times*, April 29, 1994, p. 7.

Snyder, Bill, "Spinning Down," *PC Week*, July 22, 1996, p. A1.

Spang, Kelly, "On the Rebound," *Computer Reseller News*, January 13, 1997, p. 145.

Swartz, Jon, "Sved Iftikar: His Quest and His Drive Began with a Prophet," *The Business Journal*, June 3, 1991, p. 10.

Turner, Nick, "Can SyQuest Get Fit Enough to Do Battle with Iomega?" *Investor's Business Daily*, October 8, 1996, p. A8.

Wald, Michael, "SyQuest Touts Backup Features of Its Line of Drives," *Computer Retail Week*, May 9, 1994, p. 46.

—M. L. Cohen

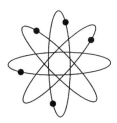

Tech-Sym Corporation

10500 Westoffice Drive
Houston, Texas 77042-5391
U.S.A.
(713) 785-7790
Fax: (713) 780-3524

Public Company
Incorporated: 1944 as Western Gold Mines, Inc.
Employees: 1,966
Sales: $246 million (1995)
Stock Exchanges: New York
SICs: 3679 Electronic Components, Not Elsewhere
     Classified; 3663 Radio & Television Communications
     Equipment; 3812 Search & Navigation Equipment

Tech-Sym Corporation is a highly diversified electronics engineering and manufacturing firm that designs, develops, and manufactures various products for use in the fields of defense systems, communications, and the exploration and production of hydrocarbons, otherwise described as geoscience. Through its principal subsidiary in the defense industry, Metric Systems, Inc., Tech-Sym provides electronic systems for the training of military pilots and crews for the U.S. Navy and Air Force, cargo handling and delivery systems, and the electronic power distribution systems for a wide variety of naval applications. Through TRAK Microwave Corporation, Tecom Industries, Inc., Continental Electronics Corporation, and Enterprise Electronics Corporation, the company's four primary subsidiaries in the communications industry, Tech-Sym provides products for navigation systems, satellites, aerospace applications, radar systems, and weather data applications. Through Syntron, Inc. and CogniSeis Development, Inc., the company's leading subsidiaries in the field of geoscience, Tech-Sym designs, manufactures, and repairs electronic data systems used in the exploration and production of oil and gas. Tech-Sym has an extensive manufacturing and marketing network around the world, with major subsidiaries located in the United States, Asia, South America, and Europe.

Early History

Although Tech-Sym had narrowed its focus during the 1980s and 1990s, for a long period of its history the company was a combination of different operations working in different fields. Initially formed and incorporated by a group of investors to take advantage of the uranium and gold deposits still undiscovered in the western part of the United States, from its inception the company was managed by a board of directors who were primarily interested in a return of their investment. This single, overriding interest led the company's management and board of directors to expand its operations. Not satisfied with the small returns garnered from collecting mineral deposits over a period of 15 years, the company began to diversify, among other fields, into the financial services industry and to engage in real estate ventures. The company changed its name to Western Equities, Inc. in 1961 and to Westec Corporation in 1966. The dizzying array of acquisitions made during the early and mid-1960s included Lee Ackerman Investment Company; Arizona Growth Capital, Inc.; Geo Space Corporation, a manufacturer of seismic products and instruments; TRAK Microwave Corporation; Pan Geo Atlas Corporation; Jet Set Corporation, a manufacturer of explosive devices; Engineers & Fabricators, Inc.; Carry Machine Supply, Inc.; Metric Systems, Inc.; and Seacat-Zapata Off-Shore Company, a gas and oil exploration firm.

By 1966, however, the company was suffering from the mismanagement of the past. Flouting such time-honored strategies as economies of scale, management had brought the firm to the brink of financial catastrophe. Many of the acquisitions made during the early part of the decade were losing money, while others had lost their traditional market share. As a result, the company was forced to file a petition in U.S. District Court under Chapter X of the Bankruptcy Act. The reorganization immediately went into effect, and the company was required to sell off many of its subsidiaries to pay outstanding debts, including Geo Space Corporation and Pan Geo Atlas Corporation. Other subsidiaries, such as Carry Machine Supply, Inc. and Metric Systems, were reorganized and merged to create more stable and profitable operations. By the time the company changed its name once again, to Tech-Sym Corporation in

1970, management seemed to have learned from its past mistakes and had implemented a reorganization strategy that was bringing the company back to profitability.

Yet the road to financial stability was a long and arduous one. With such an extensive history of varied diversification, even the new management at the company continued to delve into widely disparate businesses. In 1972, Tech-Sym purchased All Woods, Inc., a lumber company, and one year later acquired Alexander-Schroder Lumber Company. Later in 1973, management formed Coastal Lumber, S.A., in Costa Rica. These attempts to create a lumber division resulted in the opening of a retail store in Houston, Texas named "Fine Woods." Unfortunately, this foray into the lumber industry did not result in a significant financial improvement. By the late 1970s, management finally decided to focus on an area where profitability and growth were assured—the development and manufacture of electronic products for the United States defense industry.

Growth During the 1970s and 1980s

The first major acquisition during the early 1970s that introduced Tech-Sym to defense industry contracts was E&M Laboratories, a development and manufacturing firm specializing in electronic components for missiles and fighter jets. This purchase, successful both in terms of its amalgamation into the Tech-Sym corporate structure and its highly lucrative product line, helped the company complete its reorganization strategy and emerge from Chapter X in July of 1977. As management at Tech-Sym recognized the enormous profitability in procuring defense systems contracts with the United States government, and with other national governments friendly toward America, more attention was paid to possible takeover candidates in the defense industry. This shift in focus resulted in the sell-off of the company's entire lumber operation.

Although Tech-Sym was firmly established in developing and manufacturing electronic systems for the U.S. Department of Defense by the late 1970s, it was not until the election of Ronald Reagan that the company began to make a name for itself within the industry. President Reagan's commitment to the rebuilding of American armed forces around the world led to numerous contracts for Tech-Sym. During the early 1980s, Tech-Sym filled a huge contract for the development, design, and manufacture of electronic control and monitoring equipment for U.S. Navy ships. But this was only one of its contracts. The company also made airborne weapons systems and electronic countermeasure systems for the U.S. Air Force, microwave components for Navy radar, aircraft, and missiles, radar and missile simulators for training air crews, and a host of computer-based electronic systems used in air and naval defense.

The decade of the 1980s was one of the most successful financial periods in the company's history. As its cash flow continued to improve, management made strategic acquisitions that improved its position in certain fields both within and outside the defense industry. Two of the most important of these purchases included Tecom Industries, Inc. and Enterprise Electronics Corporation. Tecom Industries was a small but important California-based manufacturer of antennas and computer-controlled electromechanical components for aerospace, navigation, surveillance, and command control applications. Tecom

had garnered numerous contracts from the U.S. Department of Defense, especially in the area of naval defense systems. On the other hand, Alabama-based Enterprise Electronics Corporation was a designer and manufacturer of highly sophisticated meteorological information systems that detect and display weather patterns and other natural events through the use of Dopplar radars and innovative computer processing. Although Enterprise Electronics was well known as a firm that custom designed and installed meteorological radar systems for countries around the world, Tech-Sym expanded Enterprise's markets to encompass a wider array of customers, such as government agencies, military organizations, and meteorology departments at large universities in America, Europe, and Asia.

Transition and Development after the Cold War

With the end of the Cold War, however, the regular flow of contracts to Tech-Sym and its subsidiaries from the U.S. Department of Defense slowed to barely a trickle. The dissolution of the Soviet Union, and the growing perception within the United States Congress that appropriations for defense systems needed to be decreased, forced many companies that had relied heavily on defense business to alter their market strategy. Tech-Sym was no exception, and management at the company decided to implement a comprehensive diversification program that involved three key elements: acquisitions, new product development, and international expansion.

The transition from being primarily a designer and manufacturer of electronic systems for the defense industry to a more diversified company was not an easy one. Orders from the U.S. Department of Defense began to decline more rapidly than management could switch to commercial ventures. The area of satellite surveillance was especially hard hit and contributed to the company's earnings falling nearly 25 percent in 1991. But management had already made two important acquisitions that would help Tech-Sym ultimately break through the clouds of financial uncertainty. In 1990, Tech-Sym purchased the venerable 45-year-old Continental Electronics Corporation, the world's most famous manufacturer of high-powered radio frequency transmitters. Making transmitters that regularly produced between 500,000 and two million watts, many were used by the Voice of America and Radio Free Europe to broadcast news and various other general information programs throughout the years of the Cold War. Tech-Sym reorganized Continental Electronics and changed its focus from military radars and electronic warfare equipment to a firm that concentrated almost exclusively on manufacturing both high-powered and low frequency transmitters. Tech-Sym then began an intense marketing campaign to sell Continental's high-powered transmitters to foreign countries, including China, which employed the transmitters to broadcast radio shows to more than one billion people in rural areas. In addition, a Catholic organization in Alabama purchased $8 million worth of transmitting equipment to make religious broadcasts to people in South America. Tech-Sym also sold Continental's less powerful transmitters to numerous FM radio stations across the United States.

At approximately the same time, Tech-Sym acquired Syntron, Inc., a manufacturer of highly sophisticated, state-of-the-art seismic instrumentation and equipment. Syntron was one of the first companies in the world to design equipment that made it possible to use three-dimensional computer imaging for identifying gas and oil reserves as much as 25,000 feet below the Earth's surface. Syntron quickly became Tech-Sym's fastest growing and most profitable subsidiary. Based on Syntron's technology, Tech-Sym opened a brand new plant in Singapore in 1992 to take advantage of the growing demand in Southeast Asia for instruments used in the search for gas and oil reserves. Also during the year, the company's Enterprise Electronics subsidiary won a significant contract from the Moroccan government to custom design and install meteorological radar systems in the North African nation, as well as a contract with the Chinese government for the installation of similar radar systems. These acquisitions and sales helped Tech-Sym move away from its traditional reliance upon the defense industry. In 1989, the company derived approximately 75 percent of its total revenues from defense contracts, but by the end of 1992 defense contracts made up only 45 percent of Tech-Sym's revenues.

The Mid-1990s and Beyond

By the beginning of 1993, Tech-Sym was well on its way to succeeding in its strategy to diversify away from the previous heavy reliance on defense industry contracts. Syntron, Inc. was particularly strong, garnering numerous, ever-larger contracts for seismic information systems. One of the largest contracts during this year came from a company working along the Alaskan coastline. Contracts for meteorological radar systems, and for high-powered transmitters, were also growing more numerous, particularly from nations in Europe, Asia, and Africa. In 1994, Tech-Sym made one of its most important acquisitions to date, having purchased Anarad, Inc., an environmental instrumentation firm based in California. The purchase of Anarad was made specifically to take advantage of the impact that the 1990 Clean Air Act would have on manufacturing plants and factories stretching along the Houston Ship Channel in the Texas Gulf. More than 340 factories along the Channel were required to monitor the quality of their emissions into the atmosphere, and each of them needed environmental instruments to measure the amount of contaminated air.

In 1995, Tech-Sym acquired CogniSeis Development Inc., a seismic firm located in Houston, Texas, and Symtronix Corporation, another seismic company. These two firms were then merged with Syntron, Inc. to create GeoScience Corporation. Tech-Sym management brought the three companies together to build a major developer and manufacturer of seismic data acquisition systems used in the oil and gas exploration business.

As the demand for three-dimensional data collection grew in the field of oil and gas exploration both on land and offshore, Tech-Sym planned a public spinoff for GeoScience Corporation. Tech-Sym retained solid control of the new company through its 80 percent ownership of GeoScience Corporation stock. With seismic activity continually increasing not only in the Gulf of Mexico but throughout the world, by the end of 1996 the companies that comprised GeoScience were reporting record levels of ever-increasing revenues.

Tech-Sym successfully transformed itself from a company dependent upon defense contracts to a highly diversified firm with growing revenues from markets such as communications, meteorological data systems, and seismic instrumentation and equipment. By the mid-1990s, the company's defense contracts had leveled off at approximately 25 percent of total revenues, with the other 75 percent derived from its diversification activities. As long as management continued to focus on designing and manufacturing high profit electronic systems in the fields of communications, meteorology, and seismic data, Tech-Sym's success was most likely assured.

Principal Subsidiaries

Anarad, Inc.; CogniSeis Development, Inc.; Photon Systems Ltd.; Continental Electronics Corporation; Continental-Lensa, S.A.; TELEFUNKEN Sendertechnik GmbH; Enterprise Electronics Corporation; Metric Systems Corporation; Symtronix Corporation; Syntron, Inc.; Syntron Europe Ltd.; Synton Asia Pte. Ltd.; Tecom Industries, Inc.; TRAK Microwave Corporation; Dàden-Anthony Associates, Inc.; TRAK Microwave Ltd.

Further Reading

Byrne, Harlan S., "Tech-Sym Seismic Line Nears a Payoff," *Barron's,* March 8, 1993, p. 44(2).

Elder, Laura, "Tech-Sym Goes on Acquisition Spree To Offset Slump in Defense Spending," *Houston Business Journal,* July 15, 1994, p. 8(1).

Payne, Chris, "A Farewell to Arms: Defense Firm Comes in from the Cold," *Houston Business Journal,* April 26, 1993, p. 1A(2).

——, "Diversifying Defense Contractor Reports Strong First Quarter," *Houston Business Journal,* May 10, 1993, p. 15A(1).

Pybus, Kenneth, "Tech-Sym Spinning Off Seismic Unit," *Houston Business Journal,* April 12, 1996, p. 1A(2).

"Tech-Sym Plans Stock Buyback," *The Wall Street Journal,* June 26, 1996, p. A6(E).

—Thomas Derdak

Total System Services, Inc.

1200 Sixth Avenue
P.O. Box 1755
Columbus, Georgia 31902-1755
U.S.A.
(706) 649-2310
Fax: (706) 649-4499
Web site: http://www.totalsystem.com

Public Subsidiary of Synovus Financial Corp.
Incorporated: 1983
Employees: 2,318
Sales: $249.7 million (1995)
Stock Exchanges: New York
SICs: 7374 Data Processing Services

Total System Services, Inc. (TSYS) is the second-largest credit card processor in the world, trailing only American Express's First Data Corp. subsidiary. Under the service mark, THE TOTAL SYSTEM, and the company's TS2 computer-based processing system, TSYS offers a full line of card support services, from credit approval to production and mailing of cards, to authorizing domestic and international purchases, preparation and mailing of billing statements, and customer service support, as well as merchant accounting and other merchant support services. In 1996, TSYS handled more than 63 million consumer accounts and more than 600,000 merchant accounts for some 115 banks and other card issuers. Major clients include AT&T, Bank of America, and NationsBank Corp. TSYS has also captured more than half of the young but quickly growing commercial card market, already serving more than two million VISA and MasterCard commercial accounts since that market was created in 1994. In 1996, TSYS and VISA U.S.A.'s Merchant Bank Services formed the for-profit Vital Processing Services LLC joint venture, combining both companies' merchant processing units, which together processed nearly three billion transactions in 1995.

TSYS has also expanded into new areas to combat the increasing maturation of the U.S. credit card industry. In 1995,

TSYS, which has long serviced banks in Canada, Mexico, and Puerto Rico, took its first steps to transform itself into an international company. TSYS formed the joint venture Total System Services de Mexico, S.A. de C.V. with Controladora PROSA, an 11-bank partnership representing 75 percent of Mexico's card-issuing banks. The joint venture added four million accounts, giving TSYS de Mexico 40 percent of that country's credit card accounts. TSYS has also expanded beyond traditional credit card markets by winning the processing business of United States Medical Finance Corp.'s USMed Card, a medical credit card. An alliance with Fair, Isaac and Company subsidiary DynaMark, Inc., formed in 1995, has enabled TSYS to extend its services to its clients with dynamic database marketing capabilities.

TSYS generates revenues through the volume, rather than the amount, of transactions made on the credit cards it services. In 1995, TSYS revenues neared $250 million, producing a net income of $27.7 million. TSYS is led by Chairman and CEO Richard Ussery, Vice-chairman Kenneth Evans, and President Philip Tomlinson, all three long-time employees of parent company Synovus Financial Corp. That company, formerly known as Columbus Bank & Trust, owns 81 percent of TSYS's stock; TSYS management controls an additional ten percent of the company's shares, with the remainder trading on the New York Stock Exchange.

Started in a Basement in the 1950s

In the 1950s, it was barely possible to speak of a credit card "industry." When tiny Columbus Bank & Trust (CB&T) issued a credit card to its local depositors in 1959, it was only the second bank in Georgia, and among the very first in the country, to do so. A credit processing operation was set up in the bank's basement; processing was done manually, as computers were still rare and software was even rarer. Through the first half of the 1960s, the bank's credit department grew from processing transactions from some 200 local merchants to 3,000. In 1966, CB&T built a separate operations building, and, after attempting to form a joint venture with W.C. Bradley Company to computerize processing, CB&T installed its own computer. Finding trained computer operators was difficult and expensive;

516

Company Perspectives:

TSYS Vision: We set the standard in global transaction processing services.

instead, the bank trained some of its own personnel, establishing a computer department.

By 1969 the company was writing its own software to handle processing of its credit card accounts. Joining the team developing the bank's software programs was Richard Ussery, then in his fourth year with the bank (he joined CB&T as a teller in 1965). As more banks instituted credit cards and struggled to process accounts, they were attracted to CB&T's processing system. Ussery told *Georgia Trend* of a meeting with an executive from Landmark Union Trust, of Jacksonville, Florida, who complained of the difficulty and expense his firm was having processing its credit transactions. Ussery replied, "We can do that for you here in Columbus at half what it's costing you."

By 1973, CB&T had completed an accounting and bank card data processing software system, dubbed THE TOTAL SYSTEM, the first system in the country offering online access to credit card and bank account information. The following year, CB&T began providing processing services for other banks, starting with Landmark Union Trust. Shortly after, CB&T agreed to handle processing for two more banks, in Seattle and Kentucky. By then, the credit card industry was undergoing its first boom. CB&T's processing business took off, especially after 1976. Prior to that year, credit card issuers had been restricted to offering either one or the other of the predecessors to Visa and MasterCard, then called BankAmericard and MasterCharge. But when the card systems allowed banks to issue both cards, CB&T became the first in the country to take on processing both card systems.

CB&T began intensifying its marketing of THE TOTAL SYSTEM. As Ussery, who was named senior vice-president of the company's Operations Division in 1981, told *American Banker*, "We realized, here was an opportunity to generate some miscellaneous income." The division's revenues reached $6 million in 1980 and neared $10 million by 1982. By the end of that year, CB&T, which itself was expanding rapidly with a series of acquisitions of other banks, spun off its account and data processing operation as a separate subsidiary, Total System Services. By then, TSYS was processing more than one million accounts for more than 60 banks in 28 states. Ussery was named president and CEO, joined by Philip Tomlinson, who began working for the bank in 1974, as executive vice-president. CB&T President James H. Blanchard was named TSYS chairman. Bolstering the new company's processing capacity was the acquisition of a banking software developer, Bank-R Systems Inc., also based in Columbus, in February of 1983. In August of that year, CB&T took TSYS public, retaining 82 percent of the new company's shares. The company's revenues had passed $15 million, providing a net income of nearly $2 million.

Growing Rapidly in the 1980s

By 1984, TSYS had captured second place among the country's leading credit card processors, serving some five million accounts for more than 80 financial institutions. The addition of Michigan National Bank's processing business, among the largest credit card issuers in the United States, added another one million accounts to TSYS, raising its total to 7.5 million credit card accounts and nearly doubling its annual revenues since its initial public offering, to $28 million, with net income of more than $4.3 million.

TSYS was riding high on a new wave of credit card growth in the 1980s. Increasing numbers of banks were introducing their own credit cards, with many banks expanding their credit card business nationwide. Private label cards also began to proliferate, with department stores, airlines, oil companies, and other retail chains offering their own credit cards. Intense competition in the credit card industry lowered profit margins as the cost of processing transactions grew. Whereas larger issuers were able to achieve the economies of scale to conduct their own processing operations, smaller issuers increasingly turned to TSYS (and to rival First Data) to handle their credit card business.

TSYS made steady gains in the second half of the 1980s. Revenues passed $46 million in 1987, with more than 12 million accounts, and jumped to $56 million one year later, as accounts neared 14 million. Net income grew even faster, reaching $9.5 million by 1988. By then, the company's accounts numbered 106 financial institutions and extended into Canada, Mexico, and Puerto Rico. As the end of the decade neared, TSYS made plans to step up expansion of its account base, expecting to pass more than 40 million accounts by the mid-1990s.

To fuel this growth, TSYS moved to split its operations, turning over its banking data processing operations to its parent. CB&T, renamed Synovus Financial Corp., had continued its own rapid expansion, now combining a network of more than 20 banks in Georgia, Florida, and Alabama, and preparing an aggressive push into other states in the Southeast region. The split enabled TSYS to concentrate on its core credit card processing business and to pave the way to winning its biggest client yet.

More Than a Credit Card Processor in the 1990s

In 1990, TSYS signed a five-year contract to process AT&T's new Universal Card. The deal was expected to provide TSYS with its largest client yet as AT&T prepared to launch its Visa and MasterCard, which combined calling card features, to its 70 million household customers and 40 million calling card holders. Analysts estimated that the Universal Card could reach 35 million accounts within five years. The Universal Cards caught on quickly, growing to represent 30 percent of TSYS's total accounts, which grew to 27 million by 1992. The company's merchant account list was also growing, to 310,000 accounts. Revenues climbed from $84 million in 1990 to $112 million in 1991. In early 1992, TSYS restructured its management, with Ussery elected as chairman of the board and CEO, and Tomlinson named president.

TSYS next began to plan not only to expand the company, but also to diversify its operations, while clinging to its core processing business. In July 1992, the company acquired Mailtek, Inc., based in Atlanta, a full-service direct-mail provider of data processing and financial services beyond the financial community to health care companies, airlines, and the leisure industry. A second acquisition, of Lincoln Marketing, Inc., further enhanced the company's direct mail and marketing capacity. But the company also made a more fundamental move in September 1992, when it unveiled plans to develop an entirely new processing system, dubbed TS2. Designed to replace THE TOTAL SYSTEM, which had been expanded from a 25-million account capacity to 45-million accounts, TS2 would use the latest advances in computer technology, offering updated features, flexibility, and an account capacity of at least 250 million accounts. As Blanchard described it to the *Atlanta Journal and Constitution,* ''It is the single biggest event in the history of this company. This is like a rocket ship to the moon in terms of the technology.'' TSYS initially budgeted $27 million for developing the software system.

TSYS received a fresh boost in 1993, when it reached a new agreement with AT&T to provide processing services through the end of the century, replacing the original agreement. By then, the AT&T card had grown to 16 million accounts, making it the industry's second largest. Earlier in that year, TSYS had also signed up the processing business of PROSA, an alliance of 14 card-issuing banks in Mexico, with 3.7 million accounts. The merger of longtime clients C&S/Sovran and North Carolina National Bank as Nationsbank in 1993 helped to firm TSYS's growing client list and attract other larger card issuers as well. By October, TSYS was negotiating to take over the card processing services for BankAmerica Corp. Citing TS2 as a primary reason for signing with TSYS, BankAmerica reached agreement to add its seven million consumer accounts to TSYS in March 1994, and then added its merchant accounts as well.

TSYS's consumer accounts topped 38 million. The company moved to increase its share of the merchant processing business, forming an alliance with Deluxe Data, of Milwaukee, Wisconsin to provide enhanced merchant services. TSYS also began to see progress on TS2, testing the program in 1993 and converting the first of its clients, First Omni Bank of Millsboro, Delaware, and its 750,000 accounts to the new system in 1994. TSYS was also quick to enter the newly created corporate credit card market, as issuers sought to expand business beyond the increasingly saturated consumer market, and in 1994 became the first company to be authorized to process both Visa and MasterCard corporate accounts. Within a year, TSYS's commercial services division had captured more than half of the processing business for the new type of card. TSYS closed that year with revenues of more than $187 million and a net income of $22.5 million.

During 1995, TSYS worked to convert its clients to TS2. The company also moved into new territory when it signed with Tallahassee, Florida-based United States Medical Finance Corp. to process that company's USMed medical credit card. But 1995 proved pivotal to TSYS's expansion in other ways. In July 1995, the company announced its agreement to form a joint venture with PROSA, opening an office in Mexico, which marked the company's first international expansion. This set the stage for future plans to become a worldwide company, as credit card use itself was becoming increasingly prevalent throughout the world. Two months later, TSYS and DynaMark, the database management and marketing subsidiary of Fair, Isaac announced an alliance to provide TSYS's clients with enhanced customer data analysis. Such analysis, normally too expensive for smaller card issuers to implement for themselves, was seen as a crucial value-added element in the competition to retain customers. At the same time, TSYS was also entering negotiations with Visa affiliate Merchant Bank Services to establish a joint venture company to capture a larger share of the merchant processing credit segment. That venture, Vital Processing Services, was launched in June 1996, with first year revenues projected at $100 million.

TSYS's $250 million in 1995 revenues continued the company's secure hold on the industry's number two position. But rival First Data's aggressive diversification efforts in the mid-1990s, boosting that company's revenues past $1 billion, was seen as an opening for TSYS to capture still more of the market. Whereas processing now accounted for only around half of First Data's revenues, TSYS remained committed to enhancing its core processing business. As the industry turned to compete for the expanding global market, TSYS was well positioned to build on its base as a processing powerhouse.

Principal Subsidiaries

Columbus Depot Equipment Co.; Columbus Productions, Inc.; Lincoln Marketing, Inc.; Mailtek, Inc.; Joint Ventures: Total System Services de Mexico de S.A. de C.V., Toluca, Mexico (with Controladora PROSA S.A. de C.V.); Vital Processing Services LLC, Tempe, Arizona (with Merchant Bank Services).

Further Reading

Block, Valerie, ''Total System Stakes Claim as Purchase Card Pioneer,'' *American Banker,* June 22, 1995, p. 14.

Bunker, Ted, ''Synovus Banks on Credit Card Processing,'' *Investor's Business Daily,* January 21, 1993.

Greer, Richard, ''Total System Sees Growth in the Cards,'' *Atlanta Journal and Constitution,* May 19, 1996, p. 13G.

Hayes, Katheryn, ''How CB&T Got Big by Being Humble,'' *Georgia Trend,* October 1987, p. 50.

Jenks, Alan, ''TSYS Braces Itself for AT&T Card Business,'' *Atlanta Business Chronicle,* April 23, 1990, p. 6A.

King, Jim, ''Synovus CEO Putting Hope on 'Rocket Ship,' '' *Atlanta Journal and Constitution,* October 3, 1993, p. H1.

Klegge, Stephen, ''Total Pins Hope on New Credit Card Software,'' *American Banker,* March 31, 1994, p. 14.

Kutler, Jeffrey, ''Their Focus Is on the Core,'' *American Banker,* December 1, 1994, p. 14.

——, ''Total System Enhances Marketing Services,'' *American Banker,* September 20, 1995, p. 8.

Murphy, Daniel J., ''TSYS' Richard W. Ussery,'' *Investor's Business Daily,* February 28, 1996, p. A1.

Smith, William R., ''Best Small Company—Charge It,'' *Georgia Trend,* July 1990, p. 40.

—M. L. Cohen

Toy Biz, Inc.

333 E. 38th St.
New York, New York 10016
U.S.A.
(212) 682-4700
Fax: (212) 682-5317

Public Company
Incorporated: 1988
Employees: 106
Sales: $196.4 million
Stock Exchanges: New York
SICs: 3944 Games, Toys & Children's Vehicles; 3942
  Dolls & Stuffed Toys

Toy Biz, Inc. is one of America's most profitable toy companies. Originally founded in Montreal, Quebec, the business was reincarnated as an American firm in 1988. Since that time, Toy Biz has focused strongly on creating toys based on Marvel Comic's cast of characters, which includes the Amazing Spider-Man, the Incredible Hulk, and the Uncanny X-Men. By the mid-1990s, Marvel-related action figures and playsets generated about 50 percent of Toy Biz's annual sales. In addition to its core Marvel license, Toy Biz held short-term rights to names and symbols associated with Gerber infant goods, the Muppet characters, Coleman camping equipment, Apple computers, Revlon beauty products, NASCAR auto racing, and others. One-third owned by Ronald O. Perelman's Marvel Entertainment Group since 1993, the firm appeared poised to become a wholly-owned subsidiary of this $5-billion group of companies early in 1997.

Canadian Roots

The history of Toy Biz can be traced to Chantex Inc., a Canadian company created in the late 19th century. Sol Zuckerman, the founder's grandson, inherited the business in 1961, when it was earning $160,000 in sales. The restless 21-year-old maintained the family firm as a core interest, bringing its sales to nearly $4.5 million by 1980. In the meantime, he

devoted more of his concentration to the acquisition and operation of several Montreal nightclubs and toyed with the idea of running for public office. Zuckerman's tony discotheques were frequented by celebrities and he earned a reputation as a fast-talking, fast-moving wheeler-dealer. But Zuckerman beat a hasty retreat from the disco scene in 1980 after witnessing the assassination of a colleague by letter bomb. In the 1980s, he revisited the infants' and children's goods business that had bored him in years past.

Zuckerman transformed himself into one of Canada's highest-flying merger and acquisition artists during the ensuing decade, and his family business emerged as one of the country's fastest-growing enterprises. In 1980, he merged Chantex Inc. with Earl Takefman's Randim Marketing, Inc., a manufacturer and wholesaler of school supplies, to form Charan Industries Inc. By the time Charan went public in 1984 its annual revenues had multiplied fivefold from 1980, to $20 million. The firm's Charan Toy Co., Inc. subsidiary emerged as a leading toy company with a particular emphasis on licensing. In 1985, it held the Canadian rights to nine of the top ten toys in the North American market, including the immensely popular Cabbage Patch Kids name and logo.

Charan employed what analyst Ira Katzin of Prudential-Bache Securities Canada Ltd. (Toronto) called "a very novel approach" to consumer goods branding, an approach that would be carried on when Charan Toy was reborn as Toy Biz. The company was among the first to implement its brands—both licensed and proprietary—very broadly, applying the venerable Cooper hockey equipment brand (acquired in the mid-1980s) to Charan's existing childrenswear line, for example. This strategy would become commonplace throughout the consumer goods and entertainment industries and form a cornerstone of Toy Biz's success in the 1990s.

Pearlmutter Acquisition Reinvigorates Toy Biz

Zuckerman did not see the benefits of these strategies, however, for he sold the toy business in the late 1980s. Charan soon re-emerged as an American-owned company, Toy Biz. In 1990, Toy Biz was acquired by independent investor Isaac Pearlmutter, who installed himself as chairman and brought in Joseph Ahern as chief executive officer. Cost controls, innovative licensing agreements, and fresh toy-designing talent allowed the new management team to ride a rising tide of interest in classic comic book characters during the decade.

Trained as an accountant, Ahern had previously worked to bring toymaker Coleco Industries Inc. out of bankruptcy. Ahern's bottom-line focus was reflected in Toy Biz's low overhead. The company owned no real property, instead leasing a modest headquarters in New York City and an Arizona warehouse. It also limited costs by outsourcing most manufacturing to China and concentrating most of its sales efforts on mass merchandisers. This low overhead structure gave Toy Biz a remarkably low employee-to-sales ratio, generating nearly $2 million in annual revenues for each employee in the mid-1990s.

But low overhead was just one factor in Toy Biz's equation for success. As it had been in the 1980s, licensing continued to be an important element of the company's strategy. But this time Toy Biz forged a singular agreement with Marvel Entertainment Group, best known for its well-established cast of comic book characters. Instead of signing the short-term (one-to five-year) license typical of the industry—an agreement it had previously utilized—in 1990 Toy Biz exchanged 46 percent of its equity for an "exclusive, perpetual, royalty-free license" to Marvel's characters. Toy Biz focused its earliest efforts on just a few of the series' more than 3,500 characters, especially emphasizing Spider-Man and the Uncanny X-Men.

This strategic alliance was mutually beneficial. For Toy Biz, it eliminated royalties that would otherwise have cost the company anywhere from 6 to 12 percent of its sales of Marvel character toys. Marvel's top-ranked comic books and animated television shows amounted to free advertising for the action figures and other playthings marketed by Toy Biz. Harry De Mott, II, an analyst with CS First Boston, told *Forbes'* Suzanne Oliver that "The cartoons are like a half-hour infomercial for Toy Biz products." And Marvel's stake in Toy Biz gave it much higher returns than it would have made from mere royalties.

Toy designer Avi Arad was yet another element of Toy Biz's success. Over the course of his 20-year career, Arad had a hand in the creation of over 160 toys for such major manufacturers as Mattel Inc., Hasbro, Inc., Tyco Toys, Inc., Nintendo, and Sega. Upon joining Toy Biz on a part-time basis in 1993, Arad received

a 10 percent stake in the company in addition to his salary. His 22-person product development staff accounted for about 20 percent of Toy Biz's total employment. As executive producer of animated television programs for Marvel and the creator of toys for Toy Biz, he personally represented the intersection of Marvel and Toy Biz's interests. Arad could, for example, coordinate the launch of characters on television screens and toy store shelves. He specialized in action figures and earned a reputation for combining materials in unique ways. But Arad's creativity wasn't limited to cartoons and action figures; his resume included Baby Bubbles and Roller Blade Baby.

The combination of strict cost controls, an advantageous licensing agreement, and top talent helped Toy Biz achieve the industry's fattest profit margins. Its 24 percent margin topped giant Mattel's profit ratio by over one-fifth in 1995. Furthermore, the Toy Biz/Marvel confederation opened the door to a myriad of other synergistic business opportunities. Marvel Entertainment was just one segment of Ronald O. Perelman's diverse empire, a group that had been launched in 1978 with a $1.9 million bank loan and had by the early 1990s grown to include Revlon Inc., Coleman Worldwide Corporation, Consolidated Cigar Corporation, New World Communications Group, and First Nationwide Bank, among others. Perelman, who was appointed board chairman of Toy Biz in 1995, sought to expand cooperation among his business interests. Toy Biz soon held licenses of a more typical short-term nature for other brands in the Perelman family. The toy company designed and distributed Revlon fashion dolls (à la Barbie) and Coleman toy camping equipment, for example.

Toy Biz also licensed brands from companies outside the Marvel/Perelman universe. Its Hercules and Zena Warrior Princess action figures were based on the MCA/Universal television series shown on many New World television stations. Licensing agreements with Gerber and NASCAR expanded the company's toy-marketing realm to educational playthings for toddlers and racing-related cars, action figures, and computer games. These powerful trademarks commanded higher retail prices than generic toys, and held sway over quality- and brand-conscious parents as much as children. Popular proprietary Toy Biz toys included Baby Tumbles Surprise, Baby So Real, Wild and Wacky Painter, and Battle Builders.

Plans for the Next Century

Toy Biz boasted an impressive arsenal of growth strategies for the years leading up to the turn of the 21st century. At the core of its great potential was the largely-untapped cast of Marvel comic book characters. Noting that the company had started by promoting Marvel's best-known characters, Ahern boasted that "We have only picked the low-hanging fruit." As the marketing cachet of these personalities inevitably waned, Toy Biz looked forward to mining the potential of Captain America, the Fantastic Four, the Incredible Hulk, Ghost Rider, and literally thousands more characters. Early in 1996 the company launched its Classic Heroes candy division, which marketed candy/toy combinations featuring Marvel characters.

Toy Biz also hoped to benefit from the creation of Marvel Films, a production company expected to be launched in 1997. Led by Avi Arad, this new venture would produce both live action and animated films based on Marvel characters, adding yet another head to the Hydra-like entertainment company. Its first project was expected to feature the Incredible Hulk character.

Toy Biz entered what was expected to be the toy industry's second-fastest growing segment, electronic learning aids (ELA), in 1996. The toy company signed a licensing agreement with Apple Computer that year to produce a line of electronic and soft toys with the Apple name and logo. Toy Biz hoped to benefit from Apple's strong presence in educational computers, and Apple hoped that an association with play would cement its position in the hearts and minds of young consumers and future computer buyers. In addition, Toy Biz augmented its position in the industry through the 1995 acquisition of two toy companies, Spectra Star, Inc. and Quest Aerospace Education, Inc. Spectra Star specialized in kites and yo-yos, while Quest made small model rockets. Toy Biz expected acquisitions such as these to fuel continued growth in the late 1990s.

In spite of all these positive factors, continued prosperity was not a foregone conclusion. The toy industry was very competitive, and Toy Biz was a relatively small player in a world dominated by giants like Mattel, Hasbro, and Tyco. Like all its competitors, Toy Biz was subject to the vagaries of consumer tastes. Corporate executives realized that the leading products and characters of 1996 could be the big losers of 1997. But these general concerns paled in comparison with the issues raised by Ronald Perelman's 1996 bid for full control of Toy Biz. This apparently logical move appeared less prudent in light of Marvel Entertainment's financial difficulties mid-decade. Following a loss on the third quarter of 1996, Marvel slashed one-third of its comic book workforce and sought to restructure over $1 billion in debt. Ironically, Linda Sandler of the *Wall Street Journal* characterized the acquisition of Toy Biz as a scheme to boost Marvel's value. Whether Marvel would reciprocate was another question entirely.

Principal Subsidiaries

Toy Biz International Ltd. (Hong Kong).

Further Reading

Benezra, Karen, "Marvel Wants to Be a Movie Mogul," *MEDIA-WEEK,* July 8, 1996, p. 4.

Burke, Dan, "Hitting His Stride," *Canadian Business,* September 1987, pp. 32–43.

Chiang, Christopher, "The X-Men," *Forbes,* April 26, 1993, pp. 18–19.

Fitzgerald, Kate, "Beleaguered Apple Finds Friend in Toyland," *Advertising Age,* February 12, 1996, p. 39.

Liebeck, Laura, "Licensed, Novelty Ideas Abound as Candy Manufacturers Toy with Combo Introductions," *Discount Store News,* March 18, 1996, p. 3F.

Lippman, John, "Perelman's Andrews Group Restructures Bid for Toy Biz Amid Trouble at Marvel," *Wall Street Journal,* November 21, 1996, p. 7B.

McKay, Shone, "Charan Industries," *Canadian Business,* July 1986, pp. 58–59.

Oliver, Suzanne, "A Marvelous Annuity," *Forbes,* November 4, 1996, pp. 178–179.

"Parlaying Strengths in the Toy Field," *Mergers & Acquisitions,* July–August 1993, p. 51.

Ryan, Ken, "Toy Biz Lands 'Apple for Kids,' " *HFN: The Weekly Newspaper for the Home Furnishings Network,* February 19, 1996, p. 92.

Sandler, Linda, "Heard on the Street: Marvel Investors Find the Perils in Perelman's Superhero Plan," *Wall Street Journal,* November 18, 1996, p. 1C.

Schonfeld, Erick, "Spider-Man Spins Gold for Billionaire Perelman," *Fortune,* March 4, 1996, p. 207.

Spiro, Leah Nathans, "The Operator: An Inside Look at Ron Perelman's $5 Billion Empire," *Business Week,* August 21, 1995, pp. 54–60.

Wilensky, Dawn, "Toys Have 'License' to Thrill," *Discount Store News,* February 5, 1996, pp. 27–28.

—April Dougal Gasbarre

Toys "R" Us, Inc.

461 From Road
Paramus, New Jersey 07652
U.S.A.
(201) 262-7800
Fax: (201) 262-8919
Web site: http://www.toysrus.com

Public Company
Founded: 1957
Incorporated: 1978
Employees: 60,000
Sales: $9.4 billion (1996)
Stock Exchanges: New York
SICs: 5641 Children and Infants' Wear Stores; 5945
   Hobby, Toy and Games Shops

With sales near $10 billion, Toys "R" Us, Inc. is the world's leading children's specialty and toy store chain, with over 1,200 outlets in the U.S. and 21 international countries. Comprised of Toys "R" Us, Kids "R" Us, Babies "R" Us, and new superstore formats, Toys "R" Us, Inc. consistently beat both the industry's growth level and its own expectations. Lauded by analysts for decades, Toys "R" Us succeeded by quickly responding to customers' ever-changing demands, initiating a "no questions asked" return policy, and making toy retailing less seasonal. Long a leader in using sophisticated computer systems, Toys "R" Us centralized administrative and buying decisions so, as chairman Charles Lazarus often put it, only the selling was done in the stores.

Toys "R" Us Meets Interstate, 1952–79

Toys "R" Us founder Charles Lazarus was born above a Washington, D.C., shop where his father repaired and sold used bicycles. After a stint in the Army, Lazarus opened the National Baby Shop, a children's furniture store, in 1948, just two years after the beginning of the Baby Boom. Noting that customers often asked if he sold toys, Lazarus began adding rattles and stuffed animals to his stock within a year. In 1952 he opened the Baby Furniture and Toy Supermarket in Washington, D.C.; five years later he opened a discount toy supermarket in Rockville, Maryland, the first to bear the abbreviated Toys "R" Us name (the store's original name wouldn't fit on its sign). By 1965 Lazarus operated four such outlets in the Washington, D.C., area and the next year sold the profitable toy supermarkets to Interstate Stores Inc., but served as president of the company he created.

Founded in 1916, Interstate became publicly owned in 1927. With 46 small department stores in its fold by 1957, sales growth had dwindled to almost nothing, and profit margins were shrinking. The company sought relief for its financial woes in the burgeoning discount store arena by experimenting with a discount store in Allentown, Pennsylvania. By 1960 it had acquired two discount chains: the White Front Stores in southern California and the Topps chain, located mainly in New England.

Interstate undertook an aggressive but ill-fated expansion, overextending itself, and the 1973–74 recession aggravated its problems. In 1974 Interstate declared bankruptcy, its debt at the time the largest accumulation of liabilities in retail history. By that year Interstate had 51 Toys "R" Us stores, and it continued to open new ones during its court-ordered reorganization. Before 1974 Toys "R" Us was still ordering and counting stock manually, but that year the company streamlined its ordering and inventory system by installing its first computer mainframe. In years to come the company would upgrade its computer system many times to keep pace with its ever-growing sales volume and inventory level.

In 1978 Interstate emerged from its reorganization a vastly different company. It had closed or sold all of its discount store operations; only the 63-store toy chain and 10 traditional department stores remained. To reflect its principal business, the company had changed its name to Toys "R" Us, with Lazarus serving as its president and CEO.

Toys "R" Us Takes Off, 1980–85

Lazarus's approach to pricing was vastly different than that of his competitors: he sold the items shoppers wanted most at little or no profit. Customers then automatically assumed most of the store's items were equally well-priced and did the rest of their shopping there. By 1980 Toys "R" Us had earned a solid reputation as a retailer of great efficiency, with 101 stores around the country. Since its reorganization three years earlier, sales had more than doubled to nearly $750 million in fiscal 1981, a year in which many toy sellers suffered, especially during the holiday season.

There seemed to be no serious threat to the company's growing dominance of the retail toy market—with its 120 stores—and executives were often quoted as saying they sought not so much to boost sales as to increase market share, which Toys "R" Us did from 1978's 5 percent to 9 percent in 1981. The following year as rival Lionel Leisure, a chain of 98 toy stores, filed for bankruptcy, Toys "R" Us announced the formation of a new division to sell name-brand children's apparel at discount prices. The company had first-hand experience with the baby boom generation's willingness to spend money on their children and opened two pilot Kids "R" Us stores in the New York metropolitan area during the summer of 1983. The 15,000-square-foot exuberantly decorated stores featured electronic games and clearly marked departments. From the day the first Kids "R" Us stores opened, owners of department and specialty stores recognized them as a major threat to their survival.

All was not easy for Kids "R" Us, however. In the 1980s traditional department stores and small children's shops complained that name-brand apparel makers were selling their goods to discounters; new competition from Kids "R" Us further raised the stakes. Just a few months after Kids "R" Us opened its first two stores, Toys "R" Us filed suit in September 1983 against Federated Department Stores Inc. and General Mills Inc., charging the companies with price-fixing. The following month, the company brought a similar suit against Absorba, which had agreed to supply the new stores, but later allegedly refused to fill the orders. Toys "R" Us later dropped the suits, noting only that circumstances had made it prudent to terminate litigation.

The Kids "R" Us concept successfully implemented many of the policies Toys "R" Us had, such as discount pricing, tight inventory control, purchasing in large volume, and opening stores in low-rent strip malls along major thoroughfares. In 1983 the company surpassed the $1 billion milestone, with sales of $1.3 billion. The following year was full of firsts for Toys "R" Us, beginning with its first foray outside the U.S. in 1984, with four Toys "R" Us stores in Canada and one in Singapore; two more Kids "R" Us stores (with an additional 5,000 square feet) in New Jersey; and a generous stock option plan open to all full-time employees. Lazarus later told *Dun's Business Month*

that salaries alone were no longer enough to make people feel they had a stake in a company's success.

By the spring of 1985 there were 10 Kids "R" Us units in New York and New Jersey with an additional 15 to be opened by year's end, while five Toys "R" Us stores opened in the U.K. By the end of the year Toys "R" Us decided to try a different tack to expand its market share with the launch of *Toys "R" Us Magazine,* sold in its stores for 79¢ each. Aimed at slightly older children, the well-received magazine contained feature stories on animals, celebrities, adventure, and travel, while including ads for television shows, clothes, and toys. A second issue was offered during the summer of 1986, but the magazine was eventually phased out. At the same time the magazine was hitting stores, *Dun's Business Month* cited Toys "R" Us as one of the nation's best-managed companies and credited Lazarus with developing an extraordinary management team (most of whom were promoted from within). Between 1980 and 1985 the toy retailing industry grew 37 percent, while sales at Toys "R" Us surged by 185 percent, leading the company to estimate that it had 14 percent of all U.S. retail toy sales, an increase of 9 percent from the its share just seven years earlier when the company had emerged from its reorganization.

A Burgeoning Empire, 1986–91

Charles Lazarus believed market share was his company's number one priority; to keep increasing market share he was even willing to cut prices—at the expense of earnings. Yet perhaps earnings needn't suffer, because Toys "R" Us had the "ultimate marketing research tool," the company's highly computerized merchandising system. By January 1986 Toys "R" Us had 233 toy stores in the U.S., 13 international stores, 23 Kids "R" Us outlets, and 4 traditional department stores. And as it grew into a national chain, the company aggressively fought others using an "R" in their name—Tots "R" Us, Lamps "R" Us, and Films "R" Us were among the companies successfully sued by Toys "R" Us for name infringement, a practice the company maintained for years to come.

During the summer of 1986 Toys "R" Us and Montgomery Ward announced a joint venture to begin in Gaithersburg, Maryland, that fall. Each store would operate independently, but would share an entrance and exterior sign. The arrangement was a boon to Ward, which had restructured its business and had surplus floor space in many of its locations. Toys "R" Us found the arrangement beneficial, too, since many of the Ward stores were in excellent locations and rental rates were often quite reasonable. During the 1986 Christmas season, the company's sales far exceeded many analysts' grim forecasts. Its success was attributed to its ability to consistently offer the toys shoppers were most interested in buying. By 1987 the company had 37 additional domestic Toys "R" Us stores, 11 new overseas outlets, and 14 new Kids "R" Us stores; its market share now stood at 15 percent of the $12 billion toy industry.

Even when toy sales were sluggish, Toys "R" Us managed to perform well. In another bid to further increase its market share, the company surprised the retailing industry in 1987 by announcing that it would pass on the savings it expected from lower tax rates to customers. Two additional retailers, Wal-Mart and Target, quickly followed the company's lead. This was also the year the Toys "R" Us international division moved into the black, and the company opened four stores in as many German cities. Although there were plans to open even more stores during the year, it proved difficult to secure the required permits for a retail outlet larger than 18,000 square feet. Competing German retailers had good reason for concern; in the U.K. Toys "R" Us had captured 9 percent of the $1.8 billion toy market in just three years. The products of two prestigious German toy manufacturers, Steiff and Maerklin, were not sold in the new German Toys "R" Us stores. Steiff, maker of high-quality stuffed animals and dolls, chose not to do business with the toy giant out of loyalty to smaller-scale German retailers while Maerklin's electric trains, sold without packaging, could not be offered in a toy supermarket setting.

From the very start Toys "R" Us overseas stores were strikingly similar to those in the United States. Most were freestanding buildings, and all bulged with many of the 18,000 items for which Toys "R" Us is famous. Approximately 80 percent of the items offered were the same as those found in U.S. stores, with the remaining 20 percent chosen to reflect local interests. Sales for fiscal 1987, the first year in which Kids "R" Us earned a profit, surpassed the $3 billion mark. The company attributed part of its success to its upgraded universal product code (UPC) scanning system, which had been installed in all the Toys "R" Us stores shortly before Thanksgiving.

By January 1988 the company had 313 U.S. toy stores, 74 Kids "R" Us outlets, and 37 international toy stores. Plans to open stores in Italy and France were also in the offing. In August, Lazarus told the *Wall Street Journal* his goal was to sell half of all toys sold in the United States. While this may have sounded overly ambitious, signs abounded that Lazarus was well on the way to meeting his goal. Even though toy sales in 1986 and 1987 grew an average of 2 percent, sales at Toys "R" Us grew 27 percent during each of those years. The toy chain consistently proved itself capable of turning away all pretenders to the throne of top toy retailer. Its two nearest rivals, Child World Inc., with 152 stores and Lionel, with 78, offered similarly large toy selections in equally cavernous structures, but neither had been able to equal the success of the originator of the toy supermarket concept.

Something else Toys "R" Us had was a healthy sense of humor about itself and the industry, as when a Florida newspaper published a cartoon during the 1987 holiday season showing a couple burdened with many gifts leaving a Toys "R" Us store. The caption beneath the cartoon read "Broke 'R' Us." Company executives thought it was so funny that copies were posted throughout their offices.

The company's success was attributed to many factors, including its buying clout, great selection, deep inventories, and ability to identify the latest hot items and get them on the sales floor fast. When some companies' stores were finding it difficult to get sufficient quantities of Nintendo games in early 1988, for instance, Toys "R" Us was able to get the number of Nintendo games it wanted. It was reported in the *Wall Street Journal* that Toys "R" Us sold $330.80 worth of merchandise per square foot annually, with Child World selling only $221.70, and Lionel just $193.10. Average sales for a Toys "R" Us store

were $8.4 million; Child World, $4.9 million; and for Lionel, $4.4 million.

In the fall of '88 Toys "R" Us shed the last reminder of its connection to Interstate Stores by selling the remaining department stores in Albany and Schenectady, New York, and Flint, Michigan, to that division's management. Company sales hit the $4 billion mark in fiscal year 1988, and by the fall of the following year Toys "R" Us joined McDonald's Company (Japan) Ltd. to open several toy stores in Japan. Toys "R" Us would have an 80 percent interest in the venture to McDonald's 20 percent with an option to open restaurants at the store sites. During the holiday season in 1989, Toys "R" Us launched Geoffrey's Fun Club as a low-key, noncommercial club sending quarterly mailings featuring items such as an activity booklet with a family member's name or a storybook that presented a family child as the main character, with his or her name repeated throughout the book. The club, designed to boost the company's profile in members' homes, more than doubled original membership projections. Total sales for the year were more than $4.7 billion, with a 25 percent market share of the $13 billion U.S. retail toy market.

Lazarus told *Forbes* there would always be "room in this tightly controlled company for innovations to further decrease operating costs." An instance of this came in 1989 when Toys "R" Us completed installation of gravity-feed-flow racks in most of its U.S. toy stores for restocking fast-moving items like diapers and formula. Yet as every rose has its thorns, Toys "R" Us ran into some trouble in the early part of the 1990s. First came difficulties with the Consumer Product Safety Commission for importing toys it deemed dangerous. In the spring of 1990 the company recalled 38,000 "Press N Roll" toy boats with small parts that, if broken off, could choke a child. A few months later, Toys "R" Us was named as one of seven distributors sued by the Justice Department on charges of selling hazardous toys (including a xylophone painted with lead-based paint, and the aforementioned toys with unsafe, small parts). Yet Toys "R" Us successfully defended itself on the grounds that its safety record was excellent, and a federal judge dismissed the charges.

By the end of 1990 the company had a new $40 million distribution center in Rialto, California, that held 45 percent more merchandise than the company's other warehouses, but took up one-third less land. The company finished the year with sales topping $5.5 billion and net earnings reaching $326 million. An industry analyst, impressed by the company's solid sales and consistency, remarked to the *Wall Street Transcript*, "I can look at a slowing economy and still feel comfortable that Toys "R" Us is going to grow." And grow it did, especially overseas. Although difficulties in finding store sites and circumventing the large-scale retail law still loomed before Toys "R" Us and McDonald's, the Japanese joint venture moved ahead with plans for up to 100 stores by the end of the decade. For other U.S. retailers interested in opening outlets in Japan, Toys "R" Us became a test case in how to overcome local retailers' resistance. Japanese retailers had already felt the pinch of a declining birth rate since 1973 and didn't relish a further erosion of their market share. U.S. officials, however, persuaded Japanese officials to speed up their approval process on applications for large retail stores, and the first Toys "R" Us opened in Ami Town on the outskirts of Tokyo in 1991.

Superstores and Beyond, 1992 to 2000

Over the next few years, Toys "R" Us continued to expand in high gear, especially overseas. Once operating in a handful of countries worldwide, company stores now popped up all over the globe, in Hong Kong, Israel, the Netherlands, Portugal, Scandinavia, Sweden, and Turkey, while the heaviest concentrations were in Australia, Canada, France, Germany, Japan, Spain, and the U.K. Consequently, Toys "R" Us's annual figures reflected this steady growth: fiscal 1992 sales reached $7.2 billion; 1993, $7.9 billion; and a big leap in 1994 to $8.7 billion. Similarly, earnings climbed from 1992's $438 million to 1994's $532 million. In early 1994, there was also a changing of the guard: Charles Lazarus, the company's longtime chairman and CEO, turned the duties of the latter over to Michael Goldstein, vice chairman; and Robert Nakasone, formerly president of worldwide stores, was appointed president and COO.

In 1995 the company's sales once again soared to $9.4 billion (helped in part by the introduction of educational and entertaining computer software), yet earnings were heavily slashed ($148 million) due to restructuring costs and grand plans for the near future. As Toys "R" Us looked to the turn of the century, the company was determined to become the ultimate "one-stop kid's shop." To further this plan, the company adopted several ambitious programs to take Toys "R" Us to the end of the 1990s and beyond. First and foremost was restructuring, which included streamlining merchandise by up to 20 percent, closure of 25 underperforming stores, and the consolidation of several distribution centers and administrative facilities domestically and overseas. In addition, there would be new Kids "R" Us stores, the debut of Babies "R" Us and superstores, and the introduction of "Concept 2000," for new and renovated Toys "R" Us stores—all to provide "the ultimate kids shopping experience."

The first three Babies "R" Us stores, each measuring about 45,000 square feet, opened in 1996 with an additional seven planned before the end of the year. Like its siblings, Babies "R" Us stores were filled to the brim—with clothes, juvenile furniture, carseats, and feeding and infant care supplies. And like better department stores, Babies "R" Us also offered a computerized national gift registry. At the same time, the first Concept 2000 toy store, one of 12 announced for the year,

debuted in July. The Concept 2000 facility was a megastore of 96,000 square feet, replacing the formerly successful supermarket set up with an oval format with color-coordinated departments, lower shelving, a Bike Shop, learning centers, and special sections for Barbies, Legos, and video games.

Moreover, the company also introduced experimental superstores (the first one, Toys "R" Us Kids World, opened in November 1996 near company headquarters in New Jersey) combining the inventories of Kids "R" Us and Babies "R" Us with a multitude of top-of-the-line toys. Superstores were slated to carry fast food (similar to Wal-Mart's deal with McDonald's), candy shops, hair salons, photo studios, party rooms, possibly even rides like carousels and Ferris wheels. Two other superstores, one in Nyack, New York, and another in Fairfax, Virginia, were scheduled to open before the end of the year. With dozens of Toys "R" Us-inspired stores opening in the U.S. and around the world, the company's domination of the marketplace seemed assured. Yet with upstart chains like Zany Brainy and Imaginarium staking their claim, the future of toy-related merchandise rested firmly in the smallest of hands and most fickle of minds—children.

Principal Subsidiaries

Toys "R" Us; Toys "R" Us International; Toys "R" Us Kids World; Kids "R" Us; Babies "R" Us.

Further Reading

Barmash, Isadore, "Gains in Retail Discounting: Interstate's Story of Growth," *New York Times,* July 23, 1967.

Carmody, Dennis P., "New Jersey-Based Toys 'R' Us to Open Kids-World," *Knight-Ridder/Tribune Business News,* November 16, 1996.

Gilman, Hank, "Retail Genius: Founder Lazarus Is a Reason Toys 'R' Us Dominates Its Industry," *The Wall Street Journal,* November 21, 1985.

Halverson, Richard, "KidsWorld to Strengthen Market Position," *Discount Store News,* May 20, 1996, p. 1.

Neff, Robert, "Guess Who's Selling Barbies in Japan Now?," *Business Week,* December 9, 1991, p. 72.

Rosen, M. Daniel, "Toys 'R' Us: Taking Toys to the Top," *Solutions,* March/April 1988.

Solomon, Goody L., "Discount Toy Stores Gladden the Hearts of Toddlers and Merchants," *Barron's,* August 11, 1969.

—Sue Mohnke
—updated by Taryn Benbow-Pfalzgraf

TRM Copy Centers Corporation

5208 Northeast 122nd Ave.
Portland, Oregon 97230-1074
U.S.A.
(503) 257-8766
Fax: (503) 251-5473

Public Company
Incorporated: 1981 as TRM Copy Centers Corporation
Employees: 570
Sales: $67.5 million (1996)
Stock Exchanges: NASDAQ
SICs: 7334 Photocopying & Duplicating Services

TRM Copy Centers Corporation is the top supplier of self-service photocopying worldwide. Through its ownership of over 32,000 "copy centers," located within a wide variety of retail establishments ranging from hardware stores and pharmacies to gift shops and office supply stores, TRM services consumers in 66 metropolitan areas within the United States, Canada, France, and the United Kingdom. Identified by a prominently displayed, eye-catching trapezoidal yellow logo emblazoned with the company's initials, each TRM copy center is an ultra-efficient operation: A self-service photocopy machine, machine stand, and signs advertising its location within its host retailer are its only requirements, while TRM field service personnel monitor usage, maintain supply levels, and handle upkeep of the machines. Engaging in a symbiotic relationship with the small-scale retail establishments in which its copy centers are located, TRM pays its hosts a 24 percent cut of gross revenues. In exchange for paying TRM a monthly "location" fee for each copy center housed in its place of business, retailers are able to enhance their offerings to customers and increase traffic through their stores.

In recent years TRM has begun to expand upon its basic service of providing black-and-white photocopying. By 1995 it could boast over 400 full-color copy centers, many of which also included company-designed BisCard machines that provided design-your-own business card services to entrepreneur-ial-minded customers. Company copy centers, which charge anywhere between 3 to 10 cents per copy in the United States (depending on location), remain a bargain for consumers desiring quick, low-cost basic duplicating services.

Company Founded on Friendship in 1981

In 1981, then nineteen-year-old Matthew J. Shawcross and two other friends combined their initials over a good idea and launched TRM. Using surplus used copy machines from their existing copier sales business, Shawcross and associates started their fledgling 5-cents-a-copy photocopying business out of an office in Portland.

The company was organized around a simple contract. Under a joint agreement between TRM and the owner of each of its host retail locations, the company received a fee of $95.00 for each used, reconditioned copy machine it installed. In exchange, TRM agreed to repair and stock its machines, retaining only a percentage of the standard 5 cents per copy that it charged consumers. The first installations, which occurred in the greater Portland area, were relatively easy to keep stocked with paper and toner, and repairs were handled through arrangements with local service technicians. However, what was simple on a small scale became unwieldy as the company began to grow.

By 1984, with 100 copy machines installed in small retail locations throughout Oregon, the tiny company was floundering. Edwin S. Chan, a Chinese immigrant who had just ended a 27-year career as manager of over 80 branches of Copeland Lumber Yards, Inc., took the reins of management at the struggling TRM. "I had been managing a $100 million business," Chan would tell Dori Jones Yang of *Business Week*," and now I had to make money a nickel at a time." Foregoing a salary for the first six months in lieu of an increasing share of company equity, Chan successfully introduced several efficiency and cost-saving measures, including an automated billing system and an in-house copier repair service. Within four years Chan had turned TRM around; the once-flailing company was now experiencing an annual growth rate of 30 percent. By the end of 1988 net income was posted as $615,000 on sales of $5.9 million. At 5 cents per copy, this translated into over 118 million copies made at the company's 3,550 copy centers, totalling 236,000 reams of paper.

Expands into the 1990s

By the beginning of 1990, with the previous year's sales cresting at $10 million, Chan had already set TRM on a course down the road to major expansion. The company's steadily increasing sales volume allowed it to purchase paper, toner, and other supplies in bulk, thus benefitting from price discounts and further increasing the profitability of each sale. And by relying on a streamlined "fleet" of just two standard copier models, TRM was able to cut the cost of machine repairs by stockpiling spare parts. This homogeneity also allowed the company's repairmen to carry the most commonly used replacement parts with them when responding to service calls for individual machines. The company's increasingly centralized management and more standardized operations also minimized overhead costs. By the close of fiscal 1990, with the number of copy centers now standing at 8,307, TRM's earnings had almost doubled from the previous year's level, rising to $1 million.

In the fall of 1991 TRM opened its first copy center in English-speaking Canada; it would soon enter Quebec as well. Chan was also busy laying the groundwork for expanding TRM's markets across the Atlantic, where the company's bright yellow logo would become a familiar site in London beginning in mid-1992. And the company continued to increase the number of individual copy centers in its core domestic markets as well. Even with the increasing sales that these expansion efforts would generate, TRM's biggest stride forward was yet to come. In November 1991 the company finally made the decision to go public, offering 1.8 million shares on the NASDAQ National Market System. This stock offering raised $13.8 million worth of funding and debt reduction for the growing company, which TRM augmented during the remainder of fiscal 1991 with profits from its 11,382 copy centers in 26 metropolitan areas worldwide. By the end of fiscal 1992 TRM would post net income of $2.7 million on sales of $30.5 million. In the eight years since Chan had taken command, the copy company had grown an amazing 500 percent.

TRM Goes Color, 1992

In 1992, now with 14,000 copiers installed in 34 cities throughout North America alone, the company began to introduce color copiers in certain of its locations. By September of that year 80 color photocopy machines were available to con-

sumers in test-market cities in Oregon, Arizona, and Washington; customers were charged 39 cents a piece for full-color copies. The company also signed buying agreements with photocopy manufacturer Ricoh that enabled it to receive favorable discounts on supplies and repair parts; it would do the same with Mita in 1993.

While the company realized that its entry into the European market would require a period of adaptation to a different environment and time to acquire the requisite goodwill needed to grow sales, by August 1993 TRM had established 860 copy "centres" in London alone. In addition, plans were underway to expand northward into the industrial city of Manchester. Although management acknowledged the increased expense incurred by foreign expansion, it viewed its first overseas venture as a learning experience. Future expansion operations, both overseas and domestically, would be increasingly streamlined, with a satellite system of new copy centers receiving initial technical and managerial support from profitable, more established operations.

Meanwhile, on its own shores, the company had expanded its full-color copy centers to 298, and customer enthusiasm for this new service would continue to expand that number. 1993 also witnessed the creation of BisCard Corporation, a TRM subsidiary dedicated to developing new, business-oriented products. The BisCard self-service, design-and-print business card venture was test-marketed in 50 kiosks located throughout Portland during 1993. By year end, with expansion of both locations and product, the company employed a total staff of 365 men and women to oversee its copy centers and kiosks and manage its corporate affairs. Together, these employees helped to earn TRM sales of $38.8 million, which resulted in 1993 net income of $3.3 million.

Competition at Home, Expansion Abroad, Cut into 1994 Profits

The year 1994 would witness the first copy centers to appear on the European continent, as the yellow TRM logo became visible in various retail locations throughout northern Paris. Total copy centers now numbered 25,563 scattered over 50 metropolitan areas, the vast majority still in the United States. While company growth continued, it slowed relative to previous years, a result both of increased competition by new local vendors within TRM's core market and the disproportionate expenses associated with TRM's continuing expansion overseas. While 1994 sales in Europe increased more than 500 percent over the previous fiscal year, continental copy centres did not begin to outstep their associated costs and turn a profit until the end of the second quarter in December. By the following June—the end of fiscal 1994—the company posted sales of $47.9 million.

Despite an increasingly competitive retail environment, between 1991 and the final quarter of 1994 TRM had managed to successfully expand its network of copy centers from 26 to 41 urban areas in the United States alone. The introduction, as well, of three Canadian cities and six European metropolitan areas would result in a company presence that generated combined sales of $43.7 million in North America compared with just over $4.2 million in Europe, where the United Kingdom remained home to the majority of the company's copy center outlets.

Paper Prices Mask Rising Sales Base

Notwithstanding a dramatic worldwide increase in paper prices, 1995 would be a banner year for TRM. On the strength of its 570 employees, the company posted sales of $60.5 million, complemented by a jump in net income from $3.3 million to $3.7 million from the previous year. The company now maintained 43 service areas in the United States, three in Canada, seven in the United Kingdom, and one in France, encompassing 28,995 individual copy centers. Of these, the TRM copy centers scattered throughout the United States accounted for 80 percent of the company's total annual revenue.

In 1995 Chan would retire as president and CEO of TRM. He was replaced by Michael D. Simon, a former vice-president of Sequent Computer Systems. This changing of the guard signaled a reorganization within the ranks of the company's middle management and a renewed commitment to upgrading skills and reevaluating key operational areas. In addition to improving profitability and continuing its policy of aggressive expansion, TRM also looked to broaden its business by finding new ways to cater to its small host retailers.

The increasing automation of company systems that had been underway since Chan's first year as CEO now began to reap dividends in more ways than through heightened efficiency. From the data generated by its centralized computer system, company analysts were now able to calculate the price elasticity of various market areas throughout the world, resulting in price changes at 25 percent of TRM's copy center locations. Poorly performing machines were relocated to areas that indicated potentially higher volumes. And the servicing strategy for each of the company's photocopy machines changed from an "on-call" policy to scheduled servicing by field technicians, thereby enhancing timely maintenance, customer satisfaction, and the most cost-effective use of each technician through reduced drive-time to each service site.

Looking Ahead

By the close of fiscal 1996, TRM maintained over 32,000 copy centers worldwide and a field service network of 400 employees. With year-end net income of $4.1 million on sales of $67.5 million, the company was still burdened by the inflated costs of paper on the world market. But significant growth of its European locations—by year-end, a total of 6,552 company-owned photocopy machines were placed throughout the United Kingdom and France—and TRM's continued pricing adjustments to its domestic copy centers allowed for an 11.5 percent rise in net income over the previous year.

In the future, as in the past, TRM has anticipated a strategy focusing on the search for ways to increase operational efficiency, leverage its ever-increasing buying power, and expand its core markets in North America. 1996 marked the beginning of company-wide efforts to integrate its field service and field sales operations; TRM's new "service selling" program would provide an incentive for each service technician to promote the TRM program to retailers within his or her service areas. In addition, the company began to investigate its market potential within both larger retail chains and through stand-alone service centers. Expanding its operations throughout Europe remained another priority: by company estimates, despite the higher costs of consumables like paper, toner, and photocopier parts, the European market had the potential to be even more expansive than the U.S. market. And for TRM, expansion has always translated into profits.

Future growth was expected to continue to come from expanding not only markets, but consumer services as well. While products not related to the company's basic service of black and white photoduplication generated less than 5 percent of total sales, TRM continued to experiment with these offerings. An expanded use of color copy machines was planned. Enhanced software and an increase in user-friendly features contributed to the rising success of the BisCard kiosk network—350 sites in 1996—and prompted the planned installation of another 150 in 1997. Other product enhancements, including coin-operated machines and an electric receipt printer that makes stepped pricing (i.e., copy #1 for 10 cents, copies 2–10 for 7 cents, and so on) possible were planned for test-marketing in 1997. These enhancements were seen by management as a means to gain a winning edge in an increasingly competitive, single-price market where TRM was still the leader.

Principal Subsidiaries

BisCard Corporation.

Further Reading

Yang, Dori Jones, "TRM Makes Millions—A Nickel at a Time," *Business Week*, June 1, 1992.

—Pamela L. Shelton

Tuesday Morning Corporation

14621 Inwood Road
Dallas, Texas 75244
U.S.A.
(214) 387-3562
Fax: (214) 387-2344
Web site: http://www.tuesdaymorning.com

Public Company
Incorporated: 1974
Employees: 2,700
Sales: $210 million (1995)
Stock Exchanges: NASDAQ
SICs: 5331 Variety Stores

In spite of its name, Tuesday Morning Corporation does not always open its stores on Tuesday mornings. For about half the year the stores are closed entirely. During its four annual "sales events," which cover the peak shopping seasons, most of the company's stores are open seven days a week. Tuesday Morning sells upscale items at deeply discounted prices. Its merchandise, which the company describes as "first-quality, famous-maker giftware," generally goes for 50 to 80 percent below original retail prices. The company keeps its overhead costs in check by locking its doors during off-peak times of the year, and also by maintaining a no-frills atmosphere in its stores.

Launched in 1970s as Upscale Garage Sale

The name and concept for Tuesday Morning came from company founder, chairman, and chief executive officer Lloyd Ross. He came upon the idea for a part-year store while working for Rathcon, Inc., a manufacturer and importer of gift merchandise, in the early 1970s. Ross noticed that manufacturers had no reliable way to dispose of their surpluses of high-end inventory. He began purchasing excess merchandise from top-name manufacturers and selling it to department and specialty stores at a nice profit. The process worked so well that Ross decided to try selling a variety of products at what amounted to a single gigantic garage sale in a rented warehouse in north Dallas. The

sale was a huge success, and it left no doubt in Ross's mind that there was a place in the retail world for an operation specializing in upscale closeout items. Naming the company was easy. Ross had wanted to run a company named after a day of the week ever since he was a teenager delivering copies of the *Saturday Evening Post*. He picked Tuesday because in his opinion, "Tuesday morning is the first positive day of the week," according to company press materials.

Soon after the initial success of his concept, Ross settled on the four-sales-a-year schedule. The sales quickly gained a loyal following. In addition to offering prestigious items at low prices, limiting the time during which they were available created a sense of anticipation and excitement for many customers. For its first several years, the company continued to operate out of temporary locations, such as vacant supermarkets or warehouses. New employees were hired for each season. Before long, however, a core group of returning sales personnel made up the bulk of the staff. Tuesday Morning soon began to expand geographically, primarily in the South and West. Eventually the company settled into permanent locations. Tuesday Morning management, however, avoided locating their stores in the posh malls of the well known department stores that often sold the same merchandise for twice the price. Tuesday Morning stores have always been no-frills operations, relying on the merchandise rather than decoration to create their atmosphere. The typical Tuesday Morning customer was an upper middle-class woman who might otherwise shop at a place like Nieman-Marcus. Many of those women, purportedly, transferred their Tuesday Morning purchases into big-name department store boxes when they got home.

Profitable Throughout 1980s

Tuesday Morning went public in 1984, and by the following year there were 56 stores in the chain, generating sales of about $37 million. Sales events were handled by 1,400 part-time workers as well as 60 administrative personnel at company headquarters and 110 warehouse employees. Meanwhile, certain company policies kept Tuesday Morning on good terms with the manufacturers of their merchandise and even with the department stores that it was undercutting. Tuesday Morning generally did not include manufacturers' names in its advertising since some manufacturers felt that association with a discount chain devalued their products. If a brand name was used in an ad, it was only with the manufacturer's explicit permission. If a competing department store became upset about a markdown on a product it was still carrying, Tuesday Morning would usually take it off the shelves.

Tuesday Morning's sales and profits grew each year for the rest of the 1980s, with the exception of 1988, when earnings were held in check by a temporary increase in expenses, including the construction of a new warehouse. By 1987 there were 81 large, no-frills Tuesday Morning outlets operating in 16 states, still mostly in the South. To keep rental costs low, the company continued to locate its stores mainly in strip malls in outer ring suburbs, rather than in indoor malls or city centers. Labor costs also remained low since each store had only one permanent full-time employee, the store manager. The chain's army of part-timers were mainly housewives, who were often motivated by the opportunity to get first crack at the closeout merchandise offered at each sales event, not to mention a 20 percent discount. In 1987 the company earned $3.7 million on revenue of $66 million.

Company sales passed the $100 million mark in 1990. By the following year there were 132 stores in the Tuesday Morning chain, with locations in 21 states. Though still primarily a force in the South and Southeast, there were eight Tuesday Morning outlets in Chicago and ten in the Washington, D.C. area by this time. One of the company's strengths continued to be the loyalty of its employees. This applied not only to returning sales personnel, but to the company's growing permanent staff as well. As of 1991, ten percent of Tuesday Morning's store managers had been with the company for more than ten years, and 400 salespeople had worked there for at least five years. As the company's reputation in the retail industry grew, buying became easier as well, since manufacturers now came to Tuesday Morning with their closeout items rather than the company having to seek out bargain merchandise. Since Tuesday Morning was able to maintain high quality standards for the merchandise it sold, the stigma attached to having products sold by a deep discounter was no longer as powerful.

As the Tuesday Morning chain continued to grow, its methods became more sophisticated. Although it still relied heavily on word of mouth to generate new customers, the company also compiled a mailing list containing two million names. Attractive, four-color brochures were sent to customers on the list just before the beginning of each sales event. An experiment in television advertising a few years earlier had proven to be almost too successful. Stores in the markets targeted by the ads were cleaned out of merchandise almost immediately. New TV and radio campaigns were more carefully prepared for. Most ads featured the company's tag line, ''Gifts. 50% to 80% off everything. It's true and it's guaranteed.'' Tuesday Morning also experimented with a phone-order catalog, which was initially sent to a 170,000-name subset of its regular mailing list. In addition, the company's distribution center in North Dallas was equipped with cutting edge computer equipment, which allowed for instantaneous communications between stores, warehouse, and trucks. Unlike its stores, Tuesday Morning's distribution center was active 12 months a year.

New Technology in the 1990s

Explosive growth made it necessary to completely refurbish the company's warehouse technology during the early 1990s. Prior to the upgrade, the company had relied on sheer manpower—in the form of 400 extra employees—to handle the crush of work during peak periods. Merchandise was arriving at the company's lone warehouse in such quantities that tracking it was becoming next to impossible. By 1992 the warehouse system was in utter disarray. The transition began early in 1993, when Tuesday Morning president and chief operating officer Jerry Smith moved his office into the warehouse facility in order to observe the process more closely.

After months of examination, suggestions, planning, and design, a new computer system was unveiled in February 1994. The new system employed such up-to-date gadgetry as hand-held scanners, point-of-sale terminals, and radio frequency technology. It was now possible to locate a single specific box from among the tens of thousands of items in the system at any given time with pinpoint accuracy. With the new tracking system, which included an innovative software package called ''DC Wizard,'' worker productivity improved threefold. The system allowed Tuesday Morning's warehouse to handle up to 450,000 pieces worth $1 million per day with only 135 people, compared to the 500 people it took to process just $650,000 worth of merchandise using the old system. Once employee training was completed, the need for temporary help during peak periods, and the massive cost associated with it, was reduced dramatically. After incurring a $1.1 million loss in 1993, the first losing year in the company's history, Tuesday Morning earned $2.7 million in 1994. Company management was quick to credit the turnaround to the technological overhaul, which was completed two years ahead of schedule. For 1994 the company reported sales of about $190 million.

By 1995 the Tuesday Morning mailing list contained over three million names, and the number of stores in the chain was approaching 250. That year, sales passed the $200 million mark, and the chain's geographical range covered 31 states. There were 271 Tuesday Morning stores in operation by the middle of 1996. Amazingly, no serious competitor selling as prestigious merchandise at as deep discounts has emerged in the twenty-plus years since Tuesday Morning was established. Now that the chain is truly national in scope, it would be difficult for such a competitor to establish a foothold in the market. Until one does, Tuesday Morning seems to have a lock on those customers who still enjoy hunting for a bargain as long as their quarry sports a brand name label that they are not ashamed to display in their homes.

Principal Subsidiaries

Friday Morning, Inc.; Tuesday Morning, Inc.; TMI Holdings, Inc.; TMIL Corporation.

Further Reading

Chanil, Debra, "The Last Great Treasure Hunt," *Discount Merchandiser,* October 1995, pp. 42–44.

Fisher, Christy, "New TV Ads to Dawn for Tuesday Morning," *Advertising Age,* February 20, 1989, p. 67.

——,"If It's Tuesday Morning, The Store May Be Open," *Advertising Age,* January 29, 1990, p. S2.

Hall, Cheryl, "Controlled Chaos," *Dallas Morning News,* August 13, 1995, pp. 1H–2H.

Helliker, Kevin, "If There's Hardly Anything Left to Buy, It's Tuesday Morning on Christmas Eve," *Wall Street Journal,* December 23, 1991, p. B1.

Keefe, Lisa M., "Keep the Customers Waiting," *Forbes,* September 21, 1987, p. 74.

Mayer, Caroline E., "If It's Tuesday, This Must Be a Sale," *Washington Post,* November 19, 1984, p. 9.

Slom, Stanley, "Tuesday Morning Sells 185 Mornings," *Chain Store Age,* April 1991, pp. 26–28.

——,"Tuesday Morning DC Set for Expansion," *Chain Store Age,* May 1991, pp. 232–234.

——,"Less is More," *Stores,* January 1992, pp. 134–136.

Swisher, Kara, "Tuesday Morning, With Discounts Almost Daily," *Washington Post,* February 21, 1991, p. C10.

"Tuesday Morning Upgrade Raises Productivity," *Chain Store Age,* March 1996, pp. 36–37.

Wojahn, Ellen, "Closed for Business," *Inc.,* April 1985, p. 118.

—Robert R. Jacobson

BIG NAMES. LITTLE PRICES. GUARANTEED.℠

Ultimate Electronics, Inc.

321A West 84th Avenue
Thornton, Colorado 80221
U.S.A.
(303) 412-2500
Fax: (303) 412-2502

Public Company
Incorporated: 1968 as Pearse Electronics, Inc.
Employees: 1,307
Sales: $251.8 million (1996)
Stock Exchanges: NASDAQ
SICs: 5731 Radio, Television & Consumer Electronics
Stores; 5734 Computer & Computer Software Stores;
5735 Record & Prerecorded Tape Stores; 5999
Miscellaneous Retail Stores, Not Elsewhere Classified

Ultimate Electronics, Inc. is a leading specialty retailer of home entertainment and consumer electronics, mostly in the Rocky Mountain region. At the end of 1995 the company was operating 18 stores, including nine in Colorado under the trade name SoundTrack. Between the fall of 1993 and the spring of 1996 Ultimate Electronics opened nine large-format stores and relocated and expanded two others. It nearly tripled its sales during 1994 and 1995.

Pearse Electronics, 1968–93

Ultimate Electronics was founded by William Pearse, a business administration graduate of Western Michigan University, and his wife, Barbara. William Pearse was working as a management trainee at the Gates Rubber Co. before he and Barbara started a Team Electronics audio/video franchise store in Arvada, Colorado—a suburb of Denver—in 1968, with $15,000 in personal funds. This franchise was abandoned in 1974, when the retail business was renamed SoundTrack. The second SoundTrack opened in Denver in 1976. During the 1980s six more SoundTrack stores were opened in the Denver area and Colorado's Front Range: in Aurora (1983), Littleton (1984), Boulder and Thornton (1985), a second Littleton store

(1986), and Colorado Springs (1989). A Fort Collins store opened in 1990. Audio-related equipment was SoundTrack's core business at this time.

The SoundTrack chain grew not only by the establishment of new stores but by the expansion of existing ones and the number of products each location carried. Pearse believed his employees, about 70 percent of whom were paid through incentive compensation, could make their own decisions and direct their own efforts without much supervision; consequently, he kept down overhead by maintaining a management team of only four. All store managers were promoted from within the company. Customer service was given the highest priority: one of the company's top executives told a reporter, "The customer will generally get through [on the telephone] quicker than you would."

Pearse Electronics was willing to spend on advertising, however, publicizing SoundTrack through humorous commercials intended to distinguish the chain from such hard-sell, price-oriented rivals as Best Buy and Fred Schmid. In 1990 the company's ads featured a hippopotamus. The following year it introduced a spokesperson/ventriloquist named Taylor Mason and his puppet, Romeo, who wore different costumes, such as a white jump suit for an Elvis Presley spoof. Interviewed in the *Denver Post,* an ad-agency executive handling the SoundTrack account said, "Everybody is saying they have the lowest prices in town, so after a while there's a believability gap. We're having more fun and getting across a very competitive message as well."

Pearse Electronics had net sales of $53.7 million in fiscal 1992 (the year ended January 31, 1992) and net income of $1 million. In fiscal 1993 sales and income increased to $62.6 million and $2.1 million, respectively. The company changed its name to Ultimate Electronics in August 1993 and went public in October 1993, raising nearly $16 million by selling a minority of its common stock at $8.50 a share. The Pearse family, formerly the sole owner, retained about 60 percent of the company stock after the offering, and William Pearse continued to head the company as chairman and chief executive officer. The company said it planned to use the net proceeds of the offering to finance expansion into new markets. At this time SoundTrack was specializing in middle-market-to-upscale stereo equipment, television sets, and videocassette recorders and had about 375 employees.

Ultimate Electronics, 1993–96

In the fall of 1993 two new stores opened under the Ultimate Electronics name, in Salt Lake City and Orem, Utah—the first company outlets outside Colorado. These were also the company's largest, with about 19,000 square feet in selling space, compared to between 8,000 and 17,000 square feet for the earlier ones. One advantage of locating in Utah was that the market was yet untouched by huge retailers like Best Buy and Circuit City, although Ultimate's company president pointed out "there are lots of aggressive independents with low costs that can put products out there at low prices."

As part of a new strategy, the Ultimate Electronics stores expanded the home-office and television selections found in the SoundTrack stores. They added 100 to 200 CD-ROM titles and selections from the Top 100–selling personal-computer software titles and gave increased emphasis to PC accessories. The PC lineup was increased from four to five lines, including Packard Bell and Compaq, and from 10 to 15 models. Facsimile-machine offerings were boosted from 10 to 15 models, including products from Brother International, Murata, Panasonic, and Sharp. The number of direct-view television sets up to 40 inches was expanded from 100 to 200 models, and a big-screen viewing room had a selection of 35 rear-projection sets starting at 40 inches. Each store had two home-theater rooms packed with audio/visual receivers, speakers, and other products as well as television sets, and two cars placed on the showroom floors to display car-stereo products.

Instant acceptance in Utah enabled Ultimate Electronics to end the fiscal year with net income of $3.4 million on net sales of $88.2 million. In September 1994 the company closed its Denver SoundTrack store and opened a 31,000-square-foot superstore in the city in what had been the Century 21 movie theater. It featured 200 television sets 32 inches or smaller, 40 large-screen projection televisions, a $50,000 home-entertainment system with theater seats, and an automobile displaying a dashboard-mounted TV monitor.

During 1994 Ultimate Electronics opened new stores in Murray, Utah; Albuquerque, New Mexico; and Las Vegas, Nevada. In 1995 it opened stores in Layton, Utah; Boise, Idaho; Tulsa, Oklahoma; and a second one in Las Vegas. The new stores typically incorporated five separate audio demonstration rooms, three car-stereo demonstration rooms, two demonstration cars fully equipped with the latest in mobile electronics, two to three home-theater rooms, and a wide selection of television sets, with particular emphasis on big-screen televisions. Wall-unit furniture was among the product categories added.

Opened Thanksgiving Day, 1995, the 51,700-square-foot, $4-million Tulsa location was Ultimate Electronics' biggest one yet. It had four auto sound rooms, five home-theater rooms, and at least 45 big-screen TVs. An in-house service department accommodated all products sold by Ultimate except computers (covered by a third-party service contract) and included repairs either under warranty or out of warranty.

During 1995 and 1996 Ultimate Electronics moved its two warehouses near Stapleton International Airport, its Wheat Ridge administrative offices, and its Thornton store to the abandoned 28-acre site of a former Thornton drive-in theater. Here the company built a 285,000-square-foot, $15-million complex, including a new headquarters and distribution warehouse, a service center, and a 40,300-square-foot retail superstore. The latter, which opened in April 1996, had five audio demonstration rooms, three home theaters, two cars on the showroom floor displaying the latest in mobile-audio technology, and a children's play area named "Kid City."

For the Colorado Rockies, the expansion major-league baseball team that began playing in Denver in 1993, Ultimate Electronics sponsored an advertising display in the ballpark and player appearances. Popular manager Don Baylor became a spokesperson for the chain. In 1995, and again in 1996, the company ran commercial spots of Baylor to promote its Mitsubishi television products.

Ultimate Electronics' sales increased to $165.1 million in fiscal 1995 and to $251.8 million in fiscal 1996. Net income—a record $4.9 million in 1995—dropped to $2.8 million, but this partly reflected a charge of nearly $1 million due to a change in the accounting method for preopening expenses. A decrease of comparable-store sales of two percent in fiscal 1996 compared to a 29-percent gain for such stores in fiscal 1995 was attributed to a sluggish retail environment, increased competition in the company's markets, and the opening of new stores within markets the company already served. Ultimate Electronics expected to relocate and expand five or six of its Colorado stores in 1996 and 1997 and to open one to three new stores outside Colorado.

Ultimate Electronics adopted a shareholder-rights plan in 1995 to discourage the possibility of a hostile takeover. The Pearse family owned about 46 percent of the stock in 1995. Long-term debt, chiefly to finance expansion, grew from $3.3 million at the end of fiscal 1994 to $33.7 million at the end of fiscal 1996.

Ultimate Electronics in 1995

During 1995 Ultimate Electronics was offering more than 6,000 stock-keeping units (SKUs) representing about 200 brand names, thereby carrying, it claimed, a larger selection of full-featured, high-quality products than was generally available at its competitors. Its store format emphasized mid-to-upscale products, with displays allowing customers to make extensive side-by-side product comparisons. The company also emphasized competitive pricing and offered a 60-day price guarantee.

During the fiscal year ended January 31, 1996, television accounted for 27 percent of the company's sales; audio for 23 percent; home office for 16 percent; video for 15 percent; automotive (car stereo) for 11 percent; and other products for eight percent. Sony and Mitsubishi each provided more than 10 percent of the merchandise.

Ultimate Electronics was supporting its product sales with many important customer services, including guaranteed same-day home delivery, home-theater and audio installation and design, digital-satellite-systems (DSS) installation, mobile-electronics installation, extended service contracts, and regional service centers that offered in-home and carry-in repair services. Virtually all merchandise could be taken to any of the company's stores for repair, whether or not the product was under the manufacturer's warranty or an extended-service contract. The company's sales employees were receiving a minimum of two weeks of initial intensive classroom training and later were attending in-house training sessions on an ongoing basis. About 32 percent of all fiscal 1996 sales were purchased through the company's private-label credit card or manufacturer-sponsored credit cards.

Further Reading

Baca, Stacey, "Thornton Lands Ultimate Power," *Denver Post,* January 30, 1995, p. B2.

Mahoney, Michelle, "Hippo Catches Attention for Evans, Sound-Track," *Denver Post,* June 18, 1990, p. C3.

——, "SoundTrack Projects Humor," *Denver Post,* February 10, 1992, p. C2.

McGovern, Tim, "SoundTrack Eyes Top Slot in 2 States," *HFD,* September 19, 1994, p. 122.

Nesland, Matt, and Simpson, Bill, "1993 Entrepreneur of the Year Awards: William Pearse," *Denver Business Journal,* Sec. 2, p. B12.

Parker, Penny, "Newest SoundTrack May Be Last in Colorado," *Denver Post,* September 24, 1994, pp. D1–D2.

Seavy, Mark, "SoundTrack Expands into Utah," *HFD,* August 16, 1993, p. 83.

"Shareholder-Rights Plan Approved to Fight Takeovers," *Wall Street Journal,* February 2, 1995, p. A8.

"SoundTrack Parent to Go Public, Raise $16 Million," *Denver Post,* September 3, 1993, p. C2.

Vasquez, Beverly, "SoundTrack Benefits from Home Team Link," *Denver Business Journal,* April 12, 1996, p. A20.

Zulpo, Margarett, "Colorado's Ultimate Electronics Set to Open Friday in Tulsa, Okla.," *Knight-Ridder Tribune Business News,* November 22, 1995, p. 11220183.

—Robert Halasz

United Video Satellite Group

7140 S. Lewis Ave.
Tulsa, Oklahoma 74136-5422
U.S.A.
(918) 488-4000
Fax: (918) 488-4979
Web site: http://www.uvsg.com

Wholly Owned Subsidiary of Tele-Communications, Inc.
Incorporated: 1965
Employees: 1,100
Sales: $437.17 million (1996)
Stock Exchanges: NASDAQ
SICs: 4841 Cable & Other Pay Television Services

Look up in the sky—or on your television, your web browser, or your company's intranet—and there is a good chance one of the affiliate companies of United Video Satellite Group will be there. United Video oversees a diversified group providing information and communication services to cable television systems, home satellite dishes, radio networks, data communications networks, and private business and government agencies. United Video's Prevue Networks provides on-screen cable program guides, including the Prevue Channel, pay-per-view's Sneak Prevue, Prevue Interactive, and Prevue International, to more than 70 million cable subscribers in 18 countries. Superstar Satellite Entertainment—which merged in 1996 with parent company TCI's Liberty Media Netlink arm—provides programming services to some 40 percent of the domestic C-band (large) satellite dish market; Superstar also provides software and marketing services to Hughes Corp.'s DirecTV subscribers. In late 1996, however, the company announced its intention to sell its Superstar affiliate. UVTV, the oldest company in the United Video group, is a domestic and international marketer, distributor, and deliverer of television networks, including WPIX in New York, KTLA in Los Angeles, and CBS, NBC, ABC, PBS, and affiliated stations.

United Video's 70 percent ownership of SSDS adds that company's expertise in designing, building, and maintaining information infrastructure services, such as corporate networks, intranets, and web sites, with an emphasis on electronic commerce capabilities. SSDS clients include Federal Express, Fleet Financial Services, Capital One, Time Warner, TCI, and government agencies, including organizations within the Department of Defense, and the Department of Veteran Affairs. SpaceCom Systems is United Video's satellite transmission technology and services arm providing satellite services to paging companies, financial data networks, radio networks, weather information services, and private business networks.

United Video is a separately traded public subsidiary of Tele-Communications, Inc. (TCI). The two companies merged in 1996 with a trade of stock; TCI owns approximately 36 percent of United Video, but controls 83 percent of United Video's voting stock. Long-time company leaders Lawrence Flinn and Roy L. Bliss both left United Video in late 1996. Revenues for that year were $437 million, representing a 66 percent increase over the previous year and generating a net income of $33 million.

A Cable Pioneer's Offshoot in the 1960s

Founded in 1965 as a division of United Cable Television Corp., United Video could already trace its roots back to the origins of cable television. United Cable was started by Gene Schneider, who had pioneered the industry in 1953 when he helped his brother design and build the country's first cable television system in Casper, Wyoming. In the mid-1960s, Schneider moved to Tulsa, Oklahoma, to start his own cable company, United Cable. Tulsa was wired for cable by 1973; but Schneider had also formed a second division in the company, which later became United Video, to build a larger microwave-based television distribution network. Roy Bliss joined United Cable in 1969, and was placed in charge of building the United Video division. Bliss had known Schneider as a child; Bliss's father had also been involved in the cable television industry, and as a youth Bliss was employed in painting the various buildings and structures used for housing the collection, processing, and transmission equipment for microwave transmissions. In college, Bliss worked for a company making equipment for the cable industry, eventually joining the company's marketing department before joining United Cable's microwave division.

Company Perspectives:

Prevue Networks: To create and deploy an international, multi-channel, multi-tiered distribution network to maximize affiliate distribution and optimize spectrum space for the purpose of achieving a profit.

Superstar Satellite Entertainment: Having made our mark as a leading satellite programming provider and developer of specialized computer services, in 1996 we plan to take advantage of new opportunities in the telecommunications field. Our broad direct-to-home experience will benefit both our consumer and commercial customers, as we live up to our pledge. We answer to you.

UVTV: UVTV is a team of highly motivated individuals with the mission of profitably developing and marketing valuable programming-related services to customers— program resellers and the general public—while achieving a superior level of customer satisfaction.

SSDS: SSDS' mission is to help companies and government agencies utilize information technology to compete in their markets based on the relationship they form with their customers.

SpaceCom Systems: To provide innovative, cost-effective mass communications technology to the information industry and solve real-world information delivery problems for wireless and broadcasting companies.

Microwave transmission was an important element to the early years of cable television. A microwave network, which required placement of relay towers every 30 miles, carried the programming of independent stations and emerging cable networks to the cable television system provider, which then delivered the programming to its customers. Cable systems were most attractive to smaller cities and rural areas, typically underserved by the broadcast networks, affiliates, and independent broadcast stations. United Cable began building its microwave network to bring programming to its own and other small cable systems. In many places, as Bliss, who became president of United Video, explained to *Tulsa World*, "you either had cable or you didn't have television." Cable television found less success in larger cities, where broadcast television was more readily available. The addition of high-profile cable programming—such as the new movie network HBO—was essential to cable systems, and especially those in larger urban areas, for signing up subscribers for their services.

By the mid-1970s, United Cable's United Video division had built a 300,000-mile microwave network covering most of the Midwest and West. United Video was already providing HBO to United Cable's Tulsa cable network, and began making plans to bring that and more programming to other cable systems. But in 1975, HBO began sending its signal via satellite transmission; other programmers would shortly follow suit, including Turner Broadcasting, which began satellite transmission in 1977. This new availability of programming prompted cable television's first boom; but the satellite technology also quickly replaced microwave networks as the primary means of transmission. Bliss saw the technology's potential early—and also saw the need for a company that could distribute the satellite signals to cable sys-

tems. In 1976, Bliss, backed by financing from Lawrence Flinn, bought out the United Video division from United Cable. Flinn, who had previously worked for the Morgan Stanley investment firm, became United Video's chairman and chief executive office, and also owner of more than 90 percent of the company. Bliss was named president.

United Video sought to enter the satellite transmission market. But the cable television industry was strictly regulated by the Federal Communications Commission (FCC). As Bliss explained to *Tulsa World*, "[The FCC] had a theory that you had to have a certain receive signal level which required a 10-meter antenna—a $120,000 investment." That price was too high for the newly independent company. But when deregulation of the cable industry came in 1977, the cost of building an antenna, as well as the size requirement, dropped. With a 15-foot receiver now priced at $20,000, United Video made its move. In 1978, the company rented a satellite transponder—the last one available on the only commercial satellite in orbit at the time—at a cost of $100,000 per month. The company's plans hinged on FCC approval of its application to broadcast one of three television stations, including WGN of Chicago. "We were certain enough that we were going to get [approval] and we went out on a limb and rented [the] transponder," Bliss explained to *Tulsa World*, "which would have sunk us if we hadn't gotten the approval."

FCC approval came a month after the company's transponder lease began. Another month later, United Video began transmitting WGN, and its Chicago Cubs coverage, a relationship that would last until 1996. The company struggled for its first year as a satellite transmission company, as cable systems were slow to add satellite reception capacity. But by 1979, the company had begun to recoup its investment, building revenues to $2 million per year.

Growth into the 1990s

Led by the popularity of superstation WGN, United Video rapidly expanded its number of cable system customers during the 1980s. But the company early on began to add other satellite-based services to complement its transmission capacity. Bliss and Flinn saw a need for more services in order to fuel cable television's future growth. As Bliss told *Tulsa World*, "My vision of cable television has always been more—more services, more entertainment, more technology-driven." United Video formed as a holding company, called United Video Holdings, Inc. and began the in-house development of new services. The first added service developed by the company brought United Video into providing content, in the form of the on-screen cable program guides. Originally named Trakker, Inc., the unit later became known as the Prevue Network.

By the mid-1980s, as the launching of more commercial satellites opened up more opportunities, the company expanded into two new areas. Prior to 1986, owners of large-dish (C-band) home satellite dishes could pull in any satellite signal. But HBO began scrambling its signal in 1986, and soon other satellite-based networks followed suit. United Video recognized a new market for its distribution services, and formed Superstar Entertainment, which packaged programming and sold it as subscriptions to home satellite dish owners. Superstar quickly became profitable and proved a strong engine for

United Video's revenue growth, despite the fact that the scrambling technology employed at the time was relatively easy for dish owners to defeat. United Video's SpaceCom Systems brought the company into a fourth area: providing audio and data transmission for radio stations, government agencies, corporations, and others.

By 1990, the company's Cable Video Services Group distributed superstation WGN, which lagged only Turner Broadcasting in subscriber numbers, New York's WPIX, Los Angeles's KTLA, and the Dallas/Ft. Worth station KTVT, as well as radio stations including WFMT of Chicago and KKJZ of Los Angeles. Meanwhile, Prevue Networks had expanded onto 800 cable systems, reaching more than 20 million homes, and soon added a sister channel, Sneak Prevue, which offered an on-screen program guide for pay-per-view programs. Together, United Video's companies reached more than 41 million homes through some 14,000 cable systems. The company's sales had reached $46 million, and United Video showed a strong profit, of $4.5 million.

By 1993, the companies revenues had more than doubled, to $114 million. In November of that year, United Video reorganized as United Video Satellite Group, combining its ownership positions in its four major units. The following month, United Video went public, selling 4.1 million shares and raising $60.4 million in the offering. Flinn remained in control of 90 percent of the company. The company was branching out again, now into the promising arena of interactive services, which offered the home viewer, among other potential services, the ability to search the company's onscreen program guide. The United Video group added its fifth service, Prevue Interactive, in 1993. Meanwhile, United Video was receiving a big boost on another front. In 1993, satellite transmitters implemented a new scrambling technology that made it more difficult to pirate satellite transmissions. Paying subscriptions quickly tripled, to some 1.9 million homes, and United Video picked up a strong share of the new subscribers, building from 150,000 to 540,000 and passing TCI as the number one provider of C-band satellite transmission services. Superstar's growth helped boost the company's 1994 revenues to $196 million. Superstar also offered United Video an opportunity to gain a share of the newly emerging—and competing—direct broadcast satellite market. Using marketing software developed by Superstar, the company was able to offer telemarketing and subscription services to direct satellite providers U.S. Satellite Broadcasting, and Hughes Electronics' DirecTV, gaining a share of the revenues from this fast-growing market. By 1995, Bliss told *Investor's Business Daily*, "Over half of the DirecTV subscriptions come from us."

United Video began adding the sixth piece of the group in 1994, with purchase of a 10 percent stake in SSDS, Inc., a Colorado-based systems integrator that numbers among its customers such high-profile names as First Data Corp., Sun Microsystems, and the White House. By 1995, United Video had exercised its option to increase its share in SSDS, raising its stake to a controlling 70 percent interest. SSDS, a fast-growing company with $33 million in revenues, offered United Video enhanced technological and especially software-development capacity. United Video's revenues continued to grow strongly, reaching $263 million and bringing net earnings of more than $23 million in 1995.

Flinn, by then 60 years old, began looking at retirement. His stock—trading at $33 per share—in United Video was by then worth some $500 million. But these shares were not easily marketable—as chairman and chief executive, Flinn's attempts at selling part of his holdings would have had a negative reception from the market, and sent United Video's share price falling. United Video was also facing pressures from within the cable and satellite industries, not only from the growth of the direct broadcast satellite market—which threatened to make C-band satellite dishes obsolete within a few years—but also from recent startups, particularly by TCI, of rivals to the company's Prevue revenue engine.

In June 1995 United Video announced the agreement with TCI that gave the cable giant control of United Video. The transaction, completed in early 1996, formed United Video as a separate, publicly traded subsidiary of TCI. It also involved an exchange of stock, giving Flinn shares of the more marketable TCI stock. Prevue Networks survived, as TCI dropped development of its own onscreen program guide. Later that year, TCI also merged its own C-band satellite programming arm, Liberty Media's Netlink, into Superstar, moving Netlink's operations to Tulsa. Flinn, who retained 36 percent of United Video's stock, remained chairman and chief executive until November 1996, when he stepped down for health reasons.

Bliss remained as president and chief operating officer. But when TCI announced in November 1996 its plans to drop transmission of WGN, Bliss complained, as reported by *Tulsa World*: "This is obviously a decision made by corporate executives out of touch with local markets." The following month, Bliss left the company he had founded. By then, however, he had helped lead United Video on an impressive growth spurt, raising revenues by 66 percent in one year. As a nearly $500 million company United Video remained a relatively small player in an industry, as Flinn described it to the *New York Times*, with "a lot of elephants walking around." But with the TCI merger, United Video moved into its future with the backing of one of the largest "elephants" of them all.

Principal Operating Units

Prevue Networks; Superstar Satellite Entertainment; UVTV; SSDS, Inc.; SpaceCom Systems.

Further Reading

Curtis, Bruce, "United Video's Growth Tuned to Industry Trends," *Tulsa World*, November 2, 1992, p. G1.

Finnerty, Brian, "On Screen," *Investor's Business Daily*, August 1, 1994, p. A6.

Foisie, Geoffrey, "United Video: Making Money as Middleman," *Broadcasting & Cable*, October 18, 1993, p. 36.

Norris, Floyd, "How United Video's Chairman Can Look Like a Loser and Still Win," *New York Times*, June 26, 1995, p. D6.

Parets, Robyn Taylor, "Orbiting," *Investor's Business Daily*, July 26, 1995.

Tuttle, Roy, "Bliss Resigns USVG Posts; Exec Ripped TCI on WGN," *Tulsa World*, December 5, 1996, p. E1.

—M. L. Cohen

Uno Restaurant Corporation

100 Charles Park Road
West Roxbury, Massachusetts 02132
U.S.A.
(617) 323-9200
Fax: (617) 323-4252

Public Company
Incorporated: 1943 as Pizzeria Uno
Employees: 6,000
Sales: $172.1 million (1996)
Stock Exchanges: New York
SICs: 5812 Eating Places; 6784 Patent Owners and
    Lessors

Uno Restaurant Corporation is the controlling body for a group of companies that operate and/or franchise a chain of casual dining restaurants known as Pizzeria Uno . . . Chicago Bar & Grill. Specializing in Chicago-style deep-dish pizza, Pizzeria Uno restaurants are full-service establishments which also offer a broad range of other menu items, including pastas, appetizers, salads, and desserts. In addition to its responsibility for approximately 150 restaurants around the United States, Canada, Puerto Rico, and Korea, Uno Restaurant Corp. also controls a consumer food products division which produces and distributes Uno food items for retail sale in supermarkets and convenience stores.

Deep-Dish Pizza: A New Concept for the 1940s

The Uno concept dates back to 1943, when Ike Sewell decided to open a pizzeria in Chicago with his friend, Ric Riccardo, founder and owner of Riccardo's Restaurant. Riccardo had just returned from a trip to Italy, and was hoping to capitalize on a relatively new item on the American scene: pizza. The two men utilized space in the basement of a Chicago mansion to create Pizzeria Uno, where they began showcasing a pizza creation that came to be known as Chicago-style deep-dish.

For 12 years, Sewell and Riccardo's establishment continued to perfect its pizza, which was a thick-crusted version baked for almost an hour in a deep pan. While Sewell continued at his position as an executive for Standard Brands and Riccardo managed his other restaurant endeavor, their deep-dish pizza product gained immense popularity throughout Chicago. In 1955 they opened another restaurant just blocks away from the original, naming it Pizzeria Due.

Ten years later both restaurants were undeniable successes, and Sewell retired from his position with Standard Brands at the age of 62. He decided to open a third restaurant in the Chicago area, this time with a different focus. Su Casa began operating in 1965, and was regarded by many to be the first upscale Mexican restaurant in Chicago.

Nationwide Expansion in the 1970s and 1980s

In 1975, a man by the name of Aaron Spencer was in Chicago on business and ate dinner at Pizzeria Uno. As the owner of 24 New England Kentucky Fried Chicken units, Spencer was well-versed in the restaurant industry, and recognized that Sewell and Riccardo possessed a product capable of success on a national level. He contacted them with an offer to purchase franchise rights for Pizzeria Uno, but was initially rejected, as had been all other franchise offers throughout the years.

Three years later, however, Spencer was still interested in expanding Pizzeria Uno nationally. He finally convinced Sewell to allow one test unit to be opened in Boston; it was an immediate success. Based on that unit's proven prosperity, Sewell agreed to sign a full franchise deal giving Spencer complete expansion rights, and by 1979 the deal was set. Sewell maintained control of his three restaurants in Chicago, while Spencer created a company called Pizzeria Uno to manage his new restaurants in Boston, and Uno Restaurants, Inc. to manage all other franchised units. Although Sewell never took an active part in the management of the newly-formed Uno chain, he continued to manage his own restaurants and served as a director for Spencer until his death in 1990.

In 1984, Spencer decided to sell his Kentucky Fried Chicken units in order to concentrate solely on strengthening his blossoming Uno business. Three years later, Uno had expanded so much that Spencer formed a new body called Uno Restaurant

Corporation to preside over the two existing divisions housing the company-owned and franchised operations. Stock in the new Uno Restaurant Corp. was offered to the public, helping to earn approximately $6.2 million to fund future expansion efforts.

By 1988, Uno Restaurant Corp. had grown to include 15 company-owned restaurants and 26 franchised units, with a strong concentration in the Boston area. Prospective franchisers were continuing to make offers to Spencer, whose company made efforts to select new owners based mainly on the potential of the location. After choosing new sites, Uno Restaurants, Inc. collected a one-time $40,000 fee from new franchisees, and then offered them support in starting operations and implementing the Uno concept program. The program, known as "Going For the T.O.P.," (an acronym for Train, Operate, and Promote), was created in an effort to ensure a consistent level of service and management throughout the rapidly growing chain. The program was instituted by a committee known as the Number One Club, composed of three of the top franchise operators and three company owners.

Diversification in the 1990s

After ten years of building Pizzeria Uno into a strong presence across the eastern seaboard, Spencer began to widen the restaurant's scope. A diverse assortment of new items designed to satisfy a wide variety of customers was added to the Uno menu. The decision was also made to begin selling Uno's prepackaged deep-dish cheese pizza in supermarkets and convenience stores throughout the New England area.

Entering the 1990s, the restaurant industry was hit especially hard by a weakened economy, which meant less money was available for consumers to spend on dining out. Pizzeria Uno, however, fared extremely well in comparison to its competitors, which had come to be other full-service chains such as Chili's and Applebees, rather than other pizza makers. Uno and its prospects looked so good, in fact, that it began to attract other important players in the restaurant industry as franchisees. New owners included Art Gunther, former Pizza Hut president; J. Jeffrey Campbell, former Pillsbury Restaurant Group chairman; Jeff Grayson, former president of General Mills; Louis Neeb, former chairman of Burger King; and Stanley Nippon, a former executive at McDonald's.

By mid-1990, Uno Restaurant Corp. was responsible for the operation of 75 restaurants, after experiencing a remarkable 84

percent increase in profits over the previous four years. Average per-unit sales were well over $1 million, and the demand for Uno's retail pizza product was rapidly increasing. The company made attempts to keep pace by purchasing a processing plant near Boston, which enabled it to expand its retail pizza offerings to include pepperoni and sausage varieties as well as the cheese pizza already being sold. Prior to that acquisition, all retail production had been done out of the kitchen of one of the Boston restaurants. This new division began operating as Uno Foods, Inc.

Meanwhile, in response to a recession brought on by the Gulf War, Uno tried to counter the downturn in sales within its major markets of Boston and New York by offering different specials and promotions. It advertised specially-priced deals during the lunch hours, and lowered prices on its children's menu in an effort to capture more families as patrons. Furthermore, the restaurants continued to expand their menu items, serving pizza, pasta, sandwiches, and salads, in addition to a full array of appetizers and desserts. One popular addition to the menu was the plizzetta, a light, thin-crusted gourmet pizza which accounted for 15 percent of the chain's sales by 1992.

Based on the success of the Uno pizza retail line following the purchase of the new production facility, the company decided to test a new take-out concept in selected restaurant locations. It began offering fresh, refrigerated unbaked pizzas for customers to pick-up and take home, which allowed people to enjoy the product at home without Uno having to implement a delivery service. Another benefit of the take-out pizzas was the availability of all topping combinations, as compared to the limited offerings available in supermarkets.

The End of the Century and Beyond

In 1992, almost 50 years after Sewell and Riccardo entered the pizza business, Uno Restaurant Corp. acquired all of the outstanding shares of the three original restaurants in Chicago. The Pizzeria Uno chain had grown to include 109 restaurants throughout the United States, Canada, the U.K., and Australia. Uno was also experimenting with the hotel food service market by offering its pizzas as room-service items at selected Hiltons and Marriotts in the U.S.

Unfortunately, the chain's push to expand its menu beyond its pizza roots had not yet proved as successful as had been anticipated. While Uno's signature deep-dish pizza was a unique high-quality item, many of the restaurant's additional items did little to set Uno apart from other restaurants. Therefore, in 1993 Uno launched a $2.5 million effort to upgrade its units' kitchens, adding sauté stations, charbroilers, grills, and fryers, enabling them to produce dishes of the same high-quality as the pizza. The menu shifted slightly from its "Italianized" base, and the chain's restaurant units took on the name Pizzeria Uno . . . Chicago Bar & Grill.

Meanwhile, franchise expansion slowed for a short time while Uno tried to deal with an unsolicited $100 million acquisition bid by Morrison Restaurants, owner of the successful Ruby Tuesday restaurant chain. When Morrison originally initiated the offer, Uno's yearly sales were approximately $84 million; by the time Morrison backed away a year later, Uno's sales figures had far surpassed the $100 million mark for the first time in the company's history. Also, Uno Foods, Inc. had just landed a contract with American Airlines to put its pizza aboard selected flights, and was benefitting from increased distribution into supermarkets in the east.

In 1994, as Uno was completing its restaurants' kitchen renovations and beginning to see success from marketing Uno as an eatery with a diversified menu, the company made an acquisition that coincided with the new focus. Uno Restaurants, Inc. purchased all rights to three Bay Street seafood restaurant units in Illinois, New Jersey, and Pennsylvania. A far stretch from Uno's early beginnings in pizza, the restaurants further diversified the company's offerings in the dining industry.

Entering the late 1990s, Uno Restaurant Corp. was well positioned for continued growth in each of its divisions. The company was composed of 150 full-service restaurants, including 86 company-owned and 64 franchised establishments, and was finalizing plans to enter new markets. In 1996, Uno formed an agreement with the Kolon Group in Seoul, Korea, to open 10 Pizzeria Uno restaurants. Due to the increase in international activity, the company created Pizzeria Uno International, and hired Bruce Raba to act as president of the division. Later that year, Spencer passed down his duties as CEO to Craig Miller, who had been president since 1986. Spencer retained his position as chairman. With increasing consumer acceptance for Uno's position as a full-service restaurant with a diverse "bar and grill" menu, and with many market areas still open and sales steadily rising, the company headed into the next century poised for even greater success in the future.

Principal Subsidiaries

URC Holding Company, Inc.; B.S. Acquisition Corp.; B.S. Intangible Asset Corp.; Pizzeria Uno Corp.; Uno Restaurant Securities Corp.; Uno Foods, Inc.; Uno Restaurants, Inc.

Further Reading

Autry, Ret, "Companies to Watch: Uno Restaurant," *Fortune,* July 16, 1990, p. 75.

Bell, Alexa, "Betting on Pizzeria Uno," *Restaurant Business,* July 20, 1989, p. 170.

Frumkin, Paul, "Growth Gurus: Pizzeria Uno's Strong Operations and Phenomenal Growth Have Wooed Industry Luminaries," *Restaurant Business,* July 20, 1989, p. 164.

——, "Pizzeria Uno Charts Its Course for Smoother Times Ahead," *Nation's Restaurant News,* April 15, 1991, p. 35.

——, "Pizzeria Uno Eyes Retail Expansion," *Nation's Restaurant News,* May 28, 1990, p. 1.

Frydman, Ken, "Pizzeria Uno: More than Just Another Fast-Food Pizza Place," *Nation's Restaurant News,* November 16, 1987, p. 3.

Hodges, Dave, "Public's Appetite for Pizza Keeps Franchise Searching for Sites," *Orlando Business Journal,* October 1, 1989, p. 1.

Mehlman, William, "Boston Doldrums Not Likely to Derail Uno Restaurants," *Insiders' Chronicle,* April 23, 1990, p. 1.

Paul, Ronald N., "Going for the Top," *Restaurant Hospitality,* April 1988, p. 162.

"Pizzeria Uno to Open 10 New Locations in Korea," *Nation's Restaurant News,* July 15, 1996, p. 92.

Prewitt, Milford, "Pizzeria Uno Founder Sewell Dies," *Nation's Restaurant News,* September 3, 1990, p. 3.

—Laura E. Whiteley

VeriFone, Inc.

3 Lagoon Drive, Suite 400
Redwood City, California 94065
U.S.A.
(415) 591-6500
Fax: (415) 598-5504
Web site: http://www.verifone.com

Public Company
Incorporated: 1981
Employees: 2,800
Sales: $387 million (1995)
Stock Exchanges: New York
SICs: 3578 Calculating Machines Except Computers

VeriFone, Inc. has long dominated the market for electronic point-of-sale (POS) transaction systems—those little gray boxes found on sales counters everywhere used for authorizing credit card purchases. Since the late 1980s, VeriFone has held more than 60 percent of the U.S. market, and during the 1990s the company captured more than half of the international market for such systems. VeriFone manufactures the devices, which are actually small computers with their own processors, memory, and display, and develops the software to drive their application. The company does not sell directly to merchants; instead, VeriFone markets its products to banks and other financial institutions, which then place them on their customers' retail counters. In 1996, the company placed its five millionth system. Domestic and international sales of POS systems continue to form the majority of VeriFone's annual sales, which hit $387 million in 1995 and were expected to top $500 million in subsequent years.

But POS systems are only part of VeriFone's future. With the increasing saturation of the domestic POS market, the company has turned its attention to emerging markets to fuel its future growth. If VeriFone has its way, "transaction automation," as the company calls its industry, will become increasingly less reliant on physical products and instead turn to a virtual realm where cash will become obsolete. VeriFone has been at the forefront of this transition, shifting its own emphasis from manufacturing hardware to designing complete software solutions. Toward this end, the company has focused on two primary areas: the "smart" card and the Internet.

Smart cards replace the magnetic stripe of typical credit cards with tiny processors. The chips, which may contain as much as one megabyte of RAM, can be encoded with a variety of information, such as the amount of money available to the cardholder. Purchases made using a smart card are automatically deducted from the holder's account. Transactions are immediate, require no authorization, and thus enable the card to be used in low denomination purchases that would be too expensive or time-consuming with the typical credit or debit card. In addition, smart cards can be encoded with much more information, including a person's health insurance information, as well as that person's various credit card accounts.

The sudden growth of the Internet, and especially the World Wide Web, in the mid-1990s created a demand for secure online financial transaction applications. VeriFone has taken the lead in designing applications conforming to the Secure Electronic Transactions (SET) standards developed by Visa and Master-Card. With the $28 million 1995 acquisition of Enterprise Integration Technologies, the company that developed the Secure HyperText Transfer Protocol (S-HTTP), and a $4 million equity investment in CyberCash Inc., led by VeriFone founder William Melton, and with 1996 partnership agreements with Internet browser leaders Netscape, Oracle, and Microsoft, VeriFone has rolled out a suite of software products targeted at consumers, merchants, and financial institutions allowing secure purchases and other transactions online. Purchases over the Internet, which still produced as little as $10 million in 1995, are expected to reach into the billions by the turn of the century. VeriFone has also been working to marry the smart card to the Internet; in 1996, the company introduced the Personal ATM (P-ATM), a small smart card reader designed to be attached to the consumer's home computer, which will enable the consumer not only to make purchases over the Internet, but also to "recharge" the value on the card. VeriFone has also partnered with Keytronics to incorporate a P-ATM interface directly into that company's computer keyboards.

Company Perspectives:

VeriFone's Mission Is To Create and Lead the Transaction Automation Industry Worldwide.

VeriFone's own infrastructure, developed under Chairman, President, and CEO Hatim Tyabji, gives it a distinct competitive edge in the inevitable, and impending, explosion of electronic commerce. As one of the world's first truly "virtual" companies, VeriFone has no headquarters; its offices in Redwood, California house only about 120 of the company's 2,800 employees, primarily in administrative and financial functions. Instead, VeriFone's employees are deployed throughout the world, attached to a network of research and development centers, manufacturing facilities, and sales offices. VeriFone's sales staff travel constantly. This includes Tyabji, who typically logs 400,000 air miles per year. Communication is performed almost entirely by e-mail; indeed, paper-based communication has been banned by the company. All sales, marketing, financial, and other information is made available to employees over the company's network. Product development is also global, and the company's network enables the development of a product to be performed 24 hours a day, without subjecting employees to the grueling, often 18-hours-or-more-per-day schedules of other software developers. A software application may be initiated at the company's Dallas R & D center. When the Dallas employees have completed their eight-hour day, the code for the application can be forwarded to VeriFone's Hawaii facilities, where employees are just beginning their workday, who in turn send the code to the company's Bangalore, India center. When the Dallas employees return to work the following day, they pick up where the other centers left off, allowing the development, testing, and implementation of new products to be completed far faster than the typical development cycle.

Pioneering Transaction Automation in the 1980s

William Melton already had more than a decade of experience in payment processing before founding VeriFone in 1981. Ten years earlier, Melton had founded Real-Share, Inc., in Hawaii, a pioneer in the use of computers and other database and telecommunications systems for check authorization and guarantees. In 1980, Melton sold Real-Share to TeleCheck Services, later part of First Financial Management Corp., for some $3 million. Melton used this money to start up VeriFone in Honolulu the following year. Initially, the company provided retailers with access to information on people known to have written bad checks. The company started at the local level, but soon spread throughout the islands. Part of Melton's operating philosophy was to place his sales and support staff close to the company's customers. To maintain contact among his widely dispersed employees, Melton turned to the nascent networking and portable computer industries, outfitting the company with early e-mail messaging and online database capabilities.

A development in the still-young credit card industry, however, caused Melton to change the focus of the company. The use of credit cards first became widespread during the 1970s. By the beginning of the 1980s, the major credit card companies began seeking methods to reduce processing costs and losses due to fraud. In 1981, Visa and MasterCard began offering merchants discounts on their transactions if they agreed to use newly developed automated transaction technology for all credit card purchases greater than $50. This move opened the way for the creation of an industry devoted to producing POS authorization systems. Early systems typically had starting prices of $900.

VeriFone introduced its first POS product in 1982. By slashing operating costs and lowering manufacturing costs by outsourcing production, VeriFone brought its first system to the market at $500. In financing this effort, Melton received help from Lexis-Nexis founder William Gorog, who had sold that company and founded Arbor International to produce credit card authorizations systems under contract for Tymnet. When Tymnet decided not to pursue the POS market, Gorog agreed to finance VeriFone with letters of credit. He next brought VeriFone in contact with a venture capital firm for additional financing. In return, Arbor received the right to sell VeriFone products east of the Mississippi.

Working with Visa, VeriFone quickly captured a strong share of the POS market. In 1984, however, the company took a major step toward achieving industry dominance with the introduction of its ZON credit card authorization system, which, taking advantage of improvements in processor speeds and the lowering cost of both processors and memory, cost as little as $125, making it easier to convince retail merchants to install the system in their stores. The following year, the company's revenues grew to $15.3 million, earning a net profit of $864,000. In that year, VeriFone moved its headquarters to Redwood, outside of San Francisco, to be closer to that area's software and hardware engineering talent pool, as well as to its customers and investors.

The company doubled revenues, to about $30 million, in 1986. But VeriFone's products were beset by quality problems, the company was barely producing profits, while in constant need of new financing, and investors were critical of the company's management. As one early investor told the *New York Times,* VeriFone was led by "management by reactive panic mode." The venture capitalists behind VeriFone urged Melton to bring in a new president and CEO.

Melton chose Hatim A. Tyabji. Born in Bombay, India, Tyabji had moved to the United States at the age of 22 to attend graduate school, eventually earning two graduate degrees. Tyabji joined Sperry Corp. as a junior project manager, but in 13 years rose to become president of information systems products and technologies. When Sperry was bought up by Burroughs Corp., forming Unisys Corp., Tyabji decided to leave. Named president and CEO of VeriFone, Tyabji worked to turn the company around. Quality problems were quickly addressed; by 1988, Tyabji moved to create manufacturing as a core competency, opening VeriFone's first manufacturing plant in Taiwan. The company also acquired Arbor International, for an exchange of stock, giving it full control of marketing and sales of its products. Tyabji sought to transform the company into Melton's original vision of a virtual operation. Laying down a corporate philosophy, Tyabji encouraged the growth of the company's computer network, outlawing paper-based communications and mandating that employees make constant use of the network's e-mailing and database functions. Employees and operations were placed close to the company's customers, enabling Tyabji to institute what the company calls its "culture of urgency," allowing for 24-hour-per-day product development and sales and marketing efforts.

By January 1988, VeriFone controlled more than 53 percent of the POS systems market. Revenues had reached $73.4 million, with net earnings of more than $6 million. The following year, the company increased its dominance in the industry with the purchase of the transaction automation business of Icot Corp., then second in the market with a 20.5 percent share. The acquisition boosted VeriFone's revenues to $125 million. By then, VeriFone had entered the international market, starting with Australia in 1988 and placing its millionth ZON system in Finland in 1989. Tyabji added chairman to his titles after Melton retired from the company in 1989, taking a seat on the company's board.

New Directions for the 1990s

VeriFone went public in March 1990, raising more than $54 million. As the credit card industry matured, VeriFone pushed to install its systems into new markets, such as restaurants, movie theaters, taxis, and fast food restaurants, while developing software capacity to bring its systems into the health care and health insurance markets and to government functions, such as state welfare systems. International sales also began to build, as use of credit cards became increasingly accepted in foreign markets. VeriFone was also building its global operation, opening facilities in Bangalore, Singapore, England, Dallas, and Ft. Lauderdale, in addition to its Hawaii and California facilities. Rolling out its Gemstone line of transaction systems, which added inventory control, pricing, and other capabilities, VeriFone was aided by announcements from Visa and MasterCard that the companies would no longer provide printed warning bulletins, while requiring merchants to seek authorization for all credit card transactions by 1994.

These moves further stimulated demand for VeriFone's products. Revenues jumped from $155 million in 1990 to $226 million in 1992. By then, VeriFone had placed its two millionth system (in Fouquet's restaurant, near Paris, in 1991); by 1993, VeriFone systems were in place in more than 70 countries, including its three millionth system, in Brazil, representing the company's expansion in the Latin American market. International sales, which had contributed less than ten percent of revenues before 1990, now accounted for more than 30 percent of the company's nearly $259 million in annual revenues.

New opportunities arose as banks began rolling out debit cards in the mid-1990s. VeriFone was quick to launch itself into this new market, producing terminals designed with key pads for customers to punch in their PIN numbers. But as the domestic credit and debit card markets neared saturation, VeriFone made ready to launch itself in new directions. While continuing its international expansion, topping four million installed systems in 1994, and maintaining its manufacturing capacity, doubling production capacity with a new plant near Shanghai in

China in 1994, VeriFone had already evolved its primary focus to producing software applications, offering vertically integrated systems solutions, including applications for standard computer operating systems.

VeriFone moved to take the lead in the coming smart card revolution, teaming up with GemPlus, a France-based maker of the cards, and MasterCard International to form the joint venture SmartCash. To place the company close to technological developments in France and the rest of Europe, VeriFone opened its Paris research and development center in 1994. The company launched its smart card in May 1995. The company introduced its Personal ATM, a palm-sized smart card reader capable of reading a variety of smart card formats, in September 1996, with the product expected to ship in 1997. Among the first customers already signed to support the P-ATM were American Express, MasterCard International, GTE, Mondex International, Visa International, Wells Fargo Bank, and Sweden's Sparbanken Bank. Contracts for each called for the purchase of a minimum of 100,000 units; the total market potential for the device was estimated at more than 100 million households. In addition, VeriFone began developing smart card readers to supplement and eventually replace its five million credit and debit card authorization systems.

In 1995, VeriFone began the first of its aggressive steps to enter an entirely new area, that of Internet-based transactions. In May 1995, the company partnered with BroadVision Inc., a developer of Internet, interactive television, computer network, and other software, to couple VeriFone's Virtual Terminal software—a computer-based version of its standard transaction terminal—with BroadVision's offerings, thereby extending VeriFone's products beyond the retail counter for the first time. In August 1995, however, VeriFone took an even bigger step into the Internet transaction arena, with its $28 million acquisition of Enterprise Integration Technologies, developer of the S-HTTP industry standard for safeguarding transactions over the World Wide Web. VeriFone followed that acquisition with a $4 million investment in William Melton's latest venture, CyberCash Inc., also working to develop Internet transaction systems.

By 1996, VeriFone was ready with its Payment Transaction Application Layer (PTAL) lineup of products, including the Virtual Terminal interface for merchants conducting sales with consumers; Internet Gateway or vGATE, to conduct transactions between merchants and financial institutions; and the Pay Window interface for consumers making purchases on the Internet. After securing agreements from Netscape, Oracle, and Microsoft to include VeriFone software in their Internet browsers, VeriFone and Microsoft announced in August 1996 that VeriFone's virtual point of sale (vPOS) would be included in the Microsoft Merchant System to be released by the end of the year. VeriFone's announcement of the P-ATM, able to be attached as a computer peripheral, wedded the company's smart card and Internet transaction efforts.

The success of these ventures depended on the long-term acceptance of the new technologies, and VeriFone faced powerful competition as the industry struggled to achieve international standards and specifications. But with Hatim Tyabji leading the company in its culture of urgency, VeriFone hoped to become as ubiquitous on the screen as it had become on the store counter.

Principal Subsidiaries

TIMECORP Systems, Inc.; VeriFone Finance, Inc.

Further Reading

"An ATM in Every Home Is VeriFone's Platform," *Bank Network News,* October 11, 1996.

Daly, James J., "Out of the Box," *Credit Card Management,* November 1995, pp. 102–108.

Daniels, Jeffrey, "Payment Systems Firm VeriFone To Go Public in $56 Million Offering," *Investor's Daily,* March 2, 1990, p. 28.

Epper, Karen, "Money Creators: Point of Sales Pioneers Setting Sail on the Internet," *American Banker,* February 10, 1995, p. 14.

Freedman, David H., "Culture of Urgency," *Forbes,* September 13, 1993, p. 25.

Kutler, Jeffrey, "Terminal Maker Stakes Future on the Net," *American Banker,* December 5, 1995, p. 5A.

——, "VeriFone's Unconventional Chief: 'Lucidly Crazy,'" *American Banker,* April 20, 1995, p. 12.

Louis, Arthur M., "No Place To Call Home: VeriFone Is a 'Virtual' Workplace," *San Francisco Chronicle,* October 22, 1996, p. C1.

Nee, Eric, "Hatim Tyabji," *Upside,* September 1996, pp. 84–93.

Pollack, Andrew, "Company's Rise Is Built on Credit," *New York Times,* August 3, 1990, p. D1.

Taylor, William C., "At VeriFone It's a Dog's Life (And They Love It!)," *Fast Company,* http://www.fastcompany.com/fastco/issues/first/Vfone.htm, June 6, 1996.

—M. L. Cohen

Vivra, Inc.

400 Primrose
Suite 200
Burlingame, California 94010
U.S.A.
(415) 348-8200
Fax: (415) 375-7550

Public Company
Incorporated: 1989
Employees: 3,600
Sales: $350.5 million (1995)
Stock Exchanges: New York
SICs: 8092 Kidney Dialysis Centers; 8082 Home Health
Care Services

Vivra, Inc. is the second-largest provider of dialysis treatment services in the United States, while also holding active shares in the markets of diabetes treatment and allergy and asthma care. Vivra, whose name is translated to "will live" in the French language, serves almost 12,000 patients throughout the country who need kidney dialysis treatment, through its chain of Community Dialysis Centers. The company also provides intravenous nutritional and pharmacy support to these patients through its Associated Health Services subsidiary. Another division called Health Advantage handles the company's many diabetes management centers, while the Vivra Specialty Partners subsidiary (VSP) manages physicians' practices that deal in the care of allergies and asthma, as well as other chronic medical conditions.

The Early Years

Although Vivra, Inc. was created in 1989, its beginnings can actually be traced back 16 years earlier. In 1973, a company called Community Psychiatric Centers (CPC) purchased three outpatient medical units that specialized in providing patients with hemodialysis treatment, a process that used artificial kidney machines to rid blood of toxins. CPC's primary focus lay in the psychiatric field, however, so it created a separate division to handle operations of the newly-acquired hemodialysis units. This new operating division, which would one day become Vivra, began developing a program to manage the continuum of care for high-cost chronic dialysis patients. The dialysis services provided to patients were primarily reimbursed by Medicare under the End-Stage Renal Disease Program.

Through the Vivra division, CPC continued to provide (and expand) its dialysis services for the next decade. Then in 1983, CPC decided to purchase six health care offices in southern California that provided in-home nursing services for patients with chronic medical needs. The Vivra division became responsible for the operation of these offices as well, and within five years Vivra was generating annual revenues of over $80 million between its two subdivisions. Even with this great success, in 1989 CPC decided to focus solely on its psychiatric business, and made plans to divest the Vivra subsidiary. In August of that year, CPC distributed stock in Vivra to its own stockholders, giving out one share of Vivra for every ten shares of CPC held. To make the transition smoother, Vivra retained the services of CPC's management until August of the following year, and paid a fee for the support it received.

Shortly after the split from CPC occurred, Vivra's home health care division (now called Personal Care Health Services) received accreditation by the Joint Commission on Accreditation of Health Care Organizations. The operation also expanded from its original six offices in California to include four more offices, all of which supplied extended care (ranging from 4 to 24 hours per day) to patients in their own homes. But even with this new expansion and accreditation, Vivra's home health care remained a somewhat small part of its total business. In 1989, Personal Care Health Services accounted for only 18 percent of the yearly revenues (and only 2 percent of the actual yearly profits), while the dialysis services generated the other 82 percent of revenue (and 98 percent of profits). Therefore, Vivra decided to focus on expanding its dialysis business, and spent approximately $875,000 purchasing two units in New Mexico.

Expansion in the Early 1990s

Entering the 1990 fiscal year, Vivra was composed of 91 dialysis centers around the United States, in addition to its home health care offices in California. Already the country's second-largest provider of dialysis services, Vivra continued its efforts at expansion and growth. 1990 marked the expenditure of approximately $5.2 million to acquire dialysis units in five Virginia locations, as well as units in Washington, D.C., and West Virginia. This was paid for in part by income generated when the company issued a secondary offering of its stock in August of that year.

Meanwhile, Vivra was searching for another line of services to add to its repertoire that could be developed without bringing on too much financial strain and without compromising the care already being provided in the dialysis and home-care segments. Two new ventures arose. Vivra decided to form Associated Health Services, which would operate two pharmacies in California and Georgia that would supply specialized nutritional intravenous infusion therapy to dialysis patients. The company also began to explore the niche of diabetes treatment. 1990 also saw the company donate money to Moncrief Mountain Ranch, a recreational summer camp for kids with chronic and severe medical problems, such as kidney failure.

The year 1990 was not only a busy and varied one for the newly independent company, but a successful one as well. Revenues topped off at $115.7 million, surpassing the $100 million mark for the first time since the Vivra division was formed by CPC in 1973. The company had also increased the number of dialysis units in its Community Dialysis Center chain to 104, and had added one more home health care office to its Personal Care Health Services chain in California. Through 1991 and into 1992, Vivra continued to augment its dialysis service chain through new acquisitions. Revenues for 1991 rose to $140.7 million.

In 1992, Vivra more actively pursued its entrance into the diabetes treatment market. In April of that year, the company acquired a diabetes management service company called Health Advantage, Inc., in exchange for shares of Vivra's common stock. The company also purchased 11 more dialysis treatment centers around the country, bringing its Community Dialysis Center unit count to 115. Possibly the most notable move, however, was the company's sudden push into the operation of surgical centers. First came the formation of a new subsidiary, called Surgical Partners of America, which was created to operate ambulatory surgery centers. Then came the purchase of the Green River Surgical Center in Auburn, Washington, and the Physicians Plaza Surgical Center in Bakersfield, California. These moves, along with Vivra's mainstay dialysis and home

care business, helped the company achieve $182 million in 1992 revenues.

The following year was notable for more than one reason. First, Vivra was recognized in *Barron's* as a top investment pick by Richard Aster, manager of the Meridian Mutual Fund, due to the company's reliable yearly growth and return on equity. Second, the company's 1993 revenues surpassed the $200 million mark, topping off at $216.8 million. In the four years since Vivra had split from CPC and become its own entity, the company had more than doubled its annual income. However, in 1993 Vivra finally sold its Personal Care Health Services division, making an exit from the home health care business. The division was sold to National Medical Care, the United States' number one kidney dialysis company and a wholly-owned subsidiary of the chemical and health care firm W.R. Grace & Co.

The Mid-1990s and Beyond

Immediately following the divestiture of Personal Care Health Services to National Medical Care, Vivra actually made a bid to merge itself with the company. Such a merger would have joined the number one and number two kidney dialysis companies in the country, giving them control of the vast majority of dialysis centers throughout the United States. But Vivra's merger bid was rejected in early 1994, and so the company began plans to reevaluate its many holdings and divest those which were either unsuccessful or inconsistent with the company's main focuses.

Interestingly enough, though, the first moves made by Vivra following the merger bid's rejection were three different acquisitions that expanded the company's range of services, rather than deleting inconsistencies. Vivra first purchased a partial interest in South Coast Rehabilitation Services of Laguna Hills, California, a provider of occupational, speech, and physical therapy services. Next came the acquisition of Celsus, Inc. and Celsus of Louisville, Inc., which dealt in the management of physician practices. Vivra also purchased AllergyClinics of America, Inc., an allergy and asthma care service company.

Vivra spent the rest of the year organizing its holdings. By the end of 1994, Vivra was well-positioned in three main areas related to chronic disease medical care: dialysis/nephrology, asthma and allergy care, and diabetes treatment. Revenues for the year had jumped once again, to $284.6 million. Entering 1995, the company finally began to divest the divisions that did not fit into one of the above three areas. The Surgical Partners of America subsidiary was sold, as well as Vivra's stake in the South Coast Rehabilitation Services business. Also, the Vivra Physician Services division was restructured and became Vivra Specialty Partners (VSP), with a focus on the management of physician practices and networks.

Entering the end of the decade, Vivra was responsible for the operation of over 150 dialysis centers around the country, under the name Community Dialysis Centers. 1995 revenues were at the highest level in the company's six-year history, this time surpassing $350 million and generating an actual year-end profit of almost $38 million. Since its inception as an independent entity in 1989, Vivra had achieved substantial increases in both yearly revenues and profits every year. As the company continued to restructure its holdings and maximize its success, both in the medical care provided and in the economic environment, Vivra's potential for future growth looked promising.

Principal Subsidiaries

Associated Health Services, Inc.; Associated Medication Services, Inc.; Asthma & Allergy CareAmerica, Inc.; Vivra Renal Care, Inc.; Community Dialysis Supply Corp.; Vivra Health Advantage, Inc.; VNS (75%); Specialty Care America, Inc.; Vivra Heart Services, Inc.; Vivra OB-GYN, Inc.; Vivra Orthopedics, Inc.; Vivra Specialty Partners, Inc.; VPSL Corp.; Celsus of Louisville; Vivra Physician Services of Colorado Springs, Inc. (83%); Vivra Laboratories, Inc.

Further Reading

Burns, John, ''Two Large Dialysis Chains' Earnings Rise,'' *Modern Healthcare,* February 15, 1993, p. 28.
''Taking Stock: Vivra, Inc.,'' *San Francisco Business Times,* May 21, 1990, p. 28.
Zipser, Andy, ''Value Off the Balance Sheet,'' *Barron's,* August 2, 1993, p. 28.

—Laura E. Whiteley

Wassall PLC

Wassall Plc

39 Victoria Street
London SW1H OEE
United Kingdom
(44) 171 333 0303
Fax: (44) 171 333 0304

Public Company
Founded: 1956 as J.W. Wassall
Employees: 4,534
Sales: £972.9 million (US$1.5 billion) (1995)
Stock Exchanges: London
SICs: 3496 Miscellaneous Fabricated Wire Products;
3351 Copper Rolling and Drawing; 2891 Adhesives
and Sealants; 2521 Wood Office Furniture; 3466
Crowns and Closures

Ranked among the United Kingdom's top 500 companies, Wassall Plc is a "mini-conglomerate" with interests in an evolving amalgam of manufacturing interests. After more than 30 years in the retail shoe business, new management reincarnated the firm as a holding company in 1988. Within less than a decade, this new executive team used a series of acquisitions to transform Wassall from a small domestic retailer into a multinational manufacturing group. By the mid-1990s, over 82 percent of its sales were generated in North America, and less than 14 percent came from the U.K.

The company is often compared to Anglo-American conglomerate Hanson Plc, and in fact CEO J. Christopher Miller and director Philip G. Turner were executives with that company before moving to Wassall. Their holding company's diverse interests in cable, sealants, travel goods, bottle closures, and furniture all ranked among the leaders of their respective markets. Having multiplied its market value from £3 million in 1988 to more than £700 million by 1996, the company set its sights on Asia, acquiring a controlling interest in a Singaporean manufacturer of axles for semi-trailers.

Post-World War II Origins

The company was established in April 1956 in Leicester, England, and presumably named for its founder, J. W. Wassall. The retail shoe store went public seven years later as J.W. Wassall Ltd., and was reorganized as a public limited company, Wassall Plc, in 1982. Several factors likely explain a lack of published information on this firm's rather obscure first 32 years in business. First, Wassall was a relatively small company, having less than £3.5 million in annual sales by 1987. And while its stock was publicly traded, it probably did not warrant much attention from British analysts. Conversely, Wassall's track record since 1988 was so remarkable as to make the previous years pale in comparison. The company's operations in the 1990s had virtually nothing to do with its origins; in fact, Wassall's footwear interests were sold off in 1989. And finally, the company's new managers seemed far more interested in their creation's apparently unlimited future as a mini-conglomerate than its limited past as a mere retailer.

Advent of New Management in 1988

In September 1988, former Hansonites J. Christopher Miller and Philip Turner, along with investment banker David Roper and James Miller, merged their nascent investment firm into the shoe retailer, transforming Wassall into a holding company in the process. Their basic plan was to raise the value of their new property by trimming overhead and boosting productivity, then leverage this added value via new equity offerings on the stock market. Funds raised would be coupled with borrowings and used to purchase new makeover candidates. Like their strategic forebears at Hanson, Wassall executives did not necessarily seek out synergies among their conquests. Nor did they target businesses whose components were worth more than the whole. As an analyst for Hoare Govett Investment Research Ltd. noted in a 1992 report on the company, "Wassall is not just a 'buy, restructure, and run for cash conglomerate . . . .'" Instead, they concentrated on basic manufacturing businesses with leading market shares that seemed to be in need of a shape-up. As David Roper told *Crossborder Monitor* in 1996, "We want something we can put right by means of hard work and straightforward management techniques." At the core of Wassall's management methodology was an emphasis on lean operations and tight-fisted finances, but this frugality did not preclude investments in equipment or research and development. Instead of limiting themselves to businesses within their own fields of expertise, they concentrated on managing the holding company, delegating day-to-day management of the subsidiaries to their respective executives.

The team started out small, locally, and quickly, acquiring Evertaut, a British manufacturer of office furniture, for £11.2 million in 1988. Two acquisitions totaling £29.3 million followed in 1989: Hille Ergonom, a producer of office and auditorium seating and Antler, a leading brand of luggage in the U.K. By the end of 1989, Wassall's earnings nearly matched its pre-takeover revenues. Sales had multiplied from £3.3 million in 1987 to £38.9 million, and pre-tax profits burgeoned from £56,000 to £3.2 million.

International Expansion Begins in 1990s

Wassall commenced the 1990s with the £47 million acquisition of Metal Closures Group Plc, a bottlecap company with factories in the United Kingdom, Italy, and South Africa. Exhibiting another "Hansonesque" strategy, Wassall recovered £5.3 million of the purchase price with the sale of MCG Venus Packaging Ltd. that fall, and generated another £1.7 million via the divestment of Alucaps Italiana S.p.A. in February 1991.

With the U.K. acquisitions market fairly well "picked over," Wassall turned its attention to the New World in 1991. That year, it acquired DAP Inc., an Ohio-based manufacturer of caulks and sealants, for £50 million (US$90 million). DAP was an ideal takeover candidate for Wassall. With over 100 years in business, a leading market share, and the category's most widely recognized brand, it was unquestionably well-established. And despite two previous changes in ownership in less than ten years—during which time one might have expected the new parents to "clean house"—the company exhibited good potential for reorganization. Wassall wasted no time before grabbing its broom and dustpan, starting with a clean sweep of DAP's top layer of management. The new parent also shuttered four of DAP's nine plants, trimming 10 percent of the employee roster and 25 percent of its product line in the process. But in accordance with Wassall's philosophy, the restructuring was

not just about cuts. The new parent re-emphasized product development and invested in state-of-the-art production equipment, for example. Within a year, Wassall had cut DAP's overhead by millions and boosted its profitability by over two-thirds.

Apparently hoping to augment its global position in adhesives and sealants, Wassall mounted a hostile £94.3 million bid for Britain's Evode Holdings late in 1992. Offended at the implied and blatant criticism inherent in Wassall's offer—any acquisition brought by the company insinuated that Wassall's executives viewed the target as "undermanaged"—Evode's executives rebuffed the offer as "unwelcome and wholly inadequate." Evode was able to convince its shareholders to hold out until early 1993, when Laporte Industries Holding brought a much more attractive, £129.4 million offer.

Wassall's executives settled for "organic" growth in 1992 and 1993, during which time sales more than doubled from £130.1 million (1991) to £277.8 million (1993). The budding mini-conglomerate's pre-tax income grew even faster, from £7.6 million to £27.6 million, boosted by ongoing efficiency and productivity enhancements.

Analysts would wait until 1994 for Wassall's "quantum leap acquisition," and when it came, many doubted its prudence. The holding company made its largest acquisition to date with the £177 million (US$269.8 million) purchase of General Cable Corp., a subsidiary of Cincinnati financier Carl Lindner's American Financial Corp. One of the world's largest wire and cable producers, General Cable tripled Wassall's size. Nevertheless, some industry observers questioned the wisdom of this purchase, pigeonholing General Cable as essentially a commodities dealer. The new parent cut employment by ten percent, closed three factories by 1995, and projected the rationalization of three more by 1997, and eliminated one warehouse. Wassall seemed to have little trouble "digesting" this major acquisition; its revenues increased from £277.8 million in 1993 to £972.9 million in 1995, and its pre-tax profit more than doubled from £27.6 million to £55.1 million.

Asia Targeted in Mid-1990s

Faced with fewer prime acquisition targets in Europe and North America, Wassall joined many multinational firms in conquest of Asian markets in the mid-1990s. In 1994, the company established an office in Singapore with the intent to cultivate export markets for its existing subsidiaries, but soon began applying its acquisitive methods to this high-potential region. But the firm soon found that it was not much easier to find "bargains" in Asia than it had been in the U.S. or U.K. due to a run-up in the local stock market. In 1995, however, Wassall paid £17.4 million (US$26.3 million) for a controlling interest in York Pacific Holdings Ltd., a manufacturer of truck axles. Renamed Wassall Asia Pacific Ltd., this new member of the family gave Wassall the top share of this niche market in Singapore, Malaysia, and Australia. The parent company hoped not only to use its newest conquest as a launchpad for its existing product lines, but also to exploit the region's notoriously low overheads via joint ventures and wholly-owned manufacturing sites.

The May 1996 divestment of four of its smallest affiliates to generate £11.5 million seemed to indicate that a new acquisition could be right around the corner.

Principal Subsidiaries

General Cable Corporation; DAP Inc. (U.S.A.); Antler Limited; MCG Closures Limited; Metal Closures Group South Africa Limited (South Africa); MCG Plascaps S.p.A. (Italy); Techno Pack Limited; Bentley Photo-Litho Co Limited; Evertaut Limited; Hille Limited; Ergonom Limited; Hille Auditorium Seating Limited; Wassall Asia Pacific Limited.

Principal Divisions

Cable; Consumer; Closures; Industrial and Commercial.

Further Reading

"Evode Fight Over," *Manufacturing Chemist*, January 1993, p. 8.

"Evode Hldg: Defends Against Hostile GBP94.3 Mil Bid From Wassall," *DIY Week*, December 18, 1992, p. 2.

Greig Middleton & Co. Ltd., "Wassall—Company Report," The Investext Group, October 25, 1995.

"Growth By Acquisition," *Business Asia*, January 29, 1996, p. 12.

Hamilton, Sally, "Sons of Hanson," *Business London*, July 1990, pp. 53–57.

Hoare Govett Investment Research Ltd., "Wassall—Company Report," The Investext Group, November 2, 1992.

"Joint Venture Fiber Optic Cable Company Formed By General," *Cambridge Telecom Report*, December 30, 1996.

Kane, Frank, "Wassall Seals Long-Awaited Deal with £178m for US Cables Group," *Guardian*, May 6, 1994, p. 17.

Milstead, David, "General Cable Cuts HQ Staff," *Cincinnati Business Courier*, October 3, 1994, pp. 1–2.

SBC Warburg, "Wassall—Company Report," The Investext Group, April 2, 1996.

"U.K. Company Shops for Asian Firms," *Crossborder Monitor*, April 3, 1996, p. 8.

"Wassall Sets $269.8 Million Acquisition of Lindner-Controlled General Cable," *Wall Street Journal*, May 6, 1994, p. B4.

—April Dougal Gasbarre

Waterhouse Investor Services, Inc.

100 Wall Street
New York, New York 10005
U.S.A.
(212) 806-3500
Fax: (212) 809-0274
Web site: http://www.waterhouse.com

Wholly Owned Subsidiary of Toronto-Dominion Bank
Incorporated: 1979 as Waterhouse Securities, Inc.
Employees: 1,000
Sales: $131.2 million (1995)
SICs: 6021 National Commercial Banks; 6211 Security
    Brokers, Dealers & Flotation Companies

Waterhouse Investor Services, Inc. provides, through its principal subsidiary, Waterhouse Securities, Inc., discount brokerage and related financial services, primarily to retail customers throughout the United States. It was the nation's fifth-largest discount brokerage house in 1995. Through another wholly owned subsidiary, Waterhouse National Bank, a "virtual" bank with only one office, it electronically offers a variety of financial services and products, primarily to the customer base of Waterhouse Securities. Waterhouse Investor Services grew rapidly in the bull market of the early 1990s, a period that saw commissions collected by discount brokers rise from $613 million in 1990 (and $48 million in 1980) to almost $1.5 billion in 1994. The company was purchased in 1996 by Toronto-Dominion Bank for $525 million U.S. ($715 million Canadian) and became a wholly owned subsidiary of Toronto-Dominion.

Private Brokerage House, 1979–86

The company was founded by Lawrence M. Waterhouse, Jr., a former Chemical Bank employee who had become a financial adviser. After the Securities and Exchange Commission ended nearly 180 years of fixed-rate commissions on the stock exchanges in 1975, Waterhouse placed a small advertisement in a newspaper offering his services at a discount from the standard rate. He did well enough to incorporate in 1979 as Waterhouse Securities, Inc. In the company's first, partial fiscal year, operating out of a Manhattan office, its four account officers amassed $230,000 in commissions. In 1980 the company opened an office in San Francisco and ended the fiscal year with 13 officers and $1.36 million in commissions. The following year it opened an office in Los Angeles and ended the fiscal year with 17 account officers and $2.36 million in commissions.

After a relatively stagnant 1982, Waterhouse Securities raised its commissions to $6.9 million in fiscal 1983 (ended August 31, 1983) and earned $499,090 in net income. The following fiscal year the company opened a Chicago office, but commissions fell to $5.6 million, and it lost $42,638. In fiscal 1985 Waterhouse Securities added branches in Dallas and Washington, D.C., raised its commissions to $7.1 million, and had net income of $223,575. During fiscal 1986 it opened a Philadelphia office and ended the period with 57 brokers and nearly $11.5 million in commissions. Net income was $668,128.

Public Holding Company, 1987–90

The company reincorporated as Waterhouse Investor Services, Inc., a holding company with three subsidiaries, including Waterhouse Securities, in 1987. It went public the same year, collecting $5.7 million from the sale of nearly 40 percent of the outstanding shares at $7 a share. Most of this money was used to open a self-clearing operation in 1988 so that the company no longer would have to depend upon an unaffiliated clearing house to execute its transactions. During fiscal 1987 Waterhouse opened branches in Seattle and Miami and had net income of nearly $1.4 million. It ended the period with 70 brokers and $15 million in commissions.

During fiscal 1988 Waterhouse added branches in Atlanta, Boston, Detroit, and St. Louis, bringing the total to 13 in 11 states and the District of Columbia, serving about 80,000 customer accounts. It was reaching potential customers through a combination of referrals and advertisements in newspapers and financial publications. Its three-part marketing plan consisted of a simple, level-discount commission schedule; services by personal-account officers in regional offices; and free investment and financial-publication information (but not investment advice) to customers with active accounts. In October 1987 the Dow Jones index suddenly fell 25 percent in a wave of panic selling; as a result trading was down for the rest of fiscal 1988, and Waterhouse's revenues dropped to $14.8 million. The company lost $88,000 that year, not only because of the drop in commission revenue but also due to the start-up costs of the self-clearing operation.

Although commissions were still below the fiscal 1987 level in fiscal 1989, Waterhouse had record total revenue of $19.6 million because interest income came to almost $5 million, primarily from a new service—loans to customers who wanted to trade on margin. The company's net income for the year was $1.1 million. Waterhouse added a Cleveland branch in fiscal 1989, raised the number of its accounts to about 100,000, and declared its first dividend. During fiscal 1990 Waterhouse raised its revenue to $23.5 million and its net income to $1.3 million. It acquired a small brokerage operation in Kansas City, opened a branch in Houston and its second office in New York City, and increased its number of accounts to about 115,000.

Wall Street Favorite, 1991–93

In 1991 Waterhouse became a hot stock, rising about sixfold from its average value of approximately $4 a share in 1990. Its customer base expanded to about 150,000 accounts and its number of branches to 30 in 20 states and the District of Columbia. Net income soared to $3.2 million on total revenue of $31.4 million. During fiscal 1992 Waterhouse nearly doubled its business, earning $8.5 million on revenue of $55.4 million. It added no-load mutual funds and fixed-income securities to its offerings and ended the calendar year with 420 employees and 39 offices in 24 states.

Waterhouse was now in fourth place among discount brokers, behind Charles Schwab & Co.—by far the largest—Quick & Reilly Inc., and Fidelity Investments. Unlike the graduated commissions offered by most discount brokers, Waterhouse was offering a standard commission about 70 percent lower than that charged by full-service firms, on top of a minimum fee of $35. By the end of 1992 it was test-marketing a telephone brokerage service on the West Coast and working to develop an online service based on personal computers.

During fiscal 1993 Waterhouse's revenues grew to $84.4 million and its net income to $14.4 million. The number of offices increased to 55 and the number of active customers to 180,000. The company's stock reached $36.50 a share in September 1993, making it the most highly valued brokerage stock on the market. Even with a late-fall decline in price, Waterhouse's total stock-market value was nearly three times the fiscal year's revenue, and its share price was 6.7 times book value. *Overpriced Stock Service,* the short-sellers' newsletter, dubbed Waterhouse its overpriced stock of the month, vulnerable to the first glimmer of a bear market. Just before the end of the year Waterhouse took on $50-million worth of long-term debt by issuing 10-year convertible notes at six-percent interest.

Expanded Product Line, 1994–96

Although there was no bear market in 1994, Waterhouse's stock came back down to earth, averaging about half the level of

its 1993 peak. In the fiscal year it again set records, with total revenues reaching $107.6 million and net income $15.7 million. The number of branches reached 60 in 31 states and the District of Columbia, and the number of customers, 221,000. In October 1994 the company received federal clearance to open a new unit, Waterhouse National Bank, in White Plains, New York. This bank became operational in 1995, offering certificates of deposit and money-market accounts. It was planning to introduce a credit card and other products and services during 1996, including home-equity loans. At the end of 1995 Waterhouse National Bank had deposits of $362 million, total assets of $386.1 million, and net income of $517,000 for the year.

During fiscal 1995 the total revenue of Waterhouse Investor Services reached $143 million and its net income $19.4 million, both records. The number of Waterhouse Securities branches rose to 72 in 37 states and the District of Columbia. The number of its account officers had grown to 551, compared to 103 in 1991. Waterhouse Securities was serving more than 400,000 individual investors and had about 300,000 active accounts. Of its revenue, some 79 percent came from commissions and clearing fees; 12 percent from net interest; and seven percent from mutual fund fees.

At the end of fiscal 1995 Waterhouse Securities was offering a wide array of investment vehicles, including stocks, bonds, options, and mutual funds. (Among its most lucrative products were loans to customers for trading on margin, which grew to $365 million in fiscal 1995.) According to the parent company's description of its business, by maintaining a low-cost structure and utilizing a highly automated order-processing system, Waterhouse Securities could charge commission rates substantially lower than those charged by other leading nationwide discount brokers as well as full-service brokerage firms. The minimum commission of $35 a transaction had not been increased since the company's inception. The parent company, Waterhouse Investor Services, was also operating a deep-discount subsidiary named Washington Discount Brokerage Corp.

During the first three quarters of fiscal 1996 Waterhouse was on a pace to shatter its previous record revenues and earnings by a considerable amount. For nine months it had total revenue of $171.9 million and net income of $22.3 million. It regained fourth place among discount brokers in the United States, opened seven more offices by April 1996, and raised its number of accounts to 500,000. Waterhouse announced in June 1996 that it planned to open eight more offices by the end of the fiscal year and to introduce the Waterhouse Investors PC Network, offering investment and portfolio-management software. This would give customers direct access to the financial markets, including real-time quotas, trading, account information, and news. In addition the company would be introducing services that would allow customers to access account information and place trades 24 hours a day, seven days a week.

1996 Acquisition by Toronto-Dominion Bank

In April 1996 Toronto-Dominion Bank, Canada's fifth-largest bank, agreed to acquire Waterhouse for $525 million ($715 million Canadian) in cash and stock, or $38 a share—an extraordinary amount three times Waterhouse's 1995 revenue and nearly six times its book value. Lawrence M. Waterhouse, Jr., the company's chairman and chief executive officer, was to continue heading the firm, which would be a subsidiary of the bank. Toronto-Dominion also was operating Green Line Investor Services, Canada's largest and most successful discount broker, which had expanded to the United States in 1995 under the name Green Line USA.

The agreement called for payment in either cash or Toronto-Dominion shares, but there was a ceiling of about 35 percent in cash. Waterhouse shareholders electing to receive Toronto-Dominion (TD) common stock were to receive 1.87046 TD shares for each Waterhouse share, with fractional shares paid in cash. The other shareholders were to receive 67.14162 percent in cash and the remainder in TD stock, with fractional shares paid in cash. The principal beneficiary of the sale was the Waterhouse family, which held about 23 percent of the stock, and other officers and directors, who held about 18 percent. Ten thousand dollars invested in Waterhouse stock five years earlier would now be worth $488,606.

The transaction also enabled Toronto-Dominion to enter U.S. retail banking by acquiring Waterhouse National Bank. However, a New York City–based consumer-activist group, Inner City Press/Community on the Move, challenged the takeover on the grounds that the Waterhouse bank had not met the requirements of the Community Reinvestment Act (CRA), which mandates U.S. banks to invest in low- and middle-income neighborhoods. In response, Toronto-Dominion vowed to increase the bank's CRA annual budget—only $350,000 in October 1995—to $7 million in 1997. Waterhouse National Bank bought $2-million worth of New York City housing bonds in August 1996 and committed itself to making $1 million in community-development loans before the end of the year. Community protests continued nonetheless, but the Federal Reserve Board cleared the acquisition in October. With the closing of the merger on October 15, 1996, Waterhouse Securities and Green Line together constituted the third-largest discount broker in the world, with more than a million customers.

Principal Subsidiaries

L.M. Waterhouse & Co., Inc.; National Investor Services Corp.; Washington Discount Brokerage Corp.; Waterhouse Asset Management, Inc.; Waterhouse National Bank; Waterhouse, Nicoll & Associates, Inc.; Waterhouse Securities, Inc.

Further Reading

Blackwell, Richard, "TD Defends $715-Million Takeover of Waterhouse," *Financial Post-Toronto,* July 16, 1996, p. 9.
——, "TD Pays Top Dollar to Play in the Big Leagues," *Financial Post-Toronto,* April 11, 1996, p. 1.
Greenberg, Larry M., "Toronto-Dominion Bank to Pay $525 Million for Discount Broker," *Wall Street Journal,* April 11, 1996, p. B6.
Holliday, Kalen, "New York Discount Brokerage Firm Is Forming a Bank in the Suburbs," *American Banker,* June 22, 1994, p. 10.
Khasru, B. Z., "Inner City Targets White Plains Bank," *Westchester County Business Journal,* September 16, 1996, p. 9.
Parker, Marcia, "Discount Broker Driving the Bulls," *Crain's New York Business,* December 21, 1992, p. 19.
Power, William, "Waterhouse Investor Services Learns Firsthand What Can Happen to 'Momentum' Stocks," *Wall Street Journal,* December 2, 1993, p. C2.
Seiberg, Janet, "Amid Protest, Fed Stalls Canadian Bank's Deal and Seeks Detailed CRA Plan," *American Banker,* August 23, 1996, p. 2.
——, "Over Protests, Takeover by Toronto-Dominion Is Approved," *American Banker,* October 3, 1996, p. 2.
Siklos, Richard, "Waterhouse Has Reason to Smile," *Financial Post-Toronto,* April 11, 1996, p. 3.
"Toronto-Dominion Bank and Waterhouse Investor Services, Inc. Close Merger," *PR Newswire,* October 15, 1996, p. 1015TO004.

—Robert Halasz

WD-40 Company

WD-40 Company

1061 Cudahy Place
San Diego, California 92110
U.S.A.
(619) 275-1400
Fax: (619) 275-5823

Public Company
Incorporated: 1953
Employees: 149
Sales: $130.9 million (1996)
Stock Exchanges: NASDAQ
SICs: 2992 Oils & Greases, Lubricating Type

Since the 1950s, the San Diego-based WD-40 Company has dominated the U.S. market for its namesake multipurpose lubricant. The WD-40 substance is a petroleum-based lubricant, moisture retardant, and rust preventative. It is used in over 75 percent of American households, and is ranked in the top three percent of all brands in consumer awareness by Landor Associates. One of the product's strengths is its versatility: it has been found to improve the performance of sewing machines, attract fish, loosen rusted nuts and bolts, and unfreeze door locks and handles. Sold through industrial distributors, automotive stores, mass merchandisers, hardware and home improvement centers, WD-40 is found in over 148 countries worldwide. A one-product company until the early 1990s, WD-40 Company now also produces 3-In-One Oil and T.A.L. 5, a premium heavy-duty lubricant aimed at the industrial market.

The Birth of WD-40, 1953

Although WD-40 has been a household name for several decades, it did not begin as a household product. In 1953, Norm Larson of Rocket Chemical Company developed WD-40 as a corrosion protector for missile covers for the San Diego-based Convair, an aerospace and defense contractor and a division of General Dynamics. Eventually, WD-40 was intended for use on NASA's Atlas missile. The name WD-40 stands for "water displacement, formulation successful in 40th attempt," because

it was on the 40th try that Larson perfected the product. Employees at General Dynamics discovered that WD-40 was perfect for a variety of home uses, and they began sneaking the lubricant home from work. By 1955, Larson began experimenting with putting WD-40 in aerosol cans, and in 1959, Rocket Chemical Company responded to the consumer market for a home lubricant by contracting with an aerosol packager and preparing WD-40 for commercial sales.

Rocket Chemical Company, which was founded in 1952 by Larson and three investors, was a one-room operation with a three-person staff. In addition to WD-40, the company produced rust resistors and removers for metal parts and tools for the aerospace industry. In 1960, the company grew to include 7 employees with sales of about 45 cases per day. Rocket Chemical Company sales representatives sold the product out of their cars to San Diego sporting goods and hardware stores. A slight recipe change in 1961—adding a dose of mineral spirits to the original formula to cover the petroleum scent—is the only adjustment ever made to Larson's original formula as of the late 1990s. Hurricane "Carla," which ravaged the Florida coast in 1961, increased WD-40's business dramatically, as it was used by hurricane victims to recondition water-damaged vehicles and machinery.

One Product Transforms a Company, 1960s

By 1965, WD-40 sales were so successful that Rocket Chemical Company ceased production of all other products to focus solely on the lubricant. Sales surpassed $1 million in 1968, and when John Barry became president the next year, the company officially changed its name to WD-40. In 1969, sales reached $2 million. Between 1969 and the 1990s, sales growth has been continuous.

With a mandate to accelerate both revenues and earnings, John Barry would pilot WD-40 to a position of prominence as an untouchable one-product company. The brother-in-law of one of the three original investors in Rocket Chemical Company, Barry garnered his marketing know-how working at companies including 3M, Avery Label, and Adams Rite. With a virtually unknown product and no working capital, Barry's marketing strategies were straightforward and simple, emphasizing free samples (including 10,000 WD-40 samples each month sent to soldiers in the Vietnam War to keep their weapons dry), trade shows, and magazine advertising. Product awareness was built through manufacturers' representatives, who worked on commission and sold the product to wholesalers only. No written contracts were held between WD-40 and the manufacturers' representatives, and the relationship could be terminated with 30-day notice. The underlying philosophy behind these strategies was to market the company's one product to its full potential, diversifying the uses of the product, not the product itself, while keeping costs down.

Going Public, New Growth, the 1970s

In 1973, WD-40 went public. Prior to this first offering, the company was a Subchapter-S corporation. Shareholders gave up this election by going public, receiving looser restrictions on their estates and tax benefits in exchange. Heavy demand escalated the initial price of a 40,000 share offering to $16.5 from the originally intended $15 a share, and later in the year shares surged at $34, dropping again to $15 at the end of the year. The initial offering generated net proceeds of approximately $590,000, of which $350,000 was used for a new plant, with the remainder added to working capital. The company paid half its earnings in dividends, increasing dividends with earnings growth. The next year, the company moved its headquarters to its present location on Cudahy Place in San Diego. Prices in 1974 were raised by 10.6 percent.

In 1978, after 25 years of business, sales reached $25 million. The following year, sales increased to $34 million, with earnings of $5 million. Sales and earnings had increased at a 10-year compounded rate of approximately 35 percent. The company remained tightly held, with over half of the stock held by officers, directors, and relatives of the original three Rocket Chemical Company investors. The wholesale price of the company's product rose 43 percent between 1969 and 1981, while the U.S. wholesale price index increased 132 percent during this period. Costs at WD-40 had always been low, since the focus on one product meant there were no research and development costs. The company at this time had only 32 employees, with a

sales force of 65 manufacturers' representatives selling the product to about 14,000 wholesalers. The entire manufacturing operation was staffed by one part-time employee, who created the WD-40 concentrate from a mixture of off-the-shelf chemicals. About 28 percent of sales were spent on selling, marketing, and administration. Also, because the company had no debt, minimal overhead, and rented its office space, WD-40 paid about five percent back to investors.

In 1979, 35 million cans of WD-40 were said to reach consumers each year, with 55 percent sold to homeowners and sportsmen and the remainder purchased by commercial and industrial users. The first price increase since 1974 raised the cost of the cans by 15 to 16 percent. Half of the company's total assets were held in cash, with after-tax net earnings around 16 percent. In 1981, the company was selected by *Forbes* as one of the small, emerging growth companies on its "Up-and-Comers List." Continuing to experiment with innovative sampling as a marketing strategy, WD-40 entered into a partnership that year with Wagner Spray Tech, a spray gun manufacturer in Minneapolis. WD-40 samples were included in spray gun packages, along with instructional brochures. Both companies shared equally in the costs and profits of the sample program.

International Expansion, Mid-1980s

By 1985, sales had increased to $57.3 million, with a 21 percent increase the following year to $69.4 million. Earnings in 1986 were $11.6 million, and shares were sold at a new all-time high of $33½, a 44 percent gain. Having already achieved great success with its one product in the U.S. in the 1980s, it was time for WD-40 Company to expand its presence in the world market. International sales at this time represented less than 5 percent of total sales (not including Canada). In 1986, rather than renewing its contract with its United Kingdom Distributor, the company built its own plant in Milton Keyes (near London). The next year an official subsidiary, WD-40 Company Ltd. (United Kingdom), was established to manufacture, produce, and oversee distribution of WD-40 in Europe, the Middle East, and Africa. Since that year, when sales for the United Kingdom and Europe were $10 million, earnings have grown rapidly. By 1992, sales attributed to France, Spain, and the Middle East had reached $17.5 million. Continuing to emphasize overseas expansion, the company bolstered its sales force in Europe by adding new sales representatives in France, Spain, and Italy. Shortly thereafter, Barry began sales expansion to Australia and the Pacific Rim. By 1988, European, Australian, and Asian markets would account for 21 percent of revenues.

Sales reached $71 million in 1987, and stock hit a high of 46. However, the October 19, 1987 crash of the stock market, causing a 508-point drop in the Dow Jones Industrial Average, caused WD-40's stock to drop to the mid-20s in November. With fewer than 100 employees, the company was still able to net $11 million in 1987. Every dollar of that $11 million was paid in dividends. At this time, the company had no debt and $18 million in cash, with a market value of $231 million.

In 1988, WD-40 changed its sales strategy, shifting from salesperson commissions to direct sales. This policy was implemented as a means to increase business with large retailers, who now formed a significant portion of the company's sales, with 40 percent of sales originating in 50 of the company's 12,000 accounts. Large retailers preferred the elimination of intermediary distributors, as a cost-cutting factor. Responding to this desire, WD-40, using a contract clause allowing the termination of the hiring agreement on either side with 90 days notice, decided to eliminate twelve distributors and instead hire direct salespersons to cater to the large accounts. Good earnings prospects and an increased dividend brought WD-40's stock to an October high of 33.25, and sales rose to $80 million, with net income increasing 40 percent to $25.4 million. However, the new sales strategy would prove dangerous to the company's earnings in the long run.

Eight of the 12 distributors sued WD-40, claiming that the company had promised them job security in exchange for company loyalty. In 1992, the distributors were granted a $10.3 million settlement. WD-40 appealed the decision. In the meantime, two additional distributors—who had not joined the original suit—filed a separate lawsuit in 1992, using the same lawyers. In 1993, this second suit was settled, granting the distributors $2.5 million. In 1994, the original case was again decided in favor of the distributors, costing the company $12.6 million. It is possible, since sales had skyrocketed from $80 million in 1988 to $100 million in 1992, due in part to the new sales strategy, the settlement fee may not actually have presented a real loss to the company. 1994 was the first year in a decade in which WD-40 had flat earnings, but profits still totaled $12.6 million on record sales of $112 million.

Competition has never presented a challenge to WD-40. Though the formula for the lubricant is a guarded secret, the company has chosen never to patent it. Although WD-40 is physically indistinguishable from other products—such as 3M's Q4, Borden's Ten*4, and Valvoline's 1-2-99—no contender has presented even a minor challenge, and WD-40 has buried over 200 competing products over the years. This included, as of 1988, 14 billion-dollar companies, whose economic clout was unable to unseat WD-40s blue-and-yellow can.

After over two decades of leadership, John Barry retired to become chairman of the board in 1990, replaced by Gerald Schleif as president and CEO. Schleif was previously WD-40's executive vice president and CFO and had served the company for 21 years. In 1990, WD-40 increased the price of its product for the first time in 9 years, raising it by nine percent. The company was named among "100 of America's Best Companies" by *Fortune* magazine in 1991. A new international subsidiary, WD-40 Ltd. (Australia), was established that year, to market the product in New Zealand, Southeast Asia, and the Far East, and a sales manager was employed to handle Hong Kong in 1992.

By 1992, WD-40 had an 83 percent share of the multipurpose lubricant market, with sales of $99.9 million (an 11.3 percent increase over the previous year's sales of $89.8 million). Stock was trading at 52. Two-thirds of those sales were generated in the United States, and WD-40 Company targeted international expansion as the key to increased growth, setting a goal of a 50:50 ratio.

The 1990s, Cause for Celebration

WD-40 celebrated its 40th anniversary in 1993, breaking the $100 million sales mark with sales of over $108 million. Plans for the anniversary bash included a commemorative anniversary can. The company was featured among the *Top Ten Most Profitable* companies on the 1993 NASDAQ exchange. Statistics revealed that 4 out of every 5 American households used WD-40, and that 81 percent of industrial and trade consumers also chose the product. Weekly sales in the U.S. amounted to over one million cans of the petroleum-based lubricant.

A major new direction was implemented in December 1995. After over 30 years as a successful single-product company, WD-40 acquired 3-In-One Oil from Reckitt & Coleman (UK). The following year a new product, T.A.L. 5 (a premium, extra-strength lubricant), was developed and launched. A new corporate logo was designed, to reflect the integration of two new products. In that same year, WD-40 changed its propellant from hydrocarbon to CO2, reducing Volatile Organic Compounds content to comply with new environmental regulations. In 1996, WD-40 continued its growth, with sales of $131 million and income of $21.3 million. International sales grew in 1996 to $51.4 million, a 28 percent increase over the previous year, with international business accounting for 44 percent of sales, and with WD-40 marketed in over 135 countries and 30 different languages.

The WD-40 Company, then, has achieved practically unparalleled success in the first two phases of its executive identity: first, as a one-product company on the domestic sphere, and second, peddling the same multipurpose lubricant to world markets. In the late 1990s, the company is launching Phase Three in what it intends to be an uninterrupted story of growth. The integration of new products ends over 30 years in which WD-40's success was routinely linked with its status as a one-product company, and its colossal standing as the "generic" brand in its market. WD-40's stated goal, at the beginning of 1997, is to achieve a dominant market share of the entire category worldwide. This juncture, then, is a major turning point for the San Diego-based company, requiring an overhaul of long-trusted marketing formulas and strategies. The company's leadership has been cautious over the years, not prone to risk-taking in sales and marketing. It is unlikely, therefore, that the new product lines will destabilize the continued reign of WD-40 as the leading multipurpose lubricant. Whether the WD-40 Company will achieve further growth through the acquisition of new products, however, remains to be seen.

Principal Subsidiaries

WD-40 Company Ltd. (U.K.); WD-40 Products (Canada) Ltd.; WD-40 Company (Australia) Pty. Ltd.

Further Reading

Cowan, Alison Leigh, "Terminating Outside Sales Staff Proves Costly to WD-40," *The New York Times*, July 23, 1993, p. C4 (N).
"How to Be Happy in One Act," *Fortune*, December 19, 1988, p. 179.
Johnson, Greg, "Some San Diego Firms Join Rush to Buy Back Stock After Market Dive," *Los Angeles Times*, November 3, 1987, p. 4-2A.

Katz, Irving, "How San Diego Firms Handled the Ups and Downs," *Los Angeles Times*, January 13, 1987, p. 4–2A.

Kichen, Steve, and Jon Schriber, "Life in the Fast Lane," *Forbes*, November 9, 1981, pp. 188–189.

Lazo, Shirley A. "WD-40 Does It Again," *Barron's,* July 3, 1995, p. 38.

Murray, Thomas, "The 5 Best-Managed Companies," *Business Month*, December 1989, pp. 27, 43–43.

"Now 35 Million Consumers Push WD-40's Profit Button," *Inc.*, October, 1979, pp. 64–68.

Perry, Tony, "This Company is No Squeaky Wheel When It Comes to Self-Promotion," *Los Angeles Times*, December 16, 1992, p. B-1.

Repaci, Louis, "Sampling Program Meets Marketing Objectives of 2 Different Companies," *Marketing News*, April 16, 1982, p. 3.

Richman, Louis S., "What America Makes Best," *Fortune*, Spring/Summer, 1991, pp. 78–87.

Ritter, Bill, "WD-40 Announces Record $11.6 Million Earnings," *Los Angeles Times*, October 17, 1986, p. 4–3.

"Schleif Named to Two WD-40 Executive Posts," *Los Angeles Times*, September 26, 1990, p. D-7.

Tivenan, William, "WD-40," in *Encyclopedia of Consumer Brands*, Vol. 2, edited by Janice Jorgensen, Detroit: St. James Press, 1994, pp. 572–574.

—Heidi Feldman

Weru Aktiengesellschaft

Zumhoferstraße 25
Postfach 160
73635 Rudersberg
Baden-Württemberg
Germany
(49) 7183 3030
Fax: (49) 7183 303370

Wholly Owned Subsidiary of Caradon Plc
Incorporated: 1974
Employees 2,084 (1995)
Sales: US$352.74 million (1995)
Stock Exchanges: Stuttgart Frankfurt
SICs: 2821 Polyvinylchloride Resins, Manufacturing;
3089 Plastic Window Frames, Manufacturing; 3442
Metal Doors, Sash, Frames, Moldings, and Trim,
Manufacturing; 5031 Windows and Doors, Wholesale

Weru Aktiengesellschaft (AG) is the largest manufacturer of high-end windows and doors in Germany as well as the largest producer in continental Europe as a whole. It makes, markets, and distributes wood, aluminum, and polyvinylchoride (PVC) windows, window units, doors, glass residential conservatories, and related systems and accessories for new homes and the renovation of older buildings. Emphasizing American-style quality control, teamwork, data processing, flexible manufacturing, and creative marketing concepts and technology, Weru by the mid-1990s was offering electronic keyless entry doors, composite window systems, and so many door forms, colors, and materials that customers could choose from more than 70,000 distinct door products alone. With main plants in Rudersberg, Triptis, and Heilsbronn, Germany, Weru maintained facilities and sales offices throughout Western and, by the mid-1990s, Eastern Europe.

Glass, Christian Eppensteiner, and the Window-Maker's Trade: 1843–1917

In the early years of the 20th century, the Swiss-born architect Charles-Edouard Le Corbusier famously remarked that the history of architecture was largely the story of the window. Perhaps no other architect did more to prove Le Corbusier right than the German architect Walter Gropius, whose design for a light-flooded, all glass-exterior factory in Alfeld, Germany, in 1911 is generally credited with the birth of the Bauhaus movement that later transformed nonresidential architecture. That Gropius was German was perhaps no historical accident either, for since the Middle Ages German craftsmen had contributed much to the development of the glassmaking craft.

In 1843 one such craftsman, Christian Friedrich Eppensteiner, opened a small workshop for fitting windows with glass, a process known as glazing, in Rudersberg, Germany, a small town near Stuttgart. At the time Eppensteiner began his business, the manufacture of windows was in a period of transition. Although early windows had almost all been casements, that is, windows that opened out or in from side hinges like doors, the Dutch had introduced the now common vertically sliding, double-hung sash window around 1680, and it soon became an accepted style.

The biggest change in window design in Eppensteiner's day, however, was the amount of glass that could be used for the pane. Until the 19th century, the technology of glassmaking allowed only small panes to be fashioned, limiting the size of the average structure's windows. Improvements in both industrial machinery and glassmaking methods were already altering the window-making craft when Eppensteiner's first products began to establish his reputation in mid-century. In 1830, an Englishman named Lucas Chance brought home from Germany a new glassmaking technique that represented a significant advance over the traditional method. In this technique, a glassblowing pipe was dipped into molten glass, extracted, and manipulated into a cylindrical shape. While still hot, the cylinder was then flattened on a sand-covered iron plate and allowed to cool. Chance's German teachers had discovered that if the molten glass cylinder was allowed to cool, cut with a diamond, and then reheated and flattened on a bed of smooth glass, the surface imperfections caused by the old iron plate method could be eliminated.

By the turn of the century the artisan's craft of Eppensteiner's small workshop had evolved into a factory-based—though still labor-intensive—operation. Window panes were

Company Perspectives:

Form follows function. Doors and windows are by nature products which must be more than simply functional, they must please the eye too. And since the architectural landscape is such a broad field and because tastes must be catered down to the smallest detail, our range of forms, colors, and materials is accordingly wide and extensive. However, despite the subjective nature of aesthetic judgment, our company always puts one principle first: no form without a functional purpose.

still formed from glass melted in large *Schmelzofen* (melting ovens), from which globules of molten glass were drawn by the glassmaker through a five-foot-long pipe.

A Future for Glass: 1918–54

After World War I, an enormous demand for modest residential homes propelled the window-making industry decisively into the mass manufacturing age. As Gropius and his colleagues were revolutionizing the design of the modern high-rise, new standardized steel windows in a variety of preformed sizes and models were altering the craft of designing windows from an ad hoc art, determined by the dimensions of the existing structure, to an assembly-line industry in which a growing number of new homes were designed to accommodate the standardized windows becoming available. Window manufacturers were also soon delivering not only the window itself to the construction site but also the complete window unit, with casements preinstalled and the fittings already fixed in place.

In the years before World War II, Gropius's Bauhaus method was leading to dramatic attempts to exploit the light-giving characteristics of modern architectural and window manufacturing technology: entire walls could be filled with a single sheet of glass and even glass bricks began to be used in place of traditional construction brick. Although the sheer number of older residences in Germany's housing stock ensured that Eppensteiner's legacy of crafting glass windows to fit the particular dimensions and construction of existing structures would survive, the introduction in the late 1930s of galvanized (dipped in zinc) all-steel window frames further cemented the advances made by the newer technologies.

Roller Shutters, PVC, and the Rebirth of Weru: 1955–88

For all the advances transforming the window and construction industries in general, the family-run, artisan's approach Eppensteiner had established in 1843 continued to rule his firm even into the postwar years of German reconstruction. New construction materials—from natural or colored aluminum alloys and stainless steel to vitreous enamel—continued to alter Eppensteiner's ancient craft, however, and knowing that a larger market could be gained if the firm modernized its business, in 1955 the company's owners reformed Eppensteiner's family firm as Weru Rolladenwerk (roller shutter works). Like traditional window blinds, roller shutters were often wooden

and later synthetic slats that could be closed to protect homes from sunlight, noise, heat loss, and vandalism.

Weru's reincarnation as Weru Rolladenwerk represented its definitive entrance into the postwar homebuilding industry, and, significantly enough, it occurred just at the time when a new window manufacturing technology was revolutionizing the industry. In the early 1930s, the German industrial giant BASF began producing polyvinylchloride (PVC), or vinyl, a rigid polymer resin that because of its durability and flexibility showed promise for such applications as film, magnetic tape, and electric insulation. PVC was also a perfect material for windows: whereas metal conducted heat or cold transparently, PVC maintained a moderate temperature year-round; while wood rotted and metal rusted, PVC resisted sun erosion, pollution, and rain; and while metal and wood required periodic painting, even when scratched PVC displayed the color in which it had been manufactured.

In 1955, the German company Dynamit Nobel produced the first window system made of PVC, which was followed by the introduction by Fiberlux of the first vinyl windows in North America in 1959. A year later, another American company, B. F. Goodrich, introduced the first PVC storm window. Weru saw the potential of the new material, and in 1960 it also began using *Kunststoff*—or plastic/synthetics—for its roller shutter products.

Throughout the 1960s, PVC increased its foothold in the window manufacturing industry. In 1963, for example, Fiberlux unveiled a system for mass-producing rigid vinyl window products, by 1964 had introduced its own vinyl storm doors, and by 1967 had developed its first PVC double-hung replacement window and PVC replacement window manufacturing system. With its line of roller shutters thriving, in 1969 Weru itself began manufacturing synthetic windows and window elements, and it completed its transformation from a small "handicraft" supplier to a national industrial operation when the brand name Weru was registered as a trademark in 1969. In 1970 it began a partnership program to build a network of individual businesses identified by its trademark that by 1990 numbered 1,350. Four years later, Weru became a *Kommanditgesellschaft*, or limited partnership, and established several companies to expand its market reach. In 1975 it branched out again into aluminum PVC windows and by 1979 was manufacturing house doors. By 1985 Weru's 750 employees were producing 455,000 windows and 8,100 house doors a year, and sales had reached DM 158 million. Window and door production as well as the company's administration and management continued to be run out of the "ancestral seat" at Rudersberg, but new manufacturing technology was transforming the traditional window-making business. By the late 1980s manufacturing surplus material was being recycled to avoid wastage and reduce costs and computerized systems were used in product design to manage the flow of raw materials (primarily aluminum, plastic/synthetics, and steel), production planning, and the precision machinery that fashioned Weru's ever more complex product lines. The company also marketed two major lines of security-enhanced aluminum-frame house doors with 2,000 possible design variations as well as a steel-reinforced PVC door.

A "quality circle" program to increase the quality of its windows and doors through worker feedback had been adopted in 1986, and an educational program for keeping employees up to date in sales, product technology, application technology, and assembly techniques had also become an integral part of Weru's corporate culture. In 1988 Weru introduced its Weru Partner Software (WPS) program for settling accounts and accelerating accurate cost estimates; by 1991, 70 percent of its sales were being processed on it. Bolstered by a boom in the construction market for new homes in Germany, Weru between 1985 and 1989 saw its annual window and door output rise 26 percent and 36 percent, respectively. More importantly, between 1985 and 1988 sales had vaulted 32 percent to DM 208 million. Weru was now Germany's leader in the manufacture of doors and windows, with close to 11 percent of the market.

Going Public: 1989–95

In 1989, Weru responded to its new dominance of the German market by converting itself into a publicly owned company, selling 400,000 shares in the "highpoint" event of the company's long history. Three separate Weru operations—Weru Beteiligungsgesellschaft mbH (a holding company), Weru GmbH & Co. KG, and Weru GmbH & Co. Fensterfabrikations-KG (a window manufacturer)—were consolidated as Weru AG and merged with the window and door export distribution firm TEAM Fenster + Türen of Leonberg. Weru's sales network now extended from the United Kingdom and the Netherlands to Austria, Switzerland, and France, and 3,500 window units and 60 door systems were being manufactured every day. The fall of the Berlin Wall opened a huge new German market for Weru's products, and in November 1989 Weru reached an agreement with representatives from the East to develop Weru's market there. It also began planning its entry into new product areas including "wintergärten" (glass residential conservatories), projecting roof or eave systems, and security systems, among other lines.

With the potentially vast eastern German market now open and with only limited growth opportunities remaining in Rudersberg, Weru built a new facility in Triptis, south of Leipzig, in 1991, and its network of German sales bureaus now totaled 16, with another five international bureaus. With windows still accounting for 89 percent of its sales (windows 11 percent), Weru continued to search for alternatives to the use of PVC, which was coming under increasing assault by environmental groups as a carcinogen. It was also building a reputation for taking on challenging and public-interest projects: for a mountain cable railway station in the Karwendel mountains it transported windows and doors to the mountain site during a blizzard and completed the installation five days later; it delivered and installed windows and doors for a school in mountainous Cuernavaca, Mexico; and it donated windows and facades for the renovation of an historic church in Halbertstadt-Wehrstedt, Germany.

Weru was becoming adept at modern marketing techniques as well, salting the German media with ads, sponsoring sporting events, and participating in industry trade shows. With burglars breaking into German homes at the rate of once every two-and-a-half minutes—usually unimpeded by standard front door locks—Weru's solid, high-security door designs found a captive audience. Its marketing strategy was also tailored to two other unique aspects of German life: only 40 percent of Germans owned their own homes and when they did buy them

typically stayed put for life. Many homes were therefore elaborate and expensive and thus ideally suited to Weru's range of high-end, customizable door designs. Similarly, in the early 1990s, Germany faced a severe apartment shortage, which the federal government addressed by launching expensive new apartment construction programs. By 1992, Germany was still short about two million housing units, but by marketing to both the new housing market and the renovation market Weru could solidify its share of the German window and door industry.

With Weru pouring investment capital into the Triptis facility, by the end of 1992 its capacity had risen to 2,900 window casements a day, and a new network of suppliers enabled it to pare its inventory to a cost-saving minimum. With its new Triptis facility, sales to the new eastern German states rose 80 percent over 1991, and the company introduced higher-quality colored wood-grain PVC windows and launched a new canopy product line to complement its front door range. In technology, new computer-controlled saws and welding machines were brought on line in Weru's factories, with their data fed directly to each machine by satellite. And WPS II, an upgraded version of Weru's sales and administrative support program, was installed and made operational on 344 company systems the same year.

With sales closing in on DM 294 million, Weru celebrated its 150th anniversary in April 1993 by renting Europe's largest exhibition ship for a four-week cruise, with stops in Germany, France, and the Netherlands. Twenty-five thousand customers, dealers, and guests participated in a floating trade show-cum-party under the banner "Architecture & Living, Weru Visions." The construction of a new corporate headquarters in Rudersberg was also announced, new subsidiaries were added in Italy, Poland, and Hungary; and Weru Bouwelementen was established in Eindhoven, Holland, as a sales, training, and customer service center. A new acquisition, Selnar GmbH, of Heilsbronn near Nuremburg, reflected Weru's awareness of the growing demand in Europe for wood architectural products, the second most important raw material for windows after PVC. A new series of pine wood products ("Die Baumfenster" [wood window] and "Die Baumtüre" [wood door]) was launched for the high-end home products industry to be sold through Weru's specialist dealers.

Other new products were developed internally: the Weru "climate window" used specialized glass that yielded improved energy savings, a new window element featuring an integrated roller shutter and electronic shutter control ("Servo-Lift"), and a new "composite" window that combined the strength of aluminum with the stability and safety of PVC. Weru's soundproofed, thermally insulated door line now counted 70,000 potential variations, and a new Servo-Lock electronic door locking mechanism that used an identification chip rather than a key offered a further advance in home security. Weru also reorganized its distribution network into seven regions, expanded its WPS II software system, and laid plans for a front door design service, an interactive door selection CD, and a special financing and special event service. At the end of the year Weru founded Weru-VITTON/Warsaw to produce PVC windows and other components in Poland and eventually throughout Eastern Europe. Weru's physical plant was also improved with an expanded line of wood varnishes, new wood crafting equipment, a more efficient machining center, an expanded glass insulation manufacturing facility, and a fiber-optic-based data network.

Between 1991 and 1993 Weru's sales had climbed 41 percent to DM 486 million and its stock, roughly half of which was held by non-German stockholders, had become among a select few German stocks rated a "buy" in the world's stock markets. The first few months of 1994 seemed to promise more of the same. Weru's new Rudersberg headquarters was opened; it unveiled a house door design service that enabled customers to select three door models and have them superimposed on a photo of their home for comparison purposes; and its new Polish operation, Weru VITTON, was quickly producing 100 window units a day and had been expanded with the acquisition of a Polish plastic window production facility. A new quality and customer-sensitive service program named KLIK was launched, a steel bar reinforced high-security product named Protecdor was introduced, and a new projected-frame window surround that enabled Weru's windows to be installed in the state-protected historical buildings of the Netherlands was also unveiled.

By the end of the first quarter of 1994, however, Weru's orders had fallen 10 percent from their 1993 levels. They recovered between April and September, but Weru's attempts to get its workers (many of whom were Turkish *Gastarbeiter* or guest workers) to fill Saturday shifts, in addition to a two-shift workweek schedule, was vetoed by their union, and Weru's order backlog began to expand dangerously. Moreover, the demand for new homes was far outstripping the market for repairing existing homes, which represented two-thirds of Weru's business and yielded its widest profit margins. Weru's stock suffered a dramatic drop in price and a subsequent selloff, and at the end of the year Weru's earnings had increased only about 5 percent—versus the 20 percent most of its shareholders had taken for granted. Although Weru insisted its long-term prospects still looked good, in late 1995 it fired chief financial officer Bernd Grenner as a gesture to shareholders for the company's disappointing performance.

Caradon plc: 1995–97

Weru officials were still protesting the bad press heaped on their stock when in April 1995 the British conglomerate Caradon plc announced the purchase of almost 25 percent of Weru's shares, for DM 245 million. Established in 1921 as Allied Tin Box Makers Ltd. and for many years known as Metal Box plc, Caradon's door and window division produced wood, steel, aluminum, and PVC doors and windows under such brand names as Everest, Peachtree, Better-Bilt, Celuform, Duraflex, Alpine, and Thermal-Gard. The seeds of the deal had been planted five years before when Caradon's CEO, Peter Jansen, visited Weru's headquarters and liked what he saw. Announcing that Caradon's and Weru's door and window lines were "highly complementary," Caradon then increased its holdings in Weru shares to 50.1 percent, giving it a controlling interest in Weru's business. The new ownership meant Weru's Selnar wood window business would get needed reinforcements while Caradon's sheer size would result in Weru paying lower raw materials prices.

The German housing market continued to decline in 1996, however, and with its 1995 pretax profits down a full 43 percent from 1994, Weru was forced to announce a restructuring that led to cost-cutting and the elimination of 1,630 jobs. Eager to gain an even firmer hold in the German window market, in September 1996 Caradon increased its shareholding in Weru to 72 percent, giving it complete control of the company under German law.

Principal Subsidiaries

Weru Fenster und Türen GmbH; Weru Beteiligungs-GmbH; Selnar GmbH.; Weru-VITTON Sp.zo.o. (Poland); E.P.E.M. Maschinenvertriebs GmbH; Reform Fenster & Türen Vertrieb GmbH; Weru Bouwelementen B.V. (Netherlands); Weru Building Components Ltd. (United Kingdom); Weru Conservatory Centre Ltd. (United Kingdom); Soproner Holzindustrielle Aktiengesellschaft (Hungary); Weru Magyarország Kft (Hungary); Weru OKNA + DRZWI (Poland).

Further Reading

Ascarelli, Silvia, "Weru Forecast, Trust Issue Put Pressure on Firm's Shares," *Wall Street Journal*, October 25, 1994.
——, "Hope for Weru Raised by Deal May Not Last," *Wall Street Journal*, April 12, 1995.
——, "Germany's Market, Hit by Unpleasant Surprises at Smaller Companies, Is Going Nowhere Fast," *Wall Street Journal*, November 1995.
"Caradon Buying 43% of German Competitor," *New York Times*, April 1995.
Cook, F. Palmer, *Talk to Me of Windows: An Informal History*, South Brunswick and New York: A.S. Barnes & Company, 1971.
"Weru AG: Stock Price Sets 1995 Low as Sales of Windows Slow," *Wall Street Journal*, October 16, 1995.

—Paul S. Bodine

The Wet Seal, Inc.

64 Fairbanks
Irvine, California 92718
U.S.A.
(714) 583-9029
Fax: (714) 583-0715

Public Company
Incorporated: 1962
Employees: 4,630
Sales: $266.6 million (1996)
Stock Exchanges: NASDAQ
SICs: 5621 Women's Clothing Stores

A nationwide specialty retailer of moderately priced apparel for women, The Wet Seal, Inc. operates two chains under the "Contempo Casuals" and the "Wet Seal" banners. During the mid-1990s, Wet Seal operated 363 retail stores in 34 states and Puerto Rico, with the majority of the company's stores located in California. After decades of unassuming growth, Wet Seal recorded explosive growth during the 1980s, but faltered during the early and mid-1990s. To restore profitability the company acquired a 237-store retail junior women's chain named Contempo Casuals, Inc. in 1995. The acquisition nearly tripled the size of Wet Seal and greatly expanded the company's geographic scope, creating a dominant national force for the late 1990s.

Wet Seal was established in late 1962 in California as a beachwear retailer, though its development into the 300-unit retail chain in operation during the mid-1990s occurred only after the company had significantly broadened its beachwear merchandise mix. During the first two decades of its existence, Wet Seal had developed into a $5-million-in-sales, 17-store chain, with all retail units located in California. Size, however, was not the chain's problem. Although Wet Seal's diminutive stature left it lost among the larger apparel retailers in California, its profitability stood out as its most glaring handicap. The company was awash in debt. The sweeping changes that transformed the company into one of the darlings of the California retail apparel industry during the 1980s occurred midway through the decade when the struggling chain gained new management and a new owner. In 1984, a Canadian retail store chain named Suzy Shier acquired Wet Seal, paying $2 million for the struggling and little-known business. The purchase marked the beginning of years of robust growth and Wet Seal's ascendancy to prominence in the fiercely competitive California retail market.

1980s Growth

The chief architect of Wet Seal's prolific rise was Ken Chilvers, head of Suzy Shier's operations. When Suzy Shier acquired Wet Seal in 1984, Chilvers left Toronto and moved to California to steward the fortunes of money-losing Wet Seal. For assistance in arresting the chain's financial slide, Chilvers turned to Kathy Peckham, a former Jordan Marsh merchandising executive. Peckham's changes were pervasive, essentially abolishing the strategy that had guided Wet Seal's existence during the 1960s and 1970s. She put together a merchandising mix designed to attract a much larger customer base, adding junior sportswear apparel items that quickly drew flocks of customers through the stores' doors. Flowered denim, mini-skirts, colorful Aztec prints, and psychedelic bikinis graced Wet Seal's racks and shelves from the mid-1980s forward, drawing teenage girls in packs. Surprisingly, their mothers came as well, unafraid to don the youthful fashion trends of the day.

The metamorphosis worked, bringing in teenage customers and women in their late 40s. During the exponential growth that ensued, Chilvers was granted autonomy from his silent partners at Suzy Shier, gaining full control over all Wet Seal operations. Peckham, meanwhile, ascended to Wet Seal's executive vice-president and general merchandising manager posts, earning recognition for sparking growth that dazzled industry analysts. While describing the chain's meteoric rise, one member of the business press who cited Joseph Magnin and Contempo Casuals as the retail success stories of the 1960s and 1970s, respectively, hailed Wet Seal as the "retail phenom" of the 1980s, a distinction that few could discount given what the company had achieved during the latter half of the 1980s. Between 1985 and

1989, annual sales mushroomed more than 900 percent, approaching the $100 million plateau; the number of stores jumped from 17 to 78; and sales per square foot rose from $150 to $420. Most important, the company's profitability was restored, underscoring the importance of Chilvers' and Peckham's work.

By the end of the 1980s, Wet Seal's stature within the California retail industry had grown dramatically and Chilvers was intent on keeping the momentum. He invested heavily in increasing the size of each store, raising the average square footage of a Wet Seal unit from 2,500 to 4,000. Inside the stores, considerable capital had been invested as well. The enlarged units contained wide center aisles flanked by walls with merchandise stacked to the ceiling. Behind the central cash registers, massive computer-driven video walls played the latest rock music videos, accentuating the trendy appeal of Wet Seal merchandise.

By all accounts a successful formula had been created, but it was a formula that had yet be tested outside of California. That changed in 1989 when Wet Seal established its first stores outside of California, opening stores in Las Vegas and Phoenix that registered success commensurate with the company's California stores. Not stopping there, Chilvers looked to expand elsewhere and signed a lease in the summer of 1989 for a store in Hawaii, announcing concurrently that he planned to establish at least five stores in Hawaii by the following year. Ambitious plans were slated for Florida as well, where Chilvers anticipated establishing a minimum of 30 stores. For Chilvers, the success achieved during his first five years as Wet Seal's leader prompted him to map out ambitious plans for the company's future. But for those industry pundits alarmed by the chain's rapid expansion, Chilvers had an answer. "We are taking a cautious approach," Chilvers explained to a *Women's Wear Daily* reporter in 1989. "We will do 25 to 30 new stores next year and, let's face it, there were a lot of people who came before us that went from 65 stores to 100 and then were dinosaurs at 300."

As the company entered the 1990s, it appeared the only hazard on the horizon was Chilvers' fear of expanding too rapidly. Store sales continued to climb, the company's merchandise was widely popular, and its march across California's borders was meeting with encouraging, uninterrupted success. As Chilvers perceived it, the greatest danger of excessively rapid expansion was sacrificing the quality and "look" of Wet Seal stores in order to save money to finance the establishment of additional stores. To combat this potential problem Chilvers refused to cut corners while expanding. He invested roughly

twice the industry average for each store opening and continued to create hip havens for his customers. To fuel expansion, Chilvers took the company public in July 1990, raising $37 million from an initial public offering that was used to trim debt and finance the establishment of additional stores. By the end of the year, 20 new stores had been added to the chain, giving Wet Seal a total of 93 stores scattered across five states.

One year after moving out of California—where the company had been confined for 27 years—Wet Seal operated in Arizona, Nevada, Hawaii, and Florida. The 20 stores opened in 1990 helped lift sales over $100 million for the first time and the company's net income reached a record $7.1 million, providing tangible evidence that the prodigious expansion completed during the year had not negatively affected Wet Seal's performance. The company's financial performance, in fact, was particularly remarkable considering the state of the national economy during the early 1990s, as the first stirrings of a national recession signalled the beginning of hard times for retailers across the country. By 1991, the severity of the recession was intensifying, but unlike many of its competitors Wet Seal was moving forward, unchecked. *Time* magazine featured the company as one of the few retailers able to buck the trend spreading across the country that left many retailers pulling at their wrists as store sales plummeted and profits sagged. By constantly turning over its merchandise, which Wet Seal executives dubbed "multigenerational," and by awarding weekly bonuses to employees for inventory turnover, Wet Seal was exhibiting a financial vibrancy that distinguished it from rivals and lent credence to the statement that the company might be the "retail phenom" of the 1990s as well.

By the end of 1991 there were 112 stores composing the Wet Seal chain. Sales were up from the $107 million generated in 1990, climbing to $120 million, and although profits slipped to $4.2 million the company's financial health was sound. As the company continued with its expansion plans in 1992, adding 13 stores during the year, industry observers were surprised by the announcement of Chilvers' departure in March. Forty-five years old at the time, Chilvers had opted to take early retirement, explaining that his reasons for leaving were "private and personal, relating to my health and my family, and do not bear upon my relationship with Wet Seal or its directors, which had always been excellent." Chilvers exit paved the way for Kathy Peckham, now Kathy Bronstein.

Financial Woes During the 1990s

With Bronstein in charge, Wet Seal pressed on with expansion for the remainder of 1992, but by the end of the year, when the company reported its second consecutive decline in annual profit totals, signs of trouble were evident. Sales for the year reached $150 million—an all-time high—but Wet Seal's net income slipped from $4.2 million to $3.6 million. Following this disheartening news, the company expanded only modestly in 1993, adding four stores as sales throughout the chain began to dip. By the end of the year, alarms were blaring loudly at the company's headquarters. Annual sales dropped to $140 million and, most disconcerting, the company's net income slipped into the red. Wet Seal lost $2.4 million in 1993 and another $1 million in 1994, as the years of explosive growth shuddered to a stop.

"It was a huge shock to be that hot and then turn sour," Bronstein reflected to a reporter from *Women's Wear Daily.* "It taught that even when you're doing well," she went on to explain, "there's only a limited time you have before you have to change. You've got to know when to pull the plug." During the two-year financial malaise, Bronstein and other Wet Seal executives searched for a solution, a way to restore the company's former luster. While expansion had continued, bringing the company's store count total up to 133 by the end of 1994, consumers had lost interest in junior apparel, sending a shock wave throughout the industry. Fashion tastes had changed and Wet Seal had not foreseen the shift, a mistake that thrust the company into a precarious position as it entered the mid-1990s.

In early 1995, the company discovered what it perceived as a solution to its financial woes, a solution Bronstein described as an "unbelievable break." In April, Chestnut Hill, Massachusetts-based Neiman Marcus Group agreed to sell its floundering Contempo Casuals chain to Wet Seal. Wet Seal, as its 1995 annual report declared, "went shopping for just the right fit" and Contempo Casuals, a specialty women's retail chain that had flourished during the 1970s, was selected. With 237 stores scattered throughout 34 states and Puerto Rico, Contempo Casuals represented a significant addition to Wet Seal's operations, nearly tripling the company's size and immediately transforming it into a genuine national retailer. Expected to be completed by the end of May, the deal was concluded in July for stock valued at $1 million.

Although some industry analysts questioned the benefits of combining Contempo Casuals, which lost $37 million on $303 million in sales in 1994, and Wet Seal, a money loser itself, Bronstein was confident the right move had been made, noting in *Women's Wear Daily,* "We saw that without adding signifi-

cant overhead we could make ourselves instantly profitable." On the heels of the Contempo Casuals acquisition, the company continued to tinker with its business approach, testing a new concept store during late 1995 called "The Girl's Room," which featured apparel and accessories such as novelty toys, cosmetics, candles, and books. Positive early results prompted the company to push forward with the concept and make plans to incorporate "The Girl's Room" into 160 stores nationwide. Other plans for the late 1990s included the establishment of as many as ten new stores in 1996, but the primary focus after the Contempo Casuals acquisition was on improving sales and profitability. With this as its chief objective, Wet Seal entered the late 1990s intent on wielding its new-found national power to become a dominant force in the U.S. retail industry.

Principal Subsidiaries

Contempo Casuals, Inc.

Further Reading

"Bronstein Succeeds Chilvers as Wet Seal's President, CEO," *Women's Wear Daily,* March 24, 1992, p. 20.

Fallon, Kathryn Jackson, "Wet Seal and Whale Songs," *Time,* June 3, 1991, p. 45.

Ginsberg, Steve, "Wet Seal Makes Waves," *Women's Wear Daily,* August 9, 1989, p. 14C.

Kolbenschlag, Michael, "Ken Chilvers Knows How to Manage a Fast-Growing Company," *California Business,* November 1989, p. 80.

Marlow, Michael, "West Coast Junior Chains: Trend Catchers," *Women's Wear Daily,* June 29, 1995, p. 6.

"Neiman's to Sell Contempo Casuals," *Daily News Record,* April 4, 1995, p. 11.

—Jeffrey L. Covell

Zippo Manufacturing Company

33 Barbour Street
Bradford, Pennsylvania 16701
U.S.A.
(814) 368-2700
Fax: (800) 362-3598
Web site: http://www.zippomfg.com

Private Company
Incorporated: 1932
Employees: 1,085
Sales: $150 million (1996 est.)
SICs: 3421 Cutlery; 3423 Hand & Edge Tools, Except
   Machine Tools & Hand Saws; 3827 Optical
   Instruments & Lenses; 3951 Pens, Mechanical Pencils
   & Parts; 3999 Manufacturing Industries, Not
   Elsewhere Classified

Zippo Manufacturing Company is world famous for its Zippo windproof lighter and its lifetime guarantee. The company has sold more than 300 million lighters since its founding in 1932 and currently makes more than 100 different models, including ones aimed specifically at collectors. The dominant maker of refillable lighters in the United States, with a 40 percent market share, Zippo also sells its lighters in more than 100 other countries, with Japan being by far its largest export market. Since diversifying for the first time in 1962 (when a tape measure was introduced), Zippo now manufacturers and sells pocket knives, key holders, money clips, writing instruments, tape measures, and pocket flashlights in addition to its flagship lighters.

Entrepreneurial Beginnings

George Grant Blaisdell, Zippo's founder, had a checkered career in business prior to focusing on lighters. His father ran a machine shop in Blaisdell's hometown of Bradford, Pennsylvania, where Blaisdell started work as a machinist at age 16

(working a 56-hour week at 10 cents an hour), then became a salesman, and at age 20 took over the business. He managed to keep the business afloat during World War I through government contracts, then sold out in 1920. Blaisdell headed for New York; having failed to strike it rich playing the stock market, he returned to Bradford and invested what money remained in local oil wells (through his co-ownership, with his brother Walter, of Blaisdell Oil Company), making a modest living over the next ten years from the proceeds. Thereupon, in the early 1930s he was waiting for the right business opportunity.

On a muggy summer night in Bradford in 1932, Blaisdell and a friend stepped out on the terrace of the Pennhill Country Club. Blaisdell's friend used a cumbersome-looking Austrian lighter with a removable brass top to light a cigarette. Blaisdell proceeded to chide his friend: "You're all dressed up. Why don't you get a lighter that looks decent?" In an enthusiastic reply, his friend said: "Well, George, it works!"

Blaisdell was suitably impressed and decided to try to sell the lighters himself. He obtained rights to distribute the product in the United States, imported them for 12 cents each, and attempted to sell them for $1 each. But this venture failed, mainly because of the clumsy nature of the lighter's design. Blaisdell then decided to design his own lighter, one that was attractive, easy to use, and dependable.

The resulting original model was rectangular in shape—made from brass tubing with soldered tops and bottoms and square corners—with a chrome-plated hinge soldered on the outside for easy opening and closing. Sized to fit comfortably in a hand, the lighter featured a windhood to protect the wick. Blaisdell liked the name of another recent invention, the zipper, so he christened his lighter the "Zippo" (and his new firm, Zippo Manufacturing Company).

Production of Zippos began in 1932 in a $10 per month rented room over the Rickerson & Pryde garage in Bradford. The shop had $260 in equipment and two employees, from which came lighters retailing for $1.95 with the backing of a lifetime guarantee.

Struggling Early Years

Sales of the lighters got off to a slow start, with only 1,100 sold during the inaugural production year. Blaisdell tried all kinds of methods to move his brainchild. He gave away samples and gifts to long-distance bus drivers, jewelers, and tobacconists. In 1937 he paid $3,000—mostly borrowed money—for a full-page ad in *Esquire* magazine after he found that retailers shied away from products that were not advertised. Unfortunately, Blaisdell did not yet have sufficient distribution to take advantage of the effect of such advertising so this gambit failed to pay off.

While handling sales himself and struggling to develop a market for his windproof lighter, Blaisdell also tinkered with the design. The lighter was shortened by a quarter inch in 1933, decorative diagonal lines were added in 1934, the hinge was placed on the inside of the case in 1936, and rounded tops and bottoms replaced the square corners of the original design in 1937. This last alteration was important from a production standpoint as the lid and bottom could now be formed as a whole, eliminating the soldering process.

Blaisdell achieved his first big sales break starting in 1934 when he started selling Zippos on punchboards, two-cents-per-play gambling games popular in U.S. tobacco and confectionery shops, poolrooms, and cigar stands. Before punchboards were outlawed in 1940, more than 300,000 Zippos were sold through this game of chance, enough for Zippo Manufacturing to achieve its first profits, modest though they were.

While punchboards were a short-lived chapter in Zippo history, another of Blaisdell's marketing methods had a much longer-lasting impact. In 1936 an Iowa life insurance company ordered 200 engraved lighters that it gave to its agents as contest prizes. And Bradford's own Kendell Oil Company ordered 500 engraved lighters for its customers and employees. Thus began Zippo's specialty advertising business, which would become an increasingly important venture in the coming decades.

With sales increasing thanks to the punchboards and the special markets deals, Blaisdell expanded his operations. First, the production facility expanded into the entire second floor of the Rickerson & Pryde building; Blaisdell also added a new office elsewhere in Bradford. Then in 1938 the factory and offices were both moved into a former garage on Barbour Street

in Bradford. That same year, Zippo's first table lighter debuted, a four-and-a-half inch tall model that held four times the fuel of a pocket lighter. The following year Zippo introduced a sophisticated new lighter model, the 14-karat solid gold Zippo, available in both plain and engine-turned models.

World War II Brought Zippo Fame

With the onset of U.S. involvement in World War II, the U.S. government forced the halt in production of many consumer products. Blaisdell continued Zippo production, but as he had during World War I, he again moved into government contracting—all Zippos became destined for the U.S. military. With brass reserved for military uses only, the wartime lighters were made of a low-grade steel. Since this provided a poor finish, they were spray-painted black then baked, which produced a crackle finish.

Blaisdell sold some of these Zippos to the military post exchanges at such a low price that they were then resold for $1.00, making them the most affordable lighter available. He also sent hundreds of lighters to celebrities, including the famous war correspondent Ernie Pyle who then gave them away to servicemen overseas. Through these actions, the Zippo became the favorite lighter of GIs, whose loyalty to the product would help fuel postwar sales. Numerous war stories also helped cement the Zippo as an American icon—the Zippo that stopped a bullet, that cooked soup in helmets, that illuminated the darkened instrument panel of an Army pilot's disabled plane, enabling him to land safely. Zippos also began making frequent appearances in Hollywood movies—notably war movies at first but later films noir—enhancing their iconic status. Meanwhile, wartime production peaked in 1945 when 3 million Zippos were made.

Postwar Design Improvements, Expansions, and Diversification

The Zippo repair clinic became famous in its own right by backing up the Zippo guarantee. Repaired lighters were returned at no cost to the customer, not even return postage. The clinic provided more than just customer goodwill; it also provided invaluable information about design flaws. Over the long run, the repair clinic found that a faulty or broken hinge was the most common reason for a Zippo to be returned. But soon after World War II, in 1946, Blaisdell discovered that the most frequent repairs were for worn striking wheels—wheels that had been coming from an outside supplier. Blaisdell immediately stopped production to address the problem. He decided to bring production of the wheels in-house and spent $300,000 on a new flint wheel capable of firing a lighter as many as 78,000 times. This top quality wheel was produced by a knurling operation that remained a company secret.

Zippo continued to develop new lighter models following the war. In 1947 Town and Country designs were introduced that featured images of pheasants, mallards, geese, sailboats, trout, setters, and horses. Three years later, full cover leather lighters and sterling silver lighters made their debuts.

Meanwhile, Blaisdell sought to improve his sales force. From 1939 to 1950 Zippo's entire sales operation consisted of two cigar salesmen, who sold Zippos as a sideline mainly to tobacco wholesalers. The two men each were charged with a vast selling territory. In 1950 Blaisdell set up his own sales force, with district managers assigned specific regions. This sales force was not restricted to tobacco wholesalers, but also called on jewelry, drug store, and grocery wholesalers.

Also in 1950, Zippo set up its first foreign subsidiary, Zippo Manufacturing Company of Canada Limited. Located in Niagara Falls, Ontario, the company consisted of a small production facility that helped increase overall Zippo capacity, which reached 20,000 lighters a day by 1952. Annual revenues had reached $9.5 million and the company enjoyed healthy after-tax profits of almost 10 percent.

Zippo continued to expand its facilities in the 1950s and 1960s to meet the growing demand, both domestic and foreign. In 1954 a new building for chrome plating and fabricating, located on Congress Street in Bradford, was completed. New corporate offices were built in 1955 next to the Barbour Street factory in Bradford. During the 1960s the Congress Street plant underwent a series of additions and eventually became the main location for fabricating and assembling Zippo products.

After 30 years as a lighter-only company, Zippo in 1962 diversified for the first time when it introduced a six-foot flexible-steel pocket rule. This was followed by a compact pocketknife and nail file, a money-clip knife, a golf ball, a key holder, a magnifier, and a letter opener. Unlike Zippo lighters, however, none of these products were made available for retail purchase; they were only available through Zippo's specialty advertising operation, which by the mid-1960s accounted for 40 percent of overall company volume. Zippo boasted of more than 27,000 commercial accounts at the time. All of Zippo's metal products were backed by the same Zippo pledge: "If for any reason your Zippo will not work, regardless of age or condition—we'll fix it free." (For unfixable items, the company sent the customer a replacement.) Zippo even guaranteed its golf ball as playable for 180 holes.

End of Blaisdell Era in the 1970s

After introducing the first of a series of lighters with space designs in 1969—the first honoring the landing on the moon—Zippo ushered in the 1970s appropriately enough with a Zodiac lighter series. In 1976 a commemorative Bicentennial lighter hit the market, as did an in-fashion denim-like lighter.

The year 1978 marked the end of an era when Blaisdell died. Ownership of Zippo Manufacturing passed to Blaisdell's daughters, Harriett Wick and Sarah Dorn, who had worked for the company for years and would continue to do so for years to come but did not wish to run it. They entrusted the presidency to a long-time employee, Robert Galey.

Unfortunately, throughout the 1970s and into the early 1980s, Zippo's sales stagnated at about $30 million a year. The firm was manufacturing-oriented and needed to become more marketing-focused in order to get past this plateau. As it turned out, Galey's stint as president was short-lived since he retired in 1986. Zippo's third president was Michael Schuler, who had joined the company as controller shortly after Blaisdell's death and then was promoted to vice president and controller in 1982.

Under Schuler's leadership, Zippo's revenues would increase fivefold within ten years.

Schuler Era, 1986 Through Mid-1990s

The spectacular growth of this period was generated by a combination of increased exports, the aggressive targeting of the collector's and gift/souvenir markets, and creative line extensions. On the export front, Japan remained the top market—one of every four Zippos made in the late 1980s went to Japan—and Western European sales were strong also, but Schuler targeted such emerging areas as China and South Asia and Eastern Europe following the fall of communism. Many of these emerging nations had high percentages of smokers, making them prime Zippo territory. This contrasted sharply with Zippo's domestic market, where antismoking crusades continued to gain momentum throughout the 1990s. Overall, while exports constituted only 40 percent of total company sales in the mid-1980s, by 1995 65 percent of sales originated outside the United States.

Credit for Zippo's "discovery" of the collector's and gift markets for Zippo lighters goes to the person Schuler hired in 1991 as head of sales and marketing, James Baldo. Soon after taking the job, Baldo commissioned customer surveys that showed that 30 percent of Zippo's customers defined themselves as "collectors." The surveys also showed that many buyers gave the lighters away as gifts. In response, Zippo began offering premium-priced—$19 to $40—gift/souvenir lighter sets, including ones with licensed brands (Harley-Davidson, Corvette) or images of tourist destinations (Niagara Falls, Empire State Building).

Then Zippo began offering limited edition "collector" Zippos, directly targeting the collector's market. In 1992, a 60th anniversary lighter appeared, followed by 1993's Varga Girl lighter, 1994's D-Day commemorative lighter, 1995's Mysteries of the Forest, and 1996's Zippo Salutes Pinup Girls. Zippo also began producing a collector's guide and, starting in 1993, sponsored an annual July swap meet at the Bradford headquarters. In 1994 the company took the further step of opening in Bradford the Zippo Family Store and Museum, highly popular with collectors, which was expanded to five times its original size in 1996.

Zippo had been criticized at times throughout its history for being too conservative, in particular in regard to line extensions. But under Schuler, Zippo began a more aggressive diversification approach, beginning in 1993 with the acquisition of the crosstown W.R. Case & Sons Cutlery Company, a firm with annual sales of $15 million. Case was founded in 1889 in Little Valley, New York, but relocated to Bradford in 1905, where it developed a line of pocket knives, hunting knives, household cutlery, and commemoratives. The company had filed for bankruptcy after a difficult period and then was bought out of bankruptcy by a limited partnership, River Associates, in 1990. Case's products meshed well with Zippo's and provided Zippo with another avenue into the retail market. Soon after the acquisition, in fact, dual gift sets that included a Case knife and a Zippo lighter were soon being retailed at prices ranging from $50 to $200.

A much more dramatic extension came via the 1993 license agreement with Japanese clothing manufacturer Itochu Fashion System Co. Itochu gained the right to the Zippo name and soon offered Zippo jeans, gloves, and leather jackets in Japan. Zippo began to consider offering such clothing in the United States as well.

With antismoking forces gaining steam in the United States, Zippo came up in 1995 with a creative way to keep its brand strong. It introduced the ZipLight pocket flashlight, which was simply a traditional lighter casing with a replaceable battery pack inside. Zippo spent $500,000 on a television advertising campaign to launch this new product, one of its largest campaigns ever.

By the late 1990s, the Zippo brand, prematurely declared dead by *USA Today* in 1989, was clearly alive and well and seemed as ubiquitous as ever. The future for Zippo, still family owned, may include George Blaisdell descendants for some time, since four Blaisdell grandchildren are actively at work for the company. Secure in its core lighter market, Zippo seemed sure to continue to grow into the new century through creative marketing and line extensions.

Principal Subsidiaries

W. R. Case & Sons Cutlery Company; Zippo Manufacturing Company of Canada Limited; Zippo Europe S.A. (France; 50%).

Further Reading

Amster, Robin, "Zippo Lighter: American Classics," *Popular Mechanics*, August 1994, pp. 44–46.

Baker, Stephen, "How Zippo Keeps the Flame Lit," *Business Week*, November 20, 1995.

Brown, Christie, "Flaming Success," *Forbes*, November 18, 1996, pp. 214–16.

Carlino, Maria, "Zippo Manufacturing Co.," *Journal of Commerce and Commercial*, February 3, 1995, p. 4A.

Collins, Lisa, "Keeping Zippo's Flame: Name Is Hot, Marketing Lacks Spark," *USA Today*, August 11, 1989, pp. 1B–2B.

Galloni, Alessandra, "Lighter Lovers Flip Their Tops at a Zippo Collectors' Convention," *Wall Street Journal*, August 4, 1995, p. B1.

Kaplan, Andrew, "Scorching Demand for Lighters," *U.S. Distribution Journal*, April 15, 1996, p. 14.

Levy, Robert, "The Mark of Zippo," *Dun's Review*, October 1966, pp. 53–54, 59.

McGrath, Molly Wade, *Top Sellers, U.S.A.: Success Stories Behind America's Best-Selling Products from Alka-Seltzer to Zippo*, New York: William Morrow and Company, 1983, pp. 156–57.

"Mr. Zippo," *Fortune*, October 1952, p. 220.

Poore, David, *Zippo: The Great American Lighter*, Atglen, Pennsylvania: Shiffer, 1997.

"Zippo: A History of Progress," Bradford, Pennsylvania: Zippo Manufacturing Company, 1995.

"The Zippo Lighter Collector's Guide," Bradford, Pennsylvania: Zippo Manufacturing Company, 1996.

—David E. Salamie

Zoom Telephonics, Inc.

207 South Street
Boston, Massachusetts 02111
U.S.A.
(617) 423-1072
Fax: (617) 423-9231
Web site: http://www.zoomtel.com

Wholly Owned Public Subsidiary of Zoom Telephonics,
Inc.
Incorporated: 1977
Employees: 251
Sales: $97 million (1995)
Stock Exchanges: NASDAQ
SICs: 3661 Telephone & Telegraph Apparatus

Zoom Telephonics, Inc. is a leading designer, manufacturer, and marketer of products that link personal computers and people through the international telephone network. Designed for both home and office use, Zoom products allow people to transmit data, fax messages, portray voice and video images, and to access on-line services such as the Internet and corporate computer networks. Presently offering a broad line of fax-modems, with transmission speeds ranging from 14,400 bps to 28,800 bps, the company was one of the first manufacturers of faxmodems and voice faxmodems. Zoom Telephonics is at the forefront of the emerging trends in computer connectivity, and is preparing the way for new products that will be used for Internet access, computer telephony, video telephony, and simultaneous voice and data transmission. A wholly owned public subsidiary of parent Zoom Telephonics, Inc., located in Canada for legal reasons, the company's entire business is conducted through the operations of the U.S. office in Boston, Massachusetts.

Early History

During the late 1960s, Frank B. Manning and his roommate, Bruce Kramer, would stay up late into the night discussing how to start their own business. After graduating with doctorates from the Massachusetts Institute of Technology in the mid-1970s, the two young men decided that the timing was finally right. Taking a suggestion from T. Pat Manning, Frank's brother, the ambitious entrepreneurs settled on a product idea that they thought would be marketable and inexpensive to produce. The company was incorporated and began operations in March of 1977 under the name of Zoom which, according to the founders, would symbolize the quick growth of the business.

Manning and Kramer could not have started their business under more auspicious circumstances. The company's first product, dubbed The Silencer, was a switch that could be easily installed on a phone to keep it from ringing. This simple yet revolutionary idea lessened the frustration of callers who continually dialed a number when the phone was off the hook expecting to get through after a few attempts. The introduction of The Silencer fortunately coincided with the breakup of AT&T's monopoly of the telephone equipment industry. Marketed in such magazines as *Esquire, Vogue,* and *Playboy* as the perfect solution for an undisturbed "romantic evening at home," the new product was welcomed in newly opened independent phone stores selling non-AT&T equipment.

Although The Silencer generated approximately $200,000 during the company's first few years of operation, Frank Manning and Bruce Kramer knew that they would have to expand their product line in order to remain in business. While the two were students at MIT, they had designed an automatic dialer that would continuously dial a busy phone number. Avid tennis players, Manning and Kramer had originated the idea in order to get tennis court reservations at the campus courts, which only took reservations on a first-come, first-served basis beginning at noon. Confident of the dialer's success, Manning devoted himself to its electronic design and programming while Kramer concentrated on the mechanical design and packaging.

During the late 1970s, both Sprint and MCI entered the long distance business, attempting to attract customers by offering discounted long distance service. However, AT&T was the only company that could offer "one-plus" long distance dialing. Sprint and MCI were required to make customers dial an access code and a security code before the actual telephone number, which brought the total number of digits necessary to dial any long distance phone number to a minimum of 23, and sometimes even more. Aware of the potential demand for a product that would make using discount services like Sprint and MCI practical, in 1980 Zoom introduced the Demon Dialer. For use in both the home or office, the Demon Dialler could memorize and dial 176 telephone numbers, of up to 32 digits each. Recognized by the telecommunications industry for its innovative design and market potential, the Demon Dialer won the design award at the 1981 Consumer Electronics Show. More importantly for Zoom, however, the new product helped sales leap from $200,000 to an impressive $6 million annually.

Retrenchment and Reorganization

With the success of the Demon Dialer, Zoom not only began to hire more people and stock large amounts of inventory, but Manning and Kramer decided to go into debt in order to finance Zoom's projected expansion. The budding company hit their first major stumbling block when equal access within the telephone industry ended AT&T's monopoly on one-plus dialing and customers became free to choose their one-plus long distance carrier. It was no longer necessary to dial 23 digits to save money and the Demon Dialer became obsolete overnight. Sales dropped precipitously from $6 million to $1.5 million from 1984 to 1986, and the company lost nearly $1 million during each of those years. Manning and Kramer were forced to get rid of unused inventory, rearrange the financing for their debt payments, and reduce the number of Zoom employees from 56 to 16.

With the insight that separates the successful entrepreneur from the amateur investor, Manning and Kramer had already started to diversify Zoom's product line in 1983. By a stroke of good luck, a field applications engineer who worked for National Semiconductor had developed and designed a 300 baud modem for one of Apple Computer's first products. Aware of Zoom's reputation as a new and innovative company, he approached Manning and Kramer with the proposal that Zoom license, manufacture, and market his original design. Without much income from sales, however, Manning and Kramer convinced the Massachusetts Technology Development Corporation, a quasi-public venture capital company, to underwrite the cost of manufacturing and selling the new product.

In 1983, Zoom introduced the new product based on the licensing agreement. Dubbed the Networker, it was Zoom's first modem product, but, with the personal computer industry on the verge of expansion, the two entrepreneurs thought it expedient to take a chance on the new technology. The Networker was more successful than Manning and Kramer could ever have imagined. As the company's annual sales volume for dialers continued its downward spiral, the modem business started to grow—and grow dramatically. Unable to arrange sufficient retail distribution for its modem, Zoom hit upon the idea of selling their product through direct mail advertising. With their successful modem, Zoom began to garner a higher profile in the telecommunications industry. Soon the company was able to forego its reliance on direct mail, and focus on selling modems to distributors, personal computer manufacturers, and high-volume retail stores.

By 1985, Zoom began to design and market its own line of modems. Since the issue of compatibility was uppermost on everyone's mind, especially with IBM introducing its personal computer during the same year, the modems at Zoom were designed to provide a high level of compatibility and related enhancements, including such features as Demon Dialing. Sold at reasonable prices, Zoom's modems quickly captured a large share of the market. In just three years, sales at the company had surpassed the $5 million mark, almost all of which had been generated from the design and sale of new modems. By 1989, sales had topped the $8 million milepost and, in 1990, the company began trading shares on the NASDAQ exchange. During the same year, sales jumped to just over $13 million, and in 1991 sales skyrocketed to approximately $25 million.

International Expansion and the Emergence of the Internet

With the growth of the company through sales of modems, and in control of a significant share of the market, Manning and Kramer decided it was time to expand the company's product line overseas. As the communications network among personal computer users began to grow, the demand for high-technology, state-of-the-art, faxmodem products also rose. People found that they could keep in regular contact with their business associates, even between the most remote locations around the world, as long as they had a reliable source of electricity and a faxmodem. Zoom established distribution channels and sales offices in Belgium, Finland, Germany, Hong Kong, Italy, Korea, Poland, Portugal, Spain, and the United Kingdom. The company's major European distributors included Criterium, Computer 2000 and its Frontline division, and Northamber. Zoom's major European retail customers included Schadt and Vobis. In the Far East, the company's major distributor of its faxmodems was Nippon Polaroid, one of the largest retail stores for software and computer support technology. By 1994, Zoom reported that its international sales accounted for nearly 20 percent of its total revenues.

With the rise in interest in on-line services, personal computer users were increasingly looking for easy and quick connections to the Internet. This development alone created an enormous demand for high-speed modems. High volume production shifted from modems with a top transmission of 2400 bps in 1987 to a maximum transmission speed of 28,800 bps by 1995. The primary advantage in increasing transmission speed was that the less time it took to transmit text files and graphics, the less expensive phone call costs would be. In addition, high speed transmission modems facilitated data intensive applications such as World Wide Web browsing, remote access to corporate computer networks, and video telephony.

Recognizing the ever-increasing demand for modem-related technologies, Manning and Kramer decided to concentrate entirely on developing products to meet the needs of consumers. Zoom developed modems that provided a range of services. These included functions that digitalized incoming voice signals, stored them in memory, and then retrieved and sent these signals through the telephone network to a remote computer or person. The company's advanced modems could facilitate two-way voice conversations between employees working on the same project but in different locations. The advances in computer software during the early and mid-1990s also increased the demand for high speed transmission modems. Microsoft's introduction of its Windows 95 included capabilities such as remote access, faxing, and Internet access that could only be used with a high speed transmission modem such as Zoom's ComStar. ComStar's key features included a top data speed of 28,800 bps, voice mail, full-duplex speakerphone, VoiceView, Caller ID, Plug & Play, Internet Software, and a maximum fax speed of 14,400 bps.

The Mid-1990s and Beyond

By the end of fiscal 1995, Zoom had sold over 920,000 faxmodems on the North American continent alone. New products and savvy marketing techniques helped to expand the company's market share. One of its most successful new product marketing methods was the Zoom Business Products Line. Created specifically to meet the demands of institutional and corporate users, the company introduced the Zoom/Multiline, a collection of eight non-related high transmission faxmodems packaged in a single case. For use in situations that require multiple modems in a high-density, low-power format, and with remote access capabilities, this line of products was an immediate success.

At the beginning of 1996, Zoom renewed its commitment to developing highly innovative products and product enhancements. New products included: ISDN modems, a communication service that permitted current phone lines to transmit data digitally; simultaneous voice and data capabilities that allowed two people using personal computers to engage in a conversation at the same time as data is being transferred; combined faxmodem/LAN PCMCIA cards, which combined both faxmodem and LAN capabilities in one card and allowed one PCMCIA slot in a notebook computer to serve both functions; and multi-line faxmodems, to be used for bulletin boards, UNIX servers, and LANs that employ a variety of modems. Also in 1996, Zoom entered into an agreement with Hewlett-Packard and Rockwell to design and develop a product that would allow a printer to function as a fax receiving device, whether or not the computer is turned on.

In the mid-1990s, Zoom also reached agreements with numerous high volume retailers in the personal computer market to sell its products, including Best Buy, Circuit City, Computer City, Office Depot, OfficeMax, Staples, and Wal-Mart. In January of 1996, Zoom had secured the second largest amount of retail space set aside for modems throughout North America. In 1995, nearly 20 percent of the company's total revenue was generated from sales at the high volume retailer Best Buy, which is located in most urban and suburban areas across the United States.

As sales for the company continued to increase, Zoom management became convinced that the time was right for the implementation of an acquisition program. In July of 1996, Zoom purchased Tribe Computer Works, a private corporation based in California that manufactures remote access systems and routers for branch office environments such as banks. In 1995, the remote access systems market grew by an astounding 120 percent, and Zoom was well placed to sell remote access products in the high volume retail stores already distributing the company's products.

Zoom has received recognition from such eminent publications as *Forbes Magazine, Financial World, Fortune, PC World, Windows Magazine, ComputerLife, NetGuide, Windows User,* and *PC Professionell* in Germany. Best Buy awards have come from such distant countries as the United Kingdom and Brazil. With such rave reviews from sources all over the world, Manning and Kramer, still managing the company's development and direction in the mid-1990s, were confident that Zoom's best years lay ahead.

Principal Subsidiaries

Tribe Computer Works, Inc.

Further Reading

Brown, Bruce, ''Zoom/FaxModem V.34X,'' *PC Magazine,* October 24, 1995, p. 403.

Farrell, Craig S., ''Review: Leading 28,8K Notebook Modems Pass Muster,'' *Computerworld,* July 8, 1996, p. 86.

Laville, Stacy, ''Remote Access Expansion Plans Flurry of Buyouts,'' *PC Week,* June 24, 1996, p. 121.

——, ''Volume Rises For Voice/Data Modems At Comdex,'' *PC Week,* November 6, 1995, p. 6.

Pickering, Wendy, ''New V.34-Based Modems Join The Comdex Crowd,'' *PC Week,* November 14, 1994, p. 26.

Robinson, Earle, ''Zoom/FaxModem V.34X,'' *PC Magazine,* March 14, 1995, p. 271.

Sparks, Debra, ''The Second Time Around,'' *Financial World,* May 24, 1994, p. 59.

Wildstrom, Stephen H., ''Thoroughly Modern Modems,'' *Business Week,* July 31, 1995, p. 18.

Yang, Jae, ''Zoom/FaxModem VFX 28.8,'' *PC Magazine,* September 13, 1994, p. 308.

''Zoom Telephonics Turns Fax Machines Into Scanners,'' *PC Week,* March 6, 1995, p. 35.

—Thomas Derdak

INDEX TO COMPANIES

Index to Companies

Listings in this index are arranged in alphabetical order under the company name. Company names beginning with a letter or proper name such as Eli Lilly & Co. will be found under the first letter of the company name. Definite articles (The, Le, La) are ignored for alphabetical purposes as are forms of incorporation that precede the company name (AB, NV). Company names printed in bold type have full, historical essays on the page numbers appearing in bold. Updates to entries that appeared in earlier volumes are signified by the notation (**upd.**). Company names in light type are references within an essay to that company, not full historical essays. This index is cumulative with volume numbers printed in bold type.

S.D. Cohn & Company, **10** 455
S.D. Warren Co., **IV** 329–30
S-E Bank Group, **II** 351–53
S.E. Massengill, **III** 66
S.F. Braun, **IV** 451
S.G. Warburg and Co., **II** 232, 259–60, 422, 629; **14** 419; **16** 377. See also SBC Warburg.
S. Grumbacher & Son. See The Bon-Ton Stores, Inc.
S.H. Benson Ltd., **I** 25–26
S.H. Kress & Co., **17** 203–04
S.I.P., Co., **8** 416
S-K-I Limited, 15 457–59
S.K. Wellman, **14** 81
S. Kuhn & Sons, **13** 221
S.M.A. Corp., **I** 622
S.R. Dresser Manufacturing Co., **III** 470–71
S.S. Kresge Company, **V** 110–12. See also Kmart Corporation.
S.S. White Dental Manufacturing Co., **I** 383
S. Smith & Sons, **III** 555
S.T. Cooper & Sons, **12** 283
S.T. Dupont, **III** 28
Sa SFC NA, **18** 163
Sa SFC NV, **18** 162
SAA. See South African Airways.
SAAB. See Svenska Aeroplan Aktiebolaget.
Saab-Scania A.B., I 197–98, 210; **III** 556; **V** 339; **10** 86; **11 437–39 (upd.)**; **16** 322
Saarberg-Konzern, IV 196–99
Saarstahl AG, **IV** 228
Saatchi & Saatchi plc, I 21, 28, **33–35,** 36; **6** 53, 229; **14** 49–50; **16** 72
SAB. See South African Breweries Ltd.
Sabah Timber Co., **III** 699
SABENA, **6** 96; **18** 80
Saber Energy, Inc., **7** 553–54
SABIM Sable, **12** 152
Sabine Corporation, **7** 229
Sabine Investment Co. of Texas, Inc., **IV** 341
Sachsgruppe, **IV** 201
Sacilor, **IV** 174, 226–27
Sackett Plasterboard Co., **III** 762
Sacks Industries, **8** 561
SACOR, **IV** 250, 504–06
Sacramento Savings & Loan Association, **10** 43, 45
SAE Magnetics Ltd., **18** 250
Saeger Carbide Corp., **IV** 203
Saes, **III** 347
SAFECO Corporation, III 352–54; **10** 44
Safeguard Scientifics, Inc., 10 232–34, 473–75
Safeskin Corporation, 18 467–70
Safety Fund Bank, **II** 207
Safety Rehab, **11** 486
Safety Savings and Loan, **10** 339
Safety-Kleen Corp., 8 462–65
Safeway Stores Incorporated, II 424, 601, 604–05, 609–10, 628, 632, 637, **654–56**; **6** 364; **7** 61, 569; **9** 39; **10** 442; **11** 239, 241; **12** 113, 209, 559; **13** 90, 336, 340; **16** 64, 160, 249, 452
Safmarine, **IV** 22
Safrap, **IV** 472
Saga Corp., **II** 608; **III** 103; **IV** 406
Sagebrush Sales, Inc., **12** 397
Saginaw Dock & Terminal Co., **17** 357
Sagitta Arzneimittel, **18** 51

Sagittarius Productions Inc., **I** 286
Sai Baba, **12** 228
Saia Motor Freight Line, Inc., **6** 421–23
Saibu Gas, **IV** 518–19
SAIC, **12** 153
Saiccor, **IV** 92
Sainrapt et Brice, **9** 9
Sainsbury's. See J Sainsbury PLC.
St. Alban's Sand and Gravel, **III** 739
St. Andrews Insurance, **III** 397
St. Charles Manufacturing Co., **III** 654
St. Clair Industries Inc., **I** 482
St. Clair Press, **IV** 570
St. Croix Paper Co., **IV** 281; **9** 259
St. George Reinsurance, **III** 397
St. Helens Crown Glass Co., **III** 724
St. Joe Minerals Corp., **I** 569, 571; **8** 192
St. Joe Paper Company, 8 485–88
St. John Knits, Inc., 14 466–68
St. John's Wood Railway Company, **6** 406
St. Joseph Co., **I** 286, 684
St. Jude Medical, Inc., 6 345; **11 458–61**
St. Lawrence Cement Inc., **III** 702; **8** 258–59
St. Lawrence Corp. Ltd., **IV** 272
St. Lawrence Steamboat Co., **I** 273
St. Louis and Illinois Belt Railway, **6** 504
Saint Louis Bread Company, **18** 35, 37
St. Louis Refrigerator Car Co., **I** 219
St. Louis Troy and Eastern Railroad Company, **6** 504
St. Paul (U.K.) Ltd., **III** 357
St. Paul Bank for Cooperatives, 8 489–90
St. Paul Companies, **15** 257
St. Paul Fire and Marine Insurance Co., **III** 355–56
St. Regis Corp., **I** 153; **IV** 264, 282; **9** 260; **10** 265
St. Regis Paper Co., **IV** 289, 339; **12** 377
Saint-Gobain. See Compagnie de Saint Gobain S.A.
Saint-Quirin, **III** 676; **16** 120
Sainte Anne Paper Co., **IV** 245–46
Saipem, **IV** 420–22, 453
Saison Group, **V** 184–85, 187–89
Saito Ltd., **IV** 268
Saiwa, **II** 543
Saks Fifth Avenue, **I** 426; **15** 291; **18** 372
Sakurai Co., **IV** 327
Salada Foods, **II** 525; **13** 293
Salant Corporation, 12 430–32
Sale Knitting Company, **12** 501. See also Tultex Corporation.
Salem Carpet Mills, Inc., **9** 467
Salen Energy A.B., **IV** 563
Salim Group, **18** 180–81
Sallie Mae. See Student Loan Marketing Association.
Sally Beauty Company, Inc., **8** 15–17
Salmon Carriers, **6** 383
Salmon River Power & Light Company, **12** 265
Salomon Inc., I 630–31; **II** 268, 400, 403, 406, 426, 432, 434, 441, **447–49**; **III** 221, 215, 721; **IV** 80, 137; **7** 114; **9** 378–79, 386; **11** 35, 371; **13** 331, **447–50 (upd.)** Inc.; **18** 60, 62
Salora, **II** 69; **17** 353
Salsåkers Ångsågs, **IV** 338
Saltos del Sil, **II** 197
Salvation Army, **15** 510–11
Salzgitter AG, IV 128, 198, **200–01**; **17** 381

Sam Goody, **I** 613; **9** 360–61
Sam's Clubs, **V** 216–17; **8** 555–57; **12** 221, 335; **13** 548; **14** 393; **15** 470; **16** 64
Samancor Ltd., **IV** 92–93
Sambo's, **12** 510
Sambre-et-Moselle, **IV** 52
Samcor Glass, **III** 685
Samedan Oil Corporation, **11** 353
Samim, **IV** 422
Samkong Fat Ltd. Co., **III** 747
Samna Corp., **6** 256
Sampson's, **12** 220–21
Samsonite Corp., 6 50; **13** 311, **451–53**; **16** 20–21
Samsung Electronics Co., Ltd., 14 416–18; **18** 139, 260
Samsung Group, I 515–17; **II** 53–54; **III** 143, 457–58, 517, 749; **IV** 519; **7** 233; **12** 211–12; **13** 387; **18** 124
Samsung-Calex, **17** 483
Samuel Austin & Son Company, **8** 41
Samuel Meisel & Co., **11** 80–81
Samuel Montagu & Co., **II** 319; **17** 324–25
Samuel Moore & Co., **I** 155
Samuel Samuel & Co., **IV** 530, 542
Samwha Paper Co., **III** 748
San Antonio Public Service Company, **6** 473
San Diego Gas & Electric Company, V 711–14; **6** 590; **11** 272
San Gabriel Light & Power Company, **16** 496
San Giorgio Macaroni Inc., **II** 511
San Miguel Corporation, I 221; **15** 428–30
SAN-MIC Trading Co., **IV** 327
Sanborn Co., **III** 142; **6** 237
Sanders Associates, Inc., **9** 324; **13** 127–28
Sanderson & Porter, **I** 376
Sanderson Computers, **10** 500
Sanderson Farms, Inc., 15 425–27
Sandoz Ltd., I 632–33, **671–73,** 675; **7** 315, 452; **8** 108–09, 215; **10** 48, 199; **11** 173; **12** 388; **15** 139; **18** 51
SandPoint Corp., **12** 562; **17** 254
Sandusky Plastics, Inc., **17** 157
Sandvik AB, III 426–27; **IV 202–04**
Sandwell, Inc., **6** 491
Sandy's Pool Supply, Inc. See Leslie's Poolmart, Inc.
SANFLO Co., Ltd., **IV** 327
Sangu Express Company, **V** 463
Sanichem Manufacturing Company, **16** 386
Sanitary Farm Dairies, Inc., **7** 372
Sanitas Food Co., **II** 523
Sanitation Systems, Inc. See HMI Industries.
Sanjushi Bank, **II** 347
Sanka Coffee Corp., **II** 531
Sankin Kai Group, **II** 274
Sanko K.K., **I** 432, 492
Sanko Steamship Co., **I** 494; **II** 311
Sankyo Company Ltd., I 330, **674–75**; **III** 760; **8** 153
Sanlam, **II** 91, 93, 535
Sano Railway Company, **6** 430
Sanofi Group, I 304, **676–77**; **III** 18; **IV** 546; **7** 484–85
Sanseisha Co., **IV** 326
Santa Ana Savings and Loan, **10** 339
Santa Ana Wholesale Company, **16** 451
Santa Cruz Operation, **6** 244
Santa Cruz Portland Cement, **II** 490

INDEX TO INDUSTRIES

Index to Industries

CONSTRUCTION

CONTAINERS

DRUGS

ELECTRICAL & ELECTRONICS

FINANCIAL SERVICES: NON-BANKS

FOOD PRODUCTS

FOOD SERVICES & RETAILERS

HEALTH & PERSONAL CARE PRODUCTS

HEALTH CARE SERVICES

HOTELS

INFORMATION TECHNOLOGY

INSURANCE

MATERIALS

RUBBER & TIRE

TELECOMMUNICATIONS

UTILITIES

WASTE SERVICES

NOTES ON CONTRIBUTORS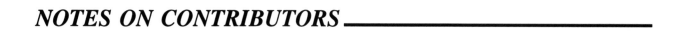

Notes on Contributors

BIANCO, David P. Freelance writer, editor, and publishing consultant.

BODINE, Paul S. Freelance writer, editor, and researcher in Milwaukee, specializing in business subjects; contributor to the *Encyclopedia of American Industries, Encyclopedia of Global Industries, DISCovering Authors, Contemporary Popular Writers,* the *Milwaukee Journal Sentinel,* and the *Baltimore Sun.*

BOYD, Karen Leslie. Freelance manuscript editor, proofreader, and writer in Homewood, Illinois.

BOYER, Dean. Newspaper reporter and freelance writer in the Seattle area.

BURGMAN, Terri L. Freelance writer currently living in rural Iowa.

COHEN, M. L. Novelist and freelance writer living in Paris.

COVELL, Jeffrey L. Freelance writer and corporate history contractor.

DERDAK, Thomas. Freelance writer and adjunct professor of philosophy at Loyola University of Chicago.

DORGAN, Charity Anne. Detroit-based freelance writer.

FELDMAN, Heidi. Los Angeles-based freelance writer.

GASBARRE, April Dougal. Archivist and freelance writer specializing in business and social history in Cleveland, Ohio.

GOPNIK, Hilary. Ann Arbor-based freelance writer.

HALASZ, Robert. Former editor in chief of *World Progress* and *Funk & Wagnalls New Encyclopedia Yearbook*; author, *The U.S. Marines* (Millbrook Press, 1993).

INGRAM, Edward C. Lawyer and freelance writer based in Columbia, South Carolina.

INGRAM, Frederick C. Business writer living in Columbia, South Carolina; contributor to the *Encyclopedia of Business,* the *Encyclopedia of Consumer Brands,* and *Global Industry Profiles.*

JACOBSON, Robert R. Freelance writer and musician.

MONTGOMERY, Bruce P. Curator and director of historical collection, University of Colorado at Boulder.

PEIPPO, Kathleen. Minneapolis-based freelance writer.

PFALZGRAF, Taryn Benbow. Freelance editor, writer, and consultant in the Chicago area.

SALAMIE, David E. Part-owner of InfoWorks Development Group, a reference publication development and editorial services company.

SHELTON, Pamela L. Freelance writer and editor.

WERNICK, Ellen D. Freelance writer and editor.

WHITELEY, Laura E. Freelance writer based in Kalamazoo, Michigan.